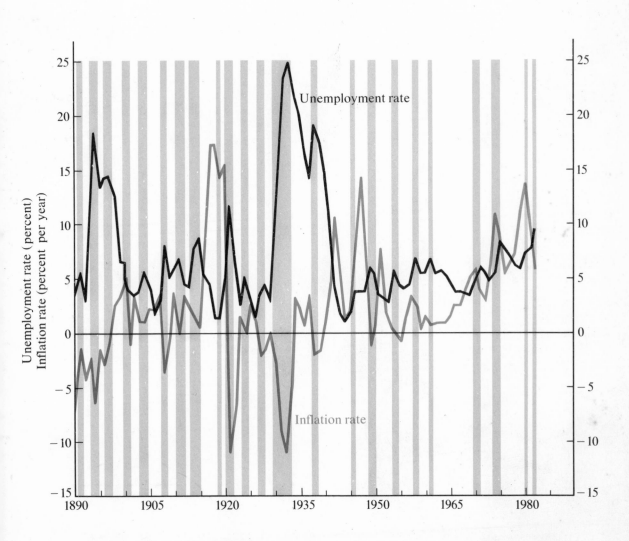

(*Sources*: Inflation rate: see sources for price level data on opposite page; unemployment rate: *Historical Statistics of the United States*, vol. 1, p. 135, and *Economic Report of the President, 1982*, Table B-33.)

Stanley Fischer

Rudiger Dornbusch

Professors of Economics
Massachusetts Institute of Technology

McGraw-Hill Book Company

New York | St. Louis | San Francisco | Auckland
Bogotá | Hamburg | Johannesburg | London
Madrid | Mexico | Montreal
New Delhi | Panama | Paris | São Paulo
Singapore | Sydney | Tokyo | Toronto

Economics

To

Michael, David, and Jonathan
and
Sergio

Economics

Copyright © 1983 by McGraw-Hill, Inc.
All rights reserved.
Printed in the United States of America.
Except as permitted under the United States Copyright Act of 1976,
no part of this publication may be reproduced
or distributed in any form or by any means,
or stored in a data base or retrieval system,
without the prior written permission of the publisher.

1234567890 DOCDOC 89876543

ISBN 0-07-017757-0

This book was set in Caledonia by Progressive Typographers.
The editors were Peter J. Dougherty, Marjorie Singer, and James B. Armstrong;
the designer was Nicholas Krenitsky;
the production supervisor was Dominick Petrellese.
The drawings were done by Fine Line Illustrations, Inc.
R. R. Donnelley & Sons Company was printer and binder.

Library of Congress Cataloging in Publication Data

Fischer, Stanley.
   Economics.

   Includes index.
   1. Economics. I. Dornbusch, Rudiger. II. Title.
HB171.5.F458 1983   330   82-22911
ISBN 0-07-017757-0

Contents

Suggested Outlines for a One-Semester Course

THIRD OPTION: One-Semester Course Emphasizing Macroeconomics

We have written this book with two notions about the level and range of material covered. The first is that there is an essential, simple, usable body of economics that has to be learned in any principles course. The second is that modern economics is more interesting and more readily applicable to analysis of the real world than traditional approaches suggest.

Preface

The Core Chapters

The material covered in the core of both the microeconomics and macroeconomics parts of the book is fundamental and traditional. In microeconomics we start with an overview of supply and demand. We then go more deeply into demand and into the cost curves that underlie the supply side of the market. Market structure and factor markets are covered in detail. In macroeconomics we start with national income accounting and go on to present aggregate demand, fiscal policy, money and banking, monetary policy, and international trade.

Even in these core chapters, our approach to economics emphasizes a blend of theory, applications, and policy discussions that brings economics across as the relevant and live social science that it is. Whenever possible—and it is almost always possible —we illustrate the usefulness of the analysis developed in each chapter by applying it to an example from the U.S. economy or the economy of a foreign country. From the start we emphasize the view that economics can be used in understanding and analyzing real-world problems.

Beyond the Core

In both micro- and macroeconomics we show how to use and extend the material of the core chapters. In microeconomics we discuss regulation and antitrust, thereby extending the material on market structure. We discuss human capital, discrimination, and labor unions, thus extending the material on factor markets. Other topics include the role of government in resource allocation, urban economics and the problems of the cities, and uncertainty in economics and economic life. While all these chapters are of independent interest, they serve to reinforce the lessons learned in the earlier chapters. For example, Chapter 16, "Applied Economics in Action," presents in simple form the reasoning and evidence in recent studies of the economics of work restrictions, the economics of time use and the family, search and information, and crime and punishment.

In macroeconomics we extend the traditional material by developing, at an appropriately simple level, the theory of aggregate supply and demand. Thus we present a complete analysis of the determination of output and of the price level and the rate of inflation. *Supply side economics* is introduced in discussing the determinants of full employment output. There are separate chapters on unemployment and on the costs and effects of inflation. Chapter 32, on money, deficits, and inflation, discusses topics of current interest in a lively way—and at the same time presents evidence from the German hyperinflation that emphasizes the basic links between money and inflation in extreme circumstances. Chapter 33, on growth and investment, continues the discussion of supply side economics and productivity growth. This material is both topical and of fundamental long-run importance, and it is presented at a level that is easily understandable by the student.

With exports now accounting for 12 percent of GNP and imports a growing policy problem, it is time that international trade be moved out of the shadows. Chapter 34 introduces trade and the balance of payments, presenting facts and definitions. This chapter is supplemented by Chapter 35, which analyzes the real side of trade—comparative advantage, intra-industry trade, and tariffs and export subsidies—and by Chapter 36, which examines on exchange rates and international finance. In these three chapters, as in the remainder of the book, we draw continually on the real world for examples to illustrate concepts and analyses.

The book concludes with chapters on big questions. We start with the problems of

developing economies and the new international economic order, explaining the issues and assessing the likely outcomes. Chapter 38 examines income distribution and poverty in the United States, and Chapter 39 discusses alternative economic approaches and systems.

Economics for the Eighties

Most of our examples, applications, and extensions of the basic material are drawn from and apply to the economic environment of the 1980s. We give extensive treatment to such issues as government deficits and inflation, the merits of balanced budgets and the limits of both Keynesian economics and monetarism, the economics of racial and sex discrimination, the role of government in antitrust and regulation, problems of the international monetary system, competition from foreign producers of automobiles, income distribution and poverty in the United States and abroad, and interest rates and inflation.

Level of Exposition

We cover the essential principles material slowly and thoroughly. Even where we discuss topics that are usually thought of as more advanced—for instance, aggregate supply—we believe we succeed in keeping the exposition at a level appropriate to the beginning student. We do not rely on algebra, or the geometry of maximization, or macroeconomic general equilibrium.

Instructor's Manual

Professor Michael Morgan of Western Kentucky University has prepared a comprehensive instructor's manual to accompany the text. He has written the questions, while we have written the introductions to the chapters.

Split Volumes

This book comes also in two split volumes. The microeconomics split contains Chapters 1–20 of this volume, along with Chapter 38, on income distribution. The macroeconomics split contains Chapters 1–3 as introductory material, and then Chapters 21–39, excluding Chapter 38.

Alternative Courses and Orders of Chapters

On pages xxiii and xxiv we set out three options for a one-semester course. Although the book begins with microeconomics, the instructor who prefers to do so can move over to macroeconomics after Chapter 3, and then return to micro.

TO THE STUDENT

There is no denying that it takes many years of study to become a complete economist with a professional's command of the subject. Most of you probably have no wish to become professional economists. But fortunately the basic issues studied by economists, the framework of analysis, and many of the conclusions can be understood very quickly in an introductory course. Our emphasis on applications is designed to convince you that the economics you are learning is about the real world and is not just a set of textbook exercises.

There is an old complaint that economists never agree about anything. This complaint is simply wrong. The press, cab drivers, and your uncle and aunt love to talk about topics on which there is disagreement. It would be a boring news show to put on two people with the same view, so the directors of TV programs search for economists who will disagree. But economics is not a field in which there is always an argument for everything. There *are* answers to some questions. One of the aims of the book is to show why we understand some issues, and what the disagreements are about others. In choosing the applications in this book, and especially in policy discussions, we have tried to develop this perspective.

How to Study

There is a world of difference between reading about economics and actually *doing* and understanding economics. The aim of the book is *not* to tell you what economics is about. Rather, we hope the book will enable you both to learn how to use economics and to understand how to attack and analyze problems.

To *do* economics you have to learn *actively*. Reading is not enough. You should be questioning the text. When the book says "clearly," ask yourself why. When the text makes three points, check back to the first when you hit the third. Above all, when the text applies the analysis, follow the application with care. When a line is drawn one way, ask why. See if it can be drawn differently. Do the problems.

Be on guard against our attempts to make the text clear. Each paragraph may be easy reading, but you also have to keep check on how the paragraphs add up to a complete picture. At the end of each section ask yourself what you have learned. And to make sure, you may want to jump ahead to the chapter summary.

Study Guide

Professor Michael Morgan of Western Kentucky University has prepared an excellent study guide that accompanies the textbook. It briefly reviews each chapter and then provides many questions that enable you to learn actively the material of the chapter. The questions in the *Study Guide* in effect take you step by step through the analysis of the chapter.

Anyone who has worked through the *Study Guide* will understand the material in the book.

ACKNOWLEDGMENTS

In writing this book we have been helped by friends and colleagues, by a large group of professors who read through earlier drafts and gave us the benefit of their own teaching experience, by students who used and commented—quite frankly—on earlier drafts, by the McGraw-Hill team, and by our assistants.

We owe special thanks to colleagues who devoted time and effort to provide us with critical feedback on earlier drafts, pointing out inaccuracies, suggesting better examples, and gently noting things that needed smoothing. We would like to mention especially Eliana Cardoso, Henry Farber, Kathleen Feldstein, Nan Friedlaender, Zvi Griliches, Jerry Hausman, Paul Joskow, Thomas Moore, Michael Morgan, Robert Pindyck, Richard Schmalensee, and Yoram Weiss.

Our acknowledgments to the many professors who offered advice and suggestions for improving the manuscript of this text appear on pages xxix–xxxi. These individuals will recognize the major differences that have resulted from their comments.

We were again extremely fortunate in the assistance we had. Alex Zanello, Andy Kaufman, and Donald Deere provided early research assistance; Susan Collins, Mike Gavin, and Jeff Miron were invaluable at the most exacting stages. Tere Bautista, Carol McIntire, and Elizabeth Walb typed many drafts with speed and accuracy, and helped manage the book and us.

We would like to give special thanks to members of the McGraw-Hill team. Marjorie Singer taught us everything she knows about principles books and the people who read them, and made many helpful suggestions. Jim Armstrong saw the book through the press with speed and calmness. Bonnie Lieberman maintained her composure under considerable pressure. The book is much the better for their help, and for the help of the many others we have mentioned and thanked above.

A final clarifying note: We are each fully and equally implicated in the virtues and faults of this book and the companion volumes, *Introduction to Microeconomics* and *Introduction to Macroeconomics*. The order of our names was decided upon to ensure that there is no confusion between these books and any other book by the same authors.

Stanley Fischer
Rudiger Dornbusch

Acknowledgments

Norman D. Aitken
University of Massachusetts

James W. Albrecht
Columbia University

Joseph Alexander
Babson College

Kenneth O. Alexander
Michigan Tech

Roy Andersen
Knox College

Richard Anderson
Texas A & M University

Mostapha H. Baligh
Bergen Community College

Maurice B. Ballabon
Baruch College

Richard Ballman
Augustana College

Robert Barry
College of William and Mary

Peter S. Barth
University of Connecticut

R. C. Battalio
Texas A & M University

G. C. Bjork
Claremont Men's College

Dwight M. Blood
Colorado State University

Frank J. Bonello
University of Notre Dame

Allan J. Braff
University of New Hampshire

Philip E. Brotherton
Los Angeles Pierce College

M. Northrup Buechner
St. John's University

P. D. Burdett
University of Wisconsin

H. Richard Call
American River Community College

Thomas F. Cargill
University of Nevada

Mabel Chang
Bronx Community College

F. C. Child
University of California–Davis

Robert Christiansen
Colby College

Donald Coffin
Illinois State University

Donald R. Connell
University of Nebraska–Omaha

C. S. Cox
St. Louis Community College

Donald Cummings
University of Northern Iowa

J. Ronnie Davis
University of South Alabama

Ernest M. DeCicco
Northeastern University

David Denslow
University of Florida

George M. Eastham
California Polytechnic State University

Kenneth G. Elzinga
University of Virginia

Yiu-Kwan Fan
University of Wisconsin–Stevens Point

Paul G. Farnham
Georgia State University

Claude H. Farrell
University of North Carolina–Wilmington

Charles Fischer
Pittsburg State University

James Frew
University of North Carolina–Greensboro

George Garman
Loyola University

Otis Gilley
University of Texas–Austin

Richard M. Gillis
Williamette University

Frank W. Glodek
Denison University

Jack Goddard
Northeastern State University

Rae Jean B. Goodman
U.S. Naval Academy

Craufurd D. Goodwin
Duke University

A. R. Gutowsky
California State University–Sacramento

U. B. Henderson
Central State University

William L. Holahan
University of Wisconsin

Robert Holland
Illinois State University

Phyllis W. Isley
Norwich University

Habib Jam
Glassboro State College

George Jensen
California State University–Los Angeles

John H. Kagel
Texas A & M University

Timothy Keely
Tacoma Community College

Ziad K. Keilany
University of Tennessee

Greg Kilgariff
Marist College

James T. Kyle
Indiana State University

Kathleen M. Langley
Boston University

Allen Larsen
Florida Southern College

Gary Lemon
DePauw University

Alan C. Lerner
New York University

Lester E. Levy
Northern Illinois University

Francis McGrath
Iona College

Allan Mandelstamm
Virginia Polytechnic Institute

James Marlin
Western Illinois University

David A. Martin
State University of New York–Geneseo

Walther P. Michael
Ohio State University

Gerald M. Miller
Miami University

D. Morawetz
Boston University

Michael Morgan
Western Kentucky University

John S. Murphy
Canisius College

Frank Musgrave
Ithaca College

Karen Nelson
Smith College

R. D. Norton
Mount Holyoke College

John Olienyk
Colorado State University

Henry Orion
Fairleigh Dickinson University

Mack Ott
Penn State University

D. Ounjian
Tufts University

Patricia L. Pacey
University of Colorado

Peter Parker
Lafayette College

George M. Perkins
University of Wisconsin–
Milwaukee

Martin M. Perline
Wichita State University

H. Craig Petersen
Utah State University

Carol Pfrommer
University of Alabama–
Birmingham

James V. Pinto
Central State University

Bette Polkinghorn
California State University

Lawrence B. Pulley
Brandeis University

Rama Ramachandran
Southern Methodist Uni-
versity

Michael Reed
University of Nevada–
Reno

Christopher C. Rhoden
Solano Community College

Roberto Rios
Lehman College

Steven M. Rock
Illinois Institute of Technology

Allen Sanderson
Princeton University

Todd Sandler
University of Wyoming

Hyman Sardy
Brooklyn College

Leslie Seplaki
Rutgers University

John C. Shannon
Suffolk University

Richard U. Sherman, Jr.
Ohio State University

Marvin Snowbarger
San Jose State University

Clifford Sowell
Eastern Kentucky Univer-
sity

George A. Spiva
University of Tennessee

Lawrence Steinhauer
Albion College

Alan C. Stockman
University of Rochester

Houston H. Stokes
University of Illinois

Robert C. Stuart
Douglass College

Eugene M. Swann
University of California–
Berkeley

Michael K. Taussig
Rutgers University

Lloyd B. Thomas
Kansas State University

William O. Thweatt
Vanderbilt University

Timothy D. Tregarthen
University of Colorado

John Vahaly
University of Louisville

Dale W. Warnke
College of Lake County

Bernard Wasow
New York University

Michael W. Watts
Indiana University–Purdue
University at Indianapolis

J. Wetzel
Virginia Commonwealth
University

Samuel Williamson
University of Iowa

Jeffrey Wolcowitz
Harvard University

Mahmood Yousefi
University of Northern
Iowa

William J. Zahka
Widener College

1

Introduction

Every group of people must solve three basic problems of daily living: *What* goods and services should be produced? *How* should those goods and services be produced? *For whom* should the goods and services be produced?

Economics is the study of how society decides *what* gets produced, *how*, and *for whom*.

The definition emphasizes the role of society and in so doing places economics among the social sciences—the sciences that study and explain human behavior. The subject matter of economics is that part of human behavior that relates to the production, exchange, and use of goods and services.

The central economic problem for society is how to reconcile the conflict between people's virtually unlimited needs and desires for goods and services and the scarcity of the resources (land, labor, and machines) required to produce those goods and services. In answering the questions *What? How?* and *For whom?* economics explains how scarce resources are allocated among competing demands.

1 THREE ECONOMIC ISSUES

Trying to understand what economics is about from definitions is like trying to learn to ride a bicycle by reading an instruction book. It's much better to get going. In this section we discuss three specific economic issues which show how society deals with the allocation of scarce resources among competing demands. In each case, we see how the questions of What? How? and For whom? appear.

The Oil Price Increase

The American economy uses petroleum products in countless ways. Most chemical products contain petroleum in some form; automobiles and airplanes use gasoline; plastic materials from kitchen utensils to sweaters contain petroleum. From the 1950s through 1973 petroleum use increased steadily, both in the production of fuel and in the manufacture of industrial products. Over that period the price of petroleum fell compared with the prices of other products. People were becoming used to that state of affairs.

In 1973–1974 all this changed very abruptly. The main oil-producing countries in the world, mostly located in the Middle East but also including Venezuela and Nigeria, belong to OPEC—the Organization of Petroleum Exporting Countries. Recognizing that among them they produced most of the world's oil, they decided to raise the price they charged for their oil. OPEC knew that users of oil would try to cut back on their oil use when the price increased. But they believed that other countries were so dependent on oil for basic transportation, heating, and industrial use that they could not cut back much. OPEC thus figured that if it raised the price substantially, it would end up selling only a little less oil than before, but at a much higher price. That way it would make a lot more money.

Figure 1-1 shows the price of oil in the period from 1969 to 1980. The OPEC price increase shows up in 1973–1974, when oil in the world market went up from $2.90 to $9 per barrel—the price *tripled*. The price increased more slowly from 1974 to 1978. Then there was another sharp price increase, from $12 per barrel to nearly $30, between 1978 and 1980. The dramatic price increases of 1973–1974 and 1978–1980 were called the OPEC *oil-price shocks*. They were called shocks because they took the world by surprise, and also because they inflicted an enormous upheaval on the world economy. The world that had become accustomed to falling oil prices somehow had to handle two very large price increases within a few years.

Much of this book teaches you that people respond to prices. When a price increases, consumers of the good that has become more expensive try to use less of it. Producers want to sell more when the price goes up and will expand production. These responses, guided by prices, are an essential part of the process by which most societies determine what should be produced, how, and for whom.

Consider first *how* the economy produces goods and services. Firms in the

economy use machines, labor, land, and materials, including petroleum, to produce goods and services. When the price of petroleum products increases as it did in the 1970s, every firm will try to reduce its use of petroleum or gasoline. Firms will be looking for petroleum-saving ways of producing chemicals; airlines will look for more fuel-efficient planes; everybody will think of buying a car that uses less gasoline. The first response, then, is that higher oil prices make the economy produce in a way that uses less petroleum.

How does the oil-price increase affect *what* is being produced? When firms and households try to conserve on the use of oil because of higher oil prices, they look for products that are fuel-efficient and less oil-dependent. Households install solar and gas heating for their homes, and they buy small cars. Airlines look for new planes that consume less fuel. They also modify existing planes, scraping off paint to save weight and installing lighter-weight seats. Tourists look for vacation spots that are closer to home so that less gasoline is used getting there. Throughout the economy firms and households shift away from petroleum- or gasoline-related products to other goods and services.

Producers, too, respond to the higher price of oil. Car designers discover that 20 percent of the gasoline used by cars can be saved by making the cars more streamlined. Textile producers return to wool sweaters, airplane producers design new planes, architects develop sun-heated housing, and research labs develop alternatives to petroleum for chemical products. Throughout the economy what is being produced is a range of goods that replace expensive oil-using products.

The *for whom* question in this example has a particularly clear answer. The vast increase in the oil revenues of OPEC meant that its buying power was greatly increased.

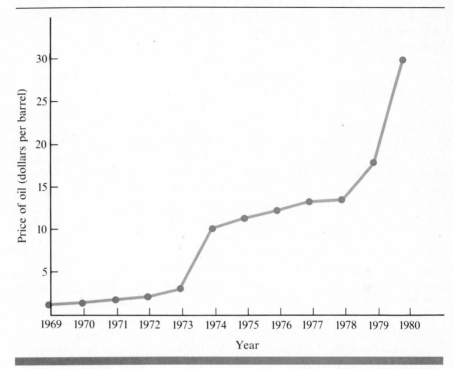

FIGURE 1-1 THE PRICE OF OIL, 1969–1980. The price is that of Saudi Arabian oil. (*Source:* International Monetary Fund, *International Financial Statistics,* 1981 Yearbook, p. 81.)

Its revenues from oil sales increased from $35 billion in 1973 to nearly $300 billion in 1980. Much of that increased revenue was spent on goods produced by American firms and firms in other industrialized countries such as Germany and Japan.

As a consequence of the oil-price increase the whole world was producing more goods for OPEC and less for everyone else. But the economy is a very intricate system with interconnected parts. A disturbance anywhere ripples through the entire economy. Thus when OPEC countries spent more on some American goods, the firms producing those goods had an increase in their sales, and the owners of the firms and the workers shared to some extent in the OPEC gains. They, too, therefore, were among those for whom the economy was producing as they themselves spent their increased revenues. But, of course, OPEC spending was not limited to industrial countries. Large construction projects in Saudi Arabia, the main OPEC country, attracted workers from Pakistan. They earned high wages, which in turn enabled them to spend in a way they had been unable to before. They, too, shared in the OPEC revenues, as did many others, from Swiss bankers to belly dancers in Beirut.

The OPEC oil-price shock gives a clear example of how society allocates scarce resources among competing uses.

A *scarce resource* is a resource that is not available in unlimited quantities at a zero price.

Any resource for which we have to pay is scarce. We can think of oil as having become scarcer when its price rose. We could have handled the scarcity in many different ways. For instance, private-car use could have been stopped entirely and all other uses of oil continued exactly as before. Or we could have forced everyone using oil to reduce oil use by some given proportion, such as 10 percent. In fact, society, guided by the higher price of oil, cut back on all uses of oil, but not in the same proportion. The idea of cutting back on all uses by the same proportion is appealing to someone with a neat mind, but that approach is certain to be a bad way of doing things. We shall see why later in the book.

One of the reasons we study economics is to evaluate policy options. For instance, what were the choices the United States faced when OPEC raised its price, and what were the benefits and disadvantages of those policy choices? Should the federal government have controlled the price of oil in the United States by not allowing gas stations to charge more than a specified amount per gallon? This is what was done, in fact. Would it have been better to ration oil, sharing the available supplies, with no one allowed more than 40 gallons per month? Or should the federal government have done nothing? That is, should it have allowed the price of oil to rise?

Income Distribution

The second issue is the distribution of income. You and your family have an annual income that allows you to enjoy various goods and services, to live in a particular neighborhood, and to maintain a certain standard of living. Your standard of living will include what you think of as the necessities of life—food, shelter, health, education—and also something beyond, such as recreation, for example. Your income might be less than that of your neighbors who have three cars and take a long vacation every year, but it is certain to be more than that of other people, both in this country and abroad. There are others who have far smaller incomes and therefore a much lower standard of living. Differences in income determine the standard of living people can afford. A poor worker might spend most of his income on food and shelter, whereas the son of a rich oilman would

spend only a small fraction of his income on these essentials and would have much left to spend on comfort, pleasure, and luxury.

Nations, just like individuals within each country, have different levels of income. A nation's income, or national income, is the sum of the incomes of all the people living in that country. A country where most of the people are poor, therefore, will be a poor country, or a low-income country. That is true even if there are a few people in the country who are rich or very rich. Conversely, a country where most of the people have a high income will be a rich country, or a high-income country.

Going beyond the level of countries, we can think of world income as the sum of all the individual countries' incomes or as the sum of the incomes earned by all the people in the world. We want to look now at the distribution of world income and national incomes to ask who in the world gets what share of these incomes.

The *distribution of income* (in a country or in the world) tells us how income is divided among different groups.

Income distribution, as we will show, is closely linked to the what, how, and for whom questions.

Table 1-1 shows the percentage of world population in different groups of countries. More than 50 percent of the world's population lives in poor countries, including the three largest such countries: India, China, and Indonesia. A little over 20 percent lives in middle-income countries, a group that includes, for example, Thailand, Brazil, Mexico, Israel, Turkey, Rumania, and Korea. The major oil countries, Iraq, Saudi Arabia, Kuwait, and Libya, account for less than 1 percent of world population.[1] The rich countries, or industrial countries,

---

[1] The major oil countries here are those large-scale oil producers whose economies are dominated by oil. There are other large-scale oil producers, such as Nigeria.

TABLE 1-1

DISTRIBUTION OF POPULATION AND INCOME IN THE WORLD, 1979

	LOW-INCOME COUNTRIES	MIDDLE-INCOME COUNTRIES	MAJOR OIL COUNTRIES	INDUSTRIAL COUNTRIES	SOVIET BLOC
Percentage of world population	52.6	22.9	0.6	15.6	8.2
Income per person in U.S. dollars	230	1420	5470	9440	4230
Percentage of world income	5.3	14.1	1.4	64.1	15.1

Note: The sum of the percentages is not necessarily 100, due to rounding.
Source: World Bank, *World Development Report, 1981,* Table 1.

include the United States, Western Europe, Canada, and Japan and account for over 15 percent of world population. Finally, the Soviet bloc has under 10 percent of the world's population. We want to discuss now how incomes differ between these groups of countries.

To have a comparable number with which to study income differences, we look at average income, or the income per person in each group. Income per person is calculated by taking all the incomes earned in a group of countries and dividing by the population of that area. The second row of Table 1-1 shows income per person for each group. In poor countries the average person earns only $230 *per year,* or just above 60 cents *per day.* In the industrial countries the income per person is nearly $10,000, or more than 40 times larger. These are striking differences. They are differences not between the poorest person in the world and the richest but between the average person living in India and the average person in the United States.

The differences between the average incomes in the different groups of countries are emphasized when we look at the last row of Table 1-1, which shows each group's *share* of world income. Over half the world's population, in the low-income, or poor, countries, receives only 5 percent of total world income. By contrast, the 15 per-

cent of the world's population that lives in the industrial countries, including the United States, receives over 60 percent of world income.

Now we want to see what light Table 1-1 sheds on our three questions: What? How? and For whom? Starting with the question of *for whom* the world economy produces, we realize that it produces mostly for people in the rich countries. People in the rich countries receive over 60 percent of the world's income, whereas the poorest earn only 5 percent. With this distribution of income, the world will be producing mostly for the people living in the rich countries, because those are the people who can afford to buy goods. The answer to the question of for whom also suggests the answer to the question of *what* is produced. World production will be directed mainly toward the goods that are consumed in the richer countries.

The most interesting question Table 1-1 suggests is why there are such large differences in incomes. This relates to the question of *how* goods are produced. In the poor countries there is very little machinery in relation to the size of the population, and the proportion of the population with professional and technical training is small. Without machinery and training, workers cannot produce very much. While in the United States a worker uses power-driven

TABLE 1-2
INCOME DISTRIBUTION IN FOUR COUNTRIES
(Percentage of Total Income)

COUNTRY	RECEIVED BY POOREST 20% OF FAMILIES	RECEIVED BY MIDDLE 60% OF FAMILIES	RECEIVED BY RICHEST 20% OF FAMILIES
United States	4.5	52.7	42.8
Brazil	2.0	31.4	66.6
Sweden	6.6	56.4	37.0
Yugoslavia	6.6	54.7	38.7

Source: World Bank, *World Development Report, 1981,* Table 25.

earth-moving equipment, in a poor country there will be many workers moving the earth, only some of them with shovels.

Low skill levels in low-income countries, along with the abundance of people in relation to machinery, have two implications. First, workers will not be very productive. This means that they will produce much less per hour of work than will a worker in the United States or Sweden, for example, who has the advantage of skill and machinery. And because the worker in a poor country is so much less productive per hour of work, less output is produced, and therefore less income is earned. In sum, workers in poor countries are not very productive because they work under highly unfavorable conditions—with little training and machinery—and for that reason they produce few goods per hour of work and thus earn little per hour or per year.

Poverty is difficult to escape and tends to perpetuate itself. Poor nutrition reduces worker productivity. The family does not have enough income for its members to take time out of working to acquire education. And poverty makes it difficult to buy the machinery and materials that would make everybody more productive.

Income is unequally distributed within each country as well as among countries. A very large share accrues to a very small portion of the people in most countries. Table 1-2 brings this out by showing the shares of

income received within four countries by the poorest 20 percent of families, the middle 60 percent, and the top 20 percent. In the United States, for example, the richest 20 percent of families receive 42.8 percent of total income. In Brazil the top 20 percent receive an even higher share, 66 percent, of national income.

The inequality in income distribution seen in the table reflects, in part, differences in the income people receive for the work they do. Managers of large factories earn more than plumbers, and plumbers earn more than assistant professors. But in addition the differences in income shares reflect differences in the ownership of wealth, or assets (land, buildings, stocks). Rich people derive a substantial part of their income from these assets, while poor people have only their labor income.

The distribution of income thus reflects how production is organized. In economies where assets such as factories or land are owned privately and are highly concentrated in the hands of a small group, income distribution is very unequal. Brazil would be an example. But it is also possible that, as in Yugoslavia, factories are owned by their workers or by the government. In that case wealth is quite evenly distributed, and thus income, too, is distributed more evenly.

The degree to which income is or is not equally distributed will in turn affect what is produced in the economy and for whom.

FIGURE 1-2   FAMILY INCOMES IN NEW YORK,
1979. (*Source:* U.S. Bureau of the Census, *Provisional
Estimates of Social, Economic, and Housing Characteristics,* supplementary report PHC-80-S1-1.

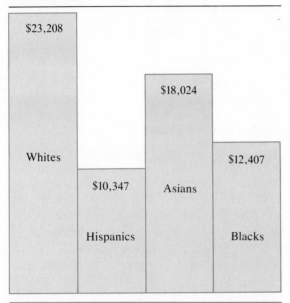

In Brazil many people work as domestic servants, chauffeurs, and maids. In Sweden
there are very few people who can afford to
hire servants.

Income distribution within a country is
shaped not only by work effort and ownership of assets but also by the amount of discrimination and inequality of opportunity
within the society. Figure 1-2 shows the
family income that was typical for each of
four groups in New York City in 1979. Why
is it that blacks and Hispanics earn lower incomes than whites or Asians? A good part of
the answer is that they have poorer jobs,
less skill, and less education. Partly it is because black and Hispanic families are, on
the average, younger and thus have fewer
more experienced (and higher-paid) workers in them. But studies that we discuss
later in this book show that there is more to
it than this. Racial discrimination does account for part of these income differences,
and through the differences in income it has

further effects on the future opportunities
and incomes of the children of the discrimi-
nated-against families.

Figure 1-2 raises important questions
about the interaction of people's attitudes,
in this case discrimination, and economics.
It illustrates that economic analysis of the
distribution of income must reach for a very
comprehensive set of explanations, ranging
from ownership of assets to racial attitudes,
to explain income differences between
groups.

The Role of Government

Our third issue deals with the role of government in society. In every society governments provide such services as national defense, education, police and fire protection,
and the administration of justice. In addition, governments make transfer payments
to some members of the society.

> *Transfer payments* are payments made
> to individuals without their providing a
> service in return.

Government transfers are payments such as
Social Security benefits, unemployment
benefits, and food stamps. To pay for the
goods and services it provides, such as national defense, and to pay for its transfer
programs, the government imposes taxes.

Table 1-3 compares the role of government in four countries. In each case we look
at three numbers: the percentage of the
country's total income that is collected in
various forms of taxes, the percentage the
government spends directly on goods and
services, and the percentage that consists of
transfer payments.[2] The four countries show
very different patterns. On one side, Japan
collects only a quarter of income in taxes

---

[2] You will notice that transfers plus purchases by the
government are not equal to tax collections in Table
1-3. The reason is that governments sometimes *borrow*
rather than tax in order to raise revenues for spending.
When taxes are less than spending, the government has
a budget deficit.

TABLE 1-3

GOVERNMENT TAX COLLECTION, PURCHASES OF GOODS AND SERVICES, AND TRANSFER PAYMENTS
(Percentage of Country's Income in 1979)

COUNTRY	TAX COLLECTION	PURCHASES OF GOODS AND SERVICES	TRANSFERS
United States	32.5	17.4	14.4
Japan	26.6	9.8	13.5
Sweden	57.4	28.4	26.6
United Kingdom	39.0	20.0	21.7

Source: *OECD Economic Outlook,* December 1981, Tables R6, R7, and R9.

(you might well say that a quarter is a lot!), whereas Sweden collects nearly 60 percent. There are also large differences on the side of government spending for goods and services and transfers. Sweden again is a "big-government" country. These differences in the share of government reflect differences in the ways the countries allocate their resources among competing uses.

Governments spend part of their revenues on particular goods and services, such as tanks, schools, and public safety. They thus affect *what* is produced. Japan's low share of government purchases of goods and services in Table 1-3, for instance, reflects the very low level of Japanese defense spending. Governments affect *for whom* output is produced through their taxes and transfer payments. By taxing the rich and making transfers to other people, usually the poor, governments ensure that the poor get more of what is produced than they would otherwise get, and the rich less.

Governments also affect *how* goods are produced, mainly through the regulations they impose. For instance, safety rules have to be obeyed in factories and mines; firms are not allowed to pollute the atmosphere and rivers freely; offices and factories can only be located in certain parts of the city.

The scope of the government's role in the modern economy is highly controversial. With government in the United States taking nearly a third of income in taxes, and

with governments in other countries going even above the 50 percent mark, many people argue that government interferes with the efficient working of the economy.

The argument is that the taxes that the government levies and the transfers it makes reduce incentives to work. If 50 cents of every dollar we earn goes to the government, then often we prefer to go to the beach rather than work another hour. With taxes so high, it's just not worthwhile working hard. That is the argument, and there may be something to it. But there is another possibility. It may be that people work harder when the government increases taxes so that they can make up some of the income lost as a result of the taxes. Whether, on balance, taxes cause people to work more or less and by how much remain matters for ongoing study by economists, as we shall see later in the book.

Similar arguments are made about the effects of government transfer programs, including unemployment benefits, on incentives to work. People on welfare might make almost as much for doing nothing as they could by working. Therefore, it is argued, government transfer programs reduce the amount that people want to work. There is undoubtedly some merit to this argument, and we shall have to see whether it is an issue of alarming proportions.

The entire argument about disincentives is interesting because it shows how the government, through taxes and social programs, affects the way society allocates its scarce resources. Taxes are needed to reconcile the government's desires to spend—possibly for good reasons—on goods and services and transfer payments with private individuals' desires to spend. But the taxes may also reduce society's total production of goods and services.

This discussion of the role of government puts government clearly into the picture as one of the means by which society determines what should get produced, how, and for whom. It also raises a question. What is the alternative to the government's deciding how society should allocate resources? This question is at the heart of economics, and we come back to it shortly when we examine the role of markets in economic life.

Before doing so, we develop an important concept and tool of economics: the production possibility frontier (or schedule).

2 SCARCITY AND COMPETING USES OF RESOURCES: THE PRODUCTION POSSIBILITY FRONTIER

Our discussion of the three economic issues emphasized society's problem of choosing what gets produced, how, and for whom in the face of the central economic problem of scarcity. In this section we develop the production possibility frontier, a basic tool of economics, which emphasizes the notions

of scarcity and the problem of choosing what is to be produced.

We develop the production possibility frontier in a hypothetical economy in which there are two types of goods, food and entertainment (or fun). There are four workers in the economy. A worker can produce in either the food industry or the fun industry.

Table 1-4 shows how much of each good can be produced per month depending on how many workers are employed in each industry. In each industry, the more workers there are, the greater is the level of output. Adding workers to the work force in an industry increases production by that industry. That is certainly reasonable.

In addition, the numbers in Table 1-4 show that the increase in output obtained by adding one more worker declines as more workers are added. For instance, take the food industry. The first worker in the industry increases output from 0 to 10, an increase of 10. Adding one more worker gets output up to 17, an increase of only 7. The third worker increases output by only another 5, and so on. Why? There is only a certain, or fixed, amount of land, water, and other resources available for the production of food. The first worker gets to work with as much of those resources as he wants. When the second worker is added, both workers have to share the land, water, and other resources. Each worker who is added gets less of the land and other resources with which to work, because those resources are being

TABLE 1-4

PRODUCTION POSSIBILITIES IN A HYPOTHETICAL ECONOMY

EMPLOYMENT IN FOOD INDUSTRY	OUTPUT OF FOOD	EMPLOYMENT IN ENTERTAINMENT INDUSTRY	OUTPUT OF ENTERTAINMENT (FUN)
4	25	0	0
3	22	1	9
2	17	2	17
1	10	3	24
0	0	4	30

shared among more people. Thus the amount each additional worker adds to output will decrease the more workers there are already in the industry.

The idea that the more workers there are in an industry, the smaller the amount each extra worker adds to output, is called the *law of diminishing returns*. We have outlined the reasoning behind the law above, and we come back to it in greater detail later. We show diminishing returns in both industries in Table 1-4. In the case of fun, the first worker adds 9 units of output, the second adds 8, and so on.

Looking at the top row of numbers in Table 1-4, we see that if four workers were working in the food industry, they would produce 25 units of food. With four workers in the food industry, there are none left to work making fun, and so the corresponding output of entertainment is zero. In the second row of numbers, one worker is taken out of the food industry and put into the entertainment industry. The output of food drops from 25 to 22, but the output of fun rises from 0 to 9. Another worker moving from food production to the entertainment industry would result in output being only 17 units of food. There would also be 17 units of entertainment produced. The table shows all possible allocations of labor between the two industries and the corresponding combinations of food and entertainment outputs.

These combinations follow a simple pattern. Higher output of food services goes along with the lower output of fun. This is the *trade-off* that society faces. Given its four workers and the assumption that they are all working, society can have more fun only if it reduces the output of food. In moving down the rows of Table 1-4, society is trading off food for fun, giving up food in order to obtain more entertainment.

The trade-off becomes clearer when we show it in a diagram, Figure 1-3. In Figure

FIGURE 1-3   THE PRODUCTION POSSIBILITY FRONTIER. The production possibility frontier shows the maximum combinations of outputs that the economy can produce using all available resources. The frontier represents a trade-off; more of one commodity implies less of the other.

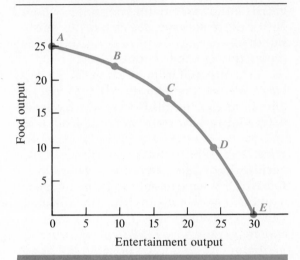

1-3 we show the combinations of outputs in the two sectors. On the horizontal axis the diagram has the output of entertainment, and on the vertical axis it shows the output of food. The first point we plot, A, corresponds to the first row of numbers in the table, with 25 units of food and zero of entertainment.[3] Similarly, point B corresponds to the second row of numbers in the table. With three workers in the food industry and one in the entertainment industry, the output of food is 22, and that of entertainment is 9. Proceeding in a similar way for the other rows in the table, we obtain the other points—C, D, and E—and we join all the points with a curve.

The curve joining points A and E is the production possibility frontier (or schedule).

---

[3] If you are unfamiliar with plotting points in a diagram, just follow the general argument. We show in detail how to plot these points in Chapter 2. At that time you should return to the present argument to be sure you have a firm grasp of the production possibility schedule.

The *production possibility* frontier shows, for each level of the output of one good, the maximum amount of the other good that can be produced.

We have drawn the production possibility frontier as bowed out, or *concave* to the origin. It has that shape because of diminishing returns.

To explain the definition, we look at Figure 1-4, specifically at point *G*. That is the point at which society is producing 10 units of food and 17 of entertainment. Society *can* produce that combination of outputs. It takes one person in the food industry and two in the entertainment industry to produce the output combination shown at *G*. With only three people working, one will be unemployed, not working. But *G* is not a point on the production possibility frontier. That is because given the level of output of entertainment, namely, 17, the output of food is not at the maximum possible. There is one unemployed person who could be put to work in either industry. If he were put to work in the food industry, society would be producing at point *C* on the production possibility frontier. Point *C is* on the frontier because given the level of output of entertainment, 17, it shows the maximum level of output of food, also 17, that society can produce. Point *G* is *not* on the frontier because given the output of 17 units of entertainment, society is not at *G* producing the maximum possible output of food.

The production possibility frontier shows the points at which society is producing output *efficiently*. At all points on the frontier, society is doing the best it can to produce output. Anywhere inside the frontier, for example, at *G*, we say that society is producing inefficiently because it is wasting resources. It could be producing more of at least one good. The waste at *G* is reflected in the unemployment of part of the work force.

Points outside the production possibil-

FIGURE 1-4 EFFICIENT PRODUCTION, INEFFICIENCY, AND UNATTAINABLE OUTPUTS. The production possibility frontier joining points *A* and *E* shows the combinations of outputs at which society is producing efficiently, maximizing the production of one good at a given level of output of the other good. Points such as *G* inside the frontier represent inefficient production. Society could move to *C* and have more output of food. Points such as *H* are unattainable. Society would like to be there rather than, say, at *D*, but it does not have enough resources to produce that combination of outputs.

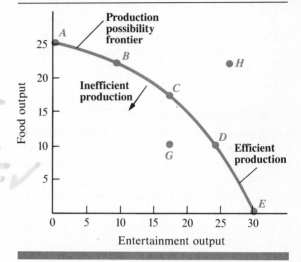

ity frontier, such as *H*, are said to be *unattainable*. Society would like to have more of both food and fun, but given the amount of labor available, there is nothing it can do to produce the output combination at *H* or anywhere else outside the frontier. Society's inability to produce at points outside the frontier emphasizes the notion of the scarcity of resources. Society has to accept the scarcity and find ways of allocating its resources in the face of the scarcity.

Society's problem of allocating resources is summarized by the trade-off shown by the production possibility frontier. Given that people want goods, society would never want to produce inefficiently. If it were producing inefficiently, inside the frontier, it could have more of everything. It should certainly take advantage of any such opportunities. But once it gets to the frontier, it can only have more of one good by accepting less of the other. It trades off increased production of one good for reduced production of the other good.

The essential point is that more of one good implies less of another, so long as resources are limited and being used efficiently. This point has been made in an easily remembered line:

There is no such thing as a free lunch. The meaning is that it takes resources to produce a lunch. Using those resources to produce the lunch means that less of something else is produced.

Society's problem is to choose where to be on the production possibility frontier. In choosing where to be, it chooses *what* to produce. It could decide on point A, with no fun at all but lots of food. Or it might take a more balanced mixture of food and fun at point C. Any of the points on the production possibility frontier can be chosen. In choosing a specific point on the frontier, society also chooses *how* to produce, because as Table 1-4 shows, corresponding to any of the points on the frontier is a given number of workers in each industry. It is not possible at this stage to show *for whom* society produces using only the production possibility frontier.

Now, how does society decide where on the frontier to produce? One possibility is that the government decides. For instance, in Figure 1-5 we show a production possibility frontier where the two goods are private goods (lawn mowers, cars, vacations) and social services (police protection, education, street sweeping). Society decides what combinations of outputs of private goods and social services to produce through the political process. A country such as Sweden (refer back to Table 1-3) would choose to be at a point such as B. Here the output of social services is high and that of private goods low. A country

FIGURE 1-5 SOCIETY'S CHOICE BETWEEN SOCIAL SERVICES AND PRIVATE GOODS. This production possibility frontier shows the choices society faces between social services and private goods. A choice is made through the political process. A big-government country such as Sweden chooses a point such as B, with a lot of social services and few private goods. A country such as Japan chooses a point such as D, where the output of private goods is large and that of social services small.

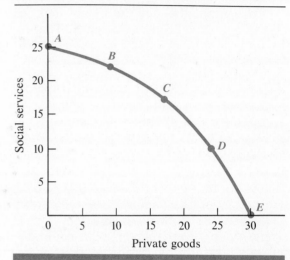

such as Japan would choose to be at a point such as D. Here the output of social services is low and that of private goods high. The choice is made through the political process.

That is one way of allocating resources. But in most economies, *markets* play the major role in determining what gets produced, how, and for whom.

3   THE ROLE OF THE MARKET

In countries outside the Soviet bloc and China the market plays a central role in allocating resources among competing uses. We can think of markets as particular places where some people bring goods to sell and others come to buy—for example, the produce markets in many cities. Or we can think of a market such as the stock market, where people call on the telephone to buy and sell stocks. The particular organization of each market varies. But we do not need to go into these details. We use instead a general definition of a market that fits those cases and others.

> *The market* is a shorthand expression for the process by which households' decisions about the consumption of alternative goods, firms' decisions on what and how to produce, and workers' decisions on how much and for whom to work are all reconciled by adjustments of prices.

Prices of goods and of resources such as labor, machines, and land adjust to ensure that the limited supplies of resources are used to produce those goods and services that society demands.

Much of economics is devoted to studying how markets and prices enable society to solve the basic what, how, and for whom problems. We do not go into the question in any detail until Chapter 3. But in the meantime you can get a feeling for how markets and prices work by thinking about any of your typical daily purchases. For example, suppose that you buy a hamburger for lunch at a fast-food restaurant. What do the market and prices have to do with that?

There is first your side of the deal. You chose that restaurant because it was convenient and fast and because the price was low. Given your desire to eat and your limited resources, the low price of a hamburger told you this was a good way to satisfy your appetite. Probably you prefer steak, but that has a higher price. The price is high enough to ensure that society answers the for whom question about lunchtime steaks in favor of someone else.

Then there is the seller's side. The restaurant owner is in the business because given the price of hamburger meat, the rent, and the wages he has to pay, he can sell the hamburgers for a price that is high enough to produce a profit. If the rent were much

higher, he could not operate a hamburger restaurant in this place. He might want to be in the same business somewhere else or maybe in some other business. As it is, though, the prices at which he can sell his product and buy the resources he needs to produce hamburgers are at levels that lead him to put his money into this business.

The student behind the counter is working there because the wage he receives is the best wage he can get for the type of part-time work he wants.[4] The best wage he can get is still pretty low because there are many people who want this type of job. If the wage were much lower, though, he would probably look for a different job. Or perhaps he might stop working altogether and try to borrow money to pay his way through college.

Prices are guiding your decision to buy a hamburger, the owner's decision to sell hamburgers, and the counter help's decision to take the job. Society is allocating resources—the meat, the building, the labor—into the production of hamburgers through the price system. If no one liked hamburgers, they couldn't be sold at a price that covered costs, the owner of the restaurant wouldn't be in the hamburger-selling business, and society wouldn't be devoting any resources to hamburger production. It is people's desire to eat hamburgers that guides resources into hamburger production. If the price of beef rose very high, the price of hamburgers would increase, and people would begin to eat more tuna fish sandwiches. Thus we get some idea of how prices enable society to allocate resources.

What about markets? Our definition is a very general one, emphasizing the role of prices in allocating resources. There were several markets involved in your purchase

---

[4] Throughout the book we refer to individuals as "he." This is done for brevity. It's easier to say "the consumer . . . he . . . his" than "the consumer . . . he or she . . . his or hers."

of a hamburger. You and the restaurant owner were in the market for fast foods. The student behind the counter is part of the local labor market. The restaurant owner is also a buyer in the local wholesale meat market and in the local rental market for buildings. But this type of description of a market is not precise. For instance, you could have been described as in the market for prepared foods, because you might have thought of buying yogurt at the supermarket as an alternative to buying a hamburger. The notion of prices adjusting to allocate resources is the main idea.

The Command Economy

The role of the market is highlighted if we ask how resources would be allocated in the absence of markets. Here we are considering a command economy.

A *command economy* is a society where the government makes all the decisions about production and consumption. A government planning office decides what will be produced, how, and for whom and instruct workers and firms about what they are to produce.

Such planning is an incredibly complicated task, and there is no complete command economy where all allocations are done by orders. But there is a large dose of central direction and planning in communist countries, where the state owns factories and land and makes many of the decisions about what people should consume and how much they should work.

To appreciate the immensity of the task of central planning, you might think about how you would begin to run the city in which you live by command. Think of the food, clothing, and housing allocations you would have to make to everyone, and then wonder how you would know who should get what and how to produce it. Of course, those decisions are now being made, but chiefly by the market.

The Invisible Hand

Markets in which governments do not intervene are called *free markets*.

Individuals in free markets pursue their own interests, trying to do as well for themselves as they can without government interference. The idea that such a system could work well to solve the what, how, and for whom problems is one of the oldest themes of economics. The most important statement is that of Adam Smith, the famous Scottish philosopher-economist, whose book *The Wealth of Nations* (1776) remains a classic in free-market economics. Smith argued that individuals pursuing their self-interest are led "as by an invisible hand" to do things that are in the interests of others and society as a whole.

How does this work? Suppose that you wish to become a millionaire. This is a goal that appears entirely in your self-interest. To achieve this goal you discover a new way to produce a good that improves the lives of all those who use it. (Think of TV, the Model T Ford, and hand calculators.) Not only do you contribute to the well-being of society, but you make society better off by creating jobs and opportunities. You move society's production possibility schedule outward and become a millionaire in the process.

Smith theorized that a group of individuals, each pursuing his self-interest *without central direction,* could produce a coherent society rather than a jungle. This unguided action was described as the invisible hand.

Smith's insight was remarkable. Modern economists have analyzed the conditions under which the invisible hand works well and also those where it does not.

The Mixed Economy

The free market and the command economy are two completely opposed means for resolving the basic economic questions. The free market leaves complete freedom to the individual household or firm to pursue its self-interest. It is assumed not to use force to interfere with other people's rights, and it is limited by the resources, however large or small, it has. In a command economy the room for personal freedom and economic freedom is small, and these freedoms are often deliberately suppressed.

There is an intermediate regime, the mixed economy.

In a *mixed economy* the government and the private sector interact in solving the basic economic questions. The government controls a significant share of output through taxation, redistributes income, and regulates the extent to which individuals may pursue their self-interest.

In a mixed economy the government may well be a producer of private goods, such as steel, or banking services, or automobiles.

Most countries have a mixed economy. Some are nearer the command economy, and some are nearer the free-market end of the line. Figure 1-6 gives examples. The Soviet bloc is near the command economy end, while the United States is on the free-market side. But the absolute extremes—complete direction from the center with no freedom to choose jobs or goods in the command economy and complete freedom and lack of government interference in free-market economies—do not exist. The Soviet-bloc economies let consumers choose some of the goods they buy and allow private agricultural markets to some extent. Some of those economies, such as Hungary, have been experimenting with a much greater use of markets. And the role of government in the major industrial economies has already been described above. Governments in those economies typically take well over a quarter of total production in taxes to spend on goods and services and to make transfers.

FIGURE 1-6 DEGREES OF MARKET ORIENTATION. The role of the market in allocating resources differs vastly between countries. At one extreme there is the free-market economy, with virtually no government intervention in production, consumption, and the exchange of goods. At the other extreme is the command economy, where government decisions and planning replace private choice and the market. In the center sits the mixed economy, where market forces play a large role but where the government intervenes extensively. The countries listed on the line are there as examples. There is no scientific way of deciding exactly where they should fit. For instance, it is arguable that Yugoslavia has more of a free-market orientation than Sweden.

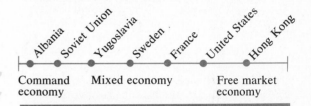

Command economy   Mixed economy   Free market economy

Although it is widely accepted in the major industrial countries that there is bound to be government intervention in the economy and that some government action is necessary, the extent of that intervention remains a live issue. Enthusiasm for the free market is strong. The following quote from President Reagan's 1982 *Economic Report* is fully in the tradition of Adam Smith.[5]

Political freedom and economic freedom are closely related. Any comparison among contemporary nations or examination of the historical record demonstrates two important relationships between the nature of the political system and the nature of the economic system:

All nations which have broad-based representative government and civil liberties have most of their economic activity organized by the market.

Economic conditions in market economies are generally superior to those in nations (with a comparable culture and a comparable resource base) in which the

[5] *Economic Report of the President,* 1982, p. 27.

government has the dominant economic role.

The evidence is striking. No nation in which the government has the dominant economic role . . . has maintained broad political freedom; economic conditions in such countries are generally inferior to those in comparable nations with a predominantly market economy. Voluntary migration, sometimes at high personal cost, is uniformly to nations with both more political freedom and more economic freedom.

The reasons for these two relationships between political and economic systems are simple but not widely understood. Everyone would prefer higher prices for goods sold and lower prices for goods bought. Since the farmer's wheat is the consumer's bread, however, both parties cannot achieve all they want. The most fundamental difference among economic systems is how these conflicting preferences are resolved.

A market system resolves these conflicts by allowing the seller to get the highest price at which others will buy and the buyer to get the lowest price at which others will sell, by consensual exchanges that are expected to benefit both parties.

Much of this book studies the workings of the market and shows how markets solve the what, how, and for whom questions of society. But it also discusses situations where free markets do not work well and where there is a case for government intervention. Most economists in the United States tend to favor the free market, but there are also areas where many of them will call for government to play a role.

4 POSITIVE AND NORMATIVE ECONOMICS

Economics is, in the first place, a science that explains how society makes decisions about consumption, production, and the exchange of goods. To make the explanation possible, a body of knowledge is developed that helps predict how firms, households, and markets respond to changes in conditions, such as OPEC's change in the price of oil in 1973.

In explaining how the economy works we do positive economics.

Positive economics deals with objective or scientific explanations of the workings of an economy.

Positive economics is distinguished from normative economics.

Normative economics offers prescriptions for an economy based on personal value judgments.

The distinction between positive and normative economics is important to keep in mind whenever you read or do economics. In positive economics we are detached scientists. Any one of us, of whatever political persuasion, would look at a set of facts and would probably offer the same evaluation of the observed phenomenon. Positive economics deals with statements such as if . . . then, just as we have them in physics or geology.

Here are some examples of positive economics in action. An economist, any economist, will predict that if the government imposes a tax on a good, the price of that good will rise. Thus if the government were to impose a tax on liquor and on cigarettes, the prices of those goods would rise. An economist will also predict, to give another example, that superb weather conditions, producing a bumper crop of wheat, will lead to both a fall in the price of wheat and a fall in farmers' incomes, as we shall see later. Any economist will predict substantially the same outcomes for a very large range of questions because there is little professional disagreement over a large range of issues.

Of course, just as in any other science, there are unresolved questions where some disagreement remains. The disagreements are at the frontiers of economics. Active research is under way with the aim of narrowing the disagreements, and it is quite likely that there will eventually be agreement on these issues. But at the same time new issues will come up, and there will always be something to disagree about and to study at the frontiers of the field.

All this is quite different from normative economics. Here the economist makes prescriptions for the economy on the basis of his own value judgments, not on the basis of objective scientific grounds. An example of a statement an economist might make that is a mixture of positive and normative economics is this: "The medical expenses of the elderly are very high compared with the medical expenses of the rest of the population; therefore, the government should pay the medical expenses of the elderly." The first part of the statement—the fact about the medical expenses of the elderly—is a positive economics statement; it is true. The second part, about what the government should do, is not a scientifically established fact. It is a value judgment based on the feelings of the person making it about society's obligations.

Other examples of normative statements are the recommendation to establish income tax systems that take relatively more from the rich than from the poor, recommendations to subsidize the high price of gasoline to avoid a large burden on the poor, and recommendations to cut taxes on the rich to achieve faster economic growth. In each instance the economist looks at a particular goal that he favors on the basis of personal preferences (equality, growth, freedom) and recommends a particular policy.

Much of everyday economics is normative. Most economists have views on how society should function, and they make no secret of them in recommending policies. But this *advocacy role* of the economist as a private, involved, informed citizen should

be kept apart from the scientific role of evaluating how the economy works. In practice it is hard to keep the two apart—not because we cannot see the difference between explaining a fact or an if-then relationship and explaining a value judgment, but because any discussion of economics involves an evaluation of facts, and facts, very often, are open to more than one interpretation. By that time our own preferences may easily come to influence our perception of how the economy actually works.

There is no avoiding some overlap between positive and normative economics. The boundaries are not sharply drawn, and when the issues are important, boundaries become all the more blurred. But it is important to know the distinction and to check, at least in others, when it is that they practice positive economics and where normative economics starts.

5 MICROECONOMICS AND MACROECONOMICS

There are many kinds of economics: labor economics, monetary economics, urban economics, Soviet economics, energy economics, defense economics, development economics, and international economics. In each area general principles of economics are applied to particular segments of economic life. Despite all the special areas, nearly all economic issues fall into two broad groups: *micro*economics and *macro*economics.

In microeconomics we study the economic behavior of individual economic agents—households, firms, perhaps cities or clubs—and of *particular* markets or industries. In microeconomics we focus on the *relative* prices of particular goods and services and the relative levels of production of particular goods and services. In microeconomics we study why a gallon of gasoline costs less than a gallon of milk but more than a gallon of water. What is the effect of rent controls on the supply of housing? Does a labor union have the ability to raise the wages of its members in relation to those of nonmembers? These are typical questions of microeconomics, with the focus invariably being the relative price or relative availability of a particular good or service.

In macroeconomics we look at economywide problems. Whereas in microeconomics we look at a specific market, such as that for oil or hamburgers, in macroeconomics we consider problems that apply to the economy as a whole. Some macroeconomic concepts are used so frequently that it is worthwhile defining them here and thus giving some idea of the scope of macroeconomics (or macro).

Gross national product (GNP) is the value of all the goods and services produced in the economy in a given period. GNP is the basic measure of the economy's total output of goods and services. When the total output of goods and services in the economy goes up, GNP signals the increase.

The *aggregate price level* is a measure of the average level of the prices of goods and services in the economy in relation to their levels at some given base date.

The aggregate price level thus tells us whether prices are, on the average, rising or falling. Of course, the prices of some goods will be falling, the prices of other goods will be rising, and the prices of still other goods will be rising even more, but the aggregate price level gives us an idea of how prices are changing on the average.

Inflation and Unemployment The economy experiences *inflation* when the aggregate price level is rising. Occasionally the economy experiences *deflation*, when the aggregate price level is falling.

The third major macroeconomic concept is unemployment.

The *unemployment rate* is the percentage of the individuals in the labor force who would like to find work but cannot. When times are bad, the unemployment rate is high. People want work but cannot find it. That is a macroeconomic problem. It is one of the central issues: Why is there unemployment, and what, if anything, can be done about it through government policy?

Inflation is the other major macroeconomic problem. Prices in most industrial economies rose over the past 20 years, despite repeated declarations by governments that they wanted to stop the inflation, and despite the fact that the public was very upset about inflation. Why has inflation persisted, and what, if anything, can be done about it through government policy?

There is obviously a difference in focus between microeconomics, studying particular markets, and macroeconomics, studying the behavior of the economy as a whole. But these are not really different brands of economics. The same concepts and the same basic ideas appear in both micro and macro, and understanding one helps in understanding the other.

SUMMARY

1   Economics is the study of what gets produced, how, and for whom. The central economic problem is how to reconcile the conflict between people's virtually unlimited demands and society's limited ability to produce goods and services to fulfill those demands.

2   The production possibility frontier shows the maximum amount of one good that can be produced for each given level of output of the other good. The frontier shows the trade-offs that society has to make in deciding what goods to produce. It also illustrates the central problem of scarcity, because points outside the frontier are unattainable. It is inefficient for society to produce within the production possibility frontier, since it can have more of at least one good by moving to the frontier from any point within it.

3   Modern industrial economies rely extensively on markets to allocate resources. The market is the process by which firms' and households' decisions about what they want to produce and consume are coordinated through the adjustment of prices. The role of prices is central to this definition.

4   In the command economy, decisions on what to produce, how, and for whom are made by a central planning bureau. There is no economy that relies entirely on command, but there is extensive planning in some Soviet-bloc economies.

5   A free-market economy is an economy in which there is no government intervention. Resources are allocated entirely through markets, in which individuals pursue their own interests. Adam Smith argued in *The Wealth of Nations* that individuals pursuing their own interests in free markets are led by an invisible hand to reach a good allocation of resources.

6   Modern economies in the western world are mixed, relying mainly on the market, but with a large dose of government intervention. The extent to which the government should intervene in the economy is a matter of ongoing controversy.

7   Positive economics is the study of the way the economy behaves. Normative economics makes prescriptions about what should be done. The two should be kept separate as far as possible. All economists should eventually be able to agree on positive economics questions. Normative economics involves value judgments, and there is no reason why economists should necessarily agree about normative economics statements.

8   Microeconomics is the study of the workings of particular markets in the economy and the relative prices of goods and resources. It deals with questions such as why one good is more expensive than another. Macroeconomics is the study of problems at the level of the entire economy. Major macroeconomic concepts are GNP (the value of total production), the aggregate price level (and the inflation rate), and the unemployment rate.

KEY TERMS

Scarce resource	Free market
Income distribution	Mixed economy
Transfer payment	Positive economics
Law of diminishing returns	Normative economics
Trade-off of goods and services	Microeconomics
Production possibility frontier (schedule)	Macroeconomics
Efficient production	Gross national product (GNP)
Command economy	Inflation
Invisible hand of Adam Smith	Unemployment

PROBLEMS

1 (*a*) Suppose you lived by yourself on an island. Which of the economic problems would you not have to solve? (*b*) Do you think that people have virtually unlimited wants, or do you think that one day we will be producing so much that people will then all have as much as they want of everything? (*c*) Why is there no economic problem when people already have everything they want?

2 How are the what, how, and for whom problems settled within an individual family?

3 There are five workers in the economy. A worker can make either four cakes or three shirts per day. Each worker makes the same number of shirts or cakes no matter how many others are in the industry. (*a*) Draw society's production possibility frontier. (You should start by setting up a table like Table 1-4.) (*b*) How much cake could society consume if it was willing to do without shirts? (*c*) Indicate which points on your diagram represent inefficient methods of production. (*d*) Explain why points outside the frontier are unattainable.

4 Suppose that a new method of producing shirts is invented. Now one worker can make five shirts per day. There has been no improvement in the making of cakes. (*a*) Show society's new production possibility frontier. (*b*) How does it relate to the old frontier? (*c*) Can you guess what will happen to society's choice of what to produce? (You can only guess because there's no way of telling for sure at this stage.)

5 We say that there's no free lunch. But when society is producing inefficiently, it can get more of all goods. In that sense there is a free lunch; nothing is lost by producing one more lunch. Is there any sense to the no-free-lunch statement? Explain.

6 In 1981 oil prices fell for a time, after the huge rise from 1978 to 1980. Describe three responses to the oil-price fall that you either know about or can imagine.

7 Soviet-bloc economies rely on prices to allocate production among different consumers. Goods are put into the stores, and the prices are set by the planners, but then anyone can buy, so long as the goods are available. Why don't the planners go all the way and allocate the goods to particular people?

8 Describe how the invisible hand works when people decide they want to work and go out looking for a job. How does a free market respond when there are more people looking for jobs? (Think of the wages that a firm pays to workers, new and old.)

9 Which of the following is positive, and

which is normative? Explain. (*a*) The rate of inflation has fallen to close to zero. (*b*) The rate of inflation has fallen to close to zero, and it's time to get the economy moving again. (*c*) The level of income is higher in the United States than in the Soviet Union. (*d*) Americans are happier than Russians. (*e*) Because people should not drink, we should tax liquor more. (*f*) If we tax liquor more, we will reduce the amount of drinking in society.

10 Explain whether the following are statements about macroeconomics or microeconomics. (*a*) The inflation rate has fallen again. (*b*) Because the inflation rate has fallen, it's time to get the economy moving again. (*c*) The price of food is down this month. (*d*) Farmers' plantings of wheat are high, and the weather looks good; therefore, there should be a large harvest. (*e*) Unemployment in Michigan is high in relation to the level in the rest of the country. (*f*) The oil-price shock in 1973–1974 caused a great deal of both inflation and unemployment in the United States.

The aim of economics is to understand how the economy works. In Chapter 1 we described three major economic issues: the effects of oil-price increases, the distribution of income, and the role of government. Economists analyze these issues for two reasons. The first reason is to understand why particular economic relationships exist. For instance, we want to understand how oil-price increases affect the economy, what determines the distribution of income, and what roles government plays in economic life.

2

The Tools Economists Use

The second reason for analyzing these issues is that society may want to do something about them. Perhaps we want motorists to use less gasoline or want the middle class to get a larger share of income. Perhaps we want to reduce the size of government. The first step here, too, is to understand how these economic variables—the amount of gasoline used, the distribution of income, and the size of government—are determined. Then we will be better able to predict the effects of actions such as reducing income taxes or taxing gasoline.

To analyze economic issues we use both models and data.

A *model* is a simplified description of reality.

Models, which we discuss in more detail later in this chapter, are frameworks for organizing thinking about a problem. They simplify by leaving out some details of the real world in order to concentrate on the essentials. From this simplified picture of reality we develop our analysis of how the real world works.

The data, or facts, interact with models in two ways. First, the data themselves sometimes suggest relationships among variables. For instance, in this chapter we will see that people with more education on average have higher incomes. A model is needed to provide a framework in which to think systematically about that relationship. Second, once the economist has built a model, the data are useful for measuring the different relationships suggested by the model. Many interpretations are possible, and data are needed to sort out the significant relationships from the less important ones.

In this chapter we introduce the tools economists use. The emphasis is not on learning economics but on gaining mastery of some of the tools of the trade. We start with economic data and the way they are shown in tables, charts, and diagrams. Then we show how data and models are used in practice. We do this by describing the approach an economist takes to a specific problem. We show how to build a simple model, how to gather data and evidence, and how to test a theory.

By the end of this chapter you should be familiar with and able to use figures and diagrams as a matter of routine. Indeed, after reading Chapter 1, you have already started using these tools. Because total familiarity comes only with practice, you may find it useful to come back to this chapter as you study later material, to refresh your understanding of the basic tools as you begin to apply them.

1 ECONOMIC DATA

For the present we set aside the interaction of models and data to focus entirely on data —the facts. We want to know where data come from, how to read the tables or figures in which data are reported, and how to organize data as a first step in analyzing a problem in economics.

Where Do Data Come From?

There are many tables and figures in this book with data from different sources. Anyone presenting data has to explain where they come from, and you will find the sources of our data listed with each table or figure. Typically the source is a government publication, which in turn collects the data from government sources, such as the Bureau of Labor Statistics, or from private sources, such as the American Newspaper Publishers Association.

There are two very useful basic refer-

ence books for finding data. *The Statistical Abstract of the United States*, published each year by the U.S. Department of Commerce, contains an extraordinary range of facts. It is the first place to which economists turn. Even if it does not have the facts we are looking for, it usually points to where they can be found. The second source is the *Economic Report of the President*, published each year by the White House. It contains many macroeconomic data, often going back as far as 50 years.

Tables and Charts

Suppose you are interested in the price of silver, perhaps because you are thinking of buying some silver in the hope that its price will go up rapidly or perhaps just because you're curious. As a first step you want to find out what the price of silver has been in the recent past.

Data on the price of silver are contained in the *International Financial Statistics*, published by the International Monetary Fund in Washington, D.C. Data on silver prices in the second half of 1981 are shown in Table 2-1. First, the title of the table gives us the general facts that are reported. The parentheses under the title contain necessary specific information, telling us that prices are quoted in U.S. cents per troy ounce,[1] not in dollars per ton, for example, or in Canadian dollars per kilogram. Without this information we would not really

---

[1] A troy ounce is just less than 1.1 regular (avoirdupois) ounces. Troy ounces are used in measuring precious metals.

TABLE 2-1

THE PRICE OF SILVER IN 1981
(U.S. Cents/Troy Ounce, New York, Monthly Averages)

JULY	AUGUST	SEPTEMBER	OCTOBER	NOVEMBER	DECEMBER
863.1	892.3	1003.6	925.1	854.7	843.2

Source: International Monetary Fund, *International Financial Statistics,* various issues.

know what we are looking at. Thus it is essential to report the details of price and quantity precisely. For some purposes we also want to know whether the quoted price is for silver today in New York or today in Australia. It may make a difference, especially if we are interested in knowing whether prices of a particular good are the same in different places. Finally, the table tells us that the prices are monthly averages. That means each number that is reported is an average of the prices prevailing on different days (and possibly hours) during the month.

Time Series Data

We show the months, July through December, in the headings above the top row of the table and the prices in the row below the headings. In July 1981 the price was 863.1 cents per troy ounce, or $8.631 per troy ounce. In September it was 1003.6 cents per troy ounce, or $10.036 per troy ounce. Thus each entry in the table reports the price in a particular month. The collection of data in the table is called a time series.

> A *time series* is a collection of measurements of a variable at different points or intervals of time.

The time series here shows monthly data, but we also have hourly time series, for example, for the price of stocks on the New York Stock Exchange, and time series of quarterly or annual data. A time series shows how a particular variable, or several different variables, changes over time.

Time series can be represented in tables, such as Table 2-1, or in charts. A chart is simply a diagrammatic representation of a table; it is another way of representing the same information. Figure 2-1 shows the monthly time series of silver prices. The horizontal axis shows time, measured here in months and running from July to December. Equal distances are marked

FIGURE 2-1 THE MONTHLY PRICE OF SILVER, 1981. The figure shows the price of silver in each of the last 6 months of 1981 (U.S. cents/troy ounce, New York, monthly averages). It presents exactly the same information as Table 2-1 but in a form that makes the general pattern of price changes stand out much more easily. The high price in September 1981 is especially noticeable. At the same time, the figure is less precise because it is difficult to see the exact values for the prices in each month. (*Source: International Financial Statistics,* various issues.)

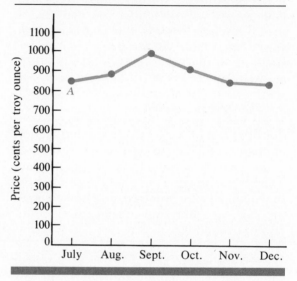

off on the horizontal axis, each of which is labeled with one of the successive months: July, August, and so on.

On the vertical axis we measure the price of silver in U.S. cents per troy ounce. Again we divide the axis, marking off equal distances, each of which represents 100 cents. Thus each mark on the vertical axis shows 100 cents, and we measure price vertically, running from zero to 1100 cents.

Next we *plot* the data from Table 2-1 on Figure 2-1. That means we put points in Figure 2-1 to show the entries from the table. The first point in Table 2-1 is the price of 863.1 cents for July 1981. On the horizontal axis we start at July and, moving up vertically, locate the point corresponding to 863.1 cents on the vertical axis. We mark off the point with a dot, as shown in

Figure 2-1 and labeled point *A*. Point *A* shows graphically that in July 1981 the price of silver was 863.1 cents.

Similarly, we plot the observations for the following months. In each case we locate the month on the horizontal axis and then move up vertically to mark off the price for that month. Then we place a dot at that price. Finally, we connect all the dots and have a chart of a time series of monthly silver prices. The chart, or figure, contains precisely the same information as Table 2-1, but the information is easier to take in at a glance. For instance, Figure 2-1 immediately draws our attention to the high September 1981 price, whereas we have to look more carefully at the table to see that.

Presenting data in the form of charts may be very suggestive, but it also has its dangers. For instance, the eye can be misled by simple changes in the presentation of the data. Consider Figure 2-2, which plots the same monthly price observations for silver as Figure 2-1. The only difference is that on the vertical axis we choose a much larger *scale*. In Figure 2-1, one inch represents 500 cents. In Figure 2-2, one inch represents 125 cents. On this scale the monthly price series seems to show much more movement, and the September price seems to be much more out of line with the other months than it is in Figure 2-1. The figure does contain a warning, though. The gap in the vertical axis warns us that the scale is not continuous and that most of the area between 0 cents and 800 cents has been left out. The effect could have been reinforced even more if we had shrunk the horizontal scale. Note that charts can be manipulated to convey information in very suggestive ways, sometimes to the point of distorting facts. This is well known in advertising and politics.[2]

---

[2] See Darrell Huff and Irving Geis, *How to Lie with Statistics*, W. W. Norton & Company, Inc., New York, 1954.

FIGURE 2-2 THE PRICE OF SILVER IN 1981. The figure contains exactly the same information as Figure 2-1 (U.S. cents/troy ounce, New York, monthly averages). However, the vertical scale is increased. The price now seems to vary much more than it does in Figure 2-1. (*Source: International Financial Statistics,* various issues.)

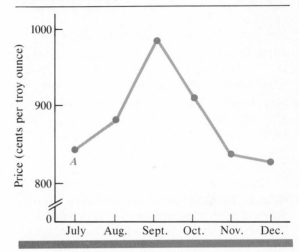

Some data are collected very frequently. For example, silver prices are available on a daily or even hourly basis. But for many purposes the hourly or daily data contain too much detail. We therefore might prefer to look at averages of prices over weeks or even months. Table 2-1 shows a monthly average of daily prices. But even that may contain too much information if we are interested in longer time periods such as quarters, years, decades, or centuries. To show how data for longer periods are calculated, Table 2-2 presents quarterly data for 1981. The quarters of the year are of course the four 3-month periods, starting January–March and ending October–December.

Table 2-2 again shows silver prices, except that we are now looking at quarterly and annual averages. For the third (July–September) and fourth (October–December) quarters, the data in Tables 2-1 and 2-2 overlap. Consider the last 3 months, or the fourth quarter of 1981, in Table 2-1. The

TABLE 2-2

THE PRICE OF SILVER IN 1981
(U.S. Cents/Troy Ounce, New York, Quarterly Averages)

ANNUAL AVERAGE, 1981	QUARTERLY AVERAGE			
	I	II	III	IV
1052.1	1338.2	1076.2	919.7	874.3

Source: International Monetary Fund, *International Financial Statistics.*

prices there are 925.1 cents, 854.7 cents, and 843.2 cents, respectively. The average of these three values is 874.3 cents = [(925.1 + 854.7 + 843.2)/3]. Thus 874.3 cents is the quarterly average of silver prices in the fourth quarter of 1981. The data reported for the other quarters are calculated in the same manner. Table 2-2 also shows the annual average. This is calculated as the average of the four quarterly data: 1052.1 cents = [(1338.2 + 1076.2 + 919.6 + 874.3)/4].

Because it is an average of the quarterly data, the annual average lies between the highs and lows of the four quarters. The same point can be seen by comparing the quarterly average with the underlying monthly observations. The longer the period (minutes, days, months, quarters, years) over which we average, the more the short-term fluctuations are smoothed out.

Whether we want to look at annual averages or data for shorter periods of time in selecting our time series depends on the problem at hand. If we want to get some idea of how much the price can change within a week, it of course does not make sense to use long-term averages. Annual data conceal week-to-week fluctuations of prices. But annual averages are useful if we want to look at long-term trends in silver prices, say, over 50 years.

Cross Section Data

Time series data allow the economist to measure the same variable (say, the price of silver) at different points in time. But the economist also uses cross section data.

Cross section data are measurements of a given variable for different economic units.

For example, cross section data might be wage rates in different industries. Or we might look at spending by households of different income levels or at income levels in different countries. The data in a cross section all relate to the same moment of time but apply to different economic units: industries, firms, households, or countries, for example.

Table 2-3 shows typical cross section data. Here we look at average wages in different industries. Table 2-3 is useful for a study of wage differences across sectors. For example, after examining the data, you might ask why the pay is nearly twice as high in construction as it is in wholesale and retail trade. When we study wage differentials in later chapters about the labor market, we will use tables such as Table 2-3 as our basic facts and starting point.

Another example of cross section data is given in Table 2-4. Here we look at income levels organized by years of education. The table shows how differences in the level of education affect income. As you might expect, men (and also women, though that is not shown in the table) with higher education levels earn higher incomes. Before we discuss the table, though, we have to define the term "median income."

The Mean and the Median   The median of any set of data is the point in the middle when the data are organized by size. The difference between the median and the mean or average can be understood most easily through an example. Suppose in the group of people with less than 8 years of schooling there are three people with incomes of 2.8, 5.6, and 111.0 (thousands of

TABLE 2-3

HOURLY EARNINGS BY INDUSTRY
(Dollars/Hour, December 1981)

SECTOR	WAGE
Mining	10.42
Construction	11.16
Manufacturing	8.26
Transportation and public utilities	10.08
Wholesale and retail trade	6.00
Financial and real estate	6.48
Services	6.66

Source: Survey of Current Business, January 1982.

TABLE 2-4

**EDUCATIONAL ATTAINMENT AND INCOME,
MEN, 1979**

EDUCATIONAL ATTAINMENT, years completed	MEDIAN ANNUAL INCOME, $000
Elementary school:	
Less than 8	5.9
9	7.9
High school:	
1–3	9.1
4	13.3
College:	
1–3	13.9
4	19.1
5 or more	22.8

Source: Statistical Abstract of the United States, 1981,
Table 236.

dollars), respectively. Average income of the three people is $39.8 = [(2.8 + 5.6 + 111.0)/3]$. The average is strongly influenced by the one exceptionally high income.

Median income, by contrast, is the point in the middle, namely, 5.6. We present the median of income or any other variable rather than the average when we want to show a typical situation and when it is possible that some extreme data will distort the statistics.

To verify your understanding of the difference, suppose incomes were 3.1, 4.8, 9.2, 12.2, and 56.9. What are the mean and median income levels, respectively? (One an-

swer is 9.2, and the other is 17.24. Which is which?) Returning to the table, we read a cross section table like a time series table. The heading identifies the general subject and gives details of the units in which the data in the table are measured. Within Table 2.4, the first column gives years of schooling completed rather than the calendar year as in a time series table. The action in this table is in the second column, which gives the income level for each category of years of school completed. For example, the median income in 1979 for a man with 1 to 3 years of high school was $9,100, whereas men with 5 or more years of college had a median income of $22,800.

Information like this is used in studies that attempt to explain differences in income among people. We look at such data in studying discrimination and the economic benefits of education in Chapter 14.

2   INDEX NUMBERS

In economics we often want to compare data without emphasizing the precise units in which they are measured. Returning to silver, we might want to know whether the price of silver has increased over time more or less rapidly than the price of another metal, say, copper. Such a comparison is most conveniently made by calculating an index number rather than by looking at the dollar prices.

An *index number* expresses data relative to a given base value.

This definition will become clear from an example.

Table 2-5 shows the annual average prices of silver and copper for selected years. From the price data it is immediately clear that the prices of both metals have risen over time. But which has risen more? An easy way to make such a comparison is to express the price in each year as a multiple of a common base year price. Suppose we

TABLE 2-5

PRICES OF SILVER AND COPPER
(Silver in Cents/Troy Ounce, New York; Copper in Cents/Pound, U.S. Refining Price, Annual Averages)

	1960	1970	1980
Silver:			
¢/troy ounce	91.40	177.10	2057.79
index 1960 = 100	100.0	193.76	2251.41
Copper:			
¢/pound	32.05	57.70	101.40
index 1960 = 100	100.0	180.03	316.38

Source: International Monetary Fund, *International Financial Statistics,* 1981 Yearbook, pp. 78–81.

select 1960 as the base year and assign a value of 100 to each index in the base year. Thus for both copper and silver we show the price index in 1960 to be 100.

Consider next 1970. What are the values of the indices for silver and copper in that year? The silver price is 177.10 cents, which is a multiple (177.10/91.40 = 1.9376) of the 1960 price. With the index set at 100 in 1960, it is equal to 1.9376 times the base year index of 100 in 1970, or (1.9376 × 100) = 193.76. Our entry for the silver price index in 1970 therefore is 193.76, as shown in Table 2-5. In the same way we calculate the 1980 value of the index. Again we divide the 1980 price by the base year price (91.40 cents) and multiply by 100 to obtain (2057.79/91.40) × 100 = 2251.41 as the 1980 value of the price index for silver. The price index for copper is calculated exactly the same way; we express each year's price as a multiple of the base year (1960) price and multiply by 100.[3]

What information do we obtain from a price index that we do not readily get from

---

[3] To check your understanding of index numbers, figure out the value of the indices in 1981, given the following data and using 1960 as the base year. Silver's 1981 average price was 1052.10 cents per troy, and copper's was 84.02 cents per pound. (Answers are 1151.09 and 262.15. Be sure you know how to get them.)

the price data themselves? Why go to the trouble of calculating an index? One use of an index is to provide a convenient comparison of changes in different series, say, copper and silver. Comparing the price indices in Table 2-5, we see that the price of silver increased much more than that of copper. The index for silver rose from 100 to more than 2000, while the index for copper increased only from 100 to somewhat more than 300. The same information can be discovered from the original price data, but not as quickly and conveniently.

Like time series data, index numbers can be plotted on a graph to present information in a more eye-catching way. Figure 2-3 shows annual price indices of silver and copper over the period 1960–1981. The base year is again 1960. Figure 2-3, like the data presented in Table 2-5, shows that silver prices increased much faster than copper prices over the period; it draws attention immediately to the strikingly different behavior of the two indices during the years 1979–1981. A figure like this is much better for depicting any unusual behavior of variables than a table containing the same information in written form.

Index Numbers as Price Averages

A more important use of index numbers is to describe the behavior of several different economic variables in terms of a single summary number. For instance, instead of being interested in the price of silver or the price of copper, we might want to know how the prices of metals have changed over time.

To talk about the prices of all metals, we must express the behavior of *all* metal prices in terms of a *single* number. But as we can see from copper and silver prices, metal prices do not all change the same way. Some prices go up, some go up more, and others may fall in any given year. How can we get a single number to describe the behavior of all metal prices? The only way

FIGURE 2-3 INDICES OF THE PRICES OF SILVER AND COPPER, 1960–1981 (1960 = 100). The two curves show price indices for silver and copper, using annual average data. The price of copper was rising over the period, with some periods of decline. The silver price reached an extraordinarily high level in 1980. The changes in the price of silver from 1979 to 1981 stand out very clearly in this figure. (*Source: International Financial Statistics,* 1981 Yearbook.)

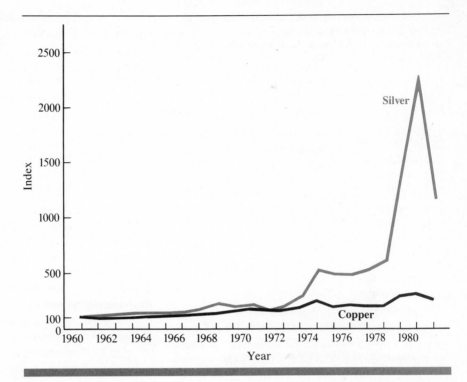

is to ask how the prices of metals have behaved *on average.*

We have to build an index number that describes the behavior of several variables. For simplicity we stay with the example of copper and silver, and we refer to them as "metals." Our aim is to construct an index that represents the behavior of the prices of metals. We therefore have to make a *single* series out of the *two* series in Table 2-5. This is done by giving the price index for each metal a share, or weight, in a price index for metals as a whole. Normally the weight to be given is suggested by the purpose for which the index is being made. For example, the weights may be the shares of copper and silver in the value of the total use of the metals in industry. We assume that silver has a weight of 0.2 and copper a weight, or share, of 0.8, reflecting the more important industrial role of copper.

Now we calculate how the price of a basket of the two metals—80 percent by

value of copper and 20 percent by value of silver—changed. The answer is provided by forming an index that is the *weighted* sum of the two indices in Table 2-5, as shown in Table 2-6.

We start with the base year, 1960. The value of the metals index is $(0.2 \times 100) + (0.8 \times 100) = 100$. Thus the basket, too, has a base year value of 100. For 1970 we repeat the calculation, which gives us the following number for the index: $(0.2 \times 193.76) +$

TABLE 2-6

PRICE INDICES FOR SILVER, COPPER, AND METALS
(1960 = 100, Silver Share = 0.2, Copper Share = 0.8)

	1960	1970	1980
Silver	100.0	193.76	2251.41
Copper	100.0	180.03	316.38
Metals index	100.0	182.78	703.39

Source: Calculated from data in Table 2-5.

$(0.8 \times 180.03) = 182.78$. Thus the price index for metals in 1970 is 182.78.

Note that this is a weighted average of the indices of silver and copper prices, respectively, and therefore lies between the two. The relative weights (0.8 for copper and 0.2 for silver) determine the extent to which the index for metals more nearly reflects copper or silver prices. In our example copper has a much larger share, which is most striking in 1980. Here the value of the index for metals is 703.39. It includes the very high price of silver to some extent, but not as much as would be the case if silver had a larger share and copper a smaller share in the index.

The Consumer Price Index

The use of indices to represent the behavior of a group of prices is very common. Probably the most famous price index is the *consumer price index* (CPI). The CPI is announced monthly and is watched closely by the news media. It is an index number of the prices of goods that households consume, including everything from food and housing to entertainment and medical care. Currently, it includes the prices of 224 different goods and services.

The purpose of the CPI is to measure changes in the cost of living, or the cost of buying the usual basket of goods, for a typical household. As such, the CPI is one of the basic indices used to measure inflation. Recall from Chapter 1 that the inflation rate is the rate at which prices in general increase. Because the CPI measures the cost of a typical basket of goods bought by consumers, it gives us a good idea of how prices of goods in general are changing. We do not want to go into a long discussion of inflation here, but we note that inflation has been one of the major economic problems of the last 20 years in the United States and in most of the noncommunist world. And inflation is nothing other than generally rising prices, a

TABLE 2-7

WEIGHTS IN THE CONSUMER PRICE INDEX

ITEM	WEIGHT (percent)
Food	19.2
Housing	44.3
Apparel and upkeep	5.5
Transportation	17.8
Medical care	5.0
Entertainment	4.0
Other goods and services	4.3

Note: Sum of weights not equal to 100 because of rounding.
Source: Business Statistics, 1979, notes to page 33.

phenomenon with which we are all familiar.

The CPI is formed, like our metal prices index, by first constructing a price index for each component (food, housing, etc.) and then calculating the weighted average of those indices. Table 2-7 shows the weights of the components of the CPI. These weights are equal to the share of the typical household's spending on that group of goods. The weights thus reflect the relative importance of the prices of the different components to the household's cost of living. If the price of food rises by, say, 20 percent, that increases the household's cost of living much more than a 20 percent rise in the price of apparel and upkeep would—because the household spends nearly four times as much on food as on clothing.

There are many goods within each category in Table 2-7. For instance, the food and beverages component of the index is made up by computing indices for the prices of coffee, tea, bread, apples, tomatoes, and so forth, weighting them, and adding them together. That way the index is used to give a picture of how prices on average are changing.

Other Indices

Indices are used to show the behavior of many different groups of variables. For instance, there is an index of wages in manufacturing, which is a weighted average of wages in different industries. Another example is the Dow Jones index, which is a weighted average of prices of different stocks.

Indices are not confined to wages and prices. We can look at the time series of any other type of data, for example, *quantities* such as chicken production in Maine or the number of workdays lost to strikes. In each case we form an index by setting the value of the series at 100 for some base date and expressing other values relative to the base value. Index numbers are routinely constructed and reported to summarize the behavior of data series, and we shall be using them throughout this book.

3 NOMINAL AND REAL VARIABLES

Table 2-8 presents data on hourly earnings in the construction industry. In the first row of the body of the table we give average hourly earnings in the industry. The next row gives the same information in the form of an index with 1960 = 100. Earnings per hour increased fivefold over the period 1950–1980, starting at below $2 and ending very close to $10 per hour.

This looks like a large increase. But it can be very misleading to look at amounts earned in dollars without at the same time asking how much goods those earnings

could buy. The prices of goods, as measured by the CPI, went up rapidly over the period 1950–1980, which is to say there was *inflation* over that period. The $10 per hour earned in 1980 certainly did not buy five times as much in 1980 as in 1950. This is the reason we distinguish between nominal and real earnings.

Hourly earnings measured in dollars are *nominal* earnings. Earnings measured in terms of the goods they buy are *real* earnings.

Real earnings are calculated by adjusting nominal earnings for changes in the amount of goods a dollar will buy, that is, by adjusting for inflation.

The calculated index of real hourly earnings is shown in the last row of Table 2-8. The index of real earnings is obtained by dividing the index of nominal earnings (second row) by the price index (third row) and multiplying by 100. Obviously the index of real earnings is 100 for 1960, when both the nominal earnings index and the CPI are equal to 100. In 1950 the real earnings index is $74.5 = [(60.6/81.3) \times 100]$. By 1970 the index has climbed to 130.2. Thus between 1950 and 1970 real earnings in the construction industry increased. A construction worker could buy more goods in 1970 with the earnings from an hour of work than would have been possible in 1950 with an hour's earnings.

The reason for concentrating on real

TABLE 2-8

NOMINAL AND REAL HOURLY EARNINGS IN THE CONSTRUCTION INDUSTRY
(1960 = 100 for All Indices)

	1950	1960	1970	1980
Hourly earnings, dollars	1.86	3.07	5.24	9.92
Hourly earnings index	60.6	100.0	170.7	323.1
Consumer price index	81.3	100.0	131.1	278.2
Index of real hourly earnings	74.5	100.0	130.2	116.1

Note: Hourly earnings include wages and fringe benefits, such as medical insurance and contributions to pensions made by the firm.
Source: Economic Report of the President, 1982, Tables B-38 and B-52.

earnings becomes clear when we look at the real earnings index for 1980. At 116.1, it is well below the real earnings index for 1970. Construction workers could buy *fewer* goods with their earnings from an hour of work in 1980 than they could in 1970. If we had looked only at the nominal earnings index, which rose from 170.7 to 323.1 over the 10 years from 1970 to 1980, we might have been misled into thinking that the worker was doing very well. In fact, the real earnings index shows that workers' wages fell behind inflation during the seventies. Their wages went up in dollar terms, but prices went up even faster, and the workers' real earnings therefore fell.

The distinction between real and nominal values is widely used and is essential to understanding what is happening in the economy when there is inflation—when prices in general are increasing. For instance, we distinguish between real and nominal incomes, where nominal income is the amount earned in any given period in dollars, and real income is nominal income adjusted for the change in prices. Or we can use the concept of *real* government spending, where nominal (dollar) spending by the government is adjusted for changes in prices.

Real or Relative Prices

The distinction between nominal and real applies not only to incomes or government spending but also to prices. In Tables 2-1 and 2-5 we looked at how the price of silver has changed over time. The price of silver measured in dollars or cents is the *nominal* price of silver, just as earnings or income measured in dollars are nominal values.

We also define the *real* or *relative price* of silver by adjusting the price of silver to account for changes in prices of goods in general. If all prices are going up and the price of silver goes up in the same proportion, the real price, or the price of silver rel-

TABLE 2-9

NOMINAL AND REAL PRICE INDICES FOR SILVER
(1960 = 100)

	1960	1970	1980
Index of nominal silver price	100	193.8	2251.4
Consumer price index	100	131.1	278.2
Index of real silver price	100	147.8	809.3

Source: See Tables 2-5 and 2-8.

ative to the prices of other goods, has not changed.

> A *nominal* price is a price measured in dollars. The *real* price, or *relative* price, is the price measured relative to the prices of other goods.

Table 2-9 illustrates the distinction between nominal and real prices for the case of silver. The indices are all set at 100 for 1960. Then the real price index for silver in 1970 is calculated by dividing the nominal index 193.8 by the CPI and multiplying by 100. The real or relative price index for silver for 1970 is 147.8. A similar calculation is made for 1980.

Why make the distinction between nominal and real prices? For most purposes what matters to purchasers is not prices measured in dollars but rather the price of one good relative to the prices of other goods. If silver prices rise along with all other prices, silver is not more expensive or valuable relative to other goods. Someone who wanted to use silver in industry would not change that decision if silver prices rose along with all other prices. But he might well reconsider the decision if the price of silver increased *relative* to the prices of other goods that could be used in its place.

The adjustment of the price of silver to take account of changes in other prices, as seen in the last row of Table 2-9, does not change the impression that silver prices increased very rapidly over the period 1960–1980. But the increase is much smaller when measured in real or relative terms rather than nominal terms. Nominal silver prices increased by a factor of more than 22. The real price of silver increased by a factor of just over 8, from 100 to 809.3.[4]

The Purchasing Power of Money

The distinction between nominal and real earnings (or nominal and real variables in general) is sometimes made by saying that real earnings are measured in terms of constant purchasing power of money.

> The *purchasing power of money* is an index of the amount of goods that can be bought with a dollar.

When prices of goods rise, the purchasing power of money falls, because a dollar buys fewer goods.

The distinction between real and nominal variables is sometimes made by using the terms *current dollars* and *constant dollars*. If we measure variables in current dollars, we measure them in the dollars of the year when they were earned (in the case of income) or the year when they were in action (in the case of prices). Thus current dollar measures are nominal.

Incomes or prices expressed in *constant* dollars are expressed in *real* terms. A constant dollar income or price expresses a nominal variable from one year by its purchasing power in the base year. Thus we could express, say, hourly earnings in Table 2-8 in 1960 dollars. This translates the nominal hourly earnings for each year to the amount they would have bought in goods in 1960. Take the 1980 nominal hourly earnings of $9.92. How many dollars would it have taken in 1960 to buy as much as $9.92 bought in 1980? Note first that the CPI in 1980 was 278.2, on a base of 1960. That

means it took $2.782 in 1980 to buy as much as $1.00 bought in 1960. Accordingly, $9.92 in 1980 bought only as much as $3.57 (9.92/2.782) would have bought in 1960. We therefore say that hourly earnings in 1980 were $3.57 in terms of 1960 dollars or that constant (1960) dollar earnings in 1980 were $3.57 per hour.

The 1980 hourly earnings of $3.57 in 1960 dollars are compared with actual 1960 dollar hourly earnings of $3.07. Thus 1980 real earnings were higher than 1960 real earnings. Indeed, the ratio of 1980 earnings in 1960 dollars (3.57) to 1960 hourly earnings (3.07) is 1.163. It is no accident that this, except for rounding, is exactly the index of hourly earnings for 1980 seen in Table 2-8. Expressing variables in constant dollars is just another way of expressing them in real terms.

4 MEASURING CHANGES IN ECONOMIC VARIABLES

In Table 2-8 we showed, using an index of real hourly earnings, that real wages increased from 1960 to 1970 but declined from 1970 to 1980. Usually, though, we want to say how much a variable changed rather than indicating only that it went up or down.

Percentage Changes A common measure of the change in a variable such as prices or real earnings is the *percentage* change. This measure is attractive because it does not use any units (pounds, feet, baskets) and therefore is readily comparable to changes in other series. For example, we might compare the percentage change in U.S. population to the percentage change in the production of beef. Such a comparison is normally more informative than a comparison of the absolute increase in population (say, 1.2 million people) with the increase in beef production (say, 55,600 cattle).

Percentage changes in real wages can

---

[4] If you need further practice on these calculations, look at Problem 9 at the end of this chapter.

be calculated from the data in Table 2-8. For instance, we work out the percentage increase from 1950 to 1960. Over that period the index increased from 74.5 to 100.0. The percentage increase is given as

$$\text{Percentage increase in real wage} = \frac{\text{index in 1960} - \text{index in 1950}}{\text{index in 1950}} \times 100$$

$$= \frac{100.0 - 74.5}{74.5} \times 100$$

$$= .342 \times 100\%$$

$$\doteq 34.2\% \tag{1}$$

A similar calculation shows the increase from 1960 to 1970 to be 31.1 percent. Finally, 1980 compared to 1970 gives an increase equal to $[(116.1 - 130.2)/130.2] \times 100$ percent. This is an increase of *minus* 10.8 percent, or a fall of 10.8 percent. Over the entire period 1950–1980, real wages rose by $[(116.1 - 74.5)/74.5] \times 100$ percent, or 55.8 percent.

These percentage changes are good summaries of the behavior of the time series of real wages. They tell us, for instance, that from 1950 to 1970 the purchasing power of wages rose. From 1970 to 1980 there was a decrease. In 1980 the purchasing power of wages was just over 55 percent higher than it had been 30 years before.

Is that a lot? The question cannot be answered without some standard of comparison. One way of comparing would be to look at other countries and compute indices of real wages and long-term percentage increases there. Another would be to look at other periods in U.S. history.

Growth Rates   When we study time series data, it is often useful to look at increases per period of time rather than over long periods such as 10 years or 30 years. Typically we measure the growth rate of a variable per year.

The *growth rate* is the percentage rate per period (typically per year) by which a variable is increasing.

A growth rate is also a percentage change, but it is a percentage change *per period*.

For example, the consumer price index was 272.4 in 1981 and 246.8 in 1980. The growth rate of consumer prices between 1980 and 1981 is given by

$$\text{Growth rate of prices} = \frac{272.4 - 246.8}{246.8} \times 100\%$$

$$= 10.4\%$$

Thus the growth rate of consumer prices between 1980 and 1981 was 10.4 percent. More familiarly, the growth rate of prices is the *inflation rate*.

Similarly, we measure *economic growth* by the rate at which the economy's total production of goods increases. If someone refers without qualification to economic growth, he means the growth rate of total production in the economy. And inflation means the growth rate of prices. "Growth" and "inflation" are the buzzwords that describe two of the significant problems in today's economy. We need to prevent prices from rising rapidly, and we want the economy's rate of production to grow rapidly. Not only that, we want both these things to happen at the same time.

5 MODELS

Now that we have discussed data and methods of presenting them, we give an example of economics in action. Suppose we are interested in the relationship between subway fares in Boston and the revenue that the subway system takes in. Specifically, our question is whether a hike in fares would increase revenue.

To answer that question we have to organize our thinking or, as the economist calls it, build a model. As we noted at the beginning of this chapter, a model is a simplified picture of reality. We turn now to the subway fare and revenue issue and try to organize our thinking. What sort of model do we need? Our aim is to answer the question, Does a rise in fares increase total fare collection? This question makes us view total fare collection as the fare times the number of rides people take.

To emphasize this point, we state it as an equation:

**Total fare
collection = fare × number of rides**   (2)

Equation (2) immediately highlights and helps us organize our thinking about two factors: the fare and the number of rides. The fare is under the control of the Transportation Authority. But the number of rides is not, and indeed, the problem is that the number of rides may change when the Transportation Authority changes the fare.

One view of the number of rides might be that it is determined by habit, convenience, or tradition and is unresponsive to changes in fares. This is *not* the view or model that an economist would adopt. To the economist the choice of means of transport—car or bus versus subway—is in good part an economic decision based on the relative costs and convenience of the alternative means of transport. Changes in the relative costs, the economist would assume, affect the decision to use one or the other. This way of thinking leads us to fill in the "number of rides" in equation (2) with a theory, or model (we use these terms interchangeably), of the number of rides people want to take on subways. This is their *demand* for subway rides.

In later chapters we study the theory of demand in detail. We see there that the quantity demanded of any good (subway rides, food, clothing, or vacations) depends not only on the price of the good in question but also on the prices of other goods as well as on income.

The demand for subway rides will make this clear. First the fare matters. If subway rides were free, *other things equal* (we ex-plain soon what this means), more people would use the subway rather than walk or drive. But if subway rides were extraordinarily expensive—say, $15 each—most people would do without subway rides and choose other means of transport instead. Of course, what matters is the price of subway transportation compared with other means of transport, such as cars, buses, and taxis. These are the prices we capture in the term "other things equal."

We now have the bare bones of a model of demand for subway rides. The quantity of subway rides demanded depends on the fare and on the prices of other means of transport. We summarize this model in a formal statement:

$$\text{Quantity of subway rides demanded} = f(\text{subway fare, taxi fare, gasoline price, } \ldots)$$
(3)

The statement reads as follows: The quantity demanded of subway rides "depends on," or "is a function of," the subway fare, the taxi fare, gasoline prices, and so on. The notation $f(\ )$ is shorthand for the statement "depends on." Inside the parentheses we place all the things that determine the quantity of subway rides demanded. Since we are not concerned here with an exhaustive list, including weather and the cleanliness of the subway cars, we place the dots . . . to stand for all other things not mentioned.

To get anywhere in answering our question, we have to be more specific than to say that the quantity of subway rides demanded depends on various prices. We have to say how the number of rides people want to take depends on those prices. We assume that an *increase* in the subway fare will *reduce* the number of rides people want to take, other things equal. That means an increase in subway fares, holding constant bus fares and gasoline prices, will reduce the quantity of rides demanded.

The model of demand will also state that a rise in gasoline prices or bus fares, *given* the subway fare, will raise the quantity demanded of subway rides because they will become *relatively* cheaper. The model of demand thus reminds us that ridership on the subway changes not only when the subway fares change but also when other prices change. Of course, we would probably have figured out that both the subway fare and other prices affect ridership even if we had not written out a formal equation such as equation (3). But writing down a model is a safe way of forcing ourselves to look for all the relevant effects. Otherwise, we might easily have forgotten about bus fares, and that could be an important omission in predicting the number of rides on the subway.

The next step is to combine the equations to predict revenue. Combining equations (2) and (3), we have

$$\begin{aligned}\text{Total fare}\atop\text{collection} &= \text{fare} \times {\text{quantity of subway}\atop\text{rides demanded}}\\[6pt] &= \text{fare} \times f(\text{subway fare, taxi fare,}\atop\text{gasoline price, }\dots) \qquad (4)\end{aligned}$$

Models in Perspective   We now have written down our complete model of what determines the total fares collected by the subway system. The most appropriate reaction is to ask what all the fuss is about. Anyone who thinks about the problem would probably organize his thoughts the same way. That is precisely the right reaction. Models can be simple, though they may be elaborate for some purposes. Their main purpose is to get us thinking systematically about the problem we are trying to solve.

Models inevitably simplify because the real world is too complicated to model in all its detail. But how far should a model go in simplifying? There is no easy answer. Learning to use models is more an art than a science. Too much simplicity, and the analysis can easily go wide of the mark. Too much detail, or the wrong details, and the analysis can get bogged down because it is too difficult or concentrates on the wrong things.

One of the main reasons for studying economics is precisely to learn how to build simple models of the immensely complicated real economic world in which we live. Doing that takes experience in building simple models. But it also requires an interaction with real-world data, as we now see.

6 MODELS AND DATA

Equation (4) is our complete model of the factors that determine the subway system's total revenues. But we immediately encounter a problem with it. An increase in the fare, holding constant all other fares and prices, does two things. First, each rider pays more. That tends to increase revenues. But second, people choose to take fewer rides, and that tends to reduce the subway system's revenues.

Because these two effects work in opposite directions, it is not clear what the total effect on revenue of a raise in fare will be. We naturally think that raising the fare will increase revenue. But higher fares may reduce ridership so much that an increase in fares will reduce revenue.

We have come to the point where we cannot determine, using only theory, whether in fact higher fares will raise or lower total fare collection. We are back where we started, and it looks as if all the modeling was a waste of time. But this is not the case. What the model tells us is that we are facing an *issue of fact,* or an *empirical issue.*

Theory alone does not tell us the balance of the two effects: higher fare versus reduced ridership. But we can look at the relevant facts. The value of the model in equation (4) is that it tells us what the relevant facts are. The relevant facts we want to look at are the relationships between fares and total fare collection, holding constant all other relevant prices.

The Facts

Where do we get such facts? It is very difficult in economics to get facts in precisely the form desired—namely, the facts on the relationship between fares and total fare collection, holding constant all other relevant prices. Economics data come mostly from the real world, not from experiments. In physics and some other sciences it is possible to do experiments in which all factors but one are held constant and then see the effects of varying just that one factor. But evidence on relationships between subway fares and the subway system's revenues does not come from controlled experiments.

Nonetheless, we do want to look at the facts, bearing in mind that perhaps factors other than changes in the fare have also been affecting subway revenues. For the moment we will ignore those other factors and come back to them later.

Where do we get the facts?

The Massachusetts Bay Transportation Authority keeps information on fares and total revenue. Their records give us the data shown in the top two rows of Table 2-10. These rows show the number of passengers and the fare in cents. The fare was raised in both 1980 and 1981. The fare for 1980 is the average fare during the year. The fare started out the year at 25 cents and ended up at 60 cents, and the average during the year was 37.5 cents.

We want to get some idea of the relationship between the fare and the number of riders. But to do that we must look at the *real* subway fare, not the fare measured in cents. All other prices were rising over this period, and we should adjust the subway fare to reflect those changing prices. Accordingly, in the third row of the table we write down the CPI, expressed as the value of 100 for 1978. In the bottom row we give the real subway fare.

To show the calculation of the real subway fare, we illustrate for 1979. The subway fare in cents for that year was 25 cents. The price index was 111.3, with 1978 as the base year. Therefore, the real subway fare was equal to (25 cents/111.3) × 100, which is 22.5 cents, measured in terms of the value of money in the base year (1978). We therefore say the 1979 fare was 22.5 cents *in 1978 cents*. Similar calculations show the real subway fare to have been 29.7 cents in 1980 and 43.0 cents in 1981. Note, incidentally, how inflation distorts the picture shown by the two top rows of the table. In those rows it looks as if the subway fare more than doubled from 1978 to 1981, whereas we see in the bottom row that it less than doubled in real terms.

From Table 2-10 we see that the number of passengers rises when the real subway fare falls and that the number of pas-

TABLE 2-10

SUBWAY FARES AND PASSENGERS

	1978	1979	1980	1981
Passengers, millions per year	95	102	92	79
Fare, cents per ride	25	25	37.5	60
Consumer price index, 1978 = 100	100	111.3	126.3	139.4
Real fare, 1978 cents per ride	25	22.5	29.7	43.0

Source: Top two rows based on data from Massachusetts Bay Transportation Authority. CPI from *Economic Report of the President, 1982,* p. 291.

FIGURE 2-4 SCATTER DIAGRAM OF SUBWAY FARES AND NUMBER OF PASSENGERS. A scatter diagram shows the combined observations on two data series. Each dot is one joint observation. The dot for 1978, for example, represents the fact that the fare in 1978 was 25 cents and that there were 95 million passengers that year.

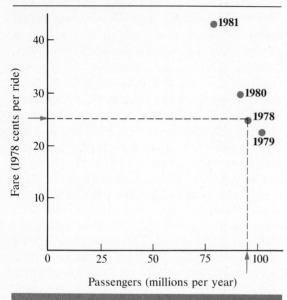

Fare (1978 cents per ride)

Passengers (millions per year)

the table a fare of 25 cents and 95 million passengers. We plot this observation as one point in Figure 2-4. To do so we note that the fare is measured in cents on the vertical axis. On the horizontal axis we measure passengers in millions.

First we look on the vertical axis for the point corresponding to a 25 cent fare; this point is indicated by an arrow. From that point we draw a line parallel to the horizontal axis. Next, on the horizontal axis we locate the point corresponding to a passenger number of 95 million; this point is also indicated by an arrow. From that point we draw a vertical line running upward. The intersection point of the two lines is marked by a dot and labeled 1978. This point corresponds to 95 million passengers and a 25 cent fare, which is the 1978 observation. Similarly, we proceed to plot the other observations for 1979, 1980, and 1981.

We emerge with four points that describe the relationship between fares and passengers. Higher fares historically have been associated with fewer passengers. The figure goes some way toward answering our question about fares and revenue by showing that indeed, higher fares mean a loss in ridership and thus tend on that account to cut into revenue. But we need to know more about the revenue-price relationship.

For that purpose we return to Table 2-10 to calculate the revenue (measured in millions of 1978 dollars) earned by the Transportation Authority each year. The data are shown in Table 2-11. The calcula-

sengers falls when the real subway fare rises. This is what we expected when we wrote down equation (3).

Scatter Diagrams

The evidence presented in Table 2-10 stands out well in a *scatter diagram* such as Figure 2-4. A scatter diagram shows how two variables are related. It is constructed as follows. For 1978, for example, we see in

TABLE 2-11

SUBWAY FARES AND REAL REVENUE

	1978	1979	1980	1981
Passengers, millions per year	95	102	92	79
Real fare, 1978 cents per ride	25	22.5	29.7	43.0
Real revenue, millions of 1978 dollars	23.75	22.95	27.32	33.97

Source: Based on Table 2-10.

FIGURE 2-5   SCATTER DIAGRAM OF SUBWAY FARE AND REVENUES OF THE SYSTEM. This diagram shows the relationship between subway revenues and the fare. Over the period 1978–1981 changes in total revenues were in the same direction as changes in the fare. (Note that both the fare and revenues are measured in 1978 dollars or cents.)

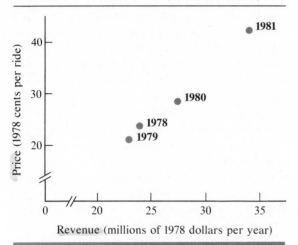

clearly. The gaps in the axes are there to remind us of the missing parts of the scales.

Figure 2-5 shows graphically that increases in subway fares have gone along with increases in the subway system's total revenues. This suggests that a fare hike would increase the system's revenues. The reason we cannot be absolutely sure about this conclusion is that something else might have been happening at the same time that the fares changed. We shall come back to that possibility later, but in the meantime we can be reasonably confident that we have the answer to the question with which we started: Will an increase in fare increase revenue? The answer is yes.

7 DIAGRAMS, LINES, AND EQUATIONS

Both Figure 2-4 and Figure 2-5 are scatter diagrams. But because there are only few points in each, we show a few more examples in Figures 2-6 and 2-7. We start with a definition.

> A *scatter diagram* shows the *combined* observations on two variables. It reveals whether there is an obvious relationship between the two variables that are plotted.

The scatter diagrams in Figures 2-6 and 2-7 are hypothetical observations on price and revenue in some market, showing alternative possibilities. In Figure 2-6 we have the appearance of a negative relationship. If price is high, revenue is low. This is different from Figure 2-5, which shows a positive relationship: when price is high, revenue is high. Finally, Figure 2-7 does not give any clear impression. The observations are all over the place, and there is no clear indication of a positive or negative pattern.

Fitting Lines

We draw scatter diagrams because they may suggest a pattern of relationships between

tion of the revenue figure for 1979 is done as follows. There were 102 million passengers, each paying 22.5 cents (measured in 1978 cents) and therefore paying in total $22.95 million (in 1978 dollars). The same type of calculation gives us all the data in the bottom row of the table.

Table 2-11 shows that the Transportation Authority's real revenue fell from 1978 to 1979, when the real fare fell, and rose from 1979 to 1980 to 1981, when the real fare increased. This strongly suggests the answer to the question of whether an increase in the fare reduces ridership enough to reduce total revenue. The evidence suggests the answer is no.

The same evidence can be seen in Figure 2-5, which is another scatter diagram. The fare is again shown on the vertical axis, but this time the real revenue earned by the system is shown on the horizontal axis. In Figure 2-5 we omit part of both the horizontal and vertical scales so as to show the relationship between fare and revenue more

FIGURE 2-6   A HYPOTHETICAL SCATTER DIA-
GRAM: NEGATIVE RELATIONSHIP BETWEEN TWO
VARIABLES. The relationship between price and revenue seen with these hypothetical data is the opposite of that in Figure 2-5. Here total revenues fall
when price rises. This is called a negative relationship between price and revenue, because they move
in opposite directions.

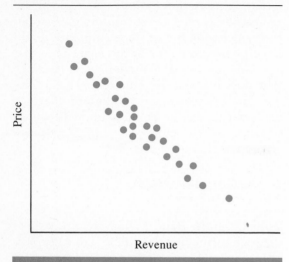

FIGURE 2-7   A HYPOTHETICAL SCATTER DIA-
GRAM: NO APPARENT RELATION BETWEEN TWO
VARIABLES. The hypothetical data in this figure
show no clear relationship between price and revenue.

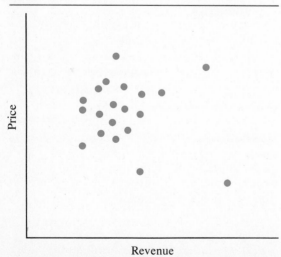

two variables we are investigating. For example, in the case of subway fares the scatter suggests that the fare and the system's revenues are positively related, even though
there are very few observations.

If we had many observations on price
and revenue, as in the scatter diagram on
Figure 2-8, we might go even further. We
could try to quantify the relationship between the two variables, for instance, by
saying that when the price goes up by 1
cent, the revenue goes up by so many million dollars.

Quantifying relationships, or putting
numbers to them, is one of the tasks of *econometrics*. Econometrics is a branch of economics devoted to measuring the relationships among economic variables. This is
done by "fitting a line" to a set of observations as well as can be done.

In Figure 2-8 we show a straight line labeled *EE* that captures the positive relationship in the figure between price and revenue. Obviously, not all the points in the
diagram are exactly on the line. Therefore,
it is not an *exact* representation of the relation. But the offsetting advantage is that it
does tell us for any price, read off the vertical axis, what is approximately or on average
the associated revenue. It thus summarizes
the quantitative relationship between the
two variables. That is very useful because
in most economic decisions we want dollar
and cents estimates of what will happen in
the event we do this or that. The relationship *EE* provides us with such estimates.

For instance, in the subway fare case,
the public transportation authority would
want to know how much to raise fares if the
objective is to get an extra $2 million of rev-
enue. They need to learn what the *quantitative* relationship between fare and passengers is, whether they call their technique
econometrics, intuition, or in-house expertise.

FIGURE 2-8 A LINE FITTED TO A SCATTER OF OBSERVATIONS. If there were sufficient data, we could summarize the relationship between price and revenue by fitting a line that describes the average relationship shown by the data. A line such as *EE* would show, for instance, that revenues rise by $1.5 million for every 1 cent rise in price.

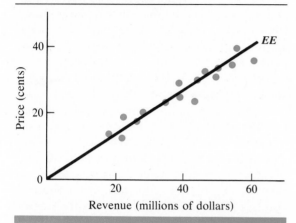

Equations

Fitting a line to the observations in a scatter diagram gives us a quantitative relationship. A line such as *EE* in Figure 2-8 represents a numerical relationship between two variables, or an *equation*. For the hypothetical case drawn in Figure 2-8 the equation is

Revenue = 1.5 × price   (5)

Revenue is measured in millions of dollars per year and price in cents per ride. This equation tells us that if price is, say, 20 cents, revenue is $30 million; if price is 30 cents, revenue is $45 million; and so on. The fitted line, or the equation that is an algebraic statement of the same relation, thus describes an exact relationship between two variables.

Whether it is possible, in fact, to establish such an exact relationship in any particular circumstance is quite another matter. The data may not be available, or as in Figure 2-7, it may not be clear what the relationship is. In this book we do not make use of equations to any great extent, but it is well worth noting that there is nothing mysterious about quantifying relationships between variables as exactly as possible and that equations specify such relationships.

Reading Diagrams

Although we do not rely a lot on equations, we will use diagrams very extensively. It is therefore worthwhile to develop a clear understanding of how to read a diagram, or understand the message a diagram conveys. Consider Figure 2-9, where we show a relationship between two variables X and Y—say, X is price and Y is revenue—to be concrete. On the vertical axis we measure Y and on the horizontal axis X.

The positively sloped schedule $Y = f(X)$ is a statement of a relationship between the variable Y and the variable X. The statement $Y = f(X)$ reads "variable Y is a function of or depends on the value taken by variable X." Thus for any value of X (for example, 1, 2, 3, or 50) the relationship $f(X)$ tells us what the corresponding value of variable Y is. For example, as we have drawn the schedule, if $X = 1$, we can read off the schedule that the corresponding value of Y is 200. We do so by first finding on the horizontal axis the point $X = 1$ and then going up until we hit the schedule $Y = f(X)$. The point on the schedule, read off to the left on the Y axis, is $Y = 200$. Thus for $X = 1$, the relation $Y = f(X)$ tells us that the corresponding value of Y is 200. Similarly, if $X = 3$, we can read off the schedule that the corresponding value of $Y = 400$.

A schedule such as Figure 2-9 is entirely described by two characteristics: the *intercept* and the *slope*. The intercept is the point where the schedule starts on the vertical axis, or where it crosses (intersects) the vertical axis. The schedule shown has its intercept at $Y = 100$. Another relation might have an intercept at $Y = 500$ or $Y = -50$. (Where is $Y = -50$ on the diagram? Can we extend the graph to show such a point?)

FIGURE 2-9 A POSITIVE LINEAR RELATIONSHIP BETWEEN TWO VARIABLES *X* AND *Y*. The diagram shows a straight-line, or linear, relation between the two variables *X* and *Y*. The schedule $Y = f(X)$ describes the relation between *X* and *Y*. The statement $Y = f(X)$ says that to every value of *X*, say, $X = 1$, there corresponds a particular value of *Y* that can be read off the schedule. For example, with $X = 1$, we can read off the value $Y = 200$.

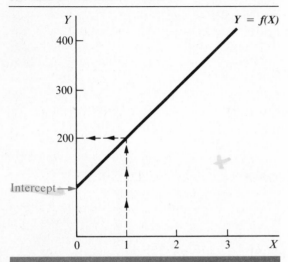

The other characteristic is the slope. You can imagine different schedules, all passing through the same intercept on the vertical axis, but some might be flatter and others much steeper than the schedule we show. The slope measures the steepness of the schedule. It measures how much *Y* increases for every 1-unit increase in *X*. For instance, the slope in Figure 2-9 is 100. For every 1-unit increase in *D*, *Y* goes up by 100. A very steep slope, as you can verify by drawing one, tells us that as *X* rises, *Y* rises a lot. A flat schedule implies that *Y* rises only a little as *X* increases.

In Figure 2-9 we have shown a positive relation between two variables *X* and *Y*. Of course, there are also many cases where the relationship is negative. A negative relationship is suggested in the scatter diagrams in Figures 2-4 and 2-6, for example. With a negative relationship, higher values of one variable imply lower values of the other

variable. This is shown in Figure 2-10, where we have a schedule $Y = f(X)$—read this again as "*Y* depends on *X*"—with a *negative* slope. As *X* increases from 1 to 2, 3, and so on, the corresponding value of *Y* declines. Again the schedule is located by two characteristics: the intercept and the slope. The schedule could be flat or steep or it could intersect the vertical axis high up or near zero.

Figures 2-9 and 2-10 showed straight-line, or *linear*, relationships between two variables. Economic relationships need not be linear, however. In some cases they may look like Figure 2-11. There we show the case of a function or relation between *Y* and *X* that is nonlinear. As *X* rises, starting at zero, *Y* first increases too. But then *Y* reaches a maximum, as shown by the arrow.

FIGURE 2-10 A NEGATIVE LINEAR RELATIONSHIP BETWEEN TWO VARIABLES *X* AND *Y*. The diagram shows a negative linear relationship between two variables *X* and *Y*. For every *X* we can read off the schedule $Y = f(X)$ the corresponding value of *Y*. For instance, for $X = 100$, the corresponding value of *Y* is 2.3. The location of the schedule is determined by its intercept and its slope. The slope tells us how rapidly *Y* declines as *X* increases. The steeper the line, the more *Y* falls for any given increase in *X*.

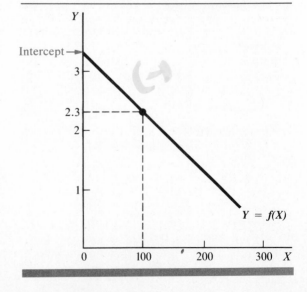

FIGURE 2-11 A NONLINEAR RELATIONSHIP BE-TWEEN X AND Y. The diagram shows a nonlinear relationship between X and Y. As X first starts rising from zero, Y increases. As X continues to increase, Y first reaches a maximum and then begins to decline.

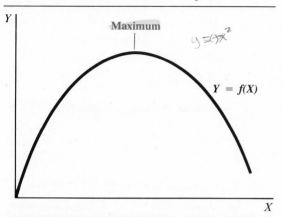

Further increases in X now lead to a reduction in Y.

We will see later that such relations exist, for example, between taxes and revenue collection. Suppose, for instance, that the tax is on movie tickets. If the tax is zero, there is no tax revenue. Then as tax rates increase, total revenue rises, but beyond a point raising tax rates still further makes movie tickets so expensive that very few people go, and tax revenues actually fall. In this example X would represent the tax rate and Y the revenue.

Another example is the relationship between ticket prices for a football game and revenue. If the tickets are free, there is no revenue. If the price is extremely high, nobody will buy a ticket and revenue will also be zero. In between there are prices that do generate some revenue and some price at which revenue will be largest. Again we would be talking about a relation like the one in Figure 2-11. The point of the two examples is to show that real-life economic problems and relations can often be readily captured by simple, though not necessarily linear, diagrammatic representations.

8 THE PROBLEM OF OTHER THINGS EQUAL

In analyzing evidence we frequently simplify by assuming "other things equal." We assume that other economic factors that might affect the relationship we are studying remain constant. For instance, in examining the relationship between subway fares, the number of rides, and revenue, we presented the data in Figures 2-4 and 2-5. We argued that those diagrams showed that increases in fares reduced the number of riders (Figure 2-4), but not enough to reduce total revenue when the fare rises (Figure 2-5).

But our model of subway revenue, summarized by equation (4), draws attention to several other variables that should affect the demand for subway rides. Among them is the price of gasoline. If the price of gasoline was also changing when subway fares changed, the evidence of Figures 2-4 and 2-5 would be harder to interpret.

Table 2-12 contains the earlier data on subway revenue and fares along with real gasoline prices measured in 1978 dollars. The price of gasoline rose rapidly over this period. Increases in the price of gasoline cause people to use the subway more, since car use becomes relatively more expensive. Thus when subway fares were raised in 1980, they were raised against a background of a rising price of gasoline that in itself was probably bringing more riders to the subway system.

Hence there is some doubt whether an increase in the subway fare would indeed increase total revenue at a time when the price of gasoline is constant. Perhaps the positive effects seen in Table 2-12 and Figure 2-5 are really a reflection of the rising price of gasoline.

What is the lesson of this section? It is not that we can never interpret evidence because something else may have been going

TABLE 2-12

SUBWAY REVENUE, FARES, AND GASOLINE PRICES, 1978–1981

	1978	1979	1980	1981
Total revenue, millions of 1978 dollars	23.8	23.0	27.3	34.0
Subway fare, 1978 cents per ride, annual average	25.0	22.5	29.7	43.0
Gasoline price, 1978 dollars per gallon	0.63	0.77	0.94	0.94

Source: Table 2-11 and *Monthly Energy Review,* July 1982.

on in the background. Given enough evidence, for instance, 20 years of data like the data in Table 2-12, we can actually figure out with considerable confidence how changes in the subway fare and the price of gasoline *each* affect the number of rides. That can be done by using econometrics or statistics to isolate the effects of each variable separately. The evidence, when it is interpreted properly, might indicate that subway fare increases reduce ridership but not enough to reduce revenues, which is what we concluded from Figures 2-4 and 2-5.

The moral is *not* that the world is too complicated for evidence to be meaningful. Rather, it is to keep on guard for variables that should be included in our models but are excluded. Also, in interpreting evidence, we should always be on guard that what we are seeing is not caused by a factor we have omitted.

9 THEORIES AND EVIDENCE

We started this chapter by saying that the aim of economics is to understand how the economy works and why particular economic relationships exist. It is an open secret that economics, like medicine, engineering, or any other live area of study, doesn't yet have a full understanding of the field. How does the economist go about understanding economic problems?

There is a three-step procedure that is more or less consciously and formally followed. First, a phenomenon is observed. For example, suppose we observe the relationship shown in Table 2-4 between years of schooling and income. People with more schooling have higher incomes on average. We wonder why this relationship exists.

The second step is to develop a theory that attempts to explain the phenomenon. A theory, or model, will try to explain what factors affect people's incomes and then focus on the relationship between education and income. The simplest model would be that education teaches useful skills. The model then makes predictions, for instance, that a given individual will have a higher income if he gets an extra year's schooling.

Of course, this sounds as though it is certain to be true. Isn't that what Table 2-4 shows? It is not. Perhaps people with more education get higher incomes because they are more able to begin with. Perhaps people go to college for fun, but colleges take in only people who will do well in later life. Or perhaps the people who go to college came, on average, from richer homes and have higher incomes because their parents have high incomes. Thus the prediction that a given individual will have higher income if he gets an extra year's schooling is not necessarily true.

The third step is to *test* the predictions of the theory by confronting it with the data. The data in Table 2-4 do *not* necessarily show that education teaches useful skills, since those data are consistent with the view that it is ability that determines both whether people go to college and the income they later receive. The tests with actual data try to standardize for IQ or some other measure of ability, for parents' income, and for luck. But we do not want to go into the details here.

Rather, we want to emphasize two points. First, economics, unlike the physical sciences, for example, does not have much scope for laboratory experiments. There has been some experimentation with animals (we describe some of this work in Chapter 5) and some large-scale experiments about how people react to welfare payments. But by and large we have to take our data where we find them. That makes testing difficult, because of the "other things equal" problem.

The second point is that there is nevertheless much evidence from both the United States and abroad that can be looked at when we study our theories. Microeconomists have been extremely ingenious in trying to isolate the effects of ability on income. For example, there are some identical twins who grew up in different families and had different educations. The data on their incomes have been used in an attempt to hold constant the level of ability as a determinant of income. In macroeconomics there is a wide range of foreign experience. For instance, the inflation, or rising prices, of the last 20 years in the United States averaged about 7 percent per year. In Germany in 1923 prices rose by a factor of *10 billion*. That was almost like a laboratory experiment in how economies behave when there is inflation. That experience is studied in Chapter 32.

Once the theory has been confronted with the data and has not been rejected, we begin to get some confidence in it. Any theory that stays alive over a long period after being subjected to many tests and not being rejected by the data tends to become accepted. As the theory becomes accepted, we believe that we better understand that aspect of the behavior of the economy. There are many widely accepted theories, for instance, that higher prices discourage demand or that extra education raises income.

But there are also many areas where economists are still trying to figure out how the world works. How can we stop inflation? Can we prevent it from coming back? Are differentials in wages between blacks and whites due to discrimination? There is bound to be uncertainty about the answers, because the field of economics is a live one and because fresh ideas and new data throw new light on old theories and facts.

SUMMARY

1   Economics has two aims. The primary aim is to understand the way the economy works, or to explain the relationships we observe among economic variables. The second is to use the knowledge of these relationships to solve everyday problems ranging from how to stop inflation to what fare to set for a subway system.

2   There is a continuing interplay of models and facts in explaining relationships or solving problems. A model is a more or less formal, simplified framework for organizing thought about the problem being analyzed. Models may be extremely simple or highly complex, but they are needed to make sure our analysis of a problem is systematic.

Models have to simplify because the real world is too complicated to analyze in anything like full detail.

3   Data, or facts, are essential for two reasons. First, the data provide relationships we are trying to explain. Second, once theories have been formulated, we turn to the data to test the hypotheses suggested by the theory and to measure more carefully the relationships on which the predictions of the theories depend.

4   Tables and charts organize data so that they are easily understandable. Time series data are values of a given variable at different points of time or for different intervals of time. Cross section data report on the same variable, at a point in time, but differing by source or characteristic of the reporting unit. The price of silver in different months in 1980 is a time series. Hourly earnings in different industries in December 1981 constitute a cross section.

5   Index numbers express data relative to some given base value. In time series, an index number expresses the value for each period relative to the value in some particular base year.

6   Index numbers are most often used to summarize information about the behavior of several different variables. For instance, the consumer price index summarizes the changes in the prices of all goods that households buy. The CPI is a weighted average of indices for the prices of goods bought by a typical household.

7   The consumer price index is a basic index used to measure the rate of inflation, or the rate at which prices in general are increasing.

8   Nominal or current dollar variables are variables measured in terms of the prices of the period to which they apply. Real, or constant dollar, variables adjust nominal variables for changes in the general level of prices. For instance, real hourly earnings are calculated by dividing an index of nominal earnings by the consumer price index.

9   Scatter diagrams show the relationship between two variables contained in the data on those variables. Scatter diagrams sometimes suggest a relationship that can be fitted to those variables by using econometrics. The fitted relationship, or line, summarizes the average relationship between the two variables, but it is not an exact description of the facts.

10   Analytical diagrams are often used in building a model. Diagrams are very widely used in economics.

11   To understand how the economy works we need both theory and the facts. We need a theory in order to know what facts to look for; there are too many facts for them to speak out clearly. Facts without theory are useless, but theory without facts does not go very far either.

KEY TERMS

Model
Data
Time series data
Cross section data
Median and mean
Index numbers
Consumer price index (CPI)
Nominal and real variables
Real (relative) prices

Purchasing power of money
Current and constant dollars
Percentage change
Growth rate
Inflation rate
Scatter diagram
Function
Other things equal

PROBLEMS

1 Use the data in Table 2-4 to plot a scatter diagram of the relationship between years of education and income.

2 The following data refer to total consumption (spending by households) and total income received by households in the United States.

	1975	1976	1977	1978
Consumption*	.976	1.084	1.206	1.349
Income*	1.096	1.194	1.312	1.463

	1979	1980	1981
Consumption*	1.511	1.673	1.858
Income*	1.642	1.822	2.015

* Trillions of dollars.
Source: Economic Report of the President, 1982, p. 261.

(*a*) Plot the two time series on a chart where time is represented on the horizontal axis. (*b*) Plot the scatter diagram of the data. (*c*) What would a "fitted line" look like in (*b*)? (*d*) What do your answers in (*b*) and (*c*) suggest about the relationship between households' income and their spending?

3 Express the hourly earnings data for 1950, 1960, 1970, and 1980 in Table 2-8 in constant 1960 dollars and then in constant 1980 dollars.

4 Draw a diagram that shows on the vertical axis the variable X measured in dollars and on the horizontal axis the variable Y measured in tons.

	1975	1976	1977	1978
Y	40	33	29	56
X	5	7	9	3

	1979	1980	1981
Y	81	19	20
X	1	11	10

(*a*) Using the table, plot the scatter diagram. (*b*) Is the relation between the variables positive or negative? (*c*) Would a fitted line be straight or more nearly curved?

5 Draw a diagram with X on the vertical axis and Y on the horizontal axis. You are told the following: for $X = 10$, $Y = 0$; for $X = 3, Y = 4$. (*a*) Draw the two points corresponding to these observations. (*b*) Connect the points by a straight line. What is the intercept in your diagram?

6 You are on the university football stadium advisory board and have to help set the price for tickets. You want to increase the amount of revenue taken in by the football team. Describe what your "model" for this problem would look like. (Note that this problem is very similar to that of the subway.)

7 You have the idea that crime is not just something that happens but may well have to do with economic factors. In particular, you believe it may have to do with people not getting jobs. (*Note:* The unemployment rate measures the proportion of the work force unable to find a job.) (*a*) How would you test your idea? What data would you want? Where would you look for them and what would you do with them? (*b*) What "other things equal" problems would you want to bear in mind?

8 You are given the following data on prices of gold and silver.

	1975	1976	1977	1978
Gold, $/oz	161	125	148	193
Silver, $/oz	4.42	4.35	4.62	5.40

	1979	1980	1981
Gold, $/oz	307	608	460
Silver, $/oz	11.09	20.58	10.52

Source: International Monetary Fund, *International Financial Statistics,* 1982 Yearbook.

(*a*) Construct an index (1975 = 100) for each of the series. (*b*) Plot the time series data of the indices derived in (*a*). (*c*) Construct an index of the ratio of gold price to silver price (1975 = 100).

9 You are given the following information.

	1979	1980	1981
Wages in manufacturing, dollars per hour	6.70	7.27	8.0
Consumer price index, 1979 = 100	100	113.5	125.3

Sources: Economic Report of the President, 1982, and *Survey of Current Business.*

(*a*) Construct an index of wages (1979 = 100). (*b*) Construct an index of real wages (1979 = 100). (*c*) What was the growth rate of real wages in 1980 and in 1981?

10 In discussing the problem of other things equal in Table 2-12 we pointed out that the increases in the price of gasoline made it difficult to be sure that increases in subway fares raised revenues. Suppose the data on gasoline prices reported in Table 2-12 had turned out to be falling, from $1.03 in 1978, $1.00 in 1979, and $0.86 in 1980 to $0.69 in 1981. How would that have affected your confidence that an increase in the subway fare would increase total revenues of the system, other things equal?

11 The accompanying table gives price indices (1973 = 100) for the CPI and for energy prices. The energy price index measures the prices of a basket of energy products including fuel, gas, and electricity. (*a*) Calculate the index of real energy prices, using these data. (*b*) Plot the three time series: the CPI, the energy price index, and the real energy price index. (*c*) Are there any years in which the nominal and real energy prices change in opposite directions?

	1973	1974	1975	1976	1977
Energy price index	100	129	143	153	168
CPI	100	111	121	128	136

	1978	1979	1980	1981
Energy price index	178	223	292	332
CPI	147	163	185	205

Note: All indices rounded.
Source: Economic Report of the President, 1982, Table B-52.

The basic questions in economics—What should be produced? How? and For whom?—have to be decided by society in *some* way. One way of making these decisions is through the use of markets and the price system. Buyers and sellers in markets, each responding to prices, effectively decide among themselves what gets produced, how, and for whom.

In this chapter we will define *markets* and see how the responses of buyers and sellers to prices determine what goods are produced, how, and for whom. The framework of analysis is a very general one that can be applied to the markets for cars, labor, and nuclear reactors as well as the markets for banana splits, haircuts, and baseball players. In each case the interplay between *demand* (the behavior of buyers) and *supply* (the behavior of sellers) determines the price and the amount of output produced and sold.

The U.S. economy and most other economies rely heavily on markets to allocate resources. To take only two examples: the quantity of cars produced and their prices are determined in the market for cars, and the wages of labor are determined in the market for labor. Because of the heavy reliance on markets and prices, the information contained in this chapter is a basic element of economics and a vital tool for the analysis of economic issues. It has to be mastered by anyone who wants to understand the economies in which we live.

3

Demand, Supply, and the Market

1 THE MARKET

At the center of the analysis of the allocation of resources through the price system is the notion of a market. We can readily think of a market as a place where people get together to buy and sell, haggling over the prices of goods such as food, clothing, or jewels. But the term "market" has a broader meaning.

A *market* is a set of arrangements by which buyers and sellers of a good are in contact to trade that good.

Here are some examples. The market for used cars operates with dealers and private sellers on the selling side. Buyers come into contact with sellers by reading newspaper advertisements, by visiting dealers, by looking at notices on bulletin boards, and by hearing from friends about people who want to sell. Some markets, such as the New York Stock Exchange, operate through intermediaries or traders.

Buyers and sellers call in their orders from all over the country and can have the orders carried out within minutes or even seconds. The markets for internationally traded commodities such as wheat or copper work largely over the telephone, with potential buyers and sellers talking to each other from anyplace in the world. Still other examples are auctions, where buyers compete against each other, and supermarkets, where the sellers fill the shelves and post the prices at which the buyers do the shopping.

These situations all describe different setups by which buyers and sellers get together and by which the price and amount to be traded are determined. An auction, where people bid for a good, is clearly different from a supermarket checkout counter, where prices are read off the boxes, jars, and cans. But once we look beyond the features of a particular market, we will see that all markets have a common, basic economic core. All help determine the answers to the what, how, and for whom questions. They determine why a box of cornflakes costs $2 rather than 20 cents or $20, who will supply cornflakes, and who will buy them. They determine why it is possible for top baseball players to receive over a million dollars a year and top football players much less.

To understand how prices are determined and resources allocated, we have to build up a model of the market. Such a model will enable us to identify the factors that matter in a market—for determining both price and the quantities bought and sold—and the precise way in which they affect price and quantity. Demand and supply are the basic ideas. By "demand" we mean the behavior of buyers. By "supply" we mean the behavior of sellers. This behavior is summarized by the amounts of goods buyers want to buy at each price and sellers sell at each price. We will now set out the determinants of demand and supply.

2 DEMAND, SUPPLY, AND EQUILIBRIUM

Demand is the amount of a good buyers want to purchase at different prices. Thus demand is not a particular quantity, say, three six-packs of beer, but rather a full description of the amount of beer the buyer would want to buy at different prices for a six-pack. In Table 3-1 we take the hypothetical example of fish. The first column shows a range of prices, from $0 (when fish is free) to $7 per pound of fish. The second column shows the quantities demanded by buyers at the different prices. For each price there is a corresponding quantity of fish demanded. When fish is free, the quantity demanded is 50 million pounds. At $4 per pound, the quantity demanded is only 10 million pounds. The first and second columns together describe demand.

Supply is the amount of a good sellers want to sell at different prices. Supply, too, is not a particular quantity. Rather it is a complete description of the amount sellers would want to sell at different prices. In the third column of Table 3-1 we show the quantities suppliers in the fish market want to sell at the different prices of fish. For each price there is a corresponding quantity of fish supplied. When fish is free, the quantity supplied is zero. When the price of fish is $5 per pound, the quantity supplied is 40 million pounds. The first and third columns together describe supply.

There is an important distinction between *demand* and *quantity demanded*. *Demand* describes consumer behavior at different prices. But at any given price, such as $2, there is a particular *quantity demanded*. Thus the term "quantity demanded" makes sense only in relation to a particular price. The term "demand" describes consumer behavior—the entire relationship between quantity demanded and price—rather than a particular quantity of goods at a particular

TABLE 3-1 ▰▰▰▰▰▰▰▰▰▰▰

DEMAND FOR AND SUPPLY OF FISH

PRICE, $/lb	DEMAND, millions of lb	SUPPLY, millions of lb
0	50	0
1	40	0
2	30	10
3	20	20
4	10	30
5	0	40
6	0	50
7	0	60

price. Exactly the same distinction applies to *supply* and *quantity supplied*.

It is important to make the distinction between demand and quantity demanded and between supply and quantity supplied even though it is not common in everyday language. In everyday language we would say that the demand for football tickets exceeded the supply, so some people couldn't get in. Not so, the economist would say. Rather, the *quantity demanded* at the price that was set for the tickets exceeded the *quantity supplied*. At a higher price the quantity demanded might have been much smaller, and the stadium half empty. There is no change in demand between the two situations even though the quantity demanded changes as the price rises.

The reason for emphasizing the distinction between demand and quantity demanded (and between supply and quantity supplied) is that in economics much of the focus is on finding prices that will balance the quantity demanded with the quantity supplied. To find this balance, it is necessary to allow the price to change. Noting the distinction between supply and demand and the quantities supplied and demanded at particular prices drives home the lesson that prices guide the allocation of resources.

Demand

Consider now the demand side. Suppose fish were free. Most households would choose a diet with plenty of fish and relatively little meat or poultry. The quantity demanded of fish would be high. But it would not be unlimited. Nobody would want to eat only fish or have huge amounts of fish lying around the house, possibly spoiling. Table 3-1 accordingly shows that with a zero price, the quantity demanded is 50 million pounds.

Suppose next that the price was $1 per pound. The table shows that the quantity demanded would be lower: only 40 million pounds. Other foods find a larger place in the diet as fish becomes more expensive and households want to purchase less fish, consuming it perhaps only 4 days per week. The table shows that at progressively higher prices of fish, there is an increasing substitution toward other foods. The quantity of fish demanded falls off rapidly; it is down to 10 million pounds at a $4 price and all the way down to zero at $5, where even the most fish-enthusiastic household eliminates fish entirely from the menu. Table 3-1 exhibits the pattern of demand: *The lower the price, the higher the quantity demanded of a particular commodity.*

Supply

On the supply side, as the third column of Table 3-1 shows, the opposite holds true. The quantity supplied increases as the price increases. On the supply side we have to ask what persuades people to devote labor and machinery (such as boats and ships) to catching and marketing fish rather than doing something else with their time and equipment. The higher the price at which fish can be sold, the more resources will be used in fishing and the more fish will be offered for sale. As the price of fish rises, fishermen use their boats more intensively, and new fishermen come into the market. Also, it becomes profitable for sellers of fish to expand their supply by importing fish from other parts of the country and even from other countries.

Accordingly, Table 3-1 shows the quantity supplied rising as the price increases. At a price of zero there will be no fish offered for sale; indeed, the price has to rise above $1 per pound before any fish appears on the market. At $2 per pound there is already some quantity supplied, and the quantity supplied increases further as the price rises. The third column shows supply behavior: *The higher the price, the higher the quantity supplied of a particular commodity.*

The Market and the Equilibrium Price

In talking about a market, we need to specify not only what is traded in the market but also what area the market covers and the length of time being considered. To be concrete, we will talk about the market for fish in Chicago and about the weekly supply and demand. We will want to know what determines the price of fish and the quantity sold per week.

Consider now supply in relation to demand, and look at Table 3-1. At low prices the quantity demanded exceeds the quantity supplied, and at high prices the quantity supplied exceeds the quantity demanded. At an intermediate price the quantity demanded and the quantity supplied are equal; in other words, there is a price that *equates* demand and supply. That price is the equilibrium price.

The *equilibrium price* is the price at which the quantity demanded and the quantity supplied are equal.

Table 3-1 shows that the equilibrium price is $3 per pound. It is only at that price that the quantity buyers want to buy is equal to the amount sellers want to sell. At any price below $3, the quantity demanded is greater than the quantity supplied, and so there is an unsatisfied demand, or a shortage, or *excess* demand. If the price somehow fell below $3, sellers would want to

sell less than the amount demanders would want to buy. Fish would be sold out before everyone who wanted some could buy it. If the price were above $3, however, sellers would want to sell more than the amount buyers would want to buy, and at the end of the day the sellers would be left with unsold fish. In this situation there is *excess* supply, or a surplus. Only at a price of $3 do the quantities supplied and demanded match; as it is put alternatively, only at the $3 price does the market *clear*.

Corresponding to the equilibrium price of $3 is an equilibrium quantity, in this case 20 million pounds. That is the amount bought and sold when the market is in equilibrium—when the quantity supplied equals the quantity demanded.

Will the price in fact be $3, and if so, how does the price get there? The price will, indeed, tend toward the equilibrium price because if it is not at the equilibrium level, there is reason for it to change. Suppose that sellers set the price at $5 and correspondingly brought 40 million pounds of fish to market. At a $5 price they would face a zero quantity demanded and therefore find themselves with more fish than they know what to do with. Their reaction would be to lower the price. If the price were below $3—say, at $2—sellers would want to sell only 10 million pounds. Buyers would want 30 million pounds. The sellers would be overwhelmed in the rush for the small quantity of fish. They would react by raising the price and trying to obtain more fish to meet the demand. Only at the price of $3, with the quantities demanded and supplied equal (at 20 million pounds), are there no forces tending to change the price. For that reason we expect the actual price to be close to the equilibrium price.

Of course, on any particular day it is quite possible that the quantity demanded and the quantity supplied are not exactly equal and that the price is not equal to the equilibrium price. Perhaps there is a sudden increase in the demand for fish and suppliers do not adjust prices quickly enough. In this case they sell out. Or perhaps the weather keeps customers away, and some fish goes unsold. But in each case there is an incentive for the price to change and to move toward the equilibrium price. Thus on the average we expect the price to be at about the equilibrium level.

We have talked about the fish market as if the sellers of fish set the price. But the actual arrangements about who sets the price in any market differ. In some markets there is an auctioneer—an individual who calls out prices until the quantity available for sale is sold. Auctioneers may be found in wholesale markets for fish, in many agricultural markets, or at auctions of household objects or used cars. In other markets prices are set by a process of haggling. The particular methods differ enormously, but in most cases we can think that the price is set so as to equate the quantity supplied and the quantity demanded.[1]

Summary

To summarize the essential points of this and the previous section:

1   Demand is the quantity of a good buyers want to buy at each price. The lower the price, the greater the quantity demanded.

2   Supply is the quantity of a good sellers want to sell at each price. The higher the price, the larger the quantity supplied.

3   The market clears, or is in equilibrium, when the price is at the level at which the

quantity demanded and the quantity supplied are equal.

4   If the price is not at the equilibrium level, it will tend in a free market to move toward it. On the average, therefore, the price will be at the equilibrium level.

3   DEMAND AND SUPPLY CURVES AND THE EQUILIBRIUM PRICE

Table 3-1 shows demand and supply conditions in the fish market and allows us to find the equilibrium price and quantity. For further applications we introduce another way of looking at supply and demand, namely, supply and demand curves.

We start by drawing the demand curve in Figure 3-1. Prices corresponding to the first column of Table 3-1 are measured on the vertical axis. Quantities, in millions of pounds per week, are measured on the horizontal axis. From Table 3-1, the quantity demanded at a price of $1 is 40 (million pounds). We show this with point A, at which the price is $1 and the quantity is 40. Consider next a price of $4 and the corresponding quantity demanded of 10. This is shown with point B. Clearly we can continue plotting all the prices and the corresponding levels of demand. This is done in Figure 3-1, where we have connected the points to show the *demand curve*.

> The demand curve or demand schedule shows the quantity demanded at each price.

Supply conditions are similarly shown by the *supply curve* or supply schedule.

> The supply curve shows the quantity that would be supplied at each price.

The points corresponding to the third column of Table 3-1 are shown in Figure 3-2 (for example, price = $4, and quantity supplied = 30 million pounds). Again, the points have been connected.

The demand and supply curves can be combined in the same diagram and used to

---

[1] Veteran economists often say that price equates supply and demand rather than that it equates quantity supplied and quantity demanded. This should be thought of as a way of saving words. But it is not strictly accurate and should not be said until you have been practicing economics for at least 8 years.

FIGURE 3-1 DEVELOPING THE DEMAND CURVE. The diagram shows how the prices and quantities demanded specified in Table 3-1 can be translated into a demand curve. The vertical axis measures price and the horizontal axis quantity demanded. We can pick a price in the table, say, $1, and observe the corresponding quantity demanded, 40 million pounds. Point *A* represents the price-quantity combination. Similarly, point *B* represents a price of $4 and the corresponding quantity demanded of 10 million pounds. Plotting all the data in the table and connecting the resulting points yields the demand curve, shown as the negatively sloping schedule.

FIGURE 3-2 THE SUPPLY CURVE. The data in Table 3-1 include for each price the corresponding quantity supplied by sellers. The price-quantity pairs can be plotted to yield the supply schedule, *SS*. The supply schedule is upward-sloping, showing that as price increases, so does the quantity supplied.

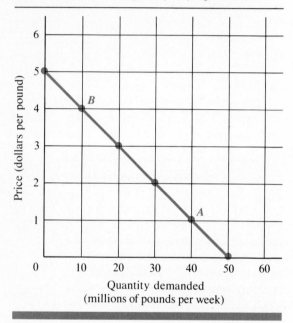

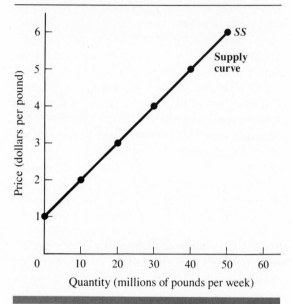

reexamine the discussion of excess supply, excess demand, and equilibrium. This is done in Figure 3-3. Now we have labeled the demand schedule as *DD* and the supply curve as *SS*. When the quantity demanded exceeds the quantity supplied at a given price, the horizontal distance between the demand and supply curves is the *excess demand*. At a price of $2, for example, the quantity supplied is only 10, and the quantity demanded is 30. There is an excess demand of 20, shown by the distance *AB* in Figure 3-3. When the quantity supplied exceeds the quantity demanded at a given price, there is an *excess supply*. Thus at the

price of $4, the quantity supplied and the quantity demanded are 30 and 10, respectively. There is an excess supply of 20, shown by the distance *CF*.

When there is an excess supply, we can say that there is a *surplus*. Suppliers want to sell more than buyers want to buy. The suppliers will be out looking for customers to buy, but the customers can get all they want at the going price, and they do *not* want to buy as much as sellers would like to sell. When there is an excess demand, we say there is a *shortage*. Buyers look for sellers, hoping to find someone who has the needed goods. But the total quantity demanded exceeds the quantity supplied, and buyers cannot buy as much as they would like.

Price Determination Now we will look at price determination. Suppose that the price is set below $3. At any price less than $3

FIGURE 3-3 EXCESS DEMAND AND SUPPLY. At point *E* the market price is such that the quantity demanded by buyers is equal to the quantity supplied by sellers. The market is in equilibrium. At a higher price there is an *excess supply* or a *surplus* of the quantity sellers want to sell over the quantity demanded. At a lower price there is a *shortage* or an *excess demand,* as the quantity demanded exceeds the quantity supplied.

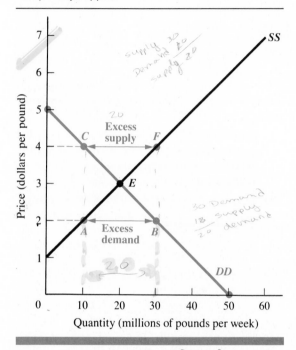

4 BEHIND THE DEMAND CURVE

To get a firmer idea of the determinants of the equilibrium price and quantity, we ask what is behind the data in Table 3-1 and in the diagrams. In concentrating on the relationship between the quantity demanded and the price, we are implicitly assuming that other things are constant. What are those other things? Similarly, in saying that the quantity supplied increases with the price, we are assuming that other things are given, or *ceteris paribus*. What are the relevant factors that are taken as given?

Three factors are important on the demand side: the prices of related goods, consumer income, and consumer tastes. We now look at each of these factors.

Prices of Related Goods

Changes in the prices of related goods will affect the demand for a good. Let us think about the demand for automobiles and ask what are the other relevant prices that affect the demand for automobiles. One price that matters is the price of public transportation, which is an alternative form of transportation. Another price that is relevant is the price of gasoline, for it affects the cost of using an automobile and therefore the desirability of owning an automobile. How could a change in either of these prices affect the demand for automobiles? A rise in the price of public transportation would shift people from using buses and subways to owning and using automobiles. The demand for automobiles increases when the price of public transportation rises. That is, at each *given* price buyers stand ready to buy more than they did at the *same price* before. Next consider a rise in the price of gasoline. The increased cost of using an automobile (given other things, including the price of public transportation) would shift people from owning and using cars to using public transportation, bikes, or their own two feet.

there is an excess demand. Sellers find themselves running out of fish before all the customers who want to buy at that price can obtain the quantities they want. The price therefore rises. At any price above $3 there is an excess supply. Sellers find that they cannot sell as much as they want at that price and are left with unsold fish. They therefore reduce the price. Only at point *E* in Figure 3-3 is there neither excess demand nor excess supply. At point *E* the quantity demanded at the $3 price is equal to the quantity supplied, the market clears, and there is no reason for the price to change. Thus $3 is the equilibrium price, and 20 (million pounds per week) is the equilibrium quantity.

In everyday language we think of public transportation as a substitute for automobiles. When people switch away from public transportation, they use instead (or substitute) cars. We can say that using public transportation is a *substitute* for automobile use because an increase in the price of public transportation leads people to use cars more. Economists use a more exact definition of substitutes, which will be introduced in Chapter 5.[2] But the everyday language certainly gives the right idea of what a substitute is. We can also use everyday language to say that gasoline and cars are *complements,* for when the price of gasoline rises, people reduce the use of cars. Again, the economist's definition is slightly different, but the everyday language gives the right idea.

How do these ideas about substitutes and complements relate to the demand for fish? Clearly, other foods (meat, poultry, etc.) are substitutes, and a rise in their prices will shift people toward fish consumption, raising fish demand. It is harder to think of fish complements—commodities whose rising prices would reduce the demand for fish. In some countries where fish-and-chips (fried fish and french fries) is a typical dish, one might expect potatoes to

be a complement for fish. The difficulty in thinking of a complement for fish correctly suggests that goods are typically substitutes and that complementarity, while present in many instances, is a more special feature (hats and feathers, coffee and nondairy cream, hammers and nails, shoes and shoelaces, screws and screwdrivers).

Income

The second important factor underlying the demand curve, in addition to the prices of other goods, is income. When income goes up, the demand for most goods will increase. But there are exceptions.

A *normal good* is a good for which demand increases when income rises. An *inferior good* is a good for which demand falls when income rises.

Inferior goods are typically goods for which there are alternatives of higher quality or greater convenience. For instance, bus riding is an inferior good. As income rises, people reduce their use of buses and switch to taxis or their own cars. Margarine is another inferior good.[3] As incomes rise, households buy more butter and less margarine.

Tastes

The third determinant of demand that we take as given is tastes. Consumer tastes are shaped in part by convenience, society, and habits. The demand for haircuts is determined in part by social conventions about how long hair should be worn. The demand for textiles to produce skirts depends on fashions and the length of skirts. The health and fitness consciousness of today has expanded the demands for jogging equipment, health centers, natural foods, and tennis facilities while reducing

---

[2] In the text we say that using public transportation is a substitute for using cars because an increase in the price of public transportation leads people to use cars more. But does an increase in the price of cars lead people to use public transportation more? Sometimes these questions have different answers. For instance, think of sugar and coffee. An increase in the price of sugar leads people to drink less coffee (suggesting that sugar and coffee are complements). But an increase in the price of coffee could *increase* the consumption of sugar (suggesting that coffee and sugar are substitutes). How could this happen? Suppose that people use more sugar in tea than in coffee. Then when the price of coffee goes up, they switch to tea and use more sugar.

We wouldn't want to have a definition that says coffee and sugar are substitutes in one sense and complements in another. They should be either substitutes or complements. The economist's definition introduced in Chapter 5 avoids this difficulty.

---

[3] Studies of the demand for margarine show that margarine is inferior. It might be that the concern over the amount of cholesterol in the diet has transformed margarine from an inferior good to a normal good. But there are not yet enough years of data to show this possibility.

cially soft-drink producers, substituted away from refined sugar and toward corn syrup and corn sugar. Once the technology for the alternative sweetener had been developed, there was a permanent reduction in the demand for refined sugar. Accordingly, even though by 1977–1979 the price of refined sugar was below the initial level, there was no recovery in demand. But we note from Table 3-3 that in the market for corn syrup and corn sugar there was a sustained increase in the quantity demanded.

The example illustrates some points about the operation of markets and the function of prices. In the short run, disturbances such as a reduction in supply lead to sharp price increases. But these price increases, which reduce the quantity demanded, lead consumers and industrial users of a good to look for substitutes. Thus a disturbance spreads to other markets, where demand and the equilibrium price will be affected.

Coffee

The second example is, if anything, more

TABLE 3-4
THE COFFEE MARKET

	1976	1977	1978	1979
Coffee:				
Price, $/lb	2.01	3.31	2.52	2.18
Quantity, lb	12.8	9.4	10.9	11.5

Note: Prices are in 1976 dollars; quantity is in pounds per head per year.
Source: Statistical Abstract of the United States, 1980, Tables 211, 806, and 811.

striking. In Table 3-4 we show data for the coffee market. A frost in Brazil, the main world supplier of coffee, sharply reduced the coffee harvest in 1977 and therefore, as shown in Figure 3-10, shifted the world supply schedule for coffee to the left, from SS to SS'. The resulting excess demand for coffee led to a sharp price increase, from E to E'. In Table 3-4 we see that the price rose from $2.01 per pound to $3.31 and that there was an accompanying reduction in the quantity demanded from 12.8 pounds (per person per year) in 1976 to only 9.4 pounds. Once the supply recovered in 1978–1979,

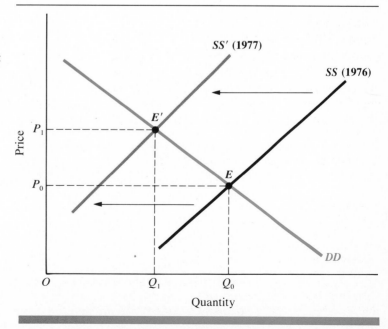

FIGURE 3-10 A FROST IN BRAZIL REDUCES COFFEE SUPPLY AND RAISES THE EQUILIBRIUM PRICE. The harvest failure due to frost in 1977 reduces the supply of coffee. At each price of coffee, the quantity supplied declines as the supply schedule shifts to SS'. The equilibrium price of coffee rises from P_0 to P_1, while the quantity demanded declines from Q_0 to Q_1.

BOX 3-2

ANATOMY OF PRICE AND QUANTITY CHANGES

The accompanying table and Figure (*a*) show indices for the real price of lumber and for the quantity of lumber shipped by producers. We know that these changes in price and quantity were caused by shifts in the supply and/or demand curves. But can we *identify* what actually happened? Was it a shift in demand or a shift in supply that led, for example, to the low 1981 real price and quantity? Or were a shift in demand and a shift in supply both at work? This question comes up often, when the economist is confronted with just the observed prices and quantities and has to determine what led to changes in the market. The question is known as the *identification problem.*

LUMBER PRICES AND QUANTITIES, 1977–1981
(1979 = 100)

	1977	1978	1979	1980	1981
Price index	91	99	100	84	77
Quantity index	101	102	100	85	80

Source: Survey of Current Business, various issues.

The first step in analyzing the data is to assume that each observation is the intersection of a demand schedule and a supply schedule.

The next step is to ask what changes in the "other things being equal" determinants of demand and supply could have caused the movements in prices and quantities seen in Figure (*a*). One possibility is that all movements are the result of shifts in the supply curve. That possibility is shown in Figure (*b*), where the demand curve is *DD,* and supply shifts from *SS* to *SS'* to *SS"*. Equilibrium shifts from *E* to *E'* to *E"*. Another possibility is that all the shifts come from the side of demand, as in Figure (*c*). Here the supply curve remains at *SS* throughout, and the demand curve shifts from *DD* to *DD'* to *DD"*. Equilibrium shifts correspondingly from *E* to *E'* to *E"*.

In practice, shifts in both the supply and demand curves are likely to happen and cause price and quantity movements. But one or the other may dominate. In the case of lumber, the observed pattern is more consistent with shifts in demand than shifts in supply. The observed points in Figure (*a*) look more as if they were produced by Figure (*c*) than by Figure (*b*).

We can easily discount the source of the price and quantity movements in the lumber market. One of the chief determinants of the quantity of lumber demanded at each price is the amount of housing construction. An index of housing construction shows that in 1980–1981 housing starts had fallen to only 60 percent of the level in 1977–1979. It is this decline in housing construction that shows up in the lumber market as a leftward shift in the demand schedule.

In many cases we can identify whether it was the supply curve or the demand curve that shifted and changed price and quantity because demand and supply have different determinants: lumber supply (*not* the equilibrium quantity supplied) has nothing to do with housing construction; lumber de-

mand has nothing to do with forest fires, which may be a determinant of supply. It is these differences in the basic determinants of demand and supply
that often allow us to unscramble the market price and quantity data to find
out what were the chief disturbances at work.

Figure (b) shows the combinations of price and quantity that would be observed if
the cause of price changes were shifts in the supply curve. In that case we would
see points like E, E', and E'', which, joined together, show the demand curve. Figure
(c) shows what would be observed if shifts in demand caused price and quantity
changes. Points E, E', and E'' in that case form a supply curve when joined together.
The pattern in Figure (a) is closer to that in Figure (c), indicating that shifts in demand were mainly responsible for the observed changes in lumber prices and quantities in the 1977–1981 period.

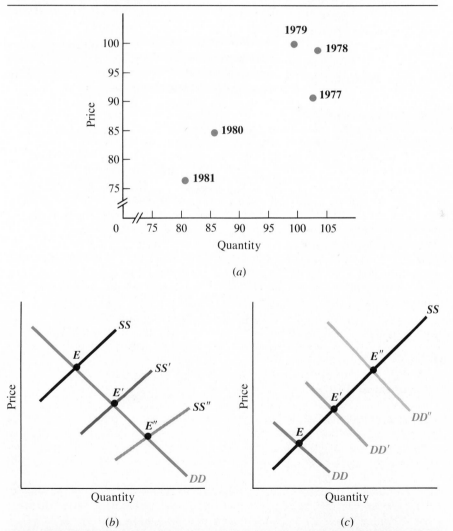

(a)

(b)   (c)

the price dropped back toward the initial level, and accordingly, the quantity demanded increased.

The increase in the equilibrium price of coffee should have affected the demands for other goods and thus spread to other markets. We would have expected the demand for tea, which is a substitute for coffee, to shift. The quantity of tea demanded at any price of tea should have risen. Thus there should have been an increase in the price of tea and an increase in the quantity of tea consumed. In fact, this is what happened. The quantity of tea consumed in the United States in 1977 was slightly higher than the quantity consumed in 1976. The price of tea in 1977 was nearly double the price in 1976.

Thus the increased price of coffee shifted the demand curve for tea, leading to a higher price for tea and a higher quantity demanded.

Digital Watches

The third example we will consider involves technological innovation and cost reductions on the supply side that work to shift the supply schedule. We will take the case of digital watches. Table 3-5 shows the relevant data.

The price of digital watches declined from $76 to only $33 between 1975 and 1979. The reduction in price led to an increase in the quantity demanded from 4.2 million watches to 19.7 million. Once again, demand is seen to be responsive to price.

TABLE 3-5
DIGITAL WATCHES

	1975	1977	1979
Price $/unit	76	44	33
Quantity, millions	4.2	15.6	19.7

Source: Statistical Abstract of the United States, 1980, Table 1488.

10 WHAT, HOW, AND FOR WHOM

The free market is one method society uses to solve the three basic economic problems: What is produced? How? For whom? This chapter has shown how supply and demand determine price and output. We now explain how supply and demand working through markets thereby solve the basic economic problems.

In Figure 3-11 we show once more a demand schedule and a supply schedule and, at point E, the equilibrium, or free-market, price and the equilibrium quantity traded. The free market "decides" how much of a particular good to produce by finding the price at which the quantity demanded equals the quantity supplied. In our example the equilibrium quantity is Q_0. That

FIGURE 3-11 THE FREE MARKET ANSWERS THE BASIC ECONOMIC QUESTIONS. The free-market price is P_0, and the equilibrium quantity demanded and supplied is Q_0. Consumers who are willing (and able) to pay at least P_0 per unit will receive the output; consumers who are willing to pay only less will receive none.

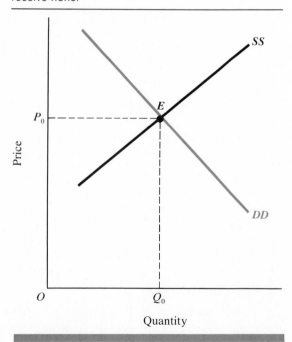

amount depends both on the position of the supply schedule and on the position of the demand schedule. If at each price consumers demanded a larger quantity, *DD* would be located farther to the right, and the equilibrium quantity would be higher. If at each price the quantity supplied were lower, the supply schedule would be farther to the left, and the equilibrium quantity would be lower. Thus the free-market answer to the question of how much of a good to produce is determined by both supply and demand conditions. Other things being equal, more of a good will be produced in market equilibrium the higher the quantity demanded is at each price (the farther to the right the demand schedule) and the higher the quantity supplied at each price (the farther to the right the supply schedule).

The free market tells us for whom the goods are produced. They are produced for all those willing to pay the price P_0 per unit of the good. The free market also tells us how goods are produced, but to understand the answer to that question we have to learn more about the production side of the economy.

It is worth emphasizing that although the free market solves the basic economic problems, its answers may be controversial. The free market does *not* provide enough food for everybody to go without hunger, and it does not provide enough medical care for everybody to be healthy. It provides enough food for those willing *and able* to pay, and it also provides enough medical care for them. The answers given by a free market, therefore, may differ very radically from what society may want to see as an allocation of resources. It is for this reason that government intervention in the free market through regulation, taxation, and the redistribution of income is so pervasive throughout the world.

SUMMARY

1   Demand is the quantity of a good buyers want to buy at each price. The lower the price, the greater the quantity demanded. The demand curve shows graphically the relationship between price and the quantity demanded. It slopes downward.

2   Supply is the quantity of a good sellers want to sell at each price. The higher the price, the larger the quantity supplied. The supply curve shows the relationship between price and the quantity of the good sellers want to sell. It slopes upward.

3   The market clears or is in equilibrium when the price is at the level at which the quantity demanded and the quantity supplied are equal. This is the point at which the demand and supply curves intersect. At prices below the equilibrium price there is an excess demand (or a shortage), and this tends to raise prices. At prices above the equilibrium price there is an excess supply (or a surplus), and this tends to cause prices to fall. Thus in a free market, prices tend to move toward the equilibrium level.

4   The factors that are assumed to be constant along a given demand curve are the prices of related goods, consumer income, and consumer tastes and habits.

5   An increase in the price of a substitute will increase the quantity of a good demanded at each price, and an increase in the price of a complement will reduce the quantity demanded. An increase in income increases the demand for the good if the good is normal. If an increase in income reduces the demand for a good, the good is inferior.

6   The main factors determining the position of the supply curve are technology, input costs, and government regulation and taxation. An increase in input costs will reduce the quantity supplied at each price.

7   Any factor increasing demand causes the demand curve to shift to the right and increases both the price and the quantity bought and sold. Any factor reducing supply causes the supply curve to move to the left, increasing price and reducing the quantity bought and sold.

KEY TERMS

Demand	Normal goods
Supply	Inferior goods
Quantity demanded	Shift of demand curve
Quantity supplied	Shift of supply curve
Equilibrium price	Free market
Excess demand (shortage)	Price controls
Excess supply (surplus)	Floor price
Equilibrium quantity	Ceiling price
Substitute	Movement along demand curve
Complement	

PROBLEMS

1   Hypothetical supply and demand data for toasters are shown below. Plot the supply and demand curves for toasters, and find the equilibrium price and quantity.

SUPPLY AND DEMAND FOR TOASTERS

PRICE, $	QUANTITY DEMANDED, millions	QUANTITY SUPPLIED, millions
10	10	3
12	9	4
14	8	5
16	7	6
18	6	7
20	5	8

2   In Problem 1, what is the excess supply or demand (a) when the price is $12? (b) when the price is $20?

3   How will the price of toasters change in situations (a) and (b) in Problem 2?

4   What happens to the demand curve for toasters when the price of bread rises? Show in a supply-demand diagram how the equilibrium price and quantity of toasters change.

5   (a) How is the demand curve for toasters affected by the invention of the toaster

oven, which to many people is a better device for toasting? (*b*) What effect would this have on the equilibrium quantity of toasters bought and sold and on the price of toasters? (*c*) Why?

6   Returning to the toaster data, suppose that the quantity supplied at each price rises by 1 million. (*a*) Calculate the new equilibrium price and quantity. (*b*) Does the equilibrium quantity sold increase by more or less than 1 million, that is, by more or less than the increase in the quantity supplied at each price? Why?

7   (*a*) Suppose that cold weather makes it more difficult to catch fish. What happens to the supply curve for fish? What happens to the price and quantity? (*b*) Suppose that the cold weather also reduces the demand for fish, because people do not go shopping. Show what happens to the demand curve for fish. (*c*) What happens to the quantity of fish bought and sold when the cold weather sets in? (*d*) Can you say what happens to the price of fish?

8   Show, using demand and supply schedules, how an increase in income would affect the demand curve for a product that is inferior. What happens to the price and quantity?

9   Suppose that a ceiling price is imposed on a good and that the ceiling is above the equilibrium price. What effect, if any, would such a ceiling have on the price and quantity?

10   When the federal government gave away 300 million pounds of cheese at the end of 1981, some supermarkets were upset; they claimed that the government's action would have a bad effect on their business. How would the supermarkets' business have been affected?

11   *Extra credit.* Using the toaster data, suppose that a tax of $1 is put on toasters. For convenience, assume that the seller pays the tax. Thus if a seller charges $16 for a toaster, he receives only $15, and the government gets $1. Similarly, if he charges $18, he receives only $17, and the government gets $1. (*a*) What happens to the quantity of toasters sold when the tax is imposed? (*b*) What happens to the price the consumers pay? (*c*) What happens to the price the sellers receive after paying the tax? (*Suggestion:* There is now a difference between the amount the buyers pay and the amount, net of tax, that the sellers receive. Interpret the demand curve as describing the amount buyers want at the price they have to pay, and interpret the supply curve as describing the amount suppliers want to sell at the price they receive. Remember that there is a gap of $1 between the amount buyers pay and the amount sellers receive.)

2

Microeconomics

You are the manager of the Old State University football stadium. You have to set the prices of tickets before the season begins, and you aim to take in as much revenue as possible—to support OSU in general and the football program in particular. Should you set a low price for the tickets, ensuring that every game is sold out, or should you set a high price, leaving the stadium with empty seats during some games? If you charge a low price, you sell more tickets. But at a high price, each ticket brings in more money. Which is the better strategy?

4

The Demand Curve: Adjustments to Price and Income Changes

Your answer depends on how responsive the quantity demanded is to changes in price. If it takes a large cut in price to increase the quantity demanded by enough to fill the stadium for each game, it will not make sense to try to fill the stadium. But if by cutting the price just a little you could keep the stadium full, you would want to set a price that ensures a sellout for each game.

In this chapter we introduce *price elasticity of demand,* a measure of the responsiveness of the quantity of a good demanded to changes in price. Price elasticity is the key piece of information in many economic problems, such as the one facing the manager of the stadium, and it is frequently used by economists.

Here are two more examples to illustrate the use of the concept of price elasticity.

The Boston subway system is running a deficit, that is, losing money. Its costs of operation do not change much as the number of riders changes. Maybe the system can reduce the deficit by changing the price of a ride. Should the fare be raised or lowered? The obvious answer is to raise the fare. But that may not be the right answer. With a higher fare, everyone who continues to use the subway pays more per trip, but the gain could be more than offset by the loss of passengers who decide to switch to other means of transportation.

To answer the question, we have to know how responsive the quantity demanded is to price. If the number of riders falls very little when the fare goes up, then the right strategy is to raise the price. If the number of riders falls a lot when the fare goes up, then *lowering* the price will reduce the deficit. The reduction in price will bring in a lot more riders, and the system's revenues will increase. We will see in this chapter that the price elasticity of demand for subway rides is the fact we need to decide whether to raise or lower the price to reduce the deficit.

Or take the example of energy. In 1973–1974 and on several later occasions, the oil-producing countries raised the world price of oil. What was the effect on their revenues? With oil prices higher, the quantity of oil demanded fell. But by how much? In fact, the quantity demanded declined very little, at least in the first few years after the oil price increase. Accordingly, oil producers sold nearly unchanged amounts of oil at much higher prices. Their revenues were immensely higher.

But how will the strategy work in the long run? Here the issue is whether there are differences between the responsiveness of the quantity demanded in the short run (say, a year or two) and in the long run (say, 5 or more years). There are indeed differences, as we will see later in the chapter—and as the glut of oil that developed in 1982, years after the price of oil first increased so sharply, suggests.

Much of the chapter deals with the responsiveness of the demand for a good to changes in the good's own price, as measured by the price elasticity of demand. But the demand for a good depends also on the prices of other goods. For instance, the quantity of coffee demanded at any given price of coffee depends on the price of tea. The higher the price of tea, the greater will be the quantity of coffee demanded. The responsiveness of the quantity of a good demanded to changes in the price of another good is measured by the *cross price elasticity of demand*. We introduce cross price elasticity in this chapter and illustrate its use.

In addition, we define *income elasticity of demand*. The income elasticity of demand is a measure of the response of the quantity of a good demanded to changes in consumer income. We discuss differences in the responsiveness of demands for different goods to changes in income. Goods for

TABLE 4-1

THE DEMAND FOR FOOTBALL TICKETS

PRICE, $/ticket	QUANTITY DEMANDED, thousands per game
22.50	10
20	20
15	40
12.50	50
10	60
5	80
2.50	90
1	96
0	100

which demand grows fast with income will take up a larger share of spending in the future, when incomes are higher. Growth prospects for those industries are good. Growth prospects are less exciting in industries where demand will not grow much as income rises. Investors and businesses are certainly interested in differences in the income elasticity of demand among goods.

1 THE PRICE RESPONSIVENESS OF DEMAND

The downward slope of the demand curve shows that quantity demanded increases when price falls. But as the examples in the introduction suggest, we often need to know more. We need a measure of how much the quantity demanded responds to price changes. We develop that measure, the price elasticity of demand, in this section.

We use the example of the demand for football tickets. The first column of Table 4-1 shows a range of prices for the tickets. The second column shows the total number of tickets demanded per game at each price. (We assume that all tickets are sold at the same price.) These data are plotted in Figure 4-1 to show the demand schedule, *DD*. The schedule has the usual downward

FIGURE 4-1 THE DEMAND
CURVE FOR FOOTBALL
TICKETS. The demand schedule
for football tickets has the conventional downward slope. A reduction in price increases the
quantity of tickets demanded.

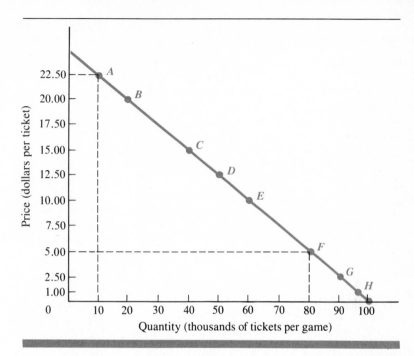

slope. Each of the labeled points (such as *A* or *F*) corresponds to a price-quantity pair in Table 4-1. By drawing a line through all the points we obtain the entire demand schedule for the hypothetical football ticket market. Note that the demand curve is a straight line and that the quantity of tickets demanded increases by 4000 for every $1 reduction in price.

The Price Elasticity of Demand

We now develop a measure of the responsiveness of the quantity demanded to price. One seemingly natural measure of price responsiveness is the increase in the number of tickets sold when the price is cut by $1. From Table 4-1, the answer is 4000 tickets.

But suppose we were interested in comparing price responsiveness in different markets. In some other market—for example, the market for chewing gum, where the average price of a packet of gum is about 30 cents—it might make no sense to discuss the effects of a $1 cut in price. Or in the market for automobiles, a $1 cut in price wouldn't even be noticed. We therefore have to adjust for the existing price in the market. We do that by asking about the effects of a given *percentage* change in price on the quantity demanded. We also want to adjust for the size of the market. Selling 4000 more units (tickets) in a market where 40,000 are now being sold is very different from selling 4000 more units (of gum) in a market where millions are being sold. We adjust for the size of the market by looking at the *percentage* change in quantity resulting from a price change.

These arguments lead economists to use the price elasticity of demand as the measure of price responsiveness.

The *price elasticity of demand* is the ratio of the percentage change in quantity demanded to the percentage change in price.

TABLE 4-2
THE PRICE ELASTICITY OF DEMAND

PRICE, $/ticket	QUANTITY DEMANDED, thousands per game	PRICE ELASTICITY OF DEMAND
22.50	10	−9
20	20	−4.0
15	40	−1.5
12.50	50	−1.0
10	60	−0.67
5	80	−0.25
2.50	90	−0.17
1	96	−0.04
0	100	0

The equation used to calculate the price elasticity of demand for any given change in price is as follows:

$$\text{Price elasticity of demand} = \frac{\text{percentage change in quantity demanded}}{\text{percentage change in price}} \quad (1)$$

Because the price elasticity of demand is used so often, economists frequently refer simply to the elasticity of demand when they mean the price elasticity of demand.

The equation shows that the elasticity of demand is calculated as the ratio of the percentage change in quantity demanded to the percentage change in price. Let us consider examples of how to use the equation. Suppose that the price rises by 1 percent and that, as a consequence, the quantity demanded falls by 2 percent. The elasticity in this case is −2 (−2 percent/1 percent). Suppose, to give another example, that the price drops by 4 percent and that the result is an increase in the quantity demanded of 2 percent. In this case the elasticity is −0.5 (2 percent/−4 percent). In the former case, with an elasticity of −2, demand is much more responsive to price than in the latter case, where the elasticity is only −0.5.

Note that the price elasticity of demand is always negative. Along the demand schedule a reduction in price always increases the quantity demanded, and a rise in price always reduces the quantity de-

manded. Therefore the elasticity, which is the ratio of the percentage change in quantity demanded to the percentage change in price, will always be a negative number.[1]

We can now use the price elasticity of demand to investigate the demand for football tickets. Table 4-2 shows the price-quantity data given in Table 4-1. In addition, it shows the price elasticity of demand.

The elasticities in Table 4-2 are calculated from equation (1). For instance, at the price of $22.50 and the quantity of 10, consider a price reduction to $20. This is a change in price of −11.11 percent (−$2.50/$22.50). The resulting increase in the quantity demanded is 10 units (from 10 to 20 tickets), or 100 percent (10/10). Therefore the price elasticity of demand at a price of $22.50 is −9 (100 percent/−11.11 percent). Now let us calculate the elasticity of demand at the price of $20. At that price, or at that point on the demand schedule, a reduction in price to $15, or a −25 percent (−$5/$20) change in price, leads to a 100 percent (20/20) increase in demand. Therefore the elasticity is −4 (100 percent/−25

---

[1] It is often a bit awkward to refer to the elasticity of demand as a negative number. Experienced economists for that reason tend to describe the elasticity of demand as positive. This might be confusing, so we will keep the minus sign to remind ourselves that price and quantity move in opposite directions on the demand curve.

FIGURE 4-2 THE ELASTICITY
OF DEMAND ALONG THE DE-
MAND SCHEDULE. The price elasticity of demand measures the
responsiveness of quantity demanded to a change in price.
Along the demand schedule in
this diagram, the elasticity varies,
ranging from a very large value at
high prices to almost zero as
price drops toward zero. The portion of the demand schedule
above the point where elasticity is
−1 (the point of unitary elasticity)
is called *elastic*. The portion
below the point of unitary elasticity, where the absolute value of
the elasticity is less than 1, is
called *inelastic*.

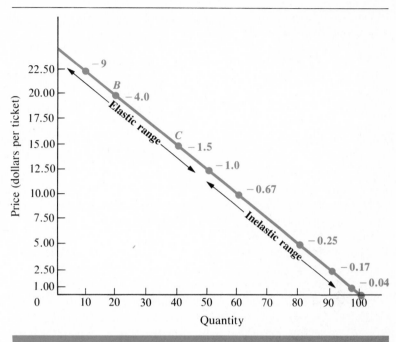

percent). The other elasticities in the table are calculated in the same way.

In Figure 4-2 we again show the demand schedule, along with the price elasticities at different points on it. There are two things to notice. First, the elasticity is not a constant, say, −5 or −10, all along the demand curve in Figure 4-2. On the contrary, elasticity varies along the demand curve. Second, elasticity is large at high prices and drops to close to zero as the price falls toward zero.[2]

Elasticity: Two Special Points

Arc Elasticity In Figure 4-2 the elasticity of demand is different at every point shown on the demand curve. This has an awkward im-

plication, which is that elasticity appears to differ depending on whether we are moving up or down the demand curve. To illustrate, let us consider price and quantity changes between points *B* and *C* in Figure 4-2.

The elasticity of demand at point *B* is shown as −4.0. This is because from point *B* to point *C* there is a price cut of $5 and a corresponding quantity increase of 20,000. The price cut is −25 percent [(−$5/$20) × 100 percent], and the quantity increase is 100 percent [(20,000/20,000) × 100 percent], giving an elasticity of −4 (100/−25). Now consider the reverse direction. Suppose we start at point *C* and raise the price by $5, moving up to point *B*. The price rises by 33.33 percent [($5/$15) × 100 percent], and the quantity falls by 50 percent [(20,000/40,000) × 100 percent], giving an elasticity of −1.5 (50/−33.33). This is, of course, the elasticity of point *C*.

It thus seems that the elasticity for a given move, such as between points *B* and *C*, depends on whether we are heading up

---

[2] We shall refer to elasticities that are large in absolute value as large. (To get the absolute value of a number, drop the minus sign.) The mathematically minded will recognize that −9 is less than −1, and thus we should say that an elasticity of −9 is small compared with an elasticity of −1. We have adopted the more convenient though less accurate language.

or down the demand curve. The notion of *arc elasticity* was invented to avoid this difficulty. The arc elasticity measures the elasticity of demand between two points on the basis of the average price between those two points—the reference price—and the average quantity—the reference quantity.

Let us look again at points B and C. The average price is $17.50, the average of $15 and $20. The average quantity is 30,000, the average of 20,000 and 40,000. The percentage change in price is then ($5/$17.50) × 100 percent = 28.6 percent, and the percentage change in quantity is (20,000/30,000) × 100 percent = 66.7 percent. The arc elasticity is −2.33 (−66.7/28.6). This will be the same whether we consider an increase in price from C to B or a fall in price from B to C.

As we should expect, the arc elasticity (−2.33) is between the elasticities at points B (−4) and C (−1.5). The equation for the arc elasticity is as follows:

Arc elasticity of demand
$$= \frac{\text{change in quantity}}{\text{average quantity}} \div \frac{\text{change in price}}{\text{average price}} \quad (2)$$

Other Demand Curves   We have defined the elasticity of demand for the straight-line demand curve shown in Figures 4-1 and 4-2. But not all demand curves are straight lines. Equation (1), for the elasticity of demand, applies for *all* demand curves, straight-line or curved. The elasticity is always defined as the ratio of the percentage change in quantity to the percentage change in price. And the arc elasticity can be used on any demand curve to avoid the ambiguity to which the standard definition may lead.[3]

Elastic Demand and Inelastic Demand

On the demand curve in Figure 4-2, elastic-ity ranges from a very large number all the way to zero. But there is an important dividing line: the elasticity of −1.

Demand is *elastic* if the absolute value of the price elasticity is more than 1. For example, demand is elastic if the price elasticity is −4. Demand is *inelastic* if the absolute value of the price elasticity is less than 1. For example, demand is inelastic if the price elasticity of demand is −0.67.

The dividing line—where elasticity is −1—is referred to as the point of *unitary* elasticity. In Figure 4-2, demand is elastic at all prices above $12.50 and inelastic at all prices below $12.50. Demand is unit-elastic at the price of $12.50.

The distinction between elastic demand and inelastic demand is important because, as we will show later in this section, a cut in price raises total consumer spending on a good when demand is elastic. However, when demand is inelastic, a cut in price reduces total consumer spending on the good. You will notice that this takes us close to answering the questions about subway fares and football tickets raised at the beginning of this chapter.

Economists frequently talk about goods with high or low elasticities of demand as if the elasticity remains fixed instead of varying, as in Figure 4-2. For instance, they will say that the demand for oil is price-inelastic or that the demand for foreign travel is highly price-elastic. Such statements always refer implicitly to parts of the demand curve around the current price and prices that have been observed in the past. They do not necessarily describe elasticities at prices very different from those seen in the past.

The Determinants of Price Elasticity   What determines the price elasticity of demand for any particular good bought by consumers? When should we expect demand to

---

[3] There are some demand curves on which the elasticity of demand is constant. Such curves are bowed toward the origin.

be very elastic—say, an elasticity of -1.5 or even -5—and under what conditions would elasticity be small?

The ultimate determinant of price elasticity of demand is consumer tastes.[4] In discussing what determines price elasticity of demand, we are really asking how consumers change their purchases when they are faced with price changes, and that clearly depends largely on their tastes for different goods. Nonetheless, we can point to some considerations that are likely to affect consumer responses to price changes of goods.

The most important consideration is the ease with which consumers can substitute from the good in question to other commodities. Consider two extreme cases. In one case we look at the market for all foods (meat, bread, fish, poultry—everything you can imagine). Suppose the prices of all these food items rise by 1 percent. Should we expect a drop in the quantity demanded of 10 percent or 0.5 percent? The answer is more nearly 0.5 percent. The reason is that consumers have no ready substitutes for food in general and cannot really do without it. They can adjust their diets, using food more efficiently and getting slimmer, but basically they will find few ways to economize on food.

By contrast, suppose there is a 1 percent rise in the price of a particular brand of cornflakes. Here consumers have plenty of substitutes. They can consume other brands of cornflakes, other kinds of cereal, or any of a variety of other breakfast foods, including eggs, steaks, fruits, and even bread. With so

much ease of substitution we would expect a very substantial demand response. The price elasticity of demand for a particular brand of cornflakes may well be -3, -5, or more.

Ease of substitution and the number and convenience of alternative goods that satisfy the same consumer demand imply a higher elasticity of demand for a good. This suggests that a more narrowly defined commodity (a particular brand of cornflakes as opposed to cornflakes in general, or cornflakes as opposed to breakfast foods, or oil as opposed to energy) typically has a larger elasticity of demand than a more comprehensive group.

Measuring Elasticities   Beyond these general principles, one has to turn to measurements of demand elasticities for particular goods or groups of commodities. Table 4-3 shows estimates of price elasticities.

The table confirms that the demand for groups of basic commodities, such as food or shelter, is inelastic. By contrast, for more

TABLE 4-3

ESTIMATES OF PRICE ELASTICITIES OF DEMAND

GOOD	PRICE ELASTICITY OF DEMAND
Food	−0.63
Clothing	−0.51
Transportation	−0.60
Shelter	−0.56
Medical care	−0.80
Toilet articles	−2.42
Sports goods	−2.40
Taxicabs	−1.24
Flowers, seeds, plants	−2.70

Source: E. Lazear and R. Michael, "Family Size and the Distribution of Real Per Capita Income," *American Economic Review,* March 1980, Table 2, for rows 1–4, and H. Houthakker and L. Taylor, *Consumer Demand in the United States,* Harvard University Press, Cambridge, Mass., 1970, Table 3.2, rows 5–9.

[4] We are talking here about the price elasticity of demand by consumers. But the concept is used much more widely. For instance, there is a price elasticity of demand for labor; it describes how firms change their inputs of labor when the wage changes. In such cases, there is more than the tastes of consumers underlying elasticity; the degree to which other factors of production can be substituted for labor in production is also important.

narrowly defined goods such as sports goods the elasticity can be quite large. An interesting comparison is between the elasticity of demand for all forms of transportation, which is -0.6, and the elasticity of demand for a particular means of transportation, namely taxicabs, which is -1.24. The larger elasticity for taxicab transportation reflects the availability of substitutes, which range from buses, private cars, and feet to no travel at all. Table 4-3 provides only a small sample of the many estimates made of demand elasticities for all sorts of goods. Such estimates are widely used by government and business.

Using Price Elasticities

How can information on price elasticities of demand be used? A typical application is the following. Suppose the price elasticity of demand for public parking in the municipal lots is -1.5. From equation (1), a 1 percent increase in parking fees would lower the quantity demanded (hours of parking space) by 1.5 percent. Suppose that at the municipal lots the current price is $2.50 per hour and that the shortage of space is about 15 percent. This means there are long lines in front of every garage and other cars driving around the block waiting for a vacancy.

By how much must the price be raised to eliminate the lines? A 1 percent increase in price will reduce the quantity demanded by 1.5 percent, and a 10 percent increase in price will reduce the quantity demanded by 15 percent. We therefore need to raise the price by 10 percent, from $2.50 to $2.75.

How does the price increase eliminate the queue? Some people will now use the bus, others will park farther away from downtown, and still others will form car pools. The elasticity of demand summarizes all these possibilities of substituting for the use of municipal parking lots. Note that if the elasticity of demand had been much smaller, say, only -0.5, a greater increase in

price would have been necessary, namely 30 percent. Thus the higher the elasticity of demand, the smaller the increase in price required to eliminate a shortage. And the smaller the price elasticity of demand, the larger the price increase required to eliminate excess demand.

The relationship between the size of the elasticity of demand and the change in price required to eliminate a shortage has a useful application in markets where supply disturbances occur. In Chapter 3 we saw that a leftward shift in the supply schedule —perhaps because of a harvest failure, or a strike, or a storm that keeps the fishermen at home—creates an excess demand and leads to an increase in the equilibrium price. What we learn here is that the size of the price increase depends on the elasticity of demand. The lower the elasticity of demand, the larger the increase in price. But in which markets do such supply disturbances occur? One is clearly the food market, which is affected by harvest failures. Because the elasticity of demand for food is very small, a harvest failure produces a large increase in the price of food. On the other hand, a bumper crop leads to an excess supply of food, which brings about a very large drop in price.

2 PRICE, QUANTITY DEMANDED, AND TOTAL EXPENDITURES

The next relationship we discuss is the one between the price of a good, the quantity demanded, and the total spending or expenditure on the good. The total spending on a commodity is the product of the price and the quantity demanded:

Total spending on a commodity
$$= \text{price} \times \text{quantity demanded} \quad (3)$$

The total spending by purchasers is, of course, also the amount of revenue received by the sellers of the good.

TABLE 4-4
PRICE ELASTICITY OF DEMAND AND TOTAL SPENDING ON TICKETS

PRICE, $/ticket	QUANTITY DEMANDED, thousands per game	ELASTICITY	TOTAL SPENDING (PRICE × QUANTITY DEMANDED)
22.50	10	−9	225
20	20	−4.0	400
15	40	−1.5	600
12.50	50	−1.0	625
10	60	−0.67	600
5	80	−0.25	400
2.50	90	−0.17	225
1	96	−0.04	96
0	100	0	0

We return now to the football stadium. The fourth column of Table 4-4 shows the total spending at each price. For example, at a price of $20 per ticket the quantity demanded is 20 (thousand), and hence the total spending on tickets is $400 (thousand) ($20 × 20). Note that the demand conditions in the second column imply that total spending first rises and then decreases as the price falls.

Equation (3) shows the source of the dilemma facing the Old State University stadium manager. When the price falls, total spending falls if the quantity demanded does not fall. But when the price falls, the quantity demanded rises, tending to raise total spending. If the quantity demanded *rises enough* when the price falls, then total spending increases when the price falls.

Figure 4-3 shows graphically how total spending changes as the price changes. Consider first Case A. The initial price, P_A, is reduced to P_B. As a consequence, the quantity demanded rises from Q_A to Q_B. The initial spending is equal to price times quantity demanded, $P_A \times Q_A$, or the rectangle $OP_A AQ_A$. At the new and lower price, total spending is equal to $P_B \times Q_B$, or the rectangle $OP_B BQ_B$.

What is the change in spending? The reduction in price implies that spending falls by the shaded area marked with a minus sign, but an increase in the quantity demanded raises spending by the shaded area marked with a plus sign. The net result in this case is an increase in spending, since the (+) area is larger than the (−) area. In other words, in the elastic range of the demand curve (toward the upper end) a cut in price raises not only the quantity demanded but also total spending. The increase in the quantity demanded more than offsets the drop in price.

Case B shows the opposite result in the inelastic part of the demand curve. Here a cut in price, while of course raising the quantity demanded, leads to a fall in total spending. Demand does not rise sufficiently to compensate for the lower price. The (+) area is smaller than the (−) area, and total spending is lower at the lower price. Now if at high prices a cut in price raises spending while at low prices a cut in price lowers spending, then there will be some price in between where a fall in price leaves spending unchanged. Case C shows that possibility: the extra spending due to higher quantities demanded exactly offsets the lower prices. This occurs, as we will now show, at the point of unitary elasticity of the demand curve.

To understand that with a unit-elastic demand, spending remains unchanged as the price changes, we return to the definition of total spending in equation (3): total spending = price × quantity demanded.

FIGURE 4-3 RELATIONSHIPS BETWEEN ELASTIC-
ITY OF DEMAND AND EFFECTS OF PRICE
CHANGES ON EXPENDITURE. The diagrams illustrate the effect of a reduction in price on total
spending. They show the effects on revenue of a reduction in price and an increase in quantity demanded. Case A shows elastic demand; a cut in
price raises total spending. Case B shows inelastic
demand; the increase in quantity demanded is proportionately less than the cut in price, and hence
total spending falls. Case C is the borderline case of
unit-elastic demand; spending remains constant,
with the price and quantity changes exactly offsetting each other.

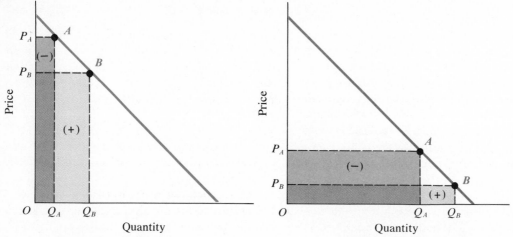

**Case A: Demand is elastic and
expenditure increases when price falls**

**Case B: Demand is inelastic and
expenditure falls when price falls**

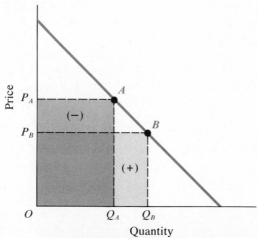

**Case C: Demand elasticity is 1 and
expenditure stays the same when price falls**

Now if the price falls by 1 percent and the quantity demanded rises, as a consequence, by 1 percent, then the product of price times quantity demanded remains unchanged.[5] If the quantity demanded increases by more than 1 percent, spending rises, and if it rises by less than 1 percent, spending falls. Thus the unit-elastic point on the demand curve is the dividing point below which further price cuts reduce spending.

Table 4-5 shows how the relationship between price changes and consumer spending on a good depends on the price elasticity of demand.

Total Revenue, Elasticity, and Price

The total spending on a good by consumers is equal to the total revenue received by sellers. From the viewpoint of the sellers—the manager of the stadium or the subway system—elasticity is useful in describing how revenue changes with price.

From Table 4-4 it is clear that the total revenue received from the sale of football tickets first increases as the price is cut; then it begins to fall as the price is cut fur-

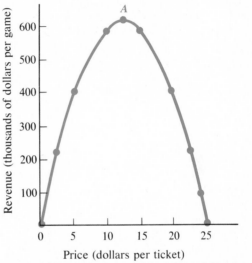

FIGURE 4-4 TOTAL REVENUE AND PRICE. As price is cut from high levels, total spending by consumers (equal to total revenue received by sellers) increases. It continues increasing so long as demand is elastic. When price hits $12.50, where demand is unit-elastic, further reductions in price will only reduce revenue. Total revenue is therefore highest at point A, where price is $12.50 and demand is unit-elastic.

ther. Table 4-5 explains why. When the price is high and demand is elastic, price reductions increase total spending on the good. When demand is unit-elastic, a small change in price has no effect on revenue. And when demand is inelastic, price cutting reduces the total spending on the good—which is, of course, the total revenue received by the seller.

In Figure 4-4 we return to the data from

---

[5] Because the price elasticity of demand is different at every point on the demand curve in Figure 4-3, a 1 percent fall in price from the point of unitary elasticity will actually slightly reduce total spending. Why? As the price is cut, the consumer moves along the demand curve to points where elasticity is slightly below 1, and spending therefore falls with further cuts in price. The price elasticity relationships in Table 4-5 apply *exactly* only for infinitesimally small changes in price. The differences are unimportant so long as only small price changes are considered.

TABLE 4-5

PRICE ELASTICITIES OF DEMAND AND SPENDING

	PRICE ELASTICITY OF DEMAND		
	ELASTIC (e.g., −4)	UNIT-ELASTIC (−1)	INELASTIC (e.g., −0.33)
Effect on spending of:			
Increase in price	Spending falls	Spending is unchanged	Spending rises
Reduction in price	Spending rises	Spending is unchanged	Spending falls

Table 4-4 to show another, equivalent way of thinking about the effects of price changes on total spending or revenue. Figure 4-4 shows the amount spent on the good, or the total revenue of sellers, at each price. From the diagram, total spending, or the amount of revenue, reaches a maximum at the price of $12.50, where the demand elasticity is −1.

Is this an accident? It is not. We know that as the price is cut from high levels, revenue increases because demand is elastic. When the price reaches $12.50, where demand is unit-elastic, further cuts in price *reduce* revenue or spending because demand becomes inelastic. *The conclusion is that spending and revenue are at a maximum at the point of unit-elastic demand.*

This piece of information is precisely what the stadium manager needs.

3 APPLICATIONS OF PRICE ELASTICITY

Transit Systems and Football Tickets

The relationship between price elasticities and spending summarized in Table 4-5 is relevant to both the question of whether we should lower or raise subway fares to eliminate a deficit and the question of pricing football tickets to maximize revenue. The subway fare question is now quite straightforward. If we know the elasticity of demand, then we know the direction in which to move prices.

Suppose we have a deficit and we know that the price elasticity of demand is −1.4. With an elasticity of −1.4, demand is elastic. Therefore a rise in price will reduce the quantity demanded *and* spending. Demand is highly responsive to prices, and therefore a price hike, while raising the price per fare, will result in the loss of so many riders that the net effect will be a reduction in total spending by consumers on subway fares. With a demand that is more than unit-elas-

tic, cutting fares will encourage demand, which is highly price-responsive, and thus increase revenue.

The example of the subway system and the right adjustment of fares effectively shows the role of the elasticity of demand. It is the number the transit system needs to know. The same is true if you set prices for the football tickets. To obtain the maximum revenue, you need to move to the point where demand is unit-elastic. If the prices currently charged are high, you may well be in the elastic portion. Cutting prices will raise revenue. However, if prices are very low, you may be in the inelastic portion, and raising prices will raise revenue.

Oil Shock

Perhaps the most dramatic application of price elasticity of demand and revenue in the last 25 years is the oil shock of the 1970s. The oil-producing countries as a group restricted the supply of oil to the world market. The shortage of oil caused the equilibrium price to more than quadruple.

What was the interest of the producers in restricting the supply? We know the answer from the relationship between price elasticity of demand and revenue changes: an increase in price raises consumer spending if demand is inelastic. And demand *was* inelastic. The price elasticity of demand was estimated to be about −0.1. Thus the effects of a price increase on revenue were hardly reduced by offsetting reductions in quantity demanded. A small restriction of the supply produced vast revenue gains. And that is, of course, what the oil-producing countries had in mind and did achieve.

The Coffee Frost

In Chapter 3 we showed that a reduction in the world supply of coffee following a frost in 1977 resulted in a sharp increase in prices. Price and quantity data for 1976 and

1977 are shown in Table 4-6. What happened to total spending on coffee when prices went up? The answer depends on the elasticity of demand for coffee. If demand is inelastic, an increase in price, while reducing the quantity demanded, leads to an increase in total spending. From Table 4-6 we find that the price rose from $2.01 to $3.31, while the quantity demanded dropped from 12.8 pounds to 9.4 pounds. Total spending per person increased from $25.73 ($2.01 × 12.8) to 31.11 ($3.31 × 9.4). Thus demand was inelastic, and the shortage and higher price led to an increase in spending.

This is a quite extraordinary result. We have just shown that a frost that destroys part of the coffee crop leads to higher consumer spending on coffee and a higher revenue for sellers of coffee. We would naturally think that a frost would hurt producers, but this is not necessarily the case. If demand is inelastic, as in the case for coffee, then a frost and a supply reduction actually increase the amount people spend on coffee, and therefore producers have higher revenues. This is a general result for commodities with low elasticities of demand.

There is one more feature of the coffee case that deserves comment. The demand for coffee turns out to be inelastic even though there are what an outside observer thinks of as substitutes, such as tea, or cola drinks with caffeine in them, or beer. This drives home the point that underlying price elasticities of demand are consumer tastes:

if consumers won't switch away from coffee, it is no use pointing out that a blend of warm tea and Coke will do the same things for a consumer that a cup of coffee will do.

Farmers and Bad Harvests

Are farmers better off when the weather is good or when it is bad? The natural answer is to think that they will be better off if the weather is good and they have bumper crops. Paradoxically, however, farmers may be better off when there is a poor harvest than when there is a good one. Figure 4-5 shows the demand for food. The demand curve in the range of prices P_A and P_B is typically inelastic, which is to say that the elasticity of demand is small.

After the farmers have planted the crop, the size of the crop depends largely on the weather. If the crop is small, as shown by supply curve SS', the price will be high. If the crop is large as a result of good weather, as shown by supply curve SS, the price will be low.[6] When do the farmers earn more? When the supply is large (SS) or when it is small (SS')? Because demand is inelastic, we know that total spending by households falls when the price falls. Therefore the lower the price, the less households spend on food, and the less farmers receive. Accordingly, the farmers receive more revenue when the supply curve is SS'—they are actually better off if the weather is bad.

Because an increase in quantity supplied lowers sellers' revenue when demand is inelastic, sellers in such markets sooner or later try to get together to manipulate the market, control the total quantity supplied, and thus prevent collapses in revenue from bumper crops.

A well-known example is the coffee ex-

TABLE 4-6

COFFEE: PRICE, QUANTITY, AND EXPENDITURE

	1976	1977
Price, $/lb	2.01	3.20
Quantity, lb	12.8	9.4
Total spending	25.73	30.08

Source: See Table 3-4. Prices are in 1976 dollars; quantities are in pounds per person.

[6] Why is the supply curve drawn with a positive slope if the crop has already been planted? The reason is that the farmers will devote more effort to harvesting the crop if the price is high.

FIGURE 4-5 BAD WEATHER MAY HELP THE FARMERS. A harvest failure that results from excessive rain or a lack of rain, for example, reduces the supply of food. This is shown by the leftward shift of the supply schedule from SS to SS'. The resulting excess demand for food raises the equilibrium price from P_B to P_A. The total revenue changes from $P_B \times Q_B$ to $P_A \times Q_A$. If the disturbance occurs at an initial price in the elastic portion of the demand curve, then a supply reduction will reduce total spending. But if demand is inelastic, a supply reduction will raise spending and farmers' revenue.

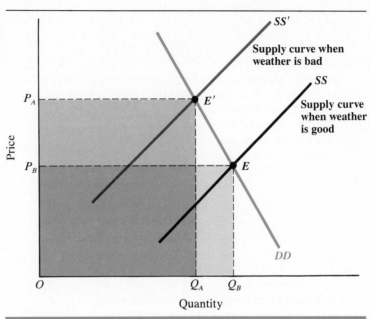

port policy of Brazil. We have already seen that coffee demand is inelastic; a bumper crop of coffee used to lead to a collapse of prices *and* revenues in the world market. Because Brazil was the chief producer of coffee, that country could prevent such a collapse simply by preventing bumper crops from coming on the market. But how? Anytime there was a bumper crop, the gov-

ernment would buy up supplies (at low prices) and simply and literally burn them.

Finally, we should note that Figure 4-5 illustrates a point that is of general importance. It shows that all farmers *taken together* will be better off if there is bad weather and the crop is small, so long as demand is inelastic. But what if any one farmer is faced with a disaster, such as a fire,

BOX 4-1

THE ELASTICITY OF SUPPLY

The elasticity of demand measures the responsiveness of the quantity demanded to a change in price. We often want also to know how responsive the quantity supplied is to a change in price. For instance, in Figure (a), supply curve SS shows a larger response of the quantity supplied to price than does supply curve SS' around point A, where they intersect.

The responsiveness of the quantity supplied to a change in price is measured by the elasticity of supply, which is defined as:

$$\text{Elasticity of supply} = \frac{\text{percentage change in quantity supplied}}{\text{percentage change in price}} \quad \text{(B1)}$$

As with the elasticity of demand, we use percentage changes to adjust for the level of the price and the size of the market.

Because the supply curve slopes upward, the elasticity of supply is positive. An increase in price increases the quantity supplied. The more elastic is supply, the larger the (percentage) increase in the quantity supplied in response to a given (percentage) change in price. In Figure (a), supply curve SS is more elastic than SS'.

Unlike an elasticity of 1 in the case of demand, an elasticity of 1 in the case of supply is not particularly important. This is because the total revenue received by a firm on the supply curve always increases as the price rises— because price and quantity increase together. The elasticity of supply is zero when the supply curve is vertical, like SS' in Figure (b). The elasticity of supply is infinity when the supply curve is horizontal, like SS in Figure (b). These elasticities are in accord with equation (B1). On the vertical supply curve, SS', the percentage change in the quantity supplied is zero when the price changes. On the horizontal supply curve, any increase in price above $\bar{P}$ would create an infinite quantity supplied.

What are the main uses of the elasticity of supply? The elasticity of supply tells us how much the price will change when there is a shift in demand. For instance, in Figure (b) we see that a shift in demand from DD to DD' increases the price much more when the supply curve is SS' than when it is SS. Hence the rule: Price goes up more in response to a shift in demand the more inelastic is supply. And correspondingly: Quantity goes up more in response to a shift in demand the more elastic is supply.

(a) SUPPLY ELASTICITY. (b) ZERO AND INFINITE SUPPLY ELASTICITIES. At point A in Figure (a), supply is more elastic on supply curve SS than on SS'. This is because a given increase in price leads to a larger increase in the quantity supplied on SS than on SS'. Figure (b) shows the extreme cases of totally inelastic supply (on SS', where the quantity supplied does not change at all when the price changes) and infinitely elastic supply (on SS, where any increase in price above $\bar{P}$ would result in an infinite quantity supplied). The figure also shows why the elasticity of supply is useful in predicting whether a given shift in demand will result in large changes in price or large changes in quantity. On the completely inelastic supply curve, the shift in demand from DD to DD' shifts equilibrium from A to A'. Price changes a lot, but quantity does not change at all. On the perfectly elastic supply curve, equilibrium shifts from E to E'. Price does not change, but quantity increases a lot.

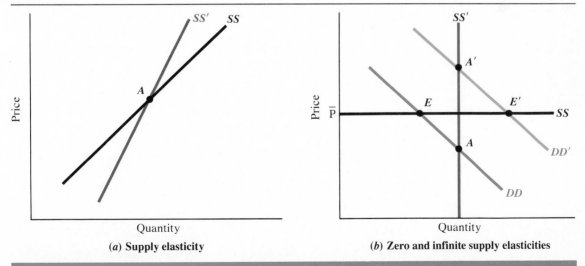

(a) Supply elasticity

(b) Zero and infinite supply elasticities

that reduces his crop, while no one else's crop is affected? Then that individual will indeed be worse off as a result of the crop reduction. The reduction in the amount he sells will have very little effect on the market price; that price will be unaffected by his bad luck. He will therefore lose from his own fire, but he would have gained had everyone's crops been reduced.

The important lesson is this: *What is true for the individual is not necessarily true for everyone taken together, and what is true for everyone taken together does not necessarily hold for the individual.*

4   THE LONG RUN AND THE SHORT RUN

The response of the quantity demanded to a change in price depends on how long the consumer has to adjust to the change. As a first example, consider changes in the price of gasoline that started becoming rapid in

1973. In 1973 most Americans had big cars, and when the price of gasoline went up, there were few ways of economizing. Certainly they decided that they would buy smaller cars in the future, but in the meantime they still had their big cars. Thus in the *short run* (of a few years), the demand for gasoline did not fall much after the price increase of 1973–1974.

Over a longer period—5 or 6 years— most consumers had time to sell their old cars and buy new ones with better gas economy. Therefore they were able, over this longer period, to reduce the demand for gasoline much more than they were in the short run. This situation is shown in Figure 4-6. The short-run demand curve is steeper than the long-run demand curve through the same point. If we start from point E and assume that the price is raised from P_B to P_A, we see that in the short run the quantity demanded is cut only to Q_S, whereas in the long run it is cut to Q_L.

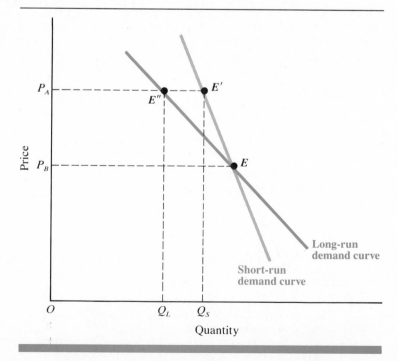

FIGURE 4-6   GASOLINE DEMAND IN THE SHORT AND LONG RUNS. The short-run demand schedule is steeper than the long-run demand schedule. This is because in the short run there is less opportunity for the consumer or purchaser to shift patterns of consumption. Over longer periods the purchaser can adjust more completely to a price change. A rise in price from P_B to P_A leads consumers in the short run to point E'. In the long run they move to E'', where all adjustments have been made, and quantity demanded therefore falls by more than in the short run.

The argument can be put in familiar elasticity terms by saying that the elasticity of demand for gasoline is lower in the short run than in the long run. The demand is more sensitive to price over a longer adjustment period than over a shorter period.

How Long Is the Long Run?

"Long run" and "short run" are fairly imprecise terms. The long run is the period that is long enough for making a full adjustment to a price change. Its length depends on the types of adjustments that have to be made. In the case of gasoline, we expect to see the long-run elasticity only after people have had a chance to choose new cars on the basis of the new price of gasoline. Thus the long run will be a period of at least several years. The short run is any period less than that, before adjustment is complete.

Table 4-7 shows actual data on the adjustment of energy demand in response to the price increases of the 1970s. The table shows that in each of the three countries energy prices increased and, as a consequence, the quantity of energy demanded decreased. The elasticities in each case are small—demand is very inelastic. But interestingly, the short-run elasticities are in some cases much smaller than the long-run elasticities.[7] In the United States, for example, the short-run elasticity of demand is −0.10, while the long-run elasticity is

nearly twice as large. For Japan the difference is even more striking.

The table shows that with an inelastic demand even huge changes in price lead only to small changes in the quantity demanded. Consider Japan. The price of energy increased there 176 percent—it nearly tripled—but the quantity of energy demanded decreased, even after 8 years, by only 19 percent. The small elasticity reveals that there are no ready substitutes for energy and that even the 8-year period may have been too short for achieving a complete adjustment through purchasing smaller cars, constructing more energy-efficient housing, and adopting more energy-conserving production processes and consumption habits.

5 THE CROSS ELASTICITY OF DEMAND

The demand for a good is affected not only by its own price but also by the prices of related goods. For instance, the quantity of movie tickets demanded at a given price depends on the price of television sets. The

[7] Obviously, we are defining the long run here as 8 years and the short run as 4 years. But we don't really know whether full adjustment to the energy price increase has been made within 8 years. Indeed, considering how long it takes to get permission to build energy-processing plants such as power stations, it is doubtful that even 8 years is long enough.

TABLE 4-7
ADJUSTMENT OF ENERGY DEMAND

	1973–1976			1973–1981		
	% CHANGE			% CHANGE		
	QUANTITY	PRICE	ELASTICITY	QUANTITY	PRICE	ELASTICITY
United States	−2.7	27.2	−0.10	−14	76.7	−0.18
Japan	−0.3	79.6	−0.02	−19.1	176.1	−0.11
Canada	−5.1	13.2	−0.11	−9.3	55.9	−0.17

Source: OECD, *Economic Outlook,* December 1981.

cheaper television is, the more people will watch TV, and the smaller will be the quantity of movie tickets demanded at any given price. The quantity of video games demanded at any price is also affected by the price of television sets, but in the opposite direction. The lower the price of television sets, the more people will have access to a television, and the more people will buy video games at a given price.

We need a measure of the responsiveness of the quantity of a good demanded to changes in the prices of related goods. This measure is the *cross elasticity of demand*, which is defined as follows:

$$\text{Cross elasticity of demand} = \frac{\begin{array}{c}\text{percentage change}\\\text{in quantity of}\\\text{good } i \text{ demanded}\end{array}}{\begin{array}{c}\text{percentage change}\\\text{in price of good } j\end{array}} \quad (4)$$

We use "good *i*" and "good *j*" in the equation to emphasize that we are interested in the effects of a change in the price of *one* good on the quantity demanded of *another* good.

The cross elasticity of demand may be either positive or negative. The cross elasticity is positive if the quantity of good *i* demanded rises when the price of good *j* rises. For instance, suppose that good *j* were coffee and that good *i* were tea. We would expect the quantity of tea demanded to rise when the price of coffee increases. This is likely to happen for goods that are *substitutes*.

The cross elasticity of demand may be negative. For instance, an increase in the price of gasoline (good *j*) may reduce the quantity of cars (good *i*) demanded. This is likely to happen when goods are *complements*, which tend to be used together.

Table 4-8 shows for some goods both the price elasticity of demand and cross price elasticities of demand. For instance, the price elasticity of demand (sometimes called the "own price elasticity") for meat is

TABLE 4-8

OWN PRICE ELASTICITY AND CROSS PRICE ELASTICITIES

	ELASTICITY OF DEMAND WITH RESPECT TO THE PRICE OF:		
	Meat	Fish	Tobacco Products
Meat	−0.48	0.01	−0.04
Fish	0.06	−0.72	−0.03

Source: A. P. Barten, "Consumer Demand Functions under Conditions of Almost Additive Preferences," *Econometrica*, January–April 1964, Table XV.

−0.48. The cross price elasticity of the demand for meat with respect to the price of fish is 0.01, which is positive, implying that the quantity of meat demanded rises when the price of fish rises. However, when the price of tobacco products rises, the demand for meat falls. You should check the second row of Table 4-8 to see whether the elasticity of demand for fish and the cross elasticities of the demand for fish with respect to the price of meat and the price of tobacco products make sense. Note in particular that the response of the quantity demanded of each good to a given percentage change in the good's own price is much larger than the response to a change in the price of other goods.

6 THE EFFECTS OF INCOME ON DEMAND

So far we have looked at the effects of changes in a good's price and changes in the prices of related goods on the quantity demanded. The final important factor affecting demand is the income of consumers. As incomes change, consumers' demands for goods change. Typically, the demand for a good rises when income increases. But even as the quantity demanded increases with income, the proportion of the consumers' income that is spent on a particular good may change as income rises. Some goods will take a larger portion of the consumers' budget as income rises, and some will take a smaller part of the budget.

We define the expenditure share or the budget share of a good as the fraction of income or household spending on a particular commodity. (For the moment we are not concerned with any possible difference between income and spending.) The expenditure share or budget share is defined as:

$$\begin{array}{c} \text{Budget share} \\ \text{of a good} \end{array} = \frac{\begin{array}{c} \text{price} \times \text{quantity} \\ \text{demanded} \end{array}}{\text{total consumer spending}} \quad (5)$$

Table 4-9 shows the share of consumer income spent on food and durable goods, respectively. The data are for different years over the last 30 years, during which period income was growing. The share spent on food has been falling over time, and the share spent on durables has been rising over time. The tendency for the share of food in the budget to fall as income rises was noticed initially by a nineteenth-century German economist and statistician, Ernst Engel, and it is certainly a tendency that has held up for a long time. The share of food falls because food is a necessity; people have to buy food even when income is low. But when income is higher, they have enough to spend on other things besides food, and the share of income spent on food therefore falls.[8]

The response of demand to changes in income is measured by the income elasticity of demand. As we should by now expect, the income elasticity of demand is defined as follows:

$$\begin{array}{c} \text{Income elasticity} \\ \text{of demand} \end{array} = \frac{\begin{array}{c} \text{percentage change} \\ \text{in quantity demanded} \end{array}}{\begin{array}{c} \text{percentage change} \\ \text{in income} \end{array}} \quad (6)$$

In words:

> The *income elasticity of demand* is the percentage change in the quantity demanded (at a given price) due to a percentage change in income.

Normal, Inferior, and Luxury Goods

In terms of the demand curve, the income elasticity of demand measures how far the curve shifts when there is a change in income. For instance, Figure 4-7 shows two possible shifts caused by a given percentage increase in income. The income elasticity of demand is much higher if a given percentage change in income shifts the demand curve from *DD* to *DD"* than if that same percentage change in income shifts the demand curve only from *DD* to *DD'*. The shift

---

[8] Changes in the share of food in the budget or changes in the share of any other good are caused by changes in both consumers' income *and* the price of the good. The numbers in Table 4-9 thus reflect the influence of both income and price changes on the budget share of food and consumer durables.

TABLE 4-9

SHARES OF INCOME SPENT ON FOOD AND DURABLES

	INCOME, billions of dollars	% OF INCOME SPENT ON FOOD	% OF INCOME SPENT ON DURABLES
1950	206.6	26.1	1.3
1960	352.0	23.0	1.6
1970	695.3	20.0	2.0
1980	1821.8	18.9	2.0

Note: "Durables" represents durable goods other than automobiles and furniture.
Source: Economic Report of the President, 1981, p. 259 for the first row and p. 248 for the second and third rows.

is always measured at a given price P_0 in Figure 4-7).

In Chapter 3 we discussed the difference between *normal* goods and *inferior* goods. The demand for a normal good increases when income rises. The demand for an inferior good falls when income rises. We can now define normal and inferior goods in terms of the income elasticity of demand.

> A *normal good* is a good for which the income elasticity of demand is positive. An *inferior good* is a good for which the income elasticity of demand is negative.

The income elasticity of demand is useful for making another distinction: the distinction between luxury goods and necessity goods.

> A *luxury good* has an income elasticity of demand greater than 1. A *necessity*, or *nonluxury*, *good* has an income elasticity of demand less than 1.

FIGURE 4-7 CHANGES IN INCOME SHIFT THE DEMAND CURVE. The figure shows how an increase in income shifts the demand curve to the right. The demand curve is initially *DD*. An increase in income shifts the demand curve either to *DD'* or to *DD''*. The income elasticity of demand measures how far the curve shifts when there is a change in income. In the figure, the income elasticity of demand is much larger if the demand curve shifts from *DD* to *DD''* when income changes by a given percentage than if it shifts only to *DD'* from *DD*, given the same percentage change in income.

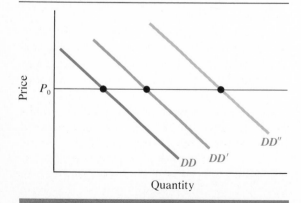

The share of consumer spending on luxuries rises with income, and this accounts for the name "luxuries." The share of necessities in consumer spending falls with income. This means that the poor spend a larger part of their income on necessities than do the rich; hence the name "necessities." However, among the necessities are likely to be goods such as cigarettes and beer. These may be necessary for mental cheer, but they are not necessities for physical survival.

Table 4-10 presents a summary of the relationships between changes in the quantity demanded and changes in income. Which goods are inferior? As income increases, consumers will tend to shift toward higher-quality types of any kind of good—from cheap shoes toward more expensive ones, from cheap cuts of meat toward steaks, from cloth coats to mink coats. Low-quality types of any kind of good are thus likely to be inferior. As income rises, the demand for these goods actually declines, and therefore total consumer spending on these goods falls. Their share in the budget therefore certainly falls.

In the group of normal goods, high-quality items tend to be luxury goods: platinum watches as opposed to steel watches, Mercedes cars as opposed to GM cars, foreign travel as opposed to an evening at the movies. Since the quantity demanded of luxuries rises proportionally more than income, as income grows the share of luxuries in the consumer budget increases. By contrast, the quantity demanded of nonluxury goods rises proportionally less than income, and so as income rises, the share of nonluxury goods in the consumer budget decreases. Food is a nonluxury good. Although the *proportion* of income spent on nonluxury goods, or necessities, falls as income rises, *total spending* on such goods will rise as income increases, so long as the good is not inferior.

TABLE 4-10

A SUMMARY OF THE DEMAND RESPONSES TO INCOME CHANGES

TYPES OF GOODS	CHARACTERISTIC	INCOME ELASTICITY	CHANGE IN BUDGET SHARE AS INCOME RISES	EXAMPLE
Normal goods:	Quantity demanded rises with income	Positive		
Luxuries	Quantity demanded rises proportionately more than income	Larger than 1	Budget share rises	Sports goods
Necessities	Quantity demanded rises proportionately less than income	Less than 1	Budget share falls	Food
Inferior goods	Quantity demanded falls when income rises	Negative	Budget share falls	Low-quality shoes

Table 4-11 gives estimates of income elasticities of demand for a variety of commodities. Note that transportation is given as a luxury good (it includes the possibility of graduating from a bus to a Rolls-Royce), while food and shelter are normal, nonluxury goods, since their elasticities are less than unity. The table lists a number of goods with income elasticities that are quite high. Included are obvious luxury items such as taxi rides and sports goods. An income elasticity of 3.7 for sports goods, for example, implies that for every rise in income of 1 percent the quantity demanded of sports equipment rises by 3.7 percent.

Quality and Income Elasticity of Demand

Changes in the quality of goods bought by consumers help account for the response of demand to income. For instance, Table 4-11 suggests that a family with an income of $30,000 will spend more than twice as much on food as a family with an income of $10,000. With an income elasticity of 0.77 and an increase in income of 200 percent [(20,000/10,000) × 100 percent], food consumption goes up 154 percent (200 × 0.77 percent).

How can the rich spend more than twice as much on food as the poor? Certainly they do not consume twice as many calories than the poor. The higher amount spent on food by the rich reflects their spending on higher-priced goods—steaks as opposed to hamburgers, for example, and restaurant food as opposed to home cooking. Even so, food in the aggregate is not a luxury good but a necessity, since spending on food falls as a percentage of income when income rises.

TABLE 4-11

INCOME ELASTICITIES OF DEMAND

GOOD	INCOME ELASTICITY
Food	0.77
Clothing	0.82
Transportation	1.10
Shelter	0.89
Medical care	1.9
Toilet articles	3.6
Sports goods	3.7
Taxicab transportation	2.8

Source: E. Lazear and R. Michael, "Family Size and the Distribution of Real Per Capita Income," *American Economic Review,* March 1980, Table 2, for rows 1–4, and H. Houthakker and L. Taylor, *Consumer Demand in the United States,* Harvard University Press, Cambridge, Mass., 1970, Table 3.2, rows 5–8.

Using Income Elasticity

What questions are answered with information on income elasticities of demand? These elasticities are essential ingredients in any forecast about consumer demand in various sectors of the economy. Suppose we know that consumer income will grow by 3 percent per year over the next 5 years and we want to know in which sectors the demand for goods will grow most rapidly. This is a natural question for a firm to ask as it plans its investment and expansion. It is also a question the government might ask as it makes plans for the allocation and direction of public investment.

Data on income elasticities of demand will tell us which goods are the high-growth sectors—in Table 4-11, taxicab transportation, sports goods, toilet articles, shelter—and which industries have low income elasticities and therefore will show smaller growth of demand.

SUMMARY

1   The price elasticity of demand, or just elasticity of demand, measures the sensitivity of the quantity demanded to changes in price. It is defined as the percentage change in quantity demanded divided by the percentage change in price, and it is negative. In general, the elasticity of demand changes as we move down a demand curve. On a straight-line demand curve, elasticity falls as the price falls.

2   If the elasticity of demand is larger than -1 (for example, -3), total spending on the good increases as the price falls. Since total spending is equal to the total revenue, or receipts, of the sellers, revenue rises as the price falls if the elasticity of demand is larger than -1. Demand is said to be elastic if the elasticity of demand is larger than -1.

3   If the elasticity of demand is less than -1 (for example, -0.5), total spending and revenue fall as price falls. In this case demand is described as inelastic.

4   The price elasticity of supply measures the responsiveness of the quantity supplied to a change in price. It is defined as the ratio of the percentage change in quantity supplied to the percentage change in price. It is positive.

5   The response of demand to a change in price depends on how long consumers have to react to the price change. Typically, in the short run the change in the quantity demanded in response to a change in price will be less than the change in the quantity demanded in the long run, after consumers have had time to adjust to the price change. In other words, the long-run elasticity of demand is typically larger than the short-run elasticity.

6   The cross elasticity of demand measures the sensitivity of the quantity of one good demanded to changes in the price of another

good. The cross elasticity of demand tends to be positive when goods are substitutes and negative when goods are complements.

7   The income elasticity of demand measures the sensitivity of demand to changes in income. It is defined as the percentage change in quantity demanded divided by the percentage change in income.

8   Goods for which the income elasticity of demand is less than 1 are described as necessities. The share of income spent on these goods falls as income rises. Goods for which the income elasticity of demand exceeds 1 are called luxuries; the share of income spent on them rises as income rises.

KEY TERMS

Price elasticity of demand	**Substitutes**
Arc elasticity of demand	**Complements**
Elastic demand	**Own price elasticity**
Inelastic demand	**Expenditure share (budget share) of a good**
Unitary elasticity of demand	**Income elasticity of demand**
Elasticity of supply	**Normal good**
Long run	**Inferior good**
Short run	**Luxury good**
Cross price elasticity of demand	**Necessity (nonluxury good)**

PROBLEMS

1   Consider the market for potatoes. The supply curve is assumed to be vertical—farmers supply a given quantity of 1000 tons at each price. The demand schedule slopes downward. The initial equilibrium price is $4 per ton. (*a*) Suppose a harvest failure reduces the available supply by 10 percent—to 900 tons. Show diagrammatically the effect of the supply reduction on the equilibrium price. (*b*) Suppose the elasticity of demand at the initial equilibrium price ($4) is −0.5. By how much must the price increase to restore market equilibrium? [You don't have to use a diagram for this. Equation (1) will be enough.]

2   Consider the following goods: (*a*) milk, dental services, beverages; (*b*) candy, chewing gum, food; (*c*) entertainment, movies, travel. For each of these goods, state whether you expect demand to be price-elastic or price-inelastic. In addition, rank the elasticities of demand within each group of goods, where possible. Explain your answer.

3   (*a*) Explain where consumer spending is at a maximum on a straight-line demand curve, and explain why. (*b*) How can this information be used by the manager of the football stadium?

4   Go back to Table 4-2 and calculate the arc elasticity of demand between the price of $15 and the price of $12.50. Explain why some people prefer to use arc elasticity.

5   The accompanying table shows estimates of price elasticities of demand and income elasticities of demand for food and for consumer durable goods (such as toys, sports equipment, TVs, and pleasure aircraft). Characterize the demand for the goods in each group as elastic or inelastic, and say whether the goods in each group are necessities or luxuries. Explain.

| | ELASTICITIES OF DEMAND | |
	PRICE	INCOME
Food	0.5	0.7
Consumer durable goods	2.4	3.72

6 Suppose the weather has been good and a big harvest has been predicted. Explain why individual farmers will continue to work hard in order to bring in the big crop, even though they know they would all have been better off if the weather had not been good.

7 Use a diagram to show how the elasticity of supply helps determine the response of price and quantity to a shift in demand. Also, explain your answer in words.

8 *Extra credit.* When costs go up, automobile manufacturers usually raise prices to help cover the higher costs. Explain whether this makes sense if the demand for their products is elastic.

9 The table at the bottom of the page shows hypothetical levels of income and hypothetical levels of spending on clothing and shoes and on housing for years 1 and 10. Calculate the share of income spent on each of the goods in the two years. Then say whether the goods are necessities or luxuries. (Assume that the prices of these goods

did not change over the period and that real income rose from year 1 to year 10.)

10 Explain the following: If the elasticity of demand for a good is not 1 and income is fixed, then a change in the price of the good must affect the demand for at least one other good.

11 Use the data in the table at the top of the next page to compute own price and cross price elasticities of demand. Are goods 1 and 2 more likely to be complements or substitutes?

12 Compare two countries: Mexico (which has lower incomes) and Canada (which has higher incomes). In which country would you expect a higher expenditure share of (*a*) food? (*b*) electricity? (*c*) cosmetics?

13 In the United States, medical costs rose very sharply in the last 20 years. Can you explain why?

14 Movie tickets are currently sold at $4, and the Golden Twenties movie theater attracts 200 customers per day at that price. The manager has reason to believe that demand is highly elastic——4. He therefore decides to cut the price to $3.50 to fill the 100 seats that are presently vacant. (*a*) Is there any reason to believe that the elasticity of demand facing the Golden Twenties movie house might be as high as −4? Explain. (*b*) If the elasticity of demand is indeed −4 and the price is cut from $4 to $3.50, by how much will the quantity demanded rise? (*c*) What will happen to the total revenue? (*d*) *Extra credit.* What would happen to the quantity demanded if other movie houses in the area followed Golden Twenties' move and reduced their prices?

YEAR	DISPOSABLE INCOME	SPENDING ON CLOTHING AND SHOES	SPENDING ON HOUSING
1	600*	50	100
10	1500	100	270

* The numbers in the second, third, and fourth columns represent billions of dollars.

	PRICE OF GOOD 1	PRICE OF GOOD 2	CONSUMPTION OF GOOD 1
Situation A	16	10	40
Situation B	12	10	50
Situation C	12	12	52

15 *Extra credit.* Suppose the price of oil rises. Think about the market for coal. How will the increase in the price of oil affect the demand curve for coal (*a*) in the short run and (*b*) in the long run? What will happen to the price of each substitute for oil as a result of the increase in the price of oil? (If you get this right, you can say that you have described what happened after the oil price increase of 1973.)

Suppose the price of wheat doubles. What happens to the quantity of wheat demanded? How does the quantity of corn demanded change? What happens in the market for other consumer goods, such as clothing and beverages?

Our study of demand in the last chapter gave us some of the answers. There we saw that a rise in the price of a good reduces the quantity demanded. The larger the price elasticity of demand, the greater the decrease in the quantity demanded. We also saw that the effect of a change in the price of wheat on the quantity demanded in other markets is measured by the cross elasticity of demand. If the cross elasticity of demand for corn with respect to the price of wheat is positive, as we expect it to be, the quantity of corn demanded increases when the price of wheat rises.

In this chapter we go behind the elasticities of demand by building a simple model of consumer behavior. The model of consumer behavior, or consumer choice, increases understanding of the demand curve. It emphasizes the constraints imposed on the consumer by the amount of income available for purchasing goods and by the prices of those goods.

In this chapter we compare the model's predictions with actual data and show how it helps explain the price and income elasticities measured by economists—such as those in Chapter 4. The chapter concludes with several applications of the model of consumer choice developed in it.

5

Special Topics in Demand

1 THE THEORY OF CONSUMER CHOICE

In this section we develop a model of consumer choice. The model organizes the factors relevant to the consumer's choice. It allows us to predict how the consumer responds to changes in the market conditions that he faces.

The model of consumer choice has four elements that describe the consumer and his market environment:

1   The consumer takes as given the prices at which he can buy any amount of the existing goods and services.

2   The consumer has a given income available for spending.

3   The consumer has tastes that allow him to evaluate, or rank, alternative combinations, or baskets,[1] of goods by the satisfaction they yield. The consumer prefers more of any one good to less.

4   The consumer chooses his consumption basket so as to maximize satisfaction, or, as it is called, utility.

Each of these items requires detailed discussion.

The Budget Constraint

Items 1 and 2 are combined to define the consumer's budget constraint.

> The *budget constraint* describes the combinations of goods the consumer can afford to buy.

The consumer in making his choices in the market has only a limited income to spend on the goods, which are not free. Thus income and the prices of goods restrict the possible combinations of goods the consumer can buy.

To see how these constraints work, assume that the consumer has to choose between only two goods: food and entertainment. Table 5-1 presents the price and income data that determine the consumer's budget constraint.

We can think of the problem in terms of a student who has a weekly budget (income, allowance) of $100 to spend. The budget can be allocated to the consumption of food or fun. The price of food is $5 per pound, and the price of entertainment (say, a concert) is $10 per ticket.

What are the combinations of goods the student can afford to buy? One possibility is to spend the entire budget on food. The student's $100 will buy a total of 20 pounds of food at a price of $5 per pound. Alterna-

TABLE 5-1

PRICE AND INCOME DATA

CONSUMER INCOME	PRICES	
	FOOD	ENTERTAINMENT
$100	$5/lb	$10/ticket

tively, the consumer might spend the entire budget on entertainment, buying a total of 10 tickets ($100/$10). Of course, in between those two extremes is a whole range of combinations of food and entertainment that use up the student's entire budget. These combinations are given by the budget constraint.

The budget constraint states that the sum of the amounts spent on each good (price times quantity for each good) is equal to income.[2]

$$\frac{\text{Spending}}{\text{on food}} + \frac{\text{spending}}{\text{on entertainment}} = \text{income} \qquad (1)$$

Table 5-2 shows some of the possible combinations of goods the consumer can buy with his income. We have already seen that if he devotes his entire budget to food, he buys 20 units of food and, of course, zero entertainment. This is shown in the last line of the table. Alternatively, if he spends all his income on entertainment, he gets 10 units of entertainment (and, of course, zero food). This is shown in the top row. The entries in between are obtained from the budget constraint. For instance, if he buys 4 units of food, he spends $20 (at $5 per unit) on food. He has $80 of income left, and with that he can buy 8 units of entertainment (at $10 each), as shown in the second row of the

---

[1] Economists often refer to the "consumption basket," meaning the combination of goods bought by the consumer.

[2] Throughout this chapter we use the terms "consumer budget," "consumer income," and "consumer expenditure" interchangeably. In fact, there is a distinction between consumer income and spending that arises from the possibility of saving. The part of income that is saved is not spent. Only in Chapters 20 and 23 do we come to the saving-consumption choice that makes this distinction important.

TABLE 5-2

ALTERNATIVE, AFFORDABLE CONSUMPTION BASKETS

FOOD		ENTERTAINMENT	
QUANTITY (Q_F)	FOOD SPENDING $(\$5 \times Q_F)$	QUANTITY (Q_E)	ENTERTAINMENT SPENDING $(\$10 \times Q_E)$
0	$ 0	10	$100
4	20	8	80
8	40	6	60
12	60	4	40
16	80	2	20
20	100	0	0

table. The other entries are obtained by making similar calculations.

Table 5-2 shows the *trade-off* the consumer has to make between food and entertainment.[3] The more food the consumer chooses, the more is spent on food, and the less is left to buy entertainment. Thus the budget constraint shows how more of one good comes at the cost of less of the other. Because there is a trade-off and the consumer cannot have as much as he wants of all goods, there is a problem of consumer choice.

The Budget Line A different, useful way of looking at the budget constraint is to use the *budget line* shown in Figure 5-1. The budget line shows the maximum combinations of food and entertainment that the consumer can buy, given his income and the prices at which he buys. The budget line is constructed by plotting the alternative consumption baskets that are calculated in Table 5-2.

The position and slope of the budget line is determined by the two intersections

with the axes, points A and F, respectively. These points have a simple economic interpretation. Point A shows the maximum amount of entertainment the budget can buy. The maximum amount of entertainment, given an income of $100 and a price of entertainment of $10, is equal to 10 units. Thus point A shows 10 units of entertainment as the one extreme of the budget line. The other extreme is point F, where all the income is devoted to food. Here the budget buys a maximum of $100/5 = 20$ units of food. Points A and F, respectively, show the purchasing power of the given income, at the going prices, in terms of entertainment and food. These two points locate the budget line.

Figure 5-1 shows a whole range of intermediate combinations between points A and F. Points such as B or C represent different quantities of food and entertainment. The budget line shows the trade-offs the consumer can make between food and entertainment.

How many units of food must he sacrifice to get 1 more unit of entertainment? The answer is given by the slope of the budget line. It shows how many units of food must be given up to acquire an extra unit of entertainment. To move from point F to point E in Figure 5-1, the consumption of food must be reduced from 20 units to 16 units; the consumption of entertainment rises from 0 unit to 2 units. Thus the con-

---

[3] Interesting choices involve trade-offs. Some good thing has to be given up to get more of another good thing. Leisure has to be sacrificed to earn income to buy goods; in the short run, inflation can be reduced only by trading off for more unemployment; increasing future consumption means saving more now—trading off current consumption for future consumption. Economists love to look for trade-offs, as we noted in Chapter 2.

FIGURE 5-1   THE BUDGET LINE. The budget line shows the maximum combinations of goods the consumer can afford, given his income and the prevailing prices. Line *AF* shows possible combinations (such as *A, B,* and *C*) that use up the entire consumer budget. Points above and to the right of the budget line (such as *G*) are unattainable—out of the consumer's reach. Points inside the budget line (such as *K*) are affordable—but points on the budget line allow the consumer to buy more of at least one good or even more of both than he buys at *K*.

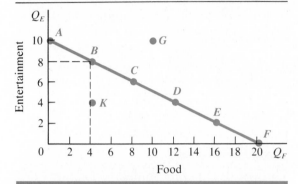

sumer has to sacrifice 4 units of food to be able to buy 2 more units of entertainment. Or—he has to trade off 2 units of food for 1 unit of entertainment. Note that this trade-off is constant along the budget line. The reason is that giving up 2 units of food (at a price of $5 per unit) saves $10, which is the price of an extra unit of entertainment.

The idea of the budget line as a trade-off between the maximum amounts of the two commodities the consumer can afford to buy draws attention to the role of prices. *In fact, the slope of the budget line is the ratio of prices.* The higher the price of entertainment *relative* to the price of food, the more units of food we must forgo to buy 1 extra unit of entertainment. If a unit of entertainment cost $25 rather than $10 and the price of food was still $5 per unit, the consumer would have to give up 5 units of food rather than only 2 units of food in order to buy an extra ticket.

So far we have argued that the position of the budget line is determined by the purchasing power of income in terms of the two

goods, points *A* and *F*, and that the budget line represents a trade-off for the consumer. The terms of that trade-off are given by the relative prices of the two goods.

Two more facts must be noted. The first is that any point above the budget line, such as *G*, is out of reach. The consumer can dream about those baskets, but economically they are out of his reach. Second, points inside the budget line, such as point *K*, are affordable. But they leave the consumer with some unspent income. At point *K*, for example, the consumer has enough income to move to *B*, buying more entertainment, or to *D*, buying more food, or to any other point on the budget line in between. Because more goods are better than fewer goods, *K* is not a relevant point for the consumer's choice. That leaves points on the budget line as the only relevant points from which to choose.

We will return later to the budget line to investigate the effects of changes in income and prices on the consumer's optimal purchases. Before getting there we have to bring the consumer's behavior into the model. We will therefore turn now to tastes and consumer maximization of utility.

Tastes

We assume that the consumer can rank, or evaluate, alternative bundles of the two goods by the satisfaction, or *utility,* they give. We do not actually require that the consumer be able to measure his happiness or well-being, for instance, by saying that a particular commodity bundle gives him four times as much utility as some other one. We require only that he know whether one bundle yields more or less utility than another.[4] These ideas are explained with the help of Figure 5-2.

---

[4] We also assume that the consumer is consistent. If bundle A yields more utility than bundle B and B yields more utility than C, then the consumer should regard A as yielding more utility than C.

FIGURE 5-2 CONSUMER RANKING OF ALTERNA-
TIVE CONSUMPTION BASKETS. The consumer eval-
uates alternative baskets, which are identified by
points *a, b, c, d,* and *e.* With respect to point *a,* any
point to the northeast is preferred, and any point to
the southwest is dominated by *a.* Points in the other
two regions, such as *d* or *e,* may or may not be preferred to *a,* depending on the consumer's tastes.

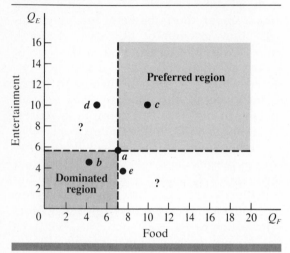

Figure 5-2 shows quantities of entertainment and food consumption on the axes.
Any point on the diagram represents a combination of goods which would yield a certain amount of utility to the consumer if he
consumed them. Our point of reference is
point *a.* Vertical and horizontal lines are
drawn through that point to divide the
space. Recall that more is better than less
for the consumer. Therefore, any point to
the northeast, such as *c,* is preferred to *a.*
This is because a point such as *c* offers more
of *both* goods. By contrast, a point such as *b,*
with smaller quantities of both goods, is
clearly worse than *a.* Thus the consumer
would rather be at point *a* instead of anywhere to the southwest (for example, *b*).

Without knowing the consumer's preferences, we cannot, in general, rank points
in the remaining two regions. Knowing that
more is better than less does not help us
rank *a* with respect to *e* or *d.* These bundles
differ in that they have more of one commodity and less of another. Here the partic-

ulars of consumer taste must be used to rank
them. Someone who favors entertainment
might prefer *d* to *a,* and someone who favors
food might prefer *e* to *a,* even though the
little extra food involves a large sacrifice of
entertainment. It is also possible that the
consumer might be indifferent between *d*
and *a* or between *a* and *e* in the sense that
he would be equally happy with either combination of goods. Even though we cannot
say anything about how the consumer will
rank these two quadrants without knowing
more details about the consumer's tastes,
we will still be able to reach quite strong
conclusions about the consumer's reactions
to price and income changes.

Utility Maximization and Consumer Choice

The last item in our model of consumer demand is the assumption of utility maximization. The consumer will choose his consumption basket so as to achieve the
maximum level of utility, or well-being,
given the budget constraint. The budget
constraint is indicated by the budget line in
Figure 5-3.

The consumer's optimal consumption
point must be on the budget line. Because
more is better than less, the consumer will
not choose any point that is inside the budget line. And he does not have enough income to be outside the budget line. Thus he
must choose a point that is on the budget
line.

But how does the consumer choose a
point on budget line *AF* in Figure 5-3? Any
point between *A* and *F* is available, and a
choice has to be made. The consumer will
not be indifferent between these points.
Point *A* involves a basket of entertainment
only and no food. At such a point the consumer would be happy to give up some entertainment in exchange for some food. On
the other hand, at point *F,* with only food
and no entertainment in the consumption
basket, food will be valued very low relative

FIGURE 5-3   THE BUDGET CONSTRAINT AND CONSUMER CHOICE. The budget line (constraint), in conjunction with tastes and utility maximization, determines the consumer's optimal consumption point. The point *must* lie on the budget line. It cannot lie above because that region is unaffordable, and it will not lie inside because that region is dominated by points on the budget line. The position on the budget line that the consumer will choose depends on tastes.

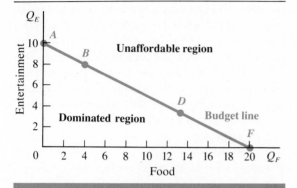

to entertainment. The consumer would be willing to give up some food in exchange for some entertainment. The question is, How far will the consumer go away from *A* or *F* ?

The consumer aims to maximize utility. A simple way to think about how the consumer makes his choice is by examining the increment in total utility that is gained as he moves, hypothetically, along the budget line from *F* to *A*. Shifting a dollar of spending from food to entertainment means that less food is to be consumed; on that account, utility is reduced. But there is an offsetting compensation because a dollar of spending is shifted toward entertainment; increased consumption of entertainment increases utility.

Diminishing Marginal Utility   How does utility change as the consumer increases spending on entertainment and reduces spending on food? Each extra unit of food or entertainment consumed adds to the consumer's utility. We make the basic assumption of diminishing marginal utility.

The consumer has *diminishing marginal utility* from a good when each extra unit of the good consumed adds less to utility, the more of that good the individual is already consuming.

For instance, think of the consumer at point *F* in Figure 5-3, consuming all food and no entertainment. The person who has no entertainment will obtain a large increase in utility from buying 1 unit of entertainment. But the more entertainment he has, the less each extra unit adds to utility. The person already going to six concerts a week does not increase utility much by going to a seventh. The assumption of diminishing marginal utility is the natural idea that the more we have of a good, the less extra satisfaction 1 more unit of it yields.

The Consumer's Optimum Position   Now, what happens to the consumer's utility or satisfaction as spending is shifted from food to entertainment? Giving up the first dollar's worth of food causes very little loss in utility, because the consumer is already consuming a lot of food. But the first dollar's worth of entertainment gives him a large amount of extra utility, since at point *F* he is not consuming *any* entertainment. Thus the first dollar of spending should be moved toward entertainment and away from food.

As each extra dollar is moved from food toward entertainment, the cost in terms of utility lost from lower food consumption increases. Why? Because the more that is being spent on entertainment, the less food is being consumed and the higher its marginal utility. And the gain in utility from each extra unit of entertainment falls progressively because of diminishing marginal utility. Thus as dollars of spending are shifted progressively from food to entertainment, the cost in utility lost from each $1 reduction in spending on food rises, and the gain in utility from each $1 increase in spending on entertainment falls.

The consumer should continue shifting spending toward entertainment and away from food up to the point where the utility gain from an extra dollar's worth of spending on entertainment exactly matches the cost in terms of the utility sacrifice of $1 reduction in food spending.

This equilibrium condition, or optimal position, of the consumer is the cornerstone of demand theory and is worth a more formal statement:

The *marginal utility of entertainment* is the increase in the consumer's utility resulting from a 1-unit increase in the consumption of entertainment. It is identified as MU_E. Similarly, the *marginal utility of food* is the increase in the consumer's utility resulting from a 1-unit increase in the consumption of food. It is identified as MU_F. The consumer's optimum condition is:

$$MU_E \times \text{dollar's worth of entertainment} = MU_F \times \text{dollar's worth of food} \quad (2)$$

In other words, at the optimal consumption point, the marginal utility from an extra dollar's worth of spending on entertainment should be equal to the marginal utility from an extra dollar's worth of spending on food.

This condition becomes clearer if we imagine that the consumer can measure utility in "utils."[5] Suppose the consumer is at a point where one dollar's worth of spending on food increases his utility by 40 utils, whereas one dollar's worth of spending on entertainment increases utility by 60 utils. Then the right thing to do is to reduce spending on food by $1, losing 40 utils, and increase spending on entertainment by $1, gaining 60 utils. There is a 20-util gain.

After moving the dollar of spending to entertainment, the consumer is spending less on food and more on entertainment. There, the marginal utility of food consumption will be higher, say, 45 utils. And the marginal utility of entertainment consumption will be lower, say, 55 utils. Once again he should move one dollar's worth of spending from food to entertainment. As long as the marginal number of utils per dollar from one good is not equal to the marginal number of utils from the other good, the consumer can come out ahead by changing his consumption bundle. Therefore, at the optimum consumption point, marginal utility per dollar is equalized among goods.

In summary, the consumer will choose the optimal consumption point on the budget line. The point will be chosen by following this rule: Arrange spending among goods so as to use the given income most effectively in "buying utility." That happens when an extra dollar's worth of spending buys the same increment in utility in every market.[6]

2 ADJUSTMENT TO INCOME CHANGES

We will now use the model of consumer choice to investigate the effects of changes in income and, in the next section, the response to changes in prices. In Chapter 4 we argued that an increase in income leads to a shift in the demand curve for a good, with the magnitude of the shift depending on the income elasticity. Now we can develop this result in the model of consumer choice.

Figure 5-4 shows the adjustment to a change in income. The initial situation is

---

[5] The notion of utils is in no way needed to develop the theory of the consumer's choice, but it does help in understanding the consumer's optimal choice. Indeed, the entire theory of consumer choice can be developed without bringing in the idea of diminishing marginal utility. But it is harder to understand without diminishing marginal utility.

[6] In the appendix to this chapter we will see that there is another way to state the consumer equilibrium condition: $MU_F/MU_E = P_F/P_E$. Here P_F/P_E is the ratio of the price of food to the price of entertainment. In this form the optimal rule for the consumer is to equate the ratio of marginal utilities to the prevailing ratio of prices.

FIGURE 5-4 AN INCREASE IN CONSUMER INCOME SHIFTS THE BUDGET LINE.
An increase in consumer income from $100 to $160 raises the purchasing power of
income in terms of both goods. Maximum entertainment consumption rises to 16
and maximum food consumption to 32. The slope of the budget line is unaffected.
    The initial equilibrium is at point e. If both goods are normal, then a rise in in-
come will increase the quantity demanded of both goods so that the new equilibrium is on the new budget line, to the northeast of e. Since entertainment is a luxury and food a necessity, the equilibrium is likely to be at a point such as e', where
the quantity demanded of entertainment has increased *relatively* more than the
quantity demanded of food.

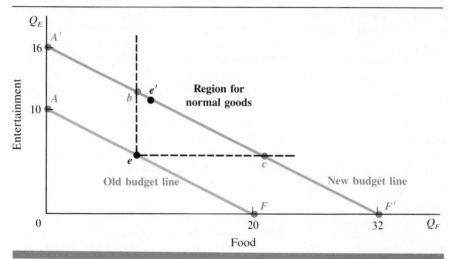

shown by the budget line AF; the consumer
maximizes his utility at point e. We call this
the consumer's equilibrium position, because this is the point at which he will stay
unless his income, or prices, or his tastes
change.

    Now suppose consumer income rises
from $100 to $160. The prices of food and
entertainment remain unchanged at $5 and
$10, respectively. With income higher the
consumer can now afford to buy more of either or both goods. Some combinations that
were previously unaffordable are now
within the consumer's reach. The budget
line shifts outward from AF to $A'F'$.

    To find the exact position of the new
budget line we have to calculate the purchasing power of the new, higher income
in terms of the two commodities. If the entire $160 income were spent on entertain-
ment, it would buy $160/$10 = 16 units of
entertainment. Therefore, one point on the

new budget line is point A'; it shows consumption of no food and 16 units of entertainment. If the entire income were spent
on food, the consumer would buy $160/
$5 = 32 units of food. This is shown at point
F'. Connecting A' and F' (or calculating all
the other possible combinations) gives us
the new budget line.

    Where will the consumer choose to
move in response to the increased income?
Suppose that both goods are normal. We defined normal goods as those goods for which
the quantity demanded rises with income.
If both goods are normal, consumption of
both goods will increase; the consumer will
move to the northeast of e. But we also know
that the new consumption point will lie on
the new budget line, $A'F'$. Therefore, the
new consumption point will lie on the
stretch bc, that is, to the northeast of e *and*
on the new budget line.

    Can we say more? For our example of

food and entertainment we can indeed say more. Food is a necessity—a good with an income elasticity less than unity. Entertainment, in contrast, is a luxury good—a good with an income elasticity larger than unity. We therefore expect that the quantity of food demanded will rise proportionately less than income. The quantity of entertainment demanded will rise proportionately more than income. We will therefore move to a point such as e', where the ratio of entertainment to food is greater than at e.

Suppose that one of the goods is inferior —the quantity demanded decreases as income rises. In this case, we would move to either of the outside segments—$A'b$ (if food is inferior) or cF' (if entertainment is inferior). With an inferior good, the quantity demanded of one good falls absolutely while the quantity demanded of the other good rises all the more when income rises.

The effects of a fall in income are, of course, exactly the opposite of the effects of an increase in income. With a fall in income, the budget line shifts inward, toward the origin. The lower consumer income will buy fewer goods. In the case of normal goods, the new consumption point corresponding to a fall in the income will lie to the southwest of the initial equilibrium position. Problem 1(c) asks you to show this case diagrammatically.

3 THE ADJUSTMENT TO PRICE CHANGES

In Chapter 4 we argued, relying on common sense and data, that an increase in the price of a good must reduce the quantity demanded. We further argued that the reduction in the quantity demanded is bigger the larger the price elasticity of demand. That elasticity, in turn, is larger the easier it is to substitute toward other goods. In this section we will expand on those results. We will consider not only the change in the quantity demanded of the good whose price has risen but also the change in the quantity demanded of the other good. That is, we will be looking not only at the own price elasticity of demand but also at the cross price elasticity of demand.

Recall from Chapter 4 that the own price elasticity of demand is the ratio of the percentage change in the quantity of a good demanded to the percentage change in the price of the good. The cross elasticity of demand for good i with respect to price j is the ratio of the percentage change in the quantity demanded of good i to the percentage change in the price of good j.

Table 5-3 shows estimates of the price elasticities of demand of various commodities with respect to their own prices and with respect to the prices of other commodi-

TABLE 5-3

OWN AND CROSS PRICE ELASTICITIES OF DEMAND

| | ELASTICITY OF DEMAND WITH RESPECT TO THE PRICE OF: | | | |
	Food	Clothing	Transportation	Shelter
Food	−0.63	−0.03	−0.01	−0.09
Clothing	−0.09	−0.51	−0.01	−0.09
Transportation	−0.12	−0.05	−0.60	−0.12
Shelter	−0.10	−0.04	−0.02	−0.56

Note: Numbers in color are own price elasticities for each good.
Source: E. Lazear and R. Michael, "Family Size and the Distribution of Real Per Capita Income," *American Economic Review,* March 1980, Table 2.

ties. Some of these data were presented in Chapter 4, in Table 4-3. These are the numbers in color on the diagonal; they are the own price elasticities of demand. For instance, the price elasticity of demand for food is −0.63, and that for shelter is −0.56.

Table 5-3 also shows cross price elasticities. For example, the cross price elasticity of the demand for food with respect to the price of clothing is −0.03. The cross price elasticity of the demand for transportation with respect to the price of food, as another example, is −0.12. We expect the own price elasticities to be negative—an increase in price reduces the quantity demanded. But what about the cross price elasticities? The table shows that for this particular group of goods, *all* the cross price elasticities are negative. A rise in the price of one good, say, clothing, reduces the quantity demanded of each of the other goods in the table. In Chapter 4 we did find some positive cross elasticities of demand. Now we will have to see why negative cross elasticities appear to be more common.

There is a second point to note about Table 5-3. In comparing the sizes of different elasticities in any one row we find that the own price elasticity is always larger than the cross price elasticities. For example, the own price elasticity of demand for shelter is −0.56, whereas the cross price elasticity of the demand for shelter with respect to, say, the price of food is only −0.10. Thus demand is more responsive to an increase in the own price than to an increase in the price of some other commodity. Again, is this a general result, or is it the case only for the group of goods we have picked? We turn now to a discussion of the sign and size of these price elasticities.

Price Changes and the Budget Line

In Figure 5-5 we show the budget line, AF, that corresponds to a consumer income of $100 and prices of entertainment and food equal to $10 and $5, respectively. Suppose

FIGURE 5-5 THE EFFECT OF AN INCREASE IN FOOD PRICES ON THE BUDGET LINE. The consumer is initially at point *e* on budget line *AF*. Food prices double—from $5 to $10—and therefore the purchasing power of income in terms of food is reduced. This is shown by a rotation of the budget line. With income and entertainment prices unchanged, maximum consumption of entertainment remains at point *A*. But maximum consumption of food falls from 20 to 10. Accordingly, the new budget line is *AF'*. Along the new budget line the consumer can no longer afford the initial consumption basket (at point *e*). Consumption of either or both commodities must be reduced.

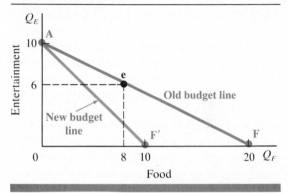

the consumer, given this budget line, chooses point *e* as the optimal consumption bundle. At *e* the consumer chooses 6 units of entertainment and 8 units of food.

Next let the price of food increase. Specifically, assume that food prices double, from $5 to $10 per unit. What is the effect on the consumer's budget line? In Figure 5-5 we show that the budget line rotates around point *A* and that the new intersection with the food axis is at point *F'*. The maximum amount of food consumption possible has fallen from 20 units to 10. The diagram must show point *F'*—10 units of food—as one point on the new budget line.

To confirm that the budget line remains anchored at *A*, we observe that the purchasing power of the $100 income in terms of entertainment is unchanged. With an unchanged $10 price of entertainment, $100 of income still buys 10 units of entertainment. Accordingly, maximum entertainment consumption, with no food, remains at point *A*.

Our new budget line, therefore, will be the schedule AF'.

We can look at that schedule from two points of view. For every level of entertainment consumption we can now afford fewer units of food. Before the increase in the price of food we could afford 6 units of entertainment and 8 units of food. Now the same entertainment consumption, with the reduced purchasing power of income in terms of food, leaves us only 4 units of food. Another way of looking at the new budget line is to note that every point except point A lies inside the old budget line. This means that the price increase has reduced the household's consumption opportunities, or standard of living. The standard of living has fallen because the household can no longer afford the initial consumption basket, wherever it may have been on AF. The only exception would be if the consumer had been at A, not consuming any food. In that special case the increase in the food price would have left him totally unaffected. The diagram shows how a price increase makes the consumer worse off by reducing his consumption opportunities, or standard of living.[7]

Income and Substitution Effects

When the price of a good rises, with the consumer's income remaining fixed, the purchasing power of his income—the possible combinations of goods he can buy—is reduced. In this sense, the effect of a price increase is similar to the effect of a reduction

in income. But the price increase really has two effects. First, it shifts the budget line inward. Second, it changes the slope of the budget line.

The consumer is faced with two changes in his situation. First, he can, except at point A in Figure 5-5, consume less of all goods, as he would if his income fell. But in addition, the relative prices of the goods have changed, and the terms under which he can trade off marginal utility between the goods by shifting spending between the goods have changed.

Economists therefore break up the effects of a change in price on demand into two parts, one corresponding to the change in the purchasing power of income and one corresponding to the change in relative prices.

> The *income effect* of an increase (fall) in price is the adjustment in the consumption of goods to the reduced (increased) purchasing power of income. The *substitution effect* of a price change is the adjustment in the composition of the consumer's spending to a change in relative prices.

We will now use Figure 5-6 and the distinction between income and substitution

FIGURE 5-6 ADJUSTMENT TO A PRICE CHANGE. An increase in food prices lowers the consumption of food. It may raise (e'') or lower (e') the consumption of entertainment depending on the relative importance of the income and substitution effects.

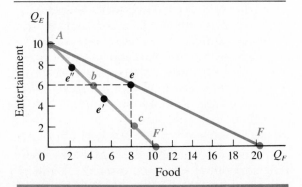

---

[7] We note here, briefly, a few results. First, a rise in the price of entertainment will rotate the budget line inward. It will leave the maximum consumption of food unchanged at point F in Figure 5-5 while reducing the maximum consumption of entertainment. Second, a fall in the price of food will rotate the budget line around point A—but outward, since now the purchasing power of income in terms of food rises. Third, a fall in the price of entertainment will rotate the budget line outward, this time increasing the maximum consumption of entertainment. Problem 1 asks you to show the last two results.

effects to analyze the effects of an increase in the price of entertainment on the quantities of food and entertainment purchased.

The Income Effects   We saw earlier that if there is a fall in income and both goods are normal, the consumer will move to the southwest of point *e* in Figure 5-6, to a position on the stretch *bc*. With both goods normal, the income effect of a price increase is the same—the consumer moves to the southwest of *e*, to the range *bc*. But this means that when we look only at the income effect, a price increase reduces the demand for *both* goods.

The Substitution Effects   In talking about substitution effects, we think of a consumer who is faced with a change in relative prices but no change in the purchasing power of his income. He can still, if he wants to, consume the same goods he consumed before. In that sense there is no change in his purchasing power. But now food has become relatively more expensive. How, if at all, does he change his consumption pattern? The consumer *must* now change his consumption pattern. Before the change in relative prices, he was equating the marginal utility received from one good per dollar spent on the good with the marginal utility from the other good per dollar spent on it. But now the relative price of food has risen.

At the original price ratio—$10 for a unit of entertainment to $5 for a unit of food—the ratio of the marginal utility of entertainment to that of food was 2 to 1. For example, suppose the marginal utility per dollar's worth of entertainment used to be 50 utils. In that situation the marginal utility of 1 unit of entertainment, which cost $10, was 500 utils (50 utils per dollar times $10). A unit of food used to cost $5; therefore, the marginal utility was equal to 250 utils.

With the new, higher price of food, the consumer can buy 1 unit of entertainment by giving up 1 unit of food. By giving up 1 unit of food he loses 250 utils. By buying 1 unit of entertainment he gains 500 utils. He will certainly want to trade—getting 1 unit of entertainment and giving up 1 unit of food, and coming out ahead by 250 utils. And he will keep doing this until the marginal utility per dollar spent on one good is equal again to the marginal utility per dollar spent on the other good.

By reducing his consumption of food and increasing his consumption of entertainment, the consumer makes himself better off. Therefore, as far as the substitution effect is concerned, a rise in the price of food will cause the consumer to substitute entertainment for food.

The substitution effect of a rise in the price of food on the quantity of food demanded is negative. This is a general result. It is always true that the substitution effect of a rise in the own price is to reduce the quantity of a good demanded.

In addition, in this case of food and entertainment, the substitution effect of an increase in the price of food on the demand for entertainment is positive. This, however, is not a general result. Where there are more than two goods, the substitution effects on some other goods may be negative rather than positive.[8]

Net Effects of a Price Increase   What do the income and substitution effects taken together tell us? If both food and entertainment are normal goods and they are the only two goods, the results are as summarized in Table 5-4.

The income and substitution effects on the demand for food of an increase in the price of food are both negative. Therefore, as shown in Figure 5-6, the total effect of the

[8] This is explained below under the heading "Complements and Substitutes."

TABLE 5-4

EFFECTS OF AN INCREASE IN THE PRICE OF FOOD ON THE QUANTITY DEMANDED

GOOD	INCOME EFFECT	SUBSTITUTION EFFECT	TOTAL EFFECT
Food	Negative	Negative	Negative
Entertainment	Negative	Positive	Ambiguous

price rise on the quantity of food demanded must be negative. This holds whether the consumer moves to a point such as e'' or to a point such as e'.

However, the total effect on the quantity of entertainment demanded is ambiguous. If the consumer moves to a point such as e'', where the substitution effect predominates, an increase in the price of food has raised the demand for entertainment. If the consumer moves to a point such as e', where the income effect dominates, an increase in the price of food has reduced the demand for entertainment.

Where the consumer moves depends on how large the income and substitution effects are. If the demand for entertainment is very income-elastic, the cut in the purchasing power of income will result in a large fall in the demand for entertainment, and the consumer will probably end up at a point such as e', with a lower consumption of entertainment. If, contrary to fact, the demand for entertainment is not very income-elastic, an increase in the price of food will increase the demand for entertainment. Then the cross elasticity of demand for entertainment with respect to the price of food

will be positive. We thus see that there is a link between income elasticities of demand and cross price elasticities.

4 THE DEMAND CURVE

We have now provided the theoretical foundations of the downward-sloping demand curve for a good as a function of its price. We have just shown, in Table 5-4, that an increase in the price of food will reduce the quantity of food demanded. This is precisely the relationship shown in the regular demand function, which we have used so far and justified on the basis of intuition and data.

Note that it did not take very much to derive the downward-sloping demand curve. We started with a simple, reasonable model of the consumer. Then we broke down the effects of an increase in price on the quantity of a good demanded into income and substitution effects. If the good is normal, the income effect reduces the quantity of the good demanded when its price rises. And the substitution effect is certainly negative. Thus both effects taken together are negative if the good is normal. And both

BOX 5-1

SUBSTITUTION: EVEN RATS DO IT

The diagram shows the substitution effect in action. In an experiment a consumer was offered a choice between a Tom Collins mix and root beer. The price of the root beer was equal to the price of the Tom Collins mix. This is illustrated by budget line AF. The consumer chose to be at point e.

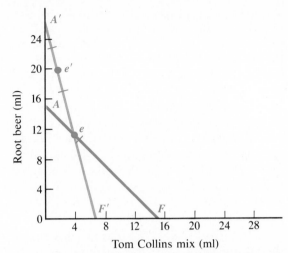

Then the price ratio was changed so that a unit of Tom Collins mix cost four times as much as a unit of root beer. The consumer's income was adjusted so that the budget line went through point e, the combination of the two drinks chosen before the price change. This is illustrated by budget line A'F', the new budget constraint.

In the new situation it is possible to continue consuming e. But of course the relative price of root beer has fallen, so the consumer will want to substitute root beer for the Tom Collins mix. Indeed, this is precisely the choice that was made. The consumer moved to e', where the consumption of root beer is higher than at e and the consumption of the Tom Collins mix is lower.

The consumer who illustrates so well how the substitution effect works was a white male albino rat "between 90 and 120 days of age at the beginning of the experiment and . . . (with) . . . no previous experimental history." The results described were obtained by Professors John H. Kagel, Raymond C. Battalio, Robert L. Basmann, and W. R. Klemm of Texas A&M University and Howard Rachlin and Leonard Green of the State University of New York at Stony Brook. The results were reported in their paper "Experimental Studies of Consumer Demand Behavior Using Laboratory Animals" (*Economic Inquiry,* March 1975).

The article presents two arguments for studying the economic behavior of animals. First, it is interesting to see to what extent behavioral principles cross the lines of the species. Second, if animals appear to behave like humans with respect to economic problems (as they do in this case), it will be much easier to do economics experiments in the future.

The authors, of course, also describe in detail the experimental procedure followed. For instance, the rat's budget constraint was the number of times he was required to push on two levers to get the two types of drinks. Each push on a lever gave the rat some amount of one drink, but the amount obtained per push changed with the price of one drink.

The authors reported one other fascinating finding. When large changes were made in relative prices, there were "severe disruptions" in consumer behavior. Many humans feel the same way.

effects taken together are precisely what determines the slope of the demand curve.[9]

The Individual Consumer's Demand Curve and the Market Demand Curve

In earlier chapters we discussed and used the downward-sloping market demand curve. In this chapter we have developed the theory of the consumer and shown that it leads to a downward-sloping demand curve for the individual consumer. We have not explicitly discussed the market demand curve.

The market demand curve is just the sum of the demand curves of all the individuals in the market. The market demand curve is obtained by asking, at each price, how much each person in the market would want to buy. By adding the quantities demanded by all consumers at each price, we obtain the total quantity demanded at each price. Thus we have the market demand curve. And since the quantity demanded by each person in the market increases as the price falls, the quantity demanded by all people in the market taken together also rises as the price falls, given the incomes of the individuals in the market.

Figure 5-7 shows how the market demand curve is put together from the demand curves of the individuals (in this case, just two of them) in the market. This process is known as *adding the demand curves horizontally*. It means that the market demand curve is obtained by adding the quantities demanded at each price.

Many Goods

Table 5-4 showed that the effects of a rise in

[9] The careful reader will note that we cannot be sure that the demand curve slopes downward unless the good is normal. It is *theoretically* possible with inferior goods for the demand curve to slope upward. (Check Table 5-4 to confirm this.) Such goods are named *Giffen goods* after the nineteenth-century British economist who is said to have raised the possibility. Giffen goods have not been observed in practice.

the price of one good on the quantity demanded of other goods are ambiguous. This means that cross price elasticities may be either positive or negative. For that reason we have to turn again to the data to get some idea of the typical sizes of these effects.

We will start by going back to Table 5-3. The cross price elasticities in that table are all negative. An increase in the price of each good in the table lowers the quantity demanded of each of the other goods. In terms of Figure 5-6, a rise in the price of a good moves consumers to equilibrium points such as e' rather than e''.

This result indicates that for the goods shown in Table 5-3, the income effect is substantial, while the substitution effect, by comparison, is relatively small. The reason why the income effect is so large is that each of these goods accounts for a very substantial share of the household budget. Food, for example, accounts for about 20 percent of the household budget. A 10 percent rise in food prices therefore reduces the purchasing power of household income by 2 percent (20 percent × 10 percent), and this reduction in the purchasing power of income depresses the quantity demanded of all (normal) goods.

Substitution effects are relatively small because food and housing are very poor substitutes, certainly by comparison with blue and green VWs, to take an extreme example. Blue and green cars are very good substitutes, because the slightest change in relative prices between blue and green cars (all other things being constant) will shift most consumers toward the lower-priced model. But food and housing are not like that. They do not satisfy identical consumer needs and are poor substitutes. Therefore the substitution response to a change in relative prices, while clearly present, is in no way sufficient to compensate for the substantial income effects.

Table 5-5 offers additional data, some of

FIGURE 5-7 INDIVIDUAL DEMAND CURVES AND THE MARKET DEMAND CURVE.
The market demand curve is the horizontal sum of the individual demand curves.
For instance, if the price is $5, the quantity demanded by consumer 1 is 11 units,
and the quantity demanded by consumer 2 is 13 units. The total quantity demanded
in the market at the price of $5 is thus 24 units, as shown on the market demand
curve. The market demand curve is kinked at point *A* because at *A*, at the price of
$8, consumer 2 comes into the market. At higher prices, the quantity demanded by
consumer 2 is zero, and the entire market demand comes from consumer 1.

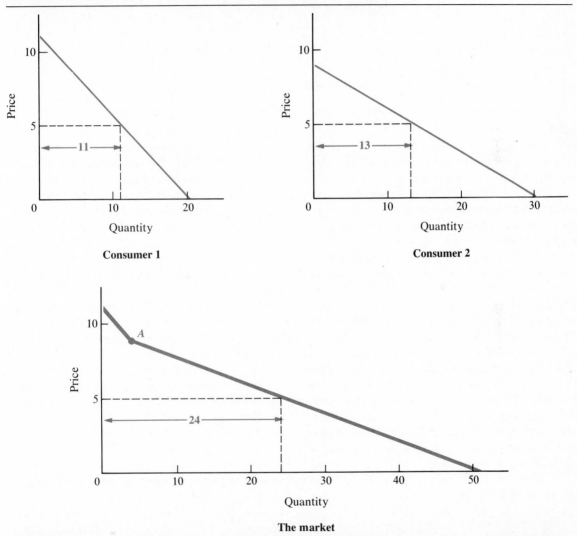

which (for meat and fish) were given in
Table 4-8. This time we will look at much
narrower commodity groups. They are not
quite as substitutable as green and blue
VWs; nevertheless, they are goods that we

can think of more nearly as substitutes.
Also, each of these goods commands a very
small share in the consumer budget compared with such broad groups as food and
shelter. Because the goods are probably

TABLE 5-5

OWN AND CROSS PRICE ELASTICITIES OF DEMAND FOR NARROWER COMMODITY GROUPS

	ELASTICITY OF DEMAND WITH RESPECT TO THE PRICE OF:				
	Meat	Fish	Tobacco products	Drinks	Candy
Meat	−0.48	0.01	−0.04	−0.02	−0.03
Fish	0.06	−0.72	−0.03	−0.02	−0.03
Tobacco products	−0.04	0.00	−0.42	0.03	0.04
Drinks	−0.06	−0.01	0.03	−0.61	0.10
Candy (including ice cream and chocolate)	−0.04	0.00	0.05	0.11	−0.51

Note: Entries in color are own price elasticities.
Source: A. P. Barten, "Consumer Demand Functions under Conditions of Almost Additive Preferences," *Econometrica,* January–April 1964, Table XV.

substitutes and because the income effects are small, the substitution effects may now outweigh the income effects.

Table 5-5 shows once more that own price elasticities (shown in color) are always negative. A rise in the price of a good reduces the quantity demanded of that good. But the cross price elasticities now show more variety. Some are approximately zero, such as the elasticity of the quantity demanded of tobacco products or candy with respect to the price of fish. Others are negative, such as the elasticity of the demand for meat with respect to the price of drinks or tobacco products. But we also have some positive entries. A rise in the price of candy raises the demand for both drinks and tobacco products. A rise in the price of fish raises the demand for meat (the elasticity is 0.01), and a rise in the price of meat raises the demand for fish. Here we have come to substitution possibilities that show up in positive cross price elasticities.

Complements and Substitutes

We have argued that in response to a change in relative prices the consumer rearranges the composition of his consumption, substituting toward the good whose price is now relatively lower and away from the good whose price is now relatively higher. In a two-good world, this is the only pattern of adjustment. But when there are many goods, there is the possibility that some of them are consumed jointly—pipes and tobacco, bread and cheese, electric stoves and electricity. We therefore have to recognize the possibility of *complementarity.*

In a world of many goods, an increase in the price of one commodity, say, tobacco, will lead consumers to substitute away from that commodity and toward other goods in general, but not necessarily toward *all* other goods. Indeed, besides substituting away from the good whose price has risen, the consumer will substitute *away* from the goods that are used jointly with the higher-priced good, even though the prices of those goods have not changed.

Pipes and tobacco are an example. Suppose the price of pipes goes up. What happens to the demand for tobacco? (We will ignore the income effect, which we know reduces the demand for all normal goods.) Pipes and tobacco are used jointly, and therefore we should expect that the demand for tobacco will fall along with the quantity of pipes demanded. How much the demand for tobacco will decline depends on how easily consumers can substitute from pipe smoking to smoking cigarettes or cigars. If that substitution is very easy, there might be only a small reduction in the demand for to-bacco but a very large reduction in the quantity of pipes demanded as many people switch from pipes to cigarettes.

Now consider the other case: tobacco prices (including the prices of cigarettes and cigars) rise, and pipe prices are un-changed. An increase in tobacco prices raises the relative price of smoking com-pared with the prices of other sources of utility, and therefore the consumer substi-tutes away from smoking and toward other goods. Now we expect the demand for pipes to fall along with the quantity demanded of tobacco. At each price of pipes, the higher tobacco prices reduce the quantity of pipes demanded; the higher prices shift the de-mand schedule for pipes to the left.

The possibility of complementarity—originating from the notion that certain goods are consumed jointly—arises quite frequently and represents a potentially im-portant part of the adjustment of demand in response to price changes. Whenever goods are complements, an increase in the price of one good will reduce the demand for the complement both through the substitution effect (substituting away from the higher-priced activity) and, of course, through the income effect. In Problem 12 at the end of the chapter (page 125), the reasoning about complements and substitutes is used to discuss the effect of higher gasoline prices on the demand for weekend motel rooms in Vermont.

Household Gas and Electricity Demand: An Example

We have seen the way in which the con-sumer adjusts to changes in prices through income and substitution effects. The elastic-ity estimates in Tables 5-3 and 5-5 indicate the responsiveness of demand to price changes. One common feature is that the elasticities are all quite small. Own elastic-ities of demand are less than 1 in each case,

implying that a rise in price will reduce the quantity demanded but raise spending on the good. The cross price elasticities are ex-tremely small in the cases where they are positive. It takes, for example, a 33¹/₃ per-cent (1/0.03) increase in the price of tobacco products to raise the demand for drinks by 1 percent.

But not all elasticities of demand are small, as Table 5-6 shows. Table 5-6 pre-sents long-run price elasticities of house-hold demand for electricity and natural gas.

The elasticity estimates in Table 5-6 show that once we come to quite narrow commodity groups and goods that are close substitutes in the sense of satisfying the same needs, the elasticity of demand can become very large. Note, as we might ex-pect, that natural gas and electricity have positive cross price elasticities. A rise in electricity prices raises the demand for nat-ural gas as a source of energy (for heating, cooking, etc.)

One important implication of Table 5-6 is worth drawing out. The own price elastic-ity of demand for natural gas, −3.4, is very large indeed. It indicates that there are large adjustments in the quantity demanded in response to an own price change. But what happens if natural gas and electricity prices rise together? Then the adjustment in the quantity of natural gas demanded is

TABLE 5-6

LONG-RUN PRICE ELASTICITIES OF HOUSEHOLD DEMAND FOR ELECTRICITY AND NATURAL GAS

| | ELASTICITY OF DEMAND WITH RESPECT TO THE PRICE OF: | |
	Natural gas	Electricity
Natural Gas	−3.4	1.7
Electricity	0.4	−2.2

Source: J. Beierlein, J. Dunn, and J. McConnon, Jr., "The Demand for Electricity and Natural Gas in the North-eastern United States," *Review of Economics and Statistics,* August 1981, Table 4.

much smaller. Part of the adjustment—substitution from natural gas toward electricity—will not take place because the price of electricity has also risen. The net effect on the quantity of natural gas demanded of a rise in the prices of both goods (in the same proportion) is an elasticity of only -1.7 $(-3.4 + 1.7)$. This point is worth bearing in mind because often the prices of close substitutes rise together. This has surely been the case in the field of energy, for example.

5 SPILLOVERS OF MARKET DISTURBANCES

Our consumer demand model has shown that the quantity demanded of one commodity depends on consumer income and on the prices of the good itself and of other goods. Income and substitution effects are the channels through which a disturbance in one market spills over to other markets. The idea that the effects of an event in one market spread to other markets helps us understand how the economy absorbs shocks, such as the oil price increase in 1973. We demonstrate the idea here with the case of refined sugar and corn sweetener.

Table 5-7 shows price and quantity data for the two commodities. The analysis starts with an increase in the world price of raw and refined sugar in 1973 and especially in 1974. The world price increased from only

7.00 cents in 1970–1972 (measured in 1973 cents) to 28.49 cents in 1974. As we would expect, the quantity demanded of refined sugar declined from 102 pounds in 1970–1972 to only 96 pounds in 1974. Just as our analysis suggests, there is evidence of a negative own price elasticity. It is also the case that the reduction in the quantity of sugar demanded was only on the order of 5 to 6 percent, which is quite small given a price increase of more than 300 percent. Thus the price elasticity is certainly small.

But the interesting fact is what the increase in the price of refined sugar does in other markets, especially in the markets for close substitutes such as corn sweetener. Corn sweetener is used in industry as a substitute for sugar—for example, in the preparation of soft drinks. The data for corn sweetener demand show a 25 percent increase in the quantity demanded—from 20 pounds in 1970–1972 to 25.1 pounds in 1974. Figure 5-8 explains this adjustment.

The demand and supply schedules for corn sweetener are shown as DD and SS, and the initial (1970–1972) equilibrium is shown at point E. The increase in the price of refined sugar shifts the demand schedule for the substitute corn sweetener to DD'. Excess demand results, and accordingly, the equilibrium price in the market for corn sweetener rises. A new, short-run equilibrium occurs at E', where both the price and

TABLE 5-7

REFINED SUGAR AND CORN SWEETENER: SUBSTITUTION EFFECTS AND SPILLOVERS OF MARKET DISTURBANCES

| | CANE AND BEET SUGAR | | CORN SWEETENER | |
	PRICE	QUANTITY	PRICE	QUANTITY
1970–1972	6.99	102	6.52	20.0
1973	10.99	100.8	7.06	21.1
1974	29.08	95.6	10.51	25.1
1975	18.45	89.1	12.95	27.5

Note: Prices are in 1973 cents per pound; quantities are in pounds per person per year.
Source: U.S. Department of Agriculture, *Sugar and Sweetener Report,* various issues.

FIGURE 5-8   THE EFFECT OF HIGHER SUGAR PRICES IN THE MARKET FOR CORN SWEETENER. A rise in the price of refined sugar shifts the demand for corn sweetener, which is a close substitute. The demand schedule shifts from *DD* to *DD'*, and the equilibrium price and quantity consumed both rise. In the long run further demand adjustment may occur as consumers find more ways to replace refined sugar with corn sweetener. Accordingly, the demand schedule shifts further, to *DD''*, and this leads to more price increases and increases in the quantities consumed.

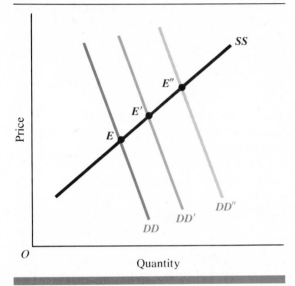

this kind of clear and dramatic episode that we can study to see the price system in action.

6 TRANSFERS IN CASH AND IN KIND—WHICH DOES THE CONSUMER PREFER?

In this section we use the model of consumer choice and especially the budget line to ask whether the consumer prefers transfers in cash or in kind. A transfer is a payment, usually made by the government, for which no corresponding service is provided by the recipient. Welfare payments and Social Security payments are examples of transfers. Wages are not transfers because the recipient is providing labor services in exchange for the wage.

Some transfers are in cash. But transfers *in kind* are common. For example, the poor receive food stamps that entitle them to buy food. But these food stamps are not cash, because they can only be used to buy food; they cannot be spent, for example, on education or entertainment. The question we ask in this section is whether an in-kind transfer program is preferred by the consumer to a cash transfer program, where the cash is equal in value to what is paid in kind.

Figure 5-9 helps develop the argument. We assume that the consumer has an income of $100 that can be spent on food or entertainment, the price of either of these goods being $10 per unit. Thus the budget line *AF* shows the maximum consumption of either food or entertainment as 10 units. Now we will consider a government program that issues to the consumer a food ration of 4 units. How will this food ration affect the budget line?

In Figure 5-9 we show that at each level of entertainment consumption the food program allows the consumer to have 4 more units of food. Where before 10 units of en-

the quantity demanded and supplied have risen. We thus see that an increase in the price of refined sugar spills over to the market for the substitute commodity and raises the price there too.

Over time, with the price of refined sugar remaining high, purchasers explore additional channels of substitution. In this case firms found that corn sweetener could be used as an ingredient in place of refined sugar. This further substitution leads, once more, to a shift in the demand schedule for corn sweetener, further raising prices and the equilibrium quantity demanded and supplied. In Table 5-7 we observe that within a few years the use of corn sweetener had expanded more than 30 percent in response to the change in relative prices. It is

FIGURE 5-9   TRANSFERS IN CASH AND IN KIND. The diagram shows that a transfer of food (a transfer in kind) may leave the consumer less satisfied than a transfer of cash of the same value. The reason can be seen by considering a consumer whose initial equilibrium is at point e'. Such an individual might want to spend less than the full in-kind allowance on food. For instance, he might prefer being at point c to being at any point on the budget line ABF' that is actually available to him. If the allowance were in cash, he could move to the budget line $A'BF'$ and thus choose a point such as c.

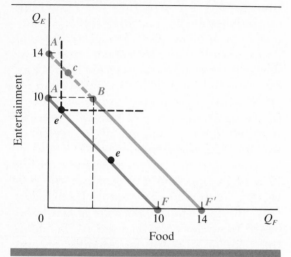

food and entertainment. The fact that the government program supplies food in kind does not bother him, because he wants to consume more food than is provided by the food program. He can consume the government rations, use some income to purchase food, and allocate the remainder to entertainment.

However, it is possible that the food program will leave the consumer with a lower level of welfare than if he were given the equivalent amount of cash, $40. With a cash allowance of $40 the budget line would include the dashed segment $A'B$, where the extra income in cash can be used to buy additional units of entertainment. The diagram shows that such a possibility is important for a consumer who is initially at point e'.

In response to the higher income he would move in a northeasterly direction to a point such as c on the segment $A'B$. He would use most of the extra income not to buy food but to buy more entertainment. With an in-kind program, without the possibility of selling the ration for cash, the consumer could at best wind up at point B. But if the preferred point is c, then the in-kind program would leave the consumer less well off than he could be at the same cost to the government. In-kind programs thus give some consumers less of a gain in utility or welfare than they could give at the same cost if there were unrestricted cash transfers. Giving cash transfers allows the consumer to purchase what he wants; giving in-kind transfers limits his options.

Transfers in kind are politically popular. The electorate wants to know that tax dollars are spent "wisely." Voters are willing to give the poor food stamps but not cash to buy liquor, entertainment, or any other goods. Indeed, those who favor transfers in kind will argue that the poor really do not know how to spend money and that it is much more important that everyone be

tertainment meant zero food, now there are 4 units of food from the government program. Accordingly, the budget line now starts at point B, with 10 units of entertainment and 4 (free) units of food. Because the food is free, point B does not lie on the vertical axis. Note next that the maximum amount of food consumption is 14 units, 10 purchased with the $100 income plus 4 free units coming from the government. Therefore, our budget line under the in-kind food program is ABF'. Any point on this line is attainable by the consumer.

Where will the optimal consumption point be in the presence of the program? If initially the consumer is at point e, for example, the new consumption point, with both goods normal, will be to the northeast on the segment BF'. This means that the consumer will increase his consumption of both

adequately fed and housed than that everyone have good entertainment. Therefore, we should undertake programs to ensure that there is adequate food and housing instead of just handing over money. Furthermore, they argue, people are typically responsible for children, and the program ensures that the children will be well fed and properly housed rather than allowed to spend a lot of time at the movies.

You will recognize that one group says people can best choose for themselves and their children how to spend their money, whereas the other group says people may spend their money unwisely. The issue is at bottom philosophical; it cannot be decided by economics alone. But the thrust of the economic analysis is clear: people will be better off or at least no worse off in light of their own tastes if they are given transfers in cash rather than in kind.[10]

7 USING PRICE AND INCOME DATA TO DETERMINE WELFARE CHANGES

Each year incomes change and prices change. At the end of the year, and indeed every month, the government announces whether average real income, or the standard of living, has risen over that period or fallen. How can we tell from data about incomes and prices whether a consumer is better off or worse off when prices and income both change? The model of consumer behavior provides the right way of thinking about the question.

---

[10] In the 1970s, the Department of Housing and Urban Development undertook a major experimental program in which people were given either money or different types of subsidies designed to improve the standard of their housing. Some people were effectively given an in-kind transfer; it ensured that they would consume at least the amount of housing the program was providing. Others were effectively given cash. Many of those given cash decided not to spend all the cash on housing—that is, they chose to move to points to the left of B in Figure 5-9. The program is described in Bernard J. Frieden, "Housing Allowances: An Experiment That Worked," *The Public Interest*, spring 1980.

TABLE 5-8

INCOME AND PRICES: HYPOTHETICAL DATA FOR 1982 AND 1983

	1982	1983	% CHANGE
Income	$100	$120	20%
Food price	5	7.50	50
Entertainment price	10	10	0

Suppose that between 1982 and 1983 a consumer's income increased by 10 percent, food prices rose by 50 percent, and the price of entertainment remained constant. Was the consumer better off in 1983 than in 1982? Table 5-8 summarizes the available information.

A simple way to determine whether the consumer was better off under the new income and price conditions is shown in Figure 5-10. The two budget lines correspond respectively to the income and price data for 1982 and 1983. Note that the 1983 budget yields a higher purchasing power in terms of entertainment, because income is higher and entertainment prices are unchanged. But the purchasing power in terms of food has declined. Thus at first sight, it is unclear whether the consumer was better off in 1983 than in 1982.

Suppose that the initial 1982 consumption point was e and that the 1983 point was e'. In this case there was clearly an improvement in welfare. The reason is that e lies inside the new budget line. This means that in 1983, given the 1983 income and prices, the consumer could have afforded the 1982 consumption bundle. The fact that he chose e' in preference means that e' yielded higher utility. Therefore, consumer welfare improved between 1982 and 1983. The criterion for welfare improvement, then, is simply whether the consumer in 1983 could have bought the 1982 consumption bundle. If the answer is yes, his *real* income, or purchasing power in terms of goods, given his particular tastes, increased.

FIGURE 5-10 A CHANGE IN INCOME AND PRICES THAT IMPROVES WELFARE. The budget lines *AF* and *A'F'* correspond respectively to the hypothetical 1982 and 1983 price and income data. If the 1983 consumption point is at *e'* (or anywhere to the northwest of point *c*) *and* if the 1982 consumption point, *e*, lies inside the 1983 budget line, the consumer must be better off. The reason is that he could in 1983 have chosen to be at *e*, but he preferred instead to be at *e'*. Since he prefers *e'* to *e*, he is better off at *e'* than at *e*.

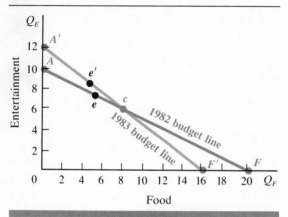

If point *e* (1982 consumption) were instead on the stretch *cF*, outside the new budget line, we would not be able to make a welfare judgment. The 1982 budget would not be enough to buy the 1983 consumption bundle, and so we couldn't say the consumer preferred his 1982 situation to the 1983 situation. The 1983 budget would not be enough for the 1982 consumption basket, and so we couldn't say whether the consumer preferred his 1983 situation to that of 1982. We wouldn't be able to say that he preferred his situation in either year to the situation in the other year. Here is a case where observations of income, prices, and consumption are not enough to allow us to make an inference about welfare.

The analysis presented in this section is the basis for the construction of cost-of-living index numbers, which attempt to measure changes in real income or prices.

SUMMARY

1   The theory of demand is based on the assumption that the consumer, given the budget constraint, seeks to reach the maximum level of utility.

2   The consumer has a problem of choice because his income and the prevailing prices limit the amounts of goods he can buy. More of one good means that less income is left to spend on other goods. The budget line represents the consumer's budget constraint and shows the maximum combinations of goods available to the consumer.

3   For the consumer more is better than less. Therefore, the consumer will always consume on the budget line.

4   The consumer optimizes the allocation of spending among goods by moving to the point on the budget line where an extra dollar's worth of spending on any good yields the same increase in utility. In that position, no reshuffling of the spending pattern can increase utility.

5   A change in prices changes the position of the budget line. This is because it changes the purchasing power of income in terms of the good whose price has changed. An increase in a price has both an in-

come effect and a substitution effect. The income effect reduces the demand for all (normal) goods. The substitution effect involves a re-shuffling of the spending pattern—the consumer moves away from the good whose price has risen and toward substitutes.

6   A rise in the price of a good must lower the demand for that good so long as the good is normal. It may raise or lower the demand for some other good depending on the relative size of the income and substitution effects.

7   Disturbances in any one market can spill over to other markets. One of the channels is the cross price elasticity of demand. A rise in the price of cane sugar, for example, increases the demand for corn sweetener and therefore leads to a rise in the equilibrium price of corn sweetener. This channel implies that prices of close substitutes tend to move together.

8   Consumers prefer to receive transfers in cash instead of transfers of equal value in kind. A transfer in kind may limit the choices the consumer can make, compared with the choices he has with a cash transfer.

9   In some cases data on income, prices, and consumption baskets allow us to judge whether consumer welfare has improved from one year to the next. We can make that judgment whenever the consumer can still afford last year's consumption bundle, given the current income and prices. If last year's consumption bundle is still affordable but the consumer prefers another one, then he must be better off.

KEY TERMS

Consumer choice	Income effect
Consumption basket	Substitution effect
Budget constraint	Market demand curve
Budget line	Complement
Tastes	Substitute
Utility maximization	Spillovers of market disturbances
Diminishing marginal utility	Transfer in kind
Marginal utility	Cost-of-living index numbers

PROBLEMS

1   Suppose that a consumer's income is $50. Food costs $5 per unit, and entertainment costs $2 per unit. (a) Draw the budget line corresponding to these data, and choose a position for the initial optimal consumption (point e). (b) Suppose now that the price of food falls to $2.50. Draw the new budget line, and indicate what can be said about the new consumption point, assuming that both goods are normal. Label

the new consumption point e'. (c) Suppose that the price of entertainment also falls and is now only \$1. Draw the new budget line, and indicate where the consumer is now, with both prices having changed. Label the new consumption point e''. (d) How does the new consumption point, e'', in (c) differ from e in (a)? Explain your answer.

2 Suppose that a consumer's initial income is \$100, the price of food is \$5 per unit, and the price of entertainment is \$20 per unit. Let the price of food now rise to \$10. (a) Calculate how much income we would have to give the consumer to allow him to buy the initial consumption bundle of 12 food units and 2 units of entertainment. (b) Draw the new budget line, $A'F'$, so that at the new prices the consumer has just enough income to buy the initial consumption basket. (c) Where on the new budget line, $A'F'$, would the consumer now place himself relative to the initial equilibrium? (d) Compare this situation with the case of the rat.

3 The own price elasticity of demand for food is, of course, negative. It is also the case that the demand for food is inelastic. (See Table 5-3.) This implies that an increase in food prices raises spending on food. Therefore, higher food prices imply that less is spent on all other goods and that the quantity demanded of each of the other goods must fall. Discuss carefully these statements, and identify any that you think might be wrong.

4 Draw the budget line corresponding to the following data: price of good 1 = \$2, price of good 2 = \$6, income = \$300 per week. Now draw the budget line corresponding to these data: price of good 1 = \$6, price of good 2 = \$18, income = \$900 per week. Can you say anything about the consumer's choices in these two situations?

5 Draw a budget set (i.e., the combina-tions of goods an individual can buy) on the basis of the following information: the price of good 1 = \$4, the price of good 2 = \$8, income = \$400 per week, and there is a limit on the amount of good 2 that can be bought —no more than 20 units per week. Can you say anything about where the consumer will probably choose to be?

6 In wartime, ration coupons are some-times given for the purchase of different goods. To buy goods requires both money and coupons. Suppose that an individual has an income of \$300 per week and that good 1 costs \$2 and good 2 costs \$6. Sup-pose also that the individual receives 100 coupons per week and that it takes one cou-pon to buy 1 unit of good 1 and one coupon to buy 1 unit of good 2. Show the choices that are open to the consumer in this situa-tion. Shade in his *budget set*, the combina-tions of goods he can obtain.

7 As an alternative to the food stamp pro-gram as a means of making people eat more food, the federal government could subsi-dize the price of food. (Indeed, bread is sub-sidized in many countries.) This subsidy would effectively reduce the price of food. Show how a subsidy program would affect the budget constraint and therefore food consumption. Compare it with a food stamp program.

8 Suppose that there are two goods, trans-portation and entertainment. Assume that transportation is an inferior good—as in-come rises, the demand for transportation declines. Show graphically the effect on the consumption pattern of a rise in income. Use the budget line diagram to study this question.

9 If an increase in the price of drinks raises the demand for chocolate, then an in-crease in the price of chocolate must raise the demand for drinks. Discuss this state-ment. Explain why it is correct or incorrect.

10 Use Table 5-6 to analyze the following problem. The Municipal Electricity Board (MEB) has decided that the large deficits must be reduced by an increase in electricity rates. At the same time, the Regional Gas Council (RGC) has announced that it is willing and able to supply increased amounts of gas at unchanged prices. Assume that the electricity rates are raised from $4 to $6. (*a*) What will happen under this pricing policy to the quantity of electricity demanded? (*b*) What will happen to the quantity of gas demanded? (*c*) What will happen to the spending on electricity? (*d*) What would happen to the quantity of electricity demanded if the RGC matched the percentage price hike of the MEB?

11 Consider a consumer with an income of $100. Draw the budget lines corresponding to the following four situations.

	FOOD PRICE	ENTERTAINMENT PRICE
(*a*)	$10	$20
(*b*)	5	20
(*c*)	10	10
(*d*)	10	25

Discuss in each case the change in the budget line compared with situation (*a*).

12 Suppose that consumers have a given income. They consume a large variety of goods, including gasoline and weekend vacations in Vermont (a 3-hour drive away from the urban centers). Now let the price of gasoline double. (*a*) What is the effect of higher gasoline prices on the quantity demanded of gasoline? (*b*) What is the effect of higher gasoline prices on the demand for motel rooms in Vermont? Be certain to discuss both income and substitution effects. (*c*) Use a demand and supply diagram to show what happens to the price of motel rooms in Vermont. (*d*) Suppose that in addition to Vermont there is a vacation place that is closer to the urban centers. What happens to the demand for motel rooms there?

13 The following is a newspaper report on the use of electricity.

> "People in some parts of the country use electricity like there's no tomorrow because it only costs them about a penny a kilowatt hour," says a spokesman for Midwest Research Institute after a nationwide survey of electrical rates. It was indicated that those with very high rates tend to keep their bills low by more careful use of their electricity. In Huntsville, Ala., for example, the average monthly bill is $46.01, based on a cost of about three cents per kilowatt hour. In New York City, the average bill is $31.72, at nearly 12 cents per kilowatt hour.

Can you explain the findings in the report by using the material presented in this chapter?

APPENDIX: INDIFFERENCE CURVE ANALYSIS

This appendix extends the discussion of consumer choice by using the tool of indifference curves. Figure 5A-1 shows food and entertainment consumption on the axes. The schedules UU_1 and UU_2 are called indifference curves.

> An indifference curve shows all the consumption baskets among which the consumer is indifferent because they yield the same level of utility.

Along UU_1 we have different combinations of food and entertainment. For example, point C is a basket with lots of entertainment and little food. Point A, by contrast, offers a more balanced mix. Point B is richer in food and has less entertainment. The consumer ranks all possible combinations in terms of the utility they yield and identifies the combinations that yield the same level. UU_1 is one set of equal-utility baskets.

Point D is on another indifference curve, UU_2. We know that for the consumer more is better than less. Accordingly, a point such as D *must* yield higher utility than A, because at D the consumer has more of both goods than he has at A. This means that utility is higher on UU_2 than on UU_1. Any point on UU_2 yields the same level of utility, but one that is higher than the level of utility along UU_1.

We have not drawn more indifference curves, but there is a whole map of them. Some lie below UU_1, since they correspond to lower levels of utility than the consumer baskets along UU_1. Others lie between UU_1 and UU_2, and still others lie above UU_2. Indeed, every point in the diagram represents a consumption basket and can be assigned a utility value. Therefore, every point lies on one *and only one* indifference curve.

The Shape of Indifference Curves

There are four rules about consumer tastes or preferences that are reflected in the way we draw indifference curves. Each is important. First, indifference curves cannot cross. The reason is that each indifference curve corresponds to a particular level of utility. If the curves crossed, this would imply that the consumption basket at the crossing point had not one level of utility but two, one corresponding to each of the indifference curves. Clearly that does not make sense, and so indifference curves cannot cross.

Second, higher indifference curves correspond to higher levels of utility, or welfare, because the consumer can have more of both goods on higher indifference curves than on lower indifference curves.

Third, indifference curves are negatively sloped. Moving along an indifference curve, the consumer is willing to sacrifice some entertainment if in exchange he receives some more food. If there is less of one, then to be indifferent there *must* be more of the other.

Fourth, as we move along an indifference curve, giving up some entertainment in exchange for some more food, we find that the indifference curve is first very steep and then gradually flattens out. At point C, for example, the consumer is willing to give up a lot of entertainment to acquire another unit of food. At point B, by contrast, he is willing to sacrifice only a very small amount of entertainment for another unit of food. We call this flattening out of the indifference curve the *diminishing marginal rate of substitution*. "Diminishing marginal rate of substitution" means that the consumer's willingness to give up entertainment in exchange for extra units of food declines as more and more food and less and less entertainment is in the basket, as the consumer moves from C toward B.

FIGURE 5A-1   INDIFFERENCE CURVES. The schedule UU_1 is an indifference curve. It shows all the
combinations of food and entertainment, such as
points A and B, among which the consumer is indifferent because they yield the same level of utility.
UU_2 is another indifference curve. It corresponds to a
higher level of utility. Any point on UU_2 is preferred
to any point on UU_1 because the former indifference
curve corresponds to a higher level of utility than the
latter.

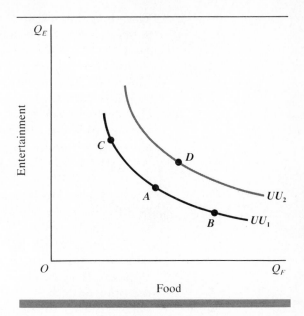

The notion of diminishing marginal rate of substitution ties in
with the idea of diminishing marginal utility. As we move to the right
along an indifference curve in Figure 5A-1, the consumption of food is
increasing, and the consumption of entertainment is decreasing.
Therefore, the marginal utility of food is decreasing, and that of entertainment is increasing.

Now we want to ask what determines the slope of the indifference
curve. Along the indifference curve, the consumer's utility is constant.
Therefore, he gives up as much utility by reducing the consumption of
entertainment as he gains by increasing the consumption of food.

The slope of the indifference curve tells us how many units of entertainment the consumer is willing to give up to get 1 unit of food.
Suppose the answer is 3. Then the ratio of the marginal utility of food
to that of entertainment must be 3. Why? Suppose 1 extra unit of food
brings in 30 utils. The consumer is willing to give up 3 units of entertainment to get those 30 utils. Therefore, the marginal utility per unit
of entertainment must be 10 (30/3). Accordingly, the marginal rate of
substitution is equal to the ratio of the marginal utilities of the goods.

$$\begin{matrix} \text{Slope of} \\ \text{indifference} \\ \text{curve} \end{matrix} = \begin{matrix} \text{marginal rate} \\ \text{of substitution} \\ \text{of food} \\ \text{for entertainment} \end{matrix} = \frac{\text{marginal utility of food}}{\begin{matrix}\text{marginal utility} \\ \text{of entertainment}\end{matrix}} \qquad \textbf{(A1)}$$

Equation (A1) provides an explanation of the shape of the indifference curve. As we move to the right along the indifference curve, the
marginal utility of food is falling, and that of entertainment is rising.

Therefore, the slope of the indifference curve is decreasing. That is precisely what the notion of diminishing marginal rate of substitution says.[11]

The Consumer's Equilibrium

Indifference curves are used to show the consumer's optimal consumption choice. The consumer wants to get to the highest possible indifference curve. That's how he maximizes his utility, or satisfaction. Given budget line AF in Figure 5A-2, the best he can do is to reach indifference curve UU_2. There is no reason for him to choose a point on a lower indifference curve, such as UU_1, because he can do better. But he cannot reach the points above point e—the points on indifference curves such as UU_3—because he does not have enough income to do so.

Note that at the optimal consumption point, e, the budget line is tangent to (just touches) the indifference curve. This means that the slopes of the two lines are the same. The slope of the budget line is the price ratio, as we learned in the chapter. The slope of the indifference curve is the marginal rate of substitution.

From equation (A1), the marginal rate of substitution is equal to the ratio of the marginal utilities of the two goods. Thus the condition

---

[11]In the text we noted that the theory of the consumer's choice can be developed without using the idea of utils or diminishing marginal utility. The alternative approach starts from the assumption that the marginal rate of substitution between goods behaves in the way implied on the indifference curves in Figure 5A-1.

FIGURE 5A-2   CONSUMER EQUILIBRIUM. The diagram shows the consumer's budget line, *AF*, and three indifference curves. The consumer can reach any point on the budget line, but no point beyond. Among the points on the budget line is point *e*. It represents the consumption bundle that yields the highest attainable level of welfare. It yields a higher degree of welfare than points *b* or *c*, which are also attainable.

At the optimal point the budget line is tangent to an indifference curve. This means that the rate at which the consumer is willing to trade food for entertainment is equal to the ratio of the prices of the two goods.

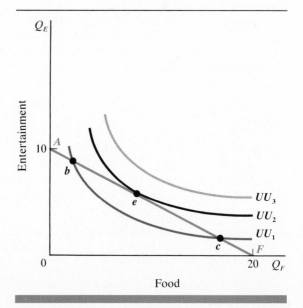

for the consumer's maximum utility is as follows:

$$\frac{\text{Marginal utility of food}}{\text{Marginal utility of entertainment}} = \frac{\text{price of food}}{\text{price of entertainment}} \qquad \text{(A2)}$$

In symbols:

$$\frac{MU_F}{MU_E} = \frac{P_F}{P_E} \qquad \text{(A2)}'$$

Now we can rearrange equation (A2)' to get a commonsense reading of the consumer's equilibrium condition:

$$\frac{MU_F}{P_F} = \frac{MU_E}{P_E} \qquad \text{(A3)}$$

Condition (A3) says that the ratios of the marginal utility of each good to the good's price are equal at the consumer's equilibrium position. But this is simply the condition that a dollar spent on any good yields the same marginal utility—the condition we used in the text.

Suppose, for instance, that MU_F is 50 and that the price of food is $5. The marginal utility per dollar spent on food is then 10 (50/5), which is equal to the left-hand side of (A3). Now suppose that the price per unit of entertainment is $10. If the consumer is in equilibrium, according to (A3), the marginal utility of entertainment must be 100 utils per unit. But that says the marginal utility per dollar spent on entertainment is 10 utils. Hence (A3) is simply the condition that the marginal utility per dollar spent on any good has to be the same at the optimum position.

The Effects of a Price Increase

Indifference curves can be used to show the effects of a price increase. In Figure 5A-3 the consumer is initially at point e on budget line AF, which corresponds to $100 of income and a price of $10 for each unit of food and entertainment. When the price of food doubles (becomes $20), the new budget line is AF'. The consumer can no longer reach point e. What is the highest level of welfare the consumer can attain given the change in the budget constraint?

The diagram shows that the new equilibrium is at point e' on AF'. The new equilibrium is at the point where the budget line is tangent to an indifference curve—or, to put it differently, where the budget line which the consumer *must* be on touches the highest available indifference curve. At that point the consumer does maximize utility (being on the highest available indifference curve) while still satisfying the budget constraint (being on the budget line).

PROBLEM

In Figure 5A-3, we show the case of positive cross price elasticity. At e' the quantity demanded of entertainment is greater than at e. This

FIGURE 5A-3 THE EFFECT OF AN INCREASE IN FOOD PRICES ON THE QUANTITIES DEMANDED OF FOOD AND ENTERTAINMENT. The consumer is initially at point e on budget line AF, which corresponds to a $100 income and a price of $10 for each of the goods. When food prices increase to $20, the budget line rotates to AF'. Point e is no longer attainable. The new equilibrium must lie on the new budget line, AF'. Indifference curve UU_1 is the highest indifference curve the consumer can now reach, given the new budget line. Any other point on AF' would be on a lower indifference curve. Therefore, point e' is the new consumption point. Because of the way we have drawn the indifference curves, the quantity demanded of food declines, but the quantity demanded of entertainment is higher at e' than at e. Thus this case involves a positive cross price elasticity; substitution effects dominate income effects.

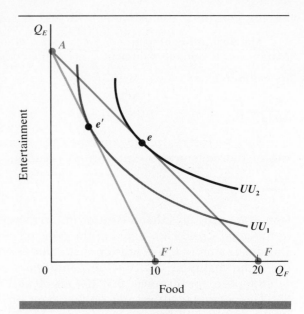

means that the substitution effect in response to the change in relative price more than offsets the income effect. (*a*) Explain why the consumer cannot in the initial situation do better than to be at point *e*. (*b*) Why can the consumer not remain at *e* when the price of food rises? (*c*) Is the consumer better off or worse off at *e'* than at *e*? (*d*) Draw a diagram for the case where the quantity demanded of entertainment falls at the new equilibrium.

Demand and supply together determine the amount of a good produced and its price. We analyzed demand in the last two chapters. Now we move on to supply and study firms' decisions on how much to produce and sell. The firm decides how much to produce on the basis of both its costs of production and the revenue it earns from its sales. The main focus of the chapter, illustrated in Figure 6-1, is on firms' *production costs* and the *revenues* firms earn by selling goods.

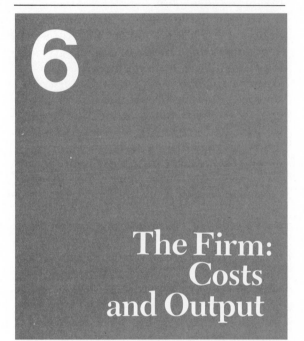

We start the chapter by describing different types of firms, from the giant corporations such as General Motors, IBM, and Exxon to the corner grocery store or the lemonade stand kids set up on a hot summer's day. What do such different firms have in common? How can a single theory of supply behavior apply to all these firms?

The key to the theory of supply is the assumption that all firms have the same aim: firms want to maximize their profits. Profits are the excess of revenues over costs. To understand how firms maximize profits, we have to analyze the meanings of revenues, costs, and profits. We also discuss the assumption that firms try to maximize their profits, and we examine alternative views of what firms' aims might be.

Two essential concepts are introduced in this chapter. The first is *marginal revenue*, and the second is *marginal cost*. These two concepts are the key to understanding how a firm chooses the level of output so as to maximize its profits. This chapter is only an introduction to the theory of supply. Later chapters present more details. But once the concepts of marginal revenue and marginal cost are mastered, the theory of supply is largely under control.

Before we define marginal revenue and marginal cost, though, we describe the different types of firms found in the economy.

1 BUSINESS ORGANIZATION

There are three types of business firms in the United States: individual proprietorships, partnerships, and corporations. Table 6-1 gives the details for 1977. There were nearly 15 million firms, the vast majority of them individual proprietorships. On the average the revenue of an individual proprietorship was only $34,000.

The revenue of a business is the amount of payments it receives from selling its output of goods or services.

The Firm: Costs and Output

6

FIGURE 6-1   THE THEORY OF SUPPLY. Firms' decisions on how much to produce and supply depend both on the costs of production and on the revenues they receive from selling their output. This is the essence of the theory of supply. In the rest of this chapter and in the next chapter we fill in the details of this picture.

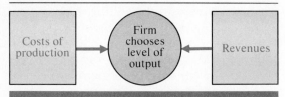

The average revenues of partnerships were nearly five times those of individual proprietorships. Corporations had, on the average, revenues of nearly $2 million in 1977.

An *individual proprietorship* is a business owned by an individual. That individual is fully entitled to the income earned by the business and is fully responsible for any losses the business suffers. The individual may, for instance, open a health food store. He rents the premises, buys the goods to put on the shelves, possibly hires someone to stand at the cash register, and keeps whatever profits are earned. Perhaps the business will show a loss, as many individual proprietorships do. In that case, the losses have to be paid for out of the proprietor's pocket. If the losses are large, the proprietor may be unable to pay. He then has to go into bankruptcy, allowing his assets to be divided up among the people to whom he owes.

But not all individual proprietorships fail. Many provide a tough living for their owners, who work long hours, frequently earning less than the average wage earner. And sometimes they provide handsomely for their owners.

If a business prospers, the owner may want to expand. To do so, he has to move to bigger premises, buy bigger stocks of goods to have available for sale, and purchase a delivery truck and office furniture. He needs financial capital, or money up front, to pay for all the new equipment and stocks. Where will that come from? One possible source is another individual, a person who goes into partnership with the original owner.

A *partnership* is a business arrangement in which two or more people jointly own a business. They share in the income of the business, and they are jointly responsible for any losses the business incurs. Perhaps one of the partners runs the business and the other merely puts up the money, or perhaps both are active in the business. There are some very large partnerships, with hundreds of partners. Examples are law firms and accounting firms.

But the partnership form has two big disadvantages. First, the partnership is very specific. If a new partner is taken in, or if an existing partner dies or wants to get out, a new partnership has to be set up. Second, partnerships (like individual proprietorships) have *unlimited liability*. This means

TABLE 6-1

BUSINESS FIRMS, 1977

	NUMBER OF FIRMS, thousands	AVERAGE REVENUES, $
Proprietorships	11,346	34,700
Partnerships	1,153	157,000
Corporations	2,241	1,830,900

Source: Statistical Abstract of the United States, 1981, Table 896.

that if the firm loses money, each partner is individually responsible for its debts. If there are two partners and one of them goes bankrupt, the other is responsible for all the debts of the firm, up to their full value. A partner in a firm puts his own wealth on the line, not only that of the firm. It is for this reason that firms where trust is involved— such as law firms and, in earlier times, some banks—are partnerships.[1] It is a signal to the customers that the people running the firm are willing to put their own personal fortunes behind the firm's obligations.

Any business needs to have some financial capital—some funds or money to spend, to begin operations, and to finance growth. The equipment and the stocks of goods the firm needs typically have to be paid for well before the income that they generate is available to pay for them. In businesses such as law or medicine where there is not much equipment and no need for large amounts of goods to have on the shelves for sale, the necessary funds can be obtained from the wealth of the individual owner or the partners—maybe with the aid of loans from banks or other individuals. But the larger the business, the more equipment and supplies it needs to operate, and the more difficult it is to provide the funds in those ways. A rapidly growing business, in particular, needs to be able to mobilize large amounts of funds. Because of the legal complications, it does not make sense to keep taking on new partners. Instead, it makes sense to form a corporation.

A *corporation* is an organization that is legally permitted to carry on certain activities, such as running a railroad, or making and selling computers, or producing a newspaper. A corporation, unlike a partnership, has an existence separate from that of the people who own it. A corporation does not

go out of existence when one of its owners —a shareholder—decides to sell his shares or dies.

Ownership of a corporation is divided up among the shareholders (also called stockholders). The original shareholders are the people who contributed money or other resources (perhaps the idea for the product the company is producing) when the corporation was set up. The shareholders are the people who have rights to a share in the company's earnings.

A corporation obtains funds to run the business by selling these rights of ownership. A person who owns shares can typically resell them to someone else. For most large corporations, the shares can be sold to anyone who can buy them. Thus the current owners of a corporation are not necessarily the people who bought the original shares. Most likely, the current owners bought their shares from previous owners through a broker working in the stock exchange. For some small companies, however, there are restrictions on the rights of an owner to sell shares. These restrictions prevent outsiders from acquiring control.

Shareholders in a corporation earn a return on their personal investment in two ways. First, the corporation makes regular, usually quarterly, payments to its stockholders. These payments are called *dividends*. A corporation is not obliged to pay dividends, but most large corporations do, and they do so regularly. The rate at which dividends are paid, both as a percentage of the firm's profits and as a percentage of the price of a share, varies from firm to firm.

The second way shareholders hope to earn a return is through *capital gains*. There is a capital gain when the price of a share rises. Thus someone who bought shares in U.S. Widget at $40 per share has a capital gain of $10 per share if the price is now $50.

The shareholders who own a corporation have *limited liability*. This means that

---

[1] State laws may *require* that law firms and accounting firms be partnerships, with the partners personally responsible for the firm's debts.

they are not liable for more money than they committed to the corporation. In contrast, a proprietor or partner is liable for any debts the business cannot pay. A shareholder can lose as much money as he commits in the first place, but no more. If you buy shares in U.S. Widget, Inc., you may lose your entire investment. But if U.S. Widget, Inc., cannot meet its debts, no one can get you to pay them. A shareholder in a corporation therefore has much less to worry about than a partner. At worst the shares become worthless.

Two advantages of owning shares in a corporation are that the shares can be quickly and cheaply transferred and that the shareholders have limited liability. These advantages have made corporations the main form of organization of big business. The firms whose names are household words are corporations. The largest private employer in the United States in 1980 was AT&T, with over 1 million employees, or 1 percent of the total work force. It is a corporation. Its revenues in 1980 were $50.8 billion, and its profits were $6.1 billion.[2] In 1980 there were in the United States 159 corporations that each employed more than 50,000 people. Total employment in those corporations was 20.8 million, or nearly 20 percent of the work force. Thus a few large corporations account for a very substantial portion of total employment and output in the United States. By contrast, the more than 11 million individual proprietorships produce less than 20 percent of total output.

We will now take a more detailed look at how firms operate.

2 REVENUES, COSTS, AND PROFITS

A firms's *revenue* is the amount the firm makes by selling its goods or services

during a given period (say, a year). The firm's *costs* are the expenses of producing the goods or services sold during the period. *Profits* are the excess of revenues over costs.

The relationship between profits, revenues, and costs can be expressed as follows:

Profits = revenues − costs   (1)

The general idea of revenues, costs, and profits is simple. In practice, calculating revenues and costs for a large business is complicated—otherwise the world would not need so many accountants. We will approach the difficulties by starting with a simple case.

Rent-a-Person, Inc., is a firm that does what its name suggests. It hires people whom it can rent out to other firms that need help. Rent-a-Person charges $10 per hour per worker and pays the people it hires $7 per hour. During one year it rented out 100,000 hours of labor. The expenses of running the business included leasing an office, buying advertising space in newspapers, and paying office workers and telephone and postage bills. All these expenses came to $200,000. Figure 6-2 shows the *income statement,* or *profit and loss statement,* for Rent-a-Person for 1983. Rent-a-Person had a net income, or profits, before taxes of $100,000 for 1983. It had to pay taxes to the federal government and to its state government totaling $25,000. Thus Rent-a-Person's 1983 profits after taxes were $75,000.

Now we can discuss some of the complications in the calculation of profits.

Outstanding Bills Very often, a firm is not paid within the year for all the goods or services it sold. Nor does it pay within the year for all the goods or services it bought. Rent-a-Person rented out $100,000 hours of labor during the year, but the renters still have not paid for services received during December. Similarly, Rent-a-Person probably

---

[2] In 1982–1983, AT&T was broken up into smaller firms as a result of antitrust actions by the Justice Department. It thus lost its position as the largest corporation.

FIGURE 6-2
RENT-A-PERSON, INC.
INCOME STATEMENT
FOR THE YEAR ENDED DECEMBER 31, 1983

Revenue		$1,000,000
(100,000 hours rented out at $10 per hour)		
Deduct expenses (or costs)		
Wages paid to people rented out		
(100,000 hours at $7 per hour)	$700,000	
Newspaper advertising	50,000	
Office rent	50,000	
Wages for office workers	80,000	
Other office expenses	20,000	
		900,000
Net income (profits) before taxes		$ 100,000
Taxes paid		25,000
Net income (profits) after taxes		$ 75,000

has not paid its telephone bill for December.

How should this complication be handled? From the economic viewpoint, the right definition of revenues is the value of the goods or services sold or rented out during the year. Similarly, the right definition of costs is the value of the goods or services used during the year.

Thus revenues and costs relate to the activities of the firm during the year and not to the dates on which payments are made for them. The difference between revenues and costs, and payments received and made, is part of the important concept of cash flow.

A firm's *cash flow* is the net amount of money it actually receives in a given period.

Cash flow may be low even though profits are high—for instance, if people haven't yet paid their bills. And, of course, a firm that is making profits but has no cash flow may eventually find it difficult to operate, since it can't keep paying for the goods and services it needs without having some cash flowing in.

Indeed, part of the problem of running a business is that the cash flow is bound to be low at the beginning, before the firm has succeeded in finding customers. This is why firms need financial capital, or money, to start up a business. With financial capital they can continue to pay expenses for a while, even with little cash flowing in. Eventually, if the business does well, cash will flow in, and there will be a net cash inflow.

Capital and Depreciation   Rent-a-Person is quite special in owning no physical capital.

Physical capital is the machinery, equipment, and buildings used in production.

Rent-a-Person rents its office space, typewriters, and desks. In practice, businesses frequently buy physical capital, such as typewriters, lathes, or trucks. The equipment is called *capital* equipment if it lasts more than a year. For instance, a firm that owns its typewriters will certainly have them available at the end of the year, and they will be good for service for several more years. How should the cost of the typewriters be treated in calculating profits and costs?

The essential idea is that the cost of *using* rather than buying a piece of capital equipment is properly treated as part of the firm's costs within the year. If a firm is like Rent-a-Person and leases all its capital equipment, its costs include the rentals it paid.

But suppose that Rent-a-Person buys eight typewriters at the beginning of the year, each for $1000. It should *not* count $8000 as the cost of typewriters in calculating its profits. Instead, it should figure out how much value the typewriters lost during the year in the process of being used for typing and then count that as a cost. Suppose the wear and tear on the typewriters reduced their value from $1000 at the beginning of the year to $700 by the end of the year. Then the cost of using the typewriters during the year was $2400 (8 × $300), and it is that amount of depreciation that should count as a cost during the year. Why? Because the typewriters can now be sold for $700 each, so having them and using them for the year reduced their value by $300 each.

Depreciation is the loss of value resulting from the use of machinery during the year. The general principle is that it is only the depreciation of capital equipment, *not* the initial cost of the equipment itself, that counts as a cost during the year. Some capital equipment, such as a calculator, lasts for only a short period of time and depreciates fast.

The existence of depreciation points once again to the difference between profits and cash flow. When a firm buys a piece of capital equipment, it has a large cash outflow. But its costs of using that machine during the year will be less than the cash outflow. Thus the firm may be making profits in a year when it actually pays out much more in cash (paying for the machine) than it receives from sales. In terms of calculating profits, though, the size of the cash outflow during the year is not relevant; it is the

costs of *using* the equipment that are deducted from revenue in calculating profits.[3]

Inventories A firm that makes goods may add to its inventories during the year.

> *Inventories* are goods held in stock by a firm for future sales.

Within a given year, the Chrysler Corporation may make, for example, 1 million cars and sell only 950,000. It adds 50,000 cars to its inventories—its stock of unsold cars.

What is the complication in calculating profits here? There is no question that the firm's revenue is the amount earned by selling 950,000 cars. Should the firm figure out its costs on the basis of what it takes to make the 950,000 cars it sold or on the basis of what it takes to make 1 million cars?

The answer is that the costs should relate to the 950,000 cars the firm sold. The 50,000 cars added to inventory are like capital that the firm made for itself; it will be selling them off during the next year. Once more, the distinction between cash flow and profits is important. There was a cash outflow during the year to pay for making 1 million cars. But part of that cash outflow was for the purchase of inventories. They are useful to the firm because next year it will be able to sell 50,000 cars without having to pay in that year to produce them.

Borrowing Firms usually borrow in order to finance their start-up and expansion activities. They need funds to buy capital equipment, to buy inventories to have available for sale, to pay lawyers' and accountants' fees for the paperwork involved in setting up the business, and so on. There is interest

---

[3] The depreciation discussed here is *economic* depreciation, the reduction in the value of the capital equipment. There are very complicated rules about how much firms can deduct from revenues for depreciation before calculating taxes. This tax depreciation is not usually the same as economic depreciation.

to be paid on the borrowing. The interest is part of the cost of doing business and should be counted as part of costs.

The Balance Sheet

The income statement, or profit and loss statement, in Figure 6-2 tells us how well a firm did during a given year. But we also want a picture of where it is at a particular time, such as the end of the year. The *balance sheet,* a list of the assets of a firm and its liabilities, gives this picture.

Figure 6-3 is the balance sheet for U.S. Snark, Inc., on December 31, 1983.

Assets are what the firm owns. They are shown on the left. U.S. Snark has some cash in the bank. It is owed money by its customers, and this is entered as "accounts receivable." It has large inventories of Snarks in its warehouse. The firm also has a factory building, now worth $200,000. Originally the building cost $250,000, but it has depreciated since it was built. The firm's other equipment, worth $180,000, is listed as one item. That equipment, too, has depreciated since it was bought. The total value of Snark's assets is $590,000.

Snark also has liabilities.

Liabilities are what the firm owes. They are shown on the right in Figure 6-3.

U.S. Snark has unpaid bills, and it has to pay some salaries for work already done. In addition, it borrowed through a mortgage to finance the construction of its factory, and it has a bank loan for its short-term cash needs. The total value of its debts is $350,000. The total value of its assets is higher by $240,000 than the value of its debts, and it therefore has a *net worth* (excess of assets over liabilities) of $240,000.

One puzzling feature of the balance sheet is that net worth—the excess of the value of assets over liabilities—shows up on the liabilities side. Why? Because the firm is owned by its shareholders, the net worth is really owed to them. It is thus a liability of the firm.

Suppose now that some other firm wants to buy Snark, Inc. Snark appears to be a promising company with an enthusiastic management and good morale among its work force. Will the right amount to offer be $240,000, the net worth of the company? In general, the answer is no. Snark, Inc., is a live company with good prospects for future growth. It has proved that it knows how to earn profits, and it looks as if it will do well in the future. The company trying to buy Snark is buying not only the factory and premises, the cash in the bank, and the

---

FIGURE 6-3
U.S. SNARK, INC.
BALANCE SHEET
DECEMBER 31, 1983

ASSETS		LIABILITIES	
Cash	$ 40,000	Accounts payable	$ 90,000
Accounts receivable	70,000	Salaries payable	50,000
Inventories	100,000	Mortgage from insurance company	150,000
Factory building (original value $250,000)	200,000	Loan from bank	60,000
			$350,000
Other equipment (original value $300,000)	180,000	Net worth	240,000
	$590,000		$590,000

other assets minus liabilities but also the firm as an operating company. Therefore, it will probably pay more than $240,000. It will base the higher payment on how much profit it thinks Snark will make in future years. This value of the company as a going and proven business is called *goodwill,* and the buying company will pay something for goodwill. But if the accounting has been done right and all those assets and liabilities on Snark's balance sheets can be sold off at the values shown, Snark should certainly be worth at least close to $240,000.[4] Anyone who buys the company can always try to sell off the pieces.

The Balance Sheet and the Income Statement

The balance sheet takes care of the complications we discussed in examining the income, or profit and loss, statement. The firm's goods that have been sold but that have not yet been paid for show up in the accounts receivable part of the balance sheet. The firm's purchase of capital equipment and the depreciation of the capital equipment appear in the balance sheet. So, too, does any change in the firm's inventories. The amount the firm has borrowed also appears, under liabilities.

Earnings

The last question we have to ask is, What does the firm do about its profits after taxes? It has two choices. First, it can pay them out to the shareholders as dividends. Second, it can keep them as retained earnings.

Retained earnings are the part of after-tax profits that the firm does not pay out to its stockholders. These earnings are kept in the firm.

Retained earnings affect the balance sheet.

[4] Why not exactly $240,000? Because it takes time and expense to sell off the assets of the company.

For instance, if the retained earnings are kept as cash, the amount of asset cash increases. If the retained earnings are used to pay off the loan at the bank, that liability is reduced. If the retained earnings are used to buy more machinery, then the assets of the firm rise. Whatever is done with the retained earnings, they will either increase assets or decrease liabilities and thus increase the firm's net worth—the difference between assets and liabilities—or the value of the firm.

Opportunity Cost and Accounting Costs

Our focus has been on revenues, costs, and profits from the accounting viewpoint. This is useful for understanding actual income statements and balance sheets, and is usually a good guide to the correct economic measures of costs. But accounting methods can be seriously misleading in two ways.

The economic notion of costs is that they represent the costs of resources used in producing the particular goods or services that are sold. Economists identify these costs as opportunity costs.

Opportunity cost is the amount lost by not using a resource (labor or capital) in its best alternate use.

It is the right measure of economic costs. To make the point clearly, we turn to two examples, starting with labor costs.

Anyone working in his own business should always take into account the costs of his own labor time spent in the business. An individual proprietor might draw up an income statement like the one in Figure 6-2, find that profits were $20,000, and decide he has a good business going. But he also has to take into account the opportunity cost of his own labor—the amount his labor would have brought in if used elsewhere. Suppose he could get an income of $25,000 elsewhere. Then if he is working full-time in his own firm, he is *losing* $5000 ($25,000 − $20,000), because that is how much less he is making by running his business rather than taking a job.[5] If he includes the opportunity cost of his labor as part of the costs of the business, he will reach the right conclusion.

The second place where opportunity cost has to be counted is with respect to capital. The individual proprietor (or partners, or shareholders) puts up financial capital to get a firm going. In calculating accounting profits, no cost is attached to the use of owned (as opposed to borrowed) financial capital. But of course the financial capital could have been used elsewhere. It could have been invested in the stockmarket, in

---

[5] Such a person might still continue to run the business, deciding that it's worth $5000 per year to him to be his own boss.

FIGURE 6-4 ACCOUNTING AND OPPORTUNITY COSTS: TWO IMPORTANT ADJUSTMENTS. Economic costs represent the opportunity costs of the resources used in producing the firm's goods or services. Accounting costs include most economic costs—although these may be difficult to measure. But they probably do not include the cost of the owner's time and also the opportunity costs of the financial capital used in the firm. These adjustments have to be made to the accounting profit in order to get the right economic measure of costs.

ACCOUNTING: INCOME STATEMENT	
Revenues	$80,000
Costs	50,000
Accounting income (or profit)	$30,000

OPPORTUNITY COSTS: INCOME STATEMENT		
Revenues		$80,000
Costs:		
Accounting costs	$50,000	
Cost of owner's time	25,000	
Opportunity cost of financial capital ($20,000) used in firm, at 15%	3,000	78,000
Economic profit		$ 2,000

another firm, or even in a long-term savings account. The opportunity cost of that financial capital is included in the *economic* costs of doing business, even if it is not included in the accounting costs. Economic costs should therefore include an allowance for the opportunity cost of capital, perhaps an amount such as 15 percent per year. Once that opportunity cost has been included and profits have been recalculated, we have a measure of the economic profits from running the business.

These are the two most important differences between accounting and economic notions of costs and profits. In practice there are many other areas where accounting is very difficult. For instance, the depreciation of capital is hard to calculate, and the correct valuation of the inventories a firm holds is not straightforward. But we need not worry about those complications here.

We summarize in Figure 6-4, showing the adjustments made to accounting costs and profits in order to get to economic measures of costs and profits.

3 FIRMS AND PROFIT MAXIMIZATION

Firms are in business to make money. Economists assume that firms behave so as to make their profits as large as they can—in other words, to *maximize profits*. In developing the theory of supply, which is the theory about how much output firms produce, we assume that firms choose the level of output that makes their profits as large as possible (or losses as small as possible).

Some economists and businessmen question the assumption that maximizing profits is the only aim that firms have. What different aim might they have? One example was given in the last section, where we described the owner of a firm who makes $20,000 per year. He could make $25,000 per year in a different job. But even so, if he values his independence, he might keep his business running. Such a firm is not maximizing profits. Even so the owner is maximizing his utility or happiness.

Ownership and Control

A more significant reason to question the assumption of profit maximization is that large firms are not run by their owners. A large corporation is owned by many shareholders, who in principle control the firm through the board of directors. The board of directors, in turn, appoints the managers and is supposed to make sure they run the firm in the interests of the owners—the shareholders.

In practice, however, many firms are run by the managers, with the board of directors rubber-stamping management decisions. The reason is that a large corporation is a very complex organization, and it is difficult for a part-time board of directors to control the managers, who are in full-time operation in the firm.

Managers' salaries are usually higher the larger the firm. Therefore it is argued that managers aim to make the firm grow rather than to maximize profits. The larger the firm, the more they can hope to earn.[6]

Under what conditions would the different aims of profit maximization and growth imply different types of behavior? One case is that of retaining earnings. If a firm does not have any very good investments to make, the best thing to do with profits might be to give them to the shareholders, perhaps through dividend payments or by buying back the company's shares.[7] But to make the company grow, the managers might instead use the retained earnings to build more factories.

There are clearly other situations in which managers act in ways that are not obviously in the interests of the shareholders. For instance, when one firm wants to buy another, the managers of the firm to be bought are usually opposed—in part because they are likely to lose their jobs. Typically, they oppose being bought even when the price being offered to the shareholders for their shares in the firm is high. This, too, is a case where the interests of managers and shareholders differ.

Because the interests of managers and shareholders may differ, a good board of directors will try to be sure the managers have an interest in the firm beyond merely their salaries. Senior managers are given stock in the company in the hope that in acting in their own interests as stockholders, they also act in the interests of the other shareholders.[8]

Social Objectives of the Firm

Firms frequently make donations to charity, or provide funds for public television, or act in other ways that do not obviously increase their profits. One view is that such actions are just a devious way of maximizing profits, with the firm trying to make sure that the community in which it works thinks well of it. Perhaps it will need approval from the city for a new building, or perhaps there will be an accidental discharge of pollution that will be forgiven because the corporation has been acting as a good citizen.

The alternative view is that the corpora-

---

[6] A theory of this type is advanced in William Baumol, *Business Behavior, Value and Growth*, 2d ed., Macmillan, New York, 1959.

[7] This may sound like a strange way of behaving, but what it does is to distribute the firm's cash to the shareholders as they sell their shares back to the firm in exchange for the cash.

[8] Recently economists have studied this problem under the heading of "the principal-agent problem." The principal (shareholder) wants to get something done but has to work through an agent (manager), who has a different aim than the principal. The principal cannot exactly control what the agent does. You will recognize this as a very general problem. It applies, for example, when you take your car or TV set in for repair.

tion is indeed acting more like a person than a profit-maximizing machine and that it in fact has a social conscience. No doubt many people would think this a good thing. But critics say corporations have no business behaving in that way. The money they give away belongs to the shareholders. The critics say that the shareholders can give money to charity if they want to, but the corporation should not try to be generous by giving away other people's money.

As we analyze the behavior of firms in the remainder of the chapter, we shall assume that firms attempt to maximize profits, despite the indications that they also have other aims. The profit-maximization assumption is certainly the place to start, because if firms do not earn any profits, they eventually have to go out of business. Other views of the aims of firms are interesting and suggestive, but they usually do not have very different predictions about the way firms will behave.

4 THE FIRM'S PRODUCTION DECISIONS: AN OVERVIEW

To begin the analysis of supply, we first take a careful look at the way in which firms decide how much output to produce. Many details are left for later chapters, but the important ideas of marginal cost and marginal revenue are introduced here.

Think of a firm going into business to manufacture snarks. The firm knows that there are different ways of making snarks. Some ways use lots of labor and hardly any machines. Others are very machine-intensive and require hardly any labor. Not only does the firm know the different techniques for making snarks, it also knows how much it costs to hire each factor of production. It knows what the wage rates for a skilled snark lathe operator are, and it also knows how much it costs to rent a snark lathe.

The firm also is assumed to know the demand curve it faces. It knows how much it would earn by selling different quantities of snarks. It might be able to sell as many snarks as it wants at the current market price of $20. Or the market for snarks may be very small, and the firm may be able to increase its sales only by reducing price below the current level. Whatever the facts about the demand facing it, the firm knows them.

The firm's aim is to maximize profits by choosing the best level of output to produce. This level of output will depend on the costs of production and on the demand curve facing the firm.

We now show how costs of production and demand conditions interact to determine the firm's level of output.

Cost Minimization

Any firm that is maximizing profits will certainly want to produce its output at as low a cost as possible. Why? Suppose that a firm is producing a given level of output and *not* producing it at the lowest possible cost. In this case profits can be increased just by producing that level of output at a lower cost. A firm that is maximizing profits is therefore a firm that is also minimizing the costs of producing any given level of output.

The Total Cost Curve

With their knowledge of methods of production and the costs of using labor, physical capital, and other factors of production, a firm's managers and engineers figure out the lowest cost at which each level of output can be produced. Probably the cheapest way to make just a few snarks per year is to use a lot of labor and not much machinery. As output rises, it makes sense to use more machinery per worker.

Table 6-2 shows the minimum cost at which each level of output can be produced. The firm incurs a cost ($10) even when it is not producing any goods. This is the cost of simply being in business—running an of-

TABLE 6-2
COSTS OF PRODUCTION

OUTPUT, goods produced/wk	TOTAL COST, $/wk
0	10
1	25
2	36
3	44
4	51
5	59
6	69
7	81
8	95
9	111
10	129

FIGURE 6-5 TOTAL COSTS OF PRODUCTION. The chart shows the minimum cost of producing each level of output. The total cost depends on both the technology available to the firm and the costs of using the factors of production. At low levels of production, costs rise quite fast. Then when 4 to 5 units of the good are being produced, costs rise slowly. As output continues to rise, costs begin to increase more rapidly again.

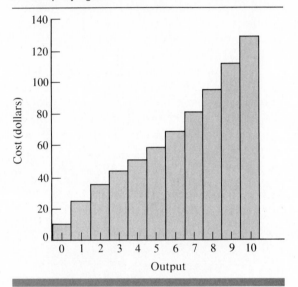

fice, renting a telephone, and so on.[9] Thereafter, the costs rise with the level of production. The costs shown in Table 6-2 are calculated including the opportunity costs of all resources used in production.

Figure 6-5 shows total costs of production for each level of output, as specified in Table 6-2. The total cost of production rises as more goods are produced, but the costs do not increase smoothly as the level of output rises. At intermediate levels of output, such as 4 or 5 units per week, costs rise quite slowly as output increases. At high levels of output, such as 9, costs rise sharply as output increases.

Total Revenue

Costs are one half of the information needed for the firm to calculate profits. The other half is revenue, to which we now turn. Then we will be able to find the level of output at which the firm's profits are maximized. The firm's revenue depends on the demand for its product.

Table 6-3 shows the prices at which the firm can sell snarks. This is the demand curve facing the firm. It receives $21 per snark if it sells only one. But the more snarks it sells, the lower the price it receives

for each one. This is because the demand curve it faces slopes downward. The firm can get only $12 per snark if it is selling 10 units per week. Given the prices at which each quantity can be sold, we can calculate the firm's total revenue from selling different quantities of snarks per week. Total revenue is just price times quantity, as shown in the third column of Table 6-3.

Table 6-3 also includes, in the fourth column, the firm's cost of producing each level of output. The difference between revenue and cost is shown in the last column. Each difference is, of course, the firm's profit per week. There is a profit level for each level of output. At low levels of output, profits are negative. Similarly, at the highest level of output shown, 10, profits are again negative. But at other levels of output the firm is making profits.

To choose its level of output, the firm

---

[9] It makes sense to think of the numbers for both output and total cost in Table 6-2 as being in thousands. To keep things simple, we have left out the thousands.

TABLE 6-3
REVENUES, COSTS, AND PROFITS

OUTPUT, goods produced/wk	PRICE RECEIVED PER UNIT, $	TOTAL REVENUE, $/wk (PRICE × OUTPUT)	TOTAL COST, $/wk (FROM TABLE 6-2)	PROFIT (TOTAL REVENUE MINUS TOTAL COST)
0	–	0	10	−10
1	21	21	25	−4
2	20	40	36	4
3	19	57	44	13
4	18	72	51	21
5	17	85	59	26
6	16	96	69	27
7	15	105	81	24
8	14	112	95	17
9	13	117	111	6
10	12	120	129	−9

goes down the last column and finds the level of output at which profits are highest. The highest level of profits is 27 (dollars per week[10]), and the corresponding level of output is 6 units of snarks per week. To maximize profits, the firm produces 6 units of snarks per week. It sells them for $16 each, receiving total revenue of $96. Costs of production, properly calculated to include the opportunity costs of all resources used in production, are $69 per week. Profits per week are therefore $27. The level of output and profits the firm determines are shown in color in Table 6-3.

Could the firm earn higher *revenues* per week? Certainly it could. For example, it could sell 10 units of snarks per week and take in $120 instead of $96. But that does not increase the firm's profits, because when it is selling 10 units per week, the firm is actually losing money. The total cost of producing 10 units per week is $129, which is more than the total revenue. Thus maximizing profits is *not* the same thing as maximizing revenue.

We now summarize this overview of how a firm chooses its level of output. The firm calculates the profit level that corre-

sponds to each level of output. To do this, it must know the total revenue it receives at each level of output and also the total cost of producing each level of output. Once it knows revenues and costs, it calculates the profit for each level of output. It produces that level of output at which the profit is highest.

5 MARGINAL COST AND MARGINAL REVENUE

The firm's decision about how much output to produce can be described in another, equivalent way. In this second approach, we ask at each level of output whether the firm should increase output. Suppose that the firm is producing 3 units of output and is considering moving to 4 units. Table 6-4 shows the relevant cost and revenue data from Tables 6-2 and 6-3. Increasing output from 3 to 4 units will raise the total cost from $44 to $51; that is, there will be a $7 increase in the total cost. On the revenue side, we have an increase from $57 to $72, or a $15 rise. Therefore, increasing output from 3 to 4 units will add more to revenue than to costs. Profits will rise by $8 ($15 in increased revenue less $7 in increased costs).

Having decided that the firm would increase profits by moving production from 3

---

[10] Recall that you may get a better feeling for the numbers if you think of them as being in thousands.

TABLE 6-4

EFFECTS OF OUTPUT CHANGES ON COSTS AND REVENUE

OUTPUT, units/wk	TOTAL COST, $/wk	INCREASE IN COSTS, $/wk	TOTAL REVENUE, $/wk	INCREASE IN REVENUE, $/wk
3	44		57	
		7		15
4	51		72	

to 4 units, we can repeat the exercise, asking whether a move from 4 to 5 units is profitable and, if so, whether it is profitable to go on to 6, and then 7, and on.

This way of thinking about the level of output—determining how the production of 1 more unit of output will affect profits—focuses on the marginal cost of producing 1 more unit and the marginal revenue.

Marginal cost is the increase in the firm's total cost when it increases output by 1 unit. *Marginal revenue* is the increase in the firm's total revenue when it increases sales by 1 unit.

The crucial point is that so long as marginal revenue exceeds marginal cost, the firm should increase its level of output. Why? Because if marginal revenue is larger than marginal cost, the firm's profits are increased when it increases output.

If marginal cost is larger than marginal revenue, it does not make sense to increase output. Profits will be reduced by doing so. It thus seems that we can use the notions of marginal cost and marginal revenue to figure out the level of output at which the firm maximizes its profits. So long as marginal revenue exceeds marginal cost, the firm should keep increasing output. As soon as marginal revenue becomes less than marginal cost, the firm should stop increasing output. To make that argument clearer, we now look more closely at marginal revenue and marginal costs.

Marginal Costs

Table 6-5 shows the output and cost data

from Table 6-2 and also the marginal cost of producing each extra unit of output. Producing 1 rather than 0 unit of output increases the total cost from 10 to 25 (dollars per week); the marginal cost of increasing production from 0 to 1 unit of output is therefore $15. In Table 6-5 we show the marginal cost on a line between the 0 and 1 levels of output to make it clear that it is the cost of increasing output from 0 to 1. All the other marginal costs shown in the table are calculated in the same way. For instance, the marginal cost of increasing output from 6 to 7 units is $12.

The marginal cost of increasing output by 1 unit at each level of output is shown in Figure 6-6b. The marginal costs can be taken directly from Table 6-5. They can also be figured out from Figure 6-5, which is the basis for Figure 6-6a. In Figure 6-6a we show the total cost of producing each level of output, as in Figure 6-5. Marginal cost is the amount by which costs rise when output is increased by 1 unit. For instance, in going from 0 to 1 unit of output, costs rise by $15. This is indicated by the shaded area *ABCD*. The shaded area at each level of output is the amount by which costs are higher, because that level of output is being produced rather than 1 less unit of output. The shaded areas thus show the marginal cost of producing 1 more unit of output. Accordingly, the marginal costs in Figure 6-6b could be taken from Figure 6-6a as well as from Table 6-5.

From both the figure and the table we see that the marginal cost of producing an

TABLE 6-5

TOTAL AND MARGINAL COSTS OF PRODUCTION

OUTPUT, units/wk	TOTAL COST, $/wk	MARGINAL COST, $/wk
0	10	
		15
1	25	
		11
2	36	
		8
3	44	
		7
4	51	
		8
5	59	
		10
6	69	
		12
7	81	
		14
8	95	
		16
9	111	
		18
10	129	

FIGURE 6-6 TOTAL AND MARGINAL COSTS OF PRODUCTION. Figure 6-6a, like Figure 6-5, shows the total cost of production for each level of output. The shaded parts show the amount by which the total cost goes up when the level of output increases by 1 unit. Thus the total cost rises from 10 to 25 when output is increased from 0 to 1 unit. The increase in the total cost at each level of output is the marginal cost of increasing output by 1 unit. The marginal costs are shown in Figure 6-6b, which uses a larger vertical scale. But it can be seen that the pattern of marginal costs in Figure 6-6b is precisely the pattern shown in Figure 6-6a: marginal costs are first high and decreasing; then they reach a minimum and start increasing.

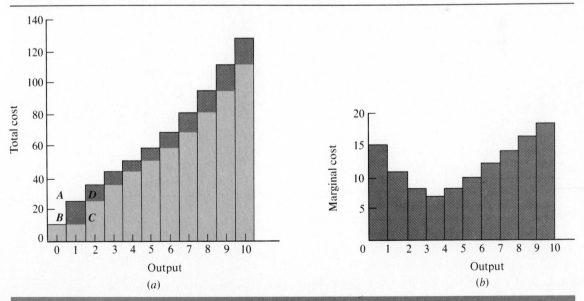

extra unit of output is high both when output is low and when output is high. Marginal cost is lowest for producing the fourth unit of output; that adds only $7 per week to costs.

Why do marginal costs start high, fall, and then rise? This depends mainly on the production techniques available for making and selling snarks. When the firm is producing only one or two snarks, it is probably using quite simple techniques of production, employing labor and simple machines. As the level of output rises, it makes sense to use more sophisticated machines, and extra units of output can be produced quite cheaply. When levels of output become high, though, the difficulties of managing a large firm begin to show. Top management finds it difficult to control production and has to add managers. Increasing output is now expensive and hard to accomplish. Marginal costs begin to increase.

This is one possible explanation of how marginal costs change as the firm's level of output changes. But there is no law of economics that says that marginal costs change the same way with output for all firms. For each firm, the pattern of marginal costs depends mainly on the production techniques used in making the goods. For instance, marginal costs may have the pattern shown in Figure 6-7: they start out high and then become constant. In this case the firm can eventually make extra units of output at the same marginal cost, however much is produced. The pattern shown in Figure 6-7 does apply for some firms. Typically, though, marginal costs are assumed to have the pattern seen in Figure 6-6.

Marginal Revenue

The firm's marginal revenue is shown in Table 6-6. Marginal revenue is the increase in revenue the firm makes by selling one more unit of output. Table 6-6 shows the price and total revenue data from Table 6-3

FIGURE 6-7 MARGINAL COSTS—A DIFFERENT PATTERN. In Figure 6-6, marginal costs first decline as output increases and then begin to increase. A different possibility is that marginal costs at first decline as it becomes possible to use more efficient methods of production with a larger output. But then marginal costs become constant; any further increases in output can be produced at the same addition to cost per unit. (In this figure, the marginal cost is 7 for all units of output beyond 3.) The pattern that actually applies in practice depends mainly on the techniques of production available to the firm. The pattern of marginal costs will vary from firm to firm and industry to industry.

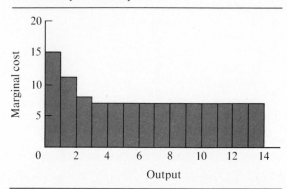

as well as marginal revenue. Marginal revenue is calculated as the increase in total revenue obtained by increasing output by 1 unit. For instance, when output increases from 0 to 1 unit, revenue rises from 0 to 21 (dollars per week). The marginal revenue from producing the first unit of output is thus $21. This is shown on the line between 0 and 1 unit of output. Similarly, as output increases from 7 to 8, total revenue rises from $105 to $112, and so the marginal revenue is $7. Both total revenue and marginal revenue depend on the demand for the firm's product.

Marginal revenue is shown also in Figure 6-8. Marginal revenue is shown as falling throughout. The more the firm sells, the lower the price at which it sells, and the lower the increase in revenue obtained by selling 1 more unit.[11] Indeed, marginal rev-

[11] Marginal revenue was already mentioned in Chapter 4.

TABLE 6-6
PRICE, TOTAL REVENUE, AND MARGINAL REVENUE

OUTPUT, goods/wk	PRICE RECEIVED, $/good	TOTAL REVENUE, $/wk	MARGINAL REVENUE, $/wk
0	—	0	
			21
1	21	21	
			19
2	20	40	
			17
3	19	57	
			15
4	18	72	
			13
5	17	85	
			11
6	16	96	
			9
7	15	105	
			7
8	14	112	
			5
9	13	117	
			3
10	12	120	

FIGURE 6-8 MARGINAL REVENUE. Marginal revenue is the increase in the firm's total revenue resulting from an increase in sales by 1 unit. In this diagram, the firm can sell more output only by reducing its price. Marginal revenue therefore decreases as output rises.

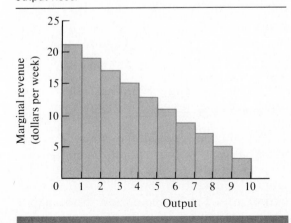

enue could easily become negative, meaning that the firm has lost more by having to lower its price than it has gained by selling more.

We now look more closely at the reasons why the firm's total revenue changes when output changes. To do this we write the equation:

$$\begin{aligned}\text{Marginal} \atop \text{revenue} &= \text{increase in revenue from selling} \atop \text{1 more unit of output}\\ &= \text{additional revenue from selling} \atop \text{1 more unit of output}\\ &\quad - \text{revenue lost by selling existing} \atop \text{level of output at a lower price} \quad (2)\end{aligned}$$

When the firm increases its output or sales, it gains revenue from selling 1 extra unit. But it loses revenue because it has to cut the price on *all* its existing output.

To take a specific example, consider the level of output of 5 and the marginal revenue from increasing sales from 5 to 6. The firm can sell 6 units of output at $16 each and 5 units at $17 each. Thus when the firm increases sales from 5 units to 6, it makes $16 by selling 1 more unit at that price. But the firm also loses $5 by having to cut the price on the 5 units it was already selling. Thus marginal revenue is equal to $11 ($16 − $5), as can be seen in Table 6-6 and Figure 6-8.

From equation (2) we see why marginal revenue keeps falling. First, the additional revenue from selling 1 more unit of output is lower the more the firm is selling already. And second, the term "revenue lost by selling existing level of output at a lower price" becomes larger as the level of output rises. When the firm is selling 8 units already, it loses $8 from having to cut the price by $1 per unit. When it is selling only 1, it loses only $1 that way. These are the reasons marginal revenue falls as the level of output rises.

The Shape of the Marginal Revenue Schedule Figure 6-8 shows the marginal revenue schedule; it gives the level of marginal revenue corresponding to each level of output. In the figure, marginal revenue falls as output rises. Is that always so? The answer is not necessarily. The shape of the marginal revenue curve depends on the demand curve facing the firm. A small firm in a big market may be able to sell as much output as it can produce at the existing market price. For instance, a wheat farmer thinking about how much revenue he would make at different levels of his own output would not have to worry about the effects of his own production on the market price of wheat. For this firm, the marginal revenue schedule is horizontal. In effect, the firm faces an unlimited demand for its output at the existing market price. Each extra unit of output can be sold for the same price. Thus each extra unit of output brings in the same extra amount of revenue. In terms of equation (2), the term "revenue lost . . ." is zero in this case, and the first term is constant. The marginal revenue schedule for such a

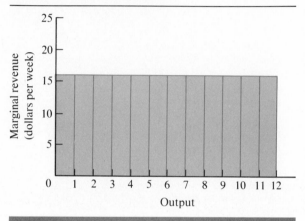

FIGURE 6-9 MARGINAL REVENUE: AN ALTERNATIVE PATTERN. In this figure the firm has the same marginal revenue no matter how much it sells. This means that it can sell goods at the existing market price without having to cut the price. The existing price is $16. The firm will have a constant marginal revenue if its output is very small in relation to the total amount sold in the market.

firm is shown in Figure 6-9. The firm can sell as much as it wants to at the existing market price of $16.

Using Marginal Revenue and Marginal Cost to Determine the Level of Output

In Table 6-7, we put together the marginal revenue and marginal cost schedules from Tables 6-5 and 6-6 and use them to determine the level of output that maximizes the firm's profits. The table shows the difference between the marginal revenue from increasing output by 1 unit and the marginal cost. Increases in output from 0 to 1 all the way up to the 1-unit increase from 5 to 6 units result in higher profits. That is because marginal revenue is bigger than marginal cost.

So long as marginal revenue exceeds marginal cost, output should be increased. This is shown in the last column of the table. Suppose that the firm has increased output from 5 to 6 units. It now thinks about increasing output from 6 to 7 units. But as the table shows, the increase in revenue

TABLE 6-7

USING MARGINAL REVENUE AND MARGINAL COST TO DETERMINE OUTPUT

OUTPUT	MARGINAL REVENUE, $/wk	MARGINAL COST, $/wk	MARGINAL REVENUE MINUS MARGINAL COST, $/wk	OUTPUT DECISION
0				
1	21	15	6	Increase
2	19	11	8	Increase
3	17	8	9	Increase
4	15	7	8	Increase
5	13	8	5	Increase
6	11	10	1	Increase
7	9	12	−3	Don't increase
8	7	14	−7	Don't increase
9	5	16	−11	Don't increase
10	3	18	−15	Don't increase

would be less than the increase in costs, and so profits would fall. Therefore, the firm should *not* increase output from 6 to 7 units. The same decision applies to all levels of output above 6.

Since the firm should increase output so long as it is producing fewer than 6 units and *not* increase output when it is producing 6 units or more, it is clear that output should be 6 units. This is the level of output at which profits reach a maximum—as we already know from Table 6-3.

Total Cost and Revenue versus Marginal Cost and Revenue

This time we reached the conclusion that profits are maximized when output is 6 units by working with marginal revenue and marginal cost rather than with total revenue and total cost. These are equivalent ways of looking at the problem, but the analysis based on marginal revenue and marginal cost is used more often. Why? Partly because it suggests a useful way of thinking about any situation in which firms or consumers find themselves. In any situation a firm (or a consumer) should ask whether any small change can be made to make it (or him) better off. If the answer is yes, then the current situation cannot be the best possible, and the change should be made.[12]

The marginal analysis does have to be supplemented, though, by checking whether the firm should be producing at all. This additional question is necessary because certain costs (in Chapter 7 we call them *fixed costs*) do not depend on the level of output but are inevitable if the firm is to be in business. For example, a bakery will need an oven whether it produces 1000 or 2000 loaves, and it will need a phone whether 10 or 100 calls are made. These fixed costs have to be covered, and it is therefore essential to check whether at the output level where $MR = MC$ it is *also* the case that profits are not negative. If they are, the owner would be better off closing down. In Chapter 7 we look in more detail at the decisions whether to stay in business but not produce for a while or go out of business entirely.

---

[12] Critics of economics sometimes argue that economists mislead themselves and others by relying so much on marginal analysis. Maybe there is no small change that can be made to improve the situation. But there may be some really large change in the economy that will be an improvement. Someone thinking only of marginal changes—Will it be better to produce one more unit of output? Should the government increase spending by a little?—may miss the important changes that should be made. Perhaps the government budget should be cut in half or doubled; perhaps there is some entirely new way of doing things; etc.

In summary, the firm chooses its output level by increasing output so long as marginal revenue exceeds marginal cost; it stops increasing output at the point where marginal revenue is less than marginal cost. At this output level, the firm should check to see if it is making a profit. If not, it should check whether it can reduce the losses by temporarily not producing. It may even decide it should go out of business permanently.

Marginal Cost and Marginal Revenue in Pictures

Figure 6-10 presents the firm's choice of output level in a diagram. The marginal revenue and marginal cost schedules are taken from Figures 6-6 and 6-8. The marginal revenue schedule starts out at $21, which is the marginal revenue obtained by producing the first unit of output, and drops to $3, the marginal revenue from increasing output from 9 to 10 units. The marginal cost schedule starts out at $15 (the marginal cost for producing the first unit), drops to a minimum of $7 for increasing output from 3 to 4 units, and then rises to $18 (the marginal cost of adding 1 more unit of output, when 9 units are already being produced).

The firm chooses the output level at which the marginal revenue and marginal cost schedules cross. That level of output is 6 units. When output is less than 6 units, marginal revenue is more than marginal cost. Therefore, profits rise when output is increased. At any point above 6 units of output, marginal revenue is less than marginal cost. This means that profits would be higher if output were lower.

The conclusion is that the firm's output level is determined by the crossing of the marginal revenue and marginal cost curves. In Figure 6-10 this is shown at the output level of 6. Of course, we have to remember to check that profits are indeed being made at that output level. If they are not, it is pos-

FIGURE 6-10 MARGINAL COST AND MARGINAL REVENUE DETERMINE THE FIRM'S OUTPUT LEVEL. The figure shows both the marginal revenue schedule and the marginal cost schedule for the firm. The schedules intersect at the output level of 6. That is the level of output at which the firm maximizes its profits, and it is therefore the level of output the firm produces. If the firm is experiencing losses at the output level of 6, it might cut those losses by not producing at all.

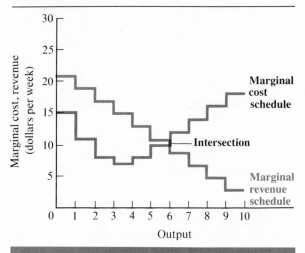

sible that the firm should not be producing at all. But if the firm does produce, it will choose to produce 6 units per week.

6 MARGINAL COST AND MARGINAL REVENUE CURVES MR = MC

So far we have assumed that the firm can produce only an integer number of goods, such as 0 or 1 or 7, per week rather than 1.5 or 6.7. But in most cases it makes sense to think that the firm is not confined to integer levels of output per week. There are two reasons for this. First, for goods such as milk or wheat or even loaves of bread, there is no particular reason to think that only 1-pound or 1-gallon or 1-bushel units can be sold. The firm can sell in odd amounts. Second, for commodities such as cars, where it is hard to think of fractional units, the rate of output could easily be something like

1243.33 per week if the firm is making, on the average, 3730 cars every 3 weeks. Thus we can conveniently think of the firm as being able to vary its production level and rate of sales almost continuously. Certainly, it is not bound to produce integer numbers of units of output per week or per year.

Now we can draw marginal revenue and marginal cost schedules smoothly, as in Figure 6-11. The marginal revenue schedule is shown as *MR*. It falls continuously because the firm can only sell larger amounts at lower prices. The marginal cost curve, *MC*, has the same general shape as the marginal cost schedule in Figure 6-10. After starting out high it falls and then rises.[13]

We use the diagram to show how the firm's level of output is determined. The firm's profits are maximized at the point where the *MR* and *MC* curves cross in Figure 6-11, at point *E*. Corresponding to point *E* is output level Q_1, the level of output at which profits are maximized. How do we know that profits are maximized at output level Q_1? We use the same logic as before. If output is less than Q_1, marginal revenue is greater than marginal cost. This means that an increase in output increases revenue more than it increases costs, and so profits increase. Therefore, output should be increased anywhere to the left of Q_1, as we show with the arrows in the diagram.

At points to the right of Q_1, marginal revenue is less than marginal cost. This means that any increase in output raises costs more than revenues and reduces profits. In other words, reducing output raises profits, because costs are reduced by more

---

[13] When we draw marginal cost or marginal revenue curves on the basis of actual data such as those in Table 6-7, the marginal cost of or marginal revenue from increasing output from, say, 2 to 3 units is shown halfway between 2 and 3, at a value of 2½ units of output. For instance, if the smooth *MR* curve in Figure 6-11 were based on the data in Table 6-6, it would show *MR* = 21 at an output of ½, *MR* = 19 at an output of 1½, and so on.

FIGURE 6-11   MARGINAL COST AND MARGINAL REVENUE DETERMINE THE FIRM'S OUTPUT. The marginal cost and marginal revenue schedules, or curves, are shown changing smoothly here. The firm's optimal level of output is Q_1, the output level at which marginal revenue is equal to marginal cost. Anywhere to the left of Q_1, marginal revenue is larger than marginal cost, and so the firm should increase output, as shown by the arrows. Where output is greater then Q_1, marginal revenue is less than marginal cost, and profits are increased by reducing output. This is shown by the arrows pointing to the left. Once again, if the firm is losing money at Q_1, it has to check whether it might be better not to produce at all than to produce at Q_1.

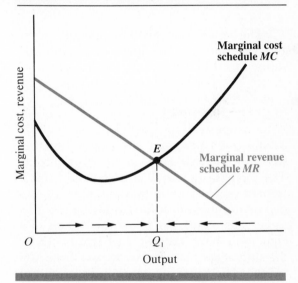

than revenues are reduced. We show this with the arrows pointing to the left, where output exceeds Q_1.

The firm chooses output level Q_1. At that level, profits are maximized, and marginal revenue is equal to marginal cost. This is important enough to deserve a formal statement:

$$MR \text{ (marginal revenue)} = MC \text{ (marginal cost)} \tag{3}$$

Equation (3) is the condition for determining the firm's level of output. When $MR = MC$, the firm's profits are maximized; therefore, the firm chooses the level of output at which $MR = MC$.

TABLE 6-8
DETERMINING THE FIRM'S LEVEL OF OUTPUT

MARGINAL CONDITION	DECISION	CHECK
Marginal revenue exceeds marginal cost ($MR > MC$).	Increase output.	
Marginal revenue is less than marginal cost ($MR < MC$).	Cut output.	
Marginal revenue is equal to marginal cost ($MR = MC$).	This gives the optimal output level.	Check that profits are positive. If they are not, determine whether losses can be reduced by not producing. If so, produce zero. Otherwise. produce so that $MR = MC$.

The conditions for maximizing profits and determining the level of output are summarized in Table 6-8.

The Effects of Changes in Costs on Output

What happens to the firm's optimal level of output if its marginal costs of production shift upward, rising at every level of output? The increase in marginal costs could result from an increase in the wages the firm has to pay or an increase in the price of a raw material such as oil. We show the effects of a change in marginal costs in Figure 6-12 by the shift of the marginal cost curve from MC to MC'. The firm now determines its output level from the new intersection point, E'. The level of output corresponding to E' is Q_2, which is less than Q_1. The firm chooses to produce less when its marginal costs of production increase.

The Effect of Shifts in the Marginal Revenue Curve on Output

What happens to the firm's level of output when there is a shift in the marginal revenue curve? Perhaps there are now more customers in the market, and the amount the firm can sell at any given price is higher. The quantity demanded of the firm's output at each price is higher. The demand curve has shifted. In Figure 6-13 the marginal revenue curve shifts outward, from MR to MR',

and the firm therefore wants to produce more output. This is shown by the shift of the intersection point from E to E''. The firm now produces output level Q_3 instead of Q_1.

Figures 6-12 and 6-13 show how the marginal revenue and marginal cost curves

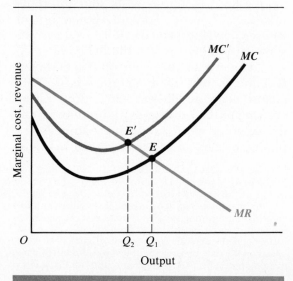

FIGURE 6-12 AN INCREASE IN MARGINAL COSTS REDUCES OUTPUT. The marginal cost curve shifts upward, from MC to MC', as a result of an increase in the costs of using a factor of production. For instance, wages may have risen. This upward shift changes the intersection of the marginal cost and marginal revenue curves from E to E' and results in a lower level of output. Output falls from Q_1 to Q_2. Thus when the firm's marginal costs rise, the firm decides to produce less.

FIGURE 6-13 AN UPWARD SHIFT OF THE MARGINAL REVENUE CURVE INCREASES OUTPUT. When the marginal revenue curve shifts upward from MR to MR', the intersection point for the marginal revenue and marginal cost curves shifts from E to E''. The firm's optimal level of output increases from Q_1 to Q_3. An upward shift of the marginal revenue curve can result, for instance, from an increase in the number of customers in the firm's market.

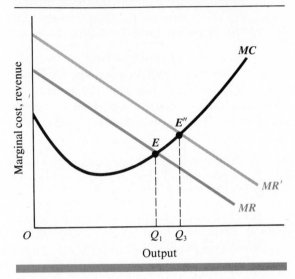

can be used not only to determine the level of output but also to see how changes in demand conditions (shifts in the marginal revenue curve) or cost conditions (shifts in the marginal cost curve) affect the level of output.

In this chapter we have presented only an overview of cost and revenue conditions. There is more to come in the next chapter. But we have explained the essential points about output determination. First, firms choose the level of output that maximizes profits. Second, that choice can be described by using marginal revenue and marginal cost curves—firms maximize profits by choosing the level of output at which marginal revenue equals marginal cost.

SUMMARY

1   The theory of supply is the theory of how much output firms choose to produce.

2   There are three types of firms: individual proprietorships, partnerships, and corporations. There are over 11 million individual proprietorships in the United States, but most of them are very small firms. The large business firms are corporations. The 159 largest corporations employ nearly 20 percent of the labor force.

3   A corporation is an organization set up to conduct a particular type of business. Corporations are owned by their shareholders (or stockholders) and run by management. A board of directors is responsible for controlling the firm and its managers in the interests of the shareholders.

4   Shareholders in a corporation have limited liability. They are not liable for any debts of the corporation or for any amount greater than their initial investment in the corporation. Partners and people who own individual proprietorships have unlimited liability.

5   Revenues are the amounts that a firm makes by selling its goods or

services during a given period. Costs are the expenses of producing the goods or services sold during the period. Profits are the excess of revenues over costs.

6   Costs should be calculated by including the opportunity costs of all the resources used in production. Opportunity cost is the amount that a factor of production could earn in its highest-paying alternative employment. In particular, economic costs include the costs of the owner's time and effort in running the business. Economic costs also include the opportunity cost of the financial capital used in the firm.

7   Firms are assumed to have the aim of maximizing profits. There is some reason to think firms may have some other aims—particularly because the managers who control a firm may not have the same aims as the stockholders—but profit maximization is a good place to start in understanding the behavior of firms. If firms do not make profits, they cannot continue in business.

8   Firms that have the aim of maximizing profits will also produce each level of output as cheaply as possible. Thus profit maximization implies minimization of costs.

9   Firms choose the optimal level of output to produce by calculating the level of profits they make at different output levels. They choose the level of output at which profits are highest.

10   Alternatively, a firm's output decision can be described in terms of marginal revenue and marginal cost. Marginal revenue is the increase in revenue from selling 1 more unit of output. Marginal revenue depends on the demand for the firm's product. Marginal cost is the increase in the firm's total cost from increasing output by 1 unit. Profits are maximized at the level of output at which marginal revenue equals marginal cost ($MR = MC$).

11   An increase in the marginal cost of production at every level of output results in an upward shift of the marginal cost curve and a reduction in output. An increase in marginal revenue at every level of output produces an upward shift of the marginal revenue curve and an increase in the firm's output.

KEY TERMS

Individual proprietorship	Limited liability	Retained earnings
Partnership	Profits	Opportunity cost
Corporation	Income statement	Total cost
Shareholder (stockholder)	Cash flow	Total revenue
Dividends	Depreciation	Marginal cost
Capital gains	Balance sheet	Marginal revenue

PROBLEMS

1 (*a*) What are the main advantages of the corporation over a large partnership as an organization for doing business? (*b*) List five corporations whose products you buy. (*c*) Do you buy goods or services from any partnerships or individual proprietorships? If so, list the items and the firms. (*d*) Is the college or university you attend a corporation? Is it a firm? Explain your answer.

2 How would each of the following affect the income statement for Rent-a-Person presented in Figure 6-2? (*a*) Rent-a-Person still owes $70,000 to the people it rented out during the year. (*b*) Instead of renting an office the company owns its office. (*c*) During the year Rent-a-Person was paid by one of the people who owed it money at the end of 1982.

3 (*a*) Suppose that Rent-a-Person is run by a hard-working owner and that this person would be paid $40,000 per year if he had a management job in another firm. Suppose also that he has invested $200,000 of his own in the company and that he could earn 12 percent on the investment elsewhere. What are the economic profits earned by Rent-a-Person? (Use Figure 6-2.) (*b*) What is the general principle underlying the adjustments made to accounting costs?

4 (*a*) Suppose that U.S. Snark, Inc., borrows another $50,000 from the bank and increases its inventory holdings. Show how its balance sheet is affected. (Refer back to Figure 6-3.) (*b*) Explain how the interest paid on the loan would appear in the income statement of U.S. Snark.

5 (*a*) Do you think that firms aim to maximize profits? Explain. (*b*) Do you think that firms *should* aim to maximize profits, or should they instead have a social conscience and support charities, the arts, political campaigns, etc.? Explain.

6 Define profits, and explain how the knowledge that firms aim to maximize profits makes it possible to figure out the level of output they will produce—if we know total costs and total revenue.

7 Refer to Table 6-3. Assume that the total costs of producing the different levels of output are higher by $20 than the costs shown in the fourth column. What level of output should the firm produce? Explain. (Figure out the answer by using the table. There is no need to draw graphs.)

8 Explain why the condition $MR = MC$ determines a firm's level of output. Be sure to explain what the firm should do to its output level if MR is greater than MC. Explain also how the output level should be changed if MR is less than MC.

9 Suppose that a firm that has the same costs as those shown in Table 6-5 can sell as much output as it wants at a price of $13. (*a*) Draw the marginal revenue and marginal cost curves. (*b*) Show the level of output that the firm will produce.

10 Table 6-3 shows the level of output produced by a firm. (*a*) What price is the firm charging? (*b*) Is the price above, below, or equal to the marginal revenue? Explain why, using equation (2).

In 1980 and 1981, U.S. automobile producers suffered record losses. Sales of U.S.-produced automobiles fell in 1981 to their lowest level in 20 years—6.3 million cars, as compared with 9.2 million in 1977 and 1978. From July to September of 1980 alone, General Motors lost $567 million, while selling 1.4 million cars at an average loss of $400 per car.[1]

Despite these losses, GM planned to stay in the automobile business. In 1982 workers agreed to lower wages, and the firm announced plans to introduce robots to further reduce costs. Analysts of the automobile industry believed the company had a good chance to survive and again show profits, and management remained confident of its future role in the automobile business.

7

Production, Costs, and the Firm's Output Decisions

GM's continuation in business despite its large losses raises several questions that are analyzed in this chapter. First, under what conditions will a firm decide to go out of business rather than continue to produce? Second, what is the relationship between the choices of techniques open to the firm—for example, the use of robots—and the firm's costs of production? Similarly, how do changes in wages affect costs and the firm's production method?

To answer these questions we have to extend the analysis of the firm's output decision begun in Chapter 6. There we started from the general notion, shown in Figure 7-1a, that the firm's output decision depends on its costs of production and on the revenue it makes by selling goods. By the end of the chapter we had filled in details of that general idea, as seen in Figure 7-1b.

On the revenue side we started with the demand curve facing the firm and derived from it the firm's marginal revenue curve. On the cost side we started with the total cost curve, which shows the cheapest way of producing each level of output. From the total cost curve we moved to marginal cost. The firm chooses the output level that maximizes its profits by determining where marginal revenue is equal to marginal cost. We also noted that the firm should check whether it is making a profit at that level of output. If it is not, maybe it can reduce its losses by not producing at all.

How does this apply to General Motors in 1980–1981? General Motors was no doubt trying to maximize its profits—or, in this case, keep its losses as small as possible—when it decided to stay in busi-

[1] These are data for GM's worldwide operations, including overseas sales.

FIGURE 7-1 DEVELOPING THE THEORY OF SUPPLY. Figure 7-1*a* shows the broad outline of the theory of supply, or the firm's output decision. The firm's choice of output level depends on the revenues it receives from sales of its product and on the costs of production. Figure 7-1*b* shows the details that were filled in in Chapter 6. The firm chooses the output level at which marginal revenue is equal to marginal cost. It has to check at that point whether profits are positive. If not, it checks whether it can reduce losses by not producing.

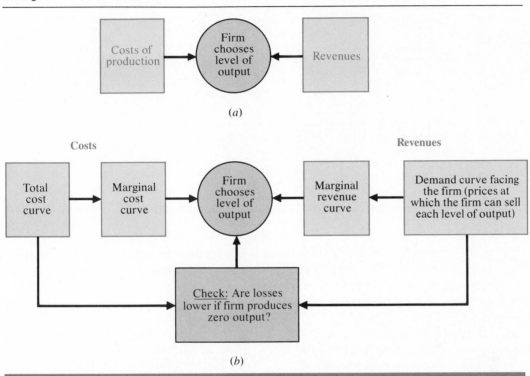

ness and produce 1.4 million cars between July and September of 1980. It decided that it would lose even more money if it produced none at all. And it certainly decided that it was better to stay in business than to close down for good.

In this chapter we develop the analysis that explains these decisions. We do so by distinguishing between the *short-run* and *long-run* output decisions of firms. No firm can stay in business if it makes losses year after year, or in the long run. GM must have regarded its 1980–1981 losses as temporary, or short-run. We will show in this chapter how and why a firm's cost curves differ be-

tween the short run, in which the firm cannot fully react to changed conditions, and the long run, in which the firm can fully adjust to changes in the demand for its product or its costs of production.

We noted in Chapter 6 that the total cost curve shows the cheapest way of producing each level of output and that its shape depends on the technology the firm can use for production. Now we will introduce the *production function*, which describes the firm's technology, or technical methods of production, and explain how the firm chooses the cheapest way of producing each level of output. We will also show why

FIGURE 7-2 THE COMPLETE THEORY OF SUPPLY. The new material to be developed in this chapter is shown in red. There are two main developments from Figure 7-1*b*. First, short-run and long-run cost curves and output decisions are carefully distinguished. Second, we go behind the total cost curve to show how the firm chooses the cheapest way of producing each level of output, given the technology available to it and the costs of hiring factors of production.

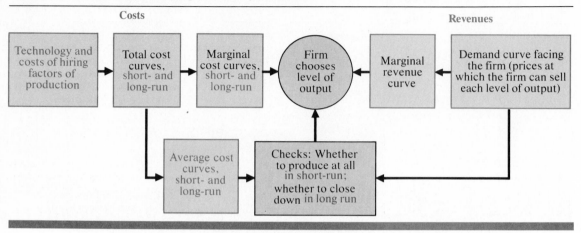

short-run and long-run cost curves differ. The differences between short-run and long-run cost curves account for the differences between short-run and long-run output decisions of the firm.

Figure 7-2 summarizes the material of this chapter. It should be compared with Figure 7-1*b*. The new material, shown in letters in color, is all on the cost side of the diagram. We now distinguish between short-run and long-run total and marginal cost curves and between short-run and long-run decisions on whether to produce at all or stay in business. In addition, we show how the firm's technology determines the shape of the total cost curve. Finally, we introduce the average cost curve, which is useful in analyzing the firm's decisions on whether to produce at all or stay in business.

Because there are many different cost curves, it is easy to get lost in the forest when using them. To find your way out, it will be useful to refer to Figure 7-2. We start on the left side of Figure 7-2 by introducing

the production function, which describes the firm's technology.

1 INPUTS AND OUTPUT

> An *input* (or *factor of production*) is any good or service that the firm uses to produce output.

Inputs thus include labor, machinery, buildings, materials such as steel or rubber or even paper clips in the office, and energy. The list is not exhaustive, but it does give the idea that the term "input," or "factor of production," is used very broadly to cover anything from senior management to the Band-aids in the company first-aid department.

A firm uses inputs to produce output. Suppose that our firm produces snarks. How does it go about making snarks from its inputs? This is an engineering and management problem. The recipe for making snarks is largely outside the field of economics and is a matter of technology and on-the-job experience. The economist takes the recipe as given, subject to one important qualification: *no waste*. We explain this qualification in discussing the production function.

The Production Function

The *production function* specifies the maximum amount of output that can be produced using any given amounts of inputs.

The production function summarizes the technically *efficient* methods of combining inputs to produce output. We emphasize the term "efficient," because the firm is not interested in production methods that waste resources.

For example, one way of producing one snark, method A, may require the firm to use 2 hours of labor and 1 hour of machine time. Another method, method B, may require 2 hours of labor and 2 hours of machine time. Method B is then less efficient than method A. It produces the same amount of output but uses more inputs. It is thus not considered by the firm as one of the methods of production summarized by the production function. Table 7-1 shows the types of information provided by a production function for snarks that involves only two inputs, physical capital (machines) and labor. The production function tells us what level of output corresponds to any specified combination of factors of production. For example, with four machines used per week and four workers, the firm can produce 100 snarks per week.

The first two lines of Table 7-1 show two different ways of producing 100 units of output. The firm can use four machines along with four workers to produce 100 snarks per week. Or it can use fewer machines and more labor, namely, two machines with six workers.

The third line shows the effect of adding one worker when the firm already has two machines and six workers. The extra

TABLE 7-1

THE PRODUCTION FUNCTION GIVES THE OUTPUT LEVELS PRODUCED BY DIFFERENT QUANTITIES OF INPUTS

OUTPUT LEVEL, snarks/wk	CAPITAL INPUT, number of machines*	LABOR INPUT, number of workers*
100	4	4
100	2	6
106	2	7
200	4	12

* Machines and labor are each used 40 hours per week.

worker increases output by 6 units per week. The fourth line shows what happens to output when the firm uses twice as much of both labor and capital as in the second line. Output should certainly go up, and in this case it exactly doubles.

Table 7-1 could be made much larger by putting in other combinations of capital and labor inputs. For each such combination, the production function tells us the maximum output the firm can produce. How does the firm discover the production function? In other words, how does it find out the highest level of output that can be produced by any given combination of factors of production? Because the production function summarizes engineering and technical information about the firm's production possibilities, the information is obtained from engineers. The firm probably does not find it worthwhile to ask the engineers to provide complete information about all the technical possibilities. Instead, the firm will in practice obtain information about a few different methods of producing several different levels of output.

Using the Production Function to Run a Business

The production function helps economists summarize a firm's production possibilities. But it does not provide enough information for anyone to open a business. Someone who wants to make snarks has to know more than that it takes machines and labor. He has to know what machines to use, how to use them, and how to hire and manage labor. He has to know how to sell snarks. The production function tells him none of these vital details.

The relationship between the production function and running a business is like the relationship between a list of ingredients for a recipe and actually producing the dish promised by the recipe. Knowing the ingredients is necessary, but not enough to enable you to prepare the food. You also have to know what to mix with what; whether to fry or boil, for how long, and at what temperature.

2 COSTS AND THE CHOICE OF PRODUCTION TECHNIQUE

In Chapter 6, we showed how a firm's output level is determined by the marginal cost and marginal revenue curves. But we did not fully discuss where the marginal cost curve and the total cost curve from which it is derived come from. The firm's cost curves are obtained from the production function and the costs of inputs.

We want to go behind the cost curves so we can understand what changes will cause them to shift and thereby cause the firm to change its output level. Why does a change in wages, such as GM faced in 1982, affect the firm's output decisions? How does the possibility of using robots affect costs and output?

From the production function and the costs of inputs, the firm calculates the minimum cost at which each level of output can be produced. Once it has calculated the minimum cost of producing each level of output, it knows its total cost curve. In this section we show how the firm calculates costs and chooses its lowest-cost production methods.

Minimizing Costs: The Choice of Technique

To find the lowest-cost way of producing any given level of output (say, 100 snarks), a firm uses its production function to calculate the costs of using different combinations of inputs that yield that level of output. If the firm is small, the owner probably does the calculations. A large firm will ask engineers to give it cost estimates for the different possible ways of producing a particular level of output.

We return to Table 7-1 and consider the cheapest way of producing 100 snarks per week. The table shows two techniques for producing 100 units of output per week. They are given again in Table 7-2 and described as techniques A and B. To simplify our analysis, we assume there are no other combinations of factors that can be used to produce 100 units of output.

The calculations made in Table 7-2 are as follows. The firm knows how much labor and capital are used in each method of production. It knows the costs of renting a machine ($320 per week) and hiring labor ($300 per week). With this information, it calculates the costs of the capital and labor it uses for each method, and then it adds those amounts to get the total cost of production. The total costs of production differ. It costs $2480 per week to produce 100 snarks using technique A. It costs only $2440 to produce 100 snarks per week using technique B, which therefore has a cost advantage of $40. The firm will choose technique B, and the total cost of producing 100 snarks per week will be $2440. We now have one point on the total cost curve for producing snarks: corresponding to the output level of 100 is the cost of $2440. Technique B is the *economically* most efficient (lowest-cost) method for producing 100 snarks, given the rental and wage rates in Table 7-2.

The total cost curve is constructed by doing the calculations for each level of out-

TABLE 7-2
CHOOSING THE LOWEST-COST PRODUCTION TECHNIQUE

	CAPITAL INPUT	LABOR INPUT	RENTAL RATE PER MACHINE, $/wk	WAGE RATE, $/wk	CAPITAL COST, $/wk	LABOR COST, $/wk	TOTAL COST, $/wk
Technique A	4	4	320	300	1280	1200	2480
Technique B	2	6	320	300	640	1800	2440

put. Given the different possible ways of producing each level of output, the firm does the same calculations as in Table 7-2 and then chooses the lowest-cost method of production. The marginal cost curve is derived from the total cost curve by calculating the increase in total costs as output is increased by 1 unit.

Factor Intensity In comparing methods of production, it is common to describe some as capital-intensive and others as labor-intensive. When a method of production uses a lot of capital and relatively little labor, it is capital-intensive. When there is heavy use of labor and little use of capital, the production method or process is labor-intensive. In terms of Table 7-2, we can say that technique A is more capital-intensive than technique B. In technique A, the ratio of capital to labor is 1 to 1 (4 units of capital to 4 units of labor). In technique B, the ratio of capital to labor is 1 to 3 (2 units of capital to 6 of labor). Thus the first production method is more capital-intensive than the second. Conversely, the second production method is more labor-intensive than the first.

Changes in Factor Prices and the Choice of Technique

Using the production function data in Table 7-2, the firm chooses the more labor-intensive technique of production, because that is cheaper. But suppose now that the cost of using labor rises. Specifically, suppose that the wage rate goes up from $300 to $340 per week. Labor has become more expensive, while the rental rate for machines has not

changed. Thus the *relative* cost of using labor has risen.

We must ask two questions. First, what happens to the total costs of producing 100 snarks per week? Second, is there any change in the preference for technique B? To answer the second question, we have to figure out the costs of production again, using the new factor prices. Table 7-3 shows the calculations.

As one should expect, the total cost of producing 100 snarks per week has risen. It now costs $2640 to produce 100 snarks, compared with $2440 (as shown in Table 7-2). This means that the total cost curve shifts *upward* at each output level when the price of any input rises.

In addition, in this case, the firm uses a different production method, technique A instead of technique B. There is a substitution of capital for labor. Before the increases in the wage rate, the firm used six workers and two machines. Now the higher wages lead it to substitute two machines for two workers. Labor use is down from six to four workers, and machine use is up from two to four machines.

The GM case works the opposite way to this example. When GM's workers agreed in 1982 to accept lower wages than they would normally have received, GM was assured that its costs of production would rise by *less* than they would have risen otherwise. The workers in turn were assured that GM would use more labor-intensive methods of production than it would have if wages had risen.

The use of robots represents a new

TABLE 7-3

THE EFFECTS OF AN INCREASE IN THE WAGE RATE

	CAPITAL INPUT	LABOR INPUT	RENTAL RATE, $/wk	WAGE RATE, $/wk	CAPITAL COST, $/wk	LABOR COST, $/wk	TOTAL COST, $/wk
Technique A	4	4	320	340	1280	1360	2640
Technique B	2	6	320	340	640	2040	2680

method of production. It would appear in a table such as Table 7-3 as very capital-intensive. Probably because wages at GM were rising at a lower rate than they would have without the agreement, GM did not introduce robots as rapidly as it would have otherwise.

Now we discuss how costs change as the firm changes its level of output.

3 LONG-RUN TOTAL, MARGINAL, AND AVERAGE COSTS

Suppose a firm is faced with an increase in the quantity demanded of its product. It will want to expand production. But it takes time to adjust production to the new demand. For short periods—say, a week or a month—the firm can get its existing work force to work overtime. With a bit more time it can begin to bring in new machinery. And over an even longer period it may build itself a new factory.

The *long run* is a period long enough for a firm to adjust *all* its inputs completely to a change in conditions.

In the long run the firm is able to vary the size of its factory, install machines best suited for its level of output, and hire the labor and management it needs at the going wage rate.

The short run is defined by contrast with the long run.

The *short run* is a period in which the firm can make *some*, but not complete, adjustment of inputs to a change in conditions.

In the short run the firm has to work with given amounts of some inputs, like the machinery. Only after time has passed, in the long run, is the firm able to fully adjust to changed conditions.

In this section we deal with long-run cost curves. These are cost curves that describe the firm's costs of producing when it is not in any way limited in choosing input levels.

The long-run total cost curve thus describes the lowest-cost way of producing each given level of output when the firm is able to adjust all its inputs optimally.

Long-Run Total and Marginal Costs

Table 7-4 shows the long-run costs of production for alternative output levels. Total costs of production are calculated as described in the previous section. The lowest-cost method of production is chosen at each output level, and the resulting cost of production is shown in the second column of Table 7-4. Since the costs in the second column are long-run costs, the cost of producing 0 unit is zero. The firm fully adjusts in the long run to an output of zero by not hiring any factors of production. A firm that produces zero in the long run is out of business.

Table 7-4 also shows the long-run marginal costs of production. These represent the increase in costs at each level of output needed to produce 1 more unit of output.

The total costs of production certainly rise with output. It must cost more to pro-

TABLE 7-4
LONG-RUN COSTS

OUTPUT, goods/wk	LONG-RUN TOTAL COST, $/wk	LONG-RUN MARGINAL COST, $/good	LONG-RUN AVERAGE COST, $/good
0	0		—
1	30	30	30
2	54	24	27
3	74	20	24.67
4	91	17	22.75
5	107	16	21.40
6	126	19	21.00
7	149	23	21.29
8	176	27	22.00
9	207	31	23.00
10	243	36	24.30

duce more output than less. But how fast do total costs increase with output? Is there any advantage to being big, in the sense that a large firm can produce goods at a lower cost per unit than small firms? Or might it be a disadvantage to be large, in the sense that a big firm produces at a higher cost per unit?

Long-Run Average Costs

To find out how costs of production change with the level of output, it is most convenient to look at the cost per unit of output, or the average cost of production.

> The average cost of production is equal to the total cost divided by the level of output.

The last column of Table 7-4 shows long-run average costs. These are equal to long-run total costs divided by output.

The long-run average cost data in Table 7-4 are shown in Figure 7-3 as the long-run average cost (*LAC*) curve. The curve starts out high, at an average cost of $30 per unit for the first unit, and then falls to an average cost of $21 per unit when output is 6. After that point the curve rises, reaching $24.30 at an output of 10. This pattern for average costs is called the *U-shaped average cost curve*. The U has very gently sloping sides,

but it's still possible to see in Figure 7-3 how the shape of the curve got its name.

Economists often draw the long-run average cost curve as U-shaped. To see why, we have to introduce the concept of returns to scale, or economies and diseconomies of scale.

FIGURE 7-3   THE LONG-RUN AVERAGE COST CURVE. This long-run average cost (*LAC*) curve represents the data in the last column of Table 7-4. The *LAC* curve has the typical U shape. The minimum average cost of production is at point *A*. At that point, the output level is 6, and the average cost is $21.

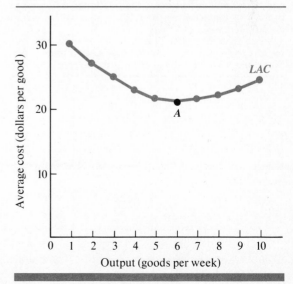

4 ECONOMIES AND DISECONOMIES OF SCALE

There are economies of scale (or *increasing returns to scale*) when long-run average costs decrease as output increases. Figure 7-4*a* shows a case of economies of scale. There are *constant returns to scale* when long-run average costs are the same at all levels of output, as in Figure 7-4*b*. There are diseconomies of scale (or *decreasing returns to scale*) when long-run average costs increase as output rises, as in Figure 7-4*c*. "Scale" in these definitions means the size of the firm as measured by its output.

In Figure 7-3 the U-shaped cost curve shows increasing returns to scale up to point *A*, where the average cost is lowest. At higher levels of output, there are decreasing returns to scale. In asking why the average cost curve is drawn as U-shaped, we are asking why economists assume that there are economies of scale, or increasing returns, at low levels of output and diseconomies of

scale, or decreasing returns to scale, at high levels of output.

In discussing economies of scale we are really talking about the production function of the firm. The average cost curve is directly related to the total costs of production, which depend on the production function. When we ask whether average costs fall or rise as output increases, we are asking whether firms can produce each unit of output more or less cheaply as output rises. For given costs of using factors, we are asking whether the firm has to use fewer or more inputs per unit of output as output rises. This is a technological question about the most efficient methods of production. So although we talk about economies of scale in terms of the cost function, they are directly connected to the production function.

Economies of Scale

There are three reasons for economies of scale. The first is *indivisibilities* in the production process of the firm. The firm has to

---

FIGURE 7-4 RETURNS TO SCALE AND THE LONG-RUN AVERAGE COST CURVE. (*a*) Increasing returns to scale, or economies of scale; (*b*) constant returns to scale; (*c*) decreasing returns to scale, or diseconomies of scale. The three long-run average cost (*LAC*) curves show the relationship between returns to scale and the shape of the *LAC* curve. When the *LAC* curve is falling, average costs of production fall as output increases, and there are economies of scale. When the *LAC* curve is rising, average costs of production increase as output increases, and there are decreasing returns to scale. In the intermediate case, Figure 7-4*b*, the average costs are constant, and there are constant returns to scale.

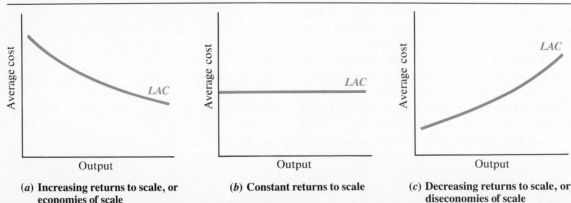

(*a*) **Increasing returns to scale, or economies of scale**

(*b*) **Constant returns to scale**

(*c*) **Decreasing returns to scale, or diseconomies of scale**

have minimum amounts of some inputs if it is in business, but it does not have to increase those inputs much as output rises. For instance, provided a firm is in business at all, it needs to be managed, has to keep its accounts in order, and probably needs a telephone and a desk. These requirements are indivisible in the sense that the firm can't keep only half its accounts or use half a telephone. As the business grows, these inputs do not have to be increased much. Management can organize three workers as well as two, there is no need yet for a second telephone, and the accounts take just as long to do as they did at a lower level of output. There are economies of scale because the indivisible factors are being spread over more units of output. Eventually, though, this source of economies of scale will die out as the firm has to hire more managers and acquire more telephones and desks.

The second reason for increasing returns to scale is *specialization*. As the firm gets larger, each worker can concentrate more on one task and handle it more efficiently. Adam Smith, the father of economics, made a strong point about the gains from specialization within a firm in his famous *The Wealth of Nations* (1776). His example is, as he calls it, a "very trifling manufacture"—the pin industry. Smith says:

> A workman not educated to this business . . . could scarce . . . make one pin in a day, and certainly could not make twenty. But in the way in which this business is now carried on, . . . it is divided into a number of branches. . . . One man draws out the wire, another straights it, a third cuts it, a fourth points it. . . .

There were then 18 stages for making a pin, and Smith estimated the average output per worker at 4800 pins per day. The economies of scale from specialization in this case are impressive. Similar benefits from specialization occur in assembly line work—for instance, in the automobile industry.

The third reason for economies of scale is closely related. In many industries, particularly those producing goods rather than services, large scale is needed to take advantage of better machinery. Engineers have a rule of two-thirds that applies to many factories and machines. The rule states that the costs of building a factory or machine rise by only two-thirds as much as the output of the factory or machine. In some cases the physical basis for this is clear. For instance, oil tankers are essentially cylinders. The amount of oil that can be carried depends on the volume of the cylinder. As the volume increases, the surface area needed to enclose the volume increases by only about two-thirds. There are, therefore, large economies of scale in tanker and storage operations.

Diseconomies of Scale

With these three good arguments for economies of scale explaining the downward-sloping part of the *LAC* curve in Figure 7-3, is there any reason to think there are ever diseconomies of scale? The first point to note is that the second and third arguments for the existence of economies of scale apply mainly to manufacturing firms. Economies of scale are likely to be less significant in service firms, such as restaurants or laundries, beyond low levels of output.

The main reason there may be diseconomies of scale is that management becomes more difficult as firms became larger. These are described as *managerial diseconomies of scale*. To begin with, the firm needs only one manager, who is likely to be the owner. As the firm grows, the owner hires vice presidents and other middle level management—which has itself to be managed. The company becomes bureaucratic, coordination of different departments is complicated, and average costs of production *may* begin to rise.

The argument that lies behind the U-shaped average cost curve (*LAC*) in Figure 7-3 is that economies of scale dominate at low levels of output but that eventually, as the firm becomes very large, managerial diseconomies of scale outweigh the economies and average costs start to rise.

However, the shape of the average cost curve for a firm is not determined by general arguments about what is likely to happen. Rather it is a matter of *fact* that depends largely on the production function. It is worthwhile looking at some facts.

Returns to Scale in Practice

Figure 7-5 shows actual data on average costs. Figure 7-5*a* is based on a study of cement factories. Figure 7-5*b* is based on a

study of the average costs of brewing beer in factories of different sizes in England. Average costs fall with the level of output in each case. No part of the cost curve shows decreasing returns to scale. Indeed, most studies of costs in manufacturing industries show a similar pattern of average costs falling with the level of output.[2]

For such firms the typical pattern of the *LAC* curve is the one shown in Figure 7-4*a*.

---

[2] C. F. Pratten, *Economies of Scale in Manufacturing Industry,* Cambridge University Press, Cambridge, 1971, presents data for 25 industries, including steel, bread, oil, soap, socks, and newspapers. F. M. Scherer, *Industrial Market Structure and Economic Performance,* 2d ed., Rand McNally, Chicago, 1980, pp. 81–118, has an excellent description of the relationship between average costs and output in practice.

FIGURE 7-5 AVERAGE COST CURVES IN THE LONG-RUN. The figure shows long-run average cost curves for (*a*) cement and (*b*) beer brewing. In both cases, average costs fall as the level of output rises. (*Sources:* Cement—Mark E. McBride, "The Nature and Source of Economies of Scale in Cement Production," *Southern Economic Journal,* July 1981, pp. 105–115; beer—C. F. Pratten, *Economies of Scale in Manufacturing Industry,* Cambridge University Press, Cambridge, 1971, p. 75.)

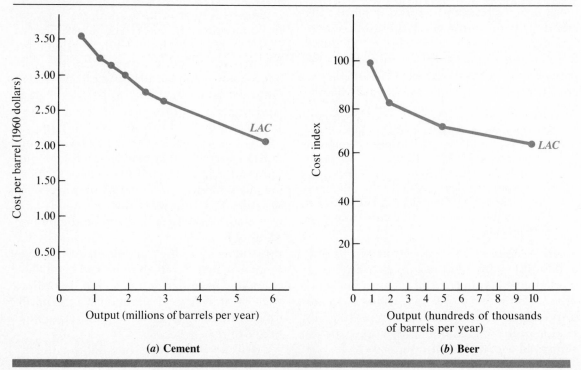

(*a*) **Cement**   (*b*) **Beer**

At low levels of output, average costs are falling rapidly. As output rises, average costs continue to fall, but less rapidly. Thus there are economies of scale at higher levels of output, but they are very moderate.

Economists have attempted for some industries to measure the level of output at which economies of scale become relatively unimportant for an individual firm. The definition that has been used is that of *minimum* efficient scale (MES), which is the scale of production at which any further doubling of output reduces average costs by less than 5 percent.

Table 7-5 contains some estimates of minimum efficient scale for several industries. Scale is given both as an output level and as a percentage of U.S. output. The estimates apply for the year 1967, but there is no reason to think that the story would be very different with newer data. Of the industries shown, only the household refrigerators industry has a MES that is more than 10 percent of total U.S. output. There are other such industries, not shown in the table, including diesel motors and automobiles.

We can thus summarize by saying that for many firms, particularly in manufacturing, there are indeed economies of scale,

but those economies stop being significant at output levels that are small relative to the output of the entire industry.[3] Essentially the *LAC* curve becomes almost flat for those firms, and their average costs of production become almost constant. It is as if the upward-sloping part of the conventional U-shaped *LAC* curve has been cut off.

For other firms, especially those not in manufacturing, the U-shaped *LAC* curve is probably a good estimate of cost conditions. From now on we will work mainly with the U-shaped *LAC* curve, but we will also refer at several places in the book to the type of *LAC* curve shown in Figure 7-4a and Figure 7-5. It has increasing returns to scale and is most likely to apply to firms in manufacturing industry.

5 AVERAGE AND MARGINAL COSTS

Table 7-4 presents long-run marginal costs along with long-run average costs. We now want to connect those two cost measures,

[3] A word of caution. The MES may be small relative to the size of the vast U.S. market. But in smaller markets, such as those in many developing countries, even a single plant may be unable to get up to an optimal production level. This means that attempts by small countries to develop self-sufficiency in production may be very expensive.

TABLE 7-5
OUTPUT LEVELS AT WHICH ECONOMIES OF SCALE BECOME SMALL

INDUSTRY	OUTPUT LEVEL (MES)	MES AS % OF U.S. OUTPUT IN 1967
Cigarettes	36 billion cigarettes per year; 2275 employees	6.6
Paints, varnishes, and lacquers	10 million gallons per year; 450 employees	1.4
Shoes (other than rubber)	1 million pairs per year; 250 employees	0.2
Household refrigerators	800,000 units per year	14.1

Source: Data are from L. W. Weiss, "Optimal Plant Size and the Extent of Suboptimal Capacity," in R. T. Masson and P. D. Qualls (eds.), *Essays in Honor of Joe S. Bain,* Ballinger, Cambridge, Mass., 1976. They are originally from work by F. M. Scherer, Alan Beckenstein, Erich Kaufer, and R. D. Murphy, *The Economics of Multi-Plant Operation: An International Comparisons Study,* Harvard University Press, Cambridge, Mass., 1975.

whose behavior is closely related. Because the relationship between long-run marginal costs and long-run average costs applies also to short-run marginal and average costs, we refer in this section simply to average and marginal costs.

The data on average and marginal costs in Table 7-4 are plotted in Figure 7-6. We plot marginal costs at output levels that are halfway between the levels for which average costs are computed. For example, the marginal cost of $30 for the first unit of output is plotted in Figure 7-6 at an output level of one-half.

Two facts from the table and diagram stand out.

1   *LAC* is falling so long as *LMC* (long-run marginal cost) is less than *LAC*, and *LAC* is rising when *LMC* is above *LAC*.

2   At the level of output where the *LMC* curve cuts the *LAC* curve, *LAC* is at its lowest level, or minimum.

Neither of these facts is an accident. There is a relationship between marginal and average costs (and, indeed, between marginal and average anything). To understand the relationship it is best to start with baseball. Suppose that a batter has been hitting .300 to date. He goes 3 for 4 in his next game. For that game, he hits .750. What happens to his overall average, taking into account all games played, including the last one? It must be that his average goes up, because he did better in the last game than he had been doing on the average so far. We can think of the .750 as his marginal score, or score on the last game, and the .300 as the average score to date. And because the marginal score is above the average, we know that the average has to rise.

Exactly the same relationship holds between average and marginal costs of production. If the cost of making 1 more unit of the good (the marginal cost) is above the av-

FIGURE 7-6   AVERAGE AND MARGINAL COST CURVES. These cost data are plotted from Table 7-4. There are two special features of the relationship between the marginal cost curve (*LMC*) and the average cost curve (*LAC*). First, *LAC* is falling wherever *LMC* is below *LAC*, and *LAC* is rising wherever *LMC* is above *LAC*. Second, the *LMC* curve cuts the *LAC* curve at the minimum point of the *LAC* curve—in other words, at the point where output is produced at the lowest cost per unit.

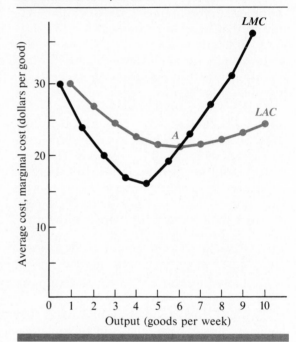

erage cost of production, then the average cost of production has to increase when 1 more unit of output is produced. If the marginal cost is less than the average cost, then the average cost falls when output is increased by 1 unit. It follows also that if the marginal cost is equal to the average cost, the average cost will not change when 1 more unit of output is produced.

Fact 2, that the average cost is at its minimum when marginal cost is equal to average cost, follows from fact 1. Figure 7-7 shows this with smooth versions of the *LMC* and *LAC* curves seen in Figure 7-6. Point *A*, where the *LMC* curve cuts the *LAC* curve from below, must be the point where the av-

FIGURE 7-7 THE *LMC* CURVE CUTS THE *LAC* CURVE AT MINIMUM *LAC*. These cost curves are just smooth versions of the cost curves in Figure 7-6. The figure presented here shows more clearly that the *LMC* curve cuts the *LAC* curve exactly at the point of minimum *LAC*, point *A*. The relationship shown here holds for *any* average and marginal cost curves, not just for the *long-run* curves.

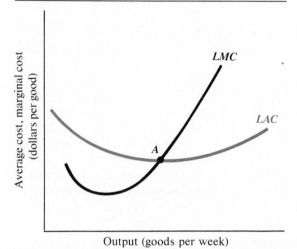

erage cost is lowest. Why? Anywhere to the left of point *A*, *LMC* is below *LAC*. Therefore, the average cost is still falling—it cannot have reached its lowest point. Anywhere to the right of point *A*, *LMC* is greater than *LAC*. Therefore, the average cost is rising—it must have been lower at some lower level of output. This means that *LAC* must be lowest where the *LMC* curve cuts the *LAC* curve, as seen at point *A* in Figures 7-6 and 7-7.[4]

---

[4] A word of warning. In Figure 7-6 the *LMC* curve cuts *LAC* exactly at the point of minimum *LAC*. But it is possible if you plot *LAC* and *LMC* curves from a table similar to Table 7-4, which gives values of costs only at particular levels of output, like 0, 1, and 2, and not in between, that *LMC* does not go *exactly* through the point of minimum long-run average cost. The reason is that the table omits information on what costs are at levels of output between 1 and 2, etc., and that minimum *LAC* could be somewhere between the levels of output actually shown. However, the *LMC* certainly in any event crosses *LAC* very close to the lowest cost shown in the table.

The relationship between marginal and average costs is important enough to be emphasized in a separate table, Table 7-6. We have omitted the *L* from *MC* and *AC* because the relationships in Table 7-6 apply to both short-run and long-run marginal and average costs. To figure out how the table works, always think about baseball.

6 THE FIRM'S LONG-RUN OUTPUT DECISION

With the concept of the long run, as well as the long-run average and marginal cost curves, we can analyze fully the firm's long-run output decision. The first requirement for profit maximization is always the same: set output at the level at which marginal revenue is equal to marginal cost. Thus in the long run, if the firm is in business, it will be at point *B* in Figure 7-8, with output level Q_1. At that level of output, *MR* is equal to *LMC*.

But there is also a second condition for profit maximization. The firm has to check whether it might do better by not producing at all. In the long run, the question for the firm is whether it should be in business. It should be in business only if it is not making losses.

Profits are, of course, equal to total revenues minus total costs. Therefore, the firm has to be sure that at output level Q_1 total revenue is not less than total cost. We will now put that same condition in terms of price and average cost.

A little common sense gives us the right answer. Suppose that the firm is selling its output at a price of $6. This is the price at which output Q_1 can be sold, for example. Now suppose that the firm's average cost of production is $7. Then the firm is losing $1 on every unit it sells. That is a bad idea. The firm should leave the business. But if the average cost is $5.99, then the firm is not making losses; it is even making a slightly

TABLE 7-6

THE RELATIONSHIP BETWEEN MARGINAL AND AVERAGE COSTS

WHEN →	MC IS LESS THAN AC	MC = AC	MC IS GREATER THAN AC
Then AC is →	falling	at its minimum	rising

above-normal profit. (Remember that costs are *economic* costs, which include an allowance for the return on the owner's investment in the firm.) Thus the condition that the firm should not make losses in the long run can be stated in another way: *In the long run the firm will continue in business only if price is not less than long-run average cost.*

Someone thinking about going into a particular line of business will make the same calculation. If there is no level of output at which the price received for output exceeds the average cost, the business will not ever be able to cover cost. There is no point in even starting.

How does this commonsense condition relate to total revenue and total cost? We know that profits must not be negative—that *total* costs must not be larger than *total* revenues—if the firm is to be in business in the long run. Equivalently, the cost *per unit of output* must be less than the revenue *per unit of output*. The cost per unit of output is

FIGURE 7-8 THE FIRM'S LONG-RUN OUTPUT DECISION. In the long run the firm chooses its output level at point B, where MR is equal to LMC. It then has to check whether it is making losses at that output level, Q_1. If price is equal to or more than LAC_1, the long-run average cost corresponding to output Q_1, the firm is not making losses and stays in business. If price is less than LAC_1, the firm's long-run output decision should be zero—it closes down permanently.

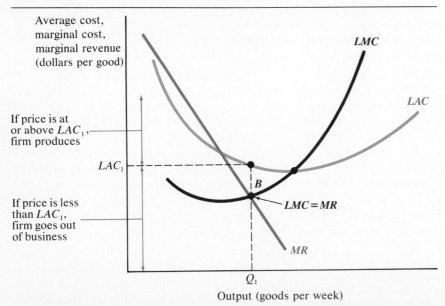

TABLE 7-7
THE FIRM'S LONG-RUN OUTPUT DECISION

MARGINAL CONDITION	DECISION ABOUT WHETHER TO BE IN BUSINESS
Choose the output level (Q_1) at which $MR = MC$.	If price is not less than LAC, at output level Q_1, produce Q_1. If price is less than LAC, go out of business.

just the average cost. The firm's total revenue is equal to the price it receives per unit sold times the quantity sold. Revenue per unit sold is thus equal to price. Accordingly, once again, profits will not be negative so long as price is not less than average cost.

This is shown in Figure 7-8. If, at output level Q_1, price is less than LAC_1, then the firm should go out of business, because it is not covering costs. If price at output level Q_1 is at or above LAC_1, then the firm should stay in business and produce Q_1. The condition for long-run profit maximization is also shown in Table 7-7.

7 SHORT-RUN COST CURVES AND DIMINISHING MARGINAL RETURNS

The short run is a period in which the firm cannot fully adjust to a change in conditions. Suppose that a firm is faced by an unexpected increase in the quantity demanded of its output. This increase shifts its marginal revenue curve. In the long run it would build a larger factory and install new machines to meet the increase in the quantity demanded at the lowest possible cost. But in the short run it cannot increase the size of its factory or obtain new machines. It can only expand output by changing its labor input.

In the short run the firm has some fixed factors of production.

A *fixed factor* of production is a factor whose input level cannot be varied.

In the long run there are no fixed factors because the firm can expand or contract by changing all its inputs. By definition, there are fixed factors in the short run.

There is no hard-and-fast rule about the amount of time that distinguishes the short run from the long run. The length of the long run depends on the industry. In the electric power industry, where it can take over 10 years to get a power station built, the long run is very long. In contrast, someone planning to enter the restaurant business may think of the long run as only a few months—as long as it takes to locate and decorate the room, set up the kitchen, hire the chef and waiters, and print the menu.

The existence of fixed factors in the short run has two implications for a firm's costs. First, the firm has some fixed costs of production in the short run.

Fixed costs are costs that do not vary with the level of output.

The firm has to pay for the fixed factors it has, whatever the level of production—indeed, even if production is zero. The costs of these factors are the firm's fixed costs. Second, because the firm cannot in the short run adjust all its inputs, its short-run costs of production will be different from the long-run production costs.

In this section we develop the firm's short-run cost curves.

Short-Run Fixed and Variable Costs of Production

Table 7-8 presents data on short-run costs of production for the firm. The second column shows short-run fixed costs, which are independent of the level of output. This is the amount the firm has to pay for the use of its fixed factors, such as the factory and the machines.

The third column shows short-run variable costs.

Variable costs are costs that change as the level of output changes.

Variable costs are the costs of hiring variable factors of production, which are typically labor and materials. In the short run the firm is most likely to change output by changing the amount of labor and raw materials inputs. It does this mainly by having its workers work overtime, but it may also hire more workers and buy more materials.

The sum of short-run fixed and variable costs is short-run total cost of production. This point is expressed in the following equation:

$$\begin{matrix} \text{Short-run} \\ \text{total cost} \\ (STC) \end{matrix} = \begin{matrix} \text{short-run} \\ \text{fixed cost} \\ (SFC) \end{matrix} + \begin{matrix} \text{short-run} \\ \text{variable cost} \\ (SVC) \end{matrix} \qquad (1)$$

Short-run total costs are presented in the fourth column of Table 7-8. Finally, short-run marginal costs are given in the last column. Short-run marginal cost is the increase in the short-run total cost from increasing output by 1 unit.

The *SFC*, *STC*, and *SMC* data in Table 7-8 are plotted in Figure 7-9. The *SFC* curve in Figure 7-9*a* is flat because fixed costs do not change at all as output changes. Short-run variable costs and therefore short-run total costs (*STC*) both increase with output. Short-run marginal costs (*SMC*) are plotted separately in Figure 7-9*b*. Note that the vertical scales of the two parts of Figure 7-9 dif-

FIGURE 7-9   SHORT-RUN COST CURVES. (*a*) Short-run fixed and variable costs; (*b*) short-run marginal costs. These cost curves are based on the data in Table 7-8. Short-run total cost (*STC*) is the sum of the fixed and variable costs. The short-run marginal cost curve (*SMC*) in Figure 7-9*b* represents the increase in total costs required to increase output by 1 unit at each level of output. The *SMC* curve can be read off the *STC* curve by calculating the increase in *STC* as output increases by 1 unit. However, the scale of the *SMC* curve is larger to make its shape stand out better.

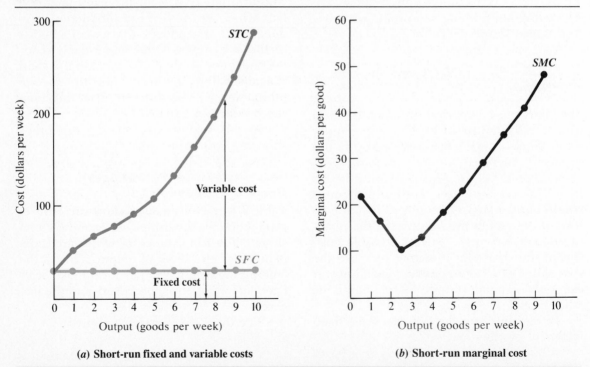

(*a*) **Short-run fixed and variable costs**

(*b*) **Short-run marginal cost**

TABLE 7-8

SHORT-RUN COSTS OF PRODUCTION

OUTPUT, goods/wk	(SFC) SHORT-RUN FIXED COST, $/wk	(SVC) SHORT-RUN VARIABLE COST, $/wk	(STC) SHORT-RUN TOTAL COST, $/wk	(SMC) SHORT-RUN MARGINAL COST, $/good
0	30	0	30	
1	30	22	52	22
2	30	38	68	16
3	30	48	78	10
4	30	61	91	13
5	30	79	109	18
6	30	102	132	23
7	30	131	161	29
8	30	166	196	35
9	30	207	237	41
10	30	255	285	48

fer. Short-run marginal costs first decrease as output rises and then increase.

Now we have to ask the usual question. Why do the cost curves have the shapes shown in the figure? To answer this question we work with the marginal cost curve. We also assume that there is only one variable factor of production: labor. In the short run the firm has given quantities of fixed factors, the factory and the machines. Varying amounts of labor cooperate with the fixed factors in production. Output varies and costs change as the firm hires different quantities of labor.

The short-run marginal costs of production are shown falling and then rising. Why?

The Marginal Product of Labor and Diminishing Marginal Productivity

The only way output can be changed in the short run is by changing the inputs of the variable factors. We are assuming that there is only one variable factor: labor. Table 7-9 and Figure 7-10 show how output increases as the input of labor is increased. All other inputs remain constant. When no labor is employed, there is no output at all. Employing 1 unit of labor increases output from 0 to 0.8 unit. The first unit of labor thus increases output by 0.8 unit.

The *marginal product of labor* is the increase in output obtained by increasing the input of labor by 1 unit.

The marginal product of the first unit of labor is 0.8 unit of output. The marginal product of the second unit of labor is 1 unit of output, and the marginal product of the third unit of labor is 1.3 units.

Why is the marginal product of labor increasing at these low levels of labor input? The reason is that the workers have a given factory and set of machines with which to work. The first worker has too many switches to control to be able to produce much. Adding a second worker is a big help, and a third one is an even bigger help. The three workers together can handle most of the machines in the factory. The marginal product of the fourth worker is lower, because the machines are already just about fully manned. The marginal product of labor continues to fall as more workers are added. Thus beyond a labor input of 3, the marginal product of labor decreases as the number of workers increases. At these higher levels of labor input, we say that there are diminishing returns to labor.

The *law of diminishing returns* is that the marginal product of a factor will, beyond some level of input, begin to fall.

FIGURE 7-10 THE PRODUCTIVITY OF LABOR AND DIMINISHING MARGINAL RETURNS. (*a*) The total product of labor; (*b*) the marginal product of labor. The data that are plotted are from Table 7-9. The total product of labor increases as the input of labor is increased. But the marginal product of labor first increases and then decreases. Beyond point *A* in Figure 7-10*b* the marginal product of labor is decreasing; that is, there are diminishing marginal returns to labor. This is because more and more workers are being put to work with the same stock of machines.

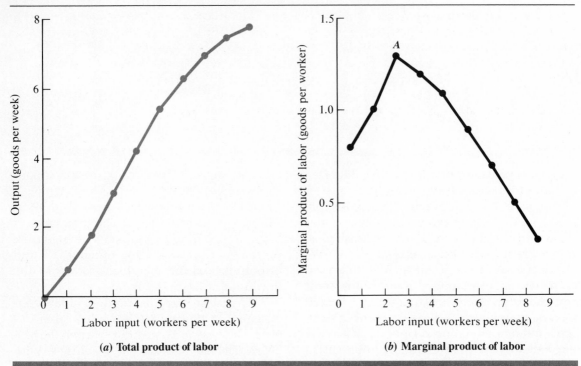

(*a*) **Total product of labor**   (*b*) **Marginal product of labor**

TABLE 7-9

TOTAL AND MARGINAL PRODUCTS OF LABOR

LABOR INPUT, workers/wk	OUTPUT, goods/wk	MARGINAL PRODUCT OF LABOR, goods/wk
0	0	
		0.8
1	0.8	
		1.0
2	1.8	
		1.3
3	3.1	
		1.2
4	4.3	
		1.1
5	5.4	
		0.9
6	6.3	
		0.7
7	7.0	
		0.5
8	7.5	
		0.3
9	7.8	

This is a law about technology. It says that adding more and more workers to cooperate with a given amount of the fixed factors will eventually result in the marginal product's falling. The first few workers who are added are able to match themselves to the existing machinery. Adding more workers is less useful. The ninth worker's main use in production is to get coffee for the people operating the machinery. This contributes to output, but not a great deal. Hence eventually there are diminishing returns to a single factor.

Short-Run Marginal Costs

The shape of the short-run marginal cost curve in Figure 7-9*b* is implied by the shape of the marginal product of labor curve in Figure 7-10*b*. Why? Every unit of labor employed by the firm costs the same. But so long as the marginal product of labor is increasing, every unit of labor employed adds more to output than the previous worker. Therefore, the extra cost *per unit* of the good being produced must be lower when the marginal product of labor is higher. Thus so long as the marginal product of labor is increasing, the marginal cost curve must be falling—for the extra cost per unit of the good being produced is the marginal cost of production. *SMC* is falling when the marginal product of labor is rising.

However, once the stage of diminishing marginal productivity is reached, *SMC* starts to rise. Now successive additions of labor add progressively less to output. But hiring one more worker adds the same amount, the wage, to total costs. Therefore, as the marginal product of labor falls, the extra amount of goods obtained by paying out the wage to each extra worker falls. And marginal costs, the increases in the total cost associated with an increase in output, are rising.

The shape of the marginal cost curve and thus also the shape of the total cost curve are determined by the shape of the marginal product of labor curve (in Figure 7-10*b*). But the behavior of the marginal product of labor is determined by the production function, which describes how output changes when inputs are changed. Thus again, the shape of the cost curves is determined by the technology facing the firm.

Short-Run Average Costs

Table 7-10 presents short-run *average* cost data corresponding to the data in Table 7-8.

> *Short-run average fixed cost* (*SAFC*) is equal to the short-run fixed cost (*SFC*) divided by the level of output. Similarly, *short-run average variable cost* (*SAVC*) is equal to *SVC* divided by the

level of output, and *short-run average total cost* (*SATC*) is equal to *STC* divided by the level of output.

Each of the three columns of average cost data in Table 7-10 is obtained from the data in Table 7-8 by dividing by the level of output. There is no average cost corresponding to an output of zero because the notion of the average cost per unit of producing 0 unit does not make sense. The table also includes short-run marginal costs.

Figure 7-11 is based on the data in Table 7-10. Figure 7-11*a* shows the three short-run average cost measures. Short-run average total cost is, of course, equal to short-run average fixed cost plus short-run average variable cost. This corresponds to equation (1) and is expressed in equation (2):

$$
\begin{matrix}
\text{Short-run} \\
\text{average} \\
\text{total cost} \\
(SATC)
\end{matrix}
=
\begin{matrix}
\text{short-run} \\
\text{average} \\
\text{fixed cost} \\
(SAFC)
\end{matrix}
+
\begin{matrix}
\text{short-run} \\
\text{average} \\
\text{variable cost} \\
(SAVC)
\end{matrix}
\quad (2)
$$

The shapes of the three curves in Figure 7-11*a* are readily understood. The *SAFC* curve falls all the way because the same fixed cost ($30) is being spread over more and more units of output as output increases. The firm would say that it is spreading its overhead, or fixed costs. The *SAVC* curve starts out falling and then rises. Its shape is a direct result of the shape of the short-run marginal cost curve, as we shall explain shortly.

The *SATC* curve is obtained by adding short-run average fixed and variable costs at each level of output. It starts out falling and then rises. It starts out by falling because both the *SAVC* and *SAFC* curves are falling. But then the *SAVC* curve turns up. The shape of the *SATC* curve is then the result of the contest between the falling *SAFC* curve and the rising *SAVC* curve. First the falling *SAFC* curve wins out, and the *SATC* curve is falling. But then the reduction in costs obtained from spreading the overhead

TABLE 7-10

SHORT-RUN AVERAGE COSTS OF PRODUCTION

OUTPUT, goods/wk	(SAFC) SHORT-RUN AVERAGE FIXED COST, $/good	(SAVC) SHORT-RUN AVERAGE VARIABLE COST, $/good	(SATC) SHORT-RUN AVERAGE TOTAL COST, $/good	(SMC) SHORT-RUN MARGINAL COST, $/good
0	—	—	—	
1	30.00	22.00	52.00	22
2	15.00	19.00	34.00	16
3	10.00	16.00	26.00	10
4	7.50	15.25	22.75	13
5	6.00	15.80	21.80	18
6	5.00	17.00	22.00	23
7	4.29	18.71	23.00	29
8	3.75	20.75	24.50	35
9	3.33	23.00	26.33	41
10	3.00	25.50	28.50	48

FIGURE 7-11 SHORT-RUN AVERAGE COST AND MARGINAL COST CURVES. These diagrams are based on the data in Table 7-10. Two separate figures are used to avoid clutter. Figure 7-11a shows the relationship between short-run average fixed, variable, and total costs. SATC is equal to SAFC plus SAVC. The shape of the SATC curve is a result of the shapes of its two components. When both SAVC and SAFC are falling, so is SATC. When SAVC starts rising, the shape of the SATC curve depends on whether SAVC is rising more rapidly than SAFC is falling. In Figure 7-11b the relationship between marginal and average cost curves established for the long run applies also to the short-run curves. The SMC curve goes (almost exactly in this case, but exactly when the curves are drawn continuously rather than just with the points at output levels 1, 2, etc.) through the minimum point of both the SAVC curve, at B, and the SATC curve, at A.

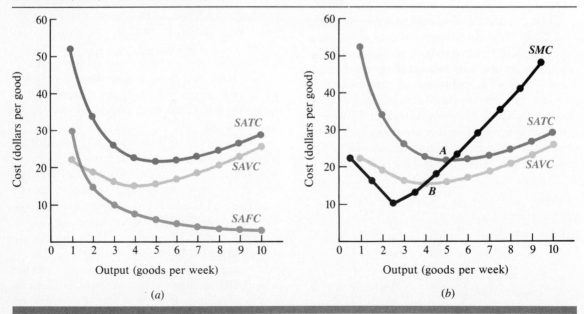

over more units of output begins to tail off (the *SAFC* curve does not fall rapidly), and the *SAVC* curve rises sharply as a result of diminishing returns to labor. Eventually the *SAVC* curve wins, and the *SATC* curve slopes upward.

There are two special features in Figure 7-11*b*. First, the *SMC* curve intersects both the *SAVC* curve and the *SATC* curve at their respective minimum points. Second, we can understand the shape of the *SAVC* curve from that of the short-run marginal cost curve.

Why does the *SMC* curve cut *both* the *SATC* curve and the *SAVC* curve at their lowest points? We have to remember the baseball player and Table 7-6. The *SMC* curve shows the change in costs when output goes up by 1 unit. If the marginal cost is above the average cost, the average cost is rising. If the marginal cost is below the average cost, the average cost is falling. It is clear from this argument that the *SMC* curve must cut the *SATC* curve at its lowest point. The argument is *exactly* the same as the argument we used to show that the *LMC* curve cuts the *LAC* curve at its minimum point.

One more step is needed to understand why the *SMC* curve cuts the curve for short-run average *variable* costs at its minimum, point *B*. The step is to note that the *SMC* curve shows the amounts by which *variable costs* as well as total costs change when output is increased by 1 unit. Why? Because the only reason why total costs change is that variable costs change. Fixed costs by definition do not change when output changes. Thus the *SMC* curve shows how much variable costs change when output rises by 1 unit. It follows that if *SMC* is above *SAVC*, *SAVC* is rising, and if *SMC* is below *SAVC*, *SAVC* is falling. Thus the *SMC* curve must cut the *SAVC* curve at its minimum point.

We can use Figure 7-11*b* to explain the shape of the *SAVC* curve. Recall that the shape of the *SMC* curve depends on the way the marginal product of labor changes with output. At low levels of output, marginal costs are declining, and at higher levels of output, diminishing returns to labor cause *SMC* to rise. This accounts for the shape of the *SAVC* curve. At low levels of output, when *SMC* is below *SAVC*, *SAVC* must be falling. But then diminishing returns to labor set in, and *SMC* starts to rise. As the marginal returns to labor diminish sharply, *SMC* rises above *SAVC*, which in turn begins to rise. Thus the shape of the *SAVC* curve reflects the marginal productivity of labor—or, in general, the marginal productivity of whatever factors of production can be varied in the short run.

By now any reasonable person is asking two questions: How can anyone remember all these cost curves? And of what use are they? The answer to the first question is, Go back to Figure 7-2, which shows that there are three basic cost curves: total, marginal, and average. Two distinctions have to be made. First, cost curves differ between the short run and the long run. And second, in the short run there is a distinction between fixed and variable costs. Putting the three basic cost curves together with the two distinctions—between the short run and the long run and, in the short run, between fixed and variable costs—generates the cost curves with which we have worked.

The second question is the more serious one. There is no point in remembering cost curves just to exercise the mind. The cost curves developed in this chapter are required for analyzing a firm's output decisions. We have already used the long-run cost curves to analyze a firm's long-run output decision. Now we will use the short-run curves to analyze the firm's output decision in the short run.

8 THE FIRM'S SHORT-RUN OUTPUT DECISION

The rule by which the firm chooses its output level in the short run is, of course, to find the point at which marginal cost is equal to marginal revenue. But since this is the short run, the period in which the firm cannot adjust all its inputs freely, the firm sets *short-run* marginal cost equal to marginal revenue. The firm's choice of output level is illustrated in Figure 7-12.

Next the firm determines whether it is better to produce at output level Q_1 in Figure 7-12 than to produce zero. This will again involve the relationship between price and average cost. If at output level Q_1

the price is above $SATC_1$, then revenues exceed costs, and the firm is making a profit. It should certainly produce Q_1.

But what if the price is less than $SATC_1$? The firm is losing money, because price does not cover costs. In the long run, the firm closes down if the price is less than the average cost, but here is where the difference between the short run and the long run appears. The firm has its fixed costs in the short run even if it produces no output. It has to pay for its fixed factors even if it does not use them in production. Thus the question it should ask if the price is less than $SATC_1$ is whether its losses would be smaller if it produced zero output rather than Q_1.

FIGURE 7-12   THE FIRM'S SHORT-RUN OUTPUT DECISION. The firm sets output at level Q_1. At that level short-run marginal cost (*SMC*) is equal to marginal revenue. Then the firm has to check whether it should produce at all. If price is above $SATC_1$, the short-run average total cost at output level Q_1, then the firm is making a profit and should certainly produce Q_1. If price falls between $SATC_1$ and $SAVC_1$, then the firm is partly covering its fixed costs, even though it is losing money. It should still produce output Q_1. Only if the price is below $SAVC_1$ should the firm produce zero. At any price below $SAVC_1$ the firm cannot even cover its variable costs, and it therefore does better to produce zero and not incur the variable costs.

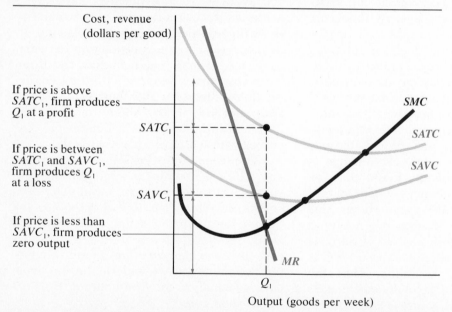

Cost, revenue (dollars per good)

If price is above $SATC_1$, firm produces Q_1 at a profit

If price is between $SATC_1$ and $SAVC_1$, firm produces Q_1 at a loss

If price is less than $SAVC_1$, firm produces zero output

SMC

$SATC_1$

SATC

SAVC

$SAVC_1$

MR

Q_1

Output (goods per week)

It will produce so long as doing so helps it pay for its fixed factors. This means that it will produce so long as it at least covers its variable costs. If its revenues exceed variable costs, it is earning something toward paying for its fixed factors. Thus the firm will produce Q_1 even if it is making losses, provided its revenues exceed the variable costs. The criterion for the decision to produce is that the price must exceed $SAVC_1$. If it does not, the firm produces zero.

The firm's short-run output decision is to produce Q_1, the output level at which $MR = SMC$, so long as the price is at least equal to the short-run average variable cost ($SAVC_1$) at that level of output. If the price is less than $SAVC_1$, the firm produces zero.

In commonsense terms, the condition for the firm to produce in the short run is that the price it receives must at least help to cover *some* of its fixed costs. For example, suppose that at output level Q_1 the short-run average fixed cost is $2, and the short-run average variable cost is $4. The short-run average total cost ($SATC$) is therefore $6. If the firm receives any price above $6, it makes a profit and certainly produces. But so long as the price exceeds $4, the firm reduces its losses by producing Q_1. Only if the price is below $4 should the firm not produce.

The analysis of the firm's short-run output decision applies directly to the GM situation with which we began this chapter. GM stayed in production even though it was losing $400 per car. Our analysis of the firm's short-run output decision says that was a perfectly sensible thing to do. To maximize its profits, GM set output at the level at which marginal revenue was equal to SMC. At that output level, the price covered the short-run average variable cost but did not cover the short-run average total cost. But the company still came out ahead by choosing to produce rather than shutting

down. It contributed toward covering its fixed costs.

The short-run and long-run output decisions of a firm are summarized in Table 7-11, which includes the information in Table 7-7. Box 7-1 draws attention to two principles used in analyzing a firm's output decisions that come up often in other areas as well.

Staying in Business in the Short Run and in the Long Run

If price covers $SAVC$, the firm produces in the short-run, even if it is losing money. But the firm cannot go for very long with fixed costs that are only partially covered by sales revenues. In effect, the firm would be making losses all the time. Naturally, the managers would have to look ahead and ask why the future should be any different from the present. Why stay in business rather than sell off any remaining assets (plant and equipment) and either use the proceeds in another line of business or distribute them to the shareholders?

There are three possibilities. First, the firm may expect more favorable demand conditions in the future. If this is the case, it is worth staying in business, making losses for some period of time but expecting to re-

TABLE 7-11
THE FIRM'S OUTPUT DECISIONS

	MARGINAL CONDITION	CHECK WHETHER TO PRODUCE
Short-run decision	Choose the output level at which $MR = SMC$.	Produce that level of output if price is not less than $SAVC$. If price is less than $SAVC$, produce zero.
Long-run decision	Choose the output level at which $MR = LMC$.	Produce that level of output if price is not less than LAC. If price is less than LAC, go out of business.

BOX 7-1

MARGINAL CONDITIONS AND SUNK COSTS

Two principles of economics used in the analysis of supply keep coming up both in economics and in life. The first is the *marginal principle.* In deciding how much to produce, the firm asks itself how producing 1 more or 1 less unit of output will affect its profits. It sets output so that profits cannot be increased by changing the level of output. If profits cannot be increased, they must be as big as they can be, or at a maximum.

The general principle is that in any situation consumers or producers or government officials can find the best position to be in by asking whether the situation can be improved by varying, at the margin, purchases or output or government spending, as the case may be. How much labor should the firm employ? It compares the cost of an extra worker with the value of the output the worker will produce. If the value of the output the extra worker will produce is more than the wage, the firm hires him. How wide should a bridge be built? Should it have four lanes or six? To get the right answer, compare the extra cost of building a six-lane bridge instead of a four-lane bridge with the benefits drivers have from the extra two lanes. These are marginal conditions, and the question is whether to do or have a little bit more or a little bit less. Following this rule will lead to an optimal situation.

Of course, it is also necessary to look at the big picture. Not only does the firm have to set marginal cost equal to marginal revenue; it also has to be sure it is earning a profit. Should it close down completely, for instance? Should a bridge be built at all? The marginal conditions and the big picture, or *total conditions,* go together.

The second general principle is that *sunk costs are sunk.* If certain costs have been incurred and cannot be affected by your decision, ignore them. They should have no role in your decision. In deciding how much to produce in the short run, the firm pays no attention to its fixed costs. Those costs are there no matter what the firm does. They are therefore irrelevant to the firm's decision. Suppose that we are halfway through building a bridge and we are told that completion will cost four times as much as originally budgeted. Should we proceed? The answer is quite independent of the amount that has already been spent to get half the bridge built. We need to compare the benefits of having the bridge with the marginal cost of completing it.

The *sunk cost fallacy* is the view that sunk costs should matter. Whenever issues involving sunk costs arise, it always seems natural to think that it would be a pity to waste all the money that has been spent already. But that natural tendency does not lead to the best decisions. Bygones should be bygones.

cover those losses in the future when demand is more favorable. This happens frequently. Perhaps because of a recession in the economy (when demand is generally low), firms may find demand unfavorable; they may fail to cover their fixed costs, but they are sufficiently optimistic about the future. This was certainly one reason for GM to stay in business, since its 1980 losses came at a time when the economy was indeed in a recession.

The second possibility is that the firm

does not expect any changes in demand but can foresee favorable changes in its costs. For example, if demand has become less favorable, the firm might shift in the long run to a smaller plant that has correspondingly lower costs and could thus be profitable. Or perhaps the firm expects new methods of production—such as GM's use of robots—to reduce its costs of production.

The third possibility is the pessimistic one: the firm cannot see any way of reducing costs, and the managers cannot look forward to better demand conditions. If that is the case, the firm should go out of business immediately since any day wasted is a day of losses.

We now look in greater detail at the second possibility: reductions in average costs due to a more suitable plant size. We approach the subject by comparing the firm's average cost schedule in the short run, with a fixed plant size or capital stock, with the average cost schedule in the long run, where all factors are flexible, or adjustable.

We thus compare the firm's short-run and long-run average cost curves.

9 SHORT-RUN AND LONG-RUN COSTS

Suppose that there is a reduction in the quantity demanded of a firm's output. The firm reacts to the fall in demand in the short run by adjusting its variable factors. But it has to continue paying for its fixed factors. The cost of the fixed factors may cause it to lose money in the short run. Over a longer period the firm can build a new, smaller factory with fewer machines and thereby reduce its costs. It may be able to make profits again in the long run, even though it is losing money in the short run. If so, it will want to remain in business despite its current losses.

In this section we compare the firm's short-run and long-run average cost curves and show why a firm may be able to make higher profits in the long run than in the short run—and thus why a firm suffering losses in the short run may stay in business.

Short-Run and Long-Run Average Cost Curves

Figure 7-13 shows a U-shaped *LAC* curve. At each point on the curve, such as A, B, or C, the firm is producing a given level of output as cheaply as is possible. The combination of factors of production used at each point on the *LAC* curve minimizes the cost

FIGURE 7-13 SHORT-RUN AND LONG-RUN AVERAGE COST CURVES. The *LAC* curve shows the lowest average cost for producing each level of output. Corresponding to each point on the *LAC* curve there is a combination of factors of production that minimizes the costs of producing the corresponding level of output. For the plant size at each point on the *LAC* curve, such as A, B, or C, there is a short-run average total cost curve. This curve shows the average costs of producing different levels of output, using the particular plant size and varying inputs of the variable factor. The *SATC* curves are always above the *LAC* curve except at one point. This means that the costs of producing a given level of output, such as Q_4, are bound to be no lower in the long run than they are in the short run. If the firm is initially at point A and conditions then change so that it wants to produce Q_4, it will be more costly to do so in the short run (at point G) than in the long run (at point H).

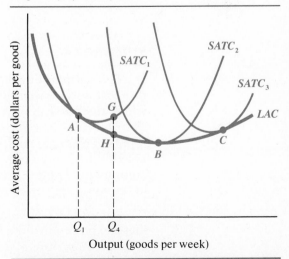

of producing the output. All factors of production, including those which are fixed in the short run, vary in quantity along the *LAC* curve.

For convenience we call the fixed factors "plant." Corresponding to points *A*, *B*, and *C* on the *LAC* curve are the three *SATC* curves shown. There is a different plant size on each of the *SATC* curves. Indeed, there is actually an *SATC* curve corresponding to *every* point on the *LAC* curve. At every point on the *LAC* curve there is a plant with a given size. Given a plant size, we can draw a corresponding *SATC* curve which shows how costs change in the short run as the variable factors are adjusted to change the level of output.

On each of the *SATC* curves—such as $SATC_1$, which touches the *LAC* curve at *A*—the firm has a given plant size. The plant size on $SATC_1$ is the size which is optimal when the firm is producing at output level Q_1. For any other output level, such as Q_4, the costs of production are higher on the *SATC* curve than on the *LAC* curve. This can be seen by comparing short-run costs at point *G* with long-run costs at *H*. Costs are higher on the *SATC* curve because the plant is the wrong size for producing Q_4 at the lowest possible cost.

This means that the *SATC* curve is *above* the *LAC* curve at every point but one. This makes sense because the firm is limited in the short run in the combinations of factors it can employ to produce output. In the long run, any technically feasible combination of factors can be used to produce a given level of output. It must thus be that long-run average costs of producing any given level of output are below the short-run average total costs of producing.

A firm's profits cannot be any lower than they are in the short run if the firm has time to adjust to a change. In the short run the firm does its best to maximize profits, but it cannot adjust plant size. Thus the short-run costs of producing Q_4 in Figure 7-13 are higher than the costs of producing Q_4 in the long run, as comparison of points *G* and *H* shows. A firm's profits will be higher in the long run, when the firm has time to adjust fully to changed circumstances, than they are in the short run, when plant size is fixed.

This means that a firm that is currently suffering losses because demand has fallen may well be able to look forward to future profits after it has had time to build a plant that is more suitable for its new level of output.

SUMMARY

1   This chapter develops the distinction between short-run and long-run cost curves and output decisions. The long run is a period over which the firm can fully adjust all its inputs to a change in conditions. The short run is a period in which the firm cannot fully adjust all its inputs to changed conditions. In particular, in the short run the firm is not able to change the quantity of the fixed factors, such as plant and equipment, that it is using. The length of calendar time corresponding to the long run varies from industry to industry.

2   The production function specifies the maximum amount of output that can be produced using any given quantities of inputs. The inputs are machines, raw materials, labor, and any other factors of produc-

tion. The production function summarizes the technical possibilities open to the firm, but it is far from being a sufficiently detailed description of technology for anyone to use in actually setting up a firm.

3   The total cost curve is derived from the production function for the given wages and rental rates for factors of production. The long-run total cost curve is obtained by finding for each level of output the method of production that minimizes costs, allowing full flexibility of all inputs. When the relative price of using a factor of production rises, the firm substitutes away from that factor in choosing production techniques. For instance, if wages rise, the firm tends to use more machines and less labor.

4   Average cost is equal to total cost divided by output. The long-run average cost curve is derived from the long-run total cost curve.

5   The long-run average cost (LAC) curve is typically drawn as U-shaped. The falling part of the U is the result of indivisibilities in production, the benefits of specialization, and some advantages of large scale from an engineering standpoint. There are increasing returns to scale on the falling part of the U. The rising part of the U is a result of difficulties of coordination, or managerial diseconomies of scale.

6   Data from manufacturing usually show that LAC decreases at all levels of output; in other words, there are economies of scale. For most industries the economies of scale become small at levels of output that are only a small percentage of total industry output in the United States.

7   The relationship between average cost and marginal cost is as follows: When marginal cost is below average cost, average cost is falling. When marginal cost is above average cost, average cost is rising.

8   In the long run the firm produces at the point where long-run marginal cost (LMC) equals MR, provided that price is not less than the long-run average cost at the particular level of output. If price is less than long-run average cost, the firm goes out of business.

9   In the short run the firm cannot adjust some of its inputs. But it still has to pay for them, and so it has short-run fixed costs (SFC) of production. Other factors of production, such as labor, are variable in the short run. The cost of using the variable factors is the short-run variable cost (SVC). Short-run total costs (STC) are equal to SFC plus SVC.

10 The short-run marginal cost (SMC) curve reflects the marginal productivity of labor. The variable factor, labor, has a given plant size with which to work. When very little labor is being used, the plant is too big for labor to produce much output. Increasing the labor input

therefore leads to large rises in output, and SMC is falling. Once the machinery is fully manned, though, each extra worker adds progressively less to output, and SMC is rising.

11   Short-run average total costs ($SATC$) are equal to short-run total costs (STC) divided by output. $SATC$ is equal to the short-run average fixed cost ($SAFC$) plus the short-run average variable cost ($SAVC$). The $SATC$ curve is U-shaped. The falling part of the U results both from a drop in $SAFC$ as the fixed costs are spread over more units of output and from a drop in $SAVC$ at low levels of output. The $SATC$ continues to fall after $SAVC$ begins to increase, but eventually the rising $SAVC$ outweighs the falling $SAFC$, and the $SATC$ curve slopes upward.

12   The SMC curve cuts both the $SATC$ curve and the $SAVC$ curve at their minimum points.

13   The firm sets output in the short run at the level at which SMC is equal to MR. It produces that level of output so long as the price is not less than the short-run average *variable* cost. In the short run the firm is willing to produce when it is losing money if that contributes to covering its fixed costs.

14   The LAC curve is always below the $SATC$ curve except at one particular point. At that point the plant size on the $SATC$ curve is the right size for producing the given level of output at the lowest possible cost. This implies that a firm will have higher profits in the long run than in the short run if it is currently producing with a plant size that is not best with regard to the long run. A firm may be producing with a plant size that is inappropriate (with regard to the long run) if it has recently faced a change in demand or cost conditions.

KEY TERMS

Inputs	Long-run marginal cost (LMC) curve
Output	Diminishing marginal returns
Production function	Fixed factors
Choice of production technique	Short-run fixed costs (SFC)
Factor intensity	Short-run variable costs (SVC)
Long run	Short-run total costs (STC)
Short run	Marginal product of labor
Long-run total cost curve	Law of diminishing returns
Long-run marginal cost curve	Short-run marginal costs (SMC)
Long-run average cost (LAC) curve	Short-run average fixed costs ($SAFC$)
Returns to scale	Short-run average variable costs ($SAVC$)
Economies of scale	Short-run average total costs ($SATC$)
Diseconomies of scale	Sunk cost fallacy

PROBLEMS

1 (*a*) What information does the production function provide? (*b*) Explain why the production function does not provide enough information for anyone actually to run a firm.

2 (*a*) What are economies of scale, and why might they exist? Discuss the evidence, and to what types of firms this applies. (*b*) The following table shows how output changes as inputs change. Assume that the wage rate is $5 and that the rental rate for capital is $2. Determine the lowest-cost (economically most efficient) method of producing 4, 8, and 12 units of output. (*c*) Do you have increasing, constant, or decreasing returns to scale between those output levels? Which applies where?

CAPITAL INPUT	LABOR INPUT	OUTPUT
4	5	4
2	6	4
7	10	8
4	12	8
11	15	12
8	16	12

3 (*a*) For each output level in the above table, say which technique of production is more capital-intensive. (*b*) Does the firm switch toward or away from more capital-intensive techniques as output rises? (*c*) Which way is more likely to apply in the real world? Explain.

4 Suppose that the rental rate for capital in Problem 2 rose to $3. (*a*) Would the firm change its method of production for any of the levels of output? Say which, if any. (*b*) How do the firm's total and average costs change when the rental rate for capital rises?

5 (*a*) Calculate the marginal and average costs for each level of output from the following total cost data. (*b*) Show how mar-

ginal and average costs are related. (*c*) Are these short-run or long-run cost curves? Explain how you can tell.

OUTPUT, goods/wk	TOTAL COSTS, $/wk
0	12
1	27
2	40
3	51
4	60
5	70
6	80
7	91
8	104
9	120

6 (*a*) Why does a firm have fixed costs of production in the short run? (*b*) Explain the typical shapes of the *SAFC*, *SAVC*, and *SATC* curves. (*c*) Why does the law of diminishing marginal productivity have anything to do with short-run cost curves?

7 (*a*)Explain why it might make sense for a firm to produce goods which it can only sell at a loss. (*b*) Can it keep on doing this forever? Explain.

8 GM lost $567 million in 3 months in 1980. Explain why this means that GM's fixed costs must have been at least $567 million during that period if it was maximizing profits.

9 Explain in words why the condition *MC* = *MR* (marginal cost equals marginal revenue) always has to hold in the long run and in the short run when a firm is maximizing profits, providing it is producing some output.

10 (*a*) Why is a crash program to achieve anything likely to be more expensive than a slower-moving program? (*b*) Does this mean that the best program of all is the program that takes the longest?

There are very few suppliers in some markets and many suppliers in other markets. For instance, there are only five automobile manufacturers in the United States. The largest of them, General Motors, produced over 60 percent of the cars made in the United States in 1981. The local power company accounts for 100 percent of the electricity sales in the city and is a *monopoly*.

A *monopolist* is the only seller of a particular good in a market. The local telephone company is also a monopoly—it is the only company from which you can buy your local telephone service.

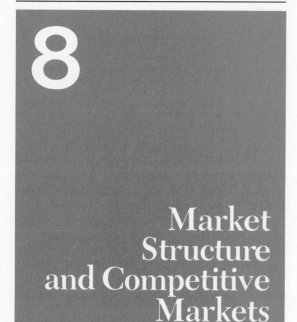

In contrast, there are 252,000 food stores in the United States, 68,600 barbers, 75,400 laundries, and 7,100 detective agencies. If you live in a town of any size, you have a choice of places to buy your food, or have your hair cut, or hire a detective.

What difference, if any, does the size and number of firms in an industry make? Do monopolists behave differently than firms that have to compete with other firms in their industry? How does the consumer benefit when there is competition between the firms from which he can buy?

These are questions about *market structure*.

The structure of a market is a description of the behavior of buyers and sellers in that market.

In this chapter we introduce market structure and define "monopoly" and "competition," everyday words to which economists give precise meanings. We also describe market structures that fall between the extremes of monopoly and competition. Then in this chapter and the next two chapters we discuss the effects of market structure on price and output in an industry, starting with perfectly competitive markets.

A *perfectly competitive* market is one in which buyers and sellers assume that their own buying or selling decisions have no effects on market price.

For this to be true, each buyer must be only a small part of the market. Thus a perfectly competitive market must have many buyers and sellers in it. This conforms to commonsense ideas about competition. We shall also see, though, that other commonsense ideas about competition—for instance, that firms should be fighting each other vigorously, like Hertz and Avis—do not fit the description of perfectly competitive markets.

8

Market Structure and Competitive Markets

FIGURE 8-1   DEMAND CURVES AND MARKET STRUCTURE. A competitive firm can sell as much as it wants at the market price, P_0. It therefore faces a horizontal demand curve, as shown in Figure 8-1a. Imperfect competitors face downward-sloping demand curves. They have to take into account the effects of their sales on the price they receive when deciding how much to produce.

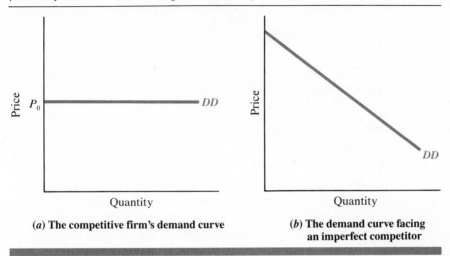

(a) The competitive firm's demand curve

(b) The demand curve facing an imperfect competitor

1   MARKET STRUCTURE

A perfectly competitive industry, in which all firms and consumers believe that their own actions have no effect on market price, is one extreme of the range of market structures. Agricultural markets are the main examples of perfectly competitive markets. The individual potato farmer in Idaho knows that his decision on how many potatoes to send to the market has essentially no effect on market price. Similarly, the consumer buying potatoes does not believe, reasonably enough, that his decision to buy this week will affect the market price of potatoes.

All market structures other than perfect competition are cases of imperfect competition.

Markets where either buyers or sellers take into account the effects of their own actions on market price are *imperfectly competitive.*

Firms in a perfectly competitive industry and those in imperfectly competitive industries can be distinguished by the demand curves for the firm's output, as shown in Figure 8-1. The perfectly competitive firm can sell as much as it wants at the going market price. This means that it faces a flat or horizontal demand curve. This is shown in Figure 8-1a. No matter how much output the firm wants to sell, it receives the same price, P_0. Imperfectly competitive firms, by contrast, face downward-sloping demand curves. When they increase sales, prices fall, other things equal. This is shown in Figure 8-1b. Why do we say "other things equal"? The answer is that an imperfectly competitive firm may be able to increase sales without reducing its price if it increases its advertising.

The extreme case of imperfect competition is monopoly, where there is a single seller of a good. The demand curve for the monopolist is the demand curve for the entire industry, and is downward-sloping. In choosing his output level a monopolist must take account of the fact that, other things equal, higher sales lead to lower prices.

TABLE 8-1
MARKET STRUCTURE

| | | MARKET STRUCTURE | | |
| | | IMPERFECT COMPETITION | | |
CHARACTERISTIC	PERFECT COMPETITION	MONOPOLISTIC COMPETITION	OLIGOPOLY	MONOPOLY
Number of sellers	Many	Many	Few	One
Ability to affect price	None	Limited	Some	More
Limitations on entry	None	None	Some	No entry
Example	Agriculture	Drugstores	Automobiles, breakfast cereals	de Beers diamonds

Between perfect competition and monopoly are two other cases of imperfect competition, *monopolistic competition* and *oligopoly.* The distinction between the three types of imperfect competition involves mainly the number of firms in the industry.

> An *oligopoly* is an industry in which there are only a few sellers.

Such firms are bound to take into account the effects of their decisions on output on the industry's price level. Cigarette manufacturers in the United States constitute an oligopoly, as do the automobile manufacturers. General Motors knows that when it changes its price, it is likely that Ford and Chrysler will change theirs.

> *Monopolistic competition* is a situation in which there are many sellers of goods which are close substitutes, and each seller has a limited ability to affect the price at which it sells.

The corner drugstore is a monopolistic competitor. It can charge a few cents more for a prescription or a tube of toothpaste than the drugstore down the road and still keep some customers. But it has only limited room for maneuver.

As with most definitions, the lines between monopolistic competition, oligopoly, and monopoly are a little blurred. We define a monopoly as the only seller of a good,

but the definition of a good is not totally clear. For instance, the local electric company is a monopoly because it is the only seller of electric power. But gas and oil can be used for heating, and so the electric company is not the only seller of heating energy. One of the most enduring monopolies has been the de Beers Company, which controls the marketing of diamonds in the western world.

Similarly, the line between oligopoly and monopolistic competition is not clearcut because the line between few firms (oligopoly) and many (monopolistic competition) is ambiguous. Large manufacturing industries, such as the automobile and television set industries, have relatively few firms and are oligopolies. Retailing has many imperfect competitors and is the preserve of monopolistic competition.

Table 8-1 presents some characteristics of the different types of market structure. The main criterion is the number of firms in the industry. But that is related to the second criterion, the extent to which the actions of the typical firm in the industry can affect price.

Perfectly competitive firms do not affect market price through their own supply decisions. We should think, therefore, of firms supplying a reasonably standard product, such as wheat or potatoes, and supplying only a small part of the market. Perfectly competitive firms do not compete in the sense that firm A's main object in life is to do better than firm B. Neither A nor B is able by itself to affect price, and nothing that B does will have an effect on A's profits. Thus perfectly competitive firms do not compete in the sense we are familiar with from sports, where the aim is to win by getting ahead of the other player or team. The way for the firms in a competitive industry to get ahead is by running as efficiently as they can and selling the amount of output which maximizes their own profits.

We show also a third criterion which helps define the different types of market structure. That is the ease with which new firms can enter the industry. If existing firms in an industry have to worry about the possibility of new firms coming in, they cannot raise their prices so high as to make very large profits. If existing firms make large profits, new firms will enter the industry to try to get some of those profits for themselves by selling at a lower price. Thus the harder it is for new firms to enter an industry, the greater the freedom the existing firms in the industry have to choose a price to charge.

Buyers and Sellers

In Table 8-1 we define market structure according to the behavior of sellers of goods. But market structure is also defined by the behavior of buyers. Corresponding to oligopoly and monopoly are *oligopsony* and *monopsony*, words that are almost never used. They mean few buyers and a single buyer, respectively. For instance, the U.S. government is frequently a monopsonist in the market for weapons. Because situations with relatively few buyers in goods markets are less frequent than situations with few sellers, we concentrate on the supply side of the market in discussing market structure. We assume that typically there are many

buyers, none believing that he can affect market price.

Why Do Market Structures Differ?

In this chapter we discuss how perfectly competitive markets work, and in the next two chapters we examine the behavior of imperfectly competitive markets. In doing so, we also ask why market structures differ across industries. The first reason is technological: there may be economies of scale in an industry, so that one or only a few firms can supply goods more cheaply than many firms. This accounts for monopolies such as the local gas and electricity companies and for oligopolies such as the automobile manufacturers.

A second reason is political and legal. Some industries have enough political power to limit entry. For example, some economists argue that the American Medical Association for many years restricted entry into the medical profession and therefore indirectly reduced the supply of medical services and raised the incomes of doctors.[1] Entry was limited by licensing requirements that were supported by legislation. Licensing requirements for other industries, such as undertaking, may have the same aim and effect.

Perfect Competition and Free Markets

> *Free markets* are competitive markets in which the government does not intervene.

Free markets are rare. Governments intervene in many markets—for example, by setting health or quality standards for restaurants, foods, and the housing industry; by imposing pollution controls on the automobile industry; and by guaranteeing minimum prices for dairy products.

[1] For a discussion of this argument, see Thomas D. Hall and Cotton M. Lindsay, "Medical Schools: Producers of What? Sellers to Whom?" *Journal of Law and Economics*, April 1980, and the extensive references given there.

Competitive markets are not necessarily free markets. For instance, the market for dairy products is competitive even though the government subsidizes milk production. Both buyers and sellers know that they cannot affect prices through their own decisions on how much to buy and sell. The dairy farmers as a group can use their political power to affect the amount of subsidy given by the government, but that does not mean their later decisions on how much to produce are based on the effect of their own output on market price. So long as individual suppliers and demanders believe their own supply and demand decisions do not affect price, the market is perfectly competitive.

2 THE FIRM'S SUPPLY DECISIONS UNDER PERFECT COMPETITION

What is special about the behavior of firms under perfect competition? In Chapter 7 we developed a complete analysis of the firm's output decisions in the short run and in the long run. We saw that firms maximize profits by producing at a level of output where marginal cost is equal to marginal revenue. This conclusion is summarized in the following equation:

Marginal cost = marginal revenue   (1)
$$MC = MR$$

Recall that a firm should also check whether not producing at all might be better than producing at the level of output where marginal revenue is equal to marginal cost. In the short run, the firm will cease production if the price is less than the short-run average variable cost ($SAVC$). In the long run, the firm will leave the industry if the price is less than the long-run average cost (LAC).

Firms under perfect competition follow the same rules in choosing their output level. They produce at the level of output where marginal cost is equal to marginal revenue, provided it is more profitable to produce something than not to produce at all. *The special feature of perfect competition is the relationship between marginal revenue and price.*

Price and Marginal Revenue under Perfect Competition

A firm in a perfectly competitive industry faces a horizontal demand curve, as shown in Figure 8-1a; it can sell as much as it wants at the market price. Every extra unit of output is sold for the same price. This means that for a perfectly competitive firm, marginal revenue is equal to price.

Marginal revenue = price   (2)
$$MR = P$$

It is equation (2) that distinguishes perfectly competitive firms from other firms. Perfectly competitive firms can sell as much as they want at the going market price; therefore, marginal revenue is equal to price. Imperfectly competitive firms believe that changes in their sales affect the market price, and therefore marginal revenue is *not* equal to price. We will see as we proceed through the next few chapters why this makes a difference to price and output determination.

The Firm's Short-Run Supply Curve

Figure 8-2 shows short-run marginal and average cost curves for a firm. It is the same as Figure 7-12. $SATC$ is the short-run average total cost curve, and $SAVC$ is the short-run average variable cost curve. We know that any firm will want to produce at the output level where marginal revenue is equal to marginal cost.

But the special feature of a perfectly competitive firm is that marginal revenue is equal to price. Therefore, to figure out how much a perfectly competitive firm wants to sell at a particular market price, we only have to see where price is equal to marginal cost. Then, as usual, we have to check

FIGURE 8-2 SHORT-RUN SUPPLY DECI-
SIONS OF THE PERFECTLY COMPETITIVE
FIRM. The perfectly competitive firm produces at the level of output where price is
equal to marginal cost, provided it makes a
greater profit by producing some output
rather than none at all. At any price above
P_3 the firm makes profits because price is
above average cost. At any price between
P_1 and P_3, such as P_2, the firm is not
covering all its costs, for price is below
average cost. But price is above *SAVC,* and
so the firm is covering its variable costs. It
therefore should continue in operation in
the short run, as long as price is above P_1.
Thus the firm's supply curve in the short
run is the *SMC* curve above point A.

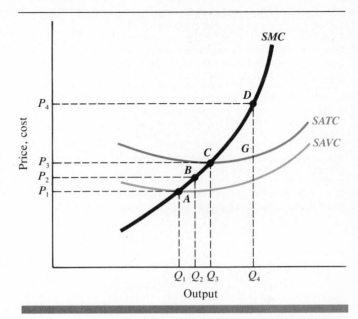

to determine whether the firm would rather
produce that level of output than not produce
at all.

Putting together equations (1) and (2),
we have for the perfectly competitive firm:

$$\frac{\text{Marginal}}{\text{cost}} = \frac{\text{marginal}}{\text{revenue}} = \text{price} \qquad (3)$$
$$MC = MR = P$$

To develop the firm's supply decision, suppose that it faces a market price equal to P_4.
This is the price at which it can sell its output. It chooses the output level by setting
marginal cost equal to price, as equation (3)
shows. This means that it wants to produce
output Q_4, as shown by point D on the SMC
curve.

Now the firm has to decide whether it
would rather shut down production in the
short run. But we know from Chapter 7 that
if price is above short-run average variable
cost ($SAVC$), a firm would rather produce
in the short run than shut down. So long
as price is above $SAVC$, the firm is contributing toward covering its fixed costs and
should produce.

We can see that in the short run the firm
should produce positive amounts of output
for any price above P_1. Given any price,
such as P_2, it chooses to produce the quantity, in this case Q_2, shown by the SMC
curve.

The curve showing the quantity the
firm wants to produce at any given price
level is the firm's *supply curve.*

The short-run supply curve is thus the SMC
curve above the $SAVC$ curve, or above point
A in Figure 8-2.

Between points A and C, or prices P_1
and P_3, the firm will be making losses in the
short run, for price is less than average cost.
But since the firm is more than covering variable costs at those prices, it certainly wants
to produce despite the losses. At any price
above P_3 the firm is making profits. Profits
per unit of output are equal to the difference
between price and average cost. For instance, at price P_4, the profit on each unit
sold is equal to distance DG, the difference
between price and average cost at output
level Q_4. We have to keep reminding ourselves that these profits are above normal

FIGURE 8-3 LONG-RUN SUPPLY DECISIONS OF THE PERFECTLY COMPETITIVE FIRM. The perfectly competitive firm produces at the level of output where price is equal to marginal cost, provided it makes a greater profit by producing some output rather than none at all. It therefore chooses points on the *LMC* curve, the long-run marginal cost curve. At any price above P_3 the firm makes profits because price is above long-run average cost (*LAC*). At any price below P_3, such as P_2, the firm suffers losses because price is below long-run average cost. It therefore will not produce any output at prices below P_3. The long-run supply curve is the *LMC* curve above point *C*.

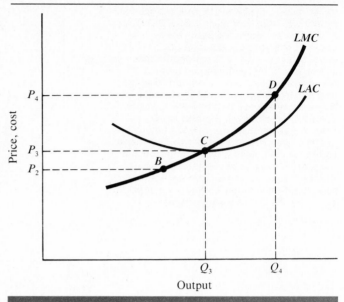

profits, for the economic costs summarized by the *AC* curve include the opportunity costs of the owners' capital and work effort.

Price P_1 is called the shutdown price.

The *shutdown price* is the price below which the firm will choose not to produce any output in the short run.

At any price below the shutdown price, the firm reduces its losses by choosing not to produce at all.

The Firm's Long-Run Supply Curve

Almost exactly the same principles apply in deriving the firm's long-run supply curve as in deriving the short-run supply curve. The firm still wants to set marginal cost equal to price. Figure 8-3 shows the firm's long-run cost curves. The average and marginal cost curves are different from the corresponding short-run curves. In particular, the long-run marginal cost curve, *LMC*, is flatter than *SMC*, reflecting the firm's ability to adjust more factors of production in the long run than in the short run.

Suppose that the competitive firm faces a price, P_4, at which it can sell its output. It

maximizes profits by choosing the level of output where the price is equal to the long-run marginal cost. This is shown by point *D* in Figure 8-3, with output level Q_4. Again we have to consider whether the firm wants to produce this amount or would rather not produce at all. If the firm does not produce in the long run, it leaves the industry.

We recall from Chapter 7 that a firm will stay in operation in the long run so long as price is not below long-run average cost, *LAC*. If price is below *LAC*, then the firm is losing money and should leave the business, or exit. For instance, at price P_2 in Figure 8-3, the firm should in the long run produce zero and go out of business.

The firm's long-run supply curve is therefore the *LMC* curve above point *C*, corresponding to price P_3. Price P_3 is the lowest price at which the firm will be willing to stay in the industry in the long run. At that price it is earning normal profits, which are of course counted in the economic costs measured by the *LAC* curve.

Exit and Entry In looking at price P_3, and

FIGURE 8-4 SHORT-RUN AND LONG-RUN SUPPLY CURVES OF THE COMPETITIVE FIRM. The short-run supply curve (*SRSS*) and the long-run supply curve (*LRSS*) are taken from the previous two figures. *SRSS* is the firm's *SMC* curve above point *A*, while *LRSS* is the firm's *LMC* curve above point *C*. The *SRSS* and *LRSS* curves intersect at point *C*, which in this figure is the point of minimum long-run average cost. This is because the firm is assumed to be operating in the short run with the stock of fixed factors (machinery, buildings, etc.) it uses to produce at the minimum average cost in the long run. For this stock of fixed factors, the short-run shutdown price is P_1. The long-run exit or entry price is P_3.

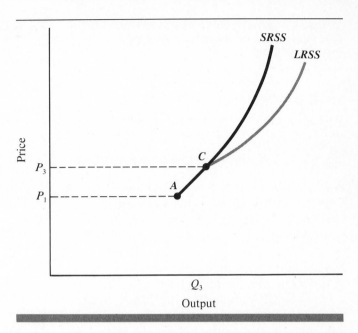

at point *C*, we see that the firm will not produce in the long run if price is below the *minimum* long-run average cost of production, at point *C*. If the price in the industry is below the lowest average cost at which the firm can produce, then the firm is certain to make losses and should not be in this business.

Price P_3, equal to the price at which the firm is just making normal profits, is sometimes called the *exit* or *entry* price for a firm. If the price falls below P_3, the firm will leave the industry, or exit, in the long run. If the price rises above P_3, the firm will want to enter this industry so that it can make above-normal profits.

What determines whether any particular firm will enter an industry? Think of someone who wants to start a business and is looking around for the best opportunity. He considers the profits he could earn in each industry. We can think of him comparing the price in an industry with the average cost at which he could operate. Of course, no one in practice knows exactly what his cost curves would look like in every possi-

ble industry, but an individual probably narrows the range of industries by looking around to see where firms are currently profitable. Then he can make more careful calculations about costs for a few promising industries and enter the industry in which he expects to do best.

The Long-Run and Short-Run Supply Decisions of the Competitive Firm

In Figure 8-4 the short-run and long-run supply curves of the competitive firm are put together. There is a different short-run supply curve corresponding to each given level of fixed factors. In Figure 8-4 we assume that the firm is operating in the short-run with a quantity of fixed factors—the machinery and buildings—corresponding to point *C*, the point of minimum long-run average cost.

The long-run supply curve, *LRSS*, is flatter than the short-run supply curve, *SRSS*. This is because of the extra flexibility the firm has in the long run; in the long run it can adjust more of its factors of production in response to price changes. But the *SRSS*

TABLE 8-2

THE PERFECTLY COMPETITIVE FIRM'S OUTPUT DECISIONS

	CHECK	
BASIC CONDITION	SHORT RUN	LONG RUN
Produce at the level of output where $P = MC$	If $P < SAVC$, shut down	If $P < LAC$, exit from the industry

curve starts from a lower shutdown price than the $LRSS$ curve. This is because the firm in the short run will continue in operation so long as it covers its average variable costs. But in the long run all costs are variable, and the firm will only stay in business if it covers total average costs.

Table 8-2 summarizes the firm's output decisions. For the competitive firm the supply curve is always the marginal cost curve —so long as it makes sense for the firm to produce some output rather than no output at all.

3　THE INDUSTRY SUPPLY CURVES

A competitive industry is made up of many firms. In this section we show how to build up the industry's short-run and long-run supply curves from the supply curves of the individual firms. There is one major difference between the industry's short-run supply curve and its long-run supply curve. In the short run, the number of firms in the industry and their fixed factors are constant. In the long run, the number of firms in the industry can change through the entry and exit of firms, and each firm in the industry can adjust all its inputs to produce as cheaply as possible.

The Short-Run Supply Curve

Figure 8-5 shows how to derive the industry supply curve. Because the short-run and long-run supply curves are derived in similar ways, we do not in Figure 8-5 indicate

whether the supply curves for the firms, SS_A and SS_B, are short-run or long-run. The same basic analysis applies.

In the short run the number of firms in the industry is given. We will start with a case where, for simplicity, there are only two firms, A and B. Each firm is competitive, taking the price as given. Each firm's supply curve is its marginal cost curve above the shutdown price. We have drawn the supply schedules in Figure 8-5 to show that firm A has a lower shutdown price than firm B. The flat parts of the supply curves show that the amount of output supplied by each firm becomes zero at the shutdown price.

We add supply curves by adding together the amounts produced by each firm at each price.[2] For instance, at price P_3, firm A supplies quantity Q_3^A, and firm B supplies Q_3^B. The industry supply is the sum of the quantities supplied by the two firms; in other words, $Q_3 = Q_3^A + Q_3^B$. Q_3 is the industry supply at price P_3. We obtain the complete supply curve of the industry by adding together the amounts produced by the firms in the industry at each price.

The industry supply curve in Figure 8-5 has a peculiar shape. It starts off with a flat segment at price P_1. The output supplied then increases with price. Up to price P_2, the industry supply curve is the same as the supply curve of firm A, since firm A is the only firm producing. At price P_2, firm B enters production, and the industry supply curve flattens out. Now both A and B are supplying output.

When there are many firms in an industry, each with a different shutdown price, the steps in Figure 8-5 become very small. With many firms the industry supply curve is smoother, because a shutdown or opening

---

[2] This process is known as adding the supply curves horizontally. Recall that in Chapter 4 we derived the market demand curve by adding horizontally the demand curves of individual consumers.

FIGURE 8-5   FIRMS' SUPPLY SCHEDULES AND INDUSTRY SUPPLY. The industry supply schedule, *SS*, shows the total quantity supplied at each price by all firms in the industry. The schedule is obtained by adding at each price the quantities supplied by the firms in the industry. This is shown for price P_3 by the horizontal arrows. Since firms can have different shutdown prices, different firms enter at different prices, and therefore the industry supply schedule can have steps such as at points *C* or *D*.

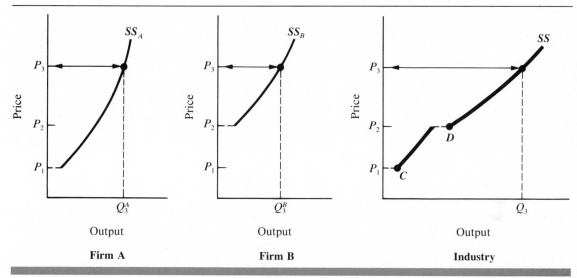

Firm A   Firm B   Industry

by one firm does not make much of a difference to the total quantity supplied.

Short-Run and Long-Run Industry Supply Curves Compared

The derivation of the supply curve in Figure 8-5 basically applies for both short-run and long-run supply curves. The differences arise because of the fixed number of firms and fixed factors in the short run, compared with the fact that both the number of firms and all factors can vary in the long run. In the long run we derive the industry supply curve by using the long-run supply curves of all firms *potentially* in the industry. Every potential producer's *LMC* curve is drawn in a figure such as Figure 8-5. Then the long-run industry supply curve is obtained by adding the firm's supply curves horizontally, with each firm entering the industry at its point of minimum long-run average cost.

Figure 8-6 shows both the short-run and long-run industry supply curves. The long-run supply curve, *LRSS*, is flatter than the short-run curve, *SRSS*. There are two reasons for this. First, the long-run supply curve is flatter for every firm in the industry than the short-run supply curve. A firm can fully adjust its factors of production in the long run. Therefore, a given change in price leads to the adjustment of more inputs in the long run than in the short run and to a greater change in output.

Second, in the long run more firms can come into an industry in response to an increase in price. Entrepreneurs will see profit opportunities in this industry and move in resources in the long run. They do not have time to make these adjustments in the short run.

Similarly, when the price falls, there is a bigger output adjustment in the long run than in the short run. Firms will start to

FIGURE 8-6 SHORT-RUN AND LONG-RUN INDUS-
TRY SUPPLY CURVES. The long-run industry supply
curve, *LRSS,* is flatter than the short-run industry
supply curve, *SRSS.* There are two reasons for this.
First, the supply curve of each firm is flatter in the
long run than in the short run, because the firm can
adjust its inputs more appropriately in the long run
than in the short run. Second, in the long run more
firms can enter the industry in response to an increase in price, or more firms will leave the industry
in response to a fall in price.

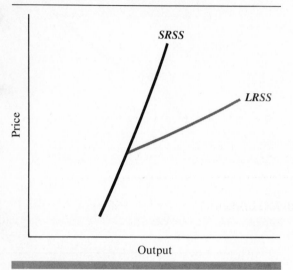

leave the industry. In the long run they
leave if price does not cover average cost;
in the short run they leave only if the
price does not cover variable costs. A firm
that is going to leave the industry in the
long run may stick around in the short run,
producing some output that helps cover its
fixed costs of operation. In the long run it,
too, will leave the industry. Thus output
falls more in the long run than in the short
run in response to a given price change.

The Marginal Firm If there are many different firms with different entry or exit
prices, there will always be a firm or firms
for which the current price is very close to
the entry or exit price. The firm that is just
on the border line in that case is called the
marginal firm. When the price falls, it is the
marginal firms that leave the industry.

When the price rises, the marginal firms
enter the industry. These firms are operating on the margin of entering or leaving the
industry. They are marginal, too, in the
sense that they just cover the average cost
of production and are not making any above-
normal profits.

**The Industry Supply Curve and Marginal
Cost** The industry supply schedule is obtained by adding together the quantities
supplied by firms at each price. At each
price, firms choose an output level such that
marginal cost is equal to price. The implication is that on the industry supply
curve, price is equal to the marginal cost of
production of every firm that is supplying
output.

> The *industry supply curve* can thus be
> defined as the marginal cost curve of the
> industry.

The Horizontal Long-Run Supply Curve
So far we have shown the long-run supply
curve as upward-sloping. But under certain
special conditions it is possible that the
long-run supply curve of a competitive industry is horizontal, or completely flat.

Suppose that all the firms in the industry have the same production technology
and also the same average and marginal cost
curves. The long-run marginal and average
cost curves for a typical firm are shown in
Figure 8-7. The minimum cost of producing
output is with plant size Q^* and a long-run
average cost of LAC^*.

Suppose that the price settles at P_2 in
this industry. At price P_2, every firm in the
industry is making a profit, since price is
above average cost. This means that other
firms will come into the industry to get
some of the profits for themselves. How
do we know that other firms will want to
enter? On the average, owners of firms in
the economy are earning normal profits.
Since profits in this industry are above

FIGURE 8-7 THE MINIMUM-COST PLANT SIZE. Output is produced most cheaply at an average cost equal to LAC*, the minimum point on the long-run average cost curve. The corresponding output level is Q^*, with price P^* being just sufficient to call forth that amount of output. If price were higher, say, at P_2, the firm would be making profits, since price exceeds average cost. The profits would attract new firms into the industry, and these firms would drive price back down toward P^*.

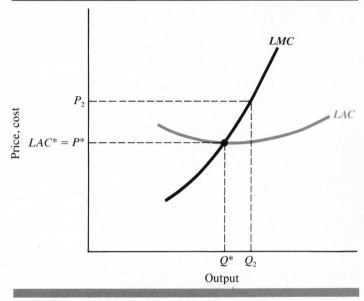

FIGURE 8-8 SHORT-RUN AND LONG-RUN SUPPLY CURVES. When firms have identical cost conditions, as shown in Figure 8-7, then the long-run supply curve, *LRSS,* is horizontal at price P^*. In the short run the supply curve, *SRSS,* slopes upward because the number of firms is fixed. *SRSS* has the same shape as the *SMC* curves of the individual firms. P_1 is the short-run shutdown price at which price falls below short-run average variable cost and firms close down.

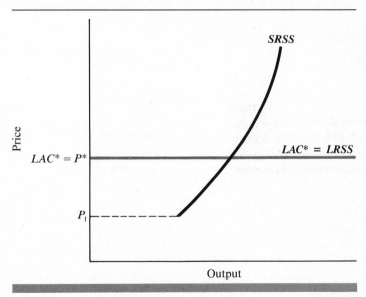

normal (remember, the cost curve includes normal profits), this industry is more attractive than the average one and will attract new firms. As they enter, they will increase the industry's output, thereby causing the equilibrium price to fall. Thus the price cannot in the long run remain at P_2. The only price at which the industry can be in

equilibrium in the long run is where $LAC^* = P^*$. At this price no firm in the industry is making above-normal profits, and none is making a loss. This is therefore a long-run equilibrium for the industry.

The short-run and long-run supply curves for an industry in which the long-run supply curve is horizontal are shown in Figure 8-8. In the short run the number of firms in the industry is fixed, and the supply curve, SRSS, is therefore upward-sloping. Indeed, its shape is precisely that of the short-run marginal cost curve (SMC) of each individual firm, since all firms are identical. The supply curve starts at price P_1, equal to the firm's shutdown price. In the long run the price in this industry will be P^*, because that is the only price at which there is neither entry into nor exit from the industry. The long-run supply curve is thus the horizontal line, LRSS.

Do we expect long-run industry supply curves to be flat in practice in a competitive industry? First let us consider the possibility that the supply curve slopes downward, implying that larger quantities are supplied at lower prices. This suggests that there are economies of scale. But we saw earlier that an industry is not likely to be competitive if there are economies of scale, since then one large firm can produce more cheaply than many small ones, and the industry will not end up with many firms in it. So suppose that economies of scale become unimportant at relatively low levels of output. Thus a downward-sloping supply curve is ruled out.

There are two reasons why long-run supply curves may slope upward. First, not all firms are identical. Management in one firm may be better than in another. Or the factors of production, especially raw materials, may differ in quality from one firm to another. Second, the prices of the inputs used by the industry may rise as industry output rises. Industries typically use some resources that are in short supply in relation to the scale of production. These may be raw materials, such as coal or copper, or some specialized types of labor. As an industry expands, the prices or wages of these factors will rise, and the industry supply curve will therefore have a positive slope.

Thus whether the long-run supply

curve for a competitive industry is horizontal or not cannot be decided purely on logical grounds. It is a matter of fact, which depends on the conditions in each industry.

Profits and Entry

In the short run, when the number of firms is fixed, the firms may be earning profits or suffering losses, depending on whether price is above or below short-run average cost. If price is above average cost for potential entrants, then they will be attracted into the industry by the possibility of earning profits. If the firms are suffering losses, some of them will elect to leave the industry in the long run.

If the cost conditions for all the firms are the same, then no firm will be earning above-normal profits in the long run. Above-normal profits are competed away by entry in a competitive industry. If an industry is not competitive and entry is blocked, then profits can continue to be made even in the long run. For instance, liquor stores may earn above-normal profits in the long run because entry is controlled through licensing.

If the long-run supply curve of a competitive industry is not horizontal—for example, because some firms are more efficient than others—then the more efficient firms will have (above-normal) profits in the long run. It is only the marginal firm which does not earn any profits in the long run. It is precisely because it is not earning any excess profits that it is marginal. If there is any drop in price, it leaves the industry. The owner will prefer to go into another line of business.

4 ADJUSTMENT TO A SHIFT IN THE DEMAND FOR COAL

Figure 8-9 represents the market for coal. The demand curve is shown as DD. The short-run supply curve is SRSS, and the

FIGURE 8-9 A SHIFT IN DEMAND IN A COMPETITIVE COAL MARKET. The demand for coal shifts from *DD* to *DD'*. In the short run, price rises from P_0 to P' as the equilibrium moves from *A* to *A'*. Then over time, as new mines come into operation and the capacities of existing mines are increased, the long-run supply schedule becomes relevant. In the long run, the industry moves to point *A''* on the long-run supply curve, *LRSS*. In the short run, then, output increases and price rises as the industry moves from *A* to *A'*. Thereafter, output expands and price falls; the industry moves from *A'* to *A''*.

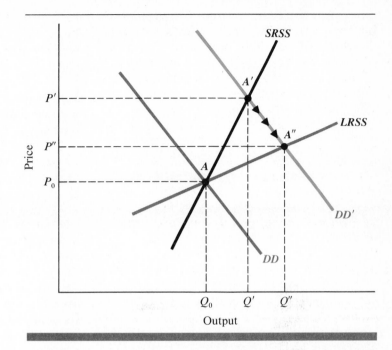

The long-run supply curve is *LRSS*. The short-run supply curve is very steep because, in the short run, increases in the amount of coal supplied have to come from existing mines. We assume that there are sharply increasing marginal costs of production for the existing mines in the short run.

The long-run supply curve is much flatter. This is because new mines can open in the long run, and workers in the existing mines can drill new shafts, install new machinery, and train new miners. But it is not horizontal, because the quality of the coal deposits varies, and not all firms have the same cost conditions.

We will now see how coal output and the price of coal are affected by a shift in the demand for coal. Specifically, we will look at the effects of the increase in oil prices in 1973–1974. The increase is shown by the shift of the demand curve from *DD* to *DD'* in Figure 8-9. Demanders want more coal at each given price.

As a result of the shift in demand, the equilibrium price of coal rises from P_0 to P' in the short run. Coal output rises from Q_0 to Q'. This simple model of the coal market therefore predicts that with the increase in the price of oil, we should see increases in both the price of coal and coal production in the short run.

Table 8-3 shows that the prediction is borne out by the facts. The table includes indexes of coal output and of the real price of coal. The real price of coal is the dollar price adjusted for inflation. The indexes are set equal to 100 for the 1970–1973 pre–oil shock period.

In 1974–1977, after the price of oil tripled, there was a 50 percent increase in the price of coal and a modest 12 percent rise in the production of coal. This is the type of response our analysis in Figure 8-9 predicted in the move from *A* to *A'*.

Table 8-3 tells us more. For the period 1978–1980, output rises a lot, and the price falls back. This is a reflection of the long-run adjustment of a competitive industry. In this case more mines are opened, increasing long-run supply and therefore reducing

TABLE 8-3

U.S. COAL OUTPUT AND REAL PRICES OF COAL
(Bituminous Coal)

PERIOD	REAL PRICE OF COAL*	COAL PRODUCTION*
1970–1973	100	100
1974–1977	152	112
1978–1980	145	129

* Index for 1970–1973 = 100.
Source: Survey of Current Business, various issues.

TABLE 8-4

ADJUSTMENT IN THE COAL-MINING INDUSTRY

YEAR	REAL PRICE*	NO. OF ESTABLISH-MENTS	EMPLOYEES
1972	102	3365	155,000
1977	147	5275	242,000

* Index for 1970–1973 = 100.
Source: Statistical Abstract of the United States, 1981,
Table 1306.

price. This is the shift in the equilibrium from A' to A''.

The shift from A' to A'' takes place slowly, as new mines come into operation. The supply schedule is shifting all the while, starting with the *SRSS* curve, and eventually ending up as *LRSS*. But in between, before the full adjustment has been made, there are "intermediate-run" supply curves for the industry. These lie between *SRSS* and *LRSS*. The intersections of these curves with the *DD'* curve result in the shifting equilibrium between points A' and A'' in Figure 8-9.

Table 8-4 shows some more details of the adjustment in the coal-mining industry. Here we compare two years (1972 and 1977) for which data are available on the number of coal-mining establishments and the number of people employed in the industry.

Table 8-4 shows that along with the 45 percent increase in price over the period,

there was a very substantial expansion of the mining industry. The number of mining establishments increased more than 50 percent, as did employment in the mining sector. We have already seen that output expanded substantially. Table 8-4 shows that a large part of the increase in output resulted from new mines coming into operation.

5 MORE ON SHORT-RUN AND LONG-RUN ADJUSTMENT IN A COMPETITIVE INDUSTRY

The pattern of price and output adjustment in the coal industry to a shift in demand is shown in Figure 8-9. An alternative way of viewing that adjustment is shown in Figure 8-10. Here we plot price and quantity against time, showing how price and quantity change in response to a shift in demand at time T_0 (1973 in the case of coal).

The initial response is that the price rises from P_0 to P', and the quantity rises as well, from Q_0 to Q'. Then as time goes on, existing firms expand their capacity, and new firms come into the industry. The price begins to fall back from P' as output increases. The price continues to fall until it reaches the new equilibrium at P''. The quantity that corresponds to this new, long-run equilibrium level is Q''.

Note that the price changes more in the short run than in the long run. Price P' is above P'', the price that is eventually reached. The price is said to overshoot its long-run value in this case. The overshooting is an essential part of the adjustment of the market to the shift in demand.

Prices, Profits, and Adjustment

When prices, such as the price of coal, increase sharply in response to a shift in demand, existing users regard the price increases as undesirable and perhaps intolerable. Anger over price increases is greater if higher prices just mean higher

FIGURE 8-10 THE ADJUSTMENT OF PRICE AND QUANTITY OVER TIME. A shift in demand—an increase in the demand for a good—results in an immediate increase in the price of the good and in the quantity produced. Then as capacity is expanded and new firms enter the industry, price begins to fall, while quantity continues rising. Because price initially rises above the level it ultimately reaches, it is said to *overshoot* its long-run value.

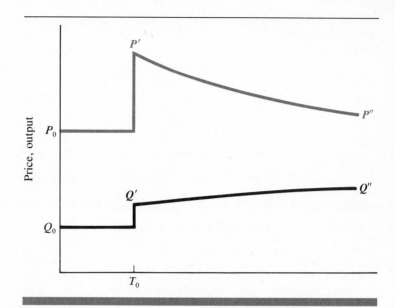

profits for existing producers and there is not much of an increase in the quantity supplied—as in the case of the coal industry in the short run. You can easily imagine consumer advocates and coal users arguing that the higher coal prices represent an unjustified transfer from the poor users to the undeserving owners of the coal mines.

It is largely true that in the short run, certainly in industries with sharply rising marginal costs, an increase in demand will lead mainly to an increase in profits. The situation will be one in which every firm in the industry is producing at prices well above average costs. But these short-run profits—they are often called *windfall profits*—are an important element in the adjustment process. They serve as a signal to potential entrants that this is an industry that can profitably be entered. Entry is the means by which the long-run supply is increased and by which the price moves toward a lower level. Policies that attempt to deprive the industry of its short-run profits may well do long-run harm by preventing entry and the expansion of supply.

6 ADJUSTMENTS TO DEMAND CHANGES IN THE MARKET FOR WOOL

In the remainder of this chapter, we use the model of the competitive industry to study real-world problems. We have already studied the effects of a shift in the demand for coal. Our second application is to study long-run changes in the wool market. The principles here are similar to those used in studying changes in the coal industry.

Throughout the post–World War II period, synthetic fibers have made large inroads on the markets for natural fibers. Indeed, even before World War II, the invention of the nylon stocking devastated the silk industry. In the case of wool, acrylic and other artificial fibers are cheaper and easier to wash than wool and have displaced wool in socks, sweaters, and other garments.

The invention and use of synthetic fibers must have had an impact on the market for wool. This is a market where we can certainly use the competitive model. There

TABLE 8-5

**WOOL AND SHEEP
(U.S. Data)**

YEAR	SHEEP, millions	CONSUMPTION OF WOOL FOR APPAREL*	REAL PRICE OF WOOL*
1955	27.1	100	100
1965	25.1	98	72
1975	14.5	33	51
1980	12.7	40	59

* Index for 1955 = 100.
Source: Statistical Abstract of the United States, 1981, Table 1246, and *Survey of Current Business,* various issues.

FIGURE 8-11   THE LONG-RUN DECLINE IN THE DEMAND FOR WOOL LOWERS THE REAL PRICE OF WOOL. Synthetic fibers replace wool in the production of clothing. The demand schedule for wool therefore shifts to the left. With less wool demanded at each price, there is a decline in the price of wool and in the quantity supplied.

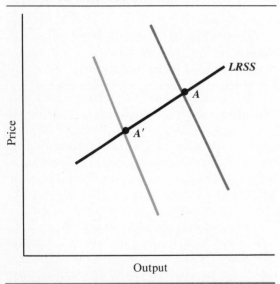

real price of wool is also shown, as well as the number of sheep on U.S. farms.

Table 8-5 shows that from 1955 to 1975 the real price of wool fell by 50 percent, while the consumption of wool decreased to only 33 percent of the 1955 level. We show the relevant analysis in Figure 8-11. The initial demand schedule is *DD*, and point *A* represents the 1955 equilibrium. Over time the demand gradually shifts away from wool and toward synthetic fibers. Therefore, at each price, the quantity demanded falls. By 1975 the demand schedule is in a position such as *DD'*. But over time the farmers also adjust, reducing the number of sheep. They are therefore on their long-run supply schedule, *LRSS*, and they reach a point such as *A'* in 1975. The table confirms that over the 20-year period there was a decrease in the demand for wool, a drop in the real price of wool, and a large fall in the number of sheep on farms.

There was an interesting reversal of the consumption and real-price patterns at the end of the 1970s. In this period there was an increase in the use of wool for apparel, accompanied by a rise in the price. Two factors interacted here. One was the rise in the price of oil, which made artificial fibers more expensive. This increase in the price of a substitute shifted the demand curve for wool to the right, raising both the price and the quantity. Second, Australia (the world's

are many sheep farmers producing wool, and none of them is able to affect the market price, because each taken separately is only a small part of the industry.

Table 8-5 shows key data for the U.S. wool market. The amount of wool consumption (apparel class) in the United States is shown as an index; it is 100 in 1955. The

largest wool producer) experienced a drought. This reduced the quantity of wool supplied to the market, and thus the price rose. The net result of the two factors was a rise in price (due to shifts in both demand and the quantity supplied) and a rise in the quantity used for apparel (with the shift in demand outweighing the results of the drought in Australia).

In the next section we will look in more detail at interactions between the domestic market for a good and foreign markets. We will see how a drought in Australia affects wool prices in the United States.

7 COMPETITION IN WORLD MARKETS

Changes in conditions in domestic markets are often the results of events taking place in other countries. Oil prices in the United States change when foreign oil producers change their prices. Wool prices in the United States change when Australia suffers from a drought. U.S. gold prices rise when Middle Eastern demand increases. In this section we show how competitive markets in different countries are linked and why shifts in supply or demand curves abroad affect domestic supplies and demanders.

One implication of international trade is that price movements in markets in different countries are related.

> The law of one price in international trade is that if there were no obstacles to trade and no costs of transporting goods, the price of a given good would be the same all over the world.

Why would the price be the same everywhere if there were no costs of transporting goods and no other obstacles to trade? The behavior of both suppliers and demanders would ensure this. Suppliers would want to sell only where the price was highest. If the price in one country was higher than the

price somewhere else, suppliers would shift supply to the country with the higher price, driving down the price in that country. Similarly, demanders would buy only where the good was cheapest, driving up the price in that country and driving down the price in other countries. There could be an equilibrium only if the price were the same everywhere.

In practice, transportation costs and restrictions on trade such as tariffs (taxes applied specifically to imports) make the prices of goods differ internationally. In practical terms, the law of one price suggests that the prices of a given good in different countries tend to move in the same direction. There are links between markets in different countries that ensure that prices in one country are affected by events in other countries.

We will now develop a supply-demand model for two countries that trade with each other to show how events in one country affect the market in the other country.

Equilibrium in the World Market

We start with two countries, the home country and the rest of the world, each considered in isolation. (We talk of the rest of the world as if it is a single country.) Figure 8-12*a* shows the home country's demand and supply curves for a commodity— say, wool. The supply and demand schedules of the foreign country (the rest of the world) are shown in Figure 8-12*b*.

If the two countries cannot trade with each other, each market reaches equilibrium independently of the other. Equilibrium in the home country is at point *A*. Abroad, equilibrium is at point *B*. With the two markets in isolation, wool is more expensive in the United States than abroad.

Now suppose we open up the possibility of trade in wool. There will be immediate trade. Every foreign producer will want to sell in the high-priced U.S. market, and

FIGURE 8-12   AN INTEGRATED WORLD MARKET. Many of the events that change prices in domestic markets occur abroad. Domestic firms compete not only with each other but also with firms abroad. The diagram shows how price is determined in a world market in which there are no obstacles to trade. The price must be the same at home and abroad in equilibrium. At that price, the amount foreigners want to export (or import) has to be equal to the amount we want to import (or export). The diagram shows an equilibrium in which we are the importers of a good and foreigners are the exporters. With trade, price at home ($\overline{P}$) is lower than it would be if there were no trade (P_h). Price abroad ($\overline{P}$—the world price) is higher than it would be if there were no trade (P_f).

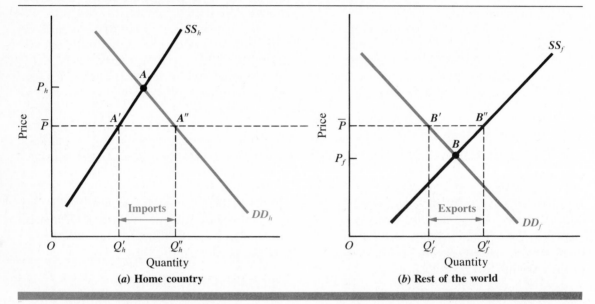

(a) **Home country**   (b) **Rest of the world**

our consumers will want to buy the low-priced foreign wool. Our market will be flooded with imports, and these will immediately drive down our price. But the quantity supplied to foreign buyers will be reduced because the foreign firms are selling in the U.S. market rather than in their own country. Therefore, the reduction in the quantity supplied in the foreign market must raise the price.

Where is the new equilibrium? The only possible equilibrium in the absence of barriers to trade is where the price is exactly equalized so that any producer is indifferent between selling here and selling there. Similarly, no buyer can get a better deal in one country than in the other. But in equilibrium, world quantity demanded must also be equal to world quantity supplied.

Thus the new equilibrium will be at the point where the world quantity demanded is equal to the world quantity supplied at the world price. Figure 8-12 shows how to find the new equilibrium. In the new equilibrium, the price will be somewhere between the prices at home and abroad before the opening of trade (P_h and P_f, respectively). Foreign suppliers will be selling some of their output to us. We will be importing wool from abroad, and foreign producers will be exporting wool to us. Equilibrium in the world market will be at the price level where the amount foreigners want to export to us is equal to the amount we want to import.

In terms of Figure 8-12, our demand for imports is equal to our excess demand for wool. For instance, at price $\overline{P}$ in Figure

8-12a our demand for imports is equal to the distance shown by the arrows between Q_h' and Q_h''. At price $\overline{P}$, the domestic quantity supplied is equal to Q_h', and the quantity demanded is equal to Q_h''. The difference is made up by imports.

At the same price, $\overline{P}$, foreigners want to sell the amount of exports shown by the arrows in Figure 8-12b, the difference between Q_f' and Q_f''. Q_f'' is the amount foreign suppliers want to sell at price $\overline{P}$, and Q_f' is the quantity demanded by foreigners at that price. The difference, or excess supply, is equal to the amount foreigners would like to export at that price.

Price $\overline{P}$ is the new world equilibrium price of wool. At that price, and only at that price, the amount foreigners want to export to the United States is equal to the amount we want to import. The total world quantity supplied by American and foreign producers together is equal to the total world quantity demanded by American and foreign producers.

You might want to check the logic of the argument. We started by saying that the world price will be between the prices that existed in the two countries before the opening of trade. But why? The reason is that if the price is not between P_h and P_f, both countries will want to be either exporters or importers. If the price is above P_h, both countries will want to export. If the price is below P_f, both countries will want to import. Such prices cannot be equilibrium prices, because the imports of one country are the exports of the other. We can't have both countries in a two-country world exporting. Nor can we have both countries importing. This means that the world price in the new equilibrium has to be between the two closed-economy prices.

Opening ourselves to trade is a two-sided affair. If we are initially the high-priced country, as in Figure 8-12, then domestic producers will be hurt by the opening of trade because prices will be competed down by the low-cost foreign producers. Therefore, at home, some firms will suffer losses and have to go out of business; they will be displaced by competition from imports. But there is an offsetting advantage. Domestic purchasers will be able to spend less for wool; therefore they will buy more of it.

Abroad, we have the other side of the coin. Foreign producers will benefit by selling abroad at a higher price than they previously received. Foreign purchasers will be hurt as their own suppliers divert goods that used to be sold at home to markets abroad.

Effects of Changes Abroad on the Home Market

When our industries compete in world markets, any change in supply or demand conditions anywhere in the world is communicated to our own market and affects the prices we pay. Suppose a drought in Australia reduces the production of Australian wool. The quantity of wool supplied in the world market at each price is reduced. The world prices of wool, including the price paid in our market, rise.

Figure 8-13 shows how higher world wool prices affect our market. The figure is just Figure 8-12a. We start in equilibrium with world price $\overline{P}$. In the domestic market, the quantity demanded is Q_d, and the quantity supplied is Q_s. The difference is made up by imports; it is equal to $Q_d - Q_s$.

Now suppose that there is a drought in Australia and the world price rises to $\overline{P}'$. At the higher world price, our consumers buy the amount Q_d'. Domestic production rises to Q_s'—our producers respond to the higher world price by increasing their output. At the higher world price, we have fewer imports. Now the quantity of imports is equal to $Q_d' - Q_s'$. There are two reasons for the drop in the quantity of imports. The first

FIGURE 8-13 THE IMPACT OF HIGHER WORLD PRICES IN THE HOME MARKET. Initially the home country faces the world price $\bar{P}$. At that price, quantity demanded is Q_d, and quantity supplied is Q_s. The amount of imports is equal to $Q_d - Q_s$. Then the world price rises, because of a drought abroad, to $\bar{P}'$. In response, quantity demanded at home falls, and quantity supplied increases; therefore, the amount of imports falls. The home country thus participates in the adjustments to changes in world supply or demand conditions.

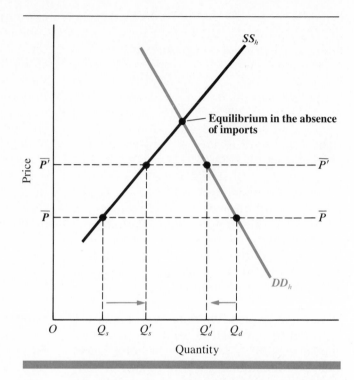

reason is that consumers demand less at the higher price. The second reason is that domestic production and the quantity supplied rise in response to the higher price.

The effects of world market conditions on domestic prices are particularly clear in the case of agricultural commodities. Whenever there is a harvest failure in Russia, the increase in Russia's wheat imports pushes up the equilibrium price in the world, including the prices U.S. consumers pay. Of course, while that is a blessing for U.S. farmers, it is a blow to U.S. consumers of wheat.

The Rest of the World as a Shock Absorber

It is easy to conclude from the discussion of drought in Australia and harvest failure in Russia that the rest of the world is mainly a nuisance for domestic consumers. Prices go up and down because of problems in the rest of the world. But trade is always a two-way street. It is also true that foreign trade is a shock absorber for the United States as well as a source of disturbances that change the prices U.S. consumers pay.

Foreign producers and demanders act as shock absorbers for shifts in U.S. supply and demand. For instance, suppose that the U.S. supply curve for a commodity shifts upward because of a drought. The price begins to rise. As the price rises foreigners cut back their purchases, and foreign suppliers increase their production. U.S. consumers draw on both foreign producers and foreign consumers to help make up for the decrease in the quantity supplied in the domestic market. That is, there is an increase in the quantity U.S. consumers import. The result is a smaller price increase than would have happened without trade.

Of course, the same principles apply to trade within the United States. If the United States were not united and each state did not trade with the others, the prices in each

FIGURE 8-14　ELASTICITY OF DEMAND AND PRICE FLUCTUATIONS. This figure shows the effects of the elasticity of demand on price changes in response to shifts in supply. Demand is less elastic on demand curve DD' than on demand curve DD. Initially the market is in equilibrium at point E, with price P_0. The supply curve then shifts to SS'. Price rises to P' if the demand curve is DD and to P'' if the demand curve is DD'. Price thus rises more on the less elastic demand curve. The point of the diagram is to show why prices fluctuate a lot in agricultural markets, where demand is typically inelastic.

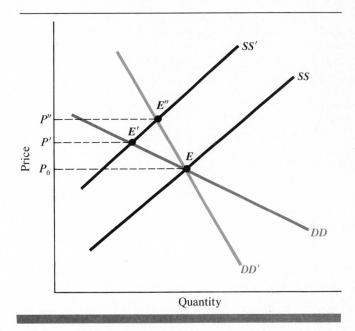

state would fluctuate much more than they do now. For example, think of Florida and California citrus products. When there is a freeze in Florida, the prices of oranges increase. But California citrus products help to soften the effects of the freeze, as an alternative source of supply is available to consumers.

8　AGRICULTURAL PRICE PROGRAMS

In many countries governments have programs to affect the prices of agricultural products. The aims of these programs differ. In some countries the price of bread is kept low so that there is at least one food that even the very poor can afford. In other cases, farmers are politically powerful, and governments try to keep them happy by making sure the prices they receive don't fall too much. Also, governments feel that the fluctuations in food prices that would occur if the prices were not controlled would be excessive—and politically unpopular.

Agricultural Price Fluctuations

Agricultural prices in free markets fluctuate a lot. The reason is that the demand for many agricultural products is inelastic. Figure 8-14 shows why the elasticity of the demand curve affects the extent to which the price changes in response to a given shift of the supply curve.

In Figure 8-14 we show two demand curves, DD and DD'. Suppose that the market is initially in equilibrium at point E, with price P_0. Then the supply curve shifts from SS to SS'. If the demand curve is DD, the more elastic demand curve, the equilibrium shifts to point E', with price P'. If the demand curve is DD', which is less elastic, the price rises to P''. The price rises more when the demand curve is less elastic; that is, price P'' is above P'.

In addition, the short-run supply curves of agricultural products are quite inelastic. As we saw in Chapter 5, with inelastic supply curves there are larger price changes in response to shifts in demand. Because both producers and consumers prefer stable

FIGURE 8-15 A GOVERNMENT PRICE SUPPORT PROGRAM. In the absence of government intervention, the competitive market would clear at price P_e. But the government supports the price at level $\overline{P}$, standing ready to buy or sell any amount at that price. The diagram shows the case where there is excess supply. The government has to buy up the amount $Q_s - Q_d$ and add it to its stocks. Alternatively, the government could sell off all its purchases (Q_s) to consumers at price P_c. The government would lose ($\overline{P} - P_c$) on each unit (gallon of milk, for example) sold.

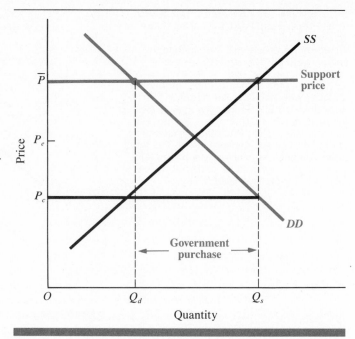

prices to the uncertainty of fluctuating prices, governments frequently attempt to stabilize the prices of agricultural goods.

How a Price Stabilization Scheme Works

Figure 8-15 shows how a government price stabilization program works in an otherwise competitive market. Without government intervention, price would be P_e. But the government decides a higher price is appropriate. It fixes a price, $\overline{P}$, for the commodity. It announces that it is willing to buy or sell the commodity at that price. As we have drawn the diagram, the government has to buy amount $Q_s - Q_d$ of the commodity, since at price $\overline{P}$ the quantity supplied is Q_s, while the quantity demanded is only Q_d.

What does the government do with its purchases? One possibility is to store them in case there is a shift in supply or demand that results in an excess demand for the commodity at price $\overline{P}$. If there is a drought and the supply curve shifts sharply to the left, then the government will be in the fa-

vorable position of being able to sell off its stocks of the good at the price it has fixed, $\overline{P}$. If the government succeeds in fixing its support price at about the average free market price of the commodity, it may on the average come out about right—buying in years when the price would otherwise be low and selling in years when the price would otherwise be high.

Of course, the government may make mistakes. If in some years it runs out of stocks of the good, then it will let the market price rise. If it sets the support price so high that year after year it has to buy up the good, then it will find itself with increasing quantities of the commodity, and it will have to figure out what to do with its stocks. We read in the newspapers about the mountains of butter that European governments have been building through their dairy price supports. They try to get rid of the butter by selling it to other countries. For instance, in 1981 the European Common Market sold butter to the Russians at very low prices in order to get rid of the huge amounts they didn't have any place to keep. Similarly, in 1981 and 1982 the U.S. government distributed free cheese and butter to some people to reduce government stocks.

Stabilization for Suppliers Only

A second plan is for the government to sell off the excess amount of its purchases to consumers. Thus in Figure 8-15, the government could set a price for consumers of P_c and sell off its purchases at a lower price than it paid for them. The government would lose $(\overline{P} - P_c)$ on each unit sold to consumers. Such a scheme stabilizes prices for producers, but it does not stabilize prices for consumers. When the supply curve shifts, consumers find the price they pay changing.

If $\overline{P}$ were ever below the market clearing price—for instance, in a year when the demand curve shifted to the right or the supply curve to the left—then the government would buy up products from the farmers at $\overline{P}$ and sell them to consumers at a higher price.

Under this scheme, the government would not have to store the goods. In some years it would make a profit, and in others it would suffer a loss. With luck, it could even set the price so that it comes out even.

Such schemes have been used in countries that export most of a single, major (in terms of the economy's total production) crop. The government guarantees price $\overline{P}$ and sells the crop at the world price. The world price changes from year to year, and in any given year the government may come out ahead or behind. But it takes the risks of price changes in place of the farmers.

U.S. Agriculture Support Programs

The U.S. government, like many others, intervenes actively in setting agricultural prices. Two methods are used. For some commodities there is a loan program. The main commodities here are wheat, corn, cotton, sugar, and tobacco. For others the government makes direct purchases of goods. The dairy program is one example of this method.

The Loan Program The government announces a target, or support, price. If the market price falls below the target level, farmers can borrow from the government, giving their output as collateral. Collateral on a loan is given in case the borrower does not repay. Then the lender gets the collateral instead. The output given as collateral is valued at its target, or support, price.

Under such a program a borrower in effect gets money from the federal government in exchange for his goods at the target price. The farmer then stores his output—wheat or corn—and waits until the loan has to be repaid. If in the meantime the value of the goods given as collateral rises (e.g., if the price of wheat rises), the farmer sells the goods, repays the loan, and comes out ahead. If the value of the goods does not rise, the farmer does not repay the loan. The government gets the goods and decides what to do with them—it either stores them or sells them.

In this way the government helps farmers by allowing them to store goods in years when the price is low and sell them in years when the price is high. This tends to stabilize the price. But if the price is low for a number of years, a government agency, the Commodity Credit Corporation (CCC), ends up with the goods, since the farmers are better off not repaying the loans. Instead, they sell the goods to the government at the target price.

Direct Purchases For some commodities, such as milk, the government makes direct purchases to prevent the price from falling below the target level. The program works as follows. The government determines a price for milk that will assure a given standard of living for the farmers.

Historically, the price that the government sets has been determined by the so-called parity ratio.

The *parity ratio* expresses the purchasing power of agricultural products in terms of the prices farmers pay for goods and services. The index for the base years 1910–1914 is 100.

Presently, the dairy parity ratio is just above 80, meaning that the government maintains the purchasing power of dairy products at 80 percent of what it was 70 years ago. The government makes its support policy work by purchasing storable dairy products—butter, cheese, dry milk—when the quantity supplied exceeds the quantity demanded.

The risk of picking too high a support price and thus encouraging excess production is very large. According to a congressional report:

The dairy price support program has increased farm milk prices at the expense of consumers and tax payers, but it also has helped to stabilize the dairy industry, resulting in an assured supply of milk and dairy products. In the past two years, however, high milk prices have contributed to a sharp expansion in milk production. In 1981, the commercial milk supply exceeded commercial use by about 10 percent, and the federal government purchased the excess at a cost of almost $2 billion. The government inventory of cheese, butter, and nonfat dry milk is nearly three times as large as commercial stocks.[3]

The study concludes that Congress should gradually reduce the support price to avoid a *growing* imbalance between supply and demand and therefore the continuing growth of government stocks. The study expresses the fear that if the support price is not reduced, the industry will keep growing, and government purchases and stocks of dairy products will reach ever higher levels.

The government's fixing of prices under dairy support programs and the consequent buildup of government stocks is in contrast to how a free market would work. If price rose in a free market, more suppliers would enter the market. Price would be driven down and eventually reach its equilibrium level. That could, of course, take a while. But with government programs for fixing prices, nothing checks the increase in the quantity supplied. The government has to buy up output; it builds up its stocks and ends up giving away dairy products to get rid of its stocks.

[3] Congressional Budget Office, *Reducing the Federal Deficit*, part III, February 1982, p. 95. See, too, Bruce L. Gardner, *Governing Agriculture*, The Regents Press of Kansas, 1981.

SUMMARY

1   The structures of markets differ according to the behavior of the firms and purchasers in each market. If both suppliers and demanders believe they have no effect on the market price in the industry, then the market is competitive. Each seller and each buyer takes the price as given. If either buyers or sellers believe their own actions influence the market price, the market is imperfectly competitive.

2   The three chief forms of imperfect competition on the side of the firms are monopolistic competition, oligopoly, and monopoly. The

main feature that distinguishes each of these forms of market structure is the number of firms in the industry. There are many firms under monopolistic competition and one under monopoly.

3   A competitive firm, like any other firm, chooses the level of output where marginal revenue is equal to marginal cost. The difference is that for a competitive firm, marginal revenue is equal to price. A competitive firm is small in relation to the size of the market.

4   The supply curve of a competitive firm is the marginal cost curve, provided that at those output levels, the firm makes more profits (or has smaller losses) by producing than by shutting down. This means that in the short run, the competitive firm's supply curve is its short-run marginal cost curve for prices above short-run average variable cost. In the long run, the supply curve is the long-run marginal cost curve above long-run average cost.

5   The industry supply curve is derived by adding, at each price, the quantities supplied by all the firms in the industry. As the price rises, industry output supplied rises, both because existing firms supply more and because firms that had not been able to earn profits at a lower price can now cover average costs and enter operation.

6   The long-run industry supply curve is more elastic than the short-run supply curve. In the long run each firm can choose its optimal plant size, and new firms can enter the industry. If the industry does not use specialized resources (for example, oil or coal deposits) or face increasing input prices as the demand for factors of production increases, and if all the firms have the same technology, then the long-run industry supply schedule is flat at the level of minimum long-run average cost. Otherwise, a competitive industry will have an upward-sloping long-run supply curve.

7   A rightward shift of the demand curve in a competitive market will lead in the short run to an increase in price. The short-run price increase is larger the less price-elastic are demand and supply. But in the long run, industry supply expands through entry and an increase in plant size. The long-run adjustment of supply results in a reduction of any profits that firms make in the short run. The short-run profits are the signal for entry and expansion.

8   A leftward shift of the demand curve leads in the short run to a large reduction in price. Existing firms are willing to operate even at some loss as long as fixed costs are partially covered. But in the long run, losses cannot be sustained, and marginal firms will leave the industry. Thus there will be a reduction in the quantity supplied at each price. This reduction in the quantity supplied implies that in the long run, the price falls less and output more than in the short run.

9   In the wool market the appearance of synthetic fibers reduced the

demand for wool and led to a long-term decline both in the real price of wool and in production. This is a typical case of adjustment in a competitive market; declining demand forces the industry to contract.

10   Markets are linked through international trade. Our firms have access to the world market, and foreign firms compete with ours in the domestic market. This integration with the world market, although it is hampered by transportation costs and often by tariffs, implies that prices in different countries move in the same direction. It implies that supply shortages are alleviated by the possibility of imports. But it also implies that foreign shortages result in fewer imports for us or more exports from us—and ultimately, therefore, in higher prices at home.

11   Free, competitive markets may show large fluctuations in price in response to harvest failures or bumper crops. These price fluctuations upset consumers and producers. Various government price-support programs attempt to stabilize prices. But here is a good example of how competitive adjustment works. If the government sets a price that is too high, then in the long run there will be a great increase in supply. Ultimately, the government will have to purchase output year after year from the firms which it has itself put into business.

KEY TERMS

Monopoly	Entry (of new firms into the industry)
Market structure	Exit (of existing firms from the industry)
Perfect competition	Marginal firm
Imperfect competition	Overshooting
Oligopoly	Law of one price
Monopolistic competition	Shock absorbers
Free markets	Price stabilization
Shutdown price	Parity ratio

PROBLEMS

1   Draw a diagram of two firms and the industry supply curve such as the one shown in Figure 8-5. Draw also the demand curve for the good. (a) Show the industry equilibrium, and trace back from the equilibrium price to show each firm's output level and profits. (b) Suppose that demand shifts to the right. Show the new equilibrium in the market and for each firm. (c) Which firm is the marginal firm?

2   (a) Why is the long-run supply curve of a firm more elastic than the short-run supply curve? (b) Why is the long-run supply curve of an industry more elastic than the short-run supply curve?

3   Assume that the market for cigarettes is in long-run equilibrium. The surgeon general then warns people that cigarette smoking is hazardous to their health. People are

very scared about smoking at first and less scared in the long run—but they are still more scared than they used to be. (*a*) Describe what happens to the price of cigarettes and the quantity smoked in the long run. (*b*) Describe the adjustment in the price and quantity over time. Take into account the fact that people's fears were greatest when the surgeon general's warning was first issued.

4   Describe the effects of the surgeon general's warning on (*a*) the market for chewing gum and (*b*) the market for matches in the short run and in the long run. In each case, do you expect more of an adjustment in the price or in the quantity? Why?

5   Suppose that the wheat crop is hit by a drought. (*a*) Explain the adjustment in the price of wheat in the short run and in the long run. (*b*) How is the price of bread affected in the short run and in the long run?

6   In the 1950s and 1960s, the U.S. government paid farmers not to use certain areas of their lands for production. Why would such a program be an alternative to providing price supports for farmers?

7   Suppose that a country is very small and has no effect on the world price of a good it produces and consumes. (It is like a perfect competitor in the world market.) Draw the demand and supply curves for that good for domestic consumers and producers. Show in a diagram how the amounts of the country's exports and imports are determined. In particular, show the world price at which the country would neither import nor export—that is, the price at which it would just consume the amount it produces.

8   (*a*) Distinguish between a competitive market and a free market. (*b*) Suppose that in a market that is currently free, with an upward-sloping long-run supply curve, the government fixes the price below the long-run equilibrium level. No firm is allowed to charge more than the government's price. Show what happens to the quantity produced in the short run and in the long run. (*c*) Does your analysis throw any light on the question of whether the worst effects of price controls are likely to show up in the short run or in the long run?

9   In the text we assumed that the buying side of the market is competitive. Sometimes, though, buyers try to get together to affect price. For instance, in 1973 there was a large increase in the price of meat. Consumers got together to organize groups to boycott (that is, to not buy) meat at the existing prices. They hoped that the boycott would drive the price down. (*a*) Explain what they were trying to do in terms of shifting the demand curve. (*b*) Suppose that meat supply is inelastic. Does an attempt to get everyone to agree to buy less meat at the existing price make sense? (*c*) Why don't consumers organize themselves in this way to affect prices more often?

10   The 1981 *Economic Report of the President* includes the following statement: "One way to reduce the economy's vulnerability to disruptions of foreign oil supplies would be to increase the short-run responsiveness of domestic production and consumption to short-term changes in price and supply" (page 93). (*a*) What does the report mean by "short-run responsiveness of domestic production and consumption"? Use supply and demand curves. (*b*) Why would an increase in the short-run responsiveness of domestic production and consumption reduce our vulnerability to disruptions of foreign oil supplies? (*Note:* This is not an easy question.)

The competitive firm can sell any amount of the good it produces at the market price. It is too small to worry about the effects of its own output decision on market price. An individual wheat farmer deciding how much to plant certainly tries to figure out what the price of the wheat will be when harvested—he tries to guess, for instance, whether the Russians will be buying heavily and what the weather will be. But he does not have to take into account the effect his own output decision will have on price. That effect is negligible.

9

Monopoly and Imperfect Competition

In many industries, though, firms know they are too big a part of the market for their actions not to affect price. Further, firms in such industries are likely to pay careful attention to what other firms in the industry are doing: Ford worries about General Motors's new models and prices; the Kellogg Company worries about General Mills; and one supermarket chain worries about the other's specials for the week.

The competitive model of the last chapter is extremely useful, as the applications to the coal industry, wool, imports, and agriculture showed. But the competitive model cannot be used when firms know that their own output decisions affect price and set their prices accordingly. When firms set output taking account of their own influence on price, there is *imperfect competition*.

Table 9-1 reminds us of the three main forms of imperfect competition, which were described in more detail in Table 8-1. The monopolist provides *all* the supply in his industry. Since the industry demand curve slopes downward, a monopolist can only sell more output—the industry's output—by reducing the price. For that reason, as we shall see, the monopolist will restrict supply, selling less than would be sold if the industry were competitive.

Oligopoly means few sellers. An oligopolistic industry is one where only a few sellers constitute the supply side of the market. The automobile industry is oligopolistic. In such markets there is indeed much "competition," in the sense of *rivalry* between the firms. Each company is acutely aware of what the other firms are doing, what prices they charge, and what styling they are working on. Although they are, in the popular sense of the word, competing, trying to get ahead of each other, they are not in a competitive industry in the economist's sense of the word. In oligopolistic industries, there is typically both influence over price by the individual firms and strategic interactions among the firms—each firm has to work out not only how its

TABLE 9-1 ▓▓▓▓▓▓▓▓▓▓▓▓
MARKET STRUCTURE WITH IMPERFECT COMPETITION

	NUMBER OF FIRMS		
	ONE	FEW	MANY
Description of industry	Monopoly	Oligopoly	Monopolistic competition

TABLE 9-2 ▓▓▓▓▓▓▓▓▓▓▓▓
CONCENTRATION RATIOS FOR REPRESENTATIVE PRODUCTS
(Shipments by Four Largest Suppliers as Percentage of Total Shipments)

PRODUCT	FOUR-FIRM CONCENTRATION RATIO
Passenger cars	99+
Chewing gum	93
Electric lamps (bulbs)	89
Cigarettes	88
Breakfast cereals	81
Household television receivers	70
Bottled beer and ale	68
Guided missiles and space vehicles	65
Aircraft	61
Doughnuts	60
Phonograph records	60
Farm machinery and equipment	46
Petroleum refining	30
Newspapers	20
Bottled and canned soft drinks	14
Screw machine products	7

Source: U.S. Bureau of the Census, "Concentration Ratios in Manufacturing," *1977 Census of Manufacturing,* MC 77-SR-9, Washington, D.C., 1979, Table 9.

customers will react to what it does but also how other firms in the industry will respond.

Oligopoly is especially common in manufacturing industries, where a few large firms are the producers of most of the output. A common measure of the extent to which a few firms dominate an industry is the *concentration ratio,* which is the percentage of sales in an industry made by the largest firms. Table 9-2 presents four-firm concentration ratios—the percentage of sales made by the four largest firms in several industries.

For most industries, these ratios are not surprising.[1] Perhaps the concentration ratio for soft drinks is lower than would have been expected and that for doughnuts higher. The main point to notice is that there are several industries where only four firms account for well over half the total production. We should thus think of oligopoly as a major form of industry structure.

Although Table 9-2 shows that there are several major industries that are highly concentrated, U.S. industry is not on the whole dominated by extreme concentration. Table 9-3 shows the degree of concentration of U.S. industrial production. It shows the shares of total manufacturing output accounted for by industries with differing de-

grees of concentration. Only 7.5 percent of all output comes from industries where the four largest firms account for more than 80 percent of sales. By contrast, nearly 20 percent of total output comes from industries where the four largest firms account for less than 20 percent of production. The table shows that the sectors with high concentration do *not* account for the lion's share of economic activity. Most (52.9 percent) of the manufacturing output is produced in industries where the four-firm concentration ratio is 20 to 49 percent.

Finally, we have monopolistic competition, a setting in which there are many firms, each selling a slightly different product than the others. A local ice cream parlor selling homemade ice cream is a monopolis-

---

[1] The concentration ratios refer to domestic producers only. They thus can give a misleading idea of the number of suppliers in an industry when there is competition from foreign suppliers. Foreign competition is certainly significant in the automobile industry and in the television industry, for example.

TABLE 9-3

SHARE OF INDUSTRIAL OUTPUT CLASSIFIED BY CONCENTRATION

| | FOUR-FIRM CONCENTRATION RATIO* | | | | |
	20−	20−49	50−69	70−79	80+
Share of total manufacturing output, %	19.2	52.9	15.4	3.8	7.5

* Percentage of output of the industry produced by four largest firms.
Source: U.S. Bureau of the Census, "Concentration Ratios in Manufacturing," *1977 Census of Manufacturing,* MC 77-SR-9, Washington, D.C., 1979.

tic competitor. Because its product is a bit different from the competitors', it can charge a higher price and not lose all its customers. It can also cut its price below the competition's, but it will not thereby get the whole market as would a perfect competitor whose price was below the market price. Monopolistic competitors have *some* control over price, but they do not have much control because other firms sell similar products, and customers can switch.

In this chapter we concentrate on the purest of the imperfect competitors, which is the monopolist. In the remainder of the chapter, we are dealing with a market in which there is only a single seller. As we noted in Chapter 8, monopoly should be thought of as a matter of degree rather than absolute, since it is always difficult to define a market or an industry. For instance, there may be only a single newspaper in town, and we would be inclined to call the newspaper publisher a monopolist. But, of course, if there is also television in town, the newspaper is not the only firm in the news-selling business. Similarly, the telephone company is the monopoly seller of local telephone services, but it is not the only firm in the market for communications. If phone rates are set high, people begin to write letters again. Despite the difficulties of defining a market, the concept of monopoly is very useful, and we proceed to discuss

how a monopolist behaves. In particular, we compare the behavior of a monopolist with that of a perfect competitor.

1 PROFIT MAXIMIZATION, MARGINAL REVENUE, AND MARGINAL COST

The monopoly firm has the same goal as other firms. The monopolist wants to maximize profits, as does a perfect competitor. The difference is that the monopolist is the only seller in the industry, and he chooses his output level taking account of the effect of his sales on market price. Indeed, as we shall see, the monopolist sets the price at which the firm's output is sold. By contrast, the perfect competitor knows that market price is outside his control and independent of his actions.

In this section we analyze the monopolist's output and price-setting decisions. We have already covered the essential material in Chapter 6, where we described the general rule for maximizing profits that applies to all firms: *choose the output level at which marginal revenue is equal to marginal cost.* In Chapter 8 we saw that the competitive firm is special in having marginal revenue equal to price. We see in this section that for the monopolist, marginal revenue is not equal to price and is, in fact, below price.

We now briefly review the concepts of marginal revenue and marginal cost and

TABLE 9-4

DEMAND AND TOTAL REVENUE FOR A MONOPOLIST

QUANTITY DEMANDED, 000s of units/week	PRICE, $/unit	TOTAL REVENUE (QUANTITY × PRICE), $000/week	MARGINAL REVENUE, $000/week
0	16	0	
			14
1	14	14	
			10
2	12	24	
			6
3	10	30	
			2
4	8	32	
			−2
5	6	30	
			−6
6	4	24	
			−10
7	2	14	
			−14
8	0	0	

their role in determining the monopolist's output and price.

The Demand Curve and Total and Marginal Revenue

Table 9-4 shows a demand schedule faced by a monopolist. At a price of $14, the quantity demanded is only 1 (thousand units per week); at a price of $2, the quantity demanded is up to 7 (thousand units per week). The third column shows the total revenue received by the monopolist at different levels of price. Total revenue is just price times quantity. It first increases as the price is cut and then decreases when the price gets low.

The data in the first three columns of Table 9-4 are shown graphically in Figure 9-1. The demand curve facing the monopolist, DD, is in the top panel. Total revenue, which equals price times quantity, is shown in the lower panel. For instance, when price is $12 ($P_0$), quantity demanded is 2 (thousand units per week), and total revenue is $24. (From now on we leave out the reminder that we're measuring quantities and total revenue in thousands per week.) Total revenue at the output level of 2 is shown by the shaded area $B + C$ in the upper panel. When price is lowered to $8, total revenue is equal to area $A + C$. Since that area is

larger than $B + C$, we can see from the diagram that total revenue must increase as output rises from 2 to 4. This is confirmed in the lower panel, where total revenue is shown to be $32 when output is 4.

The last column of Table 9-4 shows marginal revenue.

Marginal revenue, MR, is the increase in revenue obtained by selling 1 more unit of a good.

At each level of output in Table 9-4, except for the first unit, marginal revenue is below price. The reason is that for each extra unit sold, the monopolist gains the price of that good but loses from having to sell the previous level of output at a lower price.

A specific example from Table 9-4 makes the point. The demand schedule shows that 2 units of output can be sold for $12 each, whereas 3 units are sold for only $10 each. The increase in total revenue when sales increase from 2 to 3 units is $6 ($30 − $24), which is, of course, less than the price of $10. To see why, ask how much the monopolist obtains by selling the third unit ($10), and then ask by how much the price falls on the 2 units previously sold. Each of the 2 units previously sold now brings in $2 less than before, because its price has fallen from $12 to $10. Thus the monopolist makes $10 on the third unit and

FIGURE 9-1 THE DEMAND CURVE AND TOTAL REVENUE OF THE MONOPOLIST. The demand curve facing the monopolist is DD in the upper panel. As price is cut from P_0 ($12) to P_1 ($8), the monopolist's total revenue changes from area $B + C$ to area $A + C$. Because area A is bigger than B, there is an increase in revenue when price is cut from P_0 to P_1. This is seen in the lower panel, which shows total revenue (price times quantity) for every level of quantity. Total revenue is maximized at price P_1 ($8), with a corresponding quantity of 4 and a total revenue of $32.

tween marginal revenue and price in the following equation:

Marginal revenue = increase in total revenue from selling 1 more unit of output
= price at which the extra unit of output is sold *minus* the loss in revenue because each unit previously sold is now sold at a lower price   (1)

In Figure 9-2 we add the marginal revenue (MR) schedule to the diagram of the demand curve. Marginal revenue, being the increase in total revenue obtained by selling 1 more unit, can be read off the total revenue curve. To determine marginal revenue, just calculate from the total revenue curve the change in revenue when output is increased by 1 unit. For example, in Figure 9-2, the marginal revenue from increasing output from 1 to 2 units is $10. This is shown by point G on the MR curve. Point G is shown at an output level of $1\frac{1}{2}$, between 1 and 2.[2]

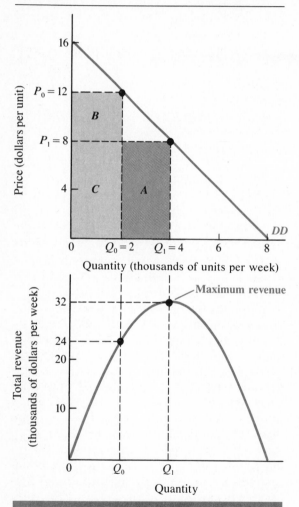

Note now the position of the MR schedule. First, it starts at the same point on the vertical axis as does the demand schedule. Second, at every quantity level except the vertical axis, MR is less than the price. Third, the MR schedule crosses the horizontal axis at the point where total revenue is at a maximum.

We now explain each of these features, which between them really describe what MR is all about. First, MR starts out at the same level as the demand curve. To see that, go back to equation (1). It says that marginal revenue is equal to the revenue obtained from selling the extra unit of output minus the amount lost because the price at which existing units are sold falls. But when

loses $4 from the lower price at which the existing output of 2 units is sold, giving a marginal revenue of $6.

We emphasize the relationship be-

---

[2] Why at $1\frac{1}{2}$? Since we are increasing output from 1 unit to 2, the appropriate place to show the corresponding marginal response is in between output levels of 1 and 2 units.

FIGURE 9-2 PRICE, TOTAL REVENUE, AND MARGINAL REVENUE. Marginal revenue is the change in total revenue as output is increased by 1 unit. For instance, the marginal revenue from increasing output from 1 to 2 units is $10 ($24 − $14). This can be read off the curve in the bottom panel. It is also shown as point G in the top panel. The marginal revenue curve, labeled MR, shows the increase in total revenue from increasing output by 1 unit for all levels of output. For output levels below maximum revenue, marginal revenue is positive; at maximum revenue output, marginal revenue is zero. Beyond maximum revenue output, marginal revenue is negative.

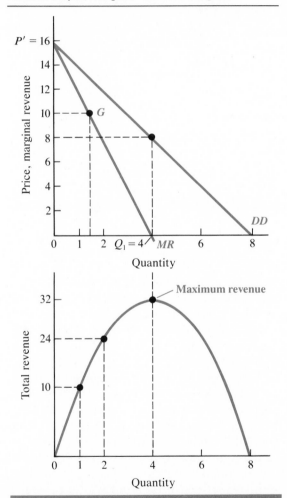

the MR curve starts out at the same point as the demand curve, which is point P′ in Figure 9-2.

Second, marginal revenue is below the price at all other levels of output for the reason specified in equation (1). Whenever 1 more unit of output is sold, the price on existing units falls. The increase in revenue is therefore less than the price.

Third, the MR curve crosses the horizontal axis at the point where total revenue is at a maximum. Marginal revenue tells us the increase in revenue from selling 1 more unit of output. If total revenue can be increased by selling 1 more unit of output, MR is positive. But if total revenue can be increased, it cannot be at its maximum possible level. Whenever marginal revenue is positive, total revenue can be increased by increasing sales. And whenever marginal revenue is negative, the same logic says that total revenue can be increased by reducing sales.

Thus the MR curve crosses the horizontal axis and is zero at the point of maximum total revenue.

Marginal Cost

Figure 9-3 shows the demand curve, DD, and the marginal revenue curve, MR, from Figure 9-2. It also includes the firm's marginal cost curve, MC. MC shows the increase in the firm's total cost when it increases output by 1 unit. The MC curve for the monopolist is the same as the MC curve for any firm. The monopolist, like any firm, tries to minimize the costs of producing any level of output. The MC curve shows the increase in cost required to increase production by 1 unit when the monopolist is producing each level of output as efficiently (cheaply) as possible.[3]

zero units are being sold, and we ask about marginal revenue from the first unit, that is just equal to the price. There were no units that were already being sold. Hence

---

[3] The average and marginal cost curves in Figure 9-3 and elsewhere in this chapter are the long-run cost curves. We leave out the L from LAC and LMC because we do not discuss short-run adjustment in the chapter.

FIGURE 9-3 THE MONOPOLY EQUI-LIBRIUM: $MR = MC$. The monopolist's marginal cost schedule is MC. An increase in sales of 1 unit yields MR as the increment to total revenue and MC as the increment to total cost. Therefore, profits rise by the difference, $MR - MC$. The monopolist expands output as long as MR exceeds MC and contracts output when MC exceeds MR. Therefore, the monopoly equilibrium, where profits are maximized, is at the point where $MR = MC$. But we have to be sure that price exceeds average cost at that point. This is the case in Figure 9-3, with price P_1 and AC equal to AC_1. Total monopoly profits are represented by the shaded area, $(P_1 - AC_1) \times Q_1$.

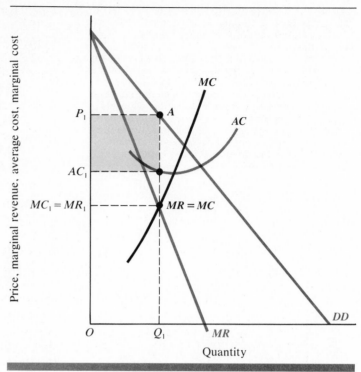

Maximum Profits

The aim of the monopolist is to maximize profits. This is achieved by producing the level of output at which marginal revenue is equal to marginal cost. Why? We already discussed this in Chapter 6, but we review the discussion here.

When output is raised by 1 unit, the increase in revenue is equal to marginal revenue. The increase in cost is equal to marginal cost. If marginal revenue exceeds marginal cost, total revenue goes up by more than total cost, and profits therefore increase. So output should be increased. But if the extra revenue from producing 1 more unit of output, MR, is less than the extra cost incurred by producing 1 more unit, MC, profits decrease. Then output should be reduced. Thus profits will be maximized if marginal revenue equals marginal cost. Table 9-5 summarizes the monopolist's criteria by which to set output.

But there is a final criterion to consider. Even when the marginal decisions are right, the monopolist still has to check whether to be in business at all. He has to make sure he is covering costs. He has to compare average costs with price.

Figure 9-3 shows the average cost schedule, AC, with its usual U shape. At the optimal output level, Q_1, we can read off the average cost as AC_1. The firm's profit per unit will be equal to the price, P_1, less the cost per unit, or average cost, AC_1. Therefore, for the case shown, the firm does make a profit. In fact, total profits can be read off as the shaded area $(P_1 - AC_1) \times Q_1$.

In looking at total profits we have to remind ourselves of two points. First, even if the monopoly were making short-run losses, covering only part of its fixed costs, it would be profitable to operate as long as variable costs at least were covered. Thus in the short run the firm should produce if the

TABLE 9-5

MONOPOLIST'S CRITERIA FOR MAXIMIZING PROFITS

| | OUTPUT DECISION | | | DECISION ABOUT STAYING IN BUSINESS | | | |
				SHORT RUN		LONG RUN	
CONDITION	$MR > MC$	$MR = MC$	$MR < MC$	Price $\geq$ SAVC	Price $<$ SAVC	Price $\geq$ LAC	Price $<$ LAC
DECISION	Increase output	Optimal output level	Reduce output	Produce	Produce zero (shutdown)	Stay in business	Close business (exit from industry)

price is not less than the short-run average variable cost (*SAVC*). In the long run, it should shut down if the price is less than the long-run average cost (*LAC*). Otherwise, it stays in business.

Second, the area $(P_1 - AC_1) \times Q_1$ shows the *monopoly profits*, or excess profits. We remember that average costs already include the alternative costs of *all* resources involved in producing output, including the alternative cost of the capital used. Thus profits here are excess profits, above the normal profits that are already included in average costs.

Price Setting   The monopolist is often described as a *price setter*, someone who sets price. Competitors are described as *price takers*, firms which cannot control price. Now in what sense is the monopolist a price setter? If we look back at Figure 9-3, we can see that the monopolist chooses output level Q_1, at which marginal revenue is equal to marginal cost.

At what price is quantity Q_1 sold? The monopolist will sell Q_1 at the price shown at point A on the demand curve, which is P_1. The monopolist will set the price at P_1 and allow customers to come buy his product. The demand curve tells us they will demand quantity Q_1 at price P_1. Thus by setting the price at P_1, the monopolist ensures that he will sell the amount of goods that maximizes his profits.

Monopoly Power   We noted in the introduction that monopoly is a matter of degree —that it is always difficult to define precisely the market in which a particular firm is selling. For that reason, economists have developed a measure of *monopoly power*, which is an index of the control a firm has over the price it charges.

The precise measure of monopoly power is not as important as the general idea. The idea is that monopoly power is said to be greater the higher the price is in relation to marginal cost. A competitive firm has price equal to marginal cost and is said to have zero monopoly power.

Elasticity and Marginal Revenue   There is a close relationship between marginal revenue and the elasticity of demand facing the monopolist. In particular, recall from Chapter 4 that we showed that so long as the elasticity of demand is above 1, a firm's total revenue increases when it cuts its price. If total revenue increases, marginal revenue is positive. Recall also that total revenue is at a maximum when the elasticity of demand is 1. But total revenue is also at a maximum when marginal revenue is zero. It follows, therefore, that the elasticity of demand is 1 when marginal revenue is zero.

This relationship has an interesting implication. A monopolist will never produce at a level of output at which demand is inelastic. Why? When demand is inelastic, marginal revenue is negative. But since the monopolist sets marginal cost equal to marginal revenue, and since marginal cost is positive, marginal revenue for the monopolist always has to be positive. Hence we know that a monopoly firm always produces at an output level at which the elasticity of demand is above 1.

Price and Marginal Cost Figure 9-3 shows that marginal cost (MC_1) is below price (P_1) at the monopoly equilibrium. Indeed, this relationship must follow from equation (1), which says that price exceeds marginal revenue, together with the fact that marginal revenue is equal to marginal cost at the optimum. In the next section we see the significance of the fact that price exceeds marginal cost in the monopoly equilibrium.

2 OUTPUT AND PRICE UNDER MONOPOLY AND COMPETITION

In what ways does the equilibrium of a monopoly firm differ from that of a competitive firm? A competitive firm operates at a level of output at which price is *equal to* the marginal cost of production, whereas a monopolist operates where price *exceeds* marginal cost. This is a clear and important difference. It arises because the competitive firm believes it can sell as much as it wants at the going market price, whereas the monopolist knows that each extra unit sold requires a reduction in price.

Suppose that a competitive industry is taken over by a monopoly. Where there were many competing sellers before, now there is only a single seller. How are the equilibrium price and quantity affected? We already have a good guess at the answer —the monopolist will charge a higher price and will therefore produce less. But we want to make the comparison between a competitive industry and a monopoly more exact. And we want to find out if monopoly in a market is a bad thing. After all, why

does monopoly have an unpopular connotation?

To be able to compare a monopoly and a competitive industry, we narrow down the difference to just one factor, namely that firms in the competitive industry take the price as given, while the monopolist is a price setter. We therefore assume that demand conditions—the demand curve, DD, in Figure 9-4—are the same whether the market is monopolized or competitive.

We also assume that cost conditions are the same for the monopolist and for the competitive industry. Here a word of explanation is necessary. We saw that for the

FIGURE 9-4 COMPARING THE COMPETITIVE EQUILIBRIUM AND THE MONOPOLY PRICE. In a competitive market, equilibrium occurs at the price where quantity supplied by the industry equals quantity demanded by consumers. In the case of monopoly, output is chosen at the level where $MR = MC$. The price, P_m, is read off the demand curve at that output level. Under a monopoly, the price is higher and output is restricted by comparison with the price and quantity that would occur under competition.

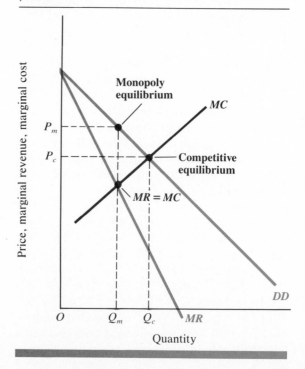

competitive industry, the supply schedule of the industry is the industry marginal cost schedule. The industry supply schedule shows the increase in costs, or MC, from producing 1 more unit of output in the industry. Likewise, the monopoly MC schedule shows the increase in costs from producing 1 more unit of output. Thus if the industry and the monopoly use the same technique of production and face the same input prices, they will have the same MC schedule. This helps in our comparison because now for both the monopoly and the competitive industry, the MC schedules are the same, and so are the demand curves. The only difference is, then, the equilibrium in the market.

Figure 9-4 shows the situations to be compared. The MC curve is the monopolist's marginal cost curve and also the competitive industry's supply curve. When the industry is competitive, equilibrium output is given by Q_c and price by P_c. This is the point at which quantity supplied is equal to quantity demanded.

When the industry is monopolized, output is given by the intersection of the MC and MR curves. Equilibrium output for the monopolist is Q_m, and equilibrium price is P_m.

When both a monopoly and a competitive industry face identical demand and cost conditions, output is lower and price is higher under the monopoly than in the competitive industry. This is the basic charge against monopoly: *monopoly restricts output and raises price.*

3   THE SOCIAL COST OF MONOPOLY

In the preceding section we showed that a monopolist restricts output and raises price above marginal cost. What is the cost—if any—to society of monopoly pricing compared with competition?

In Figure 9-5 we show a market demand curve as well as the marginal cost curve for a

FIGURE 9-5 THE SOCIAL COST OF MONOPOLY: $P > MC$. The demand curve shows at each quantity the price consumers are willing to pay for an extra unit of the good. At Q_m consumers value an extra unit of output at P_m. The MC schedule measures the marginal cost of producing an extra unit of this good. Thus if price exceeds marginal cost, as is the case at output Q_m, society would benefit from an expansion of output in this market. But the monopolist, realizing that he would lose some profits, finds it in his interest to restrict output below the social optimum at point E.

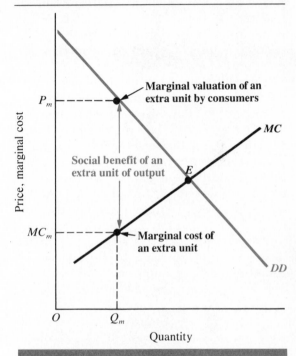

particular good, say, diamonds. Point E would correspond to the competitive equilibrium where the industry supply curve, which is the MC curve, intersects the demand curve. Normally we think of a demand curve as telling us the quantity demanded at each level of price. Now it is convenient to look at the demand curve as follows: at each quantity level, the demand curve tells us the price which consumers are willing to pay for an additional unit of the good. Thus at quantity Q_m consumers are willing to pay P_m for an additional unit of the good. The price, P_m, measures the worth to the consumer of an additional unit of the good.

What is the cost of producing an additional unit of the good? To get an additional unit of output, resources have to be withdrawn from other industries and put to work to produce the additional output. The increase in costs is given by the MC schedule. At quantity Q_m the marginal cost of producing an extra unit of output is MC_m. Thus at quantity Q_m the valuation by society of the extra unit of output, given by price P_m, exceeds the marginal cost to society of the extra unit of output, MC_m.

In a situation like that shown in Figure 9-5, an expansion in output benefits *society*. It may not benefit the *monopolist*, though. That is why monopolists restrict output, and that gives rise to the social cost of monopoly.

In Figure 9-6 we show again the competitive equilibrium, E, and we also show the monopoly equilibrium at point A. At the competitive equilibrium, price equals marginal cost. At E, the valuation of an extra unit equals the marginal cost of producing the extra unit. No gain to society would come from raising output beyond the competitive equilibrium or by cutting it below that level.

The competitive equilibrium, therefore, is socially optimal: the marginal valuation by consumers equals the marginal cost to society of the good.

This is not the case at the monopoly equilibrium. The price faced by consumers is P_m, whereas the marginal cost is only MC_m. The marginal valuation by consumers exceeds the marginal cost associated with an extra unit of output. Expanding output by drawing resources from other industries, reducing consumption there and increasing it here, would raise benefits more than costs and thus raise society's welfare.

At the monopoly equilibrium, the failure to expand output by *1* unit costs society the difference between price and marginal

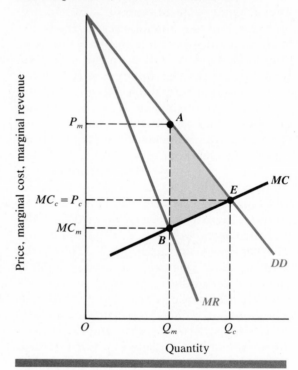

FIGURE 9-6   THE SOCIAL COST OF MONOPOLY TRIANGLE. The competitive industry produces at point E, where the marginal cost of an additional unit of output exactly equals price, or the marginal valuation of an extra unit by consumers. The monopoly, by contrast, restricts output to a level where price exceeds marginal cost. The total cost to society of a monopoly is the cumulative excess of price over marginal cost, which is the shaded area.

cost, or $(P_m - MC_m)$. But we would like to have a measure of the total cost of being at an output level restricted to Q_m rather than being at the socially optimum point, E. This total cost is given by the shaded triangle, EAB. Here is the explanation. Start at the competitive equilibrium, E, and consider a small reduction in output. With $P_c = MC_c$ there is no social cost for a *very* small reduction. But with the second unit reduction there is already a gap $(P - MC)$ equal to the vertical distance between the demand schedule and the MC schedule. For a further reduction in output, going toward Q_m, we again incur a social cost. Moreover, that social cost, $P - MC$, is growing. Taking the sum of these vertical gaps between valuation on the demand side and marginal cost, we arrive at triangle EAB. The welfare cost, or the social cost of monopoly, thus is equal to the cumulative excess of marginal valuation over marginal cost, from the monopoly output level to the competitive level.[4]

The idea that a monopoly creates a social cost by restricting output is particularly obvious if we consider the case of a no-cost monopolist. Suppose that a monopolist controls the supply of a commodity that is costless to produce. For instance, the commodity may be access to a beautiful mountain view. Because the view can be made available at no cost, the public should enjoy as much of the view as it wants, taking enough glimpses so that the marginal valuation is exactly zero. In other words, we should be at a consumption point where consumers are willing to pay precisely zero, no more and no less, for an additional peek. Of course, the monopolist would charge people to see the views. That would restrict output to a lower level. The social cost arises because access to the mountain view that would have given satisfaction at no cost is restricted by the profit-maximizing monopolist; he restricts access to preserve the scarcity of the view.

Can we say anything about how the social cost of monopoly varies with demand and supply conditions? The larger the reduction in monopoly output in relation to competitive output, $Q_c - Q_m$, and the larger the excess of price over marginal cost, $P_m - MC_m$, the larger the total cost imposed on society by a particular monopoly. There have been several attempts to measure the total social cost to the economy of reductions in output caused by imperfect compe-

tition. We will review these studies in Chapter 11, but their main finding is worth reporting now. Surprisingly, these studies find that the costs of monopoly are a relatively small percentage of the GNP, perhaps less than 1 percent. We ask in Chapter 11 whether such estimates are plausible.

4 EFFECTS OF CHANGES IN COSTS AND DEMAND

In the case of a competitive industry, we know that a rightward shift of the demand curve usually increases both output and price. If the supply curve is horizontal—totally elastic—only output increases. If supply is totally inelastic—the supply curve is vertical—only price increases. Otherwise, both price and output rise.

The effect of a rightward shift of the demand curve on price and output in a monopolized industry is basically also to increase both price and output. Figure 9-7 shows the initial equilibrium at E, which is disturbed by an increase in the quantity demanded that shifts the demand curve outward from DD_0 to DD_1. There is a new marginal revenue curve, MR_1. The new equilibrium at E_1 is at a higher level of output, Q_1, and a higher price, P_1.

The monopolist will increase output whenever a shift in demand raises marginal revenue compared with marginal cost. Whenever MR exceeds MC, the monopolist realizes that an extra unit sold will raise total profits, and he therefore increases output. However, demand changes that reduce marginal revenue in relation to marginal cost will lead to a contraction in equilibrium output. The competitive industry responds to an increase in *price* by increasing the quantity supplied. The monopolist reacts to an increase in *marginal revenue* by increasing the quantity supplied.

An increase in marginal costs, shown by an upward shift of the MC curve in Figure

---

[4] Area EAB in Figure 9-6 is the sum of consumers' surplus and producers' surplus. These concepts are defined and explained in the appendix to this chapter.

FIGURE 9-7 A SHIFT IN DEMAND INCREASES MONOPOLY OUTPUT AND PRICE. The initial equilibrium is at point E. An increase in quantity demanded at each price shifts the demand schedule to DD_1 and gives a new MR schedule, MR_1. With these new demand conditions the monopolist selects a new price and quantity, P_1 and Q_1, which are found by looking at the intersection of the new MR schedule and the MC curve.

FIGURE 9-8 AN INCREASE IN THE MONOPOLIST'S COSTS. An increase in marginal costs shifts the MC schedule to the left, to MC', and leads to a higher monopoly price and reduced monopoly output. The initial equilibrium is at point A, corresponding to the initial MC schedule. The leftward shift of the MC schedule to MC' leads to a new monopoly equilibrium at point B.

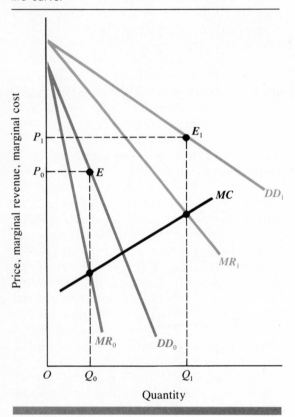

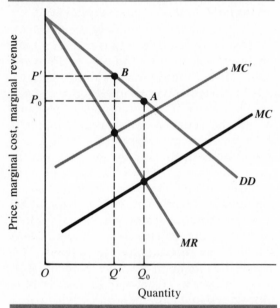

9-8, has a predictable effect on price and output: an increase in the monopolist's marginal costs will increase price and reduce output. Equilibrium shifts from A to B. The direction of the effects is the same as that for a competitive industry.

5 DISCRIMINATING MONOPOLY

Sometimes monopolists have two or more groups of customers, with different demand curves. For instance, an airline with flights between two cities may have business customers whose demand is inelastic and also vacation customers with a more elastic demand. If the monopolist can separate the two groups in some way or set up prices that will distinguish between the two groups, he can increase profits. In the airline case, there will be a high price for the business customers, since their quantity demanded will be cut back relatively little by a high price, and a lower price for the vacationers, since their quantity demanded will be more affected by a high price. The means by which the airline discriminates between the two sets of passengers is to require that those who get the cheaper ticket must stay away at least 1 week or 21 to 45 days.

A monopoly that charges different prices to different groups of customers is a *discriminating monopoly*.

A discriminating monopolist will try to identify groups that have different elasticities of demand and charge them different prices. We have to answer two questions about discriminating monopoly. The first is why customers might have different elasticities of demand. The second is why discriminating among customers increases profits.

Now why do different groups of customers have different elasticities of demand? Why should a tourist respond differently than a business passenger to a cut in the price of an airline ticket? The reason is that the air fare represents only a minor part of the cost of doing business for the business passenger, whereas for the tourist a cut in the air fare may represent a large change in the relative cost of a vacation. A special on air fares to Acapulco will not persuade many more business people to travel to Mexico to try to drum up business there. But it will persuade tourists to spend a week there rather than at the local beach. Thus business travelers will be relatively unresponsive to air-fare cuts, whereas vacation travelers will not.

Suppose then that the demand for airline flights by tourists is more elastic than that by businessmen. Here is an example that shows how price discrimination works: Happy Skies Airline is charging the same price to all its customers, but its planes fly half empty. It is making profits but would like to do better by filling empty seats. To fill the seats it has to cut the price. Would it do better, in terms of increasing its profits, by cutting the price for business people or for tourists?

Travel demand by businessmen is relatively unresponsive to price. But the demand by tourists may be much more sensitive to price. Cut price for tourists a little, and the revenue from tickets sold to tourists increases a lot. Thus the airline will cut the price for tourists, offering a vacation special.

The business people will lose out. The reason is that the airline can fill empty seats with tourists with a smaller price cut than is needed to fill them with business people.

The airline will consider cutting the price for *any* group only if the demand of that group is elastic. Why? Because when the special low fare is offered, everyone in that group flies at the lower price. The airline would lose by cutting fares for that group unless the demand of the group is elastic. The low fare must attract enough extra customers to offset the reduced revenue the airline receives because all the customers of that type it already had are flying more cheaply. Thus rule number 1 in price discrimination is to look for groups with elastic demand.

Price discrimination is common. For another example, think of subscriptions to journals and magazines. There is typically a high rate for businesses and institutions — which are assumed to have a low elasticity of demand — and a relatively low rate for individuals and an even lower one for students. In setting different prices for different groups the publisher manages to extract the most from each group taken by itself. Say, for example, that a journal called *New Energy Review* is published. To firms in the energy business a $200 subscription is nothing provided the review offers first-rate information. For a student the review can easily be read in the library and would never be bought at that price or anything above $10. Thus price discrimination is a perfectly sensible policy to exploit the low price elasticity of firms while still having sales and profits in the student market.

Here is another example. Any reputable museum offers a special low entry fee for students and a higher fee for other visitors. Once again we see price discrimination. Is this an attempt by the museum to bring culture to the young, or is it an attempt to maximize museum revenue? Fortunately, there is no conflict between those two aims, and we will not have to answer the question, but the fact is that students have a much higher elasticity of demand for museum visits than grown-ups. Cutting the entry fees for them (and for families) brings in more of them and does so without impairing the revenue from higher prices charged to the less price-sensitive groups.

Splitting the markets, if it can be done, implies that benefits are transferred from the group with inelastic demand toward both the monopolist and the group with elastic demand. The group with elastic demand will be able to buy more at a lower price and yet leave the monopolist with increased profits. Someone must pay. That someone is the group whose demand is relatively unresponsive to price, which therefore can be squeezed. This idea of separating markets is pervasive and can be found in many everyday situations.

The difficulty for the monopolist is to keep the markets separate. When the monopolist charges two different prices for the same good, there is an incentive for people who can buy the good at the lower price to find a way of selling it to the higher-price group at a price below that charged to the higher-price group by the monopolist. If the monopolist cannot prevent the resale of the good by the lower-price customers, the discriminating monopoly breaks down.

6 REASONS FOR THE EXISTENCE OF MONOPOLY

A successful monopoly earns profits that are attractive to other firms too. How, then, do monopolists keep other firms out? What are the reasons for the existence of monopolies? There are three chief reasons.

One of the examples of monopoly given at the beginning of this chapter—the telephone company—points to the main reason for the existence of monopolies, which is

FIGURE 9-9 A MONOPOLY IN A DECREASING COST INDUSTRY. The diagram shows an industry where AC is declining and where, accordingly, MC is below AC. The monopoly moves to the point where $MC = MR$, producing Q_m and making profits equal to the shaded area. Point C is *not* a possible competitive equilibrium because at that point price is below average cost, and the competitive industry would make losses. Decreasing costs are a reason for monopoly because one firm alone can produce at a lower average cost than two firms sharing the market.

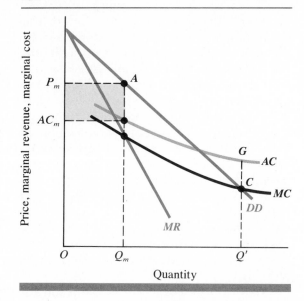

economies of scale. Frequently output can be produced more cheaply when there is only one firm rather than more. To understand this case, we show in Figure 9-9 the demand and cost curves for an industry in which there are economies of scale. The higher the level of output, the lower is average cost, and therefore, as we recall from Chapter 7, marginal cost is below average cost.

Monopoly price and output are at point A, where $MR = MC$. At point A the monopoly is earning profits equal to the shaded area, $(P_m - AC_m) \times Q_m$. What would be the equilibrium if this were a competitive industry? Our first instinct is to look for the point where the marginal cost curve crosses the demand curve. We would take the MC

curve as the competitive industry supply curve and look for the point where the supply and demand curves cross. That is point C in Figure 9-9. But that would not be the competitive equilibrium, because we recall that the competitive industry supply curve consists of that part of the marginal cost curve *above* the point of minimum average cost. In Figure 9-9, there is no part of the MC curve above the AC curve. Equivalently, we can see that if the industry were at point C in the figure, with price equal to marginal cost, the firms or firm in the industry would be losing money. If the industry were at point C, average cost would be higher than price, and there would be a loss equal to the distance CG on every unit of the good sold.

This industry, therefore, could not have a competitive equilibrium. The industry cannot be operated competitively, and we therefore have one reason why there might be monopoly. Now we want to go further by noting that a single producer in this industry can always produce more cheaply than several separate producers.

For example, suppose that we had two firms in the industry, each producing half of the industry's total output. How would the average cost with two firms compare with the average cost if the same level of output were produced by a single firm? Because average costs fall as output rises, we would always have the two firms each producing at a point where average costs are higher than they would be if one firm alone produced the output. Because a single seller can produce more cheaply—due to economies of scale— it will be difficult for this industry to avoid becoming a monopoly. If there were more than one firm in the industry, one of them by expanding output could cut prices and make it difficult for the others to make a profit. Of course, we are here discussing how an industry with a few sellers—an oligopoly—behaves, and we defer further discussion to the next chapter. But it is clear

that increasing returns to scale make it very difficult to have more than one firm in the industry.

The second reason for the existence of monopoly is that a single firm may have control over some scarce and essential resource, in the form of either raw materials or knowledge covered by a patent. In the case of diamonds, for instance, de Beers Consolidated Mines until the early 1980s had virtual control over *all* sources of supply in the non-Communist world. Or, for many years, Polaroid had control over instant photography simply because it had superior technical knowledge and patents.[5]

Third, monopolies may exist because they are given or buy the right to be the single sellers of a good. Or if they are government monopolies, the state takes the right to be a monopoly. This is the example of the tobacco monopoly in many countries or the liquor monopoly in some states. In other countries a single company is given monopoly rights to sell or market a good and therefore does not need to worry about other firms selling the same good. Particularly in the case of imports, a government may grant the right to import a good to a single company. Why would the government give a monopoly right to import? That could be a matter of politics or payoffs or both.

These reasons are not necessarily independent. In particular, the government may give a company the right to be a monopoly if there are economies of scale. But in return the government may at the same time seek to regulate the behavior of the company so that the major inefficiencies of monopoliza-

---

[5] Could we then have called Polaroid a monopolist? Clearly Polaroid had to compete with makers of noninstant film. If Polaroid raised its price very much, it would lose sales to conventional films. Thus it faced a reasonably elastic demand curve. We would say that Polaroid was a monopolist in the sense that it was the only seller of instantly developing film but that it had limited monopoly power because it faced a quite elastic demand curve.

tion—the social loss from the restriction of output—are reduced.

7 REGULATION OF MONOPOLY

Suppose that there are economies of scale in an industry, so that the industry is what is called a *natural monopoly.* Then as we have seen, the industry cannot sustain many competitive firms, because they would lose money if price were equal to marginal cost. What can be done?

Figure 9-10 is simply Figure 9-9 plus a few extra details. So long as price exceeds marginal cost, there are gains to society from increases in output. We would therefore want to increase output above the monopoly level, Q_m, because at that output level there is a gap equal to distance AH between price and marginal cost. Indeed, we would want to increase output all the way to Q', the level of output where the demand curve and the marginal cost curve intersect. At that output level, consumers' marginal valuation of the good is equal to society's marginal cost of producing it. But as we already noted, the monopolist is losing money at that point.

Now there are two alternatives. One is to try to get the monopolist to produce Q' and then to subsidize production by the amount GC per unit. This would be the economic case for subsidizing, say, the railroads if it could be established that they have increasing returns to scale. They would be told what routes to operate, with what frequency, and at what price. And then they would be subsidized.

The second possibility is to find some way of inducing the firm to produce at point B, or in any event to produce more than Q_m. Here there are again two possibilities. The simplest is to tell the firm to charge a price that just covers costs, or—in other words— to set price equal to average cost. That would take the monopolist to point B. Of

FIGURE 9-10 REGULATION OF MONOPOLY. A monopoly would produce at point *A*, restricting output. The socially optimum point is point *C*, where *P = MC*, but the monopoly could not cover costs at that point. One possibility is to force the monopolist to produce *Q′* and pay a subsidy equal to *GC* per unit of output.

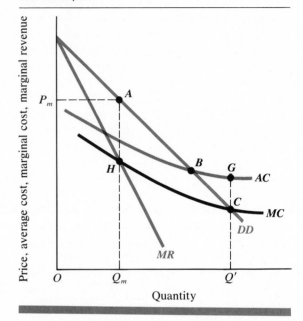

course, there is still a gap between price and marginal cost, but the gap is much smaller than it was at Q_m. Further, the monopoly does not need a subsidy from the government, because it is not losing money.[6]

Regulation whereby price is set equal to average cost (including an allowance for normal profits) is the typical way of regulating monopolies. The electric company or the telephone company normally has to get permission to raise prices, and when it does so, it justifies the request by explaining how its costs have risen.

There is one major difficulty with regu-

[6] It is quite possible, though, that there is *no* price at which the monopolist makes a profit. Looking at Figure 9-10, it is possible that the *AC* curve is above the *DD* curve at all levels of output. In this case the monopoly would have to be subsidized to be in business at all.

lation that sets price equal to average cost. The incentive to minimize costs disappears. When the monopoly is unregulated and maximizing profits, it has every incentive to minimize costs. At any level of output, the profit-maximizing monopoly can increase profits by reducing costs. But when price is set to cover costs, a firm that reduces costs has to reduce the price it charges. There is thus no guarantee that by minimizing its costs, the firm increases its profits. Without the incentive to minimize costs so as to increase profits, such a firm might be producing inefficiently. It might also not fight very hard to keep its costs low. For instance, in bargaining with its unions, the firm will not have a reason to drive a hard bargain.

Price Ceilings The second way to regulate a monopoly is to impose a price ceiling. Suppose we want the monopoly to be viable so that it can stay in business without a subsidy. But we also want to avoid as far as possible the output-restricting effects of an unregulated monopoly. A price ceiling at level P_B in Figure 9-11 will achieve that target. If the monopolist can only sell at P_B or below, then anywhere to the left of point B he will lose money because AC exceeds P_B. Only at output level Q_B can the monopolist cover costs, exactly and without excess profits. To the right of point B the demand curve sets the maximum price, and with demand prices below AC, again only losses can be made. Hence a monopolist restricted to sell at P_B or below would indeed move to point B, exactly covering costs and selling the maximum output possible without needing a subsidy. At point B the monopolist, just like a competitive firm, would make no excess profits.

Regulation of the monopolist by setting the price at P_B therefore looks like a good compromise. The level of output is not quite socially optimal, because price still exceeds marginal cost, but it is closer to the

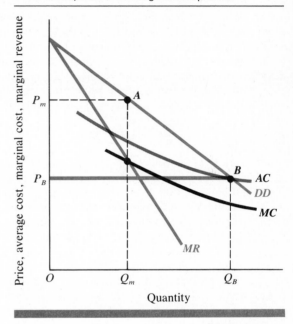

FIGURE 9-11 A PRICE CEILING, P_B, LEADS THE MONOPOLIST TO PRODUCE AT POINT B. The unregulated monopolist would reduce output to Q_m. But if a price ceiling is imposed, the monopolist cannot charge price P_m. Instead, the monopoly maximizes profits given the price ceiling. It does this by producing at point B. Here profits are zero for the monopolist. But recall that normal profits are included in costs, and so at B the monopolist is earning normal profits.

optimal level than under unregulated monopoly. In addition, the monopolist has the incentive to minimize costs. Unfortunately, there is one serious problem: it will be very difficult, indeed, for a regulator to know what price P_B actually is. To discover P_B, we have to know both the firm's average cost curve and the industry demand curve. No doubt the regulatory authority that has the job of setting prices can obtain some information about both costs and demand, but it is unlikely to be able to determine them accurately, particularly since information on costs will have to come from the firm. Thus the setting of price ceilings also cannot in practice be a perfect way of controlling the monopoly.

MONOPOLY AND SUPPLY

Controlling the price the monopolist can charge leads to a conclusion that is remarkable considering the effects of price controls on a competitive industry. Putting a ceiling on price in a competitive industry, below the competitive equilibrium price, results in a lower level of output for the industry. But now go back to what happens in Figure 9-11 when a price ceiling at level P_B is imposed on the monopolist. The monopolist *increases* output from Q_m to Q_B when the price ceiling is imposed. Thus a price ceiling below the monopoly price leads to an increase in output (if the monopolist stays in business).

To understand the difference, we should think of the price ceiling as shifting the monopolist's marginal revenue curve. Before the price ceiling, marginal revenue is less than price. With the price ceiling, the monopolist sells *every* additional unit up to quantity Q_B at the ceiling price; marginal revenue is thus equal to price P_B. At output level Q_m, the imposition of the price ceiling shifts the marginal revenue curve *above* what it was originally and leads to an increase in output.

The effect of the price ceiling on monopoly output shows that *there is no supply curve for a monopolist.* In what sense is that true? There is no supply curve in the sense that we cannot draw a schedule, independent of the demand curve, showing how much the monopolist wants to sell at each level of price. When the demand curve shifts, the amount the monopolist wants to sell at any given price changes, even if there has been no change in cost conditions. Therefore, we cannot draw a supply curve that is independent of demand conditions for a monopolist.

We thus cannot say that monopoly price and output are determined by supply and demand. But we can say that output and price in a monopoly industry are determined by demand and by cost conditions, which is true also for a competitive industry.

We are thus left with no easy way of regulating a monopoly. Subsidies may be necessary to get the socially optimal level of output. All methods of control require substantial knowledge of the firm's costs and demand conditions in the industry, or else they reduce the incentive to minimize costs. In Chapter 11, where we discuss regulation, we come back to these issues. But there is another method of handling the monopoly problem, which is to let the state run the monopolies—in the full knowledge that they will require subsidies, but in the hope that they will nonetheless be run efficiently. The post office is a typical example in most countries.

The obvious can be said immediately: experience with such control of industry varies widely. In many cases the state-run industries appear to operate very inefficiently. But sometimes they appear to be as well run as any other industry.

8 MONOPOLY AND CHANGE

The discussion so far has dealt with a monopoly operating with unchanging technology. We took the monopolist's marginal cost curve as given and assumed that the monopolist minimized costs. Under these circumstances, with given technology, there is not much to be said for monopoly beyond the fact that technology may sometimes make monopoly unavoidable because of decreasing average costs.

However, arguments have been made, notably by Joseph Schumpeter (1883–1950), that monopolies, or at least bigness, are desirable because they are good for technical change. The argument is that an industry that is monopolized, or has only a few big firms, will undertake more research and development and introduce new techniques of production more rapidly than would a competitive industry. Schumpeter argued that small competitive firms do not have the resources to devote to research and development that large firms have. Also, small firms have no guarantee when they introduce a new good or a new technique of production that they can capture the resulting profits. Instead, their competitors might imitate them and capture part of the gains.

Of course, if a firm invents a truly new product, the patent system will provide some protection. Indeed, it is the purpose of the patent system to ensure that incentives for invention exist. But it is possible to invent around a patent, and so other firms can often find ways of doing almost, if not exactly, the same thing as the inventing firm.

There are two parts to the Schumpeter argument. The first implies that more research and development will take place in large firms than in small firms. Schumpeter probably had in mind institutions such as Bell Labs, a research institution within the Bell System. Bell Labs has been the source of many innovations and inventions in telecommunications and other fields. It even has a fine economics research group.

Schumpeter's argument appears to be supported by the fact that very small firms do not do much, if any, research and development. But once a certain size of firm is reached, there appears to be little relationship between the size of the firm and the amount of research and development spending.

The second question is to what extent innovating depends on firms being monopolies rather than just having reached a certain size. Here the evidence is that monopolies are not fast at introducing new products. It seems that firms need the threat of potential entry into the industry by new firms to keep them on their toes. A totally well established monopoly, with no threat of competition, would not see any need to innovate very quickly.

The conclusion, then, is that while firms have to be of a reasonable size to undertake research and development efforts, they do not have to be monopolies. The protection of the patent laws, which offer the prospect of having a temporary monopoly if a new product is invented, probably encourages innovation. But actually having a monopoly already does not increase the incentive to innovate.

SUMMARY

1   A monopoly is a single seller of a good. Pure monopoly, in the sense that the firm does not have to worry at all about actions potential competitors may take, is rare. It is often convenient to talk of the extent of a firm's monopoly power, meaning the amount of freedom the firm has in setting its price.

2   The profit-maximizing level of output for a monopolist is the level at which marginal revenue equals marginal cost. If the monopolist is to stay in business, the price at that level of output has to cover average costs.

3   The monopolist does not have a supply schedule, but he does have a supply rule: Supply the quantity of output at which MC equals MR. Supply behavior is thus *not* independent of demand conditions.

4   Output in a monopoly industry is smaller than output in a competitive industry with the same demand and cost conditions. The monopoly price is higher than the competitive price.

5   The monopolist's restriction of output is not socially desirable because the value consumers place on increased production exceeds the cost of increasing production—but production is kept from being increased by the monopolist.

6   A discriminating monopolist charges different prices to different groups of customers, thereby increasing profits. The price is higher for groups with a lower elasticity of demand.

7   There are three main reasons for the existence of monopoly. First, there are economies of scale, meaning that production in an industry is most efficient when only one firm is producing. Second, the monopolist may have control over a source of raw materials or some special technical knowledge. Third, the government may have given monopoly rights to the firm.

8   Monopolies can be regulated so that the gap between the output they produce and the socially optimal level of output is reduced. They can be told what level of output to produce and to sell. Or they may be given a price ceiling. In some cases, it might be necessary to subsidize the monopoly to get it to produce the socially optimal level of output. In all cases, substantial knowledge of demand and costs is needed for successful regulation.

9   The imposition of a price ceiling on a monopoly at a level below the monopoly price will lead it to *increase* output (or go out of business).

10   There is no strong evidence that monopolies undertake more innovation than other big firms.

KEY TERMS

Imperfect competition	Monopoly power
Monopoly	Social cost of monopoly
Oligopoly	Discriminating monopoly
Concentration ratio	Industries with economies of scale
Monopolistic competition	Regulation of monopoly
Total revenue	Natural monopoly
Marginal revenue	Technical change (innovation)

PROBLEMS

1 The table shows the demand schedule facing a monopolist who produces at a constant marginal cost of $5.

DEMAND SCHEDULE FACING A MONOPOLIST

PRICE, $	QUANTITY
9	0
8	1
7	2
6	3
5	4
4	5
3	6
2	7
1	8
0	9

(a) Calculate the firm's marginal revenue curve. (b) What is the equilibrium output for the monopolist? (c) What is the equilibrium price for the monopolist? (d) What would the equilibrium price and output be for a competitive industry? (e) Explain in words why the monopolist produces less and charges a higher price than a competitive industry.

2 Suppose now that in addition to the constant marginal cost of $5, the monopoly incurs a fixed cost of $2 just to be in business. (a) What is the monopolist's equilibrium level of output? (b) What is the monopolist's equilibrium price? (c) What effects do fixed costs have on the monopolist's profits, and why?

3 Under the same demand assumptions as in Problem 1, assume now that the monopolist's total costs are as given in the table to the right. (a) Calculate the marginal cost schedule. (b) What are the optimal price and quantity for the monopolist? (c) How much profit does the monopolist make?

4 (a) What is the social gain in Problem 1 from moving from the monopoly equilibrium to the competitive equilibrium? (b) In what sense exactly is this a gain, and to whom? (c) How much does the monopolist lose as a result of the move to the competitive equilibrium?

5 Suppose now that the marginal cost decreases to $3 in Problem 1. (a) What is the effect on the equilibrium price and quantity? (b) Does the price change by more or less than the change in cost? (c) How does that compare with the effects of a change in marginal cost on price in a competitive industry?

6 (a) Name three monopolies with which you deal. (b) What determines the prices charged by each of them? (c) What procedures are followed when the monopolists want a change in price? (d) Do the monopolists in question make profits? (e) Why are these firms monopolies?

7 Suppose that a price ceiling of $6 is imposed on the monopolist in Problem 1. (a) What level of output will he produce? (b) How does it compare with the unregulated level of output? (c) Explain why a price ceiling may increase a monopolist's output.

8 Three major inventions which affect us daily are (a) the photocopier or Xerox machine, (b) the telephone, and (c) rayon. With what type of company (monopolist, oligopolist, etc.) are these products now associated? Did they originate with large or small companies or with individual inventors?

MONOPOLIST'S TOTAL COSTS

QUANTITY	TOTAL COST, $
0	4
1	9
2	13
3	16
4	20
5	25
6	31
7	37
8	44

9 Looking at Figure 9-3 you can see that in the monopoly equilibrium we have drawn, AC is above the minimum average cost. Why does the monopoly not expand production to reach a lower level of average costs? Would the reduction in average costs not raise profits?

10 Draw for yourself Figure 9-4, and add the average cost curve, AC, that is the same for the monopolist and the competitive industry. (Remember that the MC schedule passes through the minimum of the AC schedule.) Now show the profit $[(P_m - AC_m) \times Q_m]$ of the monopolist and the profit $[(P_c - AC_c) \times Q_c]$ of the competitive industry. Who has the higher total profit, the monopolist or the competitive industry?

11 The American Economics Association charges different membership rates according to the professional status of the member: (*a*) student, (*b*) assistant professor, (*c*) associate professor, (*d*) full professor. Discuss what possible motives the association might have for following this policy.

12 Recall the manager of the OSU stadium in Chapter 4. At what level of marginal revenue would the OSU stadium maximize revenues?

APPENDIX: CONSUMERS' SURPLUS AND PRODUCERS' SURPLUS

The analysis of the social costs of monopoly uses a measure of social costs, consumers' surplus, that is very often used in applied economics.

> *Consumers' surplus* is defined as the excess of the amount that individuals would be willing to pay for a good over the amount they actually pay.

We have to ask three questions:

1 How can it be possible for people to be willing to pay more for the amount of a good they consume than they actually pay?

2 How do we measure consumers' surplus?

3 Is consumers' surplus a good measure of social cost?

The first two questions are answered at the same time. Figure 9A-1 shows the demand curve for a good. For convenience the demand curve has steps in it, but that is not essential. Suppose that the price of the good is P'. The total measure of consumers' surplus is the shaded area under the demand curve. That represents the excess of the amount individuals would be willing to pay for the amount of the good they consume over the amount they actually pay. Why?

The demand curve shows the price consumers are willing to pay for each unit of the good. For the first unit, they are willing to pay price P_1. They actually pay amount P' for that good. Hence they have a surplus of $P_1 - P'$ on that unit of the good. This is shown by the shaded area labeled A. For the second unit of the good, they would be

FIGURE 9A-1 CONSUMERS' SURPLUS. The step schedule, *DD*, is the demand curve. It shows at each level of output the price that consumers are willing to pay for an extra unit of the good. Consumers are willing to pay P_1 for a first unit, but at market price P' they only have to pay P'. Therefore $(P_1 - P')$, shown as the shaded area labeled A, represents consumers' surplus on the first unit. For a second unit consumers are willing to pay P_2 but only need to pay P'; thus area B represents the consumers' surplus on the second unit, and so on. The entire shaded area represents the total consumers' surplus associated with a market price of P'.

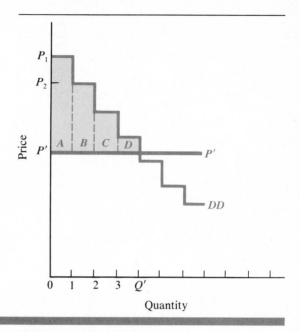

willing to pay P_2, but again they pay only P'. There is a surplus of $P_2 - P'$ on that unit, shown by the shaded area labeled B. Now the total shaded area is made up of areas like A plus B. Thus the total shaded area represents the amount consumers would be willing to pay to have a given amount of the good over and above the amount they actually pay. There is a surplus or bonus to the consumers, and it is known as consumers' surplus.

The third question is the real issue: Why would this be a measure of social cost? The idea here is that a person's money valuation of a change is a measure of the benefit to society of making the change. If society does something for which we are willing to pay $100 (even though we do not pay that amount), the value to society is $100. And the shaded area shows how much all individuals taken together would be willing to pay.

When we think about this further, we also see some of the questions that are raised about consumers' surplus[7] as a measure of social cost. The main difficulty is that everyone is weighted equally. If a billionaire is willing to pay $100 for something, that gets the same weight in the computation of consumers' surplus as would the fact that a very poor person is willing to pay $100. Everyone counts the same in consumers' surplus, and that ignores questions about whose surpluses

---

[7] The discerning student always pays close attention to the placing of the apostrophe in consumer's (consumers') surplus. Consumer's surplus, for a single consumer, is free of the difficulty discussed in this paragraph as a measure of gain to the individual. Consumers' surplus, for all consumers taken together, is not free of this difficulty, as a measure of gain to society.

FIGURE 9A-2 PRODUCERS' SURPLUS. The marginal cost schedule is shown with steps. Price is P'. If the firm produces 1 unit of output at MC_1 but sells the output at P', it realizes a surplus equal to the shaded area, $(P' - MC_1)$. If a second unit is produced, surplus on that unit is shown by the area labeled B, and so on. If the firm or industry produces at Q', the total producers' surplus is represented by the entire shaded area.

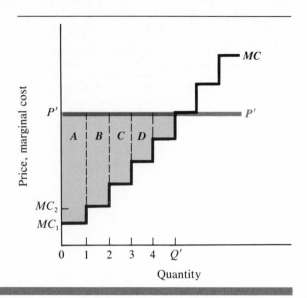

are being added. Hence some economists are reluctant to use consumers' surplus measures of social benefit. Others argue that consumers' surplus can be measured and therefore has one major point in its favor. They suggest that adjustments can be made to the consumers' surplus measure to take care of the fact that different consumers' valuations are added together in the shaded area. In practice, consumers' surplus measures are widely used, and without adjustment.

Corresponding to the notion of consumers' surplus is the concept of producers' surplus. This is shown in Figure 9A-2. A first unit of output can be produced at a marginal cost equal to MC_1, but it is sold at price P'. There is, accordingly, a surplus equal to the shaded area labeled A. The actual cost of producing the output is only MC_1, but the price received is higher.

Similarly, a second unit can be produced at a marginal cost of MC_2, but it is also sold at price P', giving rise to a surplus equal to the area labeled B. The same reasoning applies to further units, and so the total producers' surplus is the shaded area between the MC schedule and the given price, P'. (Note that producers maximize producers' surplus by moving to the point where the price equals the marginal cost.)

Producers' surplus thus equals the cumulative excess of price over the marginal cost of production.

In Figure 9A-3 we look again at the cost of a monopoly to society. The restriction of output and the increase in price, compared with the output and price in a competitive market, are shown once again. The monopolist restricts output to Q_m and raises the price to P_m. The change in total surplus is equal to the reduction in the area between the demand curve and the MC schedule.

In terms of Figure 9A-3 we lose the two triangles, $A + B$; area A is

FIGURE 9A-3 THE SOCIAL COST OF MONOPOLY: LOSS OF CONSUMERS' AND PRODUCERS' SURPLUS. The monopoly restricts output to Q_m and raises price to P_m. There is a net loss of welfare to society equal to the area $A + B$. In addition, there are losses to consumers that are collected as increased profits by the monopolist. These are transfers, as opposed to the net loss to society of $A + B$.

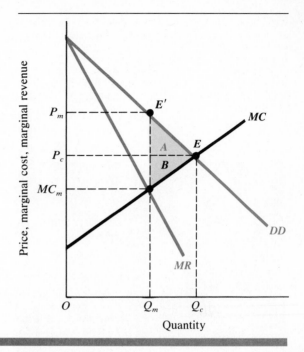

a loss in consumers' surplus, area B a loss in producers' surplus. These are losses by one group or the other that are *not* captured by someone else. They are *net* social losses or *deadweight losses* to society from monopoly.

We emphasize that the deadweight losses are total losses *to society*. There are losses also for the consumer of the good, who pays a higher price under monopoly for the goods he consumes than he would otherwise have paid. Consumers pay amount $(P_m - P_c)$ more for each unit of the good consumed under monopoly than they would pay under competition. But that does not count as a social loss. Those payments go to the monopolist. From the viewpoint of society, these payments are just a *transfer*, a payment from one group to another. Such transfers may or may not be bad, but they are not a total loss to society. One group's loss is another group's gain.

But a deadweight loss is a total loss. Both consumers and producers lose, and nobody in the economy has an offsetting gain. Whenever that happens, society would be better off preventing the distortion or misallocation of resources. We return to this important issue in discussing welfare economics in Chapter 20.

An oligopoly is an industry that has only a few sellers or is dominated by only a few sellers. The automobile industry, breakfast cereals, and television broadcasting, for example, are all industries dominated by a few large firms whose brand names are household words (General Motors, Ford, Kellogg's, NBC, CBS, etc.).

The focus of this chapter is on the behavior of oligopolists. We will ask: How do oligopolists behave? Why is there oligopoly? And do oligopolists earn high profits? We also discuss the behavior of monop-

10

Oligopoly and Monopolistic Competition

olistic competitors, firms that are small and have many competitors but yet have limited monopoly power that allows them to set their own prices at a level that is different from the market average. They may sell slightly different products or draw on slightly different sets of customers. The local movie theater can choose its own price, but it cannot set its price too far above the prices in the rest of the market. One restaurant can charge different prices than the others and still keep customers, because it provides a different type of service.

With respect to market structure, oligopoly and monopolistic competition fall between monopoly and perfect competition, which we studied in the two preceding chapters. Unlike perfect competitors, oligopolists and imperfect competitors do *not* take the prices they receive as given. On the contrary, like a monopolist, each recognizes that he faces a downward-sloping demand curve for his product. But unlike the monopolist, both the oligopolist and the monopolistic competitor are not alone in the industry.

The difference between oligopoly and monopolistic competition is that the oligopolist takes into account the reactions of the other firms in the industry to his own actions. Here is a typical problem faced by an oligopolist. Happy Skies Airline wants to expand its sales on the Houston-Miami route. It decides to offer a 25 percent discount below the fares charged by the other two airlines serving the same route. The other carriers respond by offering the same discount so as not to lose customers to Happy Skies. As a result of the discounts offered by all three airlines, there is some increase in the total number of passengers flying the route. But Happy Skies's plan to take customers away from the other two lines did not work. Instead, all the carriers lost by cutting prices. Perhaps next time Happy Skies will anticipate that its rivals will match its price cuts and will not start the process at all by cutting prices.

This illustrates the main theme of the chapter. *There is a constant tension in oligopolies between competition and collusion.*

Collusion is an explicit or implicit agreement among firms in an industry not to compete with each other.

If Happy Skies and the other airlines had kept prices high to begin with, all three would have been better off. This is the pressure to collude. But each airline also wants to improve its own position by taking customers away from the others. This is the pressure to compete.

With relatively few firms dominating the industry, oligopolists have to take into account their competitors' reactions to any moves they make. Thus oligopoly is dominated by strategic issues; one firm calculates or guesses how the others will react and acts accordingly. In monopolistic competition, by contrast, there are so many firms that each individual firm assumes that its own actions do not affect the actions of the competition. Like competitors, each monopolistic competitor believes it is too small to affect other firms. But monopolistic competitors, unlike perfect competitors, have some freedom to set their own prices.

After analyzing the behavior of oligopolists and monopolistic competitors, we end the chapter by discussing two issues connected with imperfect competition. The first is product variety, the availability to the consumer of similar but not identical products. The second is advertising. The issue here is whether advertising is a social waste or whether, on the contrary, it serves a useful social as well as private function.

1   WHY DO OLIGOPOLIES EXIST?

Oligopolies exist because there are barriers to entry.

Barriers to entry are factors that keep potential competitors from entering an industry.

The barriers may be economies of scale that mean that the total output of the industry is most cheaply supplied by only two or three producers. Or the barriers may be created by the government or by the firms in an industry. In the latter case they enable the firms to reap for themselves the benefits of colluding to increase profits.

We start by showing why firms in an industry can benefit from colluding. Then we go on to discuss the barriers to entry that enable them to maintain their collusion.

The Profits from Collusion

The existing firms in an industry can, as a group, make profits if they agree to behave as if they were a single monopolist. Figure 10-1 shows how this works. We assume that in the industry there are constant average and marginal costs, and so the industry supply schedule is horizontal at the level $AC = MC$. The market demand schedule is DD. If the industry were competitive, the equilibrium price would be P_c, with output Q_c. But now oligopolists realize that they can together make profits by restricting output. As a group they sell only Q_m and charge price P_m, just as if they were a single monopoly firm. They therefore make total profits equal to the shaded area. Behind the scenes they have to figure out how much each firm will produce and what share of the profits it will receive.

There are thus profits waiting for firms that can get together. But it is very difficult for many firms to get together without one of them cheating on the agreement. Any firm that shades price just a little below the agreed-upon price will take away business from the other firms, increasing its own profits at the expense of the others. So an industry with many firms will find it difficult to keep price and profits up.

One way to prevent the price-cutting is to have some firm buy out the others. It is easier for a few firms to keep and police an

FIGURE 10-1 OLIGOPOLISTS SHARE A MARKET TO OBTAIN "MONOPOLY PROFITS." The existing firms in a market get together to restrict output and obtain monopoly profits equal to the shaded area. This result is attained by moving away from the competitive equilibrium and deciding not to supply, as a group, more than quantity Q_m.

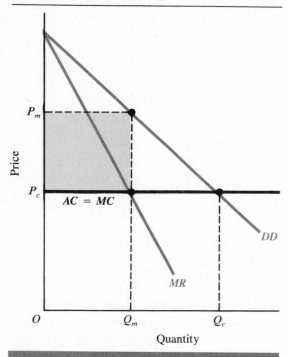

agreement than it is for many firms. It was by buying out other firms that John D. Rockefeller put together the Standard Oil Company at the end of the nineteenth century. At one time he controlled 90 percent of all oil refining in the country.

Barriers to Entry

An industry may *become* an oligopoly without there being barriers to entry. The lure of the profits from collusion and the ability of a John D. Rockefeller may create an oligopoly where there was not one before. But once an oligopoly is established, it cannot survive without barriers to entry. The profits attract new firms into the industry. These would enter by cutting their price below the

price charged by the existing firms. They would thus undercut the oligopoly and spoil the rigged market. Unless there are barriers to entry, the entry of new firms would destroy the oligopoly.

Barriers to entry can take a number of forms. First, existing firms in an industry may own essential raw materials or essential technology that is not available to potential competitors. Second, the existing firms may be protected from competition by government regulations. For instance, a license may be needed to fly a particular route or import certain goods. Third, economies of scale are often a significant barrier to entry, as we now describe.

Economies of Scale   Large firms may be able to produce more cheaply than small firms. In industries where there are decreasing costs, the market may support only a few firms of a reasonably efficient size. Thus technology, reflected in decreasing costs, arises as a barrier to keep new firms from entering. To be able to offer its output at a competitive price, the entrant has to produce on a large scale. But it is difficult for a firm at the outset to start producing on a large scale that takes a significant part of the industry's total output.

Of course, the existence of economies of scale was the main reason given in Chapter 9 for the existence of monopoly. Natural monopoly exists when it is most efficient for there to be only one firm in an industry. Similarly, we can say that an industry is a natural oligopoly if total industry output can be most cheaply produced by only a few firms. The other two sources of barriers to entry—control over raw materials and technology, and government regulation—are also reasons for the existence of monopoly.

How big are the most efficient firms? This depends on the industry. Table 10-1 shows for a number of industries estimates of the most efficient size of a plant (i.e., de-

do not produce at all. These firms receive payments from a pool of revenues contributed by the firms that are producing.

Why do the other firms pay the firms that are not producing? It is to keep them from producing and selling at lower prices, thereby lowering the price received by all the firms in the industry. This was made explicit in a quote from correspondence seized by the U.S. government in its investigation of the pool in the paper market organized by the Fiber and Manila Association at the beginning of this century:[1]

G. H. P. Gould
President, Gould Paper Company, etc.

Dear Sir:

The theory of a pool, however, is that the active members must contribute to the passive members. To induce members to refrain from making cut prices in order to market their products a "pool" properly organized, will yield them as much in profit if their mill is shut down; and therefore such members are usually satisfied to take their contributions from the pool rather than to endeavor to obtain it through sales in the market. The direct result of this is to tone up prices. . . .

Yours truly,
J. H. Parks

The Bertrand Model

A second model of oligopoly pricing, the Bertrand model, shows what can happen if firms fail to cooperate.[2] In this model, oligopolists can end up charging the competitive price. How? The Bertrand model focuses on the temptation for firms to cheat on an agreement. Suppose that there are only two firms in an industry, which is therefore called a *duopoly*. Assume that the firms are

---

[1] Quoted by Myron W. Watkins, *Industrial Combinations and Public Policy*, Houghton Mifflin Company, Cambridge, Mass., 1927, p. 196.
[2] Joseph Bertrand was a late-nineteenth-century French economist.

identical, and call them A and Z. Suppose that both firms start off by charging the monopoly price.

Now firm Z has the idea of charging a lower price to get more customers, and it believes that A will continue to keep its price at the monopoly level. As Z lowers its price a little it will get most or all of A's customers. (How many customers switch depends on whether A and Z are selling exactly the same good or slightly different goods and on how well informed the customers are.) Because firm Z believes it will get so much more business from a small cut in price, it goes ahead and reduces its price. But now firm A sees itself losing business and responds. Firm A now believes that Z will keep its price fixed, and so it cuts to a little below Z's price, taking business from Z.

Where does this process end? It will end only when the price reaches the competitive level. At that stage any further price cuts drive the firms out of business. Thus, Bertrand argued, if each firm believes the other will keep the price it charges fixed, the duopoly price eventually falls to the competitive level.

Of course this story strains our belief. Why should each firm believe that the other will not cut the price when the evidence is clear that each firm does in fact respond to its rival's price cuts? Well before the competitive price is reached, each firm realizes that it would make sense to stop in the hope that the other firm will follow suit—and perhaps even work the price back up to the monopoly level. So we should not take the Bertrand model as describing oligopoly pricing in the long run.

The Bertrand model does, though, provide a good explanation for the occasional price wars that break out in oligopolistic industries. Firms follow each other in cutting prices, and customers have a bonanza for a while. Then the firms realize they are all better off without the low prices, and they cooperate to move the price back up. Price wars break out sporadically among service stations and supermarkets, for example.

3 COOPERATION AMONG OLIGOPOLISTIC FIRMS

In this section we discuss how cooperating oligopolistic firms behave and the factors determining whether they can cooperate or collude successfully. We have already seen that the best that firms together can do is to produce like a monopolist would, with industry marginal cost equal to marginal revenue. They have to agree also on some method for allocating both production and profits among themselves.

What sorts of agreements are observed among firms in oligopolistic industries, and how do the firms in an agreement make sure that no firm is cheating? In this section we discuss in turn cartels, the dominant-firm model (which well describes the OPEC cartel), and price leadership, all of which are models of how industries achieve output levels below, and prices above, competitive levels.

Cartels

Cooperation among firms is easiest when it is legally permitted and there is explicit agreement among the firms in the industry. Such an agreement is called a *cartel*. The most famous and successful cartel is OPEC, the Organization of Petroleum Exporting

FIGURE 10-3 THE PRICE OF SAUDI ARABIAN LIGHT CRUDE OIL, 1953–1980. The data are from OECD, *Economic Outlook,* 27, July 1980, p. 115.

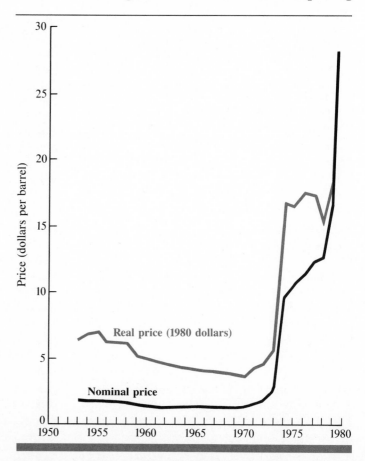

Countries. It was set up in 1960, but it has been active only since 1973. The 12 member countries of OPEC get together regularly to decide on the prices they will charge. Up to 1981 the members of OPEC stuck close to the agreed-upon prices. But in 1982 there were signs that OPEC members were beginning to cut prices below the agreed-upon levels.

Figure 10-3 shows that OPEC prices rose sharply twice since 1973. The first occasion was in 1973–1974, when the cartel exercised its muscle for the first time, quadrupling the price of oil during 1973, mostly during and after the Yom Kippur war, which was in October. OPEC maintained the price, and then in 1979–1980 it doubled the price. OPEC's total oil revenues increased by 340 percent from 1973 to 1980, even after adjusting for the general increase in prices over that period.

When OPEC first succeeded in raising prices in 1973, many economists predicted that the cartel would soon collapse, as had every cartel before that time. The reason for collapse before had been that some firm in the cartel always broke the rules by beginning to cut the price so as to increase its own profits, and then the other firms followed suit once they discovered what was going on. What, then, accounts for the success of OPEC in maintaining its price over so long a period?

The success of OPEC results mainly from the dominant role of Saudi Arabia, which acts as the shock absorber for the actions of other countries in the cartel. OPEC has a *dominant firm*, Saudi Arabia, which essentially determines the price and output for the group as a whole.

OPEC and the Dominant-Firm Model

We use Figure 10-4 to examine the dominant-firm model of an oligopolistic industry. The industry consists of a single large firm, providing a major part of total supply, to-

gether with a *competitive fringe* of firms selling as much as they want at the going price. The dominant firm is large enough to maintain the price above the competitive level.

Figure 10-4a shows the demand curve for the industry, DD, and the supply curve of the competitive fringe, SS. All the firms in the competitive fringe sell as much as they want at the going price, and so they can be thought of as having a supply curve. Now the demand curve facing the dominant firm is the difference between market demand and supply by the competitive fringe at each price, or the excess demand curve, ED, in Figure 10-4b. The dominant firm knows that at each price that it sets, other firms will sell as much as they want. So it is left only with the difference between market demand and competitive fringe supply.

The ED curve in Figure 10-4b corresponds to the distance between the DD and SS curves. Distance AB is the same in the two parts, for instance. With demand curve ED facing the dominant firm, profits are maximized by equating marginal revenue and marginal cost, setting price P_{df}, and producing output Q_{df}. Other firms sell at price P_{df}, and they sell as much as they want to at that price.

In what sense can we interpret OPEC according to the dominant-firm model? The idea is that the OPEC price is enforced by Saudi Arabia's[3] willingness to maintain the cartel agreement. Once a price has been agreed upon, the other countries sell as much as they want. So long as Saudi Arabia holds the price, and demand conditions are stable, there is no incentive for other firms to cheat by cutting the price. Saudi Arabia, the biggest producer, decides on the price

---

[3] Actually, Saudi Arabia is not the only country in OPEC which is not in the competitive fringe. Certainly Kuwait and some of the emirates are coordinating actions with Saudi Arabia. When we say Saudi Arabia, we really mean this larger group of countries.

FIGURE 10-4 (a) THE COMPETITIVE FRINGE and (b) THE DOMINANT FIRM. The industry includes a dominant firm and a competitive fringe of small firms that behave as perfect competitors. The competitive fringe has a supply curve, *SS* in part *a*. Market demand is *DD*. The dominant firm therefore faces demand schedule *ED*, the difference at each price between the quantity demanded and the quantity supplied by the competitive fringe. The dominant firm chooses output level Q_{df}, at which *MR* = *MC*. The total quantity demanded at price P_{df} is Q_d, of which Q_{cf} is produced by the competitive fringe and the rest by the dominant firm.

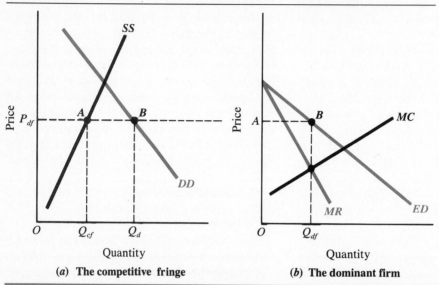

(a) **The competitive fringe**   *(b)* **The dominant firm**

at which all the firms will sell and adjusts its production so that total demand is equal to the supply from all the countries in the cartel taken together at that price.

The bargaining that goes on in meetings of OPEC is the process by which the competitive fringe and OPEC decide how much profit they and Saudi Arabia respectively will make. The countries that make up the competitive fringe prefer a high price, since they will sell as much as they want, and the higher the price the better, while Saudi Arabia has reason for worrying that the price can go too high. The price is too high for Saudi Arabia when its revenues would be higher at a lower price.

The level at which the dominant firm can maintain the price depends on the supply curve of the competitive fringe and on the total demand for oil. If the competitive fringe's supply curve shifts to the right,

the price will fall. Or if the demand curve for oil shifts to the left, the price will fall.

OPEC's inability to maintain the price of oil in the early 1980s, when oil prices fell for a time, was the result of shifts of both the supply curve of the competitive fringe and the world demand curve. The many oil discoveries made in the previous decade increased the amount supplied by the competitive fringe at each price. And the demand curve for oil shifted to the left as consumers installed energy-saving equipment and switched to energy sources other than oil.

These shifts increased the share of the competitive fringe in total supply, and thus reduced price. The dominant firm—Saudi Arabia, along with Kuwait and some other suppliers—became less dominant and price accordingly fell.

OPEC is not the only cartel, though it is

the most successful. For a long time most international air travel was controlled by an international cartel, the International Air Transport Association (IATA), to which almost all international airlines belonged. U.S. airlines with international flights were allowed to belong to IATA even though membership in cartels is usually against antitrust laws. IATA set prices and divided up the international routes among airlines. Airlines' profits were determined by their efficiency in keeping costs low and their ability to persuade customers to use their services. They could attract customers through service but not with much else, for IATA controlled even the price of drinks and earphones and the quality of the food that could be served. The IATA rules began to crumble because of price-cutting from within and competition from without, as non-IATA airlines grew. IATA still exists, but it is less powerful than it used to be.

Legal attitudes toward cartels differ among countries. The Sherman Act in the United States, passed in 1890, says that "every contract, combination . . . , or conspiracy in restraint of trade or commerce . . . is hereby declared to be illegal." U.S. corporations can enter legally into explicit agreements that determine price and output only if they have specific legislative sanction. Baseball, for instance, enjoys special legal exemption from the provisions of antitrust law. Attitudes toward cartel and other agreements among firms abroad are generally more lenient, though the trend in Europe has been increasingly to make such agreements illegal. Cartel behavior is more common in Japan.

Implicit Agreements: Price Leadership

Because explicit agreements about price among private corporations are frequently illegal, firms find ways to cooperate without explicit agreement and communication. For instance, steel prices in the United States were for a long time kept to a common level among the major steel producers, who met regularly to discuss the state of the industry without necessarily formally agreeing on the price they would charge. Another famous case is that of cigarettes. Between the two world wars, the three major cigarette producers of the time—Reynolds (Camel), American Tobacco (Lucky Strike), and Liggett and Myers (Chesterfield)—had essentially the same price for their brands. Keeping the same price did not require explicit collusion; instead, firms found ways of agreeing on a price without talking about it.

How? Any implicit agreement involves two things. First, the chosen price has to be communicated to the firms in the industry. Second, a way has to be found of checking that firms are not cheating by secretly cutting the price and thereby increasing their share of the market.

The price is typically communicated by one of the firms becoming a price leader.

> A *price leader* is a firm that, by changing its price, gives the signal to other firms in the industry to change their prices.

The price leader judges when to change the price. If it is right, the other firms follow suit, and the leader effectively changes the industry's price without having explicitly colluded with the other firms. If the other firms do not follow suit, the leader will get back into the pack by withdrawing the price increase. Such price leadership with subsequent signaling by the other firms in the industry was commonly observed in the steel industry in the post-World War II period. Price leadership is also observed in the automobile industry—General Motors's price-setting decisions usually set the tone for the other two firms.

The price leader may be the largest firm in the industry, as in the GM case. Or it may be what is called a *barometric* price leader, a firm that is regarded as measuring the pressure of demand in the industry and able to figure out how to adjust price in the industry in a way that other firms in the industry would want to if they were explicitly cooperating.

Conditions Favorable to Cooperation

Under what conditions is it easy to collaborate? The collaboration will be easiest when it is legally permitted and when no new firms can enter the industry to disturb the comfortable monopoly arrangements. Thus the ideal for an oligopolistic industry is both to be allowed to fix price and to have control over new entry to the industry.

Licensing arrangements are a typical form of control over entry. Many professions—for example, the medical, dental, and haircutting professions—have attempted to control entry through licensing and then to control price by arguing that it is unethical to compete by cutting price. For a long time the medical profession succeeded in preventing price-cutting and in controlling entry.[4]

When it is illegal to cooperate, collusion is still possible. Collusion will be successful when it is easy to communicate the agreed-upon price and when it is easy for the firms in the industry to detect cheating. Thus collusion is more likely to be successful the smaller the number of firms in the market. Collusion is also easier when the good sold is homogeneous—the firms cutting price cannot plausibly claim that the price difference reflects quality differences. The stability of the cigarette price agreement was in part based on this homogeneity. Collusion is also easier when cost and demand conditions are stable—thus the optimal price does not change often.

Although collusion is possible, it may

still be illegal even if there is no explicit communication among the firms. Companies have been accused of violating the antitrust laws without its being claimed that they explicitly got together to fix prices. For instance, in 1946 the major cigarette manufacturers were convicted of price-fixing in violation of the Sherman Antitrust Act, even though there was no explicit agreement among them on prices. We discuss the antitrust laws in detail in Chapter 11.

4 NONCOOPERATIVE OLIGOPOLY BEHAVIOR

Collusion among oligopoly members breaks down under a variety of circumstances. It is difficult to keep price discipline when there are many firms in an industry, when their products are not the same, or when cost and demand conditions change rapidly. It is also difficult to maintain collusive behavior if firms do not know the prices being charged by other firms or the quantities sold. It is much easier to cheat on an agreement when there is no public information about prices and quantities.[5]

When firms cannot collude, the essential problem of oligopoly becomes one of strategies: each firm makes an assumption about the demand it faces and about its rivals' reactions to its own actions. The firm then makes a price and output decision on the basis of its beliefs about what other firms will do. Given that decision, the initiative passes to the next firm, which makes its move in a similar fashion. The process continues until some long-run equilibrium is reached.

There are no general predictions about

---

[4] See Paul J. Feldstein, *Health Care Economics*, Wiley Medical, New York, 1979, chap. 15, for a discussion of the licensing of doctors. In this chapter there is also an interesting discussion of the discriminating monopoly in medicine, which is an application of material covered in Chapter 9.

[5] This fact led Professor Morris Adelman of M.I.T. to suggest that the United States should sell the right to export oil to the United States in secret auctions. His idea was that countries in the OPEC cartel wishing to sell more would take advantage of the secrecy to cut prices in an effort to get into the U.S. market. The scheme has not been tried.

the outcome of such interactions among noncooperating oligopolists. What happens depends critically on what each participant assumes the others' reaction will be. We have already seen the Bertrand model, in which each firm assumes that the other firms will not match price cuts. Then each firm thinks of itself as gaining very substantially by cutting price and shifting demand away from all the rivals and toward itself. But with everybody taking a turn at cutting price, all oligopoly profits disappear because there is no mechanism that looks after the firms' common interest of restricting industry output to preserve the profits.

Now we look at two other models, each making different assumptions about what the firm thinks its rivals will do.

The Cournot Model

An alternative assumption about rivals' reactions is that rivals will maintain the quantity of output they plan to sell but will sell at whatever price is charged by the firm that takes the initiative in setting the price. This assumption about rivals' reactions is the core of the Cournot model of oligopoly, named after the 1838 analysis by the French economist Augustin Cournot.

The Cournot model shares the flavor of the Bertrand model. Because none of the rivals look after the firms' common interest, the final equilibrium in the oligopoly market is not that of a monopoly but one with a higher output and a lower price. In fact, the larger the number of rival firms, the closer the industry equilibrium moves to that of a perfectly competitive industry. Each firm only looks at the fact that cutting price will increase total quantity demanded from it, and thus it provides increased sales and profits for itself. None of the rivals worry because they are at the same time cutting industry profits and expanding industry output.

In the Cournot model the challenger

and the established firms adjust their respective optimal output levels to the point where their marginal revenue, given the output level of other firms, is equal to their marginal cost. Now consider a new firm coming into the industry. As a new firm enters an industry, the only way for it to get customers, given its assumption that other firms will continue to sell the same amounts as before, is by setting a price below the existing price. This immediately drives the equilibrium in the direction of the competitive equilibrium.

But now the existing firms will find that their marginal revenue is below their marginal cost, because the price at which they are selling has fallen. They therefore raise price partway back to where it started. Then the challenger responds. The final result is that the industry equilibrium price after the challenger has entered will be lower and nearer the competitive price than the price before the challenger appeared on the scene.

In moving the price toward the competitive level, the challenger increases its own profits (which were zero before, because it was not producing at all) but reduces the profits of the other firms. Indeed, the challenger actually reduces total profits earned by all the firms in the industry, because it reduces the price of output toward the competitive price at which zero profits are earned in the industry.

The Cournot model predicts that with only a few firms in an industry, price will be above the competitive level, and each firm will be earning above-normal profits. The more firms there are in the industry, the closer the predicted price will be to the competitive equilibrium price. This is because each firm acts entirely in its own interest, given its assumptions about how the other firms will react. There is no explicit or implicit agreement among the firms to try jointly to maximize profits.

The Kinked Oligopoly Demand Curve

The Bertrand and Cournot models show how price and output in an oligopolistic industry depend on the assumptions each firm makes about the way other firms will behave. In the Bertrand model, each firm believes that the other firm will hold its price constant, and price and quantity end up at the competitive level. In the Cournot model, each firm acts on the assumption that other firms will hold quantity constant and meet price cuts, and price ends up between the monopoly and competitive levels. The exact place where it ends up depends on how many firms there are in the industry.

The kinked oligopoly demand curve model makes a particularly interesting assumption about the responses of rivals to a price change by a competitor. The assumption is that when a firm cuts its price, all existing firms go along, but if a firm raises its price, none of the rivals follow suit.[6] These ideas are shown in Figure 10-5. With these beliefs, the oligopolistic firm has a kinked demand curve. When price is raised, the firm loses a lot of business because the rivals keep their prices low. The demand facing this firm in response to a price increase is therefore very elastic. When price is reduced, however, the firm does not gain much business, because the rivals cut their price. Figure 10-5 shows the implied kinked demand curve for the firm; it is more elastic at prices above the current price, P_0, and less elastic at prices below P_0.

Figure 10-5 also shows the firm's marginal cost curve, MC, and the marginal revenue curve, MR. The MR curve has a gap. At prices above P_0, marginal revenue is high because demand is elastic. At prices below P_0, marginal revenue is much lower because demand is less elastic. The MC curve goes through the gap in the MR curve,

---

[6] The theory was invented almost simultaneously in 1939 by Paul Sweezy in the United States and R. L. Hall and C. J. Hitch in England.

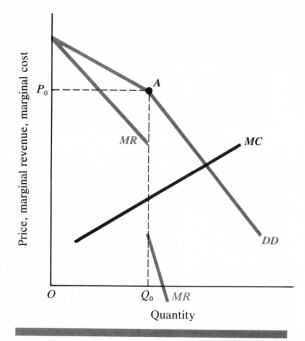

FIGURE 10-5 THE KINKED OLIGOPOLY DEMAND CURVE. An oligopolist assumes that rivals will match his price cuts but not his price hikes. Therefore, the demand schedule that the oligopolist faces is more elastic for price hikes, which result in a loss of customers, than for price cuts, which all rivals follow, with the result that relatively little is gained at their expense. With marginal cost schedule MC and initial price P_0 the oligopolist has no incentive to expand, because with all rivals following suit there is little gain in sales but a large sacrifice in price. The gap in MR stemming from the asymmetric response of rivals leaves the oligopolist at point A.

and the firm therefore will not move the price from P_0. At any price above P_0, marginal revenue exceeds marginal cost, and the firm should therefore reduce price and increase quantity. At any price below P_0, marginal revenue is less than marginal cost, and the firm should therefore increase price and reduce quantity. The conclusion is that the firm maximizes profits by keeping price at the current level.

Alternatively, we can say that it will take really big shifts in either the demand curve facing the firm or its cost conditions for it to want to change price. The theory

TABLE 10-2 ▮

MODELS OF OLIGOPOLY PRICING

TYPE OF BEHAVIOR	FACTORS INFLUENCING BEHAVIOR	PRICING MODEL	STRATEGIC ASSUMPTIONS	PRICE OUTCOME
Cooperative	1. Legal support 2. Product homogeneity 3. Stability of demand and costs 4. Ease of communication 5. Difficulty of entry	1. Full collusion: monopoly behavior in a cartel framework 2. Price leadership	All firms maintain the agreement Firms follow the leader but may signal disagreement by not following	Approximately monopoly price
Noncooperative	1. Illegality of collusion 2. Nonhomogeneity of products 3. Secrecy about price and output levels 4. Free entry	1. Cournot 2. Bertrand 3. Kinked demand curve model	Each firm assumes that the others will keep the quantity unchanged Each firm assumes that the others will keep the price unchanged Other firms follow price cuts but not price increases	Between monopoly and competitive prices; closer to competitive price the more firms there are in the industry Competitive price Prices are stable, but theory does not predict level of price
Mixed	1. Presence of one or a few large firms and many small ones	1. Dominant-firm model	The competitive fringe sells as much as it wants to at the going price; the dominant firm sets the price to maximize its profits	Price is between monopoly and competitive levels; closer to competitive level the larger the competitive fringe

predicts that oligopoly prices will be quite sticky.

To judge the model we must ask whether it does a good job of explaining the way the world works and predicting the effect of changes in the environment on the way firms respond. Evidence from antitrust suits does support the view that oligopolists are reluctant to cut prices because they believe that all that will happen is that rivals will do the same. This provides some support for the kinked demand curve model. Another prediction of the model is that price in oligopoly industries should be more stable than price in monopoly indus-

tries. Why? Because monopolists do not have to worry about the price responses of rivals, since they have no rivals. This second prediction is not supported.[7] Thus evidence on the kinked oligopoly demand curve is mixed.

Table 10-2 summarizes the previous discussion about oligopolistic markets. Unfortunately, there are no simple, well-estab-

[7] George J. Stigler, in "The Kinky Oligopoly Demand Curve and Rigid Prices," *Journal of Political Economy*, October 1947, examined the relative stability of prices in monopolies and oligopolies, arguing strongly both that we do not see more rigidity in oligopoly and that we should not expect to. Subsequent research has backed up Stigler's findings.

lished patterns of behavior in oligopolistic industries. Each of the types of behavior described in the different models can sometimes be observed.

5   ENTRY AND LIMIT PRICING

Now that we have discussed theories of oligopoly pricing, which are summarized in Table 10-2, we return to emphasize the necessity of barriers to entry for the success of an oligopoly. In particular, we discuss barriers to entry that are created by the firms in the industry rather than by economies of scale.

If there are constant costs of production, then an oligopoly that cannot control entry is certain to be undercut by firms coming into the industry and willing to sell at a price below the current industry price but above the cost of production. Even when there are economies of scale, the possibility of entry still puts some limits on the behavior of existing firms in an industry.

Firms in the industry cannot charge too high a price without making it possible for other firms to come into the industry and sell at a lower price. The price they will charge is a price that will be just low enough for it not to be profitable for other firms to enter the industry. This practice is known as *limit pricing*.

Existing firms may also use predatory pricing to prevent and deter entry.
Firms engage in *predatory pricing* when they adjust their prices with the aim of causing competitors to lose money and leave the industry.
Typically the predator cuts prices very sharply, to a level where he is losing money but where he hopes the competition is suffering more and cannot long survive.

A case in point is the Hankow Shipping Conference of the late nineteenth century. This was a group of shipowners who had fixed freight rates in shipping between China and the United Kingdom and who also had a clear policy toward new entrants. Here is the flavor of the agreement:[8]

> In 1885 the Conference decided that "if any non-Conference steamer should proceed to Hankow to load independently, any necessary number of Conference steamers should be sent at the same time to Hankow to underbid the freight which the independent shipowners might offer, *without any regard to whether the freight they should bid would be remunerative or not.*"

This says that if any other ships tried to get in on the shipping business, members of the conference would undercut them, no matter how much they might lose in the process. The aim was to prevent anyone else from coming in. The members of the conference were willing to take losses in the short run to keep out other entrants and thereby make excess profits from their monopoly position in the long run.

Whether predatory pricing succeeds in keeping out the new firms depends on how long the old and new firms can ride out the losses. If the old firms are bigger, they may well stand a good chance of winning. Sometimes a new entrant in an oligopolistic industry is a subsidiary of a firm that is itself large, though in another industry. Then it may have resources to ride out the initial period of losses that will accompany entry.

The possibility of entry is a powerful force in restricting monopoly pricing by existing firms. Indeed, even if there is only one firm in an industry, if it has no cost advantages over potential entrants and no way of keeping them out, it will have to keep its price virtually at the competitive level if it wants to remain the only firm in the industry. It will be a monopoly in name but not in power or profits.

[8] Quoted from B. S. Yamey, "Predatory Price Cutting: Notes and Comments," *Journal of Law and Economics*, April 1972, p. 139. Italics added. Copyright © by the University of Chicago.

6 OLIGOPOLY, PRICES, AND PROFITS

In this section we ask briefly what the relationship is between prices, profits, and the extent of competition in an industry. Table 10-3 shows the average rate of profits for firms of different asset sizes in the 4-year period 1977–1980. For each asset class, we look at the ratio of net profits to assets, determined on the basis of tax returns filed by corporations in the manufacturing industry. If bigness pays, larger firms will have higher rates of return.

The evidence in Table 10-3 is mixed. Surprisingly, the smallest firms, those with assets less than $10 million, show the highest rate of return, 7.7 percent. But beyond these small firms, for which the data are in fact incomplete, we do observe that profitability rises with size. Firms in the $10 million–$25 million asset size, for example, have a lower rate of return than the next group, and so on. Firms with assets in excess of $1 billion have the highest rate.

More sophisticated analyses have related profit rates in industries to concentration ratios, and also to the presence of barriers to entry.[9] Although these studies are controversial, the weight of the evidence is that profits are higher in industries with higher concentration ratios, suggesting that

oligopoly does lead to high profits—as theory predicts it will.

There is also some evidence on the *price* performance of oligopolies. Our theory clearly indicates that a particular industry would charge higher prices under oligopoly than would prevail in the same industry if it were fully competitive. An interesting test of this hypothesis has been included in a study by the University of Wisconsin Food Research Institute. The researchers looked at the prices of brand-name grocery products sold by three chains in 36 U.S. cities. The question posed was whether the price of a *given* basket varied systematically with the degree of concentration in the different local markets. Table 10-4 summarizes some of the findings.

The table shows an index of the cost of a given basket of brand-name groceries as it varies with two characteristics of oligopoly. These are, first, the particular chain's share of sales in a given local market, which is shown in the left-hand column, and, second, the overall concentration in a particular market as measured by the four-firm concentration ratio.[10] Each entry in Table 10-4 thus represents a combination of a chain's local market share and a given local market's overall extent of concentration. The index is 100 for the combination where the four leading firms account for 40 percent of local grocery sales and a particular chain has 10 percent of the market.

[9] Leonard Weiss, "The Concentration-Profits Relationship and Antitrust," in H. J. Goldschmid et al., *Industrial Concentration: The New Learning*, Little, Brown, Boston, 1974.

[10] The four-firm concentration ratio is the total share of sales of the four biggest producers in the industry.

TABLE 10-3

CORPORATE PROFITABILITY IN MANUFACTURING BY ASSET SIZE, 1977–1980
(Net Profits as Percentage of Assets, Average of Annual Data)

	ASSET SIZE, $ millions					
UNDER 10	10–25	25–50	50–100	100–250	250–1000	1000+
7.7%	6.1%	6.5%	6.6%	6.8%	7.2%	7.5%

Source: Calculated from *Statistical Abstract of the United States, 1981,* Table 922.

TABLE 10-4

OLIGOPOLY PRICING IN GROCERIES
(Index of Prices Charged)

CHAIN'S SHARE IN LOCAL MARKET, %	FOUR-FIRM CONCENTRATION RATIO IN LOCAL MARKET*		
	40	60	70
10	100	103	105.3
40	102.4	105.4	107.7
55	103.6	106.5	108.9

* Percentage of total sales by the four leading stores.
Source: Leonard Weiss, "The Structure-Conduct-Performance Criterion and Anti-Trust," in Oliver Williamson (ed.), *Antitrust and Economics,* Dame Publications, Houston, 1980, p. 245.

The theory of oligopoly suggests that the prices of the same goods should be higher under oligopoly than under competition, the more so the larger the degree of monopoly enjoyed by a given firm or by the group of oligopolists. Thus the price of the standard basket should increase both with the four-firm concentration ratio and with the individual firm's share. The table very strongly confirms that hypothesis.

A given firm with, say, a 10 percent market share will charge prices that are 3 percent higher if it works in a local market with a four-firm ratio of 60 percent rather than 40 percent. It will increase the price of a standard basket by 5.3 percent if concentration reaches 70 percent.

The table confirms also that a given chain will set *higher* prices if it has a larger market share. Thus in a market with, say, a 40 percent concentration ratio, a firm will charge prices that are 2.4 percent higher if it has a share of 40 percent rather than only 10 percent. If its market share were 55 percent, the price differential would rise to 3.6 percent. The overall impact of oligopoly can be judged by comparing the two extremes, the upper left-hand and lower right-hand entries. There is nearly a 9 percent differential between a chain with a small share in an un-

concentrated market and a chain with a large share in a heavily concentrated market. A 9 percent differential in the case of buying the *same* basket of groceries is certainly a large differential.

There is a growing body of evidence from careful industry studies showing that the prices charged by oligopolies vary with the extent of oligopoly. This is true not only for the prices of groceries but also for the interest charged by banks and the prices of gasoline, for example.[11]

7 MONOPOLISTIC COMPETITION

The theory of monopolistic competition[12] describes a situation in which there is a variety of goods, with each firm producing a good that is a close substitute for its neighbors' goods. We should be thinking of firms that compete by choosing to sell at different locations, or firms that produce different brands of toothpaste or ice cream. Everyone knows that ice cream is good, but not everyone agrees about which is best. Each ice cream parlor faces a downward-sloping demand curve.

The individual monopolistic competitor faces a downward-sloping demand curve for its own product. A cut in price increases the quantity demanded of this particular product by shifting demand away from competing firms that produce close substitutes, but not identical products. If products were strictly identical, consumers would only buy from one seller, the cheapest. But with some product differentiation every firm has its own demand curve and its own market. A cut in price increases quantity demanded, mostly by diverting demand from other

[11] Leonard Weiss, "The Structure-Conduct-Performance Criterion and Anti-Trust," in Oliver Williamson (ed.), *Antitrust and Economics,* Dame Publications, Houston, 1980.
[12] This is the title of the famous book published by E. H. Chamberlin in 1933 (Harvard University Press) that develops the analysis that follows.

firms, but also in part by inducing consumers to substitute away from entirely different goods and toward the commodity whose price has fallen. Because its demand curve slopes downward, a monopolistic competitor can choose the price that maximizes its profits.

The theory of monopolistic competition analyzes both the short-run equilibrium and the long-run equilibrium of a typical firm. At all times the individual firm acts as a monopolist, faced with a downward-sloping demand curve. It maximizes profits by setting marginal revenue equal to marginal cost. The individual firm is small and assumes in setting its price that competitors do not react to its own actions.

In the short run there are a given number of firms in the industry. Existing firms may be making profits. But the demand curve facing each firm depends on the prices and the number of close substitutes for the firm's output. The more competing models there are and the lower their prices, the smaller the demand for output. If monopolistic competitors are making profits in the short run, other firms come into the industry. As they move in, the demand curves of existing firms shift to the left. The long-run equilibrium is reached when firms in the industry are making zero profits.

We now analyze both the short-run equilibrium and the long-run equilibrium in more detail.

Short-Run Equilibrium

In Figure 10-6 we show the average and marginal cost curves for a single ice cream parlor, firm K, which faces a downward-sloping demand curve. The average cost curve has the U shape that is familiar from earlier chapters. The firm sets price at the level of output at which marginal revenue is equal to marginal cost. Initially, the firm is making profits at this point equal to $(P_0 - AC_0) \times Q_0$.

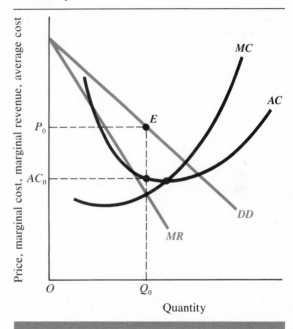

FIGURE 10-6 SHORT-RUN EQUILIBRIUM UNDER MONOPOLISTIC COMPETITION. The monopolistic competitor faces a downward-sloping demand curve. Increasing output and sales will therefore cause the price to fall. The monopolistic competitor takes this effect into account the same way a monopolist does, choosing output level Q_0, where $MR = MC$. Profits are equal to $(P_0 - AC_0) \times Q_0$. These profits in turn invite entry.

Long-Run Equilibrium

The profits attract other ice cream parlors into the business. As they enter, the demand curve for firm K is shifted to the left because customers move over to the new firms. New competitors continue to enter so long as firm K and similar firms are earning profits. Entry stops when firm K and other firms in the industry are earning zero profits, or, in other words, when price is equal to average cost. This situation is shown by the tangency equilibrium at point F in Figure 10-7.

The *tangency equilibrium* in monopolistic competition is the point of long-run equilibrium, at which the demand curve is tangent to (touches) the AC

FIGURE 10-7 LONG-RUN EQUILIBRIUM FOR A MONOPOLISTIC COMPETITOR. Under monopolistic competition, the entry of new producers continues as long as there are profits in the industry. The entry of new firms shifts the demand curves of existing firms to the left, reducing profits. Entry stops when profits are zero. That happens when a double condition is satisfied: for each firm marginal revenue is equal to marginal cost, *and* price equals average cost. This special equilibrium in which firms choose their prices the same way monopolists do but have no monopoly profits characterizes long-run equilibrium under monopolistic competition at point *F*. The demand curve has shifted all the way from *DD* in Figure 10-6 to *DD'* here.

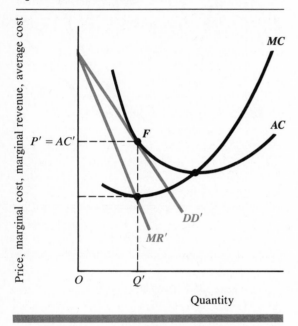

its are counted in the cost curve.) At that point, marginal revenue is equal to marginal cost, price is equal to average cost, and price exceeds marginal cost.

The equilibrium of the typical monopolistically competitive firm has a number of interesting characteristics. First, the firm is *not* producing at the point of minimum average cost. The firm could be producing more cheaply. Second, price exceeds marginal cost, and so there is a gap between the value consumers place on the good and the marginal cost of production. Third, because price exceeds marginal cost, each firm would willingly sell more than it does at the existing price. If new customers showed up wanting to buy at the existing price, the firm would profit from selling to them.

This last observation helps explain why firms are usually eager for more customers. As Professor Robert L. Bishop of M.I.T. has put it, the theory of monopolistic competition explains "why we are a race of eager sellers and coy buyers, with purchasing agents getting the Christmas presents from the salesmen rather than the other way around."[14] Remarkably enough, firms in a competitive industry that are selling just as much as they want to basically do not care if an extra customer shows up and wants to buy at the existing price. The perfect competitor tells the customer that he is not interested in selling more, because he is quite happy with his current level of output. But the monopolistic competitor would be happy to sell more at the existing price, because price is above marginal cost for him.

The theory of monopolistic competition is of considerable value both for explaining what equilibrium is in situations where there are many firms selling slightly different products and for bringing product variety squarely into the picture.

curve at the level of output where *MR* = *MC*. At the tangency equilibrium profits are zero (*AC'* = *P'*), and there is therefore no entry into the industry.

The emphasis of the theory is that firms producing close but not perfect substitutes for existing goods are attracted into the business as long as existing firms are making profits. They keep coming in until all firms have been driven to the point of zero profits.[13] (Remember, as usual, that normal prof-

---

[13] If firms differ in efficiency, some firms may be earning profits.

[14] This quotation is from Professor Bishop's unpublished magnum opus, "Microeconomic Theory," on which generations of M.I.T. students were raised.

Despite these attractions, it has been argued vigorously that the theory of monopolistic competition is unnecessary.[15] The argument is that the theory does not make predictions that are different from the ones that could be made about a competitive industry. For instance, suppose that a tax is imposed on a good. What will happen? Price will rise, says the competitive model. So does the monopolistic competition model. No matter that the theory of monopolistic competition seems more realistic, say the critics; it is not realism but predictions that matter. And, they add, monopolistic competition adds little in the way of prediction.

Despite the criticisms, the theory deserves attention because it focuses on situations where there are many different goods, close but not perfect substitutes for each other, and because it shows how equilibrium is reached in such situations. And in predicting that price is typically above marginal cost even though profits are zero, it does say something that is important and quite different from what the competitive model says.

8 VARIETY

How much does variety matter? And does the free market provide the right amount of variety, or do firms try too hard to distinguish their goods from their competitors' goods, creating wasteful excesses of variety?[16] These are questions suggested by the theory of monopolistic competition.

The essence of the problem is that the provision of variety may not be cheap. Suppose that goods are close substitutes. Suppose also that there are increasing returns to

scale at low levels of output, as on the U-shaped average cost curve. Then if we tried to produce all goods, they would be produced at a high cost because we would make just a few of each and not get the benefit of economies of scale. It is likely to be better to restrict the number of goods produced, compensating by producing goods more cheaply by benefiting from scale economies. Looking around in the shops we often have the feeling that there is too much variety, with needless expense incurred by manufacturers who need to differentiate their product from others. But economists as yet have no strong evidence to present showing whether we have enough, too much, or too little variety.

We now interpret the variety issue using the theory of monopolistic competition. Under monopolistic competition the industry equilibrium is one where each firm produces with AC above the minimum average cost (see Figure 10-7) and where price exceeds marginal cost. Therefore, each firm underproduces. There are too many firms and not enough output. But it is also the case that the equilibrium of an industry in monopolistic competition offers product variety as compensation.

Consumers value both variety and low prices. They could have lower prices and less variety if the government promoted policies that led to concentration, for example, by licensing a maximum number of firms or product variants. With a restriction on entry by licensing, the individual firm would not be forced by competition to contract output to low-volume, high-unit-cost levels. Each plant would be more nearly used at its minimum cost level, and consumers would get goods at the lowest possible prices. But, of course, along with the lower prices, there is a smaller variety of goods.

The larger the total market, the more variety is possible. As the economy grows and people become richer, more variety be-

---

[15] George J. Stigler, in "Monopolistic Competition in Retrospect," reprinted in his book *The Organization of Industry*, Irwin, Homewood, Ill., 1968, takes this view.
[16] Kelvin J. Lancaster, *Variety, Equity, and Efficiency*, Columbia University Press, New York, 1979, presents a modern analysis of these questions.

comes possible because demand for all goods is rising. In a very poor country, there may be only enough demand to buy the output of one firm, which would certainly be a monopoly. As the economy grows and consumers' demand expands, there is room for entry by more firms, and the market structure evolves into monopolistic competition, giving consumers the benefits of variety.

The same gain can be achieved by taking advantage of international trade. Much of the trade between the advanced industrialized countries takes place in the same industry. We sell them cars, and they sell us cars. This trade in differentiated products makes people in both countries better off by giving them access to a broader range of products, each of which is produced for the world market and can therefore be produced on a reasonably large scale.

9   ADVERTISING

Advertising is usually associated with oligopoly and monopolistic competition. Expenditures on advertising in the United States come to about 2 percent of the GNP. They are divided among the media as shown in Table 10-5. Perhaps the most surprising fact is that far more is spent on newspaper advertising than on TV advertising.

Much of the advertising that we see appears to be pure waste. Consider, for example, the beer industry. In 1981 the leading firm spent about $200 million on advertising and promotion, and even third- and fourth-place firms were spending as much as $100

million. Is there any reason to believe that society is any better off for having spent so many resources on learning what kind of beer which company sells?

The part of advertising that is associated with the sale of competing brands of virtually identical goods is undoubtedly socially wasteful. Much of the advertising cancels itself out. By the time brand X has told us what is wrong with brand Y and vice versa, we are convinced only that we need neither. (This may be good information to have, though it is not what the advertisers had in mind.)

But much of the advertising serves a socially useful purpose. It provides information on the availability and prices of goods that consumers otherwise would have to spend resources to obtain in some other way. Think of the Yellow Pages and your walking fingers, saving shoe leather and gasoline. Much of newspaper advertising is informative rather than persuasive, and newspaper advertising makes up a quarter of all advertising.

An interesting study by Professor Lee Benham of Washington University, St. Louis, examined the prices of eyeglasses in different states, where advertising was or was not permitted.[17] Benham found the prices of eyeglasses to be about 25 to 30 percent lower in states that permitted advertising than in states that did not. In this case advertising certainly increased competition

[17] Lee Benham, "The Effect of Advertising on the Price of Eyeglasses," *Journal of Law and Economics*, October 1972.

TABLE 10-5

ADVERTISING EXPENDITURES IN 1979
(Percentage of Total in Specified Category)

| NEWSPAPERS | | MAGAZINES | TV | | RADIO | DIRECT MAIL | OTHER |
NATIONAL	LOCAL		NETWORK	OTHER			
4.2	25.0	5.9	9.3	11.2	6.7	13.4	24.3

Source: Statistical Abstract of the United States, 1981, Table 983, p. 572.

BOX 10-1

A CONCENTRATED BREW: OLIGOPOLY IN THE BEER INDUSTRY

The beer industry is an excellent example of an oligopolistic market. It has all the features: product differentiation, brand names, advertising, a high concentration of sales, and price leadership. The following table shows the concentration ratios of the industry in the past 25 years. It is quite apparent that concentration has vastly increased and is still growing, as the 1982 figures will show when they become available. The interesting change is not only in the growing share of the 4 top companies but also—and especially—in the data for the 8 largest and 20 largest firms. Now the 8 largest firms account for more than 80 percent of the market, while they accounted for less than 50 percent in 1958. The 20 largest firms make up practically the whole market.

CONCENTRATION RATIOS IN THE BEER INDUSTRY

	% OF SHIPMENTS ACCOUNTED FOR BY			
	4 LARGEST COMPANIES	8 LARGEST COMPANIES	20 LARGEST COMPANIES	50 LARGEST COMPANIES
1958	29	45	69	88
1967	40	59	87	98
1972	52	70	91	99
1977	65	83	98	99

Source: U.S. Bureau of the Census, *Census of Manufacturing: 1977, Concentration Ratios in Manufacturing,* 1979.

The concentration in the last 25 years resulted from several large regional firms in the midwest setting up local plants in other parts of the country, thus avoiding transportation costs, and successfully outcompeting the small local brands. The small local brands were bought up. Their factories were used to produce the large national brands. The survivors were names such as Budweiser, Michelob, and Miller, whereas the victims were hundreds of smaller local breweries.

The table below shows the very sharp increase in the market share of the few leading brands. Most impressive is the rise of Miller, which dates back to the purchase by Phillip Morris, cigarette producer, of a 50 percent share of

MARKET SHARES IN THE BEER INDUSTRY
(Percentage of Total Beer Production)

	1970	1977	1981
Anheuser-Busch	17.7	22.7	29.8
Miller	4.1	15.0	22.0
Schlitz	12.1	13.7	7.8
Pabst	8.4	9.9	7.4
Coors	5.8	7.9	7.2

Source: Reprinted from *Beverage Industry,* Feb. 5, 1982, © by Harcourt Brace Jovanovich, Inc.

the Miller beer company. It then embarked on a major advertising campaign.*

Advertising is an important feature of the industry. In 1981 the leading firm spent $200 million, and firms not even among the top three spent between $50 million and $100 million. The advertising is devoted to creating brand recognition and identification on the part of customers, to introducing new products, and to stopping defection to rival products.

Pricing in the beer industry follows the pattern of price leadership. A particular firm in the industry will normally initiate price changes, and other firms follow suit.

Product diversification is yet another characteristic feature of the industry. The major producers innovate by bringing out new products—light beer, heavy beer, all kinds of beer—and they imitate each other in attempts to shift consumers between major brands. In the meantime, concentration continues on a large scale, and the Justice Department is starting to take an interest in preventing possible collusion.

---

* An informative article is "The Battle of the Beers," *Newsweek,* Sept. 4, 1978.

---

and was socially useful. Similarly, we can be sure that the opposition of the legal and medical professions to advertising by their members has less to do with a desire to prevent wasting resources on advertising than with a desire to prevent competition.

There are additional questions about advertising. First, it is often asserted that massive advertising serves to keep existing firms in an oligopoly safe from competition. By spending heavily on advertising, the existing firms make it expensive for other firms to enter the industry and thus keep them out. Thus advertising is often described as a barrier to entry—one of the mechanisms by which firms keep their industry noncompetitive.

The second issue is whether advertising is used to manipulate consumer tastes. Are we, as many feel, the greedy consumers we are despite human nature and because of advertising? Or is it merely human nature that ensures that we are serious consumers of even frivolous goods? We are asking whether advertising is mainly informative or manipulative. The answer must be that it is both. The important question is, To what extent are we being informed, and to what

extent are we being manipulated?[18] Important as that question is in judging the performance of the economic system, we do not have a good answer to it.

This is an important question because we judge the economic system by its ability to satisfy our wants and needs. If part of the system is manipulating our wants, it is difficult to say what sort of a job the system is doing in satisfying them. If we want the latest in electronic watches with a 12-tone alarm only because a clever advertising agency has persuaded us that everyone should have one, it is difficult to be impressed by the economy's success in providing us with such a watch.

The questions to be answered here are deep, and there are no ready answers from economics. But we should be on guard against the simpleminded notion that all our wants are the creation of advertising and manipulation. Many new and heavily advertised products do indeed make life easier.

---

[18] J. K. Galbraith emphasized these issues in his book *The New Industrial State,* Houghton Mifflin, Boston, 1967. See, too, William S. Comanor and Thomas A. Wilson, "The Effect of Advertising on Competition," *Journal of Economic Literature,* June 1979.

SUMMARY

1   Oligopolies exist because, first, it is profitable to keep the price above the competitive level, and second, there may be substantial scale economies in an industry. The second reason for the existence of oligopoly says that there are natural oligopolies.

2   There are two basic forces at work in determining the behavior of oligopolists. By *colluding*, firms can keep price above the competitive level and make profits. By violating the agreement, individual firms can do better for themselves so long as the other firms do not respond.

3   The collusive model of oligopoly behavior says that oligopolies will choose the monopoly price and output. The Bertrand model says that they will choose the competitive price. The difference in results stems from the differing assumptions that the individual firms make about their rivals' responses to their own actions.

4   Cooperation among firms is easiest when it is legal and firms set up cartels to agree on price and the division of the market. OPEC is the biggest and most successful cartel. The success of OPEC is largely due to the presence of a dominant firm or a few dominant firms.

5   When explicit collusion is illegal, firms sometimes find ways of cooperating on pricing decisions anyway. In a typical situation, one firm acts as a price leader. Implicit collusion is also illegal in the United States.

6   There are a variety of oligopoly models describing the behavior of firms that cannot collude. Two of the best known are the Cournot model and the kinked oligopoly demand curve model. The Cournot model predicts that an industry's behavior is more nearly competitive the larger the number of firms. The kinked oligopoly demand curve model predicts that prices in an oligopoly are very stable.

7   If an industry is not a natural oligopoly, the possibility of entry puts limits on the prices that existing firms in the industry can charge. If they set a price that is too high, new firms will enter the industry and compete away their profits. Thus many oligopolistic industries try to get legal control over entry.

8   Monopolistic competition exists when there are many firms selling similar products, with each firm facing a downward-sloping demand curve. The entry of new firms selling substitutes for the goods drives down profits. The monopolistic competition equilibrium occurs where firms have zero profits. At this point price will exceed marginal cost, unlike the situation in a competitive industry.

9   Advertising is usually associated with oligopoly and monopolistic competition. As much as 2 percent of GNP is used for advertising. The key question is whether this advertising is informative or manip-

ulative. Much of it is undoubtedly informative, as evidence that advertising is associated with lower prices shows. But we do not know how much of advertising is socially wasteful.

KEY TERMS

Collusion
Barriers to entry
Bertrand model
Cartel
Dominant-firm model
Competitive fringe

Price leader
Cournot model
Kinked oligopoly demand curve
Limit pricing
Predatory pricing
Tangency equilibrium

PROBLEMS

1 The demand curve facing an industry is as follows:

PRICE	QUANTITY	PRICE	QUANTITY
10	1	5	6
9	2	4	7
8	3	3	8
7	4	2	9
6	5	1	10

(a) Suppose that the industry is a monopoly and that the monopolist has a constant marginal cost of production equal to 3 (also equal to the average cost). What price and output level will the monopolist choose? (b) Now suppose that there are two firms in the industry, which is therefore a duopoly. Assume that each can produce at a constant average and marginal cost of 3. What price and output level will maximize their joint profits if they decide to get together? (c) Why do the two firms have to agree on the level of output that each will produce? (d) Why might each firm be tempted to cheat if it can avoid retaliation by the other? What does this tell you about the behavior of oligopolists?

2 Suppose that one of the firms in the industry (call it firm Z) decides to cheat on the agreement and believes that the other firm (firm A) will continue to keep its price fixed.

(a) What will firm Z do? (b) How do you expect firm A to react? (c) Where might a process like this end?

3 Suppose now that the firms are back together, each charging the monopoly price. Once again firm Z decides to cheat. This time it assumes that firm A will try to keep its sales constant. (Assume that A and Z were originally sharing the market equally.) (a) Supposing that A in fact did not adjust its quantity sold, show how much Z would sell at each price. This is the demand curve Z believes it faces. (b) Given the demand curve it believes it faces, what price and output level will Z choose? (c) How is A likely to respond? (d) Whose oligopoly models are described in Problem 2 and in this problem? (e) What are the weaknesses of these theories?

4 (a) For any five of the industries for which concentration ratios are specified in Table 9-2, explain whether you think economies of scale are likely to be important in explaining the share of the four largest firms. (b) How would you try to find out whether your explanations are correct?

5 In many countries there are dairy or fruit marketing boards. These are organizations to which the farmers who grow a particular type of fruit or who produce dairy products belong and through which they sell their output. In some cases, the marketing board tells its members how much of the product they will be able to sell to it in that year. In other cases, the board merely buys as much as the farmers wish to sell, and it pays the farmers the amount it obtains by selling the product, with an adjustment for its costs. (a) Under which one of these arrangements is the board likely to be acting as a cartel? (b) Why might the cartel-like arrangement be unstable unless the board had legal powers to require all farmers to sell their products only to it?

6 This question is about the importance of entry. Go back to Problem 1. Assume that one firm can produce more cheaply than any other, at a constant marginal and average cost of 3. Suppose that all the other firms that potentially can enter the industry can produce at a constant average and marginal cost of 5. (a) What price will the single firm in the industry charge? (b) What price would the firm charge if there were no threat of entry? (c) What, therefore, has the threat of entry done to the price?

7 Service station and automobile repair shop dealers have sometimes suggested that mechanics should be licensed to ensure that repairs are done by qualified people. Some economists have argued that there is no need for licensing. So long as the mechanics are trained at a reputable institution (frequently the automobile manufacturers provide training courses), any customer who cares will be able to find a qualified mechanic by asking about his training. (a) Why should those economists argue against licensing? (b) Evaluate the arguments for and against the licensing of auto mechanics. (c) Are the arguments different in the case of doctors? Why or why not?

8 Table 10-5 in the text gives the percentages of total advertising expenditures accounted for by different media in 1979. (a) Can these expenditures be classified in any way as informative versus persuasive? (b) Why does the distinction between informative advertising and persuasive advertising matter? (c) Do you think the distinction is a useful one? (d) Is there a case to be made on economic grounds for banning certain types of advertising?

9 In the dominant-firm model in the chapter, what is the effect on the price of an increase in the size of the competitive fringe, in the sense that the supply curve of the competitive fringe moves outward and to the right?

10 The table below describes the demand curve that an oligopolist thinks he faces. His marginal cost of production is constant and equal to 3.

A KINKED DEMAND CURVE

PRICE	QUANTITY	PRICE	QUANTITY
20	0	15	5
19	1	12	6
18	2	9	7
17	3	6	8
16	4	3	9

(a) What is the firm's price and level of output? (b) To what level would the oligopolist's cost of production have to rise before he would increase the price?

On January 9, 1982, an article in *The New York Times* stated:

U.S. SETTLES PHONE SUIT, DROPS I.B.M. CASE;
A.T. & T. TO SPLIT UP, TRANSFORMING INDUSTRY

The American Telephone and Telegraph Company settled the Justice Department's antitrust law suit today by agreeing to give up the 22 Bell System companies that provide most of the nation's telephone service.

On a landmark antitrust day, the Justice Department also dropped its marathon case against the International Business Machines Corporation, a suit that had sought to break up the company that has dominated the computer industry.

The A.T. & T. agreement, if finally approved by a Federal Court, would be the largest and most significant antitrust settlement in decades. It is likely to be compared with the 1911 settlement that divided the Rockefeller family's Standard Oil Company into 33 subsidiaries, some of them huge oil companies in their own right. . . .[1]

This chapter discusses the economics of antitrust and natural monopolies. We study how the government attempts through law and regulation to reinforce, maintain, or restore competition in the face of attempts to monopolize markets.

The IBM and AT&T cases are outstanding examples of government concern with competition. But there are more, ranging from price fixing in grocery stores in Cleveland to oligopolistic practices in the market for breakfast cereals. The interesting point, in all these cases, is that the law does try to prevent monopoly collusion between firms.

The law does not have an easy time, because some of the key economic questions in the area do not have clear-cut answers. At what market share does monopolization of an industry start—30 percent, 50 percent, or higher? Should we prevent mergers of firms that gain monopoly power by joining but that also achieve significant cost reductions? Is the cost of monopoly and oligopoly large enough to be a matter of concern at all?

We start with a discussion of the costs of monopoly.

11

Antitrust and Regulation of Natural Monopolies

1 THE COSTS OF MONOPOLY AND OLIGOPOLY

Experts disagree on the costs of monopoly and oligopoly. Professor F. M. Scherer of Yale has argued that the losses in the United States from a lack of competition are large enough "to treat every family in

---

[1] Ernest Holsendolph, *New York Times*, Jan. 9, 1982, p. l. Copyright © 1982 by the New York Times Company. Reprinted by permission.

FIGURE 11-1   THE SOCIAL COST OF MO-
NOPOLY. The industry has a horizontal long-
run average and marginal cost schedule.
Under perfect competition, equilibrium would
be at B. Under monopoly, output is restricted
to the point where $MR = MC$, and thus only
Q_M is produced. The monopolist earns excess
profits equal to the rectangle $P_M P_C CA$, but society suffers a welfare cost equal to the triangle ABC.

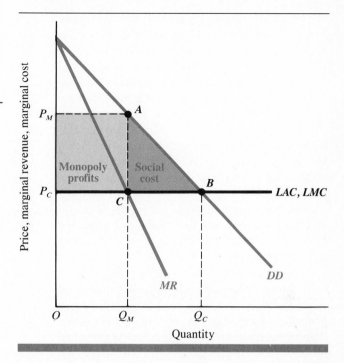

the land to a steak dinner at a good restaurant." In contrast, Chicago's George Stigler
recommends that "economists might serve a
more useful purpose if they fought fires or
termites instead of monopoly."[2]

There is no disagreement on what monopolies or oligopolies do: they restrict output and raise price as compared to a competitive market. What is at issue is the size of
the losses that result for society.

In earlier chapters we showed that monopolies—or oligopolies, for that matter—
tend to keep output below the competitive
level. The restriction of output allows the
firms in the industry to earn abnormally
high profits. But it also creates a social loss
by opening up a difference between the

marginal cost of output and the value of an
additional unit to the consumer. In Figure
11-1 we show the triangle ABC, which represents the welfare cost, or the cost to society, from monopolistic output restriction.

In Figure 11-1 we assume that there is a
constant long-run average and marginal cost
schedule. Under perfect competition the
industry equilibrium would be at point B,
where the long-run supply schedule, LMC,
intersects the demand schedule, DD. But
under monopoly, output is restricted to the
level where $MR = LMC$. Monopoly output,
therefore, is only Q_M, and monopoly price is
P_M, which is higher than the competitive
price, P_C. The restriction of output implies
that the value of an extra unit of the good to
consumers exceeds the cost of an extra unit
to society. The triangle ABC represents the
welfare cost of output restriction.

How large are the social, or welfare,
costs of monopoly, obtained by adding together triangles such as ABC in all industries where output is restricted by monop-

[2] F. M. Scherer, *Industrial Market Structure and Economic Performance*, Rand McNally, Chicago, 1980,
and George Stigler, "The Statistics of Monopoly and
Merger," *Journal of Political Economy*, February
1956. The quotations come from J. Siegfried and T.
Tiemann, "The Welfare Cost of Monopoly: An Interindustry Analysis," *Economic Inquiry*, journal of Western Economic Association, June 1974.

oly or oligopoly? Estimates in the literature have placed the costs to society from monopoly anywhere between some fraction of 1 percent of GNP—this is the traditional estimate due to Arnold Harberger—and an amount as high as 7 percent.[3] Since these economywide estimates depend largely on the precise assumptions of the author, the issue is not likely to be settled soon. Even so, two questions are relevant. First, why do most calculations produce a relatively low number, like 1 percent of GNP? Second, should we conclude that monopoly is not a serious problem and that there is no reason to have antitrust legislation and regulation of monopolies?

The reason for the relatively low number is that there are very few firms around earning huge profits. Or, at least, there are not many firms that report huge profit rates. The basic measure of welfare cost is related to price minus marginal cost (the distance AC in Figure 11-1). Because there are no data on marginal cost, it is usually assumed that costs are constant, as in Figure 11-1, and so marginal cost equals average cost—and there are data on average cost.

Given the assumption that marginal cost equals average cost, the costs of monopoly will arise only for those firms whose price is above average cost (including the allowance for normal profits). In Figure 11-1, the costs of monopoly will be high only if the

TABLE 11-1

BREAKDOWN OF THE WELFARE COST OF MONOPOLY IN THE UNITED STATES
(U.S. Industry and Manufacturing, 1963)

INDUSTRY	% OF TOTAL WELFARE COST
Motor vehicles	43.94
Petroleum refining with extraction	8.53
Plastic materials and synthetics	6.14
Drugs	4.90
Office and computing machinery	3.91
Photographic equipment and supplies	2.83
Tobacco manufactures	2.60
Electrical transmission and distribution equipment	1.21
Communications equipment	1.16

Source: John J. Siegfried and Thomas K. Tiemann, "The Welfare Cost of Monopoly: An Interindustry Analysis," *Economic Inquiry,* journal of Western Economic Association, June 1974.

distance AC, equal to P_M-LAC, is large. Thus only if there are large differences between price and average cost, or high profit rates, will we get large estimates of the social costs of monopoly. And we really do not find evidence of many firms earning extremely high profits over extended periods.

Although estimates of the social cost of monopoly and oligopoly remain tentative, it is interesting to look at a study of the United States that identifies the industries responsible for large parts of the total cost. The data in Table 11-1 are from a study in which the total cost of monopoly in U.S. industry and manufacturing in 1963 was calculated to be somewhat less than 1 percent of the GNP. Nearly half of that total came from the motor vehicle industry; other important contributions were plastic materials, drugs, and petroleum refining.

The second question is whether we should think that the monopoly problem is small and that we should not waste our time dealing with it. Here we want to look at two factors. First, the costs of monopoly might

---

[3] Arnold C. Harberger, "Monopoly and Resource Allocation," *American Economic Review,* May 1954. The 7 percent estimate comes from Keith Cowling and Dennis C. Mueller, "The Social Costs of Monopoly Power," *Economic Journal,* December 1978. They provide a detailed discussion of possible alternative assumptions about the demand curve and cost curves, and show that estimated costs of monopoly can differ substantially depending on the assumptions. Their modifications in one case would increase the Harberger estimates to close to 7 percent of GNP. Their article is quite difficult reading. So is the follow-up discussion in S. C. Littlechild, "Misleading Calculations of the Social Cost of Monopoly Power," *Economic Journal,* June 1981.

be small because we have antitrust laws and regulation, preventing firms from exercising monopoly power. Second, there may be several other costs of monopoly.

We briefly discuss three other costs. First, monopolies may not minimize costs as carefully as other firms. Without the threat of competition, monopolies can lead an easy life. Indeed, cost calculations may include items that should really count as profits. The owners of the firms may be able to conceal some of their income as costs and thus lead us to underestimate their profits. For instance, the staff may travel first-class, or the company may provide exceptional rest and recreation facilities for the staff. Similarly, as we discussed in Chapter 9, monopoly firms may not innovate as vigorously as competitive firms—though we recall that this is a disputed point.

Second, monopoly may cause waste. As firms try either to obtain monopoly positions or to engage in wasteful (from society's viewpoint—not their own) attempts to prevent competition, they incur the costs of lobbying and bringing lawsuits to protect patents. And perhaps there are costs of maintaining extra capacity, so that any potential competitor knows that he will be undersold by the existing firm if he enters the industry.

A specific form of unnecessary costs is advertising. As we discussed in Chapter 10, much of advertising is socially wasteful. Since advertising expense is about 2 percent of GNP and much is undertaken in monopolistic industries, the cost of advertising may be a sizable extra cost of monopoly.

Third, there is the political issue of whether monopoly creates an excessive concentration of political power. The antitrust laws were in part a reaction against the growing role of monopoly combinations and trusts in political and economic life at the end of the nineteenth century. Thus when President Theodore Roosevelt brought antitrust action against the giant Northern Securities Trust of J. Pierpont Morgan, the monopolist told the President of the United States, "If we have done anything wrong, send your man to my man and they can fix it up."[4] Clearly, he had the notion that he and the President could settle matters between them, without the intervention of the law. Such power, it was strongly felt, was entirely incompatible with a well-functioning democracy.

The Distribution of Monopoly Profits

Closely related to the issue of economic power is the distribution of monopoly profits. In Figure 11-1 the rectangle $P_M P_C CA$ represents the monopoly profits that arise from restricting output. These profits exceed the normal return to capital that is already embodied in the LAC schedule. They therefore represent returns over and above the required rate of return.

These excess returns are a "transfer" from consumers to the monopolist or oligopolists, a redistribution of income that has been called a privately collected tax. Monopolists raise prices above costs and in that way tax income away from consumers and toward themselves. Should society tolerate such privately collected taxes? One answer is to say that if consumers choose to buy the monopolist's products, then who is to argue about the prices they pay. Another is to say that monopoly profits represent a rip-off of society that should be taken away and used in the public interest. Both positions represent value judgments. Both are very forcefully represented in our political process.

Note that the issue of the distribution of monopoly profits is different from the issue of the social cost of monopoly as measured by triangle ABC in Figure 11-1. The monop-

---

[4] Quoted in Andrew Sinclair, *Corsair: The Life of J. Pierpont Morgan*, Little, Brown, Boston, 1981, p. 141.

oly profits are not part of the social cost measured by the triangle because they are merely amounts transferred from one group in society (the consumers) to another (the owners of the monopoly). That transfer may or may not be a good thing—for instance, the monopoly may be owned by an orphanage. Any argument about the distribution of monopoly profits is bound to involve the value judgments summarized above.

2 ANTITRUST ACTION IN THE UNITED STATES

The first major law to control monopoly and other anticompetitive practices was the Sherman Act of 1890. The act was passed during the first large merger wave in the United States—when firms merged to form giant corporations. Among the most famous are the (Rockefeller) Standard Oil Company, which at its peak controlled 90 percent of oil refining; the U.S. Steel Corporation (organized by J. P. Morgan), which controlled 70 percent of steel production; and Duke's American Tobacco Company, which controlled 90 percent of the U.S. cigarette market. The estimate is that the merger movement at the turn of the century turned 71 industries which had previously been reasonably competitive or at least oligopolistic into near monopolies.[5]

The Antitrust Laws in the United States

Legal restrictions on monopoly and oligopoly practices in the United States come primarily from two federal statutes, the Sherman Act (1890) and the Clayton Act (1914). The Clayton Act was significantly amended

by the Robinson-Patman Act (1936) and the Celler-Kefauver Act (1954).[6] In addition, the Federal Trade Commission, or FTC, was established in 1914 when the Clayton Act was passed. The acts, taken together, prohibit the pursuit of anticompetitive practices.

The Law Sections 1 and 2 of the Sherman Act contain the most important provisions. Section 1 prohibits contracts, combinations, and conspiracies that restrain trade. Any agreement between firms to fix prices, for example, would be an offense under the act. In Chapter 10 we discussed cartel agreements on prices as one means by which firms in an industry achieve abnormal profits. Whatever form a cartel takes, it is a restraint of trade and would be illegal.

Section 2 of the Sherman Act provides that

> . . . every person who shall monopolize, or attempt to monopolize, or combine or conspire with any other person or persons, to monopolize any part of the trade or commerce among the several States, or with foreign nations, shall be guilty of a misdemeanor. . . .

The act thus seeks to prevent the establishment of *new* monopolies. The current interpretation of section 2 is that it applies to firms that have, or are likely to obtain, monopoly power *and* that have acquired that power illegally by using anticompetitive practices. It is essential to recognize that monopoly itself is *not* illegal. If you are the inventor of a patented new product and your firm is the only firm in the market and thus has a monopoly, nothing is illegal.

The Clayton Act, with its subsequent amendments, and the FTC Act increased

---

[5] See Ralph L. Nelson, *Merger Movements in American Industry, 1895–1956*, Princeton University Press, Princeton, N.J., 1959, and Jesse W. Markham, "Survey of the Evidence and Findings on Mergers," in Universities-National Bureau Committee for Economic Research, *Business Concentration and Price Policy*, Princeton University Press, Princeton, N.J., 1955. Subsequent major merger movements took place in the late 1920s, the late 1960s, and (perhaps) the early 1980s.

[6] For a legal and economics treatment of antitrust action, see Richard A. Posner, *Antitrust Law: An Economic Perspective*, University of Chicago Press, Chicago, 1976, and Terry Calvani and John Siegfried (eds.), *Economic Analysis and Antitrust Law*, Little, Brown, Boston, 1979.

the range of legal remedies against anticompetitive behavior. Section 2 of the Clayton Act, amended in the Robinson-Patman Act, addresses *price discrimination*.

> . . . it shall be unlawful . . . to discriminate in price between different purchasers of commodities of like grade and quality . . . where the effect of such discrimination may be substantially to lessen competition or to create a monopoly in any line of commerce, or to injure, destroy, or prevent competition. . . .

The act specifically exempts differences in the prices charged to different customers that result from differences in the costs of providing goods to them. For example, a seller may charge small customers more per unit than large customers, provided that there are differences between the costs of supplying small customers and the costs of supplying large customers. Sellers are allowed to match the price cuts of competitors.

Section 7 of the Clayton Act, amended in the Celler-Kefauver Act of 1954, restricts mergers of existing firms that lead to excessive concentration in an industry.

There are three remedies for monopolistic practices under these laws. First, some anticompetitive practices are criminal. For example, price fixing is a criminal offense punishable by a fine and/or a prison sentence. Second, other practices are countered by injunctions by the courts or the FTC. An injunction instructs the offending firm to cease certain practices or to sell some of the companies it holds, thus breaking up a concentration of market power. Third, and very important, the legislation provides for *private* action to recover damages suffered as a consequence of anticompetitive practices. Specifically, a firm that suffers losses as a consequence of another firm's price fixing can ask for *treble damages*, three times the amount of damages actually suffered.

The purpose of these laws, we recall, is to deter and reverse monopolistic and oligopolistic behavior by firms.

Enforcement of Antitrust Laws How are the antitrust laws enforced, and what is their history? Antitrust activity is pursued for the government by the Department of Justice and by the FTC. But there are also private damage suits that are part of the enforcement of antitrust laws. Indeed, about 90 percent of the suits are brought by the private sector and only 10 percent by the government. Table 11-2 presents a survey of antitrust activity in the courts.

The table shows that antitrust activity was slow to start. In the last 20 years there has been a substantial increase in private antitrust suits. The maximum fines under the Sherman Act were raised in 1974 to $100,000 for an individual and $1 million for a corporation. The maximum prison sentence is 3 years. Thus the law does provide for stiff sentences. This is very much reinforced by the scope for private damage suits. That lesson was learned in the great electrical conspiracy (price fixing by major firms in the electrical equipment industry), in which nearly 2000 private suits were filed and $400 million in damages was awarded to firms that had suffered losses as a result of uncompetitively high prices fixed by the conspirators.[7]

Examples Under Section 1 of the Sherman Act price fixing is illegal. For a long period, ending in the early sixties, Westinghouse and other electrical equipment producers fixed the prices of electrical equipment. Contracts were shared among the price fixers, and a complex system was figured out to ensure that each firm got a "fair" share. A major antitrust suit led to conviction, substantial fines, and even the imprisonment of senior executives.

---

[7] Posner, *Antitrust Law*, pp. 32–35.

TABLE 11-2
ANTITRUST ACTIVITY IN THE COURTS

PERIOD	JUSTICE DEPT. SUITS	AVERAGE FINE FOR PRICE FIXING	PRISON SENTENCES	PRIVATE SUITS
1890–1899	15	$ 0	0	N.A.
1900–1909	42	20,000	0	N.A.
1910–1919	126	20,000	4	N.A.
1920–1929	121	98,000	8	N.A.
1930–1939	80	61,000	7	N.A.
1940–1949	358	52,000	0	1874*
1950–1959	345	40,000	4	1144†
1960–1969	402	131,000	4	6179
1970–1974	234	N.A.	6	5334

* 1937–1954. † 1955–1959.
Note: N.A. means not available.
Source: Richard A. Posner, *Antitrust Law: An Economic Perspective,* University of Chicago Press, Chicago, 1976. Tables 1–4. Copyright © 1976 by University of Chicago Press. Used by permission.

But price fixing need not involve major corporations. An interesting case is that of price fixing by three grocery chains in Cleveland. The three chains (Stop-N-Shop, Fisher Foods, and Pick-N-Pay) controlled about 55 percent of the business in the area and had conspired to fix prices and advertising and to ban trading stamps. Here is a report from the *Wall Street Journal:*[8]

The two periods of alleged price collusion in Cleveland were separated by a bitter price war. The indictment says the price cutting was instigated on June 13th, 1977 by Fisher, which said it had been losing market share in northern Ohio in the preceding months. Pick-N-Pay, in particular, immediately responded with extensive price slashing. Three or four months later the wounded, battle weary chains allegedly called a truce, which the Justice Department contends began a second conspiracy that lasted at least until October 1978.

The verdict in this case is particularly

[8] Margaret Yao, "Three Grocery Stores in Cleveland Face Trial on Charges of Price-Fixing Plot," *Wall Street Journal,* Aug. 13, 1981, p. 44. © copyright by Dow Jones & Company, Inc., 1981. All rights reserved. Reprinted by permission.

interesting. There were $2 million in fines and suspended prison sentences. Most interesting, there was compensation for the customers. The violators had to provide $20 million in scrip (coupons good for general purchases in particular stores). The scrip had to be distributed to 1 million consumers for use in 7200 stores over 5 years, and the unused portion had to go to charity.

Legal Issues It is difficult to establish anticompetitive behavior under the Sherman Act. For most prosecutions the government wants to prove that there was a conspiracy (people meeting in a hotel room, or at dawn in a parking lot) to set prices. But much of oligopoly pricing takes the form of "conscious parallelism," where one firm sets the prices and other firms simply follow the price leader.

From the economic viewpoint, such price setting is as costly as an open conspiracy, but its existence is difficult to establish in court. It is much easier to have a case such as the electrical conspiracy, where the offending parties agreed explicitly on a set of prices for all standardized machinery and had an elaborate system based on phases of the moon for deciding which firm would put in a low bid on a particular project. The illegal behavior lasted more than 30 years. Once it came out, there was enough detail and evidence for conviction.

Attempts to monopolize a market may take the form of predatory pricing.

> In *predatory pricing*, one firm or several firms charge prices below average variable cost in an attempt to discourage actual or potential competitors from operating in a particular market.

In the government's case against IBM, which was dropped in 1982, one of the charges was predatory pricing. The government charged that in introducing a new computer model, IBM had planned to sell it below cost. The government also charged that IBM had announced the introduction of the product before completion in an effort to prevent Control Data's development in the computer market.

One of the important issues in this case was the question of whether IBM did or did not have a monopoly in the *relevant* market. The government, in arguing that a monopoly did exist, defined the market narrowly as one of mainframe computers only, thus giving a large market share to IBM. IBM, in contrast, argued that the relevant market included software and peripheral equipment, since in that broader market its share is significantly smaller and a monopoly case is harder to establish. The problem of market definition is an important issue in section 2 of the Sherman Act. It is quite clear that there is no tight definition of a market in many cases where substitution between products potentially includes a large variety of goods and firms.

In the AT&T case, also mentioned in the quotation at the beginning of this chapter, the government charged that AT&T monopolized the telecommunications business in part by not allowing other long-distance phone services to have access to AT&T local networks. The government also charged that AT&T exploited its monopoly of the industry to create a demand for the equipment produced by Western Electric, a company owned by AT&T.

The agreement between AT&T and the Justice Department involves a breakup of the company. AT&T will divest itself of (set up as separate companies) all the local phone companies and retain only long-distance phone operation as well as the production of telecommunications equipment. With local phone companies independent, various long-distance phone services will now become more accessible to customers, and the market for equipment may likewise become more competitive.

In the cereals case, dropped by the FTC in 1981, the issue involved the allegation that the main producers made the market uncompetitive by providing a full range of products, leaving no gap for potential entrants. The large companies—Kellogg, General Mills, and General Foods—were also alleged to have practiced price leadership in setting their cereal prices.

Mergers Two rules are in effect when firms want to merge. First, mergers involving large firms are subject to review by the Justice Department. Second, in 1982, the Justice Department issued detailed criteria determining which mergers are acceptable in a particular industry. These criteria are described in Box 11-1.

Has Antitrust Worked?

There are a number of questions to be raised about the antitrust laws. First, how have they affected competition? Second, are the effects desirable? Third, what are the practices in other countries? Fourth, what are the prospects for further vigorous enforcement of the antitrust laws in the United States?

To know what the effects of the antitrust laws have been, it is necessary to know

BOX 11-1

LIMITS TO MERGERS

In 1982 the Justice Department challenged the proposed merger of two breweries, Pabst and Heileman, on the grounds that the merger would lead to excessive concentration in the beer industry.

What are the criteria by which mergers are judged? First, there is a distinction between a *vertical* merger and a *horizontal* merger. The former involves different firms at *different* stages of production of a given good, say, steel producers, car manufacturers, and car dealers. The latter involves different firms at the *same* stage of production or distribution of a given good, say, breweries. In the context of antitrust action, particular attention focuses on horizontal mergers that increase market power or increase the extent of concentration in an industry.

The new merger guidelines of 1982 replace the older criterion of a four-firm concentration ratio by an indicator called the *Herfindahl index.* The Herfindahl index measures market concentration. The fewer firms there are in the industry, and the more the industry is dominated by large firms, the higher the value of the index.

The index is calculated by summing the market shares, each squared, of all the firms in the industry. Thus if there are two firms in an industry, each with a 50 percent share, the index is $50^2 + 50^2 = 5000$. But if one firm has a share of 80 percent and the other firm only 20 percent, the index is $80^2 + 20^2 = 6800$. Thus the index yields larger values when the industry has an uneven distribution of firm size. It yields lower values when there are many firms. For example, if there are three firms each with a 33 percent share, the index is $33^2 + 33^2 + 33^2 = 3267$; if there are 10 firms each with a 10 percent share, the index is only $10 \times 10^2 = 1000$. The index weighs both the number and the relative size of firms and is therefore a more complex measure than, for example, the four-firm concentration ratio.

The new merger guidelines establish the following criteria:

	HERFINDAHL INDEX	
LESS THAN 1000	1000–1800	MORE THAN 1800
Market is unconcentrated No challenge to mergers	Market is moderately concentrated Challenge to mergers that raise the index by more than 100 points	Market is highly concentrated Challenge to mergers raising index by more than 50 points

The new procedures challenge mergers in markets that are moderately or highly concentrated. In a moderately concentrated market a challenge is brought if the merger leads to an increase in the market share of more than 100 points. In the example of the proposed merger of Pabst and Heileman, each had a market share of about 7.5 percent in an industry with a Herfindahl index of 1772 (see Box 10.1). The merger would have yielded a combined market share of 15 percent and would have raised the index by $15^2 - 2 \times 7.5^2 = 112.5$ points, thus moving the beer industry into the high-concentration range.

The calculation of the increase in the index is as follows: The new firm would contribute $15^2 = 225$ points to the index, because it would have 15 percent of the market. Each of the old firms contributed $7.5^2 = 56.25$ points to the index, because each had a 7.5 percent share of the market. The merger adds one firm, with an index of 225, to the industry, and removes two firms, with combined indexes of $2 \times 7.5^2 = 112.5$ from the industry. The merger therefore raises the index by $225 - 112.5 = 112.5$ points.

In a highly concentrated market there will be some firms that have a very substantial share, say, 35 or 40 percent. The merger guidelines preclude *any* merger activity of these large firms as can be seen from the following calculation: Suppose a merger is considered by a firm with a 35 percent share and another with 1 percent only. The increase in the index is $36^2 - 35^2 - 1^2 = 70$ points, which is in excess of the limit of 50. Thus the guidelines work strongly against super-large firms expanding, but they do *not* prevent minimergers of two very small firms, even if the market is highly concentrated.

what would have happened without them. That is hard to tell, but it is probable that without the antitrust laws, firms would have engaged far more frequently in price-fixing agreements, and there would have been more collusion between firms. As we have seen in earlier chapters, it is in the interest of firms in an industry to get together if they can to fix prices.

The question of whether the antitrust laws have had desirable effects deserves a reasonably complicated answer. Agreements to fix prices by oligopolies are not beneficial to consumers, or to the economy as a whole, and laws against price fixing have had a good effect. There is more debate about monopoly itself, since it is sometimes argued that monopolies generate more rapid technical change and innovation than competitive firms. Here we believe that in general the existence of the antitrust laws has had a good effect by inhibiting attempts to monopolize.

There was until recently comparatively little formal antitrust law in other countries. Governments in other countries have tended to take a more generous view of cartel arrangements. Now the European Common Market has formal antitrust laws. But governments in some countries still work hand in glove with their local manufacturers to keep out foreign competition and enable the local firms to act more as monopolies.

Finally, the degree of effort in enforcing the antitrust laws has changed over time. Initial efforts in the 1890s were quite weak, and there was again little enthusiasm for the laws during the pro-business 1920s. Enforcement activities picked up in the post–World War II period, with the government showing a willingness to try out new theories of monopolization as the basis for its cases. With the change in sentiment about business in the early 1980s, it is likely that there will be fewer government antitrust cases in the coming few years. But for the private sector, antitrust litigation for damages has definitely become an established pattern.

Doubts about Antitrust Action

Antitrust action has always been a divisive issue—between different firms in a business and between business and the consumer. It is not surprising, therefore, that arguments are made on all sides and that

FIGURE 11-2 MONOPOLIZATION WITH COST REDUCTION. An industry is initially competitive, with an equilibrium at point E, price P_C, and output Q_C. The industry is then monopolized, and this brings about a reduction in the long-run average and marginal cost from LMC to LMC'. The monopolized industry produces Q_M and charges P_M. Consumers lose from the higher prices the amount represented by triangle A, but society gains because output OQ_M is now produced at a lower cost. The cost savings are represented by area B. The *net* result depends on the relative sizes of A and B. In the diagram, monopolization involves a net gain.

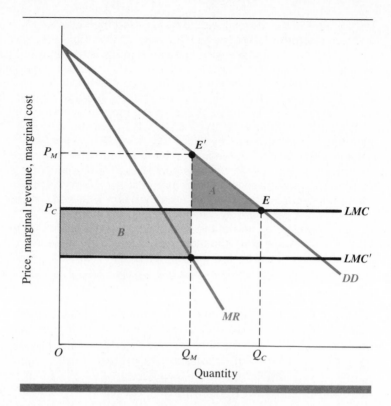

there are some arguments in favor of concentration.

There are three serious arguments. The first is that an increase in concentration, even if it implies a move to monopoly pricing, may still leave society ahead because the merged firms can produce more cheaply. We will explore this argument with the help of Figure 11-2.

Figure 11-2 shows the long-run marginal cost schedule, LMC, for a competitive industry. Equilibrium for the competitive case is at point E, with output Q_C and price P_C. Now the industry is monopolized. The monopoly firm operates more efficiently. We show this with a downward shift of the long-run marginal cost schedule to LMC'. Because the industry is now monopolized, the equilibrium output falls to Q_M, where $MR = LMC'$. The monopoly price rises to P_M.

The monopolization of the industry has led to a fall in output and an increase in price. We have to be careful in measuring the welfare cost of the monopolization. There is the loss of consumer surplus, given by the triangle labeled A, but that is offset by cost savings. The output OQ_M previously was produced at a cost of LMC, but now, because of the cost reduction it is produced at a lower cost LMC'. There are, therefore, cost savings equal to the area labeled B. These cost savings, which are collected as monopoly profits, represent also a social saving, since it takes fewer resources to produce the output OQ_M. Since area B is larger than A, the monopolization, because and only because of the accompanying cost reduction, actually involves a net gain in welfare for society. Of course, consumers of this particular good are worse off.

The question this argument raises is whether monopolization will, in any particular case, lead to substantial cost savings. If so, the antitrust law could prevent a socially desirable change.

A second concern about antitrust enforcement is that it may ignore foreign competition. Although U.S. firms may have extremely high concentration in some markets—for example, in the market for motor vehicles—there is still serious competition from foreign firms. In the motor vehicle industry there are only four U.S. firms, but there are another four or five important foreign competitors. Taking foreign competition into account gives an altogether different picture of the market; it makes increased domestic concentration look much less serious. Professor Lester Thurow of MIT has strongly argued that U.S. zeal in enforcing the antitrust laws may be misplaced in view of this foreign competition.[9]

> IBM has some of the same problems that plague General Motors—in a less acute form. Whatever its monopoly power may have been in 1969, in 1982 competition is a fact of life. Prime, Wang, Digital, Fujitsu, Hitachi, Siemens, Phillips, Olivetti—the list of effective competitors rolls on and on. It is not at all obvious that IBM, or even an American firm, will dominate the computer market in the future. The millions spent on the IBM case would have been better spent if they had been plowed back into research and development on keeping America No. 1 in computers. . . .
>
> The same competitive situation is looming on the horizon in telecommunications. . . . If America is to survive economically, it needs the strongest possible competitors in this industry. A strong A.T. & T. will undoubtedly crush some weak American firms, but these firms were going to be crushed by other strong competitors in any case.

The third concern involves the dividing line between vigorous competition and monopoly. This issue came out strongly in the titanium dioxide (a paint ingredient) case. The FTC charged that Du Pont had engaged in practices that created a monopoly. Specifically, it was charged that Du Pont had kept prices at a level that permitted its own expansion but discouraged entry. The charge was dropped, and the reasoning was as follows:[10]

> The essence of the competitive process is to induce firms to become more efficient and to pass the benefits of the efficiency along to consumers. That process would be ill-served by using antitrust to block hard, aggressive competition that is solidly based on efficiencies and growth opportunities, even if monopoly is a possible result.

This is a very important change in emphasis for antitrust enforcement. It makes the point that being big is not the issue; instead, the issue is how the consumer is served or hurt by the industry. It is interesting to note that increasingly, with the growth of private antitrust litigation and the important government cases, antitrust is slipping out of the hands of lawyers and becoming the domain of economists. In that process the basic concerns for efficiency gain in emphasis at the expense of purely technical legal issues such as concentration, size, or the appearance of monopoly.

3 REGULATION OF NATURAL MONOPOLIES

In Chapter 7 we saw that industries with decreasing average costs pose a very special problem: output is most efficiently provided by a single firm, not by a competitive, multifirm industry. A single firm operating on a big scale can produce any given level of out-

---

[9] Lester C. Thurow, "A New Era of Competition," *Newsweek*, Jan. 18, 1982, p. 63. Copyright © 1982 by Newsweek, Inc. All rights reserved. Reprinted by permission.

[10] Burt Schorr, "FTC Dismisses Charges against Du Pont in Major Statement of Its Antitrust Policy," *Wall Street Journal*, Oct. 28, 1980, p. 5. © copyright by Dow Jones & Company, Inc., 1980. All rights reserved. Reprinted by permission.

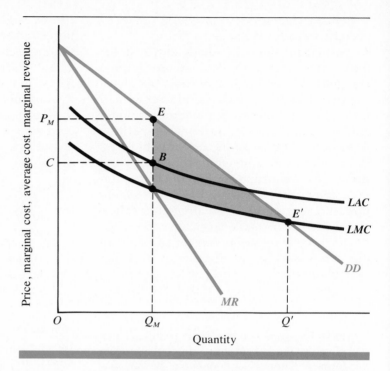

FIGURE 11-3 A NATURAL MONOPOLY. The diagram shows an industry with economies of scale, reflected in the falling *LAC* curve. A monopoly would set output at Q_M, where $MR = LMC$. But that would involve a social loss, shown by the shaded area, compared with the optimal output Q' at E'. At E' the marginal valuation, shown by the demand curve, *DD*, is equal to the marginal cost. However, the monopolist would not even be able to cover costs at E' because the price would be less than *LAC* at that level of output. The case calls for regulation that exploits the advantage of economies of scale but ensures a more favorable price and output than at the monopoly level.

put at a lower average cost than several firms, each of which produces on a small scale. But there is a conflict. If an industry is left to a monopoly, how can we be sure that customers will receive the benefits of the economies of scale? Figure 11-3 presents once more the issues involved in a decreasing-cost industry or a natural monopoly.

The Natural Monopoly Problem

In Figure 11-3 we show an industry with decreasing long-run average costs. If the industry were operated by a monopoly firm, output would be set at Q_M and price at P_M. The monopoly would earn profits equal to the area $P_M EBC$. Even though there are decreasing average costs, the industry can profitably be operated by a monopoly. In the monopoly equilibrium, costs are covered and monopoly profits are made.

Now look at the socially optimal point, E', where *LMC* is equal to the valuation by consumers, which is indicated by the de-

mand curve. Output level Q' is socially optimal because further expansion would raise *LMC* above the demand price, while less output would imply that *LMC* is below the demand price. For society, then, point E' is optimal.

But how can that output level be achieved? We cannot get there through competition because with many firms we would fail to take advantage of the economies of scale. Prices and output would be set competitively, but each firm would operate at a lower volume and thus with higher average costs than can be achieved by a single monopoly producer. We need monopoly production to exploit the technical efficiency of economies of scale, but we want to avoid the disadvantage or loss from monopoly through output restriction and high prices. Regulation of the monopoly is therefore a possible solution.

Examples of natural monopolies are water, gas, and electricity supply, as well as sewer services. The characteristic of these goods is the importance of economies of scale in transmission. Widening the sewer pipes to accommodate twice as many users less than doubles the necessary sewer capacity and costs. Running two sets of wires for electricity is more than twice as expensive as having one system. The existence of economies of scale makes it desirable to have a monopoly supplier. But regulation is introduced to control the supplier's use of the monopoly situation. The supplier's prices are controlled by the regulatory body.

State or local authorities (depending on the service) administer and regulate the provision of the service. Regulatory authorities are appointed in some states and elected in others. Their job is to regulate the provision of the service in the public interest.

Sometimes a service is provided by the government itself rather than by a regulated supplier. Thus sewer services are usually provided by the local government. In some cities the utilities are provided by the city. In others private, but regulated, companies provide the services. In either case there is a need to decide on the terms under which a service is to be supplied. That is the task of the regulatory authority or commission, which is set up to determine the prices to be charged by the monopoly.

The Task of a Regulatory Commission

The regulatory commission's job is to represent the public interest in the prudent operation of the private company that provides a service.

The regulatory commission must strike the balance between the interests of consumers—low prices, product variety, and quality of service—and the economic viability of the program. A program that favors consumers through excellent service, a large variety, and low prices will probably lead to a rapid bankruptcy of the regulated firm that provides the product. Regulators need guidelines to achieve a viable and efficient program. Three rules look helpful:

1 Marginal cost pricing should be followed as closely as possible.

2 Pricing and service should be such that the utility company has a normal rate of return on its capital.

3 Care should be taken that output is produced efficiently.

The rule of marginal cost pricing is there to ensure that consumers' valuation of a good is brought in line with the cost of an additional unit of output. Large deviations from marginal cost pricing result in waste. If the marginal cost is below the price, not enough of the good is being produced; if it is above the price, too much is being produced. But full marginal cost pricing, as we saw in Figure 11-3, implies that the utility would suffer losses, because at point E' the marginal cost, which is equal to the price, is below the average cost. Therefore, a way must be found both to use marginal cost pricing *and* to generate enough revenue to cover costs fully.

One way this might be done is through a two-part tariff.

A *two-part tariff* is a price system for public utilities in which users pay a fixed sum for access to the service and then pay the marginal cost for units of the service.

For example, in the case of electricity there would be a fixed fee, say, $4 per month, for being connected to the municipal electricity system and then a separate, metered charge for each kilowatt-hour of electricity consumed. The revenue from the fixed fee makes it possible for the company to cover costs even when marginal cost pricing is used for additional units of output. Of

FIGURE 11-4 A REGULATED NATU-
RAL MONOPOLY. The social optimum at
point E' cannot be attained because
with marginal cost pricing there would
be losses, since LAC exceeds LMC at
output Q'. A possibility is to set price P
for the regulated monopoly. At point E
price covers costs, although output is
underproduced, since price, P, exceeds
LMC at output Q. The social loss when
output is Q is shown by the shaded
area.

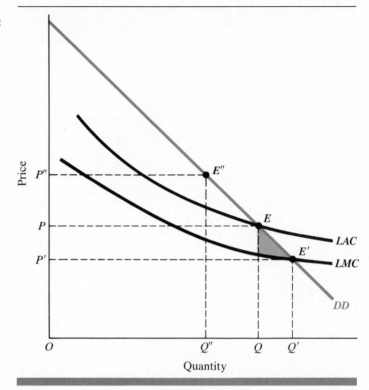

course, regulated telephone companies also use a two-part tariff.

A two-part tariff may get the regulators very close to the best allocation of resources. An alternative that does not go quite as far is to fix a regulated price that is not far from the optimum and that does cover costs. This is illustrated in Figure 11-4. We again have decreasing long-run average costs, and marginal costs are below average costs. The demand schedule is DD. The optimal point is E', where the price equals LMC, but as we have seen, that price is not sufficient to cover long-run average costs. The alternative is price P, which yields an equilibrium at point E. At that point the utility exactly covers its costs. Of course, at output Q there is underproduction of the good, since the price exceeds LMC. The social loss is shown by the shaded area.

The second rule concerns excess profits earned by the utility—that is, profits in excess of the normal return on capital. This is illustrated in Figure 11-4 with a regulated price, P'', and an equilibrium at point E''. In this case the utility would make substantial excess profits, and we would be far from the social optimum at E, much farther than is required for the utility to earn normal profits. At point E'' consumers pay more for the service than they do at E, they obtain less output, and the output is produced at a higher average cost. The equilibrium at E'' is in no one's interest except the utility company's, since the company is making excess profits. Thus it is apparent that a normal rate of return—a price covering long-run average costs—is a desirable criterion for avoiding excessive underproduction.

The third point is that a utility company may increase costs through inefficient pro-

---

TABLE 11-3
EXAMPLE OF RATE DETERMINATION FOR A PUBLIC UTILITY

1 Machinery is assumed to be in operation 50 percent of the time, generating a total of 15 billion kilowatt-hours per year.

2 The cost of operation (labor, fuel, maintenance, but excluding the return on capital) is 5.0 cents per kilowatt-hour, or $750 million.

3 The value of the asset base (machinery, buildings, etc.) is $2500 million.

4 The allowed rate of return (before tax) is 15 percent, implying that the total return to capital should be 15% × $2500 million = $375 million.

5 The total amount to be charged to customers = (2) + (4)
$$= \$750 \text{ million} + \$375 \text{ million}$$
$$= \$1125 \text{ million}$$

6 Price per kwh $= \dfrac{(5)}{(1)} = \dfrac{\$1125 \text{ million}}{15 \text{ billion kwh/yr}} = 7.5 ¢/\text{kwh}$

---

duction because it knows that regulators will guarantee prices that cover long-run average costs. If a firm cannot make excess profits *and* there is no risk of going out of business because regulators set prices that cover costs, then what guarantees that utilities will look for the cheapest techniques? There is nothing that prevents cost inflation —large salaries for executives, swimming pools for the staff, a cafeteria with subsidized lunches. Cost inflation ultimately is borne by the consumers of the products of the regulated industry. It is therefore essential that the regulators take an active interest in the efficiency question. There is a need to supervise efficiency through comparisons with utilities providing the same service elsewhere. In addition, regulators should consider the possibility of switching to alternative suppliers who are prepared to offer the same service at a lower cost.

Rate of Return Calculation

We now study the calculations involved in setting prices that guarantee a normal (or "fair") rate of return in a public utility. We take the example of an electricity company that has to set the price per kilowatt-hour. Table 11-3 presents the calculations. For a given capacity we can calculate the quantity of electricity produced and the total

cost—variable costs, including labor and fuel, plus the required return on capital.

The price to be charged per unit of output is given by the ratio of total cost to output. In our example, a price of 7.5 cents per kilowatt-hour will cover the variable costs as well as the opportunity cost of the capital tied up in the plant and machinery. The calculation can be performed for different output levels. In this way we develop the long-run average cost schedule, which tells us for each level of output what price to set to cover both the variable costs of production and the opportunity cost of the capital used by the utility.

Problems of Rate Regulation

An important problem in public utility regulation is how to ensure that the rate of return on capital in the public utility is kept in line with the opportunity cost of capital.[11]

---

[11] The *Averch-Johnson effect* concerns the consequences for the way a public utility operates of a rate of return on the firm's investment that is set too high. In this case the firm is likely to choose a combination of factors that is too capital-intensive. The idea is that if the regulatory agency allows a high rate of return on investment, then in effect it is subsidizing the employment of capital, and so the firm will use more capital in relation to labor. The A-J effect, however, does not seem to be very important empirically.

A decline in the rate of return would lead the utility to contract capacity or allow service to deteriorate. By contrast, excess returns might well lead to higher costs through less efficient production or splashy service. This is an important issue because changes in costs and demand over time require a frequent reassessment of the optimal prices to be charged.

In the 1960s the problem for electric utilities of getting the price right arose from the falling real costs of generating electricity. Rate commissions then had to lower the real price of electricity periodically to avoid excess profits. By contrast, in the 1970s and early 1980s the problem arose from increasing real costs of production, mainly because of higher fuel prices, but also because of inflation. With all prices (and costs) rising, a failure to increase utility prices would lead to losses for the operating companies, deteriorating service, insufficient construction of new plants, and inadequate maintenance of old plants—which ultimately means bottlenecks and shortages.

The delay involved in setting new prices for the services provided by regulated utilities is called *regulatory lag*. Regulatory lag is a serious problem whenever unpredictable rates of inflation or cost changes make it necessary to adjust utility prices frequently. Delays are inevitable because the work of the regulatory commissions is time-consuming—the commissions must pass judgment on the cost increases claimed by the operating firms, and they must hear the testimony of expert witnesses and consumer groups. These delays may lead to declining profitability. The decline in profitability, in turn, adversely affects the quality of service as well as investment in the industry.[12]

---

[12] For a recent discussion of the evidence, see Andrew S. Carron and Paul W. MacAvoy, *The Decline of Service in the Regulated Industries*, American Enterprise Institute, Washington, D.C., 1981.

SUMMARY

1   The welfare costs of monopoly arise from the monopolist's restriction of output. The social cost of monopoly is measured by the cumulative difference between the value consumers place on the lost output and its marginal cost of production.

2   Estimates of the social costs of monopoly tend to be small, typically less than 1 percent of the economy's total output. Costs other than those arising from the restriction of output may increase this amount. Monopolists may not minimize costs as carefully as other firms, and much of the advertising undertaken by both monopolies and oligopolies may be wasteful.

3   The first major law to control monopoly was the Sherman Act of 1890, passed at a time of extensive mergers. The act prohibits attempts to monopolize industries and combinations to restrain trade. The Clayton Act of 1914 prohibits price discrimination between customers unless the price differences result from cost differences. It also sets out penalties for violation of the antitrust acts.

4   The antitrust acts permit both government lawsuits to prevent monopolization and lawsuits by private individuals or corporations who have suffered as a result of illegal action by monopoly and oligopoly

firms. In such cases the violating company may have to pay treble damages to the suffering customer.

5   Enforcement of the antitrust laws by the government has been sporadic. Recently, private antitrust actions have become increasingly common. Given the fact that it is in the interest of existing companies in an industry to combine, the antitrust laws have probably prevented some oligopoly behavior that would otherwise have taken place.

6   Doubts are expressed about antitrust action on the grounds that large firms may be able to produce more efficiently than small ones and that large firms may be needed to compete with foreign firms.

7   When there are economies of scale, monopoly production is more efficient (cheaper) than competition. These are cases of natural monopolies. To obtain the benefits of the lower costs without the higher monopoly prices, natural monopolies are typically regulated in the prices they charge and the type of service they provide. Examples of natural monopolies are the utilities: electricity, gas, and telephone service.

8   The regulatory agency's job is to get the natural monopoly to produce as close to the socially optimal level of output as possible. It cannot do this merely by setting marginal cost equal to price, because with declining average costs, marginal cost is below average cost. Therefore, when marginal cost equals price, price is below average cost, and the utility is losing money.

9   Two-part pricing, in which there is a charge for access to the service and also a charge for each unit of service used, is one good way out of this problem. Allowing the utility to charge a price that just covers costs is another way out. In this second case, however, output is not at its socially optimal level. But the social loss is much smaller than it would be if the monopoly were not regulated.

10   Regulatory commissions that allow utilities to cover costs have to make sure that the utilities are at the same time trying to minimize costs. They also have to avoid allowing prices to lag behind changing cost and demand conditions, because they need to provide the right price incentives so the utilities will install new capacity and maintain existing service.

KEY TERMS

Social cost of monopoly	Mergers
Sherman Act	Natural monopoly
Clayton Act	Marginal cost pricing
Price discrimination	Public utility
Predatory pricing	Regulatory lag

PROBLEMS

1   Use the following data to find the price for a public utility that will guarantee a fair rate of return: (*a*) the existing capacity generates 10 billion kilowatt-hours per year; (*b*) the costs of operation (fuel, labor, maintenance) amount to $490 million per year; (*c*) the value of the capital (plant, equipment) is $1800 million; (*d*) the opportunity cost of capital is 10 percent per year, and this is the return to capital that must be guaranteed to keep the public utility going. What is the price per kilowatt-hour that will cover costs, including the return to capital?

2   In Problem 1 how will your answer change if (*a*) the costs of operation rise by 10 percent, (*b*) the opportunity cost of capital rises to 15 percent, and (*c*) the value of the capital in the operation increases to $2200? (*d*) Why should public utilities be allowed to cover costs?

3   Give two reasons for and two against vigorous enforcement of the antitrust laws.

4   (*a*) Explain what natural monopolies are all about, list the industries in which you expect to find them, and explain why we might be concerned. (*b*) Why not let industries in which there are increasing returns to scale operate without intervention so that the most efficient firm in an industry can drive out the others and produce output as cheaply as possible?

5   Suppose that an industry is competitive, and that the average and marginal costs of production are constant and equal to $5, which is also the price. One million units of output are sold each year. Now the industry is monopolized, and we know that the price rises to $8 and output falls to 800,000 units. The firm's costs of production are the same as they were in the competitive industry. Given only these facts, how would you estimate the social cost of monopoly, and what number do you get as the answer?

6   Consider an industry with a constant *LAC*. The industry is initially competitive. Now it is monopolized, and as a consequence, a major cost reduction takes place. Draw a diagram comparing the competitive equilibrium and the monopoly equilibrium. Is it possible for the move to monopoly to lower price and raise output?

7   What do you think are the three major problems of public utility regulation?

8   It has been argued that antitrust action is unnecessary because as soon as a monopoly is formed, other firms will come into the industry and undercut it. On the other side it is argued that as soon as a monopoly is formed, it becomes financially powerful enough to sell for a time at so low a price that the competition can never get started. Relate these arguments to the notion of predatory pricing, and explain why you think that predatory pricing may sometimes happen or why it is very unlikely to happen.

9   If a public utility is operated in the public interest, does this mean that the interests of the consumer should be protected in the following ways? (*a*) The utility must not discriminate against rural consumers by charging higher prices for gas and electricity supplied in distant areas. (*b*) There should be special rates for students and families with many children. (*c*) Needy people should receive essential utilities even if they cannot pay.

10   After the Three Mile Island nuclear plant broke down, the regulatory commission had to decide who was to pay for the cleanup of the radiation damage. (*a*) Who do you think should pay, the customers or the shareholders? (*b*) What are the economic arguments that suggest that the customers (or the shareholders—the owners of the utility) should pay?

On the brighter side, NHTSA [the National Highway Traffic Safety Administration] is reconsidering its standard to make bumpers withstand a five-mile-per-hour impact. I should emphasize that this standard has no safety effect whatsoever and is intended only to save consumers money. Yet, its costs so clearly exceed its benefits that it is hard to justify from a consumer welfare standpoint. More fundamentally, NHTSA has never provided any evidence that the market doesn't work in this area. And finally, in a classic case of bureaucratic confusion, even as NHTSA has been pursuing more durable bumpers it has also been thinking about making bumpers softer so that they won't injure pedestrians. Clearly NHTSA ought to forget about bumpers altogether.[1]

12

The Public Interest, Externalities, and Regulation

Government regulation of industry increased rapidly in the seventies. The regulation has different aims and takes many forms. For instance, government regulates industry to control pollution, to improve on-the-job safety for workers, to increase the gasoline mileage of cars, and to control the conditions under which interstate trucking firms operate. The increasing regulation, some of it contradictory like the bumper example cited above, led to arguments that the government had gone too far and that the time has come to deregulate. In the first major episode of deregulation, airlines were permitted in 1978 to begin competing with each other by reducing the fares they charged. The structure of the airline industry has since changed dramatically, as we shall see in this chapter.

Why should we have *any* government regulation of industry? In many cases the argument for regulation is based on the failure of the free market. It is from the perspective of market failure that we discuss regulation in this chapter. Regulation is justified when markets fail and market prices are not equal to the marginal social costs and benefits of the goods traded. In those circumstances, someone *can* be made better off without anyone else being made worse off.

Government intervention can potentially improve matters when there are market failures. But there is another question. Does government regulation *in fact* make things better? Here is where much of the controversy is centered. In the first place, much government regulation takes place in areas where there is no obvious market failure. And second, regulation may work poorly even where government intervention is in principle justified.

---

[1] W. Kip Viscusi, "Health and Safety," in *Regulation*, January–February 1982, p. 35.

This chapter cuts into the intervention issue by defining the concept of market failure and showing the potential improvements that can be made when markets fail. With these concepts in hand, we examine actual government intervention in the economy in the areas of pollution control and safety standards. We conclude by studying the decision-making process of the regulators and the effects of airline deregulation that was started in 1978.

1   MARKET FAILURE

Prices are the central allocative mechanism in a market economy. Prices guide consumers' choices among alternative goods, and they guide the allocation of resources among various industries. On the demand side, equilibrium prices reflect the valuation of an extra unit of the good by consumers. On the production side, they reflect the marginal cost of an extra unit of the good to producers. When competitive markets clear, the equilibrium price that equates the quantity demanded with the quantity supplied also equates the marginal valuation of a good with the marginal cost of supplying the good. When everything works out right, we achieve an optimal resource allocation because in each market costs and benefits are equated at the margin. We would lose by producing a bit more of one good, pushing the marginal cost above the marginal valuation of a good, and a bit less of another.

But it is certainly possible that although prices clear the market, they do *not* reflect the marginal valuation by consumers or the marginal cost of an extra unit of output. We have already seen one clear case—monopoly and oligopoly—where there is a distortion because firms charge prices in excess of the marginal cost, and there is therefore too little produced in the monopolized industry. But there are other departures from optimal resource allocation.

First, we need to define distortions.

A *distortion* exists where market prices are not equal to both the marginal *social* valuation of a good *and* the marginal social cost of producing the good.

The definition introduces a distinction between valuations by consumers and society. There is a difference whenever consumers do not capture the full benefits of a good or pay more or less than the full cost of producing the good. There are four sources of such distortions.

1   *Monopoly and oligopoly.* We have already seen in the previous chapter that less than perfect competition implies that market price exceeds marginal cost, and thus the output of a monopolized sector is underproduced.

2   *Externalities.* Here we consider activities (production or consumption) where there are distortions that result from spillover effects that are not properly priced. Examples are pollution, noise, and bad manners.

3   *Imperfect information about the safety or characteristics of goods or jobs.* In this category we discuss market failures associated with private undervaluation of the risks associated with particular activities or products and their consequent overproduction. An example is exposure to dangerous benzene vapors in gasoline-refining plants.

4   *Social priorities other than efficiency of production.* These occur where society prefers an outcome other than that of the free market—not for efficiency reasons, as under 1 and 2 above, but because of social targets. Examples include equality or literacy or peace.

This chapter will deal in detail with the distortions described in items 2, 3, and 4 on the list. We start with a discussion of externalities and use the issue of pollution as an example.

2 EXTERNALITIES

In this section we are concerned with externalities.

> An *externality* arises whenever the production or consumption of a good has spillover effects beyond the consumers or producers involved in the market *and* these spillover effects are not *fully* reflected in market prices.

Here are some examples that explain the notion and importance of externalities. Consider first pollution. A firm produces, say, chemicals and discharges waste into a lake. The discharge pollutes the local water supply, harms fish and birds, and creates an offensive smell. These are adverse side effects of the production of the chemicals; they are costly to society, and their costs may not be reflected in the prices of the chemicals. Unless the chemical company is charged for the pollution, the market prices of the chemicals will understate the cost to *society* of producing the chemicals, which of course includes the noxious effects of waste disposal.

Externalities are not all negative. The homeowner who repaints his house provides side benefits for his neighbors: they no longer have to look at a peeling, dilapidated house. But because the benefits the neighbors get are not reflected in the cost of repainting the house, the supply of newly painted houses will be too small.

The idea of externalities, then, is based on the fact that a particular good or bad is not priced in the market. This lack of pricing leads to a misallocation of resources, with too *little* being produced of goods that generate favorable externalities. We now turn to measuring social costs or benefits in the presence of externalities.

Social Costs and Benefits When There Are Externalities

We take the example of pollution. A firm produces chemicals and discharges its

FIGURE 12-1 A PRODUCTION EXTERNALITY FROM POLLUTION. A firm pollutes a river in the process of making chemicals. The pollution causes damage to others (society) that is not reflected in the marginal private cost to the firm, *MPC*. The *MSC* curve shows the marginal social cost of producing output. It includes both the *MPC* and the marginal cost to society of the extra waste resulting from the production of each extra unit of output. The *MSC* curve shows the marginal cost of output to *society*, but *MPC* is the marginal cost that the firm pays.

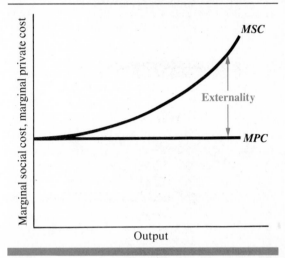

wastes into a river. There are adverse effects downstream on recreation, fishing, and water purity. We assume that the amount of waste is proportional to the amount of output. For every gallon of chemical there is a discharge of, say, 1/4 gallon of waste. The total cost to society of this waste increases with the amount of waste, and it increases at an increasing rate. For very small waste discharges, the cost is practically zero because the waste is so diluted in the river. As more waste is generated, total costs rise very sharply. The marginal cost of waste thus rises because the increasing concentration of waste in the river interferes more and more with the uses of the water.

In Figure 12-1 we show the marginal private cost to the firm. This is assumed to be constant to simplify the diagram. The marginal private cost, *MPC*, reflects the cost to the firm of the additional resources it

FIGURE 12-2 THE SOCIAL COST OF A PRODUCTION EXTERNALITY. In a competitive market, equilibrium is at point E, with output Q and price P_0. At that point the marginal valuation of the good by consumers is equal to the MPC. But the consumers' marginal valuation is below the MSC at output level Q, which is shown at point F. The externality occurs because the producers do not have to pay, and therefore do not charge for, the cost of the waste they produce. Contraction of output would yield benefits so long as MSC exceeds price. Therefore, society should move to point E', with price P'. At E' consumers' marginal valuation of the good equals the MSC. The shaded area shows the gain from moving from output level Q to Q'.

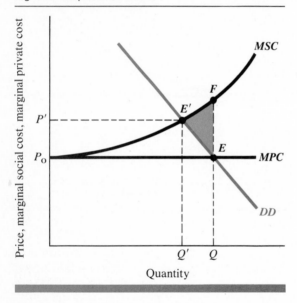

takes to produce an extra unit of the good. But it does not include the marginal cost to society of the waste being generated by the firm. The MSC schedule includes both the MPC and the marginal cost to society of waste disposal. The MSC is increasing because we assume that increasing waste leads to higher concentrations that are increasingly costly.

How much is produced under competition? In Figure 12-2 we show the market equilibrium. The firm has as its supply schedule the MPC curve. The demand schedule is DD. Therefore, equilibrium is at point E, with output Q.

But is that the appropriate level of output in the sense that the marginal cost to society of an extra unit of output exactly equals the marginal valuation of another unit by consumers? The answer is no. Figure 12-2 shows that at output level Q the valuation by consumers, given by price P_0, is far below the marginal social cost at point F on the MSC schedule. The price at which consumers buy does not reflect any of the externality, and thus the good is overconsumed or underpriced. Reducing output by 1 unit would improve welfare, because the loss to consumers is less than the gain to society in the form of reduced pollution.

We want to contract output as long as MSC exceeds price. This means that we want to go all the way to point E' where MSC equals price. The gain from the reduction in output is represented by the entire shaded area where MSC exceeds price and goods are thus underpriced or overconsumed.

Point E' is the optimum point for *society;* the costs to society of an extra unit of output exactly match the benefits to consumers of an extra unit. But point E is where the market economy takes us. Thus in the case of a market economy, goods that produce adverse externalities are overproduced. There is a market failure in the sense that the market does not lead to equality of marginal social costs and benefits. What is the exact cause of the market failure? It is that pollution is free. The firm is not charged for the adverse effects that it produces on the environment; therefore, it does not take pollution into account in its supply decision.

It is worth thinking a bit further to ask why there is no price on pollution. The answer is quite straightforward: the firm pollutes a river (or the air, or public roads), which is a common area, not a privately owned area. If pollution took place in private areas, the legal system would give the victims direct recourse against the offenders. Those who were harmed would sue for damages, and the possibility of being sued for damages would cause firms to reduce their polluting activities.

Thus the pollution externality problem can be described more narrowly as a problem of enforcing property rights for *public* areas such as rivers, the sea, and roads. We refer to all these public areas as *the commons*. Many externalities, though by no means all, result from a lack of restriction on the use of commons or a lack of enforcement of property rights.

3 POLLUTION CONTROL

We have seen that the free market will not lead to an optimal resource allocation when there are externalities. Goods that generate favorable externalities are underproduced, and goods that generate unfavorable externalities are overproduced. The market failure occurs because certain outputs—in this instance, pollution—are not priced. The obvious cure is to strengthen the free market by placing prices on all goods. This would ensure that market decisions about production and consumption reflect the marginal social costs and benefits of these activities.

The ideal solution is to charge anyone who generates an externality for the precise marginal cost of the externality. For instance, effluent charges have been recommended in the case of pollution. These are charges per unit for the amount of pollution dumped in the environment by a producer.

However, a different approach has been taken in practice, namely, regulation of pollution standards—standards that specify how much pollution firms are permitted to cause. This approach has been chosen in part because it is difficult to discover the right price to set on pollution and in part because regulators are more comfortable with setting technical performance standards than with using the price system. The upshot has been an elaborate system of environmental protection planning to reduce and reverse the increasing pollution that

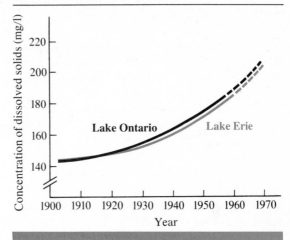

FIGURE 12-3 CHANGES IN THE CONCENTRATIONS OF DISSOLVED SOLIDS IN LAKE ERIE AND LAKE ONTARIO, 1900–1970. (*Source:* William J. Baumol and Wallace E. Oates, *Economics, Environmental Policy, and the Quality of Life,* Prentice-Hall, Englewood Cliffs, N.J., 1979, p. 16.)

has been threatening the environment for the last 100 years.

The Environmental Protection Agency (EPA)

The EPA was set up in 1970 to administer a variety of programs. At that time concern over the destruction of the environment through pollution was becoming an important social issue. Figure 12-3 shows the gradual deterioration of Lake Erie and Lake Ontario from 1900 to 1970 in terms of the solution of solids. Similar pictures can be shown for other lakes and for rivers, the high seas, the air in the city, and even the air in the country.[2] The EPA was created as a response to the awareness that pollution was out of hand and needed to be checked.

[2] Data for many types of pollution are summarized in Chapter 2 of William J. Baumol and Wallace E. Oates, *Economics, Environmental Policy, and the Quality of Life,* Prentice-Hall, Englewood Cliffs, N.J., 1979. The authors remind us that pollution has been a serious problem for a long time—in 1700 London had a worse smog problem than Los Angeles had 10 years ago.

The EPA has the tasks of controlling (*a*) air pollution, (*b*) water pollution, and (*c*) hazardous and toxic materials. The EPA has to do four things.[3] First, it must decide what levels of environmental quality are desired and set standards for the levels of air and water pollutants. Second, the EPA needs to tell firms what technologies to use to meet these standards. Third, the EPA has to monitor compliance with the standards. Finally, it has to do something about violators.

The EPA is probably best known for the setting of automobile emission standards. The agency has to certify that these standards have been met. It also has to check and certify that mileage requirements set by Congress have been met. Standards are enforced in part through fines. For instance, there is a fine of $10,000 for anyone disconnecting auto emission controls. The other important power of the EPA is its ability to deny certification for installations or equipment that does not satisfy the required standards.

With regard to water pollution, the stated purpose of the Water Pollution Control Act is to make it possible to swim in the nation's lakes, rivers, and oceans by 1983 and to stop water pollution by 1985. No one can dump wastes in water without an EPA permit, and polluters can be heavily fined.

The Optimal Quantity of Pollution

How much environmental purity do we want? In other words, how much pollution do we want? That must be a question of balancing costs and benefits. Figure 12-4 shows the cost-benefit analysis of air pollution. Suppose that the marginal benefit from cleaner air is shown by the downward-sloping schedule, *MB*. At high levels of pollution the marginal benefit from somewhat cleaner air is very high. The marginal bene-

[3] In this section we have drawn on Murray L. Weidenbaum, *Business, Government, and the Public*, 2d ed., Prentice-Hall, Englewood Cliffs, N.J., 1981.

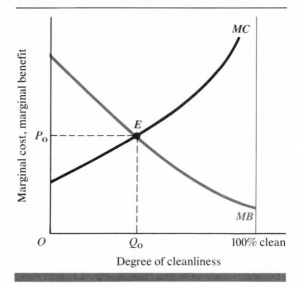

FIGURE 12-4   THE OPTIMUM QUANTITY OF POLLUTION. The marginal costs of achieving cleaner air increase with the degree of cleanliness. The marginal benefits from increasing cleanliness decline. The optimal degree of cleanliness (or pollution) is Q_0. At this level of pollution, the marginal benefit from a cleaner environment exactly matches the marginal cost of achieving increased cleanliness.

fit is low when the air is already 99 percent clean. The marginal cost behaves the other way. In general, the marginal costs of achieving somewhat cleaner air are relatively low when pollution is already high. But the costs of achieving complete purity are nearly prohibitive, and so the *MC* schedule rises sharply.

The optimal amount of pollution is Q_0. At that level the marginal cost of improving the quality of the air is equal to the marginal benefit from doing so. If there is less clean air, the marginal benefit from cleaner air is greater than the marginal cost. It is worthwhile spending more to get purer air, or reducing pollution. If the air is purer than Q_0, the marginal cost of reducing pollution is greater than the marginal benefit, meaning that there is too little pollution if purity is greater than Q_0.

The idea that there can be too little pollution may seem strange. When people think about pollution, the natural reaction is to say that the less there is, the better. But if reducing pollution means spending more on pollution-control equipment and therefore spending less on other things, it is not necessarily optimal to try to get rid of pollution entirely. Thus the aim of getting rid of all water pollution by 1985 does not make *economic* sense. And it will not be achieved.

Could we set policy by carrying out an analysis like the one in Figure 12-4, where we actually know what the benefits are to consumers of purer air? The answer is yes, in part. Some of the costs of pollution to consumers, in the form of worse health and damage to property, can be evaluated.[4] Other elements of the benefits from a cleaner environment, such as the fun of fishing or swimming in lakes or of seeing unpolluted nature, are more difficult or impossible to quantify. Curves like the *MC* curve in Figure 12-4 have been calculated. For instance, Figure 12-5 shows the marginal costs of reducing one form of pollution during petroleum refining. The interesting point is that up to 70 percent of the pollution can be eliminated quite cheaply. Getting rid of the last 30 percent is much more expensive and almost certainly should not be tried.

Similarly, it was calculated in 1975[5] that it would cost about $60 billion to eliminate 85 to 90 percent of water pollution within 10 years. Getting rid of another 10 percent of pollution would double the cost. The important point in each case is that the *MC* curve is rising very sharply when almost all pollution has already been eliminated. Thus we would not want to incur the costs

---

[4] Lester Lave and Eugene Seskin (*Air Pollution and Human Health,* Johns Hopkins Press, Baltimore, 1977) provide some of the information needed for such a calculation.

[5] Reported in Allen V. Kneese and Charles L. Schultze, *Pollution, Prices and Public Policy,* Brookings Institution, Washington, 1975.

FIGURE 12-5   MARGINAL COST OF REDUCING DISCHARGE IN PETROLEUM REFINING. (*Source:* William J. Baumol and Wallace E. Oates, *Economics, Environmental Policy, and the Quality of Life,* Prentice-Hall, Englewood Cliffs, N.J., 1979, p. 213.)

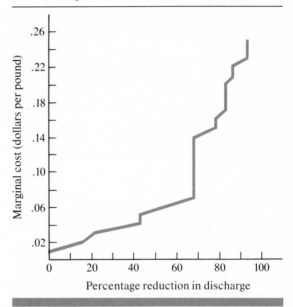

of getting rid of pollution completely. The benefits of doing so are smaller than the costs.

Has the EPA Succeeded?

Have the EPA's regulations reduced pollution? The record is mixed. Table 12-1 presents data on air pollution since 1970. Pollution is down in all but one category, that of nitrogen oxide pollution. Since GNP has grown by 37 percent since 1970, we can say that in every category there has been a sizable reduction in pollution in relation to total output. There have not been similar reductions in overall water pollution, but there are certainly many improvements. For instance, Lake Erie is coming back to life, with fish staging a reappearance.

At what cost have these improvements in the environment been obtained? Table 12-2 shows some data on expenditures for pollution abatement and control in the

TABLE 12-1

AIR POLLUTION
(Millions of Short Tons)

POLLUTANTS	1970	1975	1979
Particulates (smoke, dust, and fumes)	23.1	12.8	10.5
Sulfur oxides	31.2	27.8	27.0
Nitrogen oxides	21.0	22.3	24.9
Hydrocarbons	30.5	25.8	27.1
Carbon monoxide	124.4	108.0	100.7

Source: Statistical Abstract of the United States, 1981, Table 358.

TABLE 12-2

POLLUTION CONTROL AND ABATEMENT EXPENDITURES
(Billions of Dollars)

	1972	1979
Total	18.2	48.5
Pollution abatement	17.0	45.7
Regulation and federal monitoring	0.4	1.1
Research and development	0.8	1.7

Source: Statistical Abstract of the United States, 1981, Table 351.

United States. Total expenditure for pollution avoidance in 1979 was more than 2 percent of GNP, compared with 1.5 percent of GNP in 1972. These are large expenditures. The 1979 total is more than one-third the amount spent on national defense and of the same order of magnitude as government spending on health.

Using Prices

Economists prefer to use market mechanisms where possible, and often where impossible also. Many economists have argued that the EPA, instead of telling firms how much they can pollute and what technologies to use, should simply set a price for pollution and let the firms choose their own levels of pollution. If they have to pay, they will want to reduce costs by reducing pollution.

How would the scheme work? Go back to Figure 12-4, and suppose that the EPA knew where the MC and MB curves intersected. The EPA could then charge firms price P_0 for every unit of pollution put into the air or water. Firms would restrict their polluting activity so as to produce pollution only to the point where the price is equal to the marginal cost of reducing pollution. This would minimize the firms' costs.

Why use prices instead of regulations? One good reason is that the production would be efficiently allocated. If every firm were charged the same price for polluting, then every firm would pollute up to the point where the marginal cost of reducing pollution was equal to the price charged for polluting. This means that the marginal cost of reducing pollution would be equalized across firms, and that is the cheapest way for the economy as a whole to achieve any given reduction in pollution. To see why, suppose that the marginal cost of reducing pollution by 1 unit is lower for firm A than for firm B. Then if firm A reduces pollution by 1 unit and firm B increases pollution by 1 unit, the total cost is reduced without any increase in total pollution.

If the EPA set pollution limits for each firm, it would have a hard time ensuring that the total reduction in pollution is achieved as cheaply as possible. This is one reason for using prices. The second reason is closely related: the EPA would not have to worry about specifying regulations for each individual firm if it were regulating through price.

Several important points have to be made on the other side. First, to use a pricing scheme, it has to be possible to measure the amount of pollution being produced by each firm. And, given the importance of automobile exhaust pollution, it would also be necessary to measure the pollution caused by each car. Just reading all the meters would be quite a job.

Second, it is not really so simple to come up with the right price. But why not have the EPA experiment until it gets the right price? That is not a good policy either, because the type of equipment firms use will depend on the price charged for polluting. If the EPA chose a price that was too low and then had to raise it, firms would have to modify their machinery with new antipollution devices, no doubt at considerable expense.

One aspect of the choice between standards regulation and the use of prices deserves attention. Under standards regulation, the EPA might well force every firm—especially the worst polluters—to adjust. It is quite possible, though, that if prices were used to control pollution, the worst polluters would continue to pollute, whereas the firms that do relatively little polluting would reduce their pollution almost to zero. This would be economically efficient, but might not be politically attractive.

It is clear that the use of prices to regulate *all* pollution is impractical. But the difficulties can easily be exaggerated. For instance, emissions into rivers in Germany's Ruhr River basin, which contains 40 percent of the country's industry, are regulated through a system of effluent (outflow) charges. Although the total flow of water through these rivers is quite small, the rivers are thriving and not very polluted. The pricing system can be used in regulation and is likely to be used increasingly during the eighties.

4 QUALITY, HEALTH, AND SAFETY

The second source of market failure we discuss in this chapter occurs when households or firms cannot fully judge the attributes of the products they are buying or the working conditions in which they operate. There is less than full information because gathering information is costly. But this implies that relatively risky goods or activities might not be known as such and would therefore be overconsumed. A worker who does not know that exposure to high levels of benzene, as happens in some chemical plants, might cause cancer will be willing to work for a lower wage than if he were aware of all the risks. The firm's total cost of producing the good, therefore, will not fully reflect the true social cost of resources, and the good will be overproduced.

The federal government has over the years expanded the role of regulatory agencies in the area of health, safety, and quality standards, because it has recognized that this is a potentially important area of market failure. This belief is reinforced by an externality: jobs that are relatively risky lead to injuries or deaths, with the result that the injured and his family have to be supported by welfare or Social Security—that is, by society at large. Thus even if people correctly perceive the risks associated with products or activities, there are still costs to society that go beyond what is borne by individuals themselves.

The most important regulatory agency in this area is the Food and Drug Administration (FDA), which inspects the purity of food entering interstate commerce, governs the labeling of products, and sets standards for testing the safety and efficacy of drugs. The Consumer Product Safety Commission (CPSC) regulates the design and safety of consumer products. The National Highway and Traffic Safety Administration (NHTSA) regulates the equipment of highway vehicles to reduce accidental death and injury. The Occupational Safety and Health Administration (OSHA) regulates safety standards in the workplace.

The agencies have in common a double role. They provide information that leads to a more efficient allocation of resources by firms and consumers. More important, they set and enforce standards that are designed to reduce the risks of injury and death. In providing information and in setting standards, the agencies fill a gap where markets are not functioning with full efficiency because of imperfect information or because of externalities associated with injury and death.

Providing Information

The role of regulatory agencies as providers of useful information is shown in Figure 12-6. Suppose that a product, say, a drug, is potentially harmful, but that this is not known by consumers, or not known to the full extent. The demand is DD, the supply of the industry is SS, and the market equilibrium is at point E.

Now we ask what the equilibrium would look like if consumers had the correct information about the attributes of the product. Certainly, quantity demanded would be less at each price, since many consumers would feel that given the risks, they should buy less or none of the good. Accordingly, the "full information" demand schedule is DD', which lies to the left of DD. This is the demand schedule that gives us the *true* (i.e., full information) marginal valuation of additional units of output by consumers.

The uninformed free market equilibrium is at E, with the marginal social cost given by the supply schedule lying above the true marginal social valuation by consumers on DD'. Society gains in moving to E', where marginal social costs and benefits are equal. The free market in this instance leaves people with incomplete information and therefore leads to overproduction of the risky commodity. An agency that provides information restores efficiency by shifting the market equilibrium to point E'. In providing information the agency helps avoid a welfare cost due to misinformation. This welfare cost is represented by the shaded area.

FIGURE 12-6 PROVISION OF INFORMATION PREVENTS OVERPRODUCTION OF UNSAFE GOODS. Consumers do not know the safety risks associated with a particular good. The free market equilibrium is at E. An agency now provides information about the characteristics of the product leading to a reduction in quantity demanded. The new equilibrium is at E', where the *true* or full information valuation of an extra unit of the good is equal to its marginal social cost. Providing information prevents a welfare cost.

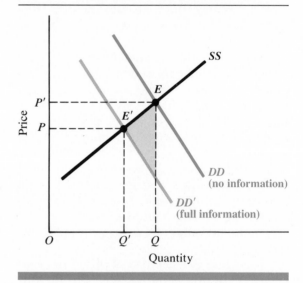

Imposing Standards

Regulatory agencies have not stopped at providing information, letting consumers and producers choose freely the risks that they want to take. On the contrary, they have imposed standards of safety and adequacy which often bore little or no relation whatsoever to economic costs and benefits. This criticism has been leveled against OSHA and also against the CPSC and the FDA.

There is a common economic analysis of the standards imposed on an industry by regulatory agencies. In all cases firms are forced to produce in a more costly way or to produce a more costly product than they would in the absence of such regulation. Thus regulation tends to shift upward the firms' marginal cost schedules, and as a result the industry supply schedule moves from SS to SS', as shown in Figure 12-7. Equilibrium output falls. Thus regulation, regardless of what its benefits are with respect to whatever is being regulated (pollution, job safety, information of consumers, etc.), will appear as a tax on the industry and for that reason will be opposed.

The FDA

One of the FDA's tasks is to set standards for the labeling of food. Ice cream must be made of dairy products, or it is not ice cream. Beef pie has to consist mainly of beef. Any soda drink containing the word "cola" or "Pepper" has to contain caffeine.

Most publicity about the FDA has been associated with the *Delaney amendment* and with the slowness of drug development and certification. The Delaney amendment requires the FDA to ban any food which causes cancer in people or animals.

The FDA banned saccharin in 1977, after experiments showed that rats fed with enormous amounts of saccharin got cancer. This ban generated much and vocal opposition. Arguments were brought to show, for example, that more people would die because of the increased risk of heart attack associated with being overweight (as a result of eating sugar instead of saccharin) than would be saved from a cancer death. The political outcry from saccharin users (including drinkers of diet soda) was so strong that a special exemption was given, and we can still drink diet soda. Similarly, the FDA discovered that red dye #2, used for making foods red, caused cancer, and so it had to ban the dye. There were alternative dyes, and so consumers of hot dogs did not suffer too much from this ban.

Critics of the FDA allege that it has been far too concerned with keeping bad drugs off the market. That is, its tests are very conservative. We can be almost sure that any new drug that is certified is OK, but

FIGURE 12-7 STANDARDS RAISE COSTS AND REDUCE THE EQUILIBRIUM OUTPUT. A regulatory agency imposes standards on an industry. This increases costs and thus shifts the supply schedule to the left. The equilibrium price rises, and the equilibrium level of output falls. The question that must be asked is whether the standards are warranted on a cost-benefit basis.

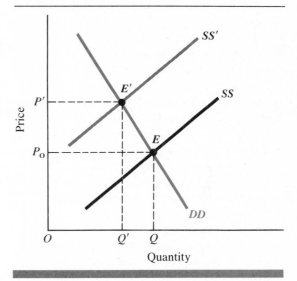

we cannot be sure that somewhere fine drugs have not been suppressed by the too rigorous tests of the FDA. And besides, the critics say, by having such a slow testing procedure (it takes about 7 years to develop a new drug and bring it to the market), the FDA deprives consumers of help they could be getting from drugs during at least 3 or 4 years of unnecessary delay.

We will now take up two questions. First, why should there be any drug regulation at all? Second, have the regulations been a good thing? Although it may seem natural to have drug regulation, there is an argument that the free market would produce the right amount of safe drugs. Any company that sold unsafe drugs would get a bad reputation. It would not be profitable to have a bad reputation, and therefore only the good drug companies could survive. Further, anyone damaged by a drug could sue the company for compensation—or perhaps the surviving family would do so. Such an argument takes a much too long-run view of the industry. It might be not only the bad drug companies but also their customers who fail to survive. And lawsuits are expensive. Some form of outside evaluation of drugs is desirable.

In the area of safety and quality certification it is important to separate two issues. One is the establishment of the objective criteria which are to be imposed—the definition of what is safe in a particular context. The other is the procedure for monitoring and enforcing the rules. The former is clearly a matter on which society does, and maybe should, take a view. It is better to ride in an elevator that has been certified as meeting government regulations than to ride in one which the owners of the building "feel" is safe. There are substantial savings for society in establishing definitions of safety or quality and in setting compulsory standards. There is a quite separate issue: how to monitor and enforce standards. The government does not always have to intervene, since in many instances of everyday life we accept private certification: Sotheby's certifies the quality of Rembrandts, private universities certify educational achievement, rabbis certify kosher food, and Moody's rates the credit standing of firms. Box 12-1 makes the case for private monitoring.

The public's interest, and therefore its insistence on standards, is particularly important when very little is known about the products to be placed in the market and when the consequences for society of any error may be catastrophic. It is entirely reasonable for society to impose its evaluation of risk on the builders of high-rises, the producers of toxic substances, or the builders of nuclear plants rather than rely on the assumption that firms, in the profit interest, will avoid unreasonable risks.

Once it is accepted that the government plays a role in defining the safety or quality

of products, though not necessarily in monitoring, we must ask this question: What will ensure that the public is kept aware of potential risks that must be avoided or an actual lack of safety that requires correction? This is an information problem which involves economies of scale, and therefore can be entrusted to government agencies that routinely patrol the goods market just as the police patrol the streets.

How effective have the drug regulations been? Professor Sam Peltzman of the University of Chicago argues that the benefits that are lost because new drugs are not introduced quickly enough and because some good drugs are suppressed outweigh the gains from keeping useless or bad drugs off the market. Such work, as interesting as it undoubtedly is, has to be highly speculative. Supporters of the FDA point to the fact that the United States avoided the thalidomide tragedy of the early 1960s. Thalidomide was a drug used in Europe; it was given to pregnant women, many of whom subsequently had deformed children. The FDA did not license thalidomide for use in the United States. It remains necessary, though, to remember that strict control can keep useful new drugs off the market, either for a time or forever.

Regulatory Abuse

Critics of the other regulatory agencies have gone far in their criticism. For example, OSHA (Occupational Safety and Health Administration) has been criticized for the enforcement of workplace safety standards that are entirely ineffective, costly, and uneconomic. Table 12-3 shows some facts about injury and fatality rates.

The data in Table 12-3 show that there were reductions in the number of deaths and injuries prior to the introduction of OSHA in 1970. It is also the case that death rates in manufacturing have not declined since 1970, although death rates in agriculture and mining have fallen substan-

TABLE 12-3

FATALITIES AND DISABLING INJURIES
(Per 100,000 Workers)

	1950	1960	1970	1980
Deaths:				
Manufacturing	17	10	9	9
Nonmanufacturing	31	25	21	15
Injuries	3396	2967	2710	2200

Source: Statistical Abstract of the United States, 1981,
Table 697.

tially. How much of the reduction in injuries is attributable to OSHA is uncertain. The reduction in mining deaths and injuries may be credited to OSHA, since regulation in the area of mining has been quite tough. In general, though, reviews of OSHA's record in the prevention of injury and death on the job conclude that the contribution has been minor.[6] The absence of a decisive impact on job safety is aggravated by the fact that OSHA has not been guided by an evaluation of the cost effectiveness of its measures.

Many of OSHA's regulations have been difficult to understand. OSHA mandated that the split toilet seat be used in wash-

[6] Albert Nichols and Richard Zeckhauser, "OSHA after a Decade: A Time for Reason," in Leonard Weiss and Michael W. Klass (eds.), *Case Studies in Regulation: Revolution and Reform*, Little, Brown, Boston, 1981, p. 217, and John Mendeloff, *Regulating Safety: An Economic and Political Analysis of Occupational Safety and Health Policy*. M.I.T. Press, Cambridge, Mass., 1979.

BOX 12-1

PRIVATE CERTIFICATION

The *Sultana* pushed out of the Memphis dock early that morning of April 27, 1865; its paddle-wheels spinning smoothly through the Mississippi water, plumes of black coal smoke pouring out of its twin funnels. On board, 2,400 Union soldiers being exchanged for Confederate prisoners. Weak from months of prison camp, the men clogged every cranny of the *Sultana* built to carry only 400 passengers.

Then, without warning, a huge explosion, estimated to have had the force of a thousand pounds of dynamite. The blast ignited an uncontrolled bonfire. At least 1,200 Union men burned to death or drowned. The steam boiler had exploded.

After 100 years of steam technology, boilers continued to explode with alarming regularity in mines, locomotives and factories. Hundreds died each year.

The news of the *Sultana*'s black day galvanized Jeremiah Allen and three of his friends. They formed the Hartford (Conn.) Steam Boiler Inspection and Insurance Co. (it still exists). They offered to insure any boiler that they inspected for safety. They put their own money on the line. Within a few decades, the idea of private boiler inspection took hold. Boiler-explosion rates plummeted.

Allen's idea holds a lesson for us today. What I am saying is that regulation is too important to be left to the government. I am talking only about regulation concerning health, welfare and safety, not economic regulation designed to fix charges by utilities, railroads, airlines, truckers, etc.

Source: Earl Ubell, "The Privatizing of Regulation," *Newsweek*, Nov. 23, 1981, p. 35.

rooms. Why should it bother anyone with such things? OSHA set maximum noise levels for factories so that the hearing of workers would not be damaged. These standards would have required an expenditure of about $18.5 billion for new machinery. It was pointed out that workers could also be protected if they were given earplugs, at a total cost of $43 million. However, for a long time OSHA would not change its mind. It argued that workers wouldn't wear the earplugs and that therefore its own regulations to reduce the noise level in factories were preferable.

The earplug case reflects a general criticism that has been made of OSHA, that it concentrates on the physical environment in trying to reduce the injury rate and does not try to affect worker behavior. Some studies suggest that worker carelessness causes the majority of workplace accidents.

Social Priorities in the Health and Safety Area

In the area of health and safety it is especially important to decide what the basis is for regulation and what precise role the government assumes. Is this an area where market failure is due to a well-defined distortion—say, a lack of information—or to externalities such that society must bear part of the costs of accidents? Is the government active in this area to further social goals that are beyond the narrow and specific issue of allocational efficiency?

Governments and politicians often proclaim that human life is undebatably beyond economic calculation and that wherever the issue arises, absolute priority must be given to preserving human life and health, whatever the cost. An economist will reply with two points. First, society cannot, in fact, afford to implement such a policy in all activities. Second, in making occupational and recreational choices, people do take risks; therefore, society

should ask how much more averse to risk it should be than the people it is trying to protect.

The task of the economist, an uncomfortable one in this area, is to point out that even when human life and health are at stake, we do need to use economic analysis to evaluate alternative approaches to achieving maximum welfare. Invariably the conclusion will be *not* to go all out in some areas. It would be foolish to spend a lot to eliminate the slightest chance of accident or disease in one area while in other areas high risks continue. The sooner we realize that society cannot afford to eliminate all health and accident risks (and will not eliminate them), the sooner we will come to a realistic regulatory approach in this area. Zero risk regulation does *not* make sense from the perspective of economics.

Economists have long called for regulatory activity to be subjected to cost-benefit analysis. We want to choose the most cost-effective ways of achieving given targets. Whenever regulation is imposed, we should know the costs of securing the benefits. Even if society does decide that certain rights (health, life) are to be set beyond economic calculation, we should still know what the cost of that luxury is. As economists become more experienced with cost-benefit analysis and acquire more information about the prices people place on risk—these emerge from studies of wages in different locations and under different conditions—there will be increasing conflicts over the value of regulation. The conflicts will involve those who argue for cost-effective regulation and those who argue that certain values are beyond economic calculation. There is no doubt that the latter case can be very persuasively stated.[7]

---

[7] See the very forceful statement by Steven Kelman in "Cost Benefit Analysis: An Ethical Critique," *Regulation*, January–February 1981.

5 THEORIES OF THE REGULATOR

We have discussed government intervention in cases of market failure, and we have seen that regulatory agencies are, in the modern economy, a chief instrument of intervention. We have also seen that they sometimes behave in economically strange ways.

This raises the question of what governs the behavior of the regulators. What are their aims? There is one sense in which the answer is quite straightforward. An agency is set up by some specific legislative act, and the act dictates the agency's tasks and criteria. In that sense, the agency has only to implement the will of Congress. But in practice, the agencies have a lot of freedom. They may, for instance, believe that their primary duty is to help consumers. Or they may believe that their duty to consumers is limited by the need to make sure the firms in the industry do not go bankrupt.

There is room, then, to explain how regulators themselves behave. Two competing theories have been advanced. One theory, due to Chicago's George Stigler, is called the *capture hypothesis.* The other theory, again from Chicago, is Sam Peltzman's theory, which has been dubbed *share the gains, share the pains.*[8] Both theories are examples of economic modeling of the political process.

The Capture Hypothesis

Many of the regulatory agencies, though not all, were set up to help consumers—to prevent problems that existed without regulation. But, the capture hypothesis asserts, no matter why the agencies were set up, they end up acting in the interests of the firms

they should be regulating. Indeed, since they have the power to control entry and pricing, they are often the ideal means for running a cartel, if only they can be captured.

Why is an industry likely to capture the regulators? There are two factors here. First, the regulators have to have some knowledge of the industry they are controlling. There is thus a good chance that they are already associated with the industry; perhaps they worked in it before becoming regulators. Second, in regulatory hearings the firms in the industry are going to have better information than the customers, and they will be willing to spend more than the customers. For the customers, the product is one of many that they buy, and no individual customer will devote a lot of energy to trying to influence what the regulatory agency decides. And it is difficult for millions of customers to get together to express their interests. However, for the firms, the regulations under which they work are vital. Thus the firms will spend more on presenting their case to the regulators than will the customers.

Share the Gains, Share the Pains

This second approach focuses on the aims of regulators. In some states, regulators are elected—for instance, those serving on state utility commissions. In other states and at the federal level, regulators are appointed by the legislature or the administration.

An elected or appointed regulator can be viewed as maximizing approval by his constituency and aiming to continue in his job. The constituency includes the legislators who established the agency and monitor it, the industry that is being regulated, and the customers who are supposed to be the beneficiaries of the regulation. Each of these groups has some say in any rating of the agency's performance and therefore will be given *some* weight. Here is, of course,

[8] See George Stigler, *The Citizen and the State: Essays on Regulation,* University of Chicago Press, Chicago, 1975, and Sam Peltzman, "Toward a More General Theory of Regulation," *Journal of Law and Economics,* 1976, as well as the comments by Jack Hirshleifer in the same place.

the difference between the Peltzman model and the Stigler view, in which only industry interests are served. The Peltzman model suggests that such a position is too risky for the regulators because it will evoke excessive opposition from consumers who are disfavored.

If regulators attach some weight to each part of their constituency, then they will typically follow policies that split the difference. When new evidence about the risks of a product emerges there will be some tightening of standards, but also some time for firms to improve the product. When an industry experiences a cost increase, there will be some adjustment of regulated rates, but also some concession to the consumer. Agencies in this model are not captured by one group or another; instead, they stand between the groups, adjusting somewhat in favor of each.

In this way of looking at an agency it becomes important to know who is most vociferous and most closely controls the appointment and budget of the agency. The FDA, for example, could not ever afford to let catastrophically dangerous drugs pass, for that would lead to an outcry from consumers. But it can afford, by contrast, steady annoyance by business. In this approach, agencies are invariably led to prevent major disasters (they close airports at the slightest indication of danger), even if in the course of doing so they *almost always* turn out to have acted with excessive prudence.

6 DEREGULATION

Regulation in the American economy goes back more than 100 years, and it increased substantially in the 1970s. At present there is a widespread sense, certainly in the business community, that regulation has gone too far, is out of control, and needs to be reevaluated. There are, in particular, proposals to *deregulate*, to remove old regulations rather than impose new ones.

The revolt against regulation is reinforced by estimates of the costs of regulation. The most prominent estimate is that reported by Murray Weidenbaum, former chairman of the Council of Economic Advisors in the Reagan administration. The estimate is shown in Table 12-4. The estimate for 1976 amounts to an astounding 3.8 percent of the GNP for that year. Updated estimates run even higher. But these data have not gone unchallenged. Perhaps more significantly, the costs have as a counterpart gains from the elimination of market failure.[9]

Economic regulation will, without any doubt, remain one of the major issues of the 1980s. On one side, social interest groups and legislators and the agencies themselves will make the case for increased regulation. On the other side, industry—and in some cases the taxpayer—will express concern and determination to stem the growth of regulation. That growth has been quite extraordinary. From 1970 to 1980 the expenditures of 57 regulatory agencies more than tripled (in constant dollars), and the number of full-time positions in these agencies rose from 28,000 to 90,000. It is against this background of growing regulatory activity, not accompanied by a perception of great success, that we should see the current movement for deregulation.

Deregulation of the Airline Industry

There are areas where deregulation does not run into moral objections involving health and life. In these areas the issue is how the consumers can best be served without doing unnecessary harm to an industry. The now classic example is the airline industry. The airline industry has been regulated since the 1920s, first by the postmaster general when airmail was one of the chief sources of revenue. Regulation increased

---

[9] See William K. Tabb, "Government Regulations: Two Sides of the Story," *Challenge*, November–December 1980.

TABLE 12-4

ANNUAL COST OF FEDERAL REGULATION, 1976
(Millions of Dollars)

AREA	ADMINISTRATIVE COST	COMPLIANCE COST	TOTAL
Consumer safety and health	1,516	5,094	6,610
Job safety and working conditions	483	4,015	4,498
Energy and the environment	612	7,760	8,372
Financial regulation	104	1,118	1,222
Industry specific	484	19,919	20,403
Paperwork	—*	25,000	25,000
Total	3,199	62,906	66,105

* Included in other categories.
Source: Murray Weidenbaum, *Business, Government and the Public,* 2d ed., Prentice-Hall, Englewood Cliffs, N.J., 1981.

especially in the 1930s, and in the 1940s the Civil Aeronautics Board (CAB) was charged with industry regulation to promote air service and prevent "unfair or destructive competitive practices." As a result, an extensive set of regulations was developed; the CAB set rates for interstate flights, fixed the frequency of flights, regulated the entry of firms into the industry, and directed every nook and cranny of the business. Indeed, there was no new entry into the business.

It is especially interesting to note that the airlines, because of restricted entry and regulated fares, shifted from price competition to nonprice competition. Instead of cutting prices to increase business and profits, the airlines competed in the quality of the meals they offered and the number of flights they scheduled. While passengers appreciate good meals and frequent flights, they also appreciate lower prices. Why was there competition in the quality of meals? Because the CAB controlled prices, competition took place on other dimensions. Competition went too far on the service front and not far enough on prices. The fares of the less regulated carriers operating only inside California and Texas, and therefore not controlled by the CAB, were much lower than those of the interstate airlines.

The belief that prices could be reduced through competition, along with the strong pro-deregulation push coming from the CAB itself, under the leadership of Alfred Kahn,[10] led Congress in April 1978 to introduce competition into the airline market. Kahn explained that the airline industry was a good place to allow competition.

> With relatively easy entry, relatively small economies of scale, and mobility of its capital equipment, the technology of aviation seems ideally suited to exactly the flexible adaptation of supply to dynamic market conditions that a market system, if unimpeded by government restrictions, can efficiently accomplish.[11]

With the support of the 1978 act, the CAB moved aggressively to allow the entry of new carriers and also to allow substantial variation in fares, ranging from 50 percent to

[10] Alfred Kahn is a onetime dean of Cornell University. He is known for his wit. An example is the comment he made on *Meet the Press:* "A dean is to the faculty what a lamppost is to a dog."
[11] Alfred Kahn, "Deregulation of Air Transportation—Getting from Here to There," in Donald P. Jacobs (ed.), *Regulating Business: The Search for the Optimum,* Institute for Contemporary Studies, San Francisco, 1978, pp. 38–39. See, too, his "Applications of Economics to an Imperfect World," *American Economic Review,* May 1979.

TABLE 12-5

AIRLINE INDUSTRY AND DEREGULATION

	1960	1970	1977	1978	1979	1980
Number of carriers	55	41	37	36	52	63
Number of aircraft in operation	1867	2437	2234	2348	2466	2505
Load factor, %	59.3	49.7	55.9	61.5	63.0	59.0
Fares in relation to costs*	N.A.	100	77	70	65	67

* Index in 1970 = 100.
Sources: Statistical Abstract of the United States, 1981, Tables 1123, 1124, and 1127, and
Statistical Abstract of the United States, 1980, Table 1161.

TABLE 12-6

COMPETITION AFTER DEREGULATION

	1977			1982		
ROUTE	CARRIERS	FLIGHTS	FARE	CARRIERS	FLIGHTS	FARE
NYC–Boston	5	53	$ 51	12	52	$ 45–107
NYC–Washington, D.C.	9	68	55	10	95	35–110
NYC–Los Angeles	3	29	294	9	28	148–488
Chicago–Denver	4	29	137	5	17	169–237
Chicago–Houston	0	0	138	4	12	90–202
San Francisco–LA	8	178	70	11	90	24–114
Houston–Dallas	3	92	57	7	112	24–92
Madison–Chicago	3	15	41	2	10	58–73

Note: Fares are in 1982 dollars; direct flights only; economy-class fares.
Source: Official Airline Guide—North American Edition, June 1977 and April 1982. Data used by special permission of Official Airlines Guide, Inc. All rights reserved.

105 percent of the official rates and beyond. There certainly was a quick response. Table 12-5 shows that there were a large number of new carriers. The competition worked to cut fares as new carriers competed with established airlines. This is shown in Table 12-5 by an index of fares in relation to costs. The index, equal to 100 in 1970, dropped to 67 in 1980, reflecting in part increased costs and the effect of competition on rates. It is interesting to note that competition worked to increase the load factor (the percentage of passenger seating capacity used) until 1980, when the generally bad business conditions in the economy lowered passenger volume.

The competitive effects of deregulation are also shown in Table 12-6. Here we see the number of carriers, the number of flights, and the range of economy-class fares for various routes. The data show an increase in the number of carriers on most routes. A wide range of fares had developed, and the lowest fare on most routes in 1982 was below the 1977 fare. Even though the price of jet fuel had almost tripled since 1977, it is today possible to fly most routes more cheaply than then. In several cases the number of flights on a given route has fallen. There are two forces at work here. The first is that there was excessive competition in the frequency of flights before. And second, the air traffic controllers' strike in 1981 led to a curtailment of the number of flights.

It is too early to judge the success of

deregulation of the airlines. The industry is still adjusting to the change. The adjustment was affected by the generally bad business conditions in 1981–1982 (air travel was sharply reduced) and by the air traffic controllers' strike, which reduced the number of flights the system could handle. Airlines have gone bankrupt. But there was no reason to believe that the transition to a competitive airline industry would be quiet and profitable for every firm in the industry.

Indeed, part of the aim of deregulation was to give the more efficient firms an opportunity to show how much better they could do than the less efficient firms. Under the umbrella of regulation, less efficient firms had stayed in business; they could not do so under competitive conditions.

Although the final word on the success of airline deregulation is not in, the early signs in the form of lower fares and more competition are encouraging.

SUMMARY

1   There are four distortions—divergences between private and social costs and benefits—that are sources of market failure. They are monopoly and oligopoly, externalities, imperfect information, and social priorities. This chapter discusses the last three as possible reasons for the regulation of industry.

2   Externalities exist when the production or consumption of a good has spillover effects on other individuals and the spillover effects are not fully reflected in prices. The key point about externalities is that they exist when some output or input is not appropriately priced. For instance, there is an externality from the pollution caused when a firm is not charged for dumping noxious waste in a river.

3   Pollution externalities can be removed if a price is put on the discharge of pollutants. Such charges, in the form of effluent charges, are used in some countries. The alternative is to limit the amount of pollution each firm can create. Economists argue for the use of prices where possible, since pollution reduction is more efficiently allocated through prices than through regulations.

4   It is not optimal to reduce pollution to zero. Rather, there is an optimal quantity of pollution. At that level the marginal social benefit from cleaning up the environment is equal to the marginal social cost.

5   There have been substantial reductions in the amount of environmental pollution in the United States since 1970. It is not firmly established how much of this is due to the EPA (Environmental Protection Agency), but it *is* the EPA that has been responsible for producing and enforcing the regulations on pollution.

6   A second role for regulation is in situations where the safety characteristics of products are unknown. Imperfect information about working conditions or products frequently is a reason for government

intervention. The government could cure the market failure merely by providing information. But typically it does more; it also imposes safety standards on products.

7   The Food and Drug Administration (FDA) is required to ban any food or medicine that causes cancer in animals. This requirement led to the banning of saccharin, and the result was an outcry that led to the lifting of the ban. The FDA has to license drugs for sale in the United States. It can make two types of mistakes. First, it can let bad drugs come on the market. Second, it might keep good drugs off the market for a long time, while they are being tested. The second type of mistake imposes costs on society, though they are not as obvious as the costs that are incurred when a bad drug is allowed on the market. Critics argue that the FDA has been too cautious and has indeed kept good drugs off the market for too long.

8   Another reason for regulation is social priorities in the health and safety area. Society, through the political process, may impose standards that, for instance, place the value of life far above the implicit value individuals place on their own lives as shown by the types of risks they are willing to take.

9   There are two chief theories of what regulators do. One is that regulators are the captives of the industry (this is the capture hypothesis). The other theory is that the regulators stand in the middle between the firms that are being regulated and the consumers who should be protected—with the legislature and administration looking on. This second hypothesis is the "share the gains, share the pains" view of regulation; the regulators always share the benefits from (or costs of) any improvements between the firms in the industry and the customers.

10   The most radical single act of deregulation has been the deregulation of the airline industry. The evidence that airline deregulation has led to lower fares and more competition is not yet definitive, but the signs are encouraging. Although deregulation has also led to airline bankruptcies, the total number of airlines has risen substantially and most fares have fallen relative to costs.

KEY TERMS

Market failure	Occupational Safety and Health
Distortions in prices	Administration (OSHA)
Externality	Delaney amendment
Property rights	Capture hypothesis
Effluent charges	Share the gains, share the pains
Food and Drug Administration	Deregulation
(FDA)	

PROBLEMS

1 (*a*) Define the term "externality." (*b*) Show why, when there is an unfavorable externality, the output of the good generating that externality should be reduced.

2 Why is it more efficient to charge prices for polluting than to fix pollution standards that have to be obeyed by every firm?

3 (*a*) Why are there regulations for the safety of the workplace? (*b*) Should the aim be to prevent all workplace accidents?

4 Some people argue that if someone knows exactly what risks he is taking in his current job, there is no reason to try to control working conditions in any way. Others argue that society should not permit people to take extremely dangerous jobs, whether they want to or not . Which side do you support, and why? (You do not have to stick to purely economic arguments, but you should bring in the relevant economic arguments.)

5 The EPA has regulated car emissions by requiring cars to meet certain standards. Suppose that a meter is invented that can be put on each car to measure the amount of pollutants emitted each year. (*a*) How might the EPA go about reducing the amount of pollution in this case? (*b*) What are the benefits of the approach outlined in your answer to (*a*) compared with the benefits of the current approach, in which the pollution levels of cars are specified by the EPA.

6 There is an ongoing controversy about the requirement that air bags must be installed in cars. The air bags will automatically inflate in the event of an accident and cushion the impact for the passengers. It is generally agreed that seat belts can do just as good a job. Seat belts are cheaper to install. The problem is that very few people wear seat belts. Proponents of air bags say that they are needed to save lives. Opponents say that people who want to save their lives can do so by buckling their seat belts. What are the economic arguments for and against (*a*) compulsory use of air bags, (*b*) stiff fines for people who don't use seat belts and the requirement that all cars must have seat belts, and (*c*) the requirement that car manufacturers must give customers the choice of having seat belts or air bags or no safety equipment in their cars.

7 (*a*) Is there any reason why society should want to keep drugs that cause no harm off the market, assuming that they do not cure the diseases they are said to cure? (*b*) It is sometimes argued (for instance, in the share the gains, share the pains view of regulation) that a regulatory agency will always tend to overregulate because it is blamed for the bad things that happen despite its regulations (e.g., a plane crash) but not blamed so much for the good things it prevents that no one knows about (e.g., a useful drug may be kept off the market for a long time). Does this argument make sense?

8 A newspaper article claims that there are 310 regulations that apply to a pizza. For example, mozzarella cheese must contain between 30 and 45 percent fat and come from pasteurized cow's milk. The tomato sauce must be of the "red or reddish" variety and contain at least 24 percent "natural tomato soluble solids." Can you see any justification for such regulations? Explain.

9 Why should the Teamsters' Union, which does not own trucking firms, be opposed to the deregulation of interstate trucking? (Think of theories of the regulatory process, and remember that truck drivers are part of the trucking industry.)

10 The quotation in Box 12-1 describes a company which both certifies and insures boilers. (*a*) How well would the company have done if it had only certified boilers? (*b*) Do you think such certification could work for drugs? Explain.

Why do the best baseball players earn over a million dollars a year and the best engineers under $100,000? Why can college students majoring in engineering expect to earn more than equally smart students majoring in history? Why does an unskilled worker in a developed country earn more than an unskilled worker in a less developed country?

The answer in each case is that it depends on the supply and demand for the particular type of labor. In this chapter and the next we discuss the supply and demand for labor. We thus begin our discussion of the markets for factors of production—capital, labor, and land. We discuss what determines the prices of factors of production—the wages of labor and the rental rates for capital and land—and what determines their allocation among different industries. The analysis is very similar for all factors of production. We start with labor and go on in later chapters to discuss capital and land.

Table 13-1 presents data on average earnings by industry that suggest the type of question that is answered in this chapter and the following chapters on factor markets. One question is why, in both 1975 and 1979, workers in the steel industry made more than twice as much as workers in the leather products industry. Why are banking wages closer to the wages in leather products than to the wages in oil and gas extraction? Why in 1979 are wages in the leather products industry less than 50 percent above the minimum wage? Do these differentials correspond to labor skills or to the attractiveness of jobs or to union activity or to foreign competition? Why are any workers, in any industry, paid more than the minimum wage?

Consider next the percentage increases in average hourly earnings, which range from only 28.7 percent in banking to 50.0 percent in steel. In light of the fact that the consumer price index rose 34.9 percent from 1975 to 1979, we realize that in both the leather industry and the banking industry, earnings adjusted for inflation actually fell. Real earnings rose in oil and gas extraction and in the steel industry. Note that there is no simple relationship between the rate of wage increase and the increase in employment in a sector. We might think that wages increased fastest in the fast-growing sectors, such as oil extraction. But we also see rapid increases in wages in sectors where employment grows little, such as steel production.

Another type of question considered in this chapter is why differ-

13

Factor Markets and Derived Demand: Labor

TABLE 13-1

AVERAGE HOURLY EARNINGS OF PRODUCTION WORKERS IN SEVERAL SECTORS

INDUSTRY	EARNINGS, $/hr		% INCREASE, 1975–1980		STATUTORY MINIMUM WAGE, $/HR	
	1975	1980	EARNINGS	EMPLOYMENT	1975	1980
Oil and gas extraction	5.38	7.72	43.5	46.6	2.10	2.90
Banking	3.52	4.53	28.7	15.1	2.10	2.90
Blast furnace and basic steel production	6.94	10.41	50.0	5.4	2.10	2.90
Leather	3.21	4.22	31.5	−1.9	2.10	2.90

Source: Statistical Abstract of the United States, 1981. Tables 669 and 684.

ent methods of production are used in different countries. Why is so much more labor used in relation to capital in developing countries than in rich countries such as Germany or the United States? For example, there is a ticket collector on a bus in a poor country and a collecting machine on a bus in a (nonunionized) rich country. A diner in a poor country has several waiters; in a rich country it has several vending machines. Five people ride on a truck in a developing country but usually only one in a rich country. The relative costs of using labor and capital in rich and poor countries have an effect on the way goods and services are produced. Why?

The economics of factor markets is, as we said above, ultimately an analysis of supply and demand. There is nothing new or surprising to be developed in this respect. What is special, though, is that the demand is not a direct or final demand but a *derived* demand. Firms demand factors of production, or inputs, to produce final goods, and the demand for a factor is influenced by conditions in the market for final goods.

By *derived demand* we mean that the demand for factors of production is derived from the demand for the goods the factors are used to produce.[1]

On the supply side, we distinguish between the total supply of labor for the economy, resulting from individuals' decisions on whether or not to work, and the supply of labor available to particular industries. At any given time, the total supply of labor for the economy and the supplies of different types of labor may be given or only slightly elastic. The skill distribution of the labor force (pilots, violinists, and plumbers) is difficult to change in the short run. The only issue is which industry attracts what types of labor and whether particular attributes, such as a violinist's skills, command a wage differential. That is, of course, a question of both technology and final demand. Unskilled labor is a poor substitute for airline pilots for flying planes, but pilots are a good substitute for unskilled labor. Thus pilots will command a premium when air traffic demand increases suddenly. In the long run, the supply of factors will be adjusted. The premium for pilots will not last very long if dentists can get themselves retrained to become pilots (so long as the pilots do not have a union that keeps the retrained dentists out).

[1] We can think of the demand for some consumer goods as also a derived demand. For instance, the demand for cars is derived from the demand for transportation.

Should we expect wages to become equalized eventually if everyone moves toward the jobs with higher pay? Obviously not. First, workers have different levels of ability. And second, not all jobs are equally attractive. There are equalizing differentials in wages between jobs.

> An *equalizing differential* in wages is a difference in wages that compensates workers for the difference in the attractiveness of jobs.

For instance, wages in mining are higher than in manufacturing because mining jobs are less desirable and riskier. Teachers' salaries are lower than the salaries in industry for people with similar qualifications because teaching jobs are more stable.

We start this chapter by studying the demand for labor in a firm and in an industry. Next we introduce the labor supply decisions of individuals and the labor supply curve for an industry. Then we combine the analyses of demand and supply by examining equilibrium in the labor market for a particular industry.

1 THE FIRM, FACTOR PRICES, AND THE CHOICE OF PRODUCTION TECHNIQUE

In Chapter 7 we studied how a firm determines the production techniques it will use and how it decides on its level of output. The choice of production technique and the choice of output level are precisely the decisions that determine the firm's demand for labor. Once the firm knows how much output it will produce and how much labor and capital it needs to produce this level of output, it knows how much labor (and capital) it wants to hire. In this section, we will review the material from Chapter 7 showing how the firm's production possibilities and the prices of factors of production determine the production technique the firm uses.

Table 13-2 includes data from Tables 7-2 and 7-3. These have to do with methods of producing snarks. The output level corresponding to the two production techniques is 100 snarks per week. We have added two columns, one showing the wage-rental ratio and the other the capital-labor ratio.

Technique A is more capital-intensive. The capital-labor ratio is 1 to 1. Technique B is less capital-intensive, or more labor-intensive. The capital-labor ratio is 1 to 3. Common sense tells us—and the calculations in Chapter 7 confirmed—that the firm will use technique A when capital is relatively cheap and technique B when capital is relatively more expensive. We will now show this, using the data in Table 13-2.

The firm chooses the production technique that will allow it to produce the snarks at the lowest cost. In the upper part of the table, the rental rate for the machines is $320 per week, and the wage of labor is $300 per week. The wage-rental ratio is 0.9375 (300/320). With technique A, the cost of production per snark is $24.80, which is equal to the total cost of $2480 divided by the output of 100 snarks. The average, or unit, cost of production with technique B is $24.40 per snark. At the factor costs shown in the upper part of the table, the firm chooses technique B in preference to technique A.

Consider next the lower part of the table, where the cost of using labor has gone up from $300 per week to $340. The wage-rental ratio has risen to 1.0625 (340/320). Again we calculate the unit cost for each technique. Of course, with higher labor costs and unchanged capital costs, the cost of producing a snark with *any* technology will increase. But it is important to recognize that the ranking changes. With labor *relatively* more expensive, technique A now becomes cheaper. Using the more capital-intensive process makes sense when the relative price of labor is higher.

TABLE 13-2

FACTOR PRICES AND CHOICE OF TECHNIQUE

	CAPITAL INPUT	LABOR INPUT	RENTAL RATE, $/wk	WAGE RATE, $/wk	UNIT COST, $*	WAGE-RENTAL RATIO	CAPITAL-LABOR RATIO
Technique A	4	4	320	300	24.80	0.9375	1.00
Technique B	2	6	320	300	24.40	0.9375	0.33
Technique A	4	4	320	340	26.40	1.0625	1.00
Technique B	2	6	320	340	26.80	1.0625	0.33

* Unit cost = total cost divided by output.

FIGURE 13-1 THE WAGE-RENTAL RATIO AND THE OPTIMAL CAPITAL-LABOR RATIO. As the wage-rental ratio rises, labor becomes relatively more expensive to use, and the firm shifts toward more capital-intensive techniques of production. This is indicated by the positive slope of the *TT* schedule, which shows the relationship between the capital-labor ratio used in production and the wage-rental ratio. The slope of the *TT* schedule represents the ease with which capital can be substituted for labor.

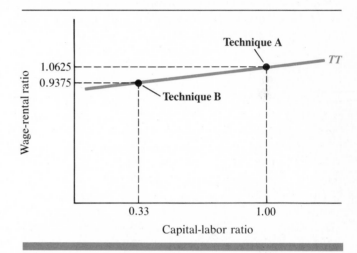

Typically, there are many techniques for producing a given level of output, not just two techniques. The results in Table 13-2 illustrate the first principle of the demand for factors of production. The principle is that a firm uses increasingly more capital-intensive methods of production as the relative cost of using labor rises. This is because the more capital-intensive techniques become relatively less expensive as the relative cost of using labor rises.

The wage-rental ratio in Table 13-2 measures the relative cost of using labor. The relationship between the wage-rental ratio and the capital-labor ratio is shown in Figure 13-1. The wage-rental ratio is shown on the vertical axis. The capital-labor ratio

of the technique the firm uses at each wage-rental ratio is shown on the horizontal axis. Schedule *TT* shows the relationship between the choice of technique and the wage-rental ratio. As the wage-rental ratio rises, labor becomes relatively more expensive, and the firm uses increasingly more capital-intensive techniques. In Figure 13-1 we implicitly assume that there are many techniques of production with differing capital-labor ratios, and so the *TT* line, representing the firm's optimal choices, rises smoothly. The facts that technique A is used when the wage-rental ratio is 1.0625 and technique B when the wage-rental ratio is 0.9375 are shown on the *TT* schedule.

Figure 13-1 provides the tool for answering the question of why there are substantial differences across countries in the capital-labor ratios used in the same industries. It predicts that the higher the wage-rental ratio is, the higher the capital-labor ratio will be. As the United States has a high wage-rental ratio relative to Mexico's, we expect U.S. firms to be using more capital-intensive techniques and Mexican firms to be opting for more labor-intensive processes. Not all industries have a complete menu of technology choices such as schedule *TT*. For certain industries, there may be only a few techniques, but still the basic idea of substitution in response to changes in relative factor prices remains unchanged.

Another important characteristic of the firm's choice of production techniques reflected in Figure 13-1 is the ease of *substitution* between capital and labor. We say that capital and labor are highly substitutable if a given change in the wage-rental ratio causes a large change in the capital-labor ratio. On the other hand, if the firm hardly changes its capital-labor ratio when there are large changes in the wage-rental ratio, we say that capital and labor are not very substitutable for each other—the firm basically has to stick to the same technique of production even as the relative prices of the factors change. The *slope* of the *TT* curve represents the ease of substitution; the flatter the *TT* curve, the more substitutable are labor and capital. In Figure 13-1, the degree of substitutability is high, because small changes in the wage-rental ratio cause large changes in the capital-labor ratio.

For a concrete example of factor substitution, consider the work of ditchdigging. At a very low wage-rental ratio, the ditches are dug by many workers with shovels. At a high wage-rental ratio, the ditches are dug by a large yellow machine operated by only one person.

2 THE FIRM'S DEMAND FOR LABOR

We have now shown how a firm faced with a given wage-rental ratio chooses the cheapest way of producing. But we have not determined what level of output it will actually produce, and we have therefore not yet shown how much labor and capital it will want to hire. Now we proceed to the demand for factors of production. We ask how much labor the firm will hire at a given wage. And we ask by how much the demand for labor will fall when the wage rises. Once more we will be reviewing and expanding on material from Chapter 7.

In the short run the firm's capital stock is fixed. With capital given in the short run, what is left for the firm to choose? The firm still has to determine how much labor to employ, and thus how much output to produce. This is the question that we discussed in Chapter 7, in looking at the firm's short-run output decision. In this section, we go through the same analysis, but we concentrate on the demand for labor.

Table 13-3 includes the information in Table 7-9, which shows the marginal product of labor for different levels of labor input. The higher the level of employment, the higher the level of output. The table also shows the *diminishing marginal productivity* of labor beyond the level of employment of three workers. The marginal product of labor increases as the first few workers are added, because it is difficult for the first and second to handle all the machinery. But by the time there are three workers employed, the diminishing marginal productivity of labor shows itself.

Now, how much labor will the firm hire? Equivalently, how much output will the firm produce? The general principle is to balance costs and benefits *at the margin*. We have to compare the cost of adding one more worker with the increase in revenue from adding one more worker. To make that

TABLE 13-3

EMPLOYMENT AND OUTPUT IN THE SHORT RUN

LABOR INPUT, no. of workers	OUTPUT, goods/wk	MARGINAL PRODUCT OF LABOR (MPL), goods/wk/worker	MARGINAL VALUE PRODUCT (MPL × $500)	WAGE RATE, $/wk	INCREASE IN PROFITS, $/wk
0	0				
		0.8	400	300	100
1	0.8				
		1.0	500	300	200
2	1.8				
		1.3	650	300	350
3	3.1				
		1.2	600	300	300
4	4.3				
		1.1	550	300	250
5	5.4				
		0.9	450	300	150
6	6.3				
		0.7	350	300	50
7	7.0				
		0.5	250	300	−50
8	7.5				
		0.3	150	300	−150
9	7.8				

calculation, we show in the fourth column of Table 13-3 the marginal value product of labor.

> The *marginal value product of labor* is the increase in the value of the firm's output resulting from hiring one extra worker.

In Table 13-3, we assume that the firm is a perfect competitor; it can sell as much as it wants at the market price of $500. The marginal value product of labor is thus $500 times the marginal product of labor. Each unit of output produced by a worker adds $500 to the value of the firm's output, and so the marginal value product is $500 times the increase in physical output resulting from hiring one more worker. The marginal value product of labor eventually declines as the number of workers increases, because the marginal product of labor is declining.

The marginal value product shows how much hiring one more worker adds to revenues. But hiring a worker adds to costs. The increase in costs is equal to the wage. Thus the total effect on the firm's profits of hiring one more worker is equal to the marginal value product minus the wage. This amount is shown in the last column of Table 13-3. Adding the first few workers increases prof-

its because revenue rises more than costs. By the time the firm already has seven workers on hand, hiring one more actually causes profits to fall (by $50 per week).

How many workers will the firm hire? It will keep adding workers so long as the marginal value product exceeds the wage. This means that the firm will hire seven workers. The seventh worker has a marginal value product of $350 and is paid only $300 per week. Hiring the seventh worker thus increases profits by $50 per week. But hiring an eighth worker adds only $250 to revenue, while the cost to the firm is $300. Profits therefore fall by $50, and the firm would not want to hire the eighth worker. The employment level of 7 is thus the optimal and equilibrium level of employment for the firm.

Note that the firm's decision on how much labor to hire is the same as the decision about how much output to produce. In deciding to hire 7 workers, the firm is also deciding to produce the amount of output—7.0 units—that is produced by 7 workers, given the capital input of 2 machines.

We can state the firm's optimal employment rule as follows: Expand employment as long as the marginal value product ex-

FIGURE 13-2 THE FIRM'S CHOICE OF EMPLOYMENT LEVEL. The marginal value product of labor declines as the level of employment rises. The firm can hire labor at the given wage rate, W_0. So long as $MVPL$ exceeds the wage, increasing employment increases profits. Thus as the arrow shows, the firm should increase its hiring whenever $MVPL$ exceeds W_0. Similarly, when the wage is above the marginal value product of labor, the firm should cut back its labor force. The equilibrium labor force is equal to L^*. At that level the wage is equal to the marginal value product of labor.

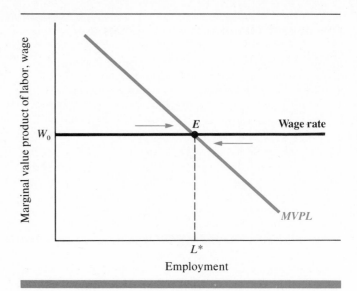

ceeds the wage, and contract employment whenever the marginal value falls short of the wage. If the labor input can be adjusted smoothly (if we are talking about hours of labor time to employ rather than the number of workers), this leads to the equilibrium employment condition:

Wage = marginal value product of labor   (1)

The firm is in equilibrium with respect to employment when the wage equals the marginal value product of labor.

Figure 13-2 shows the firm's labor market behavior, when the firm can smoothly vary the amount of labor it uses and when we assume that there is diminishing marginal productivity of labor at all levels of employment. We are thinking in Figure 13-2 about the number of hours of labor time hired per week, or even the number of minutes. Otherwise, the discussion is the same as that underlying Table 13-3. On the horizontal axis we plot the level of employment. On the vertical axis we measure the marginal value product of labor ($MVPL$). The marginal value product schedule is downward-sloping, reflecting the diminishing marginal productivity of labor.

Also shown in Figure 13-2 is the wage rate. In deciding about the level of employment, the firm compares the increase in costs from hiring one more worker with the increase in revenue. That is, it compares the wage with the $MVPL$. Note that we are assuming that the firm can obtain as much labor as it wants at the current market wage, W_0. So long as the marginal value product of labor exceeds the wage, the firm should increase its employment level. If the marginal value product of labor is less than the wage, the firm should reduce employment. Thus in Figure 13-2 the firm should hire the amount of labor represented by L^*, the amount of labor at which the marginal value product is equal to the wage. The arrows show how the firm adjusts its employment level if that level is different from L^*. At L^*, the marginal value product of labor is equal to the wage.

3 LABOR DEMAND AND THE DETERMINANTS OF EMPLOYMENT

Now that we have the rule by which the firm determines how much labor to employ, we need to ask how the amount of labor the firm demands changes when there is a change in the wage, or a change in the price of output, or a change in labor's productivity. Equation (1) or Figure 13-2 guides the analysis.

We should expect that an increase in the wage rate will reduce the firm's employment of labor. We should also expect that an increase in the price at which the firm sells output will raise its output level and therefore increase its hiring of labor. We will explain these effects by using Figure 13-3. We will also see how a change in the firm's capital stock affects the firm's level of employment.

Consider first a rise in wages as shown in Figure 13-3. Initially, the firm faces wage W_0 and is in equilibrium at point E_0. Then the wage rises to W_1, say, $10 per hour, up from $7.50. The firm now has a marginal value product that is less than the wage. Cutting employment by taking one worker off the payroll reduces wage costs by more than it reduces revenues. Accordingly, the firm reduces employment until it reaches point E_1, where the marginal costs of and benefits from increased or reduced employment are again exactly balanced. Thus in response to a rise in the wage, the firm cuts employment of labor.

Our first result, then, is that a rise in the wage, given output prices, reduces employment. We can also see that the firm's demand curve for labor is actually the MVPL curve. The demand curve for labor tells us the amount of labor the firm wants to hire at each wage level. We have seen that given the wage, the firm chooses the level of employment corresponding to the MVPL curve. Thus at wage W_0, the firm hires L_0^*. At the higher wage, W_1, the firm's quantity of labor demanded is L_1^*. For any wage, we can read the quantity of labor demanded by the firm from the MVPL curve. The MVPL curve is the firm's demand curve for labor, as a function of the wage of labor.

FIGURE 13-3 THE EFFECTS OF A CHANGE IN THE WAGE ON THE FIRM'S EMPLOYMENT LEVEL. The firm initially faces the wage rate W_0 and chooses employment level L_0^*, where the marginal value product of labor is equal to the wage. When the wage rises to W_1, it exceeds the MVPL at employment level L_0^*. The firm can therefore increase profits by reducing employment to level L_1^*, where the marginal value product of labor is again equal to the (higher) wage. The MVPL schedule is also the firm's demand curve for labor. Given the wage rate, the quantity of labor demanded by the firm can be read off the MVPL curve.

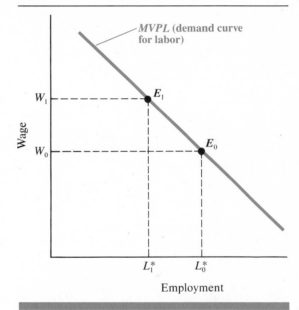

Next we ask by *how much* the level of employment changes when the wage changes. By experimenting with different MVPL (or demand for labor) curves in a diagram such as Figure 13-3, it can be seen that the fall in employment will be larger for a given wage increase the flatter the MVPL curve. The slope of the MVPL curve, in turn, depends on the extent to which labor and capital are substitutable in production.

If labor and capital are very good substitutes, then adding to the labor force and thereby reducing the capital-labor ratio does not do much to reduce the marginal product of labor. This means that a large change in employment will be needed to

FIGURE 13-4 THE EFFECT ON EMPLOYMENT OF A RISE IN OUTPUT PRICE. When the price of output rises, the marginal value product of labor rises at each level of employment. The *MVPL* curve shifts upward, from $MVPL_0$ to $MVPL_1$. The curve shifts upward by the same *proportion* at each level of employment. For instance, if the price of output rises by 50 percent, then at each level of employment, $MVPL_1$ is 50 percent higher than $MVPL_0$. As a result of the shift of the *MVPL* curve, the equilibrium of the firm moves from E_0 to E_1, given the wage of W_0. The firm's employment level therefore rises from L_0^* to L_1^*.

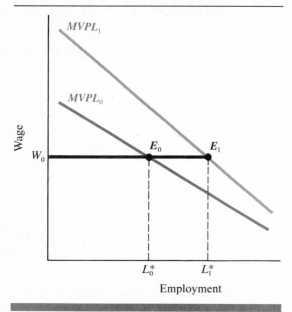

change the marginal value of labor by a given amount. But if labor and capital are poor substitutes, an increase in employment runs rapidly into diminishing returns, and the marginal value product of labor falls rapidly. In this case the *MVPL* curve will be steep.

Thus the substitutability between capital and labor, which will differ across industries, determines how much of a change in employment will be caused by a given wage change. The less substitutable capital and labor are, the less of a change in techniques the firm will implement as wages rise, and hence the less of a decline in employment it will experience. At the other extreme, with very large substitutability, a small

change in wages will bring about large changes in techniques of production and in employment.

Consider next the effects of a change in the price of output, P. Suppose that the output price increases. What is the effect on employment at the given wage rate? In Figure 13-4 we show the adjustment of employment to a change in the output price. The increase in the output price implies that at each level of output the *value* of the marginal product has risen. Labor is just as productive in physical terms as it was before, but the increase in output associated with increased employment is now worth more. Therefore, the marginal value product schedule shifts upward to $MVPL_1$. At the initial equilibrium at point E_0, the marginal value product exceeds the wage, W_0, and hence the firm finds it profitable to expand employment.

The employment expansion will proceed to point E_1, where the firm again has achieved a balance between the increase in the cost of employment, the wage, and the increase in revenue obtained by hiring one more unit of labor. How much employment will rise once again depends for a given price increase on how substitutable labor and capital are in production.

We have now seen that a rise in the wage reduces employment and that a rise in the price the firm receives increases employment. What happens if both the wage and the price increase together? Specifically, suppose that the price and the wage each go up by 50 percent. In that case, both the costs of and benefits from an expansion in employment, as calculated in Table 13-3, say, increase in the same proportion. The firm is in the same *real* position as before, and it does not change its hiring at all. In terms of Figure 13-4, a 50 percent increase in the firm's price shifts the *MVPL* curve up by 50 percent. If the wage also increases by 50 percent, then the new equilibrium for the firm will be exactly at output level L_0^*.

Of course, if the wage goes up proportionately more than the price, the firm will reduce its hiring. If the wage goes up proportionately less than the price, the firm will find labor cheaper in relation to the value of what it produces, and it will increase its hiring of labor. This is summarized by saying that the firm's demand for labor depends on the *real* wage, the dollar wage it pays divided by the price of its output. The firm increases employment when the real wage falls and reduces employment when the real wage rises.

Finally, let us examine the effects of different levels of the firm's capital stock on its employment decision. Suppose that the firm has a higher level of capital stock. With more capital, the marginal worker is more productive than when there is less capital for him to work with. Accordingly, the marginal product of labor and also the marginal value product of labor are higher at any given employment level when the capital stock is larger. An increase in the capital stock would shift the *MVPL* curve upward in Figure 13-4. This would result in a higher level of employment. Therefore, at a given wage, a rise in the capital stock leads to an expansion in employment and output.

So far our analysis has focused on the individual firm that takes as given the capital stock on hand, the wage rate, and the price of output. What are the differences at the level of the industry? Two important points emerge. First, an expansion in employment and output by all firms will change market supply and therefore affect price. Second, an industrywide expansion in response to a change in price will raise the industrywide demand for labor and therefore may affect the wage. We turn now to these questions.

4 THE INDUSTRY DEMAND FOR LABOR

In this section we move from the firm's demand for labor to the demand for labor of all

FIGURE 13-5   THE INDUSTRY DEMAND FOR LABOR. Schedule $MVPL_0$ shows the horizontal sum of the marginal value product of labor schedules of the firms in the industry. Such a schedule is drawn for a given price of output. When the wage falls from W_0 to W_1, all the firms in the industry increase their employment and output. Industry output therefore rises, and output price falls. Now the marginal value product is given by $MVPL_1$, corresponding to a lower output price. Thus when the wage falls, the level of employment in the industry shifts from E_0 to E'_1. Point E_1 is not an equilibrium point for the industry, because at E_1, the price of output is less than it is at E_0. To obtain the industry demand curve for labor, $D_L D_L$, we join together points such as E_0 and E'_1.

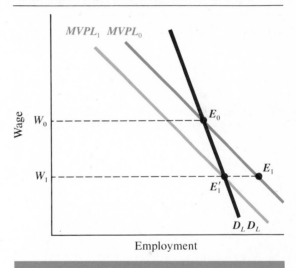

the firms in the industry together. The first step is to add together the demand for labor of all the firms. Each firm's demand curve for labor is an *MVPL* curve, as in Figure 13-3, and by adding the demand curves horizontally, we arrive at the total demand for all labor of all the firms in the industry. In Figure 13-5, we show this demand for labor schedule by the curve $MVPL_0$. This has the same shape as each firm's demand schedule. But because it is the sum of the firm's demand schedules, it has a larger horizontal scale.

It is natural to think of $MVPL_0$ as the industry demand curve for labor. But the important point about the industry demand curve is that it is *not* just schedule $MVPL_0$.

The reason is that when the industry increases the level of employment, the quantity of the good produced rises, and the equilibrium price of the good changes. Curve $MVPL_0$ expresses the demand for labor when the price of the good is given, say, at P_0. But as employment and output change at the industry level, price will change, and therefore firms in the industry will not continue to demand labor according to $MVPL_0$.

To derive the industry demand curve for labor, we have to take into account the effects of changes in wages and employment in the goods market. Suppose that the wage falls from W_0 to W_1. In Figure 13-5, we see that firms move to point E_1 on schedule $MVPL_0$, if the price of output remains at P_0. But in moving to point E_1, the firms increase employment and industrywide output. The supply curve for the goods the firms sell shifts downward because wages and costs are lower. Therefore, because the demand for goods has not changed, the equilibrium price of output will fall from P_0 to, say, P_1. Wages and costs are lower. Therefore the price of output will fall from P_0 to, say, P_1.

If price falls, every firm will experience a downward shift of the marginal value product schedule, and so will the industry, as shown in Figure 13-5. The relevant marginal value product schedule will be $MVPL_1$. At output price P_1, corresponding to wage W_1, the industry will want to be at point E_1', *not* at E_1.

By connecting points such as E_0 and E_1', we get the *industry demand for labor schedule*, $D_L D_L$, which takes into account the effect of increased employment in reducing the final goods price. Whereas the individual firm takes the price as given and moves in adjusting to wage changes from E_0 to E_1, all the firms making that adjustment together push the price down and therefore want to move only to E_1'.

What can be said about the industry demand for labor, $D_L D_L$? How is it shaped in relation to the schedules drawn for a given price level? What determines its elasticity? The industry labor demand schedule reflects the underlying $MVPL$ schedules, and thus the substitutability between labor and capital that determines their elasticities. The more substitutable labor and capital are in production, the flatter, or more elastic, the industry demand curve for labor.

The important new point is that a second factor affects the elasticity of the industry demand curve for labor. That factor is the responsiveness of the demand for the goods produced in this industry to price, or the elasticity of demand for *goods* in this industry. If the demand for final goods is very elastic, then a shift in supply will have hardly any effect on price, and so $D_L D_L$ will be almost the same as the $MVPL_0$ schedule. On the other hand, if the demand for final goods is very inelastic, a rightward shift of the supply curve will lead to a large fall in price, P_1 will be much lower than P_0, and the $D_L D_L$ schedule will be very inelastic.

The conclusion, then, is that the main factors determining the elasticity of the demand curve for labor at the industry level are the substitutability between labor and capital and the elasticity of demand for the good. This relationship between the elasticity of demand for the good and the elasticity of demand for labor of course reflects the fact with which we started this chapter: the demand for factors of production is a *derived* demand. The factors are demanded only because there is a demand for the goods they produce, and it is therefore not surprising that the elasticity of demand for labor in a particular industry should reflect the elasticity of demand for the good which the labor produces.

5 THE SUPPLY OF LABOR

In this section we will analyze the supply of labor. We start with the labor supply decision of an individual and end with the sup-

FIGURE 13-6   THE INDIVIDUAL'S SUPPLY OF LABOR. The two diagrams show two possible types of labor supply curves. In Figure 13-6a the labor supply curve slopes upward. The individual works more the higher the real wage. The labor supply curve in Figure 13-6b SS, is called a backward-bending supply curve. As the wage rises, a stage is reached where the individual decides to work less; he decides to use some of the higher income made possible by the higher real wage to consume leisure rather than work. W_p in each diagram is the wage at which the individual will begin to participate in the labor force. If the wage is below that level, the individual is out of the labor force; for any higher wage, the person is participating.

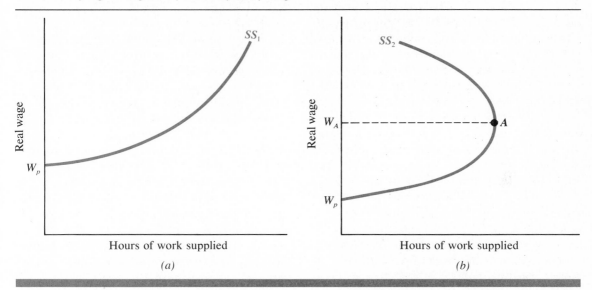

(a)   (b)

ply of labor to an industry. Then we put the industry demand and supply together to determine the equilibrium wage and level of employment.

The Individual's Labor Supply Decision

An individual's decision about whether and how much to work depends on the wage and on many other factors, such as whether the person is at college, whether he has children, whether there are aged parents to support, and whether there is a car loan to be paid off. But we will concentrate here on the effects of the wage on the individual's labor supply decision. The question is whether an increase in the wage increases or decreases the amount an individual wants to work. To start with, we assume that the individual is in the labor force and working. The question is, How many hours should he work?

Note first that the amount an individual will want to work depends on the *real wage* (W/P, the nominal wage divided by the price level) rather than on just the nominal wage, W. The nominal wage is the number of dollars per hour the individual earns. The individual works to be able to buy goods, and thus it is the real wage, which measures the amount of goods that can be bought with the wage, that will determine the amount a person wants to work. If both the nominal wage and the price level increase in the same proportion, there is no change in the real wage, and we should not expect workers to change the amount they want to work.

We show two possible labor supply curves in Figure 13-6. In Figure 13-6a the labor supply curve is upward-sloping. The higher the real wage, the more the individual wants to work. In Figure 13-6b, the pattern is more complicated. At low real wages, the labor supply curve is upward-sloping. But then at high wages, the curve has a negative slope. As the real wage rises, the individual begins to want to work less; he wants to work less at wages higher than W_A. The curve is known as a *backward-bending* labor supply curve. The question is which of these possibilities better describes the facts—or maybe there is some other type of labor supply curve that applies in practice.

The natural first guess is that the labor supply curve is upward-sloping. When the real wage goes up, the individual wants to work more; he wants to take advantage of the higher wage to earn a higher income. But then there is a second guess. When the real wage goes up, you can have your cake and eat it too. Namely, the individual can both work less and have more income. For instance, suppose that someone is working 40 hours a week at $10 per hour, earning $400 a week. Then the wage rises to $12. The individual can think of working only 35 hours, earning $420 (35 × $12) per week. The total income is higher, but the individual works less. He enjoys the extra 5 hours of leisure made possible by the higher wage, and he still has more income from work than he had before.

These two guesses suggest, correctly, that an increase in the real wage may either increase or reduce the amount the individual wants to work. There are two effects of a rise in the real wage. To get the analysis straight, think of the fact that the individual who is working is thereby giving up leisure.

When the wage rises, there is a *substitution effect* that makes the individual work more. Every hour taken in the form of leisure now costs more in terms of forgone income. Therefore, the substitution effect of an increase in the wage is for the individual to work more. But there is also an *income effect*. It is now possible to consume more leisure and more of all other goods, because

the real wage has risen. It is impossible, without looking at the facts, to know whether the income effect or the substitution effect wins out.[2]

The usual belief is that the labor supply schedule for the individual looks like SS_2 in Figure 13-6*b*. At low wage levels, the individual increases his work effort as the wage rises. At some point, though, such as point *A* in the diagram, the income effect begins to outweigh the substitution effect, and the labor supply schedule for the individual slopes backward. As the wage continues to rise, the individual works less, taking advantage of the high wage to enjoy leisure.

The empirical evidence is that for men at their prime age, the income and substitution effects just about cancel each other out.[3] The labor supply schedule for mature men who are in the labor force is almost vertical, meaning that changes in the real wage do not have much of an effect on the amount they want to work. The evidence is that for women, the labor supply schedule slopes upward, as in Figure 13-6*a*.

Participation   So far we have examined the response to a change in the wage of someone who is already working. But much of the change in the labor supply in the United States and other economies has come from changes in labor force participation.

The *participation rate* is the percentage of a given group who are in the labor force, either working or looking for work.

[2] Remember the rats of Chapter 5, who showed how income and substitution effects work? Experiments on labor supply curves for birds show that they have supply curves that look like the one in Figure 13-6*b*. See Raymond C. Battalio, Leonard Green, and John H. Kagel, "Income-Leisure Tradeoffs of Animal Workers," *American Economic Review*, September 1981. The birds are pigeons.

[3] See Jerry Hausman, "Income and Payroll Tax Policy and Labor Supply," in Laurence Meyer (ed.), *The Supply Side Effects of Economic Policy*, Federal Reserve Bank of St. Louis, 1981.

An increase in the wage can be expected to increase the participation rate. That is because for someone who is not working, not participating in the labor force, an increase in the wage has *only* a substitution effect. He is earning zero labor income, and an increase in the wage does not make it possible to have a higher income by working the same amount—his income is still zero unless he goes out to work. There is, therefore, no income effect. But there is a substitution effect. Now every hour of leisure is more expensive in terms of forgone income—income that is lost because the individual is not at work. Thus an increase in the wage will not cause anyone to leave the labor force. But it could well induce people to enter the labor force because of the substitution effect.

In terms of Figure 13-6, both of the labor supply curves slope upward at the point where the individual is doing 0 hours of work. That is because there is only a substitution effect there. If the wage had previously been below W_p (p for "participation") and now rises above it, the individual will enter the labor force.

There have been major changes in labor force participation in the last two decades. Table 13-4 gives details. The table shows the percentage of the population in each age-sex category who participated in the labor force in 1960 and 1980. Overall, male participation rates have dropped, and female rates have risen. Looking first at the males, we see the largest drop in the 55–64 age group. This is a result of increasingly early retirement by males. There is some evidence to indicate that this change resulted from changes in the Social Security law that increased payments for those retiring early.

The entire pattern of labor force participation for females has changed. In 1960 the pattern was that in all age groups most women did not work. Further, the participa-

TABLE 13-4

LABOR FORCE PARTICIPATION, 1960 AND 1980

AGE GROUP	MALES		FEMALES	
	1960	1980	1960	1980
All	83.3	77.4	37.7	51.6
16–19	56.2	60.7	39.3	53.1
20–24	88.1	86.0	46.1	69.0
25–34	97.5	95.3	36.0	65.4
35–54	96.8	93.5	46.4	62.9
55–64	86.8	72.3	37.2	41.5
65+	33.1	19.1	10.8	8.1

Source: Statistical Abstract of the United States, 1981, Table 636.

tion rate was high at ages 20–24 and then fell sharply. Women aged 25 to 34 were having children. Then after 35 some of them came back into the labor force. In 1980 the pattern was that over half the women in all age groups up to 55 were working. Labor force participation fell very little at ages 25–34. Thus we see reflected in the female labor force participation data the large change in the role of women in society that has taken place in the last 20 years.

The change is also summarized by another fact in the table. Labor force participation for men between 20 and 64 dropped between 1960 and 1980; for those same age groups, female labor force participation increased sharply.

Does Table 13-4 show the results of rising wages on participation? That would be pushing the claims of economics too far. Other social changes, in particular, preferred family size, surely have played a greater role than the increasing wage. But that does not change the fact that increases in wages tend to increase the labor supply by increasing participation rates.

Hours of Work   We have drawn the labor supply schedule as if the individual has the choice of the number of hours to work. But we know that part-time jobs are not generally available on exactly the same terms as full-time jobs. Nonetheless, we can expect that over time, firms adjust to the hours of work their labor forces prefer—so long as it is not expensive for them to do so. In manufacturing, where shift work is standard, the workweek has stayed at about 40 hours since World War II. In retailing, where it is easy to change the person standing at the cash register without bringing production to a halt, the average workweek has fallen from 40 to 32 hours since 1947. The percentage of the work force working part-time has increased in the last 15 years.

The Supply of Labor for the Economy

Taking men and women together, the evidence is that the labor supply curve for the economy as a whole is upward-sloping. This is because when the real wage rises, women want to work more, and men do not reduce the amount they want to work. In total, therefore, a rise in the real wage leads to more work from the labor force. The upward slope of the labor supply curve for the entire economy results also from the effects of changes in the wage on labor force participation.

Thus, taking everyone together, the labor supply curve for the economy is upward-sloping, as in Figure 13-6a. As the real wage rises, the quantity of labor supplied increases. It is possible that the labor supply curve for the economy as a whole might look like SS_2 in Figure 13-6b eventually. If in the year 2085 the wage is five times its current level, people might feel that they want more leisure when the wage rises further. After all, if the wage were five times higher than its current level, workers could consume just as much goods as we do by working only an 8-hour week.

The Supply of Labor to an Industry

So far we have been talking about the supply of labor to the economy in general. But the supply of labor to an industry is not the same as the supply to the economy. A very small industry that is located in an urban area and that employs no specially trained workers will have a horizontal labor supply curve. It will be able to hire workers at the going wage, or by paying very little more than the going wage in the area.

But an industry that is not small will, in the short run of several years, have a labor supply curve that slopes upward. The supply of labor to a particular industry depends on the wage in that industry *relative to* wages in other industries. In the short run, the amount of labor of the type the industry needs is limited in a particular area. Workers may also prefer to work in one industry rather than in another. To get workers to move out of other industries and from other cities, the industry will have to pay more than the going wage. To draw more workers into the industry, the wage has to rise sufficiently to make marginal workers overcome preferences for other types of jobs.[4]

The long-run labor supply curve to an industry is flatter than the short-run supply curve. This is because a given differential in wages will attract more people over a longer period, as the information about the higher wages becomes known and as people make plans to change jobs or move from areas in which they used to work. Another reason is that when the industry's wage goes up, people find it worthwhile to acquire skills the industry needs. But that, too, takes time. If people prefer to work in particular industries, the long-run labor supply curve for an industry will be upward-sloping. The more

---

[4] There is another reason why the labor supply curve for an industry is upward-sloping. As more and more workers respond to higher wages in that industry, they leave behind them sectors where labor is becoming increasingly scarce. Accordingly, firms in those sectors are willing to pay the marginal worker increasingly higher wages. The positive slope of the labor supply schedule for an industry also reflects this rising *opportunity cost* for workers of leaving other industries.

workers the industry employs, the more inducement it needs to draw them away from other industries.

Thus for most industries, we expect the labor supply curve to be upward-sloping, and flatter in the long run than in the short run. The labor supply schedule to an industry looks like the schedule in Figure 13-6a, but is a function of the wage in that industry *in relation to* wages in other industries.

6 INDUSTRY LABOR MARKET EQUILIBRIUM

In Figure 13-7 we put together the labor demand curve of an industry and the labor supply curve to that industry. The labor supply curve is upward-sloping. We will not in this section distinguish between the short-run and long-run labor supply curves to the industry; instead, we will discuss only the supply curve, S_LS_L.

Equilibrium in the labor market for the industry occurs at point E, where the demand for and supply of labor are in balance. The employment level is L_0, and the wage is W_0. The firms in the industry are all hiring the amount of labor they want to hire at that wage, and the workers in the industry are supplying the amount of labor they want to. In this connection, we should think of the wage as the whole package of work compensation, including contributions to medical insurance, the pension fund, and other fringe benefits.

This supply-demand model of the labor market is easily used to study the effects of changes in the supply or demand for labor. Suppose that we are dealing with the labor market in the lumber industry.

First we examine the effects of a shift in the demand for labor. Suppose that there has been a fall in the demand for lumber because housing construction is down. The fall in the demand for lumber by consumers results in a lower price for lumber and a downward shift of the labor demand curve

FIGURE 13-7 THE DEMAND FOR AND SUPPLY OF LABOR TO AN INDUSTRY. The supply curve of labor to the industry, S_LS_L, is upward-sloping. To attract labor into the industry, the wage has to rise relative to wages in other industries. The labor demand curve, D_LD_L, is downward-sloping, reflecting the diminishing marginal productivity of labor. Labor market equilibrium for the industry is at E, with wage W_0 and labor input L_0. When the demand for the good produced in this industry declines and the price falls, the labor demand schedule shifts downward and to the left, to $D_L'D_L'$. The equilibrium shifts to E'. The wage and the level of employment both fall.

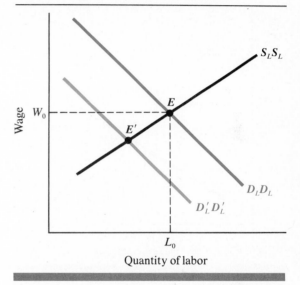

for the firms in the lumber industry. The demand curve shifts downward to $D_L'D_L'$ in Figure 13-7. The equilibrium shifts from E to E', with a lower wage and a lower level of employment in the industry. Thus a decline in the demand for the good produced by an industry affects the demand for labor, reducing both the quantity of labor employed and the wage in that industry.

Consider next the effects of a shift in the labor supply. Suppose that there has been an improvement in productivity in other sectors because capital investment has taken place there, and marginal workers there have become more productive. Wages in those sectors rise, and at any given wage level in the lumber industry, there will now be a smaller quantity of labor supplied.

FIGURE 13-8   THE EFFECTS OF A SHIFT IN LABOR SUPPLY. When wages in other sectors of the economy rise, the labor supply curve in this industry shifts upward and to the left. Workers leave the industry, and thus the amount of labor supplied at any given wage is less. As a result of the shift of the labor supply curve, the equilibrium shifts from E to E'. The wage rises from W_0 to W_1, and the quantity of labor employed falls from L_0 to L_1. A rise in wages elsewhere in the economy results in an increase in the wage in this industry. In this way, wage increases are spread throughout the economy.

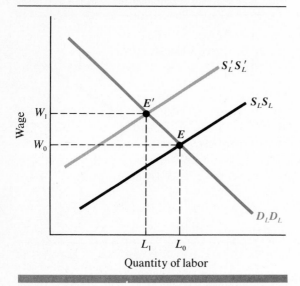

What happens to wages and employment in the lumber industry, where there has been no investment in new machinery?

We show the shift in $S_L S_L$ in Figure 13-8. Less labor is supplied to the lumber industry at each wage, and the supply schedule therefore shifts upward to $S'_L S'_L$. The equilibrium shifts from point E to E'. Accordingly, the equilibrium wage in the lumber sector rises—just as it has in other sectors—but employment declines. The capital investment in other sectors leads to an expansion in output and employment there, to an economywide rise in wages, *and* to a fall in employment in the lumber industry.

What is the key link in the mechanism by which an increase in the wage in some

sectors leads to an increase in wages in other sectors? The key assumption is that when wages elsewhere in an economy rise, some workers leave the lumber industry to work for the higher wages elsewhere. The link is thus the *mobility* of labor. If workers did not go off to try to obtain the higher wages elsewhere—that is, if they stayed behind—they would not get higher wages.

This simple model of the labor market already provides powerful insights into the behavior of employment and economywide wage patterns. The labor market is one of the chief links between various sectors of the economy. If one sector does well and can afford to pay high wages, it must, for that reason, hurt production in other sectors. In the other sectors, the higher wages are not offset by an increase in final demand that raises prices or by improved technology that cuts costs. The very fact that a particular sector can and does increase wages means that it competes away from other sectors the labor with which to expand.

We can now go back to Table 13-1 to ask how the facts shown there (and repeated in Table 13-5) relate to the analysis of industry labor markets. For comparison, Table 13-5 also shows the growth in wages and employment for the entire private sector. Two cases are easy to understand. The increase in employment and earnings in the oil and gas extraction industry between 1975 and 1979 was a result of the shift in the demand for labor in that industry—U.S. oil and gas employment rose sharply with the rise in the price of fuels that started in 1973. Similarly, the lower rate of increase for wages in the leather industry along with the fall in employment in that industry resulted from the sharp competition from foreign production faced by that industry. Wages here fell a little in real terms (recall that the consumer price index rose 35 percent over the period), but they did not fall much.

In looking at these two industries, we see the typical pattern of labor force reallo-

TABLE 13-5

COMPARATIVE WAGE AND EMPLOYMENT BEHAVIOR, 1975–1980

	GROWTH OF EARNINGS, %	GROWTH OF EMPLOYMENT, %
Total private sector	33.0	18.4
Oil and gas extraction	43.5	46.6
Banking	28.7	15.1
Blast furnace and basic steel production	50.0	5.4
Leather	31.8	−1.9

Source: Statistical Abstract of the United States, 1981,
Table 669.

cation from declining industries to expanding sectors. The wages in the expanding industries rise relative to those in the contracting industries. Thus workers are attracted to the growing industries and away from the contracting industries.

There are two facts in Table 13-5 that do not fit the simple story of expanding industries attracting labor by paying a higher wage and contracting industries losing their labor as the wage falls relative to average wages. First, employment in banking rose faster than employment in the leather industry, but the wage rose more slowly. The difference resulted from a shift in the type of labor employed in banking. During this period female participation in the labor force increased rapidly, as noted above, and the percentage of bank employees who were women increased more rapidly than the average percentage of female employees in the economy. Since women were paid less than men, the average wage of bank employees rose less than the average wage in the economy.

The second fact in Table 13-5 is that employment in the basic steel production industry rose very little, but wages rose fast. The explanation is that this is a unionized

industry. Unions were able to keep wages moving ahead during the 1975–1979 period.

The examples of the banking and steel industries raise questions about wage differentials between men and women, and between unionized and nonunionized sectors. We will turn to these questions in the next chapter. But before we do that, we still have to ask what determines the average wage level in the economy as a whole.

7   THE DETERMINATION OF THE AVERAGE REAL WAGE

So far we have explained how the wage in one industry is adjusted in relation to the wages in other industries. Now we ask what determines the average wage in the economy. The average wage is determined by the aggregate, or total, supply of and demand for labor.

In drawing the aggregate labor supply curve, as in Figure 13-9, we take the skill-sex-education composition of the labor force as given and ask how the total amount of labor supplied to the economy changes with the real wage. In Figure 13-9, we are assuming that all real wages go up or down together. Of course, some workers get more than others, but we are not concentrating now on relative wages, which are assumed to remain constant as the average wage changes. Similarly, on the demand for labor side we are assuming that the wages paid by all industries go up or down together, with relative wages being given. Thus we are concentrating in Figure 13-9 on the average real wage rather than on relative wages. The real wage is W/P, the nominal wage divided by the price level. This measures the amount of goods that can be bought with the wage.

The labor supply curve for the economy as a whole is upward-sloping, as we saw in section 5. The labor demand curve of each industry slopes downward, and therefore

FIGURE 13-9 DETERMINATION OF THE AVERAGE REAL WAGE. The aggregate labor supply curve, SS_L, is shown as upward-sloping. This reflects both the response of people already working to higher real wages and increasing labor force participation. The aggregate demand curve for labor slopes downward, reflecting the diminishing marginal productivity of labor. The equilibrium real wage, which should be thought of as the average real wage, and the equilibrium level of employment are determined at point E. When the demand for labor shifts from DD_L to DD'_L as a result of an increase in the capital stock, the equilibrium shifts to E', with a higher real wage and higher employment. The changes in wages occur in widely scattered labor markets, and they take time. Thus the economy will not shift quickly between labor market equilibrium positions.

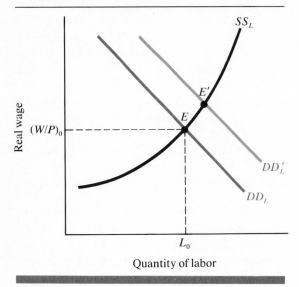

Quantity of labor

the demand curve of all industries taken together also slopes downward. Thus we have aggregate labor supply and labor demand curves of the shape shown in Figure 13-9. The aggregate labor supply curve may be very steep, and at some wage level it could even become backward-bending.

The average real wage is determined by the intersection of the supply and demand curves at point E. Now, on what does that wage depend? The position of the supply curve depends on the willingness of people to work, which in turn is influenced by their education, social customs, and health and

by similar factors. On the demand side, the demand depends on the productivity of labor in production. In particular, the higher the level of the capital stock in the economy as a whole, the larger the quantity of labor demanded at any real wage. Thus if the capital stock increases, the demand for labor will shift outward from DD_L to DD'_L, the equilibrium will shift to E', and the real wage will increase. It is partly because economies accumulate physical capital that real wages tend to rise over time.

The productivity of labor also depends on the skills the labor force has acquired. If the labor force is very skillful, there is a high marginal product of labor, and firms are willing to pay more per worker. Economists sometimes refer to the acquired skills of labor as the *human capital* of the labor force. In Chapter 14 we discuss human capital. Increases in human capital over time also help account for rising real wages over the course of decades and centuries.

Although we have drawn aggregate supply and demand curves for labor, we should realize that there is no single market where all workers and all firms get together. The labor market is highly decentralized, and adjustments of wages in response to shifts in supply and demand take place in many markets, and with different speeds. For this reason, we should think of the aggregate supply and demand curves for labor in Figure 13-9 as describing the average level to which the real wage tends to move over time. But the actual adjustments take place in many different firms and industries; they are not coordinated, and they may take a long time. It is quite possible that workers will be unable to find jobs during the period of adjustment and will be unemployed.

8 THE MINIMUM WAGE

The federal government imposes a minimum wage that has to be paid to employees.

About 85 percent of the employees in private industry and 25 percent in government are covered. The minimum wage for the years 1975 and 1979 was shown in Table 13-1, and we asked why any worker receives more than the minimum wage. Why don't employers force the wage all the way down to the minimum legal level?

The answer is that the employers are competing in the labor market. Labor is productive, and firms can earn profits by employing labor. If one employer succeeded in getting workers to work at a low wage, other firms could increase their profits by hiring those workers away and paying a slightly higher wage. Thus so long as firms are competing, the wage of labor will be driven to the value of its marginal product.

The short answer, then, to the question of why any worker is paid more than the minimum wage is that the value of the marginal product of most workers is well above the minimum wage. Because the employers are competing in the labor market and labor can work where its wage is highest, workers end up with a wage that is equal to the value of their marginal product.

But this does not mean that the minimum wage has no effect on employment or wages, because one of the central facts of the labor market is that labor is not homogeneous. Not all workers have the same productivity. There are some workers for whom the minimum wage is above the value of their marginal product. These are the young, unskilled workers.

Figure 13-10 shows the market for unskilled workers. The demand curve slopes downward. The minimum wage is $W_{\min}$, which is above the wage that clears the market, W_0. At the minimum wage, firms want to hire only L_d, while workers want amount L_s of work. The difference is unemployment, in the amount of $L_s - L_d$. Note that the reason for unemployment is that firms want less labor than the equilibrium

FIGURE 13-10 THE MINIMUM WAGE. Without a minimum wage, the labor market (for unskilled workers) clears at point E, at equilibrium wage W_0. When the minimum wage is imposed, at level $W_{\min}$, supply exceeds demand. At that wage, firms choose to hire at point F on their labor demand curve, resulting in employment of L_d. Workers would like to supply the amount of labor shown by point G, equal to L_s. The difference, or excess supply, is unemployment.

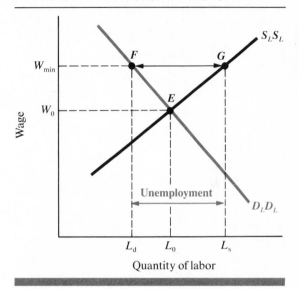

amount, L_0, while workers want more work than L_0.

The minimum wage appears to be partly responsible for the very high unemployment rates among unskilled workers, particularly teenagers.[5] The questions that have to be raised are why legislators nonetheless vote for the minimum wage and why labor unions support it. A possible explanation is that the minimum wage only damages those who cannot get work as a result. The people who remain at work get a higher wage as a result of the minimum wage. In Figure 13-10, the wage for those who remain employed increases from W_0 to $W_{\min}$ as a result of the increase in the minimum wage. It may be that both the legislators and

[5] See Donald O. Parsons, *Poverty and the Minimum Wage*, American Enterprise Institute, Washington, D.C., 1980.

the unions are more concerned about those who keep their jobs than about those who lose them. This point can be put in a very different way by noting that *all* those who are employed (not only the unskilled workers) probably have a somewhat higher wage because there is less competition from those who are now unemployed as a result of the minimum wage.[6]

9 DERIVED DEMAND AND ECONOMIC RENTS

The million-dollar-a-year baseball player is very happy to receive his income. But he would also have worked for $500,000, or probably even for $20,000 a year. The reason why the baseball star earns a million dollars a year is that he is worth it to the team's owners. He controls a scarce resource—his talent—and people are willing to pay more for the use of it than the minimum needed to get him to supply it. In this case and in similar cases we say that the owner of the resource is earning an economic rent.

> An *economic rent* is the amount of the payment to a factor of production that exceeds the minimum amount that would have to be paid to get that quantity of the factor supplied to this particular use.

Figure 13-11 illustrates the concept of economic rent for a factor in completely inelastic supply. Suppose that we are dealing with someone who loves playing baseball

---

[6] A second explanation rejects the analysis of Figure 13-10 and justifies the minimum wage as a means of increasing wages *and* employment. Recall from the analysis of monopoly that a price ceiling for a monopolist may lead the monopolist to *increase* production. Similarly, a *single* buyer of labor (a monopsonist in the labor market) may *increase* his hiring of labor if a minimum wage is imposed. It is sometimes argued that employers in effect get together in the labor market to act as a monopsony and that the minimum wage therefore improves the situation for all workers. We do not know of evidence to substantiate this view.

FIGURE 13-11 ECONOMIC RENTS. The supply curve, *SS*, shows the supply of labor (or of any factor of production) for a particular use. The supply is totally inelastic. The derived demand curve for the factor is *DD*. The wage paid to the factor is W_0. In the case shown, the entire wage is an economic rent, because the factor would have been available for use even at 0 wage. In other cases, where some minimum amount is needed to get the factor of production into the industry, the rent is the amount above the minimum needed to get the factor into the industry.

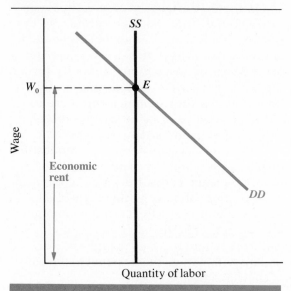

so much that he would be happy to play baseball even if he were not paid. This is shown by the supply curve, SS. The demand curve for the factor is shown by *DD*. *DD* is a derived demand curve; it depends on the amount the factor adds to the firm's revenues. The baseball player sells extra seats; therefore, there is a derived demand for his services. The wage paid to the baseball player is shown by W_0. The entire amount paid to him is an economic rent. It is the payment that he receives by virtue of being the owner of the scarce resource that is his talent. It has nothing to do with his willingness to supply his services as a baseball player.

There are three points to be made about economic rents. First, the term is used because it was originally applied to the rent paid for land. The quantity of land can, to a first approximation, be thought of as constant. The amount people are willing to pay for it depends on how productive the land is. But rent payments are not needed to induce the land to provide its services. They are there to ensure that the land gets properly allocated among alternative uses. Subsequently, the term "rent" has been applied to other factors.

Second, in cases where the factor is not in completely inelastic supply, as in Figure 13-11, rent is measured as the amount actually paid to the factor above the minimum amount it would take to get the factor into its existing use. If at any salary below $50,000 the baseball player would rather go fishing, his rent would be not $1 million but only $950,000.

Third, rents exist because the demand for the factors is a derived demand. This implies that the frequently heard complaint that the high salaries of baseball players are destroying the game should make us suspicious. The claim is that the owners can't afford to pay the salaries. But the high salaries are paid because the superstars bring in lots of extra dollars in the baseball parks in which they play. There is no simple link between high salaries for baseball players and

ruin to the game—more likely the high salaries reflect the fact that the game is making more money than ever before.

A more sophisticated analysis might find some difficulties for the game in the high salaries the players receive. For instance, if one team has a larger market than the others, the marginal value product of superstars in that city will be higher than elsewhere. This team will therefore be able to pay more for the superstars. It may end up with all the good players. Then the other owners might argue that the game is being ruined because the high salaries make it impossible for them to compete. The solution is to make sure that the revenues are spread around the league in a way that preserves competition between the teams.[7]

---

[7] Difficult footnote. Classical economists used to say that rent was not a part of the cost of production of a good. This is a subtle point; it is true from the viewpoint of society but not from the viewpoint of a particular firm. Consider again the baseball player. Does it cost the United States $1 million to employ a baseball superstar in baseball? The answer is no. The cost to society is only the opportunity cost of using the labor in baseball rather than in its next best use, say, as a college algebra teacher. Thus the cost to society of using the baseball player in baseball is not $1 million but rather the $30,000 he could have earned by teaching algebra. Of course, the firm that hires the baseball player regards $1 million as the cost of using the player, and it is right to do so.

SUMMARY

1   The individual firm can pick from a menu of techniques to produce its output. Some techniques require the use of a little capital and much labor: these are labor-intensive. Others require the use of more capital and less labor: these are more capital-intensive. The firm chooses the production technique that minimizes costs. A change in the relative prices of factors causes the firm to change production techniques. As the wage rate rises relative to the rental rate for capital, the firm tends to use more capital-intensive techniques.

2   The firm's optimal choice of technique leads to a positive relationship between the wage-rental ratio, or the relative cost of labor, and the capital-labor ratio. The same industry that works with labor-inten-

sive techniques in a low-wage country will use more capital-intensive methods of production in a high-wage country.

3   Given its capital stock, the individual firm can change output by varying its labor force. But labor is subject to diminishing returns. The marginal product of labor falls as more labor is hired.

4   In choosing the optimal level of employment, the firm compares the addition to revenue that is produced by hiring one more worker with the cost of hiring the worker. The addition to revenue is the marginal value product of labor. If the firm is a perfect competitor, the marginal value product is equal to the marginal product times the price of output. The firm expands employment as long as the marginal value product exceeds the wage. At the optimum employment level, the wage equals the marginal value product.

5   Given the price of output, an increase in the wage reduces the amount of labor the firm employs. Thus the labor demand curve of the firm is downward-sloping. A rise in output prices, given the wage, raises the level of employment. In fact, the firm's demand for labor is a function of the *real wage,* the nominal wage divided by the price of output. If both the price of output and the nominal wage rise by the same proportion, the firm does not change its employment level.

6   The extent to which a change in the real wage changes a firm's employment level depends on the substitutability of capital and labor in production. If substitutability is high, an increase in the real wage will cause the firm to substitute much capital for much labor, and the quantity of labor demanded will fall a lot for a given wage increase.

7   At the level of the firm we can take output prices as given. But that is not appropriate at the industry level. As an industry expands employment in response to a reduction in wages, the increased output can only be sold at a lower price. Thus the industry demand for labor reflects both the substitutability between capital and labor and the price elasticity of final demand. The more price-elastic final demand is, the less is the drop in price associated with an industrywide expansion, and hence the more elastic the demand for labor is.

8   An individual's labor supply decision depends on the real wage, the nominal wage divided by the prices of the goods the individual buys. An increase in the real wage has an ambiguous effect on the amount that an individual wants to work. The higher the real wage, the more expensive it is to take leisure time. Thus the substitution effect of an increase in the wage causes an individual to work more. But there is also an income effect. When the real wage rises, the individual can take more leisure time and still have a higher income left with which to buy goods. These two effects work in opposite directions,

and the overall effect is uncertain. However, for someone not working, only the substitution effect is in operation, and a wage increase, therefore, leads to an increase in labor force participation.

9   The aggregate, or total, supply curve of labor is upward-sloping: an increase in the real wage leads to an increase in the quantity of labor supplied. The response of the overall quantity of labor supplied to the real wage is determined in part by a change in the participation rate.

10   The supply of labor to an individual industry depends on the wage paid in that industry relative to wages paid elsewhere in the economy. It also depends on the workers' preferences for working in one sector rather than in another.

11   A rise in the wage paid in one sector will draw labor into that sector and therefore shift the labor supply curve for other industries. Wages will tend to rise in the other industries in response to the decline in the labor supply in those industries. Thus wage movements tend to be spread throughout the economy. An increase in the demand for labor in one sector because of increased exports or improved technology, for example, will spread throughout the labor market to other sectors, raising wages and reducing employment in those other sectors. In this way labor is freed for use in the expanding sector.

12   The average real wage is determined by the overall supply of and demand for labor. The aggregate demand for labor depends on the productivity of labor, and thus on the amount of human capital and on the amount of physical capital. Increases in either physical or human capital will lead to increases in the quantity of labor demanded at a given real wage and therefore to an increase in the real wage. Because the labor market is highly decentralized, shifts in the overall demand for or supply of labor take time to work their way through the many different industry labor markets. Adjustment in the average wage is therefore slow. The equilibrium real wage should be thought of as the level toward which the real wage tends to move over time, but it does not get there immediately.

13   The minimum wage increases the unemployment rate for unskilled labor while increasing the wage of those who remain employed.

14   Factors in inelastic supply that earn more than the minimum needed to get them into their current use are earning an *economic rent*. The rent arises from the fact that the demand for the services of the factor is a derived demand. Economic rents explain or describe the extremely high salaries paid to superstars in sports or entertainment and in related fields.

KEY TERMS

Derived demand

Compensating (equalizing) differentials in wages

Wage-rental ratio

Capital-labor ratio

Marginal value product of labor

Real wage

Backward-bending labor supply curve

Labor force participation

Mobility of labor

Human capital

Minimum wage

Economic rents

PROBLEMS

1 In what sense is it true that a firm's demand for labor and its decision on how much to produce are the same?

2 (a) Suppose that in Table 13-2 there is a third way of making 100 snarks per week. The third technique uses 4 units of capital and 5 units of labor. Would this technique ever be used? Explain. (b) Suppose that there is another technique, using 1 unit of capital and 8 units of labor. Are there any levels of the wage rate at which this technique would be used, assuming that the rental rate for capital stays at $320 per week?

3 (a) Explain why the marginal product of labor eventually declines. (b) Would the marginal product of labor be declining if a firm employed only labor? (c) Define the marginal value product of labor.

4 Suppose that a firm has to pay a tax of 5 percent of the wage that is paid to labor. (Think, for instance, of the employer who has to pay a share of an employee's contributions to Social Security.) In view of the equilibrium condition in equation (1) or Figure 13-2, how does the imposition of the tax affect employment? Explain.

5 (a) Show in a diagram the effect of an increase in a firm's capital stock on the labor demand curve. Discuss the effect. (b) What effect does an increase in the capital stock

have on the wage and the level of employment.

6 (a) Suppose that the demand curve for a final good is *completely* inelastic. Use a diagram of the market for the good to show the effect of a decline in wages on production and price. (Recall that a change in wages will shift the industry's supply curve for goods.) Now go back to the labor market, and show what the firm's labor demand curve looks like. (b) What does this tell you about derived demand?

7 Over the last hundred years, the real wage has risen, and the length of the workweek has fallen. Does this tell you anything about the labor supply curve for individual workers? Explain the two effects that determine the shape of the labor supply curve for the individual.

8 Explain how an increase in the real wage can cause everyone who is now working to want to work fewer hours but still result in an increase in the total amount of work done in the economy.

9 Why should the labor supply curve to an industry slope upward even if the aggregate labor supply curve for the economy is not upward-sloping?

10 (a) Explain how foreign competition affects wages and the level of employment in an industry. (b) How does your explanation fit the pattern of wage and employment changes in the leather industry as seen in Table 13-1? Name at least one other industry for which the analysis is relevant.

11 (*a*) Consider the market for farm labor in California. Vigorous legislation is passed that severely restricts the inflow of migrant labor during the harvest season. Discuss in detail the effect on wages in the market for farm labor and the effect on the supply and price of California lettuce and grapes. (*b*) Does the legislation make everyone worse off? (*c*) Suppose that instead the farmers are required to pay the minimum wage. (They do not do so now.) What are the effects on employment and on the supply and price of California lettuce and grapes?

12 Suppose that a movie producer says that the industry is doomed because the stars are being paid such outrageous amounts for making each film. Evaluate the argument, being sure to use the concept of economic rent.

13 This chapter opened with three questions. It is time now for you to answer them. (*a*) Why do the best baseball players earn so much more than the best engineers? (*b*) Why can engineering students look forward to higher real incomes than equally smart history students? (*c*) Why does an unskilled worker in the United States earn more than an unskilled worker in a less developed country?

APPENDIX: ISOQUANTS AND THE CHOICE OF PRODUCTION TECHNIQUE

In the text we used Table 13-2 to describe how a firm chooses the technique of production. Some techniques use relatively more capital and some relatively more labor. An alternative way of describing the production techniques the firm can choose is with an *isoquant map*. We will now describe how to read such a map.

Figure 13-A1 shows on the two axes alternative levels of the labor and capital inputs. Corresponding to any particular combination of capital (K) and labor (L) is a maximum level of output the firm can produce using those factors. Points A, B, C, and D in Figure 13-A1 correspond to different ways of producing 1 unit of output.

Technique A is, of course, the most labor-intensive process and technique D the most capital-intensive. With technique A the firm requires L_A units of labor and K_A units of capital to produce 1 unit of output. Process B requires relatively less labor and relatively more capital. Connecting points A, B, C, and D yields a schedule that is called an *isoquant* ("iso" stands for "the same," "quant" for "quantity"), meaning different combinations of capital and labor that yield the same level of output.

If there were more techniques available—between A and B, between B and C, etc.—we would get a nearly smooth schedule such as the schedules shown in Figure 13-A2. Every point on isoquant I in that diagram corresponds to a particular technique, ranging from highly labor-intensive processes to very capital-intensive ones. What

FIGURE 13-A1   AN ISOQUANT. Points *A, B, C,* and *D* show different combinations of capital and labor inputs that can be used to produce 1 unit of output. By connecting them, we obtain an *isoquant,* which shows the combinations of factors that can be used to produce any given level of output.

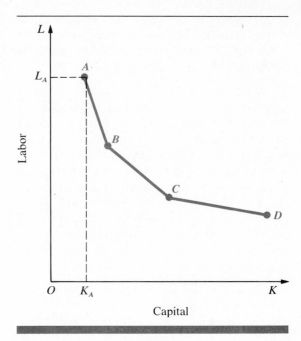

FIGURE 13-A2   AN ISOQUANT MAP. If there are many alternative production techniques, we can fill in the gaps between points such as *A, B, C,* and *D* in Figure 13-A1 to produce a smooth isoquant, such as *I.* Different isoquants show the combinations of factors that are used to produce different levels of output. The level of output on *I″* is higher than the level of output on *I′,* which is in turn higher than the output on *I.* The spacing of the isoquants represents returns to scale. For instance, at *B″,* inputs are double those at *B.* If output on *I″* is double that on *I,* there are constant returns to scale. If output on *I″* is more than double that on *I,* there are increasing returns to scale. If output on *I″* is less than double that on *I,* there are decreasing returns to scale.

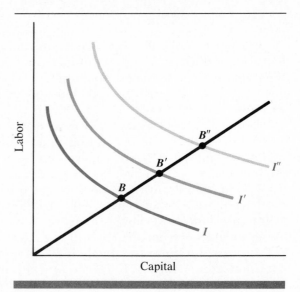

can be said about points such as *B′* or *B″*? At point *B′* both more capital and more labor are required than at point *B* on isoquant *I.* Therefore, more output is produced at *B′.* Hence *B′* lies on a higher isoquant, *I′.* Every point on *I′* corresponds to the same output, say, 2 units. Likewise, point *B″* corresponds to a still higher level of output. The successive isoquants constitute an isoquant map. Four properties of these isoquants are important. First, they cannot cross. This is because each isoquant refers to a different level of output. Second, the spacing of successive isoquants reflects returns to scale. If there are constant returns to scale, doubling both inputs will double output, tripling both inputs will triple output, and so on. The levels of output on I, I', and I'' thus reflect the ratios of inputs, say, at points B, B', and B''.

Third, isoquants are downward-sloping. This point is apparent from Figure 13-A1. Suppose that a particular technology calls for as much labor as in technique A but more capital. Such a technique, call it technique A', would sit horizontally to the right of A. *Nobody* would ever choose it because with technique A you get the same output by using the same amount of labor and less capital. The only possible alternatives to technique A that make economic (as opposed to only engineering) sense are to the northwest or southeast of A. Hence isoquants must be downward-sloping.

The fourth point also concerns the slope of an isoquant. The way we have drawn the isoquants, they are not straight lines; instead, they are curved inward. The menu of techniques, accordingly, is such that as we go toward more capital-intensive techniques, there will be progressively less of a saving on labor. Substitution, in other words, becomes more difficult as we move toward the extreme of very labor-intensive or very capital-intensive techniques.

We saw in the text that a firm chooses its optimal production technique by evaluating the total costs of producing a unit of output with different techniques. The firm picks the production method that has the lowest cost. There is a simple diagrammatic interpretation of this procedure. Suppose that the firm asks what production process will give it the most output for a given cost. Suppose that the firm spends $1000 on capital and labor and asks what process will allow the largest output. With an hourly wage of $5 and a rental for capital of $10 the firm could buy 200 units of labor (point L_0 in Figure 13-A3), or 100 units of capital (point K_0), or any other combination on schedule L_0K_0. If the firm wants to use more capital, it can trade off: starting from L_0, for every 2 units of labor (worth $2 \times \$5 = \$10$) it gives up, it can employ 1 more unit of capital.

Line L_0K_0 is called an *isocost line* ("isocost" means "equal cost"). It plays a role very similar to that of the budget line. The slope of the isocost line is equal to the rental-wage ratio. The higher the rental relative to the wage, the more units of labor the firm has to give up using to be able to pay for another unit of capital.

In Figure 13-A3, point A represents the technique that yields the most output per dollar spent or, and this is the same, has the lowest unit cost. The firm could also afford to be at points C and D on the same isocost line, but these points correspond to a lower output level than A (they are on a lower isoquant), and hence they are not chosen.

FIGURE 13-A3 MAXIMIZING OUTPUT FOR ANY GIVEN LEVEL OF COSTS. Isocost line K_0L_0 shows different combinations of labor and capital inputs that cost the same. For some given amount, say, $1000 per week, the firm could rent the amount of capital K_0, or the amount of labor L_0, or any combination of capital and labor between those points. To produce the maximum output at a given cost, the firm goes to point A, where the cost line is tangent to an isoquant. It cannot produce more than the amount on isoquant I' at the given cost. It can, of course, produce less, say, at points C or D, but that does not make economic sense.

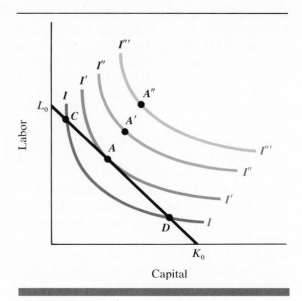

FIGURE 13-A4 THE EFFECT OF A RISE IN WAGES ON THE CHOICE OF TECHNIQUES. The firm is originally producing at point A. Then the wage rises, and the maximum amount of labor that can be bought given the same total cost of production falls from L_0 to L_1. The firm now maximizes output for the given level of cost at point C; it uses relatively more capital than at point A. Thus the increase in the wage leads the firm to move toward a more capital-intensive production technique.

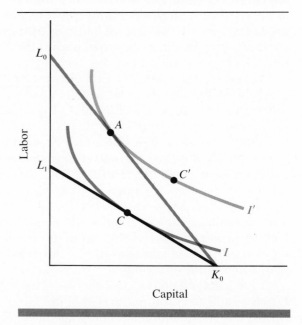

We have established, then, that the firm will choose the optimal technique by moving to the point of tangency between the isocost line and an isoquant.

A change in the relative prices of factors is now indicated by a rotation of the isocost line. If the wage rises, line L_0K_0 becomes flatter, since the given $1000 outlay now buys less labor. Accordingly, as shown in Figure 13-A4, the firm moves to more capital-intensive techniques. Whatever output the firm chooses will now be produced with technique C rather than technique A. Thus we have demonstrated that a firm responds to changes in relative factor prices by switching away from techniques that use the factor whose price has risen. The change in techniques is larger—in terms of the capital-labor mix—the flatter the isoquants or the more substitutable capital and labor are.

There is, of course, a great similarity between isoquants and indifference curves. There is also some similarity between the conditions for maximizing utility and those for minimizing costs. In each case we are looking for tangency between a straight line and an inward-curving schedule representing the same level of either utility or cost. The straight line is the budget line in the case of the consumer; it is the isocost line in the case of a cost-minimizing firm.

Males earn more than females, and whites earn more than nonwhites. The facts shown in Table 14-1 are dramatic. In 1980, white women earned, on the average, only 63 percent of what white men earned. And nonwhite men earned 75 percent of what white men earned. This chapter both describes in detail the facts about wage differentials and asks what accounts for the differentials. Are wage differentials a result of race or sex discrimination, or do they result from productivity differences between workers?

The key feature on which this chapter focuses is that labor is not homogeneous. Workers differ not only in race and sex but also in age, experience, education, and skill. In Chapter 13, we assumed that different types of labor earn different pay—for instance, baseball stars earn more than professors, and workers in declining industries receive less than those in growing industries. Now we look more closely at the facts to see what other characteristics of workers help explain actual pay differences. The interest in identifying the reasons for pay differentials arises both because everyone wants to know why other people earn more and because we want to know whether pay differences correspond entirely or mainly to productivity differences or whether they result in part from outright discrimination.

The type of result we will be looking at is shown in Table 14-2. In a study of about 1200 working male heads of households, it was found that the representative white, nonunion worker in the group earned (in 1980 prices) $8.80 per hour, while individual members earned more or less depending on the characteristics shown in the table.

The table reveals pay differentials due to personal characteristics that probably indicate the worker's skill level (education, work experience, on-the-job seniority) and also to personal status characteristics such as race, location, and union membership. The table shows, for example, that a worker with an extra year of education (beyond the average 12.7 years in the sample) earned an extra 55 cents (0.062 × $8.80) per hour. An extra year of work experience was worth 5 cents per hour, and an extra year of job seniority accounted for a pay differential of nearly 10 cents. These differentials, of course, raise the questions of why firms would pay for these personal characteristics and what determines the amount paid for them. In section 1 of this chapter, we address these issues by discussing the concept of *human capital*.

14

Human Capital, Discrimination, and Trade Unions

TABLE 14-1
**MEDIAN WEEKLY EARNINGS BY
SEX AND RACE, 1980
(Index for White Males = 100)**

	MALES	FEMALES
White	100	63
Nonwhite	75	58

Source: Statistical Abstract of the United States, 1981, Table 681.

TABLE 14-2
PAY DIFFERENTIALS

CHARACTERISTIC	PAY PREMIUM*
Extra year of education	+ 6.2
Extra year of work experience†	+ 0.6
Extra year of seniority on the job	+ 1.1
Located in the south	− 10.7
Nonwhite	− 15.1
Union member	+ 10.0

* Percentage of $8.80.
† Evaluated after 2 years of experience.
Source: J. M. Abowd and Henry S. Farber, "Job Queues and Union Status of Workers," unpublished manuscript, M.I.T., Department of Economics, Cambridge, Mass., 1980.

TABLE 14-3
**PERSONAL STATUS AND PAY DIFFERENTIALS
(1980 Dollars per Hour)**

	NONUNION	UNION
Nonwhite	7.47	8.35
White	8.80	9.68

Source: Table 14-2.

Table 14-2 also shows how pay differentials are related to location, race, and union status. Consider, for example, Table 14-3, which is derived from the information in Table 14-2.[1] Here we show that the average

pay for different workers depends on whether they are white or nonwhite and on whether they hold union jobs or jobs outside a union.

Table 14-3 shows that a white union member typically earns a third more than a nonwhite, nonunion worker. The obvious questions are why union jobs pay more and why the mere fact of being white or nonwhite should give rise to a difference in pay. In sections 2 and 3 of this chapter, we address these issues by looking at the economics of discrimination and equal opportunity and at the economics of labor unions.

1 HUMAN CAPITAL

Table 14-2 shows that education and experience both affect pay. The concept of human capital has been developed to explain why education and experience affect pay and what determines how much education people get.

Human capital is the value of the income-earning potential embodied in individuals.

Normally, when we talk about capital, we refer to an asset (machinery, houses, factory buildings) with two features: it is the result of an investment process, and it generates a flow of income over time. The human capital analogy is that a person invests in himself (or maybe his parents do the investing), paying for education and the acquisition of skills, and then he obtains a payoff in the form of higher wages.[2] In some cases, the payoff may not come in the form of wages; it might be the satisfaction the person gets from doing a particular type of work.

The idea of human capital has been

---

[1] The wage of $8.80 for the white, nonunion worker is the starting point. A nonwhite union member gets −15.1 percent for being nonwhite and +10.0 percent for belonging to a union. Thus, he is behind by 5.1 percent: his wage is equal to 94.9 percent of $8.80, or $8.35. The other calculations are similar but simpler.

[2] The idea of investing in labor is an old one. For instance, the great English economist Alfred Marshall explained in his *Principles of Economics*, written in 1890, what determines the amount of investment in training workers. Marshall emphasized that the rich invest more in their children than the poor can or do.

pushed very far. It is used to study the return to investing in education, to explain what determines the quantity and type of education that people have, and to examine the trade-off between formal schooling and learning through extra years on the job. We now take up some of these topics.

In this section, we assume that wage differentials reflect differences in the productivity of different types of labor. This is in accord with the theory that was developed in the preceeding chapter, where labor earns the value of its marginal product. Here we assume that different types of labor—workers who have different amounts of, say, education or experience—have different marginal productivities and that firms therefore pay different wages for these types of labor.

Age-Earnings Profiles and Education

We start from the observation, already reported in Table 14-2, that workers with more education have, on the average, higher incomes. Figure 14-1 shows how income changes with education. The figure shows the average age-earnings profiles for white males in the United States in 1970.

> An *age-earnings profile* is the relationship between income and age for a particular individual or group of individuals.

Each profile shows how much individuals with a given amount of education earned at each age in 1970. The years of education vary from 0 to 4 years in the lowest profile to 17 or more years at the top. The figure establishes the following facts:

1   The income of a member of the work force older than 30 is higher the more schooling he has.

2   The profiles rise very fast with age for younger people but then tend to flatten out.

Some profiles actually decline toward retirement age.[3]

3   The more schooling a person has, the later the entry into the labor force, and therefore the larger the income forgone by spending time in school.

A first question is why people with schooling should receive higher pay at all. There are at least two possible answers here. First, perhaps on the average it is the people with more ability who have more education. Second, perhaps schooling teaches special skills, such as reading, writing, and taking square roots, and also increases a person's organizing ability in ways that are useful in production.

To sort out these explanations, there have been many attempts to see if, after standardizing as best as can be done for ability, there is still an extra return to schooling. The standardizing for ability is done by comparing the earnings of individuals with the same IQ but different amounts of education. Even though IQ is an imperfect measure of ability, the evidence tends to show that there is a return to education over and above that resulting from differences in ability between those who continue with their education and those who do not.[4]

---

[3] Fact 2 has to be interpreted with care. The figure shows the earnings of individuals of *different* ages in a given year, 1970. It does not show how income changes with age for the *same* person. To see that, we would have to look at the amounts earned by the same person at different ages. Such profiles typically show income rising with age until the person retires. The difference between the profiles in Figure 14-1 and the age-earnings profile for a given person is that each generation earns, on the average, more than the previous one. Each generation starts out a little higher than the previous one.

[4] The issues here are at the frontiers of current research. The very ambitious may want to look at Zvi Griliches, "Estimating the Returns to Schooling: Some Econometric Problems," *Econometrica*, 1977, for some evidence and ideas of the techniques used in such research.

FIGURE 14-1 AGE-EARNINGS
PROFILES OF WHITE MALES,
1970, BY YEARS OF EDUCATION.
The figure shows earnings in the
United States at different ages and
levels of education. Each level of
education is represented by one
schedule. Earnings increase with the
level of education and, up to a point,
with age.

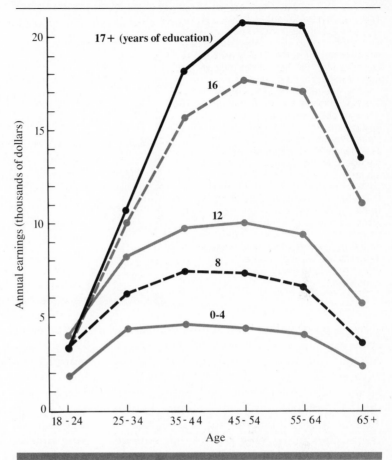

In this section, we assume that education improves productivity, and we use supply and demand analysis to see what determines pay differentials.[5] We start with the
demand for college-trained personnel by
firms.

The Market for Educated Workers
In Figure 14-2 we have on the vertical axis

the *difference* between the wage paid to
college graduates and the wage paid to high
school graduates. This is also called the *premium* paid for college graduates. On the
horizontal axis we measure the fraction of
the work force with college training.

Schedule *DD* is the demand schedule
for college-trained personnel. It shows for
each level of the wage differential the proportion of their labor force that firms want
made up of college-educated workers. For
instance, at point *B*, where the wage differential is high, firms want only a small
proportion of their labor force to be college-
educated. At point *C*, though, where college-educated labor costs only about as

---

[5] Later in this section we briefly discuss the theory of
signaling, which says that college-educated people
may be more productive but not as a result of the education. According to the theory, going to college is a
way of signaling to producers that you are good at
doing certain things, such as passing tests, that may be
useful in the workplace.

FIGURE 14-2 WAGE DIFFEREN-
TIALS AND THE MARKET FOR
COLLEGE-TRAINED WORKERS.
The demand curve for college-trained
workers slopes down. The short-run
supply curve, *SS*, shows the proportion of the labor force that has a
college education at any given time.
The *SS'* curve is the long-run supply
curve of college-trained persons.
The greater the reward for college-
trained labor, the larger the number
of people who get themselves a
college training. Equilibrium is initially at *E*. When the demand for
college-trained workers shifts to *DD'*,
the wage differential rises sharply
to *WD'* in the short run. The higher
wage differential attracts more
people into college, and the long-run
equilibrium shifts to *E"*, with wage
differential *WD"* and a larger fraction
of the population with a college
education.

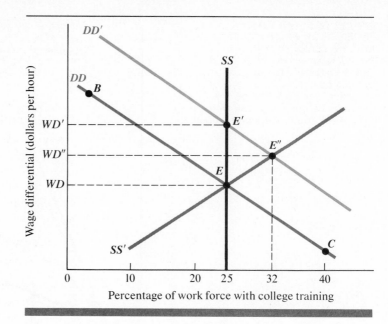

much as labor with a high school education,
firms want most of their workers to have a
college education.[6] The higher the wage
differential, the more firms will be inclined
to use non-college-educated workers instead of college-educated workers. Hence
the *DD* curve slopes downward. The basic
assumption underlying *DD* is that college
training increases the productivity of workers; therefore, firms are willing to pay a premium for workers who have a college education.

At any given time, the proportion of the
labor force with a college education is fixed.
Thus in the short run the supply of college-
trained workers is fixed, and the short-run
supply schedule, *SS*, is vertical. The position of the short-run supply schedule, *SS*, is
determined by how many people in the
population have gone to college in the past.

For instance, in the United States in 1980,
17 percent of the population aged 25 or
more had completed 4 or more years of college, and another 15 percent had completed
1 to 3 years of college.

The short-run supply schedule for college-trained workers is vertical. But in the
long run the percentage of the labor force
with a college education can change. If the
premium paid for a college education increased, we would expect more people to go
to college to put themselves in line for the
better jobs. Thus in the long run, we expect
the supply of college-trained people to increase with the wage differential paid for
such people. We will study the decisions of
individuals to go to college in more detail
below. For now, we show the *long-run* supply schedule of college-trained workers by
the upward-sloping line, *SS'*.

Given the short-run supply schedule for
college-trained labor, *SS*, and the demand
curve for college-trained labor, *DD*, the
wage differential is given at the intersection
point (point *E*); it is equal to *WD*. At this
point, the demand for college-trained per-

---

[6] We assume in Figure 14-2 that college-trained workers and other workers are not perfect substitutes. According to this view, it is quite possible that firms
would not want to pay a premium to have a 100 percent
college-trained labor force. They might say that the
work force would be overqualified.

sonnel is equal to the supply, which in this example is 25 percent of the work force. We assume that this is a position the economy has been in for a while, and so E is also on the long-run supply schedule for college-trained labor, SS'.

Now suppose that there is a shift in the demand for college-trained personnel. This might happen, for example, because the economy's mix of output changes from textiles and agricultural products to high-technology products, and college-trained personnel are more productive in firms that manufacture high-technology products. With the demand curve shifting upward from DD to DD', the equilibrium shifts in the short run from E to E'. The wage differential for college-trained people increases sharply in the short run, from WD to WD'. The increase is so large because, in the short run, there is no supply response at all. There is still only 25 percent of the population with a college education. People will have to go to college to be trained, and that takes years.

The next step is that high school graduates face the choice of entering the labor market or going to college. All those who had planned to get college training before the increase in pay for college graduates will certainly go to college. But now some of the people who had opted for a job will have second thoughts and ask themselves whether it would not be worthwhile to get some college training. More high school graduates will go to college, and the long-run relative supply of college graduates will increase, as shown by the long-run supply schedule, SS'. In the long run, therefore, the pay differential is only WD''. The differential is reduced by the revision of the educational choices of new entrants in the labor market. In the long run, 32 percent of the work force ends up with a college education. Other things being equal, the higher the wage differential, the higher the propor-

tion of the labor force with a college education. We now turn to those other things—the factors that determine how much individuals invest in higher education.

Investing in Human Capital: Cost-Benefit Analysis

Suppose we consider the decision of a high school graduate, or his parents, whether to enter college or find a job. There are basically four aspects to this investment decision excluding the family background and ability:

1   There are direct costs for college (tuition, textbooks, etc.).

2   Going to college means that there is a delay in entering the labor market and therefore a loss of income (only partially made up by summer work) for several years.

3   However, college training, once completed, leads to permanently higher incomes.

4   A college education yields nonpecuniary advantages—which is to say that people enjoy going to college, broadening their horizons, meeting new people and ideas, watching and playing football, and doing whatever else students do.

These costs and benefits have to be weighed in making the investment decision about whether or not to get college training. In Figure 14-3, we show the important economic elements in the investment decision by depicting the income pattern for a high school graduate entering the labor market at age 18 and the pattern for a college graduate who enters at age 22. The costs of going to college, represented by the gray-shaded area, are made up of direct costs and the income forgone by not working between ages 18 and 22. The benefits are given by the red-shaded income difference once the college graduate is in the labor market. On the

FIGURE 14-3 THE INCOME CONSEQUENCES OF GOING TO COLLEGE. The figure shows the effects of going to college on an individual's income. If he does not go to college, his income over his lifetime is as shown by the age-earnings profile for the high school graduate. If he does go to college, he has the profile shown for the college graduate. (We have ended the profiles at age 70, with a drop shown at the retirement age of 65. Of course, the profiles in practice continue beyond age 70.) Going to college costs an amount equal to the gray area in the diagram, which is made up of the loss of income from not working plus the direct costs of college. The benefits from going to college are shown by the red area. This is the amount of the income for a college graduate that exceeds the income of a high school graduate after age 22, the age at which the college graduate is assumed to start work.

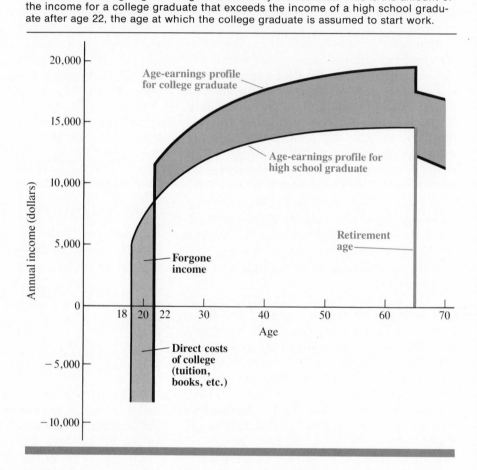

basis of this criterion, is a college education worthwhile? To figure that out, we have to have some way of comparing the costs, represented by the gray area, with the benefits, represented by the red area.

The Rate of Return The main difficulty in comparing the costs of and benefits from a college education is that the costs occur earlier and the benefits later. Later benefits are

typically worth less than earlier benefits, and so we can't simply ask whether total benefits (the red area) are larger than total costs (the gray area). We have to find some other way of determining whether a college education pays off.

The usual way of comparing the value of the costs with the value of the benefits is to treat the costs as an investment that pays interest in the future in the form of the benefits received in later years (the red area). Then we ask what interest rate would be needed, given the amount invested, to produce the benefits actually seen in practice. This is the rate of return to an investment in college education.[7] The higher the rate of return, the more worthwhile it is, from a financial viewpoint, to go to college.

The Rate of Return to College Education
Studies in the 1960s showed that the real rate of return to education was more than 10 percent.[8] On the basis of this reckoning, even before counting the "consumption value," or nonpecuniary value, of a college education, college seemed well worthwhile.

College training is worthwhile in the sense that instead of going to college, one could have invested the money (corresponding to the gray area) in bonds or in the stock market. Would the return have been higher? In the United States, the real return on stocks has averaged about 6 percent per year and that on bonds about 2 percent. Any investment with a return of 10 percent looks very promising.

However, it seems that in the 1970s the real rate of return to college education fell well below 10 percent. This reduction was in part a result of the increase in the percentage of people going to college.

Now let us consider costs and benefits in more detail. On the benefit side we have the pay differential. This, as we saw before, depends on the supply of college graduates in relation to the supply of high school graduates. The larger the relative supply of college graduates (given demand), the smaller the premium, and hence the smaller the return to a college education.

The other important aspects are the costs of college training. Suppose, for example, that tuition costs increase substantially. This would raise the direct costs of a college education and, given the pay differential, reduce the demand for college training and thus the long-run supply of college-trained personnel. In terms of Figure 14-2, a rise in tuition costs shifts the long-run supply schedule upward and to the left.

The final element to emphasize in talking about the decision to attend college is the consumption part of a college education. Many people would go to college even if it did not pay off financially. Most of the time college is interesting and fun, and that is justification enough for those who can afford to go. The investment aspect of a college education means that a college education is not only a consumption good; it may also make sense as an investment.

Education and Hog Cycles The fact that a college education takes time results in interesting time patterns of responses to changes in demand conditions. A rise in demand raises pay differentials in the short run and increases the number of high school graduates who opt for college. But once they graduate they will depress earnings and discourage college training. A drop in college training will, in turn, reduce the future supply of college graduates; once again, earnings will rise, etc. If such a process, sometimes called a hog cycle or a cobweb, gets under way,[9] the supply and the price (pay differentials and returns to education) will fluctuate around the equilibrium.

A good example of this type of cycle is provided by the market for scientists. After the Russians launched the space satellite Sputnik in 1957, there was a science boom in the United States. This sharply increased

---

[7] In the appendix to Chapter 15, we show how to calculate rates of return.

[8] A real rate of interest (or return) is an interest rate that is adjusted for inflation. If an interest rate is 12 percent and the inflation rate is 5 percent, the real rate of interest is 7 percent—that is the extra amount of *goods* that can be bought as a result of making the investment.

[9] The process was studied initially in the hog market and other agricultural markets.

TABLE 14-4

THE GROWTH OF RELATIVE EARNINGS IN PHYSICS

	1951–1954	1954–1962	1962–1968	1968–1970
Earnings growth, %:				
Ph.D. in physics*	9.2	67.7	22.3	8.8
Male professions*	20.5	40.1	36.4	17.4
Ph.D. degrees in physics:				
percentage of all				
Ph.D. degrees†	5.85	5.36	5.59	5.05

* From Richard B. Freeman, "Supply and Salary Adjustments to the Changing Science Manpower Market Physics, 1948–1973," *American Economic Review,* March 1975, pp. 27–39.
† *Statistical Abstract of the United States,* selected years.

the demand for scientists, thereby raising pay differentials and entry into science training. Later the demand for scientists fell, for firms and the government began spending less on research and development (R&D). Pay differentials collapsed, and enrollments dropped.

Table 14-4 shows the pattern of earnings growth for Ph.D. graduates in physics and, by comparison, for male professionals, along with the fraction of all Ph.D.s that were awarded in physics. We see clearly the post-Sputnik boom in earnings in the 1954–1962 period, followed by an increase in the proportion of Ph.D.s in physics in the 1962–1968 period. As the increased supply of Ph.D. graduates enters the market, relative earnings drop (in 1962–1968), and then in the period 1968–1970 there are fewer Ph.D.s in physics.

In the early 1980s a similar development may be taking place in the market for M.B.A. (master of business administration) graduates. Throughout the 1970s, the demand for M.B.A. graduates was very strong, and the salaries for M.B.A. graduates were rising steadily. There was a corresponding increase in the number of students taking M.B.A. degrees. Then in 1982, the market for M.B.A. graduates softened. Leading business schools reported that fewer firms

were showing up to interview their graduates for jobs. This change may have been a result of the poor business conditions in 1982. But it is also possible that the large increase in the number of M.B.A. graduates in the 1970s increased the supply of M.B.A. holders to the point where firms were no longer willing to pay a high premium for them. If this was the case, the number of students going on to take M.B.A. degrees will probably fall in the next few years.

On-the-Job Training and Age-Earnings Profiles

In the previous section the point was made that education is productive and that therefore there is a payoff from investing in education. But time on the job also has its payoff. A worker with experience is worth more to his firm, and indeed to any firm, than a worker who is new in the labor force. The difference between a new worker and a seasoned one is human capital acquired by holding a job—learning good work habits—or through on-the-job training. On-the-job training includes learning the routine customs of holding a job, cooperating in a production process, and acquiring specific skills.

On-the-job training is a major reason for the initially steep portions of the age-earnings profiles in Figure 14-1. Workers with some experience on the job are worth more to the firm than untrained labor; accordingly, the pay rises along with experience. But there is an interesting issue here. Who pays for on-the-job training? If the work experience makes workers acquire useful skills, why should they not pay the firm for providing that valuable experience?

We want to distinguish two types of skills. First, there is *firm-specific* human capital—knowledge of how to work in a particular firm. This skill is of no significant value elsewhere. Second, there is *general* human capital—knowledge that can move with the worker and be used elsewhere. Firm-specific training would be paid for by the firm, and so the age-earnings profile for workers acquiring specific human capital would not necessarily start out at a very low level. Generalized on-the-job training, though, which is useful in other firms, too, will be paid for by the worker: the worker will have a low starting wage and a steep age-earnings profile. This is because the firm really does not have any assurance that the worker will remain on the job after being trained.

The importance of experience and on-the-job training in determining the shape of the age-earnings profile has recently been questioned on the basis of the internal work records of a number of firms.[10] These records seem to show that older workers within a given rank are less productive than younger workers within the same rank. The question that is raised is whether this is consistent with the view that productivity increases with age—and the answer seems to be no.

The next question is what, then, accounts for the fact that the age-earnings profiles rise until workers reach their fifties, as

seen in Figure 14-1. There are no well-documented stories here, but there are some interesting suggestions. The first is that a rising profile may be a means for keeping workers interested in putting out a serious effort on the job. It is always difficult for a firm to measure a worker's effort. By having a rising earnings profile, the firm ensures that the worker will want to keep the job— the worker will want to earn the high incomes that are available only later, and so he will keep on working hard. The second idea is that workers have a feeling that a rising profile is fair—that older workers deserve more than younger ones.

This second explanation—the idea of fairness—may well be right, but it is the type of explanation that leaves economists uneasy. Economists prefer to think that the customs or ideas such as fairness that workers have are not inconsistent with their economic interests. The interesting debate on whether age-earnings profiles represent productivity differentials only or other factors is now warming up.

Human Capital in Arts and Sports

The idea of human capital—which generates a return to skills—is not limited to education or on-the-job training in ordinary industrial activity. It is used also in analyzing the more spectacular returns to talent and training in the arts and in professional sports. There is a well-developed economics of professional sports that analyzes the productivity of a baseball player in terms of the contribution his batting average makes to the team's ability to draw crowds and sell tickets, and the same analysis applies to football players or hockey players.[11]

There is little difference between music, theater, and football, at least with regard to the economics. They are team activ-

---

[10] James L. Medoff and Katharine G. Abraham, "Experience, Performance, and Earnings," *Quarterly Journal of Economics*, December, 1980.

[11] Roger Noll (ed.), *Government and the Sports Business*, Brookings Institution, Washington, D.C., 1974.

TABLE 14-5

MARGINAL RETURNS TO PUBLICATIONS AND TEACHING BY DISCIPLINE

	SOCIAL SCIENCES	LIBERAL ARTS	MATH AND ENGINEERING	BIOLOGICAL SCIENCES	PHYSICAL SCIENCES
Articles:					
1–2	$285	$212	$693	$173	$864
3–4	161	223	395	−50	425
5–10	135	163	208	7	198
11–20	113	154	179	67	119
21–50	74	97	123	56	89
50	65	90	95	77	93
Books:					
1–2	284	81	296	−284	288
3–4	407	222	307	183	179
5–10	335	228	188	69	121
10	166	185	−37	58	89
Teaching award	276	280	217	615	−246

Source: Adapted from H. Tuckman, J. Gapinski, and R. Hagemann, "Faculty Skills and the Salary Structure in Academe: A Market Perspective," *American Economic Review,* September 1977, Tables 1 and 2.

ities performed before audiences who purchase tickets and who value—in the sense of paying for tickets—exceptional performance. As in football, in music and theater we find the need for extensive training of the performers, capital costs for setting up the performance, and the costs of managerial and stagehand overheads.

There are, of course, differences in income between these fields. A good baseball player will make a substantially larger income than a good drum player in an orchestra. What accounts for the difference? Demand and supply. The good drummer does not draw an extra crowd as large as the one drawn by the good baseball player. The demand and pay for the drummer will be less.[12]

Faculty Skills and Pay

We have discussed the return to human capital in the arts and in sports. It is therefore

[12] However, since the professional life of the baseball player will, on the average, be shorter than that of the drummer, the individual with a choice might still want to become a drummer.

natural to show also the return in higher education. How do faculty skills and the ability to pitch translate into pay? In a study of pay differentials in a large group of universities, colleges, and junior community colleges the results shown in Table 14-5 were established for 1972–1973.

The table shows that a professor in the social sciences who had published one or two articles would earn $285 per year more than someone who had not published any articles. A professor who had published three or four articles would earn an extra $161. There is thus, on the average, a downward-sloping marginal value product schedule for publications. Note that publishing is worth more in mathematics and physics.

How does publishing compare with teaching? As the last row of the table shows, teaching quality, as measured by awards, is worth 1 to 4 articles, depending on the particular field.

Signaling

The basic hypothesis of this section has been that the wage structure is determined by the marginal productivities of different types of labor, as affected by education and experience—either firm-specific or general. In explaining the rising age-earnings profile, the theory argues that more experienced workers are more productive. We noted some preliminary evidence that on-the-job productivity might not increase in the same way as wages and that therefore the theory might have to be amended. The revised theory states that labor gets the value of its marginal product over the lifetime of a job, but the way in which the wage is paid over the years reflects other factors, such as ideas of fairness.

In explaining the 6.2 percent premium for an extra year of education that is shown in Table 14-2, the theory claims that the value of the marginal product is higher by 6.2 percent for each extra year of education. On the supply side, in response to the question of why there is that amount of human capital around, the theory argues that it takes a 6.2 percent premium to get workers to go to college, thus giving up earnings they could otherwise have in exchange for a higher income later.

An alternative theory of the reason for higher wages for more education is *signaling*, which says that education itself does not necessarily add to a worker's productivity.[13] Rather, says the theory, attendance at college and the passing of exams are signals to firms that the job applicant is good at doing certain things that are also useful at work, such as showing up on time and meeting targets. For a firm, evaluating all the individuals who apply in order to find out which ones are good at these types of activities is wasteful, since it means spending resources on testing. And going to college is a good idea for students because firms will be willing to pay a premium for college graduates.

The theory is that going to college is a way of sending a signal to employers. The interesting point, though, is that a college education itself may not contribute anything to the productivity of a worker under this hypothesis. We find college-trained workers earning higher incomes because they have different skills, not because they learned things at college. From the viewpoint of society, if we could find cheaper ways of sorting out those with the skills that are being rewarded in the marketplace, we could save resources. According to this view, it might be just as good to teach college students Greek and Latin (as in the nineteenth-century tradition) as it is to teach them science, math, or French—or even economics.

The signaling, or screening, hypothesis is clearly an interesting and radical thought. The empirical evidence so far is quite limited,[14] and so we cannot at this stage point to the theory as providing more than an interesting possibility about the role of education.

Signaling is a radical theory about the *economic purposes* of education. Its explanation of the observed returns to education is different from the argument of the human capital theory, namely, that education teaches students skills that increase their productivity. But the signaling approach, like the human capital approach, assumes that pay differentials arise from differences in the productivity of different types of labor. It does not relate to the possibility that pay differentials result from discrimination rather than productivity differences. We will now turn to the possibility that pay differentials result from discrimination.

---

[13] Michael Spence, *Market Signaling: Informational Transfer in Hiring and Related Screening Processes*, Harvard University Press, Cambridge, Mass., 1974, is the basic source.

[14] See John G. Riley, "Testing the Educational Screening Hypothesis," *Journal of Political Economy*, October 1979. This article presents some evidence on the issue of signaling.

TABLE 14-6

**MEDIAN WEEKLY EARNINGS BY
SEX AND RACE, 1980
(Index for White Males = 100)**

	MALES	FEMALES
White	100	63
Nonwhite	75	58

Source: See Table 14-1.

2 DISCRIMINATION

In this part of the chapter we discuss inequality and discrimination. There are large inequalities in economic status—pay, jobs, opportunities—between different members of the labor force. Specifically, female workers and nonwhite workers have fewer opportunities, lower pay, and poorer jobs than the average white male worker. Table 14-6, which is the same as Table 14-1, shows relative earnings in 1980.

The table shows that for every $100 that a white male worker earned, a nonwhite male earned only $75, a white woman only $63, and a nonwhite woman as little as $58. In this section we examine the sources of the inequality, see how inequality has changed over time, and discuss the scope for government policies to affect the differences in economic status. The emphasis in this section is on discrimination by race, because that is where most of the empirical work has been done. In terms of the analysis, the theories apply to discrimination by race or sex or, indeed, any other characteristic.

The Distribution of Employment

There are two main sources of inequalities in economic status between different groups in the labor force. First, there are differences in the share of good jobs held by each group. And second, there may be differences in the pay received for the same

job. We start by discussing the differences in the types of jobs held by different groups and the possible blame for those differences that should go to discrimination.

Who Has the Good Jobs? Table 14-7 shows for selected occupations the relative pay and the fraction of each group in each occupation. For example, 14.8 percent of white males are managers, while only 6.5 percent of nonwhite males are managers. The table shows that the best-paying jobs are those of managers, professional and technical workers, and craftspeople, while the low-paying jobs are those of service workers, clerical workers, and nonfarm labor. Managers, on the average, make twice as much as service workers.

Next consider the distribution of the different groups across jobs. More than half of the white male workers are in the top-pay job categories, while more than half of the nonwhite female workers are in the low-pay occupations. It is clear from the distribution of the groups across occupations that a very large part of the pay differentials in Table 14-6 arises from the kind of job held by the average member of each group. Only the professional jobs show an across-the-board openness with regard to both race and sex. These jobs include teachers and medical personnel.

The good jobs are good not only because they pay higher wages. They are good because they also tend to be steadier jobs. The unequal shares of good jobs help explain why blacks have higher unemployment rates than whites.

Why do a higher percentage of white males have good jobs? Why do white women have an edge over nonwhite women in getting managerial jobs? Many of the differences in Table 14-7 are the result of discrimination, past and present.

Suppose, first, that there are two jobs to be filled, a good one and one that is inferior,

TABLE 14-7

SELECTED OCCUPATIONS: RELATIVE PAY AND DISTRIBUTION OF THE LABOR FORCE

OCCUPATION	PAY*	MALES		FEMALES	
		WHITE	NONWHITE	WHITE	NONWHITE
Managers	100.0%	14.9%	6.9%	6.8%	3.4%
Professionals	91.0	15.6	10.5	16.4	14.2
Craftspeople	86.4	22.0	16.6	1.9	1.2
Nonfarm labor	59.8	6.7	12.7	1.3	1.6
Clerical workers	54.2	6.0	7.6	35.9	29.0
Service workers	47.1	7.7	15.7	16.1	24.6

* Percentage of managers' pay.
Source: Handbook of Labor Statistics, 1980, pp. 48 and 118.

and that there are two equally qualified applicants, a white worker and a nonwhite worker. If there is no discrimination, each worker, being equally qualified, has an equal chance of getting either job. But if the decision is made by a white person, and if racial prejudice is involved, then we can be certain that the white applicant will get the better job. Thus in a society where white people substantially control the jobs and where there is racial prejudice—a preference on the part of the white male majority to work with or be supervised by white male workers—it is the white male workers who will get the better jobs, given equally qualified applicants.[15]

The second kind of discrimination concerning access to jobs is more subtle; it is a matter not of outright discrimination but of "statistical discrimination." If an employer takes the view that the qualifications in a particular group, say, white females, vary more than the qualifications among white males, then applicants with the same qualifications from the two groups will still be judged differently. Although a man and a woman come with the same test scores, the woman will be downgraded because the

employer believes that the group from which she comes is a riskier group.[16]

The same kind of statistical discrimination applies if firms, in hiring labor, judge each individual person not by his own test score but rather by the average qualifications of the group he is drawn from—say, black high school students or white, 25-year-old, head-of-household college graduates. If the screening of applicants and promotions are based primarily on group qualifications, it is, of course, apparent that individual improvement becomes much less productive. The signals that matter for landing a job and for getting a promotion are largely inherited rather than acquired. In these circumstances it is not surprising that the incentives for investing in education are greatly reduced for members of a group that is seen as unqualified. Indeed, even worse, because the incentives are reduced, there will be a smaller investment in skills, and therefore the prejudice may come to be self-fulfilling.

Access to Education   The third way in

[15] See Gary Becker, *The Economics of Discrimination,* University of Chicago Press, Chicago, 1957.

[16] See Edmund Phelps, "The Statistical Theory of Racism and Sexism," *American Economic Review,* September 1972, and George Akerlof, "The Economics of Caste and of the Rat Race and Other Woeful Tales," *Quarterly Journal of Economics,* November 1976.

TABLE 14-8

MEDIAN NUMBER OF SCHOOL YEARS COMPLETED

YEAR	MALES		FEMALES	
	WHITE	NONWHITE	WHITE	NONWHITE
1959	11.8	8.1	12.2	9.4
1978	12.7	12.6	12.2	12.4

Source: Handbook of Labor Statistics, 1980, pp. 137–139.

which discrimination creates unequal shares of good jobs and economic status is through the unequal provision of good education and skills. Table 14-8 shows the strong differences that have prevailed historically. In the table we show the median number of years of schooling for male and female workers.[17]

It is apparent from the table that twenty years ago the typical black worker had only an elementary school education, while the typical white worker, male or female, had almost a complete high school education. Since then there has been much progress in equalizing the number of years of schooling that nonwhite workers receive. Still, it will take time for the improved educational opportunities—measured by years of schooling—to apply to the entire nonwhite labor force. It is an entirely different question whether the quality of education received by whites is the same as the quality of education received by nonwhites.

Equal Pay for Equal Work? The final kind of discrimination is much harder to document. It is discrimination on the job where, for the same kind of work performed, men and women or white and Hispanic workers receive different pay. While this kind of discrimination is harder to document, there is little doubt that there has indeed been a

pervasive pattern in this respect. The most impressive evidence of past discrimination of this type—different pay being given for equal work—comes from a number of lawsuits that were filed against major U.S. corporations in the last few years. The lawsuits were brought on behalf of female employees; they asked for damages for discriminatory low pay in earlier years. In most of these cases, the corporations agreed to compensate their employees for past discrimination, even before the lawsuits reached the courtroom.

Equal Opportunity

There has been substantial progress in the United States in the past 20 years in reducing discrimination and inequality in economic status by race and sex. What is the nature of that progress and to what is it due? Table 14-9 gives some measures of the relative progress that nonwhite members of the labor force have achieved. While in the 1950s the median wage of a nonwhite male worker was only 64 percent of a white worker's wage, it is now 80 percent. For women the relative earnings of nonwhites rose from less than 60 percent in the 1950s to over 90 percent in 1978. There has been a substantial narrowing of the differential even though differences remain. The same kind of progress is apparent when we take a look at access to good jobs. In the last 30 years nonwhites have increasingly gained access to the better jobs, but it is still true that a smaller fraction of nonwhites

---

[17] The median number of years of schooling is the number above which half the group has more schooling and below which half the group has less schooling.

TABLE 14-9

RELATIVE ECONOMIC STATUS: NONWHITE AS A PERCENTAGE OF WHITE
(Index for Whites = 100)

	1949–1950	1964	1978
Males:			
Median wages and salaries, full-time workers	64	65	80
Relative number of:			
Professionals	39	45	64
Managers	22	22	44
Females:			
Median wages and salaries, full-time workers	57	69	94
Relative number of:			
Professionals	47	60	87
Clerical workers	15	33	45

Source: R. Freeman, J. Dunlop, and R. F. Schubert, "The Evolution of the American Labor Market, 1948–80," in Martin Feldstein (ed.), *The American Economy in Transition,* University of Chicago Press, Chicago, 1980, p. 378. Copyright © 1980 by University of Chicago Press. Used by permission. Updated by authors.

than whites have good jobs, as seen in Table 14-7.

What accounts for the progress shown in Table 14-9? There are three especially important reasons for the move toward equality. The first, unmeasurable but important, is a general reduction in the tendency to discriminate throughout the labor market. The second is the effort, through the Civil Rights Act of 1964 and associated legislation, to use the powers of the federal government to eliminate discrimination and to improve opportunities for nonwhite workers and female workers. The third reason, in part a result of the previous two, is an improvement in the education and skills of nonwhite people. They have more access to education and a greater motivation to improve their skills. Thus they are able to get better jobs.

Sharp disagreement over the reasons for progress remains. Specifically, were government programs in the equal opportunity field successful? There are two lines of argument.[18] One view points to the important changes documented in Table 14-9 between 1964 and 1978 and credits govern-

ment programs with providing the pressure and/or the opportunities for these changes. The second view argues that the changes are really a statistical illusion.

How could the changes be a statistical illusion rather than a result of lessened discrimination? The argument is that during the sixties and seventies there was an expansion of public employment and government welfare programs. These programs either took people out of the labor force by putting them on welfare, which required that they not work, or took them out of the private labor market by giving them public employment. In general, the people in public employment programs were lower-paid workers.

There were two effects on the relative wages of nonwhite workers. First, the lowest-paid nonwhite workers were no

[18] See Richard B. Freeman, "Changes in the Labor Market for Black Americans, 1948–72," *Brookings Papers on Economic Activity,* vol. 1, 1973, and Richard Butler and J. Hekman, "Industrial Impact on the Labor Market Status of Black Americans: A Critical Review," Leonard J. Hausman et al. (eds.), *Equal Rights and Industrial Discrimination.*

longer in the labor force; therefore, the average pay of those left in the labor force rose. Second, because there were fewer nonwhite workers (as a result of some dropping out of the labor force and some working for the government), the relative wages of nonwhites rose. The overall effect was, of course, the appearance of a reduction in inequality or an increase in the relative pay for nonwhite workers.

What are examples of equal opportunity policies working in this particular way? There is some evidence that equal pay for equal job provisions, when enforced, reduce the employment of nonwhite people. Those who actually get a job are better paid and thus show up with improved relative wages, but, of course, those who are displaced show up on the welfare rolls. The example shows that antidiscrimination policy is not only important but also very tricky.

There is another direction in which interesting evidence is emerging. An important ingredient in forming human capital is not only the number of years of schooling but also the quality of schooling, which is measured by, among other variables, expenditures on schooling. Studies of the effects of the improvement in the quality of education reveal that this factor, too, has helped reduce income differentials in the last 20 years.[19]

Costs of Discrimination

Discrimination is economically costly. It is obviously costly to those who are discriminated against—to those whose income is lower than it would be without discrimination. But it is also costly to those who do the discriminating. Consider an employer who does not hire a well-qualified worker at a given wage because the worker is black or female but instead hires someone less qualified. That employer is losing profits. This has led some economists to argue that discrimination should tend to disappear without government intervention. However, it certainly showed little sign of doing so over many years.

Discrimination also imposes costs on the entire economy. If discrimination leads to misallocations of labor and causes blacks and women not to invest in human capital, output is being lost. Quite independent of any moral arguments about discrimination, there are economic arguments to be made against the practice.

3 UNIONS

In this part we discuss the purposes and functions of labor unions and their effects on wages and working conditions. Unions play a controversial role in industry. They are seen at one and the same time as organizations that protect workers against exploitation by powerful employers, as organizations that keep workers out of particular occupations and thereby raise the relative wages of their members, and also as an important institution for the smooth running of modern industry.[20] We start with the history of labor unions in the United States.

Unionization of the Labor Force

In 1978 over 20 million U.S. workers were members of labor unions. This was close to 24 percent of all employees in nonagricultural businesses. Another 3 percent of the nonagricultural workers belonged to employee associations, which are mainly in the public sector and operate much like unions.

The total number of union members in

[19] For recent research on the question, see articles by John Akin and Irv Garfinkel, Finis Welch, and Charles Link, Edward Ratledge, and Kenneth Lewis in *American Economic Review*, March 1980.

[20] See, in particular, Richard Freeman and James L. Medoff, "The Two Faces of Unionism," *Public Interest*, fall 1979, and H. Gregg Lewis, *Unionism and Relative Wages in the United States*, University of Chicago Press, Chicago, 1963.

FIGURE 14-4 UNION MEMBERSHIP AS A PERCENTAGE OF THE NONAGRICULTURAL WORK FORCE. (*Source: Handbook of Labor Statistics,* 1980, Table 165, p. 412.)

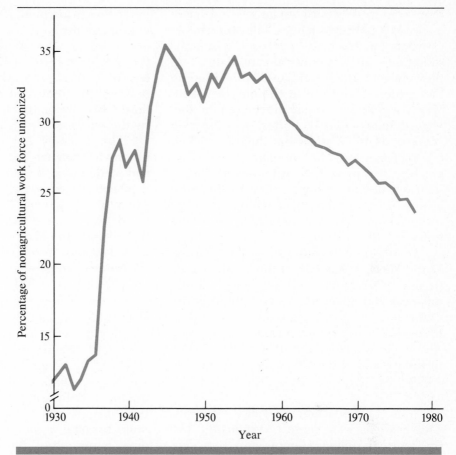

1978 was higher than it had been before, but the percentage of the labor force in unions has been falling. This can be seen in Figure 14-4, which shows the history of union membership from 1930 to 1980. Union membership doubled in just 2 years, between 1936 and 1938, during the Great Depression. It rose through World War II, with over one-third of the nonagricultural labor force being in unions at the end of that war. But the proportion of the labor force in unions has been falling almost uninterruptedly since 1955.

Trade unionism in the United States began to take its modern form in 1886, when the American Federation of Labor (AFL) was formed, under the leadership of Samuel Gompers. Unionism in the United States is different from unionism in other countries mainly because it is much less political and much more concerned with purely work-related issues. Gompers argued vigorously for two key features of U.S. labor unionism. First, U.S. unions as they exist today work within the capitalist system, and they are not working to make radical changes in the system. Second, they have—with varying degrees of enthusiasm—generally tried to stay out of political life, arguing that they can work with either or both political parties.

There is a major contrast here between American and European unions. European labor unions have typically wanted to move their countries toward socialism and have worked for political change. They tend to be associated with socialist parties. U.S. unions sometimes support political candidates, but they are not formally affiliated with either of the parties. There was at the end of World War I a political union movement in the United States—the Wobblies, or Industrial Workers of the World—but they never became a major force in unionism. The distinguishing feature of U.S. unionism has been its insistence on trying to improve the conditions of union members within the current economic system rather than by trying to change the system.

Union membership grew fast during World War I but declined during the prosperous 1920s, in no small part because both business and government were opposed to unionism. And the times were so good that there was little obvious purpose for unions. The major development of unionism came in the decade of the Great Depression, the 1930s.

The Great Depression and Legal Changes Two changes were largely responsible for the jump in union membership between 1936 and 1938 that can be seen in Figure 14-4. The first was the founding in 1936 of the Congress of Industrial Organizations (CIO), which wanted to organize labor into unions based on the industries in which workers worked. Up to that time, the unions were mainly organized on craft lines, meaning that people with specific skills belonged to a particular union, no matter what industry they were in. But once unions were organized on industry lines, it became easier to unionize large numbers of workers in each industry. That meant also that unskilled assembly-line workers became members of unions.

The second major change was the passage of the Wagner Act in 1935. This act forbade employers to engage in unfair labor practices; in particular, it forbade discrimination against workers who were members of unions or who filed complaints against the company. Firms were not allowed to interfere with their workers' rights to form unions, and they had to bargain in good faith with a union that had been established by the workers.

The Wagner Act made it easier for unions to organize the workers in a factory and made it possible for the unions to bring legal action against employers who objected to having their work force unionized. The rapid growth of unions was accompanied during and after World War II by a number of strikes and, in reaction, by a feeling that the unions had been given too much power.

The Taft-Hartley Act The reaction led in 1947 to the passage of the Taft-Hartley Act, which cut back the power of unions. One important provision is that the so-called *closed shop*, an establishment in which the employer can hire only members of the union, is outlawed. A *union shop*, an establishment in which anyone who is hired must become a union member within 30 days, is permitted. But there is a big "but" even with the union shop. The "but" is that states have the right to pass right-to-work laws—laws which outlaw the union shop. These right-to-work laws say that anyone who gets a job with a firm can have it, whether or not he joins the union. Nineteen states, many in the south, have right-to-work laws. The right-to-work states in 1978 were Alabama, Arizona, Arkansas, Florida, Georgia, Iowa, Kansas, Mississippi, Nebraska, Nevada, North and South Carolina, North and South Dakota, Tennessee, Utah, Virginia, and Wyoming. It should be clear that right-to-work laws severely weaken unions.

A second important provision of Taft-Hartley is that the President has the right to obtain a legal injunction delaying strikes for 80 days, if they would threaten the entire economy. This 80-day period is supposed to allow the two sides to cool off and reach an agreement.

The AFL-CIO　When the CIO was set up in 1936, it broke away from the AFL, with ill feeling. In 1955 the two organizations got together again and formed the AFL-CIO. The AFL-CIO is the main labor organization, but it does not have much control over the unions that make it up. The unions do the bargaining for themselves, and the AFL-CIO has little to do with the day-to-day running of unions, though it is the organization that speaks for the labor unions as a whole when that is necessary.

Declining Union Membership　Why has the proportion of the labor force belonging to unions been declining? One important factor has been the changing pattern of demand: the demand for goods has been falling, while the demand for services has been rising. The heavily unionized sectors are those that manufacture goods such as steel and automobiles. As incomes have risen, demand has shifted toward services. Correspondingly, the demand for labor has shifted from blue-collar labor to white-collar labor, which is less easily unionized. A second factor is that formal opposition has strengthened. Firms have been moving into states with weak unions and right-to-work laws and away from states with strong unions. The states with strong unions are the old industrial states of the northeast.[21]

Of course, the fact that some states have right-to-work laws, which make it difficult for unions to organize, reflects a general public attitude toward unions which is less supportive than it used to be. Part of the public sees unions as getting more for their workers than is right and as inflicting costs

[21] See Richard Freeman, "The Evolution of the American Labor Market, 1948–1980," in Martin Feldstein (ed.), *The American Economy in Transition*, University of Chicago Press, Chicago, 1980.

on other people. For that reason, legislation that is not friendly to labor is easier to pass.

The one major area of growth for unions in the seventies was the public sector. In 1970, 11.2 percent of all union members were government employees—at the federal, state, or local level. By 1978, government employees accounted for 16.7 percent of union membership. Among the unions are teachers' unions. Public sector employees are not legally allowed to strike; nevertheless, they did strike in the seventies. Early in the Reagan administration the professional air traffic controllers union (PATCO) went on strike, illegally. To the surprise of the members of the union, they were fired. This action by the Reagan administration will probably have a major impact on the number of strikes by public employees, and it may also reduce the rate at which public sector unions gain membership.

What Do Unions Do?

The first and traditional view of the role of unions is that they offset the relative power that a firm carries in negotiating wages and working conditions. If an individual worker is set against the firm, all he can do is accept the firm's terms or quit. Particularly if a worker has acquired specific human capital which will not do much for him in any other job, the firm is placed in a relatively strong position, and the worker has little protection against some exploitation and arbitrary treatment. Unions represent the interests of individual workers by presenting a common policy on working conditions and wages. They give workers strength through numbers. The firm would find it easy to dismiss and replace a single worker, but it realizes that it would be exceedingly costly to replace its entire work force on the issue of pay, hours, breaks, security, or working conditions.

A first point, then, is that unions help

FIGURE 14-5 A UNION'S EFFECT ON WAGES AND EMPLOYMENT. The *MVPL* curve shows the demand for labor in a competitive industry. The economywide wage, W_0, is the wage that labor would be paid if there were no union. A union is able to control the quantity of labor supplied to the industry and thereby raise the wage above the competitive level. In the figure, the union raises the wage from W_0 to W_1 by restricting the quantity of labor supplied to N_1.

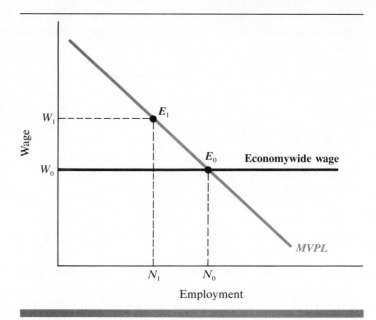

offset the strength of the firm relative to the strength of the individual worker. Of course, once a union is established, it is likely to go beyond this first task. It will try to improve the relative economic position of its members by restricting the supply of labor and thereby raising relative wages. To do this, the union must be able to restrict the firm's labor supply. If a union cannot prevent a firm from hiring nonunion labor, then whenever the union succeeds in raising wages for its members, the firm will go out to hire nonunion labor at a lower wage. It is because control over the supply of labor for a firm is crucial to a union's ability to improve its members' wages that the forbidding of union shops through right-to-work laws is so important to unions. When there is a right-to-work law, the union will have a very difficult time.

We now analyze how unions raise wages by restricting supply.

Restricting Labor Supply and Wage Differentials If a union controls the supply of labor that a firm or industry can draw on,

then the control can be used to affect the relative wage of union members. We develop the analysis in Figure 14-5. Suppose that we are looking at the construction industry. The demand for labor is given by the downward-sloping marginal value product schedule, *MVPL*. The larger the labor force employed in construction, the lower the marginal value product. Suppose also that the wage that construction workers could be earning in other sectors of the economy is W_0. If the labor supply for the construction industry was competitive, we would go to the point E_0, with employment level N_0. The wage of construction workers would equal the economywide wage, W_0.

Now suppose that the construction industry becomes unionized and that the union recognizes that restricting the supply of labor will allow it to raise the wage of the union members employed in construction. Thus if the quantity of labor supplied to the construction industry is restricted to N_1, the equilibrium wage in construction is W_1, at point E_1 on the demand for labor schedule. The union has managed to raise the relative wage of its members, and it is able to make the gain in the relative wage stick because the construction firms cannot get around using union labor by going into the free labor market. Of course, it is also true that employment in the construction industry is lower than it would be with a competitive labor market. Furthermore, with higher wages and hence higher costs, the prices of houses and structures in relation to the prices of other things will be increased.[22] Thus unions raise not only the relative wage of union labor but also the relative cost and price of goods produced by unionized labor.

The analysis raises two issues. Note in Figure 14-5 that the union can raise the wage higher the more it restricts the supply of labor for the industry. The first question is, What determines how far the union will try to go in raising the wage at the expense of less employment? The second question is, What determines how much power unions have to control the supply of labor for particular industries?

We start with the first question. Assume, to begin with, that the union has full control over the supply of labor to the firm. In this case the union acts as a monopoly seller of labor to the firm. We might think that like a monopolist, the union should aim to maximize profits, or its income. In that case it would want to set the wage at the point where the elasticity of demand for labor is 1.[23] But in the case of a union, it is far from clear what should be maximized. The union might want to maximize the income of the existing members, or it might want to maximize the per capita income of the members who remain after it has raised the wage, or perhaps it is concerned with maximizing

the size of its membership so that it can be sure of maintaining its power. These are all different objectives. Which one dominates depends largely on the extent to which the union is run in the interest of its management, in the interest of its existing members, or in the interests of existing and potential members.

The more open a union is to new members, the less effective it will be in raising relative wages. This is because as long as there are wage differentials to be had, individuals will want to get a job and enter. If the union lets them in, it cannot go far in restricting employment. But a union that restricts entry severely can raise relative wages substantially. One key issue, then, is how entry can be restricted. The techniques here vary; for example, the union can charge initiation fees or require licensing, or it can require that new members must be relatives of existing members. But it is clear that the techniques are key elements in making the restriction of the labor supply effective.

Under what conditions does a restriction of the labor supply work particularly well in raising relative wages? We are looking for firms or industries where a small reduction in the labor supply yields a large increase in the relative wage. In other words, we are talking about a low elasticity of demand for labor. Where the elasticity of demand is low, unions face a particularly favorable employment-wage trade-off.

We show the role of the elasticity of demand for labor in Figure 14-6. There are two possible demand schedules for labor, *MVPL* and *MVPL'*. The demand curve *MVPL'* is more elastic—a given change in wages generates a larger change in employment around point E_0.

Suppose that the competitive equilibrium is at E_0 and that a union succeeds in reducing employment from N_0 to N_1. Along the demand schedule *MVPL* the equilib-

---

[22] Go back to Chapter 13 to be sure you understand this point.
[23] Recall from Chapter 9 that a zero-cost monopolist maximizes profits by selling at a price where the elasticity of demand is unity.

FIGURE 14-6   WAGE DIFFERENTIALS AND THE ELASTICITY OF DERIVED DEMAND. The effect of the union on wages and employment depends on the elasticity of the derived demand for labor, as shown by the *MVPL* curve. The elasticity of derived demand is higher on *MVPL′* than on *MVPL*. This means that a given restriction in the quantity of labor supplied produces a lower increase in wages for the union members on *MVPL′* than on *MVPL*. The union prefers to face a low elasticity of *MVPL*. That way it gets large increases in wages with a small cutback in the level of employment.

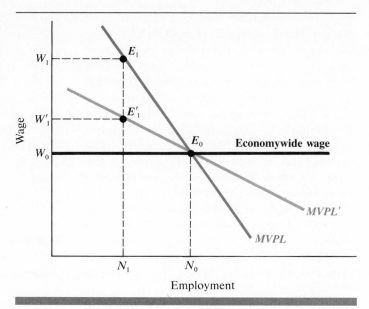

rium wage rises to W_1, while along *MVPL′* it rises only to W_1'. It is clear from the diagram that a given reduction in the labor supply raises wages more the less elastic the demand for labor is.

The demand for labor *MVPL′* might represent the case of a firm that competes with other firms that employ nonunion labor. Even a small increase in wages and costs makes that firm lose a large share of its markets as it loses out to nonunionized competitors. Accordingly, its labor demand is very highly responsive to the wage, and attempts to raise relative wages have large employment costs. The schedule *MVPL*, by contrast, represents the case of a very inelastic demand for labor and output. Even a large increase in wages does little to reduce employment, because final demand is very inelastic. Here unions can go far in raising relative wages.

We can use Figure 14-6 to consider the effects of airline deregulation on the market for pilots. Traditionally, when there were few airlines and all were unionized, pilots commanded a high relative wage—high relative to the wages of professionals. We can

assume that point E_1 is the initial equilibrium point. Deregulation opened up the possibility of new, nonunion airlines entering into competition. Now unionized carriers face more elastic demand curves on the part of passengers—passengers can substitute toward nonunion airlines. Therefore, the schedule for the derived demand for labor is more nearly like the elastic schedule, *MVPL′*. There is a very strong downward pressure on the union wage differential, since the carriers can no longer afford to pay it. Of course, it is in the union's interest to expand its coverage to the new airlines or to try to keep them out of business by lobbying for safety certification, for example. As always in a monopoly situation, the entry of new firms threatens the monopoly rents. In our case, the rents or wage differentials of unionized pilots are threatened by the entry of nonunion firms.

Another example, much along the same lines, concerns the automobile industry. Suppose that automobile workers are unionized and command a wage differential and that foreign firms start competing in the home market. The demand for cars becomes

TABLE 14-10

UNION VERSUS NONUNION DIFFERENTIALS

	% OF WORKERS UNIONIZED	UNION VERSUS NONUNION WAGE DIFFERENTIAL, %
All occupations	35.0	15.9
Craftspeople	47.7	19.5
Operatives	61.8	18.6
Transportation equipment workers	57.8	38.4
Clerical workers	28.0	2.3
Laborers	45.0	42.2
Service workers	31.6	15.5

Source: F. Block and M. Kushkin, "Wage Determination in the Union and Nonunion Sectors," *Industrial and Labor Relations Review,* January 1978, p. 189. Copyright © 1978 by Cornell University. All rights reserved. Used by permission.

more price-responsive as domestic models start competing with imports. In the labor market the derived demand for cars becomes more elastic. Car producers lose sales, and union employment falls. Unions lobby against imports, arguing that foreign cars are produced by cheap labor.

Unionization and Wage Differentials in Practice Table 14-10 shows union versus nonunion wage differentials for 1973. The first line summarizes the data. Thirty-five percent of the group examined here—white non-Hispanic males between the ages of 24 and 65 employed in the private sector—are unionized. Unionized workers earn 16 percent more, on the average. But, of course, as the table shows, there are substantial variations in unionization, and there are even more variations in the wage differential. The wage differential is largest for highly unionized, relatively low-skill jobs—for example, the jobs of laborers.

Union Wages as Compensating Differentials We have so far looked at unions as restricting labor supply and thus creating wage differentials for their members. The question that now arises is whether the differentials we see in Table 14-10 are entirely

the result of restriction of the labor supply or whether they might be, to some extent, a compensation for the kind of labor performed by union workers. Union work has certain characteristics—"notably a structured work setting, inflexibility of hours, employer-set overtime, and a faster work pace."[24] These characteristics rather than the existence of unions might at least in part be responsible for higher union wages. There are two views about the link between wage differentials and working conditions.

The first view is that after unions have taken over and raised relative wages, the employers respond by taking advantage of the presence of unions to raise productivity. Productivity is raised by establishing more standardized work patterns which can be agreed upon and enforced in cooperation with the unions. Because, other things equal, workers view these restrictions on the work pace and working time as costs, it is clear that the increase in their relative wage has in some way been eroded. They earn more, but they also work on relatively less attractive terms.

The other view is that unions are not primarily a means of restricting labor sup-

[24] G. J. Duncan and F. P. Stafford, "Do Union Members Receive Compensating Differentials?" *American Economic Review,* June 1980, p. 355.

TABLE 14-11

DAYS OF WORK LOST PER YEAR PER EMPLOYEE BECAUSE OF INDUSTRIAL DISPUTES, 1974–1978

CANADA	FRANCE	GERMANY	ITALY	JAPAN	SWEDEN	U.K.	U.S.
1.01	0.22	0.06	1.22	0.13	0.014	0.39	0.48

Source: Handbook of Labor Statistics, 1980, pp. 476–478.

ply at all but rather organizations for effective communication between employers and workers regarding working conditions. We would expect unions to emerge in industries where there are gains to be derived from the establishment of structured working conditions. The union negotiates to reconcile the workers' dislike of restrictive working conditions with the firm's need for such terms. The wage differential is the compensation for the restrictive conditions. Evidence for this view of union wage differentials as a compensation for productivity and work conditions has emerged from a number of studies.[25] These studies find that union labor has higher productivity, for example, because of lower quitting rates; that union labor enjoys less effective break time; that union labor operates in more restrictive working conditions; and so on. In sum, then, the union premium is not entirely a reflection of the union's monopoly restriction of the labor supply. Some of it represents a compensating differential. But the importance of the monopoly elements remains.

Bargaining and Strikes

When we think of unions, we probably think also of strikes. And, of course, strikes do sometimes disrupt major parts of the economy, such as the coal, steel, and trucking industries. How serious are strikes? And do they account for any significant losses of output in the economy? In total, as Table 14-11 shows, strikes cost the U.S. economy

very few workdays per year—less than half a day per year per employee, on the average. The U.S. experience is about average. Japan and Sweden lose fewer workdays, and Canada and Italy lose many more.[26]

Why are there strikes? The natural reaction is to think that a strike is the inevitable outcome of a bargaining situation in which the union and the firm are fighting each other. But it is important in thinking about unions to realize that the union and the firm have a common interest as well as opposing interests. The firm wants to make profits, and the workers want to earn income. Together they can achieve their respective aims. The workers need the firm to provide the jobs, and the firm needs the workers to provide the labor.

Typically, the bargaining process between a firm and the union is completed without a strike. And, indeed, the union and the firm are in continuing contact to operate the firm at times other than contract-negotiating time. There are always issues between workers and management that need to be settled. These issues are typically settled in a routine way between the union and management.

Sometimes a union and a firm will misjudge each other's strength or their own strength. A strike will take place, and one side or the other will give way eventually. Or sometimes a union or the firm will deliberately aim for a strike to show that it is

---

[25] See, in particular, R. Freeman and J. Medoff, *What Do Unions Do*, Basic Books, New York, 1982, and Duncan and Stafford, cited in footnote 24.

[26] The data in the table are slightly misleading because wildcat strikes—strikes which are called by the workers rather than union officials—are excluded. These are more frequent abroad than in the United States.

tough enough to resist the demands of the other party. The strike is costly to both parties when it happens, but each party believes that the strike pays off in the long run because the other party will realize the seriousness of future threats.

Sometimes leaders of unions are forced into strikes by the members. The members may be very militant and demand a large wage increase. Even though the leadership may know that such an increase is not possible, it goes through with a strike to demonstrate its toughness to the membership and also so the membership will eventually change its mind about the possibility of getting a higher wage.

Interesting as strikes are, they are not the usual means for reaching agreements between unions and firms. Typically, the bargaining process concludes with a new contract that specifies working conditions. wages, and fringe benefits for the next year or two (or three), and the union does not go on strike.

SUMMARY

1   In this chapter we have analyzed three special topics in labor economics: human capital, discrimination, and labor unions. In each case we applied principles of microeconomics to the pricing of labor services.

2   There are substantial differences in pay among workers. These reflect personal characteristics such as education, job experience, race, location, and union status. While the pay differentials differ from person to person, there are, nevertheless, distinct patterns that emerge from studies of large samples of workers. These studies allow us to determine the pay premium that, on the average, is earned for an extra year of schooling, for union status, or for other personal characteristics.

3   Skills, or human capital, are the most important source of wage differentials among workers. Human capital is a broad concept; it encompasses different sources of a person's productive ability. Human capital formation includes both formal schooling and on-the-job training and experience. Other things equal, the more schooling and/or the more job experience a person has, the higher his human capital, productive potential, and (therefore) wages are. Earnings profiles for the United States bear out the fact that more education translates in the marketplace into higher pay.

4   On the demand side, the reward for human capital depends on the substitutability between highly skilled workers and persons with less training. The less substitutable the groups are and the smaller the group with relatively more training, the higher that group's wage differential is. Thus on the demand side there is a differential for human capital because less-skilled labor is not a perfect substitute and because skilled labor is relatively scarce.

5   Skilled labor is relatively scarce because it is costly to acquire

human capital. Formal schooling, say, at the college level, involves not only direct tuition costs but also forgone income—income that could be earned by working instead of going to college. There is a payoff in terms of a wage differential for more skilled personnel. The investment decision for human capital involves balancing the direct costs and forgone earnings associated with increased schooling against the prospective rewards for more educated workers.

6   There is some evidence that the shape of age-earnings profiles may not be due entirely to the greater productivity of more experienced workers. Rather, the earnings may increase with age so as to encourage workers not to quit when quitting is costly for the firm.

7   The signaling hypothesis is another possible explanation of why a premium is paid for college-educated workers. It says that a college education itself does not add to a worker's productivity; it only shows that the worker is good at things that are useful for the firm. There is only a small amount of empirical evidence for this hypothesis.

8   Female workers and nonwhite workers are discriminated against in the U.S. labor market. They receive, on the average, lower wages and incomes than white male workers. The wage differentials reflect the facts that female workers and nonwhite workers are more heavily concentrated in relatively poor jobs (service workers rather than managers) and that within given jobs they receive less pay for identical work and have less of an opportunity for advancement.

9   Equal opportunity policies seek to eliminate the impact of discrimination on the economic status of nonwhites and women. There has been a sizable improvement in the relative position of nonwhite workers in the last decade. But it is not clear to what extent this reflects reduced discrimination and to what extent it reflects withdrawal of the lowest-paid workers from the labor force.

10 Improved education, in terms of both quality and duration, seems to be narrowing the wage differences between white workers and nonwhite workers of the same age group.

11 About one-quarter of the workers in the United States belong to unions. Union membership increased sharply between 1936 and 1938 and reached a maximum as a share of the labor force at the end of World War II. The declining proportion of the labor force in unions reflects shifts in the pattern of demand for goods—demand has shifted away from goods produced by easily unionized labor—and a changing geographic pattern of production. Public sympathy for unions has also decreased.

12 Unions in the United States, as opposed to those in Europe, have as their main aim the improvement of the wages and working condi-

tions of their members within the capitalist system. Foreign unions are more likely to be associated with socialist political parties.

13 Unions restrict the labor supply for unionized establishments and thereby raise the wages of their members in relation to nonunion wages. The wage differentials vary across industries, with the average differential being about 15 percent.

14 The wage differential that a union can achieve is larger the more effectively the union can control membership and the less elastic the demand for labor is. Union differentials will be higher or will cost less in terms of employment the less competition unionized firms face in the markets for their output.

15 Union labor tends to work under conditions that are more restrictive in terms of hours, overtime, and work pace than the working conditions for nonunion labor. This is interpreted as a reason for union differentials. The differentials are seen not as a result of the restriction of the labor supply but rather as a compensation for the kind of work performed by union labor. While that view has merit, it does not invalidate the traditional view that unions restrict labor supply and thus create differentials.

KEY TERMS

Human capital	General human capital
Age-earnings profile	Statistical discrimination
Signaling	Closed shop
Rate of return to education	Union shop
Firm-specific human capital	Right-to-work laws

PROBLEMS

1 Studies have shown that college-trained workers in the 1970s received a smaller wage differential than they did in the 1960s. (*a*) What effect would this have on the percentage of high school students going to college? Explain. (*b*) Suppose it was shown that going to college did not add at all to a person's lifetime income. Would anyone still go to college? Explain.

2 The energy shortage increased the demand for nuclear energy. Discuss in detail the labor market adjustment to the increased demand for nuclear engineers in the short run and in the long run.

3 Consider the following investment problem. A person with his existing skill can earn $20,000 a year for the next 40 years. Alternatively, he can enter a 3-year course of studies with *direct* costs of $7000 per year. If he could get an interest-free loan to finance the studies, what future income differential per year would make the investment in human capital worthwhile?

4 Suppose that economists form a union and establish certification procedures that specify who is qualified to practice economics. How would the move help to raise the relative wage of economists? (*a*) What kinds

of laws would help cement the monopoly? (b) How would the union restrict entry?

5 Apprentices are typically paid low wages. Using the concept of human capital, explain this observation.

6 Discuss whether the government should have an interest in remedying the effects of former discrimination on people currently alive.

7 Who benefits from economic discrimination against women? Explain.

8 The government enacts a minimum-wage law that requires firms to pay at least $5 per hour of labor. (a) What are the effects on unskilled workers who were earning only $4 per hour before the enactment of the law. (b) If firms discriminate against nonwhite workers, do you think that nonwhite workers will be particularly hurt or helped by the minimum wage.

9 Draw a demand schedule for labor. Assume that a union has a given number of members, $\bar{N}$, that the economywide wage is W_0, and that employment in this industry at that wage exceeds $\bar{N}$. Illustrate the different targets that the union could pursue: (a) maximize income, (b) maximize employment, (c) maximize wage.

10 Show in a diagram of the labor market how a policy of restricting flight time for pilots (to a maximum of, say, 40 hours per month) affects the wage differential of unionized pilots. Why is a restriction on the number of working hours an important part of the union's attempt to raise the wage differentials?

In the first half of the 1980s, the aim of economic policy in the United States is to increase investment, capital, and savings to get the country growing again. Industry needs to increase its capital stock—its machinery, equipment, and factory and office buildings. The automobile industry has to invest to compete with heavily mechanized foreign producers, the steel industry has to modernize its capital equipment, and the new growth industries in information processing need to invest for future production. Investment adds to the stock of capital in the economy. Thus the emphasis on investment is an emphasis on capital.

> **Physical capital is the stock of goods that contributes to the production of goods and services.**

The capital stock includes the assembly-line machinery used to make cars, the chairs in which we sit and the TV we watch while sitting,[1] houses that produce "housing services," railroad tracks, school buildings, office buildings, airplanes, and so on.

Physical capital is distinguished from land by the fact that it is produced.

> **Land is a factor of production which, rather than being produced, is naturally available.**

Older economists wrote of the "original and indestructible powers of the soil" as being land. But we do not have to worry too much about fine distinctions between land and capital. Part of the land in the United States owes its productivity to past investments made in clearing trees and rocks and in creating proper drainage. Thus part of what we call land is the result of past investments and is more like physical—produced—capital than a factor of production that was naturally available. We will see that many of the principles that apply to the economics of capital apply equally to land. Both because land and physical capital are difficult to disentangle in practice and because the economics is the same, we will discuss capital and land in the same chapter.

Capital and land together make up the *tangible wealth* of the economy. This means that they are wealth that can be touched—for example, machines and farmland. Tangible wealth and financial wealth are different. Someone who has a large bank account owns financial wealth. But the bank balance is not tangible wealth. Financial

---

[1] Why are the chair and TV set capital? Because they contribute to producing the service "watching TV," which people value.

15

Capital and Land

TABLE 15-1

VALUE SHARES OF TANGIBLE WEALTH BY ASSET CLASS, 1970
(Percentages)

	CANADA	GERMANY	JAPAN	KOREA	UNITED STATES
Consumer capital	10.6	7.6	5.5	2.4	13.7
Structures and producer durables	38.9	41.5	37.6	25.4	29.3
Residential structures	20.0	29.4	18.8	14.6	21.6
Inventories	8.4	7.8	13.9	9.0	8.9
Land	22.2	13.6	24.3	48.5	26.3

Note: Components may not add up to 100 because of rounding.
Source: L. Christensen, D. C. Christensen, and D. Jorgenson, "Economic Growth, 1947–73: An International Comparison," in J. Kendrick and B. N. Vaccara (eds.), *New Development in Productivity Measurement and Analysis,* University of Chicago Press, Chicago, 1980, Table 11-4. Reprinted by permission.

wealth has value because it is ultimately a claim on tangible wealth, but it is not the same as tangible wealth.

Similar to the distinction between tangible wealth and financial wealth is the distinction between physical capital and financial capital. A person about to open a business may say that he has capital of $10 million because he borrowed that much from the bank and his relatives. But this is *financial capital*—money and other paper assets. If the financial capital is used to buy office equipment and machinery, then the businessman has acquired physical capital, which is what this chapter is about.

1 TANGIBLE WEALTH: THE FACTS

Table 15-1 is our starting point for discussing tangible wealth. The table shows for a number of countries the composition of the stock of tangible wealth among different forms of real, or physical, capital and land. The various kinds of wealth are shown in the first column. For the most part their meaning is self-explanatory. Consumer capital includes automobiles, refrigerators, and other real assets owned by households. Structures and producer durables includes buildings, machines, and tools owned by businesses. "Inventories" refers to finished goods, materials, and goods in process that

are held by firms so that they can produce without running out of supplies and be sure goods are available when their customers want them.[2]

The table reveals interesting differences between countries.[3] The two key differences are between agricultural countries and industrialized countries and between rich or developed countries and poor countries. To see the difference between a developing agricultural country and an industrialized country, compare Korea and Germany. In Korea, nearly half of the tangible wealth consists of land; in Germany, almost half of the tangible wealth consists of structures and producer durables. The comparison between rich and poor comes out most strongly when we look at the share of consumer durables in the United States and in Korea. In the United States, consumer capital (TV sets, cars, lawn mowers, etc.) accounted for 13.7 percent of the tangible wealth in 1970; in Korea, the comparable figure was only 2.4 percent.

What is the total value of capital and land? In the United States in 1980, the total

---

[2] Why are inventories part of the capital stock? Because they are a stock of produced goods that contributes to the production of goods and services.
[3] As we will explain below, data on wealth and capital are difficult to gather; therefore, the data should not be thought of as accurate to the last decimal place.

value of tangible wealth was estimated to be $8.8 trillion, or about $40,000 per person. In Table 15-2 we examine the composition of tangible wealth in the United States over the last 30 years; the 1980 data tell us what made up the huge total tangible stock of wealth worth $8.8 trillion.

The most striking point to emerge from the table is that the composition of the stock of tangible wealth has remained quite stable over the last 30 years: plant and equipment accounts for about a quarter, as does land. Residential structures account for 30 percent, while inventories and consumer capital each account for about 10 percent.

To get a sense of the significance of capital and land in the economy, we look in Table 15-3 at three measures of the role of tangible wealth. The first is the ratio of tangible wealth to national income, or the value of all goods and services produced in the economy. The stock of wealth, in value terms, is equal to around 3 years' income. The precise value differs from year to year and varies over longer time periods, but a value of 3 for the wealth-income ratio is a useful summary number. The second measure of the role of land and capital is their share in national income. The table reveals that the income of land and capital accounts now for only a quarter of national income, having declined over the last 30 years from a level of about 35 percent.[4]

The third measure shown in Table 15-3 is the amount of land and capital per worker in the United States over the last 30 years. In 1980, the average worker had nearly $54,000 worth of land, structures, and equipment to work with. The amount of tangible wealth per worker has risen by nearly 70 percent over the last 30 years, as is apparent by comparing the 1950 and 1980 data. There has thus been a large change in

[4] The share of land and capital in national income is not exact, since it includes the labor income of the proprietors of small businesses.

TABLE 15-2

COMPOSITION OF THE U.S. STOCK OF TANGIBLE WEALTH (Percentage of Total Stock)

	1950	1980
Plant and equipment	24.3	29.2
Residential structures	29.7	28.1
Inventories	11.9	8.9
Land	21.6	22.5
Consumer capital	12.5	11.3

Source: Federal Reserve Board, *Balance Sheet for the U.S. Economy,* 1981.

TABLE 15-3

TANGIBLE WEALTH IN THE UNITED STATES

	1950	1965	1980
Tangible wealth ÷ national income	3.0	2.9	3.7
Share of land and capital in income*	34.8%	30.7%	24.7%
Land and capital per worker†	$32.3	$40.5	$53.8

* National income less compensation of employees as a fraction of national income.
† Thousands of 1980 dollars per worker, excluding consumer capital, owner-occupied housing, and household land holdings.
Sources: Economic Report of the President, 1981 and Federal Reserve Board, *Balance Sheet for the U.S. Economy,* October 1981.

the way output is produced. Over time, the average worker has been able to cooperate with an increasing amount of capital, or production has become more *capital-intensive.*

It is difficult to measure the existing stock of wealth. Capital lasts for many years. To measure the existing, useful, and operating stock of capital, we have to estimate by how much capital depreciates or wears out each year.[5] Recorded additions to the capi-

[5] For instance, think of estimating the value of all the cars in the economy. We have to figure out what new cars are worth and also what 1-year-old, 2-year-old, etc., cars are worth and how many 15-year-old cars are still around. (The value of cars is, of course, included in estimates of tangible wealth.)

TABLE 15-4
STOCK AND FLOW CONCEPTS

	CAPITAL	LABOR
Productive contribution	Capital services (machine hours)	Labor services (labor hours)
Payment for service flow	Rental rate, $/machine hr	Wage, $/hr of labor
Asset price	Price of a unit of capital, $/machine	Not available except in the case of slavery, $/slave

tal stock are adjusted for the estimated depreciation of existing capital to arrive at *net additions to the capital stock*, or *net investment*. While this procedure is not exact, the data in Tables 15-1 and 15-3 are useful estimates of changes in the composition and size of the capital stock and the value of land.

In the next few sections we concentrate on capital. We return later to a discussion of land.

2 RENTALS, INTEREST RATES, AND ASSET PRICES

In this section we set out a few definitions and concepts that help clarify the discussion of capital. The main points to be made are the distinctions between a *stock* and the *flow* of services and between a *rental payment* and an *asset price*. We make these points with the help of Table 15-4, discussing first the case of labor.

The commodity that is traded in the labor market is labor services, or hours of labor. The corresponding price is the wage per hour. We can think of the wage per hour as the price at which the firm rents the services of a worker, or the rental for labor. We do not have asset prices in the labor market because workers cannot be bought or sold in modern societies; they can only be rented. But in a society with slavery, the asset price is the price of a slave.[6]

---

[6] Robert Fogel and Stanley Engerman give data on slave prices in *Time on the Cross*, Little, Brown, Boston, 1974.

Now the application of these concepts to capital is straightforward. Where a worker provides labor services, a machine provides machine services. For example, a dentist's drill provides 1000 hours of drilling services per year, and a truck provides 3000 hours of trucking services per year.

The cost of *using* capital services is the *rental rate* for capital.

The rental rate may be a quoted market price, the amount the firm pays to rent a piece of capital from its owner. For instance, there is a rental rate for hiring a moving van from U-Haul, equal to so many dollars per hour or day. But for some capital goods there is no actual rental market. In these cases the firm has to work out how much per hour or day it spends on the use of its capital equipment. In section 4 we will discuss in more detail how a firm calculates the rental rate for the machines it uses and owns (as opposed to rents from other firms).

Finally, in the case of capital, there is an asset price as well as a price for the use of the services of capital.

The asset price is the price at which a drill or a truck or any other piece of capital can be bought outright.

What is the relationship between asset prices and asset rentals? The important point here is that the asset price represents the claim to all present and future services of the capital. Suppose we talk about a house that can be rented out for $6000 per year. What would be the price of the house? We will show that *the asset price is the present*

TABLE 15-5
INVESTMENT AND INTEREST

	YEAR 0	YEAR 1	YEAR 2	YEAR 3	YEAR 20
		INTEREST RATE = 10%			
Value of $1 invested today in year	$1	$1.10	$1.21	$1.33	$6.73
Present value of $1 to be received in year	$1	$0.91	$0.83	$0.75	$0.15
		INTEREST RATE = 5%			
Value of $1 invested today in year	$1	$1.05	$1.10	$1.16	$2.65
Present value of $1 to be received in year	$1	$0.95	$0.91	$0.86	$0.38

discounted value of the flow of rental payments. To do that, we have to start with interest rates and present values.

Interest and Present Values

We start our discussion of capital and interest by looking at a time deposit that pays interest at a given rate. Suppose that a time deposit in a bank yields 10 percent per year in interest or, in other words, 10 cents for every dollar held in the account for a year.

If we placed a dollar in a time deposit and reinvested the interest every year, the value of our investment would grow at the rate of the interest, as in Table 15-5. In year 1 we have our initial investment plus 10 cents in interest, or $1.10. In year 2 we have the year 1 investment plus interest, or $1.10 + 10 percent of $1.10 = $1.21, and so on.

The fact that the principal, or original sum, is reinvested every year together with the interest already earned means that the total value of the investment is growing, because we are earning interest on the interest that is being reinvested. After 7¼ years at 10 percent the value of the investment has already doubled;[7] after 20 years it has accumulated to nearly seven times the initial investment.

Next we look at Table 15-5 to ask how much we would pay today to receive a dollar in the future. Suppose the interest rate is 10 percent. How much would we pay today for $1 a year from now? The answer is given in the second row. One dollar today grows into $1.10 a year from now. Therefore, to get $1.10 a year from now, we have to pay $1 today. Accordingly, to get $1 a year from now, we have to pay $0.91, or $1/$1.10. Ninety-one cents invested today at 10 percent amounts to $1 a year from now. In the same way we can calculate the value today of $1 to be received 2 years from now: $1/$1.21 = $0.83. In the same way still, a dollar 20 years from now is worth $0.15 today, when the interest rate is 10 percent.

Looking at the second row of Table 15-5, we see that the value today, or the *present value,* of a payment to be received in the future is smaller the more distant the payment date. A dollar tomorrow is definitely *not* a dollar today; as long as we can invest at interest, we would never pay a full dollar today for a dollar tomorrow.

---

[7] A useful rule of thumb is the *rule of 72*, which says that the time it takes to double your money is equal to 72 divided by the interest rate. At 5 percent, it takes 14.4 years (72 ÷ 5); at 10 percent, it takes 7.2 years. The rule is good but not exact: the exact answers are 14.21 years at 5 percent and 7.27 years at 10 percent.

FIGURE 15-1 THE ACCUMULATION OF CAPITAL VALUE THROUGH INTEREST. The figure shows how $1 invested in year 0 grows in value the longer it is held. A dollar invested at 10 percent a year for 14 years ends up worth $3.80. At the lower interest rate, 5 percent, the value builds up much more slowly; it reaches only $1.98 after 14 years.

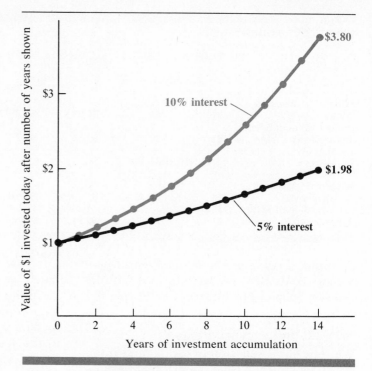

The present value of a future payment is the amount that would have to be invested today to produce exactly that payment on the payment date.

We look next at how the level of the interest rate affects the relationships we have discussed. In the lower part of Table 15-5, we assume that the interest rate is only 5 percent. With only 5 percent interest, the initial investment will grow much less rapidly. While at 10 percent it grows nearly sevenfold in 20 years, at 5 percent it does not even triple in 20 years. The interest on the interest works less rapidly in our favor when interest rates are low. For instance, if the interest rate were 20 percent, our investment would increase nearly 40 times in 20 years.[8] The counterpart is shown in the last row of the table. The present value of a $1 future payment is higher at a 5 percent in-

terest rate than when the interest rate is 10 percent. The reason is that to get $1 next year with only 5 percent interest, we have to invest $0.95 today rather than only $0.91. Therefore, we are willing to pay a higher price to receive a given future payment.

Figures 15-1 and 15-2 summarize the relationships we have derived and emphasize how they hang together. For years 1 to 3, the points in Figures 15-1 and 15-2 correspond to the data in Table 15-5. We show two results. First, in Figure 15-1, the higher the interest rate, the more rapidly a given investment grows. We show this by comparing the cumulative value of $1 invested at 10 percent with the cumulative value of $1 invested at 5 percent. Second, in Figure 15-2, we show the present value of a $1 payment to be received in the future. The present value is lower the more distant the payment date and the higher the rate of interest.

The relationship in Figure 15-2 is im-

[8] See the appendix for formulas of present value. There are tables available that give present values and financial calculators that will do the calculations.

FIGURE 15-2 THE PRESENT VALUE OF $1 TO BE RECEIVED AT A FUTURE DATE. The present value of a future payment is lower the further off the payment is and the higher the interest rate. The present value is the amount that would have to be invested now to generate the future payment. To get $1 after 14 years, it is necessary to invest $0.263 today if the interest rate is 10 percent. If the interest rate were 5 percent, it would take $0.505. There is a close relationship between Figures 15-1 and 15-2. For instance, $0.263 is equal to ($1/$3.80), and $0.505 is equal to ($1/$1.98).

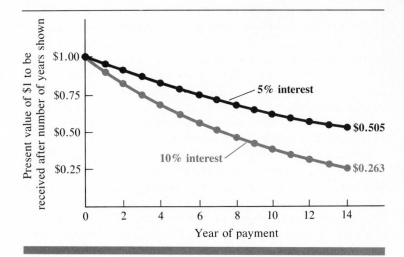

portant in understanding the general idea of asset pricing. The price of an asset is the present value of *all* future income derived from the asset. This implies, from what we have seen above, that the asset price will be higher, for a given pattern of payments, the more near term rather than distant the payments and the lower the rate of interest on alternative investments. Conversely, the asset price is lower the more distant the payments and the higher the rate of interest.

Calculating the Value of an Asset

With these general principles in mind we can look at an asset-price calculation. Suppose that we are thinking of buying a machine that yields a rental of $4000 for 3 years

and then can be sold for a scrap value of $10,000. With an interest rate of 10 percent, how much would we be willing to pay?

Table 15-6 presents the calculations for deriving the present value. In the first two rows we show receipts from rentals and the scrapping of the machine according to the year of the receipt. In the third row we have, from Table 15-5, the present value of $1 to be received in years 1, 2, and 3. The fourth row, finally, shows the present value of the receipts in each year. For example, in year 1 we have $3640 ($4000 × 0.91). The sum of the present values of each of the future payments plus the present value of the scrap value is equal to the asset price. In our example, the asset price is $17,460. This is,

TABLE 15-6
A PRESENT-VALUE CALCULATION

	YEAR 1	YEAR 2	YEAR 3	ASSET PRICE
Rental receipts	$4000	$4000	$4000	
Scrap value			$10,000	
Present value of $1 to be received in year*	$0.91	$0.83	$0.75	
Present value of receipts in year	$3640	$3320	$3000 +$7500	$17,460

* Interest rate = 10 percent.

of course, less than $22,000, the total of the cash receipts from the machine. Why? Once more, because a dollar tomorrow is not worth a dollar today. We have to convert future payments into current values by calculating present values or by *discounting* future payments.

A useful way of understanding the role of the interest rate in the present-value calculation is to note that the interest rate represents the *opportunity cost* of the resources used to buy the asset. The person who buys the asset could invest his money at 10 percent in the bank or in a bond or in some other way. Therefore, to be willing to buy the asset, he has to be sure of getting at least that much of a return on the amount needed to buy the asset.

Now we can return to the case of a house to ask how its asset price is determined. We have to go through the same calculations we performed for the machine, except that now we are looking at an asset that yields an income for 30, 40, or more years. In some cases, the asset might even last forever—for instance, in the case of land. It is a bit hard on the calculator to go through the calculation of the present value of future incomes from here to eternity. It turns out, however, that there is a useful formula. For an asset that yields a constant payment forever—say, $100 per year every year—the present value of *all* future incomes is calculated as follows:

$$\text{Present value of a perpetuity} = \frac{\text{annual payment}}{\text{interest rate}} \qquad (1)$$

Assets that yield an income forever are called *perpetuities*, and their price is equal to the (constant) annual payment divided by the interest rate.

Thus an asset that yields $100 forever, with an interest rate of 10 percent, is worth $1000 ($100/0.1). If the interest rate were only 5 percent, the asset would be worth $2000 ($100/0.05).

For long-lived assets such as houses or land, the level of the interest rate has an enormous effect on the asset price. If the interest rate rises from 5 percent to 10 percent, the asset price of a perpetuity is cut by one-half. Now formula (1) applies strictly to perpetuities only. But it actually yields a good approximation for long-lived, though not permanent, assets. The reason is that extremely distant receipts—for example, receipts 50 years or more into the future—are worth very little now.[9] It thus does not make much difference to the value of the asset. Accordingly, equation (1) is a useful formula to bear in mind for assets that last a long time, though not quite forever.

Real and Nominal Interest Rates, Inflation, and Present Values

In all the calculations that we have made of present values, all the payments in this year and in future years were given in dollars. The interest rate that we used was also expressed in dollars. When we say that the interest rate on bank deposits is 10 percent, we mean that next year we will receive 10 cents in interest for every dollar kept in the bank account for a year.

The interest rate expressed in terms of the increase in the dollar value of an investment is the *nominal interest rate*.

This tells us how much more in dollars we will have in the future if we invest dollars at that interest rate. But we are probably more interested in what those dollars will buy. For that purpose we want to look at the real interest rate.

The *real interest rate* measures the return on an investment in terms of the increase in the amount of goods that can be bought rather than in terms of the increase in the dollar value of the investment.

The distinction between real and nomi-

---

[9] For example, at an interest rate of 10 percent, the value of $100 every year forever is $1000. The value of $100 for 50 years instead of forever is $991.48.

nal interest rates is extremely important. Two examples will help make the distinction. Suppose that prices go up 6 percent per year and that the nominal interest rate is 10 percent. Consider making an investment for 1 year. At the end of the year we have $1.10 for every dollar with which we started. But each dollar buys 6 percent less than it did a year ago. Thus every dollar we have next year buys only (1/1.06) = 0.943 as much in goods as a dollar this year buys. This means that $1.10 next year is worth only $1.0373 ($1.10 × 0.943) in terms of the goods it will buy. Accordingly, we say that the *real interest rate* is only 3.73 percent —because that is how much more in goods we can buy as a result of the investment we have made.

Table 15-7 shows the calculation of the real interest rate for another example. Here the nominal interest rate is 20 percent, and the inflation rate is 17 percent. At the end of the year the investor has $1.20. However, the $1.20 buys only 1.026 times as much in goods as the $1 would have bought at the beginning of the year. The real interest rate is thus 2.6 percent. As these two examples suggest, a quick and reasonably accurate calculation of the real interest rate can be performed with this formula:

Real interest rate = inflation-adjusted
                     interest rate
                   $\cong$ nominal interest rate
                   − inflation rate   (2)

In this formula, $\cong$ means "approximately equal to." The results obtained with this formula are quite accurate so long as the inflation rate is low.

Why worry about the distinction between the real interest rate and the nominal interest rate? The reason is that in inflationary times, we can easily get a very wrong idea of the costs of borrowing if we look at the nominal interest rate. A nominal interest rate of 20 percent seems to be extremely high. But if the inflation rate is 19 percent, borrowing can be done very cheaply. Similarly, anyone who thinks that he has a good deal if he can save at 20 percent when the inflation rate is 19 percent is making a big mistake, for after saving for a year he will hardly come out ahead. And if the inflation rate is a bit higher than he expected when he made the investment, he will even come out behind in real terms. In such a case, we say that the real interest rate turned out to be negative—the saver lost in real terms by saving.

In calculating present values, it is necessary only to be consistent. So long as all payments are specified in dollars, a nominal interest rate can be used. If future payments are expressed not in dollars of the future years but rather in *real terms* (that is, in terms of the purchasing power of this year's dollars), then a real interest rate must be used for the calculation.

Real interest rates in the U.S. economy

TABLE 15-7

CALCULATION OF THE REAL INTEREST RATE

NOMINAL INTEREST RATE	$1 INVESTED TODAY BRINGS IN	INFLATION RATE	VALUE OF $1 NEXT YEAR IN TERMS OF THIS YEAR'S $	VALUE OF $1.20 NEXT YEAR IN TERMS OF THIS YEAR'S $	REAL INTEREST RATE
20%	$1.20 one year from now	17%	$\dfrac{\$1}{1.17} = \$0.855$	$\$1.20 \times 0.855 = \$1.026$	2.6% approximately (nominal interest rate − inflation rate)

have been low historically. Real rates of return on Treasury bills have averaged around 1 percent or a bit less; on long-term bonds the rates of return have been around 2 or 3 percent. It would be wrong to think that interest rates around 10 percent mean that the saver will be able to buy 10 percent more goods next year than he can buy this year, for the real interest rate is much lower than the nominal rate whenever we are in inflationary times.

What Determines the Real Interest Rate?

Interest rates are currently around 10 percent or more, and they are almost always positive. Why? A possible first answer is that the interest rate is positive because someone who borrows today will get to pay back the loan in dollars of a lower value tomorrow. The lender is compensated by receiving interest at a positive rate. But this explains why *nominal* interest rates are positive when inflation is expected. It does not explain why real interest rates are typically positive too, even though they are typically small.

A full analysis of the determination of the real interest rate will be given in Chapter 20, which is about savings and investment. But two reasons for a positive real interest rate are readily understood. First, people generally prefer to consume today rather than wait till tomorrow. People are impatient to consume. Therefore, if they make loans, they want to be compensated for delaying their consumption. This means that they want to receive positive interest. But wanting to receive positive interest is not enough. There also has to be a way of earning positive returns. And there is such a way: investing in physical capital is a way of producing net revenue in future years, even after paying back interest. Thus borrowers are willing to pay interest because they can pay the interest and still come out ahead.

The two most important forces behind a positive real interest rate are impatience and the productivity of capital. And these are the two basic forces that determine the real interest rate. Throughout this chapter we take the real interest rate as given and constant.

3 THE DEMAND FOR CAPITAL SERVICES

In this section, we analyze the demand for the services of capital for a particular industry. In the next section we turn to the supply side of the market.

The analysis of the market for the services of capital is very much in the spirit of Chapter 13's presentation of the market for labor services. The major difference between the analysis of the market for capital services and the analysis of the market for labor services is that the rental rate for capital now takes the place of the wage. The demand for capital services depends on the cost of using capital, the rental rate, just as the demand for labor depends on the cost of using labor services, which is the wage.

Throughout this section and the next two we talk about the supply of and demand for the *services* of capital to emphasize that the analysis is about the *use* of capital, such as machines and buildings, independent of who owns the capital. Someone renting the services of a truck needs to use the truck itself in production, but he does not need to own it. The examples to bear in mind when we talk about renting the services of capital are renting a building and renting a truck.

We now examine the demand for services of capital, such as industrial machinery or structures, by a firm. As in the analysis of the demand for labor, the firm asks how much 1 more hour of machine services will add to the value of the output produced. This is the marginal value product of the services of capital—of the use of a machine, a truck, or a square foot of workshop space.

> The *marginal value product of capital* is the increase in the value of output produced that results from the use of 1 more unit of capital in production.

Given the amounts of labor (and other factors) the firm employs, the marginal value product of capital declines as the amount of capital per worker rises. For a given labor force, adding more capital services increases output, but at a decreasing rate. This is shown by the downward slope of the *MVPK*, or marginal value product of capital, schedule in Figure 15-3. The larger the quantity of capital services employed by the firm, the lower the marginal value product of those services. The *MVPK* curve is, of course, just like the *MVPL* curve in Chapter 13.

We move now from the *MVPK* curve to the demand curve for the services of capital. Suppose that the firm faces a given rental rate, R_0, per unit of capital services. For instance, this might be the monthly rental for the services of a building, or the hourly rental of a car, or the cost of using the dentist's drill. How much capital will the firm want to rent? In Figure 15-3, K_0 is the firm's demand for the services of capital at rental rate R_0. If the firm rented less capital, the marginal value product of capital would exceed the rental rate, and profits could be increased by renting more. But if the firm rented more than K_0, it would find that it could reduce its use of the services of capital and increase profits.

Thus the *MVPK* curve is the firm's demand curve for the services of capital. At any rental rate, such as R_0, the firm maximizes profits by demanding the services of the amount of capital shown by the *MVPK* curve.

The marginal value product of capital services depends not only on the amount of

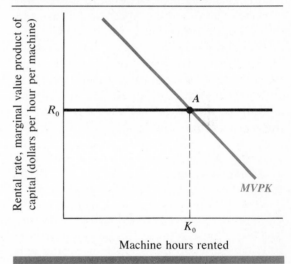

FIGURE 15-3 THE DEMAND FOR CAPITAL SERVICES. The *MVPK* schedule shows the marginal value product of capital, which declines as the firm uses more capital. This reflects the declining marginal productivity of capital. The amount of labor and other factors used by the firm is held fixed along the *MVPK* schedule. At any given rental rate, such as R_0, the firm will rent the amount of capital services such that the marginal value product is equal to the rental rate. This is the amount of capital services that will maximize the firm's profits at that rental rate. The *MVPK* curve is therefore also the demand curve for the services of capital. At rental rate R_0 the firm rents amount K_0 of the services of capital.

capital employed, as shown in Figure 15-3, but also on the demand for the firm's goods and on the amounts of the other factors employed. Since the *MVPK* curve is the demand curve for the services of capital, this is the same as saying that the demand for the services of capital depends on the demand curve for the firm's output and on the amounts of other factors it is employing.

How do these other variables affect the demand curve for capital services? As in the case of the demand for labor, the *MVPK* schedule is more elastic the more elastic the demand for the firm's output is. The demand for capital services depends also on the amount of labor employed. The more labor that is employed in relation to capital, the more productive is an extra hour of capital services.[10] Therefore, anything that increases the level of employment raises the marginal productivity of capital and shifts the *MVPK* curve upward.

Figure 15-3 describes the demand for capital services by a firm. The demand curve for the industry is obtained by adding the demand curves of the individual firms. It will have the same general shape as the demand curve of each firm. Thus the demand curve relating the demand for the services of capital to the cost of using those services slopes downward, for both the firm and the industry. The demand curve is more elastic the higher the elasticity of demand for the industry's output. And the curve is shifted upward by an increase in the amount of the other factors being used by the firms in the industry.

4 THE SUPPLY OF CAPITAL SERVICES

In discussing the supply side of the market for capital services, we distinguish between the short run and the long run. We also distinguish between the supply of capital services for the economy as a whole and for a particular industry in the economy.

The Short-Run Supply

In the short run the total amount of capital in the economy (machines, buildings, raw materials) is fixed. There are a given number of machines of each type, buildings, and stocks of raw materials, and the quantities cannot be changed in the short run. To change the stocks of capital takes time.

From the viewpoint of the economy as a whole, the short-run supply of capital services is inelastic. But from the viewpoint of an individual industry, it may be possible to vary the quantity of capital services employed. For instance, the quantity of services of trucks supplied to a particular industry can be changed in the short run by moving in trucks from other industries. For more specialized machinery such as blast furnaces, the quantity of services to an industry may be inelastic in the short run. There are a given number of blast furnaces, and there is no possibility of changing the quantity in the short run.

Figure 15-4 shows the two possible types of supply curves for the services of capital for an industry in the short run. If the industry uses a specialized type of machinery, then the quantity of services supplied is constant in the short run, and supply curve SS applies. The capital will be supplied to this industry no matter what the rental rate is, because it has nowhere else to

FIGURE 15-4   THE SHORT-RUN SUPPLY OF CAPITAL SERVICES FOR AN INDUSTRY. If all the capital used by an industry is specialized for use in that industry, then the short-run supply curve for capital services for that industry is SS. All the capital being supplied to the industry will continue to be supplied to the industry no matter what the rental rate is, because it has nowhere else to go. The quantity of services supplied cannot be increased in the short run because there is no time to build more of the capital. If some of the capital is not specialized (e.g., trucks), then a short-run supply curve like SS' will apply. New equipment can be brought into the industry in response to higher rental rates.

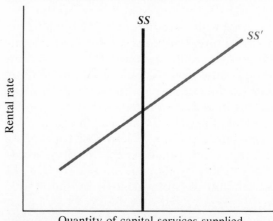

---

[10] Why? Because each unit of capital services has more workers to co-operate with it and is therefore more productive.

go. If some of the capital used by the industry is not specialized, then the supply curve for the services of capital will be upward-sloping, like SS'.

The Supply of Capital Services in the Long Run

In the long run the total quantity of capital in the economy can be adjusted. New machines and factories can be built to increase the capital stock, and machinery can be allowed to deteriorate or fall out of use to decrease the capital stock. Not only can the total stock of capital be changed; so, too, can the amounts of services of capital supplied to particular industries. In the long run it does not matter that an industry uses very specialized machinery, since new machinery of that type can be built, or the existing machinery can be allowed to deteriorate.

The Required Rental on Capital To discuss the supply side of the market for capital services, we want to think of the potential owners of capital, considering at what rates they would be willing to rent out the capital they plan to buy or build.

> The *required rental on capital* is the rental rate that allows the owner of capital to just cover the opportunity cost of owning the capital.

Before discussing the details, we develop the general idea. Anyone who buys a piece of capital incurs certain costs in renting it out. If the costs are less than the amount that can be earned by renting out the capital, there will be an expansion of the capital services offered for rent. If it costs more to maintain the machine than it earns—either from rentals or in terms of its marginal value product—there will be a reduction in the quantity of capital services used. The required rental is the rental that just covers the costs of providing the services of capital. We discuss the required rental to identify the economic forces that cause changes in the quantity of capital services supplied to an industry.

Suppose that you want to borrow from a bank to buy a machine and that you rent it out to a business. How much must you earn from that machine so as not to make a loss? Let the machine cost $10,000, which you have to borrow. First you have to cover the interest cost. Let the inflation-adjusted, or *real*, interest rate be 5 percent. The real interest cost, then, is $500 ($10,000 × 0.05) a year.

In addition, the machine will be depreciating. Therefore, maintenance expenditures are required to keep the machine in working condition. Assume that the maintenance expenditures and depreciation costs account for 10 percent of the value of the machine. Maintenance and depreciation thus cost you $1000 a year. This 10 percent is the *depreciation* rate. Thus your annual costs for renting out a machine in working condition are calculated as follows:

$$
\begin{aligned}
\text{Annual cost} &= \text{interest cost} \\
&\quad + \text{maintenance cost} \\
&= \text{price of machine} \\
&\quad \times (\text{interest rate} \\
&\quad + \text{depreciation rate}) \\
&= \$10{,}000 \times (0.05 + 0.10) \\
&= \$1500 \tag{3}
\end{aligned}
$$

The annual cost of maintaining the machine consists of the maintenance expenditures on the machine plus the interest charges. This annual cost is also the required rental that has to be charged for the use of this machine if you are not to make a loss.[11] Frequently the required rental is considered as a percentage (or a required *rate of return*)—15 percent in this case.

If you receive $1500 a year, there will be no loss from keeping the machine in operation. If you receive less, it will not pay to

---

[11] Tax policy has major effects on the required rental on capital, but we will not discuss those here.

keep the machine going like new. You will reduce maintenance spending, allowing the machine to wear out. Ultimately, you will not replace it. But if you receive more than $1500 per year, you will see that extra profits can be earned if you buy additional machines. You can borrow from a bank to finance the purchase and then use or rent out the equipment. Therefore, the quantity of capital services supplied will be expanded.

The Three Factors Determining the Required Rental   In equation (3) we see that the required rental or cost of capital is determined by three factors: the price of the capital good, the real interest rate, and the depreciation rate.[12] The depreciation rate is largely a technological matter; it depends on how fast the machine wears out through use and age. We take it as given here. In addition, we take the interest rate as given in discussing the supply of the services of capital to an industry. This leaves us with the purchase price of machines and buildings as the main variable affecting the required rental on capital.

The Long-Run Supply Curve for the Economy   The required rental on capital determines the shape of the long-run supply curve for capital services. In the long run a given amount of capital services is supplied to the economy only if it earns the required rental. If it earns more than that, people go out to build more capital. If it earns less than the required rental, owners of capital let some existing capital go out of use. Thus the long-run supply curve for capital services is the curve showing the required rental on capital at each level of capital services supplied.

In Figure 15-5 we show two possible long-run supply curves for capital services.

---

[12] If the firm using the capital also owns it, the required rental is the cost the firm should charge itself for using the capital when calculating economic costs.

FIGURE 15-5   THE LONG-RUN SUPPLY OF CAPITAL SERVICES. In the long run the shape of the supply curve for capital services reflects the way the required rental on capital changes as the amount of capital services supplied increases. We assume that the real interest rate and the depreciation rate are given. Thus from equation (3), the required rental on capital depends only on how the price of capital goods changes as the quantity changes. On supply curve *SS''* we assume that capital goods are available at a constant price. On supply curve *SS'''* we assume that the price of capital goods rises as the quantity of capital goods produced rises—that is, the supply curve for the capital goods industry is upward-sloping. We assume that supply curve *S'''* applies at the level of the entire economy, while *SS''* applies at the level of the industry.

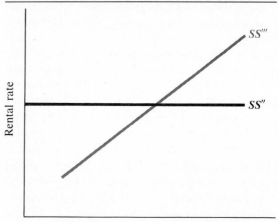

Quantity of capital services supplied

Recall that we are assuming that the real interest rate and the depreciation rate are given. Thus only the third factor, the price of capital goods, affects the required rental. On long-run supply curve *SS''* we are assuming that the economy can produce as much of the capital good as is wanted at the same price. Then the required rental is constant, as equation (3) shows, for constant real interest and depreciation rates. Any amount of capital will be supplied so long as it earns the constant required rental as calculated from equation (3)—that is, as long as the rental on capital covers the opportunity cost of owning that capital rather than a bank account or some other asset.

On supply curve *SS'''* we assume that

capital is only available at a higher price as the quantity increases. If we think in terms of the industries building the capital, such as the construction industry, the assumption is that the industry will supply more of the good only at a higher price. This means that the industry has the usual upward-sloping supply curve that we assume most industries have.

We shall work with long-run supply curve SS''' at the level of the economy, assuming that more capital services will be supplied to the economy only at a higher price. The assumption is that the more resources that are devoted to building capital, the higher will be the opportunity cost in terms of other goods given up.

The Long-Run Supply Curve for the Industry We have exactly the same two possible supply curves for capital services for the industry. If the industry is very small and the machinery is available at a constant price, then the required rental will be constant, and the supply curve for capital services will be horizontal. This is the case we shall assume in studying equilibrium in the market for capital services in an industry. For the industry, we assume that the long-run supply curve is SS''.

5 EQUILIBRIUM IN THE MARKET FOR CAPITAL SERVICES

Equilibrium in the market for capital services exists when the quantity supplied is equal to the quantity demanded. Figure 15-6 shows long-run equilibrium in the market for capital services in a particular industry.

The market for capital services is in long-run equilibrium at point E. The demand for capital services is given by the $MVPK$ curve, and the long-run supply is given by SS''. The equilibrium rental rate is R_0. Corresponding to that rental rate, amount K_0 of capital services is used in the

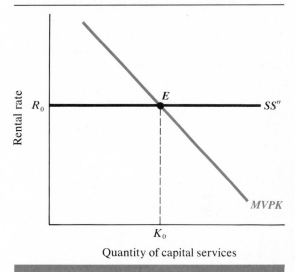

FIGURE 15-6 EQUILIBRIUM IN THE MARKET FOR CAPITAL SERVICES. The figure shows long-run equilibrium in the market for capital services. Capital services are supplied in the long run at the rental rate R_0. The demand curve is $MVPK$, with long-run equilibrium at point E. At this point the industry is using amount K_0 of the services of capital.

industry. The quantity of services, K_0, is the amount such that capital in this industry earns precisely R_0, the rental required if the capital is to stay in the industry.

Adjustment in the Market for Capital Services

To study adjustment in the market for capital services, we consider the effects of an increase in the wage on the amount of capital used in the industry and on the rental rate. Suppose that the wage rate has risen because the union in the industry has succeeded in getting a high wage settlement. We first have to ask what that does to the demand curve for capital services, $MVPK$.

The increase in wages has two effects on the demand for capital services. First, because the cost of using labor has risen, the industry's supply curve of goods shifts upward. This means that total industry output will fall because the product has become more expensive. This *cost effect* implies a

FIGURE 15-7 SHORT- AND LONG-RUN ADJUST-
MENT OF CAPITAL TO A RISE IN WAGES. The industry is initially in equilibrium at point E. Assume
wages then rise, and the *MVPK* curve shifts downward to *MVPK'*. The short-run quantity of capital
supplied is fixed, as reflected by the short-run supply
curve, *SS*. Thus in the short run, the industry moves
to point E', the intersection of the demand curve for
capital services (*MVPK'*) and the supply curve (*SS*).
At this stage the rental rate for capital is only R', and
capital therefore begins to leave the industry. As it
does this, the industry moves up the *MVPK'* curve, as
shown by the arrows pointing from E' to E''. Capital
will continue leaving the industry until the rental rate
for capital returns to R_0. This occurs at point E'',
where the new long-run equilibrium quantity of capital services used is K_1.

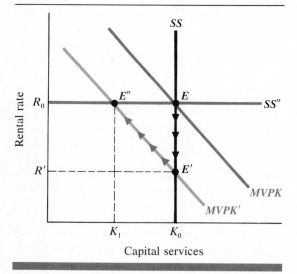

Capital services

reduction in output and therefore a reduction in the demand for capital services. But
second, because the services of capital are
now cheaper in relation to the services of
labor, the firm will use more capital-intensive ways of producing output. This *substitution effect* tends to raise the demand for
capital. The net effect depends on the relative sizes of the cost and substitution effects.

What can be said about the net effect on
the demand for capital services? The more
inelastic final demand is, the less output
will fall, and hence the more the change in
the demand for capital is likely to be dominated by the substitution effect. On the

other hand, the less substitutable capital
and labor are, the more likely the cost effect
is to outweigh the substitution effect. We
show in Figure 15-7 the case where the cost
effect dominates, leading to a fall in the demand for capital services.

Given the downward shift of the *MVPK*
curve to *MVPK'*, what happens to the rental
and the quantity of capital services employed? In the short run, we assume that the
supply curve of capital services is vertical
at level K_0, as shown by curve *SS*. The shift
in demand for capital services thus moves
the industry to point E' from point E. The
rental rate for capital services in the industry falls substantially, to level R'. The rise in
wages thus is achieved in part at the expense of consumers, who pay more for the
final good, and in part at the expense of
the owners of capital, who receive less for
the services of their capital.

Adjustment in the Long Run

The move of the industry from E to E' in
Figure 15-7 is not the final adjustment. The
short-run move to E' reduces the rental received for capital services in this industry to
below the level, R_0, at which capital is supplied to the industry in the long run. In
other words, the rental on capital in this industry has fallen below the opportunity cost
of capital, or the required rental rate.

The firms supplying the rental services
of capital—they may be separate firms, such
as Avis or Hertz, or the firms that are actually using the capital—no longer find it
worthwhile to keep up the capital stock in
the face of wear and tear. They do not replace existing capital as it wears out. Consequently, the short-run vertical supply curve
moves to the left (not shown), and the industry travels up the *MVPK'* curve. This is
shown by the arrows. The economy will end
up at long-run equilibrium at E''.

As the industry moves up the *MVPK'*
curve, its use of capital services declines
over time. At the same time, the rental price

of capital in the industry rises toward its required level. The process continues until a new equilibrium is reached at E''.

When the supply of capital services to the industry is completely elastic, as on supply curve SS'', the industry's long-run adjustment in the market for capital services is entirely in terms of the quantity of services employed. The rental rate for capital in this industry has in the long run to be equal to rates elsewhere.

These conclusions, it should be emphasized, would be the same if we were talking about labor or any other factor. If a factor can be shifted to another industry, its return will not be (much) affected by demand conditions in a specific industry, except for as long as it takes the factor to move out when demand falls or move in when demand rises.

Short- and Long-Run Adjustment: More Examples

To make clear the difference between short-run adjustment and long-run adjustment, we present another application. Suppose that competition from imports reduces the demand for domestically produced textiles. Just as we saw in Figure 15-7, the demand curve for capital services shifts to the left, since at every final price less output is demanded, and hence less capital and labor are demanded. In the short run, the rental rate for capital declines to R'. Competition from imports in this example causes losses to the owners of capital in the affected sector.

It is not profitable to maintain all the plants in existence. Over time, the capital stock contracts, as depreciating capital is no longer replaced. In the long run some of the industry's capital stock (and firms) disappears until the new equilibrium at E'' is reached.

We emphasize again the distinction between the impact effect of a disturbance—the move from E to E'—and the long-run adjustment to point E''. In the short run, capital in a firm or industry cannot easily be moved into other sectors. Much of the capital is *sector-specific*—it is of little value in other sectors, certainly in the shortest term. Over time, by contrast, much of the capital stock can be moved between industries.

This distinction between the long run and the short run is important. In the short run, capital is mostly fixed, and its rental is very much demand-determined. The rental in a given industry is high if final demand in that industry is high, and it is low if demand is low. But over a relatively long period of time, capital within the economy and even within different economies is very mobile. Capital can leave industries or countries where the rental is low.

A striking example in this context is the German textile industry in the early seventies. Competition from imports reduced the rental on the existing stock of capital, and capital moved out. How? It was literally stripped down, put on railroad cars, shipped to low-wage Greece, and installed there to produce textiles for sale in Germany.

Table 15-8 shows the share of particular sectors of the economy in total investment or capital formation. It also shows the inflation-adjusted growth in investment for the period 1970–1980. The table reveals very strikingly that a threatened industry such as textiles, subject to competition from imports, experiences very little expansion in its capital stock. Petroleum, by contrast, after the 1974–1975 oil price increase, experienced a rapid expansion of investment.

6 THE PRICE OF CAPITAL ASSETS

So far we have taken the price of the machine or capital equipment as given. But now we want to ask what determines the prices at which different types of capital goods are sold. We are now concerned with the *asset price* rather than the rental price of capital.

TABLE 15-8

INVESTMENT PATTERNS

SECTOR	SHARE OF TOTAL INVESTMENT					GROWTH IN INVESTMENT FROM 1970 TO 1980, inflation-adjusted
	1960	1965	1970	1975	1980	
All industries	100.0%	100.0%	100.0%	100.0%	100.0%	39.2%
Textiles	1.0	1.2	0.7	0.6	0.6	0.4
Petroleum	7.9	7.4	7.1	9.3	10.0	69.8

Source: Statistical Abstract of the United States, 1980.

In equilibrium, the price of any asset is equal to the present discounted value of the returns that it yields. The first step in calculating the present value of a piece of machinery or a building is to work out how much rent it brings in each year and to subtract any expenses from owning the asset, such as depreciation or maintenance expenditures for each year. That gives the amount the asset returns to the owner each year. Then to obtain the value of the asset, and the price at which it will sell, calculate the present discounted value of the stream of returns, as indicated in section 2.

The present discounted value of the stream of rentals on an asset can change for two reasons. First, the future rentals may change. Second, the interest rate at which those future rentals are discounted may change. An increase in the real interest rate reduces the present value of future payments. Thus an increase in the real interest rate will reduce the value of an asset.

We now ask how the price of a capital asset changes when the rentals it receives changes. Specifically, suppose the wage in an industry rises. This is the case examined in Figure 15-7. Recall that the increase in the wage reduced the demand for capital services in the industry. As a result, the rental rate for capital in that industry fell.

The fall in the rental rate occurs because capital in the industry is assumed to be specialized. It cannot be sent to another industry for use there. The fall in the rental rate for capital causes a corresponding fall in the asset price of capital. Whoever owns the capital will now get a lower price for it, because for some time it will not generate much income for the owner.

So long as the owner of a machine cannot sell it for as much as it costs to build a new machine, no one in the industry will be buying new machines to replace those wearing out. As the old machines wear out and the rental rate on capital rises toward the long-run equilibrium level, the asset price of the machines in use in the industry will rise to the long-run equilibrium levels.

In long-run equilibrium, the price of any capital asset (a machine or a building) will be equal to the cost at which the good can be made. If the asset price were above the cost at which the good could be made, then more of the good would be produced. Builders would increase the number of houses built, and firms would make more machines. If the asset price were less than the cost at which the equipment could be produced—as was the case in the example discussed in this section—then the existing capital would be left to wear out, and the result would be a smaller capital stock.

Thus in long-run equilibrium, the price of a capital asset is equal to the cost at which the asset can be produced. It is also equal to the present discounted value of the rentals received by the owner of the asset.

7 LAND AND RENTS

It is time to return to land. The distinguishing feature of land is that it is in essentially fixed supply[13] (in the economy at large). There is not much that can be done about increasing the quantity of land.

Figure 15-8 shows the market for the services of land. Supply is inelastic. The demand curve, *MVPT*, is derived in the same way as the demand function for capital. It represents the marginal value product of land. The equilibrium rental rate is R_0. This corresponds to land rent, dollars per acre.

Now what happens to the rental of land when the demand for farm products rises? We know that the *MVPT* curve will shift upward, because land generates a higher value of marginal product as a result of the increase in the price of agricultural crops. The rental increases from R_0 to R'. The rent is higher because the demand for agricultural products has risen.

But now consider the economic position of the farmer who does not own but rather rents the land he works. He finds that the price of his product is higher, but at the same time the rent he has to pay has risen. He finds it hard to believe that he is better off as a result of the two events together—the rise in the price of the food he produces and the increase in land rent—and he may, indeed, not be any better off. He may not even see the connection, and he may complain that the rent increase is making it impossible to earn a decent living.

Indeed, at times when agricultural prices and land rents go up together, we sometimes hear of farmers who can no longer afford to pay the rent and therefore leave the business. Can this happen? It is possible that when the demand for some food product rises, land rents all tend to

[13] Why "essentially"? Because the quantity of land can be changed a bit through reclamation of land from the sea.

FIGURE 15-8   THE MARKET FOR THE SERVICES OF LAND. The *MVPT* curve is the marginal value product of land curve; it is also the demand curve for the services of land—just as the *MVPL* curve is the demand curve for the services of labor and the *MVPK* curve the demand curve for capital services. The supply of land to the economy is fixed, as shown by *SS*. The demand for land services determines the rental rate, R_0. When the demand curve shifts to *MVPT'*, the equilibrium rental rate for land increases to R'.

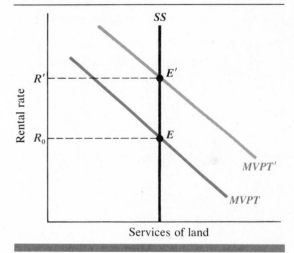

rise. Maybe someone who continues to grow the same crops as always finds he can no longer do so profitably. The market is trying to tell him to switch to another crop, the price of which is high enough to justify the rent on the land.

Because land is traditionally thought of as *the* asset in fixed supply, the word "rent" is often used to describe the return to any factor that earns a return by virtue of being in fixed supply.[14] For instance, we say that opera singers or baseball players earn rents for their ability. The demand for the services of a baseball player is a derived demand, based on the revenue he generates for the club for whom he is playing. Thus as we saw in Chapter 13, when we are told that baseball tickets cost a lot because of the high salaries that have to be paid to baseball

[14] This point was also discussed in Chapter 13.

players, we should think again. Baseball salaries are high because baseball players enable clubs to sell high-priced tickets.

Similarly, when there is an increase in the demand for food and food prices and agricultural land rents rise together, the land rents rise because food prices have risen. The food prices have not risen because the land rents are higher.

8 ALLOCATING A FIXED SUPPLY OF LAND BETWEEN COMPETING USES

Land is, of course, used for many different purposes—building roads, apartments, and houses; feeding sheep; growing alfalfa; and so on. What determines how land is allocated among its possible different uses, and how do changes in allocation affect the price and rental of land?

We simplify the analysis by assuming that there are only two industries, urban real estate and agriculture. Both use land. How is land allocated between the sectors? In Figure 15-9 we show on the horizontal axis the total amount of land in existence.

Land used in agriculture is measured from left to right, and land used in urban real estate is measured from right to left. Uses by the two sectors must add up to the total.

Now each sector, given the demand for its final goods, will have a demand curve for land as an asset.[15] Figure 15-9 shows the demand price for each type of land.

> The *demand price* of an asset is the amount that people are willing to pay for ownership of the asset.

The demand price is thus the asset price of the land.

The demand price is just the present discounted value of the rentals that will be earned on the land. The larger the amount of land employed in agriculture, the lower the marginal value product of the land and hence the lower the demand price for the land.

---

[15] We do the analysis here in terms of the asset price of the land. There is an equivalent analysis in terms of the rental rates paid for the use of the services of land. We choose to do the analysis here in terms of the asset price to illustrate the point made in section 6 that there is a close tie between the behavior of asset prices and rental rates for assets.

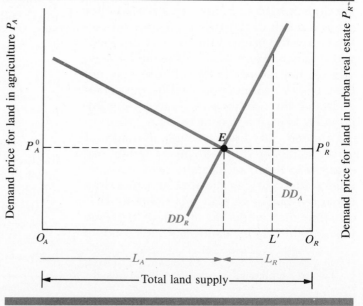

FIGURE 15-9 THE EQUILIBRIUM ALLOCATION OF LAND. The total supply of land is equal to the distance between O_A and O_R. Land may be used for agriculture or urban real estate. The demand for agricultural land is shown by DD_A. The demand curve for land in urban real estate is measured in the opposite direction. An increase in the use of land for real estate is shown by moving to the left. The demand curve slopes downward. When the sum of the demands for urban real estate and agriculture is equal to the total land supply, at E, we have equilibrium in the market. Point E gives the equilibrium price of land equal to P_A^0 and P_R^0. Amount L_A is used in agriculture, and amount L_R is used for urban real estate. With any other allocation—for instance, at L'—there would not be equilibrium. At L', the demand price for urban real estate is above that for agriculture, and land would be bid away from agriculture and toward urban real estate, with a move toward E.

FIGURE 15-10 THE EFFECT OF A TAX BENEFIT FOR HOUSING ON THE PRICE AND ALLOCATION OF LAND. The land market is originally in equilibrium at point E, with the equilibrium price for an acre of $P_R^0 = P_A^0$. A tax break is then provided for owner-occupied housing, thereby shifting the demand for urban real estate. City dwellers are now prepared to pay more per acre for any given amount of real estate in urban use. The demand curve for urban real estate shifts upward from DD_R to DD_R'. The new equilibrium will be at point E', with more land in urban real estate and less in agriculture, and with a higher price of land. In the short run, though, before the quantity of land in urban real estate can be changed, the demand price rises sharply to point B; it eventually falls as the market reaches equilibrium.

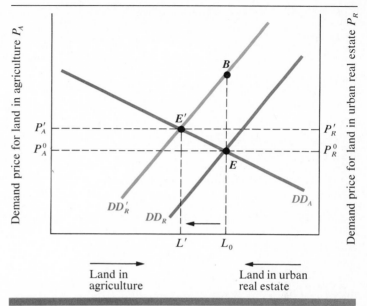

Thus schedule DD_A shows the demand price for land in agriculture, P_A, which is measured on the left-hand vertical axis. For urban real estate there is also a downward-sloping demand schedule, DD_R. The demand price for land here, P_R, is measured on the right-hand vertical axis. The quantity of land used in urban real estate is measured leftward from O_R, and so the demand curve looks backward. The slope of schedule DD_R shows that the demand price for urban real estate land falls as more land is used for urban real estate. Again, that is because the marginal value product of land in urban real estate falls as more land is used for urban real estate.

The (long-run) equilibrium allocation of land is determined at point E. At point E the demand prices, or the values, of land in the two sectors are equalized, with amount L_A of land employed in agriculture and amount L_R employed in urban real estate. If relatively more land was employed in agriculture and less in urban real estate, as at point L', the value of land to those in urban real estate would exceed the value of land to those in agriculture. Real estate businesses

would be buying up farms and using the land for residential sites until point E was reached.

In Figure 15-10 we use the apparatus to discuss the adjustment to a change. We assume that legislation is passed that gives people a subsidy for buying a home. The legislation lowers the rental cost of living in one's own home and therefore raises the demand price for homes and land in the real estate business. This is shown by the upward shift of the DD_R schedule to DD_R'.

At the initial equilibrium point, E, we now have a difference between the demand price for land in agriculture and the demand price for land in real estate. In real estate a piece of land commands a higher demand price than in agriculture because the subsidy becomes "capitalized" into the value of the land. Real estate businesses will therefore compete for land with those in agriculture, driving up the price and reducing the profitability and use of land in agriculture. The process continues until we reach point E', where demand prices are again equalized, now with a larger portion of land used for housing rather than agriculture.

BOX 15-1

THE ECONOMICS OF CAPITAL AND LAND—A SUMMARY

1   Capital and land are factors of production. This means that their use contributes to the production of goods and services.

2   The *rental rates* for capital and land are determined by the demand for and supply of their *services*.

3   The demand for the services of capital and land is determined by their marginal productivities.

4   The supply of the services of capital and land is typically fixed in the short run, both to the economy as a whole and to a particular industry.

5   The total quantity of land services available to the economy as a whole is fixed in the long run. But the quantity available to a particular industry can be adjusted by moving land out of one use and into another.

6   The total quantity of services of capital available to both an industry and the economy can change in the long run. For any particular industry, the supply of capital services may be perfectly elastic, as capital is produced and moved into the industry or taken out of it. For the economy as a whole, the long-run supply of capital services depends on the costs at which capital goods, which provide the services, can be produced.

7   The asset prices of capital and land are the present discounted values of the earnings expected to be received by holding the assets.

8   In the case of capital, where the asset can be produced, the long-run equilibrium price of any piece of capital equipment is the cost at which that good can be made. If the asset price is above the cost at which the good can be produced, then more will be produced. If the asset price is less than the cost at which the equipment can be produced, then existing equipment will be allowed to wear out.

The adjustment process of the price of land in urban real estate is interesting. In the short run the tax advantages lead to an immediate increase in the demand price from E to point B in Figure 15-10. In the long run, after some land has been converted from agricultural use to residential use, the price drops back somewhat from B to E'. The price rises more in the short run than it does eventually. There is thus a short-run *overshooting* of the price that is due to the fixed supply of land in urban use in the short run. But this overshooting of the price is precisely what provides the incen-

tive to bring about a rapid conversion of land use.

Before proceeding, you should check Box 15-1, which summarizes the economics of capital and land, to be sure you have the basic principles straight.

9   FACTOR PROPORTIONS

We have now learned how to determine the demand for capital in an industry, the asset price of capital (and land), and the allocation of land between alternative uses. Next we must ask what determines how much capital a particular industry uses. There are, of course, large differences in the amounts of capital employed in different sectors. Table 15-9 shows some examples of the amount of capital per worker in different industries.

The capital-labor ratios in Table 15-9 range from nearly $600,000 per worker in public utilities to only $14,000 per worker in the leather industry. For the public utilities, think of almost fully automated nuclear power plants. In the leather industry there is relatively little equipment per worker, and there is a relatively small requirement for structures. In between there is an entire range, with communications, for example, requiring plenty of capital (satellites and transoceanic cables), while services (barbershops and dry-cleaning establishments) and wholesale and retail businesses are typically labor-intensive. The differences in capital-labor ratios between industries at a given point in time are largely a reflection of the most cost-effective production methods.

Over time there have been interesting differences in the evolution of capital-labor ratios. Most industries have seen an increase in the amount of capital per worker. This has been so particularly in the most capital-intensive industries such as public utilities and petroleum. Innovations in technology have brought new ways of producing

output that are relatively automated and thus give rise to an increase in capital per worker. By contrast, in services and in the wholesale and retail trades the capital-labor ratio has risen only a little. This is a reflection of the fact that there has been relatively little technical progress of a kind that makes it possible to reduce the use of labor per unit of output. It still takes a barber to produce a haircut, even if there is now a faster pair of scissors around.

It may be surprising that agriculture is one of the industries in Table 15-9 with the fastest-growing capital-labor ratio.[16] Why has the capital-labor ratio for agriculture shown in Table-9 risen so fast? There has been a rapid mechanization of agriculture since 1950; by 1976 employment in agriculture had fallen to less than half its 1950 level. During the period 1950–1976 agricultural output rose by nearly 60 percent. The increasing mechanization thus produced a huge increase in output per worker in agriculture between 1950 and 1976.

As can be seen in Tables 15-3 and 15-9, there has been an upward trend in the entire economy's capital-labor ratio. Over time practically all sectors have increased the

[16] The capital-labor ratios shown for agriculture exclude the value of land. Including land would more than double the capital-labor ratios for agriculture shown in the table.

TABLE 15-9

CAPITAL PER WORKER
(In Thousands of 1980 Dollars per Person in the Industry)

INDUSTRY	1950	1976	INDUSTRY	1950	1976
Public utilities	326.5	724.2	Services	37.4	44.9
Petroleum	138.7	297.3	Textiles	15.6	36.7
Communications	95.6	272.3	Wholesale and		
Tobacco	67.2	115.7	retail	24.4	28.8
Chemicals	68.4	108.6	Construction	10.2	23.1
Agriculture	24.4	66.2	Leather	10.4	14.0

Sources: Statistical Abstract of the United States, 1980, Table 939. Agricultural data are from Federal Reserve System, *Balance Sheets for the U.S. Economy,* October 1981, and *Economic Report of the President, 1982.* (Data exclude value of land used in agriculture)

FIGURE 15-11 THE WAGE-RENTAL RATIO AND THE CAPITAL-LABOR RATIO (1980 = 100). Investment over the decades of the sixties and seventies increased the ratio of capital to labor and thereby helped increase the wage-rental ratio. Both the capital-labor ratio and the wage-rental ratio increased proportionately more in the sixties than in the seventies. (*Source: Handbook of Labor Statistics, 1980; Federal Reserve System, Balance Sheets for the U.S. Economy, 1981.*)

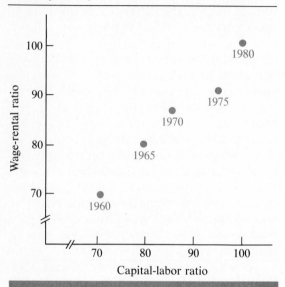

in both the wage-rental ratio *and* the capital-labor ratio over the last 20 years.

The facts in Figure 15-11 can be interpreted as follows. Over time the economy has increased its capital stock at a rate faster than the growth in the labor force. Therefore, the economywide capital-labor ratio has increased. The increase in the economywide capital-labor ratio, in turn, in combination with technological improvements, has raised the productivity of labor and thus the wage rate in relation to the rental for capital. This is the typical pattern for any economy in the course of long-term growth.

10 THE RATE OF RETURN ON CAPITAL

We have talked about the return on capital for most of the chapter. Now we look at the returns capital has earned in the U.S. economy. The rate of return on capital is defined as the income accruing to capital as a fraction of the value of the capital stock.

$$\text{Rate of return} \atop \text{on capital} = \frac{\text{income accruing to capital}}{\text{value of the capital stock}} \quad (4)$$

Since income is a dollar flow per unit of time and the value of the capital stock is a dollar amount, the ratio defined in equation (4) is a rate-per-period number. Estimates of the pretax and after-tax rates of return for nonfinancial corporations in the United States are presented in Table 15-10. "After-tax" refers to the correction for corporate profit taxes.

The first message of the table is that pretax rates of return on capital have typically been around 10 percent or more, except during the Great Depression. After-tax rates of return have been about 5 to 8 percent.

The 1930s and 1970s stand out for their particularly poor performance in the before-tax return on capital. For the 1930s this is not surprising, since the Great Depression left much of the nation's capital stock idle

amount of capital per worker, although some sectors have done so more than others. How can this upward trend in the economywide capital-labor ratio be explained? In Figure 15-11 we look at some facts. On the vertical axis we measure the economywide wage-rental ratio, and on the horizontal axis we show an index of the amount of capital per worker.[17] Both indices are equal to 100 in 1980. The figure shows an upward trend

---

[17] *Technical footnote:* There is no series available for the rental rate on capital. What we use instead is an approximation constructed by assuming that real interest and depreciation rates have stayed relatively constant. Thus interest plus depreciation times the price of capital moves approximately the same way as the price of capital. We therefore use the series for the price of nonresidential investment as our approximate index of the rental on capital.

TABLE 15-10

RATES OF RETURN FOR CAPITAL IN NONFINANCIAL CORPORATIONS
(Percent per Year)

	1929–1940	1941–1950	1951–1960	1961–1970	1971–1979
Pretax	6.3	16.9	12.4	13.3	9.7
After-tax	4.7	7.9	5.8	8.0	5.8*

* Estimate.
Sources: For 1971–1979, *Economic Report of the President, 1981,* p. 331; other data from Daniel M. Holland and Stewart C. Myers, "Trends in Corporate Profitability and Capital Costs," in Robert Lindsay (ed.), *The Nation's Capital Needs: Three Studies,* Committee for Economic Development, 1979.

and unprofitable. Part of the decline in the return on capital between the 1960s and the 1970s was a result of the higher unemployment and slower growth in the latter decade. More controversially, some blame inflation and increasing government regulation for further depressing the rate of return on capital.[18]

What is the implication of the decline in the rate of return for capital shown in Table 15-10? It might be expected that firms would be less willing to invest—to build new capital—if the rate of return on existing capital were low. Indeed, during the Great Depression, for example, there was little investment. But there was not a major decline in the rate of investment in the economy in the seventies.

Why has there been no noticeable de-

cline in investment rates in the economy? The answer lies in the distinction between the *average rate of return,* as shown in Table 15-10, and the *marginal* rate of return —the return expected on a particular new investment. In some sectors and for some projects prospective rates of return on capital may be very high even when average returns are low. For example, in petroleum there were high rates of return in the seventies and, accordingly, substantial investment. In other industries both average and marginal returns were low, and there was, accordingly, very little investment.

The distinction between the marginal, prospective return on capital and the actual, average return is essential to an understanding of the pattern of additions to the capital stock. New capital moves to the industries that have high expected returns on new capital. Thus U.S. automobile producers, for example, have negative rates of return for their present capital stock but find it profitable to invest in new plants to produce small cars, from which they expect a restoration of competitiveness and profitability.

---

[18] Martin Feldstein of Harvard and the National Bureau of Economic Research (and chairman of President Reagan's Council of Economic Advisers) has emphasized the interaction of inflation and taxation in reducing the rate of return on capital. See Martin Feldstein, "Inflation, Tax Rules and the Stock Market," *Journal of Monetary Economics,* vol. 6, July 1980, pp. 309–331. The role of regulation was discussed in Chapter 12.

SUMMARY

1   Physical (as opposed to financial) capital consists of real assets that are useful in production or in the household. Capital goods fall into four broad groups: consumer capital, structures and producer dura-

bles, residential structures, and inventories. Physical capital and land together make up tangible wealth. Tangible wealth yields a flow of services that is useful in production by firms or households or directly in consumption.

2   The value of tangible wealth in the United States is described by three numbers. In 1980 the ratio of tangible wealth to national income was about 3, the share of the national income going to the owners of tangible wealth was about one-quarter, and the value of production capital per worker was about $54,000.

3   Present value calculations allow us to translate receipts accruing in future time periods into current values. Because investments earn interest, a dollar tomorrow is worth less than a dollar today. How much less depends on the interest rate. The higher the rate of interest, the smaller the present value of a dollar tomorrow.

4   An investment grows in value over time if the interest is reinvested. It grows faster the higher the rate of interest. A dollar invested today at 10 percent will double in 7 years. At 5 percent it will double in 14 years. The fact that interest is being earned on the reinvested interest itself means that the growth of the value of the investment is accelerated.

5   The present value of a perpetuity is defined as the ratio of the annual rental to the rate of interest. A payment of $100 per year that is made indefinitely is worth $1000 when the interest rate is 10 percent.

6   There is an important distinction between real and nominal interest rates. The nominal interest rate indicates how much more *money* will be received (or paid) in the future as a result of saving (or borrowing). The real, or inflation-adjusted, interest rate is a measure of the extra goods that can be bought as a result of saving. The real interest rate is approximately equal to the nominal interest rate minus the inflation rate.

7   The demand for *capital services*, like the demand for labor, is a derived demand. The demand curve for capital services is the marginal value product of capital curve. It depends on final demand for the output and on the employment of other factors of production. The demand for capital services is higher the greater the demand for final goods and the larger the employment of other factors of production.

8   In the short term, the quantity of capital supplied to the economy is fixed. In the long term, capital is mobile between sectors either directly or because depreciating capital in declining industries is not replaced.

9   The required rental rate is the cost of operating a piece of capital. It depends on the price of the capital asset, the real interest rate, and depreciation costs. It is equal to the annual real interest plus the

depreciation costs of the asset. In long-run equilibrium in the market for capital services, the rental equals the required rental.

10   A rise in the wage rate affects the employment of capital in two ways. The wage increase raises the marginal cost of production and therefore reduces equilibrium output. This cost effect reduces employment of both capital and labor. But there is also a substitution effect that raises the demand for capital. Production methods which favor capital will be used. The net effect depends on the elasticity of final demand and on the substitutability between capital and labor in production. If there is no substitutability, the employment of capital must fall. If final demand is entirely inelastic, capital employment will rise.

11   The asset price is the price at which a piece of capital is bought and sold outright rather than rented. It is equal to the present discounted value of future rentals. In long-run equilibrium, the price of capital assets (goods that can be produced) will be equal to the cost at which they can be produced. This will be equal to the present discounted value of the rentals they earn. In the case of land, which cannot be produced, the asset price is just equal to the present discounted value of rentals.

12   There are substantial differences between sectors in the dollar value of capital per worker—more than $500,000 per worker in public utilities and less than $15,000 in the leather industry, for example. These differences in capital intensity are dictated by technology.

13   Over time there has been an increase in the capital-labor ratio in most industries, although the ratio has increased at very different rates across industries. The extent of increase in the capital-labor ratio has depended largely on innovations in technology. There has been substantial automation or mechanization in some sectors, such as agriculture, while in other sectors such as services the scope for mechanization has been relatively small.

14   Pretax returns to capital are typically around 10 percent; after-tax returns are around 5 to 8 percent. The rate of return on capital in the 1970s was lower in relation to the rate of return in the 1960s and in relation to the yield on alternative assets. This does not mean that there was an end to investment. Marginal, or prospective, returns on individual projects or in individual industries may still be high, even when the average rate of return for existing capital is low.

KEY TERMS

Physical capital	Financial wealth
Land	Rental rate
Tangible wealth	Present value (or present discounted value)

Nominal interest rate

Real interest rate

Services of capital

Marginal value product of capital

Required rental on capital

Opportunity cost of capital

Depreciation rate

Capital-labor ratio

Wage-rental ratio

Average rate of return on capital

Marginal rate of return on capital

PROBLEMS

1 Consider two countries with the following composition of employment:

	A	B
Agriculture	20%	80%
Other sectors	80	20

(a) Which economy is likely to have the higher capital-labor ratio? (b) Would you expect the employment breakdown for Korea to look more nearly like that for A or more nearly like that for B?

2 Explain why rich countries tend to have a relatively large share of the capital stock in the form of consumer capital.

3 In the U.S. economy, what part of every dollar of national income goes to capital and land, and how much goes to labor?

4 In the United States in 1980 the average member of the labor force cooperated with $54,000 worth of capital. In what way do you find this number (a) striking and (b) not representative of what is actually going on in different sectors?

5 (a) We count the stock of consumer durables—cars, TVs, washing machines, etc. —as part of the capital stock. But the consumer durables do not generate any income for their owners. Is it appropriate to regard them as part of the capital stock? (b) Consider an individual who is deciding whether to buy a washing machine or continue using a Laundromat. The cost of using the Laundromat is $2 per week. The washing machine costs $400, the interest rate is 10 percent, and other expenses of using the washing machine (including depreciation) amount to $1 per week. Does it make sense to buy the washing machine?

6 Draw the time profile of the present value of a payment to be received 2, 3, and 4 years from now with interest rates of 20 percent and 5 percent. Use a calculator to find the present values, and construct the equivalent of Table 15-5.

7 A bank offers you $1.10 next year for every 90 cents invested today. What is the rate of interest implicit in the deal?

8 It is possible for a firm to purchase a machine for $10,000. The machine yields an *MVPK* of $3600 for 2 years and can be sold at the end of the second year for $9000. Use the data in Table 15-5 to determine whether the machine is worth buying if the firm faces an interest rate of 10 percent.

9 Discuss the main determinants of the *MVPK*. First list these determinants systematically, and then use an example to illustrate the way in which they affect the response of the demand for capital services to a government tax on the final good.

10 Suppose that the interest rate increases from 10 percent to 15 percent. Discuss in detail how the increase in the interest rate affects the rental rate and capital stock in an industry in the short run and in the long run.

11 (a) Explain carefully the difference between the actual, or current, rate of return and the marginal, or prospective, rate of return. Which one affects investment? (*b*) Suppose that an industry (trucking, for example) experiences an increase in its energy costs because of an increase in oil prices. What is the effect on actual and prospective returns? Describe the investments that would take place.

12 (*a*) Suppose that a certain piece of land is suitable only for agriculture. Can it be the case that the farming industry will experience financial distress if there is an increase in the price of land? (*b*) How is your answer affected if there are alternative uses for the land?

APPENDIX: THE SIMPLE ALGEBRA OF PRESENT VALUES AND DISCOUNTING

The problem examined in this appendix is how to find a simple formula for the value today of payments to be received a year from now or at other times in the future. First we derive the formula for the 1-year case, and then we extend it.

Suppose that we invest a sum of K dollars today at an interest rate of i percent. For concreteness, assume that $K = \$100$ and that $i = 10$ percent or 0.1 per year. What will the value of the investment be after 1 year? After a year we get back the initial investment, or the *principal* ($K = \$100$), and we also receive the interest ($iK = \$10$). Therefore, we have the following pattern:

PRESENT INVESTMENT	NEXT YEAR'S VALUE
$K	$K + $iK = $K(1 + i)

Now suppose that we ask how much we have to invest, $X, to have $R next year. We fill in the entries as follows:

PRESENT INVESTMENT	NEXT YEAR'S VALUE
$X	$R = $X(1 + i)

The value of our investment next year will be our current investment plus interest, or $\$X(1 + i)$. For that to be equal to a given sum, say $R = \$100$, we can write the following:

$$\$X(1 + i) = \$R \quad \text{or} \quad \$X = \$R/(1 + i) = \$0.91R \tag{A1}$$

In equation (A1) we simply divided both sides by $(1 + i)$ to solve for the unknown current investment.

Equation (A1) is the general formula for pricing today's value of a receipt tomorrow. Today's value is equal to tomorrow's receipt ($R) divided by the term $1 + i$. We also call that division *discounting*. The term "discounting" refers to the fact that less than the face value of a future receipt is paid today for a claim on money in the future, as equation (A1) shows. The amount $R is *discounted* to $R/(1 + i)$ when a promise to pay $R in the future is sold today.

Now let us discuss the present value of a payment of $R to be received only 2 years from now. Does equation (A1) help us price that claim? It does, so long as we apply it in two steps. First we have to calculate the value next year of the payment to be received the year after next. The answer is obtained with (A1). Then we have to calculate the value *this* year of that amount. Here are the steps in the calculation:

To be received in year 2:	R
Value in year 1:	$R/(1 + i)$
Value in year 0:	$[\$R/(1 + i)]\,\dfrac{1}{1 + i}$

Example: $100
$91 (at 10% interest)
$83

The process of valuing a distant payment, then, simply involves the *repeated* application of the price of a payment to be received *one* period hence. Using the logic of the table, we find that a payment of $1 to be received 3 years from now is worth

$$\frac{1}{1 + i} \times \frac{1}{1 + i} \times \frac{1}{1 + i}$$

The present value of a payment to be received 10 years from now is equal to the term $1/(1 + i)$ multiplied by itself ten times. Any calculator will easily perform this calculation.

More generally, we can create a piece of notation. Let PV_k be the present value of a dollar to be received k years from now. Then we have the following:

**PRESENT VALUE OF A DOLLAR
k YEARS FROM NOW**

$k = 0$	$PV = \$1$
$k = 1$	$PV_1 = \$1/(1 + i)$
$k = 2$	$PV_2 = \$1/(1 + i)^2$
$k = 3$	$PV_3 = \$1/(1 + i)^3$
$k = 10$	$PV_{10} = \$1/(1 + i)^{10}$
$k = n$	$PV_n = \$1/(1 + i)^n$

It is clear from the formula that the present value of a future dollar falls as the payment date becomes more distant. At 10 percent a $1 payment to be received 10 years from now is worth only 39 cents today.

So far we have only looked at the present value of a single payment. What about a stream of payments—for example, year 1: $100, year 2: $50, year 3: $200? The present value of this stream of future payments is simply the sum of the present values of each of the pay-

FIGURE 15A-1   PRESENT VALUE OF $1.

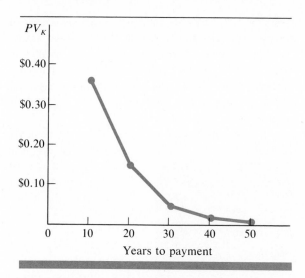

ments. If $\$R_k$ is the payment to be received in year k, the present value of the whole receipt stream is $PV_0R_0 + PV_1R_1 + PV_2R_2 + PV_3R_3$. If we use the numbers in the preceding example, we find that the sum is $\$91 + \$41.32 + \$125.60 = \$257.92$. Again we have assumed that $i = 0.1$.

Finally, we must determine the value today of a permanent stream of $\$R$ that is received year after year, from here to eternity. Clearly, we now have an infinite sum: $PV_0\$R + PV_1\$R + PV_2\$R + \cdots + PV_{100}\$R + \cdots + PV_{2500}\$R$ and so on. Even with the best of intentions you could not calculate the sum of the individual terms. Fortunately, as is known from algebra, the sum can be calculated from the formula:

Present value of a perpetuity of $\$R$ per year $= \dfrac{\$R}{i}$

If $R = \$100$ and $i = 10$ percent, then the present value of *all* future receipts is $\$1000$. In Figure 15A-1 we show the numbers for PV_k when the interest rate is 10 percent. This is an extension of Figure 15-2. It is seen in the figure that PV_{50} is only 1 cent. Most of the present value comes from payments in the near future, not from payments expected a couple of hundred years down the road. These very distant payments are worth almost nothing today.

PROBLEMS

1   How much should you be willing to pay today for an annual income of $\$5000$ for the next 5 years if the interest rate is 3 percent?

2   If the market price of a perpetuity is $\$200$ and the interest payment is $\$27$ per year, what is the interest rate?

What are the effects of limiting the workweek so that workers are not driven to exhaustion? Are the workers made better off or worse off? Why are more women working today? Why are families smaller than they used to be? Why do people marry? Does capital punishment deter crime? Should we tax cars on the basis of their size? Why is there a range of prices for the same good depending on where it is bought?

These are some of the questions that working economists try to answer. In this chapter we analyze questions like these and more—both to show how economics is used in practice and because the questions are interesting in their own right. The tools of analysis are simple and should be familiar by this stage, though perhaps the applications are unusual. At some points you may find yourself wondering whether economics is just saying what common sense said all along. But there is nothing that says common sense should not make economic sense. At other times you will wonder whether economists have a heart. But you should realize by the end of the chapter that describing some problem in economic terms does not imply that you always end up with a tough solution to the problem.

There is no unifying theme to this chapter beyond the fact that it applies the microeconomic theory we have learned to the analysis of real-world problems. Indeed, you will recognize that some of the material could easily have fitted into earlier chapters. We will take up a number of issues in turn, starting with the effects of maximum-hours laws.

16

Applied Economics in Action

1 MAXIMUM-HOURS LAWS FOR WOMEN: DOING GOOD OR TAKING ADVANTAGE?

In the period 1900–1920 many states in the United States passed laws restricting the number of hours per day and week that women could work. Supporters of the laws expressed their concern for the health of the women workers and the health and welfare of their children.

The humanitarian motivation for these laws is rarely questioned, but it takes an economist to be skeptical. Elisabeth Landes of the University of Chicago has suggested an altogether different interpretation: the maximum-hours laws were passed to reduce competition

FIGURE 16-1 INITIAL LABOR MARKET EQUILIBRIUM. Labor is supplied by both men and women, with the supply curves of each shown in (a) and (b), respectively. The total supply of labor is shown by curve SS_{m+f} in (c). It is the horizontal sum of supply curves SS_m and SS_f. The demand curve for labor is DD; employers do not discriminate between male and female employees. Demand is equal to supply at point A, with the wage equal to W_0 and total employment equal to L^o. Employment of males is equal to L_m and that of females to L_f, or the distance AB in the lower half of the figure.

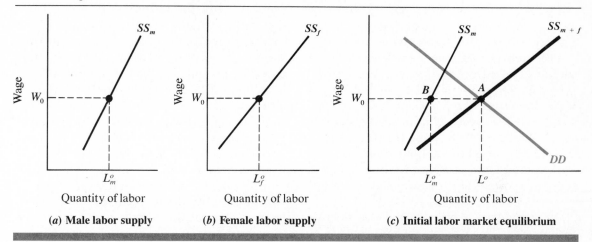

(a) **Male labor supply**   (b) **Female labor supply**   (c) **Initial labor market equilibrium**

in the labor market.[1] Rather than being considered as a reflection of humanitarian motives, she suggests, the laws should be seen as a move to reduce labor supply and thus raise wages and employment opportunities for men.

In the analysis of this issue supply and demand theory is applied to assess the effects of the laws on male and female workers. In Figure 16-1 we present the market for labor in the manufacturing sector. Both males and females supply labor, and we have to distinguish between their supply curves. On the supply side we show in part (a) the labor supply of male workers with the curve SS_m. With a higher wage there are more male workers offering their services to the industry, and each worker may want to work longer hours. Thus along SS_m male labor supplied (hours and number of workers) increases. Similarly, the supply curve

[1] Elisabeth M. Landes, "The Effect of State Maximum Hours Laws on the Employment of Women in 1920," *Journal of Political Economy*, June 1980.

for female labor, SS_f, slopes upward in part (b).

In part (c) we show the total labor supply, SS_{m+f}. This total is arrived at by adding the two supply curves in parts (a) and (b) horizontally. Thus the horizontal distance between SS_{m+f} and SS_m represents the female labor supply at each wage. Part of the increased labor supply in response to higher wages represents an increase in the number of hours worked. There is a downward-sloping demand curve for labor, DD. Firms do not care whether they employ male or female labor, so there is a single demand curve applying to all types of labor.

The initial equilibrium in the labor market is at point A, where the total quantity of labor demanded is equal to the quantity supplied at a wage, W_0, and an amount, L^o, of labor. The diagram allows us to split up the labor employed between men and women. Reading off the male supply at wage W_o we have an employment level of L_m^o. The total (L^o) minus male employment (L_m^o)

gives us the amount of female employment. This is equal to distance AB in part (c) of the figure, corresponding to the amount of female labor, L_f^o, in part (b).

We want next to look at the effects of laws restricting the number of hours women can work. Such laws were passed in many states. For example, to give a flavor of the legislation, in 1897 Pennsylvania passed a law restricting a woman's work hours to 12 per day or 84 per week.[2] Other states passed laws restricting the number of hours per day to the range of 8 to 11. How do we take these laws into account in our diagram?

In Figure 16-2 we show that the restriction on the number of hours women can work reduces the supply of labor. Women who before were offering at the given wage

to work more than the new statutory limits are now prevented from doing so. Hence the quantity of female labor supplied at each wage declines, and the total labor supply schedule shifts to the left. We have a new equilibrium in the labor market at point A' with the following features. First, the wage is higher than at A because the total supply of labor has declined. Second, women work fewer hours in total. The quantity of female labor supplied is $A'B'$, less than AB. Third, male workers supply a larger amount of labor at A' than they did at A. Previously, they supplied L_m^o. Now, at the higher wage, their supply is L_m'.

What should we make of the results? First, consider what the legislation does for men. It raises their wage and thereby makes them better off. Some of the men may work longer hours at the higher wage, but since they could always choose to work no more than before, we are sure they must be better off. What about the women? It's true that their wage has gone up, but the reason is that they no longer are able to work as long as they want.

Thus the results seem consistent with the Landes hypothesis. What appears to be protective legislation for women could be a scheme by an interested group of male workers to raise their own incomes by restricting the total labor supply. And it is done skillfully, because the restrictions are imposed on women, not men. Furthermore, as Elisabeth Landes shows, the people who were most affected were new immigrant and first-generation American women who worked long hours to try to get themselves and their families established in the United States.

In the particular instance of the maximum-hours laws, the costs of the laws were apparently borne in good part by the immigrant women who worked long hours and were then prevented by the laws from working as much as they wanted. But is it clear

---

[2] To our modern ears, 84 hours sounds like an impossibly long workweek. It was well above average in 1897, but not impossible.

FIGURE 16-2 EFFECT OF A MAXIMUM-HOURS LAW FOR WOMEN. The maximum-hours law shifts the supply curve for female labor to the left, leaving the male supply curve unaffected. The total supply of labor in the market, SS_{m+f}, therefore moves to the left, to SS'_{m+f}; the reduction in the quantity of labor supplied at each wage is due to the lower female quantity of labor. The new equilibrium is at point A', with a higher wage, W', and a lower quantity of labor supplied, L'. But the male labor supplied has risen from L_m to L_m', while the quantity of female labor supplied has fallen from AB to $A'B'$.

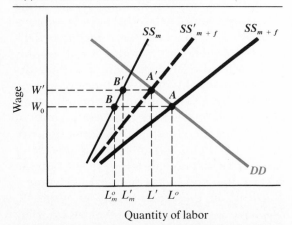

that there were actually losses for these women, and can we be sure that they were in fact worse off? Figure 16-2 shows that the women work fewer hours, but it is also true that the wage rate increases. It is quite possible that the actual incomes earned by women could increase. This is more likely the more inelastic the male labor supply and the more inelastic the demand for labor.[3] If women's incomes are higher at A' than at A and there are fewer hours of work, women are better off as a result of the passage of the law. Even if the law was intended to benefit male workers, it would in this case benefit female workers too.

To understand this result, we can think about how a trade union increases the income of its members. It does so by restricting the supply of labor. The 84-hours law also restricts the labor supply, and it is therefore not surprising that it might make all workers better off.

It is worthwhile stopping a minute to ask what might be wrong with the legislation to keep women from working more than 84 hours a week, even if it did reduce total female income. After all, is it not terrible that anyone should be working more than 84 hours a week? This is where the economist may sound heartless but where some thought will show that that is not so. If someone is working more than 84 hours a week, which is certainly undesirable, there must be a reason—for instance, to keep the children in the family from starving. Now if it is terrible that someone should work that long, then by all means do something about it—but be sure that you don't at the same time make the original problem worse. If there is no assistance available for starving children, then preventing their mothers from working is not kind but heartless.

Other Protective Legislation

There is a broader principle involved in the analysis of this section. It is the fact that standards legislation, safety legislation, or protective legislation frequently has goals or effects other than the directly apparent ones.[4] Take the example of airline pilots. There is a very large supply of commercial pilots, in part as a result of military training of pilots. But pilots' salaries are extremely high. How do the pilots' unions make sure that the services of their members do not go at a lower wage?

One effective tool for keeping up the wage is to reduce the labor supply to an industry. This could be done through licensing requirements that are sufficiently tough or costly to restrict the supply of interested people. This approach has worked well for the medical profession, which licenses medical schools and doctors and makes sure that the training process is long and expensive. Pilots have taken a different route to restricting the labor supply. They have set maximum hours that commercial pilots are allowed to fly per month. This rule, of course, reduces the labor supply in terms of hours of flying time for each individual pilot and therefore for all pilots together. In this way competition is prevented and wages are kept high.

As long as all airlines had the same union agreement, they all operated with low-hours, high-cost pilots, and therefore none of them suffered a *relative* disadvantage. However, the issue of pilots' salaries became a serious one for the existing airlines as soon as deregulation of the airline industry allowed new, nonunion carriers

---

[3] You should experiment by drawing your own supply and demand curves with differing elasticities of supply and demand to check this statement.

[4] For an example similar to that of female workers, see Howard P. Marvel, "Factory Regulation: A Reinterpretation of Early English Experience," *Journal of Law and Economics*, October 1977. Marvel argues that English legislation to control child labor was an attempt by one group of factory owners to damage a competing group.

into the business. Nonunion pilots flew twice the number of hours for about half the pay of their union counterparts. The nonunion airlines therefore had a large competitive edge. The pilots' union will no doubt press for legal standards in the industry which will set maximum hours for pilots in the interest of air safety.

2　THE ECONOMICS OF TIME USE AND OF THE FAMILY

Time is scarce, and for that reason the consumer wants to allocate time optimally or, to use less jargon, to make the best use of his time. The consumer's time allocation problem is very similar to the consumer's budget allocation problem. Time has to be allocated to various activities, just as income has to be allocated among various goods. Indeed, the allocation of time is an integral part of the consumer's optimal consumption decisions.

The theory and empirical study of the economics of time use were pioneered especially by Professor Gary Becker of the University of Chicago[5] and have been pursued in a large number of studies. In this section we briefly take up a few of the problems that have been analyzed by those working on the economics of time use and the associated economics of the family.

The starting point is that the consumer has to allocate scarce time (24 hours per day) among competing activities: enjoying life, staying alive and functional, and earning income. In other words, the choice is between leisure, household activities, and market activities. The consumer has to decide how much of his time to spend on each

[5] Gary S. Becker, "A Theory of the Allocation of Time," *Economic Journal*, September 1965. Staffan Burenstam Linder, *The Harried Leisure Class*, Columbia University Press, New York, 1970, discusses the increasing pressure on time that has come with greater affluence.

activity and how to pursue each activity in the most cost-effective way.

This is all very general. Now we examine some applications of the approach.

Time Intensity of Leisure

There are alternative kinds of leisure: going around the world on foot, spending a 3-day weekend in Paris, getting drunk on Saturday night. Who is likely to engage in leisure activities that use a lot of time? Who will take leisure intensively, using little time and many purchased inputs—airline tickets or gadgets? It is not difficult to see that people with a high opportunity cost of time —high wages—would opt for leisure activities that are time-saving and intensive in purchased inputs. Conversely, people who have no alternative use of time or a relatively low wage would be using time-intensive means of leisure.

In discussing the theory of the choice of leisure activities, we do not mean by "leisure" merely time spent not working. Instead, leisure, as we talk about it here, is measured by the satisfaction consumers get from combining goods and time to enjoy themselves.

The consumer combines time and goods to produce leisure. The cost of time for the consumer is the wage. The cost of goods is what we normally think of as the cost, namely the money price. Now if we think of someone going on vacation for a week, we should think of the vacation as costing not only the price of the hotel and the airfare but also the value of the time given up by the consumer to enjoy that vacation.

Suppose we consider two people with equal wealth, one of whom is retired and the other still working. Who is likely to take longer holidays? It will be the retired person rather than the one who is working. That is because the opportunity cost of time for the retired person is much lower. That is one reason why ocean cruises are taken more by retired rich people than by working rich people. The working rich person will probably spend as much money on a brief vacation, flying to an exotic spot for quick excitement rather than taking time for a slower vacation.

Household Appliances and Services

Another area where the economics of time is applied is in studying the production of "household services"—keeping the house clean, looking after the clothing and laundry, preparing food, and doing the shopping. Here, too, the consumer has to combine purchased inputs—goods—and time.

These activities are organized with a rational use of time in mind. The higher the wage relative to the prices of household appliances, the more appliances are owned by the household—vacuum cleaners, blenders, refrigerators, freezers, electric dental equipment, etc. These are all means by which the household can save on the use of time in producing household services. A refrigerator, for example, makes it possible to store goods and thus cut down on the number of shopping trips.

An interesting example is the washing machine. We would think that those with a relatively low opportunity cost of time (students) go to a Laundromat, spending time queuing and producing household services with rented equipment. People with higher wages own a washing machine. They do spend time, but less time because they have more exclusive and convenient access. People with still higher wages use a drop-off service and rent other people's time for the production of their household services.

In these cases it is important to distinguish between the role of the wage rate as the cost of time and the wage rate as an indication of how much income a household has. Of course, richer households are more likely to own a washing machine than to use a Laundromat. Where the theory of the allocation of time is used to make interesting predictions is, for instance, in the case of the behavior of two families, each with the same total income. In family A both the husband and the wife work, and in family B only the husband or the wife works. Family A is much more likely to use a drop-off service for its laundry than family B, because the marginal cost of the nonworking spouse's time in family B is lower than the marginal cost of time for either partner in family A. The point is that we want to isolate the wage rate as the cost of time rather than as an indication of how rich people are.

The role of the wage rate in determining how household services are produced can be seen also when we compare countries. Specifically, compare a rich country with a less developed one and consider two families with the same high income level, one family in each country. The rich family in the less developed country is far more likely to use labor- or time-intensive methods of producing household services than the rich family in the developed country. The rich family in the developed country will have a washing machine, at least one vacuum cleaner, a microwave oven, and other gadgets. The rich family in the developing country will have servants, along with much less machinery. A rich person in a developing country will have a chauffeur, whereas a person at the same income level in a developed country will use taxis. That is because time (someone else's time, to be sure) is available at a cheaper rate in the developing country.

Marriage and the Gains from Trade

One application of the theory of household time use has been in the area of marriages. The view, advanced particularly by Gary Becker, is that the nature of marriage has long been misunderstood. While marriage no doubt has something to do with affection or perhaps even love, there is an overriding economic motivation. Together the partners can run their lives better. There are economies of scale in cooking, cleaning, and living and certain complementarities that lead people to get together in a trading arrangement called marriage. They may decide to specialize if one partner has a comparative advantage in producing household services and the other has an advantage in producing market services (cash income). Or efficiency may suggest in some cases that they both engage in market activities.

To a considerable extent, this is a statement of the obvious in another language. But the theory does have predictions, particularly about how the partners in the marriage will allocate their time.[6] We should expect the partner who has the comparative advantage in market activities to work more in the market and the other partner to work more in household activities. Table 16-1 summarizes the results of a study of the use of time by households. The study confirms these predictions and others that are implied by the theory of marriage and the allocation of time.

[6] The theory does not distinguish between marriage and cohabitation.

The entries in the table show how an increase in the variables in the first column affects the allocation of time by the wife and the husband. For instance, the first minus sign in the top row of the table shows that an increase in the husband's wage causes the wife to allocate less of her time to work in the market. But, going to the next two entries in that row, the wife does not increase the amount of time spent working at home. Instead, she increases her leisure time. An increase in the wife's wage does not affect the amount of time the husband spends at work in the market, but it does make the husband work more at home. The question marks in the table mean that the particular result is probably as shown but is not statistically reliable.

Another interesting finding is that having children causes the wife to reduce her work in the market, while the husband increases market work, presumably to make up for the wife's lost income and to pay for the extra cost of the children.

Is this economics? Of course. For one thing, the analysis is performed by leading economists. In addition, the question of how the wife allocates her time bears directly on the labor supply, and this is certainly something we regard as economics.

TABLE 16-1

THE DETERMINANTS OF THE ALLOCATION OF TIME

	WIFE			HUSBAND		
	WORK IN THE MARKET	WORK AT HOME	LEISURE	WORK IN THE MARKET	WORK AT HOME	LEISURE
United States (1964):						
Husband's wage	−	0	+	+	−	+(?)
Wife's wage	+	−	−	0	+	−(?)
Nonwage income	−(?)	−	+	−	0	+
Total number of children	−	+	−	+	+(?)	−
Existence of preschool children	−(?)	+	0	+	+(?)	−

Source: Reuben Gronau, "Leisure, Home Production and Work in the Theory of the Allocation of Time Revisited," *Journal of Political Economy,* December 1977. Copyright © University of Chicago.

One of the most striking developments in the economy since the fifties has been the rapid increase in the participation of women in the labor force. In 1950 only one-third of the females over 16 were in the labor force; by 1980 over half were. The economics of the allocation of time, as in Table 16-1, is directed precisely to an understanding of such trends.

Children

By now you will not be surprised to learn that people nowadays have fewer children, because children are a time-intensive means of producing consumer utility. The continuing rise in real wages has shifted demand toward more market-purchased sources of utility and away from home- or self-produced activities such as home singing, knitting, carving, or childrearing.

It is customary in the approach we are now reviewing to measure the quantity of children by the amount of utility they yield. Fewer children receive more individualized attention and more inputs from the parents, and so the total amount of children consumed in this view does not fall as much as the number of children falls. The quality of children rises: they are better educated, healthier, and, in sum, better providers to their parents of "child services." Instead of having five brats the family has two semi-brats.

Can this be serious? It obviously has its lighter side, but even here there is an important point. The amount of investment in human capital that parents undertake in their children will depend on family size, which is indeed affected by economic variables such as the wage rate.

To summarize the material of this section, what we see is simple price theory in action to attack problems that might not at first reaction be thought of as economic. But in each case a problem of the allocation of resources is being analyzed, wages and

other prices are relevant, and the economist's tools can be applied. Insofar as the focus of the theory is on the allocation of time between home and market activities, the theory does give a basis for studying changes in market participation rates. Similarly, this approach to child raising provides a basis for studying parents' decisions on how much human capital to give their children—for instance, by paying for their education. Also, in the analysis of fertility, which is a natural extension of the material being discussed here,[7] the theory can be expected to shed light on future population trends.

3 THE ECONOMICS OF SEARCH AND INFORMATION

In the economics we have done so far, the consumer or producer knows everything there is to know about the environment in which he operates. In Chapter 19, we will discuss behavior under uncertainty, but that relates to things that will happen in the future—things that the consumer or producer can't know about now. In this section we will look at several problems of *imperfect information*, which is different from uncertainty about the future. Here we will be dealing with information that is in principle available, though in practice it does not pay to get it.

We start with the topic of price dispersion. A particular good can typically be bought at different prices in different places. Why? And how much do the prices vary?

Price Dispersion

Someone went shopping for sand for his kids' playground and thought that the

---

[7] See, for instance, Michael P. Ward and William P. Butz, "Completed Fertility and Its Timing," *Journal of Political Economy*, October 1980.

quoted price was high. Even though he had thought that sand was basically sand, he did some more shopping and to his surprise found that prices were far from equal across sellers, even for a commodity as standardized as sand. To find out more, a systematic study was conducted; the Boston Yellow Pages and a telephone survey were used to find the distribution of prices among sellers for a sample of 39 goods. Table 16-2 shows some of the results. In each case the table shows the number of sellers sampled and an index which is the ratio of the maximum price to the minimum price multiplied by 100. This index is a rough measure of the spread of prices.

Faced with the evidence in Table 16-2 of price differences of up to 567 percent (a value of the discrepancy index of 667), we are at first inclined to think that the goods

are not identical. A canvas good could be a Gucci handbag or a coal bag, and the prices would therefore differ. But in fact an attempt was made in the telephone survey to standardize as far as possible, and we therefore accept for the present the idea that the goods are homogeneous, more or less. This is our question: Why, in markets that we would think are not particularly oligopolistic or in markets where there is no reason to suspect product differentiation, do prices differ?

This dispersion, if it indeed applies to identical products, contradicts our model of the competitive firm, which takes price as given and produces at the point where marginal cost is equal to the given price. The evidence in Table 16-2, on the contrary, shows that prices can differ widely, whether they are for horoscopes or skates.

TABLE 16-2

PRICE DIFFERENCES AMONG 20 PRODUCTS

PRODUCT	NUMBER OF FIRMS	MAXIMUM ÷ MINIMUM (×100)
Bicycle	7	111
Boat	15	197
Service stations	15	148
Lumber	14	137
Cameras	15	142
Pet washing	8	150
Liquor stores	11	123
Carnations	7	250
Horoscope	4	500
Vocal instruction	12	265
Canvas goods	14	638
Diamond appraisals	12	200
Peanuts	8	209
Auto tune-up	15	183
Styling brush	12	667
Turntable	9	130
Repair clarinet	8	233
Skates	15	139
Board poodle	13	183
Calculator	12	142

Note: For detailed product descriptions, see original article.
Source: John W. Pratt, David A. Wise, and Richard Zeckhauser, "Price Differences in Almost Competitive Markets," *Quarterly Journal of Economics,* May 1979.

Search Costs and Imperfect Information

Much of the modern theory of market structure emphasizes the role of imperfect information. Consumers do not know all the prices that all potential suppliers of a product are currently charging. The consumer may not be aware of the existence of some sellers or of the fact that a particular seller may have a sale while another has just raised prices. Moreover, in multicommodity stores, prices will not differ uniformly. It is most unlikely that all prices in one store will be, say, precisely 10 percent higher than prices in another store.

We ask now why consumers have incomplete information about prices and why prices are widely dispersed. To answer the questions we first have to formulate the consumer's problem in figuring out how to look for low prices and where to buy. This is the consumer's *search problem*.[8]

The first point to make is that there is a great difference between commodities that are bought often and commodities that are very infrequently purchased. We look first at the search problem of a consumer who plans to purchase a turntable. This is not an everyday event, but it was undertaken by the authors of Table 16-2.

Figure 16-3 shows the marginal cost MC and the marginal benefit MB of search. First think of the marginal cost. There are two elements to this cost. There is the time cost of sampling different shops, inspecting the goods, and getting price quotations. This time cost is quite real because in the case of an item that is purchased infrequently, the consumer will not think of the item as a standard product that can be readily telephone-sampled. The second item on the cost side is purchased inputs that facilitate

---

[8] See George Stigler, "The Economics of Information," *Journal of Political Economy*, June 1961. Stigler received the 1982 Nobel Prize in economics in part for his work on information and search.

FIGURE 16-3   OPTIMAL SEARCH IN A MARKET WITH PRICE DISPERSION. The cost of visiting one extra firm to discover its price is constant; it is labeled *MC*, the marginal cost of search. The expected benefit from each given number of searches is shown by the *MB* curve. The benefit is positive, since the minimum price that is expected to be found is lower the more firms that are visited. But the marginal benefit declines; as more firms are visited, it is less likely that the price in the next firm will be lower than the minimum price that has already been discovered. This is shown by the *MB* curve. The optimal number of firms to visit is shown by N_0, the point at which the marginal benefit from searching is equal to the marginal cost.

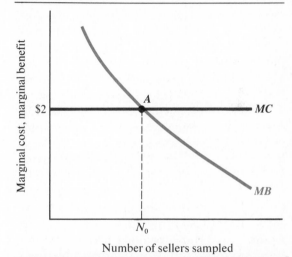

Number of sellers sampled

search—for example, gasoline, the Yellow Pages, phone calls, and a shopping guide. We assume that the marginal cost of searching is constant. That is, sampling yet another supplier neither increases nor reduces the marginal cost. For concreteness we will assume that the marginal cost of sampling one more seller is $2.

The marginal benefit of search takes the form of a reduction in the price at which we expect to buy the product. The more sellers that are sampled, the lower the minimum price the consumer is likely to get. But there are also diminishing returns to search. As we sample more and more sellers, it becomes increasingly unlikely that the next seller will have a price that is lower than the lowest price we have already found. Therefore, the marginal benefit of sampling more sellers is declining.

The optimal search will stop at point A, where the marginal cost of search, or sampling another seller, exactly matches the marginal benefit that is expected from making a visit to yet one more seller. At that point we look over our whole sample and go back to the shop that quoted the lowest price. But since the consumer stops without looking at all possible sellers, there is room for price divergences. Only if every consumer sampled every seller and then bought from the cheapest could nobody afford to charge more than the cheapest. So long as the search stops short of being complete, there is room for price dispersion.

This discussion raises two points. The first is that we once again see in this context the role of time as a scarce resource, because time costs are the main reason why consumers do not search the whole market. The other point worth raising is this: Even if sellers can, because of imperfect information, get away with charging different prices, why would they? Here we must make a distinction. Are there sellers who *always* charge a higher price than other sellers, or are there random differences in prices where some shops are high sometimes and others are high at other times? The second possibility is always present. It arises because sellers themselves find it hard to stay informed of the prices that are charged by all other sellers in a world of changing costs for their products. Whatever stops the consumer from being completely informed must also be happening to some extent to the seller.

The more interesting situation concerns one seller who consistently charges higher prices. This does not seem to be compatible with the notion of competition in an integrated market. Two possibilities arise. One is that the seller has a locational advantage

—selling cigars in the lobby of the best hotel in town, for example. The convenience of the location allows the seller to charge higher prices, but the location itself has to be paid for with a higher rent. Thus the goods are really not identical because of the location of the seller. If there were no locational considerations at all and no other differences between goods—such as the quality of the service—we would expect that in the long run competing firms would enter the market to take away the profits of the high-price firms.

Price differences can persist, though, if different firms cater to different groups of customers. This is the phenomenon of the tourist trap, whose customers are mostly from out of town, versus the high-quality neighborhood restaurant, whose customers are mostly local. Tourists pay more for restaurant food, transportation (the wandering cab driver), and other goods than the locals do. Why? Tourists are the best example, as Stigler has pointed out, of customers who do not find it worth their while to sample different sellers at any length. Unlike local inhabitants, they go to the restaurants for only a few meals, not for a lifetime, and therefore have much lower expected returns from search. But how can sellers take advantage? Why do they not compete prices down to the level of costs? Here we are on the borders of imperfect competition with no simple answers.

It is worth saying a few words about price dispersion with regard to goods that consumers habitually buy. Do we expect a larger dispersion for items that occupy a large or a small share of the budget? Clearly, continuing search pays more the larger the expected saving from finding the low-cost seller. But the saving is larger the larger the budget share of the item we are considering. If you can save 10 percent on an item that takes 30 percent of your bud-

TABLE 16-3
PRICE DISPERSION

	FREQUENCY OF PURCHASE	
BUDGET SHARE	HIGH	LOW
High	Low	?
Low	?	High

get, you gain more than if the budget share were only one-half of 1 percent. For goods with repeated purchase, prices should show less dispersion when those goods have a relatively high budget share.[9]

To summarize, we look at Table 16-3, which—given search costs—identifies the two main determinants of the price dispersion that we would expect to observe. Commodities with a high frequency of purchase and a high budget share have the highest payoff for search and should have the least dispersion of prices. Items with a low budget share and a low frequency of purchases are at the other extreme and should have a high price dispersion.

Search for Employment

Search is an important issue in labor markets, just as in the market for consumer goods. We will discuss labor market search in the part of this book that covers macroeconomics, but it is worth introducing the issue here. Suppose that someone loses a job and wants to find a new one. If information were complete, the person would immediately move into a new job; the person would know where to find the employer who has the best opening at the right pay.

[9] For an empirical investigation of these ideas applied to food prices in New York, see Roger E. Alcaly, "Information and Food Prices," *The Bell Journal of Economics,* autumn 1976, and Howard P. Marvel, "The Economics of Information and Retail Gasoline Price Behavior: An Empirical Analysis," *Journal of Political Economy,* October 1976.

Information about the availability of jobs is poor in two respects. Potential workers do not know where jobs are available. Nor do they know the wage and other conditions of employment. Therefore, workers have to search for potential employers, have interviews to gather information about jobs, and keep on searching until they find the job they think it best to take. The process is, of course, two-sided: firms that have openings are searching for the right workers; they are trying to get the right person for each job. The process is known as job matching. Search in the job market is likely to be particularly difficult because the average worker in a well-functioning economy does not look for a job very often and therefore has little information.

The issue of search in the labor market is important because it has been argued that a good part of observed unemployment is not unproductive waste but rather the pursuit of efficient search activities. Moreover, it has been argued that because unemployment benefits lower the cost of search for the unemployed, they raise search time and unemployment. More on these issues when we come to macroeconomics.

Lemons

Incomplete information changes our views of how competitive markets work. We expect price dispersion and search unemployment as part of the process by which resources are allocated efficiently, given the costs of gathering information. For instance, in a well-functioning rental market for apartments, we expect there to be vacant apartments waiting for an occupant. We could even think of an apartment as being passively engaged in search.

But problems with incomplete information may be so serious as to destroy markets altogether. In a famous paper Berkeley's George Akerlof has drawn attention to the information problem posed by markets where buyers and sellers do not have the same information about product quality.[10]

Suppose we take the example of cars and for the moment think of a world in which there is complete information. In this world there would be a price structure for used cars that would reflect solely the known characteristics of each car. An older car would be cheaper than a newer car because of more wear and tear, and a car that is known to have a cough would go for less than a car that is well behaved. Each car would be priced in accordance with its objective qualities.

Now depart from these assumptions and go to a world where sellers know the qualities of their car but buyers do not. Suppose, to make the story realistic, that there are two kinds of sellers. There are those who would like to buy a new car fairly often and are willing to part with their used car at the objective value—a value based on, say, age and mileage. They would not sell for less; they would prefer instead, to go on using their vehicle. The other group consists of owners of lemons. They would love to sell at a price based on mileage and age, thus concealing that they are trying to get rid of a lemon to replace it with a well-functioning car.

The buyer faces these sellers and does not know whether he is talking to the owner of a good car or to the owner of a lemon. If the chances of acquiring a lemon are sufficiently high, and the costs of establishing the quality of the product are sufficiently high, the market for good used cars may disappear altogether. Buyers know there is a chance that they might get a lemon, and certainly they are not willing to pay a price equal to the full value of a car that is not a lemon. Therefore, the sellers of the good used cars do not sell. All that is left in the market are lemons. Asymmetric information has destroyed the market for good used cars.

Where exactly does the problem arise? It is apparent that if sellers gave a money-back guarantee, the entire information problem would be resolved. Failing such a guarantee or a cheap way of checking out the quality of the good, the buyer has no way of establishing whether he is buying fair value or a lemon. Carrying our story a bit further, we know, of course, that not all 1-year-old cars in the used-car market are lemons, contrary to the result above. Part of the reason is that there are owners of used cars who will be prepared to take *some* loss below the fair replacement value of a good car when they want to sell. This may be because they are about to move or because they want to get a flashy new car. We can say, though not accurately, that some people "have to" sell even good used cars.

Because some people must sell and therefore set the price below the fair replacement value, other people enter the secondhand market. In part these are people who buy secondhand cars because they may not be able to afford new cars. In part they are speculators who are willing to gamble on acquiring either a lemon or a good car; they are induced to come into the market because prices are below fair replacement costs.

The secondhand market is thus a place where the poor, sellers of lemons, speculators, and distress sellers mingle. Order is restored by dealers who establish a "reputation" and create a market. The dealers can use their expertise to distinguish between lemons and better cars. Their reputation is earned if they sell at the right price —lemons go for less than good cars. The consumer's problem, then, becomes one of knowing whether a dealer is reputable. Dealers have a variety of devices for trying to

---

[10] See George Akerlof, "The Market for 'Lemons': Quality Uncertainty and the Market Mechanism," *Quarterly Journal of Economics*, November 1970.

establish that they are reputable—for instance, 90-day guarantees. But, of course, the buyer always has to beware, because of the fact that all dealers prefer to be thought of as reputable.

In this section we have seen that taking account of imperfect information substantially modifies the way we expect markets to work. Imperfect information may even make it impossible for some markets to exist. Imperfect information persists because it is overwhelmingly costly to gather all relevant information, and it may in any event be impossible to process the information, because human capabilities are limited. The economics of imperfect information helps make sense of phenomena that we meet in our daily lives. For instance, do sellers advertising on radio or TV typically offer a money-back guarantee?

4 EXTERNALITIES AND INTERVENTION

Failures of the marketplace occur whenever there are *externalities*. We talk of externalities when prices do not lead individual households or firms to take into account the full *social* costs or benefits of a private action. Firms and individuals use resources to the point where the marginal private cost equals the price. If the private cost is equal to the social cost, private individuals will be doing the socially optimal thing. But when there are spillover effects that are not priced—congestion, littering, deforestation, hazardous driving, drunkenness, poverty, pollution, noise, manners, and customs—then private maximization does not lead to optimal resource allocation, and society can be made better off by placing corrective taxes or subsidies on the activities that involve externalities. We will now look at some examples to illustrate the very general principles of resource *mis*allocation.

Optimal Car Size

Individuals choose their car size in a highly rational manner. Other things equal, they tend to prefer a larger car because of the comfort, space, and power it affords. But they do take into account that total automobile cost, both for purchase and operation, increases with size. They also recognize that the more congested the area in which they operate their vehicle, the larger the disadvantage of a larger car in terms of ability to park and squeeze through traffic. What is the optimal car size that emerges from these considerations?

In Figure 16-4 the schedule MB shows the marginal benefits of car size. These marginal benefits are positive, at least up to a

FIGURE 16-4 CHOOSING THE OPTIMAL CAR SIZE. The marginal cost of buying bigger cars is shown by the *MC* curve: the bigger the car, the higher the cost. We show the *MC* curve upward-sloping. The marginal benefit of buying a larger car is positive but decreasing, as shown by the *MB* curve. The larger the car the better, but the marginal benefit becomes small when the car is large. The consumer initially chooses a car of size S_0. If the marginal cost of buying a car of a given size were higher, as on curve *MC'*, the consumer would choose a smaller car size *S'*. In each case the marginal cost curve should be thought of as showing the *private* marginal cost—the increase in cost to the consumer.

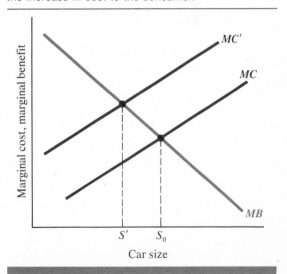

point, and they are diminishing. As car size grows, the advantages of extra comfort and space diminish. The marginal cost of operating a car depends on size, and we assume that the marginal costs MC are both positive and indeed increasing. As we increase car size from, say, a compact to the next size, operating and driving costs increase, and the increase is greater the larger the car. Thus MC is upward-sloping. Note that the MC schedule is drawn for a given level of congestion in the area. The higher congestion is, the higher the marginal cost of operating a car of a given size. That is, an increase in congestion shifts the MC curve upward.

The optimal car size in Figure 16-4, S_0, is determined by the owner's tastes—the MB schedule—and by the operating costs, MC. The higher the marginal cost of operating a larger car, the smaller the optimal car size.

Now we consider the effects of higher congestion in the area. In Figure 16-4 the MC schedule shifts upward to MC'. Optimal car size is now S'. Optimal car size is therefore smaller in more congested areas. Thus there *is* a private sector response to congestion. The individual owner of a car recognizes that in a more congested environment he is better off choosing a smaller car. But that is not enough.

In Figure 16-4 we show that if congestion raises the *private* marginal cost of car size, then owners choose smaller cars. But the extent to which they adjust car size depends only on their own increase in marginal cost, not on the fact that their choice of car size affects the overall level of congestion. If every person thinks his choice of car size does not affect the level of congestion, then all car owners together will create too much congestion. Each fails to take into account the congestion effects he imposes on others. Figure 16-5 considers the socially optimal choice of car size, given

FIGURE 16-5   THE PRIVATE AND SOCIAL COSTS OF CAR SIZE CHOICE. The MC_p curve shows the private marginal costs to the consumer of larger car sizes. But because private consumers do not take into account the effect on other drivers of their larger car, the marginal *social* cost, MC_s, is higher for any given car size. The difference is the extra cost of congestion that results from increase in car size. Individuals choose to be at point A, with car size S_o. Society should be at point A', with smaller cars. At point A', the marginal social cost is equal to the marginal benefit. Taxes or licensing requirements could be imposed to try to get consumers to point A' rather than A.

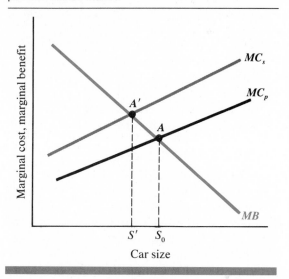

the owners' tastes as represented in the MB schedule.[11]

In Figure 16-5 the schedule MC_p shows, as before, the marginal private costs of operating automobiles of different sizes. As before, it is assumed that these costs are increasing. In addition, schedule MC_s shows the marginal *social* costs of the choices of car size. The marginal social costs of car sizes exceed the private costs because when

---

[11] You might be worried about how the analysis is affected if some people dislike larger cars. If you think about it, you see that it means MB is negative beyond some point. People would never choose to be where MB is negative. They buy smaller cars. But so long as there is some size range over which there are benefits to larger car sizes, the analysis of this section applies.

everyone picks a larger car, congestion costs go up for all. If you do not believe it, ask yourself what happens if someone tries to operate a 1960-style giant car in a congested area. The driver himself is bothered, but he does not take into account everybody else's aggravation. After all, that is why people shout in traffic congestion. It is clear from the argument that the optimal car size should reflect the full social marginal cost of size, both the congestion costs to the operator and the addition to operating costs that is inflicted on everyone else by the choice of car size.

The optimal car size is at point A'; the car that is chosen is smaller than the car chosen at A by private optimization. Society should, in congested areas, tax the use of large cars—for example, through appropriately steep license charges.

What would be the result of a license fee based on car size? Essentially, it would raise the private marginal cost of car size. Thus people would opt for smaller cars and move to point A'. They would choose smaller cars because the MC of larger cars would be higher through license fees. But that is exactly what society wants to achieve in order to "internalize" congestion costs.

Noise

Nobody enjoys noise, at least not other people's noise. Yet there is very little restriction on the amount of noise we are allowed to inflict on others. There are some restrictions on using a chainsaw at night in an apartment building and on playing a stereo after hours, but by and large people can make the noise they find privately optimal to produce.

It is apparent that we are once again in a situation like the one in Figure 16-5. There is a divergence between the private and social costs of noise. Privately there may indeed be zero cost to making noise, and thus people choose the noise levels that they prefer. But, of course, the noise level we choose affects society, and therefore we have a misallocation of resources.

In this case, unlike that of cars, there is no feasible pricing scheme that gets us just the right level of noise. Accordingly, society has to respond through two mechanisms. First, for commercial noise making we simply set standards. Here the question is, of course, whether some use of the price system could be introduced just as we have discussed in connection with pollution in Chapter 11. For private noise there is a more interesting solution: society adopts conventions or *manners* in order to induce people to internalize the social costs of their own actions.

Property Rights and Resource Exploitation

Any resource—grassland, fisheries, forests, game—that is not owned will be overused. The private firm or person going into fishing or hunting carries the activity to the point where the marginal private cost equals the marginal benefits or the price at which the output can be sold. But private costs do not include the fact that catching fish or hunting animals leaves fewer fish or animals for others to catch, making the activity more costly for other fisherman or hunters. Thus the social cost is higher than the private cost when someone uses up an unowned resource.

For optimal use, resources need management. There must be enough whales around to prevent extinction. Hunting during the mating season is therefore certainly the worst idea. Deforestation, while privately profitable, fails to take into account the effects on water supplies, soil stability, and forest growth itself. Again we have a divergence between private and social costs. The divergence arises only because those exploiting the resource do not have a sufficient interest in the long-run viability of the industry. This is because they do not get for themselves the benefits of managing the resource better.

Again society tries to find a way of overcoming the absence of property rights to make users behave in the socially appropriate way. Different methods can be applied—for example, regulating hunting seasons or the number of animals killed, or setting fees for using federal lands. Again the combination of a price system and regulation is required to restore efficiency where the absence of ownership leads people not to internalize the social effects of their actions.[12]

5 CRIME AND PUNISHMENT

The study of crime has traditionally been the property of the law and of sociology. But increasingly, economists have been analyzing the subject, using applied economics to study crime control and deterrence. Economic applications here range from the cost-benefit study of sentencing policy and prison systems to the optimal arrangements of law courts and, indeed, the law. How, then, does an economist think about crime?

The starting point is to think of criminals as rational, maximizing people who look at the costs and benefits of crime. Suppose we talk about larceny or some other common commercial crime. The burglar has the aim of maximizing the expected payoff from crime. This leads to two considerations. First, the criminal will want to seize goods having the maximum value, where value is measured by what the goods can be sold for, not what they cost the owner. Second, the criminal will want to minimize the chances of being caught. There is obviously a tradeoff here. The criminal will be willing to

forgo tempting major heists and attempt smaller, less risky burglaries. These considerations also apply to the choice of area in which to commit the crime. In areas where the rich live, there is plenty to steal, but policing and protective devices are plentiful too. Criminals and their victims find an equilibrium of theft and apprehension where the marginal costs of carrying out crime and of preventing it equal the marginal benefits.

How do the legal consequences of catching a criminal affect the willingness to carry out a crime? In other words, as the jargon goes, what is the crime supply function? The potential criminal looks at three aspects: first, the chances of being caught; second, if he is caught, the chances of being convicted; third, if he is convicted, the severity of the penalty. Now it is immediately obvious that a very severe penalty— hanging and quartering after flogging— does not deter crime if there is a negligible probability of being caught or convicted. Here is a key insight of economics or common sense: society, in its concern for crime prevention through the legal system, should concentrate resources on both apprehension and conviction because what matters for deterrence is the probability of being apprehended *and* convicted, as well as the punishment following conviction.

In studying the supply function of murder across states in the United States, Isaac Ehrlich[13] applied these ideas to determine whether the probability of conviction and the severity of punishment affect the supply of murder. Ehrlich studied the role of three main variables: the length of sentence, the probability of conviction, and the probability of execution given a conviction. The question asked is whether capital punish-

---

[12] For an early and clear discussion of these ideas, see H. Scott Gordon, "The Economic Theory of a Common-Property Resource: The Fishery," *Journal of Political Economy*, April 1954.

[13] See Isaac Ehrlich, "The Deterrent Effect of Capital Punishment: A Question of Life and Death," *American Economic Review*, vol. 65, no. 3, June 1975, pp. 397–417.

ment exerts by itself a deterrent effect. The study concludes that there is strong support for the hypothesis that higher probabilities of conviction, longer sentences, and a higher probability of execution given a conviction all reduce the supply of murder.

Studies such as this one are highly controversial. There is controversy about the strength of the evidence and the statistical techniques. Beyond that, such studies take economics to frontiers where many question its relevance. But here it is important to distinguish two questions. The first is whether an economist's way of looking at the issue—the theory of murder supply and the relevant evidence on supply responses to deterrents—has anything to offer. There is little doubt that it does have something to offer, if only because it is an organized way of thinking about people's actions.[14]

The second question is whether the evi-

dence that capital punishment deters crime should automatically lead us to favor capital punishment. That is not necessarily the case. Even if on the strength of the evidence it is accepted that capital punishment effectively reduces crime, someone may still argue that it is entirely unacceptable on moral grounds for society to use capital punishment as a deterrent. Here, as in many areas of applied economics, we have to distinguish between what is economically the most efficient way of dealing with a problem and what society finds just, proper, fair, or moral. Economic theory and evidence by themselves do not tell us what is fair or just.

---

[14] In a very interesting though difficult article, George Akerlof and William Dickens express some doubts about applying simple economics to the study of crime and punishment. See George Akerlof and William Dickens, "The Economic Consequences of Cognitive Dissonance," *American Economic Review*, June 1982.

SUMMARY

1   The aim of this chapter is to show price theory, or microeconomics, in action. There is no grand conclusion beyond the evident usefulness of fairly straightforward economics for analyzing many of the problems that we see around us.

2   Maximum-hours laws or other regulations that on the surface look as if they are for the benefit of the regulated group may actually be designed to reduce competition from that group. But the law of unintended consequences can also work here: legislation to reduce competition from female workers in the United States at the turn of the century may have led to higher total incomes for women, with fewer total hours of labor supplied.

3   There is an economic problem in allocating time efficiently and in combining time with other inputs to maximize consumer satisfaction. Individuals whose opportunity cost of time is high—with high wages—will pursue leisure activities that use very little time; they will use many gadgets or purchased services. Those with a lower opportunity cost of time will pursue leisure activities that use a lot of time.

4   Marriage or cohabitation can be viewed as an economic arrangement in which two people can produce more efficiently than each one separately—there are economies of scale. Within the marriage, the ef-

ficient allocation of resources predicts that an increase in the husband's income leads to less work in the market by the wife; an increase in the wife's income leads to more work by the husband at home. The facts are generally though not completely supportive of these predictions.

5   The choice of the number of children—fertility—can likewise be viewed as an economic decision. Because raising children is a time-intensive activity, the demand for them may well fall as the family's market wage rises.

6   Imperfect information has major implications for the way markets work. When information is imperfect, because acquiring it is costly, we should expect to see a dispersion of prices. It pays to shop. In the case of search in the labor market, it can be rational for workers to remain unemployed voluntarily while they look for a better job.

7   In some cases, imperfect information can destroy a market entirely. In the lemons case, the working of the market for used cars is severely affected by the likelihood that someone selling a reasonably new car wants to get rid of it because it is a lemon.

8   When there are externalities, market allocations will not be optimal. Examples are the choice of car size, noise pollution, and the use of fisheries. Society, acting through the government or through social convention, frequently finds methods for internalizing the externality —that is, producing behavior that is socially optimal. But there are also, of course, cases of market failure—for instance, those that occur when pollution can be created free.

9   Crime can be analyzed with the tools of economics. Individuals are viewed as deciding on a rational basis whether to go into crime. They are also thought of as conducting their work or criminal activities in a way that maximizes their welfare. The approach leads to some insights into the optimal design of the criminal apprehension and justice system; by and large, they agree with common sense.

10   The criminals' optimal (from their viewpoint) behavior leads to a supply of crime function. It is possible to estimate how the supply of crime is affected by aspects of the penalties: the probabilities of being caught and convicted and the type of sentence imposed upon conviction. Some controversial evidence suggests that capital punishment indeed deters murder.

PROBLEMS

1   (a) Would the men who had the maximum-workweek-for-women laws passed have been better off if they could have had the same laws passed to apply also to them-

selves? Be sure to say on what feature of the demand for labor function your answer depends. (*b*) Would it be correct to say that if the laws that were passed made women better off, similar laws should certainly have made men better off?

2   Two people have the same level of income. One lives off an inheritance. The other is an extremely highly paid lawyer; he charges $250 an hour for his time. Which one takes longer vacations, and why?

3   Over long periods, the workweek has fallen substantially. The 84 hours that were in dispute in the first section of the chapter would now be more like 40. (*a*) What does this suggest about the income elasticity of demand for leisure? (*b*) What do you expect has happened to the output of goods complementary with leisure (inputs into the production of leisure) as a share of GNP over the last 50 years?

4   How does the effective relative price of using a bus as opposed to a car change as an individual's cost of time or wage increases? (Assume that the car is faster.) Do you think that bus transportation is a normal or an inferior good?

5   Why do farmers have larger families?

6   It is often argued that the rate of population growth in lower-income countries will fall as the countries develop and thus that the problem of overpopulation that is seen if present trends continue is not serious. Present arguments for or against this statement.

7   (*a*) What effect would child labor laws have on the number of children if economic considerations were all that mattered in de-

termining family size? (*b*) Do you think that the use of economics in analyzing questions about marriage, family size, crime and punishment, etc., makes sense and contributes to an understanding of the phenomena? Explain.

8   Suppose that you are told that the range of prices for a good is large. Does that make you search more or less than if the range were smaller? Can you see a mechanism that prevents the equilibrium range of prices from becoming very large?

9   (*a*) Ads for used cars often say "Owner leaving country" or "Owner died." Why should anyone care? (*b*) What mechanisms besides dealers are there for trying to avoid the lemons problems when buying a used car? (*c*) Consider this statement: Don't buy anything from him that he wants to sell? Could this advice make sense? (This may remind you of Groucho Marx's claim that he would not want to belong to any club that would have him for a member.)

10   (*a*) Define an externality, and explain its significance. (*b*) What is the externality when ownership rights to a resource have not been assigned? (*c*) It is often said that the property of all is the property of none. What does this mean?

11   Why do we not have the maximum punishment for all crimes so as to deter criminals from transgressing at all? (*Hint:* This is a tough question. It depends, as usual, on the importance of marginal considerations. To answer it, think of the criminal caught in the course of a burglary, wondering whether to surrender or come out shooting.)

In the early 1980s a tax revolt was under way. It led in a number of states to constitutional amendments to limit the government's right to raise taxes. The tax revolutionaries argued that the government had too big a role in the economy, that people were not getting their money's worth from taxes, and that taxes were so high that private initiative and effort were being stifled. Indeed, a new economic argument emerged, suggesting that the government would actually get *more* tax revenue if it *cut* tax rates.

These ideas were not quack notions that never made it in practice. On the contrary, they quickly found their way into U.S. law, in the Economic Recovery Act of 1981. Individual income taxes were to be cut by 5 percent in 1981, an additional 10 percent in 1982, and another 8 percent in 1983. The tax cutting had a large effect on *marginal* tax rates.

The marginal income tax rate is the rate at which taxes are paid on an extra dollar of income.

Table 17-1 shows the impact of the 1981 Economic Recovery Act tax cuts on marginal tax rates for families at different income levels. The data indicate that there were large reductions in marginal tax rates, especially for the super-rich. A millionaire who in 1980 paid 60 cents in taxes for every additional dollar of income would pay only 40 cents by 1984.

Were the tax cuts designed to make the rich richer? And if so, is anything wrong with that? Or was their purpose (also) to revive hard work and initiative in the American economy? If so, will they suceed? Or, as opponents of the tax cuts argued, will they succeed only in reversing many years of social progress, sacrificing valuable government programs just to let the rich accumulate more wealth and power?

The 1981 tax discussion in the United States went to the heart of issues involving the government and resource allocation. It raised the question of what activities the government *should* be directly involved in and what is best left to the private market. It also raised questions of taxation. Who should pay taxes, and what effects do taxes have on the efficiency with which the economy operates?

The issues are of course both economic and political. In this chapter we focus mainly on the economics of government's role in the economy, but we also discuss the ways in which the political process affects government economic policy decisions.

TABLE 17-1

MARGINAL INCOME TAX RATES
(Tax Rates on an Extra Dollar of Income)

	MARGINAL TAX RATES	
INCOME*	1980	1984
5000–10,000	14.5	13.4
10,000–20,000	20.7	18.5
20,000–25,000	24.7	22.4
25,000–50,000	30.2	27.8
50,000–100,000	45.5	39.0
100,000–200,000	57.2	43.9
1 million and over	60.2	39.3

* In 1981 dollars.
Source: Joseph Pechman (ed.), *Setting National Priorities. The 1983 Budget,* Brookings Institution, Washington, D.C., 1982, p. 29.

1 TAXATION AND GOVERNMENT SPENDING IN THE U.S. ECONOMY

Governments in the United States—federal, state, and local—together collect in taxes about one-third of the GNP or total income earned in the economy. This is a smaller share than that of the governments in most industrialized countries, as the data in Table 1-2 showed. But it is a much larger share than governments in the U.S. took during peacetime in any period before World War II.

Of the 33 percent of the GNP that governments take in taxes, about 20 percent is spent on goods and services. Federal government defense spending and state and local government spending on education and fire-fighting services are examples of spending on goods and services. The remaining 13 percent of the GNP that is taken by governments is used to make transfer payments.

> *Transfer payments* are payments made for which no current economic service is provided in return by the recipient.

Unemployment benefits, or Social Security payments, are transfer payments. However, the wage received by a public school teacher is not a transfer, because the teacher is providing a current economic service in exchange for the wage. Transfer payments, such as welfare and Social Security benefits, have become an increasingly important and controversial part of the role of government.

The Composition of Government Spending

Table 17-2 shows the composition of total government spending in the United States in 1979 among the federal, state, and local governments. The data are grouped by various functions.

The table shows that over half of total government spending is done by the federal government. State governments account for less than 20 percent of the total and local governments close to 30 percent. At the federal level, national defense, Social Security and welfare, and interest on the national debt are the major spending categories. Interest on the national debt means payments of interest by the federal government to those from whom it has borrowed in the past. Education, highways, and social welfare are most important for state governments. Education is the most important function for local governments.

We will not comment in detail on each of the expenditure categories. Instead, we will ask a set of questions. First, taking any of these expenditure categories (highways, health, etc.), why should the government be involved at all? Why do we not provide these goods and services through the private market in the same way we provide automobiles, recreation, or haircuts? Further, how do we decide how much to provide of those goods that government does provide? Second, how do we decide whether the government should itself produce the goods and services (government schools, government hospitals, government parks) or whether they should be provided by the

TABLE 17-2

COMPOSITION OF GOVERNMENT SPENDING IN THE UNITED STATES, 1979
(Percentage of Total Government Spending)

FUNCTION	FEDERAL	STATE	LOCAL	TOTAL
Total	54.3	17.9	27.8	100.0
National defense and international relations	15.4	—	—	15.4
Education	1.2	3.8	10.6	15.5
Health and hospitals	1.1	1.7	1.7	4.5
Transportation and highways	0.6	2.1	1.7	4.3
Police	0.2	0.2	1.2	1.7
Social Security, welfare, etc.	20.0	5.9	1.8	27.6
Interest on debt	5.9	0.7	0.9	7.4
Other	9.9	3.6	9.9	23.6

Note: The totals for the components may not add up to 100.0 because of rounding.
Source: Facts and Figures on Government Finance, 1981, p. 17.

government but produced by the private sector (government pays for private garbage collectors, rents private security guards, provides for private towing of illegally parked cars)? A dose of economics and a good helping of political science are needed to deal with these questions about decision-making processes in a democracy.

The Financing of Government

The government is financed primarily by taxes. A small part of government revenue comes from fees and charges for government services, but most of the revenue is from taxes. Table 17-3 shows the composition of government revenue by source. Over 65 percent of all government revenue is collected by the federal government and only about 35 percent by state and local governments. But the federal government transfers large amounts to state and local governments, leaving itself with only 55 percent of total revenue.

The chief source of government revenue is the personal income tax, which now accounts for more than one-third of total revenue. Next in importance are Social Security taxes or payroll taxes on labor income, and then sales or excise taxes. Sales or excise taxes are taxes levied on the sale of

specific goods. At the federal level there are excise taxes on specific goods, including telephone calls and airline tickets. At the state and local level general sales taxes (with some goods exempted) are an important source of revenue.

Two taxes in Table 17-3 deserve more comment. The corporate profits tax is levied on the accounting income (defined in Chapter 6) of corporations. Although corporate taxes are very much discussed in the newspapers and in Congress, they account for only 8 percent of total government revenue, much less than the personal income tax. The property tax is also a controversial tax; it has already been at the center of the tax revolt in several states. The property tax is a tax on houses and land, and it provides much of the revenue for local governments. It accounts for less than 8 percent of total government revenue. The final category in the table, "nontaxes and other," includes traffic tickets, government revenue from selling its publications, and anything else not already in the table.

The U.S. tax structure has changed radically in the last 80 years. In 1902, as shown in Table 17-4, most of the tax revenue came from property taxes and sales and excise taxes. There was no income tax or tax on cor-

TABLE 17-3

COMPOSITION OF GOVERNMENT REVENUE IN THE UNITED STATES, 1981
(Percentage of Total Government Revenue)

SOURCE	FEDERAL GOVERNMENT	STATE AND LOCAL GOVERNMENTS	TOTAL
Taxes on income and property:			
Personal income tax	30.2	5.4	35.6
Social insurance	21.2	3.8	25.0
Corporate profits tax	6.9	1.2	8.1
Property tax	—	7.6	7.6
Estate and gift taxes	0.7	—	0.7
Taxes on goods:			
Excise taxes (including sales tax)	5.0	9.7	14.7
Customs duties	0.9	—	0.9
Nontaxes and other	0.6	6.8	7.4
Total	65.5	34.5	100.0
Federal grants to state and local governments	−9.1	9.1	0

Source: Survey of Current Business, March 1982.

TABLE 17-4

COMPOSITION OF TAX REVENUE IN THE UNITED STATES
(Percentage of Total Tax Revenue)

	INCOME TAX, PAYROLL	CORPORATE PROFITS	SALES, EXCISE, CUSTOMS	PROPERTY	OTHER
1902	—	—	30.4	41.7	27.9
1927	7.8	11.1	12.8	38.8	29.5
1981	60.6	8.1	15.6	7.6	8.1

Sources: Historical Statistics of the United States, 1970, p. 1119, and *Survey of Current Business,* March 1982.

porate profits. Not only was the structure of taxation different, so was the *amount* of tax revenue. The total tax revenue in 1902 was only 8 percent of total income or the GNP, compared with one-third today.

With the facts on government spending and revenue given in this section, we can now move on. First we will discuss the reasons for government spending, and then we will examine how the government should pay for that spending. We will be asking what a good (or least bad) tax is, which taxes should be avoided, and why. To answer those questions we will have to analyze the effects of taxes on the allocation of resources.

2 THE GOVERNMENT IN THE MARKET ECONOMY

Why should governments intervene in a market economy? Is there any reason to think that they can improve the allocation of resources? There are three broad areas where government intervention can help. The first is in minimizing or eliminating *distortions* arising from natural or artificial monopoly, from externalities, and from a lack of information about the safety of products or workplaces. We discussed the roles of antitrust legislation, regulation of natural monopolies, pollution controls, and standards legislation in Chapters 11 and 12. That is one area for government intervention in a market economy.

In this section we concentrate on two other areas where there is a case for government intervention. The first is in the provision of public goods, and the second is in the distribution of income.

Public Goods

Most of the goods we consume are private goods.

> A *private good* is a good that, if consumed by one person, cannot be consumed by another.

Ice cream is a private good. When you eat your ice cream, I don't get to consume the same ice cream. My clothes are private goods. When I wear them, you are precluded from wearing them at the same time.

But there are some goods that we can consume simultaneously, without my consumption in any way reducing your consumption. These are public goods.

> A *public good* is a good that, even if it is being consumed by one person, is still available for consumption by others.

Clean air is a public good. Your consumption of clean air does not interfere with my enjoyment of it. So, too, is national defense. If the defense forces are protecting the country from danger, your being safe in no way prevents my being safe. Radio programs and the views in the national parks are other public goods.

In discussing public goods we shall assume that there is no possibility of *excluding* anyone from the consumption of a good. Exclusion may be possible. For instance, suppose that someone has a beautiful garden that others enjoy looking at. Other people's consumption of the beauty of the garden can be excluded if the owner builds a wall around the garden. This is not the sort of public good we are discussing. We are considering public goods such as defense or clean air, where excluding others from consuming the goods is impossible or prohibitively expensive.

Free Riders Private markets have difficulty in ensuring that the right amount of such public goods is produced. This is because of the *free-rider* problem. A free rider is someone who gets to consume a good that is costly to produce without paying for it. The free-rider problem applies particularly to public goods because the amount of a public good consumed by everyone is the same. All citizens have the same level of national defense. If the amount of national defense that I have is the same as you have, I might as well wait for you and others to buy it rather than contribute my own money toward buying it. I will get a free ride on your purchase.

To get a better understanding of the nature of public goods, think of there being strong externalities in the consumption of such goods. Externalities exist when actions by one person or firm affect the welfare of others without any action on the part of those affected. Your purchase of a public good certainly affects my welfare, since it automatically increases my consumption of that good. This externality is beneficial, unlike some externalities that we can think of. For instance, there is an externality when you play your stereo loudly next door to my apartment. But in both cases the private allocation of resources is not socially optimal.

Since the market allocation of public goods cannot be optimal, because any one person is concerned only with his own utility, there is a case for government intervention to determine the output of such goods. How much of a public good *should* be produced? Here we use the general principle that society should produce goods up to the point where the marginal cost to society is equal to the marginal social benefit from those goods.

FIGURE 17-1   THE DEMAND FOR A PUBLIC GOOD.
There are two people, each of whom has a demand
schedule for the public good, DD_1 and DD_2. What is
the value that the group places on an additional unit
of output? At each level of output we add up *vertically* the price each is willing to pay for another unit.
Thus at output Q we add P_1 and P_2 to arrive at the
combined valuation of another unit of the public
good. In this way we generate the demand schedule
DD. The demand schedule is special because consumption by one person does not preclude consumption of the same good by the other. Therefore,
the *sum* of their valuations of another unit represents the price they are willing to pay as a group for
an extra unit.

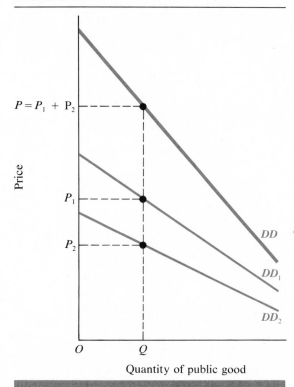

The Demand Curve for Public Goods We
start by developing the demand curve for
public goods, which gives the marginal social benefit. Suppose that the public good is
public safety and that there are two people
in the society. The valuation placed on each
specific amount of public safety by the first
person is shown in Figure 17-1 by demand
curve DD_1. The demand curve shows how

much safety he would buy at each price if
there were no game playing in which he
waits for someone else to buy first. DD_2 is
the demand curve of a second person.

Society's demand curve for public
safety is DD. It is derived by adding the
prices that individuals in society are willing
to pay for a given amount of safety. For instance, at amount Q of safety, the first person is willing to pay P_1, and the second is
willing to pay P_2. Society, consisting of the
two of them, is willing to pay P_1 plus P_2. The
sum is the value that society places, at the
margin, on that amount of safety. This is
shown by the corresponding price, P, on society's demand curve for safety, DD.

The total demand curve for a public
good differs from that for a private good.
With a public good, we add the demand
curves *vertically*. At each level of output,
we add the prices that all the individuals in
the economy taken together are willing to
pay. This is because each person gets to
consume *all* of the public good that is produced. With a private good, we add the demand curves *horizontally*. With a private
good, the amount supplied at each given
price will have to be split up among all the
people in society, each equating the marginal benefit from consuming his portion to
the amount he pays, the price. There is a
difference between the demand curves because there is excludability in the consumption of private goods, meaning that when
someone consumes a private good, he
thereby excludes other people from also
consuming it. That is not possible with a
public good.

In Figure 17-2 we combine the demand
(DD) for the public good, say, safety, with
the supply schedule. The supply schedule
is given by the marginal cost of producing
safety. The way we have drawn the MC
schedule, there is an initial phase of declining MC, but ultimately MC is rising. The social optimum is at point E. At that point the
marginal social valuation of an extra unit of

FIGURE 17-2   THE OPTIMAL SUPPLY OF A PUBLIC GOOD. Schedule *MC* shows the marginal cost of supplying an extra unit of the public good. *DD* is the demand schedule; it shows the group's marginal valuation of each unit. The social optimum is at *E*, where marginal cost equals marginal benefit.

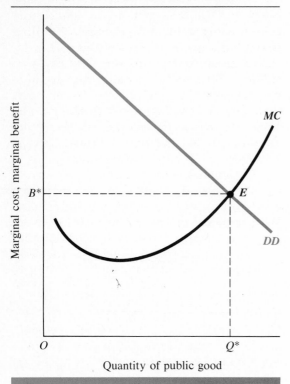

Quantity of public good

mand curves, such as DD_1 in Figure 17-1. The problem here is that if payment will be demanded according to the demand curve, individuals will have an incentive to lie. If everyone else tells the truth about his willingness to pay, say, $1000 per year for national defense, then we are not going to have appreciably less defense if I say I am willing to pay only $20 or, for that matter, nothing. I become a free rider. But if everyone thinks that way, it will be very hard to get the truth.

What if we separate the demand for public goods from the requirement that people must pay for public goods? If the amount people have to pay is unaffected by the amount of a public good they say they would like, they may announce a quantity demanded that corresponds to the case where the price is zero. If the city asks whether I want safer streets, at no cost to me, I am for it—the safer the better, so long as I don't have to pay. So this approach is also not foolproof. Mechanisms that will get a truthful response from people interested only in their own well-being have been suggested, but these are costly to operate and are not the means by which decisions on public goods expenditures are made in practice.

We should point to one more optimistic view: the possibility that most people will, if asked the right question, give an honest answer. The right question is, How much of the public good should society produce, given that you and the rest of society will have to pay for it through the tax system? If honesty is a social convention—that is, if people believe that honesty is the best policy, which it is in this case from the viewpoint of society—then people will give the honest answer.

safety (which is equal to the value all people together place on an extra unit) is equal to the marginal cost. If there was less output of the public good, society would gain from an expansion.

We have now determined what the optimal supply of the public good is. Next we need to find out how society can decide which public goods to provide and how much of them.

Revelation of Preferences   How would a government find out how much to spend on public goods? Why not ask people how much they would be willing to pay for different levels of output of a public good. In other words, ask people to reveal their de-

Government Provision of Goods   Governments in the United States provide health services, national defense, the Library of

Congress, the services of the FBI and CIA, the national parks, state liquor stores, training at state universities, and much more.

Are all these goods public goods? Are any of them public goods? National defense and the services of the CIA and FBI are indeed public goods in the sense that your consumption of the services of the defense and police forces is not reduced by my also consuming them, and in the sense that it is difficult to exclude any residents of the United States from consuming them. The national parks are a mixed case, since enjoyment of the views in the parks is a public good, but use of the eating facilities is a private good. Liquor sales are not a public good, and liquor could perfectly well be sold through private markets.

These examples show that the production of public goods does account for a large part of government spending, with defense as the most obvious case. At the same time, the liquor store example makes it clear that governments are involved in the provision of some goods that have nothing to do with public goods.

Government Production   It may seem that the government *should* produce public goods and *should not* produce any other goods. Neither conclusion is correct. Government does not have to *produce* public goods. It only has to specify how much of them should be produced. It may rely on private contractors to do the actual production, as it does, say, with regard to defense equipment. Indeed, it used to be common for countries to have private contractors provide armies on a commercial basis.

There is no reason, in principle, why governments should not produce goods, even if they are not public goods. There is no reason, in principle, why governments should produce any good less efficiently than the private sector would. There are government-owned firms in many countries, particularly in Europe, and some of them appear to be commercially successful and efficient.

Nonetheless, the general presumption from experience is that government is more likely to be inefficient in production than is the private sector. This is probably because government firms are under pressure to do things that the government wants and frequently are given financial aid when they lose money. Private firms could not continue in production if they continued to lose money. Thus inefficient government firms frequently can continue in business too long from an efficiency viewpoint.

The existence of public goods is one argument for government intervention in the workings of markets. Another such argument concerns the distribution of income.

Income Redistribution

The distribution of income that is generated in a competitive equilibrium has no ethical claims to being right. Depending on who starts out with what resources, private markets can produce many different final allocations of resources and welfare. A private market may produce a distribution of income in which the top 1 percent of the income earners get 40 percent of the total income in the economy, or it could perhaps end up with an even distribution of income. Either way, government might want to intervene to affect the distribution of income —by taxing some and giving to others.

The most difficult question that has to be answered is how society or the government decides what a good distribution of income is. Any one person can have a perfectly sensible viewpoint on what a good distribution of income is—for instance, that the more even the distribution of income the better, or that the distribution of income we have is best, or that people who work harder should be rewarded, or that people who need more should get more, or that the person in society who is worst off should not starve. Translating these different opinions into a consistent view that is taken by the government and implemented in taxation and transfer policy is not simple. In the next section we discuss some of the difficulties of reaching decisions in these situations.

There is a difference between government intervention to affect income distribution and government intervention to ensure the correct production level for public goods or to remove distortions. In the latter cases, the government is taking actions that at least in principle can improve the situation for everyone in society. But when the government intervenes to affect the income distribution, it is making some people worse off to make others better off. By talking about "society" we may only be covering up the fact that the majority is putting its interest ahead by manipulating the tax system. It is sometimes said that in a democracy the poor make the laws and the rich pay the taxes. A modern version of this complaint is that the middle class pays the taxes and the rich have lawyers and accountants who enable them to avoid paying taxes. In any event, the general point is that there is no independent economic criterion which says that one distribution of income is better than another. The question of the desirable distribution of income is settled by the society's choices reached through its political decisions.

The Equity-Efficiency Trade-off No matter how society reaches decisions on a desirable distribution of income, government taxes and spending will be used to try to achieve that distribution. Once we introduce the notion that the distribution of income is something to worry about, we also have to face up to the possibility that there is a trade-off to be made by society between *equity and efficiency.*

With efficient allocations of resources,

prices are equal to both marginal costs of production and individuals' marginal valuations of goods. As we shall see below, it is not possible in practice to raise taxes and to maintain the marginal conditions that are necessary for an efficient allocation of resources. Thus as soon as the government starts using taxes to redistribute income (or for any other purpose), it is introducing inefficiencies into the allocation of resources. Since taxes are used to redistribute income in the interests of equity, there is a trade-off between equity and efficiency.

Redistribution in Practice Governments do in practice engage in redistributions of incomes. For instance, the 13 percent of the GNP that is spent by governments on transfer payments mainly represents government attempts to redistribute income—toward the elderly (through Social Security), the unemployed (through unemployment benefits), tobacco farmers (through tobacco subsidies), and other beneficiaries.

Merit Goods

Merit goods are goods that society thinks people should consume or receive, no matter what their incomes are. They typically include health, education, shelter, and food. Thus we, society, might think that everyone should have adequate housing and take steps to provide it. Is there an economic justification for the government to provide merit goods? We can always say that there is, because the sight of someone who is starving or homeless creates an externality, making everyone else very unhappy. By providing housing for those who would otherwise be homeless, the government makes the rest of us feel better. Government provision of merit goods is closely related to a concern over the distribution of income.

In the case of merit goods, we want to be sure about what is being justified. The argument justifies policies that ensure that individuals consume the specified amounts of the merit goods. The argument does *not* say that the government should produce the goods itself, and it does not specify any other way of making sure that individuals consume the right amounts of the goods. One way would simply be to require that the right amounts of the goods be consumed. For instance, in the case of education, everyone has to go to school up to a certain age. But a person does not have to go to a government school—any accredited school will do. In the case of housing, the government could build low-income houses and rent them at a subsidized rate, or it could provide rent supplements, or it could simply announce required minimum housing standards and specify that violators must pay the penalty.

We now see that some of the items that the government produces or in which the government intervenes are merit goods. Some of these items were listed earlier—for example, health and education.

Let us summarize the ground covered so far. The question was, What in the free market approach to economics justifies government intervention in the economy? There are three basic answers. First, there may be distortions in the market equilibrium. Second, government intervenes in setting the output levels for public goods. And third, society may worry about the distribution of income. Merit goods are partly a reflection of a concern over welfare distribution and are, in part, public goods. Each of these justifications for government intervention can be regarded as a special case of an *externality*—a situation in which market and social valuations differ.

The discussion here has provided some theoretical justification for government intervention in a market economy. But governments do not make their tax and spending decisions on the basis of what economic

theory says their role should be. Only with imagination could we say that in fact all government purchases of goods are purchases of public goods or merit goods. And it would take even more imagination to see government intervention that affects the distribution of income as resulting from a consistent view of the optimal distribution. We now discuss the mechanisms that governments use to make their tax and spending decisions.

3 PUBLIC CHOICE

We need a theory of how governments actually behave. Governments are large—in some modern economies they dispose of a larger share of the GNP than is generated by all the large manufacturing firms in the economy taken together. They are run by people, and these people, like everyone else, try to maximize their own well-being. The theory of public choice tries to understand and predict how people in the political system will end up allocating resources, given the structure of the system and their own aims. It does not view the political system as a magical machine through which we, the people, successfully achieve our common goals. Instead, it looks at the design of the machine and the cogs in it to see how their interactions affect the allocation of resources.

The process by which government tax and spending (and other) decisions are typically made is shown in Figure 17-3. Voters express their preferences for decision makers. These are legislators and elected members of the executive branch, like the President and governors. Their job is to make the decisions and laws. The legislators, in turn, tell bureaucrats (including the executive) what to do, and the bureaucrats collect the revenues or administer the spending of revenues. Throughout the process of making and implementing a tax or

FIGURE 17-3   PUBLIC DECISION MAKING.

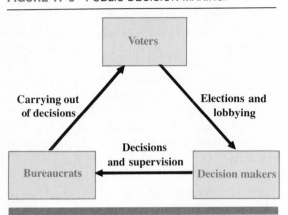

spending decision, interested voters will be lobbying to move the decision their way.

The most serious question that has to be raised about this process is whether the final result has much to do with the preferences of the voters. Certainly there are many points at which things can go off the track. To show this, we will take up in turn voting as a means of making decisions, the objectives of legislators, and the objectives of bureaucrats.

Voting

If everyone was identical, public decision making would not be difficult. The most important problem that a society solves through the political process is how to reconcile the different views and interests of its members. The difficult issues are not the issues on which everyone would agree about what should be done but the issues on which voters have different views.

In this section we discuss two features of majority voting. The first is the *paradox of voting*, which concerns cases in which society is unable to rank policy choices consistently through a majority voting process. The second is the *median-voter result*, which concerns cases in which majority voting leads to consistent choices and the choice is that of the voter in the middle.

The paradox of voting is illustrated in Table 17-5. Society chooses among three possibilities: A, B, and C. There are three voters: 1, 2, and 3. The table shows how the voters rank the three possibilities. Voter 1, for example, likes A best, B next, and C least. Now let the group choose *by majority vote* between A and B. The result is 2 votes to 1 in favor of A, since voters 1 and 3 both prefer A to B. Similarly, the vote will be 2 to 1 in favor of B over C, since voters 1 and 2 both prefer B to C. Now we know that with majority voting we will choose A over B and C. It seems, then, that A should be preferred to C. But as you can confirm, C wins in a vote against A. The conclusion is that majority voting cannot lead to a *consistent* choice among the three alternatives in the table.

Is this a serious problem or a curiosity? It is a serious problem because it means that there is no possibility that majority voting can be relied on to lead society to make consistent decisions under all circumstances.[1] It also means that the decisions a society makes may well depend on the order in which it votes on them.

The Median Voter   It is not always the case that majority voting *must* fail to come up

---

[1] Professor Kenneth Arrow of Stanford University won the Nobel award in economics in part for his work showing that society cannot find a procedure for making choices that are consistent unless the choices are effectively always left up to one person's tastes (the tastes of the dictator). The demonstration is based on the paradox of voting.

TABLE 17-5

THE PARADOX OF VOTING: VOTERS' RANKINGS

VOTERS	RANKING OF POSSIBLE CHOICES		
	A	B	C
1	1	2	3
2	3	1	2
3	2	3	1

FIGURE 17-4 THE MEDIAN VOTER. A vote is made by comparing each possible level of spending with all possible alternatives. Individual preferences are indicated by each of the 17 voters on the line ranging from 0 to $1000. Each dot represents a voter's preferred expenditure. In voting, the outcome will be the expenditure preferred by the median voter; it is indicated by the arrow. Everybody to the left will prefer the position of the median voter to anything that involves even more spending. Everybody to the right will prefer the position to any other that involves even less spending. The median-voter position is the *only* majority position that wins against all alternatives. Therefore it will win out.

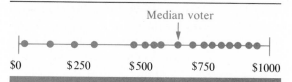

with a consistent ranking of alternatives. The model of the median voter provides a good example. Consider Figure 17-4, where we look at a majority vote on an expenditure issue. Each of 17 voters has a position on the issue, a preferred expenditure level, and the positions are indicated on the line running from $0 to $1000. Each dot thus represents the preference of one of the voters.

Further, each voter will vote for a spending level that is close to his preferred level rather than for one that is further away. If a voter's ideal spending level is $250, then in being asked to choose between $300 and $500 he will choose $300. That is closer to $250 than $500 is. These preferences are said to be *single-peaked*, meaning that there is one most desirable spending level from the viewpoint of each voter and that other spending levels are judged by how close they are to that ideal level.

Now suppose that we take each of the positions and put it to a vote against all the alternatives. The position involving near-zero spending will lose 16 to 1 against any alternative. With the exception of one voter, everybody wants higher spending and thus will vote for any alternative with a higher

level of spending. As we move along to the right, each amount specified will still be voted down in *some* vote against one of the alternatives. But when we get to the position advocated by the median voter, the person who has an equal number of voters on each side, we get a spending amount that is not beaten in any vote.

Why? Everybody to the left prefers that amount to any amount that is higher. People to the right want higher spending. But there will be a majority of 1 for the amount preferred by the median voter, since he gets people to the left plus himself. We would get the same result in any vote comparing the median with smaller amounts of spending. Thus on an issue where every voter has a well-defined (single-peaked) position, a majority vote will indeed bring a *consistent* result. The result is that the society's choice is the choice of the median individual.

Majority voting ceases to work in this way when individual voters do not have single most-preferred positions—when they are not in a situation where they dislike other positions more the further they are away from the one preferred position. Figure 17-5 illustrates two possibilities. A voter may rank different amounts of expenditure as shown by the solid line. Position A is best, anything else is worse, and the further away from A the more so. An alternative is the broken schedule that has two peaks, one at A' and one at B'. We can imagine two ways of providing, say, police protection. The voter might prefer the expenditure indicated by B', but he would rank the method indicated by A' higher than some intermediate positions.

If preferences are not single-peaked, we lose the simple possibility of getting a majority or coalition by picking the position of the median voter. Now it is entirely possible that positions to the right, say, can win out because they have the support of people who want to spend a lot, and they have

FIGURE 17-5 SINGLE- AND DOUBLE-PEAKED PREFERENCES. When voter preferences are not single-peaked, the median-voter model may break down because voters may prefer positions far from their first choice to others that are relatively closer. Position A' is preferred to some positions closer to the first choice at B'.

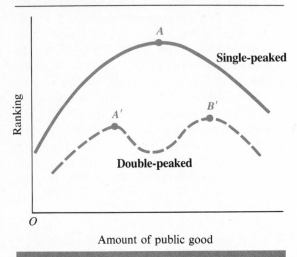

some support from people who have a second-choice preference in that range.

The median-voter model is often used to make predictions about how voting will turn out. On many issues the restriction to single-peaked preferences makes sense, and then we might expect majority voting to work as described here. That is reasonably comforting. According to the model, the choices that are made are those of the person in the middle, who almost by definition seems to be representative of the whole group. Of course, there is no particular person who is always the median voter. Depending on the issue, the median voter will be a different person.

Logrolling We illustrate the problems of majority voting with one more example, that of logrolling. In logrolling, minorities get together to decide how they will vote on a package of issues so as to emerge with an improved position from the package as a whole. Table 17-6 illustrates the problem.

There are two issues, A and B, and three voters, 1, 2, and 3. Each voter assigns to issues A and B dollar values of their gains and losses. These numbers are entered in the table. Assume that a person votes for a measure only if he gains from doing so. Thus voter 1 would vote against both A and B, while voter 2 would vote against A but in favor of B.

Consider first a majority vote on each of the issues taken separately. Both will be defeated. Issue A will be defeated by voters 1 and 2 and issue B by voters 1 and 3. Thus with majority voting neither proposal would pass. But now consider a coalition between any two voters: each one agrees that he will vote favorably on the other's preferred issue. Voters 2 and 3 can, in fact, agree to vote favorably on the two issues. Voter 2 will be ahead by 1 unit, losing 3 units on issue A but making up by winning 4 on issue B. Similarly, voter 3 will lose 1 unit on issue B but will more than recover on issue A. With majority voting, both measures are rejected, but with a coalition from logrolling both issues pass.

Legislators

The median-voter results are interesting, and the model can help us understand how society may make decisions on particular issues, especially if there is a referendum or a series of referenda on an issue. But the process of making decisions through legislative compromises is far more complicated. Decisions are not made issue by issue; there is a trading of votes between deci-

TABLE 17-6
LOGROLLING

| VOTERS | ISSUES | |
	A	B
1	−4	−1
2	−3	4
3	6	−1

sions, as in the logrolling case above. We may think that the outcome is approximately what the median, or representative, voter would prefer, but that cannot be exactly what happens.

The general question to consider is what the aims of representatives are. The representatives are, of course, human, and they have many conflicting aims. They want to do good; they want to be powerful; they want to be popular; they want to be rich; they want to be happy; and above all, they want to be reelected. These aims are not mutually exclusive. The question is whether we get from the mixture of aims and the political process a set of decisions that well reflects the goals of the society. There is, of course, a further issue of whether the society has consistent goals.

Bureaucracy

Bureaucrats, too, are part of the process by which the government affects the allocation of resources. The legislature passes the laws about spending and taxing, but the government departments and the Internal Revenue Service do the spending and receive the taxes. They are not neutral cogs in the government machine. Bureaucrats have a number of ways of influencing the allocation of resources. First, legislation may leave the administration some discretion on exactly how funds are to be spent. The bureaucrats may set the rules as to who is eligible for particular forms of government assistance, for example. Second, the politicians in charge of government departments frequently rely for advice on the civil servants in the departments and are quite likely to be influenced by their suggestions, since these are based on some expertise.

It is often argued that the government departments become the main proponents of the programs they administer. The Pentagon wants more military spending, the Education Department wants more aid for education, and so on. This raises the question of what the aims of the bureaucrats are. They, too, are human and want to do good, be powerful and respected, and all the rest. Some theories of bureaucratic behavior argue that all these aims make the bureaucrats want to expand their agencies and that bureaucracies can best be understood as having the main aim of growing. But it is difficult to believe that any large portion of the expansion of government can be blamed on the desires of bureaucrats. It is the politicians, elected by the voters, who pass the budgets.

The main point of this section is that the process through which the government makes spending and tax decisions is not one that translates society's wishes directly into action. Indeed, as the paradox of voting shows, it may even be difficult for society to have consistent aims. Eventually the theory of public choice may provide predictions about how governments will behave under different circumstances. From our viewpoint, its main feature is that it shows that there are interesting economic questions that have been raised and are being studied about the ways in which decisions on public finance are made. The simple view that public-sector decisions are made to maximize the public good is a convenient one, but it does not lead to a better understanding of how decisions are actually made—in part because the public good has to be defined.

4 PRINCIPLES OF TAXATION

So far we have discussed government spending. Now we turn to government revenue, which comes mainly from taxes. In this section we focus on three topics. First we briefly discuss different kinds of taxes. Second, we turn to the question of equity in taxation—who should pay how much. Third, we raise the issue of efficiency, analyzing how taxes distort resource allocation. In the next section we briefly talk about major issues in tax reform.

Variety of Taxes

Historically, customs duties and tolls were the main sources of tax revenue. They were easy to raise in ports and at crossroads, and there was no need for an elaborate bureaucracy to administer the tax system. We are very far from that today. Tax revenue comes from taxes on income from labor and capital, from property taxes, and from taxes on retail sales or on the sale of specific commodities such as tobacco or liquor. We can classify these taxes broadly, as in Table 17-7.

We have already discussed most of the taxes in Table 17-7. Here we single out a few taxes for special discussion.

The *payroll tax* is a tax on wages. It is actually the individual's contribution to the Social Security system, which entitles the contributor to retirement and disability payments. But because it is not voluntary, we call it a tax rather than an insurance premium. Contributing to the Social Security system is made compulsory on the argument that people may not be sufficiently farsighted to provide for their own needs in retirement and in case they become disabled.

The *capital gains tax* is a tax on the amount by which the value of an asset has risen. Someone who buys a share of Ford Motor Company for $18 and later sells it for $26 has a capital gain of $8. He has to pay taxes on that gain of $8.

Not mentioned explicitly in Table 17-7

is the *value-added tax,* or VAT. VAT is widely used abroad, especially in Europe. As the name suggests, VAT is a tax on the value added to a good in production. VAT is special because it is levied at every stage of production and sale—when goods are sold by producers to wholesalers, when retailers buy from wholesalers and ultimately when retailers sell to the final consumers. What is taxed at each stage is only the value added, which is the sales price less the cost of purchased inputs. Thus the retail store that buys goods from a wholesaler is taxed only on the retail sales price less the wholesale price.

By adding up the taxes collected at the different stages, we realize that VAT works out to be the same as a general retail sales tax levied at a common rate on all goods sold in the economy.

> Thus the VAT is equivalent to a retail sales tax, but it is collected at several stages in the production and distribution process.

Table 17-8 compares the ways in which taxes are collected in several industrial countries.[2] The United States relies relatively heavily on income and corporate profits taxes, while European countries rely relatively more on revenue through VAT. Of course, in the United States retail sales

[2] Note that the data for the United States in Table 17-8 do not quite agree with the data in Tables 17-3 and 17-4. This is partly because Table 17-8 is for the period 1965–1979, while the other two tables are for 1981. In addition, Tables 17-3 and 17-4 include "other" taxes; in Table 17-8, these are classified mainly as property taxes.

TABLE 17-7

THE MAIN TAX CATEGORIES

TAXES ON INCOMES	TAXES ON ASSETS AND ASSET TRANSFERS	TAXES ON PURCHASES
Payroll tax	Property tax	Retail sales tax
Personal income tax	Estate and gift taxes	Liquor and tobacco taxes
Corporate profits tax		Import duties
Capital gains tax		

TABLE 17-8

SOURCES OF TAX REVENUE
(Percentage of Total Taxes)

COUNTRY	TAXES ON INCOME AND PROFITS	SOCIAL SECURITY TAXES	PROPERTY TAXES	EXCISE TAX, RETAIL SALES TAX, AND VAT	OTHER
Germany	36	34	3	26	1
Italy	29	41	4	26	—
Japan	40	29	9	17	4
Sweden	45	27	1	24	3
Switzerland	43	30	7	20	—
United Kingdom	41	18	12	27	3
United States	46	25	12	17	—

Note: The entries for a country may not add up to 100 percent because of rounding.
Source: Organization for Economic Cooperation and Development, *Revenue Statistics*, p. 44.

taxes are also used at the state and local levels.

The tax system must raise a certain amount of revenue to finance government activities. It does so under two constraints. There is, first, *equity*, or *fairness*. A democratic society will not tax only the poor or only those who do not find it easy to shelter incomes from taxes. The second constraint is *efficiency*. Taxes introduce differences between market prices and individual valuations of goods and services. These are distortions that create costs for society.

We now consider these two issues.

How to Tax Fairly

Government taxes and spending affect the distribution of income, imposing burdens on some and conferring benefits on others. Economists, to say nothing of taxpayers, have long been concerned about how the benefits and the burdens should be spread. There are two main ethical precepts that are widely accepted. The first is horizontal equity, and the second is vertical equity.

The rule of *horizontal equity* is that equals should be treated equally by the tax laws.

A person who works 40 hours a week earning wages should not be taxed differently

than a person who works exactly as hard earning something which the tax laws call profits, for instance.

The rule of *vertical equity* is that unequals should be treated unequally.

Someone who earns more should be taxed more, even if somehow his reported income is artificially low. But how should unequals be treated? The oldest principle in public finance is that taxes should be based on *ability to pay*. This suggests that taxes should be based on income or wealth. An alternative is to base taxes on *benefits received* from government activities.

Defining Equals We now discuss these principles and concepts in more detail. All the principles describe ideas of fairness and reflect concern over the government's influence on the distribution of income. However, applying the principles is difficult. The first problem is defining equals. We might start with current income, but that is certainly not a reasonable measure of how well off a person is. A medical student earning the same income as a janitor is better off than the janitor, for the medical student has the higher lifetime income. Perhaps we should define equals by their lifetime incomes.

Even defining equality by lifetime income raises difficult issues. Consider two people, each of whom earned the same income while working. They had the same lifetime income. Both are now retired. One saved while he was young and lives well. One had a good time while he was young and lives very poorly now. Are they equal? Or consider two people, each working in the same factory, doing the same work, getting the same pay. One of them is married, and the other is single. Are they equals? The principle of horizontal equity does not give concrete answers in these difficult cases. But it is a useful principle to keep in mind in appraising tax systems.

Ability to Pay and the Benefits Principle
Vertical equity deals with an issue on which there is much room for dissent, namely how unequals are to be treated unequally. The ability-to-pay principle clearly takes the view that government should redistribute income. Suppose that government spending to provide, say, public safety benefits the poor more than the rich. The ability-to-pay principle says that the poor should still pay lower taxes. The benefits principle would say that the poor should pay more, since they benefit more. Those applying the benefits principle to the taxation system clearly either see the current distribution of income as appropriate or believe that the government should not engage in the redistribution of income. Such a view is typically put forward by conservatives.

Applying the benefits principle in some instances of government spending strikes many as fair. Highway users should pay more than others toward the building and maintenance of roads, it might be argued. And they do, for the highway system is financed in part through gasoline taxes. But the benefits principle cannot be applied to public goods, because we do not know how to measure the benefit of a public good to each person. The benefits principle and government transfer payments do not live well together. Should a person receiving payments from the government in the form of unemployment compensation pay the government for them in proportion to the benefit? Then why should we bother in the first place?

Let us return now to the ability-to-pay principle. The key question is by how much taxes should change with the ability to pay, no matter how it is defined. This question is about the desirable *progressivity* of the tax structure.

> A tax structure is progressive if it reduces the after-tax inequality of economic well-being.

In other words, the structure is progressive if the rich pay proportionately more than the poor in taxes.

For a long time the popular view has been that taxes should be progressive. The federal tax schedule as seen in Table 17-1 is sharply progressive in that tax rates per dollar rise as income rises. Deductions and tax loopholes reduce the progressivity of federal income taxes somewhat, but the evidence is that on balance, federal taxes reduce the inequality of income. Federal personal *taxes* do redistribute income from the richest to all others. Once we also take transfer payments, including food stamps, into account, we conclude that taxes and transfers together have a large progressive effect on the distribution of income.

Taxation and Waste
How should revenue be raised to finance the government? We have seen that equity considerations are one criterion. Another criterion involves the waste that is created as people try to avoid the taxes that are imposed. We illustrate this in Figure 17-6 with an example of the labor market. Schedule *DD* is for the demand for labor, and schedule *SS* shows the supply of labor. The labor

FIGURE 17-6 A TAX ON WAGES. A tax on wages reduces at each market wage the corresponding take-home pay. Therefore, the labor supply schedule shifts to the left from *SS* to *SS'*. To have the same take-home pay a worker requires a before-tax wage that rises in proportion to the tax. The tax of 20 percent shifts the supply schedule to *SS'* and moves the labor market equilibrium from *E* to *E'*. The number of hours worked declines, the before-tax wage increases to *W'*, and the after-tax wage falls to *W"*.

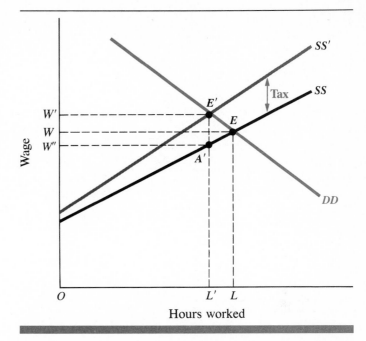

demand schedule is downward-sloping because as the real wage declines, firms are willing to substitute labor for capital, using more labor-intensive production processes. The supply schedule for labor is upward-sloping, reflecting the assumption that in response to higher real wages, workers are willing to supply a larger number of work hours. They are willing to give up leisure in exchange for wages. The initial equilibrium is at point *E*.

Suppose now that the government imposes a tax on wages, or labor income. All workers have to pay the government 20 cents for every dollar of wages they earn. At point *E* the market is now in disequilibrium. To have a $4 take-home wage, given the tax, workers will require a before-tax wage of $4.80. Similarly, to have, say, a $2 take-home pay, they need a before-tax wage of $2.40. Thus the imposition of a 20 percent tax on wages shifts the supply schedule for labor upward to *SS'*. The worker is concerned only with the amount of pay he takes home—the after-tax wage—and not with

the amount the company pays—the pretax wage.

The new equilibrium in the labor market is at point *E'*. The imposition of the tax has reduced the number of hours worked. It has *raised* the before-tax wage to *W'* from *W*, and it has *lowered* the after-tax wage to *W"*. The difference, *E'A'*, represents tax payments, or the *wedge* which the tax drives between the value of work to a firm and the amount received by the worker for working 1 more hour.

In Figure 17-7 we show the same schedules that are in Figure 17-6 and focus on two areas. Triangle *EE'A'* represents the waste created by the tax, and area *W'E'A'W"* shows the government's tax collection. We now explain these areas.

The labor market clears at the before-tax wage of *W'*. At that wage the number of hours worked has fallen from *L* to *L'*. The tax, therefore, reduces work effort. At level *L'* of work there is a wedge between the value of work to a firm, given by point *E'* on the demand for labor schedule, and the cost

FIGURE 17-7 TAX REVENUE AND WASTE. The imposition of a tax shifts the supply schedule to *SS'*. Equilibrium wages (before-tax) rise to *W'*, and the number of hours worked drops from *L* to *L'*. Triangle *EE'A'* represents the social waste arising from a discrepancy between the marginal valuation by firms of an extra hour of work and the marginal cost (or disutility) of another hour of work to workers. The area *W'E'A'W"* represents government tax collection. Taxes drive a wedge, *E'A'*, between the productivity of labor and the disutility of labor. They are a disincentive to work.

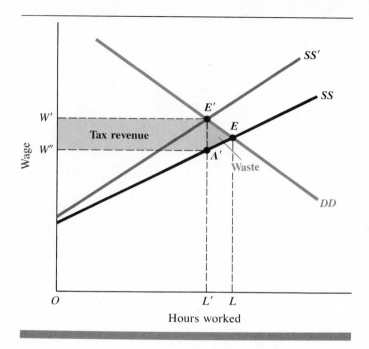

or disutility of work to workers. The marginal cost of 1 more hour of work as seen by firms exceeds the marginal benefit from another hour of work as seen by workers. Therefore, the tax has introduced a *distortion.*

Where is the distortion? With the wage paid by firms above that received by workers, the marginal value product of labor exceeds the marginal value of leisure. If workers reduced their leisure by 1 hour, society would gain an amount equal to the marginal value product of labor. It would lose a smaller amount, equal to the marginal value of leisure. But because of taxes, that extra hour of work does not get done.

Therefore the distortion is that there is too little work done. The tax acts as a disincentive to work. The total waste is equal to triangle *EE'A'*. The government collects as tax revenue the shared rectangle equal to $(W' - W") \times L'$, which is equal to the number of hours worked, *L'*, times the wage tax per hour.

Figure 17-7 shows that it is costly to raise revenue. Besides the cost to the workers, who have to share their wages with the government, there is a net waste associated with tax collection, equal to the area of the triangle. The government's tax revenue ultimately benefits someone, perhaps the very workers who pay the tax. But the triangle represents a net waste of resources due to misallocation. This waste is called the *deadweight burden* of the tax. The existence of waste makes it important to ask what design of the tax system interferes least with efficiency or creates the least waste.

A simple and important case will further understanding of the waste of taxation. Suppose, as in Figure 17-8, that the labor supply is equal to *L* at *any* wage. Thus the labor supply is totally unresponsive to the wage or totally inelastic with respect to the wage. In this case the imposition of a tax will not affect the number of hours supplied, and therefore the equilibrium remains at *E*. The full adjustment to the tax takes place through a fall in the after-tax wage. But because the labor supply is unresponsive to the wage, there is no adjustment at all in the hours worked. In this special case there is no waste because there is no attempt by workers to reduce their work effort.

We thus have as a general principle the following: Any tax on a good or factor that is in completely inelastic supply (or demand) will create no waste because there is no reduction in the taxed activity. Thus there is the possibility of having completely efficient taxes, if only we can find goods or factors that are in inelastic supply. In general, the rule is that to raise a given amount of revenue most efficiently, the government should tax relatively more heavily all those goods that are in relatively inelastic supply, the more so the more inelastic the supply.

The Welfare Cost of Income Taxes

The idea that taxes cause waste leads naturally to the question of magnitude. Is it the case that the U.S. income tax system creates a lot of waste through the process of collecting government revenue? An estimate of part of these costs has recently been made, and it suggests the following: A person who in 1975 earned $10,000 worked 9 percent less than he would have if taxes had been zero. That is a very significant labor supply response, certainly in line with Figure 17-7, not 17-8. There is also an estimate of the waste per dollar of tax collected. The amount here is 30 cents for every dollar of tax collected. Again, that is a very large number, and it certainly drives home the point that tax collection has important side costs in the form of waste.[3]

Should we conclude that if a dollar in taxes costs an extra 30 cents in waste, we are collecting too much in taxes? If the govern-

[3] See Jerry Hausman, "Labor Supply," in Henry J. Aaron and Joseph A. Pechman (eds.), *How Taxes Affect Economic Behavior*, Brookings, Washington, D.C., 1981.

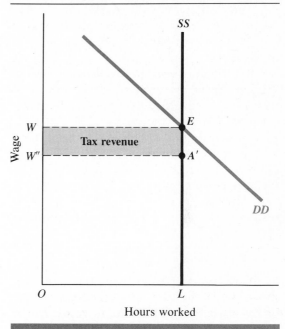

FIGURE 17-8 A TAX ON A FACTOR IN INELASTIC SUPPLY. If the labor supply is *entirely* inelastic or unresponsive to the wage, the supply schedule is vertical. A tax leaves the before-tax wage unchanged at *W*. The after-tax wage falls by the full amount of the tax. In this special case there is no waste at all.

ment must collect $1.30 worth of resources for every dollar it spends effectively, are we not losing? That conclusion is not right because we must consider the benefits associated with government spending, for example, on welfare programs or defense. The marginal benefits per dollar's worth of spending could even be much larger than $1.30.

Another Distortion: Housing and Corporate Capital

The tax system treats investment in housing and investment in capital in the corporate sector differently. Someone who invests in a corporation receives a return in the form of dividends, on which income tax is paid. Someone who buys his own home also receives a return—the value of the use of the house—but it is not taxable. If he did not own a house, he would have to rent housing and pay rent. Now he is not paying rent to anyone. It is as if he is paying rent to himself for using the house. But the *imputed rent* (the value of the use of the house) is not counted as part of his taxable income, while the return on investment in corporate capital is taxed.

Buying your own house thus has an advantage as an investment. If we add inflation, we find that the advantage of an investment in housing increases with inflation. This is mainly because of the tax treatment of depreciation (wear and tear) allowances for firms. A firm is allowed to deduct from its income certain amounts for depreciation that correspond to the cost to the firm of using up capital in production. For complex reasons, the value of the deductions falls when the inflation rate rises.

The net effects of the different treatments of housing and corporate capital are shown in Table 17-9. The effective tax rate for owner-occupied housing has been lower than that for corporate capital throughout the period since 1965. This reflects the fact that the imputed rent is not taxed. In addition, we see that in the seventies, when inflation was high, corporate capital was effectively taxed at an even higher rate in relation to the rate for owner-occupied housing. The table also shows estimates of the net of tax, real (after adjusting for inflation) return to investment in owner-occupied housing and in corporate capital. The return on capital reflects deductions for all the taxes paid en route from the firm to the private investor—taxes on the corporation and then taxes the investor pays on the income received from the corporation. The return on corporate capital has fallen in relation to the return on owner-occupied housing.

The tax system creates a distortion because investment in housing and investment in corporate capital are taxed at differ-

ent rates. What is the reason for this distortion? One simple explanation is that the favorable treatment of owner-occupied housing reflects the political power of the middle class. This sounds like a good explanation until we ask whether owners of corporate capital should be expected to have less political power.

Another possible explanation is that the tax system wants to encourage homeownership in the belief that ownership of homes contributes to the stability of society. Thus the favorable treatment of imputed rent is put into the system, and then inflation combined with the power of the middle class makes it difficult to establish reforms. The final explanation is that taxation of imputed rent would be too difficult and unpopular; therefore, it is not a good idea.

There is one final question raised by the table. The table shows substantial differences between the real net rates of return for corporate capital and those for owner-occupied housing. Can this be an equilibrium situation? Should we not expect the returns to be equalized eventually? Anyone has the choice of investing in either corporate capital or owner-occupied housing. We should, therefore, expect that investment will continue to flow more into housing until the return on housing has been pushed down and that on corporate capital raised to the point where they are equal.

In fact, investment trends in the seventies were in the direction suggested by the view that returns will ultimately be equalized. Investment in corporate capital fell in relation to investment in owner-occupied housing during the seventies.

There have been efforts to remove the distortion. In 1981 the depreciation provisions of the tax laws were reformed to allow businesses to make larger deductions. The changes reduced the wide gap between effective rates of taxation. But they did not eliminate the basic advantage to investing in owner-occupied housing implied by non-taxation of imputed rent.

Tax Incidence

Let us return to Figures 17-7 and 17-8 to ask who pays the tax on wages that the government collects. At first sight the answer seems obvious: if workers are taxed, then workers will pay the tax. But that answer is not satisfactory once we look at Figure 17-7. There we observe that the before-tax wage increases somewhat and that the after-tax wage falls somewhat. Because the after-tax wage falls by less than the full tax, the tax is only partly borne by workers; it is borne in part by firms, which have reduced profits, or by consumers of the final good, who pay more.

Are there any general rules about who pays the tax or what tax *incidence* is? The first rule is that taxes on a factor in inelastic supply are *totally* borne by that factor. This is the case shown in Figure 17-8, where the pretax wage does not change and the after-tax wage falls by the full amount of the tax.

For the rest, the incidence is split between the supply side and the demand side of the market. The more inelastic supply is in relation to demand, the larger the part of the tax borne by suppliers. You can experiment with some diagrams to see what determines whether most of the adjustment is in the pretax wage or in the after-tax wage. Problem 11 asks you to do this.

5 TAX REFORM AND TAX REVOLT

There is much unhappiness with taxation in America, and there has been much more in the last 10 years than for a long time. The dissatisfaction has been evident in a number of important directions. One is the large cut in personal income tax rates established by the Reagan administration. Another important direction is a movement to adopt constitutional amendments that limit growth in government spending at the federal and state levels. Finally, there are proposals to improve technical aspects of the tax system.

The Tax Revolt

The tax revolt of the 1970s and early 1980s started in California. Here is what one of the promoters, Howard Jarvis, had to say:

> My basic feeling hasn't changed a bit over all those years: money is much better off in the hands of the average citizen than it is in the greedy hands of those who live off the public payroll. . . . (*I'm Mad as Hell*, p. 5)

TABLE 17-9

TAXATION OF AND RETURNS ON CORPORATE CAPITAL AND OWNER-OCCUPIED HOUSING

YEAR	EFFECTIVE TAX RATE FOR CORPORATE CAPITAL, %	REAL NET RETURN ON CORPORATE CAPITAL, %	EFFECTIVE TAX RATE FOR OWNER-OCCUPIED HOUSING, %	REAL NET RETURN ON OWNER-OCCUPIED HOUSING, %
1960	66.5	3.5	32	5.0
1965	55.1	6.5	37	4.5
1970	70.5	2.8	40	4.3
1975	72.4	2.4	34	4.4
1979	74.5	2.3	32	4.3

Source: Lawrence H. Summers, "Inflation, the Stock Market, and Owner-Occupied Housing," *American Economic Review, Papers and Proceedings,* May 1981, p. 430.

Successive referenda in California sought to limit taxes.[4] Proposition 13, accepted 2 to 1 in 1978, limited property taxes to 1 percent of the value of the property. Proposition 4, accepted 74 to 26 in 1979, requires that *real* per capita state and local government spending not increase.

In 1980 a radical measure, Proposition 9, sought to cut state tax rates by 50 percent. This was defeated 61 to 39.

The swing from approval of the earlier propositions to defeat of Proposition 9 shows that voters are experimenting with the role of government but that they do not regard all government spending as being undesirable.

Table 17-10 provides some explanation of the California voting. The defeat of the state income tax cuts reflected a belief on the part of a very large percentage of the voters who were questioned in polls that education and safety would be endangered.

The Balanced Budget Amendment The California experience of legal change to reduce taxes and government spending has spread across the nation. The most important proposal currently under consideration is the balanced budget amendment to the U.S. Constitution.

The amendment seeks both to balance the budget, requiring Congress to raise as much in taxes as it spends, and to limit the amount of government spending as a percentage of GNP. Proponents argue that the record of continued federal deficits in the period since 1960 is dramatic proof that only constitutional change can reduce deficits and cut government spending. Opponents say that it is foolish to put economic policy issues in the Constitution, especially when the deficit is easily manipulated by the federal government. They also argue that it is bad economic policy to take away the federal government's ability to run budget deficits during recessions.[5]

In 1982 the amendment was rejected by the House after acceptance by the Senate and endorsement by the President. No doubt it will reappear as a major issue.

Supply Side Economics and Taxation

The Reagan administration in 1981 introduced an ambitious program of tax cuts to stimulate the economy, private initiative, and investment. At the same time it worked on eliminating excessive intrusion of the government in economic life.

One of the intellectual underpinnings of the Reagan program was the famous Laffer curve, shown in Figure 17-9. The Laffer curve—named after an adviser to the Reagan administration, University of Southern California economist Arthur Laffer—

---

[4] See Alvin Rabushka and Pauline Ryan, *The Tax Revolt*, Hoover Institution, Stanford, Calif., 1982, for a discussion of the California events.

[5] The desirability or otherwise of running budget deficits is discussed in Chapter 24.

TABLE 17-10

REASONS FOR OPPOSING TAX CUTS

	PROPOSITION 13 (ACCEPTED 1978)	PROPOSITION 9 (REJECTED 1980)
Public safety will be endangered	25%	44%
Education will deteriorate	37	59
The rich will benefit the most	57	66
Minorities will suffer the most	43	45

Source: Alvin Rabushka and Pauline Ryan, *The Tax Revolt*, Hoover Institution, Stanford, Calif., 1982, p. 178.

FIGURE 17-9 THE LAFFER CURVE. The Laffer curve shows the relationship between tax rates and the tax revenue they generate. A zero tax rate generates zero tax revenue; low rates generate some revenue; higher rates generate more. But there is a maximum at rate t^*. Increasing the tax rate further actually leads to a cut in total tax revenue because the disincentive effects outweigh the higher tax rates.

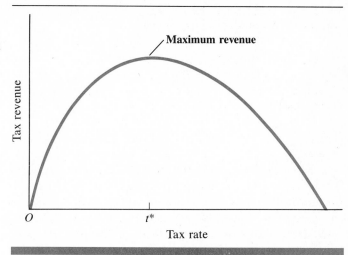

shows that government revenue from taxes need not fall when tax rates are cut. The diagram shows that at a tax rate of zero, the tax revenue is zero. But suppose, taking the example of a tax on labor income, that we increase the tax rate to a level above zero. Clearly we will now collect some revenue.

As we increase the tax rate further, say, from 5 percent to 10 percent, two things happen. People choose to work less, as we saw in Figure 17-7, and therefore some revenue is lost. But we are also taxing the remaining income at a higher rate. Initially that will lead to a net increase in tax revenue. But as we go further, the disincentive effects become larger, work effort falls a lot, and increased taxes ultimately fail to bring any more revenue. Going even further leads to a decline in tax collection. As tax rates rise more, tax revenue becomes zero—people stop working or emigrate.

The idea behind the Laffer curve is that if U.S. taxes were in the range to the right of t^*, we could perform miracles. We could cut taxes (everybody would like that), *and* we could have more tax revenue at the same time. It is clear that we would be faced with the extraordinary possibility of getting something for nothing, just by making the

economy more efficient. Nothing is wrong with the idea of the Laffer curve. What has met with the most violent professional criticism is the suggestion that the United States is, *in fact*, in the range to the right of t^*. Quite on the contrary, there is wide professional agreement that we are well to the left.[6]

The tax cuts as enacted sharply reduced high-income marginal tax rates, as shown in Table 17-1. The extent to which those cuts will affect the labor supply and tax revenues in coming years remains to be seen. The early signs in 1981 and 1982 were that tax revenues would fall, not rise, as a result of the tax cuts.

Tax Reform

There is a whole menu of changes that tax experts, if left in control, would introduce. Two stand out. The first is to make the tax system inflationproof. This change is discussed in the macroeconomics part of the book. The other major change is to simplify the tax system. The most radical proposal

---

[6] See Alan Blinder, "Thoughts on the Laffer Curve," in Lawrence H. Meyer (ed.), *The Supply-Side Effects of Economic Policy*, Center for the Study of American Business, St. Louis, Mo., 1981.

TABLE 17-11

AVERAGE TAX RATES

| | INCOME LEVEL | | | |
	$10,000	$30,000	$100,000	$1 MILLION
Flat rate*	9.5	15.8	18.1	18.9
Actual U.S. rate†	4.6	15.8	35.9	48.6

* Exemption of $5000 and a flat tax rate of 19 percent beyond.
† Based on 1982 tax table for married couple with one child, assuming standard deductions.

for simplification is the *flat-rate* tax system.

One version of this proposal has the following three key features.[7] (1) All income is taxed only once, at the same rate. (2) There is an exemption for low-income families. (3) Income tax forms are sufficiently simplified to fit a postcard. The proposed tax rate is 19 percent—for households and corporations alike. Taxes are levied only on *income*, not on capital gains. There would be no deductions for interest payments as there are now.

One advantage of the proposal is the elimination of misallocations that presently exist—for example, the misallocation of capital between housing and the corporate sector as discussed above. Of course, everyone would also value a simpler way to file returns.

But the proposal raises very serious questions about the progressivity of taxes. With a flat rate of 19 percent there is very little progressivity, and there would not be

any were it not for the exemption for low-income families. The exemption means that no tax is paid on the first few thousand dollars earned. Suppose that the exemption is $5000 and that a rate of 19 percent applies to any income in excess of that amount. What would the average tax rate be at different income levels?

The first row of Table 17-11 shows the average tax rates (taxes divided by total income) under the flat-rate proposal. The tax is progressive in that rich people pay a larger part of their income than poor people. But how does this tax structure compare with current progressivity? In the second row we show current ratios of total tax payments to *taxable* income in the United States. The data show progressivity. But many would argue that this is *not* the relevant comparison because taxable income already excludes a lot of income that benefits from some tax gimmick. The flat-raters would argue that their proposal is more progressive. At the same time, they would argue that it involves the elimination of a lot of inefficiency.

---

[7] Robert Hall and Alvin Rabushka, "A Proposal to Simplify Our Tax System," *Wall Street Journal*, Dec. 10, 1981.

SUMMARY

1   Government revenues in industrialized economies come mainly from the income tax, taxes on purchases of goods, and Social Security taxes. The sales tax and VAT may provide up to one-quarter of government revenue. The United States relies relatively more on the property tax and less on sales tax and VAT than other countries.

2   Government spending is for both the purchase of goods and services and transfers. In 1982 governments (federal, state, and local) spent 20 percent of GNP on goods and services and 13 percent of GNP on transfer payments.

3   With regard to the optimal allocation of resources in a market economy, government has a role to play in dealing with externalities. First, taxes and subsidies may reduce distortion. Second, the government intervenes to determine the output of public goods. These are goods for which consumption by one person does not reduce consumption by another. Defense is the classic example. Third, government may intervene to affect the distribution of income or welfare in the society.

4   Society is producing the optimal amount of a public good when the marginal cost of production is equal to the sum of the amounts individuals are willing to pay for the public good. Demand curves for a public good should be added vertically, since one person's consumption of the good does not reduce the consumption of others. It is difficult to get people to reveal how much they demand of a public good. This is because there is a free-rider problem. Each individual knows that he gets to consume the public good if someone else pays for it; therefore, he does not have an incentive to say he would like it.

5   The theory of public choice approaches the question of how public spending and tax decisions are made by studying the interactions of the people who make the decisions with the mechanisms that have been set up for decision making.

6   A democratic society's decision-making process is typically based on voting for legislators. They make the decisions, which are then carried out by bureaucrats under the supervision of the executive. There are no foolproof methods for obtaining or even defining a society's views about what should be done. Majority voting can lead to the paradox of voting, in which society's choices appear to be inconsistent. Provided that tastes are single-peaked, majority voting will lead to a consistent result; on any issue, society will choose according to the preferences of the median voter. Legislative decision making involves not only voting but also the complex trading of votes on different issues. The relationship between the final choices of the legislature and the underlying preferences of the voters is not easy to state.

7   Principles of vertical and horizontal equity are used in designing and evaluating tax systems. The rule of horizontal equity is that equals should be treated equally. The rule of vertical equity is that unequals should be treated unequally. One argument about how unequals should be treated is that people should pay taxes according to their ability to pay. This suggests that the wealthier should pay more. If they pay proportionately more than the poor—i.e., if they pay a

higher proportion of their income or wealth—we say that the tax system is progressive. The U.S. tax and transfer system is somewhat progressive.

8   Taxes on the scale found in modern economies inevitably create distortions in the allocation of resources. The taxes open up a wedge between market and private valuations of goods and factor supplies. When wages are taxed, the value of the marginal product of labor is higher than the take-home wage of the worker and therefore higher than his valuation of leisure.

9   The gaps between market and private valuations lead the economy away from an undistorted equilibrium and affect the allocation of resources. Taxation creates deadweight losses in that the cost of taxation to the private sector is greater than the amount of revenue raised by the government. The amount of deadweight loss depends on the elasticities of supply and demand in the market where the tax is imposed. If labor is in inelastic supply, a tax on labor income creates no excess burden. Similarly, there is no deadweight burden if the demand for a good is inelastic. The total waste of taxation is minimized if goods whose demand is inelastic are taxed relatively heavily.

10   The incidence of a tax determines who ultimately pays the tax. If a tax has no effect on the price received by buyers, the incidence must be entirely on the seller. If the tax has no effect on the price received by sellers, then the price paid by buyers must have gone up by the entire amount of the tax, and the incidence is on the buyers. The more inelastic demand is, the more the incidence is on demanders.

11   The total amount of revenue received from a tax typically rises at first as the tax is introduced, but eventually it falls when the tax rate becomes very high. If taxes were high enough, a reduction in the tax rate would both increase government revenue and reduce the deadweight burden. In the case of the U.S. income tax, the evidence is that we are nowhere near such a situation. But the income tax does appear to reduce significantly the quantity of labor supplied. An extra dollar raised through income taxes has a deadweight burden that may be as high as 30 cents.

12   The existence of distortions does not necessarily imply that government spending should be reduced. The distortions are merely part of the price that has to be paid to buy the goods the government purchases. So long as the marginal value of those goods exceeds the marginal cost to the private sector, government purchases should be made, distortions and all. If the marginal value of the government spending is less than the cost to the private sector, the spending should be cut back. It is necessary in trying to make such calculations to take into account the distributional effects of government spending and taxing.

13 High rates of taxation in the United States have led to a tax revolt and to cuts in taxes. The tax revolt is trying to use both legislative and constitutional limitations to keep taxes down. Tax reform in the shape of a vastly simplified tax system is also actively discussed and advocated.

KEY TERMS

Tax revolt	Vertical and horizontal equity
Marginal income tax rate	Ability-to-pay principle
Sales or excise taxes	Benefits principle
Public goods	Progressivity of tax structure
Merit goods	Wedge
Median voter	Waste or deadweight burden of taxes
Payroll tax	Laffer curve
Value-added tax (VAT)	Flat-rate tax system

PROBLEMS

1 Discuss what distinguishes Disneyland from a national park. Which of the two is a public good, if either? Should either or both be publicly provided? Can either or both be run privately?

2 Why does society try to make sure that every child receives an education? Discuss different ways this could be done, and give reasons for choosing one rather than another.

3 Which of the following qualify as public goods? (*a*) Fire protection, (*b*) clean streets, (*c*) garbage collection, (*d*) ambulance service, (*e*) the U.S. Marine Corps Marching Band, (*f*) the postal service. Explain and discuss alternative ways of providing the goods.

4 What reason is there for thinking that the distribution of income produced by private markets would be desirable? What is your view on the desirability of government intervention to affect the distribution of income? How does the government in fact try to intervene to affect income distribution?

5 Sweden collects 60 percent of the GNP in taxes and the United States 33 percent. What could account for the difference?

6 Explain how you would determine how much of a public good should be produced if you knew everyone's demand function for public goods. Then explain why it is difficult to discover what demand functions really are.

7 How would you apply the principles of horizontal and vertical equity in deciding how much to tax two individuals? Each one is in good health and is capable of doing the same work that the other does, but one chooses to devote more time to suntanning and therefore has a lower income.

8 Suppose that a flat rate for income tax is established. The exemption is for $10,000, and beyond that a flat tax rate of 20 percent applies. Calculate the average tax liability (taxes divided by total income) at income levels of $10,000, $20,000, $100,000, and $1 million. How does the level of the exemption affect the progressivity of the tax?

Would the tax be more progressive if the exemption were only $5000?

9 Many economists have advocated a consumption tax to replace the income tax. The tax would be based on the amount *spent* on goods and services each year rather than on the amount *earned*. The consumption tax is not identical to a sales tax, because the rate of taxation could be progressive. (*a*) What is the difference between the income tax and a consumption tax? [Think about what families do with the part of their income that is not consumed.] (*b*) What would be the major benefit of the consumption tax in that case? (*c*) In terms of horizontal or vertical equity, what is there to be said for a consumption tax? (*d*) On the basis of your answers, would you be in favor of the consumption tax replacing the income tax? Why or why not?

10 (*a*) Suppose the supply of labor is totally inelastic. Show why there is no waste or deadweight burden if labor is taxed. Show also who bears the incidence of the tax. (*b*) Now suppose that the supply of labor is quite elastic. Show the area that is deadweight burden or waste. Then discuss whether the suppliers and demanders of labor respectively bear the incidence, and explain how much. (*c*) Who ultimately bears the incidence when the pretax wage goes up as a result of taxes? [Think of what the increase in the pretax wage does to the firm's costs.]

That we face an urban crisis of utmost seriousness has in recent years come to be part of the conventional wisdom. . . . There is, however, another side to the matter. The plain fact is that the overwhelming majority of city dwellers live more comfortably and conveniently than ever before. They have more and better housing, more and better schools, more and better transportation, and so on. By any conceivable measure of material welfare the present generation of urban Americans is, on the whole, better off than any other large group of people has ever been anywhere.[1]

18

City Economics and the Problems of the Cities

High income and urbanization—the concentration of population in cities—go together. On the average, the higher the per capita income in a country, the more urbanized the country, as Table 18-1 and Figure 18-1 show. Table 18-1 shows the changes that have taken place in the last 20 years. In almost all countries the population has shifted from the country to the cities. But the shift has been going on for much longer. In the United States only 5 percent of the population lived in towns in 1790, whereas over 75 percent of the population lives in towns now.

How much of the population lives in the really big cities? The number varies from country to country. In the United States there are 18 urban areas, each with a population above 2 million. More than one-third of the total population lives in these areas. Table 18-2 gives details for 1980. The urban area around New York City, with over 16 million, still has the largest concentration in the country. The area around Los Angeles, with 11.5 million, has the second-largest concentration. But as the table shows, the population in the older cities in the north and east is declining or growing slowly, while the population in the newer cities in California and the sun belt is growing rapidly.

Cities get a bad press. Read about a city, and you read about traffic congestion, pollution, high property taxes, crime, and decay. Cities are described as having problems that need solutions. But there must be something right with cities. That's where the jobs are, as well as sports teams and the good shopping. People move to the cities, away from the country, and much less in the opposite direction.

In this chapter we discuss both the benefits of city life and the problems of the cities. We start with a simple question: Why cities? We go on to discuss population density in cities, the move to the sub-

[1] Edward C. Banfield, *The Unheavenly City*, Little, Brown, Boston, 1970.

TABLE 18-1

URBAN POPULATION AS A PERCENTAGE OF TOTAL POPULATION, AND PER CAPITA INCOME

COUNTRY	URBAN POPULA-TION, % of total population		INCOME PER CAPITA, 1979 $
	1980	1960	
Low-income countries	17	15	230
Middle-income countries	50	37	1420
Industrialized countries	77	68	9440

Source: The World Bank, *World Development Report, 1981,* Tables 1 and 20, pp. 134–135 and 172–173.

TABLE 18-2

POPULATION OF STANDARD CONSOLIDATED (METROPOLITAN*) STATISTICAL AREAS, UNITED STATES, 1980

AREA	POPULATION ON APRIL 1, 1980, millions	POPULATION CHANGE, 1970–1980, %
New York–Newark–Jersey City (New York–New Jersey–Connecticut)	16.1	−5.4
Los Angeles–Long Beach–Anaheim (California)	11.5	15.2
Chicago–Gary (Illinois–Indiana)	7.9	1.8
Philadelphia–Wilmington–Trenton (Pennsylvania–Delaware–Maryland–New Jersey)	5.5	−1.4
San Francisco–Oakland–San Jose (California)	5.2	11.9
Detroit–Ann Arbor (Michigan)	4.6	−1.1
Boston–Lawrence–Lowell (Massachusetts–New Hampshire)	3.4	−2.2
Houston–Galveston (Texas)	3.1	43.0
Washington, D.C.* (Maryland–Virginia)	3.1	5.2
Dallas–Ft. Worth* (Texas)	3.0	25.1
Cleveland–Akron–Lorain (Ohio)	2.8	−5.5
Miami–Fort Lauderdale (Florida)	2.6	39.8
St. Louis* (Missouri–Illinois)	2.4	−2.3
Pittsburgh* (Pennsylvania)	2.3	−5.7
Baltimore* (Maryland)	2.2	5.0
Minneapolis–St. Paul* (Minnesota–Wisconsin)	2.1	7.6
Seattle–Tacoma (Washington)	2.1	13.9
Atlanta* (Georgia)	2.0	27.2

Note: Data are for Standard Consolidated Statistical Areas (SCSAs) or for Standard Metropolitan Statistical Areas (SMSAs). SMSAs are indicated by an asterisk (*). An SMSA includes one or more counties that are metropolitan, as measured by the percentage of the labor force not in agriculture and by the amount of commuting within the area. An SCSA consists of several SMSAs that form a single urban area, such as the New York City area, Chicagoland, the Bay area, and other terms used by weather forecasters.
Source: Statistical Abstract of the United States, 1981, Table 23.

FIGURE 18-1 URBAN POPULATION AND INCOME PER CAPITA: INTERNATIONAL COMPARISON. (*Source:* The World Bank, *World Development Report, 1980,* Washington, D.C.)

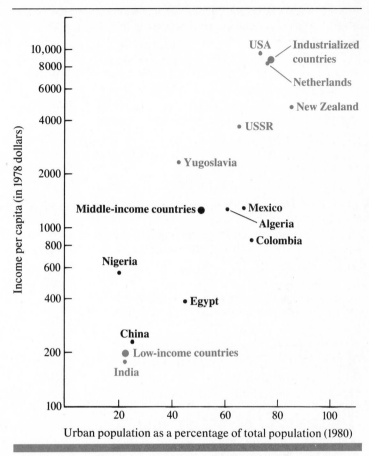

urbs and the decay of center cities, housing problems, and the funding of local government. Some of the problems that we think of as city problems—such as poverty—are actually worse in rural areas. But because they are so visible in the cities, they get more attention there.

1 WHY CITIES?

Two basic forces combine to create cities: the benefits of specialization and trade, and transportation costs. If individuals did not want to trade, there would be no reason for them to want to be in contact with each other ("trade" is used in a broad sense here). And even if they wanted to trade, but there were no costs of transporting goods or people, there would be no reason for them to live close together.

Why is there trade? There are, first, differences in skills among individuals and in the ownership of natural resources. Second, and most important, there are economies of scale in producing some goods. Average costs of production fall as output rises. Thus there is reason to produce on a large scale. Because transportation is costly, both the suppliers to an industry and the purchasers of the goods find it profitable to locate closer to the source of production. Thus economies of scale in production combined with transportation costs encourage the concentration of population.

There are also *economies of agglomeration*. These are benefits that accrue to all industries in an area as the population expands. The larger the population, the greater the range of skills in the labor force, the greater the range of available goods, the more economical and available the public utilities, and so on. One of the most quoted of Adam Smith's many famous lines is relevant here: "The division of labor is limited by the extent of the market."[2]

We want to take a broad view of production in talking about reasons for the existence of cities. Plays, rock concerts, major league sports, specialty restaurants, high- or low-class clothing shops—all of these need a large population for their support. Indeed, there is a range of services, diversity, and choice that we should expect to find in cities of a particular size, but not find in smaller ones.

Figure 18-2 shows the ranges of services found in trading centers of different sizes in a study conducted of the upper middle west in the 1960s. The smallest centers have a gas station, a grocery store, and the remaining four establishments listed at the bottom of the list on the right side of the diagram. The largest centers have all the convenience businesses listed plus the specialty establishments such as a mortuary and an antique store; in addition, they have wholesale suppliers for all the major commodity groups. Going further up the scale, we could fill in amenities such as sports teams and museums that become available in still larger cities.

In asking "why cities?" in this section, our focus has been on the benefits of urban living. But we should also ask what made cities possible and why there has been a move toward the cities over the course of history.

There are two factors here. The first is the increasing productivity of agriculture. Cities draw on other areas—largely in their neighborhood—for food. When agriculture is more productive, fewer farmers are needed to support a person living in the city. Primitive man had to devote himself almost entirely to producing food; modern man can rely on others to do so. In the United States it takes less than 4 percent of the work force to feed the population—and to have food left over to export. The second factor is lower transportation costs. Improvements in transportation made it possible for people to move around more cheaply within cities and to live further from their work. The improvements also made it cheaper for the cities to draw on more distant sources of food and raw material supplies.

2 CITY SIZE, GROWTH, AND LOCATION

The same two basic forces that create cities—the benefits of concentration and transportation costs—determine their size, shape, and location. On one side there are gains from the high concentration and density of consumers and producers. Concentration makes possible economies of scale, specialization, diversity, choice, and competition. All these are advantages that by themselves make for highly concentrated and densely populated cities.

Against the forces making for concentration is the dislike of congestion by the inhabitants of the city and their desire for space in which to live comfortably. The desire for space results in decentralization of the city. Just how far the decentralization can proceed depends on transportation costs. When transportation costs are high, the city will be concentrated but smaller in total population than when transportation costs are low.

The economics of city size are illustrated in Figures 18-3 and 18-4, which show

---

[2] Adam Smith, *The Wealth of Nations*, Modern Library ed., New York, 1937, chap. III.

FIGURE 18-2   GOODS TRADED IN CITIES OF DIFFERENT SIZES. *Note:* Values are in 1960 dollars. They should be multiplied by 3 to obtain current dollar values. (*Source:* John R. Borchert, "The Urbanization of the Upper Midwest," Upper Midwest Economic Study, Urban Report no. 2, Minneapolis, February 1963, fig. 4, p. 12; reproduced in David Segal, *Urban Economics,* Irwin, Homewood, Ill., 1977, fig. 3-7, p. 53.)

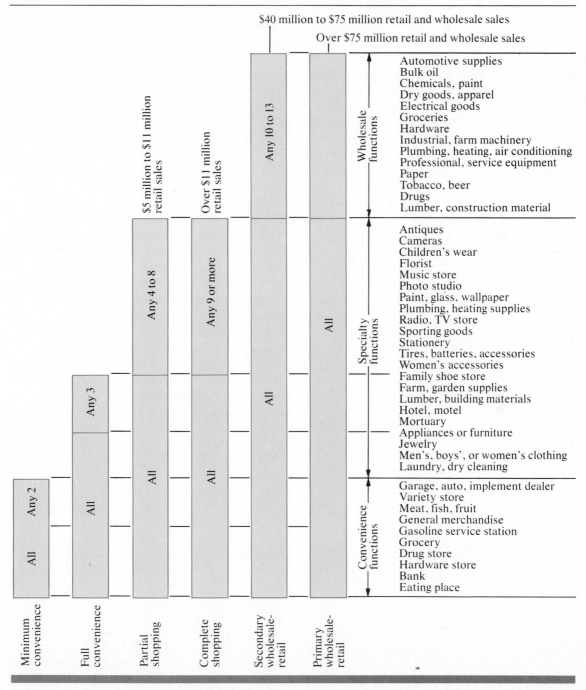

FIGURE 18-3   FORCES SHAPING
THE CITY.

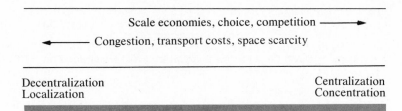

Scale economies, choice, competition ⟶

⟵ Congestion, transport costs, space scarcity

Decentralization   Centralization
Localization   Concentration

the two conflicting tendencies, one toward centralization and the other toward decentralization. On one side a larger city implies a larger population and therefore more significant economies of scale. As the city size grows, the average and marginal costs of production decline because of economies of scale. This is shown by the downward-sloping schedule *MCP* in Figure 18-4, which

FIGURE 18-4   COSTS OF PRODUCING A GOOD
AND DELIVERING IT TO THE PERIPHERY. As the
city size grows, the costs of producing goods fall
due to economies of scale, as shown by the *MCP*
curve. At the same time, the marginal cost of transporting goods to the periphery of the city rises, as
shown by *MCT*. The total marginal cost of delivering
goods to the periphery (*MCD*) eventually rises. As
MCD continues rising, it eventually makes sense to
form other cities or centers. These will, if they are
smaller, have a higher *MCP* but a lower *MCT*—the
losses from producing on a smaller scale are outweighed by the gains from lower transportation
costs.

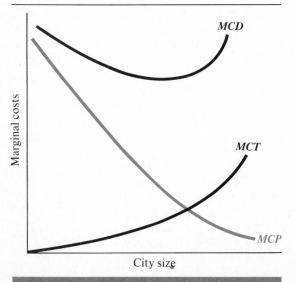

represents the marginal cost of production. The other factor is the cost of transportation. As the city size grows, the marginal cost of transportation to the farthest location—the periphery—increases because distance and congestion rise. This is shown by the upward-sloping marginal cost of transportation curve, *MCT*.

How does the marginal cost of a product delivered to the border of the city change with city size? Here we have to look at the sum of the *MCT* and the *MCP*. In Figure 18-4 the corresponding schedule, *MCD*, first falls, as the economies of scale outweigh transportation costs in the small-city range. But as the city grows, the increasing marginal transportation cost becomes more important than the cost reduction from economies of scale, and delivered products have an increasing marginal cost.

As the marginal costs of producing goods and delivering them to the periphery of the city rise, it begins to make sense to form new cities, or central locations. Then they, too, will be able to reap the benefits of economies of scale, but people living in the area will not have to pay such high transportation costs. As a city grows, there will be increasing decentralization. Local centers will spring up, with grocery stores and bank branches, supermarkets, shopping malls, and other activities that can be decentralized. This tendency leads to a flattening out of the city. Each local center can be thought of as a city in itself, with its own competitors starting at the periphery.

Cities tend to decentralize as growth leads to an increasing population that can sustain, in different centers, the economies of scale that were initially concentrated on Main Street. This means that with a growing total urban population, each city is ever growing, spreading out in little subcities. The spreading out mitigates or even eliminates the disadvantages of the city, while the benefits in terms of competition and economies of scale are maintained or even enhanced. On this account the large cities might become increasingly attractive places to live, and the result might be increasing migration toward the major cities.

However, older cities have not been able to cope with many of the problems of congestion, and in good part for that reason, there has been net migration away from the largest traditional centers in the northeast. America is becoming more urban, and the relatively smaller cities are growing rapidly, but at the same time the largest traditional cities are experiencing relatively low growth and net emigration. This was seen in Table 18-2. We turn to the decay of the central cities below.

Where Are Cities Located?

The specific location of cities depends in large part on natural resources, especially transportation. Major cities in the past were almost always located on a navigable waterway—an ocean or a river. Only with the coming of the railroad, road transportation, and air transportation do we find big cities without major water transportation. Of the 18 areas in Table 18-2, only Dallas–Ft. Worth is not on a navigable waterway. The great European cities are all located close to waterways.

The location of cities is affected also by other natural resources—cities may be centers of rich agricultural areas, or close to minerals (Kansas City, Pittsburgh), or conveniently located between mineral sources (Detroit). The location of cities may also be determined by political reasons—as was the case for Washington, D.C.

Once a city is set up, it begins to have many advantages just by being there. We would not expect the discovery of oil in western Canada to lead to the building of giant new cities near the oil fields, since most of the benefits of having cities nearby are captured already by the existing cities, such as Edmonton and Calgary. The effect of the oil development is to make the existing cities that are located nearby grow at a faster rate.

3 POPULATION DENSITY, LAND RENTS, AND MARKET EQUILIBRIUM

Cities are defined by their high density of population. Typically the population density—the number of people per square mile—is higher near the center of the city. This pattern is seen in Figure 18-5, which contains *population density gradients* for Cincinnati and San Diego.[3] A population density gradient shows how population density changes with distance from the center of the city.

Accompanying this pattern of higher population density near the center of the city is a smaller pattern of *land rents*. Land rents are rents for the use of land *alone* and not for the rental of an apartment or house. Figure 18-6 shows *land-rent gradients* for the city of Chicago for the years 1857 and 1928, respectively.[4] The land-rent gradient is a curve showing how land rent changes with distance from the center of the city. The land-rent gradients in Figure 18-6 look like the population density gradients in Figure 18-5. They all decline with distance

---

[3] These are based on data from the 1950 census.
[4] Surprisingly, data on land rents are difficult to find. This is because most urban land that is rented already has a building on it, and the rent for the land alone is difficult to determine from the rent for the land and building together. Estimated land rentals for Chicago going back well over a century are available and were used in estimating the gradients that are shown in Figure 18-6.

FIGURE 18-5 POPULATION DENSITY GRADIENTS. (*Source:* Richard F. Muth, *Cities and Housing,* University of Chicago Press, 1969, table 1, p. 142.)

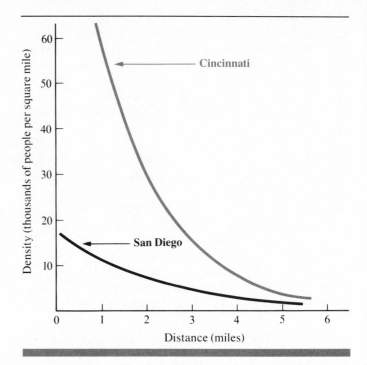

FIGURE 18-6 CHICAGO LAND-RENT GRADIENTS, 1857 and 1928. [*Source:* Edwin S. Mills, "The Value of Urban Land," in Harvey S. Perloff (ed.), *The Quality of the Urban Environment,* Johns Hopkins, Baltimore, 1969, table 1, p. 247. *Note:* Data are obtained from land value gradients estimated by Mills, assuming capitalization rate was 5% in both periods. Land values for 1857 were converted to 1928 dollars using consumer price index (all items), as found in *Historical Statistics of the United States,* series E 135–166, p. 211.]

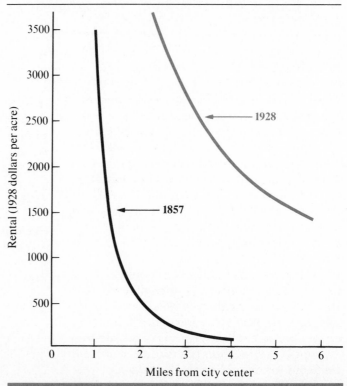

from the center of the city. Note that the Chicago land-rent gradient for 1928 is much less steep than the one for 1857.

Why do these basic population density and land-rent gradients exist? What are the economic forces producing them? We now build a simple economic model that explains the gradients.

A Simple Economic Model

This economic model, like all models, simplifies. We start with strong assumptions. Suppose that all business is done in the center of the city, that all pieces of land in the city are of the same quality except for their distance from the center of the city, that all families have the same income and same tastes, and that all families live on lots of the same size. Assume, finally, that transportation costs are proportional to distance from the center of the city.

With these very strong assumptions, all people are the same. Therefore, in equilibrium, they will all end up paying the same amount for their housing. This means that in equilibrium the benefit that people get from lower transportation costs near the center of the city must be balanced by lower rents farther from the center. To see that, suppose it were not true. Suppose that after taking account of both rents and transportation costs, people found that it was cheaper to live far from the center. Then people nearer the center would try to move out. Land rents near the center would fall, and those far from the center would rise—until the rent differences exactly balanced the transportation cost differences.

We thus already have essentially explained the patterns of land rents in Figure 18-6. They reflect in part the higher transportation costs of being farther from the center of the city. The farther out people are, the higher the transportation costs, and therefore the less the rent that is paid.

But there were two facts to explain. The

other was the decreasing population density. So far we have assumed that people live on lots of the same size; therefore, the density is the same everywhere. But with rents being lower farther out from the center of the city, people will be willing to substitute in their budgets away from other goods and toward space. Similarly, the people in the center of the city, facing a high price for space (because land rents are high), reduce their demand for space and increase their demand for other goods.

Given the demand for space, we will find people living with less space near the center of the city and more space farther from the center. And that explains why the population density decreases as we move away from the center of the city. Thus transportation costs and the desire for space together account for the basic shape of both the land-rent and population gradients in Figures 18-5 and 18-6.

Local Centers Although the general patterns shown by the population and rent gradients in Figures 18-5 and 18-6 are correct, the world is now a bit more complicated than that. There is more than one business district in most towns, and it is quite likely that there are local concentrations of population, as well as local rises and falls in the rent gradient. Indeed, if there are some people who both want to live in the city and love open space, they will prefer to live far from the center, and the rent gradient may actually rise toward the outskirts of the city. Thus we should view the simple theory outlined above as describing the main features but not the full details, of population and rent gradients.

The Slope of the Rent Gradient What determines the slope of the rent gradient? The most important factor here is transportation costs. For instance, the reason why the 1857 Chicago curve in Figure 18-6 is so much steeper than the 1928 curve is that transportation costs were much higher in 1857. The time at which a city was built is important in determining transportation costs. A city built later was probably designed for automobiles. It will have a gradient that is not as steep as the gradient for an older city because commuting is easier.

The General Level of Land Rents We have now explained the *shape* of the land-rent gradient. But we have not explained its general *level* in this chapter. Why is the land-rent gradient higher at one time than at another, for instance? What determines land rents at the edge of the city?

We have actually already answered this question in Chapter 15, where we discussed the allocation of land between urban real estate and agriculture. Figure 18-7 repeats that analysis with a simple supply and demand diagram. The rent in Figure 18-7 is the rent for land at the edge of the city.

The supply curve of land for urban use reflects the opportunity cost of the land in agriculture. The land has a rental value in agriculture because it produces crops and can be used for grazing or whatever other agricultural activity is best. The less land there is in agriculture, the higher the value of its marginal product in agriculture, and the higher the rent that will have to be paid to get it out of agricultural use and into urban use. Therefore, the supply curve of land for urban use slopes upward.

The demand for land in urban use is shown by the curve *DD*. The downward slope reflects the diminishing marginal value of land in urban use, both for industrial use and for consumption in the form of gardens and a less crowded environment. The more land there is in the city (for a given population), the less valuable is a marginal unit to the city dwellers. Therefore, the demand curve slopes downward.

The equilibrium at point *E* determines

FIGURE 18-7 DETERMINING CITY SIZE. The supply schedule for land for urban use, *SS,* reflects the marginal productivity of land in agriculture. The more land in urban use, the less land that is available for agriculture, and therefore the higher its marginal productivity. The supply curve is rising because the opportunity cost of land in urban use (in terms of forgone agricultural output) is higher the more land that is used in the cities. The downward-sloping demand curve reflects the diminishing marginal productivity of land in urban use. Equilibrium is initially at point *E*, with land rent at the edge of the city equal to R_0. An increase in urban population then shifts the equilibrium to *E'*, for the demand curve shifts to *DD'*. Rents rise, along with the size of the city.

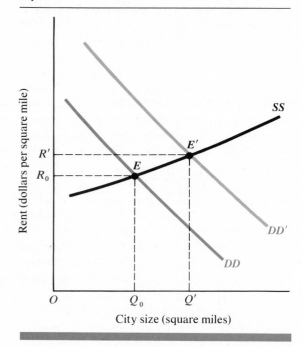

the size of the city (for a given population) and land rents at the edge of the city. The equilibrium rental for land with demand curve *DD* is R_0. This sets the level of land rents at the edge of the city. The rents rise toward the city center, as shown by the rent gradient.

An increase in the population of the city shifts the demand curve for urban land outward to *DD'*. The new equilibrium is at *E'*, with more land in urban use, higher rents at the edge of the city, and therefore higher rents also at the center of the city. Why? Because the rents rise toward the center on the basis of the level at the edge. Now with a bigger city, not only is the level at the edge of the city a bit higher, but also the distance to the center is greater. Therefore, rents in the center are higher in the larger city.

Population Densities in Practice

Population densities vary enormously both within and between cities. The population density in Manhattan in 1970 was 67,800 people per square mile; on Staten Island, also in New York City, the density was 5100 people per square mile. In Huntsville, Alabama, the population density was 1260 people per square mile. For the entire United States, the population density was only 57.[5] The average population density in Japan was 727. This figure shows how much more crowded Japan is than the United States. What is interesting, though, is that the concentration in Tokyo is about the same as that in Manhattan. The differences arise mainly from the density of population in the less urban areas.

Population density gradients of the type seen in Figure 18-5 have been studied for many cities in different countries. There are two main findings from the studies. First, population densities and the slopes of the gradients are much lower for the United States than for most other countries. U.S. cities are more spread out than others. Second, the slopes of the gradients have been flattening out over time.

The main reason why population gradients have become less steep is that transport costs have fallen with the development of the automobile. A second factor is that incomes have been growing over time. People with a higher income usually prefer to have

more land; thus they need to live farther out from the center of the city. Third, there is a clear association between the population of a city and the slope of the population density gradient: the larger the city, the flatter the gradient tends to be, given transport costs and average income in the city. This is probably a result of the opening up of additional city centers as the city grows, or efficient decentralization.

4   THE MOVE TO THE SUBURBS AND THE EFFECTS AT THE CENTER

The flattening out of population gradients over time is the same phenomenon as the move to the suburbs that has been taking place in the United States and elsewhere. The reasons for increasing suburbanization have already been reviewed above. They are lower transportation costs, rising incomes, and growing population.

Although we think of suburbanization as largely a result of the automobile, the process started well before the invention of the automobile. Transportation costs fell when trolleys were invented in the nineteenth century and, of course, subway systems too—the latter being built mostly around the turn of the twentieth century. In thinking about transportation costs, we go beyond the costs of moving goods and people. For instance, the invention of television substantially reduced the transportation costs for the individual of getting to see a good performer in action.

The Growing Suburbs

The total populations of both city centers and suburbs have been growing, but the population of the suburbs has grown much faster. A larger part of the urban population lives in the suburbs in the 1980s than did in 1950. In 1950 most of the people living in cities (57 percent) were living in the city center; already by 1970, only 46 percent of

---

[5] Data are from *Statistical Abstract of the United States, 1980*, Tables 19 and 28.

TABLE 18-3

THE SHIFT OF POPULATION AND BUSINESS TO THE SUBURBS, 1950–1970

	1950		1970	
	CENTRAL CITY	SUBURBAN RING	CENTRAL CITY	SUBURBAN RING
Population, %	57.3	42.7	43.1	56.9
Employment, %	70.1	29.9	54.6	45.4
Manufacturing	63.3	36.7	51.0	49.0
Retailing	74.4	25.6	52.2	47.8
Service	80.8	19.2	64.2	35.8
Wholesaling	87.1	12.9	65.5	34.5

Source: Edwin S. Mills, *Urban Economics*, 2d ed., Scott, Foresman, Glenview, Ill., 1980, p. 39.

the urban population was living in the city center.[6]

Accompanying the shift of people to the suburbs and out of the central city has been a shift of business and industry. Table 18-3 contains the relevant data. In 1970 it was still true that most employment (54.6 percent) was in the central city, but it is equally clear that the trend is toward increasing employment in the suburban ring. The table shows that the shift has been strongest in retailing, precisely the area in which we should most expect business to follow the population. In the other areas of employment, there is some debate about which came first, the move of population or the move of business. The same factors cause both population and business to move, so we don't have to worry which is the chicken and which the egg.

Blight Flight

We have so far explained suburbanization as the result of the increasing accessibility of the suburbs as transportation costs fell. But there is another popular explanation, called "blight flight." The argument is that

[6] The reason why some of the data in this chapter are only from 1970 is that such data are collected only every 10 years in the census—and the results of the 1980 census were not available in time.

the people—mainly whites—who moved to the suburbs were trying to escape from the blight of deteriorating city centers.

Further, by escaping from the deterioration, they were actually making it worse. Instead of maintaining their housing, they sold it to poor people, who let the housing deteriorate. As the richer people left, the tax base of the city weakened, and city services such as education and garbage collection also deteriorated.

There has indeed been a shift of poor people to the cities, as Table 18-4 shows. Before discussing the table, we have to define poverty. In the United States, poverty is officially defined by the income level of a household. For a family of four in 1979, the poverty income level was just over $7400 (in 1979 dollars). This was about one-third of the income level of the median family. The poverty level is calculated on the basis of the cost of buying a minimally adequate amount of food and other necessities. Measured in 1979 dollars, the poverty level in 1959 was almost exactly the same as in 1979.

Now, Table 18-4 shows a dramatic fall in the percentage of the population in poverty between 1959 and 1979, from 22.0 percent to 11.6 percent. But remarkably, most of that reduction comes from the fact that there are far fewer poor outside the urban

TABLE 18-4

POVERTY, BY RESIDENCE AND RACE, 1959 AND 1979
(Numbers in Parentheses Are Millions of People in the Category)

| | | METROPOLITAN AREAS | | OUTSIDE METRO-POLITAN AREAS |
	U.S. TOTAL	CENTRAL CITY	SUBURBS	
All races				
1959	22.0% (38.8)	18.3% (10.4)	12.2% (6.6)	33.2% (21.7)
1979	11.6% (25.3)	15.7% (9.5)	7.2% (6.2)	13.7% (9.6)
Blacks				
1959	55.1% (9.9)	40.8% (3.8)	50.9% (1.2)	77.7% (4.9)
1979	30.9% (7.8)	31.1% (4.4)	21.1% (1.1)	39.5% (2.3)

Note: The percentages shown are the percentages of the total number in that category who are below the poverty line. For example, the 39.5% in the bottom row, last column, means that in 1979, 39.5% of the blacks living outside metropolitan areas fell below the poverty line.
Source: Characteristics of the Population Below the Poverty Line: 1979, Current Population Reports, ser. P-60, no. 130, Table 4.

areas than there used to be. Does this mean that the people in the countryside became rich, while nothing much happened in the cities? No. The poor from the rural areas moved into the cities. Thus the proportion who were poor in the countryside fell a lot, while the proportion who were poor in the cities fell much less. But note that the proportion of poor people fell at least a little in every category shown in Table 18-4.

Turning now to the data for blacks in Table 18-4, we see both a remarkable drop in the percentage living in poverty and a fall in the number of poor from 10 million to just under 8 million. There are large drops in the number of black poor in the suburbs and rural areas. But remarkably, there is an *increase* in the number of black poor in the city centers. Even in 1979, nearly one-third of the blacks living in the city centers were living in poverty. Even though a smaller percentage of the people in the city centers were below the poverty line in 1979 than in 1959, there had been such an inflow of blacks in poverty to the city centers that a slightly greater number of them were below the poverty line in 1979 than in 1959.

Many of the urban black poor live in what we regard as inadequate housing, in slums in the centers of the cities. Now how should we think about this? Is there any explanation of how these areas came to be slums, and to what extent it is the fault of the people who left the areas and moved to the suburbs?

The first point to note is that the overall level of housing improved over the last 25 years, even though we think of that period as a time in which slum conditions worsened. Not only did the overall level of housing improve, but that of nonwhites in particular improved. Table 18-5 shows the large reduction in the percentage of housing units owned or rented by nonwhites that had incomplete plumbing facilities. Particularly in the central city, there was a tremendous improvement in the availability of plumbing between 1960 and 1975. Of course, plumbing is not everything, but other amenities improved along with plumbing. We are *not* saying that slum housing is desirable— only that the quality of housing lived in by nonwhites or blacks, including those moving from country to town, improved markedly over the last two decades.

The people who moved into the city

TABLE 18-5

HOUSING WITH INCOMPLETE PLUMBING
(Percentage of Housing for Each Category)

	1960		1975	
	NONWHITES	WHITES	NONWHITES	WHITES
U.S.	40.7	11.9	8.7	3.0
Central cities	20.7	6.7	2.4	1.9
Suburbs	39.5	5.9	7.0	1.4

Note: Each entry is the percentage of total housing falling in that category. For instance, in 1975, 7.0% of the housing units in which blacks lived in the suburbs had incomplete plumbing facilities.
Source: Edwin S. Mills, *Urban Economics,* 2d ed., Scott, Foresman, Glenview, Ill., 1980, p. 124.

centers from the countryside almost certainly improved their standard of living by doing so. Nonwhites living in rural areas were mostly poor. There were no new jobs in those areas. Agriculture was demanding less labor as it became more mechanized. Rural poverty is very severe. The jobs and better living standards were in the cities.

Because the people who moved into the city were poor, they could not afford new housing. They needed low-rent housing—and that meant older housing. As cities grow outward, the older housing is in the center, and that is why the immigrants from rural areas moved mainly into the centers of the cities. The housing continued to deteriorate because it was too expensive to maintain. To quote Anthony Downs, one of the original thinkers about urban problems:[7]

> Few people realize that a certain amount of neighborhood deterioration is an essential part of urban development in almost every metropolitan area. . . .
> Poor urban households must live somewhere. Many can afford only older units that have deteriorated enough to substantially reduce the cost of occupying them. . . .

The argument, in brief, is that there are slums because the people who live in them are poor. It is made explicitly by Richard Muth of Stanford University:[8]

> Simply stated, our fundamental urban problem is the low income, or poverty, of many of the residents of our cities.

Although the argument seems obvious, it has important implications. For instance, a favorite government policy in the sixties was urban renewal, in which slums were to be destroyed and better buildings put in their place. But if we think of the fundamental urban problem as being poverty and not deteriorating buildings, then urban renewal does not look like much of a solution to anything. We discuss housing policy for the cities again below.

The argument that the problems of the slums are largely a result of poor people living in them does not mean that there are no other reasons for urban problems. For instance, we have to ask why the cities are largely segregated by race. There were 5 million whites living below the poverty line in the city centers in 1979. They, too, could not afford good housing. They might well have lived in the same areas as the 4.4 million blacks below the poverty line. But

[7] *Neighborhoods and Urban Development,* Brookings Institution, Washington, D.C., 1981, p. 5.

[8] Richard F. Muth, *Urban Economic Problems,* Harper & Row, New York, 1975, p. 2.

they did not—the cities are strongly segregated.

This pattern of racially segregated housing is explained by the assumption that people prefer to live close to others of the same race or ethnic group. Given this preference, the whites will start moving out toward the suburbs as blacks begin moving into the older housing in the city center. This is the so-called white flight; it is associated with blight flight, the fear of deteriorating neighborhoods. The move out to the suburbs, then, is not purely the result of the greater accessibility of the suburbs through lower transportation costs. It is also a result of a search for better neighborhoods.

5 URBAN HOUSING

The low housing standards of the poor, concentrated in slums, are the most visible signs of poverty. In the post–World War II period there have been many government programs attempting to improve the housing standards of the poor. And indeed the housing standards of the poor have improved substantially. The housing problem of the poor is more visible in part because the poor have moved to the cities to improve their living standards—and urban poor are more visible than rural poor.

We start by briefly reviewing some of the policies that have been followed to affect the housing market and improve the housing standards of the poor. Then we discuss whether the government should intervene in the housing market at all.

Slum Clearance

Up to the end of the sixties, government destroyed more housing than it created. Housing was destroyed when areas were cleared to build the federal highway system. It was also destroyed when the federal government encouraged urban renewal programs. The idea here was to destroy old housing in the slums and build better housing. Some better housing was built, but the tendency was for richer people to move into that housing.

The poor were not made any richer as a result of urban renewal. They still preferred to rent lower-quality housing. And new lower-quality housing could be created by letting better-quality housing deteriorate. Thus the poor moved on from the areas that had been renewed and into other areas with deteriorating housing conditions. Slum clearance programs did not by themselves do much to improve the housing standards of the poor, though they did improve some neighborhoods in some cities.

Public Housing

Local housing authorities have built considerable amounts of housing over the period since 1937, when federal subsidies began. The federal government initially covered the building costs of the housing. The tenants were supposed to be charged rents to cover the costs of maintaining the structures.

By enouraging local authorities to provide public housing, the federal government hoped to shift the supply curve of housing, say, from SS to SS' in Figure 18-8a. The aim was to make more housing available and to lower the rents that tenants would have to pay. In Figure 18-8a the equilibrium rent falls from R_0 to R' as a result of the shift in the supply curve. There is a further reduction in rents to those actually living in the public housing, since the local authority only charges for maintenance costs. But even those living outside the public housing would benefit from the lower equilibrium rents in the housing market.

Public housing has been a limited success. There are waiting lists for places, the total amount of public housing built has been quite small, and it is claimed that the construction costs have been very high. In

FIGURE 18-8 GOVERNMENT INTERVENTION TO INCREASE HOUSING CONSUMP-
TION BY THE POOR. The diagrams show the effects of two alternative methods of
increasing the amount of housing consumed by the poor. In Figure 18-8a the government subsidizes supply, shifting the supply curve to SS' from SS. The equilibrium rental rate falls, and the quantity of housing consumed increases. (Quantity of
housing may mean either the size of the house or apartment or its quality.) In Figure
18-8b housing allowances are provided. These shift the demand curve to DD' from
DD. If supply is very inelastic, as shown here, the main effect is to increase the equilibrium rent, and there is very little effect on the consumption of housing. If supply
is elastic, the housing allowances will be very effective in increasing housing consumption.

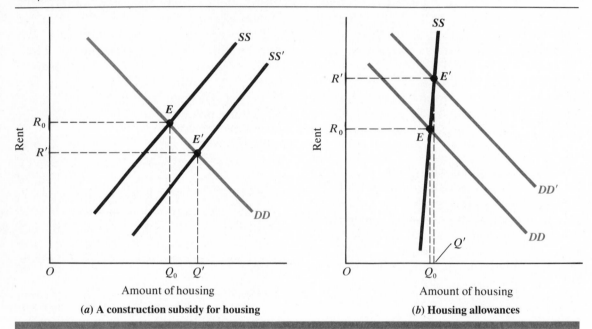

(a) A construction subsidy for housing   (b) Housing allowances

the late sixties the rules by which the federal government subsidized public housing
changed, and now there are also subsidies
for rents.[9] Those subsidies work in the same
way as housing allowances, to which we
now turn.

Housing Allowances

An alternative to subsidizing construction is
to give people money to spend on housing.
Think of the amounts as rent vouchers.
They can be spent on rents, and nothing

else. The idea is very similar to that of food
stamps. Providing housing allowances is a
way of ensuring that the spending is for a
particular commodity and that therefore the
recipients have an adequate level of that
commodity, in this case housing. Eligibility
for housing allowances is determined by the
household's income.

The major benefit of such vouchers[10] is
that the government does not have to get involved in subsidizing construction, or run-

---

[9] Details of the programs are contained in John C.
Weicher, "Urban Housing Policy," in Peter Miesz-
kowski and Mahlon Straszheim (eds.), *Current Issues
in Urban Economics*, Johns Hopkins, Baltimore, 1979.

[10] Education vouchers have been suggested by Milton
Friedman as a replacement for the provision of public
schooling. Parents would be given money to be spent
only on their children's education, but at whatever
school they wanted. Private schools would presumably
develop to meet the new demand.

ning public housing projects, or deciding which family should be allowed into what house. All the details are left to the housing market to settle. The objection that has been raised to housing allowances, compared with actual construction of more housing, is that the supply curve for housing is inelastic. Figure 18-8b illustrates this. The housing allowance shifts the demand curve to DD'. If the supply curve is inelastic, as shown, the main effect is to increase the rents, not the housing supplied. There is not much of an increase in the amount of housing consumed—but that means the program does not achieve its aims.

The choice between construction subsidies and housing allowances thus turns on the elasticity of supply. Current estimates are that the supply curve of housing is quite inelastic in the short run but elastic over the long run of several years. For this reason, and also because the evidence is that government intervention to build hous-

ing is very expensive, economists tend to favor housing allowances over construction subsidies.

Rent Controls

One apparently simple way of ensuring that people can afford housing is to make it cheap by controlling the price. Rent controls were in force in the United States during World War II and were removed in most cities. But they were kept in New York City.

Figure 18-9 shows the effects of rent controls in the short run. In the short run, the stock of housing is fixed, so the supply curve can be taken as inelastic. Indeed, the short-run supply curve in Figure 18-9 is shown as vertical. Then the imposition of rent controls at price R^*, below the equilibrium rental, R_0, forces the rent down. There is excess demand at rental rate R^* because at that price people want more housing than is available.

How can there be equilibrium with the

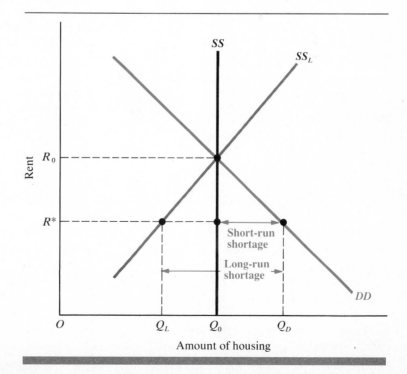

FIGURE 18-9 SHORT- AND LONG-RUN EFFECTS OF RENT CONTROLS. Rent controls are imposed to keep the rents at R^*, below the equilibrium rate, R_0. The short-run supply curve, SS, is vertical. The initial effect is the creation of a short-run shortage of housing, equal to $Q_D - Q_0$, where Q_D is the quantity demanded at the new, lower rent. The long-run supply curve is SS_L. In the long run the shortage is larger, equal to $Q_D - Q_L$. The quantity supplied in the long run drops because landlords do not maintain or replace deteriorating buildings.

existing stock of housing at rental rate R_0 and yet excess demand when the price drops to R^*? The reason is that at the lower rents, some people want to move up to better housing, children decide they can afford to leave home, and people want to take their own apartments rather than share with college classmates. Thus in the short run the rent controls create a shortage all by themselves, even with a housing stock that was adequate before the controls were imposed. People who need a house or apartment cannot find one.

But the more serious effects of rent control are in the long run. Figure 18-9 shows the long-run supply curve for housing, SS_L, along with the short-run supply curve, SS. Because rents are low, depreciating housing is not replaced. Existing buildings are not maintained. Over time the existing stock of housing deteriorates and grows smaller. This is shown by the reduction in the quantity supplied in the long run to Q_L. The excess demand will be bigger in the long run than in the short run.

Nonetheless, rent controls are popular with the people currently living in the housing. They are doing quite well, since they have the place they want at a price they can afford. For that reason, rent controls are a frequent political response to periods of rising housing rentals. But they do not do much for the supply of housing.

Why Intervene in the Housing Market?

Why should there be a particular government interest in providing better housing for poor people? Why not simply provide them with more income and let them spend it as they want? They know better than anyone else what their tastes are.

Two earlier discussions are relevant here. First, in Chapter 5 we showed why giving people money makes them happier than giving them a particular type of good of equal value. The argument is simple—maybe if given the money they would not spend as much on this good (in this case, housing) as the government is giving them.

Second, the argument against people being given money directly is that there may be *externalities* in the housing market. Perhaps prices do not guide people to set marginal social costs equal to marginal social benefits. Externalities were discussed in Chapter 12.

There are three possible sources of externalities in housing. First, slums are ugly. Perhaps others find their utility reduced by seeing or being near slums. Some evidence on the importance of this effect can be found in studies of changes in the value of property that faces slums. There is such an effect, but no estimates make it appear large.

Second, perhaps when housing is poor, the city has to spend more for health, police, and fire protection services. Here we have to try to distinguish the effects of poor housing from the effects of the people being poor. Poor housing does seem to require greater public spending on fire protection, but the effect here is small too. Other effects of this type should be blamed on the people being poor, not on the housing being poor.

Finally, we come to the notion of *merit goods*, introduced in the last chapter. There are some goods that society feels everyone should have by right, such as food, health, and shelter. People should not starve, and they should have shelter. But when we make this argument, we really have to ask whether we want to insist that people have a decent level of income, which they can allocate in the way they prefer, or whether we actually mean that they must have a particular level of housing?

Many economists contend that arguments that people should have adequate housing and other goods really mean that they should have adequate income. Therefore, they argue that the government should not attempt specifically to improve housing. Instead, it should give poor people money.

FIGURE 18-10 THE NEGATIVE INCOME TAX. Under the negative income tax the government makes payments to individuals with low incomes and receives taxes from those with higher incomes. No one receives less than Y^*. The payment made by the government falls as pretax income rises. At point A no payments at all are made. At higher levels of income, the individual pays taxes.

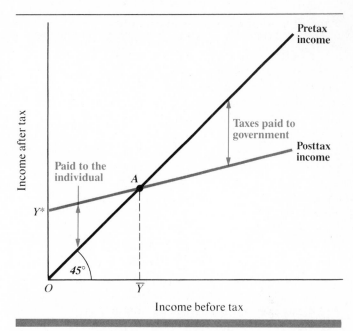

This is essentially the case for the *negative income tax.*

The Negative Income Tax Under the current tax system, individuals who earn a low income pay no taxes. As income rises, taxes begin to be paid, and then taxes rise more rapidly with income. With the negative income tax, money would be paid to low-income people.

Figure 18-10 illustrates this by showing pretax and posttax incomes. On the horizontal axis we show pretax income. Posttax income, measured on the vertical axis, is equal to pretax income plus government subsidies for people who are poor. For people with incomes above $\overline{Y}$ the government collects taxes that reduce posttax income to below the pretax income level. At low levels of income, the government pays the individual. No one gets less than income Y^*. As income rises, the government pays less. Eventually, at point A (the break-even point), no payments are made. Then at higher income levels the government receives taxes.

The negative income tax was invented by Milton Friedman and has been supported by many economists. It is a means for giving money to people with low incomes, without being specific about how they should spend it.

6 URBAN TRANSPORTATION: THE DOMINANCE OF THE AUTOMOBILE

We have seen how important transportation costs are in determining the economics of the city and how the falling cost of urban transportation has produced a move to the suburbs. We know also that a characteristic of city living is traffic congestion. In this section we look at how people travel in urban areas, focusing on the breakdown between mass transit and the automobile. Then we discuss the economics of congestion and the case for public support of mass transit.

Commuting Patterns

Although we think of commuters as people

TABLE 18-6

MEANS OF TRANSPORTATION TO WORK, STANDARD METROPOLITAN STATISTICAL AREAS, 1975

	WORKERS LIVING IN THE CENTRAL CITY	WORKERS LIVING OUTSIDE THE CENTRAL CITY
Number, millions	22.8	32.7
Means of transportation, %:		
Drive alone (private car or truck)	59.9	69.7
Car pool	17.3	18.9
Public transportation	14.0	4.4
Walk	6.0	3.4
Work at home	1.6	2.2
Other	1.3	1.4

Source: *Statistical Abstract of the United States, 1981,* Table 1099.

who move between the suburbs and the city, carrying their lunch in a little brown bag, much commuting is within the suburbs and from the city outward. And a large part of noncommuting daily travel for shopping and delivery is also from the city center to the suburbs.

The most important fact about urban transportation is that the vast majority of trips are made by automobile. Table 18-6 gives details. Both within the central city and outside, 60 percent or more of the workers drive to work alone, by car or truck. Including car pooling, over 75 percent of the workers get to work by car. Public transportation gets very little of the commuter traffic and even less of noncommuter traffic. There was a slight increase in business for public transportation after gasoline prices rose in 1973, but the use of automobiles has continued to increase despite higher gas prices.

Congestion and Mass Transit

The American love affair with the automobile is often discussed in the same disapproving tones with which elders complain about the younger generation. Since the beginning of the sixties, and especially since 1973, when the energy crisis became famous, it has been argued that automobile

travel should be discouraged and public transportation supported.

Two main arguments are made by those who want to discourage automobile use. First, they argue, the automobile is destroying the city by creating pollution and congestion and by making it possible for richer people to desert the city center—to run away from the poor and the taxes. Second, automobiles use far too much energy in relation to public transportation. The use of energy could be reduced considerably if there was a massive shift to public transportation.

The technological facts are clear. There would be far less pollution and congestion on existing roads if there was a massive shift to buses and subways and away from cars. Similarly, total energy use would fall. The average bus uses only three times as much gas per mile as the average car but carries about 40 times as many passengers.

How about the economics? A first reaction might be that if people want to get to work by car rather than by bus, that must be the socially best way for them to get to work. After all, we don't doubt that people should choose for themselves whether to eat steak or eat beans; the consumer is sovereign. But the second reaction is to think of externali-

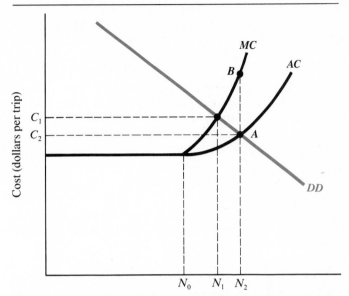

FIGURE 18-11 CONGESTION EXTERNAL-ITIES. The average cost of using a road is constant up to a certain capacity, N_0. Beyond that point the average cost begins to rise. The marginal cost, MC, is above AC for each level of use above N_0. Drivers using the road pay directly only the average cost. Their demand for trips on this road is shown by DD. They choose to travel an amount shown by N_2, with a corresponding average cost of C_2. But the marginal social cost of travel at that rate of use of the road, shown by point B, is well above the average cost and the marginal private valuation placed on travel, shown by point A on DD. Road use should be reduced to level N_1.

ties. There are indeed externalities in automobile use that arise from congestion.

Consider the economics of road use. At any one time, the supply of roads for use is given. On the demand side, there is hardly ever a direct charge for the use of roads. In some places tolls are charged for road use, but more generally road use is paid for through gasoline taxes and registration costs for cars.

We now show why the failure to charge appropriate prices for using a road can cause congestion and externalities. In Figure 18-11 the AC curve represents the average cost of a journey on a given road, which depends on the number of cars, or traffic density, within a given period, say, 1 hour. The costs are gasoline costs, the cost of wear and tear on the car, and the cost of the time of the driver. Up to a certain number of cars, N_0, the average cost is constant. But beyond that number, the average cost begins to rise. This is mainly because the congestion slows everyone down. We can think of N_0 as the capacity of the road.

Potential users have a demand curve for the use of that particular road—depending on the cost in terms of gasoline, wear and tear, and the travel time for alternative routes or means of transportation. In Figure 18-11 the demand curve is DD. The number of cars that will be used on the road per hour is N_2.

But now we come to the problem. The marginal cost of using the road is shown by the MC curve in Figure 18-11. Since AC is rising, MC is above AC beyond rate of use N_0. The increase in cost that results from one more driver using the road (MC) is *more* than the average cost, once more than N_0 drivers use the road. Why? Because the entry of one more car slows down all the drivers. The new driver is concerned only with what it costs him to get to work (that is, the average cost); he is not concerned with the increase in the commuting time he inflicts on other people using the road. That, precisely, is the externality that causes congestion.

The problem is that the cost of using the

road for the driver is not made equal to the marginal social cost of using that road. If it were possible to charge the marginal cost, then only N_1 drivers would use the road per hour, at a cost of C_1. Is there any way of charging marginal cost? On roads that have toll booths, there is no great difficulty in varying the toll, making it higher for rush hours than for off-peak time. But most roads do not have tolls, and there is no obvious way of charging the right prices.

Some thought has been given to making each car carry a sealed receiving box. This box could be triggered by transmitters on the roads on which the car travels. The box would show where and when the car traveled. Once a year or once a month, the box could be opened and the appropriate rates charged for the road use on each road for that period. This kind of device is some way off in the future. At present, trying to use a receiving box to control traffic congestion would be a clear case where it is more expensive to try to use the price system by charging exactly the right price than not to use prices at all.

Is congestion inevitable if prices are not used? It is clear from Figure 18-11 that higher gasoline taxes would raise the AC curve. If the new AC curve crossed DD at rate of use N_1, the road would be used optimally. But if the intensity of road use varies by road and time of day—as it does—a single gasoline tax cannot make all roads each be used the right amount each hour of the day. More important, where there is no market for using a commodity, it is difficult to be sure that the right amount of the commodity is used.

In fact, roads should be congested at their peak-use times, which is during rush hours. There is nothing that says society should ensure that everyone can get to work without *any* delays on the road when it is expensive to provide a big enough road for that to happen.

It is interesting to note that this is a case where the price system cannot be effectively used but where *social conventions* or habits can make a difference to alleviate some of the costs arising from the absence of a market. *Staggered hours*, which are used extensively by business, are not only a means for giving individuals a more flexible work schedule. They are also a means for avoiding some of the private and public costs of congestion, because peak-time commuting is spread over a larger number of hours. Staggered hours were introduced in Manhattan very successfully in the early seventies. One-quarter of the work force changed its work hours.

What does the discussion of congestion have to do with the question of public transportation? Here, where prices cannot be used to allocate resources, we have to use *cost-benefit analysis,* as discussed in Chapter 12, to figure out the best allocation of resources.

For public transportation, we would use cost-benefit analysis by listing the costs and benefits for society of different ways of getting people to work. A major element here is the time cost of different methods. One of the main benefits of the automobile is that it is fast and that there is no need to wait around for transportation to arrive. Cars are quicker, and that is economically valuable. Cars are usually more comfortable as well. But cars use more space and occupy more parking space downtown than would buses or subways. A full analysis would take all these factors into account and help us decide whether we should encourage further use of the automobile or raise automobile taxes and perhaps subsidize, as we do, the use of public transportation. Among the important costs of automobile travel would be the increased air pollution caused by cars.

In comparing cars and public transportation, we have to think of the different forms of public transportation. In the

United States, where cities are very spread out, subway systems are not likely to make much economic sense. The cost of building a subway line is high, and not too many lines can be built into the suburbs. Even then, people who use subways will also have to drive to and from the subway station. Such trips will mean that the costs of using the subway are higher than they seem when we look only at the costs of using the subway itself. The more likely economical means of public transportation in U. S. cities is the bus, which can use existing roads.

A complete analysis is likely to support subsidizing public transportation or taxing automobile use. If 50 cars are taken off the road and the drivers put in a bus, the total amount of congestion on the road will be reduced sharply. As Figure 18-11 shows, drivers are likely to be using cars too much in relation to the use of buses. This suggests that there should be some subsidization of buses or taxation of car use. This is the basic case for taxing car use and/or subsidizing public transportation.

Now to the second question of this section. Should we encourage the use of public transportation to solve the energy crisis by reducing gasoline use? There is a simple and correct answer here. If the price of gasoline is too low, raise the price of gasoline. If travel by private automobile becomes more expensive, people will switch. But do not overtax gasoline. The economy has to conserve on the use of *all* its scarce resources—people's time as well as gasoline. There is no sense in making transportation decisions that concentrate on conserving only one resource—gasoline—while paying no attention to other scarce resources, such as time.

7 LOCAL GOVERNMENT AND THE FINANCING CRISIS OF THE CITIES

New York City, Cleveland, and Boston are all cities that in the last 10 years have gone through exciting financial crises in which there were repeated threats that the city would go bankrupt. What is the financial crisis of the cities, and what are its causes? To understand this, we have to look at what local government does and how it finances those activities. This section is very specific to the United States.

There are many different local government organizations—municipalities, towns, counties, school boards, and more—each with its own budget and its own functions. The division of responsibilities between the state government and local governments and among the various local governments varies from state to state. For instance, New York City is responsible for most public welfare payments in the city. In Detroit those payments are the responsibility of the state of Michigan.

In the late 1970s there were nearly 80,000 local government units in the United States. Local government units spent just under 10 percent of the GNP. Their total revenues were a little higher than their expenditures, as seen in Table 18-7. The major single expenditure of local governments is on education, with welfare payments, police and fire protection, and other functions all taking a substantial but smaller part of the budget.

On the revenue side of local government budgets we see in Table 18-7 the reliance on other governments for nearly 40 percent of revenues. Federal and state revenues given to local governments have been rising in importance in the post–World War II period. At the same time, the share of revenue provided by the property tax has been falling. The utility revenue shown in the table reflects publicly owned electric companies, water supply, transit systems, and gas supplies. Among the other sources of revenue is the income from local government operation of liquor stores in some states.

TABLE 18-7
LOCAL GOVERNMENT REVENUES AND EXPENDITURES, 1979

	$ billions	%
Revenues:	234.6	100.0
From the federal government and state governments		40.4
Property tax		26.6
Sales and receipts tax		4.5
Charges and miscellaneous		15.6
Utility revenue		7.9
Other		5.0
Expenditures:	231.7	100.0
Education		38.0
Public welfare		5.0
Health and hospitals		6.2
Police and fire protection		6.7
Utility expenditure		11.4
Other		32.6

Source: Tax Foundation, Inc., *Facts and Figures on Government Finance,* Washington, D.C., 1981, Tables 225 and 233, pp. 270 and 281.

If revenues are a bit higher than expenditures, why is it said that there is a financing crisis in local governments? First, over 40 percent of the revenues comes from the federal government and from state governments. But what is more significant is the fact that the budgetary situations vary a great deal from city to city. The cities that have had financial difficulties are older central cities.

There are several reasons why such cities are likely to have financial difficulties. The first reason is one that faces all local governments. The services that are provided by such governments, such as education and fire fighting and crime prevention, are labor-intensive. These are services that we cannot expect to become highly mechanized. Thus the cost of providing such services will go up along with the general level of wages, since labor is the main ingredient in producing the services. On the average, wages rise faster than the prices of goods. Because of this fact, local government costs can be expected to increase more rapidly than other prices over time, with the result that local governments will have to raise

their budgets steadily or cut back on services.[11]

Second, turning specifically to the central cities, the cities are already substantially built up. With the heavy dependence on the property tax and the movement of population and building to the suburbs, the cities' tax revenues do not rise fast. With rising costs of providing services and not so rapidly rising revenue, the central cities are likely to find themselves in financial trouble, unless they raise their tax rates.

There is a third important factor. The central cities—particularly New York—signed generous wage and pension benefit

---

[11] This argument has been emphasized by William Baumol, who has applied it also in the context of the performing arts. As the general level of wages rises, the cost of putting on theater shows and orchestral concerts will rise along with the general level of wages. Thus putting on shows and concerts will steadily become more expensive in relation to the cost of goods. In the production of goods we can expect increasing technical progress. In the production of symphony concerts, we can hardly expect more output with fewer musicians. See William J. Baumol and Wallace E. Oates, "The Cost Disease of the Personal Services and the Quality of Life," in Harold M. Hochman (ed.), *The Urban Economy,* Norton, New York, 1976.

agreements with their workers in the sixties and early seventies. There is a fear that the pension benefits given to workers in the sixties will come back to haunt cities in the eighties, requiring them now to raise large sums of money to pay pensions that seemed an easy means for buying labor peace then.

Fourth, people who live in the central cities are, on the average, poorer than those living in the suburbs. They are therefore more likely to need the social services provided by the cities. The extent of social services offered differs among the cities, but certainly in the case of New York, a large part of the financial crisis was a result of the heavy load being placed on the welfare services.

What, if anything, can the central cities do about these problems? Why not raise taxes? There are two problems here. First, as taxes go, the property tax is an especially unpopular tax. Tax revolts in California, Massachusetts, and other states were set off by annoyance about the property tax. Someone who has to pay, say, 2 percent of the value of his house each year in taxes is likely to say that his income is not rising even though his house is rising in value. So how is he supposed to pay the increased tax? Because increases in property taxes are unpopular, politicians try to avoid them. Second, higher property taxes may only drive new buildings and potential residents out of the city center. Indeed, this second factor is very serious, for central cities already have higher taxes than the outlying suburban areas in most places. An alternative way of raising revenue is to charge for city services, such as garbage collection, but this, too, effectively raises taxes.

What else can be done? Spending and services can be cut, but this tends to reduce the population of the city. Alternatively, the city can try to get more help from the state or federal government. Should such help be given? If indeed the central city is making

welfare-type payments, the issue concerns the redistribution of income, and there is a good case for providing such aid. If the aim of the aid is to maintain the city center, then the issue is whether we should want to maintain city centers as the economy moves to more decentralized living. The case for this is not obvious.

The final possibility is for the central city and the suburbs to merge administratively. Such mergers have taken place in the newer cities of the nation. But outlying suburbs are reluctant, when they see the problems of the central city, to enter such mergers. They have to be done early in the life of the suburbs, at a time when the city still has something to offer in the form of services that the suburbs do not have.

Optimal Local Government Arrangements

Opposed to the idea of central city–suburb mergers is the argument, *the Tiebout hypothesis,* that we should have many different local governments.[12] The argument is that local government is a means for providing a package of services—education, crime prevention, parks, and so on—for the people living in the area. Once you live in an area, you get the package of services provided by the area; you cannot separately enjoy the low crime rate of one suburb and the good fire protection of another. The more local government units there are, each providing a different package of services, the more likely it is that each family can choose its location so as to buy exactly the package of services it wants. We thus get closer to the allocation of resources that people prefer. The argument is sometimes called the invisible foot—people who move between locations bring about a good allocation of resources.

[12] Charles M. Tiebout, "A Pure Theory of Local Expenditures," *Journal of Political Economy,* October 1956, is the original (nonmathematical) reference.

FIGURE 18-12   CHOICE OF HOUSEHOLD LOCA-
TION. Households get to choose between the combinations of taxes and services offered by different
cities. Because the combinations of services differ
from city to city, a bigger choice makes it possible
for each household to come closer to the combination it desires. The local services that are offered are,
of course, only one influence on a family's decision
about where to live.

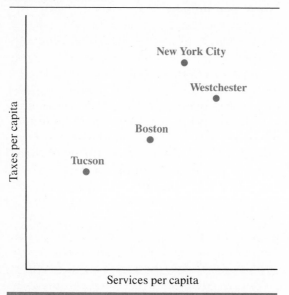

We can illustrate the Tiebout problem
using Figure 18-12. Our problem is to
choose between various packages of services and taxes. For example, the points
New York City, Boston, and Tucson represent different combinations of city taxes and
services, and the household has to decide
where to locate. For the household, services
are a "good," and taxes are a "bad." With regard to city services, a city to the southeast
of another one in Figure 18-12 is better. For
instance, Westchester has both lower taxes
and more services than New York City and
is therefore preferable with respect to city
services and taxes. Of course, living in the
city may have other advantages. Given its
income and tastes for the services provided
by local government, as well as its tastes for
other goods, the household has to decide

where to live. The point to notice is that the
household cannot choose any amount of the
services that it wants. It is confined to
choosing one of the points shown in the diagram. Maybe the household wants more services than are available in Boston, cannot afford to pay the New York City price for
them, and does not want the Westchester
County combination of services. The Tiebout proposition, then, is that the more separate local governments we have available,
the larger the choice of locations and the
more closely individuals will be able to
choose between lawless frontier towns
without schools or sewers and Westchester
County or suburbia.

There is, though, a complication which
arises from different efficiencies in providing a given basket of services. New cities
will be able to avoid many of the errors old
cities are locked into. Moreover, because
the average inhabitant is both young *and*
employed, there tend to be lots of taxes and
much less in social expenditures for health
and welfare. These cities thus are preferable for anyone who is very mobile, and for
that reason they create extra problems for
the old cities that lose the taxes with which
to pay for the services for the old and unemployed.

Zoning

One important question about the Tiebout
hypothesis is, How does a suburb that
offers, say, a better educational system keep
out people who might be able to obtain the
services provided by the suburb by moving
into an apartment or small house, thus not
paying for their share? The answer to that is
zoning.

Zoning is the regulation of land use by
  local authorities.

For instance, many suburbs do not allow
apartments or houses on lots of less than a
given size. Such zoning regulations keep
out the poor.

Is this a good thing? Here we confront the very difficult point of the distribution of income. If it is acceptable for there to be differences in income among people, then there will be differences in their consumption levels. As an economic matter, small, exclusive suburbs—with exclusion based on the ability to pay the taxes—are an efficient means for controlling access to some goods, just as prices are a means for limiting access to other goods.

Looking beyond the economics, there are two important issues. First, the economics provide no justification for limiting access on the basis of race or any criterion other than the payment that is made for the services provided by the local government. Second, there is an argument that access to some services, such as the education of children, should not be controlled by income, especially the parents' income. Access based on income only serves to perpetuate past inequalities.

The argument, in brief, is that education is a merit good. But if so, then access to public education should not be controlled by local government. Some other mechanism —for instance, education vouchers[13]— should be found.

Arguments about the ideal structure of local government are interesting, but in practice the historical accidents that have produced the existing structure of local governments have not resulted in a Tiebout-like world in which every family has access to precisely the mix of services it wants. If they had, all we would have to discuss is whether the distribution of income in the society is an appropriate one. As it is, we have to recognize that local government boundaries and activities have important effects on the allocation of resources in the society. Then it makes sense to argue that we might need cities and suburbs to form fewer, not more, local government units.

---

[13] As noted above, under this scheme parents would be given vouchers of specified value to spend on their children's education. In this way society would make sure that each child receives education worth a certain amount (at least) during each year. Schools, public or private, could compete for the education dollars provided by the vouchers, and in competing they would ensure the quality of education.

SUMMARY

1   The processes of urbanization and economic growth are related. As agriculture becomes more productive, more of the population can live in cities. Cities exist to capture the benefits of trade, which arise from economies of scale in production and economies of agglomeration. Increasing transportation costs and congestion limit the sizes of cities. As transportation costs have fallen, city size has increased.

2   A land-rent gradient shows how the rent for the use of land changes with distance from the center of the city. Land rents typically fall with distance from the center of the city. The gradients have become flatter over time.

3   The shape of a land-rent gradient reflects both the transportation costs of getting to and from work and shopping and the preference of people for having more space. Population density is therefore related to the shape of the land-rent gradient. The density of population falls

from the city center outward. Population density has been falling as the land-rent gradient has become less steep. Cities both in the United States and abroad are becoming more spread out. But U.S. cities are more spread out than most foreign cities.

4   The declining population density of the cities is the result of the move to the suburbs. Both people and businesses have been moving from the city center to the suburbs. The largest business shift has been in retailing, but all business activities have been decentralizing.

5   There are two reasons for the shift of population from the city center to the suburbs. The first is the greater accessibility of the suburbs because of improvements in automobile transportation. The second is "blight flight," the attempt to escape from the deteriorating city centers.

6   City centers have an increasing percentage of the poor people. But most of these poor people are immigrants from the country and abroad. Their poverty is not the result of the deterioration of the city centers. Rather, the city centers have deteriorated as poor people moved in. At the same time it is important to note that the total number of people falling below the poverty line has dropped remarkably in the last 20 years.

7   The federal government and local governments have actively intervened in the market for low-rent housing. Some policies subsidize supply, trying to shift the supply curve. Others encourage demand, for example, by providing housing allowances. The bang per buck from these policies, in terms of the increase in the quantity of housing consumed by the poor, depends on the elasticity of supply. The more elastic supply is, the more effective are policies that stimulate the demand for housing.

8   Rent controls are frequently used in an attempt to keep the cost of housing down. Rent control succeeds in keeping rents low for those currently in the housing but makes it difficult for new people to find housing. In the long run, it reduces the quantity of housing supplied.

9   Government intervention in the housing market may be justified on the grounds of externalities. But there is little reason to think that these are large. Rather, the problem of urban housing is that the people who live in the housing are poor. The problem can be solved by giving them more money—for example, through the negative income tax.

10   An urban transportation system has to provide trips into and out of the central city, as well as trips within the city and suburbs. The automobile is the king of urban transportation. The case for subsidizing public transportation is that automobiles create congestion and pollution and use too much gas. Because we do not use the pricing mecha-

nism directly to control access to roads, it is quite likely that there will be socially excessive congestion. If cars use too much gas, gasoline taxes should be raised.

11 There is a tremendous variety of local government bodies in the United States. Responsibility for a particular service could be with the state government in one state, the school board in another, or the city council in still another state. Education is the most important single budget item of local government. The major sources of revenue for local governments are the federal government, the state governments, and the property tax.

12 The cities that face financial difficulties or even crises are the older cities. All local governments face the problem that their expenses are likely to rise faster than the price level, because the services that they provide are labor-intensive. The central cities face the additional problem of eroding tax bases and generous pension settlements made in the past.

13 The cities can escape from the crises through federal or state aid or mergers with other local governments. They can also cut services or raise taxes, but these latter solutions are likely to make more people leave.

14 There is a general issue of how large local government units should be. The Tiebout hypothesis argues that there should be many units so that different groups of people can essentially choose exactly the package of local government services they want by locating in the right place.

15 To prevent access to their local government services by those who would not pay the full price, cities and towns have zoning regulations keeping out small houses or apartments with a high population density and low property taxes. Such restrictions are not objectionable in a world where the distribution of income has been judged satisfactory by society and where there are enough local governments so that everyone can choose his preferred package of local government services. They are problematic in a world where central cities have large populations whose access to public services is limited by the unavailability of alternatives.

KEY TERMS

Urbanization	Slum clearance
Economies of agglomeration	Housing allowances
Congestion	Rent controls
Population density gradients	Negative income tax
Land-rent gradients	Tiebout hypothesis
Blight flight	

PROBLEMS

1 What effect would each of the following changes have on the extent of urbanization of a country, and why? (*a*) An increase in the productivity of agriculture, (*b*) an increase in automobile gas economy, (*c*) the development of TV shopping, where the home-owner can view products on his home TV and order them by pushing on his telephone buttons.

2 The table shows the percentage of the urban population living in the largest city in countries according to their level of income. Why have the largest cities been growing with respect to population in the low- and middle-income countries but not in the industrialized countries?

PERCENTAGE OF THE URBAN POPULATION LIVING IN THE LARGEST CITY, 1960 AND 1980

	1960, %	1980, %
Low-income countries	14	16
Middle-income countries	29	30
Industrialized countries	19	18

Source: The World Bank, *World Development Report, 1980*, Table 20.

3 Most large cities have a central business district in which the major banks, law firms, brokerage houses, insurance companies, and so on, are located. Why?

4 Why are the central cities decaying, and what should be done about it?

5 Which policies should the government follow with regard to housing for low-income people?

6 Discuss the cases for (*a*) raising the gasoline tax, (*b*) subsidizing public transportation, and (*c*) building more roads as ways of solving the urban transportation problem. Start by saying what the problem is that needs solving.

7 It is often argued that building a new highway does not solve any congestion problems, because all that happens is that more people commute when the highway is built. (*a*) Is this true? (*b*) Would cities be better off without freeways that lead into them?

8 What government agency or agencies are responsible for the following services in the town or city in which you are studying: (*a*) school education, (*b*) public hospital, (*c*) welfare payments? Should these be handled by the same agency?

9 It is sometimes argued that city and town governments in the United States should be funded entirely by the federal government or the state governments, as are city and town governments in many foreign countries, except that they could charge directly for the services that they provide, such as garbage collection and water. (*a*) What would be the benefits of such a system? (*b*) How would funds be allocated to take into account the different needs of cities and towns?

10 There are two types of zoning regulations. Some zoning regulations allow particular activities, such as retailing, to take place only in particular parts of town. Other zoning regulations forbid entirely certain types of housing or business. Should towns be allowed to have either or both types of zoning? Explain.

11 What problems concerning municipal finance and the provision of public goods would be solved if cities could charge a direct tax—say, $1000 per person per year—for the right to take residence in a town? If you think the tax would be an effective tool for solving problems, why is it not imposed? Or is it imposed in a roundabout way? Explain.

The only certainties are death and taxes—but because the date of death is uncertain, there was over $3.5 trillion in outstanding life insurance in the United States in 1980. *Every* action we take now has an uncertain future outcome. When we add to our savings account, we do not know how much the money will buy when we want to use it, because the rate of inflation between now and then is uncertain. When we buy stocks, we do not know what they will be worth when we want to sell them, because their prices change unpredictably. When someone goes into business, he does not know whether the business will succeed or fail, or how spectacularly. An oil company looking for oil does not know what, if anything, it will find. A government that has chosen an economic policy does not know exactly how or even whether it will work. The degree of uncertainty varies, but the uncertainty is there.

How does the presence of uncertainty affect our actions? And what economic institutions are there to handle uncertainty? These are the two main questions analyzed in this chapter.

We start with some evidence on how people arrange their affairs in a world of uncertainty. There are two kinds of evidence: people buy insurance to reduce uncertainty about their future income or wealth, and people also gamble, thereby increasing the uncertainty they have to face in life. Tables 19-1 and 19-2 show the most recent relevant statistics for the U.S. economy.

Many people love to gamble—in state lotteries, at horse races or other sports events, at casinos, and with their friends and friendly local bookmaker. Table 19-1 contains some of the facts for the last year for which there are (no doubt, imperfect) data. One way to interpret the numbers in the table is to consider that the GNP in 1974 was $1430 billion, and so the estimated total gambling outlays came to 1.5 percent of the GNP.[1] The $4.4 billion shown as net outlays in the table is more relevant, since that is how much all gamblers taken together lost on gambling in 1974.

The amount of gambling revealed in Table 19-1 suggests that people—some people, at least—favor risk. But people spend much

---

[1] Of course, since the table includes illegal gambling, we might like to compare the amount spent on gambling with a measure of the GNP that includes illegal activities. There have been many arguments recently that an increasing part of economic activity is illegal and not making it into the measured GNP.

19

Uncertainty in Economic Life

TABLE 19-1

GAMBLING ACTIVITIES, 1974

TYPES	TOTAL OUTLAYS VENTURED, $ millions	NET OUTLAYS,* $ millions	PERCENTAGE OF ADULTS WHO GAMBLE
All types	22,421	4,385	48.0
Legal:	17,347	3,347	44.3
Horses	8,897	1,418	13.7
Casinos	6,076	1,004	9.4
Lotteries	639	374	24.0
Illegal:	5,074	1,039	11.2
Sports books	2,341	105	1.9
Numbers	1,064	575	3.0

* The net outlay is the amount taken out of the total outlay before paying off winners. It is thus a measure of the total amount lost by all gamblers taken together.
Source: Statistical Abstract of the United States, 1980, Table 418.

TABLE 19-2

INSURANCE FACTS, 1979

TYPES OF INSURANCE	NO. OF POLICIES, millions	NO. OF PEOPLE COVERED, millions	VALUE OF POLICIES, $ billions	ANNUAL PREMIUMS, $ billions
Life insurance	407		3222	39.1
Health insurance		183		55.9
Property and liability:				90.1
Automobiles				36.6

Source: Statistical Abstract of the United States, 1981, Tables 884, 885, 891, 892, 893.

more on insurance than they spend on gambling each year. Table 19-2 shows that total insurance premiums, the amounts paid to insurance companies, came to over $185 billion in 1979. Nearly half the total was made up of payments for property and liability insurance, much of that for automobiles. Insurance takes up a larger part of consumers' budgets than does gambling. In that sense, we can say that people tend to be risk-averse rather than risk lovers—they are willing to pay to cover themselves against a variety of losses.

From now on we shall assume that people are typically risk-averse. What does that mean about their behavior? For one thing, they will be willing to pay if they have to in order to reduce uncertainty about their future income and consumption. They will buy insurance. They will also be willing to invest in a safer asset at a lower rate of return rather than in a more risky asset at a higher rate of return, as we will see in section 4. Risk averters are willing to bear risks; they just have to be compensated sufficiently for doing so.

1 INDIVIDUAL ATTITUDES TOWARD RISK

Economists describe attitudes toward risk by defining three types of consumers: those who are *risk-averse*, those who are *risk-neutral*, and those who are *risk lovers*. How can we tell whether a particular consumer is risk-neutral or, say, risk-averse? There is a simple criterion: A *risk-neutral* consumer is not at all concerned with risk. In looking at any activity or prospect he only asks what it pays *on the average.* He is not concerned if there is a small chance of catastrophic ruin or a small chance of gigantic payoffs.

A *risk-averse* consumer requires better than fair odds to accept a bet. The *risk lover* is a strange bird. He looks for action and pays to have the privilege of taking bets that are stacked against him.

The common assumption in economics is that people are risk-averse. They will insure to reduce uncertainty, and they will undertake risky ventures only if they expect to be sufficiently compensated for taking a risk. They will never pass up a cheap opportunity to reduce their risks.

Now we illustrate the criterion for risk aversion. Suppose we are tossing a fair coin that has an even chance of coming up heads or tails. Suppose that heads pays $1 and that tails loses $1. Who would take the gamble? The risk-averse consumer sees that the average return is zero—there is a 50 percent chance of losing a dollar and a 50 percent chance of gaining a dollar. He does not expect to come out ahead from tossing the coin, and the gamble adds uncertainty to his life. Since a risk-averse person gambles only if he is compensated sufficiently, he passes up the "fair" gamble.

But suppose the payoff were $2 for heads and the loss $1 for tails, still with a fair coin. Now things get trickier, since there is a 50 percent chance of making $2 and a 50 percent chance of losing $1. Taking the gamble seems to set you ahead, since you expect to gain more than you would lose. Someone who is only moderately risk-averse will take such a gamble. Someone who is very risk-averse might need an even more favorable payoff. But who would organize the gamble? Only a risk lover would.

Attitudes toward risk and their implications are summarized in Table 19-3. We look at two tests: the kind of bet a person would take and whether or not he would buy insurance.

TABLE 19-3

BEHAVIOR TOWARD RISK

TYPE OF PERSON	BETTING	INSURANCE
Risk-averse	Demands favorable odds to bet	Will buy
Risk-neutral	Will take fair or better bets	Doesn't buy
Risk lover	Plays even if the odds are against him	Doesn't buy

Risk aversion leads to two key principles of behavior toward uncertainty. *First, risk-averse individuals will devote resources to finding ways of reducing uncertainty and risk. Second, individuals who bear risk have to be rewarded for doing so.* These two principles recur throughout the chapter.

We want next to pursue two questions arising from this section. First, is it consistent for people to both gamble and buy life insurance? After all, we argued that a risk-averse person would buy insurance but not gamble—except at better than fair odds, which are difficult to get.[2] Similarly, a risk lover will gamble but not buy insurance. One possibility is that Tables 19-1 and 19-2 describe the behavior of different groups of people, some who like risk and gamble and some who are averse to risk and buy insurance. However, we can be quite sure that many people do both—buy insurance and gamble. This can, in part, be explained by saying that people enjoy the excitement of gambling and that they probably confine their gambling to small amounts. Insurance is bought for serious matters, such as the possibility of being hospitalized or having

---

[2] There is at least one favorable gamble available. In blackjack as played in casinos, a skilled player who counts the cards can have the odds in his favor. The casinos try to keep card counters out, not regarding it as their business to lose money. It is not obvious why they do not change the payoffs to remove the favorable odds.

to pay for damage caused in a car accident.[3]

Second, how can it be that in Table 19-2, only $39.1 billion was paid in life insurance premiums in 1979, while the outstanding value of policies was over $3000 billion? The $3000 billion is the amount that the insurance companies would have to pay out to their policyholders if they all died. How can the insurance companies provide insurance of $3000 billion while receiving only $39 billion in premium payments? To understand this point we need to discuss the principles of risk pooling.

2   INSURANCE AND RISK POOLING

Buying insurance is one of the main ways of dealing with the effects of uncertainty. A person faced with the possibility of suffering a loss pays now to be compensated in case that loss occurs. If the loss does not occur, then the payment or premium is not returned. If someone faces the prospect of having his car stolen, he pays a premium of, say, $200 for protection against financial loss from car theft over the next year. If the car is stolen, he is compensated by the insurance company. If the car is not stolen, he has lost his $200. How does insurance work?

We will start with a simple example of homemade insurance. Suppose that there is a dentist who has good months and bad months and a gas station owner who has good months and bad months. There is no reason to expect that the success or failure of the gas station in a particular month has anything to do with the success or failure of the dentist's office in that month. They are entirely unrelated events. Now the dentist and the gas station owner get together and tell themselves that if they pooled their profits, they would eliminate some of the

TABLE 19-4
RISK POOLING

		DENTIST	
		GOOD MONTH	BAD MONTH
GAS STATION OWNER	GOOD MONTH	I	II
	BAD MONTH	III	IV

risks. Table 19-4 shows what things look like.

There are four possibilities. Both can have a good month, both can have a bad month, or one can have a good month and the other a bad month. Where does insurance come in? If they both have a good month, their sharing arrangement does nothing for them; nor does it harm them. If they both have a bad month, it does nothing for them. But in cases II and III there is something to be gained. Here the success of one is offset by the losses of the other. Together they have a more *stable* income than they could each have individually. If it was not too hard to set up deals such as the one between the gas station owner and the dentist, we would expect a lot of "risk pooling" or "risk spreading" arrangements.

Risk spreading is the key notion in insurance. To show how risk spreading works, we will look in some detail at life insurance. Suppose that we ask, as people in the life insurance business have to, what percentage of people of a given age will die during the next year. This information is conveniently available in mortality tables, data from which are shown in Figure 19.1. For instance, according to the data, only about 1 percent of those aged 56 will die during the next year. The deaths will result from heart disease, cancer, road accidents, and other causes in fairly predictable proportions.

Now let us take 100 people aged 56, without knowing much about their particular health conditions. According to the mor-

---

[3] A famous early attempt to explain why people both gamble and buy insurance is in Milton Friedman and Leonard J. Savage, "The Utility Analysis of Choices Involving Risk," *Journal of Political Economy*, 1948.

FIGURE 19-1   MOR-TALITY TABLE, UNITED STATES, 1978. The graph shows the probability that someone alive at an age specified on the horizontal axis will die in the next year. It is based on actual U.S. data. (*Source: Statistical Abstract of the United States, 1981,* Table 107.)

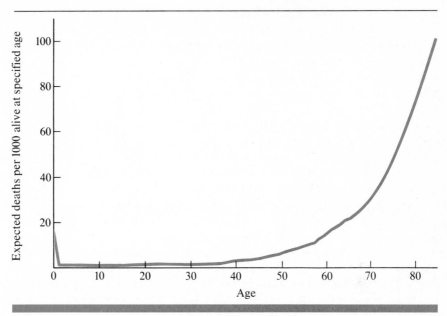

tality table, we should expect 1 percent of them, or one, to die within the next year. Dealing with 100 people, how sure can we be that 1 percent rather than 0 or 2 or more percent will die? Not very certain. Accidents and illness can happen, and it is quite possible that none or two or more will die. But suppose we have 1 million people aged 56. How sure can we be now that the percentage of deaths will be very close to 1 percent? We can, in fact, be virtually certain that the percentage of deaths will be very close to 1 percent.

The spreading of risk across many people who face that risk is called *risk pooling.*

By putting many people who each face the same risk together, we reduce the uncertainty about the average outcome. In the mortality example, uncertainty about the proportion of people who will die within the next year becomes very small as the group becomes larger. The low level of uncertainty about mortality when the group is large makes life insurance possible.

To understand life insurance, suppose that 100 people would like to leave some money to their family in the event they die in the next year. Assume further that each person puts up $100, with the proceeds to go to the families of those who are no longer alive 1 year later. One percent of the group is expected to die in the next year. Each person who puts up $100 expects that his family will receive $10,000 if he dies. With only 100 people in the scheme, it is quite possible that two or three will die during the year. If so, the families of the deceased will get only $5000 or $3333.33 each instead of the expected $10,000. That is, the payment to the family is risky. But if 1 million people enter the scheme, the families of the deceased are each virtually certain to get between $9900 and $10,000.

A life insurance company sets up a scheme in which those who wish to leave money to their family pay premiums to the insurance company in exchange for the company's promise to pay out a much larger amount if the insured person dies. The insurance company can make this promise with a high degree of certainty because it spreads its risks over many purchasers of insurance. It will charge a little bit extra for the paperwork involved and also because it inevitably bears some small remaining amount of risk—it cannot be absolutely certain that only the expected number of people and not more will die each year.

When risks can be pooled, we say there is no *social* risk—society as a whole does not face much risk, though the individual members of the society do. Mortality is an individual risk, but not a social risk. There is very little overall uncertainty about the proportion of those of each age who will die in the United States in the next year. In that sense, mortality is a very small risk for the society as a whole. But it certainly is a risk for individuals in the society.

Under what conditions does risk pooling work? The essential condition is that the risks faced by the individuals must be substantially independent. The causes of death in the 57th year of life in the United States reflect mainly individual circumstances and thus are substantially independent across individuals. If one person dies of a heart attack, that does not increase the likelihood that someone else will die.

It would be different if epidemics were a serious problem. To make the point, suppose for the moment that the 1 percent probability of death at age 57 means there is a 1 percent chance the plague will strike and wipe out all 56-year-olds over the next year. If the plague does not strike, all current 56-year-olds will survive to 57. Suppose now that everyone subscribes his $100. If the plague does not strike, everyone gets the money back, and the insurance will have been unnecessary. If the plague does strike, everyone dies, and there is only the $100 contribution from each to leave to descendants (if any). So again there was no point to the insurance. In cases where the risks are not substantially independent, insurance or risk pooling will not work.

We can now return to the question we asked at the end of the last section. In Table 19-2, how can there be over $3000 billion in life insurance outstanding with only $39 billion in premiums paid? The answer is simple. The companies can be quite sure they will not have to pay out $3000 billion; not all the lives they insure will end in the next year. How many are expected to die within the next year depends on the average age of the insured. For instance, even if all the insured were 56 years old, the companies would only expect to pay out 1 percent of $3000 billion, or $30 billion, which would be more than covered by the premium income. So $3000 billion is a misleading number when we think of the amounts the companies will probably have to pay out in the next year.

When we think about insurance, we usually have in mind an example such as life insurance, automobile insurance, or fire insurance. In each case, the risk is spread by being pooled across many individuals who each face that risk. If we ask who really provides the insurance for our car, the answer is not the insurance company but the other people who are buying insurance against the possibility of theft or damage. It is their payments that enable the insurance company to compensate us if we make a claim.

But there is another way in which insurance is provided through *risk spreading*. Insurance syndicates, such as the famous Lloyd's of London, provide insurance against events about which there is, in total, a lot of uncertainty. For instance, it is possible to buy earthquake insurance in California or insurance against damage to a movie actor's essential attractions. It is not true that each year the percentage of people suffering from earthquake damage more or less averages out.

Here is how risk is spread: many different risks are shared among many different people. When Lloyd's provides insurance, the insurance is actually provided by the many members of the insurance group. Each member agrees to provide a share of the payment that will have to be made if there is an earthquake, for example, or if a ship sinks, or if a movie actor loses an arm. In exchange, each member gets a share of the premium income. Each member of Lloyd's thus takes many different small risks, and together the members provide a lot of coverage for Californians, movie actors, tankers, and oil wells. Over the years, depending on how good they are at judging risks, the members of Lloyd's make a steady income by providing insurance against many different types of risks.

There are also cases where risk spreading will not work. These are cases where the event against which people want insurance protection will have large effects on the entire economy. Consider, for example, nuclear war. No doubt we would all be willing to pay a small amount toward an insurance policy that will pay off in the event of nuclear war. The problem here is that if I suffer from a nuclear war, you are quite likely to do so too. An insurance company selling insurance that will pay off if there is a nuclear war will have a hard time persuading people that it will be able to meet its commitments. Everyone still around who has bought the insurance will be trying to collect at the same time, and it is unlikely that the company will have enough assets to cover all the claims.

Insurance enables individuals to deal with uncertainty. But its existence affects behavior in two ways, to which we now turn.

Moral Hazard

The very existence of insurance affects people's behavior and therefore the likelihood that they will present claims. This phenomenon is called *moral hazard*. For in-

stance, a person with hospital insurance is in no hurry to get home to save on the hospital costs—he doesn't pay! Someone with car theft insurance is less careful about keeping the door locked. A person with unemployment insurance has less need to find a job quickly.[4]

What can be done about moral hazard? That depends on the circumstances. In the hospital case, the insurance companies hope to rely on doctors to make sure patients do not stay longer than necessary—but the problem is that "necessary" is not easy to define. Recently hospital cost insurance companies have even started giving incentives for leaving the hospital early. For instance, a woman leaving within 24 hours of having a baby gets a cash payment of $100. But there is not much that can be done about the increased carelessness that insurance makes possible.

There is a line between moral hazard and outright fraud. In the case of arson for profit, for example, buildings are insured and then set on fire. Here the people involved cross the line and go beyond moral hazard to crime.

Adverse Selection

Adverse selection is a problem facing insurance companies because the people who want to buy insurance against a particular loss are those most likely to actually collect the payoff. To explain, we go back to the life insurance problem. Suppose there are two types of people—the long-lived and the short-lived—and that an insurance company cannot tell the difference by examining the people. But the individuals themselves may know which type they are.

---

[4] A similar problem arises with safety regulations. It has been argued by Professor Sam Peltzman that the introduction of safety belts resulted in more accidents, since drivers thought they could safely go faster. See his article "The Effects of Automobile Safety Regulation," *Journal of Political Economy*, August 1975.

Suppose that the company bases its premiums on the average mortality of the group, which we can again take to be 56-year-olds. The long-lived people will find the premiums high, since they don't expect to die soon. But the short-lived people will consider the insurance a good deal, since the premiums are based, in part, on the life expectancy of the long-lived. So who is more likely to take life insurance in large amounts? Obviously, it is the short-lived.

Then the company, having based its pay-out estimates on average mortality, will find itself losing money. It will find more of its customers dying than the mortality tables say will die; furthermore, they will be the ones with the bigger insurance policies. So what will it do? It will probably raise the premiums—and thus drive the long-lived entirely out of the insurance market.

If the insurance company cannot distinguish among its individual customers on the basis of how risky they are, insurance is not going to work well. Those facing a small risk will probably end up not wanting insurance at the rates offered, and so they will in effect be unable to insure against the losses they might suffer. There will, though, be insurance possible for those suffering the highest risk.

What can insurance companies do about adverse selection? The only thing they can do is try to find out what types of risks they are dealing with. That is, for example, why a medical examination is needed to buy life insurance.

To understand the difference between adverse selection and moral hazard, ask which of the following cases involves adverse selection and which moral hazard. First, a person with a mortal disease signs up for life insurance. Second, a person who already has life insurance develops suicidal tendencies. Reassured by the fact that life insurance will provide enough money to take care of the family's financial needs, he commits suicide. The first case involves adverse selection; the second, moral hazard.

Discrimination or Sound Insurance Practice?

Difficult problems of fairness crop up in insurance. Two examples follow. First, in some states, car insurance rates are much higher for those under 25 than for older drivers. Insurance companies say that this is because younger drivers have more accidents (which they do) and that it would therefore be unfair to older drivers to charge them the same rates as younger drivers. Instead, a company should charge different rates by age.

But, comes the response, there are only a few reckless drivers among the young. Why should all the young have to pay merely because some of them drive badly? It is assumed in these arguments that the right thing is for every driver to pay insurance at a rate that reflects the likelihood that she will be in an accident. Given that this cannot be done, should there be as much discrimination as the insurance companies can manage, or should there be none at all? There is no decisive answer from economics. It is more a matter of fairness.

The second example is more complicated. Women live longer than men. For instance, at birth, in 1978, a male child had a life expectancy of 69.5 years, while a female's life expectancy was 77.2 years. Further, the probability of a woman of any given age dying in the next year is less than that of a man's dying. For example, at age 56 among whites, 12.49 out of every 1000 men are expected to die in the next year, but the probability for women is only 6.42 out of every 1000. This suggests that life insurance premiums should be lower for women of a given age than for men.

That seems straightforward. But now we come to pensions. A pension typically is paid to someone who has retired, for as long as he or she lives. Suppose that a man and a woman have been earning exactly the same amount each year and paying the same amount toward a pension. They retire at the same time. At age 65 a man should expect to live another 14 years and a woman another 18 years. Should the man and the woman receive the same pension each year? If so, the woman will, on the average, be getting more for each dollar that she contributed to the pension plan while she was working than the man. Is that right? Or would it be fair if both got the same amount per dollar contributed to the plan? If so, the woman would get a smaller pension, or she would have had to contribute more to the pension plan while working. It is far from obvious which is better—equal pensions per year for life or an equal amount paid out per dollar paid in. In practice, the problem has recently been handled by legislation: the same amount of pension *per year* should be received per dollar paid in while working.

To summarize so far, insurance is one of the main methods of reducing uncertainty for individuals. Some of the risks that individuals face can effectively be reduced through risk spreading. A risk may be spread over many people, in which case we talk of risk pooling. Or many people—as in an insurance syndicate—may divide a risk among themselves for a price. Either way, the consumer covers himself against a possible loss by paying an amount such that the insurer expects on the average to come out ahead. But because the insured person is risk-averse, the insurance makes him better off. Insurance almost inevitably creates moral hazard and adverse selection problems.

3 UNCERTAINTY AND ASSET RETURNS

There are many ways of carrying wealth from the present to the future. We think first

of money, but there are, in addition, bonds of various types, stocks (in many thousands of companies), housing, automobiles, antique furniture, paintings, coins, gems, stamps, and more. In this section we review rates of return that have been earned by holders of stocks and bonds in the past and reasons we are uncertain about the returns on stocks and bonds that will be earned in the future. In the next section we discuss the portfolio problem faced by a typical investor who has to decide how to divide her wealth among all the different assets she may buy.

Figure 19-2 shows, year by year, the *real* (inflation-adjusted[5]) rates of return that were earned on stocks and Treasury bills (short-term government bonds) each year since 1926. There are two components of the return on stocks: dividends and capital gains. *Dividends* are payments that a company makes to stockholders each year. The company does not have to make a dividend payment if it decides not to, but large corporations typically make regular dividend payments. The *capital gain* is the increase in the value of a stock. Both dividends and capital gains provide a return to the purchaser of the stock.

A sample calculation of the real rate of return on a stock follows. Suppose that the stock was bought at the beginning of the year for $45, that during the course of the year the company paid out $2 in dividends, and that at the end of the year the stock is worth $52. Suppose also that prices of goods have gone up 6 percent during the year. The real rate of return on the stock is calculated as follows:

---

[5] Real rates of return were defined in Chapter 15. A real rate is the rate of return adjusted for changes in the price level. Thus if the money value of my stocks goes up 17 percent, but prices have gone up 8 percent, the real rate of return on my stocks is 9 percent—that is how many more goods I can buy this year after making my investment than I could have bought last year had I spent the money then instead.

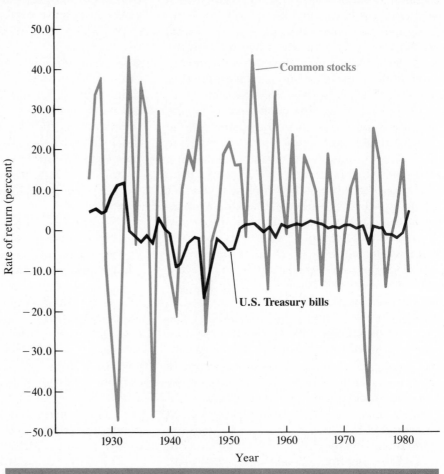

FIGURE 19-2 ANNUAL REAL RATES OF RETURN, STOCKS AND U.S. TREASURY BILLS, 1926–1981. (*Source:* Roger G. Ibbotson and Rex A. Sinquefield, *Stocks, Bonds, Bills, and Inflation: The Past and the Future,* Financial Analysts Research Foundation, Charlottesville, Va., 1982.)

$$\begin{aligned}
\text{Real rate} \atop \text{of return} &= \text{nominal rate} \atop \text{of return} - \text{inflation rate} \\
&= \frac{\text{dividend} + \text{capital gain}}{\text{purchase price}} - \text{inflation rate} \\
&= \frac{2 + (52 - 45)}{45} - 0.06 \\
&= \frac{9}{45} - 0.06 = 0.14 = 14\% \qquad (1)
\end{aligned}$$

In the case of a Treasury bill, which is a promise to pay, say, $100 at the end of the year in exchange for $91 at the beginning of the year, the real rate of return is just the nominal rate of return, 9.9 percent {[(100 − 91)/91] × 100 percent}, minus the inflation rate (6 percent), or 3.9 percent in this case.

Figure 19-2 shows how much more the real return on stocks has fluctuated than the real return on Treasury bills, especially in the period since World War II. The annual real rate of return on stocks has on several occasions been more than 40 percent and also sometimes less than *minus* 30 percent. Most of the variation in the real return on stocks could not have been predicted[6] and so we can see that there must be much un-

---

[6] Why not? Anyone who could have predicted a 40 percent increase in price would have bought stocks immediately, driving up the price. Anyone predicting a 30 percent decrease would have sold immediately, driving down the price.

certainty about the real rate of return that will be earned by buying stocks. There is also uncertainty about the real rate of return on Treasury bills, because we cannot predict the inflation rate exactly, but there is less uncertainty about real returns on bills than about stock returns.

What average rates of return correspond to the history shown in Figure 19-2? Table 19-5 gives average real rates of return on stocks and Treasury bills earned over the period 1926–1981. On the average, the real rate of return for stocks was a healthy 5.9 percent per annum. Treasury bills only barely kept up with inflation, and so the average real rate of return was basically zero. But of course, as we see from Figure 19-2, the returns on stocks were riskier. The person who prefers relative certainty and invests in Treasury bills has to pay for the certainty by expecting to earn a lower (indeed, virtually zero) real rate of return. The person who is willing to take a greater risk by buying stocks is, *on the average,* rewarded for taking that risk by earning a higher return. But there really is risk: the stock investor could lose a lot of money. Indeed, the return on stocks from 1967 to 1981 of only 1.3 percent shows just how badly a stock investor can do, even over long periods.

We want now to focus more closely on uncertainty about the returns on stocks and Treasury bills. Suppose we take $2 in 1983 and invest $1 in stocks and $1 in Treasury bills. What *average* rate of return do we expect to have earned on each investment after a year? The answer is essentially that given in Table 19-5: the historical average real rates of return—5.9 percent for stocks and 0 percent for Treasury bills.

Next we come to the important questions. To what extent could our expectations be wrong? It is clear from Figure 19-2 that stocks are not likely to yield exactly what is expected. To get a measure of uncertainty we set a standard or a confidence interval: Given the historical record, what is the

TABLE 19-5

AVERAGE ANNUAL REAL RATES OF RETURN ON STOCKS AND TREASURY BILLS, 1926–1981

	PERIOD			
	1926–1952	1926–1952	1953–1981	1967–1981
	1981	1952	1981	1981
Stocks	5.9%	7.0%	4.9%	1.3%
Treasury bills	0.0	−0.5	0.4	−0.3

Note: For calculating real returns, inflation is measured by the Consumer Price Index.
Source: Roger G. Ibbotson and Rex A. Sinquefield, *Stocks, Bonds, Bills, and Inflation: The Past and the Future,* Financial Analysts Research Foundation, Charlottesville, Va., 1982.

range of real returns that we can expect to get with 90 percent probability? If the range were plus/minus infinity, we would certainly take the view that a particular investment was risky. But if the range was 1 percent, we would think that there was very little risk.

Now what is the evidence? It is that the range of returns on stocks is much wider than the range for bills. The data are shown in Table 19-6. Someone investing in stocks may do very well indeed, gaining 42 percent within a year. But he may also do much worse. The purchaser of Treasury bills cannot expect to do as well if things go well, or as badly if things go badly. Thus uncertainty about returns on stocks is much higher than uncertainty about returns on bills. Of course, stocks are expected to yield a higher return than bills, on the average. The higher return is required to compensate for the greater uncertainty.

What accounts for the uncertainty of returns on stocks and bills? In the case of stocks, we use equation (1) and discuss separately uncertainty about dividends and uncertainty about capital gains. The part of the return that comes from dividends is uncertain because companies are not obligated to pay out any given amount (or anything at all) in dividends. How much they pay out

TABLE 19-6

RANGE OF AVERAGE ANNUAL REAL RETURNS ON STOCKS AND TREASURY BILLS THAT CAN BE ACHIEVED WITH 90% PROBABILITY

ASSET	RANGE OF RETURNS, %
Stocks	−30 to 42
Treasury bills	−7 to 7

Source: Calculated by the authors on the basis of the data in Figure 19-2.

depends on their earnings and also on their needs for cash. We do not know what capital gains will be, because we don't know how the stock market will value stocks in future years. The stock market's valuation will depend in part on companies' earnings, which in turn depend on the competition, on the invention of new technologies, on how good the management will be, on the demand for the companies' products, and more. It is easy to see why there is substantial uncertainty about stock returns.

Uncertainty about the returns on bills arises because the rate of inflation is uncertain. Bills promise to pay back a given number of dollars, but the real value of the dollars is uncertain.

To summarize, we have seen in this section typical rates of return earned on stocks and on Treasury bills, which are short-term government bonds. The average real rate of return on stocks has been about 6 percent over the last 50 years, while the average real return on bills has been about 0 percent. Real rates of return on stocks fluctuate much more than real rates of return on bills; therefore, stocks are riskier than bills. This pattern of riskier assets earning higher real returns on the average is one that we should expect, as section 6 will show.

4 PORTFOLIO SELECTION

How does a risk-averse investor decide to divide up wealth among the possible ways

of holding it? That is the portfolio (of assets) selection problem discussed in this section. There are, as we said above, many assets that are candidates—stocks, bonds, Treasury bills, gold, cocoa, antique cars, washing machines, and so on. For simplicity, in this section we will leave out assets such as washing machines for which the return earned by the owner is not in monetary form. The washing machine owner gets a convenience return in the form of having clean socks without having to use the wash basin, but we will omit those types of returns. It is not difficult to extend the theory we will present here to take account of them.

When we studied consumer demand in Chapter 5, we made a clear distinction between the opportunities available to the consumer (the budget set) and the consumer's tastes. The consumer's income and the prices of the goods together determine the possible choices that can be made. The consumer's tastes then determine the choice that is actually made.

We make the same basic distinction between the possibilities open to the consumer and the consumer's (or investor's) tastes in studying portfolio problems. But now, instead of referring to the consumer's tastes for different goods, we refer to the consumer's attitudes toward risk. Instead of referring to the prices of different goods, we refer to the returns assets are expected to yield and the risk that is attached to those returns.

The Risk-Return Choice

Tastes The risk-averse consumer (or investor) prefers a higher average return on the portfolio but dislikes higher risk. Beyond assuming that the consumer is risk-averse, we shall not be specific about tastes. We assume that consumers have to be compensated for risk by receiving a higher return when they bear more risk. By risk we mean the variability of the returns on the portfolio. For instance, the data on stocks and bills in Table 19-6 show that stocks are much riskier than bills.

Opportunities   In Chapter 5, in analyzing consumer demand, which is the consumer's choices among goods, we described the opportunities available to the consumer with the budget line. The budget line defined the combinations of goods available to the consumer. In the case of portfolio choice, the consumer's opportunities are described by the combinations of returns on assets and their risks. Each asset is described by the returns it is expected to provide and by the riskiness of those returns.

The consumer's possibilities are then defined by the differing levels of return and risk the consumer can obtain by buying different combinations of assets.

The Investor's Portfolio Choice   The simplest possible scenario is one in which there are only two assets, one riskless and the other risky. The possibilities open to the consumer are different combinations of those two assets. The risk-averse consumer will consider buying the risky asset only if it is expected to have a higher return than the riskless asset. Otherwise, the portfolio holder could have both a higher return *and* less risk by holding the riskless asset.

Suppose, then, that the risky asset has a higher expected return. What are the relevant options for the consumer? He could hold all wealth in the risky security, having a high return and maximum risk. Alternatively, he could hold all his wealth in the riskless asset, sacrificing some return in exchange for getting rid of all risk. Or he could hold some of each asset, earning an intermediate rate of return with some, but not maximum, risk.

Unless the consumer is completely risk-averse, he will not specialize; instead, he will hold some of the risky asset and some of the riskless asset. The proportions in which the portfolio is allocated between the two securities depends on the degree of risk aversion, on the amount of risk involved in the risky asset, and on the difference in returns between the two assets. In general, the following results hold, although there are unimportant exceptions. The higher the return on the risky asset compared to the return on the safe asset, the larger the share it occupies in the portfolio—the consumer, even though risk-averse, responds to yields and is willing to accept risk if the return is high enough. Second, the higher the variability of return on the risky asset (the riskier the asset, in other words), the smaller its share in the portfolio. Finally, the more risk-averse the consumer, the larger the share of the riskless asset in his portfolio. We have noted that the reactions may not always be described this way, but these three rules provide a solid benchmark for the consumer's portfolio decisions.

Diversification

We have so far restricted our attention to the case of only two assets, one risky and the other riskless. The portfolio choice made by the consumer depends on the consumer's tastes between risk and return and on the assets available.

But much of the most interesting and useful economics of portfolio choice comes from the analysis of the possibilities open to the consumer (or investor). In particular, when there are several risky assets, the consumer may be able to reduce risk without having to accept a lower rate of return. We will make the argument using Table 19-7. You will notice that the spirit of the example is not very different from that already seen in the partnership between the dentist and the gas station owner in Table 19-4.

Suppose, then, that there are two *risky* assets, say, oil stocks and bank stocks. Each

TABLE 19-7 ▰▰▰▰▰▰▰▰▰▰▰▰

PAYOFF ON A DIVERSIFIED PORTFOLIO

		BANKING	
		GOOD TIMES	BAD TIMES
OIL	GOOD TIMES	$8	$6
	BAD TIMES	$6	$4

has two possible returns: $4 if things go right and $2 if things go badly. Moreover, there is a 50 percent chance that things will go right for each industry and a 50 percent chance that they will not. Finally, we will assume that good times in one industry are entirely unrelated to good times in another, and that the returns in the two industries are independent. Suppose that the stocks cost the same and that the investor has the choice of buying one of each or two in oil or two in banking. What strategy gives the best risk-return combination? First note that both stocks have the same payoff characteristics—the same returns with the same chances. So the consumer would be indifferent between buying all oil stocks and buying all bank stocks. But the strategy of buying one of each is, in fact, superior. This is a strategy of diversifying the portfolio.

> *Diversification* is the strategy of reducing risk by spreading investments across several assets.

The principle of diversification is that of not putting all your eggs in one basket.[7]

---

[7] When Professor James Tobin of Yale received the Nobel prize for economics in 1981 for, among other things, his work on portfolio choice, reporters asked him to summarize as simply as he could what his work was about. He replied that it showed that it was not wise to put all your eggs in one basket. This reply resulted in several cartoons in which people were given Nobel prizes for other discoveries, such as "A stitch in time saves nine." Of course, Tobin's work went well beyond the simple eggs-in-one-basket example and showed precisely what trade-offs were involved in making portfolio choices and what portfolios the consumer would end up choosing.

Table 19-7 shows how to think about this. First assume that the investor specialized by holding two shares of the bank stock. There is a 50 percent chance that things go well for banking, in which case the investor earns $8. Or things go badly for banking, and he earns only $4.

In Table 19-7 we show the payoffs from the diversified investment. Now we have to recognize that a bad year in banking may coincide with a bad year in oil or that it may coincide with a good year in oil. The trick in diversification is that unless assets are such that their returns are perfectly correlated—a good year in banking is a good year in oil and conversely—a boom in one tends to offset a recession in another, thus stabilizing the return.

This is exactly the pattern we observe in the table. There are two cases where good and bad times in the two industries offset each other. Each combination of events shown in Table 19-7 happens with a probability of 25 percent. There is a 25 percent chance that both the oil industry and the banking industry will do badly, a 50 percent chance that one will do well and the other badly, and a 25 percent probability that both will do well. Now there is only a 25 percent chance each of earning $4 or $8, and a 50 percent probability of earning $6. He earns $6 when one industry does well and one badly. The diversified investor will have a less variable pattern of returns than the person who holds only one kind of asset.

We have now shown that a diversified portfolio is less risky than a specialized one. Because returns on assets do not all change together, the investor can reduce risk without reducing returns by holding a diversified portfolio of risky assets. Indeed, this leads to the key point in understanding portfolio behavior, which is that no risky asset should be looked at by itself. Instead the investor should consider how risky the *entire* portfolio is. Even if two assets each have the same returns and risk, the investor should hold some of each. If the returns on the two assets do not move in exactly the same way, the risk of the entire portfolio is reduced if the investor holds a mixture of the assets. In other words, smart investors diversify.

What happens if more stocks are added which have the same return structure as oil and banking stocks and whose returns are also independent of each other. Can we push the gains in terms of risk reduction further? The answer is yes. Think of there being three stocks. They can (with a small probability) all have a good year, and with the same small probability they can all have a bad year. But, and here is the point, *most* of the time a good year in one or two of the industries will make up for a bad year in the other one or two. Thus risk is reduced by diversification.

Indeed, as diversification is pushed further, the variability in the portfolio return declines. Risk falls more and more as the number of securities (with *independent returns*) is increased. There is thus a lot of mileage to the view that one should not put all one's eggs in one basket. The more baskets the better. To remind ourselves of this important result, we show in Figure 19-3 the relationship between portfolio risk and the number of independent stocks.

There is another aspect of diversification that is shown in Figure 19-3. It is that most of the gains in terms of risk reduction through diversification come very rapidly. It does not take many separate stocks to cut down a lot of the risk, and there are then rapidly diminishing returns to further diversification. (The result is worth remembering because it explains why people have only one spare tire in their car rather than a dozen of them.)

Because stocks are more expensive to buy in quantities under 100 shares, anyone mixing her own portfolio is advised not to

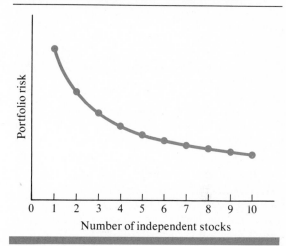

FIGURE 19-3 THE POSSIBILITY OF RISK REDUCTION THROUGH DIVERSIFICATION. The riskiness of a portfolio, measured by the variability of returns on the portfolio as a whole, can be reduced through diversification. The figure shows diminishing reductions in risk as diversification is carried further.

try to buy just a few shares of each company in order to diversify. Almost all the benefits of diversification can be obtained by buying 9 or 10 different stocks. An even more efficient way of obtaining the benefits of diversification is by buying shares in a mutual fund that has a widely diversified portfolio.

Diversification When Asset Returns Are Correlated

Up to this point we have been assuming that asset returns are independent of each other. This means, for instance, that if one stock has a high return, there is no implication that others also do. However, stock returns do move together. When there is good economic news, most stocks move up together; when there is bad news; most stocks—though not all—fall.

Asset returns are *correlated* when they move together. If returns on two assets move in the same direction, they are *positively correlated*. If the returns move in opposite directions, they are *negatively correlated*. Positive and negative correlation

TABLE 19-8

STOCK RETURNS

STOCK	RETURNS, %		
	BOOM	NORMAL	SLUMP
A	16	6	−2
B	1	4	6
$\frac{A + 4B}{5}$	4.0	4.4	4.4

have different implications for the effects of diversification in reducing risk. Suppose that two assets move together in exactly the same way and in the same direction. When stock A is unexpectedly high, so is stock B, and vice versa. In this case there is no gain at all from diversification. There is no difference between buying 1 unit of A and 1 of B and buying 2 units of either. So diversification achieves nothing.

Diversification can achieve much more when asset returns are negatively correlated. Table 19-8 gives an example. There are three possible events that determine the returns on the stocks—boom, slump, and normal times. Stock A is a cyclical stock; its returns move sharply together with the business cycle. When times are good, the stock pays a high return of 16 percent, but it does poorly when there is a slump. Stock B is a countercyclical stock. It does well when the economy is in trouble, earning 6 percent during a slump, but it earns only 1 percent when times are good. Each stock taken by itself is risky. But we can put the stocks together to get an almost riskless portfolio. Specifically, if we put 80 percent of the portfolio into stock B and the remaining 20 percent into stock A, we would get the returns shown in the third row of the table. Because of the negative correlation of the returns, the two stocks compensate for each other.

In terms of diversification, a stock that is negatively correlated with others is very useful in helping to reduce the uncertainty of the return on the overall portfolio. A stock that is positively correlated with others does less in the way of useful diversification. In the extreme situation, if two stocks have exactly the same pattern of returns, there is no benefit at all in terms of risk reduction from diversification.

Let us return once more to the consumer/investor to discuss the optimal allocation of wealth. If asset returns are independent, the answer is easy. The investor picks a very large number of stocks or a mutual fund of stocks, thus practically eliminating the risk from holding stocks because good and bad days among the various stocks average out.

What would the return on stocks be in such a world? Surely it could not be much above the return on the riskless asset because anybody can get rid of risk just by diversifying enough. Nobody needs to be paid to bear risk. Even though individual stocks are risky, a portfolio that is sufficiently diversified is not risky, and therefore even individual stocks would not bear a "risk premium." This is a quite extraordinary result that is worth thinking about.

But in the real world, asset returns are correlated. The general pattern of business cycles is one major influence on stock returns; it affects most industries in the same direction. It therefore implies that the predominant pattern is a positive correlation between stock returns. But then the consumer/investor faces a harder problem: simple diversification by holding enough different stocks will not eliminate all risk. Now it matters which stocks go into the portfolio.

What will determine which risky assets make it into the portfolio of risky assets chosen by the consumer? The characteristics that make an asset attractive are clear: high return and low risk. But when we are looking at many assets, we have to consider also how each asset does as part of a team whose aim is to keep risk low. For this reason, neg-

TABLE 19-9
STOCK RETURNS AND BETA

ASSET	RETURNS, %		
	BOOM	NORMAL	SLUMP
Market	14	6	−2
High beta	20	10	−8
Beta = 1	14	6	−2
Low beta	5	4	3
Negative beta	2	4	5

ative correlation of returns with the returns on most other assets will make an asset a very attractive prospect for the portfolio.

Beta

What is beta? Beta is a measure of the extent to which a stock's returns move with the returns of the stock market as a whole. Table 19-9 shows how the returns on stocks with different betas move with the returns of the market. We show once again only three possible rates of return for the market, though of course this is a vast simplification. The returns on the high-beta stock fluctuate a good deal more than the returns of the market as a whole. The stock with beta = 1 moves in exactly the same way as the market as a whole. The returns on the low-beta stock fluctuate in the same direction as the market returns, but there is much less fluctuation with this stock. And the negative-beta stock's returns are obviously negatively correlated with the market returns.

Betas are calculated by stock advisory services and are provided as part of their service. The desirable stocks for a given expected rate of return are low-beta stocks, for they are the least risky. Even better are negative-beta stocks, because they help reduce the risk of the overall portfolio. However, there are not too many negative-beta stocks around. Some gold stocks seem to have very low and perhaps even negative betas, but that is all. Most stocks have betas close to 1.

The reason for looking at beta, and the reason why it is computed as part of the service provided by investment advisers, is that it is a measure of how much an asset contributes to reducing the risk of the portfolio. If a stock has a high positive beta, it adds risk to the portfolio. If it has a negative beta, its inclusion in a portfolio actually reduces the portfolio's riskiness, even though it is risky by itself. We saw why that is so in Table 19-8.

Diversification in Other Situations

The idea of diversifying is important in many situations besides the consumer portfolio problem, though the principle is the same everywhere. For instance, countries try to diversify their sources of supply of raw materials. We prefer not to be entirely dependent on one country for our oil. If we were dependent, that would give the other country potential power over us; furthermore, we would be in big trouble if there was a change of circumstances there—such as the formation of a new government that refuses to sell to the United States, or the outbreak of war with its neighbors.

Similarly, an individual farmer will be anxious not to rely too much on a single crop. He will try to have different products in case the market for one of them or the crop itself is bad one year. Then he can always turn to the other products and hope that they have a good year. Risk is reduced by diversifying.

Consider a navy that is deciding whether to build a few expensive aircraft carriers as opposed to many smaller vessels. The aircraft carriers will make it possible to increase the total force, but there will be a greater risk of sustaining major damage if the enemy should successfully attack them. Many smaller vessels are more likely to sustain some damage, but they are less likely to run into major trouble when considered as a group. The choice will again be one where diversifying over the number of ships is an important consideration.

5 RISK, RETURN, AND EQUILIBRIUM

The real return on stocks in the past 50 years has been 6 percent, and that on Treasury bills has been about zero. What determines these rates of return? Why is the stock return so much higher than the Treasury bill rate of return? The considerations discussed in this chapter, attitudes toward risk and return, cannot by themselves establish what the general level of asset returns will be. That is determined by the interaction of consumers' preferences for present over future consumption with the productivity of capital—as will be studied in Chapter 20. The material covered in this chapter can tell us only why one type of asset earns more than another.

Take the zero return on Treasury bills as the starting point. Why do stocks as a group earn 6 percent more on the average? The reason is that stock returns are much riskier and that individuals dislike risk. Therefore, they will not hold the stocks unless they are expected to yield a higher return than Treasury bills. Why 6 percent, though? That reflects the extent of the society's risk aversion. If people were less risk-averse, the premium for stocks would be less than 6 percent. If people were more risk-averse, the premium would be even higher.

Now what is it that individuals do that actually determines the real return on stocks? To see this, we need to review equation (1) in this chapter, repeated here for convenience:

$$\text{Real rate of return} = \frac{\text{dividend} + \frac{\text{capital gain}}{}}{\text{purchase price}} - \frac{\text{inflation rate}}{} \tag{1}$$

The real rate of return will be higher, given the dividend, the lower the purchase price

FIGURE 19-4 RISK-RETURNS RELATIONSHIP FOR STOCKS, 1931–1965. The diagram shows the statistical relationship found between the riskiness of stocks and the average returns they yield. It is based on data from the period 1931–1965. The data confirm that average rates of return are higher for riskier stocks, where risk is measured by the extent to which returns on a stock move in the same way as returns for the stock market as a whole. [*Source:* Fischer Black, Michael Jensen, and Myron Scholes, "The Capital Asset Pricing Model: Some Empirical Tests," in Michael C. Jensen (*ed.*), *Studies in the Theory of Capital Markets,* Praeger, New York, 1972.]

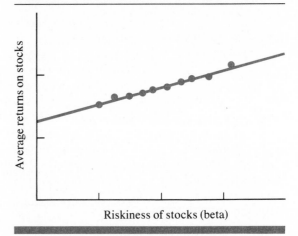

Riskiness of stocks (beta)

that people are willing to offer. So when a company tries to sell stock, the public determines the real rate of return that will be earned on a share by the amount that it is willing to pay per share. If the public decides that the real rate of return is too low, they will not buy the stock, thus driving its price down and raising the expected real return.

Consumers' attitudes toward risk therefore determine the average rate of return, but what determines the real rates of return that are expected to be yielded by individual stocks? Here we go back to the discussion of beta. Any stock with a low beta will be in high demand, consumers will be willing to offer a high price for such stocks, and their expected return will therefore be low.

We should find expected rates of return

on stocks rising with beta. This is what is found in fact. Figure 19-4 shows the results of an influential early study by Professors Fischer Black, Michael Jensen, and Myron Scholes (BJS).[8] BJS constructed portfolios of stocks with differing betas and then calculated actual average returns over the period 1931–1965 for the different portfolios. They found clearly that average returns rise steadily with beta, as the theory suggests.

The most important points of this section are, first, that the overall premium for risky versus safe assets results from the degree of risk aversion of investors and, second, that among risky assets, beta is the main measure that tells us what rate of return the market will place on assets. Now why is it beta rather than the riskiness of the stock itself? The key point is that individuals are not concerned with individual stocks as such. What they are concerned about is the riskiness of their total portfolio. And we have seen that adding an asset with a risky return to a portfolio can *reduce* the risk of the portfolio as a whole. What is important is what an asset does for the riskiness of the portfolio as a whole, and that is why beta, a measure of the extent to which an asset's returns move with the market's returns, is the right measure to use in figuring out the rate of return the market will award in equilibrium to that asset.

The last point to repeat is that the way the portfolio holders affect stock returns is the same as the way they affect prices in ordinary markets—by buying and selling. If portfolio holders think that the returns on an asset are too low, they will no longer want to hold that asset; they will try to sell it and thereby drive down its price and raise the rate of return. If a stock looks as if it will yield a high rate of return, people will try to

buy it; thus they will drive up the price and reduce the rate of return.

6 EFFICIENT MARKETS

There are two basic images of the stock market. One is that of a casino, where Lady Luck and the better gamblers reign supreme. Stock pricing is based on speculation with no rational basis. The second view —the theory of *efficient markets*—is that the stock market is a sensitive processor of information, responding quickly to each new piece of information bearing on the right price that should be paid for stocks. The second view certainly recognizes that stock prices fluctuate a lot, but the argument is that the fluctuations are the appropriate responses to changing information.

Why does it matter? And what is the right price at which a stock should sell? Stocks are claims on the income that is generated by the activities of different firms. Each firm will generate an income stream that has particular return and risk characteristics. One firm will be very cyclical, with income moving with the business cycle, and moving a lot. But maybe the firm generates, on the average, a high rate of return when it invests. Society values high returns, but it does not value returns that move together with the cycle. The stock of such a company should be priced to reflect those two characteristics. Another firm may undertake investments that generate high returns when the economy is in bad shape and that do not do especially well when the economy is booming. Such investments are valued because they reduce the riskiness of the overall stream of income for society; they reduce economic fluctuations. They should be rewarded; that is, the company's stock should sell for a high price. That would make it easy for the company to raise money by selling its stock and would encourage it to invest.

---

[8] "The Capital Asset Pricing Model: Some Empirical Tests," in Michael C. Jensen (ed.), *Studies in the Theory of Capital Markets*, Praeger, New York, 1972.

Stock prices, in brief, should give the correct signals to firms as to how much to invest. A company that can sell stock at a high price will invest a lot; other companies will be discouraged from investing if they can only sell stock at low prices.

What are the arguments for the two views of the stock market—the view of the stock market as a casino, with no fundamental economic forces determining stock prices, versus the view that the stock market is a finely tuned machine that responds to every important economic signal, and responds right?

Typical of the arguments on the irrationality side are those of the great English economist, John Maynard Keynes.[9] Keynes argued that what really dominates in the stock market is not a belief about what firms' investments will produce but only the short-run consideration of the price at which the stock can be sold in the next period. In terms of equation (1), which shows that the return on a stock consists of dividends and capital gains, Keynes says that the concentration of the market is on the capital gains part. But more than that, he says that all anyone is trying to figure out is the price at which other people will be willing to buy the stock in the next period; the individual does not believe that the price will be related to the fundamentals that determine the price at which a stock should be sold. Keynes has more claim to be believed than most, since he himself was a successful stock market investor (gambler?).

Bubbles

A market where price is based largely on expectations of what others will pay, without regard to fundamentals, is one that is said to be suffering from a *speculative bubble*. It is a bubble because everyone probably believes that it can't go on for ever and will

have to burst. But in the meantime it is foolish not to take advantage of the bubble.[10] Prices rise because everyone expects them to rise—people buy today because tomorrow the price will be higher. So long as this is believed, the price can go on rising.

Have there been speculative bubbles? It certainly seems so. The famous South Sea Bubble of 1720 in England was based on stock in a company that had no chance of producing income. The company announced that it would be selling British goods to the people who lived in the South Seas and bringing home the wonderful goods produced by those people. Yet the company's stock kept rising until finally the bubble burst. Even Sir Isaac Newton lost money in the bubble. To make it worse, the first time he invested in the South Seas company, he got out early, selling his stock at a good profit. But the temptation of the rising price of the stock was too much for him, and he invested a second time to make more money. This time he was still in there when the bubble burst. What about bubbles in more recent times? Here we must enter into disputed areas; we will return to them shortly.

What are the arguments and evidence on the side of the efficient-markets view of the world? Efficient-markets theories argue that because people realize that eventually bubbles will come to an end, they are unlikely to ever get started. And aside from bubbles, there is no reason why the market should value stocks at other than the right value. If stocks are priced too low, there are high returns to be made, and everyone will buy. If there are low returns, investors sell stocks, and the right price is reestablished.

Testing for Efficiency   Efficient-markets theorists argue that stock prices correctly re-

---

[9] John Maynard Keynes, *General Theory of Employment, Interest and Money*, Harcourt, Brace, New York, 1936, pp. 154–158.

[10] For a lively account of bubbles and other exciting forms of market behavior, see Charles P. Kindleberger, *Manias, Panics, and Crashes*, Basic Books, New York, 1978.

flect all information relevant to the price of a stock. They have tested the theory by seeing whether there is evidence that stock pricing ignored relevant information. If this had happened, it would have been possible for investors to make money by using that information.

There is very little evidence that it is possible to make money systematically by using information that is publicly available. In other words, as it is more dramatically put, there is no way of beating the market. Of course, such a conclusion must depend on the information that is used to test it. For instance, the most common test of whether the market neglects information is to ask whether, by using the past history of prices, you could find a rule that would, on the average, enable you to do better than the market. Such a rule might be "buy stock when its price has risen more than 1 percent 4 days in a row, and sell if the price falls 2 percent for 2 days in a row—otherwise hold on to it." Rules such as this do not work. The next question would then be whether some type of information other than prices—for example, a firm's income or dividends—can help you do better than the market on the average. The evidence is against this too.

But often in economics, not all the evidence is directed one way. There is, in fact, one investment advisory service that has consistently done better than the market on the average, over a period longer than 15 years. This strongly suggests that there is some information that the investment advisory service is using that is not already reflected in stock prices. This implies that the stock market is not fully efficient.

Other more recent evidence also raises some doubts about stock market efficiency. Recent research has been directed to the question of whether the stock market fluctuates "too much" in relation to the way it should move. To answer this question, we have to have a theory about how the market should move. The fundamental determi-

nants of stock prices should be the incomes earned by firms and paid out to stockholders, which is what is assumed in the recent studies. These studies, still at a preliminary stage in the process of discussion and digestion by which research becomes knowledge, do suggest that the stock market fluctuates too much, but that evidence should still be regarded as a hint rather than as a certainty.

The stock market has been the focus of most of the research on the efficiency of asset pricing. But, of course, similar questions come up in all markets where assets are traded against each other. For instance, is the exchange rate between two currencies—say, U.S. dollars and Japanese yen—in some appropriate sense correct? How about the price of gold? Research in these areas in general suggests at a minimum that there is no easy money to be made in these markets.

Buy and Hold Strategies

Suppose that the stock market prices assets appropriately and that there is no system for beating the market. This is certainly a position that can be defended on the basis of existing research. Then a fascinating question arises. What is the best thing for an individual investor to do? Should he carefully follow the market, trying to figure out whether stocks are priced right, buying a stock that looks good, and selling one he no longer likes? Or would he be better off assuming that the market has already priced all the stocks at the correct level and that he might as well hold on to his existing stocks, sit back, and relax? The latter strategy is known as *buy and hold*. If, indeed, there is no money to be made at all from carefully calculating the values that stocks should have, then a buy and hold strategy makes sense. Such a strategy keeps the costs of buying and selling stocks to a minimum, and according to the theory of efficient markets, it will do as well as any other method can be expected to. Indeed, there is much advice that individuals should decide on the type of portfolio they want and then hold on to it, avoiding buying and selling that creates income for the brokers but not for the asset holder.

There is another question. Suppose that everyone decides that the best thing to do is to buy and hold stocks and that the price set in the market is the right price. For the price to be the right price, someone has to figure out what that price should be and be buying and selling stock with a view to coming out ahead. So we seem to have a paradox: if people believe that markets are efficient, there is no incentive that will make them collect and process the information that is needed to keep the market efficient. Actually, the problem is not too serious. It is quite possible that there are small gains to be made by gathering information and that those gains are sufficient to attract the people who can do it best into the stock market. These people will try to earn a slightly higher return than others. So the people who specialize in gathering information will earn a return above the market average; the above-average return is the reward for the contribution they make in getting the market to be efficient.

Why Market Efficiency Matters: Socialism and Capitalism

It is worth reminding ourselves why all this matters—it is not only a question of how we can best make money in the stock market. The serious question is whether the stock market is an efficient means by which society can decide what to invest. Firms raise money for investing, building factories and machines. If the price signals they get from the stock market are the right ones, we can assume the investment is going in the right direction. For instance, in the early eighties firms involved with genetic engineering or personal computers had no trouble raising

money in the stock markets. Those firms expanded, using the cash they raised to build up their operation. That seems to be the case of a stock market acting sensibly.

But suppose the market were irrational. As Keynes argued, "When the capital development of a country becomes the by-product of the activities of a casino, the job is likely to be ill-done." [11] There is then a case for looking for some other way of allocating investment.

Here the case for socialism is frequently made—it is argued that state planners are better than the stock markets in figuring out what investments should be undertaken. So the issue of the efficiency of the stock market and other asset markets is extremely important. It is at the heart of arguments about whether capitalism does a good job of determining the allocation of resources.

7 MORE ON UNCERTAINTY

Uncertainty is so important as a feature of economic life that the analysis of every topic covered so far in the book—consumer demand, firms' supply functions, industrial organization, labor markets, and so on—can be extended to include uncertainty. The analysis will differ in each particular case, but the same two important features will recur: individuals try to find arrangements that reduce risk, and they have to be compensated for bearing risk.

In this section we will briefly mention two important topics. We will not go into them in the detail of the earlier parts of the chapter.

Hedging and Futures Markets

There are organized markets for the future delivery of many commodities and assets, among them corn, wheat, soybeans, rapeseed, pork bellies (bacon), coffee, sugar,

---

[11] Keynes, *General Theory*, p. 159.

TABLE 19-10
EXPECTATIONS OF WHEAT PRICES AND THE FUTURES PRICE

	TODAY'S PRICE FOR DELIVERY IN 6 MONTHS	PRICE EXPECTED TO EXIST IN THE *SPOT* MARKET FOR WHEAT IN 6 MONTHS	DECISION
Speculator A	$5.10 per bushel	$5.50	Buy wheat today for delivery in 6 months
Speculator B	$5.10	$4.73	Sell wheat for delivery in 6 months

copper, heating oil, plywood, British pounds, and Treasury bills. If you look at the financial pages of a newspaper (if not in the local paper, certainly in the *Wall Street Journal*), you will see prices quoted for the delivery of, say, wheat at given dates, which may range over a year and a half ahead. The standard wheat contract is for the delivery of 5000 bushels at the futures price quoted in the newspaper and on a specified date. When the time comes, the seller of the contract is obligated to deliver that amount of wheat at that price, and the buyer must pay the stated price for the wheat.

Who trades in the futures markets, and why? In other words, why are there futures markets? Here we need to draw a distinction between *hedgers* and *speculators*. Hedgers are people who use a market to reduce the risks they face. In the wheat market, hedgers are people whose main business is related to wheat; they either grow it, process it, or sell it. Such people use the market to get themselves some certainty about the dollar prices they will be receiving or paying for wheat in the future. The supplier who will have wheat to sell in the future is uncertain now about the price he will get then. So he may decide to reduce the risk facing him by selling some of the crop ahead of time, in the futures market. Or the baker or miller may want to lock in future supplies at a known dollar price, and so he will buy wheat today at a given price for delivery later.

As described so far, the trading in futures markets could be entirely between future suppliers of the good, who are looking for certainty about price, and future demanders, who are also looking for price certainty. In fact, most of the trading is among people who have never seen wheat and would certainly not know what to do with it if it arrived on their doorstep. These traders are *speculators*, individuals who are active in the market and who are not reducing any of their own wheat-related risk by being in the market. Such people are speculating by promising to sell wheat they do not have now or buy wheat they will not use. They are in the market because they expect to earn profits for taking risks.

At the same time they provide a service for the hedgers by being willing to buy or sell future wheat. They thereby reduce the risks faced by hedgers.

Table 19-10 shows what speculators in the wheat market might have in mind. Speculator A believes that wheat will sell for more in 6 months' time than today's futures price. The price he is speculating on is the future *spot price*, the price for the immediate sale and purchase of wheat. He is concerned with the spot price of wheat that will exist 6 months from now, compared with the present futures prices. If speculator A's beliefs in Table 19-10 are right, then every bushel of wheat that he buys today for future delivery will cost him $5.10 and can be resold in the spot market in 6 months' time for 5.50. Thus speculator A will be able to clear 40 cents on each bushel. Speculator B believes that in 6 months the spot price will be lower than the current futures price. He therefore sells wheat for future delivery. If his expectations are right, he will make 37 cents on every bushel.

The speculators have every reason to worry about getting their views on spot prices of wheat in the future right. If speculator A is right and B is wrong, then B will lose 40 cents per bushel: he receives $5.10 per bushel and has to go out to buy the wheat at $5.50 per bushel. Given this incentive, it is likely that the futures price reflects well-thought-out opinions about what the spot price of wheat will be in the future.[12]

Suppose that the futures price is now $5.10 and that unexpected news comes in that the wheat crop this year will be very large. The speculators who had hoped to sell at a high spot price in the future realize that they will not be able to do so, because there will be lots of wheat around. There are therefore fewer people buying wheat for future delivery, and the futures price falls. Similarly, if something happens that will increase the spot price of wheat expected in the future, the futures price will rise.

The futures price thus is closely related to the spot price at which wheat is expected to sell in the future. Indeed, the futures price is likely to be an estimate of the spot price at which wheat will sell in the future. Thus the futures price of wheat for delivery in March 1985 may be a reasonable estimate of what the market thinks the spot price of wheat will be in March 1985.

The pattern of prices reflects the timing of expected supplies and demands. Table

---

TABLE 19-11

FUTURES PRICES FOR OATS, MAY 20, 1982

DATE OF DELIVERY	PRICE PER BUSHEL, $
July 1982	1.94
September 1982	1.8125
December 1982	1.85
March 1983	1.8975

Note: Contracts are for 5000 bushels.

19-11, for instance, shows futures prices for oats on the Chicago Board of Trade on May 20, 1982. The July price, $1.94, is well above the September price of $1.8125 per bushel. Why? Between July and September the new crop comes in. Thus the quantity supplied rises. There are no new supplies through the following March. Any oats sold after September will have been stored. Because storage is costly, the futures price will rise.

How closely are futures prices related to future spot prices? The answer is that they are not good estimates of future spot prices. However, they are not systematically wrong. Here again there is no easy way for someone to make money. The research on the predictive ability of the futures markets suggests that the predictions are poor more because there is a lot of uncertainty about future spot prices than because the markets are inefficient at predicting.

New Futures Markets   There was rapid development of futures markets in the late seventies and early eighties. The futures markets for Treasury bills, some bonds, and heating oil are among the markets that were added, and perhaps there will soon be a futures market for coal. The economic reason for setting up futures markets is to make it possible for interested individuals or institutions to hedge against the uncertainty of the prices at which they will buy and sell in

---

[12] In practice, hedgers, too, are bound to be doing some speculating. A hedger who thinks the futures price is high relative to the spot price he expects will sell a lot of wheat in the futures markets, whereas one who thinks the futures price is too low will sell very little or none at all in the futures market.

the future. The speculators who enter a market also have a function. By putting their money on the line, they help ensure that the futures price well reflects current information about what the spot price will be in the future.[13]

Here, too, there are open questions. In futures markets, as in other markets, there is no guarantee that prices are based on the fundamentals on which they should be based—in this case, the future spot price. There have been occasions when futures prices were fixed in some way. For instance, in one episode more potatoes were bought for delivery at a given date than could possibly exist at the time of delivery. The people who had promised to sell the potatoes were then in trouble, because they somehow had to find more potatoes than existed. Another recent episode in which there was alleged wrongdoing—an attempt to "corner" the market—was in the silver market in 1980. The organizers and supervisors of the futures markets are supposed to prevent illegal or inappropriate market strategies. But they are not always successful.

Compensating Differentials in the Return to Labor

How are differences in the riskiness of different occupations reflected in wages? Given risk aversion, those with riskier jobs should be compensated with higher wages. We refer here to jobs that are physically risky, with higher than usual risk of death or injury. Second, the income associated with a job may be uncertain.

Do we in fact find that those in the riskier jobs earn more? It is necessary in answering this question to try to hold other things constant. We know that the highest-paying jobs in society—such as the job of

president of a large corporation—are not physically risky. The question is, If two jobs are the same in all respects but physical danger, does the more dangerous one pay more? The evidence, by W. Kip Viscusi, of Duke University,[14] indicates that the more dangerous jobs, with higher injury rates, do pay more. The conclusion comes from a study of the wages of nearly 500 workers. A very careful attempt was made to take account of all the other factors that might affect income. Among the other factors taken into account were age, race, health, the worker's industry, the region of the country, and whether the job required that the worker make no mistakes.

Even after all these factors were taken into account, the danger of a job (or the rate of injury associated with it) had a recognizable effect on the wage. The data were for 1970, and the workers' mean earnings were $6800. The more dangerous jobs paid an extra $375 per year, or 5.5 percent of the wage. Objectively, the risks faced by the workers were quite small, and so the compensating differential for risk was economically significant.

Viscusi found that the compensating differential for danger seemed to be associated with unionization in that the unions played a part in getting this compensation for their members. The unions were influential, Viscusi argued, because it is easier for them to identify the risky jobs than it is for the people who are taking a job for the first time.

There is also less formal evidence for compensating differentials. Among construction workers, those who work on the frames of skyscrapers (frequently they are American Indians), giving watchers below heart attacks, earn higher incomes. Combat pay is awarded in the army and has been

---

[13] A stock futures contract now exists. Essentially, a person buying this contract is betting that stocks as a whole will increase in value, while the person selling is betting that stocks as a whole will decrease in value.

[14] W. Kip Viscusi, *Employment Hazards*, Harvard University Press, Cambridge, Mass., 1979.

suggested for teachers in the tougher parts of town.

At a broader level, profits are often seen as a reward given to entrepreneurs, individuals who set up and run firms, for taking risks—they venture into the unknown, where their firms may or may not succeed. Certainly, we can point to the large fortunes of the successful entrepreneurs—Edwin Land of Polaroid, Ray Kroc of McDonald's, Steven Jobs and Stephen Wozniak of Apple Computers, and others—as the carrot that keeps many more people thinking about how to make money by producing something the public wants.

But the rewards from being an entrepreneur are very risky. The average person who sets up his own business works long hours for rewards that may well be less than the rewards he could have earned by taking a job with someone else. Thus a few win and many lose—and there is a risk-return trade-off.

SUMMARY

1   Uncertainty pervades economic life. Individuals appear both to enjoy some risk, as shown by widespread gambling, and to be risk-averse, as shown by the purchase of insurance. Risk aversion is said to exist when individuals require better than even odds to accept a risk. Risk aversion is more prevalent than risk loving in major economic activities.

2   The prevalence of risk aversion means that individuals try to find ways of reducing uncertainty and that individuals who bear risk are, on the average, compensated for doing so.

3   Insurance is one of the main means for reducing risks faced by individuals. Some risks that individuals face are not risks to society as a whole, in that the overall level of risk for society is much lower than that for individuals. Insurance schemes involving many people effectively *pool* individual risks. Examples are life, property, and health insurance.

4   Other insurance schemes operate by spreading risk across many individuals who are not themselves at risk to begin with. Here we think of earthquake insurance and insurance against other special events that may be social risks.

5   Most insurance programs suffer from problems of adverse selection, in that the people who want the insurance are those most likely to collect payments. Moral hazard is another problem of insurance. It occurs when the existence of insurance makes people behave in ways that affect the likelihood that they will have the accident against which they are insuring.

6   Historically, there has been a large difference between the returns earned on risky assets such as stocks and the returns earned on

safer assets such as Treasury bills. The average real return on stocks over the past 50 years has been 6 percent, while that on Treasury bills has been about zero. But stock returns fluctuate much more.

7   In choosing a portfolio of assets to hold, individuals are concerned with the returns they expect to get on their investments and the associated risks. Their portfolio choice depends on their tastes—the trade-offs they are willing to accept between risk and return—and the opportunities open to them—the risks and returns they can actually get from the existing assets.

8   The riskiness of a portfolio can be reduced through *diversification,* spreading risk over many different investments. As long as the returns on the assets vary independently of each other, at least a little, the riskiness of a portfolio is reduced by being spread over more stocks.

9   The risk that an asset contributes to a portfolio is not measured solely by the variability of the asset's own returns. Much more important is the *correlation* of returns on an asset with returns on other available assets. An asset that is negatively correlated with other assets may actually reduce the overall riskiness of a portfolio, even though its own returns are risky. The correlation of an asset's returns with those on other assets is measured by the asset's *beta coefficient.*

10   In equilibrium, risky assets earn higher rates of return because portfolio holders have to be compensated for bearing the extra risk. The equilibrium rates of return are established by supply and demand in the markets for assets. If an asset is expected to yield a high return, investors buy it, raising its price and ensuring that it earns the equilibrium expected return. If the expected payoffs from holding a stock fall, investors reduce their demand for the stock, the price falls, and the expected rate of return goes to its equilibrium level.

11   In an efficient market, assets are priced in a way that reflects the risk and returns associated with the incomes they produce. Efficiency of the assets markets matters because the allocation of investment depends on asset prices giving the right signals to investors. There is much evidence that asset markets are reasonably efficient, and there is some preliminary evidence that asset prices fluctuate too much, perhaps reflecting speculative bubbles.

12   In an efficient asset market, prices are right, and there is little to be gained from trying to find an investment strategy for beating the market. The best strategy may be to buy and hold a portfolio.

13   Futures markets are markets where a price is established today for the future delivery of goods. Such markets enable those active in the industry to *hedge,* reducing uncertainty about future receipts or payments by making some contracts now. Speculators are also active in

the futures markets. They try to profit by any differences that they believe exist between the futures price and the *spot price* that will exist in the market at the time of delivery. The futures price is likely to be closely related to the price that is expected by market participants to exist in the spot market in the future.

KEY TERMS

Risk-neutral consumers

Risk-averse consumers

Risk lovers

Risk pooling (spreading)

Social risk

Moral hazard of insurance

Adverse selection in insurance

Portfolio (of assets) choice

Diversification

Correlation of returns

Beta

Efficient markets

Buy and hold strategies

Futures markets

Hedgers

Speculators

Compensating differentials

PROBLEMS

1 Characterize the following individuals as risk-averse, risk-loving, or risk-neutral. Each has been offered a bet in which a fair coin (with an even chance of coming down heads or tails) is tossed. If it comes down heads, the individual wins a dollar. If it comes down tails, he pays a dollar. Each individual has been asked to choose one of three alternatives: paying to play the game, demanding to be paid for playing, and saying that he really doesn't care. Individual A doesn't care. Individual B will pay 2 cents to play the game. Individual C demands 5 cents to play. Which of the individuals would you expect to want insurance against car theft?

2 Explain why there is no social risk in the outcome of a lottery, even though each individual ticket holder in the lottery faces risk.

3 Are individuals who both gamble and buy insurance being inconsistent?

4 It is sometimes said that the family is one of the main forms of insurance available in society. In what senses is this true?

5 You hear on the radio a commercial for life insurance for anyone aged 45 and above, with no medical insurance. (*a*) Do you expect the rates charged for such insurance to be high, low, or average? (*b*) Why?

6 In which of the following are risks being pooled? (*a*) Life insurance. (*b*) Insurance for the Boulder Dam. (*c*) Insurance for an opera star's voice.

7 (*a*) Why is a bank account not a perfectly safe means for carrying your wealth through time? (*b*) It has been argued that in the period since 1953, Treasury bills have been a very safe asset, with a real return that is virtually guaranteed to be about 1 percent. Can you see the basis for that argument in Figure 19-2?

8 Why might an individual be willing to add to his portfolio a risky asset with an expected rate of return of only 0 percent?

9 What does Figure 19-3 have to do with the principles of portfolio selection?

10 Someone successfully sets up a firm to counsel unemployed people on the best way to use their time. Will the stock of this firm be expected in equilibrium to earn a rate of return of more or less than 6 percent? Why?

11 Why did the stock market fall sharply in response to the news that President Kennedy had been shot?

12 Someone gives you a tip that a company has invented a fine new product. (*a*) What do you do about it, if you are active in the stock market? (*b*) Why do the securities laws try to prevent insider trading, where people who run a firm buy and sell stock in that company on the basis of private information? (*c*) Why does it matter whether asset markets are efficient?

13 Sometimes, just before the harvest comes in, the futures price of wheat is below the *current* spot price. For example, the futures price for delivery in 3 months might be $5.05 per bushel and the current spot price $5.25. (*a*) How can this be? (*b*) (This is a difficult question.) Suppose that there is absolutely no cost for storing a good. Is it possible for the futures price to be substantially above the current spot price?

When a monopolist gets control of the entertainment industry, the price of fun rises, and the output of fun falls. But what happens to all the clowns and ushers who used to work in the entertainment industry? They go off to work at producing other goods, say, food. The monopolization of the entertainment industry therefore must raise output in the rest of the economy.

The economy is a machine with interconnected parts. Push it in one place, and it moves in many others. In this chapter we analyze the interactions of the economy's markets for goods and factors. We show how the price system connects *all* markets, simultaneously making sure that there is full employment and determining what gets produced and how.

This, in brief, is the chapter where we see the price *system* working as a system. We deal with an entire economy, keeping track of all the consequences of a change in one industry or factor market throughout the rest of the economy. This is the analysis of the *general equilibrium* of the economy.[1]

This is also the chapter in which Adam Smith's invisible hand finally emerges. Economists have a bias in favor of letting the market allocate resources, claiming that an economy in which there is competition in all markets in some way ends up producing a good allocation of resources. Many people know and rely on the argument of Adam Smith, the unmarried father of economics, that people pursuing their own interests are "led by an invisible hand" to do things that are good for everyone.

20

General Equilibrium and Welfare Economics

In this chapter we discuss welfare economics, which is the study of optimal ways of allocating resources. We will find that under some conditions, an economy in which there is competition in all markets indeed ends up with an optimal allocation of resources. We thus show in what senses Smith was right.

The welfare economics we study will answer a question that was implied in the first paragraph. If monopolization of the entertainment industry reduces the production of fun and increases the production of

---

[1] The material in this chapter is at a more advanced level than the rest of the book. We use indifference curves in the text here and nowhere else. The chapter provides a summary and extension of much of the earlier material, and if it is mastered, it will increase your economics intuition. But it is not essential for gaining a command of introductory principles of economics.

food, do we know that it is a bad thing? Maybe more food and less fun is actually an improvement.

We show the economy's general equilibrium interactions and the use of welfare economics by concluding with two applications. The first concerns the effects on price and output in a given industry and elsewhere of a tax on the industry's output. The second application is itself an important topic: we use general equilibrium analysis to study the determination of the real interest rate through savings and investment.

Some words of warning and encouragement are needed here. The warning is that we are dealing with interactions between markets, and so life may seem complicated for a while. We will be using indifference curves, introduced in the appendix to Chapter 5, but other steps of the analysis are already familiar. If you get lost, look at Box 20-1, on page 519 which summarizes the material covered. The encouragement is that once you get the idea of how markets are interconnected, you will not forget—and you will have grasped one of the essentials of economics.

The order of the material in this chapter is important. We start by asking about the *best* the economy can do—about the *optimal* allocation of resources. We do not, to start with, discuss markets at all. Once we see the optimal allocation of resources, we turn around to show that it is this allocation of resources that will result if there is competition in all markets. Thus we show in what sense there is an invisible hand. We also discuss where the invisible hand can get lost and where the market allocation of resources may not be optimal.

1 THE ECONOMY'S PRODUCTION POSSIBILITY FRONTIER

We begin by asking about the best the economy can do to make consumers in it happy.

In other words, we study the *optimal* allocation of resources in the economy. We want to know what should be produced and how factors of production are allocated among industries when the economy is doing as well for its consumers as it possibly can. Later, in section 4, we turn around and show that under certain conditions, it is precisely this optimal allocation of resources that competitive markets will produce.

On the production side of the economy, we want to be sure that the economy is producing as much as possible. We assume that there are only two goods, food and entertainment (or fun). Now we have to define *production efficiency*.

> The economy is producing efficiently if, for any given level of food output, the amount of fun that is produced is the maximum possible given the economy's resources.

This means that in an optimal allocation of resources, the economy will be on the production possibility frontier (PPF), or the transformation curve. That is because the PPF shows the maximum amount of one good that can be produced given the output of the other. The PPF is shown in Figure 20-1, where the amount of food appears on the vertical axis and the amount of entertainment on the horizontal axis. Schedule EF is the PPF.

Before showing how the PPF is built up, we need to emphasize three points. First, the PPF shows the limits of what the economy can produce. It is possible to produce any point inside the PPF, such as G, but it would certainly not be optimal to do so. On the PPF, at points such as A or B, we can have more of at least one of the goods and not less of the other. We would, of course, like to have more goods than are available on the PPF, but that is not possible. Points outside the PPF, such as point H, are *unattainable*. The economy cannot produce that much food and fun with its available resources.

FIGURE 20-1 THE PRODUCTION POSSIBILITY
FRONTIER. The production possibility frontier (PPF)
shows the maximum amount of one good that can
be produced given the output of the other. It thus
defines the economy's *efficient* combinations of output in the two industries. Points within the production possibility schedule, such as *G*, are inefficient,
because more of both goods can be produced.
Points outside the PPF, such as *H*, are *unattainable*
—the economy does not have enough resources to
produce those combinations of output.

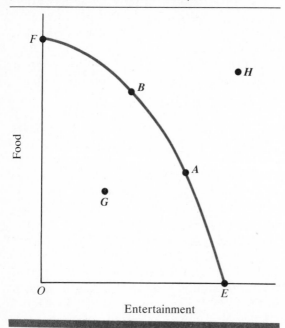

The second point is that the PPF is negatively sloped, as we recall from Chapter 1.
When the economy is producing as much
fun as it possibly can, given its output of
food, the only way of getting more fun is by
giving up some food. Thus the PPF shows
us the trade-offs between the production of
the two commodities.

Of course, if there was unemployment
of some factor, such as labor, we could have
more of both outputs. We could take some of
the labor and put it to work in each industry,
increasing output in both industries. The
negative slope of the PPF reflects the fact
that factors of production will be fully employed in an economy that is producing optimally.

The third point concerns the shape of
the PPF. As we increase the production of
food, we have to give up increasing amounts
of entertainment. There are thus increasing
opportunity costs to specializing in one
good or the other.

> The *opportunity cost* of an extra unit of
> food output is the amount of entertain-
> ment output that has to be given up in
> order to produce the food.

We will show that these increasing opportunity costs result from diminishing returns in
production. As more resources are moved
into the expanding sector, they run into diminishing returns, and thus it takes increasing amounts of resources to produce an
extra unit of output.

We now turn to a derivation of the PPF.

2 DERIVING THE PRODUCTION POSSIBILITY FRONTIER

In this section we derive the PPF. The PPF
is based on the production functions in the
economy's two industries, food and entertainment. Each sector, we assume, has
given and fixed supplies of capital and land
(machines and structures) that are used in it.
Output is produced in each industry by putting labor to work with these other factors of
production.[2] The production function tells
us how much output the labor produces.

We start our derivation of the PPF with
the production function for entertainment,
in Figure 20-2a. This is a typical production
function, showing diminishing marginal
productivity of labor. Increases in the
amount of labor used in the entertainment
industry increase the level of entertainment
output because the marginal product of
labor is positive. But because the amount of
capital and land used in the industry is

---

[2] The assumption that capital and land supplies in each
sector are fixed is a special, simplifying assumption.
Assuming that capital can be moved between sectors
would not change any essential results but would make
some of the diagrams more complicated.

FIGURE 20-2 DERIVATION OF THE PRODUCTION POSSIBILITY FRONTIER. The PPF in part *c* is built up from the production functions in parts *a* and *b*. At point *E*, all the economy's labor is used in producing entertainment; entertainment output level *E* in part *a* corresponds to point *E* on the PPF. Similarly, at point *F* on the PPF, corresponding to output level *F* in part *b*, all the economy's labor is used in producing food. The PPF is traced out as labor is moved, unit by unit, from entertainment production to food production. For instance, when 1 unit of labor is moved out of entertainment and into food production, we get to point G_1 on the PPF, with output levels of *B* in entertainment and *D* in food.

fixed, the marginal product of labor is diminishing. As more workers are added at the margin, the increase in output becomes less.

Suppose the economy's entire labor force, *L*, was used in the production of entertainment. With amount *L* of labor used in producing entertainment, the output of entertainment would be *E*. This is the maximum amount of entertainment that the economy can produce, given the amounts of capital and land in the entertainment industry and the economy's labor force, *L*.

All this applies in just the same way to the food industry, in Figure 20-2*b*. With given and fixed stocks of capital and labor in that industry, the amount of output will depend only on the labor input. The higher the labor input, the larger the level of output, but again we have diminishing returns. Furthermore, if the economy's entire labor force were used in the production of food, there would be a maximum level of food that could be produced, *F*.

Note, in looking at Figure 20-2, that we are making headway toward deriving a PPF, since we have already established the two end points, *E* and *F*. These are the points shown in Figure 20-2*c*. Point *E* corresponds to output level *E* in Figure 20-2*a*, where the entire labor force is in entertainment. Point *F* is the output level when the entire labor force produces food.

Now we have to fill in the points in the middle in Figure 20-2*c*. We start from point

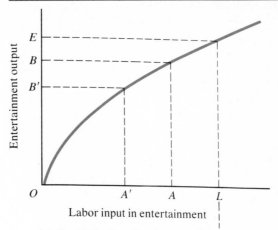

(*a*) **Production function in entertainment**

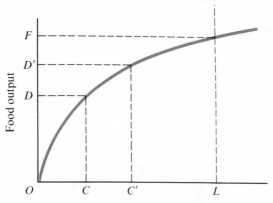

(*b*) **Production function in food**

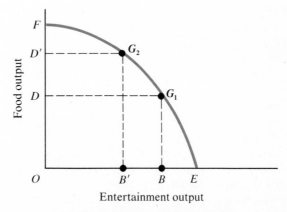

(*c*) **The production possibility frontier**

E, with the entire labor force being used in entertainment. No food at all is produced. Now we move 1 unit of labor out of entertainment and into food production. The distance AL in Figure 20-2a represents 1 unit of labor. That amount of labor is also equal to distance OC in Figure 20-2b, because that is where the labor is moved to.

There is now a new allocation of resources in the economy between the two industries. There is 1 unit of labor used in the food industry, shown by distance OC, and all but 1 unit of labor used in the entertainment industry, shown by distance OA. Corresponding to that allocation of resources are the levels of production in the two industries. Amount OB of entertainment is being produced and amount OD of food. That combination of food and entertainment production represents a point on the PPF— point G_1 in Figure 20-2c. At G_1, the amount of food being produced is OD, and the amount of entertainment is OB.

The PPF is traced out by moving labor, unit by unit, out of the entertainment industry and into food production. For instance, point G_2 corresponds to production levels in the two industries when 2 units of labor have been moved out of entertainment and into food. Amount of labor OA' is now used in entertainment and OC' in food, and the corresponding output levels in the two industries are OB' and OD'. Eventually, at point F on the PPF, all the labor is used in producing food, and none is used to produce entertainment.

The Marginal Rate of Transformation

We have now derived the PPF, which is traced out as labor is moved between industries. Each point on the PPF corresponds to a particular allocation of labor between the food and fun industries. The PPF has a negative slope because moving resources out of one industry reduces output there, and those same resources produce more output in the other industry.

The PPF is not only negatively sloped but also bowed out. Why? The short answer is diminishing returns. To show that, we see what happens to the output of food and entertainment as we move away from point E on the PPF, where all the economy's labor is employed in the entertainment industry. As we move away from E, we are moving units of labor into the food industry. Table 20-1 shows what happens to output in the two sectors.

Table 20-1 links up with Figure 20-2. The first extra worker in the food industry corresponds to amount OC of labor in Figure 20-2b, with the 3 units of extra food output for the first worker corresponding to distance OD. The 0.5 unit of entertainment output lost corresponds to distance BE in Figure 20-2a.

The second and third columns of Table 20-1 tell us how output in each industry is affected as we move labor from entertainment to food production. Food output of course grows, while entertainment output falls. But note that the extra output of food per additional worker tapers off—3 units for the first worker, 2.5 for the second, 2.2 for the third, and so on. This reflects the diminishing marginal productivity of labor in the production of food.

Indeed, the increase in output in the food sector due to an additional worker *is* the marginal product of labor in the food sector. Therefore, we also label the second column MPL_F. In the third column the diminishing marginal product of labor in the entertainment sector (MPL_E) works in the reverse direction. As more workers are withdrawn from the entertainment sector, fewer workers are left behind to work with the given capital and land stocks there. Each worker then has more capital and land to work with, and his marginal product is higher. As a result, the output loss rises as each additional worker leaves. Hence in the third column, we see a rising MPL_E.

Table 20-1 enables us to calculate the

TABLE 20-1

THE OUTPUT EFFECTS OF LABOR REALLOCATION FROM ENTERTAINMENT TO FOOD

EXTRA WORKER IN FOOD	EXTRA FOOD OUTPUT (MPL_F)	ENTERTAINMENT LOSS (MPL_E)	$MRT = MPL_F/MPL_E$
1	3.0	0.5	6.00
2	2.5	1.2	2.10
3	2.2	2.1	1.05
4	2.0	3.3	0.60
5	1.9	4.6	0.41

trade-off between the amount of extra food produced and the amount of entertainment output lost as labor is moved between the industries. As we see, to get each extra unit of food, we have to give up increasing amounts of entertainment. The trade-off, which is called the *marginal rate of transformation (MRT)*, is calculated in the fourth column of Table 20-1. The *MRT* is defined as follows:

$$\begin{array}{l}\text{Marginal rate} \\ \text{of transformation}\end{array} = MRT$$

$$= \frac{\text{change in food output}}{\begin{array}{c}\text{change in}\\ \text{entertainment output}\end{array}} \quad (1)$$

The *MRT* is calculated in the fourth column as the ratio of the quantity in the second column to the quantity in the third column. For example, the first worker who moves increases food output by 3 units at a cost of only 0.5 unit of entertainment. Therefore, the marginal rate of transformation, according to the formula above, is 6(3/0.5). The first worker who moves produces a large increase in food output at a very low cost in terms of entertainment forgone. But the *MRT* falls rapidly. When the first worker moves, the economy loses only 0.5 unit of entertainment while gaining 3 units of food—in other words, 6 units of food are gained per unit of entertainment lost. The second unit of labor moved gives us a trade-off between food and entertainment of only 2.1 (2.5/1.2), and the third

gives a trade-off that is down to 1.05. There is a diminishing marginal rate of transformation of entertainment into food.

The diminishing *MRT* shows up in Figure 20-2 in the bowed-out shape of the transformation curve. The source of the diminishing *MRT* becomes clear when we rewrite the definition in equation (1) above. We know that the gain in the output of food from moving 1 more unit of labor in is just the MPL_F—the marginal product of labor in the food sector. Similarly, the loss in output in the entertainment sector is the MPL_E. Thus the *MRT* represents the ratio of the marginal products of workers in the two industries:

$$MRT = \frac{\text{marginal product of labor in food}}{\begin{array}{c}\text{marginal product of}\\ \text{labor in entertainment}\end{array}}$$

$$= \frac{MPL_F}{MPL_E} \quad (2)$$

The source of the diminishing *MRT* is thus the diminishing marginal productivity of labor in each industry. As we move along the PPF from point *E* back toward *F*, the marginal product of labor in the food industry is decreasing because more labor is working in that industry. At the same time, the MPL_E is rising, as fewer workers are left in the entertainment business. Their ratio, the *MRT*, is therefore falling.

The slope of the *MRT* makes precise the idea of opportunity cost. The opportunity cost of producing more food on the PPF is the loss of entertainment that could have been provided instead of the food. The *MRT* measures this opportunity cost.

3 DEMAND AND THE OPTIMAL ALLOCATION OF RESOURCES

The transformation curve shows us what the economy, operating at its best, *can* produce. How do we go from here to answer the question of which of the combinations of output of food and entertainment on the PPF *should* be produced to ensure maximum happiness for the economy's consumers? That is, how do we determine the optimal allocation of resources?

To figure out the optimal allocation of resources, we have to know what consumers want. Consumers *can* be at any point on the PPF. But they prefer some points to others. We can be sure, for instance, that they would not want only food, at point F, or only entertainment, at point E. Where they actually prefer to be depends on their tastes. The analysis of indifference curves in the appendix to Chapter 5 now becomes useful, because the curves represent a complete description of consumer preferences.

In Figure 20-3 we introduce indifference curves that represent consumer preferences between food and entertainment. The consumer gets equal satisfaction or utility from all the combinations of goods on a given indifference curve. As a reminder, indifference curves are negatively sloped because when consumption of one good is reduced, the amount consumed of the other good has to be raised in order to keep the consumer as well off as he was before. Further, the indifference curves have the bowed shape shown, reflecting a diminishing marginal rate of substitution. Consumers do not want specialized consumption patterns. As the consumption of one commodity is reduced, the compensation required in terms of the other good rises.

FIGURE 20-3   THE OPTIMAL ALLOCATION. The PPF is as derived in Figure 20-2. No points on indifference curve UU_2 are attainable, given the PPF. Points on indifference curve UU_0 between M and N are attainable, but they are not optimal because the consumer can reach a higher indifference curve. The highest indifference curve that can be reached is UU_1, at point A. Thus, A represents the highest utility level that can be reached; the optimal allocation of resources is to produce amount OB of entertainment and OD of food.

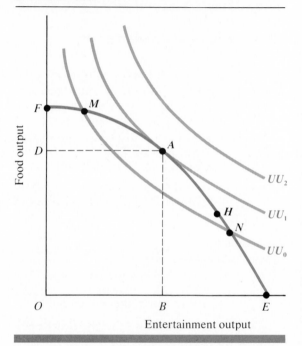

In Figure 20-3 we show three indifference curves. First observe that the level of utility UU_2 is not attainable in the economy. There are not enough resources available to produce the output combinations required to achieve that level of welfare. There are certainly enough resources to satisfy a level of welfare shown by indifference curve UU_0. That is because UU_0 passes below the PPF at some points, between M and N.

But we can do better than be on UU_0. Point A represents the best allocation of resources that the economy can achieve. Given the economy's production possibilities, represented by the PPF, and tastes, represented by indifference curves, no indifference curve higher than UU_1 can be reached. And UU_1 is reachable only at point A. At A, the indifference curve UU_1 is tangent to, or just touches, the PPF.

We now have a complete answer to the question about the best that can be done in this economy. The economy should produce at point A. The amount of fun produced should be OB, and the amount of food should be OD. Of course, these are also the amounts of food and entertainment that consumers should consume if they are to be as happy as they possibly can be. Labor should be put to work in the two sectors of the economy in the amounts that correspond to being at point A on the PPF. We can figure out how much labor should go into each sector by looking at Figure 20-2.

How should we think about this result, telling us in full detail how the economy should allocate resources? The easiest way to think about it is to say that we are dealing with the economic problem faced by a single person on a nondesert island. With a little work, food can be produced, and by using labor, it is also possible to have fun—sailing, or swimming, or sitting around the campfire thinking about better times. Such a person knows his tastes, as well as how good he is at production. Hence he knows the PPF. His problem is to make himself as happy as he can, given the technical possibilities open to him, as shown by the PPF. He does that by figuring out how much food to produce and how much fun to have. The answer is summarized by saying that he should be at point A.

Alternatively, we can think about an idealized planner for an economy. He knows how much labor there is in the economy, and he knows the production functions for each sector. He also knows what the tastes of the people in the economy are. His job, given this enormous amount of knowledge about the people, is to tell the people what to produce and how. The answer is to arrange things in the economy to

be sure it gets to point A. He directs the necessary amount of labor to each industry, tells the workers to work, and then orders the resulting output to be given to consumers (the workers and their families and whoever else is in the economy). This is a so-called command economy, discussed in Chapter 1.

Now we come to the crucial issue, which we can call Adam Smith's suggestion. We know that point A is the best possible point for this economy to be at. The question is, Is there any mechanism that will get a private economy, in which there is *no* central planner, to produce and consume the amounts of goods corresponding to A? Smith's answer, refined by later theorists, is yes. If the economy operates through a price system and has competition in all its markets—for labor and for goods—then it will indeed reach point A.

Deep down, this is the most important question that has to be asked about economies that choose how, what, and for whom to produce using markets rather than a central planner. We have a vague feeling that competitive markets lead to socially desirable levels of production and consumption of different goods. But we need to be better than vague. In the rest of this chapter, we show, for this very simple economy,[3] why

---

[3] Where is this economy simplified? There are two main places. First, and less important, labor is the only factor of production that is mobile between the sectors. To determine what gets produced, we only have to move labor between the sectors. Determining what gets produced is more complicated when there are more factors of production to move around. Second, and more serious, no real "for whom" question has been discussed so far. We have described consumers' tastes by using indifference curves. We can certainly do this if there is only one consumer. But otherwise, we have to ask whose tastes are being represented on the indifference curves. Even if all the consumers have the same tastes, we also have to ask whether they should all be treated the same, given exactly the same amounts of goods, or whether they should be treated differently. Thus the "for whom" aspects of the problem of economic organization are not seriously covered by the analysis in this chapter.

consumers who demand goods on the basis of their prices and firms that maximize profits will end up in equilibrium at point A. They get there by being put together in competitive markets.

We show how a private economy gets to point A in Figure 20-3 by breaking the issue down into two questions. First, what ensures that firms produce on the PPF rather than inside it? Second, how do we know that the economy moves to point A rather than to some other point on the PPF, such as H?

4 GETTING TO THE PPF

In this section and the next we demonstrate that the price system will move the economy to point A, given that firms maximize profits and consumers demand goods on the basis of their tastes, summarized by the indifference curves. Prices provide the signals for firms and households to end up exactly at point A, at the economy's equilibrium. What is surprising is that this complicated job of making mutually consistent employment, production, and consumption decisions is achieved through individual decisions by firms and households. It does not need a central planner.

We start by showing that with full employment equilibrium in the labor market, firms will be producing on the PPF.

In Figure 20-2 we *mechanically* derived the transformation curve by assuming that there is a given labor force, L, and given production functions. Allocating the given labor force between sectors then allowed us, from the production functions, to read off the output supplies and thus generate the PPF. But what can ensure that the entire labor force is employed? How can we be sure that we will be on the PPF in Figure 20-3, and what determines how labor is allocated between sectors? Here is the first place where wages, prices, and employ-

ment decisions by firms have to make an appearance.

From the discussion of labor demand in Chapter 13, we know that the firm expands employment to the point where the marginal value product of labor equals the money wage. If we use food as an example, we see that the firms in the food industry will expand employment up to the point where the wage is equal to the price of food, P_F, times the marginal physical product of labor in terms of food. The same is true in the entertainment sector. Therefore, we can write the firms' equilibrium conditions in the labor market as follows:

Marginal value   marginal value
   product of   = wage = product of labor
labor in food   in entertainment

or

$$P_F \times MPL_F = \text{wage} = P_E \times MPL_E \qquad (3)$$

The equilibrium condition in equation (3) draws attention to two aspects of wages. First, it points to the role of the wage rate in allocating labor between sectors. Second, it highlights the role of wage flexibility in attaining full employment. Let us look at both of these points in more detail.

We start with wage flexibility and full employment. Suppose that we have given prices of the two goods and that firms make their employment decisions on the basis of those prices. Pick any money wage. There will be a given level of employment in each industry such that at that wage, labor exactly earns its way: the marginal value product equals the wage. Firms would not want to hire either more or less labor. But, of course, there is nothing to assure us that the wage we picked, arbitrarily, will clear the labor market. If we pick a wage that is very low, both sectors' firms in combination will want to hire more labor than is available in the economy. They will compete for labor and therefore drive up the money wage. They will keep competing, raising the wage until it has increased so much, with labor demand reduced in both industries, that the total demand for labor equals the available supply. Take the other case: we pick a wage that is extremely high. At that wage, firms in both sectors want to hire only very little labor, less than is available in the economy. Workers, therefore, are unemployed and compete for jobs. The wage falls and therefore creates more job opportunities as labor demand rises in both industries. The process continues until the wage has fallen enough for everybody in the labor force to be employed.

Thus wage flexibility ensures full employment.[4] If wages were not flexible, we could get stuck inside the transformation curve with unemployment of labor.[5] But given the prices the firms face and flexible wages where on the PPF do we end up? We now show that where the economy ends up on the PPF depends on the prices the firms face. As the price of food in relation to that of fun changes, the allocation of labor between the sectors changes, and we move along the PPF.

Before we go into the technicalities, we should review what intuition would tell us. Suppose that the price of food rises in relation to that of fun. Intuitively, we think that more food will be produced. Why? Firms producing food will want to hire more labor when the price rises, and firms producing fun will want to hire less when its price falls. So it is likely that as the price of food in relation to that of fun changes, the economy moves along the PPF. We now show that in more detail.

Given the price at which it can sell food,

P_F, and given the wage it has to pay, a firm will hire labor up to the point where the marginal value product of labor is equal to the wage. It is this fact that ensures that as the price of food in relation to that of entertainment changes, we move along the PPF. We go back now to equation (3):

$$P_F \times MPL_F = \text{wage} = P_E \times MPL_E$$

Leaving the wage out of the middle, we write

$$P_F \times MPL_F = P_E \times MPL_E \qquad (3')$$

Thus firms in the two industries will have the *same* marginal value product of labor.[6]

Now we can rewrite equation (3') in a way that will emphasize that as the relative price of goods changes, we move along the PPF. We rewrite equation (3') as follows:

$$\frac{P_E}{P_F} = \frac{MPL_F}{MPL_E} = \begin{array}{c} \text{relative price of} \\ \text{entertainment in} \\ \text{terms of food} \end{array} \qquad (4)$$

Firms' maximization of profits, expressed through their demands for labor, ensures that when there is labor market equilibrium, the ratio of the marginal products of labor in the two industries is equated to the price of food relative to that of entertainment. The higher the relative price of entertainment, the higher the marginal physical product of labor in the food industry relative to the marginal physical product of labor in entertainment. That is what we learn from equation (4).

But more important, it is equation (4) which tells us that as the relative price of

---

[4] This argument takes the prices of goods as given. Later, we will have to ask what determines the prices of goods. The final answer is that the quantity of money determines the *average* price level—but that can be shown only in the macroeconomics section.

[5] Later, in the macroeconomics part of the book, we see that wage inflexibility or, alternatively, price inflexibility can be thought of as the cause of unemployment.

[6] We can see why that should be. Suppose the marginal value product of labor in the food industry was higher than that in the fun industry, and suppose the wage was equal to the marginal value product of labor in the fun industry. Then firms in the food industry would demand more labor, because by hiring 1 extra unit of labor at the wage rate, they could produce output equal in value to the marginal value product, which is more than the wage. They would increase profits. They therefore would hire more labor, driving up the wage and successfully drawing labor out of the fun industry.

entertainment rises, more labor is moved into the entertainment industry and out of the food industry. Why? Because we know that the more labor employed in food, the lower its marginal product. Thus when the price of entertainment is high relative to that of food, the marginal product of labor in food will have to be high relative to the marginal product of labor in entertainment —that is what equation (4) says. The only way the marginal product of labor in food can be high relative to the marginal product of labor in entertainment is if there is not much labor producing food and a lot of it producing entertainment. Hence labor market equilibrium, built on profit maximization by competitive firms, ensures that as the relative price of entertainment rises, labor is moved out of the food industry and into fun production.

Now we come to yet another point to remember. Recall that the slope of the PPF is equal to the marginal rate of transformation (MRT) between entertainment and food. Recall also from equation (2) that the MRT is equal to the ratio of the marginal product of labor in the food industry to labor's marginal product in entertainment. But we see from equation (4) that the ratio of marginal products is also equal to the ratio of the prices. We thus arrive at the following important conclusion: When competitive firms maximize profits and the labor market clears, the MRT is equal to the relative price of entertainment in terms of food.

$$MRT = \frac{MPL_F}{MPL_E} = \frac{P_E}{P_F} = \text{relative price} \qquad (5)$$

This means that given the price of entertainment relative to the price of food and given that we are told that firms are maximizing profits and that the labor market is in equilibrium, we know that firms will be operating on the PPF. They will be at the point where the MRT is equal to the price ratio. Thus given the relative price, P_E/P_F,

we know what levels of output of the two goods will be produced by profit-maximizing competitive firms.

MRT = Price Ratio: Another Interpretation

The result that under competition firms will produce outputs such that the marginal rate of transformation is equal to the price ratio is sufficiently important for us to drive home the message by explaining it in a different way. This time we concentrate on the result from Chapter 8 that competitive, profit-maximizing firms produce up to the point where marginal cost is equal to price.

Assume that the wage is given and that the labor market is in equilibrium. How much output will each firm want to produce, given the price at which it can sell? It will choose the production level at which marginal cost is equal to the price. Now we have to ask what the marginal cost is of producing 1 more unit of the good. More output is produced by using more labor. Hiring 1 more unit of labor increases output by an amount equal to the marginal product of labor. Suppose that hiring 1 more unit of labor increases output by 2.5 units. Then to produce 1 more unit of the good the firm has to hire 0.4 unit of labor (for example, a worker who comes in 2 days a week). That is, the amount of labor needed to produce 1 more unit of the good (0.4 in this case) is 1 divided by the marginal product of labor (2.5 in this case). And the firm will have to pay that worker the wage rate. We see, therefore, that the marginal cost of production can be calculated as follows:

$$
\begin{aligned}
\text{Marginal cost} \atop \text{of production} &= {\text{cost of hiring extra labor} \atop \text{needed to produce 1 more} \atop \text{unit of the good}} \\[2mm]
&= {\text{wage} \times \text{amount of labor} \atop \text{needed to produce 1 more} \atop \text{unit of the good}} \\[2mm]
&= \frac{\text{wage}}{MPL} \qquad (6)
\end{aligned}
$$

In each industry, firms will equate the marginal cost of production to the price they face. Thus we have

$$P_E = MC_E = \frac{\text{wage}}{MPL_E}$$
and
$$P_F = MC_F = \frac{\text{wage}}{MPL_F} \qquad (7)$$

If we leave the marginal cost term out of the middle in equation (7), we will see that it is nothing other than the condition that we used in equation (3), that the value of the marginal product of labor in each industry be equal to the wage. And from there we can get once more to the conclusion that the MRT, or the ratio of the marginal product of labor in the food industry to the marginal product of labor in the entertainment industry, is equal to the price of entertainment in relation to that of food.

Once more we have shown that profit-maximizing competitive firms will act in such a way that the economy reaches a point on the PPF where the marginal rate of transformation is equal to the price ratio.

5 THE CONSUMER AND GENERAL EQUILIBRIUM

We have now seen that given the ratio of prices, firms will act to produce outputs such that the MRT is equal to the price ratio, as in equation (5). Wage flexibility in the labor market and profit maximization by competitive firms will get the economy to the PPF, given the prices of goods.

To see which point on the PPF the economy settles at, we turn to the consumer side, to add the demand for goods. At this point we remind ourselves of the main result of the appendix to Chapter 5, in which indifference curves were introduced. We showed there that the consumer optimizes or maximizes utility by choosing to consume at a point where an indifference curve is tangent to the budget line. At that point

the marginal rate of substitution in consumption between entertainment and food, MRS, is just equal to the relative price prevailing in the market. Consumer maximization, in summary, implies the equality of relative prices and the MRS:

$$MRS = \frac{P_E}{P_F} \qquad (8)$$

Equilibrium

In Figure 20-4 we show the complete equilibrium of the economy. The slope of the pp curve is equal to (minus) the ratio of the price of entertainment to that of food. Firms

FIGURE 20-4 $MRS = MRT$ IN EQUILIBRIUM. Consumers' tastes are represented by UU_1. Given relative prices, shown by the price (budget) line, pp, consumers maximize utility by choosing a point at which pp is tangent to an indifference curve. This is point A. Similarly, given the prices represented by pp, profit-maximizing firms are led to point A. Point A is therefore the point of general equilibrium. The amounts of goods firms want to produce are equal to the amounts consumers want to buy, in both the food and entertainment industries.

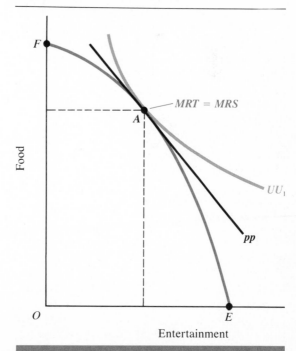

maximize by producing at a point where the *MRT* equals the prevailing relative price, and they produce on the transformation curve. The combination of labor market equilibrium and firms' maximization of their profits ensures that they end up on the PPF.

Households maximize by consuming goods in the proportion such that the *MRS* equals the prevailing relative price of goods.

In equilibrium, it has to be true by definition that the amount of goods the households want to consume is equal to the amount the firms want to produce. We know, given profit maximization by firms and labor market equilibrium, that firms want to be on the PPF. Therefore, to find the point of general equilibrium, we are looking for points on the PPF such that the *MRS* is equal to the price ratio. At such points, given the price ratio, households will want to consume the amounts the firms

want to produce. There is only one such point, namely point *A*.

If the price ratio is anything other than that implied by *pp* at point *A*, we will not have equilibrium. For instance, suppose that the price ratio is *pp'*, as shown in Figure 20-5, with a higher relative price of food. Firms want to produce at point *G*. But if the economy goes to *G* and households can buy the amount produced at *G*, they would rather at those prices have more entertainment. At *G*, an extra unit of entertainment can be bought quite cheaply in terms of the amount of food given up. Therefore, households would increase utility by giving up food in exchange for entertainment at the prices the market has set. Households want to move down price line *pp'* toward the southeast to *G'*, increasing their utility as they go. Of course, the economy cannot get there, but the prices in the economy tell the consumers they can move that way. Therefore, the price ratio shown

FIGURE 20-5 DISEQUILIBRIUM WHEN THE PRICE RATIO IS WRONG. This figure shows what happens when price ratios are wrong. Suppose that prices are as given by *pp'*, which is different from *pp* in Figure 20-4. At those prices, firms are led to point *G*. But given output at *G*, households want to consume the amounts shown at *G'*. They want more fun and less food. There is an excess demand for entertainment and an excess supply of food. The relative price of food therefore falls, and the price line becomes steeper. Only at point *A* will supply be equal to demand in both markets and the relative price remain constant.

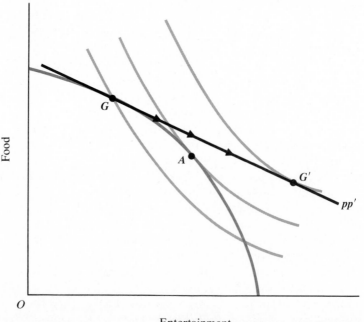

on pp' cannot be an equilibrium price ratio, and the economy cannot be in equilibrium at G.

Prices will be adjusted so that food becomes relatively cheaper and entertainment relatively more expensive. The price line becomes steeper as the relative price of entertainment rises, and production moves toward the southeast on the PPF. Prices continue to be adjusted until the economy reaches point A, at which there is no excess demand for either good.

Hence we have shown that the general equilibrium of the economy can only be at point A. But point A is precisely the point at which resources are allocated optimally. We have thus shown that the allocation of resources that results when competitive firms maximize profits, households maximize utility, and prices clear markets is the socially optimal allocation.

The argument is far from simple. We therefore repeat its essence, and in Box 20-1 we summarize it more formally. The essence of the argument is this:

1   Wage flexibility ensures labor market equilibrium with full employment, putting the economy on the PPF.

2   Given the prices of goods, profit maximization by firms leads them to a point on the PPF at which the marginal rate of transformation (MRT) is equal to the price of entertainment in relation to that of food.

3   Given the price ratio, consumers will be in equilibrium only if the marginal rate of substitution (MRS) is equal to the price ratio.

4   Given prices, firms will be producing on the PPF. Equilibrium exists, therefore, at a point on the PPF where the price ratio is such that the MRS is equal to the MRT. At any other point on the PPF, and given the price ratio, households prefer to consume some combination of goods that is different

from the combination the firms want to produce.

5   In the economy's general equilibrium, MRS is equal to MRT. But that is precisely the condition for the socially optimal allocation of resources. Hence an economy with competitive firms, using prices and markets to allocate resources, achieves the socially optimal allocation of resources.

6 GENERAL EQUILIBRIUM: A SUPPLY AND DEMAND DIAGRAM

In this section we briefly present a supply and demand diagram that embodies all the general equilibrium interrelationships of the economy. We do so by looking at supply and demand in the market for only one good, entertainment. We need to look only at one market because it is clear from Figures 20-4 and 20-5 that the market for food can be in equilibrium only if the market for entertainment is.

Figure 20-6 contains the supply and demand curves for entertainment. But these are not the usual supply and demand curves, in which it is assumed that conditions in the rest of the economy are unaffected by events in the industry we study. Rather, they take full account of the interactions within the economy.

The supply curve shows the amount of entertainment firms want to produce as the relative price of entertainment is increased along the PPF. We start at point F on the PPF in Figure 20-4, with a very low relative price of entertainment, as evidenced by the flatness of the PPF at that point. [Check back to equation (5) to see that the relative price of entertainment is high when the MRT is low.] Gradually we increase the relative price of entertainment, and the economy's production moves down along the PPF. Fun production increases. This is shown by the supply curve in Figure 20-6.

In the background, of course, is the fact

FIGURE 20-6 GENERAL EQUILIBRIUM
SUPPLY AND DEMAND CURVES. The *SS*
curve shows how the output of food
changes as the price ratio is changed and
firms move along the PPF. When the relative price of entertainment is low, firms
produce close to point *F* in Figure 20-4,
and the output of entertainment is low. As
the relative price rises, the output of entertainment rises. The *DD* curve shows the
marginal valuation consumers place on entertainment relative to food at each point
on the PPF. Near point *F* in Figure 20-4, entertainment consumption is low, and firms
value 1 more unit of fun highly relative to
the loss of 1 unit of food. As we move to
point *E*, households' relative valuation of
entertainment falls. Therefore, demand
curve *DD* is downward-sloping. Quantity
supplied equals quantity demanded at point
A. This corresponds to point *A* in Figure
20-5. A shift in demand toward fun and
away from food, shown by *DD'*, raises the
relative price of fun and the quantity of fun
produced.

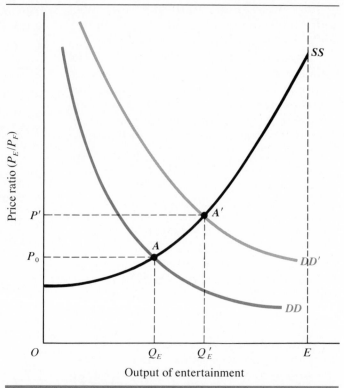

Output of entertainment

that at the same time, the production of food
is falling. Labor is being pulled out of the
food industry and into entertainment. On
supply curve *SS* in Figure 20-6, all the interactions taking place in the economy are
fully taken into account. We can thus refer
to *SS* as a general equilibrium supply curve.

On the demand side, the *DD* curve
shows the marginal valuation households
put on entertainment relative to food for
each point on the PPF. This marginal valuation is given by the slope of the indifference
curve, or by the *MRS*, at each point on the
PPF. Thus at point *F* in Figure 20-4, where
food consumption is high and there is no entertainment, people put a very high relative
value on getting 1 more unit of entertainment. The indifference curves on the PPF
at points near *F* are steep (check back to
Figure 20-4), meaning that households are

willing to give up a lot of food to have some
fun. Then as we move down the PPF, the
MRS falls, and the *DD* curve in Figure 20-6
is correspondingly downward-sloping.

Note again that this is a general equilibrium demand curve. We do not say that income is fixed, as we would for the usual demand curve. Rather, we take account of the
fact that the economy is moving along the
PPF, and we measure consumer demand
conditions on the PPF, where production
will actually be taking place.

The general equilibrium of the economy is found at point *A* in Figure 20-6. We
can say that supply is equal to demand,
meaning that the relative price consumers
are willing to pay for entertainment is precisely the price at which firms willingly
supply the quantity. In the background, we
are also aware that the market for food is in

BOX 20-1

GENERAL EQUILIBRIUM IN REVIEW

LABOR MARKET

$$P_F MPL_F = \text{wage} = P_E MPL_E$$

Firms hire labor to the point where the marginal value product equals the wage. Because labor is mobile between the sectors, it cannot be paid more in one sector than in another. This ensures that the value of labor's contribution to output in each sector is equal. Wage flexibility ensures that all labor is employed and thus that the economy produces on the production possibility frontier (PPF).

Note: We can rewrite the labor market equilibrium condition as follows:

$$\frac{MPL_F}{MPL_E} = \frac{P_E}{P_F} = MRT$$

Since the ratio of the marginal products of labor in the two industries is equal to the marginal rate of transformation, we see that the *MRT* is equal to the price ratio, P_E/P_F.

PRODUCTION

Equivalently, we can think of firms equating the marginal cost of production to the price of output. This gives in the two sectors

$$\frac{\text{Wage}}{MPL_F} = P_F \quad \text{and} \quad \frac{\text{Wage}}{MPL_E} = P_E$$

Setting marginal cost equal to price also implies that at the point on the PPF at which firms want to produce, *MRT* is equal to the price ratio.

CONSUMERS

$$MRS = \frac{P_E}{P_F}$$

Consumers optimize when they equate the marginal rate of substitution between entertainment and food (*MRS*) to the prevailing relative price of goods. The *MRS* reflects the consumer's relative valuation of the two goods, or the terms under which the consumer is willing to trade one off for the other without reducing utility. This trade-off is equated to the prevailing price ratio.

GENERAL EQUILIBRIUM

Consumers and producers face the same prices. The relative price, on the supply side, reflects the relative marginal costs of production. On the demand side, the relative price is equal to the consumers' relative valuation of the two goods. Therefore, with the same prices for consumers and producers:

$$\begin{matrix} \text{Relative marginal} \\ \text{cost of producing goods} \end{matrix} = MRT = \frac{P_E}{P_F} = MRS = \begin{matrix} \text{relative marginal valuation} \\ \text{by consumers} \end{matrix}$$

Resources are allocated optimally through the price system. Point *A* is reached.

equilibrium. Anything that happens in the market for entertainment will also affect the market for food—and the demand for labor.

For instance, suppose that there is a change in tastes. At every point on the PPF, households now place a higher relative valuation on entertainment. Hedonism has set in. The DD curve in Figure 20-6 shifts up to DD', and equilibrium is now at A'. The relative price of entertainment rises to P', and the output of entertainment rises from Q_E to Q_E'. At the same time, we know that the output of food falls. Figure 20-6 is a diagram that is an alternative to Figure 20-5 for studying the full equilibrium of the economy.

The obvious question this section raises is why we don't always do our analysis of problems in a general equilibrium setting. The answer must be pretty clear. It is more complicated that way. So long as we are dealing with an industry that is only a small part of the economy, it is reasonable to assume that the general equilibrium interactions of the industry with the rest of the economy cannot be important enough to change the basic results obtained. For most practical purposes, that is right. But it is useful to know how to do the complete analysis, taking the interactions into account, in case that is needed.

7 QUALIFICATIONS

In this section we briefly draw attention to assumptions that were made along the way in showing that the market allocation of resources is the optimal allocation.

We assumed, to begin with, that the economy was free of distortions. All firms faced the same wages, all firms were competitive, and wages and prices were adjusted to ensure equilibrium. We also assumed in drawing the PPF that there were diminishing returns to labor in each industry. Thus there were no problems of econo-mies of scale, which, as we recall from Chapter 11, always create difficulties for the existence of competition. These are all serious assumptions, many of them violated in the economy in which we live. So it is unwise to get too excited about the optimality of the market of resources without checking that the conditions necessary for optimality to apply do, in fact, exist.

On the other side, it is important also not to make the mistake of assuming that because something is wrong with the market allocation of resources, it is easy to fix the problem with a law or government intervention of some sort. Government bureaucracies also have their problems as means of allocating resources. In any particular case, it is necessary to sit down to try to figure out the best way of correcting a bad situation. (Perhaps the conclusion is that it cannot be done.)

The most serious qualification concerns the *distribution of income* or welfare that results in a market economy. We noted earlier that the economy dealt with so far is simplified because there is essentially a single consumer. When we focus on the fact that there are many different consumers, the optimality of the market solution has to be stated with care. The market solution then will imply a particular distribution of income among the workers and property owners in the economy.

That distribution of income in turn depends on how resources are distributed to begin with—that is, it depends on who owns the capital, and the land, and the human capital.

> The optimality of the competitive allocation of resources then has to be stated as follows: Given the level of welfare of every individual but one in the economy, the competitive equilibrium makes the last person as well off or as happy as is technically possible.

But because there are many different possible competitive equilibriums, each corresponding to a different initial distribution of resources, there is no way of saying that *the* competitive allocation is optimal.

The competitive equilibrium is also described as *Pareto optimal*. This is a situation where no one in the economy can be made better off without someone else (at least one person) being made worse off. Pareto optimality is a minimal requirement. If we were in a situation where someone could be made better off without anyone else being damaged, then the existing situation could easily be improved and certainly should not be thought of as optimal.

Going back to What? How? and For whom? (the basic questions of economics), we can say the following. A competitive market system solves the what and how problems optimally, given the distribution of resources—or given the for whom. The for whom produced by a competitive economy has no claims of efficiency or optimality to support it. For example, those who criticize a competitive market system because it rewards people whose parents had the good sense to be rich are not committing any errors of economics.

This says that the distribution of income that results in a market economy depends on the rules under which property and wealth ownership are treated. For instance, an economy in which all means of production except labor are owned by the state could, in principle, be a market economy. Indeed, there are some who argue that the economy of Yugoslavia is more like the competitive economy we have been studying in this chapter than is the economy of the United States, even though in Yugoslavia the workers own and operate the firms.[7]

8   THE ECONOMICS OF DISTORTIONS

The economy reaches an optimal allocation of resources when it is on the PPF, with the

---

[7] The Yugoslav economy is briefly described in Chapter 39.

marginal rate of substitution in consumption equal to the marginal rate of transformation in production. Departures from the optimal allocation of resources involve distortions—for example, taxes—that make the MRS and MRT differ. Economists say that distortions "drive a wedge" between the MRS and the MRT.

We now study the effects of the imposition of a tax on entertainment to show how distortions affect the allocation of resources.

Suppose that the government imposes a 10 percent tax on entertainment. What are the implications for resource allocation and welfare? To answer this question we first have to decide whether the measure affects the shape of the transformation curve. It does not, because there is neither a change in the production functions nor a change in factor supplies. Thus the PPF remains unaffected. Second, we ask whether firms will still produce on the PPF. The answer is yes, because wage flexibility ensures full employment.

Next we reach the question of whether firms still produce at the point where the MRT equals the *market* price ratio. Here the answer is no. Firms do not receive the market price, since they have to pay the entertainment tax. The entertainment tax introduces a 10 percent gap between the prices faced by producers and consumers. Consumers face the market price, while firms face the net of tax price, which of course is 10 percent lower. And firms produce at a point where the MRT is equal to the *net of tax price ratio*.

In Figure 20-7, we show the equilibrium at A without a tax and at A' with an entertainment tax. At point A' the indifference curve is no longer tangent to the transformation curve. The relative price of entertainment (including the tax) that consumers face is higher than the relative price that producers receive. Not surprisingly, the increase in price for consumers and the reduction in price for producers cause the

FIGURE 20-7 A TAX ON ENTERTAINMENT RE-
DUCES ENTERTAINMENT OUTPUT AND WELFARE.
The economy is initially at point *A*. A tax is imposed
on entertainment. The tax drives a wedge between
the relative prices paid by consumers and those received by producers. The relative price of fun for
consumers *rises.* The relative price of fun received
by producers *falls.* The economy moves to point *A'*,
where *pp'* shows the price ratio for producers and
pp" the price ratio for consumers. Less fun is produced and more food.

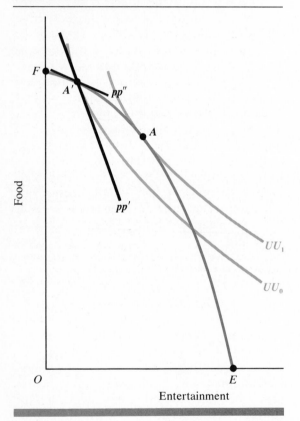

If society for some reason needs to impose taxes, it should impose taxes that do
not affect the efficiency of resource allocation. But it is very hard to find such taxes.

In our example the tax may have been
imposed because the government viewed
the amount of entertainment produced at
the optimal allocation point, point *A*, as excessive. In effect, the government was saying that consumers' tastes should be over-
ridden. Given such a government aim, a tax
on entertainment will do the trick of reducing the production and consumption of entertainment. Of course, consumers see
themselves as worse off as a result of the tax.
We do not want to go further into the interesting and important question of whether
society or the government should always accept consumers' tastes as being the criterion
for policy. What if some liked watching
gladiators fighting wild animals? What if
many liked dangerous drugs?

The point of this section is that the imposition of a tax results in a welfare cost for
the consumers in the economy because it
creates a gap between the *MRS* and the
MRT. But there may, nonetheless, be good
reasons for imposing taxes—for instance,
defense forces may have to be paid for, or
society may want to change the distribution
of income.

The analysis of distortions enables us to
answer the question raised at the beginning
of the chapter: Why is monopoly bad if the
factors of production that would have been
used in the monopolized industry go off to
work elsewhere in the economy? The reason is that the monopolist does *not* equate
marginal cost to price. Therefore, the marginal rate of substitution for consumers is
not equal to the society's marginal rate of
transformation. Indeed, we can think of the
monopolist as imposing a tax on consumers.
The difference between the monopolist's
tax and the government's tax is in who collects the revenue.

economy to produce less entertainment and
more food.

But the consequences for allocation go
beyond the shift from *A* to *A'*. First, at *A'*
consumers are worse off than at *A*. The entertainment tax has moved consumers to a
lower indifference curve than at point *A*.
Any distortion that drives a wedge between
consumers' and producers' prices will have
this welfare-reducing effect.

9 DETERMINING THE INTEREST RATE THROUGH SAVING AND INVESTMENT

Some prices are more important than others, and the real interest rate is high on any list. No serious problem involving the future can be analyzed without at least implicitly taking the real interest rate—which gives the terms at which current consumption can be traded for future consumption—into account.

The real rate of interest played a key role in our discussion of capital and land in Chapter 15. There we showed how the interest rate establishes the present value of future payments and is used to calculate the prices of assets. In Chapter 15, we also briefly discussed how the real interest rate is determined by productivity and savings.

In this section, we use the general equilibrium framework set out in this chapter to show in more detail how the interest rate is determined. We will rely again on the PPF and on indifference curves, but with a difference: instead of food and entertainment on the axes, we now have consumption today and consumption tomorrow. But that is about the only change we have to make.[8]

Investment and the PPF

In this part we introduce in Figure 20-8 a PPF showing the trade-offs that can be made between present and future consumption. How does the economy make the transformation between current and future consumption? For instance, at point A, society is maximizing today's consumption

[8] The use of the PPF and indifference curves to show how the interest rate is determined is due to Irving Fisher, the great American economist (1867–1947) who was also an investor and a health freak. Fisher's book, *The Theory of Interest*, reprinted by Augustus Kelley in 1965 (original in 1930), is a long but readable account of the theory. Its full title is *The Theory of Interest as Determined by Impatience to Spend Income and Opportunity to Invest It.*

and not providing anything for the future. How is that done? At A', society is not consuming at all today but maximizing future consumption. How is that done?

The trade-offs shown on the PPF in Figure 20-8 reflect different amounts of resources being devoted to *investment*, that is, to increases in the capital stock. The economy has a given capital stock and supply of labor. At one extreme we could use all the capital and labor for producing current consumption goods—goods to be enjoyed and used up today. We would pay no attention to the maintenance of the capital stock. Certainly we would not increase it by investing, and wherever possible we would use it to increase our current consumption. This gives us point A, where current con-

FIGURE 20-8 THE PPF CURVE BETWEEN CURRENT AND FUTURE CONSUMPTION. The PPF shows the combinations of current and future consumption that society can produce. The different combinations reflect decisions about how much to invest. At A, no provision at all is made for the future. At A', the economy is investing all its resources to produce maximum future consumption; it is not devoting any resources to current consumption. At point G, the slope of the PPF is −1. We discuss point G later, in connection with Figure 20-9.

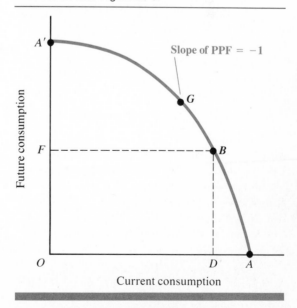

sumption is at a maximum and, we assume, the capital stock has been so neglected that no future consumption is possible.

At the other extreme is the possibility of devoting all our current resources to producing capital. We want to make future consumption as large as possible, and so we produce nothing at all for current consumption. This gives us point A', where future consumption is maximized at the expense of zero current consumption.[9] Point A' is the point that a society concerned only about the future would reach.

Between points A and A' we are moving resources from the production of current consumption goods to the production of capital and thus increasing future consumption. As we move from point A to B, current consumption is reduced by amount AD. Giving up amount AD of current consumption allows us to buy amount OF of future consumption. If we think of the amount of current consumption given up as the cost of our investment, then OF represents the return on the investment of AD.

Why does the PPF between current and future consumption show a diminishing marginal rate of transformation? Once again we meet diminishing returns. The first unit of today's consumption given up has a very high payoff in terms of future goods. At point A we are, after all, destroying the existing capital stock—in a sense we are eating the capital stock—but we cannot do much consumption by chewing on a lawn mower. So all that happens when we move from point A on the PPF to point B is that we stop doing unnatural things like that. We will lose almost nothing in current consumption and get a lot of future consumption in exchange.

As we invest more of the current output,

consuming less, we are increasing the quantities of resources put into the capital goods industry. The more resources put into that industry, the lower their marginal productivity. At the beginning all we are doing is better maintaining the existing capital stock. Later, we have to build new factories and machinery. Increasingly, the new investments produce less per unit of consumption given up today. The return to shifting resources into the production of capital and thus future consumption is diminishing.

Earlier in the chapter, when we were working with a PPF between food and fun, we interpreted the slope of the PPF or the MRT as the price ratio between food and fun. In this case of the PPF between current and future consumption, we can interpret the slope of the PPF as the return on investment.[10]

$$MRT = \frac{\text{increase in future consumption}}{\text{current consumption forgone}}$$

$$= \text{(marginal) return on investment} \qquad (9)$$

A typical number at point B might be like 1.15/1, meaning that 1 unit of current consumption forgone buys 1.15 units of future consumption.

It is easy to go from the MRT to a measure of the productivity of investment. The percentage rate of return on investment is defined as follows:

$$\text{Rate of return on investment} = \frac{\begin{array}{c}\text{increase in future}\\ \text{output} - \text{current}\\ \text{consumption forgone}\end{array}}{\begin{array}{c}\text{current consumption}\\ \text{forgone}\end{array}} \times 100\%$$

$$= \left[\frac{\begin{array}{c}\text{increase in}\\ \text{future output}\end{array}}{\begin{array}{c}\text{current}\\ \text{consumption}\\ \text{forgone}\end{array}} - 1\right] \times 100\%$$

$$= (MRT - 1) \times 100\% \qquad (10)$$

---

[9] A current consumption level of zero is impossible, since people would starve. We should therefore interpret current consumption of zero in Figure 20-8 as being the minimum amount needed for survival.

[10] The slope of the PPF is actually negative. By convention, we typically refer to the slope as being positive. As long as we remember the convention, there should be no confusion.

FIGURE 20-9 INVESTMENT AND THE RATE OF RETURN ON INVESTMENT. As the economy moves from point A, where it is producing only for consumption today, toward A', where it is producing only for future consumption, the rate of return on investment falls. Point G, where the rate of return on investment is zero, is the same as point G in Figure 20-8, where the slope of the PPF is $(-)1$.

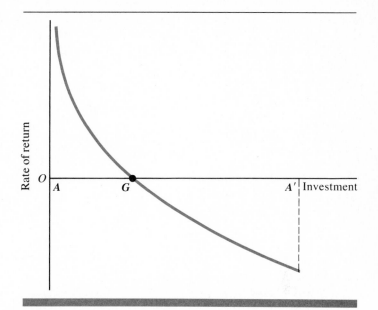

The definition of the rate of return is the increase in future consumption gained by giving up 1 unit of current consumption. For instance, at point B, if the slope of the PPF is 1.15, the rate of return on investment is $(1.15 - 1) \times 100\% = 15\%$. This means that investment yields 15 percent more in future consumption than is given up in current consumption.

In Figure 20-9, we show how the rate of return on investment changes as we move from point A to A', increasing the rate of investment from zero until all the economy's output is devoted to producing capital goods (at point A'). The rate of return starts out very high and decreases all the way. Indeed, at point G in Figure 20-9, the rate of return becomes zero, and it is negative. for higher rates of investment.

How can we have a negative rate of return on investment? This happens when more than 1 unit of current consumption has to be given up to get a unit of future consumption. We have so many resources producing capital goods that moving more resources in adds less to future consumption than the amount of current consumption

given up. Point G in Figure 20-9 corresponds to point G on the PPF in Figure 20-8, where the slope of the PPF is $(-)1$. At point G on the PPF, we get 1 more unit of future consumption in exchange for 1 unit of current consumption. At that point the rate of return on investment is zero.

In summary, we have defined a measure of the productivity of investment. Our measure is the rate of return on investment.[11] The slope of the PPF is equal to 1 plus the rate of return on investment. Near point A, with the economy nearly specialized in producing consumption goods, there is a very high rate of return on investment because the first units of consumption forgone have a high payoff in terms of future goods. Farther along AA', the rate of return falls as the economy becomes excessively specialized in investment; eventually, the economy runs into negative returns.

Indifference Curves and Saving

Figure 20-8 shows us the technical possibilities open to the economy. To determine

---

[11] The rate of return on investment is sometimes called the rate of return over cost.

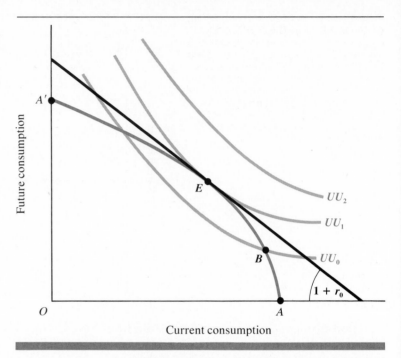

where on the PPF the economy ends up, we
have to bring in the consumer. The consumer values both current consumption and
future consumption and would be happy to
have more of either or both. The consumer's
tastes between current and future consumption are summarized by indifference curves,
as seen in Figure 20-10.

The consumer is willing to trade future
consumption for current consumption, as
shown by the negative slope of the indifference curves. But there is a diminishing marginal rate of substitution between current
and future consumption, and so the indifference curves become flatter as we move
down and to the right along the curves.

In Figure 20-10, we put the PPF and the
consumer's indifference curves together
and ask what the maximum level of utility is
—the highest indifference curve—that the
consumer can reach, given society's possibilities for trading off consumption today for
consumption tomorrow. Possible trade-offs
are shown by the PPF.

The best the consumer can do is to be at
point E. Why? No higher indifference curve
such as UU_2 can be reached, given the technical limits on how much consumption in
the two periods can be produced. On the
other side, choosing any other point on the
PPF will leave the consumer on a lower indifference curve; for example, the consumer
will be on UU_0 if he chooses point B. Thus
point E, the point of tangency between the
PPF and an indifference curve, shows the
maximum satisfaction the consumer can
achieve, given available resources and technology.

Now comes the next question. What
does point E have to do with the determination of the interest rate through productivity
and thrift? We now have to show that the interest rate will be equal to the rate of return
on investment at point E and that at point E
households want to consume today as much
as firms want to produce for today's consumption. We have to show, in other words,
that point E is a point of equilibrium for an

economy in which firms produce, deciding how much to sell today and how much to invest, and in which households make the consumption choices.

The Equilibrium Interest Rate

We will now show that the interest rate adjusts to bring the economy to the equilibrium at point E in Figure 20-10. To do so, we focus on saving and investment.

> *Saving* is the difference between income and current consumption.

The saving decision is made by the household. Investment represents the amount that firms want to add to the capital stock to provide for future consumption. It is the amount of current production they want to set aside for adding to the capital stock rather than selling for current consumption.

In equilibrium, saving will have to be equal to investment. Why? Saving is the amount of current income households want to set aside for future consumption. Investment is the amount of current production firms want to set aside to produce future consumption. We can write this out as follows:

Saving = income − current consumption   (11)

Investment = production − sales for
                           current consumption   (12)

We have to note one more thing: the income received in the economy is equal to total costs incurred by the firms plus any profits they might earn. Their costs go as income—for example, wages—to other people in the economy. The profits of the firms are income for the owners of the firms. Total costs plus profits are, of course, equal to the value of production. Thus the value of production is equal to income.

Now we can look at equations (11) and (12) and see that they can be rewritten as follows:

Saving + current consumption = income   (11)

Investment + sales for current consumption
                              = production   (12)

But production is equal to income, and so we have

Saving + current consumption = investment
               + sales for current consumption   (13)

In equilibrium, households are buying for current consumption the amount that firms want to sell, and so current consumption is equal to sales for current consumption. Finally, we reach this conslusion:

Saving = investment   (14)

In equilibrium, saving will be equal to investment.

What determines saving and investment, and in what market can we think of saving being made equal to investment? We want to think about the market for loans. Households that wish to save offer to lend. Firms that wish to invest go out to borrow in the loan market. In the real world, we think of the loan market as a place where banks make the loans, but we should realize that a bank is really acting as the agent for the lenders, such as households who make deposits in the bank. The loan market we are considering here is a simplified one in which households meet firms without the intervention or intermediation of other institutions.

Both saving and investment are affected by the interest rate. In Figure 20-10, the interest rate affects the slope of the consumer's budget line. When the interest rate is high, future consumption has a low opportunity cost in terms of current consumption. The budget line is steeper the higher the real interest rate. As the interest rate rises along the PPF, households are likely to want to save more, but we are not sure how the rate of saving (or lending) changes as the interest rate changes because income and substitution effects work in opposite directions.

FIGURE 20-11 SAVING = INVESTMENT DETER-
MINES THE INTEREST RATE. The *SA* curve shows
the amount of saving households want to do as the
interest rate rises. In the figure, it is assumed that
households' desired saving increases with the interest rate. The demand for investment goods is shown
by *ID*, which is identical to the curve for the rate of
return on investment in Figure 20-9. The intersection
of the *SA* and *ID* curves at point *E* determines the interest rate, r_0, and the rates of saving and investment, S_0 and I_0.

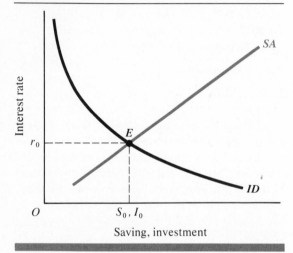

In Figure 20-11, where we study the
equilibrium of saving and investment, we
show the saving schedule, *SA*. On *SA* the
substitution effect dominates, implying that
saving increases with the interest rate.[12]

Figure 20-9 shows the investment
schedule as it relates to the interest rate. Investment decreases with the interest rate.
Why? Because given any interest rate, firms
will want to undertake investments up to
the point where the rate of return on investment is equal to the interest rate. Suppose
that they invested less, so that the rate of return on investment was above the interest
rate. Then they could borrow more, invest
the borrowing to increase future consumption, and still earn more than the interest
rate at which they borrowed. They would

---

[12] You should experiment here with a negatively
sloped schedule on which the income effect dominates.

come out ahead. So firms will certainly expand investment, at least to the point where
the marginal return is equal to the interest
rate. They will not be wise to go any further.
Suppose they invested more, driving the
rate of return below the rate of interest.
Then they would be borrowing at a higher
interest rate than they are earning on their
investment. They would increase profits by
cutting back investment. The conclusion is
that the schedule in Figure 20-9, showing
the rate of return for investment as the rate
of investment changes, is precisely the investment demand function, *ID*, we want to
have in Figure 20-11.

Equilibrium is determined at point *E* in
Figure 20-11, where saving is equal to investment. The equilibrium interest rate is
r_0.

This analysis shows how the real interest rate is determined by productivity and
thrift. The *ID* curve is determined solely by
the productivity of capital in transforming
current consumption into future consumption. We derived it in Figure 20-9 from the
PPF of Figure 20-8. The *SA* schedule is
derived from consumers' preferences between current and future consumption and
represents their willingness to be thrifty to
provide for future consumption. Any shift in
either schedule will change the interest
rate.

We want to go back now to Figure 20-10
to check that the equilibrium shown in Figure 20-11 will take us to point *E*. If the interest rate is equal to the rate of return on
investment, then we know that profit-maximizing firms will be at point *E*. That is the
only point at which the rate of return on investment is equal to r_0. Anywhere to the
right of *E* on the PPF, the rate of return on
investment exceeds r_0, and so the firms
cannot be producing there. They want to
produce more future consumption; i.e., they
want to invest more. Anywhere to the left of
E, the rate of return on investment is less
than r_0, and so the firms would not be pro-

ducing there. By cutting back on investment, they reduce their losses. Thus firms that are faced by interest rate r_0 will choose to produce at point E.

Households faced by any given interest rate will want to be at a point at which the marginal rate of substitution between current and future consumption is equal to the price ratio between current and future consumption. The price ratio is equal to $(1 + r_0)$, because giving up 1 unit of current consumption buys $(1 + r_0)$ units of future consumption. The price line with slope $(1 + r_0)$ touches its highest indifference curve at point E. Therefore, point E is the equilibrium point for the economy in Figure 20-10; it corresponds to point E in Figure 20-11.

We have now shown how productivity and thrift determine the real interest rate, which is the key intertemporal price. Movements in the real interest rate bring about the equality of saving and investment. Firms that want to invest borrow in the loan market. Households that want to save lend in the loan market.[13] The interest rate is ad-

justed to equate lending and borrowing. Suppose that the interest rate is too high. Then firms reduce their borrowing, while households at the same time try to save and lend more. There is an excess of desired lending over desired borrowing, causing the interest rate to fall. At the equilibrium interest rate, desired borrowing (equal to the firms' desired investment) is equal to desired lending (households' desired saving).

In terms of Figure 20-10, the equilibrium of saving and investment is at point E. At that point firms are investing at the rate they want to and selling as much for current consumption as they want, while households are consuming at the rate they want to currently and saving the desired amount for future consumption. The interest rate has been adjusted to equate saving and investment.

Any change in productivity—shifts in the PPF—or thrift—shifts in indifference curves—would change the real interest rate as well as saving and investment. For instance, if saving became more attractive, shifting the SA curve downward in Figure 20-11, the real interest rate would fall, but saving and investment would rise.

---

[13] Or the households may lend to banks or other financial institutions that do the lending in the loan market.

SUMMARY

1   The optimal allocation of resources in the economy occurs when the marginal rate of transformation (MRT) is equal to the marginal rate of substitution (MRS). The MRT is the rate at which society can trade off between two goods, say, food and entertainment, given the available technology and resources. The MRS is the rate at which consumers are willing to trade off one good for another while maintaining constant utility.

2   The most important result demonstrated in the chapter is that an optimal allocation of resources is achieved in a competitive market economy in which prices are used to allocate goods. This is the fundamental justification for the view that the allocation of resources is best left to "the market" to handle.

3   The details of these arguments are summarized in section 20-5 and in Box 20-1.

4   The result that the equilibrium reached in a competitive economy with clearing markets is optimal is both remarkable and subject to qualification. The result requires price and wage flexibility and competition. This latter condition also requires an absence of strongly increasing returns to scale. The distribution of income in the particular competitive allocation reached will depend on who initially owns the wealth. The for whom realized by competitive markets depends on the property rules in the economy being considered.

5   Distortions in goods or factor markets lead to a misallocation of resources in goods or factor markets. The misallocation involves a discrepancy between the marginal valuation of goods by consumers and the marginal *social* costs of producing output. For instance, a tax on a good leads to underproduction of it and to a reduction in welfare.

6   The interest rate is the key intertemporal price in economics. It affects the allocation of consumption between today and tomorrow and the allocation of capital between alternative uses.

7   The trade-off between present and future consumption on the production side is defined by the production possibility frontier. Forgoing current consumption frees resources to build capital or invest and thus raise future consumption.

8   The interest rate establishes equilibrium between borrowing and lending, or investment and saving, or current consumption demanded and current consumption supplied.

9   The equilibrium interest rate is determined by productivity and thrift. The interest rate is higher the more productive investment opportunities are and the less willing consumers are to trade off future consumption for current consumption. A high rate of interest may be as much a reflection of highly productive investment opportunities as it is a reflection of a strong preference for current consumption on the part of households.

KEY TERMS

General equilibrium of the economy	Command economy
Invisible hand of Adam Smith	Distribution of income
Optimal allocation of resources	Distortions
Production efficiency	Marginal rate of substitution
Production possibility frontier	Investment
Opportunity cost	Rate of return on investment
Marginal rate of transformation	Saving
Diminishing marginal rate of transformation	

PROBLEMS

1 (*a*) Why is it inefficient to end up producing inside the production possibility frontier? (*b*) Draw the PPF if there are constant returns to the employment of labor in only one of the economy's industries, and draw the PPF if there are constant returns in both of the industries. (For the first situation, assume that there are diminishing returns in the other industry. You should start from a diagram like Figure 20-2).

2 Define the marginal rate of transformation, and then explain what it has to do with the idea of opportunity cost.

3 Explain why profit-maximizing firms will end up on the PPF, with the marginal rate of transformation equal to the price ratio.

4 Suppose that the wage is stuck at a level that is above the equilibrium level. How would this affect the PPF?

5 What problems might face a central planner who, having absorbed the conditions for the optimal allocation of resources, decides to implement them. Think particularly of the amount of knowledge the planner might need.

6 Most of the analyses that were conducted earlier in the book can also be carried out in a general equilibrium framework. (*a*) Why do we not usually carry them out in a general equilibrium framework? (*b*) Using the PPF and indifference curve diagrams, show the effects of an improvement in the efficiency of making food on relative prices and on the outputs of food and entertainment. (*c*) Do your results differ in any way from those you would have obtained using partial equilibrium analysis of the type carried out in earlier chapters?

7 At the end of the chapter, we analyzed the effects of the imposition of a tax on entertainment. Repeat this analysis using a diagram like Figure 20-6.

8 Why is it that only the *relative* price of goods matters for determining the MRS and MRT?

9 Examine Box 20-1. Take the set of equalities at the end of the box. Explain where each of them comes from and why they establish that resources are allocated optimally through the price system.

10 Suppose that a union succeeds in raising the wage in the entertainment industry 20 percent above the wage in food production. (*a*) What effect does this have on the equality of the values of marginal products of labor in the two sectors? (*b*) Will the economy stay on the PPF? (*c*) What happens to the allocation of resources in the economy as a whole? (*d*) Do workers in the food industry benefit from the higher wages of their fellow workers?

11 (*a*) In what sense do productivity and thrift determine the interest rate? (*b*) Are we referring here to the real interest rate or the nominal rate? (The real interest rate is measured in terms of goods obtained tomorrow by giving up goods today; the nominal interest rate is measured in terms of money obtained tomorrow by giving up money today.)

12 In Figure 20-11, we show the determination of the interest rate through the *ID* and *SA* functions. Now suppose that the savings function is negatively sloped, though not very much so. (*a*) Why might the *SA* curve be negatively sloped? (*b*) Assuming that the *SA* curve is unaffected by any improvement in productivity, analyze the effects of an increase in the productivity of investment on the equilibrium interest rate and the rate of investment when the *SA* curve has a negative slope.

13 Show, using either Figure 20-10 or Figure 20-11 or both, the effects on the interest rate of an increase in the desire to save.

3

Macroeconomics

To The Congress of the United States:

One year ago, in my first address to the country, I went before the American people to report on the condition of our economy. It was not a happy occasion.

Inflation, interest, and *unemployment* rates were at painfully high levels, while real *growth,* job creation, new investment, personal savings, and productivity gains had virtually ceased. Our economy was staggering under the burden of excessive tax rates, double-digit inflation, runaway Government spending, counterproductive regulations, and uneven money supply growth.

The economy, I declared, was in the "worst mess" in half a century. . . .

Our goal was, and remains, economic recovery—the return of noninflationary and sustained prosperity. We seek a larger economic pie to provide all Americans more jobs, more after-tax income, and a better life. Quick fixes won't get us there.[1]

Ronald Reagan
February 8, 1982

21

An Introduction to Macroeconomics

Macroeconomics is the study of the operation of the economy as a whole.

In macroeconomics we focus on the *total* production of goods and services in the economy, or gross national product (GNP). Similarly, we analyze the factors that determine the *average* price of goods and services, not asking why one good costs more than another but rather asking why prices are, on average, higher or lower this year than last year. As in microeconomics, we use demand and supply curves to determine output and price. The difference is that in macroeconomics the demand curve shows the *total* demand for goods and services, and the supply curve shows the *total* amount of goods and services firms want to produce.

President Reagan's 1982 budget message sets out the major issues and problems studied in macroeconomics, particularly inflation, unemployment, and growth, and the government's ability to affect them. As his remarks suggest, the macroeconomic news of the late seventies and early eighties was mostly bad. To understand why macroeconomic performance was bad during this period, we shall in the next few chapters develop an analysis of the behavior of consumers, producers, and the government that explains how the level of GNP and the aggregate price level are determined.

---

[1] From the budget message of the President. In *The United States Budget in Brief, Fiscal Year 1983,* p. 3. Emphasis added.

Before developing the analysis in later chapters, we introduce macroeconomics here both by discussing the three major macroeconomic issues and by presenting an overview of the approach to be used in later chapters.

We have *inflation* when prices in general are rising. As we noted in Chapter 2, inflation is commonly measured by the rate of increase of the consumer price index (CPI), which is an index of the cost of the basket of goods bought by a typical consumer. The inflation rate kept rising from the fifties through the early eighties, as Table 21-1 shows. People strongly dislike inflation, which is therefore a major economic and political issue. We shall have to see not only what causes inflation but also why it presents a problem for people.

The *unemployment rate* measures the percentage of those in the labor force who are out of a job and are looking for work.

Jobs are difficult to find when the unemployment rate is high. It is therefore no mystery that high rates of unemployment are a problem for people. Those who do not have jobs worry that they will have trouble finding work. And many who have jobs worry that they will lose them.

Unemployment rates over the last 30 years are also shown in Table 21-1. The unemployment rate was higher in the seventies than in the fifties or sixties, rose higher yet in 1980–1981, and in 1982 reached 10 percent, a post-World War II peak. An unemployment rate that high means that nearly 1 in 10 people who want to work cannot find a job. When this happens, the economy is wasting scarce resources. If the unemployed people were working, they would be producing goods and services. We shall have to ask why the economy sometimes suffers from high unemployment and the consequent waste of resources and whether anything can be done about it.

TABLE 21-1

INFLATION AND UNEMPLOYMENT, 1952–1981

YEARS	INFLATION RATE, % per year	UNEMPLOYMENT RATE, % of labor force
1952–1961	1.4	4.9
1962–1971	3.1	4.6
1972–1981	8.4	6.6
1980–1981	11.9	7.4

Source: Economic Report of the President, 1982, pp. 271, 291.

The third major macroeconomic issue is *growth.* The economy is growing when its total production of goods and services is increasing. That means, in President Reagan's words, that we have a larger economic pie to share. Growth not only makes more goods available, it also generates more jobs and higher living standards. We define growth more precisely later in this chapter and review the recent historical record.

Inflation, unemployment, and growth are the major topics in macroeconomics. In what sense are these specifically macroeconomic issues? They relate to the economy as a whole. Inflation is the rate at which prices are rising *on average.* Unemployment is the percentage of the *total* labor force that cannot find a job. Growth is the rate at which the economy's *total* production of goods and services is increasing.

Macroeconomics and Policy

High inflation, high unemployment, and slow growth all make life more difficult for most people. The question then arises whether there is anything that can be done about them. When inflation is high, can the government do anything to reduce it? When unemployment is high, is there anything the government can do to make it easier to find jobs? Is there anything that can be done to make the economy grow faster so that we will have more goods to consume in the future?

It seems clear that the government, by its actions, has the potential to affect major macroeconomic variables such as unemployment and inflation. For instance, if the government increases its demand for goods, it adds to the total demand for goods and services and probably increases output and employment. But at the same time it probably increases the price level. Or if the government increases taxes, leaving people with less to spend, that probably reduces demand, output, and the price level.

Economic policy consists of government actions to affect the economy. The variables the government adjusts in carrying out economic policy, such as tax rates and government spending, are called policy variables, or policy instruments.

Partly because it is closely related to policy—to questions of what the government can do—macroeconomics is an area where there are disagreements among economists. Frequently, the disagreements result from differences in value judgments. As always, we should be on guard for these in reading any economist's advice about macroeconomic policy. But sometimes there are disagreements on positive economics, for instance, on what happens to total production and inflation when the government cuts taxes. Here we have to make up our minds on the basis of theory and data.

In presenting macroeconomic theory and evidence, we do not go out of our way to focus on controversies. Where there are differences of opinion on issues that matter, we mention and explain them. But most of the macroeconomics section develops the widely agreed-on solid core of the subject.

1 PRODUCTION, INCOME, AND SPENDING

The economy is made up of many independent units: millions of households and mil-lions of firms (and federal, state, and local governments, which we leave out of the picture for a while). Households decide how much to buy and how much to work. Correspondingly, firms decide how much to produce and sell and how many people to hire. Together, these decisions by all households add up to the economy's total spending, and the decisions by all firms add up to the economy's total level of production. We now develop this interdependence between individual decisions and the total, or economywide, levels of spending and production.

Table 21-2 classifies the different transactions between firms and households in the economy. Households own the firms, which in turn own machines, buildings and equipment, and raw materials and other goods used for production.

Goods and services useful in production are called *factors of production.* They include, in particular, labor, machines, office and factory buildings, and land.

Ultimately, all factors of production are owned by households, either indirectly through firms or directly as in the case of labor.

Table 21-2 provides a simplified picture of the transactions in the economy. Here are some of the simplifications. First, we have omitted the government, which is neither a household nor a firm but does play a role in

TABLE 21-2

TRANSACTIONS BY HOUSEHOLDS AND FIRMS

HOUSEHOLDS	FIRMS
Own factors of production, including labor, which they supply to firms	Use factors of production supplied by households to produce goods and services
Receive incomes from firms in exchange for supplying factors of production	Pay households for use of factors of production
Spend on goods and services produced by firms	Sell goods and services to households

the economy. Second, we show firms selling goods to households (in the third row) but omit sales by firms to other firms. For instance, IBM sells computers to other firms, not only to households. Third, we have not specified whether we are talking about the U.S. economy or the economy of the entire world. All these points matter, but fortunately they are easily accounted for once we have the simple ideas straight.

In Table 21-2 the top two entries describe the fact that households ultimately own all factors of production and that firms use those factors to produce goods and services. The middle entries show that in exchange for providing factors of production for use by the firms, the households receive incomes, primarily as wages and profits paid out by the firms. The households in turn use their incomes to buy the goods produced by the firms, which therefore can pay for the factors of production they use.

Figure 21-1 shows the interactions of Table 21-2 between households and firms. First we draw attention to the flow of the services of factors of production from households to firms in exchange for incomes. By the services of the factors of production we mean the use that the firms make of labor, machinery, and other factors of production. The outer loop of the figure shows the flow of productive services matched by the flow of incomes. At the same time, in the inner loop, there is a flow of goods and services produced and sold by firms to the households and matched by the spending of households on these goods and services. Figure 21-1 is called a *circular flow* diagram because in each loop there is a circular flow, starting at any point and coming back to that point.

The top and bottom halves of Figure 21-1 show two different types of transactions. The top half shows how the economy *produces* goods and services. There is a flow of services of factors of production to

FIGURE 21-1 INTERACTIONS BETWEEN FIRMS AND HOUSEHOLDS. In the outer loop, we see the flow of services of factors of production from households to firms, matched by incomes paid by the firms to households. Moving in the opposite direction in the inner loop is a flow of goods and services from firms to households, paid for by households' spending from their incomes. The nature of the flows in the top and bottom halves of the figure differs. In the top we have flows of goods and of factors of production. In the bottom we have flows of *payments* to and from firms and households.

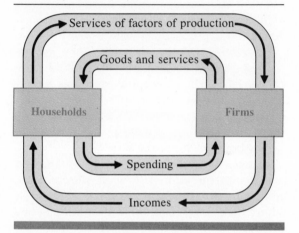

firms, from which the firms make the goods and services shown flowing in the opposite direction. The bottom half shows how the economy pays for the transactions. Firms pay incomes to households, and households in turn pay firms for the goods they buy.

Figure 21-1 is a model, or simplified picture, of the transactions in the economy. It is a useful framework for starting the analysis of unemployment, inflation, and growth.

Unemployment

To consider unemployment we look at the upper part of the figure, where firms hire productive services from households. Unemployment exists when people who are willing to work cannot find jobs. How can this happen? If firms cannot sell all the goods they are producing and find their shelves filled with unsold merchandise, they cut back on production and hire fewer workers. People lose their jobs and become unemployed.

What happens next? The economy has to find some way to put people back to work. There is a problem here because the people who have lost their jobs will have less income to spend, as we see from Figure 21-1. Thus firms will be able to sell even less, and that seems to make the unemployment problem worse.

Here we face a basic question of macroeconomics. If people become unemployed because firms cannot sell all the goods they are producing, what gets the economy back on track? How do we avoid a *continuing* fall in production and employment? We shall see that there are mechanisms that get the economy back on track, including changes in wages and prices, and government policies, but that these mechanisms may work quite slowly.

Unemployment is, of course, a problem for the people who cannot get jobs. But it is also a problem for society, because it means society is wasting its scarce labor. Figure 21-2 shows the production possibility frontier that was introduced in Chapter 1. When there is unemployment, society is not on the production possibility frontier but rather is operating at an inefficient point, such as G, inside the frontier. One of the basic questions in macroeconomics is why society sometimes has very high unemployment and thus wastes resources.

Although the term "unemployment" is usually reserved for labor, other factors of production such as machinery and factories are sometimes not used even though they are available for production. They too can be described as unemployed. The basic macroeconomic question of why society sometimes has high unemployment of labor extends also to the question of why society sometimes (usually at the same times that labor is unemployed) wastes resources

FIGURE 21-2 UNEMPLOYMENT AND THE PRODUCTION POSSIBILITY FRONTIER. The frontier shows combinations of output at which the economy is fully employing its labor. When there is unemployment, the economy is producing at some point such as G and wasting resources. One of the basic questions in macroeconomics is why the unemployed are not put very quickly back to work producing goods and services that people would like to consume.

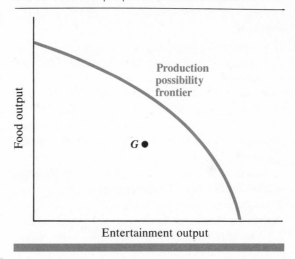

by not using its machinery and factories to produce goods and services.

Inflation

Suppose that the firms in the economy are producing a given amount of goods and that everyone is working. The economy is producing on the production possibility frontier. Now consumers decide that they would like to spend more than they used to. They demand more goods from the firms. Firms cannot produce more goods because all resources in the economy are fully employed.

Something has to give. To start with, firms may put "sold-out" signs in the windows or put customers on waiting lists. But they will also raise prices, trying to reconcile the scarcity of goods with the households' increased demand for goods. Inflation here results as firms raise prices in response to households' demands for more goods than can be produced.

But there are also times when inflation takes place even though the economy is not at full employment, or not producing on the production possibility frontier. One of the big issues in macroeconomics is to explain inflation that occurs when there is unemployment.

Growth

Economic growth is an increase in the economy's production of goods and services.

We can describe economic growth by using the production possibility frontier (PPF) in Figures 21-2 and 21-3. Economic growth occurs under two circumstances. First, growth (an increase in the production of goods and services) takes place when unemployed resources are put back to work. Thus if we moved from point G in Figure 21-2 to a point on the PPF, there would be growth.

Second, economic growth also takes

FIGURE 21-3   GROWTH OCCURS WHEN THE PRO- DUCTION POSSIBILITY FRONTIER SHIFTS OUT- WARD. Growth occurs when the PPF shifts out from *AE* to *A'E'*. Originally the economy was producing at point *C* on the PPF, the *AE* curve. As a result of the shift of the PPF to *A'E'*, production now takes place at *C'*. The output of both food and entertainment is higher at *C'* than at *C*.

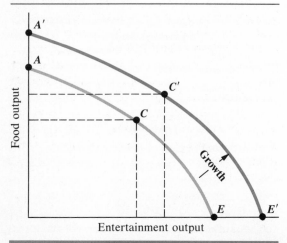

place as a result of the PPF shifting out- ward. This is shown in Figure 21-3. If the economy was initially at point C on AE, eco- nomic growth takes the economy to point C' on the new PPF, A'E'. The output of both food and fun has risen, and the economy is producing more goods and services.

There are two reasons why the PPF may shift. First, the quantity of factors of produc- tion (machines and labor) may increase. Second, existing factors of production may become more productive because of inven- tions that improve machines or because of better training of labor. In Figure 21-1 eco- nomic growth would show up in an in- creased flow of goods and services from firms to households in the upper loop and an increased flow of income to households in the lower loop. Corresponding to the larger flows of income and goods and ser- vices is more spending by households.

The central growth question is, What can be done to promote growth, to improve the standard of living by making more goods and services available for people?

Macroeconomics and Interactions

The basic framework of Figure 21-1 applies throughout macroeconomics. Decisions by households and decisions by firms between them (with the addition of decisions by gov- ernment, which will be discussed later) de- termine the economy's level of employment and rate of unemployment, its price level and rate of inflation, and the amount of goods and services produced and the growth rate of production.

Macroeconomic problems occur when these decisions do not work out in a way that ensures full employment without infla- tion. Sometimes prices rise rapidly, some- times there is high unemployment, and sometimes there is slow growth. Macroec- onomics has the task of explaining why these problems occur. At the center of the explanation are the independent decisions of firms and households, affecting one another through the interactions described in Figure 21-1.

The essential difference between macroeconomics and microeconomics consists in the *interactions* described in Figure 21-1. The fact that firm and household decisions are made independently is *not* unique to macroeconomics. Going back to the supply-demand analysis of the fish market in Chapter 3, we see that the decisions about how much to supply and how much to demand are made independently by suppliers and demanders. But macroeconomics is different in that firms' decisions about how much to produce determine the incomes of households and therefore their spending. Those interactions, or *feedbacks*, which are unimportant in microeconomics, are the essence of macroeconomics; they are illustrated by the circular flow diagram in Figure 21-1.

We follow up this overview of macroeconomics problems with a look at the facts. The following sections present definitions and a discussion of recent experience with inflation, growth, and unemployment.

2 THE PRICE LEVEL AND THE RATE OF INFLATION

In Chapter 2 we introduced price indices as measures of the cost of buying a specified basket of commodities. In particular, the CPI represents the price of a basket of 224 goods and services, each of which receives a weight that was determined by studying the spending behavior of more than 20,000 families. Weights for broad categories of goods were given in Table 2-7. Table 21-3 shows the CPI, with base 1967 = 100, for selected years.

In 1981, for example, the value of the CPI was 272.4. With the base year 1967 = 100, this means the cost of buying the basket of goods and services in the CPI

TABLE 21-3

THE CONSUMER PRICE INDEX AND THE INFLATION RATE

YEAR	CPI, 1967 = 100	CPI INFLATION, % per year
1979	217.4	11.3
1980	246.8	13.5
1981	272.4	10.4
1982*	290.1	6.5

* Estimate.
Source: Economic Report of the President, 1982, Table B-53.

was 2.724 times as high in 1981 as in 1967. Prices had, on average, nearly tripled. Similar comparisons can be made with earlier years. For instance, looking back to 1929, which is not shown in the table, we find the CPI equal to 51.3.[2] With the CPI at 100 in 1967 and 51.3 in 1929, the costs of goods bought by the typical consumer about doubled from 1929 to 1967. Thus we see that prices of goods in general have risen threefold since 1967 and sixfold since 1929.

In Chapter 2 we also discussed the inflation rate.

> The *inflation rate* is the percentage rate per period that prices are increasing.

Normally we talk about annual inflation, but we can also look at inflation rates between months, quarters, or decades. Table 21-3 reports the annual inflation rates of the prices of the goods represented by the CPI.

We briefly recall how the inflation rate is calculated. Suppose we want to figure out the inflation rate, or the growth rate of prices, between 1979 and 1980. This inflation rate is reported in the table as the entry for 1980. Inflation for 1980 is the percentage change in prices, or the growth rate of prices, from 1979 to 1980. It is calculated as in equation (1):

---

[2] The 1929 index does not measure the cost of exactly the same basket of goods as the current index, but the costs of goods bought by consumers can still be approximately compared from CPI values at different dates.

FIGURE 21-4 THE PRICE LEVEL AND THE INFLATION RATE IN THE UNITED STATES, 1861–1981. 1967 = 100. (*Sources: Historical Statistics of the United States* Series E135, and *Economic Report of the President, 1982*, p. 291.)

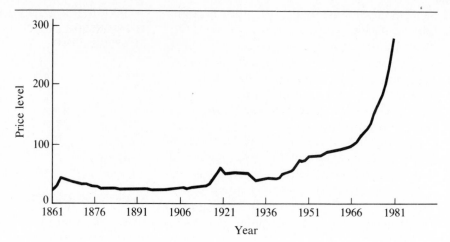

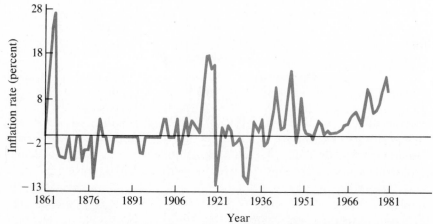

Inflation in 1980 $= \dfrac{\text{CPI in 1980} - \text{CPI in 1979}}{\text{CPI in 1979}} \times 100\%$

$= \dfrac{246.8 - 217.4}{217.4} \times 100\%$

$= .1352 \times 100\%$

$= 13.52\%$ (1)

Similarly, we can calculate the 1981 inflation rate, as we have already done in Chapter 2, as the percentage increase in price between 1980 and 1981, which is equal to 10.4 percent.

Table 21-3 shows that there has been inflation in the period since 1979, with prices rising every year. But inflation goes back

farther than that. Figure 21-4 shows both the price level and the inflation rate in the U.S. economy since 1861. Note first that there has been inflation in every year since 1954; for every year since 1954, prices have risen. The second point to note is that the inflation rate moves around a lot. It was very high in 1974 and 1980, for example. In contrast, in the early 1960s or more recently in 1970 it was low.

The third point to note is that prices can fall as well as rise. The price level was falling from 1865 to 1896 and fell again in 1920–1921 and in 1929–1933. When prices fall, there is negative inflation, or *deflation*.

Prices fell more frequently in the nineteenth and early twentieth centuries than they do now. The last time there was deflation in the United States over a period as long as a year was 1954. In early 1982 there was a period of 3 months during which prices fell. Thus deflation can happen, although it has become rare.

International Comparisons Price indices are calculated in most countries, and we can therefore compare inflation in different countries. Table 21-4 reports a comparison of average inflation rates during the 1970–1979 period in a number of countries.

The table shows large differences in inflation rates among countries. In Argentina, for example, prices on average more than doubled every year. Chile had even higher inflation than Argentina, while in the United States or West Germany, in comparison, inflation seems very low. Indeed, it might even look as if we chose the countries in the table to make the United States look good by comparison. However, the impression given by the table that U.S. inflation has been low by international standards in the period since 1970 is correct, even though our inflation in that period was high by the standards of U.S. history.

The international differences in inflation rates shown in Table 21-4 call for some explanation, to be developed as we go further into macroeconomics.

3　OUTPUT AND GROWTH

In Chapter 1 we defined gross national product (GNP) as the value of all the goods and services produced in the economy within a given period. The value of output in a given period measured in the prices of that period is *nominal* GNP. Nominal GNP in 1981 was $2.9 trillion, which means the value of total output in the economy was $2.9 trillion.

TABLE 21-4

AVERAGE INFLATION RATES, 1970–1979
(Percent per Year)

COUNTRY	INFLATION RATE, average per year
Argentina	128.2
Brazil	32.4
Canada	9.1
Chile	242.6
India	7.8
Israel	34.3
Italy	15.6
Japan	8.2
Mexico	18.3
Nigeria	19.0
Switzerland	5.4
United Kingdom	13.9
United States	6.9
West Germany	5.3

Source: World Bank, *World Development Report,* 1981.

Nominal GNP can change either because prices change or because the physical quantities of goods produced change. For example, if all prices rise 10 percent while the levels of production of goods and services remain constant, nominal GNP rises 10 percent. But if prices remain constant and the physical output of each good and service goes up 10 percent, nominal GNP also goes up 10 percent.

To have a measure of the level of production in the economy that is free of the effects of changing prices, we define real GNP, or GNP in constant prices.

Real GNP is the value of all production, calculated using prices of a given base year.

The base year is now 1972. GNP in constant prices, or real GNP, is regularly calculated and reported by the government, along with nominal GNP. We use real GNP as the basic measure of the economy's output of goods and services. When real GNP goes up, we know that total production has risen and that more goods and services are being produced. This contrasts with nominal GNP, which may go up merely because there has been inflation.

TABLE 21-5

REAL GNP AND GROWTH

YEAR	REAL GNP, billion 1972 $	REAL GROWTH, % per year
1979	1479	2.8
1980	1474	−0.3
1981	1503	2.0
1982*	1480	−1.5

* Estimated.

Source: Economic Indicators, October 1982, p. 2.

Table 21-5 presents real GNP data for recent years. The left-hand column shows that real GNP declined slightly from 1979 to 1980. In 1980 the total production of goods and services was less than it had been in 1979.

A fall in real GNP, or output, is referred to as a *recession.*

From 1980 to 1981 real GNP, or output, increased, but from 1981 to 1982 there was again a decline. Figure 21-5 shows in the upper panel the time series for real GNP over the period from 1961 to 1981. Over the extended period output has been rising most of the time. The trend of rising real GNP has some dips, though, which correspond to the recessions of 1970, 1973–1975, and 1980.

The third column of Table 21-5 shows the growth rate of real GNP. The growth rate was defined in Chapter 2 as the percentage rate per period that a variable is increasing. The growth rate of real GNP is calculated in Table 21-5 in the same way the inflation rate was calculated in Table 21-4. For example, the real growth rate of 2.0 percent for 1981 is calculated as

$$\begin{aligned}\text{Real growth} \atop \text{rate in 1981} &= \frac{\text{real GNP} \atop \text{in 1981} - \text{real GNP} \atop \text{in 1980}}{\text{real GNP in 1980}} \times 100\% \\ &= \frac{29}{1474} \times 100\% \\ &= 2.0\% \end{aligned} \qquad (2)$$

Real growth rates for the other years shown in the table are calculated the same way. The lower half of Figure 21-5 shows the real growth rate of GNP over the period since 1961. Note that real growth is positive most years but that there are several years when output declines, or real growth is negative. These are years of recession. Note also the relation between the upper and lower halves of the figure. When output in the upper panel is falling, the growth rate of GNP in the lower panel is negative.

We defined a recession as a period of falling output. This is a time when business is bad, firms find it difficult to sell goods, and people have trouble finding jobs. When business is good, we say there is a *boom.* There is no simple definition of a boom except for the general notion that it refers to a period of sustained or prolonged high real GNP, relative to trend, and low unemployment. By this definition, the period from 1965 to 1968 was certainly a boom period, since there was a long period of both high real GNP and low unemployment.

Real GNP growth, which measures increases in the production of goods and services, is by and large a good indicator of improvements in the standard of living in an economy. One adjustment must be made,

TABLE 21-6

AVERAGE PER CAPITA REAL GNP GROWTH, 1960–1979 (Percent per Year)

Chad	−1.4
Indonesia	4.1
Philippines	2.6
Egypt	3.4
Korea	3.5
Singapore	7.4
United States	2.4
Japan	9.4
United Kingdom	2.2

Source: World Bank, *World Development Report,* 1981, Table 1.

FIGURE 21-5 THE LEVEL AND GROWTH RATE OF REAL GNP, 1961–1981. (*Source: Economic Report of the President, 1982,* pp. 234–235.)

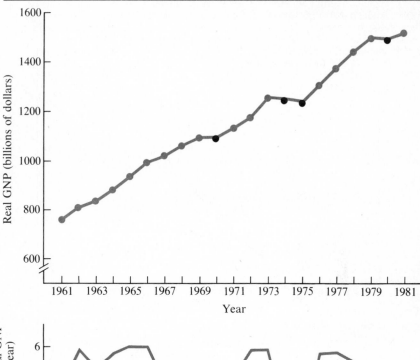

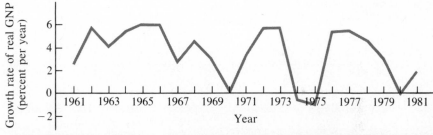

though. Since real GNP measures total output—the pie in President Reagan's remarks quoted earlier—we have to adjust for the number of people who share the pie. This is done by dividing real GNP by the population to obtain real GNP per person, or real GNP per capita.

> *Real GNP per capita* is equal to real output per person in the population.

Growing per capita real GNP means that output is growing faster than population. Rising real GNP makes it possible to improve the standard of living.

Table 21-6 shows average growth rates of per capita real GNP for a number of coun-

tries in the 1960–1979 period. Most countries show *some* growth over this 20-year period. This is the case for all the countries reported in the table except Chad, where real output has been declining. There are large differences in growth rates. There are supergrowth countries such as Japan and Singapore, and there are countries like the United States, where growth has been steady but small. Economists have explored such growth to try to understand what makes Japan grow so much faster than, for example, the United Kingdom. We will study that question in Chapter 33.

For the moment, though, we make an

FIGURE 21-6   REAL OUTPUT PER CAPITA IN JAPAN AND THE UNITED KING-
DOM. Japan is a fast-growing country compared with the United Kingdom. Al-
though Japan started with a lower level of per capita output, its rapid growth en-
abled it to catch up and overtake the slower-growing country. (*Source:* Irving B.
Kravis, Alan Heston, and Robert Summers, *World Product and Income,* Johns
Hopkins University Press, Baltimore, 1982, pp. 329, 333–335.)

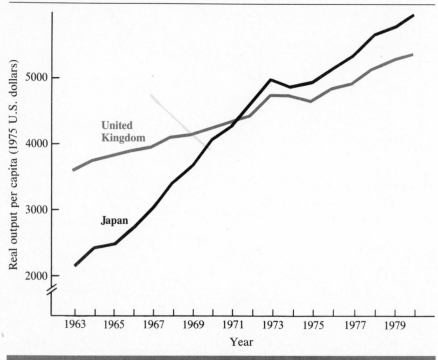

important point about growth. If year after
year a country has a higher growth rate than
another country, even though the difference
may be small, ultimately the high-growth
country gets ahead and has a higher *level* of
per capita real GNP.

Figure 21-6 shows per capita real output
for Japan and for the United Kingdom. The
data are reported in 1975 U.S. dollars. For
example, in 1980 the value of output per
capita in Japan was about $5950, whereas in
the United Kingdom it was below $5400. It
is interesting to note that the United Kingdom started off in the 1960s as the country
with higher output per capita. In 1963, U.K.
output per capita was $3605 compared with
$2060 for Japan. But Japan grew faster on
average and therefore caught up and ulti-

mately outpaced the United Kingdom. By
today, of course, Japan is ahead. Being
ahead in output per capita means that Japan
has a higher standard of living, as measured
by production of goods and services, than is
enjoyed in the United Kingdom.

4   UNEMPLOYMENT

In 1982 the unemployment rate reached 10
percent in the U.S. economy. For young
people between the ages of 16 and 19 years
it went well above 20 percent. What do
these numbers mean?

The *unemployment rate,* unless otherwise qualified, is the fraction of the civilian labor force 16 years and older that
is recorded as unable to find a job.

Unemployment rates are calculated for the entire labor force but also for particular subgroups such as teenagers, men 20 years and over, women, or heads of households. The unemployment rate is one of the chief indicators of how well the economy is doing. When unemployment is high and rising, the economy is performing poorly; human resources, instead of being used productively, are going to waste, and people who want to work and earn a living cannot do so.

Unemployment rates are calculated from estimates of the civilian labor force and from weekly surveys that determine whether people are working. The labor force consists of people who are either working or unemployed. The criterion for being counted as unemployed is that a person was available for work in the current week, did not actually work, and had made an effort in the preceding 4 weeks to find a job. Also included are people who are not working but are waiting to be called back to their jobs or are waiting to report to a new job the next month.

Table 21-7 shows the unemployment rates for different groups in 1980 and 1981. Note the large differences. Unemployment tends to be much higher among nonwhite people and young people. Note the fact that from 1980 to 1982 unemployment rates increased in every group. We shall soon link this to low growth and recession in the economy in that period.

TABLE 21-8

**YOUTH UNEMPLOYMENT RATES
IN SEVERAL COUNTRIES**
(Youth Aged 15–24, Percent Unemployed)

COUNTRY	1979	1981
United States	11.2	14
Japan	3.5	4.3
Germany	3.7	7
United Kingdom	11.3	19.6
Italy	25.6	27
Canada	13	12.8

Source: OECD, Economic Outlook, December 1981, Table 7.

Unemployment is an international, not only an American, problem. There are some data that allow international comparisons. One such comparison appears in Table 21-8, which contains data on youths between the ages of 15 and 24 in a number of industrialized countries. It is striking to see that in several countries, 1 or even 2 out of every 10 young people were out of work. At the same time the table suggests we should try to discover why Japan has so much less youth unemployment than other countries.

5 ARE THERE SIMPLE RELATIONSHIPS?

Are there any simple relationships among growth, inflation, and unemployment? We should expect the following. When households reduce their spending, firms have

TABLE 21-7

U.S. UNEMPLOYMENT RATES BY GROUP
(Percent Unemployed)

	NONWHITE	16–19 YEARS, BOTH SEXES	MEN 20 YEARS AND OVER	WOMEN 20 YEARS AND OVER	OVERALL UNEMPLOYMENT RATE
1980	13.1	17.8	5.9	6.4	7.1
1981	14.2	19.6	6.3	6.8	7.6
1982*	16.9	23.0	8.2	8.3	9.4

* April 1982.
Source: Economic Indicators, August 1982, p. 12.

FIGURE 21-7 RECESSIONS AND INFLATION, 1961–1981. The diagram shows the rate of CPI inflation in the United States. The shaded areas correspond to periods of recession. The evidence is that recessions slow inflation but do not stop it for good. (*Source:* See Figure 21-4.)

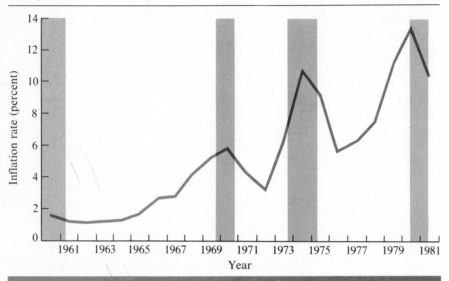

trouble selling goods. They therefore produce less, and growth slows. At the same time, unemployment rises as firms need less labor and because firms are having trouble selling. Their prices rise less rapidly or even fall. In brief, the argument is that recession, low growth, high unemployment, and slower inflation go together. In contrast, when households want to increase their purchases, firms try to produce more goods and hire more labor. Growth increases, and unemployment falls. At the same time, because the demand for their goods has risen, firms raise prices more. Thus we expect a boom, high growth, low unemployment, and more rapid inflation to go together.

Some of these relationships can be seen in the data. Figure 21-7 shows the rate of inflation again, except this time we have shaded in periods of recession, or falling output. We observe that when the economy is in a recession and shortly thereafter, inflation falls. Thus both in 1975 and again in 1980 recessions slowed inflation. But it is

also clear that inflation quickly returns and even rises above its previous peaks. This is a worrisome pattern of *accelerating inflation.* It raises the question whether we can stop inflation from continually rising unless we have recessions.

But to worry about that issue already supposes that there is something wrong with inflation. It is a fact that people complain and worry about inflation, but economists are not totally sure of the reasons for this. Here we note two points. First, inflation brings with it uncertainty about prices. If people do not know whether prices will rise by 5 percent or 10 percent, they do not know how much they will be able to buy with their wages and how many goods they can buy with their money. Second, it is quite likely that people feel cheated by inflation. When wages are increased, they can buy more goods. But if prices immediately start rising, they feel that something has been taken away from them. That feeling is likely to exist even if they can persuade themselves in some detached way that wages and prices are all rising because of inflation.

Some economists believe that there are no very good reasons for people to worry much about inflation and that therefore society should not do so either. Others argue that there are reasons, including increased uncertainty, why people get upset about inflation. We shall review the arguments later. But it is clear that whether or not there are good reasons, people regard inflation as a serious problem.

A second strong relationship exists between unemployment and growth. When the economy grows rapidly, unemployment rates fall. When the economy grows very slowly or even moves into recession, unemployment rates increase. This means that several years of successive high growth bring unemployment rates to very low levels as more and more people find jobs while production is increasing. In contrast, when real GNP is not growing much or is even falling, firms increase their employment of labor slowly, and unemployment rates increase. The high unemployment rates in 1982 are a reflection of the very low growth rates of real GNP shown in Table 21-5.

But the point goes further. Starting from an unemployment rate near 10 percent in 1982 means that it will take a number of years of high growth to get unemployment back down to lower levels, around 5 to 6 percent. It means that youngsters leaving school or college in the 1983–1984 period will have a much harder time getting jobs than those who graduated in the late 1960s, after a long period of expansion.

6 GROWTH, UNEMPLOYMENT, AND INFLATION IN PERSPECTIVE

The 1970s was a period of poor macroeconomic performance throughout the world. In virtually all countries there was a decline in real GNP growth, a rise in unemployment rates, and an increase in inflation. Table 21-9 presents data for a number of industrialized countries. For each of the four countries, the period from the 1960s through 1973 was a time of rapid growth, low unemployment, and reasonably low inflation. The period since 1973 has seen slower growth, more inflation, and more unemployment.

In the early 1980s many governments, especially that of the United States, have mounted a war against inflation. At the same time, they have proclaimed as their long-term aim the restoration of higher growth. These policies are a reaction to the poor

TABLE 21-9

INFLATION, UNEMPLOYMENT, AND GROWTH, 1960–1981
(Average Annual Percentage Rate)

	UNITED STATES	UNITED KINGDOM	GERMANY	JAPAN
Inflation:				
1960–1973	3.2	5.1	3.3	6.1
1973–1981	9.4	15.4	4.9	9.0
Unemployment:				
1960–1973	5.0	2.9	0.8	1.3
1974–1981	6.9	6.3	3.2	1.2
Growth rate of real GNP:				
1960–1973	4.2	3.2	4.8	10.5
1973–1981	2.4	0.5	2.0	4.0

Source: Economic Report of the President, 1982, pp. 355–357.

macroeconomic performance of the 1970s. The material we cover in macroeconomics aims to make it possible to understand the reasons for, and the uncertainties about, the economic policies governments are following in the eighties.

SUMMARY

1   Macroeconomics is the study of the operation of the economy as a whole. The major macroeconomic issues are inflation, unemployment, and growth and whether there is anything the government can do about them.

2   Macroeconomics is distinguished from microeconomics mainly by the interactions between the decisions made by firms and households, as summarized in Figure 21-1. Households supply the services of factors of production to firms, which use them to produce goods and services. In return for the services of the factors of production, firms pay incomes to households, which are used by the households to purchase the goods and services produced by the firms.

3   A reduction in purchases of goods by households causes firms to reduce employment of labor, reducing households' income and thereby reducing spending on goods and services even more. A question to be studied is what mechanisms exist to prevent small changes from developing into major problems.

4   Growth is an increase in the production of goods and services. Growth may occur either when unemployed resources are put back to work so that the economy moves from inside the PPF to the frontier or when the PPF itself shifts out. The PPF may shift either because there are more factors of production or because existing factors have become more productive.

5   The inflation rate is the rate at which prices of goods in general are rising. In the United States in the last 20 years prices have risen every year. The inflation rate started out around 1 percent in 1961 and has been above 13 percent since then. By international standards, U.S. inflation has been low. Prices may also fall sometimes, in which case there is deflation.

6   A country that has faster growth than another country will eventually have a larger real GNP, however far behind it started out.

7   Unemployment in the U.S. economy has risen on average in the seventies. In 1982 it stood at the highest level in the post-World War II period. Unemployment rates differ sharply among different groups. Youths and blacks have particularly high unemployment rates. Youth unemployment is high throughout the industrialized world except in Japan.

8   When the economy is in a boom, output is high, unemployment is low, and inflation tends to be rising. When the economy is in a recession, output is low, unemployment is high, and inflation tends to be falling.

9   High growth rates reduce unemployment. It would take several years of above-average growth to get unemployment down from nearly 10 percent to more normal levels, around 5 to 6 percent.

KEY TERMS

Inflation	Output
Unemployment	Nominal GNP
Growth of economy	Real GNP
Interactions between households and firms	Recession
Circular flow diagram	Boom
Deflation	Real GNP per capita

PROBLEMS

1   Draw a circular flow diagram and use it to explain why a fall in spending by households may increase unemployment.

2   (a) The consumer price index for 1973 was 133.1, and for 1974 it was 147.7. What was the inflation rate between those two years? (b) The CPI for 1931 was 45.5, and for 1932 it was 40.9. What was the inflation rate, positive or negative, between those years? (c) What name is given to negative inflation?

3   (a) Real GNP in 1980 was $1474.0 billion. Real GNP in 1979 was $1479.4 billion. What was the growth rate, positive or negative, between those two years? (b) Explain what it means for a growth rate to be negative.

4   Suppose there are only two goods in the consumer price index: food and housing. Food has a weight of 0.33. Housing has a weight of 0.67. The price of food rises 20 percent, and the price of housing rises 10 percent. (a) What is the rate of inflation ac-

cording to the CPI? (b) Suppose there are many goods in the CPI. Explain why the rate of inflation calculated according to the CPI can never be higher than the fastest rate at which the price of any of the goods in the index goes up.

5   (a) If unemployment rates for blacks and for teenagers are well above the average rate of unemployment, what is likely to be true about the rate of unemployment for older white workers compared with the average? (Check Table 21-7 for signs that your answer is right.) (b) Why do you think young people have much higher unemployment rates than older people?

6   Discuss the relationship between growth in real GNP and the rate of unemployment. (a) State in words the relationship, if any, you expect. (b) Suppose the unemployment rate is 10 percent. Suppose over the next 3 years growth was expected to be −3.0 percent, 1 percent, and 1.5 percent. Would you think that with those

growth rates, unemployment 3 years from now would be higher or lower than today?

7   Suppose today's inflation rate is 10 percent. Suppose over the next 3 years growth will be as indicated in Problem 5(*b*) above. What do you think will happen to inflation?

8   Why do you think people worry about inflation, and do you think they are right?

9   Why do economists use the concept of per capita real income and its growth rate? State in your own words why these are useful concepts, but also state in what way you think they may be too narrow or even misleading.

10 If recessions slow inflation and increase the unemployment rate, what do you think might be the relationship between inflation and unemployment?

Gross national product (GNP) is the total value of the economy's output or production in a given period, such as a year. GNP is widely used as the basic measure of the performance of the economy in producing goods and services.

The circular flow diagram (Figure 21-1) showed that the economy's output of goods and services generates the incomes received by owners of factors of production, because payments for purchases of goods and services eventually end up as wages and profits for the people who produce the goods. *National income* is the total income received by the economy's factors of production. One of the tasks of this chapter is to show how national income is related to GNP.

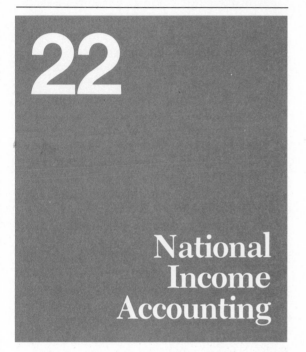

22

National Income Accounting

We study national income accounting in part because it provides us with definitions and measures of GNP and national income. But we also study it because it is necessary for our analysis of the determination of the levels of output, income, and employment in later chapters.

This chapter starts by carefully defining GNP and describing how it is measured. Then we focus on two important sets of relationships. First, there are the links between GNP, or output, and the incomes earned in the economy. Second, there are the links between expenditures on goods and services and the value of output produced. These relationships, too, are shown in Figure 21-1. The accounting relationships between output and income and between expenditures and output are the foundation for our first model of income and output determination, which will be set out in Chapter 23.

The measurement of GNP and the links among GNP, income, and spending take up most of this chapter. We also want to know how accurate our measurements are and for what purposes they are used. The chapter ends with a discussion of the uses made of GNP data, emphasizing the distinction between nominal and real (inflation-corrected) GNP and mentioning some shortcomings of GNP as a measure of the economy's total output.

1 GROSS NATIONAL PRODUCT: CONCEPT AND MEASUREMENT

Gross national product is the market value of the goods and services produced within a given period by domestically owned factors of production.

For instance, in 1981 U.S. GNP was $2938 billion. This is the value of the cars, movies, vacations, buildings, wheat, space shuttle trips, and millions of other products produced in 1981 by factors of production owned by Americans. The definition of GNP contains several features and technical terms that we must clarify.

First, in measuring production we have to avoid *double counting*, or counting the same production twice. For instance, the value of automobiles produced is part of GNP. If we include in GNP the value of automobiles produced, we do not want to include also the value of the tires sold to the carmaker, which is already included in the value of the car.

We avoid double counting by focusing on each firm's value added.

Value added is the increase in the value of goods resulting from production.

Value added is calculated by deducting from the value of the firm's production the cost of the produced goods or raw materials it buys. Table 22-1 illustrates this for the case of an automobile producer. Total sales by that producer were, say, $10 billion. Of that $10 billion, $4 billion represents the value of the steel, tires, plastics, electricity, and other produced goods that were bought by the carmaker for use in automobile production; these are also called *intermediate goods*. Deducting the cost of the intermediate goods, we see that the automobile producer's value added was $6 billion. Next we look at the tire producer, who sold $350 million worth of tires, all to the car producer. The tire producer paid $150 million for rubber, polyester cord, and other produced inputs. Value added by the tire producer was thus $200 million. We could keep going, doing the same calculation for the steel producer and all the other firms and making sure to include only value added by each firm in the value of output, or GNP. That way we would avoid double counting.

With the cost of all intermediate goods deducted, what is left to account for value added? What is left is the value of the labor services used by the firm and the services of its machinery and factories. Value added is the contribution to the value of output made by the labor and capital employed or owned by the firm.

Second, *all* output should be included in GNP. The main problem here is that some output is not sold through markets and is difficult to value. U.S. GNP measures include estimates of some output that is not sold through markets. For example, GNP includes an estimate of the value of the services homeowners receive from living in their houses. The houses produce services for the owners that would generate rent payments if the owners did not live in them. Although there are in fact no rent payments, the GNP accounts estimate the rent that would be paid for owner-occupied housing and add it to GNP. This is called *imputed rent*.

But the principle of including all production is not applied consistently. Volun-

---

TABLE 22-1
VALUE ADDED

AUTOMOBILE PRODUCER		TIRE PRODUCER	
Value of goods produced	$10 billion	Value of production	$350 million
Less: Cost of purchased produced inputs (steel, tires, electricity, etc.)	4 billion	*Less:* Cost of purchased produced inputs (rubber, cord, trucking, etc.)	150 million
Equals: Value added	$ 6 billion	*Equals:* Value added	$200 million

teer services, the value of housework, and do-it-yourself activities are not included because it is difficult to estimate the value of these services, although there are unofficial estimates. Also excluded from GNP is the value of illegal activities, such as illegal gambling, and production that is concealed to avoid taxes. For instance, when a handyman asks to be paid in cash, it is quite likely that the value of the service he performed will never be counted in GNP because he will not report the payment as income. Such activities are part of what is called the *underground economy,* or the part of the economy that escapes the official statistics. Some economists have estimated that the output of the underground economy is as much as one-quarter of official GNP, but most estimates are closer to 3 to 5 percent of GNP.

The third point to note is that it is the value of goods *currently* produced that is part of GNP. Transactions in existing assets, for instance, houses, are not included. The value of an old house when it is sold is not a current productive activity of the economy, and so the value of the house is not included in GNP. We would, though, include the value of any brokerage services associated with the purchase and sale of the house, since the broker adds to the current output of the economy by bringing buyer and seller together. By comparison, when a new house is *built,* the value of the house is counted in GNP.

Fourth, GNP measures the value of output produced by *domestically owned* factors of production. Part of the GNP is produced abroad. For instance, the income earned by an American working in Paris is part of U.S. GNP. Similarly, when an American company owns a factory in Germany and receives profits from its operation, those profits count as part of U.S. GNP. By the same argument, the income earned in the United States by factors of production owned abroad is *not* part of U.S. GNP.

Gross domestic product (GDP) measures the output produced by factors of production located in the domestic economy, whoever owns them.

For most economies there is little difference between GNP and GDP; either factor payments to and from foreigners are small or such payments roughly balance. The United States has in recent years on balance received payments from abroad equal to just under 2 percent of GNP. Thus GNP exceeds GDP. However, such payments may be more significant for other economies. Egypt, for example, receives over 6 percent of its GNP as factor payments from abroad, mostly from Egyptian nationals working abroad who send payments home. Gabon, in Africa, has a GNP that is only 87 percent of its GDP. It is an oil-producing country in which much of the production is done by foreigners who send their income home.

Finally, goods are valued at their market value, or the price at which they are sold to the final users. Goods which are taxed, for instance, through a sales tax, are valued at a price including the tax; that is the market value. But it is difficult to value goods produced by the government that are not sold through the market. Examples are defense, police protection, and public education. The value of government services is, by convention, taken to be equal to the wages paid to government employees.

Per Capita GNP   U.S. GNP in 1981 was $2938 billion. The number is so large that it is difficult to get any feeling for what it means. A number that is easier to understand is *per capita GNP,* or the value of production per person. Dividing the 1981 GNP of $2938 billion by the population in 1981, 229.8 million people, we obtain per capita GNP of $12,785 in 1981. This is the value of the production of goods and services per person in the United States, including children and others not working.

TABLE 22-2

PER CAPITA GNP IN SELECTED COUNTRIES, 1979
(Thousands of 1979 Dollars)

COUNTRY	GNP PER CAPITA
Bangladesh	90
China	260
El Salvador	670
Syria	1,030
Argentina	2,230
Hungary	3,850
Italy	5,250
United States	10,630
Switzerland	13,920
Kuwait	17,100

Source: World Bank, *World Development Report*, 1981, pp. 134–135.

The range of per capita GNPs in the world is enormous. Table 22-2 gives some estimates. Comparisons among countries are difficult, because different goods are produced in different countries and because output is measured in different currencies, such as Swiss francs in Switzerland and dollars in the United States. Even so, the numbers in Table 22-2 give some idea of the range of international output levels.

Some of the numbers are hard to believe. Whereas per capita income in the United States was above $10,600 in 1979, in Bangladesh it was only $90. Americans could not live on so low an income. Probably the value of output produced in Bangladesh is above $90, because output produced by farmers who consume their own crops is not counted accurately. But it is still true that per capita income in Bangladesh is so low that people starve, some quickly and some slowly as ill health leads to early death. At the other end of the scale is Kuwait, whose oil production leads to per capita GNP 60 percent higher than that in the United States.

Measuring GNP   GNP data in the United States are published by the Commerce De-

partment. The statistical procedures are elaborate and imperfect. The data are sometimes revised as new studies are made and new information becomes available. Estimates are made in two ways. One estimate is obtained from the value of production; the other is obtained from the value of the incomes earned by people in the economy. We recall from Figure 21-1 that the value of production and the value of income are closely related, and we shall show that more precisely. By independently estimating production and income, the Commerce Department has a check on the accuracy of its data.

Although there are published data on GNP for all countries in the world, the numbers do not all have the same reliability. The extensive record keeping expected of firms in industrial economies is not practiced in some less-developed countries. In those economies, GNP data are based on guesswork and imagination. For instance, careful study of the level of per capita GNP may be made in a particular year. For later years, the estimate is updated by assuming that per capita GNP is rising at the same rate as the economy's output of electricity. Crude estimates of this type are better than nothing for getting some idea of how much output is being produced.

Output, Income, and Spending   Given GNP as the basic measure of the value of goods and services produced by the economy, we now explore two questions.

First, how is GNP related to the incomes that various factors of production receive, and what income accrues to households that are the ultimate owners of the factors of production? Second, GNP is the value of production of final goods and services. What are those goods and services, and who buys them? This question leads to a consideration of the components of expenditures by sector.

2   GNP AND NATIONAL INCOME

The circular flow diagram (Figure 21-1) shows that GNP, or output, and income are related, because the payments made for goods produced are paid out in turn to factors of production. Now we study that link in more detail, showing how GNP is related to the income received in the economy, or national income.

There are two main adjustments in going from GNP to national income. The first is the deduction from GNP of *depreciation,* or the *capital consumption allowance.* Capital goods—machinery and buildings—wear out while they are being used to make goods. This wear and tear should be treated as a cost of production, and it is therefore deducted from GNP in calculating the income received by factors of production or their owners. GNP minus the capital consumption allowance is equal to *net national product* (NNP).

Why deduct depreciation in order to get a measure of income? Think of the owner of a machine, using it in his business to produce goods. Whatever profits the owner of the business makes are part of his income. But if the machine is wearing out during the year, the owner should regard that depreciation as part of the cost of making goods and therefore not as part of profits. The using up of the machine is a cost of production just as much as the using of labor or the using of raw materials during the course of the year. Thus we deduct depreciation in going from GNP to national income, which measures incomes earned by factors of production in the economy.

Second, in moving from GNP, which measures the market value of output, to national income, which is the income received by factors of production, we have to adjust for the excise taxes that are paid on many goods. For these goods, the market price exceeds the income received by the firm. An example is the sales tax on gasoline. If a gallon of gasoline costs $1.50, of which $0.20 is taxes paid to federal and state governments, the workers in and owners of firms producing gasoline receive only $1.30 per gallon as income. Thus indirect taxes have to be deducted from GNP to calculate national income, or the income received by factors of production.

Other goods, by contrast, receive subsidies which reduce the market price below the price received by sellers. For these goods, income received by factors of production exceeds the value of sales of the goods. In this case, we have to add the value of subsidies to GNP to calculate national income.

Table 22-3 summarizes the adjustments which link GNP and national income. Starting from GNP of $2938 billion, we first deduct depreciation of $330 billion to calculate net national product (NNP), equal in 1981 to $2608 billion. In that year depreciation was just above 11 percent of GNP, which is about average. From NNP we calculate national income by deducting indirect taxes and adding subsidies. On balance, we have to deduct $256 billion, because indirect taxes are much larger than subsidies. Thus we show indirect taxes minus subsidies to be equal to $256 billion.[1] We then have national income for 1981 equal to $2352 billion. This is the amount received as income by factors of production in the economy.

Factor Earnings

The deductions made in Table 22-3 in going from GNP to national income give us the total amount that is earned by factors of production in the economy after adjusting for depreciation. The earnings of the various factors of production are shown in Table 22-4.

---

[1] There are some other small adjustments included at this stage.

TABLE 22-3

U.S. GNP AND NATIONAL INCOME, 1981
(Billions of Dollars)

GNP			2938
Less:	Depreciation	330	
Equals:	Net national product (NNP)		2608
Less:	Indirect taxes minus subsidies	256	
Equals:	National income		2352

Source: Survey of Current Business, July 1982, p. 26.

TABLE 22-4

U.S. NATIONAL INCOME AND ITS COMPOSITION, 1981

	$ BILLIONS	PERCENT
National income:	2352	100
Compensation of employees	1768	75.2
Proprietors' income	125	5.3
Rental income of persons	34	1.4
Corporate profits	191	8.1
Net interest	236	10.0

Note: Sum of percentages not equal to 100 because of rounding.
Source: Survey of Current Business, July 1982, p. 28.

There are two basic types of income: income from labor and income from property. Compensation of employees (wages and benefits like health insurance) is, of course, labor income. This accounts for over 75 percent of national income. There is also some labor income in proprietors' income. Proprietors' income is the income of unincorporated businesses and includes the income the owners make as a return to the labor they put into the businesses.

All the rest of the income in Table 22-4 represents income from property. This makes up less than one-quarter of national income. Part of proprietors' income is a return on the owners' investment in businesses. Rental income of persons is income from patents and royalties but includes also imputed income from owner-occupied

housing. Corporate profit is the return on capital (machines, structures, patents) in the corporate sector. Finally, net interest represents the payments by businesses and the rest of the world to firms and households that have lent to them.[2]

3 NATIONAL INCOME AND PERSONAL DISPOSABLE INCOME

National income is the total amount earned by the economy's factors of production. A person's income is available for spending or saving. But not all of national income is actually available for household spending on goods and services.

Personal disposable income is the income available for spending or saving by households.

To calculate personal disposable income we have to make a few more adjustments to national income. Table 22-5 summarizes these adjustments.

Each adjustment in Table 22-5 accounts for some part of national income that is not paid to households and that households therefore cannot spend. First, firms do not pay out all their profits to the owners. Some of the profits are kept in the firm to be used in the firm's operations. The only part paid out to individuals is dividends, which cor-

---

[2] This item does *not* include interest payments by households or by the government. Neither of these interest payments is included in GNP because they are not thought to represent payments based on the production of goods and services.

TABLE 22-5

U.S. NATIONAL INCOME AND PERSONAL DISPOSABLE INCOME, 1981
(Billions of Dollars)

National income	2352
Less: Corporate profits	191
Plus: Personal dividend receipts	63
Plus: Interest adjustment	93
Less: Taxes	624
Plus: Transfers	336
Equals: Personal disposable income	2029

Note: Components do not sum to total because of rounding.
Source: Survey of Current Business, July 1982, pp. 26 and 37.

porations pay their stockholders. Thus in Table 22-5 we start by deducting profits from national income and then add back dividends paid to individuals. This ensures that only that part of profits actually received as income by the owners is included in the total of personal disposable income.

Next there is an adjustment for interest payments. We noted before that interest payments by government and households are not counted as part of national income, since these are not regarded as payments based on the production of goods and services. But households that receive interest income from the government do think of the interest receipts as income and have it available for spending. Thus we have to adjust national income for interest payments that are received by households but not ordinarily counted as part of national income. In 1981 the adjustment was $93 billion, which is added to national income to calculate personal disposable income, or the amount actually available to households.

Finally, we have to take account of taxes. Amounts that households pay in taxes are obviously not available for spending and are therefore deducted from national income to calculate personal disposable income. In 1981 the adjustment for taxes was $624 billion, as can be seen in Table 22-5.

But households receive *transfer payments* from the government and from business. Transfer payments are payments made without the recipient providing any current service in return. Government transfer payments consist of such things as Social Security benefits and unemployment benefits. Business transfer payments consist mainly of pensions.[3]

With all these adjustments, the table shows that households end up with disposable income of only $2029 billion out of a national income of $2352 billion. Recalling that GNP for 1981 was $2938 billion, we see that personal disposable income was only 69 percent of GNP. Although per capita GNP in 1981 was above $12,700, disposable income per capita was under $8900. The difference arises largely from taxes and depreciation.

The Allocation of Personal Disposable Income

Next we ask what people do with the income they have available for spending. Most of personal disposable income is in fact spent.

Consumption expenditure of households is all their spending on goods and services except for purchases of houses.

Over 90 percent of disposable personal income is consumed, as shown in Table 22-6. Another 2.7 percent goes to pay interest to businesses from which households have borrowed. The remainder—the part of disposable personal income that is neither spent on goods and services nor repaid as interest to businesses—is saved.

Personal saving is the part of their disposable income which households use to add to their wealth.

---

[3] Note that transfer payments are very large, equal to more than 15 percent of national income. Most of this total is government transfers. The increase in the federal government budget in the seventies was a result of rapidly rising transfers.

TABLE 22-6

THE ALLOCATION OF U.S. PERSONAL DISPOSABLE INCOME, 1981

	$ BILLIONS	PERCENT
Personal disposable income:	2029	100
Consumption expenditure	1843	90.8
Interest payments to business	55	2.7
Personal saving	130	6.4

Note: A small amount ($0.6 billion) of personal disposable income transferred to foreigners is omitted from the table.
Source: Survey of Current Business, July 1982, p. 37.

They save by adding to their bank accounts, stocks, or mutual funds or by buying (newly produced) houses. Saving may also be used to reduce old debts. A household that reduces its debts on balance increases its wealth. Thus using part of personal disposable income to reduce debt also increases a household's wealth and counts as saving.

> The share of personal saving in disposable personal income is the *personal saving rate.*

The personal saving rate in the United States in 1981 was only 6.4 percent. This is the lowest saving rate among the major industrial economies. The countries with high personal saving rates are Italy with around 22 percent and Japan with 18 percent during the last few years. Some economists blame U.S. economic difficulties, especially low growth, on the low personal saving rate. We return to this question later.

4 GNP AND SPENDING

The total amount of goods and services produced, GNP, is sold to the demanders of output. In this section we examine who does the buying of the goods and what categories of goods are sold to which demanders. We divide the economy into four spending sectors: households, firms, government, and the rest of the world, or the external sector.

Table 22-7 shows total expenditures on goods and services by the four sectors. We start with the household sector. Household spending on goods and services is called consumption and is denoted by the symbol C. We have already seen that consumption spending in 1981 was $1843 billion. This comes to 62.7 percent of GNP.

Business firms' spending on goods and services that are not intermediate goods is by definition investment spending. Firms' investment spending takes two forms. Firms purchase goods to add to their physical capital stocks, such as machines and buildings. In addition, firms buy or produce goods to add to their inventories. Inventories are stocks of goods that are useful in

TABLE 22-7

U.S. GNP AND ITS COMPONENTS, 1981

SECTOR	GOODS	SYMBOL	BILLIONS OF DOLLARS	PERCENT
Households	Consumption	*C*	1843	62.7
Business	Investment	*I*	472	16.1
Government	Government	*G*	597	20.3
Rest of world	Net exports	*NX*	26	0.9
	Total	GNP	2938	

Source: Economic Report of the President, 1982, p. 233.

production or are awaiting sale to consumers. Automobile producers hold inventories of steel so that they can keep the production line moving without running out of steel, and department stores hold inventories of clothing so that they can have goods available to sell to their customers. Additions to these inventories count as part of investment. We denote investment by I. In 1981, investment made up 16.1 percent of GNP.

The next major purchaser of goods and services is the government. Government buys the services of labor, provided, for instance, by soldiers, teachers, and bureaucrats, and it also buys goods such as tanks and school buildings. The government sector includes state and local governments along with the federal government. In 1981

government spending, G, accounted for 20.3 percent of GNP.

The final sector whose spending generates a demand for domestic production is the foreign sector. Recall that we are interested in spending on goods and services produced by domestically owned factors. So far we have listed spending by households, firms, and the government. Some of this spending goes to pay for imports from abroad, and so it does not constitute spending on goods produced by domestic factors. On the other side, though, we have not yet included spending on our goods by foreigners, which is exports.

We adjust for the existence of trade by adding net exports to spending on goods produced by domestically owned factors.

BOX 22-1

THE COMPOSITION OF GNP

The composition of GNP spending provides useful information about the structure of the economy. The accompanying table gives examples, shown also (except for Lesotho in Africa) in the figure. The data start with the United States in 1981. The next row shows the United States in 1944, at the height of World War II. At that time government was buying nearly half the economy's total production for the war effort. Investment was being squeezed very heavily. Indeed, during World War II there was a special system of licensing of investment. Firms needed licenses to invest, and only investment that contributed directly toward the war effort was permitted.

Algeria in 1979 represents the opposite extreme, an economy investing

COMPONENTS OF GNP IN U.S. AND OTHER ECONOMIES
(Percent)

	C	I	G	NX
United States—1981	63	16	20	1
United States—1944	51	3	46	−1
Algeria—1979	45	44	14	−3
Kuwait—1979	17	12	14	57
Sweden—1979	53	20	30	−3
Lesotho—1979	143	29	16	−88

Note: Components may not sum to total because of rounding.
Sources: Economic Report of the President, 1982, p. 233, *Survey of Current Business,* July 1982, p. 22, and *World Development Report, 1981,* pp. 142–143.

THE COMPOSITION OF GNP SPENDING. *Note:* The solid red area shows negative values of *NX*.

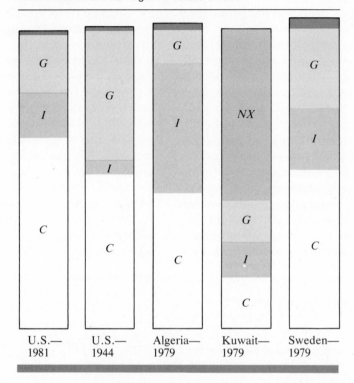

extremely heavily. The Algerians were rapidly increasing the capital stock, building roads and factories in the hope that the economy would grow fast. The heavy investment came in large part at the expense of consumption, which in 1979 took a smaller share in GNP than consumption in the United States took in wartime.

Kuwait is another special example. The Kuwaiti economy is dominated by oil. The table shows that its exports far exceed its imports, so much so that net exports make up more than half of GNP. Although Kuwait has a high GNP, in 1979 it was not spending much of that GNP on consumption, investment, or government purchases. The excess of production over spending in the economy is saving. Kuwait saved most of its GNP by buying assets abroad. Kuwait, as one of the richest oil producers, has added rapidly to its ownership of assets in other countries.

Sweden is included as an example of a country where government spending on goods and services is relatively high, and Lesotho is included to show that a country can consume more than the value of GNP. This is possible if it is buying goods abroad. As we see in Table 22-8, net exports were negative, meaning that imports exceeded exports. And the excess is enormous: 88 percent of GNP. Thus Lesotho was importing a large volume of goods and consuming more than the value of its production.

Net exports is equal to exports (the value of our goods sold to foreigners) minus imports (the value of goods we buy from foreigners).

Net exports is denoted *NX* in Table 22-7. In 1981 net exports came to 0.9 percent of GNP. Net exports were the difference between two much larger numbers: exports in 1981 were $367 billion and imports were $341 billion. Total sales to foreigners—our exports—were thus a major source of demand for the goods produced in the United States.

Foreigners accounted for 12.5 percent [(367/2938) × 100 percent] of the total purchases of the goods and services produced by Americans in 1981. A similar calculation shows that Americans spent an amount equal to 11.6 percent of GNP on goods imported from abroad. Foreign trade thus accounts for a significant part of the sales of American products and purchases by Americans.

Table 22-7 shows all the categories of spending on goods and services produced as GNP. The sum of the components is thus equal to GNP, as recorded in equation (1):

$$GNP = C + I + G + NX \qquad (1)$$

GNP and the Demand for Goods and Services It is useful to think of consumption, investment, government spending, and net exports as the sources of *demand* for goods in the economy. By demand we mean the amounts of goods each sector wants to buy. The exception is in investment. Part of the amount recorded in the national income accounts as investment may not have been desired or demanded by firms at all. Specifically, suppose that firms produced goods to sell to consumers but that no customers showed up willing to buy them. The firms then had to add those goods to their inventories of goods awaiting sale. But the firms did not want to add those goods to inventories. Because the firms misjudged how much their customers would buy, these goods were added to inventories and thus are counted as part of investment in GNP.

Thus we can think of the categories of spending shown in Table 22-7 as generating the demand for the economy's output. But we have to recognize that part of investment in inventories in any period may not have been demanded at all. Instead, it is unplanned or undesired inventory investment, a result of mistakes firms made in planning production.

5 SUMMARY OF NATIONAL INCOME ACCOUNTING

Recalling the details of national income accounting is never easy. It is therefore worth summarizing in Figure 22-1 the most important relationships studied so far. The only relationships omitted from the figure are those in Tables 22-5 and 22-6, which describe how disposable personal income is related to national income and then how personal disposable income is spent. Refer back to those tables for that information.

6 WHAT DOES GNP MEASURE?

As we noted at the beginning of this chapter, GNP is in practice widely used as a measure of the performance of the economy. Comparing countries with levels of per capita GNP varying from $90 (in 1979) in Bangladesh to over $17,000 in Kuwait, it seems natural to use GNP as an indicator of the living standards of people in different countries. And within any given economy, the growth rate of GNP is also often used to discuss the performance of the economy. Rapid growth of GNP is assumed to be good, indicating that the economy is producing more goods, and slow or negative growth is bad.

In this section we stand back from the details of national income accounting to discuss the uses and limitations of GNP data.

FIGURE 22-1 NATIONAL INCOME ACCOUNTING: A SUMMARY.

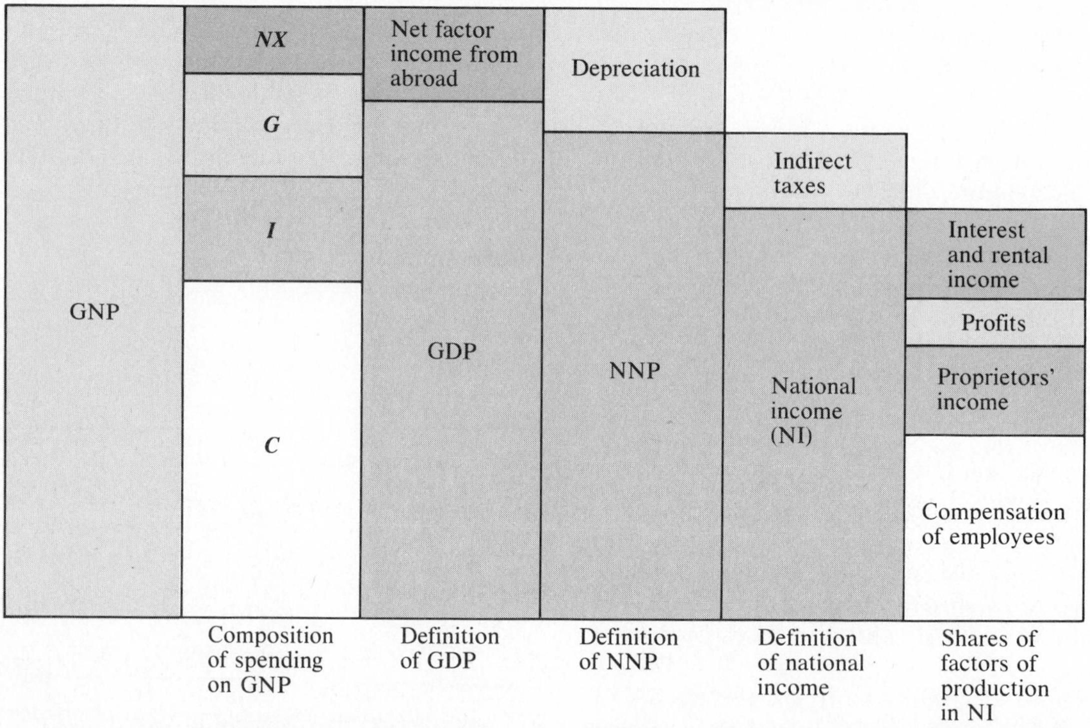

| Composition of spending on GNP | Definition of GDP | Definition of NNP | Definition of national income | Shares of factors of production in NI |

We make three points. First, we recall the essential distinction between real and nominal GNP. Real GNP corrects nominal GNP for inflation. Changes in real GNP therefore give a more accurate picture of how the economy's production of goods and services is changing than do changes in nominal GNP. Second, we show how the use of per capita GNP changes our interpretation of growth rates. The section concludes with a discussion of the comprehensiveness of GNP accounting and the existence of a substantial nonmarket sector.

Nominal and Real GNP

In Chapter 21 we introduced the distinction between nominal, or current dollar, GNP and GNP measured at constant prices, or real GNP. Table 22-8 presents an example

of the calculation of real and nominal GNP in a simple, imaginary economy producing only bananas and chickens. Nominal GNP is the value of production in each year measured in the prices of that year. But real GNP is the value of production measured in a common set of prices—the *base year* prices. In Table 22-8, the base year is 1972, and real GNP is therefore calculated using 1972 prices of goods, or in 1972 dollars.

As we see from the table, there is a substantial difference between the change in nominal GNP in our hypothetical economy from 1972 to 1985 and the change in real GNP over that period. The reason is, of course, that the prices of all goods have risen over that period. But real GNP, by using the same prices to value output in different years, does not allow price changes to

TABLE 22-8
CALCULATION OF REAL AND NOMINAL GNP

PERCENT	OUTPUT		PRICE, $/unit		VALUE OF OUTPUT, current $		VALUE OF OUTPUT, 1972 $	
	1972	1985	1972	1985	1972	1985	1972	1985
Bananas	100	150	2	4	200	600	200	300
Chickens	100	140	4	6	400	840	400	560
					600	1440	600	860
					Nominal GNP		Real GNP	

(handwritten annotations: 150×4 above 600; = 2 × 150; 4 × 140)

influence the measure of output. Thus real GNP is a measure of the economy's output that adjusts for inflation.

Figure 22-2 shows real and nominal GNP for the United States for the period since 1966. Here too there is a large difference between the behavior of real and nominal GNP. From 1966 to 1981, nominal GNP increased almost fourfold from $756 billion to $2938 billion. But real GNP measured in the prices of 1972 increased only from $985 billion to $1503 billion, or only about 53 percent. Most of the increase in nominal GNP was the result of rising prices, not of rising production of goods and services. Note also from Figure 22-2 that although nominal GNP increased every year, real GNP fell in the recessions of 1973–1975 and 1980.

Whenever we want to compare the economy's physical production of goods and services rather than the money value of output, we should use *real GNP*. That way we do not confuse increases in the quantity of goods produced with increases in their prices.

The GNP Deflator The distinction between real and nominal GNP gives us the second most widely used measure of inflation, the GNP deflator. The most widely used measure of inflation is the CPI, which was discussed already in Chapters 2 and 21.

The *GNP deflator* is the ratio of nominal GNP to real GNP expressed as an index. Expressing the deflator as an index means that the ratio of nominal to real GNP is multiplied by 100.

In the hypothetical economy of Table 22-8, the GNP deflator for 1985 is 167.4 [(1440/860) × 100]. According to the deflator, prices increased 67.4 percent [(167.4 − 100) percent] between 1972 and 1985 in the simple economy. If we look at the rates of increase of the individual prices, we see that the deflator gives us a good idea of the average behavior of prices. The price of bananas increased 100 percent over the period, while that of chickens rose 50 percent. The conclusion from the index is that prices rose on average by a little over 67 percent, giving us a reasonable picture in one number of the changes in the two underlying prices.[4]

Turning now to actual data, the rate of inflation is calculated as the growth rate of the GNP deflator. For instance, the deflator for 1981 was 193.6, while for 1980 it was

---

[4] This is a technical point. The GNP deflator implicitly uses for weights in the price index the shares of the different goods in the value of output in the *current* year (1985 in the example). An index such as the CPI uses the shares of output in the *base* year for weights. That is one reason the CPI and the deflator differ. Another reason is that the deflator includes all goods produced, whereas the CPI measures the cost of goods consumed by a typical wage earner.

FIGURE 22-2 REAL AND NOMINAL GNP, UNITED STATES, 1966–1981. *Note:* Shaded periods are recessions. (*Source: Economic Report of the President, 1982,* pp. 233–234.)

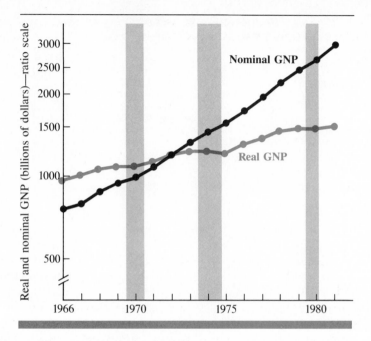

177.4. The rate of inflation from 1980 to 1981, calculated from the deflator, is

$$\text{Rate of inflation (GNP deflator)} = \frac{\text{index in 1981} - \text{index in 1980}}{\text{index in 1980}} \times 100\%$$

$$= \frac{193.6 - 177.4}{177.4} \times 100\%$$

$$= 9.1\%$$

The rate of increase of the GNP deflator is widely used to measure inflation because it applies to all goods produced in the economy. It is thus a very broadly based indicator of inflation. The CPI, by contrast, includes only the prices of goods consumed by a typical consumer.

Per Capita Real GNP

Because total or aggregate GNP numbers are hard for anyone to comprehend, we introduce the more manageable concept of per capita GNP, or GNP per person. Per capita *real* GNP data are also useful in interpreting data on the growth of real GNP. This is illustrated in Table 22-9, which

shows real growth rates for four countries during the seventies.

The first column in Table 22-9 reports growth rates for real GNP, showing substantially higher growth rates for Brazil and Mexico than for the United States or Germany. The second column shows the growth rate of population. The rate is less than 1 percent in the United States, near zero in Germany, but 2.8 and 3.5 percent in Brazil and Mexico, respectively.

What are the implications for real GNP as an indicator of the availability of goods and services? While real GNP was growing in each country, so was population. Therefore, the total production of goods had to be shared among more people. But in each country real GNP actually grew faster than population so that there was an increase in GNP per capita. It is interesting to note, though, that while the growth rate of GNP was higher in Mexico than in Germany, the growth rate of real GNP per capita was lower in Mexico. Thus adjustments for population growth are essential in interpreting

TABLE 22-9

REAL GNP AND POPULATION GROWTH RATES, 1970–1979
(Percent per Year)

	REAL GNP GROWTH	POPULATION GROWTH	PER CAPITA REAL GNP GROWTH
United States	3.5	0.9	2.6
Germany	2.9	0.1	2.8
Brazil	8.9	2.8	5.9
Mexico	5.4	3.5	1.8

Sources: *International Financial Statistics*, Yearbook, 1980, and *International Financial Statistics*, December 1981.

and comparing real growth rates across countries or time periods; a country with a high growth rate of population has to grow faster just to keep each person equally well off.

Another point must be raised about real GNP growth rates as measures of improved living standards. Although per capita income may be rising in a country, it is not necessarily true that everybody shares in that improvement. Indeed, it is quite possible that along with what looks like reasonable growth there is a change in income distribution that makes some people absolutely poorer while others enjoy more than the economywide average growth in real income.

A More Comprehensive Measure of GNP

Because we use GNP to measure the production of goods and services in the economy, it is desirable that the coverage of the GNP accounts should be as comprehensive as possible. In practice we encounter two problems in including all production in GNP. First, some outputs, such as noise, pollution, and congestion, are nuisances. We should make an adjustment for these "bads" by subtracting from the traditional GNP data an allowance for all the nuisance goods that are created in the process of producing GNP. This is a perfectly sensible suggestion, but it is almost impossible to assign a cost to these nuisance goods because they are not traded through markets and therefore their outputs and the value of the damage that they do are difficult to measure.

We noted earlier that a variety of productive economic activities are excluded from measured GNP. These include the services of homemakers, the activities of do-it-yourselfers, and illegal or unreported incomes. Estimates of the value of these activities have been made, although they are necessarily highly speculative.

Estimates of the size of the unreported economy range all the way from 3 percent to 25 percent of GNP.[5] Professor John Kendrick of George Washington University has concentrated on a few areas including unpaid household work, unpaid labor services (especially schoolwork by students), volunteer work, and the rental value of nonbusiness property that are at present unaccounted for in GNP.[6] Each of these activities is pursued for an economic purpose, but because they are nonmarket activities, they have eluded proper accounting. Were they to be included, Kendrick estimates, they would raise GNP estimates quite dramatically, by more than 60 percent.

Net Economic Welfare Deducting the value of nuisance outputs from GNP and adding the value of unreported and nonmar-

---

[5] The size of the unreported economy may be larger in some foreign countries where tax evasion is a more regular part of life. Several official organizations have tried to estimate the size of the unreported economy. One example is a work by the Organization for Economic Cooperation and Development (OECD) in Paris, *The Hidden Economy in the Context of National Accounts,* published in 1981.

[6] John W. Kendrick, "Expanding Imputed Values in the National Income and Product Accounts," *Review of Income and Wealth,* December 1979, pp. 349–363.

ket incomes would make GNP a better measure of the economy's production of goods and services. This would make us more confident about using real GNP as the basis for measuring the standard of living in the country.

But one more major adjustment has to be made. We must include the value of leisure in a measure of economic welfare. GNP tells us what goods and services are produced. But people do not live only to produce; they certainly enjoy leisure too. Thus if we want to evaluate changes in well-being, we should take account of changes in the amount of leisure people enjoy.

In 1972 Professors William Nordhaus and James Tobin of Yale estimated a measure called *net economic welfare* (NEW) which adjusted GNP by deducting "bads," adding the value of nonmarket activities, and including the value of leisure.[7] The value of NEW is larger than that of GNP.

But on balance NEW has grown more slowly than GNP. Production of "bads" (pollution) has been growing fast, and leisure has not been increasing as rapidly as the output of goods and services.[8] NEW estimates are of course crude, but they remind us that GNP is far from being a perfect measure of economic welfare.

Nonetheless, real GNP is our main measure of economic activity, and it is used in practice as an indicator of economic well-being. It's the best measure we have that is available on a regular basis.

---

[7] William Nordhaus and James Tobin, "Is Growth Obsolete?" in National Bureau of Economic Research, *Fiftieth Anniversary Colloquium*, Columbia University Press, New York, 1972. Nordhaus and Tobin named their estimate MEW, or measure of economic welfare. MIT's Paul Samuelson renamed it NEW.

[8] Two developments have affected the amount of leisure. The workweek has shortened for those at work, increasing leisure. But a greater proportion of those of working age are now at work, and that means they enjoy less leisure.

SUMMARY

1   Gross national product (GNP) is the key measure of economic activity. GNP is defined as the market value of all goods and services produced within a given period by domestically owned factors of production.

2   GDP (gross domestic product) is the value of the output of goods and services produced in the domestic economy. It differs from GNP by an amount equal to net income from abroad. Income earned by Americans from their ownership of factors of production abroad is added, and income earned by foreigners from their ownership of factors of production in the United States is deducted from GDP in calculating GNP. The United States on balance receives factor income from abroad. Thus GNP exceeds GDP for the United States. For many developing countries, GDP exceeds GNP.

3   The production of GNP generates the income earned by domestic factors of production. A number of adjustments have to be made in going from GNP to national income (NI). Not all the value of goods

and services produced accrues as incomes to the factors of production. There are two major adjustments. The first is depreciation. As the equipment and structures used in production wear out, part of output has to be set aside to replace and maintain the stock of physical capital, and this represents a deduction from income. GNP minus depreciation is net national product (NNP). The second adjustment is indirect taxes. Indirect taxes, such as a sales tax, create a difference between the market value of goods and the amount individuals receive as income for producing those goods. NNP minus indirect taxes is national income.

4   NI measures total income received by domestically owned factors of production. National income, in turn, can be split into the returns to different productive factors: labor compensation, rental income, proprietors' income, corporate profits, and net interest.

5   Disposable personal income is a measure of the income households actually receive. It differs from national income because of the deduction of government taxes (corporate profits taxes, personal income taxes, and Social Security taxes) and undistributed corporate profits, the addition of transfer payments, and the adjustment for interest. Most of disposable personal income is consumed. Most of the rest is saved.

6   Looked at from the expenditure side, GNP is equal to the components of demand: consumption, investment, government spending, and net exports. The sum of these components is identical to GNP because investment is defined to include involuntary inventory accumulation.

7   Real GNP is obtained by valuing the output of goods produced each year at the prices of a given base year, currently 1972. Real GNP is thus a measure of the economy's physical production of goods and services.

8   The GNP deflator, or the ratio of nominal to real GNP, is a widely used price index.

9   GNP as measured does not include all production of goods and services. Some nonmarket activities and unreported incomes are excluded.

10 Real GNP is in practice used as a measure of economic welfare, but it has major shortcomings in this role. First, the value of nuisance outputs such as pollution should be deducted. Second, the value of leisure should be added to GNP. This gives a measure of net economic welfare (NEW). NEW is not calculated on a regular basis and therefore serves mainly to remind us to be cautious in using GNP as a welfare measure.

KEY TERMS

Gross national product (GNP)

National income (NI)

Value added

Imputed rent

Gross domestic product (GDP)

Per capita GNP

Depreciation

Net national product (NNP)

Personal disposable income

Personal saving

Personal saving rate

Net exports

Nominal GNP

Real GNP

GNP deflator

Net economic welfare (NEW)

PROBLEMS

1   Suppose GDP is \$2900 billion. Domestic residents receive factor payments from abroad equal to \$150 billion. Foreigners receive factor payments from the United States equal to \$75 billion. (*a*) What is GNP? (*b*) What does GNP measure?

2   This question deals with value added accounting. We are interested in the contribution of automobile production to GNP. Suppose final automobile producers purchase tires, windows, and windshield wipers from suppliers and produce the remaining parts in their own firms. Suppliers in turn purchase materials from materials suppliers who we assume (unrealistically) purchase no intermediate goods themselves. Here are the raw data:

	FINAL SALES	INTERMEDIATE GOODS PURCHASES	
Automobile producer	1000	270	730
Window producer	100	12	88
Tire producer	93	30	63
Windshield wiper producer	30	5	25
Materials producers	47	0	47
			953

What is the contribution of automobile production to GNP?

3   Suppose GNP is \$3000 billion. Suppose depreciation is \$300 billion and indirect taxes are \$200 billion. There are no subsidies. (*a*) What is the value of national income? (*b*) Explain in words why and how depreciation enters in the relationship between national income and GNP. (*c*) Explain in words why indirect taxes enter the relationship between GNP and national income.

4   (*a*) Explain in words why the imputed rental income of owner-occupied housing should be part of GNP and national income. (*b*) Why is it the rental and not the fair market value of the house that should be included?

5   (*a*) Explain how government provision of services such as police protection is accounted for in the GNP accounts.

Some people argue that government spending on police protection does not really contribute to GNP. Problems (*b*) through (*d*) are designed to show why they make this argument. (*b*) Suppose standards of public behavior improve and the police force can be reduced by half. The policemen get jobs at exactly the same pay in private industry. Explain why there is no change in GNP. (*c*) Is society better or worse off with a smaller police force in this case? (*d*) What does this suggest about including police protection as part of GNP?

6   In going from national income to personal disposable income we make adjustments for taxes and transfers. (*a*) What are the main transfer receipts by the household sector? (*b*) Why are transfers not included in national income?

7 Suppose personal disposable income is equal to $2000. Net interest payments by consumers to business are equal to $50. (*a*) Assuming the personal saving rate is the same as it is in Table 22-6, calculate consumption. (*b*) Define consumption and saving. (*c*) Is there any part of what is counted as consumption that might better be counted as saving? (Think of goods households buy that may increase their wealth.)

8 Suppose GNP = 2000, $C = 1700$, $G = 50$, and $NX = 40$. (*a*) What is investment? (*b*) Suppose exports are 350. What are imports? (*c*) Suppose depreciation is 130. What is NNP? (*d*) In this example net exports are positive. Could they be negative? Explain.

9 Consider an economy with the following data:

	NOMINAL GNP	GNP DEFLATOR
1981	2000	100
1982	2400	113

(*a*) What is the 1982 GNP in constant (1981) dollars? (*b*) What is the growth rate of real GNP from 1981 to 1982? (*c*) What is the inflation rate? (*d*) Suppose 1982 nominal GNP was 2240 with all other data above unchanged. What would 1982 real GNP be? What would the growth rate of real GNP be? Explain in words what is going on.

10 Explain why the following nonmarket activities should or should not appear in a comprehensive measure of GNP: (*a*) Time spent by students in class. (*b*) The income of muggers. (*c*) The time spent by boxing match spectators. (*d*) The wages paid by the city to traffic wardens who issue tickets. (*e*) Littering.

Real GNP in the United States has grown since 1890 at an average rate of 3.2 percent per year. Figure 23-1 shows both the actual level of real GNP and the trend level for the period 1890–1981. The trend level of GNP is the level GNP would have been each year if it had grown smoothly. But the growth of real GNP has not been smooth. The figure shows large movements of real GNP relative to trend. The Great Depression of the 1930s stands out, with output falling far below trend. So does the experience of World War II, when output increased above its trend level.

Real GNP has stayed much closer to its trend level in the post-World War II period. But even here, as Figure 23-2 shows, the economy has not had steady growth. Sometimes—for instance, from 1973 to 1975, in 1980, and again in 1981—real GNP has fallen. Such falls in GNP occur during *recessions*. Recessions are typically periods in which real GNP is falling, unemployment is rising, and economic prospects are gloomy. The eight post-World War II recessions are shaded in Figure 23-2. The longest period without a recession lasted from the beginning of 1961 to the end of 1969.

A recession is one phase of the business cycle.

> The *business cycle* consists of more or less regular simultaneous movements in GNP relative to trend, unemployment, inflation, interest rates, and other economic variables.

The business cycle is described in Box 23-1. Business cycle terminology—words such as "recession," "recovery," and "boom"—is part of everyday language, and we use it extensively. One of the main aims of macroeconomics is to explain why GNP fluctuates in the business cycle and to analyze the forces that determine the level of GNP. We start that analysis in this chapter.

Figure 23-2 shows the level of potential output, or potential GNP, as well as actual output, or GNP.

> *Potential output* is the output level the economy would produce if there were full employment.

The difference between actual and potential output is called the *output gap*. The output gap measures the amount of output lost through unemployment. It dramatizes the fact that the economy sometimes does not produce efficiently, operating at a point inside rather than on the production possibility frontier.

Figure 23-2 shows periods, such as the late sixties, in which out-

23

The Business Cycle, Output, and Aggregate Demand

FIGURE 23-1 ACTUAL AND TREND REAL GNP, 1890–1981. Trend real GNP shows the level at which GNP would have been if it had grown smoothly over the entire period at the average growth rate of real GNP of 3.2 percent. The Great Depression, World War II, and the rapid growth of the 1960s stand out. (*Sources:* U.S. Department of Commerce, *Long Term Economic Growth, 1860–1970,* and *Economic Report of the President, 1982.*)

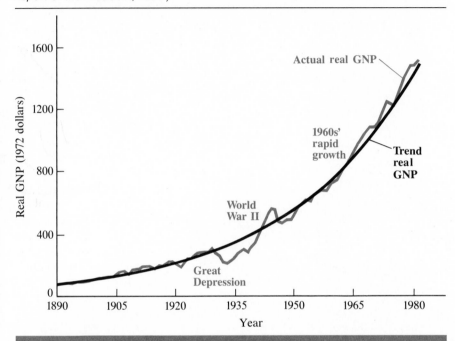

put is above its potential level. Output can be above its potential level when there is overfull employment, with firms short of workers and workers putting in overtime. Such situations drive home the point that potential output is not a physical measure of how much the economy could produce if everyone were forced to work 16 hours a day. Rather, potential output measures how much the economy would produce if everyone who wanted a job had one, allowing for normal unemployment that occurs because people cannot immediately find the jobs they want. Potential output now corresponds to an unemployment rate of about 5.5 percent to 6 percent.

In this chapter we begin our analysis of the determination of the level of output. We want to explain why GNP is not always at its potential level and why it fluctuates during the business cycle. We focus here on aggregate demand—the amount people want to spend on goods—as the main force determining the level of output. In later chapters we bring in other factors affecting the level of output and discuss the part government can play in trying to stabilize output at its potential level.

The model of income and output determination we present in this chapter was developed in the 1930s, mainly by John Maynard Keynes (1883–1946), who is widely, though not unanimously, regarded as the foremost macroeconomist of the century. The model was developed to explain the high levels of unemployment and low levels of output that persisted in most industrial economies between the two world

FIGURE 23-2   ACTUAL AND POTENTIAL GNP, 1948–1981. The gray vertical areas represent recessions. The shading between the potential and actual output curves shows situations where there is an output gap with potential above actual output. The red shading shows periods in which actual output is above potential. (*Source:* John A. Tatom, "Potential Output and the Recent Productivity Decline," in *Federal Reserve Bank of St. Louis Review,* January 1982.)

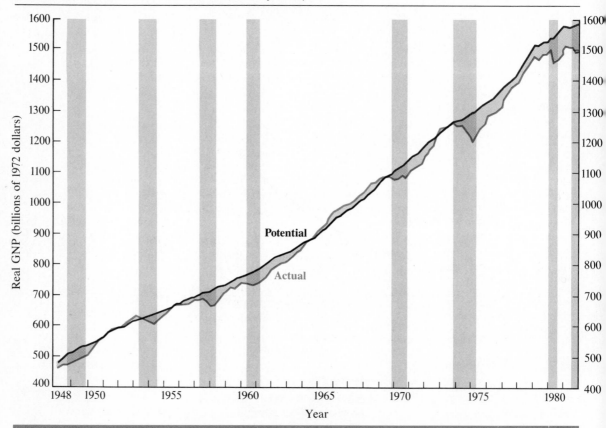

wars, in the 1920s and 1930s. In the *Great Depression* of the 1930s in the United States, unemployment reached 25 percent. One person in four who wanted to work could not find a job. The waste of output resulting from the Great Depression can be seen in the large gap between actual and trend output in Figure 23-1.

Keynesian analysis simply and definitely shows how to avoid deep depressions of the type experienced in the thirties. It is also a crucial building block in modern theories of the business cycle, which ex-

plain not only unemployment but also inflation. Our present-day ideas about the economy and economic policy still start from and build on Keynes's ideas.

After the appearance of Keynes's great book, *The General Theory of Employment, Interest and Money,* in 1936, most younger economists quickly became *Keynesians,* or followers of Keynes's economics. Later, in the 1950s and 1960s, Keynesian economics was challenged by a group of economists called *monetarists.* The intellectual leader of the monetarists was Professor Milton

Friedman of the University of Chicago. Monetarists argued that Keynesian analysis was good for understanding depressions but provided no good explanation of inflation. In this they were right. Macroeconomics today combines both the simple Keynesian model that we develop in this chapter and some elements emphasized by monetarists.

Nearly 50 years after the publication of *General Theory*, Keynesian economics has suffered the fate of all successful revolutions. It has been absorbed. Contemporary economists take a great deal of Keynesian analysis for granted as they get on with the business of analyzing how the economy works.

BOX 23-1 ▄▄▄▄▄▄▄▄▄▄▄▄▄▄▄▄▄▄▄▄▄▄▄▄▄▄▄

THE BUSINESS CYCLE IN THE UNITED STATES

Real GNP, employment, unemployment, and many other macroeconomic series show systematic patterns over time which we call the business cycle. The accompanying figure shows a sketch of the stages of the business cycle for real GNP. The cycle is made up of a sequence defined by the *peak* and *trough* in economic activity. The recession, or contraction, is the period from the peak in cyclical activity to the trough, or bottom. The recovery, or expansion, is the move up to the next peak.

THE BUSINESS CYCLE. The business cycle consists of the several-year-long movements of output relative to the trend of output and the associated movements of other economic variables. Output moves irregularly from peak through recession to trough and then into a recovery, or expansion. The business cycle is irregular both in length of time of each of the phases and from peak to peak and in the extent to which output exceeds trend output at the peak or falls short at the trough.

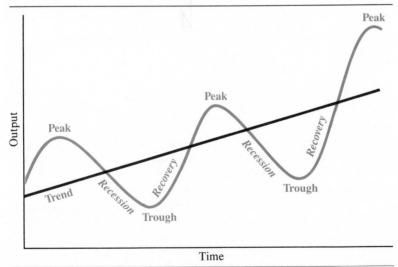

These patterns have been studied for more than 50 years for the U.S. economy by scholars associated with the National Bureau of Economic Research (NBER), a Cambridge, Massachusetts, based private, nonprofit research organization. A group of NBER wise men follows many economic time series and determines the timing of peaks and troughs in the business cycle. Their most carefully watched pronouncements are those dealing with the start of a recession, which they typically make 6 months after the recession begins. We use the NBER dating of business cycles in many figures in this book. For instance, the figure below shows the value of real GNP compared with its trend value. During recessions, which are the shaded areas between peak (P) and trough (T), real GNP is falling relative to trend. During expansions, the ratio rises and actual GNP comes to exceed its trend level.

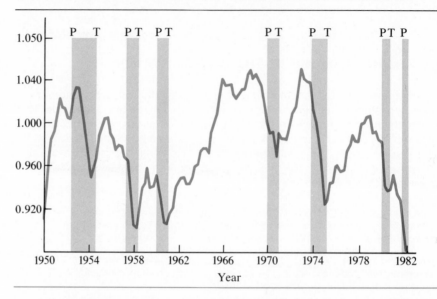

This systematic behavior of real GNP relative to trend is also shared by other time series.

A *time series* is cyclical if it shows definite patterns during the business cycle.

For instance, unemployment is highly cyclical. It rises during recessions and falls during expansions. The inflation rate, automobile sales, housing construction, the budget, and most other macroeconomic time series show cyclical patterns.

The business cycle is definitely not a matter of the past. In 1974–1975 the United States had a major recession; a recession occurred again in 1980 and yet again in 1981–1982. But even though there are still cyclical fluctuations in output, they have been much less severe since World War II.

1 THE CIRCULAR FLOW

The model of output determination that we develop in this chapter focuses on the interactions between households' spending decisions and the production decisions of firms. These interactions were shown in

Figure 21-1. Figure 23-3 presents a similar diagram that emphasizes the basic interdependence of spending decisions and production decisions.

Figure 23-3 shows how aggregate demand, or spending, determines firms' level of production or output, which in turn generates the income from which households spend. To appreciate the interactions, suppose households decide to spend less of their income. A reduction in spending confronts firms with reduced demand for their goods. Firms in turn reduce employment because they cannot sell all the goods they are producing. But that means households earn less income. With less income earned, less is spent. Therefore, the demand for goods declines even further, employment falls, income falls—and spending again falls.

Is there an end to this chain of declining demand reducing output, which in turn reduces income and demand further? The Great Depression is evidence that the economy can indeed move far from its level of potential output. We will show that there is an automatic end to the decline in activity resulting from a reduction in the demand for goods. A further question is whether government can do anything to stabilize output.

2 COMPONENTS OF AGGREGATE DEMAND, OR PLANNED SPENDING

In Figure 23-3 we emphasized household demand for goods as the source of aggregate demand. But we know from national income accounting that there are four different sectors that demand goods. Households demand consumption goods, and firms demand investment goods. The government is a source of demand, and so are foreigners. In this chapter we build a simplified model that omits the government and the rest of the world. The government is introduced again in Chapter 24, and the rest of the world in the appendix to Chapter 24.

We distinguish between the two sources of demand for goods we are examining in this chapter by writing

$$\begin{matrix} \text{Aggregate} \\ \text{demand} \end{matrix} = \begin{matrix} \text{consumption} \\ \text{demand} \end{matrix} + \begin{matrix} \text{investment} \\ \text{demand} \end{matrix} \quad (1)$$
$$AD \quad = \quad C \quad + \quad I$$

FIGURE 23-3 THE INTERDEPENDENCE OF OUTPUT AND SPENDING. The level of demand for goods determines the amount firms want to produce, as shown by the leftward-pointing arrow between aggregate demand and output. But the level of output and production determines the level of income earned by factors of production, which in turn determines aggregate spending, or demand. Change anywhere in the circle will produce change elsewhere. For instance, if households decide to spend less, firms will reduce output, and income in turn will be reduced. One question concerns what, if anything, keeps this process from continuing to reduce the level of output.

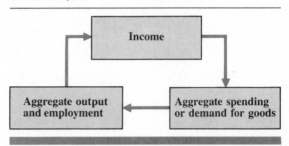

Recall from national income accounting that in the United States about 65 percent of aggregate demand, or spending, comes from consumption and about 15 percent from investment. Thus, the two sources of demand included in our simplified model account in practice for most of aggregate demand.

We distinguish between the sources of demand because each source is determined in a different way. Firms make decisions about how much to invest on the basis of how much they expect to sell in the future and how much it costs them to buy the machinery, inventories, and buildings in which they invest. Households' decisions on how much to consume are determined mainly by their income. We now discuss consumption spending.

Consumption Spending

Households buy goods and services ranging from automobiles and food to baseball bats, movie performances, and electricity. These consumption purchases amount in total to over 90 percent of their personal disposable

FIGURE 23-4   THE RELATIONSHIP BETWEEN CONSUMPTION AND INCOME, 1953–1981. (*Source: Economic Report of the President, 1982.*)

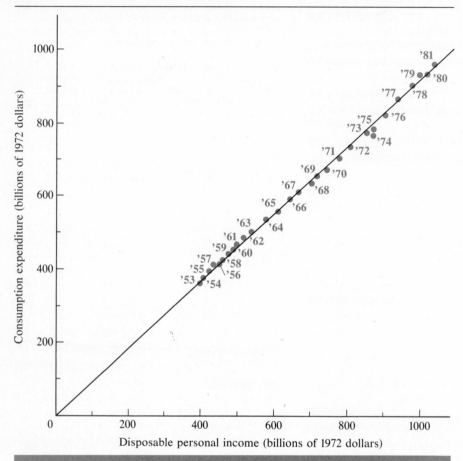

income. We recall also that personal disposable income is divided among consumption, payment of interest to firms, and saving. For simplicity we assume in this section that there are no interest payments to firms so that what households do not consume is saved. In this case, households' decisions about how much of their personal disposable income to consume are at the same time decisions about how much to save, or add to their assets.

Each household and individual has many different factors affecting its consumption and saving decisions at any particular time. One family may be saving to send its children to college. Another may be splurging because it just received an inheritance. One family has to spend large amounts on medical care and actually *dissaves*, spending more than its income by drawing down its assets, such as its checking account.

These are all specific factors affecting individual households. But each household's consumption is also systematically affected by its income. Households cannot for long spend more than their incomes unless they are very wealthy. And households with rising incomes generally want to consume more. Thus the major common influence on household consumption decisions is the level of income available for spending.

Figure 23-4 shows the relationship between consumption and disposable personal income for the period since 1953. Consumption spending rises with disposable income. The relationship is summarized by the fitted line[1] in the figure. The relationship is a strong one, as can be seen from the fact that most of the points lie close to the fitted line. Because the relationship is a close one, we shall assume in this chapter that the level of consumption demand is determined by households' income.

Although the line fits well, it does not fit exactly. Figure 23-4 shows some differences between the actual data and the fitted line. Economists have developed more refined theories that help account for the differences. The leading theories are described in Box 23-2.

The Consumption Function Figure 23-5 shows the relationship between consumption and income that we assume in the remainder of this chapter. It is based on the type of relationship seen in the line fitted to the actual data in Figure 23-4. This is the consumption function.

> The *consumption function* specifies the level of consumption for each level of personal disposable income.

In Figure 23-5 we put income rather than personal disposable income on the axis because in our simplified model we omit all the complications that create a difference between national income and personal disposable income.

As we have drawn it, the consumption function starts at the origin, showing zero consumption at zero income. Consumption is proportional to income. Consumers are

---

[1] The method and meaning of fitting lines was described in Chapter 2.

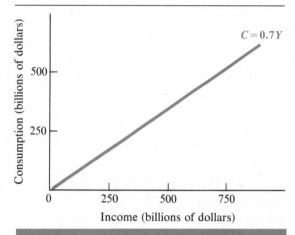

FIGURE 23-5 THE CONSUMPTION FUNCTION. The consumption function shows the level of consumption corresponding to each level of income. The consumption function shown here goes through the origin. Consumption is proportional to income. The marginal propensity to consume is 0.7, meaning that 70 cents of every extra dollar in income is consumed. The remaining 30 cents is saved.

shown spending 70 percent of income. Consumption will be proportional to income any time the consumption function is a straight line through the origin, as it is here.

Given that the straight-line consumption function starts at the origin, the only remaining characteristic to be examined is its slope. The slope of the consumption function is the marginal propensity to consume.

> The *marginal propensity to consume* is the fraction of a dollar by which consumption increases when income rises by a dollar.

In Figure 23-5 the marginal propensity to consume is 0.7. When consumers' income rises by a dollar, they increase consumption by 70 cents. We denote the marginal propensity to consume by *MPC*.

What about the part of income that is not consumed? That amount is saved. Under the assumption that there are no interest payments to business, saving is the amount of income that is not consumed. In Figure 23-5, 30 cents out of every dollar of income

FIGURE 23-6   THE SAVING FUNCTION. The saving function shows the amount saved at each level of income. The shape of the saving function is implied by the consumption function. Whatever part of income is not consumed is saved.

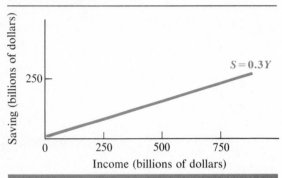

is saved. The marginal propensity to save (*MPS*) is the fraction of every extra dollar of income that is saved. The saving function is of course implied by the consumption function and vice versa. If we know one, we can figure out the other. Figure 23-6 shows the saving function corresponding to the consumption function in Figure 23-5.

In Figures 23-5 and 23-6 we write the equations that describe the consumption and saving functions. The symbol Y stands for income. The consumption function is written $C = 0.7Y$, indicating that consumption is equal to 0.7 of income, or 70 percent of income. It also implies that the *MPC* is 0.7. Similarly, the saving function is written $S = 0.3Y$, implying that 30 percent of income is saved.

Investment Spending

We have now identified income as the key determinant of household consumption or spending plans, as described by the consumption function. What can be said about the factors that determine investment demand by firms?

> *Investment demand* consists of firms' desired or planned additions to their physical capital (factories and machines) and to their inventories.

Inventories consist of goods being held for future production or sale.

Firms' investment demand is examined in detail in Chapter 27. A firm's plans to expand its production facilities by adding machinery or buildings, and its plans for inventory, depend in part on the demand it expects for its goods in the future. The demand it expects is affected in turn by current demand. If the economy is in a recession, firms probably do not expect demand to be at a high level very soon and therefore need not hurry to get factories built and new machines installed. Despite this link between the current level of income and investment demand, we make the strong assumption that investment demand is constant and independent of the level of income. Firms are assumed to have a given demand for investment whatever the economy's levels of output and employment.

3   AGGREGATE DEMAND

> *Aggregate demand* is the amount firms and households plan to spend on goods and services at each level of income.

With net exports and government excluded, aggregate demand consists, as equation (1)

BOX 23-2

THEORIES OF CONSUMPTION

The consumption function in Figure 23-4 is a good first description of the facts about aggregate consumption. But more sophisticated theories have been developed to help account for differences between actual data and the fitted line. The two leading theories are the permanent income theory developed by Milton Friedman of the University of Chicago and the life cycle theory of Franco Modigliani of MIT and Albert Ando of the University of Pennsylvania.

PERMANENT INCOME

This theory argues that consumption is proportional to income, as Figure 23-4 suggests, but not proportional to *current* income. It argues that households' consumption is determined by *permanent* rather than current income, where permanent income is defined as an average of income over periods longer than a year.

The theory is especially insightful in explaining how households react to temporary changes in income. For instance, suppose that a household's income falls because of sickness of the income earner and that the sickness is known to be of a type that lasts no more than a year. If consumption were proportional to current income, the household would cut consumption in the same proportion as its income has fallen. But permanent income theory tells us that if household income has fallen only temporarily, consumption is not cut so much. Rather, the household will run down its assets, or borrow, to maintain its standard of living. This is indeed the way people behave when income falls temporarily.

In the macroeconomic context, permanent income theory predicts that if a recession is expected to last only a short time, consumption will not fall as much as it would if the same fall in income was expected to be permanent.

LIFE CYCLE CONSUMPTION

This theory, too, argues that consumption is related to income over a longer period than a year—in this case, the period is the entire lifetime of the individual or household. People look ahead and try to estimate the incomes they will receive in the future. Future income affects current consumption. People who have high income now but expect low income in the future will save. People who expect higher income in the future will borrow now and be willing to go into debt to have a high level of current consumption.

Life cycle theory explains why, for instance, students live at a much better level than their incomes suggest. They are looking forward to higher income in the future, possibly borrowing to consume now and pay later. The theory also suggests that much saving is done specifically for retirement, when income will be low. Individuals save during their high-earning years and then draw on savings in the years when they earn little, which includes the retirement years.

The two theories share the view that individuals' consumption is affected by income over longer periods than a year. This implies that consumption may be less sensitive to current changes in income than Figure 23-4 might imply. If income changes for a year but does not much change individuals' beliefs about their permanent incomes or lifetime incomes, the income change will have much less effect on consumption than it would if it was expected to last for a long time.

Both theories have been successful in providing more accurate predictions about the consumption of individual households and about aggregate consumption than the simple theory we use. But the refinements are not needed for our analysis of income determination.

FIGURE 23-7 AGGREGATE DEMAND. Aggregate demand is the sum of the amounts households plan to spend on consumption and firms plan to spend on investment. Since we are assuming investment demand is constant, consumption is the only source of demand that increases with income. The line labeled C shows the consumption function of Figure 23-5. The demand for investment is added to consumption demand to give aggregate demand, as shown by the line AD.

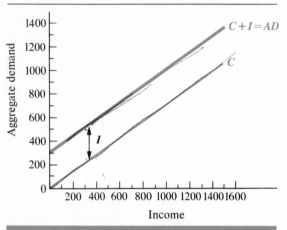

showed, of households' consumption demand and firms' demand for investment goods.

The Aggregate Demand Schedule

Figure 23-7 shows the *aggregate demand schedule*. The aggregate demand schedule shows the planned level of spending on goods and services at each level of income. Figure 23-7 starts with the consumption function from Figure 23-5. At each level of income we add the given demand for investment goods to obtain the total, or aggregate, demand for goods at that level of income.

In Figure 23-7 we assume that the amount firms want to invest, I, is equal to $300 billion. (From now on we omit both the dollar signs and the billions). Thus aggregate demand exceeds consumption demand at each level of income by 300. At an income level of zero, where consumption

demand is zero, aggregate demand is 300. At an income level of 1000, where consumption demand is 700, aggregate demand is equal to 1000 (700 + 300). At an income level of 1200, aggregate demand is 1140 [(0.7 × 1200) + 300].

Figure 23-7 shows how aggregate demand increases with income. Since consumption is the only component of aggregate demand that increases with income, the total increase in aggregate demand when income rises by a dollar comes from increased consumption. We know that consumption demand increases by 70 cents for every dollar that income rises. Therefore, in Figure 23-7 aggregate demand, too, increases by 70 cents for every dollar that income increases. With investment not changing as the level of income changes, the *MPC* tells us how much aggregate demand rises with the level of income.

We now use the aggregate demand schedule to analyze how the level of output is determined. In doing so we cut through the interactions shown in Figure 23-3, in which the demand for goods determines firms' production levels, which in turn determine the economy's level of income and thereby determine the demand for goods. Before doing so, we introduce a useful tool, the 45° diagram.

The 45° Diagram

Figure 23-8 shows income on the horizontal axis and spending on the vertical axis. It also includes a 45° line. The special property of the 45° line is that at any point on the line, the value of the variable on the horizontal axis (here it is income) is equal to the value of the variable on the vertical axis (here it is spending). For instance, look at the income level of 400. Go up to point B on the 45° line and then go across to the spending axis. Spending corresponding to point B is also 400, and we could show the same for any level of income and spending.

FIGURE 23-8 THE 45° DIAGRAM. The 45° line has the property that the value of the variable on the horizontal axis is equal to the value of the variable on the vertical axis. For instance, look at point B. Starting at the income level of 400 and going up to the 45° line and across to the vertical axis, we see that the level of spending corresponding to B is also equal to 400. The point at which the AD curve cuts the 45° line at point E is the only point at which aggregate demand (AD) is equal to income.

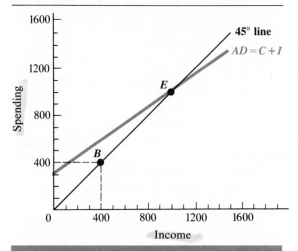

The usefulness of the diagram can be seen when we add the AD line, where AD is aggregate demand (equal to C + I). The AD line crosses the 45° line at point E. At point E, which is on the 45° line, we know that the value of the variable on the horizontal axis (income) is equal to the value of the variable on the vertical axis (spending). Thus at point E, income is equal to spending. This is the *only* point on the AD curve where that is true, because it is the only point at which the AD curve touches or crosses the 45° line. We will now use the 45° line to analyze equilibrium output and income.

4 EQUILIBRIUM OUTPUT

To show how the level of output is determined, we make two further assumptions. First, we assume that the level of output, or GNP, is equal to the level of national income, which in turn is equal to disposable

personal income. The underlying assumptions are that there is no depreciation and no taxes, that all profits are paid out to households, and that there are no interest or transfer payments.[2] Firms in this economy produce goods and services and pay out the proceeds to households, either as wages or as profits. Thus output is equal to income.

The second assumption deserves emphasis. We assume that *prices* in this economy *are given and constant*. Firms are willing to supply any quantity of goods and services demanded at the prevailing prices. The idea here is that firms have enough capacity (machinery, structures, and management) on hand to increase output. They can also hire labor at the going wage rate. With firms willing to supply any amount of goods and services at the given level of prices, the demand side of the market—namely, aggregate demand for goods and services—will determine the level of output.

We shall maintain the assumption that prices are given and constant for the next few chapters. But of course, they are not constant in the real world, and in Chapter 28 we allow prices to change. But even there we shall see that the analysis now carried out with fixed prices is useful in understanding inflation.

Definition of Equilibrium

The goods market is *in equilibrium* when, at the going level of prices, the level of output supplied is equal to aggregate demand, or planned aggregate spending.

Figure 23-9 shows equilibrium output at point E. What is special about the point that makes it a point of equilibrium? At that point, firms are producing output equal to 1000. That output in turn is equal to income.

---

[2] Check back to Chapter 22 to make sure these simplifications ensure that personal disposable income is equal to GNP.

FIGURE 23-9 THE DETERMINATION OF EQUILIB-RIUM OUTPUT. At point *E*, the demand for goods, shown by the *AD* curve, is equal to the level of output. At *E*, aggregate demand is equal to 1000. That is the amount individuals and firms together wish to purchase; it is also the amount being produced. Since the amount being produced is equal to the amount demanded, there is equilibrium in the market for goods and services at the level of output of 1000. At any other level of output (income), aggregate demand will not be equal to output. For instance, at an output level of 300, aggregate demand exceeds output. Similarly, at output levels above 1000, output exceeds aggregate demand.

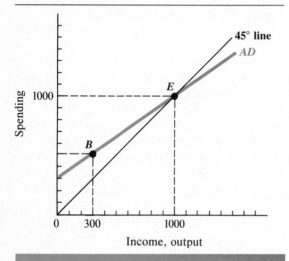

At an income level of 1000, we can read from the *AD* curve that the demand for goods is equal to 1000. Thus at point *E*, the demand for goods is exactly equal to the amount being produced. The quantity of goods supplied is equal to the quantity demanded at the going level of prices. This is the same definition of equilibrium output we used in studying demand and supply in a single market in Chapter 3.

At any output level other than 1000 in Figure 23-9, output is not equal to aggregate demand. For instance, suppose output is only 300. That amount of output is exactly what is demanded by firms for investment. But there is still more demand for goods coming from the households that are earning 300 in income and therefore want to

spend 210 (70 percent of income) on consumption. At an output level of 300, there is therefore an excess demand for goods. More goods are demanded than are being produced. Similarly, for any level of output above 1000, more goods are being produced than are demanded. Only at the output level of 1000 is output equal to aggregate demand.

Thus we have our first model of the determination of the level of aggregate output, or GNP. The model is built around the circular flow diagram in Figure 23-3. The equilibrium level of output is that level at which the demand for goods—generated in part by the income resulting from output produced—is equal to output. In terms of the figure, the interaction of spending and output is shown by the fact that equilibrium is on the 45° line, at which demand for goods is equal to income.

Adjustment to Equilibrium

To understand how the economy gets to the equilibrium level of output at point *E* in Figure 23-9, we consider what is happening at any level of output other than 1000. Suppose first that output is below the equilibrium level, say, at 300. At an output level of 300, aggregate demand is 510, as we saw above. Aggregate demand exceeds production. If firms have inventories or stocks of goods available, they can sell more than they produce for a while. But as they do, their stocks run down. If firms do not have inventories of goods, they have to turn away customers who want to buy goods but now cannot. Firms are likely to respond to declining inventories or unsatisfied customers by raising output. This is shown in the first row of Table 23-1.

At *any* output level below 1000, aggregate demand exceeds output. Firms are either running down their inventories or turning away customers, and they therefore are likely to increase production. This implies

TABLE 23-1

AGGREGATE DEMAND AND OUTPUT ADJUSTMENT

OUTPUT LEVEL, Y	I	C = 0.7Y	AD = C + I	Y − AD	INVENTORIES ARE*	OUTPUT IS
300	300	210	510	−210	Falling	Increasing
800	300	560	860	− 60	Falling	Increasing
1000	300	700	1000	0	Constant	Constant
1200	300	840	1140	+ 60	Increasing	Falling
1500	300	1050	1350	+150	Increasing	Falling

* These are unplanned or undesired inventory changes.

that whenever output is below the equilibrium level, it is increasing, as Table 23-1 shows.

Similarly, suppose output is above 1000, at a level of 1200. Table 23-1 shows that aggregate demand is only 1140, which is below the level of output. Now firms are producing more than they can sell. Production is 1200, but quantity demanded is only 1140. Firms are adding to their stocks of goods, but these are not additions to inventories that the firms want to make. If firms did want to make them, they would count as part of investment demand (recall that investment includes firms' desired additions to inventories), and we would not be in a situation where aggregate demand is less than output. When aggregate demand falls short of output, firms make *undesired* or *unplanned* additions to inventories. In response to these undesired additions to inventories, firms cut their output levels. At any output level above 1000, there will be unplanned or undesired additions to inventories, and firms will therefore be cutting output.

We have thus shown that output is cut if it is above 1000 and is increased if it is below 1000. Thus the level of output in the economy will be 1000, or the level at which aggregate demand is equal to output.

Equilibrium Output and Employment The income level of 1000 in Figure 23-9 is an equilibrium level in the sense that aggregate demand is equal to output so that firms are selling all the goods they produce and households and firms are able to buy the goods they want. But we have not discussed the level of employment or asked whether this is necessarily a situation in which everyone who wants to work is doing so.

There is nothing in the analysis so far that ensures the economy will reach a level of output at which there is full employment. In terms of potential output, in Figure 23-10 we could have actual output at level Y_o while potential output is equal to Y_p. There is an output gap at point E, but nothing in the analysis of aggregate demand suggests the gap will be closed.

Indeed, the point of our analysis is that the economy can end up with an output level below potential, without any forces being present to move output to the potential level. Firms have no incentive to hire unemployed workers to increase production, since they will not be able to sell the increased output. At the given level of prices, the lack of aggregate demand stands in the way of an expansion of output to the full-employment level.

The emphasis is on the fact that firms will not hire more workers than they need to produce the output they can sell. Aggregate demand determines the levels of output and employment. The role of aggregate demand will become more clear when we look at the effects on output of a shift in the aggregate demand curve.

FIGURE 23-10 ACTUAL AND POTENTIAL OUTPUT AND THE OUTPUT GAP. The equilibrium of aggregate demand with output does not guarantee that output is at its potential level. There may be unemployment at the equilibrium level of output Y_o, reflected in the output gap ($Y_p - Y_o$). Here Y_p is the level of potential output.

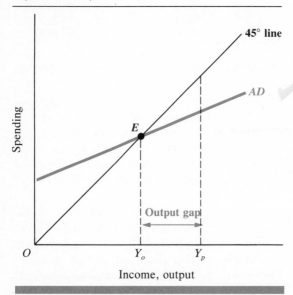

5 ANOTHER APPROACH: SAVING EQUALS INVESTMENT

Figure 23-9 shows how the equilibrium level of output is determined where aggregate demand is equal to output. An equivalent way of showing how the equilibrium level of output is determined is by noting that at the equilibrium level of output, saving is equal to investment in this simplified model that excludes the government and the foreign sector.

To show this we start from Figure 23-9, which shows that in equilibrium income equals consumption plus investment. Equivalently, income minus consumption is equal to investment:

$$I = Y - C \tag{2}$$

Next we remember that the part of income which the household does not spend on consumption is saved. Saving therefore is equal to income minus consumption, which we can write as $S = Y - C$. Using this relationship in equation (2), we see that both saving and investment are, in equilibrium, equal to income minus consumption. Thus, in equilibrium,

$$S = I \tag{3}$$

This can be stated in words: When there is goods market equilibrium, saving equals investment.

This condition has a simple interpretation in an economy where the same people do the saving and investing. For instance, think of a person managing a farm. The person consumes part of the crop and puts part aside as seeds for next year. The part that is put aside is saved. It is also invested because the farmer is adding to his desired inventory of corn. For this farmer, saving is automatically equal to investment.

But in modern economies, in which firms do the investing and households do the saving, the connection between saving and investment is not automatic. Income has to be at its equilibrium level for saving to equal investment. Figure 23-11 shows how the equilibrium level of output is determined, using the same data as Figure 23-9. The demand for investment goods is 300, and the *MPC* is 0.7. The saving function in Figure 23-11 is the same as that in Figure 23-6. Saving is equal to investment only at the equilibrium level of output, 1000.

If output is above 1000, households want to save more than firms want to invest. Saving is the part of income they do not consume. They thus are consuming too little for the given level of output to be an equilibrium level. Inventories are piling up, and firms decide to cut production. On the other side, with output below the equilibrium level, investment exceeds saving. Consumption and investment demands be-

FIGURE 23-11   THE DETERMINATION OF EQUILIB-RIUM OUTPUT: THE SAVING EQUALS INVESTMENT APPROACH. The equilibrium level of output is 1000, the level at which saving is equal to investment. This figure presents another way of viewing the determi-nation of equilibrium output shown in Figure 23-9. The saving function, $S = 0.3Y$, is implied by the con-sumption function in Figure 23-9, where the *MPC* is 0.7. The level of investment of 300 is the same as that in Figure 23-9. And saving is equal to investment at the same output level, 1000. To the right of *E*, households save more than firms want to invest. Their excess saving causes goods to pile up in in-ventories, and firms cut production. To the left of *E*, households save less than firms want to invest. In-ventories are being reduced, and firms therefore in-crease output.

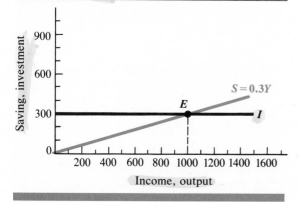

tween them exceed output, and firms are drawing down their inventories. They raise output, and output moves toward the equi-librium level.

Rather than think about saving and in-vestment in the abstract, it makes sense to think of households saving by making loans to firms, and firms having to borrow from households in order to pay for the invest-ment goods they buy. Then we can think of saving as the amount of loans households want to make to firms and investment as the amount firms want to borrow from house-holds. At the equilibrium level of output, the amount firms want to borrow is equal to the amount households want to lend.

The saving equals investment approach is logically the same as the aggregate de-mand equals output approach to the deter-

mination of output. We can use either method to get the same correct answers to the questions of how the equilibrium level of output is determined and how it changes when some component of demand, such as investment, changes. We concentrate on the aggregate demand equals output approach because it will be easier to use when we bring the government back into the picture. But either method can be used.

6   A FALL IN AGGREGATE DEMAND

We have seen how aggregate demand deter-mines the level of output. But what happens to the equilibrium level of output when ag-gregate demand changes? Specifically, sup-pose investment demand drops from 300 to 240. Firms become less optimistic about their prospects and decide to buy fewer new machines to use in producing output to meet future demand; investment demand falls. As a result of the drop in investment demand, aggregate demand for goods drops by 60 at every level of income. The aggre-gate demand curve in Figure 23-12 shifts from *AD* to *AD'*.

Before we go into the details, we want to think about what is likely to happen to the level of output. It will certainly fall, be-cause the demand for goods has fallen. But how far will output fall? When the quantity of goods demanded falls by 60, firms cut back production. That means households have lower income, and they in turn cut back their consumption demand. Firms cut production more. Thus output will probably fall by more than 60. But how far will it fall and what, if anything, brings the process of falling output to an end?

Figure 23-12 shows that a downward shift of the aggregate demand schedule by 60 reduces the equilibrium level of output from an initial level of 1000 at point *E* to 800 at point *E'*. Output does indeed fall by more than the reduction in investment demand of

FIGURE 23-12 A FALL IN INVESTMENT DEMAND REDUCES OUTPUT. When investment demand falls from 300 to 240, the aggregate demand curve shifts from *AD* to *AD'*. It shifts down by 60 at every level of output, since that is the amount by which aggregate demand has been reduced at each level of output. The shift in the aggregate demand curve reduces the level of output as the economy moves from point *E* to *E'*. The equilibrium reduction in income is 200 as output drops to 800 from its former level of 1000. Thus the drop in investment demand of 60 has multiplied (larger) effects on total spending.

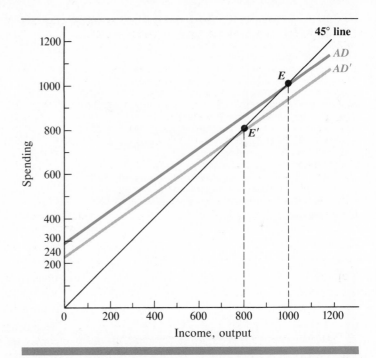

60, but it does not fall all the way to zero. There is a new equilibrium level of output at 800.

Now we want to understand both why the level of output drops by more than the 60-unit reduction in investment demand and also why it drops by 200 rather than any other amount. Table 23-2 explains. Step 1 shows the original equilibrium from Table 23-1, with investment demand still at 300 and output at the equilibrium level of 1000. In step 2 there is a drop in the demand for investment goods to 240. We assume that firms did not expect demand to change and therefore still produce 1000. But that means output exceeds aggregate demand by 60 units. Firms add these goods to their inventories and respond to the excess of output over quantity demanded by cutting production.

Step 3 shows the firms producing only 940. That is the level of output that would just meet the demand for goods at step 2. But when firms cut the level of output, in-

come falls, and therefore the quantity of consumption goods demanded also falls. Thus at step 3 consumption has fallen below its initial level of 700. The fall of 42 units in consumption is entirely due to firms' cutting back production by 60 units. Since the *MPC* is 0.7, a reduction in output and income of 60 reduces consumption demand by 42. Firms produce 940 because aggregate demand has fallen. But aggregate demand (in this case consumption) falls further as a result of the decline in income to 940. Therefore, in step 3 output is still above aggregate demand. The excess is now 42 units. Again inventories are increasing, and again firms respond by cutting output.

At step 4 we assume firms are producing enough to meet the demand for goods seen at step 3. Output is 898. But once again the cut in output reduces income and therefore reduces consumption demand. At step 4 output again exceeds aggregate demand. Firms are unwillingly adding to inventories and again decide to cut output. Note that at

TABLE 23-2
ADJUSTMENT TO A SHIFT IN INVESTMENT DEMAND

	OUTPUT, Y	I	C = 0.7Y	AD = C + I	Y − AD	INVENTORIES ARE*	OUTPUT IS
Step 1	1000	300	700	1000	0	Constant	Constant
Step 2	1000	240	700	940	60	Increasing	Being reduced
Step 3	940	240	658	898	42	Increasing	Being reduced
Step 4	898	240	628.6	868.6	29.4	Increasing	Being reduced
Step 5	868.6	240	608.02	848.02	20.58	Increasing	Being reduced
⋮							
New equi-librium	800	240	560	800	0	Constant	Constant

* This represents *undesired* inventory investment.

each step the excess of output above aggregate demand is smaller than at the previous step.

The process will keep going until it reaches the new equilibrium level of output, or 800. Only at that level of output is aggregate demand equal to output. There is no excess of output over demand, undesired inventories are not being accumulated, and output is therefore kept constant.

How long does it take for the economy to reach the new equilibrium? That depends on how well firms can figure out what is going on during the process. If they mechanically produce during each period to meet the demand they saw in the last period, it can take a long time to adjust. But smart firms will recognize that period after period they are producing too much and adding to unwanted inventories, and therefore they will adjust to the new equilibrium more quickly than Table 23-2 suggests.

We can now answer the first question we asked: Why does the level of output fall by more than 60 when investment demand falls by 60? The answer is that when firms cut output because demand has fallen, consumption demand also falls. Thus between the old equilibrium at E and the new equilibrium at E' in Figure 23-11, aggregate demand falls *both* because investment demand is lower and because the quantity of

consumption goods demanded is lower. The lower demand for consumption goods is a result of the drop in production and income that is caused by lower investment demand.

To answer the second question—Why is the drop in output exactly 200 and not some other amount?—we introduce the multiplier.

> The *multiplier* is the ratio of the change in equilibrium output to the change in investment that causes the output change.

In the example of Figure 23-12, the initial change in investment was 60, and the final change in output was 200. The multiplier is thus equal to 3.33 (200/60). We now examine the multiplier in more detail.

7 THE MULTIPLIER

The multiplier tells us how much output changes when there is a shift in aggregate demand. When the multiplier is more than 1, a 1-unit change in aggregate demand produces a larger change in equilibrium output. For instance, in Figure 23-12, where the multiplier is 3.33, a $1 increase in investment demand increases equilibrium output by $3.33.

The multiplier is larger than 1 because any given change in investment demand

TABLE 23-3

CALCULATING THE MULTIPLIER

	CHANGE IN Y	CHANGE IN C (0.7 × change in Y)	CHANGE IN I
Step 1	0	0	1
Step 2	1	0.7	0
Step 3	0.7	0.7×0.7	0
Step 4	$(0.7)^2$ or 0.49	$0.7 \times (0.7)^2$	0
Step 5	$(0.7)^3$ or 0.343	$0.7 \times (0.7)^3$	0
Step 6	$(0.7)^4$ or 0.2401	$0.7 \times (0.7)^4$	0
⋮	⋮	⋮	

sets off further changes in the quantity of consumption goods demanded. This gives us a clue about what the size of the multiplier depends on. We should expect the multiplier to be related to the marginal propensity to consume. If the *MPC* is large, a 1-unit increase in investment demand that leads to a 1-unit increase in output and income will cause a large change in consumption demand. The multiplier will be big. If the *MPC* is small, a given change in investment demand and output will cause only small changes in the quantity of consumption goods demanded, and the multiplier will be small.

We obtain an exact formula for the multiplier by going through a series of steps like those in Table 23-2. Table 23-3 starts with a 1-unit *increase* in investment demand. Firms see their inventories falling. At step 2, they react to the increase in demand in step 1 and raise output by 1 unit. Consumption accordingly changes by 0.7, or the marginal propensity to consume times the change in income and output. At step 3, firms increase output by 0.7 to meet the increased consumption demand seen in step 2. That in turn further increases consumption demanded by 0.49 (0.7 times the increase in income), leading at step 4 to an increase in output of $(0.7)^2$, or 0.49. Consumption increases again, and the process continues.

To find the value of the multiplier, we add together all the increases in output from each step in the table, and then we keep going. The total change in output is found by adding together the terms from the first column of Table 23-3:

$$\text{Multiplier} = 1 + 0.7 + (0.7)^2 \\ + (0.7)^3 + (0.7)^4 + (0.7)^5 + \ldots \quad (4)$$

The dots mean that we keep adding terms like those in equation (4) without end. An expression like equation (4) for the multiplier can be simplified. The value of the sum of all the numbers in equation (4), including the numbers not explicitly included but shown instead by dots, is known to be

$$\text{Multiplier} = \frac{1}{1 - 0.7} \quad (5)$$

This is a formula for the multiplier for the case in Table 23-3, where the *MPC* is 0.7. But a similar formula applies whatever the value of the *MPC*. Thus the general formula for the multiplier is

$$\text{Multiplier} = \frac{1}{1 - MPC} \quad (6)$$

With the *MPC* in Table 23-3 equal to 0.7, we see that the multiplier in this case is 3.33 $[1/(1 - 0.7)]$.

We can check on the formula for the multiplier by drawing another diagram. This time we assume the *MPC* is 0.5. In Figure 23-13, the level of investment is originally 300 and then rises to 400. According to

FIGURE 23-13   THE MULTIPLIER. Investment demand increases by 100, from 300 to 400. With an *MPC* equal to 0.5, equation (8) tells us the multiplier is 2. Thus equilibrium output should increase by 200 when investment demand increases by 100. The figure shows that output does increase by 200, from 600 at *E* to 800 at *E'*.

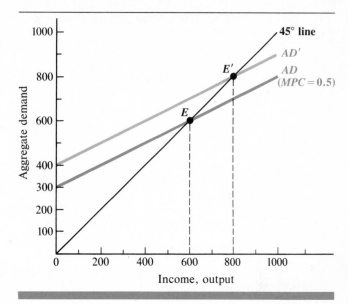

equation (6) for the multiplier, income should rise by two times [1/(1 − 0.5)] the increase in investment. Income should rise by 200. Looking at Figure 23-13, that is exactly what happens as the increase in investment causes income to rise from 600 at *E* to 800 at *E'*.

Our guess that the multiplier would be larger the higher the *MPC* is confirmed by equation (6). The equation shows that the multiplier is larger the larger the *MPC*. For instance, with an *MPC* of 0.5, the multiplier is 2. With an *MPC* of 0.7, the multiplier is 3.33. With an *MPC* of 0.9, the multiplier is 10.

The Multiplier and the *MPS*   The formula for the multiplier given in equation (6) can be written in another way when we recall that the sum of the *MPC* and the *MPS* (marginal propensity to save) is 1. Whatever part of an extra dollar of income is not consumed is saved. The term (1 − *MPC*) in equation (7) is therefore equal to the *MPS*. For instance, with an *MPC* of 0.7, (1 − 0.7) is equal to 0.3, which is the *MPS*. It follows

that we can write the multiplier as equal to 1/*MPS*.

In this form of the expression for the multiplier, we see that the multiplier is smaller the larger the *MPS*. The source of the multiplier is the increase in consumption that takes place when output rises. If the *MPS* is large, any given increase in output does not increase consumption much, and the multiplier is therefore small.

8   THE PARADOX OF THRIFT

We now use the income determination model to analyze what happens when households want to change their saving behavior. Initially the economy is in equilibrium with output equal to 1000, investment at 300, and the *MPC* equal to 0.7. Now households decide they want to save 100 less at each level of income. In terms of Figure 23-14*a*, the saving function shifts down from *SA* to *SA'*, at which saving is lower by 100 at every level of income. Equivalently, they decide to increase consumption by 100 units at each

FIGURE 23-14 SHIFT IN THE CONSUMPTION FUNCTION. Households decide they want to save 100 units less at each level of income. The saving function shifts downward by 100. The consumption function therefore shifts upward by 100, from *CC* to *CC'*, because a reduction in the amount of saving at any given level of income implies an increase by the same amount in consumption.

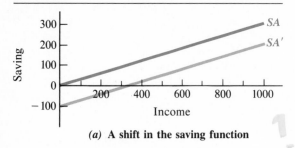

(a) **A shift in the saving function**

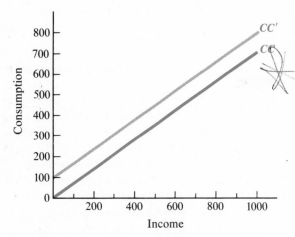

(b) **The equivalent shift in the consumption function**

income level, shifting the consumption function from *CC* to *CC'* in Figure 23-14*b*.[3]

---

[3] The consumption function *CC'* in Figure 23-14*b* shows an intercept on the vertical axis, meaning that people would spend on consumption goods even if their income were zero. That, of course, is possible only if they can *dissave*, selling off assets such as houses or cars to finance the excess of spending over income. It used to be thought that the consumption function always looks like *CC'* in Figure 23-14*b*, with a substantial intercept. Today the data suggest, however, that it more nearly passes through the origin, as seen in the plot in Figure 23-4.

What happens to the *actual* level of saving when households want to save less? Figure 23-15 shows the effects of the reduced desire to save in the shift of the aggregate demand function from *AD* to *AD'*. The new aggregate demand function is above the old one by 100 at all levels of income.

The equilibrium shifts from *E* to *E'*, and the level of income and output rises from 1000 to 1333. Income rises as a result of the increased desire to save less. But the actual amount of saving does not change at all. In the new equilibrium, saving is still equal to 300, or the amount of investment. Households started out wanting to save less. They end up with higher incomes and no change at all in the amount of saving they do.

This is the paradox of thrift. The paradox is that a change in the amount households want to save can end up having no effect at all on saving, although it does lead to a higher income level. If we had thought of the saving equals investment approach before drawing the figure, we would have realized that with investment given and equal to 300, saving would, in equilibrium, have to end up back at its original level of 300.

The paradox of thrift is more than a curiosity. Rather, it is a help to understanding an old argument about the virtues of saving and spending. One school argues that people who consume do good for society. By spending, they provide jobs for other people. The other group argues that saving is a good thing, because it enables individuals and society to provide for more consumption in the future.

The argument emerges typically in times of recession, when there does not seem to be enough aggregate demand to keep everyone employed. The paradox of thrift suggests that if the problem is a lack of demand, as it is at times of high unemployment, the private virtue of saving is not a public virtue. At a time of recession, or

FIGURE 23-15 THE PARADOX OF THRIFT. The shift in the consumption function in Figure 23-14*b* results in a shift in the aggregate demand schedule to *AD'*. The equilibrium level of income rises to 1333 from 1000. This change in income was set off by households deciding they wanted to save less. But the final result is that they save exactly the same amount, 300, with the only effect of the changed desire to save being a change in the level of income.

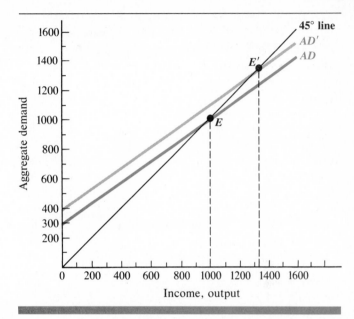

worse, depression, people who reduce saving are indeed adding to aggregate demand and increasing employment, as in Figure 23-15.

All this is very different when the economy is already at full employment. If the economy is working well, with full employment being maintained, an increase in the desire to save will lead to increased actual saving. We shall analyze the mechanisms that might maintain full employment later, when we make our simplified model more realistic by providing a role for money and considering the possibility that the price level can change. But the lesson of the paradox of thrift is indeed valid so long as we understand it applies to situations in which the economy is suffering from low aggregate demand.

9   INVESTMENT AND OUTPUT

The model of output determination in this chapter includes only consumption and investment as sources of aggregate demand. The level of investment and the consumption function between them determine the level of output. If investment demand changes or if the consumption function changes, the level of output will change.

The Keynesian tradition has been to emphasize changes in investment demand as the main source of movements in output. Consumption appears statistically to be closely related to the level of income so that the consumption function does not change much over time. But investment demand is bound to be based on expectations about the future. Firms that invest are making plans on the basis of what they think will happen to the demand for their goods in the future, sometimes the very distant future. Investment decisions about building a factory or power station depend on what firms think demand will be as much as 10 years down the road. Since there is no way of knowing for sure what demand will be, Keynes argued that investment demand was bound to be strongly affected by the pessimism or optimism of the investors—what he called the *animal spirits* of the investors.

There is another reason to emphasize

investment fluctuations as a potentially major source of changes in output. Investment is often made in response to new discoveries. Thus there were investment booms in the United States in the nineteenth century as the railroads were built and in the 1920s as the automobile and home appliances reached the majority of American families for the first time. But useful new inventions do not come along at a steady rate. When they arrive, investment demand is high, and there is a boom. When there are few new inventions, investment demand is lower, and so is output.

For both these reasons, investment demand is the more likely source of the movements of GNP shown in Figure 23-1. And certainly movements in investment demand are a major source of the cyclical movements in output shown in Figure 23-2.

Although simplified, the model presented in this chapter provides useful insights about the determination of output. The most obvious question it raises is whether anything can be done to affect the level of output, and particularly to try to keep output close to its potential level so that there is full employment in the economy. We begin to answer that question in Chapter 24, when we bring in the role of the government, introducing both government spending and taxation.

SUMMARY

1   The demand for goods comes from consumption demand by households, investment demand by firms, and the demands of the government and foreigners. In this chapter we use a simple model of aggregate demand, focusing on consumption and investment. Between them, they account for about 80 percent of total demand in the United States.

2   Consumption demand is determined in large part by households' income. The data show a strong though not perfect relationship between consumption and personal disposable income.

3   The marginal propensity to consume (MPC) is the fraction by which consumption rises when income goes up a dollar. Leaving aside personal interest payments to firms, any part of income that is not consumed is saved. The marginal propensity to save (MPS) is the fraction of an extra dollar of income that is saved. The MPC and the MPS sum to 1, since income is either consumed or saved.

4   In this chapter we treat investment demand as constant. Investment demand is firms' *desired* additions to physical capital—machinery and buildings—and to inventories.

5   Aggregate demand is the amount all spending units in the economy plan to spend on goods. The aggregate demand schedule shows the level of aggregate demand at each level of income.

6   The goods market is in equilibrium when at a given price level,

output produced is equal to planned aggregate spending, or aggregate demand. Equivalently, the equilibrium level of output, or income, is the level at which aggregate demand is equal to income.

7 Adjustment toward the equilibrium level of output takes place through firms' responses to undesired or unplanned additions to inventories. When output is above the equilibrium level, the demand for goods is below output, and inventories are being accumulated. Firms therefore cut output. Similarly, when output is below the equilibrium level, inventories are being reduced, and firms increase production.

8 Equilibrium in the goods market does not mean that output is at the potential, or full-employment, level. With prices given, output may settle at some level below potential, with firms unwilling to increase production because they do not believe they will be able to sell more.

9 The equilibrium condition that determines the level of output, or aggregate demand equal to income, can equivalently be expressed as the equality of saving and investment.

10 An increase in planned investment demand leads to a larger increase in equilibrium output. The increase is larger because the increase in output to meet higher investment demand also causes an increase in consumption demand.

11 The multiplier is the ratio of the increase in output to the increase in demand that causes output to rise. In the simple model of this chapter, the multiplier is equal to $1/(1 - MPC)$, or the inverse of the marginal propensity to save.

12 The paradox of thrift shows that a reduced desire to save may result in no change in saving at all and only a higher level of output. The paradox shows that increased saving at a time of insufficient aggregate demand is not a virtue, even though we think of saving as a good thing.

KEY TERMS

Potential output	Aggregate demand schedule
Output gap	Undesired or unplanned inventory
Consumption function	investment
Marginal propensity to consume (MPC)	Multiplier
Marginal propensity to save (MPS)	Paradox of thrift
Aggregate demand	Animal spirits

PROBLEMS

1 Figure 23-2 shows both potential and actual output. (*a*) Define potential output. (*b*) Define the output gap. (*c*) How can output be above the potential level? (*d*) Looking at Figure 23-1, do you think output was above the potential level during World War II? Explain.

2 Define aggregate demand, explaining clearly what parts of investment it does *not* include.

3 Suppose actual output is 100, households' planned consumption at this level of income is 70, and planned investment is 45. (*a*) Is there excess supply or excess demand for goods at this point, and how much? (*b*) What changes are there in inventory levels? (*c*) Show this situation graphically, assuming the consumption function is $C = 0.7Y$. (*d*) What is the equilibrium level of output and income?

4 Describe the relationship between the multiplier and the marginal propensity to save. [It is not enough to repeat equation (6).] Also explain why a higher or lower *MPS* implies a higher or lower multiplier.

5 Suppose the *MPC* is 0.6. Assume also that starting from an initial equilibrium level of income, investment demand rises by 50. (*a*) How much does equilibrium income change? (*b*) How much of that change is investment demand and how much is consumption demand? (*c*) Explain how output might in practice adjust over time to the new equilibrium level (use a table like Table 23-2).

6 Suppose people decide they want to save a higher proportion of their income at each level of income. Specifically, the consumption function shifts from $C = 0.7Y$ to $C = 0.5Y$. Investment is 150. (*a*) Show what effect the shift in the consumption function

has on the level of income. (It is easiest to use a graph.) What is the new equilibrium level of income? (*b*) Are people saving a higher proportion of their income at the new equilibrium? Explain. (*c*) Using a saving-investment diagram like Figure 23-11, show how the shift in the consumption function affects equilibrium output.

7 Continuing with the example of Problem 6: (*a*) Are people saving more at the new equilibrium than before? (*b*) Explain the paradox of thrift. (*c*) When if ever is the paradox of thrift an idea worth keeping in mind?

8 (*a*) Find the equilibrium level of income and output in an economy in which investment demand is 400 and the consumption function is $C = 0.8Y$. Use a graph if you want. (*b*) Would output be higher or lower if the consumption function were $C = 100 + 0.7Y$? (This consumption function means that individuals want to consume something even if income is zero. This is the consumption function drawn in Figure 23-14*b* as CC'.)

9 This question looks ahead to Chapter 24. Suppose there is an output gap, with output below potential. Suppose the government is back in the model as a potential source of demand for goods. Is there anything the government can do to close the gap?

10 Because demand determines the level of output, and output and income determine demand, some way must be found to cut through the interdependence. (*a*) Describe in words how the simple model of this chapter solves the interdependence problem. (*b*) Explain why the multiplier reflects this interdependence.

Governments—federal, state, and local—buy about 20 percent of the total output of goods and services in the United States. Total taxes amount to over 30 percent of GNP. Because government spending is a large component of aggregate demand and because taxes affect the amount households and businesses have available for spending, government spending and taxation decisions have major effects on aggregate demand and output.

In this chapter we begin to analyze the macroeconomic impacts of government fiscal policy.

Fiscal policy is the government's decisions about spending and taxes.

We start the chapter by using and expanding the model of income determination given in Chapter 23 to show how fiscal policy affects aggregate demand and output.

In addition we take up three fiscal policy issues. The first is stabilization policy.

Stabilization policy consists of government actions to control the level of output to keep GNP close to its potential level.

We analyze both the possibilities and difficulties of using fiscal policy for stabilization.

The second issue, which recurs throughout the chapter, is the significance of the government budget deficit.

The *budget deficit* is the excess of government outlays over its receipts.

When the government is running a deficit, it is spending more than it is taking in. From 1950 to 1982, the federal budget was in deficit in all but 5 years. The last time there was a federal government budget *surplus*—an excess of receipts over spending—was 1968. Deficits worry people. People wonder how and whether the government can keep on spending more than it receives year after year without something terrible happening. Presidential candidates routinely promise they will get rid of the budget deficit when elected and just as routinely find themselves unable to do so. We shall examine the size of the deficit and ask how much we should worry about it.

When the government runs a deficit, it has to find some way of paying for the excess of spending over receipts. Mostly it does this by borrowing from the public through selling bonds, which are promises to pay specified amounts to the holder at future dates. As a result of this borrowing, the government builds up its debts to the public.

The *national debt* consists of all government debt outstanding.

24

The Budget, Fiscal Policy, and Aggregate Demand

As deficits have continued year after year, the national debt has continued rising to apparently astronomical levels. By 1983 the national debt was well above $1 trillion, or more than $4000 per person. The third fiscal policy issue we examine is therefore the effects of the national debt.

1 GOVERNMENT IN THE CIRCULAR FLOW

Figure 24-1 shows how the government gets into the circular flow of income, output, and spending. Government spending contributes directly to aggregate demand on the right side of the figure. On the left side, taxes and government transfer payments[1] come between the amounts firms pay out to factors of production and the amount the private sector has available for spending. Before going into the ways these changes affect the determination of the level of output,

we present data showing in more detail what the government buys and what taxes and transfers it makes.

Government Spending

Government spends on defense, education, roads, hospitals, and other public services. In the United States, more spending on goods and services is done by state and local governments than by the federal government. Table 24-1 shows the 1981 breakdown of government spending. Most federal government purchases were for defense. State and local government purchases of goods and services were for education, highways, police, and hospitals.

There is one distinction to note in Table 24-1. The federal government budget in 1981 had *outlays* of $670 billion, or nearly 23 percent of GNP. But Table 24-1 shows federal government *purchases* of goods and services as only 7.8 percent of GNP. The difference arises because most of the federal government's outlays, or spending, is not for purchases of goods and services.

---

[1] Recall from Chapter 22 that government transfer payments are payments that are not in exchange for current economic services. Social Security payments and unemployment benefits are examples.

FIGURE 24-1 GOVERNMENT IN THE CIRCULAR FLOW. The government intervenes in the circular flow by taking part of income in taxes and making transfer payments, thus affecting the amount of income households have available for spending. In addition, the government purchases goods and services, thereby contributing to the aggregate demand for goods and services.

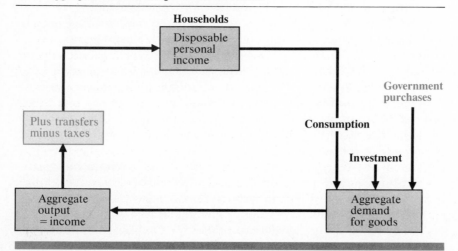

TABLE 24-1 ▐▬▬▬▬▬▬▬▬▬▬▬▬▬▬▬▬

GOVERNMENT SPENDING ON GOODS AND SERVICES, UNITED STATES, 1981
(Percent of GNP)

FEDERAL BUDGET OUTLAYS	FEDERAL PURCHASES OF GOODS AND SERVICES			STATE AND LOCAL GOVERNMENT PURCHASES OF GOODS AND SERVICES
	TOTAL	DEFENSE	OTHER	
22.9	7.8	5.2	2.6	12.4

Source: Economic Report of the President, 1982, Tables B-1 and B-76.

Rather, two-thirds of federal outlays in 1981 consisted of transfer payments to persons, grants to state and local governments, and interest payments. Federal government transfer payments include payments to Social Security recipients and unemployment benefits. The interest component of federal government outlays goes to the holders of the national debt. In 1981 interest on the national debt came to over 2.5 percent of GNP.

Taxes and Transfers

Government taxes and transfers get into the circular flow by affecting the disposable income—the income available for spending or saving—of households and the after-tax profits of firms. Thus we have to take taxes and transfers into account in analyzing the role of government in affecting the level of output.

Federal government transfer payments in 1981 came to 9.6 percent of GNP. The composition of these transfers for 1979 is shown in Table 24-2. Most are Social Security payments to people who are retired or disabled. Transfer payments by state and local governments are comparatively small.

On the taxation side, the federal government takes in about 21 percent of GNP in taxes. Table 24-3 shows the details. The major source of revenue for the federal government is the individual income tax, which in total comes to about 10 percent of GNP. The second largest source of revenue for the

federal government is Social Security contributions. State and local governments take in about another 11 percent of GNP in revenues from the private sector, with much of this coming from property and sales taxes.

2 GOVERNMENT AND AGGREGATE DEMAND

Figure 24-1 shows the two places in which the government enters the circular flow of income, spending, and output. First, government purchases of goods and services are part of aggregate demand, a fact we record as

$$
\begin{aligned}
\frac{\text{Aggregate}}{\text{demand}} &= \frac{\text{consumption}}{\text{demand}} + \frac{\text{investment}}{\text{demand}} \\
AD &= C + I \\
&\quad + \frac{\text{government}}{\text{demand}} \\
&\quad + G
\end{aligned} \tag{1}
$$

The only component of aggregate demand omitted is net exports. In the appendix to this chapter we show how the inclusion of net exports affects income determination.

We assume that government purchases of goods and services are fixed at a level G that is independent of income and output. The same applies for investment demand, I.

Government also comes into the aggregate demand picture by affecting consumption through its taxes and transfers. The difference between taxes and transfers is called *net taxes*. In the United States, taxes come to about 30 percent of GNP and trans-

TABLE 24-2

TRANSFER PAYMENTS BY FEDERAL AND STATE AND LOCAL GOVERNMENTS, 1979
(Percent of GNP)

FEDERAL GOVERNMENT						STATE AND LOCAL GOVERNMENTS
SOCIAL SECURITY, RETIREMENT, AND DISABILITY	HOSPITAL AND MEDICAL INSURANCE	FOOD STAMPS	MILITARY RETIREMENT AND VETERANS' BENEFITS	UNEMPLOYMENT BENEFITS	OTHER	
5.0	1.2	0.3	1.0	0.4	0.6	1.5

Source: Facts and Figures on Government Finance, 1981, p. 33.

TABLE 24-3

TAXES RECEIVED BY FEDERAL AND STATE AND LOCAL GOVERNMENTS, 1981
(Percent of GNP)

FEDERAL GOVERNMENT					STATE AND LOCAL GOVERNMENTS*				
TOTAL	INDIVIDUAL INCOME TAXES	SOCIAL INSURANCE TAXES AND CONTRIBUTIONS	CORPORATE PROFIT TAXES	OTHER	TOTAL	PROPERTY TAXES	SALES TAXES	INDIVIDUAL INCOME TAXES	OTHER
21.0	9.9	6.7	2.4	2.0	11.3	2.0	2.4	1.2	5.5

* Approximate, calculated assuming that ratios for fiscal year 1979–1980 apply to 1981.
Source: Economic Report of the President, 1982, pp. 321–323.

fers to about 10 percent, and so net taxes are about 20 percent of GNP. Net taxes reduce personal disposable income—the amount available for spending by households—relative to national income.

$$\text{Personal disposable income} = \text{national income} - \text{net taxes} \qquad (2)$$

We assume here that net taxes are proportional to national income. If income goes up a dollar, taxes go up by amount t, where t is the tax rate. For instance, if the tax rate is 0.2, a \$1 increase in national income raises net taxes by 20 cents.

With a net tax rate of 0.2, or 20 percent, households have only 80 percent of national income as disposable income. For instance, if national income is 1000, household disposable income is only 800. A \$1 increase in national income will increase household disposable income by only 80 cents. The other 20 cents goes to the government.

We continue to assume that consumption is proportional to personal disposable income. Figure 24-2 shows how taxes affect the consumption function. On consumption function CC, taxes are zero, and consumption is given by $C = 0.7Y$, as in Chapter 23. When we include taxes, we see that households get only 80 percent of national income as disposable income. They consume 0.7 of disposable income, but now disposable income is less than national income.

The consumption function can be written as $C = 0.7YD$, where YD is disposable income, which is equal to 80 percent of national income. It follows that consumption is a lower proportion of national income, specifically 0.56 (0.7 × 0.8). The consumption function CC' shows how consumption is related to national income when net taxes take 20 percent of income. The effect of taxes is to reduce consumption at each level of income. The propensity to consume out of *national* income can now be written as

FIGURE 24-2 THE EFFECTS OF TAXATION ON THE CONSUMPTION FUNCTION. Consumption function CC shows how consumption is related to national income when there is no taxation. CC' shows the relationship when there is a proportional tax rate of 0.2, meaning that households get 80 cents of every dollar in national income. They continue to consume 0.7 of their disposable income, but now they consume 0.7 × 0.8 of national income, or 0.56 of national income. As a result of the taxation, the consumption function shifts down from CC to CC'.

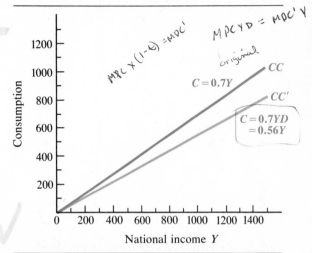

$MPC' = MPC \times (1 - t)$. The $(1 - t)$ in the case of a 20 percent, or 0.2, tax rate is 0.8. Thus the presence of proportional taxes reduces the MPC to only 80 percent of the value it used to have. The higher the proportional tax rate, the lower the marginal propensity to consume out of national income.

Proceeding one step at a time, we now show how the inclusion of government affects the level of output. We start from an example where $I = 300$ and the consumption function is $C = 0.7Y$, with MPC equal to 0.7.

The Effects of Government Spending on Output

First assume that government spending on goods and services is 200 but that there are no taxes. In Figure 24-3, we recognize that an increase in government spending from

FIGURE 24-3 THE EFFECTS OF AN INCREASE IN GOVERN-MENT SPENDING ON OUT-PUT. The economy is initially in equilibrium at point *E*. Government spending then increases from zero to 200. The aggregate demand curve shifts up by 200, from *AD* to *AD'*. As a result, the equilibrium level of income rises from 1000 at *E* to 1667 at *E'*. The increase in government spending has exactly the same effect on equilibrium output as an increase in investment demand by the same amount.

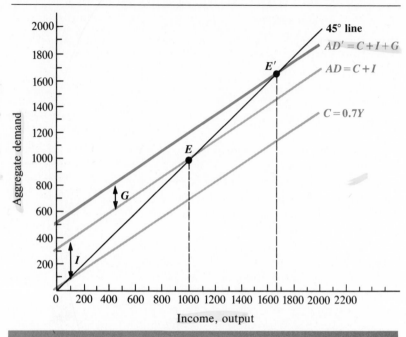

zero to 200 has precisely the same effects as an increase in investment spending from 300 to 500. With the multiplier equal to $1/(1 - MPC) = 3.33$, an increase in government purchases of goods and services from zero to 200 increases income and output by 666, or from 1000 to 1666. This is seen in Figure 24-3, where the 200-unit increase in *G* shifts the aggregate demand curve from *AD* to *AD'* and equilibrium from *E* to *E'*.

Thus increases in government purchases increase the equilibrium level of output. The amount by which they do so is equal to the multiplier times the increase in *G*. The effects of government purchases on output suggest that at times of recession, government purchases can be increased to raise output.

The Effects of Taxation on Output

Now we start from the beginning again, assuming no government purchases of goods and services and only government taxation.

Figure 24-4 shows what happens to aggregate demand when the tax rate is increased from zero to 0.2. The consumption function pivots downward, as in Figure 24-4, and the level of income falls from *E* to *E'*. The new equilibrium level of income is only 682.

Taxation reduces output because the taxes reduce consumption spending at each level of national income. The effect thus comes entirely from aggregate demand. Taxes reduce household disposable income at each level of national income and therefore reduce consumption demand. With lower consumption demand and unchanged investment demand, output and income are sure to fall.

The effects of taxes on output and income suggest that taxes can be changed to help keep output near its potential level. During a recession, taxes can be cut to increase output. During a boom, taxes can be increased when aggregate demand should be reduced.

FIGURE 24-4 THE EFFECTS OF AN INCOME TAX ON OUTPUT. An increase in the tax rate from zero to 0.2 causes consumption demand to fall at each level of income, as in Figure 24-2. The aggregate demand curve thus pivots down from *AD* to *AD'*. The equilibrium level of output and income falls from 1000 to 681. The fall is a result of the reduction in consumption demand at each level of national income.

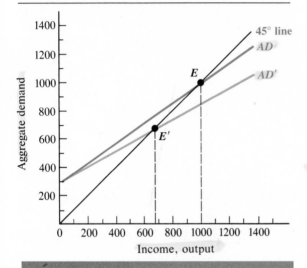

The Combined Effects of Government Spending and Taxation

Next we put the two changes together. Government spending goes up from zero to 200, and the tax rate goes up from zero to 0.2. Investment remains at 300, and the *MPC* out of disposable income is still 0.7. Of course, the presence of taxation means that the marginal propensity to consume out of national income drops to 0.56.

How do the two effects work out together? Figure 24-5 shows that national income actually rises as a result of the two effects together. The new equilibrium level of income is 1136.

The Balanced Budget Multiplier There is an interesting aspect to the result shown in Figure 24-5. The economy was originally in equilibrium at an output level of 1000. Government spending was then raised to 200.

At the same time, taxes equal to 20 percent of income were imposed. At the initial equilibrium level of income of 1000, 20 percent of income is 200, implying that at the initial equilibrium, the increase in government spending was just matched by the increase in taxes.

A natural assumption would be that if government spending and taxes go up by the same amount, the equilibrium level of income should not change. But as Figure 24-5 shows, income increases. Why does this happen? We should think of what government actions do to total aggregate demand. The increase in government spending directly raises aggregate demand by 200. The tax increase reduces disposable income by 200. But a reduction in disposable income by 200 reduces consumption demand by only 140 (0.7 × 200), or the *MPC* out of disposable income times the reduction in disposable income. The demand for goods at the initial equilibrium level of income thus increases by 200 because of government spending but falls by 140 because of the increase in taxes. Aggregate demand at the income level of 1000 thus increases by 60, and output therefore increases.

This example is closely related to the famous balanced budget multiplier.

The *balanced budget multiplier* states that an increase in government spending accompanied by an equal increase in taxes results in an increase in output.

This happens because the increase in government spending increases demand by the full amount, but the increase in taxes reduces consumption demand by less, as in the above example. The two effects together therefore actually increase aggregate demand and cause output to rise.

The Multiplier with Proportional Taxes

The effect of proportional taxes—for example, a tax that takes 20 percent of income—is to reduce the marginal propensity to con-

FIGURE 24-5   THE COMBINED EFFECTS OF AN INCREASE IN GOVERNMENT SPENDING AND TAXES. Government spending rises from zero to 200, and the tax rate goes from zero to 0.2, causing the *AD* curve to shift up but also become flatter. The *AD* curve has a slope of 0.7, but the *AD'* curve has a slope of only 0.56 (0.7 × 0.8). The new aggregate demand curve *AD'* intersects the 45° line at *E'*, which means that the equilibrium level of income is higher than it would be in the absence of government spending and taxation.

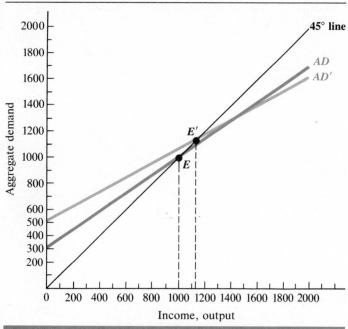

sume out of national income. The formula for the multiplier that we worked out in Chapter 23 still applies here, except that what matters now is the *MPC* taking taxes into account, that is, *MPC'*.

The multiplier is given by

$$\text{Multiplier} = \frac{1}{1 - MPC'} \qquad (3)$$

Of course, we recognize that *MPC'* in equation (3) is equal to $MPC \times (1 - t)$. Since the equation for the multiplier shows that a low *MPC'* means a low multiplier, and since high proportional taxes mean a low MPC', we see that the presence of proportional taxation reduces the multiplier. The higher the rate of proportional taxation, the smaller the multiplier. Table 24-4 gives some examples of how equation (3) works.

To understand why a high tax rate reduces the multiplier, we have to think about why there is a multiplier at all. The multiplier arises from the effects of increases in income on consumption demand. For in-

stance, when investment demand rises and production increases to meet the higher investment demand, that higher production raises income and thereby raises consumption demand. The higher the *MPC*, the larger the increase in consumption demand resulting from any given increase in output, and therefore the larger the multiplier. When the tax rate is high, any given change in income results in only a small change in household disposable income and thus only a small change in consumption demand. The multiplier is therefore small when the tax rate is high.

3   THE GOVERNMENT BUDGET

A *budget* is a description of the spending and financing plans of an individual, business, or government.

The government budget describes what goods and services the government will buy during the coming year, what transfers it will make, and how it will pay for them.

TABLE 24-4
VALUE OF THE MULTIPLIER

MPC	t	$MPC' = MPC \times (1 - t)$	MULTIPLIER $= \dfrac{1}{1 - MPC'}$
0.9	0.0	0.9	10
0.9	0.2	0.72	3.57
0.7	0.0	0.7	3.33
0.7	0.2	0.56	2.27
0.7	0.4	0.42	1.72

FIGURE 24-6 THE GOVERNMENT BUDGET DEFICIT AND SURPLUS. The budget deficit is equal to government outlays minus taxes, or government purchases of goods and services minus net taxes. Government purchases are shown as constant, independent of income, while net taxes are proportional to income. Thus at low levels of income the budget is in deficit, and at high levels of income the budget is in surplus.

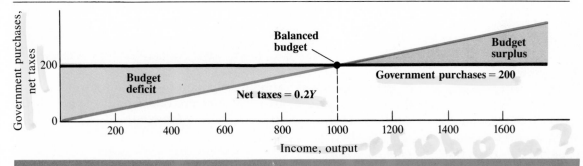

Usually the government plans to pay for most of its spending by making the public pay taxes. But taxes often do not pay for all purchases of goods and services and transfers. When government outlays exceed taxes, there is a government budget deficit. When taxes exceed outlays, there is a government budget surplus.

$$\begin{aligned}
\text{Government budget deficit} &= \begin{array}{l}\text{government}\\ \text{purchases of}\\ \text{goods and}\\ \text{services}\end{array} + \text{transfers} - \text{taxes} \\[2ex]
&= \begin{array}{l}\text{government}\\ \text{purchases of}\\ \text{goods and}\\ \text{services}\end{array} - \text{net taxes} \qquad (4)
\end{aligned}$$

Figure 24-6 shows government purchases G and net taxes tY in relation to income. Government spending is fixed at 200.

Taxes are proportional to income, with a tax rate of 0.2, and so taxes are equal to 0.2Y. Taxes are zero when income is equal to zero, are equal to 100 when income gets to 500, and are equal to government spending when income reaches 1000.

The figure shows that at income levels below 1000, the government budget is in deficit, with G larger than taxes. At an income level of 1000 the government budget is balanced, and at higher income levels there is a surplus. Thus given the level of government spending and the tax rate, the budget deficit or surplus depends on the level of income. The higher the level of income, the smaller the deficit or the larger the surplus.

The state of the budget surplus or deficit is thus entirely determined by the tax rate, the level of government spending, and

 # Difference between taxes rising & tax rate rising

the level of income. But there is a complication. We know that the level of government spending and the tax rate each affect the level of income. An increase in government purchases of goods and services increases the level of income and thereby raises the total taxes received by the government. The question arises whether it is possible for an increase in government spending to *reduce* the deficit rather than increase it. This doesn't seem possible, but could it happen? Perhaps an increase in government spending could set off so large an increase in income that taxes go up more than government spending. We now check whether that is possible.

Government Purchases, the Tax Rate, and the Deficit

Suppose government purchases are equal to 200, the *MPC* is 0.7, and the tax rate is 0.2. We know that in this case the multiplier is equal to 2.27, as shown in Table 24-4. Now suppose government spending rises by 100. Table 24-5 shows how we calculate the effects on the deficit. Because the multiplier is 2.27, income goes up by 227. Taxes go up by 0.2, or 20 percent of that amount, equal to 45.4. Thus taxes go up by less than government spending increases. In this case certainly, an increase in government spending does *not* lead to a larger increase in taxes. Increased government spending always increases the deficit, though to be sure, by less than the increase in *G*. In this example

the deficit rises only 54.6, since government spending went up by 100 and taxes went up by 45.4.

Table 24-5 also shows the calculation of the effects of an increase in government spending by 100 on the deficit in two other cases. In each example, the increase in government spending ends up increasing the deficit, which is probably what we would have expected to begin with.

The results in Table 24-5 give us the correct answer to the question of what effect an increase in government spending has on the deficit.

> An *increase in government spending* increases both the deficit and the level of income. Because the level of income and therefore taxes rise, the deficit increases by less than the increase in government spending.

Similar calculations for the case of an increase in the tax rate would confirm what we should have guessed.

> An *increase in the tax rate* reduces both the deficit and the level of income.

We obtain a better understanding of these results when we look at the relationships among saving, investment, and the government budget deficit.

Saving, Investment, and the Budget Deficit

Recall from Chapter 23 that the condition that aggregate demand be equal to output could be put alternatively by saying that

TABLE 24-5

EFFECTS OF AN INCREASE IN GOVERNMENT SPENDING ON THE DEFICIT

(1) CHANGE IN G	MPC	(2) t	(3) MULTIPLIER, FROM TABLE 24-4	(4) = (3) × (1) CHANGE IN Y	(5) = (2) × (4) CHANGE IN TAXES	(6) = (1) − (5) CHANGE IN DEFICIT
100	0.7	0.2	2.27	227	45.4	54.6
100	0.9	0.2	3.57	357	71.4	28.6
100	0.7	0.4	1.72	172	68.8	31.2

FIGURE 24-7   GOVERNMENT SPENDING AND TAXES IN THE EQUILIBRIUM
CIRCULAR FLOW. In equilibrium, income is equal to aggregate demand. This also
means that leakages from the circular flow are equal to injections. Leakages are net
taxes and saving. Injections are government purchases of goods and services, and
investment. Thus in equilibrium, saving plus taxes is equal to government purchases plus investment.

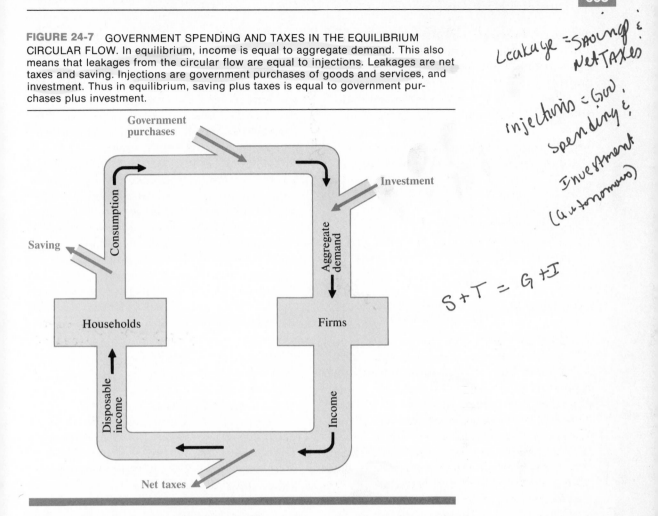

*Leakage = Saving &
Net Taxes*

*injections = Gov.
spending &
Investment
(autonomous)*

$$S + T = G + I$$

saving is equal to investment at the equilibrium level of output. This same point is
sometimes made in terms of *leakages* from
and *injections* into the circular flow of goods
and income. Saving is a leakage of aggregate
demand, a part of the flow of income that
does not get translated back into aggregate
demand for goods. Investment is an injec-
tion of aggregate demand that does not
come from the circular flow because it does
not depend on the level of income. In equilibrium, leakages out of the circular flow—
in that case, saving—are equal to the injections—in that case, investment.

Now we use the leakages equal injections approach in Figure 24-7 to show the
equilibrium relationship between the government budget and saving and investment.
We start at the right, with the firms. We
know that the inflow of aggregate demand
must be the same size in equilibrium as the
outflow of income. Part of that income leaks
out into net taxes and transfers and is unavailable for demanding goods. The rest goes
to households as disposable income. Part
leaks out as saving, leaving consumption
demand as part of aggregate demand. The
two injections of aggregate demand are gov-

ernment purchases and investment, which add to the flow of aggregate demand. In equilibrium, the leakages are equal to injections.

Thus we can write that in equilibrium, when aggregate demand equals income,

$$\text{Saving} + \begin{array}{c}\text{net}\\\text{taxes}\end{array} = \begin{array}{c}\text{government}\\\text{purchases}\end{array} + \text{investment} \quad (5)$$

$$S \quad + \quad T \quad = \quad G \quad + \quad I$$

We use the symbol T to stand for net taxes. Now we can rearrange equation (5) by moving I to the left-hand side and T to the right-hand side so that $S - I$ is equal to $G - T$. Of course, $G - T$ is the government budget deficit.

In words, we have

$$\text{Saving} - \text{investment} = \begin{array}{c}\text{government}\\\text{budget deficit}\end{array} \quad (6)$$

$$S \quad - \quad I \quad = \quad G - T$$

In Chapter 23, we warned that saving equal to investment was the equilibrium condition only in that simplified model, which did not include government. Now we see why. When the government is put into the picture, saving is not equal to investment if there is a government budget deficit or surplus. For example, if there is a budget deficit, saving will exceed investment.

To understand this relationship, think in terms of the lending and borrowing that is taking place in the economy. Households are doing the saving. Firms borrow to finance their investments. If the government is running a budget deficit, or spending more than it takes in in taxes, it too has to borrow. Equation (6) tells us that total borrowing by the government and firms together (the government deficit plus investment) is equal to total saving in equilibrium.[2]

$$G - T + I = S$$

---

[2] This relationship between saving and investment on one side and the government budget deficit on the other will be useful when we discuss the question of whether government deficits reduce investment in Chapter 27.

We use the relationship in equation (6) to show that an increase in government spending increases the deficit, which is something we only asserted before. How do we know? Look at the left-hand side of equation (6) and ask what happens when government spending increases and income increases along with it. Saving increases with income. Therefore, saving is higher as a result of the higher income. But investment is by assumption constant. Thus saving minus investment must rise. But saving minus investment in equilibrium is equal to the government budget deficit. Therefore, it too must rise when government spending increases. In Problem 11 at the end of this chapter we ask you to use the same argument to show why the deficit must fall when the tax rate is increased.

$$S' - I > S - I \qquad S - I = G - T$$
$$S' - I = G' - T$$

4 FISCAL POLICY, THE DEFICIT, AND THE FULL-EMPLOYMENT BUDGET

In early 1975, with the United States in its worst (up to that time) post-World War II recession, the government decided to give a tax rebate to the taxpayers. Taxes were reduced in an attempt to get the economy out of the recession and back to full-employment output. The tax cut increased the government budget deficit, as can be seen in Figure 24-8, which shows the government budget surplus since 1955. In 1975, there is a large drop in the surplus, or an increase in the deficit, reflecting the tax cut.

Similarly, in 1968 the economy was suffering from overfull employment and excess demand as a result of the Vietnam war. In an attempt to get output back down to its potential level, taxes were raised. This shows up in Figure 24-8 as an increase in the budget surplus. Indeed, that is the last time there was a surplus.

These changes in tax rates are examples of the active use of fiscal policy to try to get the economy to operate at a level close to

FIGURE 24-8　THE FEDERAL GOV-ERNMENT BUDGET SURPLUS, 1955–1981 (Percent of GNP). (*Source: Survey of Current Business,* April 1982, p. 26).

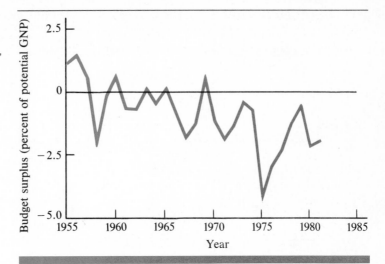

potential. They show that fiscal policy can be used to try to stabilize the economy. The active use of fiscal policy raises two sets of questions. The first involves how successfully fiscal policy can be used to stabilize output. The question can be put differently by asking why there have been so many recessions in the post-World War II period, even though Keynesian analysis shows how to use fiscal policy to avoid recessions. We look at those questions in the next section.

The second set of questions concerns whether the government budget deficit is a good measure of fiscal policy. Does an increase in the deficit mean that the federal government is using fiscal policy to try to increase the level of output? Does a decrease in the deficit mean that the federal government is undertaking contractionary fiscal policy in an attempt to reduce GNP? *Expansionary* policy aims to increase GNP; *contractionary* policy aims to reduce GNP.

The answer is that the deficit is *not* a good measure of fiscal policy, because it can change for reasons that have nothing to do with fiscal policy. For instance, if investment demand drops and income falls as a result, the budget deficit will rise. Fiscal policy—government spending and tax rates

—has not changed in any way, but still the deficit rises. The deficit thus does not give us information about how the government is manipulating fiscal policy to try to expand or contract GNP. The deficit may be changing passively in response to other forces that are changing GNP and thus tax collection.

In particular, for given government spending and tax rates, we should expect the budget to show larger deficits in recessions than in booms. For example, suppose the economy goes into a recession. The budget goes into deficit. Someone looking only at the deficit might say that fiscal policy is expansionary and there is therefore no case for cutting taxes. But that is wrong. The deficit exists because of a recession. It is not an argument against cutting taxes.

The Full-Employment Budget

The full-employment (or high-employment) budget has been invented to handle the problem of the deficit being a potentially misleading guide to the direction of fiscal policy.

The *full-employment budget* calculates the level at which the budget surplus or deficit would be if the economy were at full employment.

FIGURE 24-9 ACTUAL AND FULL-EMPLOYMENT BUDGETS. With the level of output at 800, the actual budget is in deficit by 40. But the full-employment level of output Y_p is 1300, and the full-employment budget is in surplus of 60. The full-employment budget calculates what the budget would be if the economy were at full employment, or potential output.

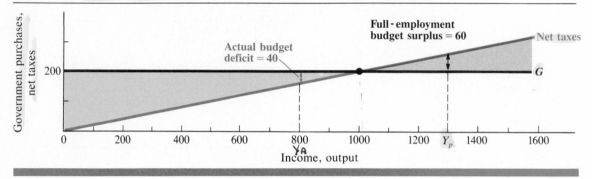

Figure 24-9 illustrates. This figure repeats Figure 24-6, showing how the actual budget surplus or deficit relates to the level of output. The full-employment level of output is Y_p. The figure shows that at Y_p, the budget would be in surplus. Y_p is equal to 1300, and the tax rate is 0.2. Thus taxes at full employment would be 260. Actual government spending is 200, and so the full-employment budget is in surplus by 60. Actual output is 800, and the actual budget is in deficit by 40.

We see in this example a clear difference between the full-employment budget and the actual budget. Anyone looking at the actual budget, with a deficit of 40, might say that fiscal policy is highly expansionary, but in fact, the budget is in deficit because the level of output is so low. If the economy were at full employment, the budget would be in surplus. Anyone looking at the full-employment surplus would say that fiscal policy is set at levels that generate a surplus at full employment and that he therefore doubts the deficit is a serious problem. He would even be willing to cut taxes despite the deficit in the actual budget, believing that when the economy comes back to full employment, the deficit will disappear.

Figure 24-10 shows the calculated full-employment surplus for the United States over the period since 1955. It also shows the actual budget deficit. For most of the period the full-employment deficit has been smaller than the actual deficit, because output has been below its full-employment, or potential, level. There are occasions when the actual and full-employment budgets give very different pictures of what is happening. For instance, in 1958, with the economy in recession, the budget deficit was as large as 2.3 percent of GNP. But the full-employment budget was in balance.

Similarly, in 1982 the federal budget was in deficit equal to more than 3 percent of GNP, and there was widespread concern that the deficit was too large. But the deficit was that large mainly because there was a recession. In thinking about the effects of fiscal policy on the economy, we should concentrate on the full-employment budget, not the actual budget.

5 ACTIVE FISCAL POLICY AND AUTOMATIC STABILIZERS

Figure 24-10 shows how the full-employment budget surplus has varied over time. There are several large changes that represent policy decisions to try to control the

FIGURE 24-10   ACTUAL AND FULL-EMPLOYMENT SURPLUSES AND DEFICITS, 1955–1981. (*Source: Survey of Current Business,* April 1982, p. 26.)

economy. We have already examined the 1968 tax increase and the 1975 tax cut.

Why, despite the active use of fiscal policy, does the economy still have booms and recessions? Why can fiscal policy not be operated to keep output precisely at the full-employment level? The main reason is that fiscal policy works slowly and uncertainly.

Suppose something happens that moves the economy into a recession. In 1973, for instance, a huge increase in the price of oil was the main factor causing the recession that persisted from the end of 1973 into 1975. We should note that the dates of a recession become clear and are announced only after the recession has actually started, sometimes months afterward. When the oil-price increase struck, no one was quite sure what would happen. There had been no such shock before, and there was uncertainty about the effect on the economy. Thus it was not even clear what should be done. The effect of the oil shock did not show up in increasing unemployment until the second half of 1974, more than 6 months after it happened. The first uncertainty, then, was over what to do. This uncertainty was so strong that in late 1974, at a White House conference of economists to discuss

the problem, only a few economists emphasized that the economy was about to go into a deep recession, even though we now know it was already in recession.

By November 1974 it became clear that the recession was under way, but again there was uncertainty about how long it would last and how bad it would be. To know how much to cut taxes or increase spending, it is necessary to know how much output should be increased. Some argued that the recession would be short and that therefore there was no need to cut taxes much. Others said the situation was so serious that massive tax cuts were essential. Again there was uncertainty, this time about where the economy was heading.

There is another source of uncertainty, which is that we do not know exactly what the value of the multiplier is. Economic data give us information that the multiplier for a dollar of taxes cut may be approximately 2, but we do not really know whether it is 1.5 or 2.5. That means we cannot know exactly how much taxes should be cut to eliminate a given output gap.

Why not cut taxes a little, see how that works, and then cut them some more if needed? The problem with this approach is that tax cuts or increases in government spending can take many months to work their way through to output. After the tax cut is passed, firms have to adjust the amounts deducted for taxes from workers' paychecks. The workers in turn may not go out to buy more goods the very next day; they may take a few weeks to react. Then, when firms see an increased demand for their goods, they may at first not increase production at all. They probably have excess inventories that accumulated as output fell. Only when the demand has been high for a while do they increase production.

Both the uncertainty and the slowness of policy, or *lags* of policy, mean that economic policy cannot be relied on to keep output at the full-employment level continuously. But policy is not impossible. When it is clear what should be done, it gets done. By early 1975 everyone could see how bad the recession was. Congress passed the tax rebate program within 2 months, and checks were in the mail by March. Why checks? It was part of an attempt to speed up the spending reaction. By sending checks, Congress ensured that people did not have to wait for the employers to adjust tax rates on paychecks. It also meant that the checks went out to unemployed people, who would react more quickly than others. The rapid turnaround of fiscal policy in 1975 helped get the economy moving quickly out of that recession.

Automatic Stabilizers

Fiscal policy affects the economy's behavior even when government spending and tax rates are held constant. To see this, think of the economy being hit by a fall of 100 in investment demand. Suppose first that the MPC is 0.7 and that there is no taxation. A drop in investment demand by 100 will cause GNP to fall by 333, since the multiplier is equal to $[1/(1 - MPC)] = 3.33$.

But now suppose there is a proportional income tax in place. We know from Table

24-4 that with a proportional income tax of 0.2 of income, the multiplier falls from 3.33 to 2.27. With the income tax in place, a fall in investment by 100 results in a reduction in output of only 227. Thus the existence of the income tax reduces the effects of the fall in investment demand on output. Similarly, if investment demand increased, the existence of the income tax would reduce the impact on output.

The proportional income tax is an example of an automatic stabilizer.

Automatic stabilizers are mechanisms in the economy that reduce the response of GNP to shocks.

By shocks we mean events like the oil-price increase in 1973, a drop in investment, or a war. The main automatic stabilizer is the income tax. Unemployment benefits are another example. If something happens to increase unemployment, the unemployed receive benefits and are not forced to cut their spending as much as they would otherwise. The multiplier effects of the initial shock are thus reduced.

Automatic stabilizers have an important advantage over active fiscal policy. They work automatically and without anyone having to decide when they should go into effect. There is no decision to be made when the income tax stabilizes the reaction of the economy to a shock. No one argues whether the shock is small or big, and no one takes 3 months deciding whether to react. It all happens automatically.

Business cycle behavior since World War II is different from what it was before. Recessions are shorter and smaller now. One reason is that the modern economy has automatic stabilizers. There were very low taxes then, and unemployment benefits were low, unlike today. One reason economists doubt that there will be another Great Depression with 25 percent unemployment is that the economy's automatic stabilizers will prevent declines in aggregate demand

FIGURE 24-11   THE NATIONAL DEBT HELD BY THE PUBLIC. (*Source: 1983 Budget of the United States Government,* part 9, p. 60.)

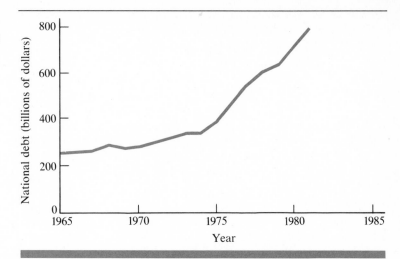

from having very large multiplier effects on GNP.

6   THE NATIONAL DEBT AND THE DEFICIT

The federal government's total outstanding debts are called the *national debt.* The national debt increases whenever the federal government runs a deficit, for then it has to borrow to pay for the outlays that are not covered by taxes. Figure 24-11 shows the national debt for each year since 1965. By the end of 1981, the debt held by the public was about $800 billion. It has continued to pile up since then.

How much should we worry about the national debt? There is a popular view that the national debt is a burden, in some way a drag on the economy's performance. The obvious concern is that everyone has a debt of about $4000 to add to his other burdens. The burden arises because debts of the U.S. government are ultimately debts of the taxpayers. At this level there is nothing to worry about. The national debt is mostly a debt that we owe ourselves. For instance, anyone who owns a U.S. savings bond owns part of the national debt. Looking at all Americans together, on average they both own national debt and owe it to themselves. Thus on that basis it cancels out, except for the part of the debt owed to foreigners.

There is a second sense in which the national debt is a smaller problem than it seems. Looking at Figure 24-11, we see the debt getting bigger year after year. But of course, the economy has also been growing over that period. Figure 24-12 shows the size of the debt relative to GNP. The picture here is much less dramatic. On average, the debt has been declining relative to GNP. In the late seventies and early eighties, the debt increased relative to GNP, but those were years of recession during which the government budget deficit was high as a result of the business cycle. There was no indication that the debt would continue increasing relative to GNP. Indeed, the pattern in the United States has been that the national debt increases rapidly in wartime because government spending is high and then gradually declines relative to GNP during peacetime.

These two arguments give reasons why the debt is not as serious a problem as might be thought from its size and the use of the word "debt." But there are two reasons why the debt may be a problem. Someone own-

FIGURE 24-12 THE NATIONAL DEBT HELD BY THE PUBLIC AS A PERCENTAGE OF GNP, 1965–1981. (*Source: 1983 Budget of the United States Government,* part 9, p. 60.)

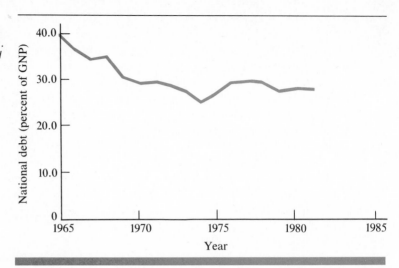

ing a U.S. savings bond, for example, could as well own stocks. Someone owning a U.S. Treasury bill has decided to hold wealth in that form instead of in real estate. It is possible that the debt displaces other forms of assets that people might hold instead; people may save by holding national debt rather than physical capital. That would mean the stock of physical capital is lower than it would be without the debt. Therefore, there is less physical capital available for production.

The second reason for worry is that interest payments on the debt can become very large. If the debt is large and interest payments the government has to make to holders of the debt are large, the government has built a very large outlay into the budget. How is it to pay? If it can raise taxes, there is no problem. But the government may have trouble raising these sums through taxes and instead have to borrow from the public. Then we see the possibility of a vicious circle. The debt is large, and therefore interest payments are high. But because interest payments are high, the government has to borrow to pay them. That means the debt is increasing, and therefore interest payments are increasing.

This situation may mean trouble. Un-

less the government can raise taxes, it has to find some other way of financing its outlays. One way is to borrow from the public. Another way, as we shall see shortly, is to print money to finance the deficit. It is the possibility that a large deficit and debt can lead ultimately to the government's having to print money, and thereby create inflation, that is probably at the bottom of popular fears about the deficit.

However, as we shall stress later, there is no automatic link between the national debt, budget deficits, and the printing of money. A government can run deficits for a long time without being faced with a calamity. Provided that the deficits are small, it can keep running deficits forever. For if the deficits are small enough, the size of the national debt may even be decreasing relative to GNP despite the deficits.

7 DEFICITS AND THE BALANCED BUDGET AMENDMENT

The history of budget deficits in the United States since 1968 and popular concern over both the deficit and the national debt have led to a political movement to ban deficit financing. The method would be to pass a constitutional amendment that requires Congress to balance the budget unless there is some very good reason not to do so, such as a war.

At times of recession, budget deficits are certainly not a bad thing. Any attempt to eliminate a recession-caused deficit by raising taxes will only make the recession worse. Thus as a first statement, there is nothing in economic analysis that suggests the budget should be balanced all the time. Keeping the budget balanced all the time may be destabilizing for the level of output. The running of deficits over longer periods raises different issues. Small deficits of 1 percent of GNP or less can certainly be run for a long time. But very large deficits of the order, say, of 10 percent of GNP cannot easily be handled for very long. Interest payments become very large, and it may eventually be necessary to start printing money to finance the deficits.

Thus economics says there is nothing inherently bad about deficits. Large deficits are not a big problem in recessions, and small deficits are easily possible over long periods. But economics does not in any way suggest that larger deficits are always better than smaller ones or that the budget should always be in deficit.

The main force behind the constitutional amendment has little to do with the economic arguments. Rather, the proponents of the amendment argue that governments that can finance themselves by borrowing tend to do so and to spend too much. They argue that the government is taking up too large a share of society's scarce resources and that therefore its spending should be restrained. One way to do that is to make the government tax people when it wants to spend. That way the voters will know how much they are paying for government.

The proposed constitutional amendments that would require budgets to be balanced also require that federal government outlays be reduced and kept to some specified percentage of GNP. This is in keeping with the view that the main force behind the balanced budget amendment is the desire to reduce the size of the government.

In the early 1980s the balanced budget amendment was making its way through Congress and the state legislatures, with supporters hopeful that the amendment would eventually be passed.

SUMMARY

1   Government enters the circular flow by taxing income, reducing the amount of income available for consumption and saving, and buying goods and services.

2   Proportional taxes in effect lower the marginal propensity to consume out of national income, because households get only a fraction of each dollar of national income to use as disposable income.

3   An increase in government purchases of goods and services increases aggregate demand and output. An increase in taxes reduces aggregate demand and output.

4   An equal increase in government spending and total taxes raises aggregate demand and output. This is the balanced budget multiplier.

5   The government budget deficit is the excess of spending over taxes. When taxes exceed spending or outlays, there is a budget surplus.

6   An increase in government spending increases the budget deficit. An increase in the tax rate reduces the budget deficit.

7   In equilibrium, and ignoring net exports, saving minus investment is equal to the government budget deficit. This relationship can be thought of in terms of borrowing and lending. Households save and lend. The borrowers are firms that finance investment goods purchases, and government, which finances its deficits.

8   The government uses taxes and spending to stabilize the economy through fiscal policy. Fiscal policy does not stabilize GNP perfectly because of uncertainty about the needed changes in taxes or purchases and because those changes affect GNP only slowly.

9   The deficit is not a good measure of the direction of fiscal policy, since it can change merely because the level of income has changed. In particular, if the economy goes into recession, the budget tends automatically to go into deficit. But that does not mean that fiscal policy is being actively used to stabilize the economy.

10   The full-employment budget calculates what the budget surplus or deficit would be at full employment. It is a better measure of the direction of fiscal policy than the actual deficit.

11   Automatic stabilizers reduce fluctuations of GNP by reducing the multiplier. The income tax and unemployment benefits act as the most important automatic stabilizer.

12   The national debt grows as a result of government budget deficits. The debt is often thought of as a burden because it is the debt of everyone in the country. But the national debt is owed mostly to ourselves, and thus the burden mostly cancels out. The debt may be a burden because it displaces physical capital as part of savings and, if the debt becomes very large, because interest payments can become a large part of government outlays.

13   Deficits are not necessarily bad. Particularly during recessions, any move to be rid of them would make the situation worse. But extremely large deficits create the possibility of a vicious circle in which large deficits increase the national debt, increase interest payments, and thereby lead to larger deficits.

KEY TERMS

Fiscal policy	Balanced budget multiplier
Budget deficit	Contractionary (or expansionary) policy
Budget surplus	Full (high)-employment budget
National debt	Automatic stabilizers
Government spending	National debt as burden

PROBLEMS

1 (a) Explain the difference between government outlays and government purchases of goods and services. (b) Describe the breakdown of both government purchases and government transfer payments between federal and state and local governments.

2 Suppose equilibrium output is 1000, consumption is 800, and investment is 80. (a) What is the level of government purchases of goods and services? (b) Suppose investment rises by 50. Assume the marginal propensity to consume out of national income is 0.8. What are the new equilibrium levels of $C, I, G,$ and Y? (c) Suppose instead that government spending has risen by 50. What would the new equilibrium values of $C, I, G,$ and Y be? (d) Suppose full-employment output is 1200. How much would government spending have to be increased to get the economy to potential output?

3 (a) Explain in words why the multiplier is lower when there is a proportional income tax than it is in the absence of income taxes. (b) Relate your answer to automatic stabilizers. (c) How do automatic stabilizers work to stabilize the economy?

4 The government makes a transfer payment of $5 billion to the elderly. The income tax rate is 0.2, and the MPC is 0.8. (a) What is the effect of the transfer payment on equilibrium income and output? (Give a numerical value if you can work it out.) (b) Does the budget deficit rise or fall as a result of the transfer? Explain.

5 Suppose the level of equilibrium output is $1000. Government spending is $G = 100$, and the income tax rate is $t = 0.2$. (a) What is the government budget deficit or surplus at the initial level of income? (b) Suppose

full-employment output is $1100. What is the full-employment budget deficit? (c) For what purposes is the full-employment budget used?

6 Initial income is at the potential output level of 1000, and the level of government spending is 50. The MPC is 0.8, and the tax rate is 0.2 (a) Investment falls by 30. What is the effect on equilibrium output and the GNP gap? (b) What is the effect of the decline in income on the actual and full-employment budgets? (c) Suppose the government increases spending to get the economy back to potential output. What happens to the actual and full-employment budgets? (You have to start by calculating how much G has to increase to get back to the output level of 1000.)

7 Explain why in an economy with a government, saving is not necessarily equal to investment in equilibrium.

8 (a) How does the national debt grow? (b) In what senses, if any, is the debt a burden on the economy?

9 Why does the federal government bother to finance itself through taxes at all, when it could borrow in order to cover its outlays?

10 "It is really quite simple to keep the economy operating at full employment. All it takes is a willingness by the government to use its fiscal policy weapons quickly whenever needed." Discuss.

11 Suppose the government raises the tax rate. (a) Show graphically why the level of income falls. (b) Explain why a tax rate increase reduces the budget deficit even though it also reduces the level of income.

APPENDIX: FOREIGN TRADE AND INCOME DETERMINATION

The model for the determination of income has as a basic condition of equilibrium that aggregate spending on goods, $C + I + G$, must equal output. We now study the changes that are required once we introduce the foreign sector and show that there is another component—net exports—which must be added to consumption, investment, and government spending to arrive at total demand for goods produced in the economy.

> *Net exports* are the excess of our exports to the rest of the world over our imports from abroad.

The new equilibrium condition in the goods market, now taking all components into account, therefore is

$$Y = C + I + G + X - Q \tag{A1}$$

where X denotes our exports, Q our imports, and $X - Q$ our *net* exports.

Consider now why net exports appear as a component of aggregate demand. First, looking at exports, we realize that part of the goods that are produced in this country are sold abroad or exported to residents in foreign countries. Exports thus represent the foreign demand for our goods. They are as much a component of demand for what we produce as government purchases of our goods. Thus exports, X, must appear in the goods market equilibrium condition. Imports must appear, too, but they appear as a correction factor. The term $C + I + G$ represents all spending by households, firms that invest, and the government. But it is not necessarily the case that all this spending is on goods that we produce. Firms may buy foreign machinery, the government may buy foreign weapon systems, and households may import their whiskey from abroad. Therefore, $C + I + G$ actually overstates how much is spent on goods made in this country. We subtract the amount that is imported, Q. With this correction, we have added exports and deducted from total spending the part that falls on imports. The two adjustments amount to adding net exports, $X - Q$.

Table A24-1 shows U.S. net exports, exports, and imports, each expressed as a fraction of GNP. There are two striking features. First, *net* exports are typically positive but are small relative to GNP. In each year shown, and indeed for all but 2 years since World War II, exports exceed imports. But net exports average less than 1 percent of GNP. Second, both exports and imports increased rapidly relative to GNP in the decade from 1971 to 1981. Most U.S. exports are manufactured goods, as are most U.S. imports. But oil imports make up nearly one-third of the total. Exports and imports as a fraction of GNP now are almost the same size as investment.

TABLE A24-1

**U.S. FOREIGN TRADE, SELECTED YEARS, 1951–1981
(As Percent of GNP)**

	NET EXPORTS	EXPORTS	IMPORTS
1951	1.3	6.0	4.6
1961	1.3	5.7	4.4
1971	0.4	6.4	6.0
1976	0.8	9.9	9.1
1981	0.8	12.5	11.7

Note: Difference between exports and imports in 1951 is not equal to net exports because of rounding.
Source: Economic Report of the President, 1982, p. 233.

How do net exports behave, and what are their determinants? We assume here that our exports are determined by demand conditions abroad and that they are constant. On the import side we recognize that import spending, like consumption spending, depends on the level of income. When income rises, households want to consume more. Part of that increased consumption takes the form of purchases of foreign goods. Thus imports rise with the level of income.

Figure A24-1 shows the behavior of exports, imports, and the difference, which are net exports, or the *trade balance.* The exports are shown by a horizontal schedule on which exports are constant. Import spending increases with income, starting from zero at an income level

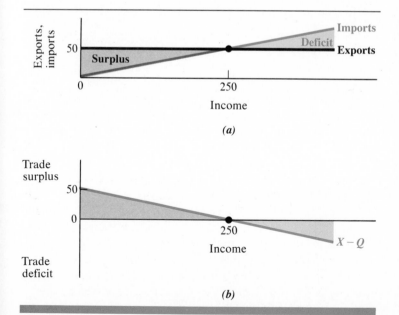

FIGURE A24-1 EXPORTS, IMPORTS, AND THE TRADE BALANCE. Part (*a*) shows the given level of exports of 50 units. Imports increase with the level of income. The diagram assumes a marginal propensity to import, shown by the slope of the import schedule, of 0.2. The difference between exports and imports is equal to the trade balance. At the income level of 250, imports are equal to 50 (0.2 × 250) and are therefore equal to exports. At a higher level of income, there is a trade deficit. The schedule labeled net exports in part (*b*) shows the difference between exports and imports, or the trade balance, at each income level. The trade balance surplus falls and ultimately becomes a deficit as income increases.

of zero and increasing as income rises. The slope of the import schedule shows the marginal propensity to import.

> The *marginal propensity* to *import* is the increase in imports per $1 increase in national income.

The marginal propensity to import, which we will denote by MPQ, is a fraction, certainly smaller than the MPC. It might take a value of $MPQ = 0.1$ or even 0.2. Note that the MPQ depends, just as MPC', on the income tax rate. Higher income tax rates lower disposable income relative to national income and therefore lower the fraction of an extra dollar of national income that is spent on imports.

The difference at each income level between exports and imports represents net exports, or the trade balance. At low levels of income, there is a trade *surplus* because import spending is low relative to exports. At high income levels, with imports high compared with exports, there is a trade *deficit*. Moreover, because it raises imports but leaves exports unchanged, an increase in income will always reduce the trade surplus or increase the trade deficit.

Net Exports and Equilibrium Income

Figure A24-2 shows how equilibrium income is determined once net exports are introduced. We start from the schedule $C + I + G$, which we analyzed in this chapter, and add to that schedule the amount of net exports at each level of income. At low income levels, net exports, as seen from Figure A24-1b, are positive. Hence $X - Q$ is a positive number, and aggregate demand exceeds $C + I + G$ at low income

FIGURE A24-2 EQUILIBRIUM INCOME IN THE OPEN ECONOMY. Net exports, or our exports minus our spending on imports, must be added to $C + I + G$ to arrive at the demand for domestic goods, or aggregate demand. This is done by adding to $C + I + G$ at each level of income the amount of net exports. At zero income, for example, net exports are 50, but as income rises, imports rise and net exports fall off. The schedule AD shows all components of demand for domestic goods. Equilibrium obtains at point E, where aggregate demand, including net exports, equals income.

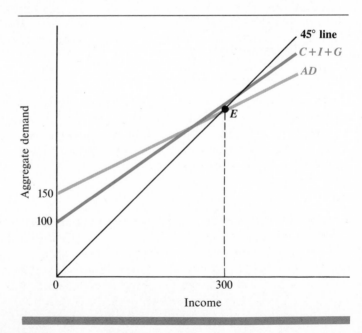

levels. As income rises, so do imports. The level of net exports declines, becomes zero, and ultimately becomes negative. At high levels of income, aggregate demand for our goods falls below $C + I + G$, because net exports are now negative.

Figure A24-2 shows aggregate demand at a zero level of income to be 150, made up of $I + G = 100$ and 50 units of exports. As income rises, aggregate demand also rises. We assume that the marginal propensity to consume out of national income is $MPC' = 0.7$, and we assume, as in the earlier figures, a marginal propensity to import or $MPQ = 0.2$. A $1 rise in income therefore raises aggregate demand, or demand for *our* goods, by $0.5 \times \$1$; of the $0.70 of increased consumption, $0.20 falls on imports and only $0.50 is spent on domestic goods.

Equilibrium income occurs at point E, where aggregate demand equals income. The level of income in equilibrium is 300. This corresponds to $100 of $I + G$, $50 of exports, and $150 ($0.7 \times \$300 - 0.2 \times \$300$) of consumer spending on domestic goods. We also note that with a marginal propensity to import of 0.2, there will be a trade deficit of $10. This is because we export $50 worth of our goods, but at an income level of $300, our import spending is equal to $60 ($0.2 \times \$300$).

The Multiplier in the Open Economy

With net exports becoming a part of aggregate demand for our goods, the multiplier will change. We already suggested in which direction. The fact that imports rise with income means that less of the increased spending falls on our own goods. A $1 increase in income leads to less consumer spending on our own goods, and for that reason the multiplier will be smaller. The amended formula for the multiplier now is

$$\text{Multiplier} = \frac{1}{1 - MPC' + MPQ} \tag{A2}$$

For the numbers we used in Figure A24-2, we have a multiplier of 2 since the MPC' was 0.7 and the MPQ was 0.2. Thus a $10 increase in government spending, for example, would increase equilibrium income by $20. The multiplier is reduced because part of increased spending falls on foreign goods.

An Increase in Exports

Foreign demand for our goods or exports is part of aggregate demand. Changes in exports therefore lead to changes in equilibrium income. Figure A24-3 shows how an increase in our exports, perhaps because of a rise in foreign income and spending, affects our income and trade balance. We assume exports increase by $20. Figure A24-3*a* shows the upward shift of the aggregate demand schedule. Increased exports raise aggregate demand by $20 at each level of income. Equilibrium

FIGURE A24-3 A rise in exports shifts the aggregate demand schedule upward at each level of income. Equilibrium income rises from E to E'. The lower panel shows that increased exports shift the export schedule upward so that the trade balance has improved at the new income level. The trade balance improvement is less than the increase in exports since imports have risen because of higher income and spending.

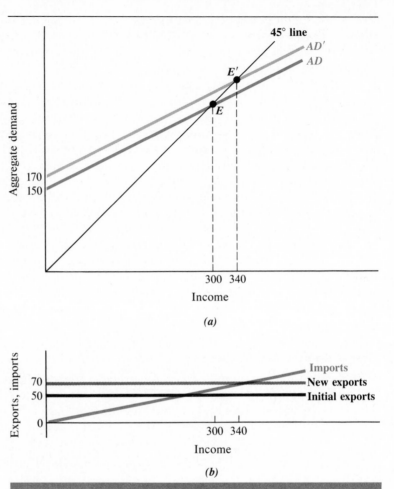

(a)

(b)

income therefore rises from E to E'. With the values assumed so far, the multiplier is 2 and income therefore rises from \$300 to \$340. Increased exports thus work in the same way as higher investment or government spending. They create demand for our goods and therefore lead to higher output, income, and employment. Exports are always good for employment.

Figure A24-3b shows the effect of increased exports on the trade balance. The export schedule shifts upward, reflecting the fact that at each level of income we now export more. Imports, of course, depend on the level of income. At the new equilibrium level of income, the trade balance is improved. But we note that the trade surplus rises by less than the \$20 improvement in exports. The reason is that the income expansion raises imports somewhat. But the trade balance must improve when exports rise, the more so the smaller the marginal propensity to import. In our example the trade balance improves by \$12, which represents $20 of increased exports minus the increase in imports of $8 (0.2 × $40) owing to higher income.

Import Spending and Employment

A common view is that imports steal jobs at home. Goods are made abroad rather than being produced by our workers. Thus by reducing imports, we can create employment at home. That view is both correct *and* dangerous. It is correct because increased consumer spending on our goods rather than on imports *will* raise demand at home and therefore increase output and employment. Whenever there is unemployment, restricting imports of goods which we can also make at home will raise employment. In terms of Figure A24-3*a*, a reduction in the propensity to import makes the *AD* curve steeper and raises equilibrium income and output.

The view that import restriction is good for employment is dangerous because it can lead to worldwide restriction of trade. Every country tries to gain employment at the expense of the rest of the world. By reducing imports we hope to gain employment at home. But we are taking employment away from foreign countries, and they will respond by reducing *their* imports. That means they will reduce their demand for our exports. In the end, nobody gains employment, and international trade disappears. Whenever the world is in recession, the need is for worldwide expansionary fiscal policies, not for policies in which each country attempts to steal employment from abroad.

SUMMARY

1　When exports and imports are brought into the income determination model, exports enter as a source of demand for our goods. Imports are a leakage from the circular flow, since they represent a demand for foreign-produced goods.

2　Exports are determined mostly by conditions abroad and are treated as constant. Imports are assumed to be proportional to disposable income, with a propensity to import out of disposable income of *MPQ*.

3　The inclusion of imports reduces the multiplier.

4　An increase in exports increases domestic output and income. An increase in the propensity to import reduces the domestic output level.

5　The trade surplus is the excess of exports over imports. The trade surplus is larger the lower the level of income. An increase in exports increases the trade surplus, and an increase in the propensity to import reduces it.

PROBLEMS

1   Draw an injections equal leakages diagram like Figure 24-7 to show how imports and exports affect the determination of income.

2   The MPC' is 0.8. The marginal propensity to spend on imports, MPQ, is equal to 0.4. Suppose investment rises by 100. (*a*) What happens to the level of income? (*b*) How does the trade balance change?

3   In Problem 2, suppose exports increase by 100. How does the trade balance change?

4   Using the data from Problem 2, assume the propensity to import, MPQ, falls from 0.4 to 0.3. Give the values of the multiplier before and after, and explain why the multiplier changed the way it did.

5   Suppose a country's trading partners have a recession. (*a*) What happens to the balance of trade? (*b*) What happens to the level of income? Explain.

Through history, money has taken many different forms: dogs' teeth (minus the dog) in the Admiralty Islands; cocoa beans in South and Central America; cowrie and wampum sea shells in Africa, Asia, and North America; gold and silver in many countries in the nineteenth century; and the U.S. dollar in parts of Latin America and Europe today.

In songs and popular language the word "money" stands for many things. It is a symbol of status and achievement and the major source of crime, and it makes the world go round. Economists use the word more precisely.

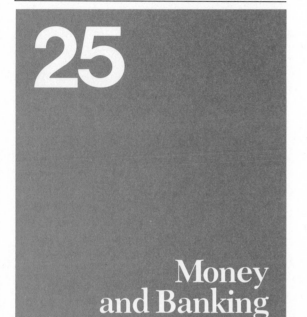

25

Money and Banking

> *Money* is any generally acceptable means of payment in exchange for goods and services and in settling debts.

The essential characteristic of money is that it is generally accepted for making payments. It does not matter what physical commodity is used for money. Dogs' teeth are money if people are willing to take them in payment, just as dollar bills are.

We introduce money in this chapter by studying the reasons society uses money and the role banks play in the monetary system. Later chapters discuss the role of central banks and the effects of changes in the quantity of money on the level of output, the aggregate price level, and the inflation rate. We emphasize historical developments to draw attention to the continuing changes in society's monetary arrangements. For instance, gold used to be money but is no longer. And the current U.S. monetary system is changing as banks begin to pay interest on checking deposits and as new forms of deposits are invented. There is even the possibility that money use will eventually disappear as electronic payments systems using credit cards are developed.

1 MONEY AND ITS FUNCTIONS

Money has four functions. It serves as a medium of exchange or means of payment, a unit of account, a store of value, and a standard of deferred payment. We now discuss these four functions in turn, but note already that the distinguishing feature of money is that it is the medium of exchange.

The Medium of Exchange

In a modern economy the medium of exchange, money, is used in one-half of almost all exchanges. When you work, you exchange your labor for money. When you buy goods, you exchange money for the goods. In the economy, people are exchanging goods and services that they produce for goods and services provided by other people. None of us wants money to consume directly. We want it only to buy goods and services now or in the future. Money is the medium of exchange because it is the means through which goods and services are exchanged between people in the economy.

The use of a common medium of exchange, serving as one-half of each transaction, makes the exchange of goods and services more efficient. The benefits of using a medium of exchange are best appreciated by thinking of a barter economy.

> A *barter economy* is one without any commonly accepted medium of exchange. Goods are traded directly for other goods.

Because there is no money in a barter economy, the only trading that can take place is between any two people *each* of whom has something the other wants. To buy a hamburger, you have to hand over something the owner of the hamburger stand wants. To visit a movie house, you have to pay something the owner wants directly. We say there has to be *double coincidence of wants* before exchange can take place in a barter economy. The seller and buyer *each* must want something the other has to offer. Indeed, each trader has to be both a seller and a buyer.

Trading becomes very costly if there has to be a double coincidence of wants, since people must spend time and resources looking for others with needs that precisely match their own. In some cases trade becomes impossible, as Figure 25-1*a* illustrates. A produces bananas and wants oranges. B produces apples and wants bananas. C produces oranges and wants

apples. Figure 25-1*a* shows that if A sells B a banana, there is nothing B can offer A in exchange. Similarly, if B sells C an apple, there is nothing C can offer in exchange, since B does not want oranges. The same applies to trade between C and A. If a double coincidence of wants is a requirement, there can be no trading in this case.

An economy in which all trading has to be direct is so cumbersome that ways will be found to make trading more efficient. People engage in indirect barter. Figure 25-1*b* shows how this can be done. A sells a banana to B, who pays with an apple. Then A sells the apple to C in exchange for an orange. Everyone ends up with the good he wants. The problem with this form of trade is that A, who wants to specialize in producing and selling bananas, ends up having to trade also in apples. A now has to become informed about the quality of the apples he is buying and about the sources of demand for apples. Indirect barter reduces the amount of specialization in the economy and requires trading that, as we now see, is unnecessary in a monetary economy.

The use of money—any object that is *generally* accepted in payment for goods, services, and debts—simplifies exchange. Figure 25-1*c* shows the exchanges that are made in a monetary economy. Each person sells directly to the buyer, and each person buys directly from the seller. Less time and effort is spent engaging in indirect trading of goods and in finding and locating barter deals. People such as A in Figure 25-1 can become more specialized and more productive.

A modern economy could not operate without a commonly accepted medium of exchange. For instance, every student paying tuition would have to find some good that the college was willing to accept in payment and that the student could in turn either provide or obtain through further exchanges. The essential benefit of using a

FIGURE 25-1 TRADING ARRANGEMENTS WITHOUT AND WITH MONEY. If a double coincidence of wants is needed for trade, no trade may take place even when everyone could be made better off by trading. Figure 25-1a shows an example where there is no trade possible even though each person has something someone else wants. In Figure 25-1b indirect trading permits the exchanges to take place but requires A to sell both bananas and apples. In Figure 25-1c monetary exchange is introduced, and each producer is able to specialize in selling only what he produces and buying only what he wants for consumption.

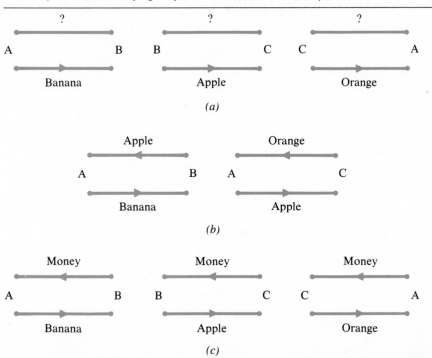

commonly accepted means of exchange is that it reduces the amount of trading of goods for other goods and therefore saves resources that would have been used in trading and can be used instead to produce more goods or leisure.

Other Functions of Money

The *unit of account* is the unit in which prices are quoted and accounts are kept. Prices in the United States are quoted in dollars and cents, and the dollar is therefore the unit of account. In France prices are quoted in French francs, and the franc is the unit of account, and so on. But prices are not always quoted in terms of the medium of exchange. In countries where inflation is high and prices in terms of the local money are changing fast, prices are frequently quoted in terms of a foreign money. For example, in the rapid German inflation of 1922–1923, firms and shops quoted prices and kept their accounts in dollars. But payments were made in the German medium of exchange, marks, at least during the earlier part of the inflation.

Money is a *store of value* because it can be used to make purchases in the future. Money *has* to be a store of value if it is to be accepted in exchange. If money could not be used to make future purchases, no one would be willing to accept it now in exchange for goods or services. But money is neither the only nor necessarily the best store of value. Houses, automobiles, stocks, savings accounts, and stamp collections all serve as stores of value. Someone who wants to store value for any length of time can almost certainly find a better way of doing so than through money.

Money serves as a *standard of deferred payment* in that payments to be made in the future are usually specified in terms of money. When you borrow from the bank, you have to pay back a given number of dollars at a future date or dates. But this is not an essential function of money. The amount of the future payment may be contracted in terms of something other than money; perhaps the amount might be specified in ounces of gold or in terms of a foreign currency. When the time comes, the payment is made in money, in an amount equal in value to the amount of gold or foreign currency specified in the agreement.

Thus, of the four functions of money, its use as a medium of exchange is the distinguishing characteristic. The use of money as a store of value is necessary for money to continue being used. Money need not be the unit of account or the standard of deferred payment, but it usually is. However, in countries suffering from rapid inflation, money stops being used for these last two purposes.

Different Kinds of Money

In prisoner-of-war camps cigarettes served as money, and in the nineteenth century gold and silver coins were money.[1] Today money generally takes the form of other-

wise valueless paper and of deposits at banks. These examples suggest the distinction among three kinds of money: commodity money (gold, silver, cocoa), token money, and IOUs.

Commodity Money

A *commodity money* is used as a medium of exchange and also is bought and sold as an ordinary good.

Commodity monies are as valuable in commercial and other uses as they are as money. When cocoa was used as both money and a drink, it had the same value in both uses. How do we know that? Ask what would have happened had cocoa been more valuable as money. Then no one would have drunk it. If it had been more valuable as a drink, people would not have used it as money. Thus it had the same value in both uses. Similarly, when gold was used as money, it had the same value as money and in its industrial uses.

Token Monies

Token monies are those means of payments whose value or purchasing power as money exceeds the cost of production and the value in alternative uses.

A hundred dollar bill, for instance, is worth far more as money than as a 3 × 6 inch piece of high-quality paper.

Coins, too, can be token monies when their value as money exceeds the worth of the copper or nickel of which they are made. Most of the time it does not pay to melt down quarters to extract the metal and sell it. On occasion, though, the value of the metal of which coins are made increases sharply relative to the value of the coin as money. As a consequence the coins disappear rapidly from circulation. This happened to silver coins and also for a time to the copper cent when the price of copper was high. At that time banks were offering $1.15 for a bag of 100 pennies.

---

[1] Cigarettes were used as a medium of exchange in World War II prisoner-of-war camps. The monetary system of such camps is described in a very interesting article by R. A. Radford, "The Economic Organization of a P.O.W. Camp," *Economica*, November 1945.

How can token monies exist? The essential condition is that there be control over the right to produce money. If people could print dollar bills, it would be profitable for them to keep printing until there were no more profits to be earned by doing so. They would keep printing until the cost of the paper plus the cost of the printing and engraving reached $1. If costs were any less than that, it would still be profitable to print more. Given that it now costs only a few pennies to make a dollar bill, how would the economy reach a situation in which it costs a dollar's worth of resources (paper, labor, machinery) to make a dollar? The answer is that the dollar would become worth less in terms of goods. As printers kept printing, the supply of money would keep rising. As the quantity supplied increases, the value, or purchasing power, of each bill falls. Token money survives mainly because private production of money is illegal and the forces of competition therefore do not drive the value of dollar bills and coins down to the cost of making them.

Modern monies are accepted in part because the law requires them to be accepted. These are *fiat monies,* or legal tender.

> *Legal tender* is money that the government has declared acceptable in exchange and as a lawful way of paying off debts.

Usually the legal tender will be the only means of payment accepted by the government, for instance, to pay taxes. With this legal support, the domestic money in each country has a strong start on being generally accepted in exchange.

Most countries produce and use their own money. But in countries with a high rate of inflation, which makes the value of money fall fast, people may start using foreign currencies even though the local currency remains legal tender. Despite the law, sellers refuse to sell goods unless payment is in gold or dollars rather than the local currency. Thus legal tender laws can take the money only so far. Beyond that, people will not use the money if its value is falling rapidly.

IOU Monies Aside from token monies and commodity monies, there is a third category which accounts for most of the money used in modern economies.

> An *IOU money* is a medium of exchange based on the debt of a private firm or person.

A bank deposit is IOU money, because it is a debt of the bank. The bank is obliged to provide dollar bills in exchange for a deposit. Traveler's checks, too, are IOU money. They are a debt of the company that issued the check and is obliged to pay dollars in exchange for the check whenever asked.

Traveler's checks are a medium of exchange because people know (or expect and trust) that they can be turned into dollars. If there is any doubt, they are not accepted in payment, just as a dollar bill that is thought to be counterfeit is not accepted. Similarly, bank deposits serve as a medium of exchange because it is easy to transfer their ownership to someone else. All it takes is a check that gives the receiver the right to demand dollars from the bank on which the check is written. If there is any doubt that the payer actually has a sufficiently large deposit, the check will not be accepted in payment.

How did IOUs of private firms such as banks come to serve as money? The answer is linked with the development of the banking system, to which we can now turn.

2 THE FABLE OF GOLDSMITHS, BANKING, AND MONEY

There is a traditional story about how banks developed that both has some historical basis and explains the role of banks in the monetary system. In the fifteenth and sixteenth centuries, gold was used as money, particularly for making large transactions. The gold was in the form of coins or bullion, (which consists of blocks of gold of specified weight). But the streets were not safe, and neither were homes.

People wanted a place to store their gold safely. Goldsmiths, who worked with gold, had vaults and guards to keep gold safe. They began to provide this service to others. A person would take gold to the goldsmith for safekeeping and then pick it up when it was needed for making payments.

Banking

Two developments turned the goldsmiths from safekeepers to banks. First, people found they did not have to transfer gold in person when making a payment. They did not have to go to the goldsmith to pick up the gold and then take it to the person from whom they were buying. All they needed to do was give the seller a letter, telling the goldsmith to transfer the money to that person. The person bringing the letter, the bearer, might either take the gold or leave it at the goldsmith's. The letter is, of course, a check.

Once checks became acceptable in payment for purchases, people felt that the gold they held at the goldsmith's was as good as gold in the pocket as a means of making payment. In figuring out how much money they had, they would count both gold in their pockets and gold held by the goldsmith.

The amount deposited at the goldsmith's for safekeeping was called a *deposit*.

People would say their money holdings were equal to gold in their physical possession plus deposits.

We can aleady begin to see how the goldsmiths affect the means of making pay-

ments. Deposits at the goldsmiths' are more convenient for making payments than the gold they represent. Thus the invention of deposits made the payments system more efficient.

The second development is more significant, though. The goldsmiths noticed that they had large quantities of gold sitting idle in the vaults. People would sometimes transfer gold to others by check, and most of the time they did not even bother to visit the bank. They never came by to see that their own gold was still there. All the goldsmith had to do was be ready whenever asked to provide gold to the people who were entitled to it.

The First Loan

Suppose a businessman approaches the goldsmith to ask for a loan. The goldsmith realizes he can give the businessman a loan of some of the gold sitting in the vault. The businessman will spend the gold, but eventually he will repay with interest. The goldsmith is confident that in the meantime everyone who wants gold from the vault will still be able to get it. He goes ahead and makes the loan, duly noting the loan in his accounts.

The account in Table 25-1 shows what happens. The left side shows the goldsmith's balance sheet before the loan is made. He has $100 worth of gold in the vault, and he owes $100 to the people who have deposited the gold with him. Those are liabilities—amounts owed by the goldsmith—recorded on the right-hand side of the T. The second T-account shows the situation after the first loan has been made. The goldsmith-banker still owes $100 to depositors. But instead of holding $100 in gold as assets, he now holds $90 in gold, and $10 is the value of the loan he has made. The loan will be repaid with interest, and so he is pleased to move from the first to the second

TABLE 25-1
T-ACCOUNTS

OLD-FASHIONED GOLDSMITH				GOLDSMITH-BANKER			
ASSETS		LIABILITIES		ASSETS		LIABILITIES	
Gold	$100	Deposits	$100	Gold	$90	Deposits	$100
				Loan	$10		

TABLE 25-2
A LOAN IN THE FORM OF A DEPOSIT

AFTER LOAN IS MADE				AFTER BORROWER BUYS A CARRIAGE			
ASSETS		LIABILITIES		ASSETS		LIABILITIES	
Gold	$100	Deposits	$110	Gold	$90	Deposits	$100
Loan	$ 10			Loan	$10		

balance sheet, even though the total amounts of assets and liabilities are the same.

A Loan in the Form of a Bank Deposit The borrower might not immediately want gold when he borrows from the goldsmith. He may be content for a time to keep the gold in the bank and instead hold a deposit in order to make payments as needed. In that case the goldsmith can make the loan by giving the borrower a deposit at the bank. The balance sheet then looks like the T-account on the left in Table 25-2. Instead of having only $100 in assets and liabilities, the goldsmith now has $110 of each.

Most likely, the borrower wants the loan to buy something, say, a carriage. He therefore uses his deposit to make a payment by check. When that happens, the balance sheet of the goldsmith-banker changes from the left side of Table 25-2 to the right side. The person from whom the borrower bought a carriage arrives with his check and asks for $10 worth of gold. As it is paid out, the amount of deposits held drops by $10 because the borrower no longer has a deposit. And assets held drop by $10 because the amount of gold held in the vaults is $10 lower. Note that the T-accounts on the right side in both tables are the same. Thus Table 25-1 summarizes what happens whether the goldsmith makes a loan by directly giving cash (gold) to the borrower or instead gives him a deposit that is only later used to make payments. From now on we concentrate on balance sheets in the form of Table 25-1 when discussing the effects of the goldsmith's lending.

Reserves

What can go wrong for the goldsmith? His only problem is that he does not have enough gold on hand to meet *all* the demands his depositors can make on him. If they all show up at once, demanding their gold, he is in trouble. He can certainly pay out $90, and he does have a claim to $10 plus interest on the borrower, but it is not certain that the borrower will have that amount of gold at a moment's notice.

The goldsmith as banker is making loans by relying on the fact that not all customers come to claim their gold simulta-

FIGURE 25-2   THE SOLVENCY-PROFITABILITY TRADE-OFF. The goldsmith-banker has to choose a reserve ratio that strikes a balance between the risk of insolvency because of reserves that are too low and the low profitability that comes from high reserve ratios.

neously. We describe the amount of gold he does hold as reserves.

> The *reserves* are the amount of gold immediately available to meet depositors' demands. The *reserve ratio* is the ratio of reserves to deposits.

If the goldsmith has a 100 percent reserve ratio, as he did before he discovered the loan business, he will never be in trouble. There is never a moment at which he is unable to meet all the claims of depositors for gold. But of course, when he holds 100 percent reserves, he is not making any profits from the lending business.

The goldsmith earns interest as soon as he goes into the loan business and reduces his reserve ratio below 100 percent. For instance, on the right-hand side of Tables 25-1 and 25-2, the reserve ratio is 90 percent, since deposits are $100 and reserves are $90. But when the reserve ratio is less than 100 percent, he opens himself up to the possibility of being unable to meet depositors' claims and perhaps having to declare bankruptcy. He thus faces a trade-off between profitability and solvency, as shown in Figure 25-2. The lower the reserve ratio, the more interest he earns. But the lower the reserve ratio, the greater the chance that one day many depositors will demand their gold and he will not have enough.

The amount of reserves needed to assure safety depends on the behavior of depositors and the types of loans that have

been made. The more unpredictable and variable the amount of withdrawals from the bank on any given day, the more reserves the bank will need to be able to meet any demands for gold from the depositors. The more quickly the bank can get gold from those to whom it has loaned, the less reserves it needs. If the borrower is willing and able to repay the loan within a day of being asked, the bank can lend out more than it could if all the loans were for the period of a year. Thus from the viewpoint of the banker, the unpredictability of demands for gold withdrawals and the types of loans that have been made determine how much reserves he will want to hold.

Goldsmith Banking and the Money Stock

> The *stock of money* is the value of generally accepted means of payment.

In the hypothetical goldsmith banking economy, the stock of money consists of gold held directly by persons plus the amount of deposits they have at the goldsmiths'. The deposits count as money because checks are generally accepted in payment. The amount of gold held directly by people is called *gold* (or currency) *in circulation*.

Thus the total value of the money stock is given by

Money stock = gold in circulation + deposits at goldsmiths'   **(1)**

Note that we are now assuming there are several goldsmiths. Looking back at Tables 25-1 and 25-2, we see that the total value of deposits at the goldsmiths' is equal to the amount of gold held by them plus the value of loans they have made. Thus we can also write

Money stock = gold in circulation + gold held by goldsmiths + goldsmiths' loans   **(1a)**

The final step is to note that gold in circulation plus gold held by the goldsmiths equals all the gold in the economy, or the total gold stock. Therefore we write

Money stock = gold stock + goldsmiths' loans (2)

Now we see the role of goldsmiths in affecting the stock of money. Before the goldsmiths went into the lending business, the total money stock consisted of the gold stock. Now the money stock consists of the gold stock *plus* an amount equal to the loans made by the goldsmiths.

It is worth emphasizing the result we have just shown. When gold is the currency in circulation and all bank deposits are claims on gold, the activities of the goldsmith-banker affect the money stock.

At what stage do the goldsmiths begin to affect the money stock? It is *not* when they first accept gold for safekeeping. At that stage loans are zero, and the money stock consists of gold in circulation plus deposits which are equal to the rest of the gold stock. It is when the goldsmiths decide they can hold less than 100 percent reserves that they begin to affect the money stock. That is when they start making loans, and the money stock rises.

We can pinpoint what happens by going back to Table 25-1. When the goldsmith made a loan of $10 to the borrower, the borrower received money. So far as he was concerned, he now had money like anyone else. But no one else in the economy had any less money than before. Everyone with a claim on the goldsmith still maintained the same amount of claims. Essentially, what the goldsmith did was take $10 out of the vaults and put it back into circulation. In that way, by making loans and putting gold back into circulation, the goldsmith increased the money supply.

The fact that the money stock (gold in circulation plus deposits) is also equal to the total amount of gold plus goldsmiths' loans has two implications. First, the amount of loans made by goldsmiths will be higher the lower the reserve ratio they are willing to keep for any given amount of gold deposited with them. Thus we expect the money stock to be higher the lower the reserve ratio of the goldsmiths.

Second, the money stock exceeds the total amount of gold in the economy. But everyone who owns money thinks it is as good as gold. Everyone either has gold or thinks he can immediately obtain it from the goldsmiths. However, the goldsmiths do not have that much gold. Part of their assets—matching deposits on the other side of the balance sheet—are actually loans made to borrowers. The goldsmiths may not be able to obtain gold instantly from the people to whom they have made loans.

Financial Panics

If holders of deposits that are in principle instantly convertible into gold become suspicious, a financial panic may develop. If deposit holders decide that the goldsmith may not be able to meet demands for gold, they will go as quickly as possible to get their own gold out before anyone else.

Once such a process starts, everyone tries to withdraw his gold. This is called a *run* on the bank. The problem with runs on the bank is that they are self-fulfilling prophecies. If people believe banks are in danger of not being able to pay out gold on demand and they all go ahead to get their gold first, they ensure that the bank *is* in fact unable to meet all the demands on it for gold. Because part of the deposits are matched on the other side of the balance sheet by loans, it is impossible to meet all demands for gold. The institution must declare itself insolvent, that is, unable to pay its debts. We call a *financial panic* a process in which people try to obtain gold or currency which is owed to them but unavailable and in the process cause banks and other businesses to go bankrupt.

Financial panics were common even early in this century. Financial panics are not confined to a goldsmith banking system. Any banking system in which banks hold less than 100 percent reserves may be subject to runs on banks and financial panic.

Runs on banks took place when it became known that some of the banks' borrowers had trouble repaying their loans. That meant that perhaps the bank would not be able to pay gold to its depositors when they demanded it. Immediately the depositors would stage a run on the bank to get cash while there was any to be had. Inevitably the bank would have to put up a sign: "payments suspended."[2] Such panics are rare today, for reasons we discuss in Chapter 26.

3 MODERN BANKING

Modern banks are profit-making financial intermediaries.

A *financial intermediary* is an institution that stands between lenders and borrowers. It borrows and then relends the funds to the borrowers.

A commercial bank borrows currency from the public, issuing a deposit in exchange. Then it uses the money it has borrowed to make loans to firms or individuals who it believes will repay them.

Banks are not the only financial intermediaries. Life insurance companies and pension funds also receive money from people who are saving or lending and in turn relend that money. The banks are distinguished by the fact that they are the major financial intermediaries, with a large share of total lending in the economy, and even more by the fact that some of their liabilities are used as means of payment and are therefore part of the money stock.

---

[2] Charles Kindleberger, *Manias, Panics and Crashes*, Basic Books, New York, 1979, provides a highly readable account of the more spectacular panics.

In this section we show what modern banks do. In the next section we show how banks help make payments. Then we define the money stock in the United States and the role of the banks in providing part of it. Throughout we refer to the present-day U.S. banking system. The details of banking systems differ around the world, but the overall picture is not very different from country to country or at different times. Indeed, we shall see that the story of the goldsmith banks provides good guidance to understanding how modern banks work.

The best place to start is the balance sheet of the banks.

The Balance Sheet of the U.S. Banking System

Table 25-3 shows the assets and liabilities of all U.S. commercial banks.

Commercial banks are financial institutions with a state or federal charter that authorizes them to accept checkable and other deposits and make loans.

A checkable deposit is, as the name suggests, one against which checks can be written.

We now discuss the entries in the balance sheet. There are three categories on the assets side: cash assets, loans and securities, and the remainder, called "other." Cash assets include dollar bills and coins but also include reserves which commercial banks hold at the U.S. central bank, which is called the Federal Reserve, or *Fed* for short. Chapter 26 discusses the operations of the Federal Reserve; here we simply note that part of commercial bank assets are held with the Fed, which is a bankers' banker. The category of cash assets is what we call commercial bank reserves.

Commercial bank reserves are assets immediately available to meet claims by the banks' depositors.

They correspond to the gold held as reserves by the goldsmiths.

TABLE 25-3

THE BALANCE SHEET OF U.S. COMMERCIAL BANKS
(Billions of Dollars, December 1981)

ASSETS		LIABILITIES	
Cash Assets:	$ 173.1	Deposits:	$1241.1
Currency and coin		Demand	
Reserves with Fed		Savings and time deposits	
Other			
Loans and Securities:	1268.1	Borrowings	190.1
Commercial and industrial		Other	222.4
Other loans			
U.S. and other securities			
Other	212.5		

Source: *Federal Reserve Bulletin*, May 1982, Table 1.25.

Loans and securities are the investments, consisting mainly of loans the banks have made with the funds they have received from depositors or from borrowing. Commercial banks make loans to business firms for any of a variety of purposes. Airlines may borrow to finance the purchase of planes, automobile companies may borrow to finance new assembly lines or robot plants, and grocery stores may borrow to finance an investment in new checkout counters or simply to pay for the goods on the shelves. Loans also include bank lending to households for purchases of cars, for example, or for a college education. But banks also hold part of their earning assets in the form of interest-bearing claims on the federal government and on foreign governments. From the point of view of banks, U.S. government securities have the advantage of safety. The federal government is unlikely to default, while commercial customers or foreign governments may default at some time. U.S. government securities are attractive also because there is a well-developed market for these securities so that they are in many cases almost as good as cash.

The last category is a group, "other," in which we put all assets ranging from typewriters to the bank buildings and parking lots as well as earning assets that do not fit neatly into the first two categories.

The assets side of the balance sheet shows how banks hold their assets. The liabilities side shows the different sources for the funds the banks hold. The main source is deposits. Banks attract deposit customers by offering the convenience of checkable deposits, interest-bearing deposits, or both. For the customers, deposits are preferred to holding and carrying around cash because of the convenience and safety of writing checks or because deposits earn interest whereas cash does not. In either case deposits are an attractive way for people to hold part of their wealth, and banks are one of the places where deposits can be held.

The balance sheet shows a distinction between demand deposits and savings and time deposits. About 30 percent of deposits are demand deposits; the rest are savings and time deposits. Demand deposits, which are checkable, are deposits on which the depositor can draw without any notice. By contrast, savings and time deposits, which are not checkable, require notice of a specified period before a withdrawal can be made. Banks are willing to pay a higher interest rate on these deposits than on demand deposits because customers cannot receive the money back immediately. We return to this point below in discussing reserves.

Deposits are not the only source of bank funds. Banks also acquire funds by borrowing directly from the public. Banks do so by selling IOUs, that is, promises to pay the holder, after a given time, a specified amount of money plus interest. The proceeds from selling these IOUs or notes are then used to make loans to the banks' customers. The difference between bank deposits and borrowings by banks is that in the case of deposits, the date at which the customer wants to use the deposit and thereby withdraw his money from the bank is up to the customer. In the case of bank IOUs, the bank knows exactly when it has to make payment.

The last category on the liabilities side, "other," includes items that are of no immediate significance.

Banks as Financial Intermediaries

In what sense are banks financial intermediaries, standing between lenders and borrowers? Think of someone or a group of people setting up a bank. A bank is a business. As in other businesses, its owners aim to maximize profits. To get the bank started, they put up some of their own money, which is known as the bank's capital. This is available to cover the costs of setting up the bank and then later as a margin of safety for depositors in case some of the bank's loans are not repaid.

How does the bank go about maximizing profits? The owners have to get people to lend them money. Since the bank has to compete with existing banks, it offers favorable terms to potential depositors. They can have free checking, perhaps free toasters, and interest rates as high as the law allows. If the bank is successful at attracting money, people will start making deposits with it. The depositors are lending money to the bank.

Next the bank has to find profitable ways of lending what it has borrowed. The balance sheet of Table 25-3 shows what banks typically do with the money they have borrowed. Some is held as reserves. Most is lent out to firms that want to buy machinery, students who need tuition loans, and people who need a mortgage to buy a house. Some of the money is used to buy securities such as Treasury bills. If the bank's management is good at choosing people to whom to lend and securities to buy, the bank will make high profits. The owners will have a high return on the money they put up.

What economic service does an intermediary provide? It creates assets for households of a type they find attractive, such as deposits. By investing the proceeds in loans, it enables the households, through the interest they receive, to benefit from the bankers' expertise in choosing among borrowers. The deposit holder and other lenders to banks indirectly get to hold a share of the bank's assets. The deposit holder is, for instance, holding a little bit of a mortgage loan to a shopping center, some part of the bank's loan to the government of Poland, and some part of the bank's loans to computer chip manufacturers. And the holder gets to hold those assets in the very convenient form of a deposit.

There is another way in which banks may make profits. Banks are not only financial intermediaries; they also help people make payments by using checks. Banks can, and sometimes do, charge for the payments services they provide. These charges would, for instance, be some flat amount per check, such as 25 cents. We shall see shortly how banks help operate the payments mechanism, but we note here that in practice almost all banks' income comes from their lending activities and very little comes from their charges for making payments. Indeed, many banks do not even bother to charge for checks, instead treating free checking as a way to attract depositors.

Fractional Reserve Banking

The balance sheet of banks in Table 25-3 reveals deposit liabilities of $1241 billion. Not shown in the table is the fact that $365 billion of these were demand deposits, repayable on demand by the depositor. Against all these deposits, the banks held $173 billion of reserves in cash assets. The reserve ratio, or ratio of reserves to deposits, is therefore 13.9 percent [(173/1241) × 100 percent]. For every $1 of deposits, the banks held only 14 cents of reserves. Total reserves even came to less than half the total amount of demand deposits. With such low reserves, banks would be totally unable to survive a run. As in the case of the goldsmith-bankers, if everyone wanted currency in exchange for deposits, banks would not have enough cash to make the payments.

What determines the reserve ratio of the banking system in the United States? Is it determined, as in Figure 25-2, by a careful weighing of the benefits in terms of higher earnings for the bank from a low reserve ratio versus the risks in terms of a greater likelihood that the bank will be unable to meet claims for money? At present, the answer is no. Existing reserve holdings are mostly determined by the Federal Reserve system.

The Federal Reserve system fixes *minimum reserve requirements*, differing by bank size and kind of deposit. Table 25-4 shows details for large banks. In 1982, for example, demand deposits at large banks carried reserve requirements of 16¼ percent. Savings and time deposits, by contrast, had reserve requirements of only 1 to 3 percent, depending on the length to maturity. Regulation of reserve requirements had as its counterpart regulation of maximum interest rates banks were allowed to pay on different kinds of deposits. These rates ranged from

TABLE 25-4

MAXIMUM INTEREST RATES AND RESERVE REQUIREMENTS AT LARGE BANKS

TYPE OF DEPOSIT	RESERVE REQUIREMENT, %	MAXIMUM INTEREST, % per year
Demand deposit	16¾	0
Savings accounts*	3	5¼
Time deposits:		
30–179 days	3	5¼–5¾
180 days–		
4 years	2½	5¾–6
4 years or more	1	7¼–8

* Savings accounts and NOW (negotiable order of withdrawal) accounts have the same treatment. NOW accounts are essentially checkable time deposits.
Source: Federal Reserve Bulletin, May 1982, Tables 1.15 and 1.16.

zero on demand deposits to 5¼ percent on interest-bearing checking accounts (NOW accounts) and up to 8 percent on time deposits. Reserve requirements and maximum interest rates set by the Fed in 1982 are shown in Table 25-4.

In Chapter 26 we discuss why both reserve ratios and interest rates are regulated. All regulation of bank interest rates is scheduled to end in 1986.

4 COMMERCIAL BANKS AND THE PAYMENTS SYSTEM

By virtue of the $1650 billion of their assets at the end of 1981, the banks are the largest single group of financial intermediaries. They play a major role in mobilizing funds from depositors and lending them to borrowers.

But their distinguishing characteristic among financial intermediaries is that their liabilities—deposits—serve as a means of payment. Checking deposits can be used to make payments throughout the country and indeed the world. The payments system operated by the banks substantially reduces the cost of trading goods compared with a system in which currency would have to be delivered directly to pay for every sale.

To understand how payments are made by banks, consider a payment of $100 made by Joan James to U.S. Widget. The payment is made by a check written by Ms. James on her bank, the First Bank of Dry Gulch. U.S. Widget's bank is Gotham City Bank. How exactly does the $100 get from Ms. James to U.S. Widget?

To start with, Ms. James sends the check to U.S. Widget. The check is written on the First Bank of Dry Gulch and constitutes an instruction to pay $100 to U.S. Widget or whomever U.S. Widget wants the payment made to. U.S. Widget deposits the check in its account at Gotham City Bank. This is shown in the T-account in Table 25-5a. Gotham City's balance sheet shows an increase in deposits by U.S. Widget on the liabilities side and an increase in assets in the form of a claim on the First Bank of Dry Gulch.

Now Gotham City Bank wants to collect the $100 owed it by the First Bank of Dry Gulch. How does it do this? In the United States, payments between cities are likely to be handled by the Federal Reserve system (the Fed). Members of this system (we discuss in Chapter 26 which banks are members) hold accounts at the Fed and can make payments from those accounts. Gotham City will send its check to the Fed and ask it to present the demand for $100 to Dry Gulch. The Fed sends the check to Dry Gulch.

When the check arrives, Dry Gulch instructs the Fed to transfer $100 from its account at the Fed to Gotham City's account. Accounts at the Fed count as reserves for the banks, and so Dry Gulch loses $100 in reserves, as can be seen in Table 25-5b. Corresponding to that change, Dry Gulch's liabilities fall by $100 as Ms. James's deposits fall by $100.

Now the transaction is almost complete.

In Table 25-5c, we see that Gotham City receives $100 in its account at the Fed. Its reserves rise by $100, and its claim on Dry Gulch has been settled. As a result of all these transactions, Ms. James was able to pay U.S. Widget simply by writing out a check. At no stage did either Ms. James or U.S. Widget have to transport currency anywhere in order to make the necessary payments.

Before the creation of the Fed, commercial banks used to operate their own systems to settle payments among themselves. A *clearing system* is a set of arrangements in which debts among banks are settled by adding up all transactions within a given period and paying the *net* amounts needed to balance the accounts.

In a clearing system, the banks might get together at the end of the day. Each bank sees how much it is owed by depositors in all other banks. Those banks in turn inform the bank of how much its depositors have paid them. The bank has to settle the differences between what it received from depositors in other banks and what its depositors paid to them either in gold or in claims on gold. Even today, in major cities there are clearing systems in which the banks at the end of the day total up and settle the various debts that have arisen among them during the day.

The payments system is now very sophisticated. If necessary, payments can be wired between two banks in a matter of a few minutes. The wire transfer is an instruction sent by cable between any two banks which will be settled immediately through transactions at the Fed. The efficiency of the payments system is a major factor in making trade among cities, regions, and states so easy to carry out. In this way the banks' efficient operation of the payments system is a factor contributing to the overall efficiency and productivity of the economy.

TABLE 25-5

THE PAYMENTS MECHANISM

(a)	GOTHAM CITY BANK			(b)	FIRST BANK OF DRY GULCH		
ASSETS		LIABILITIES		ASSETS		LIABILITIES	
Claim on First Bank of Dry Gulch	+$100	Deposits U.S. Widget	+$100	Account at Fed	−$100	Deposits of Joan James	−$100

(c)	GOTHAM CITY BANK		
ASSETS		LIABILITIES	
Account at Fed	+$100		
Claim on First Bank of Dry Gulch	−$100		

5 COMMERCIAL BANKS AND THE MONEY STOCK

In the United States today we define as money those generally acceptable means of payment that are usable for *unrestricted* payments. That means we can use them any time to pay any amount to anyone. The definition excludes, for example, time deposits, on which the owner cannot write a check and from which he can receive money only after giving notice to the bank. It also rules out money market fund shares (we discuss these below), which are checkable but only in amounts larger than $500. The definition of money, technically referred to as M1, focuses on a narrow range of assets including *currency*, checkable deposits at banks, and traveler's checks. Table 25-6 shows the components of the U.S. money supply.

Currency is issued by the U.S. government. It includes coins (pennies, quarters, nickels, dimes, Susan B. Anthony dollars, and half-dollar pieces) and all the bills. Coins are issued by the U.S. Treasury. All paper money is issued by the Federal Reserve. In terms of our earlier definitions, currency in the U.S. is token and fiat money. It is worthless except for the fact that it is acceptable in payments for goods, services, debts, and taxes. The rest of the U.S. money supply represents debts. These are either debts of banks at which the public holds deposits or the debts of companies that sell traveler's checks. The definition of M1 money then is

$$\text{Money (M1)} = \text{currency outside banks} + \text{checkable deposits} + \text{traveler's checks} \qquad (3)$$

Banks as Creators of Money

Banks play a role in the U.S. money supply because their checkable deposit liabilities are part of the money stock. In analogy with the goldsmith story, we can now ask whether U.S. banks create money. Suppose a U.S. bank makes a loan. The loan recipient

TABLE 25-6

THE U.S. MONEY SUPPLY: M1
(Billions of Dollars, December 1981)

COMPONENT	AMOUNT
Currency (paper money and coin)	$125.4
Checkable deposits at banks	321.8
Traveler's checks	4.1
Total = M1	451.3

Source: *Federal Reserve Bulletin*, May 1982, Table 1.21.

BOX 25.1 ▰▰▰▰▰▰▰▰▰▰▰▰▰▰▰▰▰▰▰▰

U.S. CURRENCY

U.S. currency consists of coins (pennies, nickels, dimes, quarters, and dollar coins) and notes issued by the Federal Reserve banks. The table below shows the composition of currency holding by value in 1980. Two related facts stand out. First, nearly half the value of currency is in the form of bills of $50 or more. Second, average holdings of currency are over $600 per person. Very few people hold that much currency. Where is it all?

THE COMPOSITION OF U.S. CURRENCY, 1980

% OF TOTAL CURRENCY VALUE OUTSTANDING							
COIN	$1–$5	$10	$20	$50	$100	$500+	CURRENCY PER CAPITA, $
9.0	6.4	8.7	30.0	10.0	35.9	0.3	602.7

Source: Statistical Abstract of the United States, 1982, Tables 2 and 869.

The large bills are probably used mostly for both legal and illegal transactions abroad and for illegal transactions in the United States. People engaging in illegal transactions or tax fraud will not use bank accounts in order to avoid leaving records of their transactions. They therefore use currency. There are no data on the amount of U.S. currency used abroad, but anyone who has traveled knows that foreign banks and black market traders in currency use large-denomination bills. There are also no data on the amount of currency used in illegal transactions in the United States.

But there is a way of getting an idea of how much illegal use there may be. The local Federal Reserve banks receive currency that is worn out, damaged, or suspicious and thus have a steady inflow and outflow of bills. Records are kept of these bills by denomination. The Federal Reserve bank offices in Los Angeles and in Miami and Jacksonville show much higher turnover of large-denomination notes than is observed in all other offices. This is shown in the following table.

COMPOSITION OF CURRENCY RECEIVED AND VERIFIED BY FEDERAL RESERVE OFFICES
(Percent of Total Dollar Volume, 1979)

MIAMI AND JACKSONVILLE		LOS ANGELES		ALL OTHER OFFICES	
$10 AND UNDER	$50 AND OVER	$10 AND UNDER	$50 AND OVER	$10 AND UNDER	$50 AND OVER
19.5	31.8	21.2	20.0	30.5	16.3

Source: Ralph C. Kimball, "Trends in the Use of Currency," New England Economic Review, September–October 1981, Table 3.

The large share of high-denomination bills in Los Angeles and Florida results from their use in illegal transactions, particularly drug traffic. There is also a demand for high-denomination currency in those areas by residents of Latin American countries suffering from high inflation. Residents of those countries prefer to hold dollars rather than their local currencies, because inflation reduces the value of the local currency in terms of goods as prices rise.

There is one apparent puzzle seen in comparing the two tables. Even in Florida the share of notes $50 and over taken in by the Federal Reserve offices is lower than their share of total currency outstanding. Why? Those notes are used much less often than the small-denomination notes, wear out less quickly, and therefore are much less often turned in to the Federal Reserve.

Another puzzle may be the column marked "$500+" in the first table. Those notes were issued before World War II and are no longer issued. What is shown in the table is the remnant of the earlier issues. The issue of high-denomination notes was stopped to make illegal transactions more difficult. Indeed, even in 1982 the Internal Revenue Service was trying to get bills larger than $20 removed from circulation.

The use of dollar bills abroad and for illegal transactions explains why the data show that the *average* U.S. resident holds $600 in currency. We understand this when we read in the newspaper that someone was arrested with a suitcase full of hundred-dollar bills and 6 tons of marijuana or when someone demands to be paid in cash.

receives the loan in the form of a deposit on which he can draw, or if he chooses, he can receive it directly in currency. Does the fact that the bank makes a new loan increase the money supply? The T-accounts in Table 25-7 show the answer: *Any time a bank makes a loan, it increases the money stock.*

In (*a*) we show the case where a loan customer takes a loan in currency. In this case the bank's reserves decline by the amount of the loan. Total assets of the bank remain unchanged, and the loan has simply reshuffled the assets from reserves to earning assets. The amount of liabilities is unchanged. Looking at the definition of money in equation (3), the money stock has risen because currency that used to be in banks and thus was *not* part of the money stock now is held by the public. In making a loan, the bank has created money by releasing some of its reserves for use by the nonbank public. This is the same process used by the goldsmith who lent gold to his customers.

In case (*b*) the bank also creates money. This time the loan customer or whoever is paid by him holds the proceeds of the loan as a deposit. Bank assets are increased through the loan, and there is an offsetting rise in liabilities with the increase in deposits. The money stock has risen because with currency outside banks unchanged, there is a rise in deposits, which are part of the money stock.

TABLE 25-7

T-ACCOUNTS FOR BANK CREATION OF MONEY

Case (*a*)   Loan customer receives currency

ASSETS		LIABILITIES
Reserves	−$10	
Loans	+$10	No change

Case (*b*)   Loan customer receives deposit

ASSETS		LIABILITIES	
Reserves	No change	Deposits	$10
Loans	+$10		

Economists have focused on the question of whether banks create money because, as we shall see in Chapter 27, the stock of money affects spending decisions of households and firms. It thereby affects output and prices in the economy. For that reason, decisions by banks to make more or fewer loans or by customers to borrow more or less will have an impact on the macroeconomy. The effects of bank creation of money on the total money stock has to be taken into account by the Fed in determining how to conduct its own policies to control the quantity of money.

6   MONEY AND NEAR-MONIES

The M1 definition of money includes a narrow range of assets that can immediately and without restriction be used to make payments. But there is a host of other assets that are "almost" as good as money. We refer to them as *near-monies*, suggesting by the name that they do not fully possess all the functions that money must fulfill. Near-monies include, for example, savings accounts at saving and loans (S&Ls).

S&Ls are depository institutions that receive savings deposits and use the proceeds to make mostly real estate loans.

These savings deposits are not quite as good as money if they cannot be readily used in making payments by writing checks on them without prior notice.

Another example of a near-money is shares in a money market mutual fund.

A *money market fund* is a financial institution that sells shares to the public and uses the proceeds to invest in short-term interest-bearing securities. The holders of shares can sell them by writing checks on the fund.

For all practical purposes money market fund shares are checkable and interest-bearing demand deposits. They are attractive to hold for making large payments because they pay a high rate of interest, indeed much higher than bank deposits pay. These shares are near-monies rather than money, because the minimum size of the checks written on the fund is $500.

Each of the examples we have given describes an asset that competes with the traditional monies: checkable deposits and currency. These assets are invented by financial intermediaries to acquire funds with which to make loans. They represent financial innovations that could have extremely large impacts on the performance of the entire U.S. economy. In 1978, for example, money market mutual funds (MMMFs) accounted for barely $7 billion of assets. By 1981 their size had grown to $150 billion. That growth occurred at the expense of other assets—in particular, checkable deposits in banks. In 1982 it was decided to allow banks to offer MMMFs to their customers.

A share in an MMMF may be almost as good for its owner as money in the form of currency or a checking account at a commercial bank. For larger payments it serves as well as a bank checking account, and it even pays interest. Thus it is not much worse as a medium of exchange, and as a store of value it is better than money since it pays interest. To a lesser extent, the same can be said of large time deposits and even U.S. government short-term bonds. They can be turned into cash because there is a ready market for them, but they certainly are not a means of payment. They are a near-money in the sense that their value in terms of dollars is highly stable and that they have a ready market and thus can easily be turned into money.

To the extent that individuals regard these near-monies to varying degrees as being close to money and serving some of the same functions, it is quite possible that the existing stock of near-monies affects inflation and economic activity. It is for that reason that we pay attention to them.

TABLE 25-8

DIFFERENT MEASURES OF MONEY AND NEAR-MONIES
(Billions of Dollars, December 1981)

	MONEY	BROADER AGGREGATES	
	M1	M2	M3
Currency	x	x	x
Checkable deposits at banks	x	x	x
Traveler's checks	x	x	x
Savings and small time deposits*		x	x
Money market mutual fund shares		x	x
Large time deposits			x
Commercial paper, liquid U.S. Treasury securities, U.S. savings bonds, other			x
Total	451.2	1829.1	2199.6

* Small time deposits are $100,000 or less.
Source: Federal Reserve Bulletin, May 1982, Table 1.21.

The *broader monetary aggregates,* M2 and M3, include, in addition to M1, near-monies that are almost as good as money from the viewpoint of the holder.

Table 25-8 indicates the components of each of the aggregates by an x in the relevant columns and also shows the totals of each aggregate.

SUMMARY

1 Money has four functions: a medium of exchange, a store of value, a standard of deferred payment, and a unit of account. The distinguishing function of money is its use as a medium of exchange.

2 Money facilitates exchange because it dispenses with the need for a double-coincidence of wants. In a monetary economy, trading is simplified because there is no need for a seller to find a buyer who has what he wants and who wants what the seller has.

3 There are two kinds of money: commodity money and token money. Commodity money is a good that has the same value as a monetary unit and as a commodity. Token money, by contrast, is a good that has a larger value as money than as a commodity. Paper money, for example, is a token money. Commodity monies can become token monies whenever the monetary value of the good rises above its commodity value.

4 Token money is accepted either because people believe they can in turn use it to make payments or because the government has specifically declared it to be legal tender.

5   The story of the goldsmith-banker illustrates the role of modern banks. Goldsmiths who make loans create money. They do so either by releasing into circulation gold previously in vaults or by increasing the value of deposits. The choice of how much reserves to hold involves a trade-off between profitability and solvency. Too much lending leaves the goldsmith unable to meet calls for gold; too little means no profits.

6   Modern commercial banks are profit-making financial intermediaries. They attract funds through deposits or borrowing and use the funds to make loans.

7   Banks facilitate, in conjunction with the Fed, the payments system. The clearing makes for rapid nationwide settlement of checks.

8   Banks hold less than 15 cents of reserves for every dollar of deposit liabilities. Like the goldsmiths, banks create money when they make loans. They do so either by reducing their cash reserves or by increasing their deposits.

9   Money is defined as those generally acceptable means of payment which can be used for unrestricted payments, including currency, checkable deposits, and traveler's checks. But there is a host of other assets that are near-monies. They are highly liquid in that they can be converted into currency at short notice. They are not included in money because they are not useable as a means of payment immediately and in an unrestricted way.

KEY TERMS

Money	IOU money
Double coincidence of wants	Financial intermediary
Unit of account	Fractional reserve banking
Store of value	M1
Commodity money	Currency
Token money	Near-money
Legal tender (fiat money)	

PROBLEMS

1   (a) Suppose a person trades in a car when buying another. Is the used car serving as a medium of exchange? Is that person engaged in a barter transaction? (b) Could you tell by watching someone buy peppermints (little white disks) with coins (little silver-colored disks) which one is money?

2   A goldsmith holds 100 percent reserves against his deposits. Use the T-accounts and the definition of the money supply to explain what happens to the money stock when a customer withdraws gold from the goldsmith's vault.

3   Which do you think is a better store of

value, gold or U.S. dollars? Explain your answer.

4 Suppose gold coins are used as money. Initially gold is a commodity money, with the monetary and commodity value of gold the same. Explain under which conditions (*a*) gold becomes a token money and (*b*) gold disappears from monetary circulation.

5 Suppose that umbrellas were too inconvenient to store in the house and that a storage house opened up for them, with people picking up their umbrellas only when needed. (*a*) Could the owner of the storage facility safely lend out a large part of his stock of umbrellas? (*b*) What is the difference between this case and that of the goldsmith?

6 Explain in words the function of commercial banks as financial intermediaries. Use T-accounts to illustrate their sources and uses of funds.

7 Explain in what sense commercial banks create money. (Use the goldsmith story if you want.) (*a*) Use a T-account to show how check clearance works. (*b*) How might payment be made between Atlanta and Los Angeles if there were no checks? (*c*) What difference does an efficient payments system make to the economy?

8 Suppose there were no reserve requirements imposed by the Fed. What would determine how much reserve banks would hold? (It might be helpful to think in terms of the goldsmith bank again.)

9 (*a*) What is the case for counting travelers' checks as part of the money supply? (*b*) Is there a case for counting subway tokens as part of the money supply? (*c*) What about credit cards? (*d*) And postage stamps?

10 (*a*) Money market mutual fund shares have rapidly become a major form in which people hold their liquid assets. In 1982 they were worth more than $150 billion, which is more than the total stock of currency. Discuss whether, as money, MMMFs are better or worse than the components of M1 which we traditionally call money. (*b*) Why should we care what is and is not money?

Money has been used for thousands of years. Central banks, by contrast, are newcomers on the stage of world history. The Federal Reserve System, the central bank of the United States, was not set up until 1913. The Bank of England and the Bank of Sweden, the oldest central banks, were founded at the end of the seventeenth century. Modern central banking goes back at most to the nineteenth century, when the functions of central banks in an economy with fiat money and banks began to be defined.

26

Central Banking and the Monetary System

Today every country of any size has a central bank. Central banks have two basic tasks. First, the central bank has to ensure that the banking and financial systems run smoothly. In particular, the central bank has to prevent financial panics, which can occur in any fractional reserve banking system. In performing this task the central bank is described as the lender of last resort.

The *lender of last resort* lends to financial institutions and firms at times when panic threatens the financial system.

We explain this function of central banks in detail in this chapter. The second task is to run monetary policy, or to control the money stock in a way that promotes full employment with low rates of inflation.

Central banks are continually criticized for their monetary policy performance. Typical of the criticism is that by Milton Friedman, the leading thorn in the side of the Federal Reserve System (the Fed).

Ever since the establishment of the Federal Reserve System, every chairman of the Federal Reserve Board . . . has proclaimed that the Federal Reserve will not be an engine of inflation. Yet the Federal Reserve System was an engine of inflation during both world wars and has been one in peacetime since at least 1960. . . .

The Federal Reserve governors, who now devote 90 percent of their time not to monetary control but to their regulatory functions, could spend 99 percent of their time on such regulatory functions. They would do far less harm that way than the harm which they have been doing with the additional 9 percent they now spend on monetary control.[1]

The regulatory functions which Friedman says take 90 percent of the Fed's governors' time are related to their first task—ensuring the effi-

---

[1] Milton Friedman, "Monetary Policy," *Journal of Money, Credit and Banking,* February 1982, pp. 102, 117.

cient operation of the banking and financial systems. We discuss both of the Fed's tasks in this chapter, starting by describing the structure of the Federal Reserve System. Central banks in other countries are organized differently but still have the same two basic functions.

1 THE FEDERAL RESERVE SYSTEM

The Federal Reserve System was created by an act of Congress in 1913 and has developed over the years with major reforms in the 1930s and again at the end of the 1970s. This section describes the organizational structure and functions of the system.

The Structure of the Federal Reserve System

There were nearly 15,000 commercial banks in the United States in 1980. Over 5000 were members of the Federal Reserve System, as shown in Table 26-1. Although a little more than a third of the banks belonged to the Federal Reserve System, those banks held nearly 75 percent of the total assets held by commercial banks. Thus on average it is the larger banks that belong to the Fed, and in fact most large banks are members.

Membership in the Federal Reserve System carries both duties and privileges. Members are required to clear checks at par, that is, for the full value written on the check. This requirement promotes the use of the banking system for making payments. If checks did not clear at par, people would tend to use currency instead. Member banks are also required to abide by a host of other regulations issued by the Fed. Members benefit by being able to use the Fed's check-clearing system, which makes it easy and cheap to settle payments between different parts of the country. In addition, member banks are allowed to borrow from the Fed if they need loans.

TABLE 26-1

MEMBER AND NONMEMBER BANKS, 1980

	MEMBERS	NONMEMBERS
Number	5422 (36.5%)	9414 (63.5%)
Assets, $ billions	1137 (74.3%)	393 (25.7%)

Source: Statistical Abstract of the United States, 1981, Table 848.

Figure 26-1 describes the organizational structure of the Federal Reserve System. The most important body in the system is the *Board of Governors*, located in Washington, D.C. There are seven members of the Board, each appointed for a 14-year term by the President of the United States. The long term of office is intended to ensure continuity, stability, and independence of the Board. The Board of Governors is headed by the *chairman*, who is also appointed by the President and who serves for 4 years. The chairman is the most powerful person in the system. He usually dominates the Board and the entire system and is occasionally—though with some exaggeration—described as the second most powerful person in the country.

The system is organized in 12 districts, each having a Federal Reserve bank. Figure 26-1 includes a map showing the Fed districts and the cities in which Federal Reserve banks are located. The 12 Federal Reserve banks operate the Fed's check-clearing system at the local level, implement Fed decisions and regulations, and carry out research on economic conditions in their districts. They also report back to the Board on economic conditions in their areas, keeping the Board informed of what is happening around the country.

The *Federal Open Market Committee* (FOMC) makes decisions about U.S. monetary policy. It consists of the seven members of the Board, the president of the New York Federal Reserve Bank, and on a rotating

FIGURE 26-1   THE STRUCTURE OF THE FEDERAL RESERVE SYSTEM.

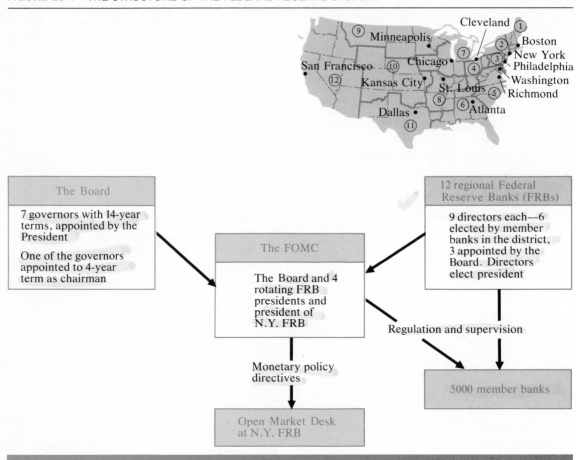

basis four of the presidents of the remaining 11 Federal Reserve banks. Monetary policy decisions, which involve purchases and sales of government securities and will be described in detail below, are carried out in New York by the *Open Market Desk*. Because the major financial markets are in New York, the president of the New York Fed is a permanent member of the FOMC and the Open Market Desk is located in New York.

Functions

The Federal Reserve System was organized to serve the two basic functions of a central

bank. First, it is responsible for the smooth running of the monetary and financial systems. In this connection it acts as both banker to and supervisor of the banking system.

The Fed is the *bankers' banker*. It is in the role of banker to the banking system that the Fed operates the clearing system by which check payments are made between depositors at member banks. As banker to the banks, the Fed also stands willing to lend to member banks that temporarily run short of reserves.

The Fed supervises the banking system by controlling lending and reserve holding practices. The Fed sets reserve requirements for all banks, not just member banks. The Fed also controls the interest rates that commercial banks can pay on their deposits, as described in Table 25-4. The Fed shares the job of supervising banks with other federal and state agencies.

The Fed's second basic task is to conduct monetary policy. It does this mainly by its instructions to the Open Market Desk, telling it how to control the money stock. As we noted above, it is the Fed's monetary policy decisions that keep it in the limelight, now and in the past. We have already seen quotations from Milton Friedman blaming the Fed for the inflation that started in the 1960s. In addition, Friedman has blamed the Great Depression of the thirties on Fed policies. We review part of that argument later in this chapter.

To understand the Fed's functions in acting as banker to the banks and in determining the money stock, we now examine the Fed's balance sheet.

2 THE FEDERAL RESERVE BALANCE SHEET

Table 26-2 shows the balance sheet of the Federal Reserve banks. This is the balance sheet of the combined or consolidated accounts of the 12 Federal Reserve banks, collecting together all their assets and liabilities. We start our discussion with the liability side.

Liabilities

There are two main liabilities: deposits and Federal Reserve notes. Federal Reserve notes are the bills we carry in our pockets. These are issued by the 12 regional Federal Reserve banks, and each carries the seal of the issuing Federal Reserve bank.[2] The other liabilities are deposits with the Fed. These deposits belong to depository institutions (mostly commercial banks) and also to the U.S. Treasury.

One crucial fact about the liabilities of a central bank underlies the operation of modern monetary systems. *There is no possibility that the Fed can go bankrupt.* The Fed is not obligated to convert its liabilities into gold, silver, or anything else. If I have a debt to you, I have an obligation to pay you money on some specific date. If I do not have the money, I will be in trouble. But if you hold a Federal Reserve note, described here as a liability of the Fed, there is nothing the Fed has to give you. If you take a $50 note to the Fed and explain that the balance sheet that the Fed publishes describes the $50 as a liability and therefore you want to be paid $50, the best that can happen is that the Fed will give you 50 dollar bills. Thus the unique feature of the Fed's liabilities is

---

[2] If you check in your pocket, you can immediately tell in what Federal Reserve district you live. Most notes you have will carry the seal of the local Federal Reserve bank; very few will have the seal of another Federal Reserve district. Paper money does not travel much.

TABLE 26-2

FEDERAL RESERVE BALANCE SHEET
(Billions of Dollars, March 31, 1982)

ASSETS		LIABILITIES	
Gold	11.2	Federal Reserve notes	128.9
Loans and acceptances	3.1	Deposits:	
Government securities	134.7	Depository institutions	26.4
Other net	9.1	U.S. Treasury	2.9

Source: Adapted from *Federal Reserve Bulletin,* April 1982, Table 1.18.

that it can create them in unlimited quantities without fear of bankruptcy.

In the days of the gold standard, dollar bills were obligations to pay specific amounts of gold to the holder. In those days central banks could have found themselves unable to meet their liabilities. But not now. For instance, suppose all the depositors at the Fed decide to withdraw their deposits. In what do they expect to be paid? They can be paid only in currency. Then all the Fed has to do is print notes fast. The only obstacle to meeting its liabilities may be the time it takes to do the printing.

Treasury Deposits On the liabilities side, both the Treasury account and the accounts of commercial banks play a role in macroeconomics. The Federal Reserve acts as a payment agent for the U.S. Treasury. The Treasury maintains an account with the Fed, and when payments are to be made, a check is written on the Federal Reserve. When payments are received by the Treasury, say, from taxes or the sale of oil leases, these are deposited in the Treasury account.[3]

Commercial Bank Deposits The deposits which the commercial banks maintain at the Federal Reserve serve two purposes. First and chiefly, they are part of the reserves commercial banks maintain against their own liabilities. Because a bank must pay its depositors or those who receive checks written on a deposit in U.S. dollars, reserves must be held in that form. Commercial banks hold the main part of their reserves as deposits with the Federal Reserve. They can draw on these deposits at the Fed either by writing a check or by asking for actual delivery of Federal Reserve notes.

The accounts held by banks at the Fed also simplify the payments system. They make it possible to use the Fed for clearing checks drawn by the depositors of one bank

and received by the depositors of another. This process was described in Chapter 25, with the relevant T-accounts shown in Table 25-4. The clearing is done by the Fed, which debits the account of the bank whose depositors have written the check and credits the bank whose customers received and presented the check. This is done with a minimum of turnaround time and therefore contributes to making the payments system more efficient.

Assets

The asset side of the balance sheet includes gold. Gold is no longer in circulation in the United States as money. Indeed, it plays no monetary role at all. But the Fed does own some gold, which appears as an asset in the Fed's balance sheet. The Fed acquired the gold mostly during the 1930s. This was a result of the impending war in Europe. Today the Fed neither buys nor sells gold, but its existing holdings appear on the books.

It is essential to remember that U.S. dollar bills that are circulating are not backed by gold and certainly cannot be converted into gold at the Fed. That possibility, as we see later in this chapter, stopped in 1934. Today's Federal Reserve notes are convertible into fresh notes or notes of other denominations or coins, or they can be used to pay taxes, but they are *not* convertible into gold.

The entry "loans and acceptances" in Table 26-2 results from the Fed's role as lender to banks. The Fed lends to banks that are short of reserves. The loan provides the borrower with Fed liabilities, typically a deposit in the account of the borrowing bank at the Fed. The deposit in the bank's account at the Fed increases its reserves and thereby enables the bank to meet its reserve requirements.

Usually the loan is provided outright, with the borrowing bank giving government

---

[3] The Treasury also maintains accounts with commercial banks. These are called tax and loan accounts.

bonds to the Fed to serve as collateral or security for the loan. If the borrowing bank is unable to repay, the Fed has the government bonds to keep instead. The Fed also in effect lends to banks by temporarily buying government securities from them and later reselling the securities. When the Fed buys a government security, it increases the deposit of the selling bank at the Fed and thereby increases its reserves. Later the bank buys back the government security at a higher price (to allow for interest to the Fed), and its deposits at the Fed go down again. Between the dates of buying and selling of the security by the Fed, the selling bank in effect had a Fed loan.

But by far the largest entry on the assets side is the Fed's holdings of government securities. These are securities (government bonds and Treasury bills) of the federal government that the Fed has acquired over the years in a way that we now study.

3 THE FED AND THE MONEY SUPPLY

The Fed plays an important role in the economy because it controls the money supply. In this section we study how the money stock is determined and what role the Fed plays in determining it. The first step is to remind ourselves of the definition of the money supply given in Chapter 25. We leave traveler's checks out of the discussion because they make up only a small part of the money stock.

The Money Supply in the United States

In the United States we define money, M1, as the sum of currency in the hands of the nonbank public plus checkable deposits.

$$M1 = currency + deposits \qquad (1)$$

The money supply thus represents in part the liabilities of the Fed (currency held by the public) and in part the liabilities of banks (checkable deposits of the public at banks).

In Table 26-3 we present simplified T-accounts for the Fed (based on Table 26-2) and the banks (based on Table 25-3). The accounts are simplified by leaving out the U.S. Treasury and gold. The items that together constitute the money stock are shown in red. The T-accounts enable us to show how the Fed's *three instruments of monetary control* affect the money stock.

We now describe the three instruments: reserve requirements, the discount rate, and open market operations.

Reserve Requirements

The *required reserve ratio* is the ratio of reserves to deposits the Fed requires the banks to hold as a minimum.

Banks can hold more than the required reserves, but they cannot hold less. They have to borrow reserves, perhaps from the Fed, if they are short.

Increases in the required reserve ratio reduce the money stock. To see this, suppose to begin with that the banks have the balance sheet shown in Table 26-4. The re-

TABLE 26-3

SIMPLIFIED T-ACCOUNTS FOR THE FED AND COMMERCIAL BANKS

THE FED		BANKS	
ASSETS	LIABILITIES	ASSETS	LIABILITIES
Loans to banks	Federal Reserve notes: Currency held by public	Reserves: Deposits at Fed	Checkable deposits
Government securities	Vault cash of banks Deposits of banks	Vault cash Loans and securities	Other deposits Loans from Fed

TABLE 26-4

EFFECTS OF AN INCREASE IN REQUIRED RESERVES OF BANKS

BEFORE RESERVE CHANGE			AFTER REQUIRED RESERVE CHANGE		
ASSETS		LIABILITIES	ASSETS		LIABILITIES
Reserves	20	Deposits 100	Reserves	20	Deposits 80
Loans and securities	80		Loans and securities	60	

quired reserve ratio is 20 percent, and the banks have exactly that amount of reserves. Now the Fed raises the required reserve ratio to 25 percent. The banks are holding $20 in reserves, and they are therefore below the new required reserve ratio.

The banks may think of trying to obtain reserves from the Fed. But the Fed raised the reserve ratio to reduce the money stock and will not turn around and lend to the banks so that they can avoid having to reduce their loans.

When there is no other way out and the banks are short of reserves, they have to start reducing their loans and securities. Suppose, for example, they reduce loans. Customers who borrowed before will not have their loans renewed, because the banks are short of reserves. The amount of loans falls. Table 26-4 shows the amount falling from 80 to 60, with the amount of reserves held by the banks not changing. The $20 of reserves now backs only $80 of deposits instead of $100. The deposit component of M1 and M1 itself are reduced.

This example shows the entire adjustment to a change in required reserves taking place through a reduction in loans by the banks. It is also possible that the banks can obtain more reserves by getting people to make deposits of currency. They do this by offering a higher interest rate on deposits. In this case the fall in the money supply will be in part a reduction in currency held by the public and in part a fall in deposits

rather than entirely a fall in deposits as implied by Table 26-4.

We have now seen how the Fed can reduce the money stock by increasing required reserves. It does this by forcing the banks to reduce their holdings of loans and securities.

The Discount Rate

The *discount rate* is the rate at which the Fed lends to banks borrowing to meet reserve shortfalls.

If the Fed announces an increase in the discount rate, say, from 10 percent to 14 percent, the banks will be concerned not to have to borrow at so high a rate. To avoid running short of reserves and having to borrow from the Fed, they will try to increase their reserves. Again, they will try to sell assets or call in loans. As they do so, they will cause the money stock to fall.

We have thus seen that any time a bank tries to increase its reserves, it causes a fall in the money stock. Conversely, when banks reduce reserves, making loans rather than calling them in, the money stock expands. The Fed can bring about changes in the money stock because it can, directly through reserve requirements and indirectly through the discount rate, affect banks' demand for reserves.

However, changes in the discount rate and reserve requirements are no longer used much as instruments of monetary policy. The discount rate is used relatively

little because the Fed is trying as much as possible to discourage borrowing by banks except in emergencies. Required reserves are not changed much because increases in reserve requirements make banks less profitable as financial intermediaries, compared with other institutions. Their profits fall because they are holding a larger part of their portfolio as reserves at the Fed and as vault cash, both of which do not pay interest. Thus when reserve requirements rise, commercial banks can hold only a smaller part of their portfolios in interest-earning form, and their profitability goes down. Because the Fed wants the commercial banks to remain competitive with other financial institutions, it does not want to raise reserve requirements and therefore usually does not change them at all.

Open Market Operations

The chief instrument of monetary policy is *open market operations*. The Open Market Desk at the Federal Reserve Bank of New York implements the instructions of the FOMC to buy or sell government securities, and in so doing it affects the money stock.

> In an open market operation, the Open Market Desk buys or sells government securities in the financial markets.

Suppose the FOMC has instructed the desk to reduce the money stock. What are the steps and channels?

The T-accounts shown in Table 26-5 illustrate the case where the Fed, through the Open Market Desk in New York, has sold

government securities worth $1 million. Suppose these securities were bought by Mr. Jones, a customer of First Security Bank in Overbrook, Kansas, who pays the Fed for the purchase with a check drawn on his bank. This is what the account looks like after the transaction, leaving out all items that are unaffected.

The desk has sold $1 million worth of securities to Mr. Jones, who now owns these securities, having paid with a check drawn on First Security. At the Fed, the transaction shows on the assets side as a reduction in security holdings. On the liabilities side, the Fed debits the account of First Security on which the check of Mr. Jones is drawn. Consider next First Security. The transaction here shows as a reduction in reserves because the bank's account at the Fed has been reduced by the amount of Jones's check. There is an offsetting debit of Jones's account which reduces the bank's deposit liabilities.

We started off with an open market sale of debt to reduce the money stock. Has this happened? Glancing at the definition of money in equation (1), it is clear that the decline in Mr. Jones's deposit at First Security means a reduction in money, because deposits are down. But we cannot really stop there. The story continues because First Security, which was precisely in balance before the transaction, holding just enough reserves to satisfy Fed requirements, now has a worse reserve deposit ratio.

Suppose total deposits were $100 mil-

TABLE 26-5

AN OPEN MARKET SALE OF SECURITIES
(Millions of Dollars)

THE FED		FIRST SECURITY OF OVERBROOK	
ASSETS	LIABILITIES	ASSETS	LIABILITIES
Government securities −1	Deposits of banks −1	Reserves: deposits at Fed −1	Deposits −1

lion and reserves had been $20 million, amounting to a 20 percent reserve ratio. Now deposits are $99 million and reserves have declined to $19 million, which is a reserve ratio of only 19.2 percent (19/99). The bank therefore is no longer meeting its reserve requirements and has to take steps to do so. Therefore, further adjustments are made to the open market operation as First Security tries to gain reserves by calling in loans or selling assets. As we have seen, this attempt to gain reserves leads to further contraction in the money stock as the loan customers pay off their loans with currency or by drawing down their bank accounts. In either case the money stock is reduced further by these secondary effects.

The Money Multiplier

The full impact of an open market operation on the money stock includes both the direct and the secondary effects. The fact that there are also secondary impacts immediately means that a $1 million sale of securities by the Fed must change the money stock by more than $1 million.

The $1 million fall happens as soon as the sale of securities is made. The extent of the final change in the money stock depends in particular on two factors: the reserve deposit ratio of banks and the way the public divides their money holdings between currency and deposits. If banks held nearly 100 percent reserves (which they do not) and if the public held nearly no currency and mostly deposits, the open market operation would have no secondary effects. Why? Because the bank, when it loses a dollar of reserves and a dollar of deposits, still has 100 percent reserves and need not adjust further. But if the reserve/deposit ratio is small, say, 10 percent, a fall in deposits and reserves by the same dollar amount reduces the reserve ratio a lot; this means banks will call in a lot of loans and thus produce a large money contraction.

The multiple by which a Fed open market operation affects the money stock is called the money multiplier.

The *money multiplier* gives the change in the money stock per dollar in an open market operation.

In the U.S. economy, the money multiplier in 1981 was about 2.7. This number is not a constant since it depends on the behavior of banks and the public, but it does remain reasonably constant over the period of a year or two. Over longer periods, though, it does change. Since 1965, for example, it has declined from a value of 3. A money multiplier of 2.7 means that for every $1 million sale of securities by the Fed, the money stock falls by $2.7 million.

To complete the analysis we also look at a Fed purchase of securities to show that it will lead to multiple expansion of the money stock. In the first step, the Fed buys securities in the open market, paying with a check drawn on itself. The seller deposits the Fed check in his own account at a commercial bank. Money, according to equation (1), has expanded because deposits have increased. But further expansion occurs because the commercial bank that deposits the Fed check in its account at the Fed now has an increase in reserves equal to the increase in deposits. The bank has excess reserves relative to deposits and will therefore buy some earning asset by making loans or purchasing securities. In doing so it further expands the money stock. Again the money multiplier tells us what the cumulative change in money is.

The appendix to this chapter shows how a Fed open market operation affects the money stock. In doing so, it shows why the money multiplier is more than 1.

High-Powered Money and the Money Stock

We have seen that Fed open market operations lead to multiple expansions or contractions in the money stock. For every dollar of securities the Fed buys, the money stock rises by several dollars. For every dollar of securities the Fed sells, the money stock falls by several dollars. This happens because an open market operation changes the stock of high-powered money.

> High-powered money is defined as the sum of currency outstanding plus bank deposits at the Fed.

High-powered money is also called *monetary base*.

When the Fed buys securities in the open market, it must pay for these securities either by actually paying Federal Reserve notes (for example, sending a truck with $1 million in notes to the seller) or by paying with a check which will be credited to the Fed account of the commercial bank with which the seller holds his account. Because a change in the Fed's liabilities leads to a multiple expansion in money, we call these liabilities high-powered money, or the "base" of the money stock.

With this definition of high-powered money—currency outstanding plus bank deposits at the Fed—we can write an equation that shows the determinants of the money stock:

Money stock = money multiplier
$$\times \text{ high-powered money} \quad (2)$$

The equation is useful because it shows the two factors that affect the money stock. First, the Fed can affect the money stock directly by open market operations that affect high-powered money. The Fed controls the quantity of high-powered money in existence. This is the chief manner in which the Fed controls the money stock. We saw that a $1 open market operation leads to approximately a $2.7 change in money.

The second channel for monetary policy is changes in the size of the money multiplier. The Fed can do this by changing reserve requirements. An increase in reserve requirements will, for example, reduce the multiplier. The Fed can also achieve this indirectly by changing the discount rate, which leads banks to change the reserves they choose to hold. Banks may well decide to hold excess reserves if the discount rate is high and borrowing is costly. In that way they reduce the money multiplier.

Money Stock Determination in Review

Figure 26-2 summarizes our discussion of money stock determination by the Fed. At the top of the figure is high-powered money, a liability of the Fed. That is divided between currency held by the public and bank reserves. The currency part of high-powered money goes directly into M1. The other part is used as reserves by the

FIGURE 26-2   MONEY STOCK DETERMINATION. The money stock (M1) consists of currency and deposits. The base of the monetary system is high-powered money, which is the liability of the Federal Reserve. High-powered money either is held as currency by the public or serves as reserves for the banking system. The reserve/deposit ratio is less than 1 so that deposits are a multiple of bank reserves. The money multiplier is larger than 1, and thus the money supply is a multiple of high-powered money.

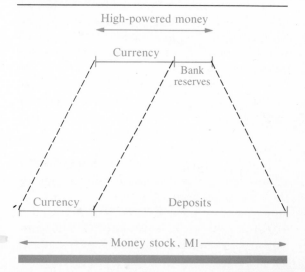

banks. As reserves, that part of high-powered money generates a larger amount of deposits (that's why it's called high-powered). The lower the reserve ratio, the more deposits are generated.

Then, at the bottom of the figure, we see that currency and deposits together make up the money stock. The ratio of M1 to high-powered money is the money multiplier. The figure makes it clear why the money multiplier is higher the lower the reserve ratio. It also shows how the Fed controls the money supply. The Fed's control comes through open market operations, which change the quantity of high-powered money at the top of the diagram, and through its ability to change the money multiplier by increasing the required reserve ratio and increasing the discount rate.

4 BANKING PANICS AND THE LENDER OF LAST RESORT

Equation (2) shows two separate sources of changes in the money stock. One is changes in high-powered money. Here the Fed has almost complete control and can prevent or minimize changes. The other source is disturbances to the money multiplier that come from changes in the reserve/deposit ratio of the banks or from changes in the amount the public wants to deposit in banks. If the public chooses to hold more currency relative to deposits, the move to cash from deposits will find banks short of reserves and force a multiple contraction of the money stock.

The Great Depression
The outstanding example of a change in the money stock that resulted from a change in the money multiplier is the decline in the money supply from 1929 to 1933. Over the 4-year period, the money supply fell 25 percent. At the same time, the stock of high-powered money increased.

Why did the money multiplier fall in this period? There were two reasons, both resulting from bank failures that started in 1930, recurred more seriously in 1931, and in 1933 led to the closing of all the banks in the country for a week in an attempt to straighten out the banking system. The first banks to fail did so because they had made loans which, in the Depression, the borrowers could not repay. But once banks started to fail, depositors feared that they would not be able to get money if their banks failed, and so they decided to hold more currency. The ratio of currency to deposits increased, and as depositors rushed to withdraw money, more banks failed.

The second reason for the decline in the multiplier was that banks themselves decided to increase their reserves in response to the increased likelihood that depositors would withdraw their money. If a bank expects withdrawals, it has to have reserves available to meet them. Therefore, the banks increased their reserve ratios, which also reduced the money multiplier.

The collapse of the banking system in the Great Depression resulted in large part from the failure of the Fed to act as lender of last resort. Instead of trying to help banks having trouble paying their depositors, the Fed closed those banks. The Fed is often blamed for making the Great Depression great by failing to act as lender of last resort.

The Lender of Last Resort
Any fractional reserve banking system can collapse if the banks do not have enough reserves to meet the demands of all their depositors simultaneously. If depositors believe banks are going to fail, they will make the banks fail as they rush in to withdraw their money. The only way to prevent the collapse of the banking system is to prevent the banks from starting to fail.

This can be done by making sure that

banks that need high-powered money to pay out to their depositors get it. And there is one institution that can manufacture high-powered money without any difficulty: the central bank. The Fed's liabilities are high-powered money, and as we saw earlier, the Fed can never go bankrupt by issuing more liabilities. Early in the period when banks started to fail, the Fed should have made loans to those banks. It should have made it clear to depositors that banks would not be allowed to fail because of bank runs started by panic; this way it would have prevented the panics.

If the Fed had taken a strong stand early, the banking failures would never have reached the proportions they did. By doing so, the Fed would have been acting as *lender of last resort,* making loans to financial institutions at a time when the financial system was threatened by panic. It could have prevented the panic instead of making it worse.

The Fed has learned the lesson of the Great Depression about the necessity for a lender of last resort to stand ready to step in very early if there is any sign of financial panic. There have been occasions in the seventies and eighties when banks were in difficulty and even bankrupt, but the Fed promptly assured financial markets that it was ready to lend to borrowers in need and to support them. That assurance has helped prevent financial panics and chain reactions that spread from one failing bank to all the others and therefore end up reducing the money stock as the money multiplier falls.

Federal Deposit Insurance

Even more important in preventing financial collapse than the Fed's ability to learn from experience was the introduction of the Federal Deposit Insurance Corporation (FDIC). The FDIC insures bank deposits, guaranteeing depositors that they will be paid off if the bank in which they deposit goes bankrupt. The insurance applies only to deposits up to a certain high maximum, but since one person can hold many insured accounts, the FDIC essentially removes the risk any depositor faces of losing his money as a result of a bank failure.

But once that risk is gone, bank failures themselves become less likely. We have seen that one cause of bank failures is that people think the bank will fail and therefore rush to withdraw their funds. However, if the funds are guaranteed, there is no reason to do this. Thus the existence of the FDIC is an unusual case in which the existence of insurance makes it unlikely that the insurance will be used.

As a result of the FDIC and the Fed's willingness to stand ready to lend as a last resort, there have been very few bank failures since the 1930s. In the period from 1921 to 1933, 14,807 banks were suspended or closed because of financial difficulties. In the entire period from 1934, the first year of the FDIC, until 1980, only 704 banks were closed. Most of these banks were insured by the FDIC, and so their depositors suffered no loss.

Is the American banking system panic-proof? It is panic-proof so long as the Fed follows appropriate central banking policy, as it has in regard to the lender of last resort function since the 1930s. And with the continuation of the FDIC, the need for the Fed to act as lender of last resort is much reduced.

5 THE FED AND THE TREASURY: FINANCING DEFICITS

The Fed is formally an independent organization which does not take instructions from the Treasury or any other part of the administration. Why does this matter? It matters because a government that cannot raise enough taxes to cover its spending has to find some way other than taxes to pay for what it buys. There are only two other ways. One is to borrow from the public; the other is to print money.

In the United States, the Treasury, which has to pay the government's bills, does not issue money. It can only finance its excess of spending over taxing—the budget deficit —by borrowing. But in other countries the Treasury, or at least the administration, may control the printing of money and decide to finance its deficits by printing high-powered money. The printing of money is an easy way of paying for goods, and to begin with it is a painless way. There is no need to raise taxes to finance spending. All that is necessary is to crank up the printing press. Governments in need have often resorted to the printing of money. As we should expect, this leads to inflation.

The Fed was given its independence to try to minimize the likelihood that the U.S. government would use money printing as a way of financing deficits in the budget. But the formal independence of the Fed is not sufficient to guarantee that deficits are not in effect financed through the printing of money. Looking at the Fed's balance sheet in Table 26-2, we see that the major category of assets is government securities. We have also seen that whenever the Fed buys a government security, it increases the quantity of high-powered money. Now suppose the federal government is running a deficit and selling bonds to finance the deficit. If those bonds are bought by the Fed, it is in effect allowing the government to finance itself by printing money. Under those circumstances, the Treasury and the Fed between them would be financing the deficit by creating high-powered money.

Formal independence for the central bank is thus not enough to guarantee that it will not use its power to create money for the purpose of financing government deficits. The central bank has to stand back to make sure that it does not end up financing government deficits indirectly by creating money. Independence of the central bank certainly helps it do this.

6 PERFORMANCE OF THE FED AND ALTERNATIVES

The behavior of the monetary system, or regime, often becomes a political issue. It has been that way in the United States throughout the period of inflation that started in the 1960s. The Fed is charged with failing to maintain low and stable money growth. The critics charge the Fed has promoted both inflation and instability —booms and recessions rather than smooth growth—in economic activity.

Critics of the Fed—in particular, Professor Milton Friedman and his followers— point to evidence such as Figure 26-3, which shows the annual growth rate of M1 in the last 20 years. It also shows as a dashed line the average growth rate in two subperiods breaking in 1972. The figure shows that money growth fluctuates a lot around the average from year to year. It also shows that money growth has increased over the years. While the money supply grew from 1952 to 1962 only at an annual rate of 1.8 percent (not shown in the diagram), the average growth rate in the 1960s and 1970s was sharply higher. This, the critics argue, is where our inflation comes from. And, they continue, the inflation is a result of the Fed's failure to pursue its task of maintaining economic stability.

We will learn more in later chapters about the Fed and the way monetary policy affects inflation and economic activity, but here we want to ask what other monetary system might be possible in place of the Fed. Two possibilities have received a lot of attention: monetary rules and the gold standard.

Monetary Rules

Milton Friedman and his followers have

FIGURE 26-3   THE GROWTH RATE OF M1, 1963–1981. The dots show the
year-to-year growth in the nominal money stock as measured by M1. The
dashed lines show average annual money growth for the periods 1963–1972
and 1972–1981. Critics of the Fed claim that money growth has been too
high and too variable. (*Source:* Federal Reserve Bank of St. Louis, *Annual
U.S. Economic Data,* May 1982.)

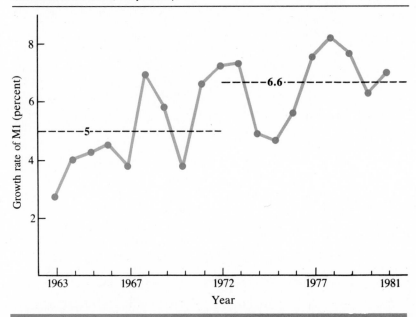

strongly argued that the Fed should *not* pursue an active monetary policy, trying to move the economy out of recessions or prevent booms. Such policies, although well intended, too often go wrong, they say, and may on balance aggravate the departure from stability of output and prices. To prevent any temptation for active monetary policy through open market sales or purchases of securities or through changes in discount rates and reserve requirements, it has been proposed that the Fed should follow a simple rule: the constant money growth rule.

> The *constant money growth rule* requires the Fed to cause the money supply to grow at a *constant* rate, low enough to avoid inflation.

Strong concern about inflation and skepticism about the success of monetary policies that try to affect booms and reces-

sions have made the constant growth rule approach very influential in many industrial countries. Today a number of central banks, including the Fed, are committed in principle to achieving more stable and lower growth rates of money. In the United States this has been the policy since 1979. Figure 26-4 shows half-yearly growth rates of nominal M1 for the period 1978–1981. Money growth became very slightly lower but does not show much stability over 6-month periods. Critics of the Fed claim that the intentions may be right but the execution is weak.

A Gold Standard

Our current monetary system relies on the liabilities of the Federal Reserve System as the monetary base. Monetary base can be created by the decisions of the Fed at the stroke of a pen. Under this system the west-

FIGURE 26-4   HALF-YEARLY M1 GROWTH SINCE 1978. In the recent past, money growth (M1) under the policy of following a monetary rule has not stabilized appreciably, nor has it declined much. (*Source:* Federal Reserve Bank of St. Louis, *Monetary Trends,* May 1982. *Note:* 1 and 2 refer to the first and second half of the year, respectively. Growth rate is for each six-month period relative to the previous six months.)

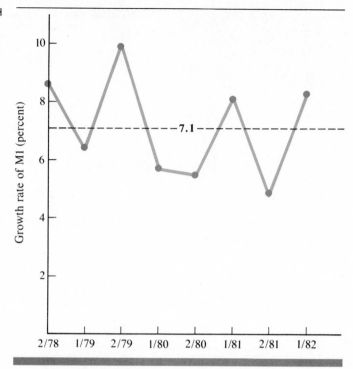

ern world has seen its most prolonged peacetime inflation in the post-World War II period. The inflation was particularly high in the 1970s.

Earlier monetary systems usually had some link with gold as the monetary base. Under the *gold standard,* the monetary base consisted of gold coins or claims on gold coins. Anyone with a British pound sterling was entitled to demand a certain weight of gold from the Bank of England. This amounts to fixing the price of gold in terms of the pound sterling, or, in the United States, in terms of the dollar. Anyone who had gold could bring it to a bank and get a certain amount of money in exchange.

A gold standard keeps down inflation, provided that gold discoveries are not too abundant, thus keeping down the amount of gold the central bank would have to purchase at the fixed price of gold. With low

growth of gold stocks, high-powered money would grow little, and so would prices. In addition, supporters of the gold standard argue, prices would be stable from year to year. In fact, the gold standard did not work that way. Figure 26-5 shows that money growth (M2, defined in Chapter 25, is shown because we have no separate series for M1) was both high and very unstable. From 1880 to 1895 gold was in short supply, and banking crises in the early 1890s interfered with stability of money growth. But then, after the South African gold discoveries in 1895, money growth and inflation picked up. Even so, inflation never reached today's levels for any length of time.

The contrast between the noninflationary experience of the gold standard world and current economies has led to some nostalgia for the gold standard. Should we go back to gold? What are the advantages and

FIGURE 26-5 MONEY GROWTH (M2) UNDER THE GOLD STANDARD, 1881–1902. Under the gold standard, money growth was neither very low nor very stable. Banking panics and gold discoveries made for instability perhaps even larger than today. But inflation, on average, was much lower. (*Source: Historical Statistics of the U.S.*, pp. 992–993.)

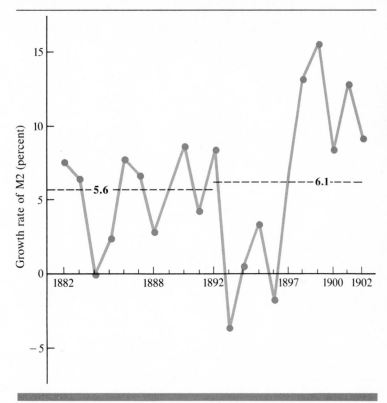

disadvantages? The chief advantage is the low average rate of inflation that would be likely to result. But we should not be too influenced by the experience of the nineteenth century, for other governments did not stick to the gold standard throughout. In particular, the gold standard was usually abandoned during serious wars. The British went off gold during the Napoleonic wars and during World War I. The United States went off gold during the Civil War. Countries went off gold precisely because they wanted to print money to finance wars, and the gold standard would not let them do that. Thus even in earlier times the gold standard was not an infallible bulwark against inflation.

The essential disadvantage of the gold standard is that it is a waste of resources. It takes people and machinery to get gold out of the ground. Using gold as high-powered money or requiring the central bank to hold reserves of gold uses up resources. There is virtually no cost to providing high-powered money when we have a fiat currency.

The second disadvantage is that changes in the supply of gold are themselves uncertain. The economy is likely to be subject to inflation and deflation depending on the rate at which new gold is found and what the industrial and other uses for gold are. The amount of gold supplied for monetary use depends on the total amount mined each year and the amount that is used for other purposes.

The gold standard is unlikely to re-emerge as a basis of modern monetary system. In 1981 Congress appointed a gold commission to investigate the merits of a return to gold. The commission strongly but not unanimously rejected the possibility and pointed to monetary rules as a more fruitful direction in which to look for monetary stability.[4]

---

[4] See U.S. Department of Treasury, *Report of the Gold Commission*, Washington, D.C., 1982.

SUMMARY

1   The Federal Reserve System contains about 5000 member banks that are regulated and supervised by the Board of Governors and by 12 regional Federal Reserve banks.

2   The Fed Open Market Committee (FOMC) is in charge of monetary policy. It sets the discount rate and reserve requirements and, most important, instructs the Open Market Desk on what open market operations to carry out.

3   Open market operations involve the purchase or sale of government securities by the Fed. Such purchases or sales affect the money stock directly because they lead to a change in currency or deposits of the buyer or seller. They also have secondary effects because they change the reserve ratio of the banking system and thus cause further adjustments.

4   The money multiplier tells us how much a $1 open market operation changes the money stock. In the United States today the money multiplier is about 2.7.

5   High-powered money is defined as currency outstanding plus bank deposits at the Fed. The Fed completely controls the supply of high-powered money. Through that control it can affect the money stock. Open market operations have an impact on the money stock because they change the amount of high-powered money, or monetary base, available for the banks and the public.

6   The money multiplier can and does change over time. Before the FDIC, banking panics could lead to huge fluctuations in the multiplier. Today there is more stability.

7   Critics of the Fed have charged that it has allowed the money stock to grow too rapidly and erratically, thereby bringing about high inflation and too much variability in economic activity. Fed monetary policy, in this view, has aggravated rather than reduced macroeconomic instability.

8   Alternatives to an active monetary policy by the Fed include a gold standard and a monetary rule. Under a gold standard, the monetary base grows only as a consequence of gold purchases or sales. If gold supplies in the world grow slowly and smoothly, so will money

and prices. Under a monetary rule, the Fed would not allow fluctuations in the money stock. The money stock would be made to grow at a low, constant rate.

KEY TERMS

Lender of last resort

Board of Governors of Federal Reserve System

Required reserve ratio

Bank reserves

Discount rate

Open market operations

Money multiplier

High-powered money (monetary base)

Federal Deposit Insurance Corporation

Constant money growth rule

Gold standard

PROBLEMS

1 Suppose the Fed conducts a $1 million open market purchase of securities. The securities are sold by Mr. Jones, who holds his bank account with Stockmens National Bank in Cotulla, Texas. (a) Show the effect of the open market purchase on the T-accounts of the Fed and Stockmens National Bank, assuming that Mr. Jones pays for the securities by writing a check on his account. (b) Show the immediate impact on the money stock. (c) What further adjustments will take place? (d) What would have happened if Mr. Jones had paid for the securities in currency?

2 Discuss the open market operation in Problem 1 on the assumption that Stockmens National Bank holds 100 percent reserves. Which part of your answer would change?

3 Do you think a system in which banks hold 100 percent reserves is necessary to stabilize (a) the money multiplier or (b) the money supply?

4 If the money multiplier suddenly falls because people become suspicious about the solvency of banks, is there anything the Fed can do to prevent the money stock from falling?

5 Suppose people decide they want to hold more currency and fewer deposits. Use the T-accounts of commercial banks to show the effect on the banks and on the money stock.

6 Here are data for December 1981: checkable deposits = 313.4, bank reserves = 45.7, currency = 123.1. Calculate (a) M1, (b) the monetary base, or high-powered money, and (c) the banks' reserve ratio.

7 Discuss how an ideal gold standard could make the economy perform better than the Fed might be able to.

8 List three instruments through which the Fed can affect the money stock. Explain how each works, using T-accounts for at least two of them.

9 Explain the sense in which banks increase the money supply. Do this by showing how the money supply is affected when a person decides to deposit some currency that previously was hidden under the mattress. Show the bank's balance sheet.

10 Should the Fed adopt a monetary rule that causes the money supply to grow by 4 percent per year?

11 (*a*) What are the two main factors determining the money multiplier? (*b*) How do they affect the multiplier? (*c*) What would happen to the money multiplier if people began to use credit cards more extensively for making small transactions?

12 Is a financial panic possible in a fiat money system?

13 The Federal Deposit Insurance Corporation insures bank deposits. If your bank is insured by the FDIC, the FDIC would pay you the amount of your deposit even if the bank went bankrupt. What is the effect of the FDIC on the likelihood that there will be a run on the bank? Explain.

APPENDIX: THE MONEY SUPPLY AND THE MONEY MULTIPLIER

In this appendix we show in greater detail how an open market purchase by the Fed affects the money supply. In particular, we analyze the process by which a $1 expansion in the stock of high-powered money leads to an increase of more than $1 in the money stock. We do so by deriving a precise formula for the *money multiplier*.

Concepts and Definitions

The money multiplier is the multiple by which a $1 increase in the stock of high-powered money increases the money stock. We start by reminding ourselves of the definitions:

Money stock ≡ currency + deposits
Monetary base ≡ currency + bank reserves ≡ high-powered money

The process by which an increase in the monetary base increases the money stock involves three groups: the Fed, commercial banks, and the public. We now describe the role of each and the assumptions we make about their behavior.

The Fed   The Fed determines the monetary base. Open market operations enable the Fed to change the base.

Commercial Banks   The banks have a fixed reserve ratio, which we assume to be 15 percent. When an extra dollar is deposited in a bank, the bank holds 15 cents of that deposit as reserves, and lends the remaining 85 cents. When a dollar is withdrawn from a bank, the bank has to call in some loans so as to get its reserve ratio back to 15 percent.

Nonbank Public   The nonbank public holds both currency and deposits. We assume people have a preferred ratio of currency to deposits equal to 35 percent. That means that, on average, for every dollar held in their bank accounts, individuals hold 35 cents in currency. Using the M1 definition of money, this is in fact close to the current U.S. ratio of currency to deposits.

When people receive an extra dollar, they hold 35 cents as currency and deposit the other 65 cents in the bank. If they receive a check for $1, they withdraw 35 cents from the bank to hold as currency; if they receive a dollar bill, they deposit 65 cents in the bank.

Multiple Expansion of the Money Stock

We are now ready to show how a $1 (billion) open market purchase by the Fed leads to a larger expansion of the money stock. The process involves interactions among the Fed, the banks, and the public.

We proceed step by step, at each stage showing the balance sheets that are affected by adjustments to the initial open market purchase by the Fed.

Step 1 The Fed makes an open market purchase of $1, increasing the monetary base by $1. The seller of the bond receives a $1 check from the Fed, written on itself. The seller takes the check to his bank and deposits it. He withdraws 35 cents in currency and holds the other 65 cents as a deposit. The bank deposits the $1 check in its account at the Fed. Since it has paid out 35 cents in currency to the depositor, it now has an extra 65 cents of reserves. Table 26A-1 shows the changes for each of the three groups who among them determine the money supply.

TABLE 26A-1
BALANCE SHEETS
(Step 1)

(a) THE FED		(b) BANKS		(c) PUBLIC	
Securities +$1.00	Monetary +$1.00 base	Reserves +$0.65	Deposits +$0.65	Securities −$1.00 Currency +$0.35 Deposits +$0.65	

Step 2 The public is now holding currency and deposits in the ratio it prefers. But the banks have an extra 65 cents in reserves. Since they want a reserve ratio of only 15 percent, they can lend 85 percent of the 65 cents, or 55.25 cents.

Specifically, suppose the deposit was made in Bank 1. Bank 1 now makes a loan of 55.25 cents, giving the borrower a deposit in Bank 1. But the borrower wanted to spend the money, and pays the 55.25 cents to someone else. That person deposits a check for 55.25 cents in his bank, Bank 2. He withdraws 35 percent of the 55.25 cents, or 19.34 cents, as currency, and leaves the rest as a deposit in Bank 2.

Bank 2 sends the check for 55.25 cents on Bank 1 to the Fed for clearance. Bank 1's account at the Fed is reduced by 55.25 cents, resulting in a loss of reserves for it. Bank 2 has paid out 19.34 cents in currency to its depositor, but still is left with an extra 35.91 cents in reserves.

TABLE 26A-2

BALANCE SHEETS
(Step 2)

(d) BANK 1		(e) BANK 2		(f) PUBLIC	
Reserves −55.25¢		Reserves +35.91¢	Deposits +35.91¢	Currency +19.34¢	Loans +55.25¢
Loans +55.25¢				Deposits +35.91¢	

Table 26A-2 shows the *changes* in balance sheets in step 2.

Before proceeding to step 3, we note that the money supply has already increased by more than $1 after the first two steps. To see this we need look only at the changes in the public's holdings of currency and deposits in balance sheets (c) and (f). In balance sheet (c), the public holds $1 extra in money. Thus in step 1 the money stock increases by exactly the same amount as the open market purchase. But after step 2 the public holds an *extra* 55.25 cents in money, of which 19.34 cents is in currency and the rest in deposits.

Therefore after the first two steps the public's holdings of money are up by $1.5525. There is already a greater increase in the money stock than the $1 increase in high-powered money. Where does it come from? The crucial change occurred when Bank 1 decided to make a loan. At that stage it took 55.25 cents out of reserves and made a loan, putting that amount back into circulation. This is exactly how the goldsmith bankers in Chapter 25 increased the money stock.

Step 3   At the end of step 2, the public is once again happy with the ratio of currency to deposits. But now Bank 2 is holding an extra 35.91 cents in reserves, and would like to make a loan of 85 percent of the 35.91 cents. The recipient of the loan uses it to make a payment to someone who banks with Bank 3.

In this step we are just matching all the changes in step 2, except that we start with a smaller loan. Now we start with a loan of 30.52 cents rather than 55.25 cents. The balance sheet changes at this step are shown in Table 26A-3.

To make sure we understand the process, we consider the public's balance sheet in Table 26A-3i. The person who took the loan has an increased liability of 30.52 cents, which shows up on the right-hand side of the balance sheet. The person who received the payment was given 30.52 cents as a check on Bank 2. He wanted to hold 35 percent

TABLE 26A-3

BALANCE SHEETS
(Step 3)

(g) BANK 2		(h) BANK 3		(i) PUBLIC	
Reserves −30.52¢		Reserves +19.84¢	Deposits +19.84¢	Currency +10.68¢	Loans +30.52¢
Loans +30.52¢				Deposits +19.84¢	

of that, or 10.68 cents, as currency, and the rest, or 19.84 cents, as a bank deposit. That deposit shows up in Bank 3.

After step 3 the money supply is up by more than the $1.5525 reported at the end of step 2. Now the public holds an extra 30.52 cents in deposits. Therefore the money stock is up by $1.8577 after three steps.

Step 4 By now the general process should be clear. At the beginning of step 4, Bank 3 is holding 19.84 cents in reserves. But it wants to lend 85 percent of those reserves, and makes a loan of 16.86 cents. After all the changes in step 4, the public will hold an extra 16.86 cents in money, so the money stock will have risen by $2.0263 after four steps. Further, another bank, Bank 4, will be holding reserves that it wants to reduce by making a loan by the end of step 4. (In the problems at the end of this appendix we ask you to fill in the three balance sheets for this step.)

The Money Multiplier

Rather than proceed through steps 5, 6, and on, we take a closer look at the changes in the money stock at each step so far. We show both the change in the money stock and the new level at the end of each step.

	STEP 1	STEP 2	STEP 3	STEP 4
Change in money stock	$1.00	55.25¢	30.52¢	16.86¢
Level of money stock	$1.00	$1.5525	$1.8577	$2.0263

The pattern is quite clear. The money supply increases at each step. But the increase at each step is smaller than the increase at the preceding step. Eventually, the increase becomes so small that it is negligible. If we kept going for more steps. we would eventually find the money stock increasing by $2.70 as a result of initial $1 open market purchase by the Fed.

To check your understanding of the money multiplier, consider two questions. First, why is the multiplier greater than 1? And second, why do the increases in the money stock become smaller with each step?

The multiplier is greater than 1 because the banks can expand the money stock by making loans using high-powered money as reserves. Whenever someone deposits high-powered money at a bank, and that bank lends part of it, the money stock increases. You can check that if at step 1 the person selling the bond decided to hold the $1 in currency, the process would end. The $1 increase in high-powered money would in that case be equal to the total increase in the money stock.

Second, the increase in the money stock becomes smaller at each step because the banks hold back part of the amount deposited with them to keep as reserves, and because the public keeps back part of their increased holdings of money as currency. The larger the amount the public wants to keep back as currency, the smaller the money multiplier will be. And similarly, the larger the banks' reserve ratio, the smaller the money multiplier is.

These effects are summarized in the formula for the money multiplier:

$$\text{Change in money stock} = \frac{1 + c}{r + c} \times \text{change in monetary base}$$

In this formula, the money multiplier is the expression before the multiplication sign. The symbol c is the currency-deposit ratio, equal to 35 percent in our case. The symbol r is the banks' reserve ratio, equal to 15 percent in our case. Therefore in our case a \$1 billion increase in the stock of high-powered money leads to a change in the money stock of (\$1.35/0.50 billion) or \$2.70 billion. With a higher reserve ratio, or higher currency-deposit ratio, the money multiplier would be smaller.

PROBLEMS

1 Show the balance sheets for Banks 3 and 4, and for the public, at step 4, assuming the currency deposit ratio is 35 percent and the reserve ratio is 15 percent.

2 Show the balance sheets for step 2 assuming the currency deposit ratio is 20 percent and the reserve ratio is 10 percent. (*Note:* you will have to work out also what happens at step 1 in this case.)

3 Calculate the money multiplier using the formula given, under the assumption that the currency deposit ratio is 20 percent and the reserve ratio is 10 percent.

4 Explain in words why the money multiplier is higher the lower the currency-deposit and the reserve ratios are.

5 *Extra credit:* (*a*) What is the ratio of the increase in the money stock at step 2 to that at step 1, using the data in the table in this appendix? (*b*) Similarly, what is the ratio of the increase in the money stock at step 4 to that at step 3? (*c*) If you know the expression for the sum of a geometric series, show where the formula for the multiplier comes from.

In Chapter 26 we showed how the Federal Reserve System controls the quantity of money by determining the stock of high-powered money. In this chapter we show why the Fed and the stock of money matter. We discuss the effects of changes in the stock of money on the economy as well as interactions between the assets and goods markets.

Figure 27-1 updates Figure 21-3 by including the Fed. The Fed controls the supply of money. The demand for money, as we shall see in this chapter, depends on the level of income, or GNP, and the interest rate. Changes in the supply of money interact with the demand for money to affect interest rates, which in turn affect consumer and business spending, which in turn affect the level of income. In this chapter we systematically introduce interest rates into our analysis of the economy.

The emphasis here is on the link between control over the money supply and the *aggregate demand* for goods. Aggregate demand, we recall, is the demand for goods in general; it consists of the demand for consumption goods, plus investment, plus government spending, plus net exports. Our focus will be mostly on investment demand and to some extent on consumption demand.

1 THE DEMAND FOR MONEY

In 1965 the amount of money (M1) per person in the United States was $850. By 1981 that amount had increased to $1909. What accounts for this rise of 125 percent in per capita nominal money holdings? Answering that question will introduce us to the factors that determine money demand, which in turn sets the stage for understanding how monetary policy works.

We single out three factors that affect money holdings: interest rates, the price level, and real income. We discuss each of these factors and then see how far they take us in explaining the 125 percent rise in per capita nominal money holdings from 1965 to 1981.

Money Demand and Interest Rates

The starting point of the discussion is to argue that people *hold* money. This may be puzzling since you rightly connect money with spending. People *spend* money when they buy beer, go to the movies, or buy a record. In fact, the only reason to have money is to spend it

FIGURE 27-1   MONETARY POLICY AND THE INTERACTIONS BETWEEN THE ASSETS AND GOODS MARKETS. The chapter shows how the Fed, by controlling the money stock, can affect interest rates and, through that channel, aggregate demand and equilibrium output and employment. It also shows that the effects of increased government spending or lower taxes on output are dampened as interest rates rise and reduce investment spending.

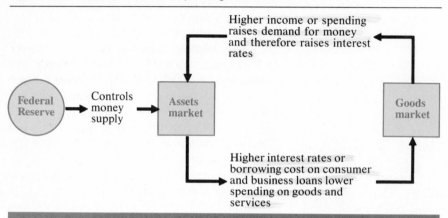

sooner or later. But it is also true that people always hold some money. The average person almost always has some money in his pocket or bank account. That money is held to be spent. When it is spent and the person's holdings of money fall, money holdings are replenished for the next round of spending. The person deposits a salary check or gets a loan. People hold money, and the amount they hold is related to the rate at which they spend.

What determines the amount of money that people choose to hold? It depends in part on the amount they plan to spend, but it also depends on the costs and benefits of holding a lot of money or relatively little. It is entirely possible to spend $1000 per month and never have more than $50 in money for any length of time.

How? You would invest all your assets in the stock market or the bond market, earning interest and dividends.[1] Any time you want to buy something, you quickly sell bonds or stocks to get money with which to pay. Thus on average you hold practically zero money balances except in the brief instant before you pay. Nobody goes to that extreme because it would be very costly. Money holdings are the outcome of a calculation of the costs and benefits of holding money, as we will see.

There are many assets that people can hold instead of money. Near-monies such as savings and time deposits and money market mutual funds, bonds, and equities are the major financial assets. Bonds are promises to pay specified amounts of money to the holders on particular dates. Equities are shares in companies, entitling the holder to a share in the profits.

For convenience we lump together all the nonmoney assets and call them bonds. We call the returns obtained by holding those assets interest. In the case of stocks, the returns may actually be dividends and also capital gains and losses,[2] but in devel-

---

[1] Dividends are payments made by a firm to its stockholders. Dividends are usually paid out each quarter. The firm is not obligated to pay them, but established firms typically do.

[2] Capital gains (or losses) are increases (or decreases) in the price of a stock. Look back to Chapter 19 for more details.

oping our model of the role of money and interest rates we have to simplify by omitting unnecessary detail. For that reason all assets other than money are described as bonds.

We start with the definition of the interest rate.

The *interest rate* is the payment, expressed in percentage points per year, made by a borrower to a lender in exchange for the use of the amount of money lent.

When a person, firm, or government sells a bond, it is in effect borrowing from the buyer. In exchange, the seller of the bond promises to make interest payments at regular intervals to the holder. When a bank pays interest on a savings account, it does so because the depositor has lent the bank money (the deposit) which the bank can use to make loans.

Interest rates in the economy vary according to the types of loans made. The interest rate on a savings deposit, for instance, is low compared with that on a Treasury bill. The savings deposit is easily bought and sold by going to the bank and making deposits or withdrawals, compared with the purchase of a Treasury bill, which can be done only in amounts of $10,000 or more. We simplify in this chapter by talking of "the" interest rate on bonds. Since all interest rates tend to move in the same direction, the simplification is not misleading.

Now we turn to the demand for money, which is based on the costs and benefits of holding it.

The *opportunity cost* of holding money is the amount of interest that is given up by holding money rather than bonds.

Suppose the interest rate on money (a checking account) is 5 percent and the interest rate on bonds is 15 percent. Then the opportunity cost of holding money is 10 percent. Anyone who reduces money holdings by $100 on average over the year and in-

stead holds that $100 in bonds will come out with $10 of extra interest.

How is it possible to reduce money holdings by, say, $100 on average? Think of the alternative asset, the bond, as being shares in a money market mutual fund. The average amount kept in the bank can be reduced by watching the bank account carefully, making sure that there is never too much money in it. As soon as there is any sizable amount in the bank account, the individual buys bonds by sending a check to the money market mutual fund. If the amount of money in the bank account is falling, the asset holder calculates carefully when to transfer funds back from the money market mutual fund, making sure not to do it too soon.

Two factors will determine how much money the individual keeps in the bank account. First, there is the opportunity cost. The higher the opportunity cost, the more worthwhile it is to run the bank account very carefully, and the smaller the holdings of money. But second, watching the bank account carefully is a real nuisance. The more of a nuisance it is, the more money and the fewer bonds will be held.

Figure 27-2 shows how the individual decides how much money to hold. The marginal benefit schedule shows the gains, as seen by the individual, from holding one more dollar of money at each level of money holdings. The benefit is the saving of time and worry gained by having more money in the account and not having to watch it so closely. The marginal benefit declines with the amount of money held. When there is almost no money in the account, any extra dollar held makes life much easier. By the time the individual is holding so much money in the account that there is no worry about running out of cash, holding an extra dollar contributes very little extra benefit. The marginal cost schedule shows that holding one extra dollar costs the same

FIGURE 27-2 OPTIMAL MONEY HOLDING. Schedule *MB* shows the benefit of holding an extra dollar of money at each level of money holding. The first dollar held brings great convenience and saving in terms of the need to coordinate spending plans. But the advantages from holding one more dollar of money decline as the amount of money already held increases. The *MC* curve shows the marginal cost of holding an extra dollar in the form of money rather than bonds. The marginal cost is equal to the interest earnings that could have been obtained by holding one more dollar of bonds. The optimum cash holdings are at *E*, where the benefit of holding one more dollar is exactly equal to the cost. A rise in the interest rate, shown by an upward shift of the *MC* schedule, leads to a new equilibrium at *E'*. An increase in the interest rate on bonds reduces optimal money holdings from *L* to *L'*

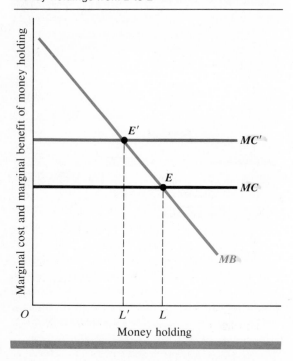

Money holding

where the marginal cost is equal to the marginal benefit. If one more dollar is held, the extra cost will be greater than the extra benefit, and so the individual should cut back money holding. If one less dollar is held, an increase in money holding will give benefits greater than the cost. Thus *L* is the right amount of money to hold.

What happens when the opportunity cost of holding money rises? We show this by shifting the *MC* curve in Figure 27-2 to *MC'*. The optimal holdings of money now fall to *L'*. This is exactly what we should expect. The more costly it is to hold money, the less money will be held. Thus the quantity of money demanded declines as the opportunity cost of holding money rises.

We have reached a first conclusion: The amount of money people hold falls when the interest rate rises. People manage their cash balances more closely, and thus manage to finance their spending by having less money in their pockets and in the bank.

How does this relate to the increase in the amount of money held per person over the period 1965–1981? Over this period, interest rates rose threefold. These higher interest rates *reduced* money holdings. Thus we have to look to the other two factors affecting money holdings—the price level and real income—for an explanation of the increase in money holdings.

Money Demand and the Price Level

People hold money as a means of payment. They hold it to buy goods and services. Suppose someone holds a given money balance, say, $100, and assume now that *all* prices and his nominal income double. With all prices and his nominal income doubled, he will want to and be able to buy exactly the same goods and services he bought before. Only now it costs twice as much in dollars.

But what about money holdings? If they are kept at $100, they buy only half as much goods and services as they used to. If before

amount, namely, the forgone interest. The marginal cost is the same whatever the level of real balances. In our example, where the checking account earns 5 percent and the money market mutual fund earns 15 percent, the opportunity cost, or marginal cost of holding one extra dollar, is 10 percent, equal to 10 cents per dollar per year.

The optimal amount of money is held

the price increases $100 lasted for 3 days' shopping, it now lasts only 1½ days. That would mean more trips to the bank or more phone calls to the broker to sell bonds to obtain money. But the interest rate has not changed, and so that does not make sense. Instead, the individual decides to double the amount of money he holds. In that way he will be able to buy exactly the same amount of goods and services with his money holdings that he bought before.

This result can be stated in a somewhat different way.

The demand for money is a demand for real balances.

People hold money for the *purchasing power* it has, that is, the amount of goods it buys. When prices double and nominal income doubles, the amount of money people hold also doubles so as to keep the real value or purchasing power of their money holdings unchanged.

Now we return to the 1965–1981 increase in money holdings. In 1981, prices of goods were more than 2.5 times higher than they had been in 1965. If nominal money holdings had not changed over that period, the purchasing power of the cash in people's pockets and in the bank would have been only 40 cents for every dollar that it was in 1965. To have the same purchasing power in 1981 that they had in 1965, people would have to hold $2.50 for every $1 they held before.

Our second conclusion, then, is that people adjust their nominal money holdings so as to maintain the purchasing power of their money holdings when the price level changes. When prices double, so does the quantity of nominal money people want to hold. Their demand for money is a demand for *real* balances. Given the increase in the price level between 1965 and 1981, this argument suggests that nominal money demand per capita should have increased since 1965.

Money Demand and Real Income

We have seen that the demand for money is a demand for real balances. We also have seen that the amount of real balances people want to hold depends on the opportunity cost. The higher the rate of interest on bonds, the lower the amount of real money balances people will choose to hold. But the amount of spending must matter too. Certainly someone who never spends need not hold any money. Someone who spends a lot will hold more money than someone who spends much less.

The level of spending, as we have seen in earlier chapters, depends on the amount of real income households earn. A rise in real income leads to a rise in the level of spending. Because increased spending with unchanged real balances means more inconvenience in managing the bank account, higher real income leads to an increased demand for real balances.

This is shown in Figure 27-3. The initial equilibrium is at point E, with real money holdings equal to L.[3] Now real income increases and with it the level of spending. Financing the higher level of spending with unchanged real balances would mean more nuisance and inconvenience. Thus the marginal benefit of an extra dollar of real balances increases, as shown by the shift of the marginal benefit schedule to MB'. With unchanged interest rates, the new equilibrium is at point E', where real balance holdings have increased.

By how much does an increase of 1 percent in real income raise the demand for real balances? The evidence is that the demand for real balances rises by about 0.7

---

[3] Now that we have introduced *real balances*, we draw the MB and MC curves in Figure 27-3 with real balances or real money holdings on the axis. That is because the demand for money is fundamentally a demand for *real* balances; people hold money to buy goods and services, and thus they are concerned with the real and not the nominal value of their money balances.

FIGURE 27-3 THE EFFECT OF HIGHER REAL IN-COME ON OPTIMAL MONEY BALANCES. Initial equilibrium is at point E, where the marginal cost and benefit of an extra dollar of money holding balance. A rise in real income raises the marginal benefit of money holding because with higher real income, the level of spending rises. The new equilibrium is at E' with larger money holdings.

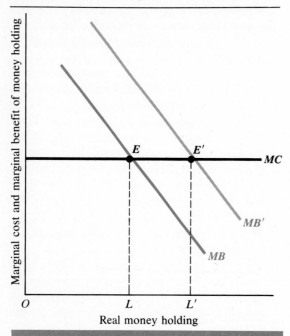

in the same proportion so as to keep real balances unchanged, *other things equal*. But there are also higher interest rates that reduce the demand for real balances and higher real incomes that raise it. Table 27-1 helps to summarize these factors. The first row gives an index of nominal per capita money holdings which have risen by 125 percent.

The second row shows what happened to the purchasing power of money holdings. Once we adjust for their higher level of prices, the 1981 money holdings have a lower real value than money held in 1965. Real balances per capita declined by 13.8 percent. We are left with the task of explaining why real balances in 1981 are lower than they were in 1965. Real income does *not* help because in 1981 it was 40.3 percent higher than in 1965, and that should have increased real balance holdings by about 28 percent (40 × 0.70 percent). The last row shows the rise in interest rates, which went from 4.1 percent in 1965 to nearly 14 percent in 1981. This *does* help explain the fall in real money demand. With so large a rise in the opportunity cost of holding money, we would expect people to try to economize on their cash holdings, spending more time managing their assets and thus being able to

percent when the level of real income goes up 1 percent. Returning again to the increase in nominal money holdings from 1965 to 1981, over that period real GNP per capita in the United States rose by a factor of 1.40. This 40 percent increase in real income would have increased the demand for real balances by 28 percent (40 × 0.7 percent).

Explaining Changes in Money Holdings

We have put together the factors explaining the change in per capita nominal money holdings from $850 in 1965 to $1909 in 1981. Our discussion identified three factors. Higher prices increase money demand

TABLE 27-1

DETERMINANTS OF REAL BALANCES

	1965	1981
Nominal balances per capita, 1965 = 100	100	224.8
Real balances per capita, index 1965 = 100	100	86.2
Real GNP per capita, index 1965 = 100	100	140.3
Interest rate on bonds, 6-month U.S. Treasury bills	4.1%	13.8%

Sources: Economic Report of the President, 1982, and Federal Reserve Bank of St. Louis, *Annual U.S. Economic Data, 1982.*

TABLE 27-2
THE DEMAND FOR MONEY

EFFECT ON:	INCREASE IN PRICE LEVEL	INCREASE IN REAL INCOME	INCREASE IN OPPORTUNITY COST OF HOLDING MONEY
NOMINAL MONEY DEMAND	Increases demand for nominal money balances proportionately	Increases demand	Reduces demand
REAL MONEY DEMAND	Leaves demand for real balances unaffected	Increases demand	Reduces demand
PER CAPITA HOLDINGS OF NOMINAL BALANCES, 1965–1981	Increased demand for nominal balances	Increased demand	Reduced demand

do with lower real balances even though real income and spending have increased.

There is no reason to expect that the three major factors—the price level, real income, and interest rates—explain *exactly* what has happened to real money balances. There may well be other factors that have an impact on people's choice of money holdings. Certainly the invention of money market mutual funds, for example, introduced an alternative to money that would explain part of the fall in real balances that we observe in the data.

Even so, for our discussion of macroeconomics we retain the three basic factors. First, higher interest rates reduce the demand for real balances. Second, an increase in the level of prices leaves real money demand unchanged. In other words, it increases the demand for nominal balances in the same proportion that prices increase so as to keep the purchasing power of money holdings constant. Third, higher real incomes raise the demand for real balances. These three aspects of money demand turn out to be important channels for the operation of monetary policy. For that reason we collect them in Table 27-2 for later reference.

2 THE MONEY SUPPLY AND EQUILIBRIUM INTEREST RATES

Our aim in this chapter is to explain the effects of changes in the money supply caused by the Fed on aggregate demand and equilibrium output. We show that when the Fed reduces the supply of money, interest rates rise, and then we show that the higher interest rates reduce aggregate demand and equilibrium output. In this section we study the first part of the channel, running from money supply changes to changes in interest rates.

Table 27-3 illustrates what our model has to explain. The table shows the changes from quarter to quarter in the real money stock, and it also shows the level of interest rates in 1979 and early 1980. We note that the real money stock started declining in the third quarter of 1979 and continued to decline in the next two quarters. What is the effect of such a fall in the stock of real balances? We observe one effect in the second row, which shows interest rates. Interest rates that had been at the level of 9.4 percent rose steadily and sharply until they reached 13.5 percent in early 1981. In this

TABLE 27-3
CHANGE IN REAL BALANCES AND RATE OF INTEREST

	1979:2	1979:3	1979:4	1980:1
Growth in real balances*	2.0%	−2.3%	−1.2%	−4.9%
Interest rate†	9.4%	9.6%	11.8%	13.5%

* Percent change over preceding quarter.
† Interest rate on 3-month Treasury bills.
Sources: Federal Reserve Bank of St. Louis, *Monetary Trends,* August 1982, and *Economic Report of the President, 1982,* Table B-67.

section we show why interest rates increase when the real money stock declines. The next section shows the further impact, linking changes in interest rates to aggregate demand and output.

Money Market Equilibrium

We have seen that the demand for real balances depends on both the level of real income and the opportunity cost of holding money, which is equivalent to the interest rate on bonds.[4] The supply of *nominal* balances is determined by the Fed, which controls high-powered money and influences the money multiplier. With our assumption that prices are given, this means the Fed controls the supply of *real* balances. The Fed can, through open market purchases or sales of securities, change the stock of real money balances in existence.[5]

We now want to examine the effects of a change in the quantity of money on interest rates. We start with equilibrium in the money market.

> The money market is *in equilibrium* when the quantity of real balances demanded equals the quantity supplied.

Figure 27-4 shows the equilibrium in the money market. The demand curve, or demand schedule for real balances, is *LL*. The schedule shows that the lower the rate of in-

FIGURE 27-4 EQUILIBRIUM IN THE MONEY MARKET. The demand schedule for real balances is *LL*. It is drawn for a given level of real income. The demand schedule shows that the quantity of real balances demanded is higher the lower the opportunity cost of holding money. The real money supply is equal to M_0, as indicated by the vertical supply schedule. Equilibrium in the money market obtains at point *E* with an interest rate i_0. At any lower interest rate, the quantity of real balances demanded exceeds the quantity supplied. At any higher interest rate, quantity supplied exceeds quantity demanded. Only at point *E* is supply equal to demand.

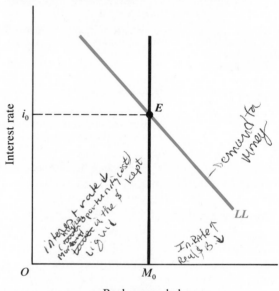

[4] Throughout, we refer to the opportunity cost of holding money as "the interest rate." We mean by that the interest rate on bonds or, if money pays interest too, the excess of the interest rate on bonds over the interest paid on money.

[5] We have to issue a serious warning at this point. We are for now assuming that the aggregate price level is given. *Under that assumption,* the Fed, by changing the quantity of nominal balances, also changes the quantity of real balances. In this section we therefore talk of the Fed affecting the quantity of real balances. But in later chapters we allow the price level to change. Then we will realize that one of the Fed's problems is that when it changes the quantity of nominal balances, the price level changes too. That means the Fed is less able to control real balances than nominal balances. We return to this important point when the price level is allowed to become variable in Chapter 28. For now, we can talk of the Fed's control over the quantity of both nominal and real balances.

terest, or opportunity cost of holding money, the greater the quantity of money people want to hold. The existing real money supply is indicated by a vertical schedule. That is the amount of real balances determined by the Fed, denoted by M_0.[6] Equilibrium is at point E, with an interest rate equal to i_0. At that interest rate, the quantity of real balances demanded is equal to the existing stock.

The first step in explaining how the Fed's control over the money stock affects the economy has now been taken. We see how the demand for the real balances schedule (LL) and the money stock—controlled by the Fed—between them determine the interest rate. We want to see next how the interest rate changes when the Fed changes the quantity of money and also how shifts in the demand for real balances affect the interest rate.

The Effect of a Change in the Money Stock

Figure 27-5 shows what happens to equilibrium interest rates when the Fed ~~reduces~~ *increases* the money stock. The initial equilibrium is shown by point E. Now the Fed conducts an open market operation, buying securities and thus increasing the amount of high-powered money and the nominal money stock. With a constant price level, the change in the *nominal* money stock is also a change in the *real* money stock. Therefore, in Figure 27-5 the supply of real balances shifts to the right from M_0 to M'. At the initial equilibrium point E, there is now an excess supply of real balances, and therefore the equilibrium interest rate must fall to i' to restore equilibrium in the money market.

We have shown that the equilibrium interest rate falls when the Fed increases the

---

[6] Just to be safe, we repeat that the Fed directly determines the *nominal* money supply. With the price level given, as we assume it to be in this chapter, the Fed thereby also determines the real money supply.

FIGURE 27-5 AN INCREASE IN REAL BALANCES LOWERS THE EQUILIBRIUM INTEREST RATE. Initial money market equilibrium obtains at point E, where the supply of real balances is equal to the quantity demanded. The equilibrium interest rate is i_0. An increase in the real money stock from M_0 to M' lowers the equilibrium interest rate to i' from i_0.

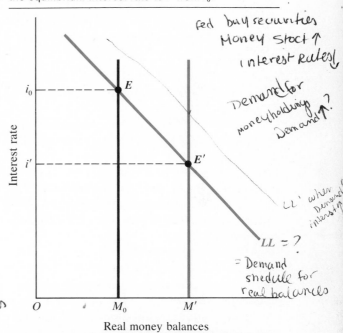

money stock. With more money available for people to hold, interest rates must fall to encourage increased money holding. Lower interest rates encourage increased holding of money because they make it less attractive to economize on money by holding interest-bearing assets. Looking back to Table 27-3, the analysis also explains why a *reduction* in real balances *raises* the equilibrium interest rate.

The Effect of Higher Real Income on Interest Rates

We complete our analysis of the money market by looking at a change in real income. When real income increases, people want to hold higher real balances because the marginal benefit of money balances rises. The

TABLE 27-4 ▰▰▰▰▰▰▰

CHANGES IN THE MONEY MARKET

	INCREASED REAL MONEY SUPPLY	INCREASED REAL INCOME
EQUILIBRIUM INTEREST RATE	Falls	Rises

increase in real income therefore shifts the demand schedule *LL* up and to the right in Figure 27-4 (not shown).

At each interest rate, the increased demand for real balances creates an excess demand for money. As you can see by drawing a diagram similar to Figure 27-4, and then shifting the *LL* curve, an increase in income therefore results in an increase in the equilibrium interest rate. Thus higher real incomes, with an unchanged real money stock, raise the interest rate. Conversely, when real income declines, so does the amount of real balances people want to hold at each interest rate. With an unchanged real money supply, that means the equilibrium interest rate will fall.

Table 27-4 summarizes these conclusions for later reference.

3 INTEREST RATES AND THE DEMAND FOR INVESTMENT

This section introduces the second link between the Fed's control of the money stock and its resulting ability to affect aggregate spending and equilibrium output. This second link involves investment spending by firms. Investment spending—additions to plant, equipment, the residential housing stock, and business inventories of goods—depends on the interest rate. Because changes in the money stock, as we have seen, change interest rates, they affect investment and thus aggregate demand. The critical link is that investment depends on

the interest rate. Before elaborating on that point, we look at some facts about investment.

Facts about Investment

Figure 27-6 shows investment spending as a fraction of GNP. The figure shows substantial fluctuations, with the ratio of investment to GNP at times being nearly 18 percent and other times being less than 13 percent.[7] We have shaded in the recessions. It is clear that investment falls relative to GNP during recessions and rises as a share of GNP during recoveries and booms. This pattern was particularly striking in the 1974–1975 recession and the subsequent recovery.

Table 27-5 shows data on the composition of investment in 1979–1981. The table deals separately with three kinds of investment: firms' additions to plant and equipment, investment in new housing, and changes in business inventories, or stocks of goods. Of these three, business investment in plant and equipment is by far the largest, followed by residential investment. Inventory changes tend to be small and quite variable. In some years firms add to their stocks of goods; in others they run down inventories.

One point to note from Table 27-5 is the large change in housing investment. From 1979 to 1980–1981 residential investment declined by over 25 percent. By contrast, the changes in business investment in plant and equipment were relatively small. We will argue that high interest rates such as those in 1980–1981 particularly affect investment in housing.

---

[7] The data in Figure 27-6 are for *gross* investment, or the total amount spent on producing investment goods. Because capital wears out through depreciation, *net* investment, which is equal to gross investment minus depreciation, is about 10 to 11 percent lower as a share of GNP than gross investment. Net investment ranges from about 3 to 8 percent of GNP. It is *net* investment that adds to the capital stock each year.

FIGURE 27-6 INVESTMENT AS A SHARE OF GNP. (*Source:* Citibank Database.)

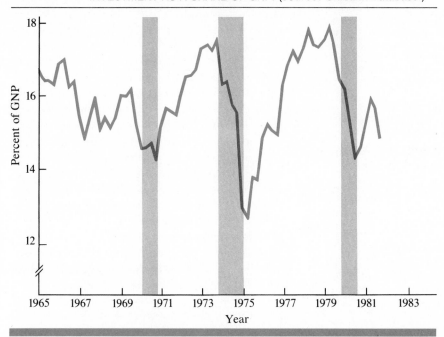

TABLE 27-5

COMPOSITION OF INVESTMENT
(Billions of 1972 Dollars)

YEAR	TOTAL	RESIDENTIAL	PLANT AND EQUIPMENT	CHANGES IN INVENTORIES
1979	233	59	163	10
1980	204	45	158	−3
1981	215	42	162	7

Note: All numbers rounded off to the nearest billion.
Sources: Survey of Current Business, March 1982, and *Economic Report of the President,*
1982.

Investment and Interest Rates

Investment spending is spending on
new production of machinery, housing,
business or farm structures, and inventories. Investment spending adds to the
economy's stock of physical capital.[8]

---

[8] Recall the distinction between net and gross investment.

Firms add to the amount of plant and equipment because they look ahead to increased
demand for their products and want to expand the scale of their operations. Sometimes investment in plant and equipment is
also a way to take advantage of more cost-effective ways of producing a particular good
or is associated with the production of a new
good. General Motors might invest in a new

FIGURE 27-7 THE INVESTMENT DEMAND SCHEDULE. Planned investment spending on plant, equipment, housing, and additions to inventories depends on the interest rate. The higher the rate of interest, the fewer the investment projects that remain profitable. Therefore, increased interest rates reduce the demand for investment. As interest rates rise from i_0 to i', investment demand declines from I_0 to I'.

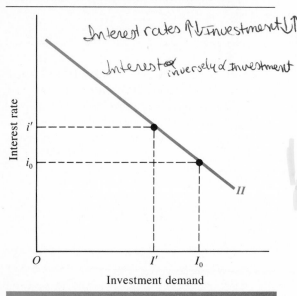

tive to the current costs to pay the interest on the loan that helps finance the investment. The higher the interest rate, the higher must be the future benefits on any project relative to the current costs of investment for it to be acceptable.

At any time there are a host of projects firms *could* undertake. Such projects would include building new factories, reequipping the telephone system, and replacing worn-out trucks. At a high interest rate very few of them will be profitable; at very low interest rates most will, because the future benefits need not be so large relative to the current investment costs. But that means high interest rates discourage the amount of investment firms wish to undertake. Conversely, at low interest rates investment spending by firms will be large.

The relationship between investment and the rate of interest just described is shown in Figure 27-7 as the investment demand schedule II.

> The *investment demand schedule* shows the amount of investment firms wish to make at each rate of interest.

The higher the rate of interest, the lower the desired level of investment spending. For example, at an interest rate i_0, the desired level of investment is I_0. If the interest rate increases to i', there will be fewer projects that remain profitable, and desired investment spending therefore falls to only I'. In drawing the investment schedule we hold constant such factors as business expectations about future demand for their goods, available technology, and the wages firms have to pay.

plant that uses robots to produce cars, or Volkswagen might construct a new plant to build cars in this country.

In each case the decision to build plants or to buy machinery and equipment depends on a cost-benefit calculation. The firm has to weigh the benefits from the new plant or equipment—the increase in profits—against the cost of the investment. But the benefits occur only in the future, while the costs are incurred immediately as the plant is built or the machine is purchased. The firm therefore has to compare the value of future income receipts with the current costs.

Here is where the interest rate comes in. The firm borrows today to finance the investment, and it has to ask whether the investment will return enough in extra profits to pay back the loan *plus* interest. The future benefits must be sufficiently large rela-

What if the firm does not have to borrow to carry out the investment project? Would the interest rate still matter? Yes, because the firm should make the best use of the money it has on hand. If it does not have to borrow, it must already have the cash that is needed to undertake the investment project. But then it has to ask whether it could not earn a higher return by using that cash to do something else, such as buy bonds or lend to other firms. The higher the interest rate, the more attractive it is for the firm to lend its cash rather than invest directly in a factory or other project of its own. Whether or not the firm has to borrow, it is less likely to want to invest in physical capital as interest rates go up.[9]

What has been said of business investment in plant and equipment also goes for investment in housing or for inventories. When interest rates rise high enough, the given future benefits from a new house or from a stock of inventories of goods will not be large enough to repay a loan plus inter-

est. The higher the rate of interest, the smaller the amount of investment in housing or inventories that will seem profitable. Thus the investment demand schedule in Figure 27-7 describes the demand for all investment.

4 MONEY, INTEREST RATES, AND AGGREGATE DEMAND

In the previous section we saw why the demand for investment is related to the interest rate. The higher the interest rate, the lower the amount of investment firms want to carry out. We also saw earlier that when the Fed reduces the quantity of money, it causes the interest rate to rise. Thus the Fed affects the quantity of investment demanded by changing the supply of money, thereby changing the interest rate, which in turn changes the quantity of investment demanded.

In Figure 27-8 we show, using the familiar 45° diagram, how a change in the

---

[9] If you have read the appendix to Chapter 15, you will recognize that we are talking here in a slightly different way about present discounted values. A firm will invest if the present discounted value (PDV) of the investment project's returns exceeds the PDV of the costs. Typically, the higher the interest rate, the more likely that the PDV of the costs will exceed the PDV of the revenue.

FIGURE 27-8 A REDUCTION IN INTEREST RATES INCREASES INVESTMENT AND AGGREGATE DEMAND. A reduction in interest rates increases investment spending from I_0 to I'. The aggregate demand schedule therefore shifts upward, and equilibrium income rises from Y_0 to Y'. Thus monetary expansion, by lowering interest rates, raises income and output.

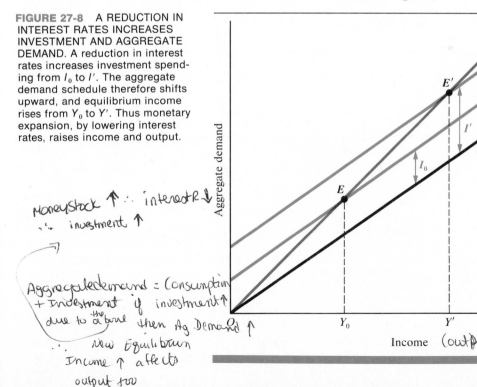

TABLE 27-6

THE EFFECT OF INCREASED REAL MONEY BALANCES ON OUTPUT

(1)	(2)	(3)	(4)	(5)
Fed increases money stock	Excess supply of money	Interest rates fall to clear money market	Lower interest rates raise investment and aggregate demand	Firms raise output, employment, and income

on borrowed $

quantity of money affects interest rates and thereby affects aggregate demand and the level of output. Initially, the economy is in equilibrium at point E, with the level of investment at I_0. Now the Fed increases the money supply, reducing the interest rate and increasing the quantity of investment demanded. Investment demand increases to I', and the aggregate demand schedule in Figure 27-8 shifts upward as shown. The new equilibrium of the economy is at point E', with a higher level of income and output Y' instead of Y_0.

Table 27-6, which should be read from left to right, gives the different steps in the move from an increase in the real money stock to a higher level of output and employment. Each of the entries corresponds to one of the linkages we have studied. The combined effect shows that the Fed can use its control over the quantity of money to affect the level of output and employment. An expansion in the money stock leads to a rise in investment, output, and employment. A cut in the money supply drives up interest rates, reduces investment, and leads to a fall in output and employment.

Box 27-1 discusses the role of monetary policy in affecting the stock markets and, through them, investment.

Money Supply ↑ Interest ↓ Invest ↑ good to borrow ↑
output ↑ employment ↑
income
∴ Demand for money ↑ which
drives interest rate ↑ ∴
counterbalances the whole thing

investment unit some up
putting $ in bank

BOX 27.1

THE STOCK MARKETS AND MONETARY POLICY

The stock markets or stock exchanges are the many markets in which shares of ownership in corporations are traded. Stocks differ from bonds because there is no promise with a stock that the company will make specified payments at particular times.

What does monetary policy have to do with the stock markets? In what sense can we lump stocks and bonds together when talking of the assets markets in general? The connection is that stocks are ultimately valued because of the dividends they are expected to pay. Someone may buy a stock hoping to sell it quickly if its price goes up, but that price rise in turn will have to be based on what other people think the stock is worth when held as an asset. And when it is held as an asset, the stock pays out dividends: so much per share every 3 months.

Now consider how the market values one share in, say, General Motors. Such a share is expected to pay a dividend every quarter, perhaps 60 cents per quarter. Given the expected dividends, the market values the stock at, say, $50. With annual dividends of $2.40 (60 cents four times a year), someone buying a G.M. share at $50 makes 4.8 percent a year [$(2.40/50) \times 100$]. Someone who holds G.M. shares has considered the alternative of buying bonds at their current interest rate and has decided he prefers the returns he expects from the shares.

Now the interest rate rises. Investors can earn a higher return on bonds than before. Therefore some people decide to hold bonds instead of stocks. This reduces the demand for stocks and causes the price of stocks to fall. Thus a rise in the interest rate causes stock prices to fall.

The next step is to see that changes in the value of stocks affect the rate at which firms are willing to invest. Suppose a firm is thinking of undertaking a particular investment project.

To undertake the project, the firm has to find cash with which to pay the costs of the investment. Sometimes firms borrow for this purpose by selling bonds. But they may also try to sell stocks or shares in the company in the stock market. The price they get for the stock will determine whether they can raise enough money to pay the costs of the investment project. If stock prices are high, the firm will raise enough money to finance the investment. If stock prices are low, the firm will not be able to invest.

Thus, there is a link between the level of stock prices and firms' willingness and ability to invest. When stock prices are high as a result of low interest rates, firms will undertake a lot of investment. When stock prices are low, so too is investment. Thus, monetary policy affects the rate of investment by affecting stock prices, as well as through the direct effects of interest rates.

Dampening Effects

Our discussion of the impact of money on output is not quite complete. We must still recognize that once a monetary expansion has led to a rise in output and income, this income increase will in turn raise the demand for money. The increase in money demand in turn will raise interest rates back up *somewhat*. Investment will not increase as much as Table 27-6 implies, and therefore the income expansion will ultimately not be as large as it would have been without these second-round adjustments in money demand. While these effects exist, we should note that they merely dampen the income expansion without changing the basic message. An increase in the money stock raises output, and a reduction in the real money stock lowers real output.

An Application Tight money raises interest rates and, through that channel, reduces investment spending. Housing construction is the component of investment that is most sensitive to the interest rate. Figure 27-9 shows the relationship between interest rates and housing starts.

The data show the number of one-family houses on which building began in each year. At low interest rates, housing starts were high. When interest rates were at their peak for the period shown (1981), housing starts were at their lowest level.

The figure shows clearly the strong effect of interest rates on housing investment. When the Fed reduces the money stock and causes interest rates to rise, it reduces housing investment.

5 FISCAL POLICY AND CROWDING OUT

In Chapter 25 we showed that an expansionary fiscal policy, through tax cuts or through increased government spending, leads to higher aggregate demand and therefore to

FIGURE 27-9 THE EFFECT OF INTEREST RATES ON HOUSING INVESTMENT.
High interest rates make it more expensive to borrow to buy a house and therefore reduce the quantity of houses demanded. The figure shows that housing starts
(the number of houses on which building commences) decline as the interest
rate rises, and rise as the interest rate declines. (Shaded areas are recessions.)
(*Source: Economic Report of the President, 1982,* Tables B-47 and B-67.)

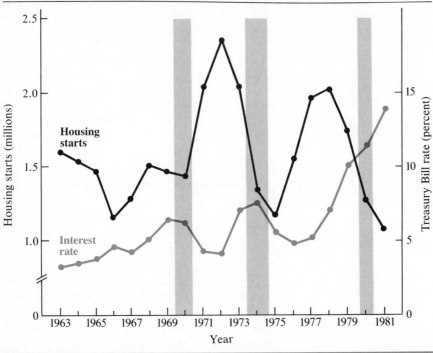

[Handwritten annotation: Fiscal expansion: AG↑ ∴ output↑]

[Handwritten annotation in left margin: Income ↑ why? money demand ↑ Due to cost-benefit]

an increase in output and income. We follow up on that discussion here by asking
whether inclusion of the money market can
lead us to qualify or modify these conclusions. As you would anticipate, there is a
modification. Once interactions between
goods and money markets are taken into account, we see that higher incomes, brought
about by a fiscal expansion, lead to increased money demand. With an unchanged real money stock and higher real
money demand, there will be pressure for
interest rates to rise. That in turn reduces
investment spending, aggregate demand,
and output, offsetting the effects of the expansionary fiscal policy. But we can already
state here, before developing the analysis,

that these repercussions from the money
market only *dampen* the expansionary impact of fiscal policy. They do not reverse the
expansion.

Fiscal Expansion and Interest Rates

In Figure 27-10 we take a look at the effect
of an increase in government spending on
aggregate demand and income. Starting
from point E, increased spending by the
government shifts the aggregate demand
schedule upward from AD to AD'. At each
level of income, spending is higher, and
therefore output expands until point E' is
reached.

But this analysis overlooks what happens in the money market. The rise in real

FIGURE 27-10 CROWDING OUT. Increased government spending shifts the aggregate demand schedule upward at each level of income from AD to AD'. Other things equal, the economy would move to point E' with income level Y'. But the rise in income raises money demand. With an unchanged money stock, there is excess demand for money, and interest rates increase. The rise in interest rates in turn reduces investment spending. This is shown by a downward shift of the aggregate demand schedule from AD' to AD". The new equilibrium, taking into account adjustments in the money market, is therefore at E". Fiscal policy with a constant money stock is less expansionary than it would be if the money stock were adjusted to keep interest rates constant.

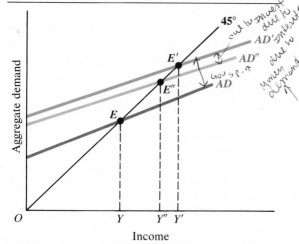

the aggregate demand schedule, owing to reduced investment, from AD' to AD". The final equilibrium therefore is at point E", where output has risen compared to E, but less than it would have if the interest rate had remained constant.

Investment demand declines but by less than the rise in government spending. This must be the case because otherwise aggregate demand and income would actually be lower and interest rates would not have risen in the first place.

But the fiscal expansion *does* increase the interest rate and thereby reduces the rate of investment, or crowds out some investment.

> *Crowding out* of investment through fiscal expansion takes place when an increase in government spending or a reduction in taxes results in a lower level of investment.

Investment is crowded out, or displaced, because higher interest rates reduce firms' demand for investment. We say that crowding out is complete when the reduction in investment demand is equal to the increase in government spending. But as we have just seen, crowding out is not complete in the model presented in this chapter. Nor is crowding out likely to be complete in practice.

Table 27-7 summarizes all the steps in the argument. We can also use the table to analyze other kinds of fiscal expansion, such as a cut in the income tax rate. The result remains the same: expansionary fiscal policy leads to a reduction in investment.

income raises the demand for real balances and therefore, with an unchanged supply of money, raises the equilibrium rate of interest. Corresponding to point E' there now are higher interest rates, and that means planned investment spending is lower. We show the effects of the lower investment demand in Figure 27-10 as a downward shift of

TABLE 27-7
GOVERNMENT SPENDING AND CROWDING OUT

(1)	(2)	(3)	(4)
Higher government spending raises output and income	Higher income raises desired real money balances	Higher real money demand and an unchanged supply lead to higher interest rates	Higher interest rates crowd out investment and thus dampen the expansion

Policy Mix

Monetary and fiscal policy have very different effects on the *composition* of aggregate demand. By lowering interest rates, a monetary expansion leads to a rise in investment. By contrast, a fiscal expansion such as higher government spending or lower personal taxes leads to increased interest rates and lower investment. Both monetary and fiscal expansion lead to increased output and employment. Table 27-8 shows the effects of different combinations of policies. For each combination, the entry shows the effect on the level or composition of demand. By tighter (easier) money we mean a decrease (increase) in the money stock; by tighter (easier) fiscal policy we mean higher (lower) taxes or lower (higher) government spending.

If both monetary and fiscal policy tighten, the Fed and the administration are putting on all the brakes. GNP will begin to grow more slowly, and the economy may go into a recession. Tighter monetary and fiscal policy between them will not have a great impact on the composition of aggregate demand since tight money tends to reduce inflation and tight fiscal policy tends to increase investment. But the combination will without doubt reduce aggregate demand. Exactly the opposite occurs when both monetary and fiscal policy are expansionary. The economy moves out of a recession or into a boom because aggregate demand is increased. Monetary and fiscal policy both moved in the direction of restraint in 1969–1970, and the economy indeed went into a recession. In 1975–1976 policymakers used joint monetary and fiscal expansion to achieve a recovery from the recession of 1973–1975. The recovery kept going for nearly 5 years.

Crowding out is shown as the effect of tighter monetary policy combined with easier fiscal policy. Because the two policies are pulling in opposite directions, total de-

TABLE 27-8
POLICY MIXES

	TIGHTER MONEY	EASIER MONEY
TIGHTER FISCAL POLICY	Recession/ slowdown 1969–1970	Crowding in; share of investment in GNP rises
EASIER FISCAL POLICY	Crowding out; share of investment in GNP falls	Boom/recovery 1975–1976

mand is relatively little affected, but the composition of aggregate demand changes. Interest rates rise and investment falls, giving way to increased consumption spending or spending by the government.

In the "crowding in" case, money eases through an expansion in the real money stock, but at the same time increased taxes or reduced government spending offset the expansionary impact on aggregate demand. Total demand and output is largely unchanged, but interest rates fall because of the monetary expansion, and thus investment takes the place of government or consumer spending.

The composition of aggregate demand is a particularly important issue when the economy is near full employment. The higher the share of investment, the more we are adding to the stock of physical capital, especially buildings and machines, and the more provision is made for increased production and jobs in the future. The larger the share taken by consumption and government, the less we invest in the future.

Subsidizing Investment

Is there a way for the government to pursue unchanged monetary policy combined with easier fiscal policy and yet not reduce investment? At first sight the answer is no because tighter fiscal policy through cuts in income taxes or higher government spending will raise interest rates. But we can also think of a special kind of fiscal policy that favors investment directly.

Suppose the easier fiscal policy takes the form of an investment tax credit.

An *investment tax credit* allows firms to deduct a percentage of the cost of an investment from the taxes they owe the government. It thus reduces the cost of investing. *Tax break for investing*

An investment tax credit raises investment and aggregate demand, causing output to expand. It is true once again that the increase in income will raise interest rates and thereby dampen the expansion as compared with a situation in which the interest rate remains constant. But this time, because of the tax benefits, investment is increased even though interest rates are higher.

An administration that wants monetary policy to be tight in order to fight inflation but is also concerned about investment for future production can run an expansionary fiscal policy that encourages investment by providing investment tax credits. This way investment is not put at a disadvantage in an expansion. In the United States in 1981–1982, the Reagan administration targeted its tax cuts in directions that it hoped would lead to higher investment even as the Fed ran a very tight monetary policy.

It turned out, though, that the tight monetary policy was so tough and powerful that the economy went into a deep recession. Even though fiscal policy tried to encourage investment, aggregate demand fell sharply.

6 KEYNESIAN ECONOMICS AND ACTIVISM

The analysis of this chapter has expanded further the Keynesian idea that aggregate demand determines the level of output and employment. The idea here is to show that not only fiscal policy but also monetary pol-

icy can help maintain the economy close to the full-employment level. During periods of recession and insufficient aggregate demand, monetary and fiscal expansion are called for to expand output and employment; during booms, tighter monetary and fiscal policies should be pursued. *expansion rectifies recession*

Keynesian ideas were very popular in the United States in the post-World War II period because the Great Depression had been so devastating. It was quite clear that more active and intelligent use of monetary and fiscal policies in the 1930s could have prevented many years of deep unemployment, lost output, and social and personal distress.

Keynesian economics came into active policy use in the 1960s, when the Kennedy and Johnson administrations pursued several years of expansionary fiscal policy, supported by a generally expansionary monetary policy. In particular the large tax cuts of 1964 were held responsible for getting the economy out of recession to full employment and beyond. At the time the policy seemed highly successful. The "new economics," as it was called, stressed *active* monetary and fiscal policies to fight recessions and achieve high levels of employment. The economists working for the administration did not express many doubts about their ability to control the economy.

But policy did not work perfectly. Keynesian policies in the 1960s reduced unemployment from nearly 6 percent in 1963 to only 3.5 percent in 1969. At the same time, though, inflation, which had been only about 1 percent in 1963, gradually increased to more than 5 percent in 1969. That build-up of inflation proved to be a lasting and costly aftereffect of the Keynesian policies. Thus today we are more doubtful about the success of the activist policies in the 1960s. Particularly, we doubt that the experience could be repeated with assurance of the same success. Here is what is at issue:

Keynesian economics proceeds on the assumption that the price level is given. Monetary and fiscal policy that induce increased aggregate spending therefore always increase the demand for goods, output, and employment. But what happens when the price level can change, for example, when the economy is near full employment? Then a monetary expansion may not lead to higher employment; it may only lead to higher prices, as it did in the late 1960s. We develop this concern in detail in Chapters 28 and 29, which discuss today's skepticism about Keynesian policies.

The skepticism is qualified, however. Few people would argue that monetary and fiscal expansion do not have *any* effect on output, even in the short run. Rather, critics fault the Keynesian analysis of this type for not allowing for the inflationary effects of changes in monetary and fiscal policy. The critics also doubt that the effects of the policies can be predicted well enough for them to be useful for stabilizing the economy.

The lessons of the past 20 years certainly suggest that the analysis of monetary and fiscal policy presented in this chapter describes well how those policies affect output and its composition. But the analysis is still only half the story. We must look at the determination of both output *and* prices. To do that we need a model that includes both aggregate demand, which we have studied so far, and aggregate supply. Supply and demand between them determine output and the price level. Chapters 28 and 29 extend macroeconomics to include determination of output and price level and bring us to a more complete understanding of the behavior of the economy.

SUMMARY

1   The demand for money is a demand for real balances. An increase in the level of prices raises the demand for nominal balances in proportion, and therefore leaves real money demand unchanged.

2   A rise in real income raises real money demand; a rise in the interest rate on bonds reduces the demand for real balances.

3   In monetary equilibrium the quantity of real balances demanded equals the quantity of real balances supplied. The interest rate adjusts to clear the money market.

4   Higher real income raises the equilibrium interest rate. A higher quantity of real balances reduces the equilibrium rate of interest.

5   Investment spending depends on the rate of interest. The higher the interest rate firms have to pay, the less likely it is that given investment projects are sufficiently profitable to repay the loan plus interest. Therefore, higher interest rates reduce investment.

6   Monetary policy works by affecting the supply of real balances, the equilibrium interest rate, and thereby investment, aggregate demand, and output. A reduction in the real money stock through an open market sale of securities raises interest rates and reduces output. An open market purchase increases output.

-645
(42)

7 A fiscal expansion crowds out, or displaces, investment through higher interest rates. The combination of easy money and tight fiscal policy will encourage investment. A combination of tight money and tight fiscal policy will lead to a slowdown, or recession.

KEY TERMS

Opportunity cost of holding money	Crowding out
Real balances	Monetary-fiscal policy mix
Nominal balances	Easy (or tight) money
Money market equilibrium	Easy (or tight) fiscal policy
Stock market	Investment tax credit

PROBLEMS

1 Explain the effects on the demand for (1) nominal money balances and (2) real money balances of (a) an increase in the price level, with real income and the interest rate staying unchanged, (b) an increase in the price level accompanied by an increase in real income, (c) an increase in the interest rate on bonds, and (d) an increase in the interest banks pay on deposits.

2 When the Fed increases reserve requirements, it reduces the money multiplier. What is the effect of an increase in reserve requirements on (a) the money stock and (b) the interest rate?

3 Why does the interest rate affect the rate of investment?

4 (a) Using diagrams, show how an increase in the money supply increases income and investment. (b) What is the effect of the increased income on interest rates? (c) Is it possible that the increase in the money supply will end up increasing the interest rate?

5 (a) Why would a company invest more if the price of its stock rose? (b) Does monetary policy affect stock prices?

6 Draw a graph showing how an increase in investment affects the economy's production possibilities schedule.

7 Suppose the government wants to reduce aggregate demand and increase investment at the same time. Can it do so?

8 Suppose the government pursues the following monetary-fiscal mix: Fiscal policy takes the form of an investment tax credit, and monetary policy involves an open market sale of securities by the Fed. What happens to GNP and to investment?

9 Suppose firms become more optimistic about their future profit opportunities. What is the effect on interest rates and equilibrium income?

10 In 1981 the full-employment deficit was reduced by $20 billion while the real money stock declined slightly. How would you describe the monetary-fiscal policy mix and what would you predict were the effects?

Inflation, along with unemployment and growth, is one of the three key macroeconomic issues. Keynesian macroeconomic models of the type we have presented so far assume a fixed price level and determine output solely from aggregate demand. These models present a correct view of part of macroeconomics, but in the form we have developed so far they cannot be used to analyze inflation. We now have to go beyond the Keynesian model of aggregate demand, bringing in the aggregate supply side to get a reasonable and complete picture of the determination of both the aggregate price level and the level of output.

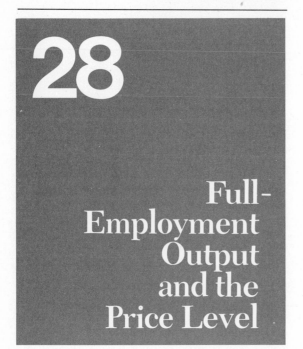

28

Full-Employment Output and the Price Level

We find two things when we include the determination of the aggregate price level. First, the entire Keynesian macroeconomics developed so far is an essential part—but only a part—of the analysis. Second, the conclusions drawn when the price level was assumed to be constant now have to be qualified. Printing money, or increasing the money supply, will sooner or later create inflation, not a continuing gain in output and employment. Fiscal expansion will sooner or later raise the price level and interest rates rather than continue to increase output. Today's uncertainties and controversies in macroeconomics deal with how quickly prices adjust to changes in monetary and fiscal policy and thus with the time frame in which Keynesian conclusions about the effects of policy are accurate.

Policies that increase aggregate demand cannot increase output indefinitely because the economy's limited resources cannot produce unlimited quantities of output. Thus we have to combine our analysis of aggregate demand with an analysis of how much output firms are able and willing to supply. By bringing in aggregate supply, or firms' decisions about how much to produce, in this chapter and Chapter 29, we complete our model of the determination of both output and prices.

We start the analysis of aggregate supply and demand in this chapter by studying how prices and output adjust in an economy where all wages and prices are perfectly flexible. This takes us away from the one extreme of a Keynesian model with fixed prices all the way to the other extreme, known as the classical model.

The *classical model* of macroeconomics describes the operation of the economy when wages and prices are fully flexible.

In this model, as we shall show, there is always full employment. Changes in monetary and fiscal policy *do* affect the price level but

FIGURE 28-1 LINKAGES BETWEEN THE MARKETS FOR ASSETS, GOODS, AND LABOR. A complete macroeconomic model determines output and employment, interest rates, wages, and prices. Such a model must take into account relations between markets for assets, goods, and labor. Goods and labor markets are related by the links between output and employment and by connections between wages and prices. Goods and assets markets are linked because interest rates affect spending decisions and because incomes and prices affect interest rates.

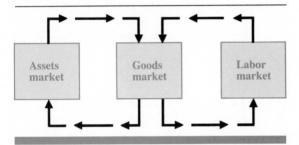

do not affect output. In Chapter 29 we combine the Keynesian analysis, with its fixed prices, and the classical analysis, with its fully flexible prices, to look at how the economy *actually* behaves as prices adjust in response to the pressures of aggregate demand and supply.

Figure 28-1 outlines the analysis of this chapter. We study the interactions among three markets: the assets market, the goods market, and the labor market. This may look alarming, but it is not. The analysis breaks down into two parts. First, there is aggregate demand, or the analysis of equilibrium in the goods and assets markets. That is precisely what we have learned so far. The new element is the introduction of aggregate supply, involving the interaction of the labor and goods markets.

1 THE PRICE LEVEL AND AGGREGATE DEMAND

In this section we develop the relationship between the aggregate demand for goods and the price level. We start by reviewing the relationship between the real money

stock and aggregate demand that was developed in Chapter 27. We showed there that an increase in the real money stock lowers the equilibrium interest rate in the money market. The interest rate has to fall so that people will be willing to hold the larger quantity of real balances. The lower interest rate in turn increases investment spending, aggregate demand, and income.

In Chapter 27 the increase in the real money stock occurred because, with a given price level, the Fed increased the nominal money stock. Now we approach the same question from a slightly different angle. We ask how aggregate demand changes when the price level changes, with the quantity of money not changing at all.

Why is this the same issue? We see this from the definition of real balances:

$$\text{Real money stock} = \frac{\text{nominal money stock}}{\text{price level}} \quad (1)$$

The real money stock can decline either because there is less nominal money—say, $250 billion instead of $500 billion—or because prices have increased—say, from 100 to 200. An increase in the aggregate price level has exactly the same effect on the real money stock as a decrease in the nominal money stock.

Now we analyze the effects of an increase in the price level on aggregate demand. For that purpose, we study how a reduction in the real money stock affects aggregate demand.

Prices and Interest Rates

In Figure 28-2a the demand for real balances is shown as the *LL* schedule. The quantity of real balances demanded rises when interest rates decline, as we recall from Chapter 27. The real money stock is indicated by a vertical supply curve. Initially, M_0 is the real money stock. Equilibrium in the money market is at point E, where quantity demanded and quantity supplied are

FIGURE 28-2 AN INCREASE IN THE PRICE LEVEL LEADS TO LOWER INVEST-
MENT DEMAND. An increase in the price level reduces the real money stock. Given
the nominal money stock, higher prices reduce the purchasing power of money.
This is shown in part (a) as a leftward shift of the supply of real balances which
leads to increased interest rates as the equilibrium moves from E to E'. Part (b)
shows that the increase in interest rates leads to a decline in investment demand
from I_0 to I'. Thus increased prices lead to lower investment once the repercussions on equilibrium interest rates are recognized.

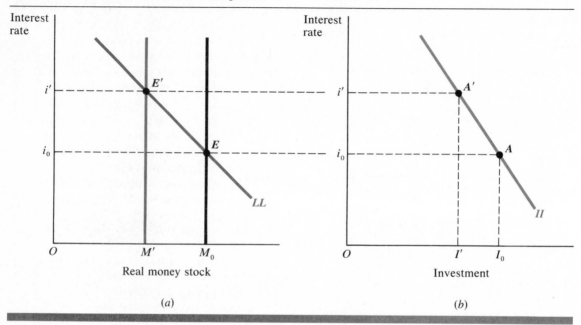

(a)   (b)

equal at an interest rate i_0. Figure 28-2b
shows the investment demand schedule II.
Investment spending is higher the lower the
interest rate firms face as they borrow to
finance projects. At an interest rate i_0, investment spending will be I_0, as shown by
point A on the investment demand schedule.

Now the price level increases, and the
real money stock declines. This is shown in
Figure 28-2a as a leftward shift of the supply
schedule from M_0 to M'. With the reduced
supply of real balances there is now an excess demand for money. Equilibrium interest rates will rise until at point E' the quantity demanded of real balances is reduced to
the lower level of supply. A rise in prices
that reduces the real money stock thus leads
to the higher equilibrium interest rate i'.
The right-hand panel shows the conse-

quences of the higher interest rate. As the
interest rate rises from i_0 to i', investment
spending declines from I_0 to I'. Thus a
higher price level leads, through the interest rate adjustment, to a reduction in investment. Lower investment, as we now see, reduces aggregate demand and income.

Aggregate Demand and the Price Level

By raising interest rates in the money market, a higher price level reduces investment. The fall in investment means a decline in aggregate demand. At each level of
income there is now a reduction in the demand for goods; hence the level of output at
which aggregate demand is equal to output
must fall. This is shown in Figure 28-3. Initial aggregate demand is AD with an equilibrium income level Y_0. At higher prices

FIGURE 28-3 HIGHER INTEREST RATES REDUCE AGGREGATE DEMAND AND INCOME. A rise in prices leads to higher interest rates, which reduce investment. The aggregate demand schedule shifts downward from AD to AD'. Equilibrium income falls from Y_0 to Y'.

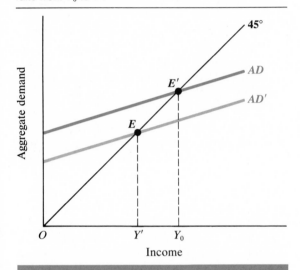

and therefore higher interest rates, investment falls, and that shifts the aggregate demand schedule downward to AD'. Equilibrium income falls to Y'.

We have now shown the links that run from the level of prices to asset markets, interest rates, aggregate demand, and equilibrium output. Table 28-1 reviews the steps for later reference. Reading the first and last parts of the table gives the basic message: An increase in prices leads to a reduction in equilibrium income and spending. Reversing all the arguments, we see that a fall

in prices of course leads to lower interest rates, higher spending, and higher equilibrium income.

The relationship identified in Table 28-1 can be presented in a diagram. Figure 28-4 shows the relationship between prices and equilibrium income on the demand side of the economy. The schedule is labeled *MD* to stand for macroeconomic (or macro) demand schedule. This reminds us that the relationship between prices and the level of output and spending that is shown arises from interactions between goods and money markets. Movements along the schedule involve adjustments in interest rates, investment, spending, and output.

Here is a definition of the schedule.

> The *macroeconomic demand schedule* shows the equilibrium level of output, corresponding to each level of prices, at which planned spending equals income.

The schedule slopes downward because lower prices mean lower interest rates, higher investment, higher planned spending, and hence higher equilibrium income. Moving up and along the schedule, income falls because a rise in prices raises interest rates, which limits spending. As a point of reference, moving up and along the schedule, say, from A to A', is the same as reading across Table 28-1.

The macroeconomic demand schedule shows the equilibrium level of income at which we have equilibrium in the money market and at the same time equality of ag-

TABLE 28-1

THE LINKAGE BETWEEN PRICES AND AGGREGATE DEMAND

(1)	(2)	(3)	(4)
An *increase* in the price level reduces the real money stock	Excess demand for real balances leads to higher interest rates	Higher interest rates reduce investment and aggregate demand	Reduced aggregate demands leads to a decline in equilibrium income and spending

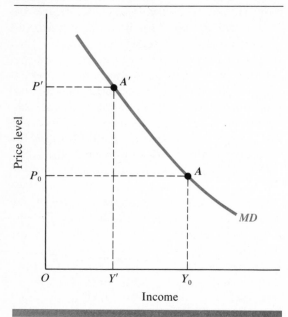

and households, which supply labor. That
interaction determines the equilibrium
levels of employment and wages. The employment level in turn determines the level
of output that firms want to sell, or aggregate
supply.

> The *aggregate supply schedule* shows
> the quantity of output firms want to sup-
> ply at each price level.

We now derive the schedule, starting from
the labor market.

Labor Demand

Firms have a given amount of machines,
structures, and land—we call these resources capital—with which to produce.
They also hire labor. Labor and capital together are used to produce the goods which
the firms offer for sale in the goods market.

Figure 28-5 shows the demand schedule for labor by firms. The real wage is on
the vertical axis, and the quantity of labor,
measured, say, in hours per week, is on the
horizontal axis.

> The *real wage* is the amount of goods
> and services a given money wage will
> buy.

We now explain why the demand curve for
labor slopes downward, meaning that firms
want to hire more labor when the real wage
falls.

The firm makes its hiring decision by
comparing the costs and benefits of hiring
extra workers. Hiring one more worker
makes it possible to produce more output
and therefore adds to the firm's revenue.
But the firm also has to pay the worker. It is
worthwhile to hire one more worker if the
amount he adds to output is worth more
than the amount it costs to hire him. The
amount he adds is called the marginal product of labor.

> The *marginal product of labor* is the in-
> crease in output produced by employ-
> ing one additional worker.

In making its decision, the firm compares the

gregate spending and income. For each
price level there is a different equilibrium
level of income and employment at which
goods and money markets clear. But
nothing has been said so far about what determines prices or about supply. To complete our analysis we have to bring in the
linkage between goods and factor markets
to get an aggregate supply schedule. Aggregate supply and demand in combination determine output *and* prices.

2 THE LABOR MARKET
AND AGGREGATE SUPPLY

On the supply side of the economy we look
at the interaction between firms, which are
sellers in the goods market and hire labor,

FIGURE 28-5 THE DEMAND FOR LABOR. Firms hire workers to the point where their addition to output—the marginal product of labor—equals the real wage. As more and more workers are employed, the marginal product of labor falls. When real wages fall from w' to w, firms want to increase employment, from N' to N. At the lower real wage, some expansion in employment is warranted because the extra workers, $N - N'$, add more to the value of output than they add to costs.

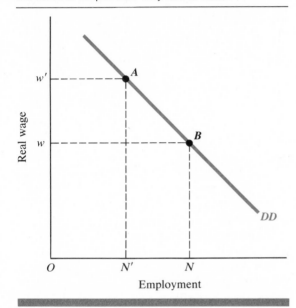

Employment

marginal product of labor with the real wage, which is the value, in terms of goods, of the wage paid to the worker.

To understand the employment decision, we can think of the firm paying workers in terms of the goods they produce. If the marginal product exceeds the real wage, adding one worker increases output by more than the amount he has to be paid—and the firm will certainly increase its labor force. If the marginal product of labor is lower than the wage, reducing the work force by one person saves the wage and costs the firm only the marginal product of labor, which is a smaller loss. The firm comes out ahead and therefore will reduce its labor force. The conclusion is that the firm will keep hiring labor up to the point

where the real wage is equal to the marginal product of labor. That is the condition that determines the firm's demand for labor.

The curve DD in Figure 28-5 is the demand schedule for labor. It shows the quantity of labor that the firm wishes to hire at each real wage. The schedule is downward-sloping because as more and more workers are hired to cooperate with a given amount of machinery, the addition to output they produce declines. The first driver of a truck, for instance, adds a lot, a second driver is useful, but the fifth driver adds hardly anything to output. Thus the quantity of labor demanded by the firm is larger the lower the real wage, because only at a low real wage is it worthwhile to employ a lot of people. Only at a low wage would an extra worker who adds relatively little to the operation bring in more revenue than he costs in wages. It is for this reason that the quantity of labor demanded increases as the real wage declines.

Labor Supply

Workers who supply labor also weigh the costs and benefits of employment. An extra hour of work gives the worker purchasing power over goods and services in the form of real wages. But working an extra hour means giving up an hour of leisure. The individual trades leisure for extra income. The higher the real wage, the more work hours workers are willing to supply. In Figure 28-6 the supply schedule SS shows the supply of labor. It is positively sloped to reflect the fact that when real wages increase, workers do with less leisure in order to earn higher wages and incomes.

Must the labor supply schedule be upward-sloping as we have drawn it? It need not be. For instance, people may decide to work 9 hours a day, no more or less, whatever the real wage. In that case the SS schedule is vertical since there are only so many work hours the given labor force will

FIGURE 28-6   EQUILIBRIUM IN THE LABOR MAR-
KET. The supply schedule of labor *SS* shows the
number of hours households are willing to work at
each level of the real wage. The higher the real
wage, or the higher the purchasing power in terms
of goods an hour of work will buy, the larger the
amount of effort households are willing to supply.
The labor market clears at a real wage *w* with a level
of employment *N*. At any lower real wage, firms want
to hire more hours of work than households are
willing to supply. At higher real wages than *w*,
households want to supply more than firms can afford to hire when labor is so expensive.

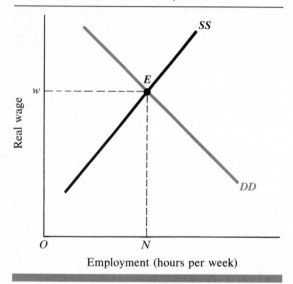

Employment (hours per week)

dence suggests that when real wages rise,
there is an increase in work hours. To a
large extent this comes from extra members
of the family joining the work force and
doing part-time work. We come back to the
question of the shape of the labor supply
curve later, when we ask how income taxes
affect the amount of work people are willing
to do.

Labor Market Equilibrium   At point *E* in
Figure 28-6 the labor market is in equilibrium. At the real wage *w* the quantity of
labor firms demand is equal to the amount
of hours people are willing to work. Therefore, *N* is the equilibrium level of employment. At any real wage lower than *w*,
quantity demanded exceeds the quantity
supplied. Firms want to hire more hours of
labor than workers are willing to supply,
and hence wages are bid up. If wages were
higher than *w*, quantity supplied would exceed the amount firms are willing to hire at
so high a wage, and wages would be bid
down as workers competed for the limited
number of jobs. Wages thus adjust to move
the economy to point *E*.

At point *E*, everyone who wants to work
is doing so. There is thus *full employment*
of labor when the labor market is in equilibrium.

Money Wages, Prices, and Real Wages   We
have so far looked at the labor market in
terms of the *real* (not *money*) wages firms
are willing to pay and households require
for a given work effort. That is indeed appropriate on the side of supply, since workers work for what they can buy with their
wages. They know that if both wages and
the prices of goods they buy double, their
real situation is unchanged, and they continue to work the same amount as before. By
the same token, if all prices double, workers
will not go on supplying the same number
of hours at unchanged money wages. The
real wage has fallen even though the nomi-

be willing to work, whatever the real wage.

It is also possible that people react to
higher real wages by reducing their work effort. If they get $12 per hour of work instead
of $10, they may decide they can afford to
work a bit less and enjoy more leisure at that
higher wage. In that case the supply schedule beyond a given wage may actually bend
backward: at a high wage, further wage increases will reduce work effort.

Although these alternatives are possible, the facts for the U.S. economy seem to
be as shown by the schedule *SS*.[1] The evi-

---

[1] For some discussion, see J. Hausman, "Labor Supply," in Henry J. Aaron and Joseph Pechman (eds.),
How Taxes Affect Economic Behavior, Brookings Institution, Washington, D.C., 1981, pp. 27–83.

nal wage has not. Workers reduce the quantity of labor supplied in response to the lower *real* wage.

Firms, too, look at real wages rather than money wages in making their employment decisions. They compare the wage measured in terms of goods they pay an extra worker with the amount that the worker adds to output. They pay in wages exactly what a worker adds, at the margin, to output.

Workers and firms who make their decisions by looking at real wages are said not to suffer from money illusion.

Money illusion is present when a change in money wages or prices leads people to alter their behavior even though real wages have not changed.

For instance, let all prices double, and suppose that money wages also double. If households work more because nominal wages are higher, they suffer from money illusion. The illusion is that real wages are higher even though, in fact, the *real wage* is unchanged.[2] Any time people respond to changes in nominal values when real values are unchanged, there is money illusion.

The absence of money illusion in the labor market and the full flexibility of wages have two strong implications. First, any change in the price level that is not caused by a shift in the labor supply or demand curves will be matched by an equivalent change in money wages, leaving real wages unchanged. Second, because real wages do not change, employment also is unchanged. We now develop these two points, which are the core of the classical model of output determination.

Suppose once again that we are in labor market equilibrium, with a given real wage

and level of employment. For some reason having nothing to do with labor supply or demand, the price level in the economy doubles, and this is clear to everyone, workers and firms alike. What adjustments will occur in the labor market? Suppose that at first the money wage remains unchanged. Firms now realize that the higher prices imply a fall in real wages and that therefore it is worth hiring more workers. Workers realize that at the going money wage they are getting a lower real wage per hour of work, and they therefore reduce the quantity of labor they supply.

Thus at the original money wage there is an excess demand for labor. Money wages will increase as firms compete for the limited amount of labor supplied. How far will the money wage increase? Money wages will have to rise until real wages are again what they were to start with. Only when money wages have increased fully to match the higher prices are real wages back to the equilibrium level where the amount firms want to hire equals the amount households choose to supply. But at that point employment also is back where it started.

We have derived a very strong result. In the absence of money illusion, changes in the price level will not change equilibrium real wages or employment. In a labor market with wage flexibility and no money illusion, any change in the price level[3] is matched by an equivalent change in money wages. Price level changes do not change equilibrium employment, because decisions in the labor market are geared to real wages.

Employment, Output, and Prices

The last step on the supply side is to link employment, output, and prices. We have shown how real wages in the labor market

---

[2] The term *money illusion* is used more generally to refer to any behavior by which individuals, firms, or governments react to changes in prices expressed in dollars even though no real change in their situation has taken place.

[3] We repeat that this refers to a change in the price level that is not caused by a shift in either the labor supply or the labor demand curve.

adjust to equate the quantities of labor supplied and demanded. Labor market equilibrium thus determines the level of employment. Because everyone who wants to work at the equilibrium real wage is doing so, there is full employment when the labor market is in equilibrium. Furthermore, the equilibrium level of employment is not affected by changes in the aggregate price level.

Given the amount of capital (machinery, structures, and land) firms have available, they are able with a given level of employment to produce a particular level of output. With full employment of the labor force, the level of output firms produce is *potential output*. Potential output, which we introduced earlier, is the level of output corresponding to full employment of the labor force.

Putting these points together—with labor market equilibrium, output is at its potential level and employment is independent of the price level—we conclude that the level of output supplied by firms is independent of the level of prices and equal to potential output. This is shown in Figure 28-7 by the vertical aggregate supply schedule *AS*.

> The *aggregate supply schedule AS* shows the amount of output supplied at each level of prices. If money wages are flexible and there is no money illusion, the amount of output supplied is independent of prices. The aggregate supply curve is vertical at the level of potential output. This is the *classical case*.

Consider once more what the vertical aggregate supply schedule tells us. Suppose we start from a price level *P*. At that price level firms are supplying an amount of output equal to Y_p, as we can read from the supply curve at point *B*. Now prices fall to *P'*. At point *B'* firms still offer output Y_p; the quantity supplied is unaffected by the decline in prices, and money wages fall enough to

FIGURE 28-7   AGGREGATE SUPPLY SCHEDULE: THE CLASSICAL CASE. When wages are flexible and there is no money illusion in the labor market, employment does not depend on the price level. Changes in prices lead to offsetting changes in money wages; real wages and employment stay unchanged. Therefore, the amount of output firms produce is also unaffected by the price level. Output is supplied at a level Y_p that is determined by technology, available capital, and the equilibrium level of employment established in the labor market.

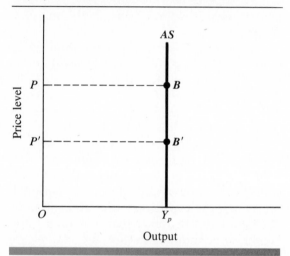

keep the real wage constant. Y_p is the level of potential output. The critical assumptions that guarantee this result are full wage flexibility and absence of money illusion. We shall, of course, have to ask at some point how realistic these two assumptions are.

3 THE EQUILIBRIUM PRICE LEVEL

We have now developed the macroeconomic demand curve *MD* and the aggregate supply curve *AS*. With these two curves, we are ready to show how the equilibrium price level is determined.

The curves are combined in Figure 28-8. The demand schedule shows the equilibrium level of output and income at which spending equals income, given equilibrium in the money market. The aggregate supply schedule shows how much output firms are willing to supply, given equilibrium

FIGURE 28-8 THE EQUILIBRIUM PRICE LEVEL.
Combining aggregate supply and the macroeconomic demand schedule *MD*, we find the equilibrium
level of prices at which *all* markets clear. At point *E*
the level of prices is such that what firms are producing with the level of employment that establishes
labor market equilibrium is equal to what demanders
want to buy, given incomes and interest rates that
clear the money market. Point *E* establishes the
simultaneous equilibrium of goods, money, and
labor markets.

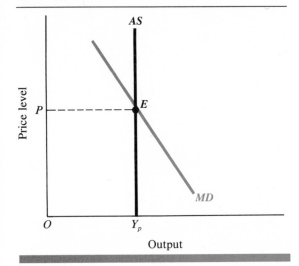

Output

in the labor market. The intersection of *MD*
and *AS* therefore gives equilibrium in the
money, labor, *and* goods markets. At point *E*
we have a price level such that the quantity
of goods demanded is equal to the amount
firms are willing to supply.

The *equilibrium price level P* in Figure
28-8 does a lot of work. It clears the markets
for goods, labor, and money. The labor market is in equilibrium because we are on the
aggregate supply schedule at point *E*. The
money market is in equilibrium and all output is sold at point *E* because that is how we
derived the *MD* schedule. Thus at the intersection of *MD* and *AS*, all three markets are
in equilibrium. The price level *P* ensures a
real value of the money stock and therefore
interest rates at a level such that people
want to spend exactly what firms are willing
to produce.

Suppose prices were somewhat higher
than *P*. The real money stock would be
lower, and therefore interest rates would be
higher. With higher interest rates, aggregate
demand is lower. Thus at a price level
higher than *P*, firms could not sell the
amount of goods Y_p. Prices would tend to
fall, and that would lower interest rates and
encourage aggregate spending. Conversely,
if prices were below the level *P*, real balances would be higher, interest rates would
be lower, and aggregate spending would exceed potential output. Prices would be bid
up to return the economy to point *E*.

What Determines Prices?

In Figure 28-8 the equilibrium price level *P*
is determined by a number of factors that
are reflected in the positions of the macroeconomic demand schedule *MD* and the aggregate supply schedule *AS*. We now want
to identify these factors and then in the next
section ask what the effects are of changes in
these determinants of the price level.

On the aggregate supply side the level
of potential output Y_p depends on three factors. First, it depends on labor supply conditions. If workers at any given wage want to
work a lot, other things equal, equilibrium
employment and hence output will tend to
be larger. But output will also depend on
the contribution the labor force makes to
production, as reflected in the marginal
product of labor. That contribution depends
on how much capital workers have to work
with. The more capital there is, the higher
the level of potential output. Thus changes
in workers' desire to supply labor and
changes in the capital stock can shift the position of the *AS* schedule and be the source
of changes in supply and therefore in the
price level.

On the demand side, two determinants
might be singled out especially. One is the
nominal money stock, which is held constant in our analysis so far but which can be

changed by the Fed. Changes in the nominal money stock mean higher real balances at each level of prices and hence lower interest rates and higher aggregate demand. The other policy variable that works on the demand side is fiscal policy. A cut in taxes or a rise in government spending, for example, affects aggregate demand and thereby disturbs equilibrium.

We now investigate these disturbances in detail. We want to study their effects in the classical model in comparison to what happens when prices are constant. Under Keynesian assumptions, with prices given and output determined *only* by demand, expansionary monetary and fiscal policies raise output and employment. This is not at all the case in the classical model, and we shall now find out what changes the outcome so much.

4 MONETARY AND FISCAL POLICY

The macro demand schedule is derived for given fiscal policy—government spending and tax rates—and a given level of nominal money balances. Changes in the price level, moving along the schedule, change the level of aggregate demand because they change real balances and interest rates. Changes in fiscal and monetary policy, by contrast, *shift* the *MD* curve, changing the level of aggregate demand at *each* level of prices. These shifts in the *MD* curve in turn affect the price level, as we now show.

An Increase in the Nominal Money Stock

Suppose that the economy is in equilibrium at point *E* in Figure 28-9 and that the nominal money stock is doubled because the Fed has purchased securities in an open market operation. At point *E*, with an unchanged price level, a larger nominal money stock means that the real money stock is higher. This implies that equilibrium interest rates

FIGURE 28-9   AN INCREASE IN MONEY RAISES PRICES, NOT OUTPUT. A doubling of the nominal money stock shifts the macroeconomic demand schedule at each level of prices to the right. At each price level real balances are higher, and therefore equilibrium income on the demand side rises. But aggregate supply has not changed. Excess demand at the initial level of prices P_0 causes prices to rise until they have increased in exactly the same proportion as nominal money at E'. At that point real balances are what they were initially, and therefore spending and income return to their initial levels.

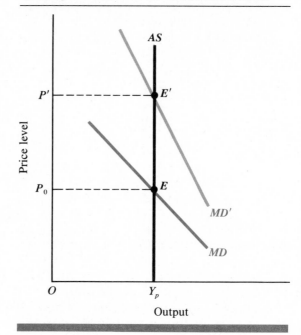

are lower and investment and aggregate demand higher; thus equilibrium income and spending on the demand side rise. This is shown by a rightward shift of the demand schedule from *MD* to *MD'*. At each price level, quantity demanded increases.

We can also look at how far the *MD* curve shifts upward at any given level of output. If prices change in the same proportion as the money stock, real balances and aggregate demand are both unchanged. Accordingly, when the money supply doubles, the *MD* curve shifts upward to *MD'*, where the price level on *MD'* is twice the price level at the same level of output on *MD*.

That way real balances are the same on both curves at each level of output. Thus at E' the price level P' is double the price level P.

This means that when the money supply increases, the *equilibrium* price level increases in the same proportion in the classical model. Further, there is no change in output, which remains at the potential level, Y_p.

Now we show the economic forces that cause the price level to rise from P to P'. A higher nominal money stock shifts the aggregate demand schedule from MD to MD'. At the initial price level P_0 there is an excess demand for goods. Interest rates have fallen, investment has risen, and thus spending plans by households exceed the level of output firms are willing to supply at the real wage that clears the labor market. By creating excess demand for goods, the increase in nominal money leads to increases in prices as people compete for the limited amount of goods supplied. There is too much money chasing too few goods. How much will the price level rise? Because output is independent of the price level, prices must rise enough to bring demand back to the level of potential output. This occurs when prices have risen enough to reduce real balances to their initial level, thus raising interest rates to a level at which spending is again in line with income.

The adjustment process to a monetary expansion thus involves a period of boom. As long as prices have not risen fully to match the rise in money, interest rates are low and spending is high. Firms have no trouble selling their goods, and competition for the limited quantity available bids up prices. Then, as the price level increases and real balances return to their initial level, interest rates rise again and spending is dampened to the level of potential output.

In the long run, when all adjustments in prices have taken place, a change in nominal money has no effect on output or interest rates, in the classical model.

Keynesian and Classical Models Compared

What causes the difference between this classical result and the result reached with the Keynesian model in Chapter 27? There we assumed unemployment and a given level of prices. Firms would supply *any* amount of goods they could sell. In that case increased nominal money increased demand, just as here, and led to an expansion in output rather than a rise in prices.

There we started with unemployment. When the demand for goods increased, there were unemployed workers available to increase output. Here the labor market clears, there is no unemployment to begin with, and the limited supply of goods does not respond to higher demand. With supply limited at the level of potential output, it is prices that respond, not employment.

The difference between the Keynesian and classical analyses comes out also when we consider the effects of a reduction in the nominal money stock. In the Keynesian analysis, this leads to higher interest rates, lower investment, and lower output. In the classical case, it leads only to a fall in the price level in the long run, when all adjustments have taken place. The difference exists because the Keynesian analysis stops short of the long run by limiting itself to given prices and wages. If wages do not fall and firms do not cut prices, a fall in nominal money is not offset by lower prices. Real balances will be lower, interest rates will be higher, and the economy will be producing at less than the full-employment level.

Fiscal Policy

Fiscal policy changes affect the level of aggregate demand and equilibrium income and spending. If the government increases purchases of goods and services, aggregate spending rises, and at each level of prices, equilibrium income must rise for spending to equal income. The same is true if the government cuts taxes, thus increasing con-

FIGURE 28-10   AN INCREASE IN GOVERNMENT
SPENDING. At each price level, increased government spending raises aggregate demand and equilibrium income and spending on the demand side of
the economy. *MD* shifts to *MD'*. At the initial price
level there is now excess demand. Prices are bid up,
and the rise continues until point *E'* is reached. Here
the rise in prices and therefore in interest rates has
been large enough to reduce investment by the full
amount of increased government spending. Output
is unchanged, the government spends more, and investment is crowded out by the same amount.

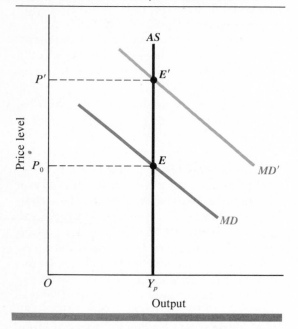

helps restore equilibrium. As prices rise,
with the nominal money stock unchanged,
the real money stock declines. The fall in
real balances raises interest rates, and that
reduces investment and aggregate demand.
Thus in the first stage a fiscal expansion, by
creating excess demand for goods, puts upward pressure on prices and thus on interest
rates. That in turn *crowds out*, or *displaces*,
investment. But how much will the price
level rise? In Figure 28-10 the new equilibrium between demand and aggregate sup-
ply is at point *E'* with a price level *P'*. Prices
thus must rise enough to reduce demand
back to the level of potential output. They
will keep rising until real balances have
fallen enough and interest rates have increased enough to lower total spending to
the initial level.

There is more to be said. At point *E'*
total spending is again equal to full-employment output, just as it was initially. But now
the government spends more because we
have had a fiscal expansion. If total output is
the same and the government spends more,
someone else must spend less by exactly
the amount. Who? We saw that the increase
in prices raises interest rates and reduces investment.

> An increase in government spending
> *crowds out* an equal amount of invest-
> ment in the long run, in the classical
> model.

In the Keynesian model we saw how fiscal expansion raises income and therefore
raises interest rates somewhat. That led to
reduced investment and a dampening of the
expansion of output. Here output does not
change at all in the long run. Consumption
is unchanged because the level of income is
unchanged. Therefore increased government spending is matched *fully* by reduced
investment. Competing demands for goods
are reconciled with the available supply by
the increase in interest rates that reduces
investment. Again the classical model has

sumer spending at each level of income.

Figure 28-10 shows the effect of an increase in government spending on goods
and services by a shift of the *MD* schedule.
With increased government spending, more
goods are demanded at each price level, and
thus *MD* shifts to the right to *MD'*. Our initial equilibrium was at point *E*, with a price
level P_0 at which all markets cleared. The increased spending by government now has
created excess demand for goods. Firms' inventories are running down, and people are
competing for the limited supply of goods
by bidding up prices.

Once again the rise in the price level

implications much different from those of the Keynesian model. The fact that output is determined by supply means that whatever the government purchases comes not from increased employment but from some other sector.

A Moment for Perspective

It is worth looking back to see what we have done. We started in Chapters 23 and 24 by looking solely at the goods market, assuming prices were fixed. This analysis gave a first view of income determination. Later we added the assets markets, examining the demand for money relative to bonds, which really means all other assets. By adding the assets markets we were able to discuss the role of the interest rate in affecting investment. Now the price level is allowed to change, and we develop a macroeconomic model that makes it possible to study the simultaneous determination of the level of output and the price level. The material we learned earlier is still useful, for instance, in telling us how the macroeconomic demand curve *MD* shifts when the money stock is changed or when there is a change in fiscal policy. But this is only part of the story. The full story includes aggregate supply along with aggregate demand.

5   SHIFTS IN POTENTIAL OUTPUT

To emphasize that price level determination in a complete model is a matter of both

supply and demand, we now look in detail at the effects of a reduction in income taxes, taking into account the effects of the tax reduction both on the supply of labor, and hence on potential output, and on aggregate demand. This analysis enables us to evaluate the arguments of *supply siders* that tax cuts have beneficial anti-inflationary effects by expanding potential output. *Supply side economists place much emphasis on the role of the tax system in determining the level of potential output.* They argue that policies, operating through the tax system, that increase potential output can have large, beneficial effects on the economy in terms of higher output, increased growth, and lower inflation.

A Cut in Income Tax Rates

Under the income tax system the government takes part of every extra dollar of income that a person earns. Proposed tax cuts that started to go into effect in 1982 and are slated to continue through 1984 would sharply reduce the marginal tax rates.

> The *marginal tax rate* is the fraction of an extra dollar of income that has to be paid in taxes.

Table 28-2 shows the changes in marginal tax rates from the new legislation.

Table 28-2 shows that a person earning $50,000, for example, used to pay 50 cents out of every extra dollar in taxes. Under the new legislation this would be reduced to 45 cents, which is a 10 percent cut in

TABLE 28-2

CHANGES IN MARGINAL INCOME TAX RATES FOR 1983
(Single Taxpayer)

	REAL INCOME, 1979			
	$10,000	$20,000	$30,000	$50,000
Old law marginal rate	24%	34%	44%	50%
New law marginal rate	19%	28%	36%	45%

Source: Economic Report of the President, 1982, Table 5-3.

taxes, or a 10 percent rise in after-tax wages on the marginal dollar earned. The tax cut would look the same to suppliers of labor as an increase in wages, because what matters to them is the after-tax wage.

> Cutting tax rates increases an individual's after tax wage rate. With the Federal Government taking a smaller share of the last dollar of earnings, the return to an individual from an extra hour of work or a more demanding job will increase, strengthening the incentive to work more hours, or accept a more demanding job.
>
> The preponderance of empirical studies suggests that the labor supply effects of a tax cut are small for married men, somewhat larger for unmarried people, and substantial for married women. The most important effect of these changes in personal marginal income tax rates may thus be to increase labor force participation rates and hours of work of married women.[4]

Figure 28-11 shows the effect of the cut in income tax rates as a shift of the supply schedule of labor from SS to SS'. With lower income tax rates, workers are willing to supply more labor because the same before-tax wage (which is on the vertical axis) now gives them a higher take-home wage. With labor supply shifted to SS', the new equilibrium in the labor market is at point E'. The equilibrium real wages firms have to pay has fallen, workers have higher take-home pay, and the level of employment is higher.

The essential element by which the income tax cut increases output is that workers' wages *rise* while wages paid by firms *fall*. How is this possible? The reason is that wages are taxed, so that some of what the firms pay out goes to the government, and the remainder to workers. When government reduces its share, workers can receive more even though firms pay less.

[4] *Economic Report of the President*, 1982, pp. 120–121.

FIGURE 28-11 A TAX CUT INCREASES LABOR SUPPLY. A cut in income tax rates leaves workers with larger take-home pay for every dollar of wages firms pay. Therefore, at each wage the supply of effort increases. The supply schedule shifts to SS'. The equilibrium real wage that firms pay declines to w', and the level of employment rises from N to N'. Workers have higher take-home wages, and firms pay less.

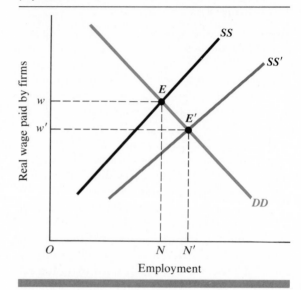

The higher level of employment means that firms are now producing a larger amount of goods. More workers are working the machinery, and hence output is larger. This is shown in Figure 28-12 as a shift of the aggregate supply schedule from AS to AS'.

The income tax cut also affects aggregate demand. Households have a larger share of national income, and less is being kept by the government. Because household spending depends on disposable income, part of the increase in disposable income will be spent. This means that at each level of prices, consumption, aggregate demand, and hence equilibrium income on the demand side of the economy will be higher. In Figure 28-12 this is shown as the shift of the macroeconomic demand schedule from MD to MD'.

FIGURE 28-12   SUPPLY SIDE ECONOMICS: A TAX CUT. A cut in marginal income tax rates raises the supply of effort and therefore shifts the aggregate supply schedule from *AS* to *AS'* as potential output rises. The tax cut also increases disposable income at each level of output, and that raises consumption, aggregate demand, and equilibrium income on the demand side. This is shown by the shift of the macroeconomic demand schedule from *MD* to *MD'*. The new equilibrium at *E'* involves higher output. Prices will be higher or lower depending on the relative shifts of the *AS* and *MD* schedules. If prices are higher than they are at *E'*, interest rates must be higher, and investment will decline.

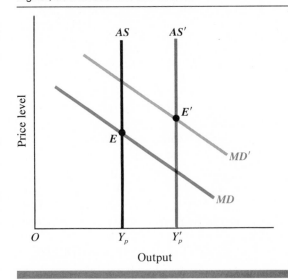

The new equilibrium, taking into account the effect of the tax cut on both the supply and demand sides of the economy, takes us to point *E'*. We cannot be certain whether prices rise or fall, but it is quite certain that potential output will be larger. The price level in the new equilibrium will be higher if the *MD* schedule shifts a lot, as we show it doing in Figure 28-12. This occurs when the marginal propensity to consume is high so that the multiplier on the demand side is large.

The effects of the income tax cut on investment depend on the relative shifts of the *MD* and *AS* curves. If *MD* shifts more, the price level rises, real balances fall, the interest rate rises, and investment falls. If *AS* shifts more, the price level falls, interest rates fall, and investment actually increases.

The key point, though, is that a tax cut will increase potential output because it increases people's willingness to work at any given level of the real wage paid by firms.

Supply Side Economics, Taxes, and Output

The policy proposals of supply side economists are not limited to personal tax cuts that shift the supply of labor and thus increase potential output. There are also suggestions for tax changes that would affect both investment and saving.

Investment   In terms of our analysis, a policy to encourage investment, such as an investment tax credit, would have two effects.[5] In the short run it would not change the capital stock by much. It takes a few years of higher investment for the capital stock to be increased appreciably.

In the short run, an investment tax credit has its major impact by affecting aggregate demand. In terms of our diagrams, an investment tax credit shifts the *MD* schedule outward and to the right. Because there is hardly any effect on potential output in the short run, the effect of the policy is to raise prices and interest rates. Now we have to ask whether the higher interest rates completely offset the effects of the investment tax credit and therefore leave the level of investment spending unchanged. The issue is this: Potential output is given at the time the tax credit is introduced; government spending is held constant. That leaves only consumption and investment. If investment is to rise, consumption has to fall. Consumption will fall only if saving increases as the interest rate rises.

---

[5] An investment tax credit is a reduction in a firm's taxes that is proportional to the amount of investment the firm does. It effectively reduces the cost of investing for firms and therefore encourages investment.

If the increase in the interest rate caused by the increase in aggregate demand raises saving, investment will rise, and the capital stock will begin to increase. Over the course of a few years, potential output will increase appreciably, and the investment tax credit will have succeeded in raising the level of output. As output rises, consumption will rise and will probably end up higher than it started before the investment tax credit.

Saving In a fully employed economy, the success of an investment tax credit in raising output rather than just interest rates thus depends entirely on the response of saving to a change in the interest rate. When the interest rate rises, the return to saving increases. Someone who was making 5 percent a year before will now get 10 percent. Since saving yields a higher return, the natural reaction is to think that people do more of it. But another way of thinking about the question makes the effect of an increase in the interest rate on saving less certain. Suppose you want to be sure of having $1000 a year to spend out of your savings in the future. When the interest rate is 5 percent, you need $20,000 total to give you $1000 a year. But when the interest rate is 10 percent, you can get $1000 per year with accumulated savings of only $10,000. In this case it seems that with a higher interest rate there is less need to save in order to guarantee a particular income in the future, and therefore there will be less saving.

These arguments show that we cannot be sure without looking at the facts whether an increase in the interest rate increases saving. Unfortunately, we cannot be sure even after looking at the facts. The data do not show any clear relationship between the interest rate and saving and certainly do not suggest a large response of saving to an increase in the interest rate. The challenge of supply side economics has opened up the question of the effects of interest rates on saving, but there is as yet no convincing new evidence.

The reason why this is a major issue can be understood by comparing the recommendations of supply side economists and those of more traditional economists. Suppose potential output is given, the economy is at full employment, or producing at the level of potential output, and investment is to be increased. The traditional analysis runs like this. Given government spending, investment can be increased only if consumption is reduced. Consumption can be reduced only if disposable income is reduced. Therefore, to increase investment, the government increases income taxation, reducing consumption spending and making room for investment.

The supply side prescription, on the contrary, is to cut taxes. Cutting income taxes will increase the supply of labor and increase potential output. Furthermore, when income taxes are cut, the rate of return to saving goes up. Suppose someone earning 10 percent on savings is being taxed at a 40 percent rate. That person gets only 6 percent after taxes from his savings. Now reduce the tax rate to 20 percent. The return to savings will rise to 8 percent after taxes. This encourages more saving, say the supply siders, thus increasing investment further.

The traditional view that income taxes should be raised to encourage increased investment when the economy is at full employment contrasts sharply with the supply side prescription to cut taxes. The issue is far from academic. The great tax cuts of 1982–1984 were initiated by an administration committed to a supply side view of the issue. The administration argued that tax cuts would lead to higher saving, which would finance increased investment and higher potential output in the future and also lead to a greater supply of labor, increasing potential output immediately. The passage of time should help give a verdict on the effects of the tax cuts.

The Wedge

The basic point of supply side economics is that taxes drive a *wedge*, or gap, between the prices, wages, and interest rates paid by users of factors of production on one side and the incomes received by the sellers on the other side. The tax is like a wedge, and removing the wedge raises potential output by inducing people to save more, invest more, and work harder. For instance, in the case of the income tax, reducing the tax wedge reduces the wage *paid* by the firm because more labor is supplied, but the wage *received* by workers rises—workers and firms split between them what used to be paid to the government. Similar good things happen in any other market when wedges are removed. The responses to re-

duced taxes may not be very large, but there can be no doubt that the basic point is sound. Removing the wedges will increase potential output.

But that raises a serious issue. Why bother to have income taxes at all since they clearly reduce output in this case? The answer is that there are things we expect government to buy, such as defense and social welfare programs, and they have to be paid for somehow. The only way is through taxes, even though the taxes put wedges into various markets. When we reduce wedges by reducing taxes, we also usually reduce the government's revenue and therefore its ability to spend. Thus not everyone is necessarily made better off by a reduction in income taxes. Those who were previously benefiting from government spending are likely to suffer even though total output rises.

SUMMARY

1   The classical model of macroeconomics assumes full flexibility of wages and prices as well as the absence of money illusion.

2   An increase in the price level, given the nominal money stock, raises interest rates and reduces investment, aggregate demand, equilibrium income, and spending on the demand side of the economy.

3   The macroeconomic demand schedule shows the equilibrium level of income and spending at each level of prices. The schedule slopes downward; at lower prices, real balances are higher, and that increases aggregate demand through lower interest rates.

4   The supply of labor depends on the real wages individuals earn. We assume that increased real wages raise the supply of effort.

5   The demand schedule for labor is downward-sloping. The lower the real wage, the larger the amount of labor the firm is willing to hire. The firm always hires workers to the point where the addition to output of an extra worker exactly equals the real wage he is paid.

6   If there is full flexibility of wages and no money illusion, the equilibrium level of employment and the real wage are independent of the

price level. An increase in prices will be matched by an equivalent rise in money wages.

7   If employment is independent of the price level, the output firms produce with the labor they employ will also be independent of the price level. Therefore, the aggregate supply schedule is a vertical line at the level of potential output.

8   The equilibrium price level is determined in the goods market at the point where aggregate supply equals the macroeconomic demand. At that price level the goods market, the labor market, and the money market all clear.

9   An increase in the nominal money stock, with no money illusion and full flexibility of wages and prices, leads to a proportional rise in prices and no change in interest rates, output, employment, or real wages.

10   An increase in government spending leads to an increase in prices, higher interest rates, and a 1 for 1 reduction in investment.

11   Supply side economics draws attention to the role of taxes in reducing the incentives to work, save, and invest. Supply siders argue that reducing marginal income tax rates would lead to increased work effort, more saving, and more investment. Potential output would increase. Some of these predictions have evidence in their favor; others, in particular the effect of tax reductions on saving, remain open issues.

KEY TERMS

Wage and price flexibility	Crowding out
Macroeconomic demand schedule	Supply side economics
Aggregate supply schedule	Marginal tax rates
Money illusion	Wedge

PROBLEMS

1   (a) Define the macroeconomic demand schedule, or curve. (b) How sould the macro-economic demand curve shift if consumers' propensity to save increased? (c) How would it shift if investment increased?

2   (a) Define the aggregate supply curve. (b) Explain why the aggregate supply curve is vertical when wage and price flexibility ensures labor market equilibrium.

3   Suppose the aggregate supply curve is vertical. The government wants to increase the rate of investment. (a) Can it use monetary policy for this purpose? (b) How about fiscal policy? (c) What effect would a reduction in income tax rates have on investment?

4   (a) What effect would an increase in the income tax have on labor supply? (b) What would the total effect of income taxes on the

price level and level of output be? (*c*) Is your analysis consistent with the view expressed in 1981 by the Reagan administration that income tax cuts will get the economy moving again and reduce inflation?

5   Explain how a higher capital stock affects the aggregate supply curve.

6   Explain how and whether an increase in the money stock affects prices and output when wages and prices are fully flexible.

7   "Supply side policies are good for growth, and demand side policies are good for controlling the price level." Evaluate this argument and explain your answer.

8   Suppose the government increases its spending in a fully employed economy. (*a*) What effect does this have on consumption and investment, respectively? (*b*) Explain what you understand by the term "crowding out."

9   Now suppose that prices are sticky and that there is unemployment (as in Chapter 27). The government increases its spending. (*a*) What effect does this have on consumption and investment, respectively? (*b*) Is there crowding out here?

10   Using your answers to the previous two questions, explain why we have to bring the supply side into our macroeconomic model.

In the economies of the United States and other industrialized countries, disturbances that reduce aggregate demand, such as a fall in the money stock or a decline in investment, are always followed by periods of unemployment. The unemployment can be very severe and persistent. Recessions last not weeks or months but often more than a year. The fact that recessions and unemployment are so persistent means that the classical model of Chapter 28, with its continuing full employment, cannot describe what happens in the short run in economies hit by disturbances. At best it can describe long-term adjustments. But the Keynesian analysis, which gives emphasis to unemployment, is also lacking. It fails to explain why prices continually rise in most industrial countries and why expansionary policies in economies that are near full employment lead to higher prices rather than increased output and employment.

Neither the Keynesian model nor the classical analysis *taken by itself* is a good way of looking at the economy. But in combination they are helpful in fixing two points of the macroeconomic adjustment process to disturbances. The Keynesian model is a good way of thinking about the short run, where prices adjust only slowly and employment varies. The classical model is a good way of thinking about the long run, in which all wages and prices have time to adjust fully.

With these two points of reference from Chapters 27 and 28, respectively, understood, the challenge is to grasp the transition between them. We want to understand the linkages between the short run of Keynesian analysis and the long run of the classical model. We also want to get a sense of whether the long run means a period of weeks, months, or years.

The transition of the economy as it responds to a disturbance such as an increase in the money stock or a tax cut comes from the interaction between output, employment, and wage and price behavior. We shall show that there is an automatic adjustment process that occurs over time —*not instantly*— by which overemployment raises wages and prices and unemployment lowers wages and prices. Because that process is not instantaneous, the Keynesian analysis is extremely useful for analyzing the short run. But the adjustment does take place, and therefore the classical model ultimately tells the right story. The interesting and controversial question is why the adjustment of wages

29

Aggregate Supply, the Price Level, and Unemployment

and prices is not instantaneous and what the implications are for monetary and fiscal policy.

The classical model assumes a vertical aggregate supply curve, as was developed in Chapter 28. Keynesian analysis assumes that firms will sell any amount of goods at the going level of prices. This chapter introduces the upward-sloping aggregate supply schedule, which represents an intermediate position. Changes in prices bring about some change in output supplied and in employment, but these changes depend on the state of the labor market. The upward-sloping aggregate supply schedule will come across as a unifying tool of the analysis of Chapters 27 and 28. Once we have command of that tool and understand the labor market adjustments that lie behind it, we will have a good tool with which to discuss today's macroeconomic policy problems.

The aggregate supply schedule is central to the adjustment process because it links the goods and labor markets. The labor market matters because wages are the major part of costs, and prices that firms charge must cover the costs they incur. It is wage behavior that makes prices respond slowly to changes in demand. Because wage behavior matters so much to the behavior of prices, we start our analysis with the labor market.

1 THE LABOR MARKET AND WAGE BEHAVIOR

In the labor market, firms hire workers and workers offer their labor services. It is here that we observe either unemployment or a shortage of workers. It is in the labor market that we must look for the answers to two questions. First, why does persistent, high unemployment not cause wages to fall rapidly so that everybody who wants to work can get a job? Second, when aggregate demand increases, why do wages not immedi-

ately adjust so that output never rises above its potential level? To answer these questions we have to look at relationships between firms and their labor force.

Long-Term Job Commitments

From the viewpoint of both firms and workers, a job is typically a long-term commitment. It is expensive for a firm to fire and hire workers. Firing an existing worker may mean the payment of severance pay or a pension and other benefits. It also means the loss of whatever special expertise the worker has built up on the job. Hiring a worker means advertising for a position, setting up interviews, checking the applicants' records and references, and training the new employee. Thus firms are reluctant to hire and fire workers quickly. The firm thinks of much of its labor force as being reasonably attached to it, at least over a number of months or even a number of years.

Similarly, from the viewpoint of the worker, the job arrangement is not a day-to-day matter. It is costly to move from job to job, and most workers expect to stay in a job for some time when they take it. They too are concerned with long-term arrangements.

Since both workers and firms view job arrangements as long-term, both want to reach some explicit or implicit understanding about the terms of the work. This includes agreements about wages and about how to handle variations in the amount of output the firm produces.

Adjustments in Labor Input

A firm and its workers have explicit or implicit labor contracts that specify working conditions. These include normal working hours, overtime requirements, regular wages, and pay schedules for overtime work. It is up to the firm to set the number of hours of work within the limits of these conditions.

FIGURE 29-1   LABOR INPUT: THE HOURS-WORKERS MIX. The firm wants to employ 1000 hours of labor input per week. It can achieve that level of labor input by different combinations of weekly hours per worker and the work force. At *A'* more hours are being worked by fewer workers compared to *A*. In the long run the number of hours is determined by the customary workweek.

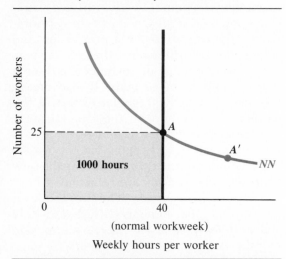

The firm has to decide on the optimal level of its labor input.

Labor input is defined as the *total* number of labor hours the firm employs.

But the total number of labor hours is the number of hours per worker (per week, say) times the number of workers the firm employs, or

Total labor input = hours per worker
× number of workers   (1)

Figure 29-1 shows the schedule *NN* corresponding to a total labor input of, say, 1000 hours (per week). The firm can achieve 1000 hours of labor input with different combinations of the size of the work force and the number of hours per worker, represented by different points on *NN*. For example, 1000 hours of work can be done by 100 workers each working 10 hours, 40 workers each working 25 hours, or 25 workers each working 40 hours. There is a normal full workweek, which we show as 40 hours in Figure

29-1. This implies that the firm's normal work force to provide 1000 hours of labor is 25 workers. Point *A* represents the long-run equilibrium of the firm.

How does the firm choose the total labor input? If the firm wishes to produce a given amount of output, given technology and *labor productivity*, there is a corresponding amount of labor input required to produce that specified level of output.

Productivity is defined as the amount of output per unit of input. *Labor productivity* equals output per unit of labor.

Higher output per labor hour thus means higher labor productivity. The higher the labor productivity, the smaller the number of labor hours required to produce the output.

Suppose the firm, because of higher demand for its goods, wishes to increase production and hence the labor input to, say, 1200 hours. We show this in Figure 29-2 as an outward shift of the *NN* schedule to *NN'*. Should the firm obtain the increased labor input through increased hours per worker or should it hire more workers? The typical adjustment pattern is to move in the short run to point *A'*, increasing hours rather than workers. Each worker works more, probably doing overtime. In the medium run and the long run, the firm progressively returns to the normal workweek, thus reducing overtime and increasing the work force to point *A"*.

In the short run the firm adjusts its labor input primarily through changes in hours rather than in the number of workers on the payroll. It does so because there is uncertainty about how long the higher level of demand and production will last. Since it is costly for the firm to hire and fire workers, the work force is expanded only when the firm believes it will be producing at the new higher level in the long run as well as the short run. In the short run it is more cost-effective to let the existing labor force work overtime, even if overtime rates are higher then normal wages. In moving from *A* to *A'*

FIGURE 29-2 LABOR INPUT SCHEDULES. Labor input is measured in work hours, or the number of workers times the number of hours per worker. The firm can vary the labor input by raising the number of hours per worker or the number of workers with unchanged hours or both. In the short run an increase in labor input typically occurs through increased hours, moving from A to A'. In the long run the firm returns to a normal workweek (40 hours) and adjusts the work force, moving to A".

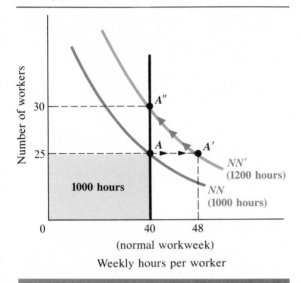

Weekly hours per worker

Figure 29-2 shows a case where initially *all* of the adjustment is in hours while in the long run all the adjustment is in the work force. The long-run adjustment is entirely sensible, but in the short run too it is possible to have some adjustment in the work force. Rapid work force adjustment is more likely when costs of changing the labor force (screening, advertising, training, and severance pay) are low relative to overtime rates and when workers are unwilling to do overtime. But the general point remains that in the short run the adjustment is primarily in hours, and in the long run it occurs almost entirely in the work force.

Layoffs and Labor Hoarding: Adjusting to a Fall in Demand

Most firms have a labor force trained to perform relatively specialized tasks. The specialization goes beyond the worker being an electrician or an accountant to include an acquired familiarity with output and routine tasks in the particular firm. Workers have firm-specific skills. These skills are valuable to the firm since they are costly to acquire, especially in terms of learning time. An accountant who is familiar with the firm's procedures, for example, is more valuable than a fresh accountant who is unaccustomed to the routines. These firm-specific skills imply that the firm will hold on to workers with particularly useful skills even when a decline in product demand reduces the firm's demand for labor. The firm practices what is known as labor hoarding.

> A firm *hoards labor* when it keeps more workers on the payroll than are strictly necessary to produce the *current* level of output.

No firm can permanently hold on to more skilled labor than is required for production. Ultimately a permanent decline in demand must end in a cut in the labor force. But in the short run, when it is not clear whether demand has fallen transitorily or

in Figure 29-2, the firm avoids the costs of advertising for and screening new workers and training them to perform specialized jobs. When changing the work force is expensive and the need for increased labor input is likely to be temporary, using the existing labor force to work overtime is the right strategy.

If the increase in demand turns out to be permanent, the firm will not stay at point A'. It would be very costly to have workers do a 48-hour week year in and year out. The use of overtime by the existing labor force is strictly a transitory adjustment. The correct adjustment to a permanent increase in demand and production is to hire more workers, moving to point A". At A" the entire work force is back to normal hours. New workers on the payroll substitute for the initial use of overtime work.

permanently, firms practice labor hoarding. They adjust the intensity of work effort of the labor force and the number of hours worked rather than dismissing valuable or experienced workers.

Even when the firm is faced with a longer-term decline in demand, it may be desirable to hold on to experienced workers in some fashion.

A *layoff* is a transitory separation of the worker from the firm.

The worker is not dismissed definitely—fired, in other words—but rather goes off the payroll for the duration of the fall in demand and is expected to be rehired when demand picks up again. To the firm, the arrangement allows the payroll to be trimmed during a decline in demand without the permanent loss of a skilled worker.

The layoff makes sense for the worker, too, because the specific skills he has acquired will give him higher wages once he is rehired than he can expect to make starting a fresh job elsewhere. Layoffs and recalls to work provide some flexibility in the short-term adjustment of the firm. When demand falls, some of the adjustment is through hours and some through layoffs. Conversely, when demand picks up, recalls provide an alternative to increased hours.

Figure 29-3 shows the U.S. layoff rate as a percentage of the labor force as well as the average number of hours worked per week for the entire labor force. The data show the

FIGURE 29-3 THE LAYOFF RATE AND THE AVERAGE WORKWEEK. This graph shows the inverse relationship between the average annual layoff rate (red line) and the average hours per workweek (black line) from 1960 to 1980. During booms, such as 1965, the workweek exceeded 40 hours while the layoff rate fell below 1.5 percent. During recessions, such as 1975, weekly hours per worker fell and the percentage of layoffs rose. (*Source:* Citibank Economic Database.)

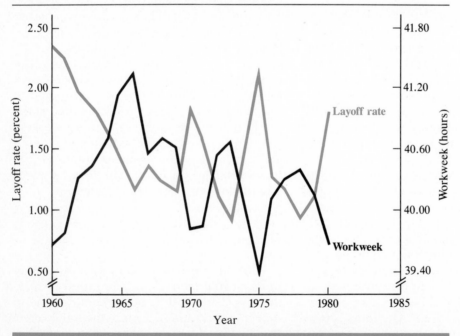

variations in the workweek depending on the state of aggregate demand. In a recession such as 1975 and 1980 hours are low, while during a boom, as in 1973, hours are high. Layoffs have the opposite pattern. During a boom the fraction of the labor force laid off is small (less than 2 percent), while in a recession the layoff rate rises substantially, as in 1975.

Wage Adjustment

As firms vary the level of production, employees vary the amount and intensity of their work. These variations in the amount of work and effort happen without much change in the wage. The wage does not change continually because the job is not a minute-by-minute arrangement. The worker does not take a job expecting to be paid by the minute according to the amount of labor supplied.

The worker knows that the amount of work on any given job varies from time to time. If he is asked to work harder for a week in a particular firm, he does not immediately go off to look for a job where they pay the same amount for less intensive work that week. Some other week there will be more work to be done in the new firm, and then he will have to move on again. The wage in each firm will be adjusted every now and then to maintain competitiveness by keeping up *on average* with wages in similar jobs.

Wages and Unemployment

Why don't wages fall when there are unemployed workers looking for jobs so that anyone who is looking for a job can find one immediately? Again the reason is that the relationship between the firm and its work force is a long-term one. New workers cannot immediately replace the existing ones and do as well, since they lack experience. The existing workers would resent a cut in their wages as a result of there being

people out there willing to do the job, and so the firm does not cut the wage of its existing workers when more people come knocking on the door looking for work. Probably, though, the firm will not raise wages as fast as it otherwise would have. Now it is less worried about losing workers, since there are more substitutes available. But the pressure of unemployment on the wages of existing workers will be slow.

On average, the firm has to maintain the attractiveness of the jobs it offers, but it need not match, minute by minute, the going wage in the market. But it cannot, for that matter, recklessly take advantage of the existence of unemployment to cut wages. Such a move would risk workers' morale and productivity. Firm-specific skills and the practices of labor hoarding, layoffs, and variations in hours of work all make the labor market moderate the effects of shifts in demand on wages. The labor market thus is very different from the market for fresh fish, where late at night the price falls until the last herring has been sold. In the labor market the unemployed provide only very gradual and indirect competition for those who hold jobs.

Summary

Table 29-1 summarizes some of our results and provides a road map for the following sections of this chapter. The table lays out the adjustment in the labor market in the short run, the medium run, and the long run. We have suggested a time period for each "run"—3 months, 1 year, 3–6 years—although these periods serve as reference points, certainly not as constants. The table shows that in the short run, variations in labor input largely take the form of changes in the workweek, supplemented by recalls or layoffs, with few new hires or fires. In the medium run, as changes in labor demand persist, the firm adjusts the level of employment to have the labor force work more

TABLE 29-1

ADJUSTMENT IN THE LABOR MARKET

	SHORT RUN (3 MONTHS)	MEDIUM RUN (1 YEAR)	LONG RUN (3–6 YEARS)
Wages	Largely given	Adjusting to unemployment	Clearing the labor market
Workweek, hours	Demand-determined	Hours/employment: mix is adjusting	Customary workweek
Employment	Largely given*		Demand- and supply-determined

* Except for recalls or layoffs.

nearly normal hours. In the long run that adjustment becomes complete (point A'' in Figure 29-2).

In the short run the wage is largely given. In the medium run it adjusts to excess demand for labor or unemployment. In the long run the wage becomes completely flexible so as to clear the labor market. The long run corresponds, of course, to the analysis of Chapter 28, where the clearing of the market resulted in a vertical long-run supply curve of output. In this chapter, by contrast, we study why the short-run slow adjustment of wages leads to a positively sloped supply curve. We also see how the medium run links the short run and long run with wage changes in response to over- or underemployment pushing the economy toward full employment. We now turn to the linkage between the labor market and the goods market.

2 WAGES, OUTPUT, AND UNEMPLOYMENT

Wages adjust only gradually as firms change the size of the work force. Figure 29-4 shows this by the WW schedule, which relates the level of wages to the level of output. The schedule shows that at potential output, or full employment, the wage will be W_0. A rise in output to Y' will raise the level of wages, but only very modestly, as shown

at A'. The major part of the increase in wages comes from overtime rates, not from changes in the base wage. Similarly, a reduction in output, to Y'', for instance, will not lead to a large cut in the level of wages. The firm adjusts mainly through changes in hours of work and layoffs, not through changes in the base wage.

We can think of the WW schedule in terms of the adjustment mechanism laid out in Table 29-1. In the short run, the wage is largely given. This fact is reflected in the very flat slope of WW. The wage is almost unresponsive to output. But saying that the wage is "given" raises a question: What is the "given" level of the wage? Is it $10 an hour, $15, or what? Here we recognize that wage setting and adjustment in the labor market take time. At any point in time the wage is made up of three parts:

Current wage = last period's wage
+ current cyclical adjustment
+ other   (2)

Cyclical adjustment means an adjustment of wages for deviations from full employment. The first two terms on the right-hand side will now be developed in detail. The term "other" will come up later and is to be disregarded now.

Equation (2) states that except for cyclical adjustment, the wage today is the wage we had last period, say, last quarter. At the

FIGURE 29-4 WAGES AND OUTPUT LEVELS. The wage along WW at any point in time is made up of two main determinants. The current wage is what it was last period plus or minus an adjustment for deviations of output and employment from full employment, Y_p. If output is Y', above full employment the wage at A' is higher than it would be at A; if output is below potential, the wage is lower than at A''. If output is at its potential level, wages do not change from where they were last period.

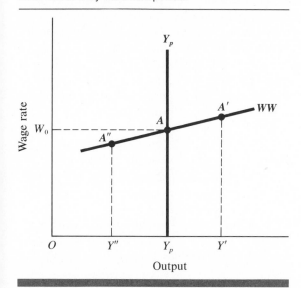

full-employment point A, today's wage is that of last period, or W_0. But if output is above full employment, the wage level will be somewhat higher because of overtime and tighter labor markets. Conversely, with unemployment, the wage may be somewhat lower than W_0. Thus last period's wage sets the level of the WW schedule in Figure 29-4. The higher last period's wage, the higher today's full-employment wage.

Table 29-1 makes a second point, this time about the medium run. In the medium run, wages adjust to labor market conditions. If output and employment are high, wages are *rising*. If output and employment are low, wages are *falling*. Thus Figure 29-4 tells us about the *level* of the wage rate (the short-run question) and the *rate of change* in wages that relates to the medium run. The wage at A' is slightly *higher* than the

wage at A because the firm is paying overtime. But because the labor market is tight, wages are *rising*. New workers receive wages above W_0, and the economywide average wage moves up.

If output is kept above normal, wages rise in every period. In every period they exceed what they were before in the same way that at point A' in Figure 29-4 the wage is higher than at A. Thus with output above normal, the WW schedule shifts upward over time. Conversely, if output is below normal, wages fall each period, and thus the WW schedule shifts downward over time. Sustained unemployment thus means falling wages; persistent overemployment means rising wages. These adjustments in wages persist as long as the economy is not at full employment. Thus wages do adjust, or keep adjusting, as long as the labor market is not in equilibrium. But there is no reason to believe that the adjustment is very rapid. We now link the behavior of wages to the prices that firms set in the goods market.

3 PRICES AND THE AGGREGATE SUPPLY SCHEDULE

In some markets, such as agricultural markets for wheat or soybeans, prices are set at an auction. But in most cases, prices are set by the sellers of the good. The price is based on the firm's costs of production. The firm figures out how much it costs to produce the good, using labor, raw materials, and capital and making allowances for mistakes and profit, and then announces its price. The price may be adjusted depending on market conditions. If there is a competitor selling a close substitute for less, the firm will have to reduce its price. If the demand for the good is high, the firm may increase its profit margin.

Labor costs constitute the major part of the costs of producing goods in the U.S. economy. Of course, materials, land, and capital also add to the costs firms incur and at times are the major source of cost changes. But we disregard these for the moment and concentrate on wages as the chief determinant of costs. Once our analysis is developed, it will be easy to introduce other cost items.

The firm incurs labor costs in producing output, and the prices it charges must cover these labor costs. Labor costs depend on how many hours of labor time it takes to produce a unit of output and on the wage the firm pays. Suppose productivity of workers does not change much so that it always takes approximately the same number of work hours to produce an extra unit of output. Then we are left with the wage rate as the only source of changes in costs.

Higher wages mean that labor costs are higher; the firm has higher labor costs in producing output and therefore will charge a higher price. Our assumptions, omitting other cost items and keeping constant labor productivity, thus leave us with a simple relationship between wages and prices. Any time firms experience wage increases, they pass them on in the form of higher prices. When they experience reductions in wages, they pass them on in the form of lower prices.

We have made very strong simplifications, and none of them exactly describes what happens in reality. Productivity does depend on output levels, firms have costs other than labor costs, and firms may in the short run sacrifice profits when wages increase and thus not raise prices. Every one of these points is correct and would be part of a broader model of the adjustment process. None, though, would substantially affect the analysis that we present now, which looks only at wages as determining prices. The gain in simplicity is large and justifies some sacrifice of realism.

In assuming that firms base the prices they charge on the wages they pay, we can move directly from Figure 29-4, which

shows wages and output, to the aggregate supply schedule in Figure 29-5, which shows prices and output. All we have done is change the label on the vertical axis, moving from wages to prices.

The vertical line Y_pY_p shows the level of *potential output*. This corresponds to the level of output when the labor force is fully employed—neither underemployed nor overemployed. As we saw in Chapter 28, full-employment output is independent of the price level. Therefore, the schedule is vertical. The Y_pY_p schedule corresponds to the *long-run aggregate supply schedule*. In the long run the economy will be producing at the level of full-employment output.

The upward-sloping schedule AS is the short-run aggregate supply schedule.

The *short run aggregate supply schedule* shows the price firms charge at each level of output.

The price is based on labor costs. Because wages do not move rapidly in response to employment changes, the schedule is very flat.

Suppose that it takes 3 work hours to produce a unit of output, say, a widget, and that last period's wage was $12 per hour. At full employment today's wage would be the same as last period's, and therefore firms would be charging a price of $36 (3 hours × $12 per hour) for a unit of output. If output and employment were higher, wages would be higher, therefore the price the firm charges would also be higher. Conversely, with output and employment at only Y'', the wage would be less than last period's $12, and therefore the price charged would be less than the full-employment price of $36. The wage might be only $11, and the price the firm charges would be $33 instead of the full-employment price of $36. Thus the cyclical position—deviations from full employment—does have *some* impact on the price the firm charges. But that impact is small because prices are based on

FIGURE 29-5 THE SHORT-RUN AGGREGATE SUP-
PLY SCHEDULE. The firm bases the price it sets on
the labor cost it incurs. At full employment, today's
wage is the same as last period's, and thus the price
today is the same as it was last period. This is shown
by point A. If output today is above potential, wages
are higher, and so is the price the firm charges. The
converse is the case at a lower output level such as
Y''. The schedule AS shows the price firms set at
each level of output and employment. The position is
determined by the wages firms pay.

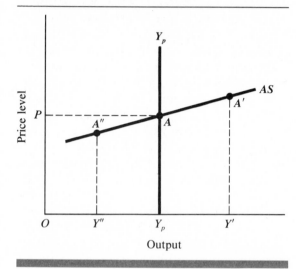

labor costs, and labor costs do not move rapidly even though there is unemployment or
overemployment.

If employment remains above normal,
wages will rise over time. This means labor
costs will be rising, and firms will pass on
these higher costs by charging higher prices
at each level of output. Conversely, a lasting
recession and unemployment will put
downward pressure on wages. Wages will
fall, slowly reducing labor costs. Firms will
pass on these cost reductions by supplying
output at lower prices period after period.
Thus the aggregate supply schedule will
shift over time. It shifts upward if wages are
rising because the economy is in a sustained
boom. It shifts downward if there is a sustained recession that keeps lowering wages.

In summary, the aggregate supply

schedule has two features relevant to the
adjustment process. In the short run it is
very flat. An increase in output will be supplied with little change in costs and therefore little change in wages. This reflects the
long-term contractual arrangements in the
labor market that we spelled out at the beginning of this chapter. But it is also the
case that a *sustained* departure from full
employment will keep changing wages,
costs, and prices. Therefore, if output were
kept away from potential, the aggregate supply schedule would keep shifting over time.

We now use these two properties to develop a realistic picture of the adjustment of
the economy to disturbances. Anticipating
our main results, we shall show the following: Because the aggregate supply schedule is flat, an aggregate demand disturbance
in the short run *will* change output and employment. This is the Keynesian feature.
But because deviations from full employment bring about ongoing wage and price
changes, the economy returns over time,
through price level adjustments, to full employment. This, of course, is the long-run
classical feature.

4 PRICES AND OUTPUT
IN THE ADJUSTMENT PROCESS

We now combine the macroeconomic demand schedule derived in Chapter 28 with
the short-run aggregate supply analysis.
The aim is to show how disturbances on the
demand side or the supply side work themselves out in the adjustment process. In this
section we study an increase in spending
brought about by an increase in the nominal
money stock.

The economy is initially at point E in
Figure 29-6. The price level is P, and output
is at the full-employment level. Therefore,
wages are not changing, and there is thus no
tendency for the aggregate supply schedule
to be moving. Now assume that long-run

FIGURE 29-6 THE SHORT-RUN EFFECT OF AN IN-
CREASE IN THE MONEY STOCK. An increase in the
nominal money stock shifts the macroeconomic demand schedule from *MD* to *MD'*. From the initial full-
employment equilibrium at *E*, the economy moves to
E'. Output and employment are higher, the real
money stock is higher, and interest rates have declined, thus supporting a higher level of income and
spending. But *E'* is not the final equilibrium because
with overemployment, wages are rising, shifting *AS*
upward over time.

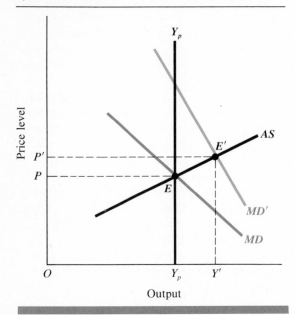

equilibrium is disturbed by an increase in
the nominal money stock. As we saw in
Chapter 28, that leads to a rightward shift of
the macroeconomic demand schedule. At
each level of prices, real balances are
higher, interest rates are lower, and therefore investment and aggregate demand have
risen. *MD'* is the new demand schedule corresponding to the higher level of the money
stock. Recall now that in our analysis in
Chapter 28, assuming full wage and price
flexibility, output was *always* at the full-employment level. An increase in the nominal
money stock would immediately lead to a
proportional rise in prices and thus return
the economy to the initial level of real balances, output, and employment.

With an upward-sloping *AS* curve
(which shifts over time), a change in the
money stock will affect both the level of output and the price level. Only in the long run
will output return to its equilibrium level.
In the meantime, output will be changing as
the effects of the increased money stock
slowly work their way through the economy. Such a framework makes it possible to
explain the facts of the business cycle.

The shift in demand from *MD* to *MD'*
confronts firms with increased sales, to
which they respond by increasing employment (hours and workers) and production.
Because the expansion of employment
raises wages somewhat, firms also respond
to increased production and sales by raising
prices somewhat. The short-run equilibrium after the monetary expansion is at
point *E'*. What has happened at *E'* is the following: Because prices have not risen very
much—certainly not in proportion to the increase in nominal money—the stock of real
balances is higher than it was at *E*. Interest
rates are lower, and therefore spending is
greater. But that cannot be the end because
at *E'* the labor force is overemployed.
People are working overtime, and that is
putting upward pressure on wages and
costs. At point *E'* the aggregate supply
schedule is shifting upward over time. The
consequences of that adjustment are shown
in Figure 29-7.

One period later the aggregate supply
curve has shifted upward to *AS'*. The demand curve remains *MD'*. The equilibrium
of the economy moves to point *E"*. The price
level is higher than it was a period ago, and
the level of output is lower. The level of
output is still above Y_p, and so unemployment is still lower than at full employment.

If we were to continue drawing in the
shifting aggregate supply curve, we would
discover the price level and level of output
continuing to change. The price level rises
steadily toward its new equilibrium level

FIGURE 29-7 THE MEDIUM-TERM ADJUSTMENT TO INCREASED NOMINAL MONEY. In the short run a monetary expansion leads the economy to point E', where output is above potential. Therefore, wages are rising, and this shifts the aggregate supply schedule upward over time from AD to AD' and farther. As the increase in costs shifts the aggregate supply schedule upward, prices are rising from P' to P'' and beyond, real balances are starting to decline, interest rates rise back up, and the initial expansion in demand is starting to be reversed.

FIGURE 29-8 ADJUSTMENT PATHS OF PRICES, OUTPUT, AND INFLATION TO AN INCREASE IN THE MONEY STOCK. When the money stock is increased at time t_0, the price level and the level of output both increase. The price level thereafter slowly increases up to its new equilibrium level P''' as the short-run aggregate supply curve moves upward. The level of output slowly falls back toward the potential output level Y_p. Also shown is the inflation rate. The inflation rate—the rate of increase in prices—is largest at the beginning and then slowly falls back down to zero as the price level gets closer to its equilibrium level P'''.

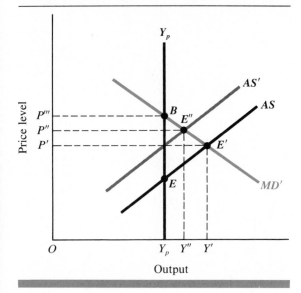

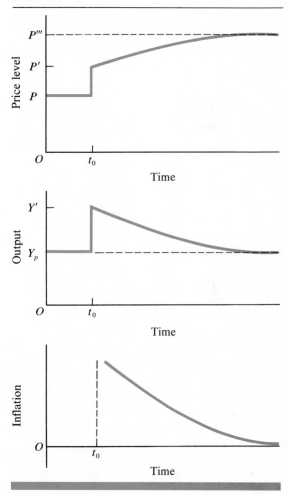

P'''. Output, after its initial jump to Y', gradually falls back toward the full-employment level. In the background, the wage is adjusting as the rate of unemployment changes.

Figure 29-8 shows how the change in the money stock affects prices, output, and inflation in the economy. The change takes place at time t_0. Output initially rises above the Y_p level and then falls back. Prices rise above the P level and continue rising. Figure 29-8 also shows the behavior of the rate of change of the price level, or the inflation rate. So long as the price level is rising, the inflation rate is positive. It is most rapid at the beginning, when the price level takes its biggest jump, and thereafter slows back down to zero.

Our aggregate supply and demand

model thus shows how the inflation rate is determined, and why the economy takes a long time to respond to changes in the quantity of money and in aggregate demand. The basic source of the lengthy process is the slow adjustment of wages.

Figure 29-8 provides a good way of seeing the comparison between the model we have arrived at and the two extreme cases: the fixed-price Keynesian view of Chapter 27 and the flexible-price classical model of Chapter 28. The realistic model we have developed connects these two extremes.

Prices are neither fully fixed nor fully flexible. A monetary expansion gradually raises the price level until prices have risen in the same proportion as money in the long run. After all adjustments have taken place, this model gives, of course, exactly the classical answers. This can best be seen from the path of output. In the long run output is back to its full-employment level.

Thus printing money cannot indefinitely increase employment above normal. But because prices do not immediately increase enough, since wages are relatively sticky, there are temporary, or transitory, real effects of an increase in nominal money. This means that in the transition, output and employment are higher and interest rates are lower than they would have been without the increase in money. Finally, in terms of inflation, the approach here differs from that of classical analysis. There the price level immediately jumps to the new higher level, and that ends the adjustment. Here inflation occurs over time, first at high rates and then winding down. There is an adjustment process over time, or an output and price adjustment path. The presence of such a path over time is the distinguishing feature of the business cycle.

Here we have seen that an increase in the money stock can lead to a business cycle: an expansion in output and then a contraction back to the level of potential output. The same would be true for a fiscal expansion or a rise in investment. In Problem 6 on page 726 we ask you to analyze the effects of a change in fiscal policy.

5 A SHIFT IN AGGREGATE SUPPLY

When aggregate demand expands, shifting the MD schedule, both the price level and the level of output rise. Higher output is associated with inflation when there is a demand shift. Now we want to see what happens when the aggregate supply curve shifts. A favorable (rightward) shift in the aggregate supply curve will reduce the price level and increase output. Thus higher output will be associated with lower inflation. Conversely, when there is an adverse supply shock, lower output will be associated with higher inflation.

To study supply disturbances we consider the case where Congress enacts a reduction in income taxes and thus increases the incentive to work.[1] The increased work incentive leads to an increase in the labor force—more people want to work, or people want to work longer hours or hold extra jobs. Thus the level of potential output in Figure 29-9 rises from Y_p to Y'_p.

The increased labor supply may also have some immediate effect on wages, causing a reduction in wages paid by firms at each output level. This would lead to a rightward shift of the short-run aggregate supply schedule from AS to AS'. Initially the economy was at point E, with full employment and a price level P. The increase in labor supply, by shifting the short-run aggregate supply schedule to AS', leads to an excess supply and thus to both a fall in prices and a rise in output and employment. In the short run, the economy moves to point E'. Next period, the AS curve shifts downward some more, to AS'', and the economy moves to point E'', with an even lower price level and a higher level of output. Gradually the aggregate supply curve will continue shifting downward and the price level will keep fall-

---

[1] We disregard here the fiscal expansion on the demand side by assuming that other taxes are raised or transfers are reduced so as to hold total taxes constant.

FIGURE 29-9 A TAX CUT INCREASES POTENTIAL OUTPUT. An increase in the supply of labor because of a tax cut causes the level of potential output to increase and shifts the long-run aggregate supply from Y_p to Y'_p. At the same time, the short-run aggregate supply curve shifts downward from AS to AS'. Because wages adjust slowly, not all the extra people who want to work get jobs immediately. As wages adjust, the short-run aggregate supply curve shifts downward gradually until the economy reaches a new equilibrium at E^*, with a higher level of output Y'_p and a lower price level P^*.

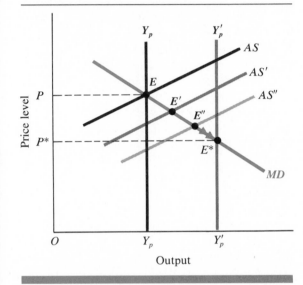

ing, until eventually there is long-run equilibrium at point E^*. Now the level of output is at the new higher potential output level, and the price level is at P^* instead of P_0. While the economy moves between E and

E^*, output is rising and the price level is falling; there is deflation, or negative inflation.

There is thus a marked difference between the effects of shifts in aggregate supply and shifts in demand. When the demand curve shifts rightward, there is a temporary increase in output accompanied by inflation. When the aggregate supply curve shifts rightward, there is an increase in the level of output accompanied by deflation. If the economy already has inflation, a rightward supply shift will generate less inflation with more output, and a demand shift will generate more inflation with more output. The differences are shown in Table 29-2.

An Adverse Supply Shock

So far wages have been the only determinant of costs and of the aggregate supply schedule. We now show that the framework can also be used to study the effect of changes in other items of costs, such as materials prices. This is done in Figure 29-10. We start in long-run equilibrium at point E. Now oil prices, copper prices, or for that matter any materials prices rise, and the firms that use the materials in production experience a cost increase. At the given wage, costs per unit of output are higher, and so the going price no longer covers costs. At the going wage and price, the firm now suffers losses. How does such a materi-

TABLE 29-2

EFFECTS OF SHIFTS IN AGGREGATE SUPPLY AND DEMAND CURVES

TYPE OF SHIFT	EFFECTS ON OUTPUT		EFFECTS ON PRICE LEVEL		EFFECTS ON INFLATION	
	SHORT RUN	LONG RUN	SHORT RUN	LONG RUN	SHORT RUN	LONG RUN
Demand curve shifts to the right	Increase	None	Higher	Higher	More	None
Supply curve shifts to the right	Increase	Increase	Lower	Lower	Less	None

FIGURE 29-10   AN ADVERSE SUPPLY SHOCK. An increase in oil prices raises firms' costs at each level of wages. The materials price increase shows up as a shift of the aggregate supply schedule from *AS* to *AS'* as firms raise prices to cover the higher costs. The economy moves from *E* to *E'* with output falling below potential. Only when wages have fallen enough to lower costs do we regain full employment.

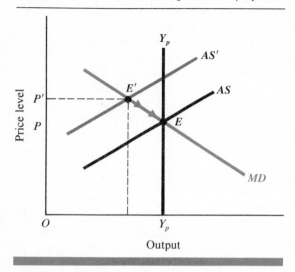

als price increase may only be transitory, and thus its reversal will help return the economy to point *E*. In any event, while it lasts and while the higher materials prices are not offset by lower wages, costs and prices are higher, and the real money stock is therefore lower, as are output and employment. This is why we call the disturbance an *adverse* supply shock.

A Wage Increase   We can also think of Figure 29-10 as showing the short-run effects of a strike by workers that leads to a new, high wage settlement far in excess of any gains in productivity that labor may have had. In terms of our analysis that would mean an increase in costs for firms and thus a shift of the *AS* schedule as shown. From an initial prestrike equilibrium at *E*, the economy moves to *E'*. Prices rise, and output falls. The wage increase leads to a contraction in output and employment along with higher prices. At *E'* workers have made some gains in real wages. But some of the wage increase they secured in the strike is already eroded by price increases, and some of the wage increase is "bought" at the cost of unemployment.

The economy will not stay at *E'*. The unemployment that prevails puts pressure on union militancy and on wages. Over time, wage settlements will soften. With wage increases falling short of productivity increases, unit labor costs will fall, and as this happens over time, the aggregate supply schedule will shift back downward toward point *E*. In the long run, after unemployment has returned unit labor costs to their initial full-employment level, the economy returns to the initial equilibrium.

Why do workers go on strike to gain higher wages if the benefits are ultimately eroded and in the transition are paid for by unemployment? Part of the answer is that those who keep their jobs will have both work and higher pay during the transition.

als price increase affect the prices of finished goods and the macroeconomy at large?

When firms experience cost increases, they pass them on in the form of higher prices. In Figure 29-10 this is shown as an upward shift of the aggregate supply schedule from *AS* to *AS'*. The increase in costs leads to a new short-run equilibrium at point *E'*. Here prices are higher and output is lower. The increase in prices has lowered the real money stock, and that leads to higher interest rates, reduced aggregate spending, and thus a lower equilibrium level of output and employment.

Thus an *adverse supply shock* reduces output and raises prices.

The economy, of course, will not stay at point *E'*. There is now unemployment, and that puts downward pressure on wages, shifting the aggregate supply schedule back downward and to the right. Also, the materi-

For them, clearly, the wage increase is a good idea. For the economy at large and particularly for those who lose their jobs, it is not a good idea. We return to these questions in Chapter 31, when we ask what happens if the government accommodates the wage increase by an expansion in aggregate demand that seeks to maintain full employment even at the higher wages and prices.

6 THE BUSINESS CYCLE

Shifts in aggregate supply and demand generate changes in the level of output and prices and in the inflation rate. As the level of output changes, so does the unemployment rate. Shifts in aggregate supply and demand are thus the underlying source of the business cycle.

When the economy is hit by many different types of changes, the level of output and the price level will be changing contin-

ually. At any one time, we can expect the macro demand curve to be shifting because monetary and fiscal policy are changing or because private sector demand for goods is changing. Perhaps the price of oil is rising or wage settlements are unusually high, thus shifting aggregate supply.

The business cycle is the result of all these many disturbances hitting the economy at different times and all taking time to work themselves out. In response to each shock, output and prices change in the short run, and then there is a longer-run process that takes place as the supply curve shifts. The business cycle is irregular because the shocks happen irregularly. The United States got through the sixties without a major supply side shock. In both 1973 and 1979, though, there were major supply side shocks in the form of the oil-price increases. Similarly, wars are major sources of disturbances to the economic system that can help set off booms and later recessions.

FIGURE 29-11 INFLATION AND UNEMPLOYMENT IN THE UNITED STATES. Inflation rate is that of GNP deflator. (*Source:* Citibank Economic Database, 1982; data estimated by authors.)

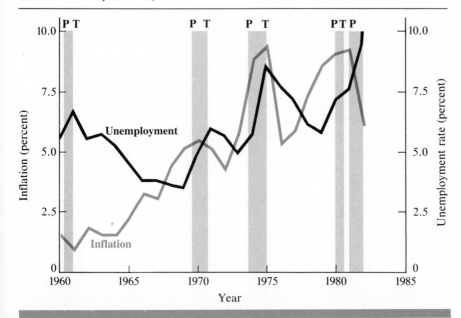

The facts of recent U.S. business cycles are presented in Figure 29-11, which shows the inflation rate and the rate of unemployment. The unemployment rate shows large swings from as low as 3.8 percent in 1969 to the 10 percent range in 1982. Inflation moves up and down but on balance shows a steady upward trend. These data are generated by shifts in the demand and supply schedules that we have studied. We could look at a particular period to see how a supply shock or a monetary or fiscal policy action changed unemployment and prices. Consider, for example, the period 1963–1969, during which fiscal policy was strongly expansionary, supported by monetary policy. As a consequence, aggregate demand was high all the time; unemployment gradually fell below normal levels; and inflation gradually built up over the period.

Another example is 1973–1975. Here we look at the supply shocks that shifted the aggregate supply schedule upward, raising prices rapidly and reducing employment and output or raising the unemployment rate. Yet another example is 1981–1982, when monetary policy turned tight to fight inflation, and that reduced aggregate demand. Unemployment increased sharply, and inflation started to decline.

Recent economic history illustrates the usefulness of the aggregate supply and demand apparatus as a simple set of tools for understanding the behavior of the economy. Of course, it is inevitable that many details are left out and that the timing of events is not exactly as predicted by the simple theory we have developed. But the big picture comes through quite clearly. The rates of inflation and output are being moved about by shifts in aggregate supply and disturbances on the demand side.

Persistent Inflation

A close look at the data in Figure 29-11 leaves us with one puzzle. It is true that there are swings in the unemployment rate, showing that there are booms and recessions induced by shifts in spending or in aggregate supply. But one thing is missing: There is *always* inflation. Prices always rise; they never fall. It is true that during booms inflation is higher and that during recessions it slows down, sometimes very much, but still, prices are always rising. Why, in an economy with, say, 10 percent unemployment, do prices rise? Prices rise because wages are rising, but that makes the issue even more of a puzzle.

We must remember the important facts of the labor market, where long-term and often implicit contracts govern the relations between firms and their workers. Inflation is persistent because even during a recession, when unemployment is high, firms will be reluctant to cut money wages or even stop giving pay increases. They will slow down the pay increases but will not deny increases to workers whom they hope to keep on the payroll.

The increases are probably thought of as compensating the workers for the ongoing inflation. Because all firms compensate their workers for the ongoing inflation, they all have increasing costs which they pass on in the form of higher prices, even during recessions. What keeps inflation alive in these conditions is that the Fed allows money to expand, thus avoiding sharp and deep recessions as a result of wage and price increases.

In Chapter 31 we study this process further to ask two questions. First, how can it be stopped? How can we break a vicious cycle in which wages are rising because prices are rising, and prices are rising because firms have agreed to pay higher wages and know the Fed will expand money to keep employment reasonably high? Second, are there any costs to such a persistent inflation process that make it important to stop it?

SUMMARY

1   Wages change slowly in response to the demand for goods and in response to unemployment since job arrangements are typically for the long run. It is costly for firms to hire and fire workers and to train them. Workers do not plan to change jobs frequently if they can help it, because moving between jobs is a nuisance and is likely to be costly in terms of lost seniority.

2   Firms and workers therefore have arrangements about wages and how to handle variations in the amount of work to be done. In the short run, workers vary the amount of work they do in accordance with how much demand there is for the firm's goods. The wage is set so that it is equal, on average, to the value of the marginal product of labor over the lifetime of a job. Workers and firms expect the wage to average out about the same as it is elsewhere in the economy.

3   Pressure on wages from the unemployed works slowly. When the unemployment rate rises, firms do not cut the wages of existing workers. Rather, they increase wages more slowly. The wage rises somewhat with the demand for labor, which rises with output. Therefore, the wage increases with the level of output. But it does not increase much as output rises.

4   Over time, the wage rate will continue to increase if output is above the level of potential output or unemployment is below the natural rate. In the long run, the wage is fully flexible.

5   Prices are based on costs, in particular, labor costs. Given labor productivity, the aggregate supply schedule has exactly the same shape as the relationship between wages and output.

6   The aggregate supply curve shifts over time if output is not at the full-employment level. If output is above its potential level, the aggregate supply curve shifts upward. If output is below the potential level, the aggregate supply curve shifts downward.

7   When the aggregate supply and demand curves are put together, we can study the behavior of output, prices, and the inflation rate. An upward shift of the demand curve results in an increase in the price level in the long run. In the short run it causes an increase in both the price level and the level of output. During the process of adjustment to the new equilibrium, there is inflation combined with output above the level of potential output.

8   A shift in the aggregate supply curve to the right results in the long run in a higher level of output and a lower price level. During the adjustment process, output is rising along with a falling price level.

9   The business cycle of booms, recessions, and recoveries is the re-

sult of the many different types of shocks and disturbances that affect the economy. Anything that affects the aggregate supply or demand curves can set off a long process of adjustment of prices and output. Because the shocks that affect the economy happen irregularly, the business cycle is also irregular.

KEY TERMS

Long-term job commitments
Labor productivity
Layoffs
Recalls
Workweek

Short-run aggregate supply schedule
Adjustment path
Adverse supply shocks
Materials prices

PROBLEMS

1   Suppose the aggregate supply curve is vertical, as in Chapter 28. (*a*) How would the economy adjust to an increase in the money supply? (*b*) To what time period, if any, is the vertical aggregate supply curve relevant in reality?

2   Explain how each of the following changes affects the short-run aggregate supply curve and how that in turn affects price and output in the short run. (*a*) A tax on labor income. (*b*) An increase in the productivity of labor. (*c*) An increase in the money stock.

3   Why do the layoff rate and the workweek move in opposite directions? Does this agree with theory?

4   It is sometimes stated that it is a law of economics that inflation must fall when unemployment rises. Is this true (*a*) when the supply curve shifts and (*b*) when the demand curve shifts?

5   Suppose the government wants to reduce the price level by using monetary policy. Using aggregate supply and demand curves, explain why this can be costly.

6   Suppose government spending on goods and services is reduced. Starting from an initial equilibrium, trace the adjustment process of output and prices. (*a*) What is the initial effect in a diagram such as Figure 29-6 (page 718)? (*b*) What happens over time in the labor market? (*c*) What happens in the long run to nominal wages? (*d*) What happens in the long run to investment?

7   The government passes legislation that prohibits the industrial use of pollutants. As a consequence, some of the machinery in existence can no longer be used. Discuss the short-run and long-run effects on output and prices.

8   The Federal Reserve decides to reduce the money stock. Discuss in detail what happens to output and prices in the adjustment process. Identify precisely what it is that makes adjustment slow. Point out, too, which components of aggregate demand will be affected by the reduction in money in the short run.

9   A nationwide sales tax is enacted by Congress. Firms have to pay 10 percent of every dollar of sales to the government. Use the aggregate demand and supply analysis to work out the effects of the measure. *Note:* The price level on the vertical axis is the after-tax, or market, price. To cover their costs, firms now have to charge prices inclusive of the tax, which are thus 10 percent higher.

10 Why has there been continuing inflation in the United States for more than 25 years, despite rising unemployment?

In 1933 one-quarter of the labor force was unemployed. Thirty-nine million people had jobs, but 12 million of their neighbors did not, and wanted them. The misery of the unemployed and the fears for the future of the United States in the 1930s dominated economic policy and thinking about the economy for most of the next 50 years.

But in the sixties and seventies a new and quite different view of unemployment began to take shape. In this new view, the unemployed looking for jobs are unemployed for only a short time. Many of them are looking for a first job or perhaps for a better job than the previous one and are taking the time to be sure to get a job they want. Some of the unemployed may be suffering real hardship, but—according to this new view—most are not in serious economic difficulty.

Part of the reason for the change in views about unemployment is that the post-1945 unemployment experience has been much less serious than the pre-World War II experience, even if we exclude the Great Depression. Figure 30-1 shows annual unemployment rates since 1890. The unemployment rate of the thirties is overwhelming. But even before that, in the 1890s and again in 1921, unemployment exceeded anything in the post-World War II period. Although the unemployment rate rose to nearly 11 percent in 1982, unemployment has been on average lower and less variable since 1945 than it was before.

30

Unemployment

1 PREVIEW

In this chapter we raise a number of questions.

1   How is unemployment defined and measured?

2   How do people become unemployed? What proportion becomes unemployed by losing a job and what proportion by deciding to look for a job or change the existing one?

3   How long do people remain unemployed?

4   Who in the labor force tends to become unemployed? What are unemployment rates among the young? How do unemployment rates vary by sex and race?

The answers to these questions help answer the main question:

FIGURE 30-1   THE U.S. UNEMPLOYMENT RATE, 1890–1982. The unemployment rate shows the percentage of the civilian labor force without a job. In the period since World War II the unemployment rate has been on average lower than it was in the 1930s or in other earlier periods. (*Sources: Historical Statistics of the U.S.,* p. 135, *Economic Report of the President, 1982,* p. 269, and estimate by the authors.)

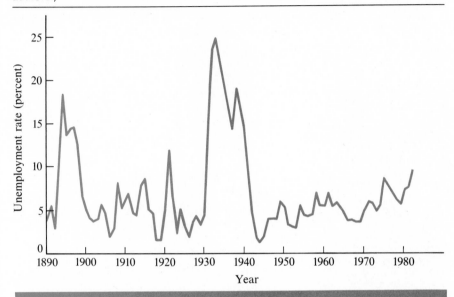

What is the correct picture of unemployment? Should we think of the unemployment rate as telling us what proportion of the labor force is in deep trouble or instead think of unemployment as a sign of people on the move to new and better things? The answer matters in deciding what if anything to do about unemployment. Of course, the answer is that neither picture is totally correct. Many of the unemployed are people between jobs or looking for a first job and not under any great economic pressure. But one of the main lessons of this chapter is that much of U.S. unemployment is indeed accounted for by people who are unemployed for a long time.

Before we go into these detailed questions of the definition and nature of unemployment, we describe basic facts about the behavior of unemployment. We ask how unemployment changes with GNP and what typical rates of unemployment are.

The Cyclical Behavior of Unemployment: Okun's Law

Unemployment rises during recessions and falls during recoveries and expansions. This is shown in Figure 30-2 for the period 1965–1982. The shaded areas show the recessions. Each time there is a recession, the unemployment rate rises. Once recovery and expansion begin, the unemployment rate comes down again. This relationship is not surprising because during recessions output falls and some of that decline in output translates into a reduction in the demand for labor. In recoveries and expansion the opposite happens. Firms experience growing demand for their output and thus are willing to hire extra workers, the more so the longer and more rapid the expansion that they anticipate.

Okun's law describes this systematic relationship between economic activity and unemployment.

FIGURE 30-2   UNEMPLOYMENT AND THE BUSINESS CYCLE, 1965–1982. The
unemployment rate is highly cyclical. During recessions (shaded areas) unemployment rises. During recoveries and expansions it declines. The longer the expansion and the higher the growth rate of output, the larger the reduction in unemployment. (*Source:* Citibank Economic Database.)

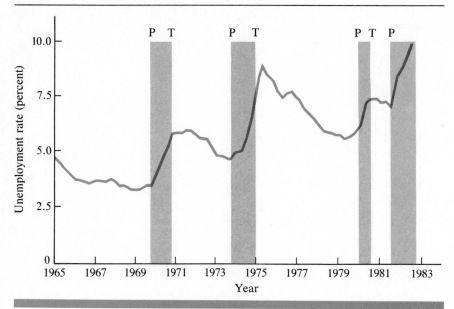

Okun's law states that annual GNP growth of 3 percent keeps the unemployment rate constant. For every 2 percentage point increase in growth (for example, 5 percent instead of 3 percent) over a year, the unemployment rate declines by 1 percentage point. For every 2 percentage point decrease in growth below 3 percent (for example, 1 percent instead of 3 percent) over a year, the unemployment rate rises 1 percent.

There are two aspects to the law. First, a certain amount of GNP growth is needed just to keep the unemployment rate from rising. The labor force is growing every year, and in addition output grows because existing workers become more productive. For these reasons, we need about 3 percent GNP growth per year to generate enough new jobs to keep unemployment from increasing. The second part of the law describes by how much the unemployment rate changes when GNP growth moves away from 3 percent per year. Higher rates of growth reduce unemployment; lower rates of growth make the unemployment rate increase.

The most useful aspect of Okun's law is the numerical relationship: the 2:1 rule.[1] The 2:1 rule gives a measure of how much growth can do to solve unemployment problems. Here is how we use the rule. Suppose we look at the mid-1982 economy, which has an unemployment rate of 9.5 percent. An election is coming up in 1984, and the administration is concerned about its showing at the polls. It decides that unemployment must be reduced. The economy must be made to grow more rapidly by monetary and fiscal stimulus.

---

[1] When Okun first examined the data in the early 1960s, the law looked more like 3 to 1 than 2 to 1. But as more data were added, especially in the seventies, the relationship became more clearly 2 to 1.

But how fast should the growth be? If unemployment is to fall to 7.5 percent by mid-1984, we need a 2 percentage point reduction in the unemployment rate over 2 years. That means we need real GNP growth rates of 5 percent per year for 2 years to get there. We arrive at 5 percent by noting that a 2 percentage point reduction in unemployment rates requires 4 percent of *extra* real GNP growth over and above the 3 percent benchmark that will keep unemployment rates constant. An extra 4 percent growth over 2 years means 2 percent more growth per year. Thus the annual growth rate would have to be 3 percent + 2 percent = 5 percent. That is a high growth rate of real GNP but one that is quite possible in a recovery. In 1976 and 1977, for example, growth was above 5 percent per year, and that indeed led to a sizable reduction in unemployment.

Okun's law implies that unemployment rates are the result of cumulative low or high growth. To get the unemployment rate to 9.5 percent, for example, it takes a few years of low growth and a recession. To get it down to less than 4 percent, as in 1969, takes many years of high growth. High unemployment rates cannot be wiped out rapidly.

The Natural Rate of Unemployment

Figure 30-3 also shows the unemployment rate for the United States. This time we draw attention to the fact that unemployment is *never* zero. When we think about people who are looking for a first job or those who have moved from one city to another and are looking for another job, it is not surprising that there are always people unemployed.

Thus *some* unemployment is to be expected even in an economy that is working well and providing jobs within a reasonable length of time for those who want them. This leads to the idea of the natural rate of unemployment.

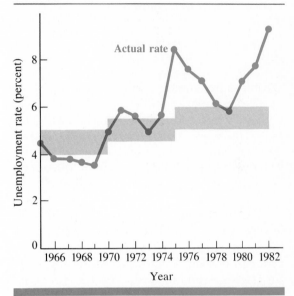

FIGURE 30-3 THE ACTUAL AND NATURAL RATES OF UNEMPLOYMENT. The shaded range shows unemployment rates broadly consistent with full employment. There is no certainty about the precise location of the range, but it is believed to be up from 4 to 5 percent in the late 1960s to 5 to 6 percent in the 1980s. (*Sources:* For actual unemployment: Citibank Economic Database; for natural rate: authors' estimates.)

The *natural rate of unemployment* is the unemployment rate that corresponds to practical full employment in the economy.

This definition of the natural rate is not complete because we have not yet studied the sources of unemployment. But it gives the right idea by defining the natural rate of unemployment as that level of unemployment at which we can say the economy is at full employment of labor.

Economists have estimated the natural rate of unemployment. The range of estimates is shown in Figure 30-3. There are three points to notice. First, there is a *range* of rates since no one knows for sure what the natural rate is. The range of estimates at any one time is about 1 percent. Second, the natural rate as estimated is large—5 percent to 6 percent in the 1980s. With a labor force of over 100 million, this means that over 5 million people are out of work even when the economy is at full employment. One of the purposes of this chapter is to explain why the natural rate is so high. The third point is that the natural rate has risen from the 1960s to the 1980s. That fact, too, we explain in this chapter.

2 THE DEFINITION AND MEASUREMENT OF UNEMPLOYMENT

To measure unemployment, we have to know how many people who want a job at current wage rates do not have one. The main measure of unemployment in the United States is obtained through a sample survey of households in which questions are asked about individuals who might be in the labor force.

The first question is whether the person worked at all (aside from work around the house) during the last week. If the answer is yes, the person is counted as employed. If the person did not work in the previous week, the next question is whether the person has looked for work during the past 4 weeks. If the answer is yes, the person is counted as unemployed. If the answer is no, the person is counted as not being in the labor force. The status of being unemployed, then, is defined from the survey questions as follows:

> A person is reported as *unemployed* if he did *not* work in the last week but had looked for work during the past 4 weeks.

As with any definition, there are tricky points. A person who didn't work in the previous week but was sick, on vacation, on strike, or unable to work because of bad weather counts as employed. A person waiting to go back to a job or waiting to take a job within the next 30 days but not working in the last week counts as unemployed. This means, for instance, that a student, not yet

working, who has lined up a summer job due to start within 30 days is counted as unemployed. The definition also means that someone who has given up looking for a job for some time is neither counted as being in the labor force nor considered unemployed. Despite some problems with the definition of unemployment, its overall purpose is clear: Count as unemployed those who want to work and whose willingness to do so has been demonstrated by a recent effort to find a job.

Flows in and out of Unemployment

The unemployment statistics classify people into one of three groups. A person may be employed, unemployed, or not in the labor force. The possibilities are shown in Figure 30-4 by three boxes. Those who are either working or unemployed count as being in the labor force. That is why those two boxes are put together.

To understand who the unemployed are and how they come to be unemployed, we concentrate on flows in and out of unemployment. We can think of unemployment as a pool, with inflows of people newly unemployed and outflows of people leaving unemployment for the only two other destinations: employment or being out of the labor force.

We start with movements between employment and unemployment. There are three ways of leaving employment and becoming unemployed. First, a person may be fired or lose a job because the firm is closing down. These people are job losers. Second, a person may be laid off. A person who is laid off expects eventually to go back to the same job, and the employer expects to be able to provide the job again in the future. Layoffs are common, for instance, in the automobile industry. When demand for cars is temporarily low, the firm tells workers there is no work, but it expects to hire them back if demand later increases. Third, a person

FIGURE 30-4 LABOR MARKET STATUS AND LABOR MARKET FLOWS. A person may be either working, unemployed, or out of the labor force. The arrows show the routes by which people move between employment, unemployment, and being out of the labor force. Each of the routes is heavily traveled. In particular, there is much movement in and out of the labor force, both between working and being out of the labor force and between unemployment and being out of the labor force. Most movements out of the labor force are temporary and brief.

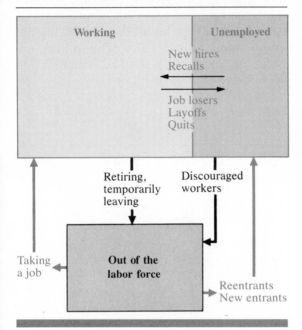

may choose to leave a job and become unemployed by quitting.

People enter unemployment not only from employment but also from being out of the labor force. People becoming unemployed who were previously not in the labor force either are new entrants who have not worked before or are entrants who used to have a job and are now coming back to look for another one.

Table 30-1 summarizes how people become unemployed, either by moving from out of the labor force to unemployment or moving from work to unemployment.

People leave the unemployment pool in the opposite directions. Some get jobs and leave unemployment for work. Of these, some are workers who formerly were laid off and now return to their old jobs. Others leave unemployment by leaving the labor force.

Movement in and out of the Labor Force

Figure 30-4 shows two routes in and out of each category in the labor force. For instance, people leave unemployment either by becoming employed or by leaving the labor force. Those who leave the labor force from unemployment because they believe they cannot find a job are called *discouraged workers.*

How important are the two routes out of unemployment? Surprisingly, they are about equally important. About the same number find jobs as are leaving the labor force. Nearly half the people leaving unemployment in a given period leave the labor force; the other half locate a new job. Most of those leaving unemployment by leaving the labor force will be out for only a short time. Soon—within 2 or 3 months—most will be unemployed or back in a job.

More generally, we want to ask how much traffic there is on the various routes shown in Figure 30-4. One possibility is that most of the movement goes between employment and unemployment, with

TABLE 30-1

UNEMPLOYED PERSONS BY REASON OF UNEMPLOYMENT (Percent of All Unemployed, June 1981)

Percentage becoming unemployed after working:		63.6
Lost job	35.7	
Were laid off	17.1	
Left job	10.8	
Percentage becoming unemployed after being out of the labor force:		36.5
Reentered labor force	24.5	
New entrants	12.0	

Note: Details do not add to totals because of rounding.
Source: Monthly Labor Review, August 1981, p. 75.

people only once in their lives moving in or out of the labor force. In fact, though, there is a large volume of movement both between employment and unemployment and in and out of the labor force. For instance, 20 percent of the unemployed leave the labor force each month. More than 70 percent of those taking a job in a given month were out of the labor force in the previous month.

How the Unemployment Rate Changes

The unemployment rate changes when people flow into the unemployment box or pool at a different rate than they flow out. When more people are flowing into the pool

than out, the unemployment rate is rising. When more people are flowing out of the pool than in, the unemployment rate is falling. The unemployment rate rises when the rate of job losses, quits, or decisions by those out of the labor force to look for a job increases. The unemployment rate falls when people who were unemployed get jobs or when they give up looking and leave the labor force.

Figure 30-5 shows the reasons for unemployment since 1978. The unemployment rate increases when the economy is in recession and falls during recoveries, as we know from Okun's law. The predominant influence on unemployment during the

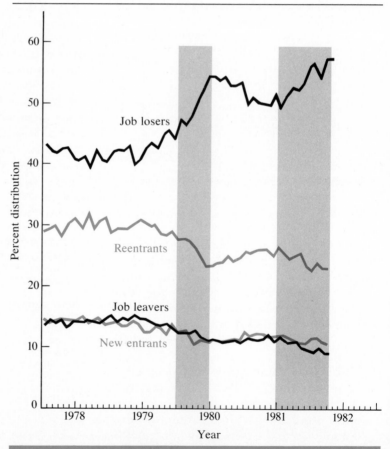

FIGURE 30-5   REASONS FOR UNEMPLOYMENT, UNITED STATES, 1978–1982. The recessions starting in 1980 and 1981, respectively, are shaded. Job loss rises during a recession. The other sources of unemployment become relatively less important. In particular, the rate at which people reenter the labor force to become unemployed and look for a job actually falls during recessions. But the dominant force is the increase in the rate of job loss. (*Source: Economic Indicators,* May 1982, p. 13.)

business cycle is the rate of job loss. The rate of job loss rises sharply during recessions and falls during recoveries.

Some of the factors responsible for unemployment move in the opposite direction. Most important, when job prospects are improving during a recovery, more people who are out of the labor force decide to look for a job, and this tends to increase the unemployment rate.

We can see the effects of good job prospects on unemployment by looking at different cities. Unemployment rates may be higher in cities that are growing fast than in slow-growing cities. That is because people go to the fast-growing cities looking for jobs. While they are looking, they count as unemployed, thus raising the unemployment rate above its level in slowly growing cities.

3 THE DURATION OF UNEMPLOYMENT AND THE IMPORTANCE OF LONG-TERM UNEMPLOYMENT

The *duration* of unemployment is the length of time a person is unemployed. We can imagine two extreme possibilities for the duration of unemployment. In one case, everyone would occasionally be unemployed for a short time. In the other case, just a few people would be unemployed all the time.

For instance, suppose the unemployment rate is 5 percent. Possibility A is that during the year *every* worker is unemployed 5 percent of the time, or about 2.5 weeks. Alternatively, under possibility B, 5 percent of the work force might be unemployed *all the time*. Table 30-2 shows the two possibilities.

Under possibility A, the duration of unemployment is low, and many people become unemployed. Under possibility B, the duration of unemployment is high, and relatively few people are unemployed. Which of these two possibilities, A or B, best describes unemployment in the United States? Seemingly, we have already had a clue, since we know there is a lot of movement on the routes between employment and unemployment and in and out of the labor force. However, the clue is misleading. In fact, much unemployment in the United States is accounted for by people who are unemployed for a large part of each year; thus possibility B accounts for a considerable part of U.S. unemployment.

Table 30-3 shows the percentage of unemployment accounted for by people unemployed for different lengths of time in each of three different years. The total amount of unemployment experienced by each individual is counted. If a person becomes unemployed three times, each time for 3 weeks, that person is counted as unemployed for 9 weeks. The year 1969 was one of low unemployment (3.5 percent); unemployment was at about the natural rate in 1974, when it was 5.6 percent, and unem-

---

TABLE 30-2

THE DURATION OF UNEMPLOYMENT: TWO POSSIBILITIES

POSSIBILITY A		POSSIBILITY B	
During the year, each worker is out of job 5 percent of the time, approximately 2.5 weeks		During the year, 95 percent of workers are never unemployed; 5 percent are unemployed for the entire year	
Duration of unemployment	2.5 weeks	Duration of unemployment	1 year
Unemployment rate	5.0 percent	Unemployment rate	5.0 percent

TABLE 30-3

PERCENTAGE OF UNEMPLOYMENT ACCOUNTED FOR BY TIME UNEMPLOYED

ALL GROUPS	1969	1974	1975
Weeks of unemployment (percent of weeks):			
1–4 weeks	5.7	4.2	2.6
5–14 weeks	27.8	22.2	15.6
15–26 weeks	31.6	31.7	27.0
27–39 weeks	19.1	21.1	22.3
40 weeks or more	15.8	20.7	32.5
Total	100.0	100.0	100.0

Source: Kim B. Clark and Lawrence H. Summers, "Labor Market Dynamics and Unemployment: A Reconsideration," *Brookings Papers on Economic Activity,* 1979, 1, Washington, D.C.: The Brookings Institution, 1979. Copyright 1979 by the Brookings Institution, Washington, D.C.

ployment was at the high level of 8.9 percent in 1975. In 1975, over half of all unemployment was accounted for by people who were unemployed at least half the year. Even in 1969, one-third of unemployment was accounted for by people who were unemployed at least half the year.

Unemployment Benefits   What difference does it make whether unemployment is a result of everyone being unemployed for a short time or a few people being unemployed for a long time? If unemployment is something that happens to everyone for a brief period each year, there is no serious problem. We do not have to worry about people living for long periods without a job. We expect people to make provision for their likely short spells of unemployment by saving while working so that they will have a financial reserve to support them for the few weeks a year they are out of a job.

But if much unemployment is long-term, there is a recognizable group in the labor force which experiences unemployment and will suffer from it. The extent to which the unemployed suffer economically depends heavily on how large *unemployment benefits* are. Unemployed people who

lose their jobs (which they had for some time) are entitled to collect unemployment insurance or benefits while they are out of a job so long as they can show that they are continuing to look for work. If these benefits are high compared with previous wages, the unemployed do not suffer much direct economic loss. If the benefits are low, the cost of being unemployed is high. In addition, there is much evidence that unemployed people suffer loss of personal esteem and undergo distress while unemployed.

Unemployment benefits in the United States vary from state to state and by individual. In cases which some politicians, some economists, and the press love to describe, some unemployed earn 95 percent of their former wages. On average, unemployment benefits have been about 36 percent of the weekly wage. The benefits are in general not taxable, and so after-tax unemployment benefits come on average to about half the income received while working.

However, there are variations. Members of some unions receive extra unemployment benefits from the union. Rates of compensation vary from state to state. Furthermore, individuals can receive benefits only for a maximum length of time, usually 6 months. About a quarter of those who become unemployed eventually stop receiving benefits before getting a new job.

In summary, unemployment benefits provide support for most people who become unemployed. The level of support varies widely by state and person but comes to between 35 and 50 percent of the former wage. People who remain unemployed for a long time eventually lose their benefits, although during recessions the government extends the period for receiving benefits. Thus unemployment benefits substantially reduce the burden of unemployment for most who become unemployed, but there remains a problem of the economic well-being of the very long-term unemployed.

BOX 30-1 ▰▰▰▰▰▰▰▰▰▰▰▰▰▰▰▰▰▰▰▰▰▰▰▰▰▰▰

WHO ARE THE UNEMPLOYED?

A portrait of unemployment and the unemployed has been drawn by Professor Robert Hall of Stanford University. Based on a careful study of the data on unemployment, he suggests that by age, education, and sex, unemployment is typically made up of the cross section of society shown here.

TYPICAL MEMBER OF GROUP	% OF TOTAL UNEMPLOYMENT ACCOUNTED FOR BY THIS GROUP
50-year-old man with a grade school education on layoff from a job on an assembly line	12
35-year-old man with a high school education who has lost a job as a mechanic and is looking for another job	33
25-year-old woman with 2 years of college who quit a job as a typist and is looking for a new job	13
17-year-old who is looking for a temporary job in the afternoon during the school year	13
Recent college graduate who is looking for full-time work	7
30-year-old woman who is looking for a job as a waitress and has not worked in the past 9 months	21

Source: Robert E. Hall, "The Nature and Measurement of Unemployment," National Bureau of Economic Research Working Paper No. 252, July 1978.

Why not reduce the burden borne by the unemployed by paying them more and for longer when they are out of a job? The reason is obvious. The higher the unemployment benefits, the less incentive an individual has to look for a job. There is therefore a trade-off between incentives, which suggest the unemployed should want to look for and find jobs, and not having those who have lost jobs through no fault of their own suffer on that account.

A useful picture of who the unemployed are is contained in Box 30-1. Much unemployment in the United States is accounted for by people who are unemployed for a substantial part of the year. It nonetheless remains accurate to say that there is much movement of people in and out of the labor force and between employment and unemployment.

4 THE DISTRIBUTION OF UNEMPLOYMENT

Unemployment is distributed very unevenly across the population. Table 30-4 shows the important facts. First, unemployment rates among blacks are about twice those of whites. Second, teenage unemployment rates are more than double those of older workers.

Table 30-4 breaks down the labor force into different groups. When workers are grouped by race, age, and sex, white males 20 or older have the lowest unemployment rates, and black teenagers have the highest rates—more than seven times the rates of white males age 20 and over. Females tend to have slightly but not substantially higher unemployment rates than males of the same age and race. Table 30-4 also shows that un-

TABLE 30-4

UNEMPLOYMENT RATES FOR LABOR FORCE GROUPS

GROUP	UNEMPLOYMENT RATE, 1979	UNEMPLOYMENT RATE, DECEMBER 1981
Total	5.8	8.8
By race, sex, and age:		
White, male, 20 yrs +	3.6	6.9
White, female, 20 yrs +	5.0	6.4
White teenagers	13.9	19.0
Black, male, 20 yrs +	8.4	14.6
Black, female, 20 yrs +	10.1	13.1
Black teenagers	33.5	39.0
By occupation:		
White-collar workers	3.3	4.5
Blue-collar workers	7.0	12.7

Source: Employment and Earnings, May 1982, Tables A-35 and A-36.

employment is distributed unevenly by occupation. Blue-collar workers suffer more unemployment than white-collar workers. Note particularly that as the economy moved into recession in 1981, the unemployment rate of blue-collar workers rose more than that of white-collar workers.

Many of the groups in Table 30-4 have unemployment rates nearly double those for whites age 20 or more. Yet the average unemployment rate is close to that for whites age 20 or more. How can that be? With all those groups having high unemployment rates, even more than 30 percent in some cases, shouldn't the average unemployment rate be higher? The average unemployment rate is close to that of whites 20 or older because that group makes up most of the labor force, almost 80 percent. Whites age 20 or more have unemployment rates below the average, and because they make up nearly 80 percent of the labor force, their unemployment rates balance the very high unemployment rates of some other groups.

There is one significant difference in the nature of unemployment between teenagers and others. Teenagers tend to have frequent short spells of unemployment, moving in and out of the labor force as well as in and out of unemployment. Older work-

ers who become unemployed tend to remain unemployed for a long time.

The facts raise an obvious question: Why do unemployment rates vary so widely? And there is a subsequent question: What can be done to reduce unemployment among those with the highest unemployment rates? To understand differences in unemployment rates by age, we want to think of the typical pattern of job holding in the United States.

People may go into the labor force when they are still at school or college, looking for temporary jobs. When they enter the labor force without planning to continue formal education, they switch around among jobs. At some stage the person and the job click, and there is little movement after that. When a person who has been in a job for a long time loses it, he is likely to be unemployed for a long time.

Some of the reasons for differences in unemployment rates are straightforward. High unemployment rates among teenagers reflect in part the types of jobs they are looking for and the fact that many of them will be planning to go to, or are at, school. On the other side, employers, knowing that teenagers are not likely to be around for a long time, do not make good jobs that require training available to teenagers. High unemployment rates among blacks are partly due to the fact that more blacks hold blue-collar jobs, which are less stable within the business cycle and have higher unemployment rates than white-collar jobs.

Unemployment rates among black teenagers still stand out as quite astonishing and require separate discussion. Before doing that, though, we examine the natural rate of unemployment.

5 THE NATURAL RATE OF UNEMPLOYMENT

We have now seen how unemployment is measured and where in the labor market it originates. Some unemployment exists because people are counted as unemployed while they wait to report for a job they have already found. Other unemployment exists because people who have lost jobs are looking for new ones or because people have entered the labor force to look for a job. And some unemployment exists because people are taking it easy for a while to think about their future, helped along by unemployment benefits.

Since people take time finding new jobs and in moving between jobs, there is always some unemployment. Even when the economy is operating at the level of potential output, we expect there to be unemployment. We call the unemployment rate that corresponds to practical full employment the *natural rate of unemployment.*

The notion that there should be some unemployment at full employment is a strange one unless we think about the fact that the economy is continually changing, with new jobs being created and old ones destroyed and with people moving into and out of the labor market. There are bound to be people out of work looking for a new job.[2]

As we showed in Figure 30-3, there is no precise estimate of the natural rate. Estimates of the natural rate are made by using as a benchmark some period when the economy had full (and not overfull) employment with reasonably stable prices. The mid-1960s would be such a period. Then the rate is adjusted for changes in the composition of the labor force since then. For instance, with more teenagers in the labor force, the estimate of the natural rate is raised to reflect the higher natural rate of unemployment of teenagers. Similarly, there has been an increase in female participation in the labor force, and the estimated natural rate has been increased because women have a slightly higher rate of unemployment than men. These adjustments to the mid-1960s rate of unemployment of about 4.5 percent get the rate up to nearly 5.5 percent.

The notion of the natural rate of unemployment is a useful one even if we do not know the exact rate. For instance, when the unemployment rate exceeds 7 percent, it is safe to assume that it still has a way to fall before the natural rate is reached. When unemployment is at 6 percent, it is a little harder to say whether the economy is at full employment. For that reason, in Figure 30-3 we show a range of unemployment rates rather than a single number corresponding to the full-employment unemployment rate.

6 REDUCING UNEMPLOYMENT

Could and should we try to get the unemployment rate down? We want to distinguish here between unemployment that is associated with recessions and unemployment that is associated with full employment.

The cyclical unemployment that is associated with recessions is also associated with lower real GNP. In that sense, the un-

---

[2] At one time economists referred to the *frictional rate of unemployment,* meaning much the same as the natural rate. The word "frictional" gives a good idea why there is always some unemployment. There is friction between old and new jobs and between deciding to get a job and actually finding one.

employment is a waste. The unemployed could be at work, producing goods. There are two amendments that qualify this view of the benefits of reducing unemployment but do not change the big picture. First, unemployed people are not working and therefore have leisure. For those who dislike working, unemployment and its enforced leisure is a gain. However, this is easily overrated. For one thing, most people like to work and do not like to be unemployed. The second reason why the unemployment associated with a recession is not necessarily all a loss is that sometimes recessions happen because there has been a real change in the economy. For instance, when oil prices changed, the structure of production and employment in the economy had to change. People who were unemployed and looking for a good job were performing a useful function by trying to find a place where they would be most productive in the future.

Despite these qualifications, the economy would be better off if economic policies could keep output and unemployment from fluctuating as much as they have in post-World War II business cycles—and certainly as much as they did in earlier business cycles.

Reducing the Natural Rate

We would prefer to do without recessions. But should we also want to lower the full-employment rate of unemployment? As already noted, some unemployment serves a useful purpose as people shop around to put themselves into jobs they fit well. Even so, unemployment rates are high, especially among teenagers.

The unemployment rate among those 20 and over was 6.1 percent in the recession year 1980, compared with 7.1 percent for the entire labor force. If the unemployment rate for teenagers could be brought down to the level for older workers, the total unem-

ployment rate would drop by 1 percentage point.

The unemployment of teenagers is marked by a very high proportion of unemployment resulting from new entrants into the labor force and from reentrants. Teenagers also leave the labor force often. If some way could be found to help teenagers get jobs more quickly and stick to them longer, their unemployment rate would be reduced. This thought has led to suggestions that there should be a youth employment service to help school leavers find jobs.

The Minimum Wage

A more controversial issue is the role of the minimum wage in causing teenage unemployment. Since 1938, the federal government has required that employers pay a minimum wage to some groups of employees. The minimum wage has in recent years been about 45 percent of the average wage paid in manufacturing. The minimum wage applies to nonsupervisory employees and now covers about three-quarters of the labor force. The extent of coverage has changed over the years. There are also some state minimum wage laws covering workers not included under federal law.

A minimum wage should, according to microeconomic theory, increase the unemployment rate. Figure 30-6 shows the supply and demand for labor. The demand curve for labor slopes downward; employers want to hire more labor the lower the real wage. The supply curve of labor is upward-sloping. Without a minimum wage, employment would be at level N_0 and the real wage would be W_0, where supply equals demand.

Corresponding to the equilibrium shown in Figure 30-6 at point E would be the natural rate of unemployment, which results from people changing jobs and looking for new ones. Now a minimum wage equal to W_{min} is imposed. The minimum is above

FIGURE 30-6 EFFECTS OF THE MINIMUM WAGE ON EMPLOYMENT AND UNEMPLOYMENT. To start, there is no minimum wage. The wage and level of employment are determined by supply and demand. The equilibrium wage is W_0, and N_0 people are employed. Then a minimum wage is imposed, at level W_{min}. At that wage the demand for labor is only N_1, and that number of workers is employed. But at that higher minimum wage, N_2 people want to work. The minimum wage therefore increases unemployment by $(N_2 - N_1)$ workers. It also reduces employment, by $(N_0 - N_1)$ workers.

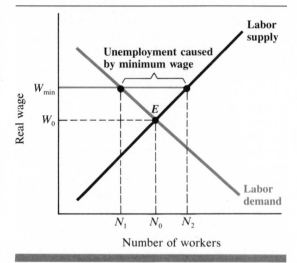

the wage at which there is equilibrium in the labor market. Employers now want to hire fewer than N_0 workers. More people want to work at wage W_{min} than wanted to work at the equilibrium at E. But employers will hire only N_1 workers. There is extra unemployment of $N_2 - N_1$. Therefore, the minimum wage has increased unemployment.

Why is this particularly important in the case of teenage unemployment? The minimum wage is low relative to the wages earned by experienced workers, but it is not low compared with wages earned by teenagers entering the job force for the first time. In 1981, the minimum wage was $3.35 per hour. At this wage many teenagers cannot find jobs because employers are not willing to pay that much to employ them.

What is the evidence about the effects of the minimum wage? Most research shows that minimum wage rates have indeed increased unemployment among those who would otherwise be earning low wages. Even more clearly, the minimum wage causes less employment among teenagers. This effect, too, would be predicted from Figure 30-6, where we see employment falling from N_0 to N_1 when the minimum wage is imposed.

One interesting question that the minimum wage issue raises is why we have such legislation when it prevents people from getting jobs. Why would politicians vote for such laws? Shouldn't all the people who can't get jobs because of the minimum wage be calling their congressmen to ask them to remove the law? But the minimum wage does not harm everyone in the labor force. In particular, those who get jobs at the minimum wage are better off than they would be if there were no law. Without the law, they would be getting the wage W_0 in Figure 30-6; with the law, they get the wage W_{min}. Thus minimum wage legislation does not make everyone worse off.

The Natural Rate Again

When we introduced the natural rate of unemployment, we asked both why it is so high and why it has risen since the 1960s. The natural rate is determined by the factors we have discussed in this chapter: the nature of teenage unemployment; the type of work patterns people have over their lifetimes with younger people taking short-term jobs; in part the rate at which firms and the jobs in them die; and unemployment benefits that affect the amount of time for which people who become unemployed remain unemployed.

The reasons for the increase in the natural rate were discussed earlier. They come largely from the changing composition of the labor force. The proportion of the labor

BOX 30-2

EMPLOYMENT AND UNEMPLOYMENT: THE DOUGHNUT AND THE HOLE

The focus on unemployment in this chapter is the standard way of thinking about the success of the economy in providing jobs for those who want them. But there is another way of looking at the situation, which considers the employment rate.

The *employment rate* is the percentage of those in a given group who are working.

In the United States about 58 to 60 percent of those 16 and over work. Those are all people who want a job, which the economy has been able to provide.

If we look at the employment rate rather than the unemployment rate, we get a more favorable impression of what has happened since the sixties. The accompanying figure shows the unemployment and employment rates since 1965. The unemployment scale is reversed to show how the employment rate and the unemployment rate move together within the business cycle. When the unemployment rate rises in recessions, the employment rate falls. When the unemployment rate falls in recoveries, the employment rate rises.

But the overall trend of the two series is different. The employment rate has been rising over the period since 1965. That seems like a good thing. The economy is succeeding in putting a larger proportion of the potential labor force to work. A closer look at the data shows that what has been happening is that an increased proportion of women are working and that the employment rate of men has actually fallen over this period.

Which should we look at, the doughnut of employment or the hole of unemployment? Both. It is a good thing that the economy has provided jobs for so many who want them, as shown by the employment rate. Furthermore, the employment rate is a useful number to look at because it does not change

FIGURE 30a   EMPLOYMENT AND UNEMPLOYMENT RATES, 1965–1981. (*Source: Economic Report of the President, 1982,* Table B-31.)

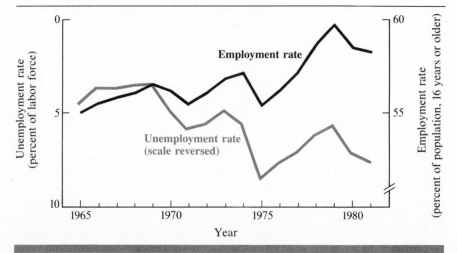

when a discouraged worker leaves unemployment because he cannot find a job. But we should look even more at the unemployment rate. A well-functioning economy should provide jobs for those who want them at the going wages. It is when the economy fails to provide those jobs that we know resources are being wasted through unemployment. Thus the unemployment rate, adjusted for changes in the natural rate, is a basic measure of the resources being wasted because the economy is not operating at its potential output level.

force consisting of males who have completed their education has fallen. Those are the people with the lowest unemployment rates. The share of young people, who have much higher unemployment rates, and women, who have slightly higher unemployment rates, has risen. Thus the natural rate has risen over the past two decades.

The emphasis on unemployment in macroeconomics has been disputed by economists who say we should focus on how many people are employed rather than the smaller number unemployed. Box 30-2 reviews this argument.

7 INTERNATIONAL COMPARISONS

Unemployment rates differ widely internationally. Table 30-5 shows average unemployment rates over 5-year periods since 1965 for a number of industrialized economies. The United States and Canada stand out, having the highest unemployment

rates. Up through 1974, most of the remaining countries had unemployment rates about half or less than half of the U.S. rate. But in the period 1975–1979 the unemployment rates abroad rose much closer to U.S. rates. Since 1979, the British unemployment rate has continued to rise, and it is now well above the U.S. level, at 12 percent in 1981.

What accounts for the differences and for the changes in some of the countries since 1974? There is a different story for each country. For instance, in Japan workers are very rarely fired and seldom quit. Instead, there is an implicit agreement between firms and workers that the workers have lifetime jobs, provided that they are male. Females who lose jobs tend not to become unemployed but rather move out of the labor force.

Germany until 1974 imported workers from other parts of Europe. Germans who wanted jobs could get them, and others

TABLE 30-5

COMPARATIVE UNEMPLOYMENT RATES, 1965–1979

PERIOD	UNITED STATES	AUS-TRALIA	CANADA	FRANCE	GERMANY	GREAT BRITAIN	ITALY	JAPAN	SWEDEN
1965–1969	3.8	1.7	4.0	2.1	0.8	2.9	3.5	1.2	1.8
1970–1974	5.4	2.2	5.8	2.6	1.0	3.3	3.2	1.3	2.3
1975–1979	7.0	5.6	7.6	5.1	3.6	5.5	3.6	2.1	1.9

Note: Unemployment rates are averages of annual rates. Definitions are on a consistent basis.
Source: Bureau of Labor Statistics, *Handbook of Labor Statistics*, December 1980, pp. 465–466.

could come only if there was a job waiting. There was therefore almost no unemployment in Germany through 1974. After the oil shock struck in 1973, the German economy began to grow more slowly, the foreign workers were sent home, and German workers became unemployed.

France decided during the 1975–1979 period to close down inefficient firms and industries and allowed workers to become unemployed when firms with large monetary losses were closed. Up to this time, the French approach had been not to allow firms to close when a large loss of employment was feared. Rather, the state provided funds to keep the firms going. Such a policy cannot keep going forever unless the firms are fundamentally sound, which they were not in the French case. The increase in Australian unemployment in the 1975–1979 period has been attributed not only to the energy shock but also to increases in unemployment benefits. In Sweden it is extremely difficult for a firm to fire a worker; the laws are such that a firm has to pay large

compensation to the fired worker, and it tends therefore not to fire. This helps keep the unemployment rate low.

The unemployment rate in any country depends on a host of factors relating to the structure of the labor market in that country. These include the stability of the demand for labor (how often and by how much firms want to change production and therefore employment), the costs to firms of firing or laying off workers rather than keeping them on the payroll not doing much work, the unemployment benefits received by workers without jobs, and institutions that have developed, such as the Japanese system of lifetime attachment of individuals to firms. But in each country it remains true that changes in aggregate demand are transmitted to the demand for labor and thus to unemployment. The natural rates of unemployment differ among countries, but unemployment in each country still is a cyclical variable that responds to changes in policy and other shocks to the economy that cause recessions and recoveries.

SUMMARY

1   The unemployment rate increases in recessions and decreases in recoveries. The unemployment rate falls 1 percentage point for every 2 percentage points of extra GNP growth above 3 percent. It takes a growth rate of real GNP of about 3.0 percent just to keep the unemployment rate constant. This is Okun's law.

2   A person counts as unemployed if he is out of a job and has looked for work during the past 4 weeks. Some special cases do not fit the general definitions; for instance, someone waiting to take a job within the next month counts as unemployed. Labor market statistics classify people into one of three groups: employed, unemployed, or out of the labor force. People who count as either employed or unemployed are in the labor force.

3   Most movements in and out of the unemployment pool are brief. There is much movement not only between employment and unemployment but also in and out of the labor force.

4   Between 40 and 60 percent of unemployment is accounted for by

people losing their jobs. Job loss becomes more important as a source of unemployment when the economy is in recession. About one-third of unemployment is accounted for by people becoming unemployed after being out of the labor force. This source of flows into unemployment becomes smaller in recessions and larger in recoveries.

5 The unemployment rate rises when flows into unemployment exceed flows out of unemployment.

6 Although there is frequent movement of people in and out of the labor force and between employment and unemployment, much of U.S. unemployment is accounted for by people who are unemployed for a large part of the year.

7 Unemployment benefits typically come to somewhat less than half the after-tax wage. Unemployment benefits are paid for only a limited period after a person loses a job.

8 Unemployment rates for blacks are about twice those for whites. Teenage unemployment rates are more than double those of older workers.

9 The natural rate of unemployment, or the full-employment rate of unemployment, is 5 to 6 percent. Policies to reduce the natural rate focus on the very high unemployment rates among teenagers. The role of the minimum wage in causing teenage unemployment is controversial. Nonetheless, the evidence is that the minimum wage does cause higher unemployment, especially among teenagers, as economic theory suggests it would.

10 There are substantial differences in unemployment rates among different nations. Until 1975, U.S. and Canadian unemployment rates were much higher than those in other large industrialized countries. Since then, unemployment rates in a number of other countries have risen relative to those of the United States and Canada.

KEY TERMS

Okun's law
Natural rate of unemployment
Quitting
Discouraged workers

Unemployment duration
Unemployment benefits
Minimum wage

PROBLEMS

1 Suppose the unemployment rate is 8 percent. How fast would the economy have to grow to get the unemployment rate down to 6 percent (a) in 1 year (b) in 2 years?

2 Which of the following people is unemployed? (*a*) A student who would like to work but hasn't yet gotten around to looking for a job. (*b*) A student who has arranged for a job to start in 6 weeks' time and therefore has stopped looking for a job. (*c*) A retired person who looks at the newspaper help-wanted advertisements every week in case some suitable job becomes available. (*d*) A person who searched for a job for 6 months and then gave up, deciding to wait until the economy improves. (*e*) A person laid off by his last employer who is waiting to go back to the same job and not looking for another one. (*f*) A person who lost a job 3 months ago and has kept looking for another one ever since.

3 From the viewpoint of society's welfare, how serious do you think unemployment or being out of the labor force is in each of the cases in Problem 2?

4 Figure 30-4 shows four sources of flows into unemployment. (*a*) Explain which of those sources of unemployment increases in recessions and which decreases in recessions. (*b*) As a matter of logic, is it possible that unemployment could increase in recoveries and decrease in recessions?

5 Explain how a given unemployment rate is consistent either with many people experiencing unemployment or with very few becoming unemployed.

6 Suppose 80 percent of the labor force are white workers and 20 percent are nonwhite workers. The unemployment rates for the two groups are 6 percent and 12 percent, respectively. What is the overall unemployment rate for the economy?

7 Shouldn't we pay unemployment benefits that are on average equal to a person's wage when working so that people don't suffer from being unemployed?

8 Why is black teenage unemployment so high?

9 It there any reason not to try to get the natural rate of unemployment down to zero so that people who want a job can get one immediately?

10 It has been suggested that it would be desirable to have a lower minimum wage for teenagers than for older workers. What difference would this make?

Persistent long-term inflation is a new problem in the United States and in most industrial countries. Thirty years ago, the idea that prices would continue to rise year after year for the next 30 years would have been extreme. But prices did rise year after year from 1955 on. Now most people expect inflation to continue on that path.

Figure 31-1 shows the inflation rate of the consumer price index in the United States since 1860. There were, to be sure, several episodes of high inflation before the 1950s, typically associated with wars. The Civil War period shows very high inflation, as do the two world wars and the Korean war. But between the inflations there were also periods of falling prices, or *deflation*. These were quite frequent in the nineteenth century, but there has also been twentieth-century experience with deflation, such as in 1921 and the Great Depression. Inflation and deflation tended to alternate in the period before World War II. This did not happen very systematically, but it did, for example, happen on a sufficient scale to make the price level exactly the same in 1905 as it had been in 1860. Of course, there were ups and downs in between.

The most interesting part of Figure 31-1 is the post-1950 period. The last time the consumer price level fell over a period as long as a year was 1955. Since then prices have risen in the United States *every single year*. A 30-year period of continually rising prices is unprecedented in the United States in the last 120 years and more. The experience of continually rising prices has brought about a large cumulative change in the price level in a short period. Thus in the years since 1950 the price level in the United States has increased more than it did in the entire preceding 100 years.

This chapter deals with the problems posed by persistent inflation such as the inflation which has now emerged in the United States. We want to find out what are the causes of persistent inflation, what are its costs (or benefits), and what can be done about it.

The chief question we ask in this chapter is why inflation is evidently so difficult to control. Why, despite the announced hopes and plans of governments, has inflation stayed with us? We pose in addition a number of related questions. Why should we care about inflation? What harm or good does it do? Can we change the structure of the economy, for instance, by moving to the gold standard, in a way

31

The
Inflation
Problem

FIGURE 31-1   THE U.S. INFLATION RATE (CPI), 1861–1982.
(*Sources: Historical Statistics of the United States,* Series E-135;
Economic Report of the President, 1982, p. 291; 1982 estimated by authors.)

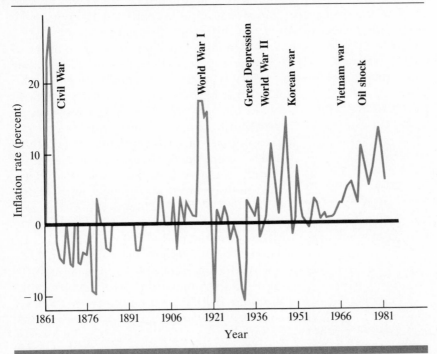

1   U.S. INFLATION SINCE 1960

that will get rid of inflation? Or should we change the structure of the economy so that inflation becomes easier to live with?

The U.S. inflation that we worry about today started in the 1960s. It is true that World War II raised the price level as had earlier wars. So did the Korean war. But the inflation rate was low during the 1950s, and by the early 1960s inflation rates were in the neighborhood of 1 percent per year. Figure 31-2 shows inflation rates for the period since 1948.

Figure 31-3 shows both inflation and unemployment in the United States since 1961. The figure shows a series of loops or spirals. In studying the inflation experience in the United States we use this figure to make three points which we then develop

in detail.[1] The first point to note is the negatively sloped segments, such as 1961–1969 and 1976–1979. These segments show a decline in unemployment accompanied by an increase in inflation, and they correspond to the 1960s concept of the inflation process as a trade-off between inflation and unemployment. The second point concerns the relatively flat parts such as 1969–1971, 1974–1975, and 1979–1981. Each corresponds to an *unsuccessful* attempt to slow inflation by restrictive monetary policy. In each case inflation stops rising, but unemployment rises

[1] The figure can also be used to make a fourth point. Note that in no year in Figure 31-3 is the inflation rate above 10 percent, whereas in Figure 31-2 the inflation rate exceeds 10 percent in 1974 and 1979–1981. The difference occurs because the inflation rate is measured in Figure 31-2 by the CPI and in Figure 31-3 by the GNP deflator. These two measures obviously do not behave in precisely the same way, for reasons we reviewed briefly in Chapter 22.

FIGURE 31-2   U.S. INFLATION RATE (CPI), 1948–1982.
(*Sources:* See Figure 31-1.)

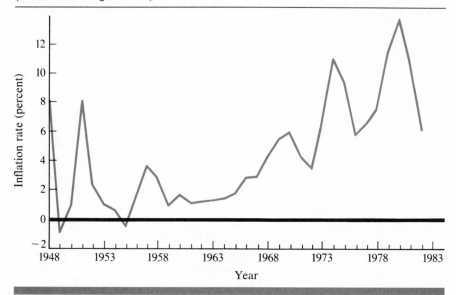

FIGURE 31-3   INFLATION AND UNEMPLOYMENT IN THE UNITED STATES, 1961–
1982. *Note:* Inflation rate is that for GNP deflator. (*Source: Economic Report of the
President, 1982*, p. 51; 1982 estimated by authors.)

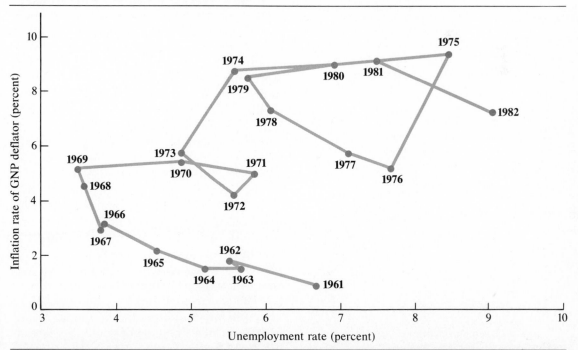

fast. The third point is the general picture from 1961 to 1982, which shows, on average, both higher inflation *and* higher unemployment. We now turn to a more detailed discussion of recent U.S. inflationary experience and prospects.

The Phillips Curve and the 1960s

In the 1960s macroeconomic policy was based on the belief that there was a trade-off between inflation and unemployment. Figure 31-4 shows that trade-off, which is called a Phillips curve.

> The *Phillips curve* shows an inverse relationship between the inflation rate and the unemployment rate. The higher the rate of inflation, the lower the rate of unemployment.

FIGURE 31-4   THE PHILLIPS CURVE. The Phillips curve represents a trade-off between inflation and unemployment. Policymakers can reduce unemployment by expanding aggregate demand. But the tightening of labor and goods markets will make for higher wage and cost increases and thus for higher inflation.

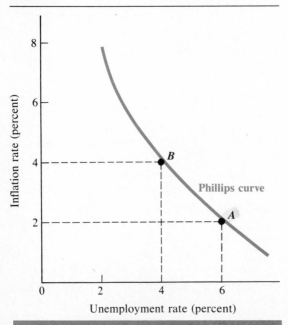

The relationship was discovered by Professor A. W. Phillips in the 1950s in the United Kingdom. Its significance is that it was eagerly accepted by policymakers in the United States and other countries as describing a trade-off that they faced in choosing a macroeconomic policy.

The Phillips curve represents a trade-off between inflation and unemployment in the following sense. If aggregate demand is expanded through tax cuts, increased money, or higher government spending, output can be increased and the unemployment rate can be reduced. But with lower unemployment and less slack in the economy, there is more pressure on wages, costs, and prices. Therefore, prices will be rising at a more rapid rate the lower the rate of unemployment. (You will note that the Phillips curve is in fact the basis of our aggregate supply schedule in Chapter 29.)

The Phillips curve tells the policymaker that there is a whole menu of inflation and unemployment combinations from which to pick. For example, one possibility is point *A* with a high 6 percent unemployment but only 2 percent inflation. Another possibility is point *B* with 4 percent unemployment but more inflation. The policymaker who starts in a situation like point *A* but is concerned with the high unemployment may choose to trade off a reduction in unemployment, say, to only 4 percent, in exchange for an increase in inflation to 4 percent by moving along the Phillips curve from *A* to *B*.

In the 1960s policymakers thought that a Phillips curve in the general shape of Figure 31-4 in fact represented their policy trade-off. And they used it. In 1961 the economy was at a point like *A* with nearly 7 percent unemployment and less than 2 percent inflation (see Figure 31-3). The story of the 1960s was an attempt to use expansionary monetary and fiscal policy to reduce unemployment at the cost of some increase in inflation. You can see in Figure 31-3 that the policy was highly successful in reducing unemployment, which fell below 4 percent by 1966 and stayed below 4 percent through 1969. But there was also an increase in inflation to more than 5 percent by 1969. Labor markets tightened, and the economy was more than fully employed.

Troubles with the Phillips Curve

By 1969 the incoming Nixon administration felt inflation was too high and should be reduced. The administration did not worry about increasing unemployment, since the economy was if anything overemployed. But how does the economy behave on the way down the Phillips curve? Figure 31-3 shows the effects of the cut in aggregate demand of that period. The restrictive monetary and fiscal policies of the Nixon administration produced sharply rising unemployment but virtually no reduction in inflation. There was a rude awakening for those who believed that the economy could turn around and simply work its way down the Phillips curve, reducing inflation at the cost of some increase in unemployment. The experience of 1969–1971 was, instead, stagflation.

> *Stagflation* is a period of continuing inflation combined with a recession or stagnation of economic activity.

What is the explanation for the failure of restrictive policy to reduce inflation in 1969–1971? A sustained period of inflation leads people to expect inflation to continue. As a result, the expected inflation is built in to the wages and other payments fixed by contract in the economy. With wages continuing to rise because of the built-in increases, restrictive monetary and fiscal policy affects mainly output and unemployment and has little effect on inflation. It takes a long period of unemployment to produce changes in the pattern of wages and get the inflation rate down.

Wage agreements are made for long periods, usually for at least 1 year and often for 3 years. Wage rates agreed on by the two sides of the bargain reflect the inflation expected over the life of the contract. At any time, part of the labor force is working for wages that were agreed on earlier and that depend on the rate of inflation that was expected at the time that the agreement was reached.

Thus for workers on long-term contracts, past beliefs about current inflation affect current wage rates. If it was believed 2 years ago that there would be a lot of inflation today, wages which were set then would be rising quickly now. This is one way inflationary expectations affect the response of the economy, particularly wages, to economic policy. Part of the behavior of wages today depends in this case on what was expected a few years ago about the inflation rate today.

There is a second way in which expectations of inflation matter. What happens to wages today depends not only on the pressure of demand today but also on what firms and workers expect will happen to policy and to aggregate demand in the future. If a firm and its workers enter a contract today that fixes wages for the next 3 years, they will think about what will affect the inflation rate over that period.

Suppose the government announces today a tough new radical anti-inflationary policy. This happens sometimes, typically at the beginning of a new administration. If everyone believes that the government will indeed carry out that policy, reducing the growth rate of money and tightening fiscal policy, today's wage agreements may reflect expectations of lower inflation in the future. But people know that many governments promised the same sort of thing in the past and gave up on the anti-inflationary policy when unemployment resulted. Therefore, everybody is less likely to reduce the rate at which wages are to be increased for the next few years.

The lesson of the early 1970s is that the Phillips curve is a tricky trade-off. It is easy to move up the Phillips curve, reducing unemployment and building up inflation. The unemployment comes back very rapidly as demand is cut, but the inflation is extremely difficult to get rid of, particularly for any government that cannot make recessions long and deep because of the fact that high unemployment hurts their prospects for re-election.

Supply Shocks

The third lesson about inflation comes from the period 1973–1975. Again looking at Figure 31-3, we observe an unusual pattern for 1973–1974: sharp rises in *both* inflation *and* unemployment. This is exactly the opposite of what the Phillips curve would lead us to expect. The explanation for the sharp increase in inflation in this period is to be found mostly in supply shocks such as the oil-price tripling of 1973–1974 and the sharp increases in food prices in the world economy. In 1973–1974 these commodity (oil, food, and materials) prices increased simultaneously and by such large amounts that they led to a sharp rise in overall inflation. Increases in materials prices acted as a supply shock, raising the costs of firms' inputs. The firms therefore increased the prices of their products.

Then came the other part of the supply shock. If firms charge higher prices and the government does not at the same time expand money or cut taxes, there will be a stagflation; that is, there will be higher inflation and reduced output with higher unemployment. The price increases reduce the real money stock, lead to higher interest rates, and thus lead to reduced demand for goods. This is the story of 1973–1975 in the United States and in most other countries around the world.

Accommodation and Acceleration of Inflation

By 1975 inflation had reached nearly 10 percent, but it was widely recognized that this sharp increase was caused mostly by a supply shock and was not a permanent state of affairs. Indeed, by 1976 the inflation rate was down below 6 percent. The main concern of the year was the very high unemployment level of nearly 9 percent, then the highest since the Great Depression. Therefore, policy turned toward expansion of demand.

In the period 1976–1979 the U.S. economy once more moved up a Phillips curve, reducing unemployment and increasing inflation. Once again the high level of inflation in 1979 led to the adoption of more restrictive policies, and we found that it is far easier to reduce unemployment than to reduce inflation. By 1982 the economy had paid for a large reduction in inflation with unemployment that was much higher even than in 1975. But even in the face of such unemployment wages continued increasing. Why does wage inflation continue even in very severe recessions?

Economists do not have a single, decisive answer to this question, but part of the answer is that policy over the last 30 years has been one of *not* tolerating long periods of high unemployment. There has not been a *credible* commitment to price stability on the part of monetary and fiscal authorities, and because of that workers and firms have not felt that they should reduce wage and price increases during recessions. They know that recessions will soon be followed by expansions and renewal of inflation.

It is the effect of policy on expectations that leads to emphasis on the *credibility* (believability) of government policy. If what the government promises is widely believed and is credible, it is likely to affect wages that are being set in contracts for the

FIGURE 31-5 ACTUAL AND CYCLICAL AVERAGE RATES OF INFLATION (GNP DEFLATOR) IN THE UNITED STATES, 1950–1982. (*Source:* Citibank Economic Database.)

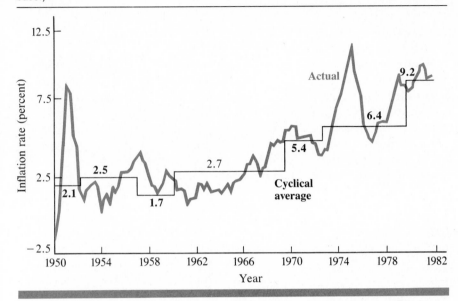

next few years. Thus a credible policy is more likely to succeed.

But how does a policy become credible? This is as much a question for political scientists as for economists. The only sure long-run way of being credible is to do what is promised.[2] But this is no great help to a new government coming to power and wanting to change things immediately. Such an administration does not start with a clean slate, even though it would like to. The public has seen many new administrations, and most of them made optimistic and tough-sounding predictions. Most of them eventually gave up on their counterinflationary policies when the going got tough.

Such a view of the inflation process

emerges when we look at Figure 31-5, which shows the actual inflation rate of the GNP deflator as well as the average rate during each business cycle. We measure the business cycle from peak to peak. The figure shows a very striking fact. In the last 20 years inflation has risen in every successive business cycle. Every time a recession starts, inflation slows down; but soon an expansion gets under way, and inflation goes above the previous peak.

With that history in mind, neither workers nor firms will show much confidence and belief when the government announces that *this* time it is serious about inflation. Of course, it is entirely possible that *this* is really the time the government gets serious, but most people think of it as a bluff as it was all the previous times. After all, there is always an election year just around the corner, and incumbent candidates do not want to face an election campaign with unemployment high and rising.

We asked at the outset of this section

---

[2] The problem of credibility has been studied in depth by those interested in nuclear war. Nuclear weapons will deter only an enemy who believes they might be used. Given that politicians on either side will be reluctant to push the button and cause such enormous death and destruction, how can one side deter the other? One way is to put your side in a situation where it seems to have no choice.

how we got to such high rates of inflation and why policymakers don't stop inflation. The answer is easy for the first part: We never had enough will or enough of a consensus to make policies sufficiently credible. This is so, in good part, because people still remember the Great Depression, with its mass unemployment and terrible nationwide despair and social unrest. The legacy of the 1930s favors high employment. But because the government is committed to high or reasonable employment levels, there is little hope for breaking inflation. And inflation worsens when unfavorable supply shocks such as those of 1973–1974 come on top of ongoing demand side inflation.

How Costly Would It Be to Stop Inflation?

We have discussed the role of credibility, long-term wage contracts, and expectations as standing in the way of inflation stabilization. The basic lesson from the U.S. experience is that if wages and prices respond little to contractionary monetary and fiscal policies, output and employment will respond a lot. Estimates for the U.S. economy

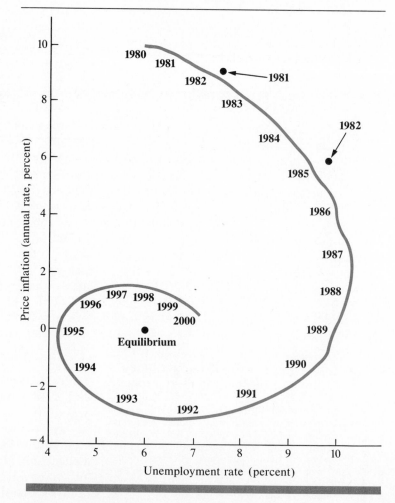

FIGURE 31-6 SIMULATED EFFECTS OF MONETARY DISINFLATION ON UNEMPLOYMENT AND INFLATION, 1980–2000. Values for 1981 and 1982 indicated by arrows were added by the authors. For 1981 this is actual unemployment and rate of increase of GNP deflator. The 1982 values are authors' estimates. (*Source:* James Tobin, "Stabilization Policy Ten Years After," *Brookings Papers on Economic Activity,* 1, Washington, D.C., 1980.)

suggest that the unemployment costs of bringing down inflation may be enormous.

Figure 31-6 shows an estimate for the U.S. economy which implies that to get inflation from 10 percent down to zero would take more than 20 years and that unemployment would have to increase to 10 percent in order to achieve this. The estimate is due to Nobel Prize winner Professor James Tobin of Yale University, who is a staunch opponent of policies that risk high unemployment.

Is There Hope?

How certain is it that the dismal message of Figure 31-6 describes how the U.S. economy would respond to anti-inflationary policy? It is not very certain. The reason again is expectations. It is quite likely that if an anti-inflation policy were undertaken and carried through, wages and prices would eventually begin to move quickly. At some stage, firms and workers would realize that inflation was indeed coming down. But that would take several years, because there is a long history of administrations keeping their policies going for a few years and then changing them. Thus we view the unemployment costs of eliminating inflation as smaller than those shown in Figure 31-6 but still very serious.

The early evidence from the 1981–1982 period, in which the Reagan administration and especially the Federal Reserve System followed extremely restrictive policies, suggests that the basic pattern predicted by Tobin was right, although the timing was too pessimistic. By 1982, the economy was about at the position Tobin had predicted for 1985. But the unemployment rate had risen to 10 percent, nearly as high as Tobin's forecasted peak unemployment for 1987–1988.

2 FOREIGN EXPERIENCE WITH INFLATION

The United States is certainly not the only country that has experienced persistent and accelerating inflation in the last 25 years. Indeed, most industrial countries have had an almost identical pattern. Table 31-1 shows inflation rates for more than 100 countries in two years, 1970 and 1979. The table shows the striking fact that throughout the world inflation rates in 1979 were significantly higher than in 1970. Whereas in 1970, 88 percent of the countries had inflation rates less than 10 percent, only 42 percent of the reporting countries had these "low" rates in 1979, and 50 percent of the countries had inflation rates in the range from 10 to 50 percent. Thus the whole world has become more inflationary.

In Table 31-2 we follow up on world inflation by comparing the period from 1960 to 1972, just prior to the oil shock, with the 1972–1980 period. We see that the U.S. experience of increased inflation is shared by other large industrialized countries and also

TABLE 31-1

INFLATION PATTERNS IN THE WORLD

YEAR	NUMBER OF COUNTRIES WITH INFLATION RATES OF:						TOTAL
	0–5%	5–10%	10–20%	20–50%	50–100%	100%+	
1970	57	33	10	2	—	—	102
1979	12	33	39	13	7	1	105

Source: International Monetary Fund, *International Financial Statistics,* various issues.

TABLE 31-2
INFLATION RATES, 1960–1980
(CPI, Percent per Year)

PERIOD	UNITED STATES	JAPAN	GERMANY	UNITED KINGDOM	ITALY	CANADA	OECD
1960–1972	2.9	5.7	3.1	4.7	4.2	2.9	3.9
1972–1980	8.8	9.9	5.0	15.1	16.0	9.1	10.9

Sources: OECD, *Economic Outlook,* and *Economic Report of the President, 1982.*

by the OECD group of countries.[3] Of these countries, Italy, for example, had an increase in inflation much more severe than that in the United States, but Germany, where inflation also increased, did much better than the United States.

The way in which prices and wages respond to policy changes differs from country to country. This is partly due to differences in the systems of wage bargaining. Wages are more flexible in Japan than they are in the United States. In Japan, there is an annual general bargaining session between employers and workers that unions call the spring offensive. During each session detailed wage arrangements, based on the national agreement, are negotiated between each firm and its workers.

Unions in Japan are organized by plant rather than by industry. With one union representing all the workers in the firm, there is some common interest between the union and the firm. If the union pushes too hard on wages, the firm won't be able to keep going. In addition, Japanese firms rarely fire workers. Most male workers have essentially lifetime jobs. This long-term tie makes it even more clear that the firm and the workers have a common interest.

[3] The OECD is the Organization for Economic Cooperation and Development, located in Paris, an intergovernmental organization grouping the major industrial countries. Its task is to coordinate policies of common concern.

Although the Japanese inflation rate shown in Table 31-2 is only 5.7 percent for the 1960–1972 period, Japan was particularly badly hit by the 1973 oil shock. Its inflation rate rose to 24 percent in 1974. The Japanese government restricted the money supply very sharply, with the result that Japanese industrial production fell 4 percent in 1974 and another 10 percent in 1975. Thus even in Japan, with its more flexible wages, it took a large loss of output to get inflation down from more than 20 percent to the 5 to 6 percent levels it is at now.

In Germany, too, where inflation performance has been good, there is a bargaining session once a year between unions and employers. The government takes part in these negotiations, announcing its intentions with respect to economic policy during the coming year. Policy thus has a chance to affect wage agreements directly.

There is one other special factor in Germany. In the early 1920s, Germany experienced extremely high rates of inflation that totally disrupted the economy and society and that have remained in the memories of Germans, even those who did not live through that period. We discuss the German *hyperinflation* in Chapter 32. The aversion to inflation in Germany is very strong. When the government warns that there will be inflation if wages rise too fast, workers listen and restrain their wage demands.

3 THE COSTS OF INFLATION

People dislike inflation and would like to get rid of it. But does the process of generally rising prices matter? This sounds like an academic question when it is so obvious that rising prices are a bad thing, but it turns out that the answers are not so obvious.

Inflation Illusion?

The chief reason people dislike inflation may be that they have an illusion about it. Certainly everyone thinks of inflation as causing the prices of goods *they* buy—food, stereos, used cars, and movie tickets, for example—to rise. That must be bad, because with less inflation we could buy more goods.

But this is a very one-sided view. Inflation usually also causes nominal income to go up. Wages rise each year partly to compensate for inflation. Interest rates are higher when there is inflation, and so lenders are compensated. Given these adjustments to inflation, we should look at both sides—income and spending—to see what inflation really does and whether it makes people worse off.

TABLE 31-3
COSTS AND EFFECTS OF INFLATION

| INFLATION EXPECTATIONS ADJUSTMENT | INSTITUTIONAL ADJUSTMENT TO INFLATION | |
	COMPLETE	INCOMPLETE
COMPLETE	Shoe-leather costs Menu costs	Distortions from interest rate controls, bracket creep, and taxation of inflation adjustments in capital markets
INCOMPLETE	Redistributions from creditors to debtors Uncertainty	Redistributions and tax effects

It is quite likely that many people look only at one side—the spending side—when they think about inflation. They think that every time their income goes up, it is because they worked hard for the increase rather than because of inflation. Then, when the prices of the goods they buy go up, they see inflation as stealing their hard-earned gains. This would certainly make people dislike inflation.

Leaving this illusion aside, what are the costs of inflation?

Expectations, Institutions, and the Costs of Inflation

The costs of inflation depend very much on the circumstances. Two questions must be asked. First, was the inflation that is occurring fully expected, or were people surprised by it? Thus if inflation in 1982 was 6.0 percent, did everybody predict *exactly* that number, or were there many people who were proved wrong because they thought the inflation rate might be only 3 percent or go as high as 12 percent? Or maybe they had no good idea of what the inflation rate would be. Second, are all institutions—in particular, government regulations and the tax system—fully adapted to the existence of inflation, or is the adaptation incomplete? We explain below how the economy adapts to inflation.

Table 31-3 shows the four combinations that are possible. The upper left-hand corner shows the case of inflation with nobody surprised and no obstacles in the economy to living with inflation. All the other cases represent mixed possibilities where people either are surprised by the inflation outcome or are living with institutions that make inflation have special effects. We now study the costs of inflation for each of these possibilities. The starting point is the case of an economy that is fully adjusted, both in expectations and institutions, to the presence of inflation.

Inflation with Complete Adaptation and Correct Expectations

Picture an economy where inflation every year, year after year, is 10 percent. Everybody knows it, and all institutions have adjusted to it. What does such an economy look like? First, all prices and incomes, including wages, are rising 10 percent per year. Therefore, all real incomes are constant, as are all relative prices.[4] Second, everybody's tax payments are unaffected by inflation. Along with the increases in prices and incomes, the dollar value of tax payments increases so that in real terms we pay the same taxes year after year.

Third, the presence of inflation has no impact on decisions to hold wealth in the form of bonds or real assets. Anyone who lends in the form of bonds and thus will be receiving a fixed sum of money at the end of the loan is compensated for the loss of purchasing power resulting from inflation by a higher interest rate on the loan. The increase in the interest rate exactly compensates for the loss in the value of money over the life of the loan. Fourth, these inflation adjustments in the capital market are correctly treated by the tax system in the sense that they are seen as inflation adjustments, not as true capital gains or real incomes.

This is a complete list of the adjustments for inflation that will occur in an economy that has totally adapted to inflation. As we shall see, some of these adjustments disappear when the economy or expectations have not adapted to inflation.

Inflation and Interest Rates   One of the conditions for complete adjustment to inflation we listed above is that interest rates can and do fully reflect inflation expectations. This point deserves elaboration because it is central to much of the costs of inflation.

Suppose someone lends $100 for 1 year provided it brings him an extra $3 worth of goods and services next year. If there is no inflation, the lender is willing to lend at 3 percent, meaning that after a year he gets back $103, an amount that enables him to buy 3 percent more goods and services than he could have bought a year earlier.

Let the inflation rate rise to 10 percent and suppose that everyone recognizes that. If the lender continues to lend at 3 percent, he gets back $103 at the end of the year. But now it is worth much less — 10 percent less than before there was inflation. The lender would *lose* approximately 7 percent rather than make 3 percent in terms of the change in the amount of goods and services he can buy.

Someone who lends $100 for 1 year and wants $103 in *real* terms at the end of the year needs an interest payment large enough to buy $103 worth of goods and services (measured in today's prices) at the prices that will exist at the end of the year. If prices will be 10 percent higher 1 year from now, the required payment is $113.30 ($=\$103 \times 1.1$). The lender will have to ask for 13.3 percent in interest at the end of the year to be compensated for the 10 percent inflation. The 13.3 percent is approximately equal to the initial 3 percent plus the expected inflation rate. It is the *nominal* interest rate, corresponding to a *real* interest rate of 3 percent and an inflation adjustment of 10 percent.

The *nominal interest rate* is the interest rate expressed in terms of the money payments made on a loan. The *real interest rate* is the return or cost of a loan expressed in terms of goods and services. The real rate is approximately equal to the nominal rate minus the inflation rate.

---

[4] To simplify our discussion we assume an economy where there is no productivity growth or changes in supply or demand conditions. Therefore, we can say real wages, for example, and relative prices are constant. Pure inflation could of course also happen in an economy where there is real growth.

leads to proposals for changes in the monetary and fiscal system that will prevent future inflation. At the end of this section we discuss the third way: learning to live with inflation.

Policies that could help restrictive monetary and fiscal policies in the fight against inflation are *incomes policies* and *tax-based incomes policies* (TIPs).

Incomes Policies The slowness of wages to respond to aggregate demand policies is the key element that makes the economy slow to disinflate. This suggests it would help if wages could be influenced directly by policy.

> *Incomes policy* is policy that attempts to influence wages and other income directly.

For instance, the government might ask trade unions to limit their wage increases in a given year to no more than 7 percent. Or the government might reach an agreement with a trade union organization that if the unions ask for only moderate wage increases, the government will keep taxes from rising.

The government might even pass laws that seek to control the rates at which wages and prices can be increased. Such laws are wage and price controls.

> *Wage and price controls* limit and regulate the wages and prices that firms are allowed to pay and charge.

Wage and price controls have been used in the United States during World War II, the Korean war, and the Nixon administration. There is little doubt that incomes policy during World War II kept prices from rising as fast as they had during earlier wars. There is also little doubt that incomes policy during the Nixon administration did not succeed.

Indeed, it is often argued that incomes policy has *never* succeeded. Part of the reason may be that incomes policies have often been seen as a substitute for macroeconomic policies to reduce inflation rather than as a useful complement to such policies. If the government is implementing tough anti-inflationary monetary and fiscal policy, that would be a good time for incomes policy to prevent wage and price rises that might occur because of expectations or momentum. But incomes policy has not usually been accompanied by tight macro policies.

Wage and price controls have also failed because they are extremely difficult to administer. The controllers are always asked to make exceptions for particular wages or prices. It is hard for anyone not in an industry to know what prices and wages should be, and the controller is at best going to be making rough and ready decisions. As time goes on, the pressures to grant more exceptions and exemptions increase, and eventually the controls become too difficult to administer.

Tax-Based Incomes Policy (TIP) Incomes policies have generally taken the form of either government advice to unions and management about wages and prices or actual government controls. TIP is an innovative alternative, advocating the use of taxes to induce firms and workers not to raise prices and wages.

> *TIP* is a system in which firms or workers are rewarded or penalized through the tax system in accordance with the increase in prices they charge.

Consider, for instance, a price TIP. Firms would be told that the taxes they pay depend on how much their prices are raised. For example, a 5 percent rise would not cause the firm to suffer any penalty. For every 1 percent the firm's prices go above that, the firm's tax rate would be increased by the government. The tax rate might rise 2 percent for every 1 percent increase in the rate at which the firm's prices are increased.

With such a TIP, it becomes costly for firms to raise prices. The firms therefore have an incentive not to raise prices too much. All firms taken together therefore raise prices less than they otherwise would have, and the inflation rate is reduced.

A similar plan could be implemented for wages. Workers could be told that their tax rates would be kept down if wages did not rise more than a certain percentage. Taxation of higher increases would be very steep. Firms would be told that their tax rates would be increased if the average rate of increase paid their workers exceeded some required norm. Wage TIPs would not be popular with workers, for they penalize the workers who succeed in getting ahead.

There is considerable interest in TIP. Indeed, the Carter administration (1977–1981) did try to get Congress to introduce a wage TIP but did not succeed. So far TIP is untried, and there is little to go on in predicting whether it could work.

Institutional and Constitutional Reform to Deal with Inflation

The second approach to the inflation problem takes a longer view. There is little doubt that we would have less inflation, whatever the costs, if money growth had been kept at lower levels in the last two decades. Therefore, according to this view, we can prevent future inflation by preventing rapid money growth in the future. But how? There are again two alternatives.

Controlling the Fed but Continuing to Use Paper Money The Fed controls the money supply; therefore, the Fed has to be controlled. One way is for Congress to instruct the Fed to make the money supply grow at some fixed low rate, such as 4 percent per year. The Fed indeed seems to have moved toward such a target during the seventies and early eighties.

Keeping to such a rule would prevent future inflations on a major scale, so long as the money stock the Fed was controlling remained the main medium of transactions in the economy. Historically, economies have continued to develop different types of money. Originally gold was the only money. Then came notes, then bank deposits; now we have money market funds. It is quite possible that while the Fed is busy controlling one set of assets, another group of assets will begin to be used as money. An alert central bank should not, however, fall asleep on the job and let control over the relevant money supply escape its grasp.

What are the chances for such a monetary rule? So long as the Fed keeps a tight control on the money stock, it is unlikely that Congress will formally vote for a rule. But if the Fed starts misbehaving, a monetary rule may appear.

Giving Up on Paper Money: Back to the Gold Standard More radical economists argue that so long as the country's money is only paper, there will be inflation. Pointing to the historical record of the United States in Figure 31-1, gold bugs say we never had inflation when the United States used gold for money, except during wartime, when the gold standard was suspended. And, they add, we have always had inflation when we had paper money controlled by the Fed. The exception is the Great Depression, which in any case reflects no credit on the Fed.

Proponents of the gold standard would make gold the money of the United States again. The Fed would be obliged to buy and sell gold at a price fixed in terms of dollars. That way the Fed would have to be sure it did not print too much money. If it printed too much money, people would start demanding gold from the Fed in the belief that it would not be able to keep the dollar price of gold fixed for long. With the supply of gold being limited, the Fed would have to take steps immediately to reduce the quantity of paper money to make sure that it remained able to meet the demand for gold at the fixed price.

The gold standard was already discussed in Chapter 27. As we noted then, the economy did not work especially well under the gold standard. Recessions were deeper than they are now. The price stability and absence of inflation that the economy enjoyed came at the price of longer recessions than we now have. And using gold for money is wasteful. There is no need to devote resources to digging gold out of the ground when money can as well consist of paper that costs almost nothing to create.

Learning to Live with Inflation

There is a third choice: learning to live with inflation. This means, in particular, that the economy's institutions should be adjusted for inflation. The process has already begun. As we noted earlier, the banking system is being freed of controls, and bracket creep is scheduled to end in 1985, when the indexation of tax brackets gets under way.

What other adjustments would have to be made? On the tax front, it would be necessary to make complicated adjustments to remove the effects of inflation on taxation of capital. On other fronts, indexation could be widely introduced.

Indexation automatically adjusts payments for the effects of inflation.

For instance, when labor contracts are indexed, wages rise automatically with the price level. When pensions are indexed, the pension (measured in dollars) goes up with the price level. Pensioners are thus safeguarded against real losses they might otherwise suffer. Loans would be indexed. The amount to be repaid would rise with the price level. Lenders would no longer suffer

from unexpected inflation, and borrowers would no longer gain.

There is already some indexation in the economy. Most important, Social Security benefits are indexed. Payments to recipients of Social Security rise with the price level. Those who rely on Social Security for retirement income are thus not affected adversely by inflation. The basic Social Security pension does not make anyone rich; instead, indexation provides a useful floor under the real value of receipts.

Should We Adapt to Inflation? Why not give up the fight against inflation and learn to live with it? In fact, this is what the economy has been doing by default during the past decade. But adoption of indexation is not a good solution to inflation, either.

Indexation is difficult to implement. There are lags between the time prices change and the time payments can be adjusted appropriately. And indexation does nothing for the shoe-leather costs of inflation. There is a second argument against learning to live with inflation. We will never get rid of inflation that way, and we are likely to suffer from an inflationary bias —in other words, we would think that the inflation rate might as well be allowed to rise since that does not have major consequences. If that is so, we would eventually find ourselves with a very high rate of inflation. And because shoe-leather costs are there anyway, and indexing adjustments are imperfect, the costs of inflation would again become high at high rates of inflation. Thus, it is argued, we would do better to fight today than fight in the future, when the inflation rate will be much higher.

There are difficulties with each of the three ways of dealing with inflation. None of them presents any quick and easy solution to the inflation problem. The most likely course of events is that we will combine the first and third approaches. When the inflation rate becomes high, restrictive monetary and fiscal policy will be used to fight it. As inflation continues, there will be continuing adaptation of the tax system and other economic institutions to reduce the distortions that inflation currently imposes on the economy.

SUMMARY

1   Prices in the U.S. economy and abroad have not always been rising. For long periods in the nineteenth century the United States experienced falling rather than rising prices. The inflation of the post-World War II period is the most serious peacetime inflation in U.S. history. The recent inflation has been worldwide.

2   Inflation in the United States is deep-rooted and persistent. The persistence of inflation results from the slowness of wages and prices to adjust to reductions in aggregate demand.

3   The slow adjustment of wages and prices results in part from the important role of expectations of inflation. Past expectations of inflation are built into today's rates of wage increases through labor contracts. Furthermore, the rates at which wages are set to rise in future years depend on what people today think will happen to economic policy in the future. The credibility of government's promises to follow anti-inflationary policies becomes important.

4   The Phillips curve shows a trade-off between inflation and unemployment. The higher the rate of inflation, the lower the rate of unemployment. This trade-off was the basis of expansionary policies in the 1960s which led to the inflation rates we have now.

5   Because inflation reacts slowly to reductions in aggregate demand, policymakers face a painful policy choice. If they reduce aggregate demand, it will take some years of unemployment to get rid of the inflation. If they do not fight the inflation, it will not get better and may well keep rising.

6   In the United States, governments have eventually chosen to accommodate inflations by allowing the money supply to grow faster rather than continue to fight inflation when the costs in terms of unemployment become very high.

7   Part of the unpopularity of inflation may be due to an illusion in which people see inflation causing the prices of things they buy to go up but do not notice inflation making their incomes go up.

8   Inflation does have real costs. Those costs depend on two factors: first, whether the inflation is expected or not, and second, the extent to which the economy has adjusted its institutions to deal with inflation.

9   The costs of expected inflation in an economy whose institutions have adapted result from shoe-leather costs of economizing on holdings of money and menu costs of changing prices more frequently. If institutions have not adapted, there will be extra costs even from an expected inflation. In particular, taxes are likely to change because of bracket creep and because capital taxation is sensitive to the rate of inflation. The financial system will respond badly to inflation if interest rates are controlled.

10   Unexpected inflation will bring about redistributions of wealth between nominal creditors and debtors.

11   To fight inflation, governments have sometimes used *incomes policies* to affect wages and prices directly. Tax-based incomes policies (TIPs) attempt to use incentives to reduce rates of inflation by penalizing firms that raise prices or wages quickly and rewarding those which raise prices slowly.

12   Suggestions have been made that the monetary system should be changed in a way that prevents the growth rate of money being high in future. The Fed should be required to increase the money supply 4 percent per year every year without exception. Alternatively, there is some support for returning to the gold standard, which kept inflation rates low in the nineteenth century.

13   As long as inflation continues, the economy learns to live with it. Adapting to inflation is a way of reducing its costs. Living with inflation would lead to widespread *indexation* of the terms of contracts to the price level.

KEY TERMS

Phillips curve	Menu costs of inflation
Stagflation	Bracket creep
Credibility	Unexpected inflation
Institutional adaptation to inflation	Monetary rules
Inflation-adjusted interest rates	Gold standard
Shoe-leather costs of inflation	Indexation

PROBLEMS

1   What have the characteristics of price level behavior of the U.S. economy been since 1860?

2   Why is there persistent inflation in the United States? Describe briefly what persistent inflation means and give at least two reasons for the persistence.

3   Using the supply and demand frame-

work of Chapter 29, show how policies in the 1960s led to lower unemployment and higher inflation. Show whether your analysis is consistent with the Phillips curve.

4   Looking at Figure 31-3, can you identify two episodes of expansion and two episodes of contraction?

5   Using Figure 31-3, how can you tell the difference between a supply shock and a demand contraction and between a supply shock and a demand expansion?

6   Suppose an economy is hit by unexpected inflation of 5 percent. Identify at least three groups that gain and show in each case who loses.

7   Which do you think is more costly, expected or surprise inflation?

8   What do you think would be a set of policies by our government to definitely stop inflation? Describe the policies exactly and indicate what risks you see in the implementation.

9   Suppose there is no inflation and lenders want to receive 5 percent interest in real terms so that on a $100 loan for 1 year, they would require payment of $105 at the end of the loan. Now suppose inflation is expected to be 15 percent. How many dollars of repayment are required to yield 5 percent interest in real terms?

10   Suppose that the loan in Problem 9 has been made in the expectation of no inflation, with the lender receiving $105 at the end of a year, but that there turned out to be inflation at the rate of 10 percent. What is the real value of the loan repayment including interest? Who gains, who loses, and how much compared to what they had expected?

11   Explain why taxation of nominal interest rates may affect real rates received by lenders even if interest rates adjust 1 for 1 for inflation.

12   What is bracket creep?

"Inflation is too much money chasing too few goods" is everyone's first definition and explanation of inflation. This view has been studied and developed by monetarist economists, the most prominent of whom is Milton Friedman. Monetarists argue that changes in the stock of money are primarily responsible for the business cycle and for inflation. Their conclusions about the causes of inflation are summarized by Friedman's statement, "Inflation is always and everywhere a monetary phenomenon."[1]

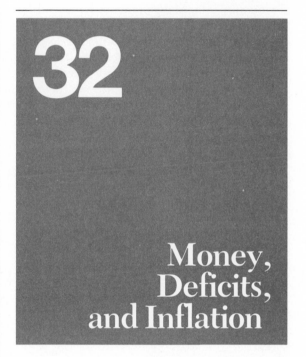

32

Money,
Deficits,
and Inflation

The aggregate supply and demand framework developed in Chapters 28 and 29 can be used to examine several possible causes of shifts in the aggregate supply and demand curves that would make the aggregate price level change. This suggests that inflation can have many possible causes, differing from country to country and time to time. But, monetarists argue, shifts in aggregate supply and demand curves can never cause prolonged inflation unless the money supply grows. If the money supply is constant, a rising price level reduces real balances and raises interest rates; eventually the inflation stops.

In this chapter we look at three issues related to inflation, starting with the link between money growth and inflation. The second issue is the relationship between budget deficits and inflation; budget deficits are the second most popular explanation for inflation. Third, we examine the relationship between interest rates and inflation that was introduced in Chapter 31. In addition, we discuss the economics of hyperinflation, or periods of extremely rapid inflation, when relationships between inflation and other economic variables stand out in full clarity.

In considering each issue, we examine both the predictions of theory and the evidence from the data. Does money growth lead to inflation, and how tight is the link? Does the budget deficit really matter for inflation in the United States and abroad? Do interest rates go up 1 for 1 with the inflation rate? In each case the theory is straightforward and the data extensive. The data show that the simple theories linking money growth and inflation and linking inflation and interest rates work well when money growth is high. But the evidence is much more mixed in countries where the inflation rate is low.

---

[1] Milton Friedman, *Dollars and Deficits*, Prentice-Hall, Englewood Cliffs, N.J., 1968, p. 39.

1 MONEY AND INFLATION

From our discussion in Chapter 27 we recall that in monetary equilibrium, the supply of real balances is equal to the demand for real balances. The demand for real balances increases with the level of real income because people buy more goods and services when their incomes are higher; hence they wish to hold higher real balances to finance their purchases. The other determinant of real money demand is the opportunity cost of holding money. The opportunity cost is the amount of interest forgone by holding money instead of other assets. The higher the opportunity cost, the lower the demand for real balances since people will economize on cash in order to earn higher interest on their assets.

The Price Level

We develop the relationship between money and inflation by starting from monetary equilibrium. In monetary equilibrium the real money supply is equal to the demand for real balances. We can write

$$\frac{\text{Nominal money supply}}{\text{Price level}} = \text{real money demand} \quad (1)$$

On the left-hand side we have written the definition of the real money stock.

> The *real money stock* is the ratio of the nominal money supply to the price level.

Equation (1) can be rearranged to read

$$\text{Price level} = \frac{\text{nominal money supply}}{\text{real money demand}} \quad (1a)$$

Equation (1a) is the basic equation of inflation economics. It states the following:

> The *price level* increases whenever the nominal money stock increases relative to the demand for real balances.

The determinants of the price level in equation (1a) allow us to discuss the quantity theory of money.

The *quantity theory of money* states that movements in the price level are determined largely by movements in the nominal quantity of money.

This theory is at least 500 years old (there are claims it goes back to Confucius), and its age attests to the fact that movements in the price level have been a source of concern for economists, statesmen, and the public for a long time. Today the quantity theory is defended by monetarists who argue that *most* movements in prices are due to changes in the nominal money stock.

To see how far we can get with the simple quantity theory approach, which argues that most changes in the price level are caused by changes in the money stock, we look at the data for several countries in Table 32-1. For each country we compare the money stock and the price level in 1980 with their levels in the base year 1962. In France, for example, the money stock in 1980 was more than five times as large as it had been in 1962. Prices were 3.5 times as large. For the United States, prices and money increased in almost exactly the same proportion. In Japan, by comparison, money increased 13-fold while prices did not even quadruple.

What do we conclude from this evidence? For most countries, there is no close relation between nominal money and the price level. This is not surprising because equation (1a) tells us that prices rise by the same proportion as the money stock *only* if real money demand stays constant. The evidence, then, is that in practice there are also changes in real money demand. The first lesson is that we rarely observe a very close relation between nominal money and prices. Changes in real money demand almost always play a significant part.

Changes in Real Money Demand Real money demand changes over time for one of three main reasons. First, there are changes

TABLE 32-1
NOMINAL MONEY SUPPLY AND PRICES, 1980
(Index 1962 = 100)

	CANADA	NETHERLANDS	FRANCE	ITALY	GERMANY	JAPAN	UNITED STATES
Money	429	519	522	1440	410	1323	270
Prices	278	297	346	503	201	368	272

Note: Money is M1. Prices are the CPI.
Source: Federal Reserve Bank of St. Louis.

in real income. Such changes may well be significant over a long period such as 20 years because real income grows year after year, and that growth accumulates into a large change in real income and hence in money demand. In terms of equation (1a), real income increases raise real money demand and therefore, other things equal, reduce prices. If nominal money is growing and real income is growing, the two influences on the price level go in opposite directions. Nominal money growth makes for inflation, or rising prices, while real income growth and hence increases in real money demand tend to make prices fall. The net effect depends on the balance of the two forces. If nominal money grows very rapidly—say, 30 percent per year—and real income grows only 2 or 3 percent per year, we are certain to have rising prices.

Returning to Table 32-1, we note that real income growth is a good candidate to explain why in most countries prices increased less than money. Real income increased in all the countries in the table, and this tended to reduce the growth in the price level relative to the growth in the nominal money stock. In particular, real income growth explains the Japanese experience, where money rose 3.5 times as fast as prices. Real income growth in Japan was nearly 7 percent a year so that over 18 years Japanese real income rose by a factor of nearly 3.5. Such a large increase in income certainly accounted for most of the differ-

ence between the increase in the real money stock and the increase in prices in Japan over the period 1962–1980.

But there are two more determinants of real money demand still to be considered. Next in importance is the opportunity cost of holding money. When the opportunity cost of holding money rises, the demand for real balances falls. From equation (1a) we note that an increase in the opportunity cost of holding money reduces real money demand and therefore increases the price level. We shall see that this effect plays a significant role in countries where inflation moves from low to extremely high rates. But it has also played a role in the United States. U.S. interest rates, as we saw in Chapter 25, rose from the 1960s to the late 1970s. Thus real money demand declined, and that contributed to increasing prices, given the growth in money.

The third source of change in real money demand is financial innovations that introduce near-monies and new methods for households to make the same amount of transactions with lower real balances. Examples are credit cards and money market mutual funds. By reducing the demand for real balances these innovations put upward pressure on prices.

In the United States innovations developed particularly rapidly over the 1962–1980 period. This helps explain why money and prices grew almost to the same extent in the United States even though real income increased over that period. The reduction in real money demand from innovations and higher interest rates in the United States just offset the growth in real income that would by itself have raised real money demand. Money and prices therefore increased in the same proportion. In countries where interest rates did not rise as much and there were fewer innovations, real money demand grew more, and therefore prices increased less than the money stock.

Inflation

So far we have discussed the price level and changes in the price level, using equation (1a). We can also talk about the growth rate of prices, or the inflation rate:

$$
\begin{array}{c}
\text{Inflation} \\
\text{rate}
\end{array}
=
\begin{array}{c}
\text{growth rate of} \\
\text{nominal} \\
\text{money stock}
\end{array}
-
\begin{array}{c}
\text{growth rate of} \\
\text{real money} \\
\text{demand}
\end{array}
\quad (2)
$$

Equation (2) is similar to equation (1a). It turns out to be a very useful equation once we learn how to manipulate it.

Suppose real money demand grows at the same rate as real income. For example, if real income grows 3 percent per year, real money demand also grows 3 percent. Suppose also that the opportunity cost of holding money does not change and that there are no financial innovations to affect real money demand. Then growth in real money demand is just equal to the growth in real income. Let nominal money growth be 10 percent and real income growth be 3 percent. Equation (2) tells us the inflation rate will be 7 percent (10 percent − 3 percent). If money growth were 15 percent, the inflation rate would be 12 percent (15 percent − 3 percent), while higher real income growth—say, 5 percent instead of 3 percent—would mean less inflation. Equation (2) is the basic inflation equation.

Now we take a real-world example: Jamaica in the period 1975–1980. From the statistics we find the following: Average an-

nual real income growth was −3.0 percent—real income fell during the period. Nominal money grew at an average rate of 19.3 percent. Using equation (2), what would we expect the inflation rate to be? Assuming only real income changes moved real money demand, we predict an inflation rate of 22.3 percent [19.3 percent − (−3.0 percent)]. In fact, inflation averaged 24.9 percent. Thus the model gets us very close to the right numbers. Note, though, that there is some error. We predicted 22.3 percent, but in fact the rate of inflation averaged nearly 25 percent. There was some other disturbance reducing real money demand and adding to the inflation over and above what is explained by the rise in nominal money and the fall in real GNP.[2]

Figure 32-1 shows the relationship between money growth rates and inflation rates for a group of countries, including some with very high money growth. Note that we have made no adjustment at all for growth in real money demand. Even so, it looks as if we have a very strong relationship. The higher the money growth rate, the higher the rate of inflation. The figure makes the following point: *When money growth rates are very high—30 or 50 or 100 percent—inflation tends to be dominated by money growth.* At high money growth rates it makes little difference whether we are adding or subtracting 2 to 3 points for real growth.

This is the valid case of the quantity theory. When money growth is very high, inflation over long periods is roughly equal to money growth. But this relationship does not hold tightly over short periods of a year

---

[2] How can you be sure we didn't cheat by finding the only country for which this method—predicting the inflation rate to be equal to the growth rate of money minus the growth rate of income—works? You can't be sure, though in fact we chose Jamaica only because of its high growth rate of the money stock. Only by looking at many more countries and time periods can we build confidence in such relationships.

FIGURE 32-1 MONEY GROWTH AND INFLATION, 1970–1980 (AVERAGE ANNUAL GROWTH RATES). (*Source: International Financial Statistics Yearbook, 1981.*)

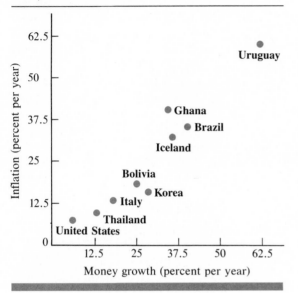

or two. Nor, as we saw from Table 32-1, does it hold at all for industrial countries, in which money growth rates in many cases are lower than 10 percent.

U.S. Money and Inflation

The absence of a close relationship between money growth and inflation in the short run and with low money growth is well illustrated by the U.S. example. Figure 32-2 shows the annual growth rate of money (M1) for the United States and also shows the inflation rate measured by the growth rate of the CPI. Two facts stand out. Over time both money growth and inflation have increased. They were lower than 3 percent at the beginning of the 1960s, and they were larger than 5 percent at the end of the 1970s. But it is also quite apparent that in the short run there is no clear-cut relationship between money growth and inflation. In 1974–1975, for example, supply shocks forced up the rate of inflation while money growth actually declined. In 1976 inflation declined while money growth increased.

Perhaps we should look for a relation-

FIGURE 32-2 MONEY GROWTH (M1) AND INFLATION (CPI), UNITED STATES, 1960–1981. (*Source:* Citibank Economic Database.)

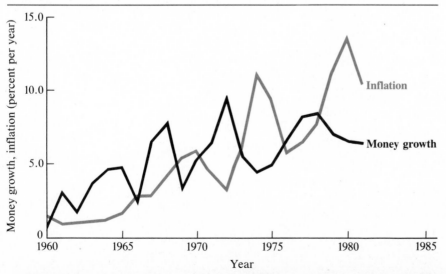

ship that involves well-specified lags. Today's inflation might, for example, be caused by money growth over the last 2 or 3 years. However, there is no evidence of such well-specified lags. Obviously, what happened in the United States was that demand shocks from money, from fiscal policy, and from investment interacted with the supply side to generate inflation and output. Money is only one factor in that equation, though an important one. It is only by looking across countries over longer periods, as in Figure 32-1, that we succeed in identifying the role of money in explaining inflation.

Another way of seeing the role of money is to look at the extreme inflations that occur occasionally. When inflation rates are not 5 or 50 percent but a few thousand percent, we can best understand the interaction of nominal money growth and real money demand in determining the rate of inflation.

2 HYPERINFLATION

Hyperinflations are extraordinary events in which the instability of money and prices becomes so vast that it dominates everyday life, disorganizing production and markets and redistributing income and wealth in society.

Hyperinflations are periods in which inflation rates exceed 1000 percent per year.

They are always associated with political dislocation and chaos; they almost invariably occur in the final stages of a war or a social revolution. Several occurred in the early part of this century and after World War II, but they continue to occur every now and then. The latest episode was the huge inflation in the final stages of the Allende government in Chile in the early 1970s. The episode we look at here is the most famous, the German hyperinflation of the 1920s.

Germany, 1922–1923

Table 32-2 shows the behavior of an index of the money supply and of prices in Germany in 1922–1923 as well as the monthly rate of inflation. Our discussion starts with 1922, although by that time prices had already risen very substantially from their level at the start of World War I in 1914. Germany had lost the war and some territory, government expenditures were large, and tax revenue was low. Therefore, there was a large government budget deficit, which was financed in large part by printing money.

Table 32-2 shows that from January

TABLE 32-2

MONEY AND PRICES IN HYPERINFLATION IN GERMANY

	CURRENCY (January 1922 = 1)	PRICES (January 1922 = 1)	INFLATION, % per month
January 1922	1	1	5
January 1923	16	75	189
March	45	132	−12
May	70	221	157
July	354	2021	386
August	5394	25515	1262
September	227777	645946	2532
October	20201256	191891890	29720

Source: Data adapted from C. L. Holtfrerich, *Die Deutsche Inflation 1914–1923,* Walter de Gruyter, New York and Berlin, 1980, Tables I and II.

1922 to January 1923 the index of the money supply rose from 1 to 16. That means the money supply increased 16-fold, or by 1500 percent. Within the next 6 months money growth accelerated sharply, and by July the money stock index was already 354, more than 22,000 percent higher than it had been 3 months earlier. As you see from the table, in the next few months money literally exploded to 20 million times the January 1922 level. For every reichsmark he held in January 1922, the average person held 20 million in late 1923. Putting this in U.S. terms, if you now have $40 of cash on you, after a money stock increase as big as the German one, you would have $800 *million* in your pocket.

You might ask, just to imagine the extent of what was going on, what a 20 million reichsmark note looked like and how the government could produce money that fast. It was not easy. The government simply stamped new numbers on old notes. At one point they had to move to high-speed printing presses. During the night money would be restamped for the higher prices of the next day.

What was the consequence of the rapid money expansion? The second column of the table shows the behavior of prices. The index of prices rose much more rapidly than the money stock. Where money had risen from January 1922 to 1923 by a factor of 16, prices rose by a factor of 75. By October 1923, a hotdog that had cost 1 reichsmark in January 1922 cost 192 million reichsmarks. How do you carry around 192 million reichsmarks? Not in small change. All bills carried gigantic numbers such as 1 billion reichsmarks, and people went shopping carrying baskets full of currency.

The third column of Table 32-2 shows the monthly inflation rate. From a low rate of 5 percent per month, or about 80 percent per year, in 1922, inflation increased to 30,000 percent per month in the final stage

of hyperinflation. A rate of 30,000 percent per month corresponds to about 40 percent per day. Thus prices at the end of the hyperinflation were doubling about every other day. But the inflation was also very uneven. In January 1923, for example, it was almost 200 percent, whereas in March prices were actually falling because there was a short-lived expectation of stabilization. People thought the government was going to change its policies and stop inflation. But it did not happen then, and soon hyperinflation was under way again.

The Flight from Money

We have noted that an increase in the opportunity cost of holding money reduces real money demand. The German hyperinflation offers striking evidence of this. When inflation reaches extraordinary levels, the purchasing power of money falls very rapidly. Anybody holding money even for a day loses relative to someone who holds real assets such as houses or land or even groceries. To avoid this loss, people try to economize on real balances. They arrange to be paid more frequently, do their shopping right after being paid, and even resort to barter.

In the final stages of the German hyperinflation, when prices doubled every other day, there was very little use of money. Workers were paid twice a day so that they could go shopping during lunchtime to avoid the depreciation in the purchasing power of their money balances that would have occurred if they waited till the end of the afternoon. Some firms even paid workers with the goods they were producing, allowing them to go out and barter the goods directly for food. In restaurants people would order two beers at the same time because beer grew stale at a slower rate than prices were rising.

This attempt to save on real balances, or to finance the same level of spending with a

TABLE 32-3
REAL BALANCES IN THE GERMAN HYPERINFLATION

DATE	CURRENCY (January 1922 = 1)	PRICES (January 1922 = 1)	REAL BALANCES (January 1922 = 1)
January 1922	1	1	1
January 1923	16	75	0.21
March	45	132	0.34
May	70	221	0.32
July	354	2021	0.18
August	5394	25515	0.21
September	227777	645946	0.35
October	20201256	191891890	0.11

Source: See Table 32-2.

smaller amount of money on hand, can be seen in the real value of the money stock. In Table 32-3 we set the real value of the money stock at 1 in January 1922. We calculate the real value as the ratio of the index of nominal money to the index of prices. By January 1923, the real money stock was down to 0.21 (16/75), just over a fifth of its value a year earlier. Thus even though inflation had increased to "only" about 200 percent per month, the real balances people held were one-fifth of what they had been under the less inflationary conditions. This is already evidence of a large reduction in real balances. Then real balances increased a bit. By October the level of real balances had declined further, to about one-tenth the value of a year before. Thus payment habits changed sufficiently for people to hold money with 11 percent of the purchasing power of their money holdings at the lower rate of inflation of 2 years previously.

This effect is described as a flight from money.

The *flight from money* is the economizing on real balances that occurs on a massive scale when rapid inflation makes it costly to hold money.[3]

The flight from money plays a significant role in inflation. In discussing equation (2), we noted that when real money demand declines, inflation exceeds the growth rate

of nominal money. The same thing can be stated in terms of price level behavior in equation (1). If there is a decline in real money demand, the price level increases more than the nominal money stock. As people try to reduce their real balances, they increase the demand for goods, and this leads to an increase in prices as too much money chases too few goods. This effect is apparent in Table 32-3, where we see that the price level increased *much more* than nominal money. This is just another way of saying that there was a flight from money, which helped propel the inflation being driven by the growing money stock.

For monetary economics this hyperinflation is almost a laboratory experiment. It shows that when money growth is extreme, practically all that matters for inflation is the growth rate of nominal money and the flight from money. Both play their role, and therefore prices rise even more than the money stock increases. When it becomes extremely costly to hold money, people try to do without it.

---

[3] The flight from money is also on occasion called an increase in the velocity of money. *The velocity of money is the ratio of nominal income to nominal money. Velocity is the rate of turnover of money.* When velocity increases, fewer dollars are held on average to finance a given flow of spending.

Hyperinflation and Society

Hyperinflation makes all nominal assets worthless. A common joke during the German hyperinflation was the story of a woman who had gone shopping carrying a basket full of currency—it took a whole basket to carry all the paper. She was queuing in a shop and had set down her basket. When she returned to look for it, the basket had been stolen—but the money had been left.

It was not only money that became worthless but also all assets fixed in nominal terms: holdings of government bonds and savings certificates, pensions, and insurance policies. The value of any contract that was not indexed to move with the price level—and virtually *no* contract was indexed—essentially became zero. If you owe $1 or even $10,000, the value of what you owe becomes almost zero in real terms if prices rise by a factor of 20 million. But that meant that anyone who had worked for many years to build up a pension for retirement was suddenly faced with the prospect of having nothing at all. Within a year the value of people's life's savings had entirely disappeared. Anyone who had bought a government bond, hoping to build up wealth by earning interest, found that the purchasing power loss outgrew the interest earnings by a huge margin and that a life's savings became worthless.

Two questions must be asked at this point. With all the holders of nominal claims (money, bonds, insurance contracts, and pensions) losing their purchasing power, who were the gainers? Second, what happens to society when fortunes are wiped out overnight? The first question is relatively easy. The beneficiaries of the hyperinflation were the debtors. An inflation that is massive and unexpected, such as the German hyperinflation, redistributes wealth from creditors, or holders of nominal claims, toward debtors. Among the chief debtors was the government, whose liabilities—money and government bonds—became worthless.

Redistributions of wealth from creditors to debtors on as large a scale as happens during hyperinflations can easily destabilize society. In the case of Germany, the middle class—the holders of bonds, money, insurance, and pensions—was ruined by the inflation. But of course, the ruin was not easily accepted but rather led to a growing support for totalitarian government. The hyperinflation was one of the chief factors responsible for the rise of the Nazi regime in Germany.

Hyperinflations are the most dramatic symptom that an economy has fallen into economic problems or conflicts that society is unable to handle within the given political system. Hyperinflations threaten anyone who has something to lose—a safe job or savings—and lead to "law and order governments" at the expense of political freedom and democracy. When a government fails to provide reasonable stability in prices and in the distribution of wealth, when property, jobs, and economic security suddenly are put in question, the doors are quickly opened to totalitarian governments. This is not a serious issue when inflation rises from 5 to 10 or even 15 percent, but it certainly will be the case when inflation runs to 100 or 500 percent. In this case inflation is the most ready barometer of a government's inability to handle matters in the accustomed way, and it eases the way for political forces that society disdains in ordinary times.[4]

3 BUDGET DEFICITS AND INFLATION

We turn next to the association between budget deficits and inflation. We know from

---

[4] See the collection of readings by F. K. Ringer (ed.), *The German Inflation of 1923*, Oxford University Press, London, 1969.

the analysis of fiscal policy in Chapter 27 that increases in government spending or reductions in taxes increase aggregate demand and tend to raise the price level. These fiscal changes also increase the deficit. Thus the earlier analysis suggests one possible link between the budget deficit and inflation. Note that this theory suggests a link between the *full-employment deficit* and inflation, not between the actual deficit and inflation.

The full-employment deficit, we recall, measures the deficit as it would be if the economy were at the level of potential output. It removes the effects of the business cycle from the measured deficit. *Actual* deficits may be high either because the full-employment deficit is high or because the economy is in a recession. If the economy is in a recession, we do not expect the inflation rate to be high, even though the budget deficit will be high. This theory suggests that we should not find in the data any close link between budget deficits and inflation that reflect the operation of fiscal policy—unless changes in the deficit are mainly the result of changes in the full-employment deficit.

Evidence   Figure 32-3 shows the relation-ship between the budget deficit in the United States and the inflation rate for the period 1965–1981. There is no very tight link between the two series. Similarly, in Figure 32-4, we look at international experience to see whether countries with larger deficits also have higher rates of inflation.

It is quite apparent that here too there is no relationship between inflation and budget deficits. Japan has a very substantial deficit—more than 5 percent of GNP—and low inflation. In the United States the budget deficit is less than half that, and the inflation rate is much higher. In Germany and the United States budget deficits as a share of GNP are the same, but U.S. inflation is twice that of Germany.

Deficits and Money Growth

In Figures 32-3 and 32-4 we looked for but did not find a direct relationship between budget deficits and inflation. But the relationship may be indirect. It is widely believed that there is a close link between the size of the government budget deficit and money growth. Given the connection between money growth and inflation, there would be an indirect relationship between budget deficits and inflation.

When there is a deficit in the budget,

FIGURE 32-3   BUDGET DEFICITS (AS PERCENTAGE OF GNP) AND INFLATION, UNITED STATES, 1965–1981. (*Source: Economic Report of the President, 1982,* Tables B-1, B-3, and B-76.)

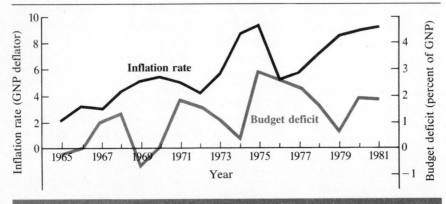

FIGURE 32-4   BUDGET DEFICITS (AS PERCENT-
AGE OF GNP) AND INFLATION, 1977–1979. The figure shows the average rate of inflation and the budget deficit as a percentage of GNP for 1977–1979. It
is not obvious that there is a close relation. (*Source:
International Financial Statistics,* May 1982.)

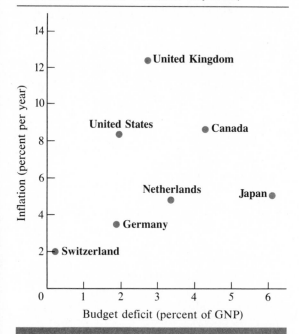

the government is spending more than it receives in taxes. But of course, it has to pay
for all its spending. How does it do that?

There are two ways of financing a budget deficit.

1   The government can borrow from the
private sector. In a year in which the budget
deficit is, say, $50 billion, the government
can borrow that amount from the private
sector. It does this by selling bonds to the
private sector: to insurance companies, pension funds, and private individuals. In exchange for the bonds, the government receives money, which it spends. Later it
repays the bonds, perhaps by borrowing
more from the private sector or by taxation.

2   The government can create money. In

some countries the government may literally print money or else pay by giving the
seller of goods a check. Such a check, which
is written against the government's account
at the central bank, changes the quantity of
high-powered money.

In the United States, the institutional
process is more complicated than item 2
suggests, in that the Federal Reserve is an
independent agency. The Treasury has to finance *all* of its deficit by borrowing. But if
the bonds are bought by the Fed, it is the
same as if the government were financing
the deficit by printing money. When the
Fed buys bonds, it increases the quantity of
high-powered money.

It is clearly possible to finance a deficit
by printing money. But does it happen?
This depends on the country. In countries
where there are no good bond markets, governments find it difficult to borrow from the
private sector. Therefore, they tend to finance their deficits directly by printing
money. We now look at some evidence.

During hyperinflations there is very
little question of what is going on. The government has a large deficit, perhaps because
a war or revolution has reduced tax collection or because a new government has an
ambitious spending program. Because tax
collection is lacking and bond finance
seems impossible, the government resorts
to printing money to finance the deficit in
the budget. Thus nominal money starts increasing at a rapid rate. But nothing has occurred to raise real money demand. Therefore, with nominal money growing and real
money demand unchanged, prices start rising. In the next stage, once the inflation gets
under way, real money demand declines as
people reduce their real balances to avoid
the opportunity cost imposed by inflation.
This is again the flight from money, which
aggravates the ongoing inflation.

The Inflation Tax   Using money creation to

finance the budget deficit is another form of taxation, the inflation tax.

The *inflation tax* is the cost to money holders of maintaining the purchasing power of their real balances in the face of inflation.

When there is inflation, we have to increase our nominal money holdings every week or month just to make sure that the real value, or purchasing power, of the money we hold stays constant. But to get more dollar bills we have to spend less than our income (or sell assets). Our spending less than our income is exactly matched by the government's printing the dollar bills to finance the budget deficit.

To take a concrete example, suppose I start this year with $200. There is 10 percent inflation during the year. In order to maintain the real value of my money holdings, I have to hold $220 by the end of the year. That means I have to add $20 to my money balances. I do that by saving $20, spending less than my income on that account. I could alternatively have been taxed directly for $20, and that also would have made me spend $20 less than my income. I am being taxed by the inflation tax because the government is making me spend less than my income.

During the German hyperinflation, the government collected 6 percent to 7 percent of GNP through the inflation tax. Even today, governments in some less-developed countries collect as much as 5 percent of GNP in the form of inflation taxes.

Budget deficits financed by money creation may be the only way a weak government can tax the private sector effectively. Keynes, writing in 1923 about hyperinflations, made this point:

> A government can live for a long time, even the German government or the Russian government, by printing paper money. That is to say, it can by this means secure command over real resources, resources just as real as

those obtained by taxation. The method is condemned, but its efficiency, up to a point, must be admitted. A government can live by this means when it can live by no other. It is the form of taxation which the public finds hardest to evade and even the weakest government can enforce, when it can enforce nothing else.[5]

Budget Deficits and Money Growth in the United States   Figure 32-5 shows the deficit as a percentage of GNP and the growth rate of money. The time series have some similarities, particularly for the years 1966–1971. But there is no simple tight link between budget deficits and money growth. For instance, in 1975 the budget deficit reached a peak and then fell, whereas money growth continued to rise through 1978. Similarly, in 1971 the deficit reached a peak and began to decline, while money growth continued rising.

Because there is no automatic link between budget deficits and money growth in the United States, the lack of a tight connection between the two series in Figure 32-5 is not surprising. As we have noted, decisions on the deficit and money growth are made separately. The deficit is the result of budgetary decisions made by the administration and Congress. Money growth is decided on by the Fed. Any links there might be would have to be a result of decisions made by the Fed.

The Fed *could* create a link between the deficit and money growth if it tried to keep interest rates constant. For instance, when the deficit rises as a result of a tax cut or increased government spending, we know from Chapter 27 that interest rates tend to rise. The Fed might try to prevent interest rates from rising by an open market purchase, but such a purchase would in-

---

[5] J. M. Keynes, *A Tract on Monetary Reform*, St. Martin's Press, New York, 1971, p. 37. This book was first published in 1923.

FIGURE 32-5 BUDGET DEFICITS AND MONEY GROWTH, UNITED STATES,
1965–1981. (*Source: Economic Report of the President, 1982,* Tables B-1,
B-61, and B-76.)

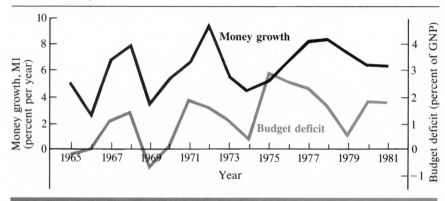

crease the money stock at a time of high deficits. This way the Fed could indirectly create a link between deficits and money growth.

The evidence of Figure 32-5 is that any such relationship in the United States is a weak one. Evidence from other developed countries shows the same thing—there is no necessary link between budget deficits and money growth. Nonetheless, the warning by Keynes should always be borne in mind. When budget deficits become very large and there is no good way of raising taxes, a weak government will resort to the inflation tax.

4 INTEREST RATES AND INFLATION

In Chapter 31 we briefly introduced the idea that interest rates on bonds will increase whenever the inflation rate rises. We now expand that discussion and look at some evidence. Figure 32-6 shows the Treasury bill rate in the United States and the inflation rate for each year since 1950. After the early years of the period, when inflation was a result of the Korean war, we see a simple relationship between the inflation rate and the interest rate. They go up together. This association between the inflation

rate and the interest rate is known as the *Fisher relationship.* It is named after Irving Fisher, a famous American economist who was interested in inflationary problems for most of his long professional career from the 1890s to 1947.[6]

The Fisher relation in Figure 32-6 is approximately 1 for 1. The interest rate goes up 1 percent for every 1 percent increase in the inflation rate. The explanation is that the interest rate is the price paid to borrow money. When prices are changing because there is inflation, the value of money is falling. Someone who borrows $100 when the inflation rate is 10 percent will pay back 1 year later with dollars that buy fewer goods. Therefore, we expect people who lend to want to be compensated for the loss in the value of the loans they have made. Those who borrow know the dollars they pay back have a lower value, and so they agree to pay back more dollars.

In more detail, we once again distinguish between the *nominal* interest rate and the *real* interest rate. We recall that the

---

[6] Fisher taught at Yale and made many contributions to economics and the understanding of the economy. He was also a health enthusiast who believed in sleeping in the fresh air and eating wheat germ. He wrote health books as well as economics books.

FIGURE 32-6 INFLATION AND THE TREASURY BILL RATE, UNITED STATES, 1950–1981. (*Source:* Citibank Economic Database.)

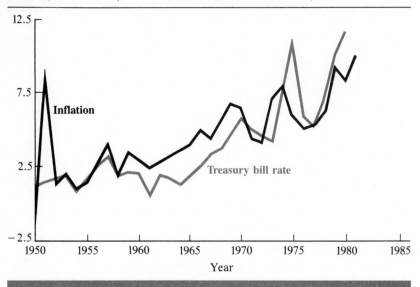

TABLE 32-4

REAL AND NOMINAL INTEREST RATES

AMOUNT LENT AT START OF YEAR	AMOUNT RECEIVED BACK AT END OF YEAR	NOMINAL INTEREST	AMOUNT OF INTEREST COMPENSATING FOR FALL IN VALUE OF MONEY	REAL INTEREST
$100	$115	$15 = 15% of $100	$10 = 10%	$5 = 5%

nominal interest rate is the amount of dollars to be paid for a 1-year loan of $100. Table 32-4 shows how a 1-year loan works. At the beginning the borrower receives $100. At the end of the year he pays back $100 plus interest. In the example in the table, the nominal interest rate is 15 percent, meaning the individual pays back $115 after having the loan for a year.

Now we do the same calculation to find the real, or inflation-adjusted, interest rate, which measures the amount of interest in terms of goods and services, not in terms of dollars. The borrower gets $100 at the beginning. Because the inflation rate for the year is expected to be 10 percent, he pays

$10 as the *inflation premium,* or the part of the interest that compensates the lender for the fall in the value of money over the year. The remaining $5 is the real interest payment.

We summarize this discussion of real and nominal interest with the following equation:

$$\text{Nominal interest rate} = \text{inflation premium} + \text{real interest rate} \quad (3)$$

The inflation premium is equal to the rate of inflation expected over the lifetime of the loan.

The distinction between real and nominal interest rates is essential for understanding both the business cycle and inflation. In countries where there is rapid inflation, interest rates may be in the three-figure range. It is hard initially to see how anyone can afford to take a loan at an interest rate of more than 100 percent. But suppose you could borrow at 100 percent at a time when prices were rising 200 percent. You would have an incredibly good deal—in fact, a real interest rate of −100 percent. For instance, imagine buying a used car at the beginning of the year with borrowed money. The car costs 10,000 continentals. At the end of the year you have to pay back 20,000. Quite likely, though, with prices rising 200 percent, you will be able to sell the car after a year and still come out with a profit.

Another way of making these points is to look at equation (3), rearranged to focus on the real interest rate:

Real interest rate = nominal interest rate − inflation rate   (3a)

In this form we see that for the real interest rate to be positive, the nominal interest rate must *at least* equal the rate of inflation. If inflation rates are 20 percent, the nominal interest rate must at least be 20 percent for lenders not to *lose* from a loan by having less purchasing power at the end than they had when they initially made the loan.

Evidence on the Fisher Effect

We can find evidence for the relationship between interest rates and inflation either by looking at the relationship between inflation and interest rates over time, or by looking across the world. Figure 32-7 shows the rate of inflation and the rate of interest on government bonds for various industrialized countries in the third quarter of 1981. The figure strongly supports the contention that the higher the rate of inflation, the higher the nominal interest rate. Italy, for example, has the highest inflation and interest rates; Switzerland has low inflation and

FIGURE 32-7 INFLATION AND INTEREST RATES, 1981. (*Source: International Financial Statistics,* May 1982.)

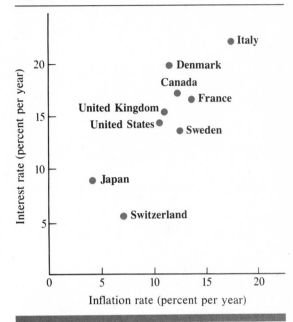

a low interest rate. The relationship between interest rates and inflation is strong, but it is *not* an exact one in which higher inflation is matched point for point by a higher interest rate. There must be factors other than inflation causing interest rates to differ between countries.

We can also look beyond the main industrial countries to take a broad sample of countries. Table 32-5 shows the short-term nominal interest rate and the inflation rate in late 1981 for a number of countries. Table 32-5 reinforces the idea that the relationship between inflation and nominal interest rates is present but not exact. Argentina and Brazil, with inflation rates around 100 percent, have interest rates near 100 percent, and Singapore, with an inflation rate of less than 10 percent, has an interest rate lower than 10 percent. But in both Argentina and Brazil inflation is still very much in excess of interest rates. Real interest rates, therefore, are

TABLE 32-5

INFLATION RATE AND NOMINAL INTEREST RATE
(Percent per Year, November 1981)

COUNTRY	INFLATION RATE	NOMINAL INTEREST RATE
Brazil	107.0	90.2
Argentina	120.7	84.7
New Zealand	15.4	11.2
Korea	16.2	17.8
Singapore	9.5	5.4
Mexico	28.5	33.3

Sources: International Monetary Fund, *International Financial Statistics,* May 1982, and *World Financial Markets,* June 1982.

very negative. By contrast, in Mexico and Korea they are positive. This evidence shows that the level of the inflation rate is only one of the various determinants of the rate of interest. Among the other determinants are current monetary policy and fiscal policy.

The data in Figure 32-7 and Table 32-5 show that it is quite possible for the real

yield on bonds to be substantially negative or to be a large positive number rather than some small positive number. In the United States the average real yield on Treasury bills in the last 50 years has been zero. But there have been periods, such as 1981–1982, when there was a very large positive real yield in the 5 to 10 percent range. At other times, for example, in the mid-1970s, the real yield was substantially negative. Figure 32-7 shows that in almost all countries the interest rate at that time exceeded the inflation rate so that real yields were positive. But that is not a rule, and we can likewise find periods when real yields are negative.

This section carries a qualified message. Other things equal, higher inflation also means higher nominal interest rates, since there is no reason why the mere existence of a positive rate of inflation should lower real interest rates. But other things equal is rarely the case. Often a sharp increase in inflation may be a surprise or may be accompanied by other macroeconomic disturbances that do affect the real interest rate.

SUMMARY

1   In monetary equilibrium, the price level is determined by the ratio of the nominal money supply to the demand for real balances. A rise in the nominal money supply or a fall in real money demand will lead to higher prices.

2   The quantity theory of money asserts that movements in prices are due primarily to movements in the nominal money stock. The theory is correct only in those cases where changes in real money demand are minor.

3   In countries with moderate increases in the quantity of money during the last 20 years, changes in the price level have not closely matched the rise in money because real money demand changed as a result of income growth, the changing opportunity cost of holding money, and financial innovations.

4   The inflation rate is equal to the growth rate of nominal money minus the growth in real money demand in monetary equilibrium. If

money growth persists at high levels over long periods, inflation and nominal money growth are closely related.

5   In the U.S. economy there is no close, short-term link between money growth and inflation.

6   A hyperinflation is a period of extremely rapid growth in nominal money and consequently of rates of inflation that reach 1000 percent per year and more. Hyperinflations enable us to study the effects of money supply changes almost as we would in a laboratory.

7   Budget deficits financed by money creation lead to inflation. In the United States and other industrialized countries, deficits are to a large extent debt-financed. There is no necessary close link between deficits and inflation or between deficits and nominal money growth.

8   During inflationary periods lenders require compensation for the depreciation in purchasing power of the money they lend. The nominal interest rate, or market rate, therefore will incorporate an inflation premium.

KEY TERMS

Hyperinflation   **Budget deficit financing**
Quantity theory of money   **Inflation tax**
Flight from money   **Nominal and real interest rates**

PROBLEMS

1   The accompanying table shows growth rates of money (M1) and rates of inflation for several countries in 1980. Plot these observations in a diagram and comment in light of your diagram on the statement "Inflation is always and everywhere a monetary phenomenon."

COUNTRY	MONEY GROWTH	INFLATION
United States	8.6	13.5
Canada	4.5	10.1
Japan	0.8	8.0
Germany	2.4	5.5
Switzerland	−5.4	4.1
United Kingdom	4.5	18.0
Spain	10.2	15.6
Italy	15.9	21.2

Source: International Monetary Fund, *International Financial Statistics,* May 1982.

2   The following are data for inflation and the nominal interest rate on Treasury bills in the United States.

	1975	1976	1977	1978
T-bill rate	5.8	5.0	5.3	7.2
Inflation	9.3	5.2	5.8	7.3

	1979	1980	1981
T-bill rate	10.0	11.5	14.1
Inflation	8.5	9.0	9.1

Note: Inflation rate is for GNP deflator.
Source: Economic Report of the President, 1982.

(*a*) Calculate the real interest rate for each year. (*b*) Point out where there is a sharp change in the real interest rate. What is the difference between 1975–1976 and 1980–1981?

3 Suppose there are three countries with the following information and that a 1 percent increase in income increases money demand by 1 percent.

	MONEY GROWTH, %	REAL GROWTH, %	VELOCITY GROWTH, %
Country A	15	3	0
Country B	2	5	−1
Country C	3	0	0

What are the rates of inflation in each country?

4 Consider the following data that refer to Chile in the period 1971–1974.

	NOMINAL MONEY STOCK, millions of pesos	PRICE LEVEL (Index 1971 = 100)
1971	15.8	100
1972	31.3	180
1973	122.3	813
1974	485.0	4923

Sources: International Monetary Fund, *International Financial Statistics,* various issues, and Banco Central de Chile, *Indicadores Economicos 1960–1980,* p. 117.

(*a*) Construct an index of the nominal money stock with base year 1971 = 100. (*b*) Construct an index of the real money stock with base year 1971 = 100. (*c*) Calculate the annual growth rates of nominal money and of prices. (*d*) How closely does inflation match money growth? (*e*) Why does the real money stock fall?

5 From 1890 to 1914 inflation in the United States averaged 0.7 percent per year. In what ways relevant for inflation might the U.S. economy at that rate have been different from what it is today? Which factors account for the much lower rate of inflation then?

6 In countries that experience hyperinflation, discuss why the price level rises much more than the nominal quantity of money. Is this in contradiction to the quantity theory of money?

7 What role do budget deficits and money growth play in explaining the U.S. inflation rate from year to year.

8 (*a*) Explain why nominal interest rates are likely to rise with the inflation rate. (*b*) Should the real interest rate also increase along with the inflation rate?

9 Is it possible that the inflation rate will just equal the growth rate of nominal money year after year?

10 If inflation hurts creditors, deflation (falling prices) must hurt debtors. Discuss.

11 *Extra Credit:* Inflation must be stopped before it can run away. Discuss.

Real income per person in the United States today is more than seven times the level it was in 1870. We are richer than our grandparents were,[1] and our grandchildren will be richer than we are. This growth in per capita income has happened all over the industrialized world, not just in the United States.

Table 33-1 shows growth rates of *per capita* income in 16 industrialized countries for the period since 1870. It also shows the ratio of per capita income in each country in 1980 to the level in 1870. In Japan, the fastest growing country, per capita income in 1980 was nearly 18 times its 1870 level. Even in Australia, the country where per capita income grew most slowly, the ratio is above 3.

Growth rates of *total* GDP[2] for the same 16 economies are shown in Table 33-2. Because their populations have increased rapidly relative to those of the other industrialized economies, the United States and Canada rise in the rankings in Table 33-2. Canada and Japan each have a ratio of GDP in 1980 that is more than 50 times the 1870 level. Production in each economy increased by a factor of 50 over the period. For the 16 countries taken together, the growth rate of total GDP per year was above 2.8 percent. Per capita income grew on average at more than 1.7 percent.

We will ask three questions about the growth records shown in Tables 33-1 and 33-2:

1   What does the growth in income mean?

2   What factors are responsible for the growth shown in the tables?

3   What economic policies can be used to change the growth rate?

For most of this chapter we concentrate on U.S. experience, but we also compare U.S. growth with that of other industrial economies. In Chapter 37 we look briefly at the income levels and recent growth experiences of the economies of developing countries, which contain

33

Growth and Investment

---

[1] Of course, some people whose grandparents were very rich (e.g., the Rockefellers) may be poorer than their grandparents. It is only on average that we are richer.
[2] Recall from Chapter 22 that GDP is the value of total output produced within the nation's borders. It is different from GNP because GNP subtracts the part of GDP that is earned by factors of production owned by foreigners and adds whatever income is earned from our ownership of factors of production in other countries.

TABLE 33-1

GDP PER CAPITA, 1980 AND 1870

COUNTRY	GDP PER CAPITA		RATIO OF 1980 TO 1870	ANNUAL GROWTH RATE, %
	1870	1980		
Australia	2600	8703	3.4	1.11
Austria	953	8398	8.8	2.00
Belgium	1822	9642	5.3	1.51
Canada	1201	10166	8.5	1.94
Denmark	1110	8332	7.5	1.83
Finland	780	8623	11.1	2.18
France	1216	9830	8.1	1.90
Germany	1038	9702	9.4	2.03
Italy	1079	6592	6.1	1.64
Japan	481	8559	17.8	2.62
Netherlands	1610	8569	5.3	1.52
Norway	949	10224	10.8	2.16
Sweden	807	9571	11.9	2.25
Switzerland	1525	9044	5.9	1.62
United Kingdom	1888	7428	3.9	1.25
United States of America	1502	11299	7.5	1.83

Note: Income is measured in 1980 dollars.
Sources: Based on Angus Maddison, "Phases of Capitalist Development," in R. C. O. Matthews (ed.), *Economic Growth and Resources,* vol. 2, St. Martin's, New York, 1979. Series updated from *International Financial Statistics,* various issues.

most of the world's people. Per capita incomes for most people in those economies today are well below the 1870 levels of income shown for the industrialized countries in Table 33-1.

1 WHAT DOES THE GROWTH IN INCOME MEAN?

Comparing incomes in different countries or in the same country at widely different times is difficult. The average American in 1870 lived in a small town and did not know what an automobile, a telephone, a television set, or processed cheese was. To say that average income today is seven times the average income in 1870 is to make a bold guess.

The income comparisons are based on GNP or GDP measurements. There are three problems with these measures that we will discuss before we use them.

1 GNP is a poor measure of economic output.

2 It is difficult to account for changes in the types of goods being produced.

3 There is no direct relationship between GNP and happiness.

GNP as a Measure of Economic Output

GNP mostly measures economic activity that is paid for with money. Alternative measures of the value of output produced in the economy start from GNP but try to get closer to a measure of economic welfare (MEW).[3] The two biggest adjustments are as follows:

Add to GNP the value of leisure enjoyed

[3] William Nordhaus and James Tobin of Yale University have put together a series of MEW in "Is Growth Obsolete?" National Bureau of Economic Research, *50th Anniversary Colloquium,* New York, 1972. See also Chapter 22 of this text.

TABLE 33-2
GDP IN 1980 AND 1870

COUNTRY	GDP, billions of 1980 $		RATIO OF 1980 TO 1870	ANNUAL GROWTH RATE, %
	1870	1980		
Australia	4.3	127.1	29.6	3.10
Austria	4.3	63.1	14.7	2.45
Belgium	9.1	94.8	10.4	2.13
Canada	4.5	243.3	54.1	3.66
Denmark	1.9	42.7	22.5	2.84
Finland	1.4	41.2	29.4	3.07
France	46.8	527.9	11.3	2.21
Germany	40.7	597.5	14.7	2.45
Italy	28.5	373.8	13.1	2.34
Japan	16.5	1000.1	60.6	3.76
Netherlands	5.8	121.1	20.9	2.77
Norway	1.6	41.9	26.2	2.98
Sweden	3.3	79.5	24.1	2.89
Switzerland	4.1	57.2	14.0	2.40
United Kingdom	59.0	415.7	7.0	1.77
United States of America	59.9	2573.0	43.0	3.44

Note: Income is measured in 1980 dollars.
Sources: Based on Angus Maddison, "Phases of Capitalist Development," in R. C. O. Matthews (ed.), *Economic Growth and Resources*, vol. 2, St. Martin's, New York, 1979. Updated from *International Financial Statistics*, various issues.

Subtract from GNP items such as pollution that impose costs on people

When the production of goods creates pollution, we want to deduct that from the value of the economy's output. But there is also a case for excluding other components of GNP. Should we include spending on the police and defense in GNP, for instance? The answer is that since GNP is a measure of economic activity, we want to count such spending. But for purposes of finding out how well off people are, it is better to look at their levels of *consumption* rather than at GNP. We still want to add the value of their leisure to consumption and subtract pollution.

How would these adjustments affect comparisons, such as those in Table 33-1, between income in 1870 and income in 1980? Leisure has certainly increased a lot since 1870. The workweek then was above 60 hours; now it is less than 40. If people sleep 8 hours a day, there are 112 hours per week available for other activities. Work used to take up more than half that time; now it takes up about a third. The adjustment for leisure would increase the *amount* by which economic output has risen since 1870, but it would not increase the ratio of output in 1980 to that in 1870. The reason is that leisure has clearly not increased by a factor of 7, which is the factor by which income per capita for the United States rose, as shown in Table 33-1.

We do not know how much pollution has changed since 1870. Certainly little attention was paid then to preventing pollution. But industrial processes were simpler and output was smaller, and so less waste was being created to be dumped into the air or the rivers. Thus we can guess that pollution may have risen more than sevenfold. Thus both the leisure correction and the pollution correction would reduce the ratio of 1980 income to 1870 income if we recalculated Table 33-1.

Finally, if we based the comparison on consumption instead of GDP, we would also reduce the ratio for 1980 relative to 1870. Consumption has fallen as a percentage of GDP. This is not because households have reduced the ratio of consumption to *disposable income*. Rather, it is because the ratio of disposable income to GDP has fallen. The rise of government has meant that more of income is taken in taxes, and so disposable income—and therefore consumption—has fallen as a percentage of GDP.

Thus all three adjustments—for leisure, pollution, and consumption—would reduce the sevenfold ratio in Table 33-1 to a lower figure, perhaps four or five. But these are still large numbers.

The Changing Composition of Production

The biggest conceptual difficulty in measuring GNP over long periods is finding a way to account for new goods. Many, if not most, of the goods we consume today did not exist 110 years ago. How can we compare the value of production today with that in 1870? When we think about it, we realize there can be no good way. In practice the comparisons are made by building up year by year comparisons.

There is no great error in comparing real GNP today with real GNP last year. If a new good has been invented, we can usually figure out roughly what it is worth compared with the goods it replaces, because both are sold in the market at the same time. We can thus compare GNP for successive years. Then the short-term comparisons are linked together to make a long series of comparisons. At each intermediate

step, there are few new goods creating difficulties of comparison. The comparisons from year to year are quite accurate, but over a century the errors can add up to substantial amounts. Thus we have to treat the long-term comparisons skeptically.

GDP as a Measure of Happiness

Even without changes in the types of goods being produced, and even if we adjust GNP or GDP for leisure, pollution, and so forth, we still will not necessarily have a measure of happiness. Man does not live by bread alone. In less elegant terms, a person's happiness is not dependent solely on consumption of goods.

This said, it is hard to believe that most people would give up today's standard of living for that of 1870. Material goods are not everything, but they help. Man does not live by bread alone, but he does not live without any bread. The claim that material goods do not make people better off is made mainly by those who already have the goods. Movements in which people try to go back to a simpler life with fewer possessions have not had much success. The burning desire of developing countries to increase their GNPs is further evidence that people want more goods.

Happiness and the Distribution of Income

We shall be using GNP and GDP measures to compare average income levels. But a given average level of income is consistent with very different distributions of income. Maybe almost everyone has close to the average income in a country such as Sweden, or most of the income may be in the hands of a very small part of the population, as in Brazil. The average levels of income for the two countries partially conceal these differences.

Over long periods, since the nineteenth century, the distribution of income has probably become more equal in the industrialized countries. Thus for the median person—the person in the middle of the income distribution[4]—income has probably risen faster than the averages shown in Table 33-1 suggest.

There is another sense in which the distribution of income matters. People may worry about their relative position in society rather than the absolute level. A person earning $2000 per year (measured in 1980 dollars) in 1870 would have had an above-average income and been quite happy about his position in life. A person with exactly the same level of income today would be a lot less happy.

This fact again reminds us that we cannot use GNP as a good indicator of how happy people are. Indeed, does it make sense to say someone is seven times happier than someone else? How do we know? Thus we want to be sure what the GNP and GDP comparisons mean. They tell us roughly the amounts of goods available to people in different periods and in different places. More is better, but we do not know how much happier people are when they get more goods.

Other Indicators of Welfare   In comparing living standards across long periods of time, we can look at statistics other than GNP. For instance, life expectancy has increased markedly since the nineteenth century. At birth in 1870, a male child in the United States had a life expectancy of about 42 years; today a male's life expectancy at birth is 70 years. For females, life expectancy at birth has risen from about 42.5 years to 77.5

years. Most of this increase has come from the decrease in childhood deaths.

How Long Can It Have Been Going On?

Simple arithmetic shows that the growth in incomes seen in Tables 33-1 and 33-2 cannot have been going on for more than a few centuries. Income would have had to start at impossibly low levels if growth had gone on at rates like those shown in Table 33-1 for many centuries.

For example, consider one of the slower growing countries, such as the United Kingdom, in which per capita income in 1870 was $1888 (in 1980 dollars). Over 100 years, income growing at the U.K. rate of 1.25 percent per year increases by a factor of 3.5. Thus going back from 1870 to 1770, income would have had to start in 1770 at $539 ($1888/3.5) for it to have reached $1888 in 1870 by growing at 1.25 percent per year. Going back another 100 years, to 1670, income per person would have had to start at $154 ($539/3.5) for it to reach $539 in 1770 by growing at that rate.

It is already difficult to believe that people could have lived on less than $154 per year,[5] and so income probably could not have grown in the United Kingdom by 1.25 percent per year from as early as 1670. But if it had, where would income have had to be in 1570? The answer is around $44, which is impossible to believe.

Thus the growth in per capita income shown in Table 33-1—which has become accepted and expected as part of the normal development of the economy—is historically exceptional. The beginnings of growth at modern rates are associated with industrialization, or the process in which produc-

---

[4] The person in the middle of a distribution is known as the *median* person. If we line up 99 people in order of increasing height, the median height is that of the fiftieth person in the line. Median income is sometimes used as a measure of average income, since it is more representative of what the average person earns than average income is.

[5] There are studies of how cheaply it is possible to live —survive—in the United States today. It is possible to survive for less than $2000 per year on a diet heavy in beans and milk powder. Clothing and shelter have to be added, and so survival costs come out to well above $2000 per year.

tion uses machinery intensively and relies less and less on individual craftsmen and on animal sources of power. Modern rates of growth are also associated with spectacular changes in technology. We come back to industrialization and new knowledge as explanations for growth later in this chapter.

2 THE PRODUCTION FUNCTION AND GROWTH

To understand growth, we start from the important idea of a production function, which can be written as

Output = f (capital, labor, land, raw materials, technical knowledge)   (1)

> The *production function* gives the maximum amount of output that can be produced using any specified amounts or inputs, or factors of production (capital, labor, land, and raw materials).

Given the quantities of factors of production being used, the amount of output that can be produced depends on the technical knowledge available to producers.

Growth results from increases in the quantities of factors of production and from improvements in technical knowledge. We first discuss the roles of the factors of production and of technology in growth. Then we examine estimates of the relative importance of the growth of the different factor inputs and of improvements in technology in accounting for growth in the United States and other industrialized countries.

Capital

Capital is the machinery, buildings, and inventories of produced goods that are used in production. The stock of houses is included in the capital stock since people living in houses benefit from the services (of shelter and comfort) provided by the houses.

The composition of the U.S. capital stock is shown in Table 33-3. The two largest components are the plant and equip-

TABLE 33-3

CAPITAL STOCK, UNITED STATES, 1980

	BILLIONS OF $
Plant and equipment	2562
Residential structures	2466
Inventories	785
Total	5813
Consumer durables	995
Total	6808

Source: Federal Reserve Board of Governors, *Balance Sheets for United States Economy,* 1981.

ment used by firms and the housing stock. The part of the capital stock that contributes to GNP as measured came to almost $6 trillion in 1980. This is about double the level of GNP. In addition, there was nearly $1 trillion in consumer durables such as cars, refrigerators, and television sets.[6]

Plant and equipment—factory buildings and offices and machinery—are factors of production because workers equipped with more machinery can produce more goods. Inventories also contribute to production. If firms do not have inventories or raw materials on hand, production cannot proceed smoothly; if a retail store runs out of inventories, customers have to waste time going elsewhere to shop. The economy operates less efficiently if inventories are too low.

Labor

Increases in labor input increase production. Part of the growth of *total* output of the industrialized economies recorded in Table 33-2 comes from the increase in the total

---

[6] These do not contribute to *measured* GNP because GNP as measured does not attribute a flow of services to consumer durables in the same way as it does for housing, though of course it should do so.

In thinking about economywide numbers, it is always useful to reduce them to per person terms. Consumer durables worth $995 billion in 1980 are equivalent to about $4400 per person in that year. That seems like a reasonable number for the average value of cars, stereos, etc., owned in the economy.

amount of raw labor input—increased total hours of work—the economies have had in the past century. However, the average workweek has fallen over the past century. Thus the increases in *per capita* output shown in Table 33-1 cannot be a result of increased hours of work.

Human Capital   Human capital is the skill and knowledge embodied in the minds and hands of the population. As a result of increasing levels of formal education and on-the-job experience, the amount of human capital per worker increases over time. The quality of the labor input has thus increased over the past century even as the average workweek has fallen.

The average level of formal education has risen dramatically over the past century. In 1870 only 2 percent of 17-year-olds were high school graduates; by 1980 more than two-thirds were high school graduates. The expansion of postschool education has been equally impressive. The stock of human capital has increased not only through formal schooling but also through on-the-job training and the experience of the labor force in working with modern sophisticated machinery.

The importance of the skill level of the labor force is brought out by the speed with which western Europe was able to recover from World War II devastation when the United States provided aid through the *Marshall Plan*. The Marshall Plan helped the west European economies rebuild their stocks of physical capital. Together with the human capital already in those economies, the new capital rapidly increased production levels.

Land

The amount of land available for production is especially important in an agricultural economy. A densely settled agricultural society in which each person has barely enough land to grow the food needed to support a family is a poor society. When agriculture dominated economic life—as it did before the industrial revolution and as it still does in many developing economies—the amount and quality of land available per person was a major determinant of the standard of living.

Malthus, Land, and Population   Economists of the early nineteenth century, living in a largely agricultural economy, worried very much about the limited supply of land available to the economy. Because the supply of land could not be expanded, they saw land as the limit on the growth of the economy. Their vision was that as population grew, more people would be living off the same land, which could not expand food production rapidly. Standards of living would fall, and starvation would eventually stop future population growth.

The most famous scenario was painted by the Reverend Thomas Malthus in 1798. He argued that population tended to grow geometrically, in a series like 2, 4, 8, 16. But there were diminishing returns in the production of food. With each additional worker adding less to output than the previous one, agricultural output, Malthus believed, would go up only arithmetically in a series like 1, 2, 3, 4, while population increased geometrically. The amount of food per person falls with the size of the population in Malthus's scheme. Eventually the pressure of population on the food supply becomes too great, there is starvation, and population falls.

This Malthusian view of the world gives important insights into the problems of some developing countries. With population growing fast and agricultural output growing less quickly, they face the risk of famine. Such countries may be caught in a *Malthusian trap*. If agricultural output rises, people become healthier, and popula-

FIGURE 33-1   THE MALTHUSIAN TRAP. Per capita food production declines as the size of the population increases, because of diminishing returns. A small population produces a food surplus and grows, as shown by the arrows to the left of N^*, until it reaches the equilibrium population. A large population cannot produce enough food to feed itself. There is therefore famine, and population declines as shown by the arrows to the right of N^*. At point E, per capita food production is just large enough for survival. Thus N^* is the equilibrium population, with the economy stuck in the Malthusian trap.

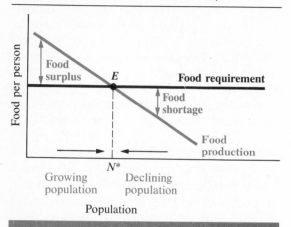

tion begins to grow. But then pressure on the available land reduces living standards back to the starvation level.

The Malthusian trap is shown in Figure 33-1. When population is small, food output per person is high, and population grows. The growth of population drives food output per person to the survival level. If population exceeds the level N^*, at which it just survives, there is starvation, and population falls back to N^*.

The Malthusian scenario turned out to be wrong for most countries. Malthus underestimated the huge increases in the productivity of agriculture that took place in the nineteenth century and continue today. There may indeed have been diminishing returns in the production of food, but they were outweighed by the improvements in technology, which made it possible for countries to feed themselves even as popu-

lations grew and the number of workers on farms declined.

Land is less important in highly industrialized economies; indeed, industry typically does not want to spread itself out as broadly as possible over the available land. Rather, there are benefits from being close to other firms. Nonetheless, given the quantities of other factors of production being used, the addition of 1 acre of land will lead to more output in the economy. The value of that output is related to the rental rate people are willing to pay for the use of the land, which depends very much on where the land is.

The total value of land in the United States in 1980 was $1974 billion. This is less than the value of plant and equipment or of the housing stock. It is about two-thirds of GNP and came to $8700 per person in 1980.

Raw Materials

The more raw materials that are used, the more output that is produced, given the quantities of other inputs. Thus raw materials are also a factor of production. It may seem that there should be very little substitution possible between raw materials and other factors of production. After all, doesn't it take a certain amount of iron and coal to produce a ton of steel?

Actually there is considerable opportunity for substituting other factors of production for raw materials. More efficient machinery (meaning more capital) or more careful methods of production (meaning more labor) make it possible to produce the same level of output using fewer raw materials. The prime example is the use of energy in the developed economies in the seventies. Since 1971 the amount of energy used in the industrialized economies has dropped 20 percent relative to GNP. The drop reflects the substitution of capital, in the form of more energy-efficient machinery, for energy and also the substitution of labor for energy—the 55 mph speed limit saves gasoline by making drivers stay on the road longer.

Raw Materials and Depletable Resources
Some raw materials, such as wood, are *renewable*. The supply of wood can be increased by planting and cutting down trees. Other raw materials, such as oil, coal, and copper, are *depletable*. The use of these resources reduces the amount that can potentially be used in the future.

The fact that there is only so much of a depletable resource available leads to fears that the world will run out of resources and that their disappearance will be the ultimate limit on growth. With a little imagination the lights can be seen going out as the last drop of fuel is burned.

The energy crisis of the seventies dramatized the depletable resource problem.[7] During the seventies there were two major oil shocks, one in 1973–1974 and the other in 1979–1980. In each case the price of imported oil more than doubled. In the United States concern over energy has centered on the supply of oil, because although U.S. reserves of oil are small—less than 10 years consumption—those of coal are enormous—several hundred years of consumption at current rates.

If depletable resources have been running out and thereby reducing economic growth, their prices should have been rising over time. The rising prices reflect the increasing scarcity and increased expense of extracting the resources: the digging of deeper mines, for instance, or the shift to offshore drilling for oil, which is more expensive than the exploitation of earlier

sources of supply. For most depletable resources, though, rates of discovery and improvements in methods of extraction have kept pace with use so that the prices of the resources have not risen much over time.

Figure 33-2 shows the prices of two depletable resources—coal and copper—every tenth year since 1800. The prices are shown relative to the wholesale, or producers', price index. The picture for the two commodities is mixed but certainly does not show steadily rising prices for each. The relative price of copper was lower in 1979 than in 1800, meaning that copper was becoming relatively less scarce over this period. The relative price of coal, though, was by 1979 at its highest level since 1800. Even here there is no pattern of a steadily increasing relative price of coal. Rather, the price has fluctuated over the years, reaching a minimum in 1870. From 1950 to 1970 there was no increase, and the entire post-World War II rise in price took place in the seventies.

What has kept the relative price from rising steadily over time? There are three factors. First, new discoveries of coal sources around the world increase the known supply and thereby tend to reduce the price. Second, technical progress takes place; it both increases the efficiency with which coal is used and develops alternative sources of energy. Finally, *substitutes* for coal, such as oil and gas or nuclear energy, are developed.

The price at which alternatives are available limits the price that will be paid for a particular source of energy. For coal and other depletable energy sources, the alternative that is essentially renewable is nuclear energy. The price of nuclear energy to generate electricity is high. But the price is even higher for such uses as powering automobiles, since it would be necessary to develop an electric automobile before nuclear energy could replace gasoline.

The question for economic growth is

---

[7] The energy crisis dramatized the problem but did not start the interest in it. Already in 1972 a widely publicized report, financed by the Club of Rome, entitled *The Limits to Growth* argued that economic growth would have to stop as the world ran out of depletable resources, which the report saw happening within 100 years.

FIGURE 33-2 REAL PRICES OF ANTHRACITE COAL AND COPPER, 1800–1979.
1970 = 100. (Source: *Historical Statistics of the United States* for data through 1970;
Energy Information Administration; *Statistical Abstract of the United States, 1980.*)

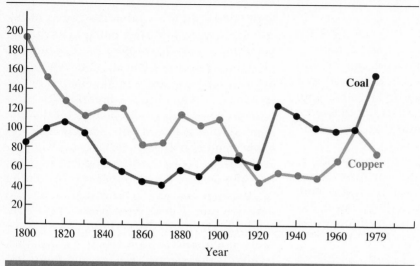

whether depletable resources have restricted or will restrict growth. There is little evidence that the cost of using raw materials increased in the period up to 1973 and no evidence that raw materials scarcities reduced growth significantly. Since 1973, the industrialized economies have all grown more slowly than before. Later in this chapter we shall discuss the role of the energy crisis in causing that slower growth.

The question of whether technical progress and the use of substitutes for depletable resources will make it possible to avoid the limits to growth will be answered convincingly only in the future. But past history gives us grounds for optimism. Technology and new discoveries have always come through in the past.

Contributions of Each Factor

How much do increases in the quantities of factors of production contribute to output? The amount contributed to production by 1 more unit of any factor is equal to the marginal product of that factor. The contribu-

tion of 1 more unit of labor is its marginal product, which is in turn equal to the wage it earns; the contribution of capital is the marginal product of capital, typically estimated to be about 10–12 percent in the United States at present. The marginal product of land is equal to the rental rate that has to be paid for the land. The marginal product of a unit of raw material is equal to the price of the raw material that is used up.[8]

Economies of Scale How do the contributions add up? For instance, what would happen if the economy somehow succeeded in doubling its inputs of all factors of production? Would output go up by a factor of 2, more than 2, or less than 2?

---

[8] All this is in accordance with the microeconomics of the demand for factors of production, which says that factors of production are used up to the point where they are paid an amount equal to the value of their marginal product. Turning this around, we can tell the value of their marginal product, which is what they contribute to output, from the amount they are paid.

There are *economies of scale* if output more than doubles when inputs double. If output doubles when all inputs double, there are *constant returns to scale*; if output less than doubles when all inputs double, there are *diseconomies of scale,* or *decreasing returns to scale.*

There is no way of knowing in general whether there are economies or diseconomies of scale in any particular economy. Frequently, economists assume there are constant returns to scale. There are certainly examples where bigger is better, such as in the building of oil tankers, where within certain ranges of capacity there are economies of scale. But there is no general presumption that big is better. Many of the serious mistakes of development policy in the developing countries have been made because of the belief that bigger is necessarily better, as, for instance, in the building of giant steel mills.

The extent to which economies of scale may or may not have been important in the growth of the U.S. economy is a question for empirical research, to which we turn now.

3 TECHNICAL KNOWLEDGE

At any given time, a society has a stock of knowledge about ways of producing goods. The knowledge takes many forms. Some of it is written down in books, journals, and blueprints; some is recorded in patents; and much has been acquired by experience and is not written down. Watch a skilled worker doing a job, and you realize that much knowledge is contained in the experience of the labor force.

Invention and innovation are two aspects of the development of technical knowledge. *Invention* is the discovery of new knowledge; *innovation* is the development of methods for applying existing knowledge. The distinction is not watertight. In developing methods of applying existing knowledge, it is often necessary to develop new knowledge.

Inventions

Spectacular changes in technical knowledge are associated with major inventions. Of these, the most important in the process of economic growth was the discovery of ways of generating more power than humans alone can generate. The use of animals is very ancient. But the generation of power from machinery, with fossil fuels as the energy source, distinguishes the industrial age from earlier periods.

We can see the role of inventions by looking around at the products we use or by thinking about the technological advances that make them possible. In transportation, railroads replaced animals and steamships replaced sails; then came the automobile and the airplane. The telegraph made long-distance rapid communication possible in the mid-nineteenth century; then came the telephone and radio. Radio and television, vacuum cleaners, and washing machines make life more pleasant or more easy. All rely on the availability of household electricity. Artificial fibers and materials including plastics are everywhere. Computers do calculations that were impossible only 30 years ago. Underlying the bringing of products to market are engineering improvements that transform small-scale experimental results to practical large-scale production techniques. And the engineering achievements were often preceded by basic scientific progress in understanding natural processes.

In thinking about inventions, we tend to focus very much on industrial products. But technical progress in agriculture has been essential to growth. So long as agriculture provided enough only for the farmer's family, there was no prospect of the development of industrial economies. Productivity gains in agriculture have been remarkable and indeed continue to be remarkable. In 1980 only 2 percent of the U.S. labor force was employed in agriculture; 70 percent of the labor force was employed in agriculture 150 years ago. In the last 50 years output per person employed in agriculture has grown fivefold.

These gains in agricultural productivity are in large part a result of industrial development: the replacement of animal power by machines, and industrial production of fertilizers. They also reflect the development of new varieties of hybrid seeds.

Embodiment of Knowledge in Capital Inventions and innovation are very important in the growth process. But typically the major inventions have to be embodied in capital, physical and human, before they have effects on production. After an invention is made and engineers figure out how to put it to productive use, investment in new machinery is necessary.

Indeed, some broad theories of economic growth associate particular eras of spectacular development with particular inventions and bursts of investment. The nineteenth century was the era of the railroad; the 1920s, the era of the automobile, the radio, and other household goods; the 1950s, the age of television; and the 1970s, the age of the microchip.

Learning by Doing Improvements in technical knowledge result not only from inventions but also from on-the-job experience. Workers get better at doing a job the more often they do it. The most famous example is known as the Horndal effect, after a Swedish steelworks which was built in 1835–1836 and then was maintained in almost exactly the same condition for the next 15 years. There were no changes in the machinery in the factory or in the size of the labor force. Over that period, output per worker hour in the factory rose about 2 per-

cent per year. Another famous example is the productivity of workers in assembling airplanes; the length of time taken to assemble a frame decreases, the more planes that have already been put together. The rate of learning by doing is typically fastest at the beginning and then slows down.

Systemwide Interactions In the process of growth, one development leads to another. To quote Professor David Landes of Harvard, describing the industrial revolution of the late eighteenth century and the nineteenth century in Britain,

> Change begat change. . . . A cheap supply of coal proved a godsend to the iron industry, which was stifling for lack of fuel. In the meantime, the invention and diffusion of machinery in the textile manufacture and other industries created a new demand for energy, hence for coal and steam engines; and these engines, and the machines themselves, had a voracious appetite for iron, which called for further coal and power. . . .[9]

A similar description fits the development of the automobile industry in this century.

Motivation for Invention and Innovation

How does technical change come about? The driving forces are the profit motive, curiosity, and laziness ("There must be an easier way to do this."). "Build a better mousetrap, and the world will beat a path to your door" explains the benefits of innovation to the innovator. Edwin Land of Polaroid, Henry Ford, and Steven Jobs of Apple Computer had the world beat a path to their doors—though, to be sure, the world needs lots of encouragement in the form of good marketing of the product even after the invention has been made.

---

[9] David S. Landes, *The Unbound Prometheus: Technical Change and Industrial Development in Western Europe from 1750 to the Present,* Cambridge University Press, London, 1969, pp. 2–3.

Some inventions are made by scientists working in universities or working for fixed salaries in research divisions of corporations. Some innovation comes from suggestions of workers on the factory floor. There are the same motivations: curiosity, the desire to do a good job, and the financial motive of hoping to get ahead.

Research and Development

What determines the amount of technical change? As with any economic activity, the results depend in large part on the resources devoted to the activity. Research and development spending is a measure of the resources being devoted by the economy to the development of changes in knowledge and technology. Total spending on research and development (R&D) in the United States has been above 2 percent of GNP in recent years.

The outcome of R&D spending is uncertain. Where basic knowledge is involved, researchers are never certain what, if anything, they will discover. Sometimes discoveries are made by accident, though the accidents come to those who have minds that can recognize the significance of what they see. Penicillin is the most famous of these accidental discoveries. In cases of development, where known methods are applied, the results of R&D spending are less uncertain.

Spending on R&D is like an investment in capital. The resources have to be committed before the outcome is known, and there is risk about the return. In the case of R&D there is an additional complication in that the ability to protect the gains from the investment has to be taken into account. If one firm invents a better mousetrap and everyone else copies it, the investing firm has less incentive to invest than it would if it got the return from its invention.

The *patent system* is designed to provide incentives for invention by promising the inventors that they will get the returns from their investment in discovering new knowledge for a period of 17 years. But there is a problem even with patents. Once knowledge has been created, society is better off if that knowledge is available to everyone, and no one has temporary monopoly on the right to use the knowledge. Patents strike a compromise by offering the right to monopoly use of knowledge for a time as encouragement to develop new knowledge.

In microeconomic terms, there is an *externality* when the costs or benefits of an action are not borne by the person carrying it out. If an invention were to become freely available as soon as it was made, the benefits would not accrue to the person responsible for the invention, and there would be externalities. In such circumstances, the price system does not give the right signals for the efficient allocation of resources.

There is therefore an argument that basic research should be financed by the government, with the knowledge becoming freely available as soon as it is discovered. Government laboratories exist in many countries; government provides research grants to both universities and private firms for the development of new knowledge.

International Comparisons　The percentage of GNP devoted to R&D in the United States has fallen since the sixties. Comparative data for the United States and other countries are shown in Table 33-4. Aside from the Soviet Union, the United States still spends as large a part of GNP on R&D as any other large country. But when defense R&D spending is removed, the United States comes third in the rankings, with Germany in the lead in 1976. This is indeed a change since the sixties. Of course, because U.S. GNP is larger than that of other countries, the United States still spends more than any other country on

R&D SPENDING AS A PERCENTAGE OF GNP

	TOTAL		EXCLUDING DEFENSE	
COUNTRY	1967	1977	1967	1976
France	2.1	1.8	1.6	1.5
Germany	2.0	2.3	1.8	2.2
Japan	1.5	1.9	1.5	1.9
United Kingdom	2.3	—	1.7	1.5
Soviet Union	2.9	3.5	—	—
United States	2.9	2.3	1.9	1.6

Source: Congressional Budget Office, *The Productivity Problem: Alternatives for Action,* January 1981, pp. 71, 72.

R&D, even excluding defense-related R&D spending.

Financing of U.S. R&D spending is split about evenly between the government and the private sector. Government-financed R&D goes mostly for defense, but there is some government financing of non-defense R&D.

The Rate of Return to R&D Spending Studies of R&D spending show very high rates of return, with 30 percent as typical for the firm doing the R&D.[10] Rates of return to society as a whole are estimated to be even higher. However, rates of return to defense-related R&D are lower.

With such high rates of return, the natural question is, Why don't firms do more R&D? Part of the answer is that the return is very uncertain, as is the ability of the inventor to capture the return.

4   U.S. GROWTH

We have now reviewed the factors that can produce growth: increases in factor inputs,

[10] For a summary of some of the studies, see M. Ishag Nadiri, "Contributions and Determinants of Research and Development Expenditures in the U.S. Manufacturing Industries," in George M. von Furstenberg (ed.), *Capital, Efficiency, and Growth*, Ballinger, Cambridge, Mass., 1980.

economies of scale, and technical change. The next question is, How much of U.S. growth and that of other countries is accounted for by the different possibilities? Is growth largely a matter of increasing capital, is it mainly technical progress, or is it a little bit of everything? The answer is that growth results from the contributions of all factors but that technical change or improvement is particularly important.

Edward F. Denison made one of the classic studies of the sources of U.S. growth. His conclusions on the sources of U.S. growth in the period 1929–1969 are summarized in Table 33-5. Denison attributes about one-third of growth over that period to increases in labor input; capital growth accounted for about one-seventh (0.50 percent out of 3.41 percent total). The remaining 1.59 percent was accounted for mainly by increased knowledge. He also suggests some growth is due to economies of scale. The entry "resource allocation," accounting for about one-tenth of growth (0.30 percent out of 3.41 percent), reflects the reallocation of factors from agriculture to industry.

The essential conclusions from Denison's study have also been reached by others. Improvements in knowledge are an

SOURCES OF GROWTH OF TOTAL NATIONAL INCOME, 1929–1969

SOURCE OF GROWTH	GROWTH RATE, % per annum
Total factor input: Labor: 1.32 Capital: 0.50	1.82
Output per unit of input: Knowledge: 0.92 Resource allocation: 0.30 Economies of scale: 0.36 Other: 0.01	1.59
National income	3.41

Source: E. Denison, *Accounting for United States Economic Growth 1929–1969*, The Brookings Institution, Washington, D.C., 1974, p. 127.

TABLE 33-6

SOURCES OF GROWTH, UNITED STATES, 1960–1979

	1960–1973, %	1973–1979, %
Overall growth rate of real gross business product	4.4	2.9
Labor input	1.3	1.8
Increase in output per unit of labor input (labor productivity)	3.1	1.1
Factors accounting for increase in labor productivity:		
Increase in capital input	1.2	0.5
Improved labor quality owing to education	0.4	0.7
Changes in composition of labor force and reallocation of labor	−0.1	−0.3
Economies of scale	0.4	0.3
Government regulation	−0.1	−0.4
Advances in knowledge	0.7	0.1
Other	0.6	0.3

Note: Details may not add to totals because of rounding.
Source: Based on John W. Kendrick, "International Comparisons of Recent Productivity Trends," in W. Fellner (ed.), *Essays in Contemporary Economic Problems,* American Enterprise Institute, 1981–1982 edition, Tables 1 and 7.

important source of growth, and capital growth accounts for a significant but certainly not dominant part of growth.

The Recent Productivity Slowdown

Table 33-6 presents the sources of growth in the United States for the periods 1960–1973 and 1973–1979.[11] There are two noteworthy features. First, the rate of growth slowed substantially between the two periods. Second, most of the slowdown resulted from a fall in the rate of increase of labor *productivity*, which is defined as the part of growth not resulting from increases in the input of labor. These two characteristics apply to all the industrialized economies since 1973.

To what is the reduction in growth and particularly in productivity growth due? The data analyzed by John Kendrick of George Washington University give a variety of explanations. First, the rate of increase of the capital stock decreased sharply. Capital accounted for 1.2 percent of growth in the earlier period and only 0.5 percent in the later period. The labor supply grew more rapidly in the later period.

The major remaining difference in productivity growth arises from two sources. First, there was a large fall in the contribution of advances in knowledge. Second, there was a substantial increase in the amount of government regulation of the economy in the seventies, in the form of pollution controls, for instance, to which Kendrick assigns part of the blame for the slower rate of productivity increase. Among the "other" factors accounting for lower productivity increase in the seventies was the higher price of oil.

The major difficulty of the economy in the seventies was the fall in the rate of increase of productivity. Table 33-6 shows that in the period to 1973 output per worker hour was increasing on average at a rate of 3.1 percent (4.4 − 1.3 percent). In the period 1973–1979 the rate of increase was

---

[11] The table refers not to GNP but to that part of GNP produced by the business sector, which comes to about 85 percent of total GNP.

only 1.1 percent (2.9 − 1.8 percent) on average. This tremendous decrease in the rate at which output per worker and average income increased is probably the single most important reason people felt the economy had gone out of control in the seventies.

Kendrick's conclusion is that there is no one factor that deserves all the blame. Certainly he puts some blame on government regulation and some on the decline in investment in capital. But part of the blame comes from the slowdown in advancing knowledge, which is difficult to control. However, there is a sense in which Table 33-6 is encouraging. Because there are many different sources of the productivity slowdown, it appears that a variety of policy measures that affect many different aspects of the economy may be able to increase productivity growth again.

The Role of Higher Energy Prices   The role of the higher price of oil in reducing productivity growth in the seventies is still being debated. The direct effect of the oil-price increase and consequent reduction in oil use accounted for at most 0.3 percent of the fall in growth. But the oil-price increase may have reduced productivity growth in other ways. First, it could have diverted R&D efforts toward attempts to save energy and thus helped account for the fall of 0.6 percent in advances in knowledge. It is also possible that the higher energy prices made part of the capital stock uneconomical to use because the capital used too much fuel. Neither of these possibilities has been shown beyond doubt to have happened, but the circumstantial evidence is strong that the energy crisis had a major role in reducing productivity growth in the seventies. The strongest evidence is the timing of the fall in productivity growth, which came soon after the rise in oil prices in the United States as well as other industrial economies around the world.

The Seventies in Longer-Run Perspective

The period 1973–1979 looks very poor indeed in comparison with 1960–1973 in Table 33-6. But there is another perspective, which is summarized in Table 33-7. We can ask how the period looks in comparison with the very long-run averages for the United States which we discussed at the beginning of this chapter. The answer is that the period since 1973 was, by historical standards, one of only slightly less than average per capita growth. Indeed, since 1980 was a recession year and 1973 a boom year, the 1973–1980 growth rate mixes in the effects of the trade cycle along with changes in the growth rate of income on average over the cycle.[12] Taking that into account, we can say that per capita GDP in the period 1973–1980 grew at essentially the average historical rate.

By contrast, the period 1960–1973 stands out as one of extraordinary growth by historical standards for the United States. If income started out at the same level in two countries and then grew 3.17 percent in one and 1.83 percent in the other, the level in the first country would be nearly four times that in the second after 100 years. The differences shown in Table 33-7 thus are very large indeed from the long-run view.

Other Countries   The picture in all the major industrialized economies is much the same as that for the United States. They all experienced large reductions in the aggregate growth rate in the seventies, and all grew more rapidly in the 1960–1973 period than they did over the long-run period 1870–1980.

What accounted for the fall in the rate of

---

[12] The same problem leads to an overstatement of the underlying growth rate of 1960–1973. There was a recession in 1960, and 1973 was a boom year. Thus the average growth rate over the period 1960–1973 exaggerates the cyclically adjusted growth rate.

TABLE 33-7
THE POST-WORLD WAR II PERIOD IN HISTORICAL PERSPECTIVE, UNITED STATES

	GROWTH RATE OF REAL PER CAPITA GDP, % per annum	GROWTH RATE OF REAL TOTAL GDP, % per annum
1870–1980	1.83	3.44
1950–1980	2.40	3.41
1960–1973	3.17	4.18
1973–1980	1.57	2.39

Sources: For 1870–1980, see Tables 35-1 and 35-2. For other data, see *Economic Report of the President, 1981*, Tables B-10 and B-26.

growth in the industrialized economies other than the United States after 1973? The answer is the same as for the United States: a little bit of everything, in varying proportions, with the rise in the price of energy in the background accounting for several of those effects.

5 POLICY AND THE ROLE OF CAPITAL

The large and rapid reduction in the rate of growth of the industrialized economies has led to a search for policies to reverse the reductions and get the large economies moving again. Having said this, it is also a good idea to remember that the large industrialized economies have even in the last few years not been doing much worse than they did on average over the last century. The question being asked is whether the extraordinary growth of 1960–1973 can be restored or whether it was good while it lasted but was not the sort of growth any country has a right to expect over long periods.

The main concern is with rising living standards, and so for most countries there is no wish to increase growth by increasing the rate of population growth and thus the rate of increase of the labor force. There are exceptions. Countries that seek military strength also encourage population growth. But the focus in the growth debate has not been on increasing the number of workers as much as it has been on capital and technical change.

The Role of Capital

How much can be expected of capital growth as a means of increasing the growth rate of output? Studies of the rate of return to capital in the United States show it to be about 12 percent for the economy as a whole. That means a dollar invested today will return 12 cents per year (after adjusting for inflation) in later years. Equivalently, if 1 percent of GNP is added to the capital stock, output next year should be higher by 0.12 percent of GNP. Thus if 4 percent of GNP is added to investment, output will be higher by about 0.5 percent of GNP.

Given that the GNP growth rate fell 1.5 percent in the last half of the seventies, it seems that investment could do a lot to improve the situation, taking us back toward the better growth performance of the sixties. But first we have to ask how large 4 percent of GNP is. The answer is that it would take a lot to get the share of investment in GNP to rise 4 percent. Gross investment in plant and equipment is now about 10 to 12 percent of GNP. Thus an increase equal to 4 percent of GNP means increasing investment by nearly 40 percent. This is a very large increase that would be difficult to achieve.

The message on investment, then, is mixed. There is no doubt that increased investment increases the economy's growth rate, but it would take a lot of investment to get the growth rate to increase rapidly. That certainly does not mean that policies to encourage investment are wrong or would not increase growth. It does mean, though, that the role of investment should not be exaggerated. More investment would increase growth, but it is not a magical process.

Encouraging Technical Progress

Since so much of economic growth has resulted from causes other than capital and labor growth, and since the rate of return to R&D spending is so high, shouldn't it be possible to increase growth markedly by encouraging the development of new technical knowledge and innovation? Surely government programs aimed at encouraging research and development will have dramatic payoffs?

There are two different types of policy issues here. First, there are government-created impediments to economic growth, such as the increased regulations shown in Table 33-6 as reducing the growth rate in 1973–1979 by 0.3 percent relative to the earlier period. Such impediments to growth can be removed or reduced through changes in regulations. For instance, rather than imposing absolute standards for pollution control that apply to all factories, it is better to charge firms for the amount of pollutants they emit. Then the firms that can most cheaply reduce pollution will do so more than firms for which control of pollution is expensive. The economy will be able to obtain a given reduction in pollution more efficiently this way than it would if all firms had to meet the same standards. In countless other ways, government could remove regulations that slow down growth.

Second, the government can actively encourage R&D. There is already considerable incentive for R&D activity. The most important incentive is that R&D spending by firms receives better tax treatment than other investment spending. It would also be possible to provide tax credits for R&D spending and thereby provide more encouragement by subsidizing R&D.

There is one other big question. If R&D spending is such a good thing, why don't we have more of it already? Why should the government subsidize and support R&D spending when the private rate of return to R&D is so high? The case for government

support arises from the difficulty for investing firms of protecting the knowledge they gain from R&D and thus capturing the fruits of their investment. This is more difficult for basic research that has no immediate applications than for applied research, suggesting a definite need for government funding of basic research. The difficulties that firms have in capturing the returns on their R&D spending—and the conflict between their interests in doing so and the desirability of diffusion of the knowledge once it exists—make the case for some government support of R&D and possibly for more government support than now exists.

How much growth can be expected from increases in R&D spending? Suppose that the rate of return is 30 percent and that the share of GNP going to R&D is increased by 2 percent, from about 2 percent to 4 percent. This would produce an increase in GNP of 0.6 percent (30 percent of 2 percent), which is substantial. It would, though, take a long time for the economy to double the number of scientists, engineers, and other researchers working in R&D.

Increases in R&D spending would increase the growth rate of GNP, as would increases in investment. But it would take massive increases in the share of GNP devoted to investment or R&D or both to increase the growth rate of GNP by as much as the 1.5 percent that it fell between 1960–1973 and 1973–1979.

Prospect for Growth

What growth can we expect through the end of the century? The answer is that the growth rate of real GNP will be somewhere between the great performance of 1960–1973 and the poor performance of 1973–1979. There are two reasons. First, it is unlikely that the economy will again be hit as hard by external shocks as it was by the oil-price increases of 1973–1974 and 1979–1980. Second, economic policy in the early eighties is aimed directly at encouraging in-

BOX 33-1 ■■■■■■■■■■■■■■■■■■■■■■■■■■■■■■■■■

MEASURES TO INCREASE PRODUCTIVITY

The Congressional Budget Office offered the following agenda for legislation to increase productivity.*

Modification of the tax laws to encourage saving and investment: Exempt savings from income taxation; offer investment tax credits; increase allowances for depreciation of capital.

Redesign government regulations to minimize their negative effects on productivity: Use incentives rather than regulations to achieve the aims of the legislation.

New measures to stimulate R&D, diffusion of modern technology, and improvement of the economic environment for small high-technology businesses: Institute tax credits for R&D spending, direct government spending for basic research, and measures to make it easier for small firms with new technologies to borrow money to get started and to keep going.

Modification of federal policies to encourage the development of workers' skills and adaptiveness: Provide for more retraining of workers who lose jobs; replace programs that merely provide unskilled jobs for the young with training programs.

Industrial policies: Encourage the development of industries in which productivity is high.

The agenda is of very mixed quality. The first three items are clearly more feasible than the last two. But the important point is that productivity growth can be changed through economic policy.

---

* Based on Congressional Budget Office, *The Productivity Problem: Alternatives for Action,* Congress of the United States, Washington, D.C., January 1981.

■■■■■■■■■■■■■■■■■■■■■■■■■■■■■■■■■

vestment and R&D and reducing regulation.

Why is that not enough to take us back to the superior growth record of the sixties? The truth is that we cannot predict whether it will or will not. The major cause of growth in the sixties was technical progress, and by its nature that is difficult to forecast. If there should be major technical progress over the next two decades, fast growth will occur. If there is no exceptional technical progress, the likelihood is for steady growth at levels that look good from the long-run perspective of the U.S economy.

SUMMARY

1   Living standards in the industrialized countries have increased rapidly over the past century. Per person GDP has risen by a factor of about 7 in the United States since 1870; in Japan per capita income has risen by a factor of 18. Total GDP rose by a factor of 43 in the United States over the same period.

2   The high growth rates of per capita income observed in the last 100 years cannot have been going on very long by historical standards. These rates are associated with the shift from agricultural to industrial economic activity.

3   The process of economic growth is best understood from the viewpoint of the production function. The level of output increases as the quantities of inputs increase and as technical knowledge improves.

4   Inputs are classified into capital, labor, land, and raw materials. The capital stock consists of factories and machinery, houses, and inventories. Both the quantity and quality of labor input matter. Increases in the quantity of human capital—the skill and knowledge embodied in the labor force—improve the quality of the labor force.

5   Classical economists feared that growth would be limited by the fixed supply of land. The most famous analysis was that of Malthus, who believed that per capita food supply would fall as population grew, as a result of diminishing returns to labor in producing food. Countries would be condemned to living at subsistence income levels. Technical progress in agriculture and industry has so far outweighed the diminishing returns resulting from the increasing pressure of other factors on the limited supply of land.

6   Technical knowledge is in part written down and in part embodied in the skills of the labor force. Technical progress takes place through inventions of new knowledge and innovations, which broaden the applications of existing knowledge.

7   Invention and innovation take place largely in response to the profit motive. Firms and government finance research and development activities. About 2 percent of GNP is devoted to R&D spending in the United States; about half of that is government-financed. Most government R&D spending is for defense. The United States devotes a large share of GNP to R&D in comparison with other industrial countries. Estimated rates of return to R&D spending are very high.

8   Over the long run, most of the increase in output per worker hour in the United States has been the result of technical progress. A large part of productivity increase is also accounted for by increases in the capital stock per worker.

9   Productivity growth in the United States and other large industrial economies was exceptionally high in the 1960–1973 period. The rate of productivity increase since then has slowed down considerably, back to levels closer to long-run historical averages.

10   Policies to improve the rate of productivity increase focus on increasing investment in physical capital and on encouraging technical progress largely through increased R&D spending. Taxes and subsidies change the incentives for investment and for R&D. It would take

truly heroic efforts to offset the total reduction in the rate of productivity increase since 1973 by increasing investment in physical capital and R&D.

KEY TERMS

Malthusian trap
Technical knowledge
Learning by doing
Research and development

Patent system
Productivity slowdown
Labor productivity
Technical progress

PROBLEMS

1 (*a*) What are the difficulties in making long-term comparisons of living standards? (*b*) How do we try to make such comparisons?

2 Explain why the high growth rates of output and income per person measured by economists must be a comparatively recent phenomenon, historically speaking.

3 What data would you need to discover how much output would increase if 1 more unit of (*a*) the capital stock, (*b*) labor, (*c*) the supply of land, or (*d*) the quantity of oil were used in production?

4 Suppose Malthus's view of the production functions is right so that as labor supply rises in a series like 1, 2, 4, 8, 16, . . . output rises in a series like 1, 2, 3, 4, 5, . . . (*a*) Draw a diagram showing output on the vertical axis and the number of workers on the horizontal axis. (*b*) Calculate the marginal product of labor per worker as the number of workers rises from 1 to 2 to 4, etc. (*c*) Are there any countries where the Malthusian trap may be working?

5 (*a*) What is the difference between an invention and an innovation? (*b*) What motivates technical change?

6 (*a*) If the return to R&D spending is so high, why does the private sector not undertake more of it? (*b*) Is there any case for government support of R&D?

7 (*a*) Over the 1929–1969 period, what were the relative contributions of capital and technical progress in explaining increases in output per worker in the United States? (*b*) For the United States, what were the contributions of increases in labor input and capital input in explaining the growth of output in the period 1973–1979? How much growth was a result of technical progress?

8 In what ways could the increase in the price of oil in the seventies have contributed to the productivity slowdown in the industrialized economies?

9 Suppose you had the job of designing a set of policy measures to increase the economy's growth rate. What would you do? (Be specific. For example, rather than saying, "Encourage technical progress," explain what tax credits or subsidies you might give.)

10 There is a powerful antigrowth movement that argues growth is destructive and does not really contribute to happiness. Explain.

4

The
World
Economy

International trade is part of daily life. Americans drive Japanese cars, Frenchmen drink Scotch whisky, Italians use Libyan oil, Russians eat American wheat. The list could be made much longer. If there is nothing remarkable about all this, why is there a separate branch of economics devoted to international trade?

There are two distinguishing features of international trade. First, the firms or consumers involved in international trade live in different countries. Thus the first question analyzed in international trade is why residents of different countries trade. There are no special principles here that do not also apply to the question of why people in different regions of the country trade. Montanans buy Florida grapefruit for much the same reasons they buy Mexican sweetmelons.

But there is a political reason for singling out international trade. Governments frequently control international trade. For example, they may impose tariffs, which are taxes on goods imported from other countries. Part of the subject matter of international trade economics analyzes the reasons for and the effects of tariffs and other government policies to control trade.

The second distinguishing feature of international trade is that the consumers and firms doing the trading may be using different monies. The American buyer of a Japanese car pays in dollars, but the Japanese workers who make the car are paid in yen. Therefore, a second major set of issues analyzed in international economics is that of international payments—how payments are made when different currencies are used in trade and what implications the use of different monies has.

This chapter introduces international trade by describing the facts about what goods are traded internationally by whom and by discussing methods of making international payments.

34

International Trade and the Balance of Payments

1 TRADE PATTERNS

In this section we look at how much trade takes place, among which countries trade occurs, and what goods are traded.

Imports are goods bought by domestic residents from foreigners.

Exports are sales by domestic residents to foreigners.

Typically, exports are goods we sell to other countries for use there, and imports are goods we buy in other countries for use here. But the

TABLE 34-1

THE VALUE OF WORLD EXPORTS

	1928	1935	1950	1973	1980
World exports, billions of 1980 dollars	$294	$123	$189	$880	$1868
World exports as a fraction of U.S. GNP	57.3%	27.1%	20.0%	39.5%	71.1%

Sources: League of Nations, *Europe's Trade,* Geneva, 1941; International Monetary Fund, *International Financial Statistics; National Income Accounts of the United States,* 1928–1949.

definitions actually describe the people doing the trading rather than where they do it. If a German tourist eats in a Houston restaurant, the meal is, strictly speaking, counted as an export by the United States and an import by Germany.

World trade in goods and services consists of imports and exports. As the example of the restaurant meal above suggests, one country's exports are another country's imports. Thus to get some idea of how much trade takes place, we can look at either exports or imports.

How Much World Trade Is There?

Table 34-1 shows the value of world exports for selected years, measured in billions of 1980 dollars and also as a fraction of U.S. GNP to provide a scale of comparison.

Two facts stand out. First, world trade has expanded very fast since 1950, at an average annual rate of 8.0 percent. Since the data are in 1980 dollars, the increases in trade shown here are *real* increases in the amount of goods being traded. Thus international trade has been playing an increasingly important part in the economies of most nations. For instance, in 1960, total U.S. exports were 5.7 percent of GNP; in 1980, U.S. exports were 9.9 percent of GNP. Similar changes can be found for most countries. Table 34-2 gives examples. At the world level, exports were about 18 percent of total world GNP in 1980.

The second fact is that the Great Depression of the 1930s and World War II virtually destroyed international trade. There was more world trade as a percentage of U.S. GNP in 1928 than there was in 1950, and it was only after 1973 that this ratio once again reached its 1928 level.

The increasing importance of trade shows that nations and economies have been becoming increasingly interdependent in the post-World War II world. Events in other economies affect us in our daily lives more than they did 20 years ago. In all countries, people are more likely now to be

TABLE 34-2

EXPORTS AS A SHARE OF GNP
(Selected Countries, 1960 and 1980)

	1960	1980
Australia	14.4%	18.2%
Belgium	32.3	60.0
Germany	20.0	28.9
India	4.2	7.0*
Italy	12.9	22.9
Japan	11.5	15.2
Mexico†	10.6	12.6
Morocco	26.4	18.5
Nigeria†	14.6	25.5‡
United Kingdom	20.0	28.1
United States	4.8	9.9

* Figure for 1979.
† GDP instead of GNP.
‡ Figure for 1978.
Sources: International Monetary Fund, *International Financial Statistics, Yearbook, 1980,* and, May 1982 (figures calculated using data rows: 90c/99a).

using products made abroad and to be selling the goods they make to foreigners than they were 20 years ago.

Next we look at the facts about who trades with whom.

World Trade Patterns

In Table 34-3 we show the pattern of trade among four major groups of countries. The first group is made up of the industrialized, or developed, countries of Western Europe and North America and also includes Japan, Australia, New Zealand, and South Africa. These are the world's rich countries, with most of the world's income and most of the trade. The oil-producing countries such as Saudi Arabia and Kuwait are shown separately because trade in oil makes up a large part of total world trade. The eastern trading area is made up of the Soviet-bloc countries —Russia, Poland, East Germany, and others. The remaining countries of the world are grouped as non-oil LDCs. "LDC" means *less-developed country*, and the term is commonly used. It covers a wide range of countries, from the very poor, such as China

and India, all the way to the nearly rich, such as Brazil and Mexico.

The entries in the table are the percentages of world exports going from countries in the left-hand column to the groups constituting the first four column heads. Thus, for example, 47.5 percent of world exports go from industrialized countries to other industrialized countries.

What are the major points to be learned from Table 34-3? First, most of world trade is among industrialized countries. Industrialized countries account for over 65 percent of world exports, just as they account for about the same share of world income. Second, the share of world exports of the other three groups is around 10 percent each, although their shares of world income differ substantially. Third, trade is very much organized around the industrialized countries. We can see this by noting that both the oil-producing countries and the LDCs export far more to the industrialized countries than to any other group. For instance, the non-oil LDCs send exports to the industrialized countries that come to 8.4 percent of all

TABLE 34-3
WORLD TRADE PATTERNS, 1979
(Percentage of World Exports)

	EXPORTS TO				SHARE OF	
	INDUSTRIALIZED COUNTRIES	OIL-PRODUCING COUNTRIES	NON-OIL LDCs	EASTERN TRADING AREA	WORLD EXPORTS	WORLD INCOME
Exports from:						
Industrialized countries	47.5%†	4.8%	9.6%	3.3%	65.2%	63%
Oil-producing countries	9.9	0.2	2.7	0.3	13.0	2
Non-oil LDCs	8.4	0.8	2.7	0.7	12.6	16
Eastern trading area	2.9	0.4	1.2	4.8	9.3	19
					100%	100%

† Figures in color show share of world trade accounted for by trade between countries within each group. For example, 2.7 percent of world trade is between non-oil LDCs; for instance, India exports goods to Zambia.
Source: GATT, *International Trade, 1980/1981*, Geneva, 1981; World Bank, *World Development Report,* 1980.

trade, but they export to other non-oil LDCs an amount that comes to only 2.7 percent of world trade. Fourth, the Soviet-bloc countries trade mostly among themselves.

The small amount of trading among the LDCs (2.7 percent of world trade) results from the nature of their exports. They export mainly raw materials that are used in production in the industrialized countries. It is not surprising that only 0.2 percent of world trade is accounted for by exports from one oil-producing country to another. The oil-producing countries mostly export oil, and they are, of course, not exporting oil to each other.

The Commodity Composition of World Trade

What goods are traded internationally? Table 34-4 shows world trade by major products for selected years. The table distinguishes between primary commodities (agricultural products, minerals and ores, and fuels) and manufactured or processed commodities (chemicals, machinery, textiles, steel, etc.). Primary commodities now account for 41 percent of world trade, and manufactures make up 59 percent.

Note in particular the sharply declining

TABLE 34-4 ▮▮▮▮▮▮▮

THE COMPOSITION OF WORLD EXPORTS
(Percentage of World Exports)

	1955	1973	1979
Primary commodities:	50.5%	35.3%	41.0%
Food, agricultural products	22.3	15.3	12.1
Fuels	11.2	11.3	20.3
Minerals (other than fuels)	3.8	2.6	2.1
Manufactures:	49.5	64.7	59.0
Road motor vehicles	3.6	7.3	7.2
Engineering products	21.4	33.3	31.7
Textiles and clothing	6.0	6.4	5.2

Source: GATT, *International Trade, 1979/1980*, Geneva, 1980, and *Networks of World Trade, 1955–76*, Geneva, 1978.

share of *nonfuel* primary commodities. These made up 39.3 percent of world trade in 1955 and only 20.7 percent in 1979.[1] The decline in this share was matched in part by the increased share of manufactures and also, of course, by the increased share of fuels after the price of oil rose 300 percent in late 1973 and 1974. The share of fuels in the value of total world trade nearly doubled between 1973 and 1979, from 11 percent to 20 percent.[2]

The main changes in manufactured goods trade took place between 1955 and 1973. Engineering products as a group have become increasingly significant, and so have road motor vehicles (cars and trucks). By contrast, textiles and clothing, typical exports of developing countries, have maintained a relatively constant share. The increased share of engineering products is one of the significant trends in world trade that we look at further when discussing theories of the gains from international trade.

Examples of Trade Patterns

Table 34-5 completes our review of trade patterns with examples of the imports and exports of particular countries. We start with the United States. Although the United States is the largest industrial country, nearly a third of its *exports* are primary commodities, mainly food and agricultural commodities. Two-thirds of its exports are manufactures, mostly engineering products such as machinery, transportation equip-

[1] Here is the calculation for 1955. Primary commodities accounted for 50.5 percent of trade and fuels for 11.2 percent. Thus nonfuel primary commodities accounted for 39.3 percent (50.5 − 11.2) of world trade.
[2] Someone comparing Tables 34-3 and 34-4 may ask why, if fuels accounted for 20 percent of world trade in 1979, Table 34-3 shows oil-producing countries selling only 12.7 percent of world exports. There are two reasons. First, fuels include coal as well as oil. Second, some oil exporters such as Indonesia are not included in the group of oil-producing countries in Table 34-3, because their economies are not dominated by oil.

TABLE 34-5
EXPORT AND IMPORT COMPOSITION: SELECTED COUNTRIES, 1978 AND 1979
(Percentage of Exports or Imports)

	UNITED STATES		JAPAN		LDCs	
	EXPORTS	IMPORTS	EXPORTS	IMPORTS	EXPORTS	IMPORTS
Primary commodities:	32.2%	46.3%	3.9%	77.5%	57.9%	36.2%
Food	19.2	9.0	1.3	15.1	28.1	12.1
Fuels	3.3	29.3	—	41.1	14.5	17.7
Other	9.7	8.0	2.6	21.3	15.3	6.4
Manufactures:	66.5	52.1	95.1	21.5	40.0	59.3
Engineering products	44.7	29.7	64.4	7.9	12.9	33.9
Road motor vehicles	8.6	11.5	20.1	0.7	0.8	5.1
Other	13.2	10.9	10.6	12.9	26.3	20.3

Note: Data for LDCs refer to 1978; data for the United States and Japan refer to 1979.
Source: GATT, International Trade, 1979/1980, Geneva, 1980.

ment (including planes), tools, and appliances.

Half of the U.S. *imports* are primary commodities, the largest part of these being fuels. Engineering products account for only 30 percent of imports, the remainder being such items as steel, chemicals, textiles, and clothing.

Consider for comparison Japan, whose trade patterns are also shown in Table 34-5. Japan is the typical industrialized country. Japan imports primary commodities—three-quarters of her imports are primary commodities, and 99 percent of her oil is imported—and she exports manufactures, most of which are engineering products. Road vehicles constitute a full 20 percent of exports, for the economy is indeed very highly specialized in exporting cars and trucks. Recall from Table 34-2 that Japan's exports come to less than 16 percent of her GNP. Japan exports and imports a smaller proportion of GNP than all the major European countries, such as Germany and the United Kingdom. That is in part because she is very far from the countries with which she trades.

The last two columns focus on the group of non-oil-producing LDCs. Less-devel-

oped countries are exporters of primary commodities other than oil and importers of manufactures, especially engineering products. This emphasis on primary commodity exports and manufactures imports contrasts them with industrial countries (compare LDCs with Japan in Table 34-5). But even though nearly 60 percent of LDC exports are primary goods and nearly 60 percent of imports are manufactures (and oil), we must not overlook the fact that manufactured *exports* (textiles, clothing, consumer goods) do make up a substantial 40 percent of the exports of LDCs.

Trade Issues

The facts set out in Tables 34-1 through 34-5 are an essential background against which we discuss international trade in this chapter and the next three chapters. There are four main facts.

1   The amount of international trade has been growing faster than GNP. In 1980 world trade was about 18 percent of the total world GNP.

2   World trade is centered around the industrialized countries. Nearly half of total

world trade takes place within this group of countries. In addition, the exports of both oil-producing countries and non-oil LDCs go mainly to the industrialized countries.

3   About 40 percent of world trade is in primary commodities (oil, agricultural products), and about 60 percent is in manufactures.

4   The LDCs mostly export primary commodities, but 40 percent of their exports are manufactured goods.

These facts also help explain several of the issues in international trade that will be discussed in later chapters and which we introduce here.

Raw Material Prices   The fact that the LDCs mainly export primary commodities and import manufactures leads them to worry that the industrialized countries are exploiting them by buying raw materials at a low price and sending them back at a much higher price after manufacturing. The non-oil LDCs want higher prices for their raw materials. The producers of coffee, sugar, and copper, for instance, would like to raise their prices. The example they have before them is OPEC—the Organization of Petroleum Exporting Countries—which, we recall from Chapter 1, tripled the price of its product in 1973.

Manufacturing Exports from LDCs   The LDCs want to make their own manufactured goods and export them to the industrialized countries. Indeed, some LDCs have very successfully developed manufacturing industries. The newly industrialized countries, or NICs (pronounced "nicks"), are countries like Mexico, Brazil, and Taiwan that have developed major manufacturing sectors in their economies. Their exports to the industrialized countries have led to complaints within the industrialized coun-

tries that jobs are being threatened by competition from cheap foreign labor.

Trade Disputes among Industrialized Countries   The third set of trade policy issues arises among advanced industrialized countries. These are issues of intraindustry (within an industry) trade. Germany, Japan, and the United States all produce the same types of goods—automobiles, TVs, refrigerators—and they trade in these goods. But some producers like Japan have increased their efficiency and come to dominate entire industries. This has caused the threat of massive job losses throughout the industries—as in the case of automobiles—in all the other countries. Should Japan be stopped for the benefit of domestic automobile workers, or should consumers have the last word and get their imported cars?

2   THE FOREIGN EXCHANGE MARKET

The second distinguishing feature of international trade is that the people trading goods may use different monies. For example, a U.S. firm that exports a computer to France wants to be paid in dollars. The French firm that imports the computer uses francs to make payments. How is the importer to obtain dollars? To start with, that importing firm goes to its bank and buys dollars in exchange for francs. The bank will tell the importer that one dollar costs 8 French francs and sell the importer the dollars it wants in exchange for francs. But that only pushes the question back a stage. Where does the bank obtain the dollars in exchange for francs?

The answer is the foreign exchange market.

> The *foreign exchange market* is the market in which one currency is exchanged for another.

For instance, the foreign exchange market

between francs and dollars is the market in which dollars are exchanged for French francs.

> The *exchange rate* is the price at which currencies are exchanged.

Typically the exchange rate is expressed as the price in our currency of 1 unit of the foreign currency. The French franc exchange rate might be, for instance, 12.5 cents, meaning that it costs 12.5 cents to buy one French franc.

Figure 34-1 shows typical transactions in the franc-dollar exchange market. On one side are people demanding francs who want to exchange dollars for francs. An American importer of French wines is one such person. So, too, is an American buyer of French antiques. He needs francs to pay the people from whom he is buying the antiques. On the other side of the market are those who want to exchange francs for dollars. The French importer of the computer is one. A Frenchman planning a U.S. vacation would also want to exchange francs for dollars so that he can pay for the hotels and Disneyland.

The exchange rate is determined by supply and demand in the foreign exchange market. We show the foreign exchange market in Figure 34-2. We should think of the good being traded as francs and the price as being the dollar price of a franc. This is exactly how we would think of the market for any good, such as bananas, where the quantity of the commodity traded is on the horizontal axis and its price in terms of dollars is on the vertical axis.

The demand curve for francs represents the demands for francs by people like the Americans importing French wine and antiques. The demand curve is downward-sloping: the cheaper francs are, the more francs the Americans want so they can buy more wine or antiques or French cars. The supply curve represents the exchanges that people like the French buyer of the computer or the tourist want to make. As the dollar price of the franc rises—for example, from 10 cents to 12.5 cents—the number of francs it takes to buy one dollar drops, in this case from 10 to 8. American goods become cheaper for Frenchmen. The supply curve is therefore shown as upward-sloping.[3] Supply and demand determine the equilibrium exchange rate, e_0, and the number of francs that are exchanged for dollars in the foreign exchange market, Q_0.

A shift in either the demand curve or the supply curve changes the exchange rate. Suppose that Frenchmen decide to import more from the United States at each level of the exchange rate. They then want more dollars, and therefore, at each exchange rate, the quantity of francs they supply is increased. The supply curve shifts to SS'. The exchange rate falls to e_1. The dollar price of francs falls.

There is a special vocabulary for changes in exchange rates.

> When the dollar-franc exchange rate drops, as from e_0 to e_1 in Figure 34-2, we say that the dollar has *appreciated*. At the same time, we say that the franc has *depreciated*.

---

[3] The supply curve for francs in exchange for dollars in Figure 34-2 might not slope upward. To see why, suppose that the suppliers of francs want only to buy a particular American computer costing $10,000. When the exchange rate is low, say, 10 cents, the Frenchman has to supply 100,000 francs. When the exchange rate is higher, say, 12.5 cents, he needs to supply only 80,000 francs. Thus at the higher exchange rate he supplies *fewer* francs to exchange for dollars.

If his demand for computers is totally inelastic, then the supply curve for francs will be downward-sloping. But note that when the exchange rate rises from 10 cents to 12.5 cents, all American computers become cheaper for a Frenchman. If he increases the dollar value of the machine he orders by enough, the supply curve for francs will slope upward. For instance, a rise in the exchange rate from 10 cents to 12.5 cents might cause him to order a $15,000 machine instead of a $10,000 machine. If so, the amount of foreign exchange offered rises from 100,000 to 120,000 (15,000/0.125) francs. It is this latter case that we assume in drawing the upward-sloping supply curve in Figure 34-2.

FIGURE 34-1 TRANSACTIONS IN THE FRENCH FRANC–DOLLAR EXCHANGE MARKET. We can divide participants in the foreign exchange market between dollars and French francs into those who want to obtain francs and are willing to pay in dollars to do so—on the left-hand side of the diagram—and those who want to obtain dollars and pay in francs—on the right-hand side of the diagram. The diagram shows some of the types of transactions that go through the foreign exchange market.

Demanding francs in exchange for dollars

U.S. importer of French wines

U.S. purchaser of French antiques

FOREIGN EXCHANGE MARKET

Supplying francs in exchange for dollars

French tourist planning U.S. vacation

French purchaser of U.S. computer

FIGURE 34-2 THE MARKET FOR FOREIGN EXCHANGE BETWEEN DOLLARS AND FRENCH FRANCS. Curve *DD* shows the demand for francs by people like the importer of French wines, who needs francs to pay the seller of the wine. Curve *SS* shows how many francs suppliers are willing to supply at each exchange rate. The equilibrium exchange rate is e_0, with quantity Q_0 of francs being traded. A shift in the supply function to *SS'*, resulting, for example, from an increase in the French desire to import American goods, causes the exchange rate to fall, or the dollar to appreciate, to e_1. Equivalently, the franc depreciates.

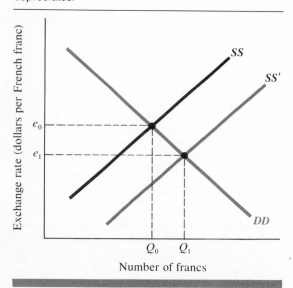

The idea is that the dollar is now worth more in terms of francs, and so we can use the word "appreciated," which means increased in value. For instance, exchange rate e_0 might be 12.5 cents, whereas e_1 might be 10 cents. At e_0 one dollar is worth 8 francs. At exchange rate e_1 one dollar is worth 10 francs. Hence the dollar is worth more francs and has appreciated. The argument goes in exactly the opposite direction for the franc, explaining why it is said to have depreciated.

Governments and the Foreign Exchange Market

In Figures 34-1 and 34-2 we show only private firms and consumers buying and selling in the foreign exchange market. Some foreign exchange markets have operated in that way. But most of them operate with continuing or frequent intervention from central banks, which buy and sell foreign exchange.

In the French franc–dollar market, the Federal Reserve System and the Banque de France, the two countries' central banks, might either or both intervene. We show first how they intervene and then discuss why they might intervene. Suppose that the Banque de France decides that the ex-

FIGURE 34-3 CENTRAL BANK INTERVENTION IN THE FOREIGN EXCHANGE MARKET. The exchange rate is originally e_0. The Banque de France decides that it would like a higher exchange rate so that the franc will appreciate in relation to the dollar. To achieve this it has to increase the quantity of francs demanded. It does that by buying francs with dollars. Distance GE' shows how much purchasing of francs with dollars it has to do to get the exchange rate up from e_0 to e'.

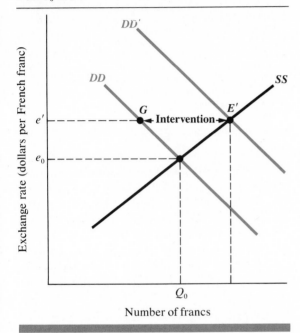

dollars. In this case it acts on the supply side. This will cause the dollar to appreciate or the franc to depreciate.

Where does the Banque de France get the dollars and the francs with which to intervene? Most central banks have reserves of foreign assets, particularly dollars, which they bought in the past. Thus the French central bank could start selling off these assets in order to get the franc to appreciate. Or it might be able to borrow dollars. In any event, the central bank needs dollars to intervene to get the franc to appreciate, or to prevent it from depreciating.

Intervention in the opposite direction is easier. The Banque de France can always create francs just by writing a check on itself. It need never run out of francs, and it can keep on intervening to drive the exchange rate down by selling more francs.

Why do central banks intervene in the foreign exchange market? The first reason is that movements in the exchange rate affect the prices at which domestic residents can export to and import from foreigners. If the franc depreciates, imports become more expensive for Frenchmen. The Banque de France might try to intervene to prevent import prices from rising. If the franc appreciates, French goods become expensive for Americans, the quantity demanded falls, and French exporters lose business. Again, the Banque de France might want to intervene to prevent this.

The second reason for central bank intervention is that changes in the exchange rate affect domestic inflation. Since movements in the exchange rate affect the prices in francs that Frenchmen pay for imports, they also affect the prices of goods made from imported raw materials. And those prices in turn affect the general price level in francs. One reason why central banks intervene in the foreign exchange market is to try to prevent higher prices for imports that would in turn produce inflation at home.

change rate is too low—say it is at 12.5 cents. The Banque de France would prefer it to be at 15 cents so that the franc will be worth more in terms of dollars.

If the Banque de France has dollars, it can raise the exchange rate by buying francs with its dollars. In terms of Figure 34-3, it shifts the demand curve for francs from DD to DD'. The exchange rate rises, as desired. The distance GE' shows how much buying of francs or *intervention* the Banque de France is doing.

Alternatively, the Banque de France may think that the exchange rate is too high and want to get it down. Then it can go into the market and sell francs in exchange for

A further understanding of the factors affecting exchange rates requires us to introduce the balance of payments.

3   THE BALANCE OF PAYMENTS

> The *balance of payments* is a systematic record of all transactions between the residents of one country (households, firms, and the government) and the rest of the world.

The easiest way to think of the balance of payments is to go through the example of an individual as shown in Table 34-6.

An Individual's Balance of Payments Accounts

Table 34-6 shows a typical picture of household finance. Mr. Morgan earned an income of $23,000 from his jobs and assets but spent $26,500. Spending exceeded income, perhaps because medical bills were high or because the vacation was extravagant or because this year's income was lower than average and Mr. Morgan did not want to cut his standard of living. The net receipts—all incomes less all expenses of Mr. Morgan in his transactions with the rest of the world—are called the current account. Mr. Morgan has a current account deficit of $3,500.

> There is a *current account deficit* (surplus) when spending exceeds (is less than) income.

Mr. Morgan has to find some way of paying for the amount of spending in excess of his income. In the terms used in international trade, the deficit must be *financed*. To understand how the deficit is financed, we turn to the capital account.

> The *capital account* shows all transactions in financial assets.

On balance, Mr. Morgan sold assets (although he bought some stocks, he was a net seller of assets), and he borrowed "abroad," namely from his aunt and the bank. The bal-

TABLE 34-6

MR. MORGAN'S BALANCE OF PAYMENTS, 1984 (US$)

CURRENT ACCOUNT:	−3,500
Exports (income from work, moonlighting, dividends, and interest)	+23,000
Imports (rent, food, upkeep, entertainment, medical expenses, paint job on the car, insurance, vacation)	−26,500
CAPITAL ACCOUNT:	+3,500
Net sale of assets (reduction in bank account + sale of GM shares − purchase of South Sea Bubble stock + sale of stereo)	+2,000
Net borrowing (increase in debt to bank + borrowing from Aunt Amy − payment of Sears bill)	+1,500
Total	0

ance of all transactions in assets is a surplus just large enough to finance the current account deficit. A capital account surplus means that Mr. Morgan, on balance, received money through his dealings in assets. His net sales of stocks plus borrowing provided him with just the amount of cash needed to finance the current account deficit.

If Mr. Morgan had spent less than his income, he would have had a current account surplus. This would have been matched by a capital account deficit. He would have increased his net claims on the rest of the world (reduced bank debts or debts to his aunt, or increased his holdings of stocks, bonds, real estate, antiques).

In summary, for an individual the current account represents the excess of income over expenditure in his transactions with everyone else, or the rest of the world. *Any current account surplus (deficit) is financed by an offsetting capital account deficit (surplus)*. Spending in excess of income means that assets have to be sold or that the individual has to borrow. A surplus in the current account means reducing debts or adding to assets. Confusing as it

TABLE 34-7
SUMMARY OF AN INDIVIDUAL'S PAYMENTS ACCOUNTS

Current account deficit
Spending exceeds income.
Deficit is financed by a net reduction in assets (increased borrowing or sales of assets) or capital account surplus.

Current account surplus
Income exceeds spending.
Surplus finances a net increase in assets (reducing debts or purchasing any kind of asset) or capital account deficit.

may be, a capital account deficit corresponds to the case of someone reducing debts or adding to assets. On net such a person is buying or importing assets.

Getting Surpluses and Deficits Straight
There is a simple rule for distinguishing surpluses from deficits. When transactions lead to an increase in money holdings, there is a surplus in that account. When income exceeds expenditures, the individual or country is, on balance, adding to money holdings, and there is a current account surplus. When sales of assets and borrowings on balance exceed purchases of assets and repayment of borrowings, the individual is increasing cash holdings through his capital account transactions, and therefore he has a capital account surplus. Table 34-7 summarizes the balance of payments accounts for an individual.

The Balance of Payments Accounts for a Country
Balance of payments accounting for an individual is quite plain. The same principles apply to balance of payments accounting for an entire country. We simply record all incomes from the sale of goods and services (income from exports of airplanes, sales of technology, assets abroad) and subtract all expenditures on imports (oil imports, im-

ports of Japanese cars, technology, insurance, payments to foreign holders of our debts). The difference is the home country's current account.

> The current account of the balance of payments is the excess of exports over imports. There is a current account *surplus* when exports exceed imports and a current account *deficit* when imports exceed exports.

In Table 34-8 we show the 1979 balance of payments for selected countries. In 1979, the United States, Germany, and Brazil all were exporting less than they imported; that is, they were running current account deficits. There is an immediate question: Can *all* countries run current account deficits? The answer is no. One country's exports are other countries' imports, and one country's imports are exports from other countries. If one country or a group of countries is importing more than it exports, then other countries must, in total, be exporting more than they import. Thus not all countries can have deficits. In 1979, the countries running the surplus were the oil producers. Their surplus was $70 billion, as shown in the last column of Table 34-8. We return to the oil producers' surplus later.

Financing of Deficits   A country, like an individual, must finance any current account deficit either by selling assets (reducing its net claims on the rest of the world) or by borrowing (increasing its liabilities to the rest of the world). On the other hand, a surplus in the current account finances an increase in net claims on the rest of the world (buying assets) or a reduction in net liabilities (repaying borrowing). Thus in 1979 the United States, Germany, and Brazil all experienced a current account deficit and a reduction in their net external assets. They all sold assets to the rest of the world—that is, reduced their claims—or borrowed—that is, increased their liabilities.

TABLE 34-8

BALANCE OF PAYMENTS OF SELECTED COUNTRIES, 1979
(US$ Billions)

	UNITED STATES	GERMANY	BRAZIL	OIL-PRODUCING COUNTRIES
Current account	−0.8	−6.3	−10.5	70.0
Increase in net foreign liabilities:	0.8	6.3	10.5	−70.0
Capital account	14.2	3.3	7.7	N.A.
Net official liabilities	−13.4	3.0	2.8	N.A.
Total	0	0	0	0

Source: International Monetary Fund, *International Financial Statistics, Yearbook, 1981.*

Who bought those assets? The answer is implied by the vast increase in the oil-producing countries' net claims on the world of $70 billion. The oil-producing countries had a surplus on current account and a deficit on capital account. Their capital account deficit was large enough to finance the current account deficits of the United States, Germany, Brazil, and many other countries that were also running current account deficits. For instance, the oil-producing countries bought stocks, bonds, and real estate in the United States, reflecting their capital account deficit.

Thinking about the relationship between the current account deficits of the non-oil-producing countries and the capital account deficits of the oil-producing countries, we see that the oil producers essentially took partial payment for their oil in the form of stocks, bonds, real estate, and other assets in the non-oil-producing countries. The remaining payments (those that did not generate a current account deficit for the non-oil producers) took the form of goods and services, such as wheat, automobiles, and consulting services.

The balance of payments data in Table 34-8 thus give an important first relationship that is worth recording as a formal equation. The current account surplus of a country has as a counterpart the increase in net claims on the rest of the world or the increase in net foreign assets:

$$\begin{array}{l}\text{Current} \\ \text{account} \\ \text{surplus} \end{array} = \begin{array}{l}\text{increase in net} \\ \text{foreign assets} \end{array} \tag{1}$$

Countries that run a current account surplus thus build up external assets—they come to own the rest of the world—and countries that run a current account deficit have to sell off assets or go increasingly into debt.

Defining the Country's Balance of Payments

The difference between an individual's and a country's balance of payments results from the use of different currencies among countries and the associated role of the government in affecting the balance of payments. In the case of the individual in Table 34-6, the current account deficit is equal to the capital account surplus. But in Table 34-8 we see that the current account deficits and capital account surpluses for the United States, Germany, and Brazil do not exactly offset each other.

The difference arises from central bank intervention in the foreign exchange market. In the case of the individual, Mr. Morgan, a current account deficit had to be matched by a capital account surplus. That meant he personally had to sell assets or borrow to finance the current account deficit. But when a *country* runs a current account deficit, it is the country as a whole, including *both* the central bank and the private sector, that has to reduce its ownership of foreign assets or increase its borrowing to finance the deficit.

Thus we can write the following equation:

Increase in net
foreign assets = increase in net foreign assets
                held by private sector
                + increase in net foreign
                assets held by central bank   (2)

Of course, equation (2) also holds when a country is reducing its asset holdings. For instance, if it has a current account deficit, the increase in net foreign assets is negative, or a decrease.

To take a specific example, in Table 34-8 we look at the case of Brazil in 1979. In that year Brazil had a current account deficit of \$10.5 billion. The private sector increased its net foreign liabilities by \$7.7 billion, largely by borrowing from foreign banks. The central bank reduced its net ownership of foreign assets by \$2.8 billion, selling off dollars in exchange for Brazilian cruzeiros so as to prevent the exchange rate from falling further than it did that year. Corresponding to the entries in equation (2), we have

$$-10.5 = -7.7 - 2.8 \qquad (3)$$

It is the last item in equation (2), the increase in the central bank's[4] holdings of net foreign assets, that we single out as *the* balance of payments.

> The balance of payments surplus (deficit) is equal to the increase (decrease) in the central bank's holdings of foreign assets.

The remaining item in equation (2), the net

---

[4] Sometimes the Treasury rather than the central bank is responsible for holding foreign assets, depending on the country. It is the change in official (i.e., government) holdings of foreign exchange that corresponds to the balance of payments.

amount of foreign assets acquired by the private sector, is the capital account deficit.

Thus we can write, corresponding to equation (2),

Current   capital   balance of
account = account + payments
surplus   deficit   surplus   (4)

Or, more conveniently, we turn equation (4) around and write

Balance of   current   capital
payments = account + account
surplus   surplus   surplus   (5)

And we recognize that the balance of payments surplus of a country is equal to the net amount of foreign assets acquired by its central bank.

To summarize, a country's balance of payments surplus is equal to the net acquisitions of foreign assets by its central bank (or Treasury). A balance of payments surplus can be generated either by a current account surplus or by a capital account surplus.

We can also see the balance of payments in Figure 34-3. The distance GE' in that diagram represents French central bank purchases of francs with dollars. If the Banque de France did not change its holdings of any other foreign currencies, then distance GE' would be the French balance of payments deficit. In practice, the Banque de France also buys and sells other currencies, such as the (German) deutsche mark, and its balance of payments deficit is equal to the value of total sales minus purchases of foreign currencies in exchange for francs.

Balance of Payments Problems

A country that is running a current account deficit has to find some way of financing the deficit. In other words, it has to pay for the excess of imports over exports.

An individual spending more than he earns can finance his deficit for a while. He can always draw down his bank account, or sell the car, or borrow. Similarly, a country can run a current account deficit for a while.

However, balance of payments *problems* arise when current account deficits are *persistent*. Persistent current account deficits cannot be financed. Neither a country nor an individual can forever spend more than its income. A country or an individual has to *adjust* or take action to get rid of a persistent deficit.

What can countries with balance of payments problems do? An individual who experiences a persistent current account deficit must take one of two actions: he can get a better-paying job so he can pay for expenditures, or he can cut expenditures. Getting a better-paying job normally means working more—longer hours or harder work—not the good fortune of getting paid more for the same amount of work. For a country the corresponding adjustment is to sell more of its goods. This can be done by working harder and producing more for sale and by cutting expenditures so that there is more left to export. For a country that means reducing consumption, investment, or government spending or working harder to produce more. Adjustment is tough. Just as for the individual, adjustment for a country implies a reduction in the standard of living. For that reason adjustment to balance of payments problems is politically unpopular. Adjustment is often delayed, and this ultimately gives rise to balance of payments *crises*.

Balance of payments crises occur when a country has for a time resisted adjusting its current account deficit and has no further ways of financing (continuing) deficits. The central bank's holdings of foreign assets are already sold; foreigners, especially banks, do not want to lend either to individuals or to the government; and no other sources of finance are available. When things have gotten that far out of line, adjustment on a quite radical scale is called for. We shall see some examples later.

There is a range of options for adjusting to current account deficits and to balance of payments crises. The country may try to reduce imports and increase exports by taxing imports (imposing a tariff) and subsidizing exports. Or it may increase income taxes in the hope of getting people to spend less on goods so that more are available for export.

One primary option is to change the exchange rate. As we shall now see, balance of payments problems can be blamed on central banks' intervention in foreign exchange markets that maintains an inappropriate exchange rate.

Central Banks and the Balance of Payments

It is frequently said that without central banks there are no balance of payments problems. This point is quite correct, at least at a superficial level. Without central banks there is no central bank intervention in the foreign exchange market, and therefore there can be no balance of payments surplus or deficit. The capital account *must* finance the current account, just as in the case of an individual, because there simply is no other way of financing the current account.

What ensures that the current account and the capital account exactly match if there is no central bank intervention? We have already seen that in Figure 34-2, where the price of foreign exchange, or the exchange rate, moves to ensure equilibrium between supply and demand in the foreign exchange market. For instance, an increased demand for dollars in exchange for francs would cause the exchange rate to fall, or the dollar to appreciate.

In practice, though, central banks do not allow exchange rates to move freely. For instance, in 1979, as Table 34-8 shows, the United States had a balance of payments surplus of $13.4 billion. Germany had a deficit of $3.0 billion, and Brazil had a deficit of

$2.8 billion. In the case of the United States, the Federal Reserve bought on balance $13.4 billion worth of foreign currency in 1979. This was done to prevent the dollar from appreciating. In the cases of both Germany and Brazil, the central banks were trying to prevent their currencies from depreciating.

A major issue in international trade is whether countries should simply allow their exchange rates to change so that there is no balance of payments surplus or deficit or whether, on the contrary, they should intervene by buying and selling foreign currencies and thereby try to affect the exchange rate. We now describe alternative exchange rate systems and the policies that central banks and governments have followed in trying to affect and control exchange rates.

4 EXCHANGE RATE SYSTEMS AND POLICIES

In this section we describe the main exchange rate systems. We start by examining Table 34-9, which shows dollar exchange rates for several countries at different times. Each entry in the table refers to the dollar price of a unit of foreign currency in the specified year—such as $0.0028 per yen in 1950.

Fixed Exchange Rates

In the period between 1950 and 1960, most exchange rates were kept constant or fixed. We can see in Table 34-9 that the yen, deutsche mark, and pound sterling (British) exchange rates were all the same in 1960 as they were in 1950. During that period the exchange rates were kept constant by the central banks of the different countries, which bought and sold foreign currencies at fixed prices.

In practice, the system worked by each country fixing its exchange rate against the dollar and buying or selling its currency in exchange for dollars. In terms of Figure 34-3, the central bank was willing to intervene on either the demand side or the supply side of the market whenever needed to prevent the exchange rate from moving from the fixed level.

Adjustable Peg

We see from Table 34-9 that both the $/deutsche mark and $/pound sterling exchange rates had changed by 1970. The exchange rate for the deutsche mark had increased, showing that the deutsche mark had appreciated, while the exchange rate for the pound had fallen, showing that the pound had depreciated. These changes reflected formal decisions by the central banks to change the exchange rates.

TABLE 34-9

DOLLAR EXCHANGE RATE AGAINST MAJOR CURRENCIES
(US$ per Unit of Foreign Currency)

DATE	US$/YEN	US$/DEUTSCHE MARK	US$/£	US$/CAN$
1950	0.0028	0.24	2.80	0.92
1960	0.0028	0.24	2.80	1.03
1970	0.0028	0.27	2.40	0.95
1980	0.0044	0.55	2.39	0.86
Percentage change, 1950–1980	57.1	129.2	−14.6	−6.5

Note: £ is the symbol for the British pound.
Source: International Monetary Fund, *International Financial Statistics, Yearbook, 1981.*

In the British case, there was a devaluation of the pound in 1967.

> A *devaluation* is a reduction in the price at which the central bank commits itself to buying and selling its currency.

The word "devaluation" is usually reserved for a fall in the exchange rate in a system where central banks are intervening to fix rates. A devaluation is a depreciation (fall in value) of the currency, but it is an official action rather than something that happens in the free market. The 1967 devaluation reduced the price of a pound from $2.80 to $2.40.

Why did the British government, or the Bank of England, devalue the pound? The current account of the balance of payments had frequently been in deficit, and the government decided it could not go on intervening to try to keep the exchange rate fixed at $2.80. The country was running out of foreign assets to sell and going heavily into debt to foreigners. In terms of Figure 34-4, very large-scale intervention, with the Bank of England buying pounds in exchange for dollars, was needed to keep the exchange rate at $2.80. Rather than continue losing its dollars, the government decided to devalue to $2.40, to let the exchange rate fall.

The change in the deutsche mark exchange rate reflects two *revaluations*, which means increases in the price of a deutsche mark in terms of dollars and other currencies, in 1961 and 1969. Germany was running large current account surpluses. Rather than continue to buy foreign assets, the government decided to revalue, to let the exchange rate (measured in $/deutsche mark) rise.

The exchange rate system in operation in the fifties and sixties and into the early seventies is known as the *adjustable peg*. In this system central banks are committed to keeping the exchange rate fixed at any one time, but occasionally, when it is obvious that the exchange rate is far from an equilib-

FIGURE 34-4 DEVALUATION. With the exchange rate at $2.80 per pound sterling, the Bank of England had to intervene with large amounts of dollars, buying pounds in exchange for dollars. The intervention could not be maintained. Instead, the rate was devalued to $2.40. At that price the Bank of England promised to buy and sell as much sterling as was needed to maintain the exchange rate. But it was no longer necessary to continue buying pounds in exchange for dollars. (Indeed, to begin with, the Bank of England had to *sell* pounds and add to its holdings of dollars in order to keep the exchange rate at $2.40.)

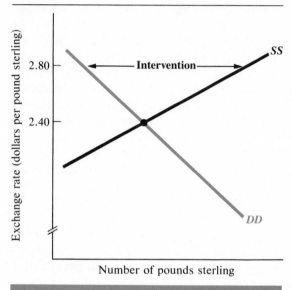

Number of pounds sterling

rium level, the rate (or the peg) is adjusted.

Flexible Exchange Rates

The adjustable peg system collapsed in the early seventies. Governments were no longer willing to commit themselves to fixing the exchange rate for any length of time. The major countries then moved to a system of *flexible*, or *floating*, exchange rates. In this system the exchange rate may change from day to day or minute to minute. Canada had already had a floating exchange rate in the 1950s and early sixties.

> If central banks do not intervene in the foreign exchange markets at all, then the system is known as *clean floating*.

This is the type of system described in Figure 34-2, where private sector supplies of and demands for currencies determine exchange rates. There is no balance of payments surplus or deficit, because the central bank is not intervening.

A system of clean floating is the opposite of a system of totally fixed exchange rates. Under clean floating the market has complete freedom to set exchange rates. Under fixed rates the government changes its holdings of foreign assets in order to prevent the market from having any effect on the exchange rate.

In practice, neither pure system exists. The fixed exchange rate system of the fifties was really an adjustable peg system, for the government eventually responded to market forces by devaluing or revaluing. Similarly, in the period since 1973 when exchange rates have been flexible or floating, central banks have in practice intervened heavily to affect them.

The current system, in which the central bank is not formally committed to fixing exchange rates but often intervenes to affect the rate, is known as *dirty floating*, or *managed floating*. Exchange rates are basically free to adjust to make the demand for foreign exchange equal to supply. But if a rate is changing rapidly, either appreciating or depreciating, the central bank is likely to intervene to prevent it from moving too fast.

Why do central banks intervene? As we have noted before, it is because changes in the exchange rate affect exports and imports and domestic inflation. When the exchange rate appreciates, foreign goods become cheaper. For instance, if the $/£ exchange rate moves from $2.40 to $2, British goods become cheaper for Americans. We import more British goods. American goods become more expensive for the British, and they import fewer American goods—or the United States exports less. Thus the demand for American exports falls, and jobs are lost in firms producing exports. But if the exchange rate depreciates, American goods become cheaper abroad, and American exports rise. The export industries increase production.

Because countries frequently want high levels of production, they are often tempted to help the currency depreciate. That way they get to export more and import less. But other countries are on the reverse side of the picture. They end up importing more, exporting less, and losing jobs.

Dirty floating thus raises the danger that countries will compete to depreciate their currencies, to increase their exports and create employment at home—at the expense of foreigners. But not all countries can depreciate at the expense of foreigners at once. To prevent competitive depreciations under dirty floating, there are attempts by all countries together to define what is good behavior in the exchange markets.

The Operation of the Current System

In the 1970s, as we noted above, flexible exchange rates with a good bit of government intervention were the rule. One of the questions we will ask is whether the system has worked well. This leads to the next question: Compared with what? The comparison that is normally made is between the adjustable peg system of the 1960s and the dirty floating of the 1970s. The questions include: Have flexible rates helped smooth the adjustment of current account deficits, and have they helped in the financing of transitory deficits? Have they helped reduce inflation, or have they aggravated inflation problems in the world or in particular countries?

These are important questions. But we have to issue an immediate warning: the questions are interesting, but the evidence is far from being complete or agreed on.

Take, for example, the case of the dollar-sterling exchange rate shown in Figure

FIGURE 34-5 DOLLAR-STERLING EXCHANGE RATE. The rates are in terms of the number of dollars per pound sterling, and they are end-of-year rates. (*Source:* International Monetary Fund, *International Financial Statistics, Yearbook, 1979,* and May 1982.)

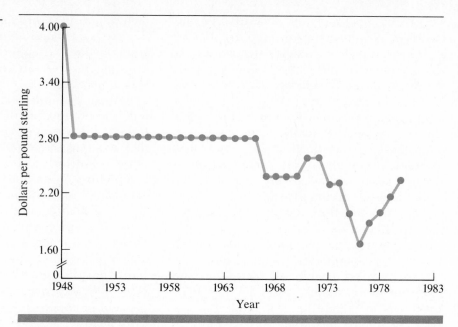

34-5. The figure shows that the dollar price of sterling fluctuated widely in the 1974–1981 period. There was a sharp depreciation of sterling in 1976—the dollar price of pounds fell to the low point of $1.68—but then the exchange rate climbed over the next few years to a high point of $2.40, only to fall again to below $2.

In the debate over fixed versus flexible exchange rates, the explanation of exchange rate movements like those in Figure 34-5 plays a key role. Those in favor of clean floating believe the market does a good job of determining the exchange rate. They argue that the movements seen in Figure 34-5 reflect the large disturbances the world economy suffered in the seventies, with oil prices tripling in 1973 and rising again in 1979. Those in favor of fixed rates say that there is no reason why the exchange rate should have moved as much as it did and that central bank intervention to fix rates would have prevented needless changes in the levels of exports and imports in response to changing exchange rates.

The Gold Standard

Some argue that a proper comparison is not between flexible rates and the system of the 1960s. They argue that the proper comparison is with an ideal system of fixed-forever rates such as the gold standard.

> The *gold standard* is a system in which the government in each country fixes the value of its currency in terms of gold and is willing to buy and sell gold at that price.

For instance, in the United States during the 1920s the price of gold was fixed at $20.67 per ounce. In Britain the price was £3.89 per ounce for the years 1926–1930.

With the value of each currency fixed in terms of gold, exchange rates are automatically determined. For instance, from 1926 to 1930, the $/£ exchange rate was $5.31. Only at that price could the foreign exchange market be in equilibrium. Suppose that the exchange rate were at some other level, say, $4. Then someone could buy an ounce of gold in London for £3.89, sell it in New York for $20.67, take the $20.67 and get £5.17 for it (20.67/4), and make a clear profit on the deal. Since everyone could do this, there would be a lot of people trying to convert dollars in pounds, and by doing this they would push the exchange rate up. Only at $5.31 could there be equilibrium in the foreign exchange market.

So long as each country is sticking to the rules and keeping the value of its currency in terms of gold fixed, exchange rates are well and truly constant. Under such a system it is almost as if the world is using just one form of money—gold. This means that one of the distinguishing features of international trade—that people engaged in it use different monies—disappears.

Those in favor of the gold standard have been for it mainly because they believe it would reduce the inflation rate. If the government is committed to a fixed price of gold, it cannot change the money supply at will, and therefore it loses the freedom to print money and thus generate inflation. But the introduction of the gold standard would certainly change the way foreign exchange markets work, and we therefore analyze the gold standard system in Chapter 36.

In the early 1980s a small but vocal group of enthusiasts for the gold standard became sufficiently influential in the United States for the President to appoint a Gold Commission to study the desirability of linking the dollar to gold. The commission reported negatively in 1982. But the appeal of gold and an automatic monetary system is strong enough that interest in the gold standard will return.

5 MACROECONOMICS IN THE OPEN ECONOMY

This section discusses the links between the state of the economy—boom or recession—and the external balance or current account. Should we expect particular links—for instance, that a boom implies a deficit or that a recession implies a surplus?

Figure 34-6 sets the stage for our discussion. On the horizontal axis we measure aggregate economic activity, say, by the GNP gap. A boom corresponds to a positive GNP gap, with actual output in excess of potential output. A recession or slump implies a negative gap, as potential output exceeds actual output. On the vertical axis we show the current account. The current account may be in surplus, or in balance, or in deficit. Figure 34-6 defines four regions, each of which is characterized by a particular combination of activity and the current account. The diagram shows examples of where countries have been at particular times.

Kuwait, for example, in 1979–1980 had an oil-led boom in demand, with domestic employment above potential employment and with a large current account surplus. The United Kingdom, by contrast, is shown in 1981 in a deep recession accompanied by a surplus in the current account. Mexico experienced a boom in 1979–1980, just as did Kuwait, but the current account was in deficit. Finally, Brazil and Germany had deficits and recessions. The examples make clear that any constellation is possible.

There are thus two interesting questions. First, what types of disturbances lead an economy to, say, a boom and surplus rather than to a boom and deficit? Second, once the economy is in a particular imbalance position, what are the adjustments that take place, and what, if anything, can policy do to help?

Internal and External Balance

Figure 34-6 shows different combinations of booms and recessions and current account surpluses and deficits. We take as our benchmark for the following discussion the concepts of internal and external balance.

Internal balance is the level of demand for our goods that sustains full employment.

FIGURE 34-6 THE EXTERNAL BALANCE AND THE STATE OF ECONOMIC ACTIVITY. The diagram classifies the situation of individual countries as regards the current account (surplus/deficit) as well as the level of employment and activity (boom/slump).

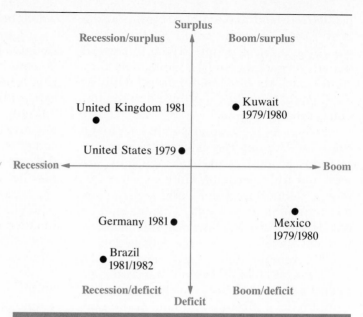

The definition of external balance is the following:

> A country is in *external balance* when the current account balances. Exports of all goods and services equal imports.

In terms of Figure 34-6 the combination of internal *and* external balance is the intersection of the two axes, where there is neither boom nor recession, neither surplus nor deficit.

The combination of internal and external balance is a useful benchmark because this is the state the economy cannot depart from for too long without taking corrective action. Countries can run deficits for some time, even a long time, by borrowing abroad, but these deficits must be closely tied to productive investments because otherwise there is no hope of ultimately repaying the debt. Thus external balance is a reasonable constraint to place on the economy in the medium term. Internal balance is a foremost policy objective. Policymakers are concerned about maintaining full employment and will react both to the inflationary consequences of an economy that is overemployed for a lengthy period and to sustained unemployment. We thus take the objectives of internal and external balance as given and ask how various disturbances affect an economy.

Disturbances to Internal and External Balance

Figure 34-7 shows the impacts of different disturbances on external and internal balance. These disturbances fall broadly into three classes:

1   Changes in domestic spending, perhaps due to changes in monetary or fiscal policies

2   Changes in world demand for our goods or in the prices at which our goods sell in world markets

3   The discovery of new export products or the development of new export markets through increased competitiveness or new products

FIGURE 34-7 DISTURBANCES TO INTERNAL AND EXTERNAL BALANCE. The diagram identifies the direction in which different disturbances affect our internal and external balance. For example, a tighter fiscal policy involving a cut in spending both on our goods and on imports leads to a slump and to an external surplus, thus moving the economy to the upper left-hand quadrant.

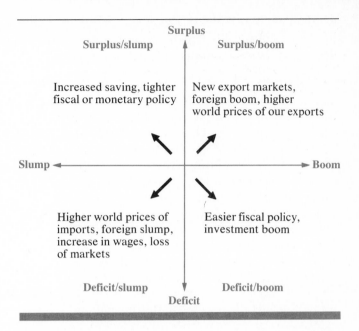

In each of these cases we can make a clear prediction about the impact of the disturbance on both the internal balance and the external balance. For example, a tax cut will lead to increased consumer spending. This raises the demand for goods at home and therefore raises employment: there will be a boom. But part of increased spending falls on imports, and therefore there will be a deficit (or reduced surplus) in the external balance. To give another example, the discovery of new export markets leads firms to increase their sales abroad. This will raise home employment, creating a boom, but will also increase export earnings and therefore create an external balance surplus. We leave you to work through the remaining examples and those in the problem section at the end of the chapter. The main point to take from Figure 34-7 is that most disturbances in an open economy simultaneously affect both internal and external balance.

The Policy Problem

Figure 34-7 shows how different disturbances take an economy away from internal and external balance to situations of surpluses and booms, deficits and slumps, or any other combination. Is there any reason for the government to intervene? For a first response we would say no. An economy that has a deficit and unemployment is one where goods are overpriced and therefore cannot be sold. Workers are asking for wages that are too high and are unemployed. Their wages have to come down to restore employment, and there is little that can be done to avoid the adjustment. At the same time the deficit means that people are spending more than their incomes. Certainly they will adjust once they realize that they are running down their assets, and in any event, their creditors will tell them in time. Thus there are forces of adjustment that will take an economy *automatically* back to equilibrium eventually.

However, how long does it take until unemployment leads to a cut in wages and thus to an increase in our competitiveness? And how long does it take before creditors stop our borrowing, and possibly do so abruptly? Here is where policy does come in. If adjustment takes a long time, and if it involves significant unemployment or, on the other side, significant inflation, then policy measures may help eliminate the imbalances in a way that works more rapidly and at a lower cost to the economy.

There are two basic adjustments that policy can promote. One is to change the *level* of spending. The other is to affect the *composition* of spending. Monetary and fiscal policy affect the level of spending. For example, a tax cut leads to higher spending and therefore, other things being equal, to higher employment and an external deficit. A tax increase or tight money, by contrast, leads to a reduced level of spending, lower employment, reduced imports, and, therefore, an external surplus. The level of spending thus matters for both internal and external balance, and it can be affected by monetary and fiscal policy.

The composition of spending between domestic goods and imports can also be affected by policy. Consumers will switch their spending away from imports if they become more expensive in relation to domestically produced goods. A tariff, for example, makes imports more expensive and therefore leads consumers to spend more on domestic goods and less on imports. A devaluation works in the same way by making imports more expensive. While a devaluation or a tariff or limits on imports reduce import spending and the deficit, they shift demand toward domestically produced goods, and thus they create employment. Policies that affect the composition of spending thus also have an impact on both internal and external balance.

The policies affecting the level *and* the composition of spending make up a *policy mix* that can restore internal and external balance from any of the situations described in Figure 34-7. In general, we need a policy mix because one tool by itself cannot cope with two targets. For example, a country with a deficit and a slump can cut taxes to get rid of the slump, but because people will spend more, the deficit will become even larger. Such a country needs a policy mix involving, for example, easy fiscal policy to eliminate the slump and, at the same time, a devaluation to improve the external balance.

SUMMARY

1   World trade in 1980 amounted to about $2000 billion, or 18 percent of world GNP. World trade grew rapidly during the 30 years to 1980.

2   Most of world trade involves industrialized countries, either trading with each other or trading with the remaining groups. This large role of industrialized countries mainly reflects their size in the world economy.

3   About 40 percent of world trade is in primary commodities (minerals, agricultural products, fuels), and 60 percent is trade in manufactures.

4   There is great variety in the trade patterns of different countries. Agricultural countries tend to export food and import manufactures. Industrialized countries, for example, Japan, import primary commod-

ities and export manufactures. The United States, perhaps surprisingly, has a substantial share of primary commodities on both the import and export side.

5   The balance of payments is a systematic record of a country's transactions with the rest of the world. There is a distinction between transactions on current account (goods, services, and transfer payments) and transactions on capital account (net sale of assets). The balance of payments surplus is equal to the current account surplus plus the capital account surplus.

6   The current account surplus is equal to a country's increase in net foreign assets. Countries with current account surpluses acquire net claims on the rest of the world (or reduce their liabilities). Deficit countries increase their liabilities abroad.

7   A balance of payments surplus corresponds to official intervention in the exchange market. Intervention means that the central bank buys the currency that is in excess supply (the currency of the deficit country) and supplies, or sells, the currency that is in excess demand.

8   Persistent current account deficits require adjustment, not financing. But current account adjustment is costly. It involves working harder or spending less. For that reason governments often delay adjustment, thus leading to payments problems or even crises.

9   There are two basic exchange rate systems, fixed rate systems and flexible rate systems. But most exchange rate practice now lies in between: some form of dirty floating, or managed exchange rates. Under managed exchange rates the central bank sets limits to the magnitude or speed of exchange rate movements. Since exchange rate movements affect trade flows, there is the possibility of using and abusing exchange rate policy to increase exports and reduce imports.

10   Under the gold standard countries fix the value of their currencies in terms of gold. This determines exchange rates. In effect, the world uses a single form of money, gold.

11   A country that has problems of internal and external balance requires a policy mix that affects both the level and the composition of spending.

KEY TERMS

Imports	Exchange rate
Exports	Currency appreciation
Less-developed countries (LDCs)	Currency depreciation
Newly industrialized countries (NICs)	Balance of payments

Current Account
Capital account
Deficits
Surpluses
Fixed exchange rate system
Adjustable peg exchange rate system
Devaluation
Revaluation

Flexible (floating) exchange rate
  system
Clean floating exchange rate system
Dirty (managed) floating exchange
  rate system
Gold standard
Internal and external balance
Policy mix

PROBLEMS

1 The dollar price of deutsche marks is 50 cents per deutsche mark. The dollar price of the pound sterling is $2 per pound sterling. What is the price in deutsche marks of a pound sterling? That is, what is the deutsche mark–pound exchange rate?

2 In 1951 the dollar price of the pound was $4 per pound. In 1980 it was around $2.40. Did the pound appreciate or depreciate from 1950 to 1981? By what percentage?

3 Give some explanations for the fact that the eastern trading area's share of world income is much larger that its share of world exports.

4 Show the impact of the world oil-price increase on the composition of world trade among three groups of goods: non-oil primary commodities, oil, and manufactures. (Refer to Table 34-4 to see which share increased and which share fell from 1973 to 1979.)

5 (a) How do you explain the differences between the composition of trade of the LDCs, in Table 34-5, and that of Japan? (b) Would you think that Denmark is more like the United States or more like Japan in terms of the composition of exports and imports? And how about Hong Kong?

6 Suppose that a country has a current account surplus of $6 billion. The capital account shows a deficit of $2 billion. (a) Is the balance of payments in deficit or surplus?

(b) Are the central bank's net foreign assets rising or declining? (c) Is the central bank buying or selling domestic currency? Explain.

7 Gold mines are discovered in a country. Machinery and prospectors pour into the country to mine gold. Would you expect the balance of payments to show a surplus or a deficit? Which factors lead you to expect a surplus, on current or capital account, and which may lead to a deficit?

8 (a) Suppose that there is a sudden decline in the demand for French francs. Show how the central bank intervenes to prevent the franc from depreciating. (b) Why do central banks intervene? What is the alternative?

9 (a) As a holder of assets, would you prefer to hold assets denominated in a currency that is rapidly depreciating or appreciating? Why? (b) Given your answer, what would you do if you found out that the newly elected government of a country intends to implement campaign pledges to stop inflation, restore free enterprise, and remove deficits in the budget?

10 The OPEC countries together have been running persistent current account surpluses ever since the 1974 oil shock. How is this compatible with the statement in the text that persistent current account disequilibriums ultimately need adjustment? Are there different rules for deficit and surplus countries, for example, that deficit countries must adjust, but surplus countries need not?

11 Suppose that a country has a trade surplus and a boom. What is the policy mix you would recommend to restore internal and external balance?

12 A country develops a new product that sells well abroad. What is the impact on internal and external balance? Are policies required to restore equilibrium?

In this chapter we discuss why countries trade and the benefits they gain from doing so. Countries trade because they can buy goods more cheaply abroad than at home. This, simply put, is the reason for international trade and the reason it makes countries that trade better off than they would be if they cut themselves off from trade.

International trade involves *specialization* and *exchange*. A country that trades with others specializes by producing more of some goods than are demanded in the home market. The excess is exported in exchange for goods desired by domestic residents but not produced in sufficient quantity at home. Specialization and exchange allow a country to use its resources more efficiently; by trading it can consume more goods than it could if it produced entirely for itself.

There are two separate reasons why trade enables a country to increase its consumption of goods. First, international differences in the availability of raw materials or other factors of production, and in technologies, mean that there are international differences in costs of production. Cold areas are poorly suited to growing wine, and equatorial areas do poorly at producing wheat, for example. International trade enables countries to specialize in producing what they can produce most cheaply.

The second reason for gains from trade is that there are scale economies. When there are scale economies, larger-scale production lowers average costs. There is no better way to increase the scale of production than to use the entire world as a market. When there are scale economies, specialization and exchange through international trade make it unnecessary to rely on higher-cost, smaller-scale production for the domestic market alone.

These arguments describing the benefits from trade are analyzed in detail in this chapter. But while countries are ultimately better off if they trade, some people may lose, especially in the short run, as the economy adjusts to changing trade conditions. American consumers are made better off when Japanese automobile production becomes more efficient. However, Detroit automobile workers are not. They have to find new jobs. And they know that foreign competition is to blame. Because foreign competition may make life difficult for some voters, governments are frequently under pressure to reduce imports, for example, by imposing tariffs. In this chapter we discuss the policies with which governments react to trade problems. We also discuss

35

The Gains from Trade and Problems of Trade

whether it might be a good idea to impose tariffs under some conditions.

1 COMPARATIVE ADVANTAGE

We start by showing the benefits from trade when there are international differences in techniques of production. We use an extremely simple model, which highlights the key role of differences in the *relative costs* of production between countries. The model demonstrates the law of comparative advantage.

> The *law of comparative advantage* says that countries specialize in producing the goods that they can make at a *relatively* lower cost.

The precise meaning of the law, formulated by the great English economist David Ricardo (1772–1823),[1] will become clear as we develop the model.

We assume that there are two countries, the United States and France. Two goods can be produced, cars and textiles. Labor is the only factor of production, and there are constant returns to scale. Table 35-1 shows the assumptions made about production. It takes 300 hours of American labor to produce one car. The production of 1 unit of textiles takes 5 units of labor in the United States. Labor in France is less productive.

----

[1] Ricardo was a successful stockbroker before retiring at the age of 40 to become a Member of Parliament and an economist. His great book is *The Principles of Political Economy and Taxation*. Ricardo's arguments have a modern ring to them, because he uses models, clearly setting out his assumptions and their implications.

There it takes 600 hours of labor to produce one car and 8 units of labor to produce 1 unit of textiles.

Costs and Prices

In addition to the assumptions about techniques of production in the two countries, we assume that there is perfect competition. This means that the prices of all goods are equal to the marginal costs. And since there are constant returns to scale, the marginal costs are equal to the average costs, and so prices will be equal to the average costs of production.

Table 35-1 shows costs of production in the two countries, in dollars in the United States and in francs in France. Because labor is the only factor of production, costs consist entirely of wages. The wage rate is assumed to be fixed at $10 per hour in the United States and 50F (francs) in France. If neither country is trading, the two goods are each produced in each country and sell for prices equal to their average costs of production.

Before we allow the countries to trade, we should note that American labor requirements are lower for *both* goods than in France. But the differences are not uniform. American labor is *relatively* more productive in making cars than in making textiles. It takes twice as many hours to produce a car in France as it takes in the United States, but for textiles the ratio is only 8 to 5. It is these relative productivity differences that are the basis for trade.

TABLE 35-1
PRODUCTION TECHNIQUES AND COSTS

COUNTRY	WAGE	UNIT LABOR REQUIREMENT, labor hr/unit		UNIT LABOR COST	
		CARS	TEXTILES	CARS	TEXTILES
United States	$10	300	5	$3000	$50
France	50F	600	8	30,000F	400F

TABLE 35-2 ▮▮
COST DATA FOR ALTERNATIVE EXCHANGE RATES

| | | | COST IN $ WHEN EXCHANGE RATE IS | | | | | |
| | UNIT LABOR COST | | 5¢/F | | 11¢/F | | 20¢/F | |
COUNTRY	CARS	TEXTILES	CARS	TEXTILES	CARS	TEXTILES	CARS	TEXTILES
United States	$3000	$50	$3000	$50	$3000	$50	$3000	$50
France	30,000F	400F	$1500	$20	$3300	$44	$6000	$80

Opening of Trade

Now we allow the two countries to trade. Since they use different currencies, an exchange market has to be set up and an equilibrium exchange rate established. Table 35-2 shows the costs of goods in dollars for three alternative exchange rates, 5 cents per franc, 11 cents per franc, and 20 cents per franc.

Two of these three exchange rates cannot be equilibrium exchange rates. If the franc costs only 5 cents, then both cars and textiles cost less in France than in the United States. Americans would want to buy *all* their products in France and none from American producers. But Frenchmen would not want to buy anything from high-priced American producers. Americans would want to be demanders of francs so they can buy goods in France, but no one would want to sell francs. The 5 cents per franc exchange rate cannot last; the exchange rate has to increase. How about an exchange rate of 20 cents per franc? That, too, cannot be an equilibrium rate. *Both* cars and textiles are cheaper in the United States at that exchange rate. In the foreign exchange market, there would be French suppliers of francs wanting dollars to buy goods at low American prices but no one buying francs. Thus the exchange rate would have to fall.

The 11 cents per franc exchange rate is potentially an equilibrium rate. At that exchange rate, cars are cheaper in the United States, and textiles are cheaper in France. Everyone wants to buy textiles in France and cars in the United States. In the foreign exchange market, the supply of francs comes from Frenchmen wanting to buy American cars, while the demand for francs comes from Americans wanting to buy French textiles. There can be equilibrium in the foreign exchange market, provided the value of the cars that Frenchmen want to buy is equal to the value of the textiles that Americans want to buy.

Because there cannot be equilibrium in the foreign exchange market if both goods are cheaper in one of the countries, the range of equilibrium exchange rates is limited. Table 35-3 shows the range of possible exchange rates, starting with 10 cents per franc, including 11 cents per franc, and ending at 12.5 cents per franc. Exchange rates starting as low as 10 cents per franc and going as high as 12.5 cents per franc *may* be equilibrium rates.

Now we will show the production and trade patterns corresponding to the exchange rates in Table 35-3 and explain why there can be equilibrium at those rates.

Production and Trade Patterns

Corresponding to each exchange rate in Table 35-3 is a particular pattern of trade and production. Figure 35-1 illustrates. We start at the exchange rate of 10 cents per franc, corresponding to Figure 35-1a. At that exchange rate, cars cost the same in both

TABLE 35-3
THE RANGE OF EQUILIBRIUM EXCHANGE RATES

| | UNIT LABOR COST | | COST IN $ WHEN EXCHANGE RATE IS | | | | | |
| | | | 10¢/F | | 11¢/F | | 12.5¢/F | |
COUNTRY	CARS	TEXTILES	CARS	TEXTILES	CARS	TEXTILES	CARS	TEXTILES
United States	$3000	$50	$3000	$50	$3000	$50	$3000	$50
France	30,000F	400F	$3000	$40	$3300	$44	$3750	$50

FIGURE 35-1   PATTERNS OF TRADE AND PRO-
DUCTION. (a) United States specializes in car production; (b) both countries specialize in production;
(c) France specializes in textile production. In part a
cars cost the same to produce in both France and
the United States, and they are produced in both
countries. Textiles are produced only in France. The
United States exports cars, and France exports textiles. In part b cars are cheaper in the United States,
and textiles are cheaper in France. Each country
specializes. France exports textiles, and the United
States exports cars. In part c textiles cost the same
to produce in both countries, and they are produced
in both. Cars are cheaper to produce in the United
States and are produced only there. The United
States exports cars, and France exports textiles.

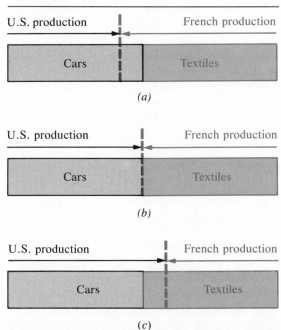

(a)

(b)

(c)

France and the United States. Textiles are
cheaper in France. This means that everyone buys textiles in France. But if Americans are buying French textiles, how can
they pay for them? How can the foreign exchange market be in equilibrium? The
United States has to be selling France *something*, and that something is cars. Therefore
the United States must be exporting cars to
France.

Figure 35-1a shows the corresponding
pattern of production. Textiles are produced
only in France. The United States produces
only cars. But France, too, probably produces some cars, since they cost the same to
make there as in the United States. We thus
expect France to produce both cars and textiles and the United States only cars.

At an exchange rate of 11 cents per
franc, cars are cheaper in the United States,
and textiles are cheaper in France. The
United States is the only producer of cars
and France the only producer of textiles,
since everyone buys where the goods are
cheapest. The United States exports cars to
France, and France exports textiles to the
United States. This case of complete *specialization* in production is shown in Figure 35-1b. Each country specializes by producing only one good.

Finally, at the exchange rate of 12.5
cents per franc, only the United States will
produce cars. Frenchmen import cars from
the United States, and Americans therefore
have to be importing textiles from France—
otherwise the foreign exchange market

could not be in equilibrium. The pattern of production is that France produces only textiles, while the United States may produce both cars and textiles, since textiles cost the same to make in the United States as in France. In this case, as in Figure 35-1a, only one country specializes.

The pattern of production can be summarized very simply. The United States always produces cars. France always produces textiles. If the United States specializes, it produces cars. If France specializes, it produces textiles. But sometimes one of the two countries will produce both goods. When it does, the other country specializes. The general rule, then, is that the opening of trade (in this model) leads to specialization by at least one country.

The trade pattern can be summarized even more simply. The United States always exports cars and imports textiles. France correspondingly always imports cars and exports textiles. Now we explain why.

Comparative Advantage

The patterns of production and trade seen in Figure 35-1 show the law of comparative advantage. The law states that countries specialize in making the goods that they can make at a *relatively* lower cost. Looking at Table 35-1, we see that in France the cost of producing textiles is 1.33 percent (400/30,000) of the cost of producing a car. But in the United States the cost of producing textiles is 1.67 percent (50/3000) of the cost of making a car. Therefore, making textiles in France costs relatively less, compared with making cars, than it does in the United States. The law therefore tells us that France will specialize in making textiles and the United States in making cars, which is what we see from Figure 35-1.

There is an emphasis on *comparative* advantage and *relative* costs because it is easy to believe that there would be no point

for the United States in trading with France when U.S. labor is more productive in *both* car and textile manufacture. After all, the argument might go, the United States is better at making both goods.

In the case of trade between France and the United States, we should ask what the best use is that the world can make of the labor in the two countries. Labor in the United States is better at making cars, compared with making textiles, and so U.S. labor should make cars. French labor is better at making textiles, and so it should make textiles.

If we are guided by the *absolute advantage* of U.S. labor, the fact that labor is more productive in both lines in the United States (see Box 35-1), we tend to forget that French labor is also a scarce resource and that the world should use it to produce goods as well. Indeed, the principle of comparative advantage is often useful in personal situations. Consider, for example, two economists writing a book. The first one both types and draws diagrams faster than the second. The second is relatively faster at drawing diagrams, though absolutely he is slower. How should the two of them divide up the responsibilities for drawing diagrams and typing? Obviously, if the faster economist both typed and drew diagrams, the slower professor's labor would go to waste. The slower professor should also do his share, and it is more efficient for him to do the diagrams. That way he can be thought of as saving relatively more of the speedy professor's time for typing.

Equilibrium Production Patterns

In Figure 35-1 we show three possible patterns of production. In each case France exports textiles and the United States cars, and in each case at least one of the countries specializes in production. But what determines which pattern is actually established?

That depends mainly on the relative sizes of the countries. Let us consider the United States, with 240 million people, and Finland, with under 5 million, and two goods, wheat and timber. The United States has a comparative advantage in wheat.

The likely pattern of production is that Finland specializes in timber, while the United States produces both wheat and timber. To see this, suppose that it is Finland that produces both goods, while the United States specializes in producing wheat. This means that Finland produces all the world's timber. But the U.S. economy is so large in relation to Finland's that total Finnish timber production cannot possibly satisfy the entire demand from the United States, let alone the entire demand from both the United States and Finland. If Finland cannot meet both countries' demand for timber, and if it has a comparative advantage in timber production, it will specialize. And the United States will produce both goods, wheat and also timber.

The Gains from Trade

We have seen that opening trade between countries will lead at least one of them to specialize. Each country will export the good in which it has a comparative advantage and import the good of which it is the relatively less efficient producer. Now we have to ask whether such trading patterns make anyone better or worse off. Can we show that one country or the other actually benefits from trade compared with a situation of no trade, or *autarky*? The answer is yes. The country that specializes will be better off, and the other country will be no worse off. Thus the world benefits from trade.

Here is the demonstration. We want to show that citizens in a country that specializes under trade can purchase with their labor time more of the importable goods than they could produce themselves

directly. Thus trade is just an indirect way of producing: we produce for export to buy imports which we are relatively less efficient at making.

Consider Table 35-3, and look at the case where the exchange rate is 10 cents per franc so that cars cost $3000 in each country while textiles are cheaper in France. American workers producing cars can buy 75 ($3000/$40) units of imported textiles for each car they produce, but they could only buy 60 ($3000/$50) units if they had to purchase the higher-cost domestic textiles. Thus U.S. workers gain through access to imports. At the same time there is no loss for French workers, who need to produce 75 units of textiles to buy a car, whether it is domestic or foreign.

Consider next the 11 cents per franc exchange rate. It is still the case that American workers can buy more textiles per car— 68.16 ($3000/$44) units—through access to imports than they could buy if they had to pay the higher domestic costs. But now French workers also gain. A unit of textiles that they produce "buys more car" if they can buy imports rather than domestically produced cars. For their textiles French workers can buy $44/$3000 = 0.0147 unit of imported cars but only $44/$3300 = 0.0133 unit of home-produced textiles. Again there are gains from trade. French workers are better off specializing in textiles and spending their income on imported cars rather than producing cars themselves.

The two examples show the general principle of the gains from trade: Any time a country specializes, it gains from trade because it increases its purchasing power, producing the good it is relatively efficient at making and importing the good that it is relatively poor at producing. A country that specializes must gain, and a country that in trade equilibrium does not specialize still will not lose. Therefore, trade benefits the world.

BOX 35-1

ABSOLUTE AND COMPARATIVE ADVANTAGE DEFINED

This box clarifies the distinction between comparative advantage and absolute advantage. The table summarizes three possibilities.

UNIT LABOR REQUIREMENTS AND COMPARATIVE ADVANTAGE

	CASE I		CASE II		CASE III	
	CARS	TEXTILES	CARS	TEXTILES	CARS	TEXTILES
United States	300	5	300	5	300	5
France	600	10	1500	10	1500	3
United States/ France	$1/2$	$1/2$	$1/5$	$1/2$	$1/5$	$5/3$

CASE I
The United States has an absolute advantage in the production of both goods. U.S. labor is *uniformly* more productive than French labor. Therefore, there is no *comparative* advantage, or relative advantage, in the production of either cars or textiles.

CASE II
The United States has an absolute advantage in the production of both goods because U.S. labor requirements are lower in both industries than French labor requirements. But the United States has a comparative advantage in the automobile industry because in that sector U.S. labor is *relatively* more productive. U.S. labor is twice as productive as French labor in textiles but five times as productive in automobiles (300 labor hours in the United States versus 1500 in France). Therefore, the United States has a comparative advantage in automobiles.

CASE III
The United States has an absolute advantage in automobiles, and France has an absolute advantage in textiles. Clearly, the United States has a comparative advantage (and an absolute advantage) in automobiles and a comparative (and absolute) *dis*advantage in textiles.

International trade hinges on *comparative* advantage, whether we have case II or case III. Even though a country may have absolutely lower labor productivity in every sector than her trading partners, she can still benefit from international trade. Exchange rates move to make every country competitive in at least one industry, the industry in which the country has a comparative advantage.

Many Goods
Our example with only two goods gives the basic principles of comparative advantage, and of the gains from trade. The same principles continue to hold when we allow for many goods. Suppose that we have, in addi-

TABLE 35-4

UNIT LABOR REQUIREMENTS: THE MANY-GOODS CASE
(Hours of Labor per Unit of Output)

	COMPUTERS	CARS	TV SETS	TEXTILES	CERAMICS	SHOES
United States	200	300	50	5	7	15
France	1200	600	90	8	6	10
United States/France relative unit labor requirements	$1/6$	$1/2$	$5/9$	$5/8$	$7/6$	$3/2$

tion to cars and textiles, TV sets, shoes, ceramics, and computers. Table 35-4 lists the unit labor requirements for each industry in the two countries, as well as the relative (United States relative to France) unit labor requirements.

The United States is relatively most efficient at producing computers, needing only one-sixth as much labor time as France. France is relatively most efficient at producing shoes; it actually takes less time in France than in the United States. The table shows the order of U.S. comparative advantage, going from left to right, from computers to shoes. French comparative advantage runs in the opposite direction, from shoes to computers.

Who will produce which goods? Since every country must produce at least one good, the United States will certainly produce computers, and France will certainly produce shoes. Just where the dividing line falls depends in part on the sizes of the two countries, as in the case where there were only cars and textiles. Figure 35-2 shows a possible pattern of production.

Both countries now gain from trade. Each is importing some of the goods it used to produce domestically. This means that those goods are now being produced relatively more cheaply than before, and therefore consumer buying power has increased in each country.

The Ricardian model emphasizes *international labor productivity differences* as the main reason for trade and the main factor determining the patterns of specialization in international trade. The model predicts that specialization takes place according to the principle of comparative advantage, and it shows that at least one country must gain from trade and that neither country will lose. We now extend our analysis to bring in other reasons for international trade and for gains from trade.

2 DIFFERENCES IN FACTOR ENDOWMENTS AS THE BASIS FOR TRADE

The Ricardian model used to present the theory of comparative advantage emphasized differences in relative labor productivity as the basis for trade. But the essential point is not so much differences in labor productivity as differences in *relative costs* of producing goods.

Relative costs of producing goods are determined not only by differences in technology but also by the relative amounts of factors of production (or the factor endowments) a country has. To take the simplest example, Saudi Arabia has a comparative advantage in producing oil because she has a larger stock of oil in the ground than other countries. Saudi Arabia can produce oil relatively cheaply compared with other countries, just as Chile and Zambia can produce copper relatively cheaply, and just as South Africa can produce gold relatively cheaply.

FIGURE 35-2 PATTERNS OF PRODUCTION WITH MANY GOODS. The goods are arranged in order of U.S. comparative advantage from left to right. The pattern of production is determined by the position of the dividing line. The United States produces goods to the left of the line, and France produces to the right of the line. The position of the line is determined in large part by the relative sizes of the countries. Each country will import the goods it does not produce.

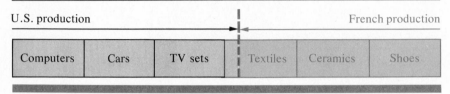

These countries therefore produce and export those minerals.

While countries that have large mineral deposits generally export them, we should remind ourselves that just having the deposits is not enough. It also has to be profitable to exploit them. For instance, the existence of vast amounts of timber in the Amazon jungles does not automatically mean that Brazil exploits that timber—most of the timber is too remote for that.

Differences in Capital-Labor Ratios

Differences in raw material endowments are one reason why relative costs of production differ among countries. But so are differences in countries' endowments of other factors of production, for instance, capital (machines) and labor.

We consider the United States and Mexico and assume that the United States has both more capital and more labor than Mexico because it is a bigger country. But the United States also has *relatively* more capital. The capital-labor ratio, or the amount of capital per worker, is larger in the United States than in Mexico. With relatively more capital, the rental rate on capital in the United States is relatively lower than that in Mexico, and U.S. labor is relatively more expensive.

We stick with cars and textiles but now assume that car production and textile pro-duction use both capital and labor. Automobile production is assumed to be capital-intensive. This means that more capital is used per worker in making cars than in making textiles. Table 35-5 summarizes the information. The table shows that the United States has twice as much capital per worker as does Mexico—that the United States is a capital-rich country compared with Mexico. The technology is such that cars are capital-intensive in both countries, while textiles are labor-intensive in both.

The two countries taken in isolation would look quite different. In the United States, where there is a lot of capital in relation to labor, cars that use relatively more capital would be produced relatively cheaply compared with cars in Mexico. Textiles would be relatively expensive. In this sense the United States has a comparative advantage in capital-intensive automobiles and Mexico in textiles that are labor-intensive.

Because cars are relatively cheaper in the United States, the opening of trade will lead the United States to produce and export cars and Mexico to produce and export textiles. Comparative advantage continues to be the basic explanation of trade patterns. Countries export the good in which they have a comparative advantage or for which they have relatively lower costs of production. In the Ricardian model comparative

TABLE 35-5

HYPOTHETICAL CAPITAL-LABOR RATIOS

	ENDOWMENTS (CAPITAL PER WORKER)	TECHNOLOGY	
		CARS	TEXTILES
United States	$5000	Capital-intensive	Labor-intensive
Mexico	$2500	Capital-intensive	Labor-intensive

advantage depends on labor productivity. In this extended model it depends on the relative availability of capital and labor. Capital-rich countries export relatively capital-intensive goods and import relatively labor-intensive goods.

Some Evidence on Factor Endowments and Trade Patterns

Comparative advantage theory based on international differences in factor endowments suggests that countries that have a lot of capital in relation to labor will export goods that use relatively more capital than the imported goods. Conversely, countries that are relatively rich in labor will tend to export labor-intensive goods and import capital-intensive goods. Figure 35-3 offers some evidence on the theory.

In Figure 35-3 we show on the horizontal axis the capital-labor ratio for different countries. The ratio is measured in U.S. dollars per worker. On the vertical axis we show the capital-labor ratio of exports compared with imports. The number 0.5 means that exports are only half as capital-intensive as imports. The number 1 means that exports and imports have the same capital-labor ratio. Now consider the evidence. A country such as India has a very low capital-labor ratio, only $300 per worker. In conformity with the theory, her exports are only half as capital-intensive as her imports. At the other end we find countries such as Sweden or Canada which have a very high capital-labor ratio—more than $12,000 per worker—and which have export sectors that

are relatively capital-intensive compared with the import sector. The positive relationship suggested by the data confirms in a broad way the comparative advantage theory based on relative supplies of capital and labor.

Comparative advantage, or lower relative costs of production, is one of the fundamental reasons for international trade. Cost differences may occur either because countries differ in productivity or because the relative supplies of factors of production in the two countries differ. Countries then specialize in producing the goods in which they have a comparative advantage.

3 INTRA-INDUSTRY TRADE

A striking fact from trade statistics, or from looking around in a street or shop, is that we do not observe a lot of specialization. The United States imports *and* exports automobiles. Germany imports *and* exports automobiles, or refrigerators, or clothes, or chemicals, or anything you care to think of. There is, in practice, a lot of two-way trade, or *intra-industry* (within an industry) trade; the same good, defined broadly, is both imported and exported.

Of course, it is not literally the same good that is traded both ways. An American car and a Japanese car are not exactly the same; U.S. wine and French wine are not exactly the same; German beer and Danish beer or Schlitz are not exactly the same. They are diversified products, highly substitutable, but enjoying some brand alle-

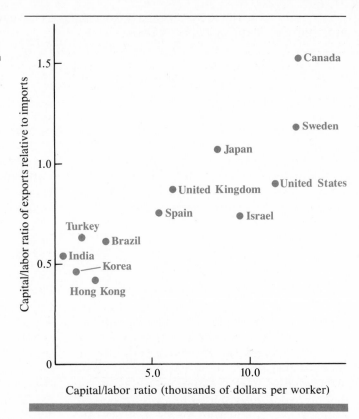

FIGURE 35-3 THE ECONOMYWIDE CAPITAL-LABOR RATIO AND THE CAPITAL-LABOR RATIO OF EXPORTS IN RELATION TO IMPORTS. The data are from U.S. Department of Labor, *Changes in the International Pattern of Factor Abundance and the Composition of Trade,* Economic Discussion Paper 8, June 1980.

giance that makes it possible for each of them to be produced and internationally traded.

Analysis of intra-industry trade suggests that there are three forces at work. First, consumer preferences for diversity create a demand for a broad range of goods. Consumers do not all want exactly the same type of car, or shirt, or radio. Second, there are economies of scale in production. In some industries, any firm that can produce on a large scale rather than only for the home market will enjoy scale economies that reduce costs and thereby make it cost-competitive in foreign markets. But the tendencies to specialization caused by scale economies and the demand for diversity are reduced by transportation costs. If two countries are producing goods at roughly the same cost, then the costs of transporting

the goods between the two countries will ensure that each produces for its own market unless scale economies are powerful.

Intra-industry trade is the outcome of these divergent forces. Now we want to measure the importance of intra-industry trade. Suppose that we define an index as zero when trade in a particular commodity is entirely one-way; a country only exports or only imports the good. The index is 1 if there is complete two-way trade in the sense that the country imports as much of a particular good as it exports. Figure 35-4 shows the index for selected commodities in U.S. trade and indicates the forces that make for one-way trade and two-way, or intra-industry, trade. For different commodities we show the value of the index of trade flows.

At one extreme is the case of fuels.

FIGURE 35-4   THE INDEX OF INTRA-INDUSTRY TRADE FOR SELECTED U.S. COM-
MODITIES. When there is no intra-industry trade, and a good is either only exported
or only imported, the value of the index is zero. When the values of imports and
exports of a good are equal, the index is 1, and then trade is dominated by intra-
industry trade. The data show the extent of intra-industry trade for a number of
industries. (*Source:* GATT, *International Trade, 1978/1979,* Geneva 1979.)

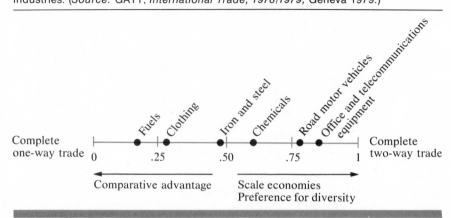

There is little two-way trade; the United States imports fuel but exports very little. At the other extreme is office and telecommunications equipment. Here two-way trade is very strong, and thus the index is as large as 0.84. Various other goods lie in between. In general, it will be true that the more the commodities are undifferentiated goods (fuel, iron, and steel), the more we expect comparative advantage along the regular lines of relative resource abundance to dictate trade patterns. As we move toward finished manufactures, product differentiation becomes dominant, and comparative advantage loses some of its overriding role. Thus intra-industry trade becomes more significant in automobiles or office equipment.

Intra-industry trade reflects economic integration among countries. The more closely markets are integrated and the lower the obstacles to trade—in terms of both distance and tariffs—the larger the extent of intra-industry trade we would expect to observe. This is brought out by a comparison of intra-industry trade indices for the United States, Japan, and the *European Community*—EC for short—(Germany,

France, Italy, Netherlands, Belgium, Luxembourg, United Kingdom, Ireland, Greece, and Denmark). For each country or group of countries we list in Table 35-6 the index of intra-industry trade.

Table 35-6 serves to make two points. First, it gives the example of a country whose trade is substantially one-way, namely, Japan. Japan imports primary commodities and exports virtually nothing in this category. She exports manufactures and imports very little in this area. Accordingly, the index of intra-industry trade for Japan is small for most goods.

By contrast, the European Community has a more diversified resource endowment. It is a more integrated market in that distance, information barriers, and tariffs are relatively insignificant. Therefore, we are not surprised to see that intra-industry trade is the rule in almost all commodity groups. Indeed, in some commodity groups, such as office and telecommunications equipment, the index almost reaches unity.

We thus see that intra-industry trade comes into its own particularly when close proximity and the absence of restrictions to

TABLE 35-6

INTERCOUNTRY COMPARISON OF THE INDEX OF INTRA-INDUSTRY TRADE, 1979

COMMODITY	UNITED STATES	EC	JAPAN
Primary commodities	0.73	0.68	0.09
Total manufactures:	0.97	0.88	0.39
Total engineering products:	0.89	0.82	0.23
Office and telecommunications equipment	0.84	0.98	0.42
Road motor vehicles	0.77	0.82	0.07
Other machinery and transportation equipment	0.64	0.81	0.33
Household appliances	0.54	0.95	0.12
Textiles	0.8	0.98	0.67
Clothing	0.28	0.84	0.33
Other consumer goods	0.6	0.91	0.82
Weighted average	0.87	0.77	0.26

Source: GATT, *International Trade, 1979/1980,* Geneva, 1980.

trade create very integrated markets. This also describes trade among different regions of the United States (although Detroit, like Japan, would have almost complete one-way trade in automobiles). The gains from such trade are that consumers are able to consume a more diverse group of commodities and consume at a lower cost than they could if producers were not able to take advantage of international markets to produce on a large scale.

4 GAINERS AND LOSERS

We have shown why countries trade and why there are gains to opening an economy to trade rather than avoiding exchange with the rest of the world. This says that allowing some trade is better than not allowing any. But it does not say that everything that happens in the international economy makes everyone better off. We give two examples here of the types of conflict that are raised by international trade and that lead to restrictions on trade.

Refrigeration

Figure 35-5 shows the chilled beef exports of the United States and of Argentina in the period 1896–1913. At the end of the nineteenth century improved refrigeration made it possible for Argentina to become a supplier of frozen meat in the world market. Exports that had been nonexistent in 1900 rose to nearly 400,000 tons by 1913 as the new technology was used to ship meat to Europe. The United States had been an exporter of beef, but U.S. exports dwindled from their 100,000-ton level to virtually zero.

Sharply rising Argentine beef exports— and similar increases in meat exports from Australia and New Zealand—provide a good example of the conflicts of interest that international trade raises. Table 35-7 shows who gained (+) and who lost (−). In Argentina the possibility of exporting implied a major change in the production structure of the entire economy. Cattle grazing and meat export attracted resources. Owners of cattle and land gained; other users of land whose costs increased lost out. Argentine consumers found their steaks becoming more expensive as meat was shipped abroad. Thus even for some Argentinians the possibility of exporting was a mixed blessing.

In the United States and Europe the main effects were on consumers and beef

FIGURE 35-5 REFRIGERATION ENABLES ARGENTINA TO BECOME A MAJOR EXPORTER OF BEEF IN WORLD TRADE. (*From* League of Nations, *The Network of World Trade,* Geneva, 1942, p. 86.)

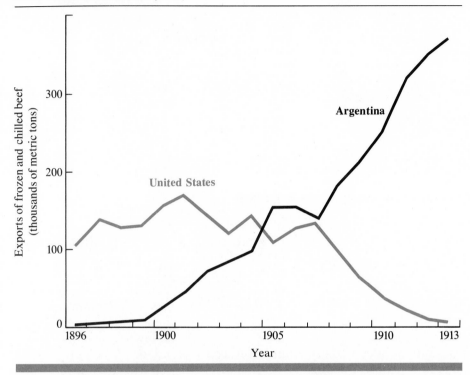

TABLE 35-7

ARGENTINE BEEF EXPORTS MADE POSSIBLE BY THE INVENTION OF REFRIGERATION: GAINS AND LOSSES

	UNITED STATES	EUROPE	ARGENTINA
Producers of beef	−	−	+
Other producers	0	0	−
Consumers	+	+	−

producers. The producers lost because beef prices fell. For that same reason consumers gained. Effects on other producers were probably small.

Did the world gain from refrigeration that allowed trade in meat? We are inclined to say yes, but we have already seen that a number of groups actually lost. How do we strike the balance?

The U.S. Automobile Industry

The second example is the U.S. automobile industry. Table 35-8 shows data for exports and imports of automobiles as well as the ratio of imports to domestic production. There is a clear trend of imports gaining an increasing share in the U.S. market, especially imports from Japan. By 1980 U.S. producers of automobiles were suffering large

TABLE 35-8

U.S. AUTOMOBILE TRADE
(Billions of U.S. Dollars)

| YEAR | EXPORTS | IMPORTS | | | RATIO OF IMPORTS TO RETAIL SALES |
		TOTAL VALUE	% FROM JAPAN	
1965	$ 2.0	$ 0.8	13.2%	6.1%
1973	6.0	10.1	21.4	15.4
1978	13.0	21.9	37.6	17.7
1979	14.7	23.6	40.4	21.8
1980	14.2	25.7	45.6	26.7
1981	16.2	26.2	N.A.	27.3

Sources: *Survey of Current Business*, May 1982; GATT, *International Trade*, Geneva, 1980; *Business Statistics*, 1979; and United Nations, *Commodity Trade Statistics, 1965*, New York, 1965.

losses. They pressured the government to prevent further increases in imports.

Again there would be gains and losses. Restricting imports of cars from Japan would raise prices—certainly of Japanese cars—to the American consumer. Restrictions would also cost jobs, or at least reduce the growth in incomes, in Japan. Against these losses American automobile workers would keep their jobs, and people owning shares in automobile companies would gain.

How should we decide whether to restrict imports or allow free trade? Should consumers have the final word or injured workers, or the stockholders of General Motors? And there is another question. Should we be free to change our import policy from one day to the next, thus changing the demand for Japanese cars and creating difficulties for the producer?

Similar issues arise in other contexts where trade is restricted. The restrictions might take the form of limits on exports of particular goods, perhaps for strategic reasons (the United States tries to prevent exports of sophisticated computers to the Soviet Union, for instance), limits on lending to countries that violate human rights, limits on wheat exports to Russia, limits on all

trade with a particular country as a measure of international warfare, or limits on imports of Cuban cigars. In each case there is a cost to the measures, and there will be side benefits or a cost for consumers or producers. To measure the costs and benefits we now develop in detail the analysis of a tariff and then extend the framework to other instruments of commercial, or trade, policy.

Commercial policy is government policy that influences trade through taxes, subsidies, and direct restrictions on imports and exports.

5   THE ECONOMICS OF TARIFFS

The most common type of trade restriction is a tariff, or import duty. A tariff requires the importer of a good to pay a specified fraction of the world price to the government. With a tariff at the rate of 20 percent on automobiles, for example, and a world price of $4000, the duty would be $800 (0.2 times $4000). The importer now has to cover not only his payment to the foreign producer ($4000) but also the duty paid to the government ($800).

The (minimum) domestic price at which the importer is willing to sell is therefore equal to the world price plus the duty, or the world price times 1 plus the tariff rate:

Domestic price of an importable commodity = $\dfrac{\text{world price}}{} \times (1 + \text{tariff rate})$ (1)

In our example with a world price per car of $4000 and a tariff rate of 0.2, or 20 percent, the domestic price is equal to $4800 ($4000 times 1.2). The tariff raises the domestic price of an importable commodity above the world price. In doing so, it provides protection for domestic producers, and it taxes consumers, as we shall see now in detail.

The Free-Trade Equilibrium

The starting point of our analysis is the free-trade situation. We look at a country that faces a given world price, say, $4000 per car. In Figure 35-6 we study the home market for automobiles. The given world price is shown by the horizontal schedule, and the home country can buy any amount at the going world price. Schedules DD and SS represent the domestic demand for automobiles and the domestic supply. Implicit in our analysis is the assumption that domestic

cars and foreign cars are identical or perfect substitutes.

Given the domestic demand in Figure 35-6 we note that at the price of $4000 consumers would wish to buy Q_d units, consuming at point G on the demand curve. Home firms would produce only Q_s units at point C on their supply curve. The difference, Q_d minus Q_s, is made up by imports. At the prevailing world price part of the home demand is satisfied by domestic production and part by imports. As long as the goods are perfect substitutes, as we assume, consumers are entirely indifferent between imports and domestically produced cars.

Equilibrium with a Tariff

In Figure 35-7 we show the effect of a 20 percent tariff. The tariff raises the price at which an importer is willing to supply goods (cars) in the home market. At a price of $4800—the foreign cost of $4000 plus the duty of $800—importers are willing to sell any quantity in the home market. Hence the new *tariff-inclusive* price that will prevail

FIGURE 35-6 THE FREE-TRADE EQUILIBRIUM OF PRODUCTION, CONSUMPTION, AND IMPORTS. *DD* is the demand curve of domestic residents for automobiles. *SS* is the supply curve of domestic producers. Automobiles are available in the world market for $4000. Therefore, no one will pay more than $4000 for a car. At the price of $4000, domestic demand is Q_d, and domestic supply is Q_s. The quantity demanded domestically is Q_d, and quantity supplied is Q_s. The difference between domestic quantity demanded and production is made up by imports, and so the quantity of imports is equal to $(Q_d - Q_s)$.

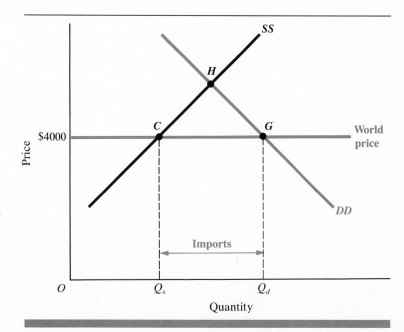

FIGURE 35-7 THE EFFECTS OF A TARIFF. The imposition of a 20 percent tariff raises the price at which cars can be imported from $4000 to $4800. Quantity demanded falls from Q_d to Q_d' as a result of the higher price, which also induces an increase in domestic production from Q_s to Q_s'. Imports fall.

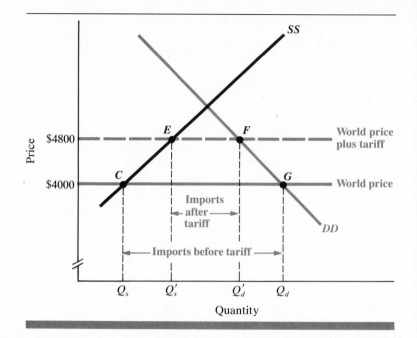

On the demand side the price increase induces consumers to reduce their purchases of cars. Consumers move along their demand curve from point F, and the quantity demanded falls from Q_d to Q_d'. For consumers the tariff is clearly a bad idea. It is like a tax. Consumers have to pay higher prices, and for that reason they reduce their quantity demanded.

is $4800, as shown by the dashed schedule. Thus the tariff raises the domestic, or tariff-inclusive, price above the world price.

What are the effects of the tariff on consumption and production? Because the tariff raises home prices, it encourages domestic production. Firms increase their production from Q_s to Q_s'. The tariff provides protection by allowing home firms to produce at a higher marginal cost than the world price. At point E on the supply schedule the domestic marginal cost is equal to $4800 and thus exceeds the world price of $4000. This is only possible because domestic producers do not have to pay the tariff and therefore can afford to be less efficient producers than their competitors in the world market. On the production side a tariff thus discriminates in favor of domestic producers. It acts like a subsidy to domestic production of cars.

A *subsidy* is a payment from the government to encourage the production or consumption of a good.

Subsidies are negative taxes.

On the demand side the price increase induces consumers to reduce their purchases of cars. Consumers move along their demand curve from point G to point F, and the quantity demanded falls from Q_d to Q_d'. For consumers the tariff is clearly a bad idea. It is like a tax. Consumers have to pay higher prices, and for that reason they reduce their quantity demanded.

Figure 35-7 shows the combined effect of the increase in production and the decline in demand, namely a fall in imports. Imports decline in part because the tariff-induced price increase lowers the quantity demanded. In part they fall because domestic production expands and replaces imports. By experimenting with the diagram we can see that the fall in imports will be larger the more responsive demand and supply are to price. With relatively flat or elastic schedules a given tariff brings about a very large change in imports. But if the schedules are very steep, the price change has little effect on the quantities demanded and supplied and hence on imports.

Costs and Benefits of a Tariff

Figure 35-8 and Table 35-9 provide a detailed accounting of the costs and benefits of a tariff. We have to be careful to distinguish net *costs to society* from *transfers* between one part of the economy and another. Recall that transfers are payments made that are *not* in exchange for economic services provided. Our earlier discussion of conflicts of interest between consumers and producers already warned us of precisely these transfers.

A starting point is to recognize in Figure 35-8 that consumers pay more for the goods they continue to purchase. The increased cost is $800 times the quantity, Q'_d. We will analyze how that amount, equal to area *LFHJ*, is divided up among the recipients. The second part is to recognize that triangle *FHG*, labeled *B*, corresponds to a loss for society.

The increased payments by consumers go in part to the government as tariff revenue. Tariff revenue is equal to the quantity of imports times the tariff, or rectangle *EIHF*. The rectangle is the product of the tariff per unit ($800) times the import volume $(Q'_d - Q'_s)$. The tariff revenue represents a *transfer* from consumers to the government. It does *not* represent a cost to

FIGURE 35-8   THE WELFARE COSTS OF A TARIFF. The imposition of a tariff creates both transfer payments and deadweight burdens, or social losses. As a result of the tariff, consumers pay a total of *LFHJ* more for the Q'_d cars they buy. Area *EIHF* of that amount is tariff revenue, equal to the $800-per-car tariff times the number of imports. Area *ECJL* is an increase in the profits of producers. Both of these amounts are transfers, from consumers to the government and from consumers to firms, respectively. Areas *A* and *B* represent losses. Area *A* represents the excess of social costs of production incurred above the level that would be incurred if the same resources used for producing cars were instead put to another use. And area *B* represents the loss of consumers' surplus from the higher price of cars.

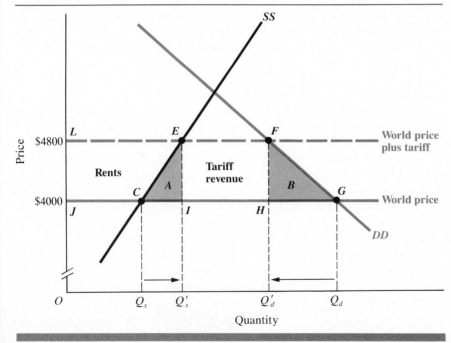

TABLE 35-9

COSTS AND BENEFITS OF A TARIFF

	CONSUMERS	FIRMS	GOVERNMENT	SOCIETY
	Pay tariff revenue (EIHF)		Collects tariff (EIHF)	0
	Pay rents to firms (ECJL)	Receive rents (ECJL)		0
	Lose surplus (FHG)			−FHG
	Pay excess cost of home production (EIC)			−EIC
Net	−LFGJ	+ECJL	+EIHF	−FHG − EIC

society because the government can use the revenue. For example, it could return the revenue to consumers as a general income tax cut.

Increased consumer payments also go in part as profits or rents to firms. This corresponds to area *ECJL*. Firms receive higher prices for their output, and their profits increase by the excess of price over marginal cost. For firms these rents or profits are a main attraction of tariffs, but to society they do not represent a *net* cost. Instead, they represent a redistribution of income from consumers to producers of import-competing goods.

The shaded area labeled *A does* correspond to a social cost. Part of the increased payment of consumers supports inefficient domestic production.

Inefficient production means that it costs more to produce a good, at the margin, than the good costs in the world market. The excess of the domestic marginal cost over the world price times the quantity wastefully produced—triangle *A*—is a social cost, or waste induced by the tariff. In part consumers and society pay for waste when a tariff is imposed. The resources drawn into the import-competing sector could have been used more efficiently in other sectors.

There is another area of social loss, labeled *B*. Here we look at the excess of valu-

ation by consumers over cost. The marginal valuation of an extra car by the consumer is indicated by the demand schedule. The marginal cost to society is given by the world price. Reducing demand when the marginal valuation exceeds the marginal cost is wasteful and gives rise to a loss of consumer surplus. This is a cost to society just as is the waste on the production side.

In summary, a tariff redistributes income from consumers to producers and to the government. Most of the increased payments of consumers represent transfers rather than social costs. They do not represent a social cost because consumers ultimately own the firms and the government. Of course, we must qualify the idea that transfers do not hurt consumers. This is only true if all consumers are alike and share equally in the ownership of firms and the benefits of government programs. Otherwise, some people surely pay the tariff, while other people enjoy the revenues. For instance, the government might use the revenues to subsidize city buses. Then car drivers would be hurt, and bus riders would benefit. Even though the transfers cancel out in total, some people may benefit while others are being damaged.

But even beyond the transfers and potential distribution effects, a tariff always involves waste. There is an excess cost of production as firms push their marginal cost to the level of the tariff-inclusive price. They produce too much in that the marginal cost of domestic production exceeds the world price. There is also a net cost on the consumption side, where consumers' marginal valuation of cars exceeds their cost to society. These two items, shown by the shaded areas, represent the social costs of a tariff. It can be seen by experimenting with the diagram that these triangles will be larger the larger the tariff is and the more elastic the demand and supply schedules are.

The analysis of the costs and benefits of a tariff has shown the distinction between *transfers* and *waste.* A tariff redistributes income from consumers to producers and the government. These transfers may or may not be controversial, but they do not necessarily involve any social costs. What does involve a social cost (and no corresponding gain to anyone) is the excess cost on the production side and the cost to consumers who value importable goods above the world cost. These are unavoidable *deadweight losses.* They create the presumption that a tariff is a bad idea.

But are tariffs *always* a bad idea, or might they sometimes be desirable? Of course, we want to be particularly suspicious of any pro-tariff argument, given that producers stand to benefit from a tariff and therefore will certainly be inclined to invent reasons for protection, whether they are socially justifiable or not. But just because someone benefits from an argument does not necessarily mean it is wrong.

6 ARGUMENTS FOR TARIFFS

The analysis of tariffs shows that there is an excess cost, or waste, that results from overproduction and underconsumption of the protected commodity. This cost must be set against any benefit claimed for a tariff in deciding whether there is a net gain from protection.

Table 35-10 lists some of the most popular arguments for tariffs. It turns out that there is only a single case where a tariff is *the* best instrument to achieve a given purpose with minimal social costs. In all other cases a tariff is either a second-best policy, only to be used when other methods are unavailable, or a policy that is entirely unwarranted.

The starting point for testing the case for a tariff is the recognition that a "good" tariff must pass a double test. First, the tariff must work in the sense that it brings about a socially desirable objective. Second, it must do so at a lower cost, in terms of waste, than any other available instrument. Most popular arguments fail the double test because other methods—consumption or production subsidies or taxes—solve the problem more cheaply.

We now examine several of the arguments for tariffs in Table 35-10, explaining both what the arguments are and why they are put into the three categories shown. "Second-best" means that there are better ways of reaching the goals that the tariff is supposed to achieve.

Way of Life

Society may want to protect the livelihood of inefficient farmers or craftsmen. Society feels that these people, with their traditional, stable way of life, are the backbone of the community and should be maintained in their accustomed lives. Therefore, it is argued, tariffs should be imposed to protect them against foreign competition.

This is a second-best argument because there is a better way of protecting the traditional way of life, at a lower cost to consumers. A tariff both raises the price for consumers and gives protection to producers. But we can protect producers by giving them a production subsidy. The production subsidy will keep farmers in business without also raising the price to consumers.

TABLE 35-10

ARGUMENTS FOR TARIFFS

FIRST-BEST (NATIONAL ADVANTAGE)	SECOND-BEST	NONARGUMENTS
Foreign trade monopoly	Infant industry, defense, scale economies, way of life, externalities, dependence, distortions, antiluxury, revenue	Cheap foreign labor, foreign subsidies(?)

Take another, similar second-best example, where society frowns on luxury consumption goods (Rolls-Royce cars, golden toothpicks). Should it use a tariff to discourage luxury consumption, or is imposing a consumption tax on luxuries the better way? A tariff, in effect, both taxes consumers and encourages producers of luxuries. Surely if we are interested in reducing the consumption of luxuries, there is no reason to encourage wasteful domestic production of luxuries. A consumption tax is the right tool.

The Infant Industry Case for Protection

The *infant industry* argument is one of the most common arguments for a tariff. The argument is that firms acquire technical know-how and low costs of production only as a consequence of being in business. There is *learning by doing.* The only way an industry can become competitive is by actually producing. But if at the outset firms cannot match foreign producers in competitiveness, how can they ever get started? Thus, it is argued, young, or infant, industries should be given tariff protection until they grow up and can compete on equal terms with more experienced foreign producers.

Society should invest in an infant industry if it ultimately has a payoff in the form of sufficiently lower costs of production. But there are two reasons why a tariff is still not a good idea. First, this is once more a situation where a production subsidy is better than a tariff. There is no reason why consumers should be taxed while domestic producers are learning how to produce. Second, there is a great danger of building up industries that remain uncompetitive even in the long run. It is always difficult to get rid of subsidies once they are introduced.

Whether a government (unwisely) imposes a tariff to help infant industries or subsidizes production, it should give the infants a definite date at which they are expected to leave home and get by on their own. But this is not often done, because once the industries are set up, reducing their protection will result in a loss of jobs, and politicians are reluctant to cause this. We come back soon to the question of why tariffs are used so often.

Revenue Arguments for Tariffs

In the eighteenth century most government revenue came from tariffs, because it was easy to collect tariffs at the ports through which goods were imported. At that time tariffs were an efficient means for governments to raise revenue. Indeed, even today in countries where the administrative system is underdeveloped, tariffs may be a good tool for raising revenue. But in modern economies with developed accounting and administrative systems, there is little to be said for the tariff as an efficient means for raising revenue. It is not harder to collect sales taxes on all goods sold than to collect taxes on imports.

Other Second-Best Arguments

The other second-best arguments all have a similar logic. For instance, it is argued that we should impose a tariff to protect industries producing for defense so that they will be strong if they are ever needed in time of war. But if we want defense industries to have a large production capacity, we should subsidize production, not impose tariffs. Or, it is argued, we should impose a tariff because production in some industries creates favorable externalities, and by keeping out foreign production, we gain the benefit of the higher level of production. This, too, is a case for a production subsidy.

Cheap Foreign Labor

It is frequently argued that home producers require protection because foreign countries use cheap labor. There are two things to be said here. First, cheap foreign labor is cheap per hour worked. But part of the reason it is cheap is that it is less productive. It probably takes more foreign labor than domestic labor to produce 1 unit of a good. Thus the foreign labor may not be cheap in relation to the total cost of production.

But arguing about how much foreign labor really costs is to miss the main point. The foreign labor may indeed be cheaper because there is more of it. One of the main reasons to trade is precisely that there are international differences in factor endowments. Some foreign country will have more and cheaper labor, or more and cheaper raw materials. We want to take advantage of that by allowing the country to produce the goods in which it has a comparative advantage. If we do not import the goods in which it has a comparative advantage, then we lose the benefits of trade.

The problem is not that foreign labor is unfairly cheap but that some domestic labor is producing goods that should be made abroad. If the domestic industry has lost comparative advantage, then it should be closed down. Its workers might be given assistance so that they can relocate in other industries and areas. Indeed, the United States does provide adjustment assistance for workers in industries suffering from foreign competition.

Foreign Subsidies and Dumping

We register foreign subsidies as a nonargument in Table 35-10 with a question mark. Foreign governments sometimes subsidize their producers, who can then export more cheaply. Domestic producers say that is unfair, because the foreign government is giving the foreign firms an advantage that has nothing to do with free markets.

If the foreign governments are providing the subsidy permanently and we can rely on it continuing, then we should take advantage of it. If some foreign government wants to make it cheap for us to consume some good that the country produces, that is fine. In that case there is no objection from us to the subsidy.

But the reason for the question mark is that subsidies are often temporary. They are part of an attempt by foreign governments to help out producers who are having short-run difficulties. In that case there is an argument for some restriction of trade. Otherwise, domestic producers first have to reduce production when the low-priced foreign goods arrive and then shortly have to increase it again when the subsidy is removed. So if subsidies are temporary, they are likely to disrupt our industry—and therefore there is a case for preventing that.

This issue is closely related to that of dumping.

Dumping takes place when producers sell abroad at a price below cost.

Dumping typically takes place in recessions, when an industry does not want to cut back production but cannot sell at home. It then turns to foreign markets, disrupting foreign production in order to stabilize its own production. If U.S. producers can establish that foreign producers are dumping, selling below cost, the U.S. government has to impose duties to prevent the dumping. For instance, in 1982 the United States imposed tariffs on European steel imports, because they were being sold in the United States below cost.

The objection to dumping is that it is bound to be temporary. If foreigners always wanted to sell at a price below cost, then we should import from them. But a private firm cannot keep doing so. Therefore, it is clear that it is disrupting another country's production to stabilize its own.

The Optimal Tariff

There is one unambiguous argument that justifies a tariff from the national point of view. Individual households or firms behave competitively in making decisions to consume or produce, taking the price as given. But a country may be able to influence prices in world trade. We may face a downward-sloping demand curve for our exports or an upward-sloping supply curve for our imports. In that case there is a *national* gain from restricting trade, reducing exports or limiting imports. The trade restriction—for example, a tariff that reduces imports—will lower the world price that we pay. We are able to exploit foreigners by making them pay part of the tariff. Note, though, that this is a tariff in the *national* interest; from a world point of view it represents a misallocation of resources, as does any exercise of monopoly power.

Why Do We Have Tariffs?

Aside from the optimal tariff argument, there is almost nothing to be said in favor of tariffs. Economists have been arguing against them for well over a century. But tariffs and other restrictions on trade are still imposed. Why do the economic arguments apparently not carry much weight?

Concentrated Benefits, Diffuse Costs Consider the American losers and gainers from Japanese competition in the automobile industry. The losers are the auto workers and the owners of stock in U.S. auto companies, GM, Ford, Chrysler, and American Motors. The gainers are the purchasers of Japanese cars.

Restriction of trade would benefit the auto workers and the companies and hurt the car-buying public. Now the auto workers are a clearly defined group with efficient union representation. Management, too, knows its way around the political arena. But the buyers of cars are not well organized. The benefits from being able to buy Japanese cars are not so large that buyers are likely to organize themselves into a lobbying group to fight the producers.

Because the benefits from restricting trade typically go to a well-defined group, and because the costs from restricting trade are borne by a larger, less organized group, the political system tends to accommodate to the pressures by imposing restrictions. This is the concentrated benefits–diffuse costs explanation for trade restrictions.

Another example of the concentrated benefits and diffuse costs of trade restrictions concerns the sugar quota. With the world price of sugar at 8 cents per pound in 1982 and imports increasing, the United States decided to keep imports out to maintain the profitability of the domestic sugar-growing industry. The U.S. price was about 20 cents. Now no one pays much attention to the price of the sugar in his coffee, and so the costs of the restrictions are barely noticed—but they are borne by almost everyone. The gainers, however, are a very concentrated group, the growers; they successfully brought strong political pressure to bear to keep the imports out.

Tariffs versus Subsidies Even given the ability of concentrated interests to achieve their goals, why do they do it more often through interference with trade than through domestic subsidies? We argued above that subsidies were usually the right tool for achieving the goals for which tariffs were proposed as the solution.

There are two main reasons why governments frequently use tariffs when they would do better to subsidize production. The first is that the problem often first arises in the context of international trade. Japanese cars are the problem for Detroit producers. The direct solution looks simple: forbid Japanese cars. The second reason for using tariffs is that it is less clear who is doing what for whom with a tariff than with a subsidy. A producer receiving a subsidy takes money explicitly from the taxpayers. A tariff appears mainly to harm foreigners and indeed to bring in money for the government. We know that consumers are paying higher prices directly to the producers, but that is less obvious than the producer actually getting checks from the government. Tariffs don't look like a giveaway, while subsidies do. But tariffs are a giveaway.

Is Second-Best Any Good?

In Table 35-10 we describe most of the arguments for tariffs as second-best, and we have argued that subsidies on production or consumption taxes would be better means for meeting the goals of the tariffs. But are tariffs justifiable if taxes on consumption or production subsidies are not used? They could be in principle, but we doubt it in practice.

To explain, we take the example of the farmers whose way of life society has decided to preserve because it adds essential stability to the nation. Suppose that the government for some reason rules out production subsidies. The question is then raised whether a tariff is an appropriate means for maintaining the farmers' livelihood. An economist would answer with an estimate

of the costs that were analyzed in Figure 35-7. Just to make sure everyone knew the facts, the economist would also include an estimate of the costs of using a production subsidy instead of a tariff.

If after seeing the cost estimates and duly considering them, democratic institutions such as Congress decided to go ahead, we would conclude that the social value of having the farmers on the farm must exceed the costs. We would also have to conclude that society has good reasons for not using better policies, such as production subsidies.

We doubt that tariffs are good in practice because we believe that tariffs are more likely to be proposed because of the concentrated benefits–diffuse costs problem than because society has made a fully informed decision to accept those costs as an acceptable price to pay for achieving some social goal. It is also likely that the production subsidy is rejected mainly because it makes the costs so explicit. Thus the economist's basic attitude toward tariffs is opposition and skepticism—conceivably they are appropriate, but more likely the arguments for them are based on self-interest at the expense of others, dressed up in fancy talk.

7 TARIFF LEVELS: IT'S NOT SO BAD AFTER ALL

Figure 35-9 shows the history of tariffs in the United States over the past 160 years. U.S. tariffs have never been lower than they are now. The United States traditionally had high tariffs, but since World War II (indeed, starting even in the 1930s) tariffs have come down. The same trends apply in the rest of the industrialized world. World trade has probably never been freer than it is at present.

Of course, there are frequent attempts to interfere with trade and frequent government restrictions. For instance, in the case

FIGURE 35-9 THE U.S. TARIFF: 4-YEAR AVERAGES FROM 1821 to 1979. (*U.S. Historical Statistics.*)

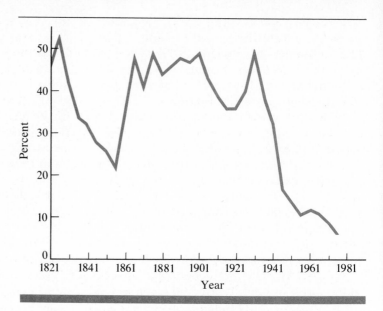

of the Japanese automobiles, the United States negotiated an informal, temporary limit of 2 million cars a year on Japanese exports to the United States in 1981. But the overall climate is not favorable to trade restrictions. Governments know that they should not impose them.

GATT   Partly this is because since the end of World War II there has been, under the General Agreement on Tariffs and Trade (GATT), an international agreement to follow rules of good behavior in not interfering with trade and in reducing tariffs. GATT has been the forum for international negotiations to reduce tariffs, and its success can be seen in the falling tariffs in Figure 35-9.

The basic force behind GATT and governments' concerns about interfering with trade is the experience of the 1930s. In that period countries raised their tariffs and cut off imports in attempts to preserve the jobs of their own workers. But with other countries imposing tariffs, countries lost jobs because exports were declining at the same time that they gained jobs by cutting off imports. The final result in the 1930s was the sharp reduction in total world trade that we saw in Chapter 34. No one gained from the tariffs, and everyone lost the benefits of trade discussed earlier in this chapter. There is a widespread fear of repeating that performance. The fear acts to restrain governments tempted to break the GATT rules, as they all do—but they know that if they go too far, all countries suffer together.

8 OTHER COMMERCIAL POLICIES

Tariffs are not the only form of commercial policy. There are three other instruments that deserve attention: quotas, nontariff barriers, and export subsidies. We comment on each in turn.

Quotas

Under a tariff importers are free to purchase *any* amount of foreign goods provided they pay the duty. Under a quota, or quantitative restriction, by contrast, the government limits the quantity or sometimes the value of imports that are allowed. Thus the government might say that car imports from Japan cannot exceed 2 million units or that shoe imports from Brazil cannot exceed 500,-

000 pairs. Typically the quota rights (the rights to import) are either auctioned by the government to the highest bidder or given away according to government priorities.

Quotas operate just like tariffs in that they restrict imports. Because the quantity supplied is reduced and further imports are forbidden, home prices rise above those prevailing in the rest of the world. Quotas differ from tariffs in two ways. One is that they exclude any impact of foreign competition on home prices. For instance, if foreigners match our tariff with a decline in their prices, imports will tend to fall less. But with a quota this is not the case, since imports cannot exceed the quota.

The second respect in which quotas are attractive to policymakers is that they provide certainty about the quantity of imports. While this is an advantage from the viewpoint of policymakers, it is at the same time one of the shortcomings as viewed by economists. Quotas are very rigid policy instruments. They in no way reflect any attempt to balance, at the margin, costs and benefits from trade in a way that an optimally chosen tariff may do. Most important, quotas remove domestic producers entirely from the threat and discipline of foreign competition. With an effective quota, foreigners cannot even give away their products in the home market if they exceed the quota. Indeed, it is for this reason that quotas were widely introduced in the 1930s. It was hoped that they would prevent foreign competitors from entering home markets through sharp price-cutting.

Nontariff Barriers

Nontariff barriers are administrative regulations that discriminate against foreign goods and in favor of home goods.

These regulations can take any of a number of overt or subtle forms. A barrier may be a government buying policy that stipulates that at equal—or even at higher—prices domestic products must be given preference. (Buy American.)

This form of discrimination is routinely practiced, American firms have charged, in Japan. The Japanese counter that American firms have not learned to do business in Japan and therefore are less than successful. The fact remains that this is an active form of trade restriction.

Nontariff barriers arise in situations other than government buying. They may also arise in specification standards for goods such as pollution equipment, in safety standards for products, or in domestic taxation that tends to fall particularly heavily on foreign-type products. Progressive road taxes, for example, are levied according to the sizes of cars. They tend to fall on relatively large cars, which tend to be American. Sanitary restrictions prohibit trade in certain agricultural commodities (fruit cannot be brought into California, for example). While these rules may well be justified as sanitary measures, they clearly act at the same time as a convenient instrument of protection for local producers.

Export Taxes and Subsidies

We have so far looked only at restrictions on imports. But there are also commercial policies directed at exports. Countries attempt to promote their exports with outright subsidies, through the exemption of certain domestic taxes, or with particularly cheap credit.

Figure 35-10 shows the economics of an export subsidy, taking now the example of computers. Suppose that we are the world's only producers of computers. Suppose also that the world price of a computer is $10,000. Under free trade consumers in the home market buy Q_d units at point G on the demand curve, and producers build Q_s units at point E on their supply curve. GE units are exported under free trade.

FIGURE 35-10 AN EXPORT SUBSIDY INCREASES EXPORTS AND CAUSES UN-
DERCONSUMPTION AND EXCESS PRODUCTION. The world price of computers, of
which we are the only producers, is $10,000. The government gives an export sub-
sidy of $2000 per computer. Domestic producers can sell as many computers as
they want in the world market at $10,000 and in addition receive $2000 per computer from the government. Thus they will not sell in the domestic market at any
price below $12,000, which is now the home price. Exports increase from $(Q_s - Q_d)$
to $(Q'_s - Q'_d)$. The loss to society is shown by the two shaded areas, H and K. H is
the loss of consumers' surplus and K the loss because computers are being sold to
foreigners at prices below their social cost of production.

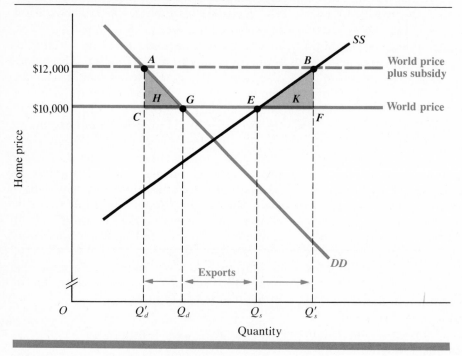

Now the government decides to push
exports of computers and for that purpose
imposes a 20 percent *export* subsidy. For
every unit *exported,* firms now receive a
subsidy equal to $2000. No firm will choose
to sell in the home market for $10,000 if it
can sell the same good for $12,000 (includ-
ing the subsidy receipt from the government) in the world market. The price in the
home market therefore must rise to $12,000
for *any* computers to be sold there. This is
shown in Figure 35-10 by the new price line
including the subsidy.

The new equilibrium under the export
subsidy finds consumers at point *A.* The increased price in the home market leads to a
decline in the quantity demanded to Q'_d. On
the production side the subsidy encourages
increased output, moving firms along their
marginal cost schedule to point *B.* With the
quantity demanded reduced and output increased there is a rise in exports.

The subsidy thus achieves the purpose
of raising exports, but of course it does so at
the social cost of the shaded areas. Firms
now produce goods at a marginal cost above
what foreigners are paying for the computers. The government, and that means ultimately the taxpayer, makes up the difference. On the consumption side there is a cost

because we are selling computers abroad for a price below what they are worth to home consumers. Just like a tariff, an export subsidy involves an excess cost. Just like a tariff, it raises domestic prices, subsidizes producers, and taxes consumers. Just as in the case of a tariff, there is rarely a first-best argument for an export subsidy.

SUMMARY

1   Countries trade because they can buy goods more cheaply in other countries. Differences in international costs of production arise because of technological differences and differences in factor endowments. In addition, scale economies make it efficient to specialize in production.

2   Ricardian trade theory shows that a country will produce those goods in which it has a comparative advantage. These are the goods it produces *relatively* cheaply. Countries benefit from trade even if one of them is more efficient than the other in making all goods.

3   Under the simplifying assumptions made by Ricardo, countries specialize in production and in importing and exporting. The dividing line between the goods they import and export depends mainly on their relative sizes.

4   Countries gain from trade if they specialize. In effect they are using their resources, embodied in the goods they export, to produce the goods they import, and they are using less labor than they would have to if there were no trade. The opening of trade benefits at least one of the trading partners and harms neither. A small country is more likely to gain from trade than a large one.

5   The extension of trade theory to more than one factor of production emphasizes *relative* factor abundance. A country that has a relatively high capital-labor ratio will export capital-intensive goods and import labor-intensive goods. Trade in goods is an indirect way of trading capital services (embodied in capital-intensive exports) for labor services (which are embodied in the labor-intensive imports). The relative abundance of raw materials such as oil is another major factor explaining patterns of world trade.

6   Intra-industry trade occurs because of scale economies and consumer preferences for diversity. By producing for the world market, firms have lower production costs. Consumers benefit from having a choice between domestic products and imported products. Intra-industry trade accounts for a large share of trade in Europe and the United States.

7   World trade creates conflicts between the interests of consumers and the interests of producers. Cheap imports benefit the consumer

but hurt the domestic producer. Export subsidies benefit the producer but hurt the consumer. The economics of commercial policy is concerned with analyzing the costs and benefits of different instruments of trade restriction or trade promotion.

8   A tariff raises the domestic price of imported goods subject to the tariff. The increase in the domestic price discourages consumption but leads to an expansion of production. Imports are in part reduced through the fall in the quantity demanded, and in part they are replaced by the expansion in production.

9   A tariff raises the cost of a good to consumers. The increased cost to consumers represents in part the government's tariff revenue and in part increased profits for domestic firms. But there are also deadweight losses—losses to the consumers that do not have a counterpart in increased revenues for other sectors. These deadweight losses arise from overproduction by firms—the marginal cost exceeds the world price—and underconsumption of the importable good. These deadweight losses represent the social cost of a tariff.

10   There are few arguments for tariffs that stand up to close scrutiny. In most instances there is instead a case for a production subsidy or for a consumption tax.

11   Export subsidies raise domestic prices to consumers and producers. They reduce the quantity demanded and increase production, thus raising exports. Just as in the case of a tariff, they involve waste because goods are exported for less than what they cost to produce (to society) or what they are worth to consumers.

12   U.S. tariffs and those in other countries have fallen substantially since World War II and are now at their lowest levels ever. The reduction in tariffs is in part a response to the disastrous collapse of world trade under tariff restrictions in the 1930s. But there is often an upsurge of protectionism in specific industries.

13   Protection is harmful from the social point of view. The persistent pressure for protection is explained by the fact that producers have more at stake (per head) than consumers and therefore find it more profitable to organize political support for their position. The countervailing force is the recognition of the advantages of an open trading system and institutions, such as adjustment assistance, that give emphasis to the reallocation of resources rather than protection.

KEY TERMS

Comparative advantage	Factor endowments
Absolute advantage	Intra-industry trade
Gains from trade	Commercial policy

Tariff
Subsidy
Deadweight loss (burden)
Infant industry tariff argument
Dumping

Optimal tariff
General Agreement on Tariffs
  and Trade (GATT)
Quotas
Nontariff barriers

PROBLEMS

1 "A country that is absolutely less productive in every line of production than its trading partners cannot compete in world trade and therefore can only lose by opening itself up to foreign competition." Discuss this assertion in detail.

2 "Large countries cannot gain from world trade." Discuss this statement, and show what is or what is not true about it.

3 Consider the case of Table 35-4, where there are many goods. Suppose that the initial equilibrium is one where the United States produces computers, cars, and TV sets and France produces the remaining goods. Suppose now that a lot of labor migrates from France to the United States. What do you think will happen to the pattern of specialization and trade?

4 This question is quite difficult but turns out to be important in practice. Take Table 35-4 and an initial trade pattern where the United States produces computers, cars, and TV sets, while France produces the rest. Suppose now that in France the unit labor requirement for TV sets falls from 90 hours to 30, or that the ratio of U.S. to French unit labor requirements rises from 5/9 to 5/3. (*a*) What happens to the order of goods in Table 35-4? (*b*) What will happen to trade patterns?

5 Explain in words why a country that is relatively capital-rich will tend to export goods that are relatively capital-intensive

and import goods that are relatively labor-intensive.

6 "The system of world trade condemns poor countries to produce goods that use unskilled labor. Therefore, they are precluded from good jobs and the potential for progress." Discuss this statement, and indicate what parts, if any, strike you as correct or wrong.

7 Consider five goods: stereo equipment, wine, cotton shirts, pocket transistor radios, and steel sheeting. Which of these goods do you think have a high index of intra-industry trade, and which have a low index? Explain your reasons.

8 It has been argued that a tariff does not represent a cost to society because it just moves money from one pocket to another—from consumers to the firms and the government. Comment carefully on this proposition.

9 Society has decided that preservation of the national heritage and arts is to be pursued. For that purpose a complete ban on the export of any national artistic product is imposed. (*a*) Do you think such a quota is preferable to an export tax? (An export tax is the opposite of the export subsidy studied in Figure 35-10.) (*b*) Who benefits and who loses from the measure? (*c*) Do you think that the measure will encourage young artists to stay in business?

10 Suppose that the TV industry has economies of scale. Therefore, manufacturers argue that society has an interest in promoting the right scale of the home country's TV industry by preventing consumers from buying imported models. Discuss and evaluate this case for a tariff.

11 Certain activities—agriculture, weapons development, the manufacture of basic materials—are essential to the national defense and military preparedness. Should a tariff be imposed to maintain these activities in the face of foreign competition? Evaluate the argument.

12 The accompanying table shows wages in the automobile industry and in manufacturing in general in the United States and Japan in 1980. (*a*) On the basis of these data and the discussion of the issue in this chapter, do you think the United States should protect the automobile industry with a tariff, with a quota, or not at all? (*b*) Also discuss whether there is any argument for providing temporary relief for the automobile industry, for example, by imposing a tariff for a few years only.

HOURLY COMPENSATION, 1980

	UNITED STATES	JAPAN
Motor vehicles	$14.71	$6.98
Manufacturing	9.92	5.65

Source: Bureau of Labor Statistics.

No aspect of economics is more mysterious to the outsider than exchange rates and international finance. Indeed, it may also be mysterious to the insider. Keynes, who speculated by buying and selling foreign currency, is said to have made three fortunes—but to have lost two.

Much of the mystery comes from the unfamiliar nature of the language. But even when the language is understood, it is sometimes difficult to see how events are related. For instance, why do people start selling a currency when they believe it will be devalued? A devaluation is an increase in the price of foreign currencies. In selling a particular currency, such as the franc, a speculator is buying another currency, say, the dollar. Before the devaluation he buys dollars at a low price. After the devaluation he will come back to buy francs, selling the dollars at a high price. There is no better way of making money than buying low and selling high. But there are more questions. For instance, why does the strengthening of the dollar make the President proud but make exporters wish the dollar would weaken?

We set ourselves three tasks in this chapter. The first is to remove as much of the mystery about exchange rates and international finance as we can by analyzing how the foreign exchange market works. In Chapter 34 we presented a preliminary discussion, which we extend here. Second, we want to show how alternative exchange rate systems, such as the adjustable peg and flexible exchange rate systems, work. The third task is to understand the role played in international financial markets by capital flows and speculation.

The sort of question we hope to answer is suggested by Figure 36-1, which shows an index of the dollar price, or exchange rate, of the deutsche mark (DM) and the pound sterling (£). Each index is equal to 100 in 1960. A rise in the index means that the exchange rate is rising, or that the foreign currency is appreciating. Conversely, when the index declines, this means the dollar price of the foreign currency is falling, the foreign currency is depreciating, or the dollar is appreciating relative to that currency.

The figure immediately reminds us of the difference between the exchange rate systems of the 1960s and the 1970s that we saw in Chapter 35. The 1960s was a period of fixed rates with occasional adjustments through devaluation or revaluation (the pound in 1967 and

36

The Economics of Exchange Rates and International Finance

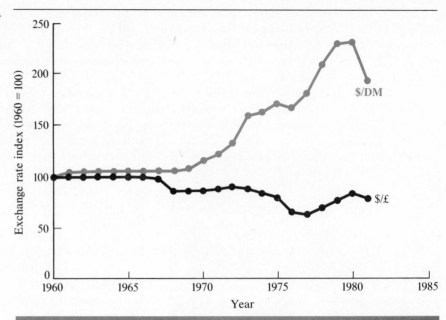

FIGURE 36-1 THE DOL-LAR PRICE OF FOREIGN EXCHANGE, 1960–1981 (Index 1960 = 100). (*Source:* Citibank Economic Database.)

deutsche mark in 1961 and 1969). The 1970s, by contrast, was a period of floating rates. We want to understand what determines the movements of rates under a floating rate system and why the adjustable peg system was abandoned.

Exchange rate systems, as we have seen, differ according to whether rates are fixed or flexible. But there is a second difference: between systems that are completely automatic and those in which governments intervene to influence the exchange rate. Table 36-1 gives the four possible combinations of fixed and flexible, free and not free exchange rate systems and gives examples.

The nineteenth-century gold standard is an example of an automatic system with fixed exchange rates. A totally free, or clean, floating exchange rate is an automatic system with flexible rates. There probably has never been any such system in practice. The adjustable peg and managed floating systems of the post-World War II periods are, respectively, fixed and floating rate systems with government intervention. We now discuss these systems in more detail.

TABLE 36-1

ALTERNATIVE EXCHANGE RATE REGIMES

GOVERNMENT INTERVENTION	EXCHANGE RATES	
	FIXED	FLEXIBLE
None (system operates automatically)	Gold standard (nineteenth century)	Fully free floating (never?)
Some	Adjustable peg (1960s)	Managed floating (1970s and 1980s)

1 FREE FLOATING EXCHANGE RATES

We begin the analysis of alternative exchange rate systems by developing in more detail Chapter 34's model of the foreign exchange market. We simplify by assuming there is no international borrowing or lending. The only way to obtain foreign currency is by exporting, and the only reason we want foreign currency is to be able to import. Thus we identify the demand for foreign exchange with imports, and the supply of foreign exchange with exports.

Figure 36-2 shows the foreign exchange market. The exchange rate is on the vertical axis. An increase in the exchange rate means that we pay more for the foreign currency and therefore that our currency, the dollar, depreciates. For variety, we show the exchange rate in this figure as being the exchange rate of dollars for deutsche marks.[1]

On the horizontal axis we measure in dollars the quantity of foreign exchange demanded and supplied. The supply of foreign exchange is the total value of export revenue. If exporters, at a particular exchange rate, earn, say, $10 billion of foreign currency, the supply of foreign exchange at that exchange rate is $10 billion. Thus on the horizontal axis we report the *value* (in dollars) of export revenue and import spending.

The schedule *XX* in Figure 36-2 shows our export revenue increasing with the exchange rate. Two features of the *XX* curve should be emphasized. First, the prices of goods both at home and abroad are held fixed. Thus the dollar price of American goods and the deutsche mark price of German goods are given. Second, we also assume that the level of income in Germany is given. We shall see below how changes in either domestic or foreign prices or changes in foreign income can shift the *XX* curve.

As our currency depreciates, our goods become cheaper for foreigners. Table 36-2 shows why for the example of a car. The car costs $5000 in the United States. At an exchange rate for the deutsche mark of 25 cents, the car costs DM20,000 in Germany. At an exchange rate of 50 cents, the car costs

FIGURE 36-2   THE MARKET FOR FOREIGN EXCHANGE. The curve *XX* shows our earnings from exports, measured in dollars. The higher the exchange rate, the cheaper are our exports for foreigners, and the more they demand. We assume that foreigners' demand for our goods is elastic, and so their spending on our goods measured in dollars rises as the exchange rate rises and the *XX* curve slopes upward. Our demand for imports is shown on the *MM* curve. As the exchange rate falls, imports become cheaper for us. The *MM* curve therefore slopes downward. Equilibrium is at point *A*, with an exchange rate of $0.50/DM. At any higher exchange rate, such as $1.00, there is an excess supply of foreign exchange and a surplus in the current account, and the exchange rate falls. At any lower exchange rate, such as 25 cents, there is an excess demand for foreign exchange, and the exchange rate rises.

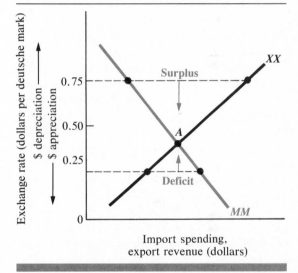

DM10,000. The fall in the DM price is a direct result of the rise in the exchange rate, or the depreciation of the dollar.

The quantity of our goods demanded by foreigners increases as the exchange rate increases and our goods become cheaper for foreigners. We make the further assumption that the demand for our goods by foreigners is elastic, and so *revenue* (dollar price times quantity purchased) from exports rises as the exchange rate increases. This implies that the *XX* curve is upward-sloping.

The *MM* curve, showing our spending on imports, is downward-sloping. As the exchange rate falls and our currency appreci-

TABLE 36-2

EFFECT OF EXCHANGE RATES CHANGE ON THE PRICE PAID BY FOREIGNERS

(1) PRICE OF DOMESTIC CAR, $	(2) EXCHANGE RATE, $/DM	(3) = (2)/(1) PRICE OF DOMESTIC CAR, DM
$5000	0.25	DM20,000
$5000	0.50	DM10,000

ates, foreign goods become cheaper for us. Therefore, the quantity demanded of the import good, along with dollar spending on import goods, increases as the exchange rate falls. The *MM* curve is drawn for a given level of income at home and for given prices of goods at home and abroad.

In the foreign exchange market, exporters sell the foreign currency they earn from their exports and importers buy the foreign currency with which to pay for their imports. The exchange rate adjusts to make quantity supplied equal to quantity demanded.

Figure 36-2 shows the exchange rate of $0.40/DM as the equilibrium rate. If the rate were higher, say, $0.75/DM, there would be an excess of export revenue over import spending. At the more depreciated level of the exchange rate our goods would be so cheap abroad and foreign goods would be so expensive in our country that the value of exports would exceed that of imports. With the quantity of foreign exchange supplied exceeding demand, the price falls, or the currency appreciates. This is shown by the downward-pointing arrow.

Conversely, at an exchange rate of, say, $0.25/DM, foreign currency is so cheap that quantity demanded and import spending are larger than export revenue. The excess of the quantity demanded of foreign currency over the quantity supplied leads to a rise in the exchange rate, or currency depreciation, to restore equilibrium.

Thus with a freely flexible exchange

rate, and the absence of international lending and borrowing, the rate moves to equate the demand for foreign exchange arising from imports to the supply of foreign exchange provided by exports. There is no government intervention in this process.

Adjustment under Flexible Exchange Rates

We now show how the foreign exchange market responds to a change when the exchange rate is fully flexible. Suppose domestic income rises and the demand for imports at any given exchange rate therefore increases. In Figure 36-3, the *MM* curve shifts to *MM'*. At the initial equilibrium exchange rate of 40 cents importers want to spend at point *A'*, but there is no change in export revenue. Export revenue is still indicated by point *A* on the schedule. The difference between import spending and export revenue, *AA'*, represents the payments deficit, or *excess demand for foreign exchange*. The initial exchange rate now is a disequilibrium rate.

The excess demand for foreign exchange drives up the dollar price of marks until a new equilibrium is reached at point *A''*. Increased import spending thus leads to a depreciation of the dollar. The depreciation, in turn, restores payments balance through two channels. First, the depreciation reduces import spending relative to what it is at the initial exchange rate. The depreciation makes foreign goods more expensive relative to our own and therefore

FIGURE 36-3   AN INCREASE IN IMPORT SPENDING LEADS TO A CURRENCY DEPRECIATION. An increase in the level of income at home causes the demand curve for imports to shift from *MM* to *MM'*; there is a greater quantity of imports demanded at each price. At the initial equilibrium exchange rate of $0.40/DM there is now an excess demand for deutsche marks, or a deficit in the current account. The excess demand for foreign currency causes the price of foreign currency—the exchange rate—to increase. The new equilibrium is at A″, with the exchange rate equal to $0.60/DM.

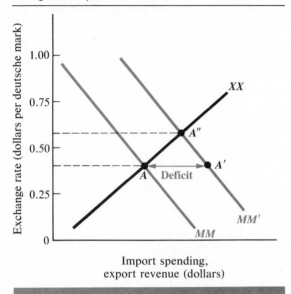

Import spending,
export revenue (dollars)

reduces the quantity demanded of imports. Second, the depreciation also reduces the prices of our goods in foreign currency to foreigners. It therefore increases export revenue and thus helps finance increased import spending.

A fully flexible exchange rate adjusts the balance of payments *automatically* by bringing about equality of the demand for foreign exchange from import spending and the supply of foreign exchange raised from export revenue. There are complications connected with borrowing from and lending to foreigners and speculation that we comment on later, but the basic principles are already established: The exchange rate moves without government intervention to restore the balance of export revenue and import spending. An entirely different but also automatic mechanism is provided by the gold standard, which we now discuss.

2   THE GOLD STANDARD

There are three distinguishing features of the gold standard. First, the government fixes the price of gold in terms of its currency.

> The *par value* of gold is the price of gold in terms of money fixed by the government.

Second, the government maintains *convertibility* of the home currency into gold. The government will on demand buy or sell home currency for gold at the par value. For a modest charge anyone can convert dollar bills into gold at the central bank. Third, the government follows a rule that links money creation to its holdings of gold. The government can issue dollar bills only by buying gold from the public. If the public converts money back into gold, the stock of dollar bills is automatically reduced. This is called *100 percent cover*, or 100 percent *gold backing*, meaning that behind the dollar bills stands an equivalent value of gold.

The idea of 100 percent cover is sufficiently important for us to take a further look. Table 36-3 shows the hypothetical balance sheet of a central bank that has 100 percent gold backing for its currency. The balance sheet differs in several respects from that of present-day central banks, which we studied in Chapter 26. There are no bank deposits with the central bank and no central bank ownership of the debts of the government, the private sector, or foreign governments. The central bank owns

TABLE 36-3
BALANCE SHEET OF A GOLD STANDARD CENTRAL BANK

ASSETS	LIABILITIES
Gold	Banknotes (currency) outstanding

only gold, acquired when it issued currency.[2]

Suppose the public decides to buy gold from the central bank, turning in its currency for the gold. With 100 percent cover, the government loses that amount of gold and also has its liabilities (currency outstanding) fall by the same amount. A reduction in the stock of gold in the central bank therefore leads to a *one-for-one* reduction in the stock of dollar bills outstanding. As we see presently, this mechanism will automatically ensure a tendency for payments balance.

Balance of Payments Adjustment under the Gold Standard

Suppose the world is made up of two countries each of which is on the gold standard in the sense that it follows the three rules: a par value, convertibility, and 100 percent cover. Specifically suppose that in the United States the par value is $20.67 per ounce of gold, and in the United Kingdom it is £4.25 per ounce of gold. These par values imply an exchange rate of $4.86/£ ($20.67 per ounce of gold/£4.25 per ounce of gold). At any other exchange rate there would be an excess supply or demand for foreign exchange as people tried to make profits by exporting or importing gold bought from the central banks.

> The exchange rate calculated from the relative price of gold in the two countries is called the *gold parity*.

Under the gold standard the exchange rate in fact stayed very close to the gold parity, differing only by the small amount it cost to transport gold between countries.

Now consider payments and adjustment under the gold standard. In Figure 36-4 we

---

[2] We are describing here a pure form of the gold standard. In practice in the nineteenth and twentieth centuries, central banks tied their money creation to gold in many different ways. Sometimes less than 100 percent cover was used; sometimes the bank did not follow any simple rule tying money issue to gold but was still committed to convertibility.

FIGURE 36-4 GOLD FLOWS LEAD TO AUTOMATIC PAYMENTS ADJUSTMENT. An increase in the demand for imports shifts the *MM* curve to *MM'*. The exchange rate stays at the gold parity of $4.86 so that there is initially a deficit equal to *AA'*. The deficit reduces the U.S. money supply as Americans buy gold with their dollars and send the gold to the United Kingdom. The *MM'* curve therefore starts shifting back. In Britain the money stock starts increasing as British exporters turn in their gold to obtain pounds. The money supply expands, and the *XX* curve starts shifting to the right as Britons increase their spending on exports. The two curves keep shifting until they meet at *A''*, at which time the deficit is eliminated.

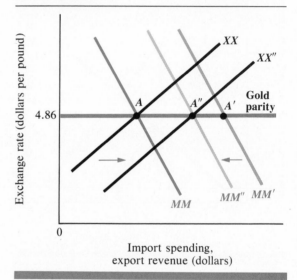

look again at the market for foreign exchange and the case of an increase in home import spending. The exchange rate of $4.86/£ is the rate implied by the par values for gold established in Britain and the United States. It is the initial equilibrium exchange rate, shown at *A*.

The increase in import spending shifts the *MM* curve to *MM'*, creating a deficit, just as in Figure 36-3. But now the exchange rate does *not* adjust. As soon as the dollar begins to move to an exchange rate above $4.86, people wanting sterling go to the Federal Reserve, using their dollars to buy gold and ship it to Britain in exchange for sterling. That way they get sterling for $4.86 per pound. The exchange rate cannot move from \$4.86 because no one will exchange currencies at any other price.

With the exchange rate unchanged, exports remain unchanged, while imports rise. There is a deficit in the balance of payments equal to distance AA'. The sterling received from our sales of exports is all traded for dollars in the exchange market. But the extra sterling needed, which is equal to the deficit AA', is obtained by people buying gold from the Federal Reserve and selling it to the Bank of England.

The payments deficit *does* lead to an automatic adjustment *over time*. As importers purchase gold from the Federal Reserve, and pay for the gold with dollars, the U.S. money stock declines. The gold is shipped to England and presented to the Bank of England for purchase of sterling. In buying the gold the Bank of England pays for it by printing sterling currency, thus expanding the English money supply.

Thus the U.S. deficit leads *automatically* to a reduction in the U.S. money supply and an increase in the British money supply. The changes in money supplies in turn affect spending, as was discussed in Chapter 27. In the United States the monetary decline leads to higher interest rates and reduced spending. In Britain the money expansion lowers interest rates and raises spending. These changes in spending in turn eventually feed back to the foreign exchange market, as we now see.

In the United States, as long as there is a deficit, the Federal Reserve is losing gold and therefore the money supply is falling. Spending, including spending on imports, falls in reaction to the tightening of money. Therefore, the import spending schedule starts shifting back from MM' toward the left. At the same time money is expanding in the United Kingdom, and therefore spending is increasing, including spending on our exports. Therefore, our export revenue will be increasing so that the XX schedule starts moving out and to the right.

We show these effects of the monetary adjustment process by the arrows in Figure 36-4. With the MM' schedule shifting to the left (our import spending falling) and the XX schedule shifting to the right (our export revenue rising), the deficit becomes smaller over time. The process continues until enough money has moved to reduce home import spending and raise foreign spending on our exports so as to restore the payments balance. This is the case at point A'', where the import demand schedule is now MM'' and the export schedule is XX''.

The automatic adjustment process of a gold standard is not instantaneous. Adjustment takes time as gold losses and monetary contraction in the deficit country lead to reduced import spending while gold gains and monetary expansion raise spending and imports of the surplus country. The process continues until the deficit is wiped out. The process is automatic because payments balance will eventually be restored by the three gold standard rules.

The Gold Standard in Action

The gold standard was in use through much of the nineteenth century and part of the twentieth. In Britain there was an established sterling value for gold from the end of the Napoleonic wars in 1816 through 1931. There were occasions during this period when convertibility of sterling into gold was suspended: during World War I and for some time further and during several financial crises. But the gold standard was the basic monetary system. The United States, too, was on the gold standard for most of the nineteenth century but suspended convertibility during and after the Civil War. United States monetary links with gold were not formally suspended until 1971, though American citizens lost the right to convert dollars into gold in 1934.

The gold standard in action was not quite the same as the idealized system described here, because the link between money and gold was not one-for-one. The system did work automatically in that the exchange rate stayed at the gold parity level while convertibility was maintained.

Questions about the operation of the gold standard are not so much related to how it handled international exchange but deal rather with its effects on the domestic economy. The gold standard period was one in which there was no major inflation except in wars during which the standard was suspended. But it was also a period in which there was, on average, higher unemployment and more variability of the price level than there has been in the post-World War II period.

Proponents of the gold standard point to the absence of major inflations as a reason for reinstating the gold standard. Opponents say the higher average unemployment and variability of inflation are reasons for not returning to gold.

3 FIXED RATES, DISEQUILIBRIUM, AND DEVALUATION

The fully flexible exchange rate and gold standard systems are pure forms of exchange rate regime. But the two regimes used in the post-World War II period—adjustable peg and managed floating—are far from pure. As Table 36-1 shows, both these systems operate with government intervention. In this section we discuss the adjustable peg system, in which countries fix their exchange rates against the dollar but occasionally change them if there are persistent deficits or surpluses at the chosen rate. We will examine later as an example the sterling devaluation of 1967.

The Adjustable Peg and the Dollar Standard

Because exchange rates in the sixties were fixed against the dollar, that period of the adjustable peg system is also known as the

period of the *dollar standard.* The name comes from the similarity with the gold standard. Under the gold standard, countries or central banks fixed the value of their currencies in terms of gold. Under the dollar standard, they fixed the value of their currencies in terms of dollars.

The second rule of the gold standard was convertibility. Under the dollar standard, currencies were supposed to be convertible into dollars rather than gold. Thus at the officially fixed exchange rate, central banks would buy or sell dollars from the public in exchange for their own currency. The third rule was the link between the money stock and the central bank's holdings of gold. Under the dollar standard, central banks were supposed to have enough dollars (and also some gold) to be able to meet the demands for dollars in exchange for their currency. These dollars were called the country's international reserves.

> *International reserves* are a country's holdings of foreign currency and other assets that can be used to meet demands for foreign currency.

The dollar thus served as the reference point of the system in the same way gold had under the gold standard.

But there was one critical difference between the dollar standard and the gold standard. There was no automatic adjustment mechanism under the dollar standard because central banks did not allow the money stock to adjust according to the balance of payments.

Under the gold standard, a deficit in the balance of payments led to a falling money supply and a surplus to an increasing money supply. Under the dollar standard, central banks changed the money supply to affect domestic unemployment and inflation without being bound by the gold standard rule that the money supply should be reduced when there is a balance of payments deficit. A country running a payments deficit but having unemployment might increase the money supply under the dollar standard. Countries in surplus, with the rate of inflation and domestic spending at levels they desired, refused to expand the money supply to increase spending. Instead, they accumulated reserves. And countries in deficit, instead of adjusting, lost reserves. The persistent payments imbalances led eventually to a need to adjust exchange rates. And the expectation of such changes in turn fed speculation, as we will see below in our discussion of capital flows.

Sterilization

How does a central bank under the dollar standard break the link between reserve losses and monetary contraction and reserve gains and monetary expansion? The central bank balance sheets shown in Table 36-4 helps explain the meaning of *sterilization.*

Suppose the demand for imports in Britain shifts, and at the fixed exchange rate Britain starts to run a payments deficit. The Bank of England has to provide the dollars demanded by importers in order to prevent the exchange rate from depreciating. This is the same thing that happens under the gold standard. Table 36-4 (*a*) shows a reserve loss of £100. Corresponding to that, the public paid the Bank of England with checks or cash, thereby reducing the quantity of high-powered money by £100.

But now the Bank of England decides it does not want spending to decline and therefore does not want the money supply to fall. It immediately reverses the effect of the balance of payments deficit on the quantity of high-powered money by buying bonds from the public in an open market purchase (as discussed in Chapter 26). By buying £100 of bonds, it ensures the quantity of high-powered money, and thus the money supply does not change. The effects on the bank's balance sheet are shown in Table 36-4 (*b*). The combined foreign exchange sale (the original £100 deficit) and the open market purchase for £100 ensure that the money supply is unchanged even though reserves have declined.

A central bank *sterilizes* the impact of reserve losses (gains) on the money supply when it undertakes open market purchases (sales) that exactly balance the changes in the reserves.

In sterilizing, the central bank prevents the automatic adjustment mechanism of the gold standard type.

Table 36-5 shows sterilization in the United Kingdom in the 1960s. The first row shows the gain or loss in reserves (net foreign assets[3]) for each year. The second row

---

[3] The Bank of England borrowed abroad during this period. *Net* foreign assets are equal to the bank's ownership of foreign assets minus the amounts borrowed from other countries.

TABLE 36-4

A CENTRAL BANK LOSES RESERVES BUT STERILIZES THROUGH AN OPEN MARKET PURCHASE

(*a*) LOSS OF FOREIGN EXCHANGE RESERVES

ASSETS		LIABILITIES	
Foreign exchange reserves	−£100	High-powered money	−£100

(*b*) OPEN MARKET PURCHASE

ASSETS		LIABILITIES	
Bonds	+£100	High-powered money	+£100

TABLE 36-5

UNITED KINGDOM MONETARY AUTHORITIES: CHANGES IN NET FOREIGN ASSETS AND CHANGES IN HIGH-POWERED MONEY
(Millions of Pounds Sterling)

	1963	1964	1965	1966	1967	1968
Net foreign assets	−87	−625	−97	−145	−774	−1390
High-powered money	103	234	346	212	177	155

Source: IMF, *International Financial Statistics, Yearbook, 1981,* pp. 434–435.

TABLE 36-6

THE BRITISH DEVALUATION OF 1967

	1965–1967 AVERAGE	1968	1969	1970
Net exports, millions of $	−780	−1637	−422	−80
Exchange rate, $/£	2.80	2.40	2.40	2.40
Budget deficit, % of GNP	1.0	1.7	−1.9	−1.3
Money growth, % per year	3.7	4.0	0.3	9.3

Source: IMF, *International Financial Statistics, Yearbook, 1981,* pp. 434–437.

shows the change in high-powered money. If the Bank of England did not sterilize the impacts of reserve losses, the changes in reserves would be matched by changes in high-powered money, as in Table 36-4(*a*).

It is quite obvious that the behavior of the money supply does not match in any way the behavior of reserves, either in magnitude or even in direction. From 1963 to 1968 net foreign assets were falling but the money supply was expanding. Throughout the period reserve losses were *more* than offset by open market purchases.

Ultimately a central bank that is sterilizing will have to admit that it cannot keep the exchange rate fixed by selling dollars, because it has no dollars left to sell. It will have used up its reserves and its ability to borrow from other countries. The exchange rate has to depreciate. This can be done either by leaving the market free to find its own equilibrium level, as under free floating, or by devaluing. In devaluing, the central bank fixes a new higher level for the exchange rate, which it hopes ensures payments balance or a surplus.

We examined devaluation briefly in Chapter 35 and now discuss the example of the British devaluation of 1967. The devaluation was necessary because as Table 36-5 shows, the government was not willing to follow the gold standard rules and contract the money supply in accordance with its reserve losses from 1963 on.

Devaluation

Table 36-6 shows the data for the United Kingdom. The trade balance in 1965–1967 was on average and in each year in deficit. Because it could not sustain the exchange rate under growing reserve losses, the government devalued in November 1967 by 15 percent. In Table 36-6 the depreciation shows up as a reduction in the dollar price of sterling from $2.80 to $2.40 per pound. Surprisingly, the devaluation did not lead to an immediate improvement in the trade balance. On the contrary, the trade balance worsened.

There is an important lesson here. The trade balance depends not only on the exchange rate but also on the level of income and spending. The last two rows of the table show that in 1968 the government budget deficit increased and the growth rate of money went up slightly. These policies raised aggregate spending and more than offset the favorable effect of the depreciation. In 1969, when the budget turned to surplus and the growth rate of money fell, the devaluation started showing its effects as the trade balance improved. Of course, with the trade balance depending both on the relative price of our goods and on aggregate spending, we cannot easily tell what part of the improvement is due to the change in monetary and fiscal policy and what part is due to the devaluation. *In general, correcting a deficit requires both a cut in spending and a depreciation or devaluation.*

To understand how a devaluation works, we need only think back to how a freely flexible exchange rate works to equilibrate the market, as shown in Figure 36-3. As in the case of the freely floating rate, the change in the exchange rate eliminates the deficit through two channels. First, the increased price of foreign currency makes foreign goods more expensive and reduces import spending. Second, the reduction in the price of domestic goods from the viewpoint of foreigners makes them increase their imports, which are our exports. Therefore, both the reduction of imports and the expansion of exports help correct the payments imbalance when a country devalues. We do not in general know whether the deficit is eliminated mainly through higher export or lower import spending. That depends on how sensitive import and export spending are to changes in the exchange rate.

Devaluation seems an effective way of coping with problems of external imbalance, but we need to ask whether anything can go wrong. Something can. A devaluation will work only if the exchange depre-

ciation is not offset by an increase in domestic prices. Suppose the pound depreciates by 15 percent. British goods therefore become 15 percent cheaper for foreigners, and demand shifts toward British goods as imports fall and exports rise. But if at the same time British prices all rise by 15 percent, the devaluation and inflation together do nothing to the relative prices of British goods. An increase in domestic prices makes British goods 15 percent more expensive for foreigners, and a devaluation of 15 percent just offsets that effect.

To work, a devaluation must be a *real* devaluation. After the devaluation, the devaluing country's goods should be cheaper relative to the foreign country's goods. If prices in the devaluing country rise by the same proportion as the devaluation, there is no change in the relative prices of its goods, and the devaluation does not achieve anything real.

To ensure that a devaluation sticks, it is essential that it be accompanied by a tightening of monetary and fiscal policy. Otherwise, the effects of the devaluation on the relative prices of exports and imports may be wiped out by inflation. In the British case shown in Table 36-6, we saw that in 1968 expansionary monetary and fiscal policy increased the deficit, despite a devaluation. Thus, to correct a deficit, the accompanying macroeconomic policies are as important as a devaluation.

In many cases it is difficult to achieve a *real* devaluation, since a real devaluation reduces workers' real wages. It makes imported goods more expensive and thus reduces the purchasing power of wages. Workers respond by claiming higher wages, which, if granted, raise costs and prices. In no time the effects of the initial devaluation are lost, and a new round of devaluation and inflation takes place.

This devaluation-inflation-devaluation spiral is not uncommon and reflects the fact

that a devaluation, if it is to be effective, requires that our goods become cheap for
foreigners and that their goods become expensive for us. That means we are willing to
work for less. Only in that way can we export more and import less, but of course that
means also that our standard of living is
lower. There is no cheap way of correcting a
balance of payments deficit.

4 FIXED RATES, SPECULATION, AND CAPITAL FLOWS

So far we have focused on imports and exports of goods and services as the sources of
the demand for and supply of foreign exchange. Now we introduce international
capital flows, which are sales and purchases
of assets, through the capital account of the
balance of payments. There is a demand for
dollars or a supply of foreign currency by
foreigners when they buy stock in American
companies or any other kind of American
assets, just as there is a supply of foreign
currency when they buy American goods.
In the adjustable peg system large capital
flows often forced the governments involved to change the exchange rate.

Figure 36-5 shows how capital flows
modify the analysis of the foreign exchange
market. We look this time at the foreign exchange market between French francs and
dollars, and we look at it from the viewpoint
of the French. The price of the dollar in
terms of francs is on the vertical axis, and
the quantity of francs traded is on the horizontal axis. MM shows the demand for foreign currency resulting from French imports. Curve XX shows the supply of foreign
currency resulting from French exports. At
the existing exchange rate, shown as F6/$,
France is running a deficit in the current account; imports exceed exports.

At the same time, though, there is a supply and demand of foreign currency from
capital account transactions. Some people
are trying to buy French assets with dollars

FIGURE 36-5 CAPITAL FLOWS AND THE BALANCE OF PAYMENTS. Curves XX and MM show the supply and demand for foreign currency when capital flows are assumed to be equal to zero. Once capital flows are included, there is a supply of foreign currency from those selling French assets in exchange for dollars and a demand for foreign currency from those buying American assets with francs. The current account deficit is equal to distance AA' at the fixed exchange rate of F6/$. Once capital flows are taken into account, the balance of payments deficit is seen to be distance BB'. This is the amount of dollars the Banque de France has to be selling to maintain the exchange rate of F6/$.

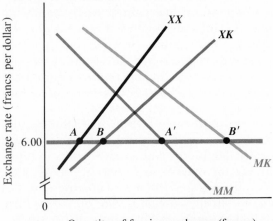

and therefore are contributing to the supply
of foreign exchange. We show the effect of
these purchases of French assets with dollars by shifting the XX curve to XK, where
XK is the supply of dollars (foreign currency
from the viewpoint of the French) in exchange for francs. Similarly, other people
are demanding dollars in exchange for
francs to buy assets, for instance, IBM
shares, in New York. We show how that modifies the demand for dollars by shifting the
MM curve to MK. As we have drawn the
curves, the shift in the demand for foreign
currency is larger than that of the supply.
This means that at the F6/$ exchange rate,
there is a capital account deficit. On balance, people are buying American assets,
demanding dollars in exchange for francs.

As a result of the capital account deficit, we see that the balance of payments deficit of the French is worse than what is indicated by the current account alone. The current account deficit is only *AA′*. The balance of payments deficit (current and capital accounts) is the larger distance *BB′*. In this case, the Banque de France has to pay out more dollars to support the exchange rate when we take capital flows into account than it would when we look only at the current account.

What determines the size of the capital account deficit, which is also often called the capital outflow?

> The *capital outflow* (inflow) from a country is the size of its capital account deficit (surplus).

The amount of assets Frenchmen on balance want to buy in the United States depends on the rates of return that are expected to be earned in the United States compared with those in France.

The rates of return earned in each country are the interest rates paid on assets held in those countries. Thus ordinarily we expect a country to have a capital inflow if its interest rates are high compared with those abroad. A country with low interest rates relative to those of foreigners is likely to have a capital outflow.

But there is one crucial factor that has to be added to the comparison of interest rates: the possibility of exchange rate changes. Suppose interest rates in France are high and an American therefore thinks of buying French bonds. Suppose the French interest rate is 12 percent compared with an American rate of 8 percent. An American investor seems to come out ahead by 4 percent a year. At the beginning of the year he buys a bond in France. At the end of the year he sells it, buys dollars again, and has 12 percent more dollars than he had at the beginning of the year, compared with the 8 percent he could have gotten in the United States.

But what if in the meantime the franc has been devalued? Suppose the devaluation is 20 percent. Then the American who bought French bonds at the beginning of the year, earned 12 percent in France, and then sold the French money for dollars would in total get *less* in dollars than he started with. The calculation is as follows. At the beginning of the year, with an exchange rate of F6/$, he took $100 and bought a bond worth F600. At the end of the year he gets back F672 (because of the 12 percent interest). But now a dollar costs F7.20 because there has been a 20 percent devaluation. Therefore with the 672 francs, he gets back only $93.33 (672/7.20). Instead of coming out ahead, the devaluation puts him behind despite the higher French interest rates.

Thus any time a devaluation is expected, capital flows will be heavily affected. Indeed, if a devaluation is expected soon, there probably will be a huge amount of capital flows away from the depreciating currency. Suppose you know that tomorrow the franc will be devalued 20 percent. Then if you live in France, you take 600 francs to buy $100. The next day $1 is worth F7.20, and you are ahead by F120.

There is one more aspect to this situation. In free asset markets such as the stock market, there is usually a good chance to lose as well as make money. But when the central bank is fixing the exchange rate and there is a deficit in the balance of payments, there is only one way the exchange rate can go—it can only be devalued. That means anyone buying American assets and selling French assets at a time when the franc is expected to be devalued has a safe bet. If the franc is not devalued, nothing bad happens to him. If the franc is devalued, he makes a lot of money.

Thus when there are capital movements, maintenance of disequilibrium fixed exchange rates becomes difficult or impossible. Everyone will be trying to move assets out of the currency in trouble. So-called hot money flows out of a currency that people expect will be devalued. The central bank, committed to the exchange rate, has to sell dollars to meet the demands made by those who are trying to buy American assets. But the amounts that can flow in response to an expected devaluation or revaluation are enormous. For instance, in 1973 the German central bank took in $10 billion within a 5-week period when speculators expected that the deutsche mark would be revalued.

When the capital flows become very large, the central bank runs out of reserves very quickly. In terms of Figure 36-5, the curve *MK* will be very far to the right when a devaluation is expected. The central bank cannot meet the demands for dollars and is forced to devalue. These episodes in which there are large flows of capital are called balance of payments crises, speculative attacks, or flows of hot money. And under the adjustable peg system, a speculative attack can force a devaluation or revaluation very quickly.

Speculative capital flows ultimately caused the collapse of the fixed exchange rate system in the early 1970s. Germany was running balance of payments surpluses at the time. It had revalued in 1961, 1969, and 1971. In 1973 there were large capital inflows once more, taking advantage of the one-way bet that Germany could only revalue, not devalue. Rather than formally revalue yet again, the German central bank decided to stop trying to fix the exchange rate and let the deutsche mark find its own equilibrium level in the market.

Other central banks, too, decided to stop trying to fix par values. The system moved from fixed but adjustable rates toward a regime of flexible rates. Looking back to Figure 36-1, we see that in the transition from the 1960s to the late 1970s there was a major realignment of exchange rates.

The DM appreciated cumulatively by 50 percent while sterling depreciated against the dollar by 40 percent. These changes are the reflection of the accumulated disequilibrium on which speculators in the late 1960s were betting when they moved out of sterling and dollars and into deutsche marks.

Controlling Capital Flows   If capital flows are so disruptive to orderly exchange markets, why do governments not simply prohibit them? This is in fact done in many countries. Residents are prohibited from holding foreign securities of any kind, and thus outflows are avoided. But such controls are not watertight. In a country where residents firmly expect a large devaluation, a thousand ways are found to get out of domestic assets and into foreign securities. Currency is smuggled out of the country in trucks and suitcases. Exporters ask their foreign customers to pay in part (and secretly) by transferring money into a bank account abroad. Importers pay more than the true price for foreign goods, asking the suppliers to put the difference in a foreign account for them. Importers pay their bills early, and exporters delay their receipts until after the expected devaluation. Thus even without authorized capital flows, there are plenty of ways in which speculation can and does take place. In the end, if the public is sufficiently certain of a devaluation, the central bank will be forced into it.

It would be a mistake to view international capital flows purely as a problem for policymakers. They also serve an important economic function. If domestic residents—firms, households, and the government—wish to spend more than current income, they have to borrow abroad. If firms want to invest more than domestic savers wish to lend, foreign borrowing will cover the difference. Conversely, if domestic residents wish to save more than home firms can profitably invest, the home country will lend abroad. International capital flows thus provide gains from trade just as international trade in goods does. Savers in one country can benefit from higher rates of return elsewhere. The world puts its investment where returns are highest, without regard to national boundaries. Thus capital flows are in principle beneficial.

Of course, things can go wrong. When capital flows become dominated by exchange rate speculation rather than by the more basic determinants of international investment and saving patterns, they can easily play havoc in the foreign exchange market. They start determining saving and investment rather than being determined by them. More often than not, however, the trouble lies not with the international investor-speculator but rather with central banks that attempt to sustain unrealistic exchange rates. We shall see more of this issue in the discussion of flexible rates to which we now turn.

5 EXCHANGE RATE MOVEMENTS UNDER FLEXIBLE RATES

In this section we extend the analysis of the floating exchange rate system by dropping some of our special assumptions. We want to see how inflation at home and abroad affects the exchange rate, how disturbances that affect trade—such as the British discovery of oil in the late 1960s and early 1970s—affect the exchange rate, and how capital flows enter the picture. We want, in brief, to understand how exchange rates have moved in the period since 1973, when the adjustable peg system was abandoned.

Purchasing Power Parity

One of the main determinants of exchange rate movements since 1973 has been differences between inflation rates in different countries. If our inflation exceeds inflation abroad, then, other things equal, our currency will tend to depreciate.

We start by looking at the example of Peru and the United States, for which Table 36-7 presents data. All indices are set to 100 for 1970. Between 1970 and 1980 the Peruvian price index increased to 1400, whereas that for the United States rose to only 210. Suppose for the moment that the exchange rate had not changed. Then American goods would have been incredibly cheap for Peruvians, and Americans would find Peruvian goods very expensive. In fact, with prices of Peruvian goods rising so fast, Peru's exchange rate kept depreciating. Indeed, by the end of the decade, the exchange rate (expressed as an index measured in terms of dollars per Peruvian sole) fell to 13 from its 1970 level of 100.

What did this do to the prices of Peruvian goods compared with the prices of American goods? Consider an American buying

TABLE 36-7

PURCHASING POWER PARITY EXCHANGE RATES
(Indices, 1970 = 100)

	(1) U.S. PRICES	(2) PRICES, local currency	(3) EXCHANGE RATE, $/sole	(4) = [(2) × (3)]/100 PRICES, $	(5) = [(1)/(2)] × 100 PPP EXCHANGE RATE
1970	100	100	100	100	100
1980	210	1400	13	182	15

Source: IMF, *International Financial Statistics, Yearbook, 1981.*

goods in Peru. For 1970 we set the index of the dollar cost of Peruvian goods at 100. By 1980 prices of Peruvian goods have risen to 1400, but the exchange rate has dropped to 13. For an American, Peruvian goods are more expensive because their price in soles has risen and cheaper because the price of soles in terms of dollars (the exchange rate) has fallen. The fourth column shows how these two forces work out. On an index of 100 for 1970, the dollar price of Peruvian goods has risen to 182. But of course the dollar price of American goods has risen from 100 to 210, as the first column shows. Thus the Peruvian depreciations actually made Peruvian goods *relatively* cheaper for Americans despite the rapid Peruvian inflation.

The fifth column shows how much depreciation would have been needed in Peru to get the relative prices of American and Peruvian goods to stay constant. On a 1970 index of 100, the exchange rate in 1980 would have had to be 15 to maintain the relative prices of American and Peruvian goods. The exchange rate was actually lower, showing that the exchange rate depreciated further than was needed to hold constant the relative prices of goods.

> The exchange rate that maintains the relative prices of goods in two countries is the *purchasing power parity* (PPP) rate.

Depreciation of the currency exactly offsets differences in inflation in the two countries when exchange rates follow PPP. With the relative prices of goods remaining constant, import and export demands are not affected by the combined exchange rate and price level changes.

We now show how price changes affect exchange rates in a flexible rate system. Figure 36-6 shows the foreign exchange market of Peru. Initial equilibrium obtains at point A at an exchange rate of 100 soles per dollar. At that exchange rate export revenue exactly

FIGURE 36-6   AN INCREASE IN HOME PRICES LEADS TO AN EXCHANGE DEPRECIATION (PPP). When domestic prices rise by 50 percent, the demand for imports shifts. Foreign goods are now relatively cheaper, and therefore more are demanded at any exchange rate. The same relative prices will exist when the exchange rate depreciates 50 percent. Therefore, the *MM* curve shifts to *MM'*, precisely 50 percent above *MM*. Similarly, when domestic prices rise, exports become more expensive for foreigners. It takes exactly a 50 percent depreciation for the quantity of exports demanded to remain the same, shifting the *XX* curve upward by 50 percent. The new equilibrium is at *A'*, where the exchange rate has depreciated 50 percent, exactly the amount that maintains purchasing power parity.

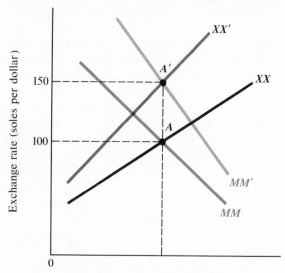

matches import spending. Suppose now that because of expansionary monetary and fiscal policies or because of an increase in wages, all prices in Peru rise by 50 percent. What happens in the foreign exchange market? Recall that our original export revenue and import spending schedules were drawn for given prices at home (Peru) and abroad (United States). A change in Peruvian prices therefore shifts these schedules. Higher Peruvian prices imply that at the initial exchange rate foreign goods are relatively cheaper. Therefore, import spending would tend to rise. This is shown as the shift of the import spending schedule to *MM'*. It is also true that with higher Peruvian prices, exporters are at a disadvantage compared with foreign competitors. Their prices are now higher, and therefore less is exported; thus export revenue is lower. This is shown by the shift of *XX* to *XX'*.

Note in Figure 36-6 that higher Peruvian prices lead to a depreciation of the Peruvian currency. Because higher prices give rise to a deficit—higher imports and fewer exports—there is pressure for the currency to depreciate up to the point where competitiveness is restored sufficiently for payments to be balanced. The required depreciation is exactly 50 percent—just as much as the price increase. That is the depreciation consistent with PPP. Our import prices will have risen in home currency just as much as domestic prices, and therefore the incentive to shift toward imports will have been wiped out. Likewise, our exporters' higher home prices are offset by a depreciation of the currency that restores the prices in terms of dollars to their initial level. Thus the figure exactly supports PPP and explains the approximate size of the depreciation of the sole in the seventies.

The role of relative inflation rates in affecting exchange rates is more obvious the larger the inflation differentials between the countries. It is also more apparent the less other factors, to which we now turn, affect the exchange rate.

Trade Disturbances and the Exchange Rate

Exchange rates can deviate quite dramatically from a path suggested by PPP. Consider the example of the United States and the United Kingdom in Table 36-8, which makes the same calculations as Table 36-7.

U.K. prices rose much more than American prices over this period. The PPP exchange rate by 1981 was only 60 on an index that was 100 in 1970. However, the actual exchange rate barely changed. Thus in relative terms British goods became much more expensive for Americans, and American goods became much cheaper for the British.

What kept the exchange rate away from PPP? There are two factors. First, there was a long-term change in Britain's demand for imports, because it began to produce its own oil in the 1970s instead of importing it. Second, Britain was running a restrictive monetary policy in an attempt to get inflation under control.

The effects of Britain's production of its own oil on the exchange rate can be analyzed by using a diagram such as Figure 36-6. The demand for imports falls, the *MM* curve shifts to the left, and the exchange rate appreciates. But we have to ask whether the reduction in British oil imports could possibly have accounted for the large appreciation (relative to PPP) of the pound seen in Table 36-8. This is extremely unlikely. It is more plausible to look for additional factors that may have been at work.

The Business Cycle and Exchange Rates

In discussing the British devaluation of 1967, we noted that monetary and fiscal policies contribute to the success or failure of devaluation. Restrictive policies reduce the demand for imports, thereby tending to reduce a payments deficit or increase a surplus. Restrictive monetary and fiscal policies also, of course, affect exchange rates under flexible rates. They reduce the demand for imports, thereby tending to appreciate the exchange rate. Indeed, restrictive policies also have some effect on exports. Firms that cannot sell at home are more inclined to try to sell abroad, thereby increasing exports at any given exchange rate.

Expansionary policies work in the opposite direction. They tend to cause deficits in the balance of payments under fixed rates

TABLE 36-8

U.S.–U.K. PRICES AND EXCHANGE RATES
(Indices, 1970 = 100)

	U.S.	U.K.			
	PRICES	PRICES	EXCHANGE RATE, $/£ INDEX	PRICES, $	PPP EXCHANGE RATE
1970	100	100	100	100	100
1981/I	230	380	96	365	60.5

Source: IMF, *International Financial Statistics, Yearbook, 1981.*

and depreciation of the exchange rate under floating rates. Thus the state of the business cycle—boom or recession—in different countries also helps explain why exchange rates deviate from a PPP path.

Interest Rate Differentials and Capital Flows

Monetary policy has a major impact on exchange rates. If the United States reduces monetary growth, this tends to raise interest rates in America compared with the rest of the world. Investors, seeing the high U.S. interest rates, shift their portfolios out of DM or sterling or French francs and toward U.S. dollars. Capital will tend to flow to the United States. Conversely, when monetary policy is tightened in Europe but not in the United States, capital will flow from the United States to Europe as investors sell American bonds to buy European securities that promise a higher yield.

How do these capital flows affect our analysis of the foreign exchange market? In discusssing devaluations and speculative capital flows, we already saw how capital inflows add to the supply of foreign currency and can be incorporated by shifting the *XX* curve in Figure 36-7 to *XK*. Similarly, capital outflows shift the *MM* curve to *MK*. The initial equilibrium exchange rate in Figure 36-7 is $2.40/£.

Now suppose the United States reduces

its money growth and raises interest rates. Worldwide, investors want to buy dollar assets. The *XK* curve shifts to *XK'*.[4] The exchange rate falls to $1.80/£. Higher U.S. interest rates, by attracting capital inflows, make the dollar more expensive in currency markets, or make foreign currencies less expensive for America.

Note from Figure 36-7 that the capital inflow and the dollar appreciation affect trade in goods, not just capital flows. With the dollar appreciating to point *A'*, export revenues fall from *B* to *B'* while U.S. spending increases from *D* to *D'*. Thus the capital inflow at the new exchange rate increases and finances the trade deficit. The appreciation of the U.S. currency raises imports as foreign goods become relatively less expensive abroad. Thus interest rate movements, by affecting capital flows, have an effect on exchange rates and thus trade flows.

This effect of interest rates on exchange rates and trade flows was evident in 1980–1982. U.S. monetary policy turned increasingly tight, and U.S. interest rates reached peaks that had not been seen before. Europe did not want to match these very high interest rates, and accordingly capital started to flow from Europe to the United

---

[4] The *MK* curve will probably shift to the left as Americans reduce their desire to invest abroad, but we do not show that shift in order to keep things simple.

FIGURE 36-7 A CAPITAL INFLOW TO THE UNITED STATES LEADS TO THE APPRECIATION OF THE DOLLAR. The demand for foreign currency is shown by *MK* when there are capital flows, and the supply by *XK*. Tight monetary policy in the United States increases U.S. interest rates and increases inflows of capital. The *XK* curve shifts to *XK′*, and the dollar appreciates (sterling depreciates). The capital inflow affects trade. Exports fall from their level at *B* to their level at *B′*, and imports increase from their level at *D* to that at *D′*.

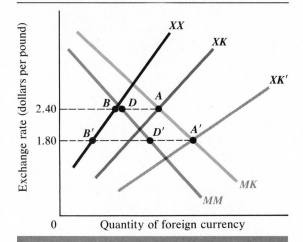

States. There was large pressure in the foreign exchange market and a huge appreciation of the dollar. Table 36-9 shows some of the data.

The striking fact that emerges from Table 36-9 is the huge deutsche mark depreciation of more than 30 percent, from DM1.78/$ to DM2.43/$ in less than a year. Inflation rates in the two countries were about the same over this period. This meant that the capital inflows to the United States, as suggested by Figure 36-7, made U.S. goods more expensive relative to foreign goods.

The high U.S. interest rates and capital inflows had effects that were regarded as undesirable by Europeans. The Europeans could have matched the American high interest rates by tightening up their own monetary policies and forcing their interest rates higher, but they did not want to have a re-

strictive monetary policy. However, they also did not want their currencies to depreciate too much, fearing that with imports becoming more expensive, their own price levels would rise. They responded in three ways. They tightened their monetary policies somewhat, raising interest rates above the levels they wanted, allowed their exchange rates to depreciate somewhat, and complained about American policy a lot.

Intervention and Dirty Floating

With capital flows affecting exchange rates, central banks have intervened in the flexible rate system to try to offset the effects of the flows. They do this by buying and selling foreign exchange, just as under the adjustable peg system. The difference is that there is no official par value.

Some central banks claim that they intervene merely to try to prevent large changes in exchange rates in the short run. But in practice it is very difficult to know at the time what is a short-term capital flow affecting the exchange rate and what is the beginning of a fundamental change in the exchange rate. Thus central banks have often intervened heavily in trying to fight what look like fundamental changes in the exchange rate.

TABLE 36-9

SHORT-TERM INTEREST RATES AND EXCHANGE RATES

PERIOD	INTEREST RATES		EXCHANGE RATE, DM/$
	UNITED STATES	GERMANY	
1980 III quarter	9.8	9.2	1.78
1980 IV quarter	15.9	9.6	1.91
1981 III quarter	17.6	12.8	2.43

Source: IMF, *International Financial Statistics,* April 1982.

Intervention that affects the level of the exchange rate rather than just smoothing out fluctuations is known as *dirty floating*.

6 FIXED VERSUS FLEXIBLE RATES

In the last 20 years the world economy has seen fixed rates in the 1960s and flexible rates in the 1970s. Fixed rates were never quite fixed—there were intermittent devaluations and revaluations of major currencies. Flexible rates were never quite flexible because there was a lot of intervention. Still, we have seen both regimes in action and should therefore be able to decide which one works better. And there are some people who argue that the choice between fixed rates as practiced in the 1960s and flexible rates as practiced in the 1970s is too restricted. They would like to return to the nineteenth-century gold standard, which, as we have seen, automatically linked the money stock to the balance of payments and produced reasonably low inflation.

The Arguments

There has been a debate between proponents of fixed exchange rates and flexible exchange rates at least since the early fifties. There is no clear-cut winner. The experience since 1973 suggests the flexible rate system is workable. The adjustable peg system broke down and thus did not seem workable. One persuasive argument says that we will have to continue with flexible rates until countries decide they want to follow policies that ensure that exchange rates can in practice be kept fixed. This will require them to follow gold standard–type rules more closely. For instance, the British experience in the sixties (Table 36-5) reflects the government's preference for conducting monetary policy to maintain full employment rather than a fixed exchange rate. Unless such preferences change, fixed exchange rates will not return.

Still, there is a question about the desirability of fixed rates. Here there are three main issues. First, do flexible rates create unnecessary exchange rate movements that would be avoided under a fixed rate system? Figure 36-8 shows the exchange rate of dollars to deutsche marks from 1975 to 1982. There are large fluctuations. These, as we know from our discussion of Figure 36-7, affect imports and exports of goods and thus have real effects. The question is whether such fluctuations reflect real forces that *should* change exchange rates or whether they are merely speculative changes without any basis in what should happen. If they are merely speculative, a fixed rate system could prevent them. If they reflect fundamentals, a fixed rate system would eventually have to react.

There is no strong evidence that convinces either side about the real cause of these fluctuations. Certainly, there were fewer fluctuations in the sixties. But then there were no massive disturbances to the international economy in the sixties, as there were from oil-price changes in the seventies. The argument remains unsettled.

The second issue concerns the discipline alternative systems require from central banks. Do central banks pursue more stable policies under fixed or flexible rates? More important, do we have less inflation, and more stable inflation, with higher employment under fixed or flexible rates? Here we do not have enough evidence. The 1960s was a period of low inflation and high growth in most industrialized countries; the 1970s, under flexible rates, showed lower economic growth with higher and more variable inflation. But as we know, the 1970s was also a period of major international shocks such as the oil-price increases.

The last issue concerns which regime provides more freedom for international trade and payments. Under fixed rates, it is argued, the need to defend the exchange

FIGURE 36-8 $/DM EX-CHANGE RATE. (*Source:* Citibank Economic Database.)

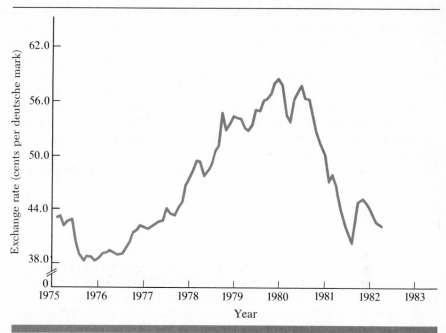

rate leads countries to restrict trade by tariffs or to curb international capital flows. Under flexible rates, depreciation becomes a ready substitute for restrictions. It is true that in the 1970s, despite the impact of the oil-price shocks, world trade and payments remained quite unrestricted, perhaps more so than in the 1960s. This evidence does point in favor of flexible rates.

Since the world will not soon go back to fixed rates, the argument between proponents and opponents of fixed rates will continue. There is one question to ask, though: Why is it that we have fixed exchange rates *within* a country? The California dollar exchanges one-for-one with a New York dollar (though they did not always do that in the nineteenth century). If flexible exchange rates are a good thing between the United States and Canada, why not between New York and California? The answer is that monetary and fiscal policies in California and New York are the same, whereas they are not in the United States and Canada.

Similarly, there is totally free movement of labor and capital within the United States, but not between Canada and the United States. Because inflation rates in the two countries may differ, it is useful to have the exchange rate available as a means of adjusting. If the two countries shared a single central bank, there would be a stronger argument for fixed exchange rates.

Back to Gold?

We have already discussed arguments for and against the gold standard. The *gold bugs*—those in favor of the gold standard—want to be sure the money supply is controlled automatically and therefore propose to tie it to the balance of payments and to the amount of gold that a country produces.

One argument decisively disposes of the gold standard. Under the gold standard, society devotes scarce resources to producing money by digging it from the ground. But money can just as well be made at a much lower cost by printing it. If it is desirable to control the money stock strictly, the same rules that the gold standard imposes can be imposed on a paper money system. We could always require the Federal Reserve by law to follow the three gold standard rules set out earlier as its basic rules for creating high-powered paper money. It would be cheaper that way.

Quite aside from the fact that the gold standard wastes scarce resources is the issue of whether we should want to control the money stock through the balance of payments. There is no convincing argument that says monetary policy is best conducted by trying to keep the balance of payments in balance. Inflation and unemployment are also serious concerns of policy. If society wants to affect them through monetary policy, it cannot follow the gold standard rules.

Arguments for the gold standard have had little support from economists.

SUMMARY

1   In the last 20 years the major industrialized countries have moved from a regime of fixed but adjustable rates to flexible rates. Under flexible exchange rates, the exchange rate is determined as the equilibrium price in the foreign exchange market. Under fixed rates, the rate is set by the central bank, which undertakes to buy or sell *any* amount of foreign exchange at the set rate.

2   Given prices at home and abroad, exchange rate movements change relative prices of domestic and foreign goods. A depreciation of the home currency makes our goods cheaper abroad and makes foreign goods more expensive in the home market. Therefore, depreciation tends to raise exports and reduce imports.

3   In a free market for foreign exchange, a deficit implies an excess demand for foreign currency and therefore a depreciation of our own currency. Conversely, a surplus implies an excess supply of foreign currency and therefore leads to an appreciation of the home currency.

4   A gold standard is a regime of fixed exchange rates. The home currency value is defined in terms of gold (say, $35 per ounce of gold), and the central bank buys or sells gold in unlimited amounts at the price. Moreover, the central bank will issue or retire money *only* in connection with gold operations. Gold inflows lead to monetary expansion; outflows lead to destruction of money. In this manner the gold standard implies an automatic adjustment process of the balance of payments.

5   The monetary adjustment process under the gold standard and under fixed rates without sterilization implies that in a surplus country the money supply expands, raising spending and prices and thus raising imports and reducing exports. In deficit countries, reserve (gold) losses lead to monetary contraction, reduced spending, and lower

prices and thus to lower imports and increased exports. Thus the monetary adjustment process tends to restore payments balance.

6   Sterilization of gold or reserve losses occurs when the central bank of a deficit country offsets the automatic decline in money by an open market purchase of bonds. The reserve loss automatically reduces the money supply, but the open market purchase reintroduces the money. Thus, with money unchanged and no other policies corrected, deficits can persist until the time that the central bank runs out of reserves.

7   A central bank that defends an overvalued exchange rate must ultimately face up to the fact that the reserve losses cannot go on and that a devaluation is called for. A devaluation restores external balance by making our exports more competitive abroad and by making foreign goods more expensive in home markets. A devaluation leads to higher exports and reduced import spending. A successful devaluation requires that domestic prices *not* rise to offset the gain in competitiveness. This typically requires a tightening of monetary and fiscal policies.

8   Capital flows internationally in response to interest differentials and expectations of exchange rate movements. Capital is attracted to countries that offer high interest rates or currency appreciation or, better still, both. Investors flee from currencies that are expected to collapse, and they like nothing better than countries where money is being tightened, leading to high interest rates and appreciation.

9   Under fixed exchange rates investors can take advantage of one-way bets. Weak currencies can easily be spotted, and the recognition that *ultimately* they must be devalued leads to speculation against them. If speculators hold their beliefs with sufficient strength, the capital outflows and reserve losses may be so large that the central bank must actually give in and devalue. The breakdown of the fixed rate regime of the 1960s took place in this form—speculation against sterling and the dollar in favor of the deutsche mark.

10   A flexible rate is determined by three factors. The first is levels of prices at home and abroad. Other things equal, an increase in money and prices at home leads to an equiproportionate exchange depreciation. Second, real factors related to trade flows influence the exchange rate. A loss in export markets, for example, will bring about a deficit and therefore a depreciation so as to restore competitiveness. The third factor is international capital flows. An increase in home interest rates will tend to draw in capital and thereby bring about a home currency appreciation.

11   The discussion about the merits of fixed and flexible rates shows no clear winners. Neither regime seems intrinsically better equipped to provide price stability and full employment.

KEY TERMS

Freely flexible (floating) exchange
   rate systems
Par value of gold
100 percent cover (100 percent gold
   backing)
Dollar standard

International reserves
Sterilization
Capital inflows and outflows
Speculative attack
Purchasing power parity (PPP)
   exchange rates

PROBLEMS

1   Suppose in a country, say, Italy, prices increase by 140 percent between 1975 and 1985. In the rest of the world prices rise by 90 percent. What should happen to the Italian currency in a free foreign exchange market?

2   Suppose the home country experiences a gain of 10 percent of export revenue because of new markets for its goods. (*a*) Use a diagram of the foreign exchange market to show the initial equilibrium and the new equilibrium under a freely floating exchange rate. (*b*) Suppose alternatively that the exchange rate was fixed under a gold standard. What would be the adjustment mechanism?

3   Suppose the interest rate in Argentina is 50 percent per year, and in the United States it is only 15 percent. What would the international investor have to know before choosing where to place his money?

4   "The fixed exchange rate system of the 1960s collapsed because central banks would not play by the rules." Discuss.

5   Suppose Mexico embarks on a tight monetary policy. What would you expect to happen to Mexican exports over the next year or so (*a*) under fixed exchange rates and (*b*) under flexible exchange rates?

6   "The fixed exchange rate system is preferred to flexible rates because it gives rise to less disturbing capital flows." Discuss.

7   "Under flexible exchange rates each country can choose its own inflation rate, entirely independent from the rest of the world." Discuss.

8   "The gold standard is the best possible exchange rate regime because it eliminates any possible tinkering with the money supply." Discuss.

9   "Under flexible exchange rates current account adjustment is costless, whereas under fixed exchange rates it requires a cut in real wages." Discuss.

10   "Under dirty floating, central banks intervene in the foreign exchange market to stabilize exchange rates. In so doing they often overstep their role, and this is why exchange rates have not moved at all in the last few years." Discuss this statement using your knowledge of the theory and facts.

11   "Balance of payments problems cannot exist in the absence of a central bank that intervenes in the market." Discuss.

12   "There is no difference between pegging exchange rates and supporting potato prices. The economics is just the same." Discuss.

13   In this chapter we said that the President is proud when the dollar is strong but exporters are unhappy. Explain each attitude.

14 Figure 36-1 shows how the pound and deutsche mark exchange rates have moved since 1960. (*a*) Explain what happened to the pound in 1967–1968. (*b*) Explain the broad movements in the rates. (*c*) Explain why in 1981 both the pound and the deutsche mark depreciated.

5

The Big
Questions

In 1974 the General Assembly of the United Nations adopted a resolution proclaiming

> Our joint determination to work urgently for the establishment of a new international economic order based on equity, sovereign equality, interdependence, common interest and co-operation among all States, irrespective of their economic and social systems, which shall correct inequalities and redress existing injustices, make it possible to eliminate the widening gap between the developed and the developing countries and ensure steadily accelerating economic and social development. . . .[1]

37 Problems of Developing Countries in the World Economy

The resolution on the *new international economic order* (NIEO) was an expression of the discontent of the developing countries with their share in the world's income and wealth and a reflection of their feeling that the way the world economy works is stacked against them. Since the resolution was passed, there have been international meetings and summit meetings to discuss the restructuring of the world economy, but there has not been much action. There are bound to be more such meetings in the years to come, perhaps leading to changes in the world economy.

In this section we will look at the facts behind the movement for an NIEO and the proposals that have been made to change the current situation. We are once more dealing with a sensitive and important topic for which economics cannot give all the answers but can certainly be used to analyze the proposed solutions.

1 WORLD INCOME DISTRIBUTION AND THE NIEO

The most important fact underlying the demands for an NIEO is the enormous inequality of income in the world. Table 37-1 gives an indication of the inequality. In 1979, there were 2.3 billion people living in the low-income countries. Their average income was $230 per person. At the same time 2.0 billion people lived in the rest of the world with an average income of $4600. Of course, we know that data on income in different countries cannot easily be compared and that the figures are subject to a wide margin of error. But the basic fact emerges strongly: *Most of the world's people live in poverty that is beyond the imagination of people in the high-income countries.*

---

[1] U.N. General Assembly Resolution 3201, May 1, 1974.

TABLE 37-1

AVERAGE INCOMES, 1979

	POPULATION, billions	AVERAGE INCOME, 1979 dollars	SHARE OF WORLD INCOME, %
Low-income countries	2.3	230	5.4
Rest of world	2.0	4600	94.6

Source: World Bank, World Development Report, 1981, Table 1.

The distribution of income in the world cannot be described only by looking at the average incomes in different countries. Even in countries with middle-income levels, many people may live in great poverty. We can certainly say that most of the world's people live way below what are regarded as poverty levels in high-income countries.

Data other than income levels suggest other dimensions of world poverty. Table 37-2 shows energy consumption, life expectancy, caloric intake, availability of medical care, and education data for countries classified by income level. The low-income countries are badly off in every dimension.

Progress, 1960–1979   Bad as the situation

in the low-income countries is, it has improved in many respects since 1960. Table 37-3 shows increases in the adult literacy rate and in life expectancy in all countries. The increase in life expectancy is most marked in the low-income countries, and this is a clear indication that the quality of life in those countries has improved over the past 20 years.

Table 37-3 shows that per capita incomes increased on average in all groups of countries. But over the 1960–1979 period the low-income countries grew more slowly than the others. Thus they fell further behind in that period. Since 1974, the relative position of the low-income countries has been improving. Their growth in the seventies was generally higher than it had been in

TABLE 37-2

WORLD WELFARE INDICATORS

	PER CAPITA GNP, 1979 dollars	PER CAPITA ENERGY CONSUMP-TION, 1979, U.S. = 100	ADULT LITERACY RATE, %, 1976	PERCENT OF AGE GROUP IN SECONDARY SCHOOL, 1978	LIFE EXPEC-TANCY AT BIRTH, 1979	POPULATION PER MEDICAL PERSONNEL (PHYSICIANS AND NURSES), 1977	DAILY CALORIC INTAKE AS % OF REQUIRE-MENT, 1977
Low-income countries	230	3.7	51	36	57	3100	98
Middle-income countries	1420	9.9	72	41	61	1300	109
High-income countries	9440	63.9	99	89	74	160	131

Source: World Bank, World Development Report, 1981, Tables 1, 7, 21, 22, and 23.

TABLE 37-3
WORLD DEVELOPMENT, 1960–1979

	GROWTH RATE OF PER CAPITA GNP, 1960–1979	ADULT LITERACY RATE, %		LIFE EXPECT-ANCY AT BIRTH	
		1960	1976	1960	1979
Low-income countries	1.6	28	51	42	57
Middle-income countries	3.8	53	72	53	61
High-income countries	4.0	—	99	70	74

Source: World Bank, *World Development Report, 1981,* Tables 1, 21, and 23.

the sixties, whereas the high-income countries' growth rates of income fell. But even if the low-income countries grow a bit faster than the high-income countries, the gap between them may be getting bigger.

How can that happen? Suppose incomes in the low-income countries rise 25 percent, from $230 (in 1979) to $287.50. At the same time, suppose incomes in the other countries rise 10 percent, from $4600 (in 1979) to $5060. To begin with, the gap between incomes in the two groups of countries was $4370 ($4600 − $230); after the growth, it is $4772.50 ($5060 − $287.50). Even though the low-income countries grow faster, they may be falling further behind in terms of the dollar gap between average incomes.

Thus there has been some progress in the past two decades, but the gap between the low-income countries and other countries is wide and continues to grow; thus the low-income countries see little hope of improvement relative to the other countries. It is this combination of enormous differences in incomes and slow or no progress in reducing the gap that is the driving force behind the NIEO.

The North and the South
The call for an NIEO is often expressed as

the difference between the north and the south. The north-south distinction is used to differentiate one set of problems from those of an east-west nature, in which the world is seen as being divided between a communist or collectivist east and a free-market west. The north–south distinction sees the world divided into the rich north (which includes the Soviet Union) and the poor south; the difference is in the level of income, not the organization of the economy. Those in the south claim the right to a larger share of the world's resources, quite independently of their political or economic organization, and their claims are on rich countries whether those countries are capitalist or socialist or communist.[2]

The north-south division is the same as the division between developed, or industrialized, economies and the *LDCs*. The LDCs, or less-developed countries, are the

---

[2] For extensive discussion of the NIEO and what might be done about existing inequalities, see *North-South: A Programme for Survival*, Report of the Brandt Commission, Pan Books, London, 1980. The Brandt Commission was a private group, headed by former German chancellor Willy Brandt, which studied world development and issued a report recommending major changes in the international economic system. The report is convincing in painting a grim picture of the economic problems of the low-income countries but does not successfully come to grips with the difficulties of changing the structure of the world economy.

countries of the south, or the third world, ranging from the poorest countries to middle-income countries such as Argentina and Yugoslavia.

The International Economic Order

The countries of the south blame many of their difficulties on the existing world economic order, or the formal and informal rules under which international economic interactions take place. Their general complaint is that the system is stacked against them. Specifically, they make the following points.

1   The markets for their primary products are controlled by the high-income countries. The prices they receive for their goods—for example, copper, tin, bauxite, coffee, and cocoa—are generally too low and certainly fluctuate too much for their economies to plan serious development. Furthermore, on average, the prices have been turning against them. They have had to pay more in terms of their own outputs for the imports they purchase.

2   The markets for industrial commodities they want to produce are closed to them by protectionism in the developed economies. Since industrialization is, they argue, the only way to grow fast, the high-income countries are shutting them out of fast growth.

3   The terms on which financial aid for development is provided are too stiff. When LDCs borrow from commercial banks and financial institutions, the loans are too short-term to make it possible to undertake important long-term investment projects. And borrowing from the major international agencies such as the World Bank is not sufficiently cheap.

4   Given the extreme poverty of LDCs and the way the world economy has operated so far, other countries should as a matter of justice provide aid for their future development. The aid may take the form of gifts— unilateral transfers of resources from the rich to the poor countries—or it may take the form of a willingness to bend the rules in a way that will help the south. For instance, the south wants the right to keep out foreign imports while being given access for their exports to the developed countries.

We shall now take up some of the complaints in more detail and discuss what might be done about them.

2   THE LDCs IN WORLD TRADE

LDCs have grievances both in the area of world trade and in the field of international

---

BOX 37-1

WHO'S WHO IN THE WORLD ECONOMY

IMF (International Monetary Fund): Located in Washington, D.C., the International Monetary Fund was intended to be the central banks' banker. The fund was set up in 1945 as part of the *Bretton Woods system* of post-World War II international finance. Bretton Woods is a country resort in New Hampshire where the international negotiations took place. The Bretton Woods system, loosely characterized, aimed for stable exchange rates and unhampered and nondiscriminatory trade.

The IMF helps maintain such a system by providing members with short-term balance of payments financing. The availability of this financing, beyond an automatic portion, depends on the acceptance of "conditionality," which is an adjustment program for monetary and fiscal policy prescribed by the IMF. Most countries are members of the IMF, although the voting power is concentrated in the hands of the major industrial countries. At the present stage of international economic integration the IMF does not play the role of a world central bank. It lacks powers of money creation, and it mostly deals with developing countries that need to borrow.

World Bank: Also located in Washington, D.C., and part of the Bretton Woods system, the bank started as a lender to industrial countries, financing postwar reconstruction with capital provided by the members. It is now an important source of development finance and of expertise and advice on development policy. In the last 10 years the World Bank has set itself the task of drawing attention to world poverty, illiteracy, malnutrition, and disease as well as financing public projects to combat these major areas of backwardness.

OECD: The Organization for Economic Cooperation and Development is located in Paris and is an organization linking 24 industrial countries. These include the European countries, New Zealand, Australia, and Japan as well as Canada and the United States. The OECD is mainly a vehicle for consultation and exchange of views on economic policy among industrial countries.

UNCTAD (United Nations Conference on Trade and Development): Part of the United Nations, UNCTAD was formed in 1964 to pay particular attention to the trade and development problems of poor countries. It has been a militant, influential body that has sponsored reform in the field of trade (preferences for LDCs, commodity stabilization, foreign investment codes, etc.) and payments.

OPEC (Organization of Petroleum Exporting Countries): OPEC is the cartel of oil producers. The countries whose oil exports are at least 1 percent of world oil exports are Algeria, Indonesia, Iran, Iraq, Kuwait, Libya, Mexico, Nigeria, Oman, Qatar, Saudi Arabia, the United Arab Emirates, and Venezuela. There is another group of 11 countries that are oil exporters on a lesser scale. OPEC burst on the world scene in 1973, when it dramatically raised the world price of oil through an agreement on supply restrictions. The real price of oil has been raised in two large steps: 1970–1973 = 100, 1974 = 395, 1980–1981 = 622. Thus there was a tripling of oil prices in 1974 and another sharp increase in 1980.

NIEO (new international economic order): This is an informal movement by developing countries, in the United Nations and in other international bodies, calling for a sharp revision of traditional economic and power relations between the north (industrial countries) and the south (poor countries). The north-south debate on new international rules involves commodity stabilization, trade preferences, debt relief, and monetary arrangements. These topics will be discussed later in this chapter. Little definite progress has been made, in good part because the south is a very diverse group including middle-income countries such as Mexico, Argentina, and Brazil and very poor countries such as India or Zaire. Their problems are very different, and the division has hampered progress. Industrial countries have shown absolutely no enthusiasm for a major review of the economic order, being basically committed to market economies and firm control on the amount of aid and transfers they undertake.

TABLE 37-4

COMPOSITION OF EXPORTS OF DEVELOPING COUNTRIES
(Percent of Total Exports)

	1960	1970	1978
Primary commodities	83.9	65.9	49.3
Manufactures	16.1	34.1	50.7

Note: Excluding petroleum exports.
Source: World Bank, *Commodity Trade and Price Trends, 1980.*

finance. We start here with an analysis of the two trade issues: the problems of exporters of primary commodities and the problems of trade in manufactures.

Before proceeding to these issues we briefly look at Table 37-4, which shows the evolution of LDC export composition. As recently as 1960 the LDCs were primarily exporters of raw materials. Now more than half their exports are manufactured goods.

There are good reasons for this shift in trade patterns, but it also creates future problems that we shall discuss.

Problems of Trade in Primary Commodities

Figure 37-1 shows the real prices of two commodities: natural rubber and cocoa. In each case we look at an index of the price of the commodity in world trade, adjusted for changes in the prices of manufactured goods in world trade. The prices of both commodities are highly volatile. In a year price may rise 20 or 30 percent or more, and in another year it may fall very sharply. Thus *volatility* of the prices of primary commodities is the first fact to bear in mind.

The second question is one of *trend.* Have the prices of primary commodities risen less rapidly than those of manufactured goods so that the purchasing power of

FIGURE 37-1   THE REAL PRICES OF COCOA AND NATURAL RUBBER (INDEX 1974–1976 = 100). (*Source:* The World Bank, *Commodity Trade and Price Trends,* 1980.)

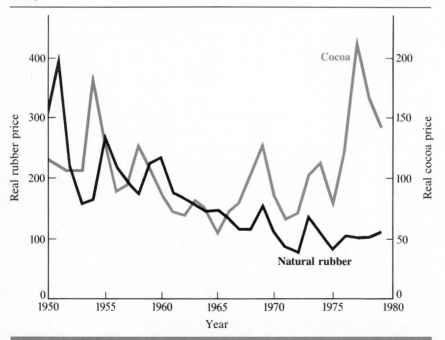

TABLE 37-5

THE REAL PRICE OF PRIMARY COMMODITIES
(1950–1959 = 100)

	1950–1959	1960–1969	1970–1979
33 commodities:	100	85.2	81.8
Agricultural commodities	100	77.0	78.6
Metals and minerals	100	100.8	84.0
Petroleum	100	69.2	188.5

Source: World Bank, *Commodity Trade and Price Trends, 1980.*

primary commodities has fallen? Figure 37-1 shows clearly that the real price of natural rubber has on average been falling, or the purchasing power of rubber has been declining. By contrast, there has been no downward trend for cocoa.

But cocoa and rubber are only two of many primary commodities. Table 37-5 examines the behavior of an index of real prices of 33 primary commodities. The table also shows the behavior of the real price for different groups of commodities.

Table 37-5 shows that compared to the 1950–1959 period the real prices of minerals and metals have been roughly stable but that prices of agricultural commodities have fallen 20 percent in real terms. For comparison, we also show the real price of petroleum. In the 1970s the real price was double that of the 1950s. By 1980 (not shown in the table) it was five times the level of the 1950s. In addition to volatility, there is, then, the issue of a general decline in the purchasing power of LDC export commodities.

Price Volatility The outstanding fact in the markets for primary commodities is the low elasticities of supply and demand with respect to *current* price. These low elasticities imply that any disturbance has a very large effect on price and revenue. The reason for the low price responsiveness on the demand side is simple. Primary commodities are either food or industrial inputs. The demand for food is relatively inelastic with

respect to price. Certainly in the short term, dietary habits are firmly established and respond little to price.

Take the example of the coffee price increase of 1977. Frosts in Brazil reduced the world supply of coffee and drove up prices. What adjustments were made by U.S. consumers? A doubling of the price of coffee reduced quantity demanded by consumers in 1977 by only 26 percent. Demand is very inelastic. The same is true for other primary commodity demands. A fall in the price of natural rubber, for example, will not greatly increase demand by industrial users. In the short run it is difficult to find new uses for rubber as an input. Given the inelastic demand, any disturbance on the supply side implies that price must move a lot to restore market equilibrium.

For different reasons, there is also short-run inelasticity on the supply side. Many commodities have very long production delays. Metals are produced from mines that take years to build. Even for agricultural goods, the short-run supply response is negligible. Once the planting has taken place, the supply is determined primarily by the weather, and there is little scope for increasing output in the short run. The short-run inelastic supply in turn implies that any demand disturbance will have large effects on price.

The volatility of commodity prices is thus explained by the low elasticities of demand and supply. But that is not enough. We also need to ask what the disturbances are that throw markets into disequilibrium in the first place. The main source of disturbances are supply disruptions arising from harvest failures or political events. On the demand side the main disturbances arise from the business cycle and from inventory speculation. Harvest failures or booms in world industrial activity raise commodity prices, while bumper crops or slumps in world industrial activity lower commodity prices.

Export Concentration   High export price variability implies revenue and income instability for the LDCs. This problem is aggravated at the macro level by the fact that many developing countries are specialized in the production of a narrow range of commodities. Table 37-6 shows some extreme cases in which the concentration of exports on a single primary commodity exceeds 60 percent.

Consider, for example, the case of Ghana, which now derives more than half its export revenue from a single commodity, cocoa. But the price of cocoa moves a lot. The high is more than three times the low. Thus if the market collapses and cocoa prices fall by, say, 50 percent, export reve-

nue in Ghana falls over 30 percent (0.63×0.5). That, of course, is a catastrophic result. It comes from the interaction of a high export concentration (63 percent) and a high price variability. Of course, things can go the other way. A boom in the commodity raises export revenue and makes for a great year. But the overriding fact is that high concentration in conjunction with high volatility implies that the entire economy is affected any time the world price of the export commodity moves. The world commodity price is *the* central macroeconomic variable.

The instability of export price and revenue is one reason why LDCs have been looking to diversification of production and exports as a goal of policy. To the extent that production and trade are diversified among different primary commodities and between commodities and manufactures, there is more stability of total export revenue. Disruption in the market for a single commodity in this case has a smaller effect on total exports. This move to diversify is apparent in the typically falling share of the single commodity in exports in Table 37-6. We return to it in the discussion of manufactures trade.

TABLE 37-6

EXPORT CONCENTRATION AND REAL PRICE VARIABILITY

COUNTRY AND COMMODITY	SHARE OF TOTAL EXPORTS, %		PRICE VARIABILITY (ratio of maximum to minimum price, 1969–1979)
	1969	1979	
Zambia (copper)	95	83	2.3
Mauritius (sugar)	92	68	5.2
Surinam (aluminum)	89	77	1.7
Chad (raw cotton)	82	54	1.7
Gambia (groundnuts)	95	71	1.8
Chile (copper)	86	48	2.3
Liberia (iron ore)	70	54	2.0
Ghana (cocoa)	66	63	3.4

Sources: International Monetary Fund, *International Financial Statistics,* various issues, and World Bank, *Commodity Trade and Price Trends, 1980.*

Trends in Prices　Table 37-5 shows that relative prices of primary agricultural commodities have fallen since the 1950s. Is this an accident or a trend? Here it is argued that technological progress in the cultivation of primary commodities and in the industrial use of these goods is such that supply is growing rapidly while demand is growing slowly. Therefore, there is a long-run tendency for the real price to fall. The tendency for the real price to fall is all the more forceful in those cases where synthetic substitutes provide low-cost perfect replacements for the primary commodity. One example is natural rubber being replaced by synthetic rubber and plastic.

The table also shows that prices of metals fell somewhat since the 1950s and that prices of petroleum products of course rose substantially. Again, the question is whether these are accidents or trends we should expect to continue. In the case of depletable resources, such as petroleum and metals, there should be a long-run tendency for a rising price to ration the remaining stocks of the resources, which are reduced as the resource is used up.

Beyond these two principles, there is no general answer to the question of how the prices of primary exports will behave in the future. Exhaustible resources will tend to have stable or rising real prices. Reproducible resources may have falling real prices, provided that technical progress is rapid in production and end use relative to the growth in demand for the goods that use these products.

Going back to Table 37-5, we see that these two observations are roughly confirmed. Agricultural commodities have had falling real prices over the past 30 years, while the real price of metals has been stable until recently. But there is, of course, a large variety of experiences among different primary commodities. Iron ore and manganese ore real prices, for example, have been falling, as have been the real prices of bananas and burlap. Real prices of coal and bauxite have been rising, while the price of cotton has been relatively constant. The general tendencies thus are not strong enough to establish that prices of all agricultural products decrease over time and that the prices of metal products rise.

Commodity Stabilization Schemes

The instability of commodity prices leads to the question whether these markets can be stabilized. Stabilization is in the interest of producers because it reduces the volatility in their export incomes and also reduces instability in their macroeconomies. Stabilization would also be helpful for the individual producers who may not easily be able to adjust consumption between years of abundant harvest and low prices and incomes, and periods of poor harvest and high prices and incomes. Remember that by assumption demand is inelastic. This means that whenever supply increases because of a bumper crop, price falls more than proportionately, and therefore revenue falls. Conversely, when there is a harvest failure, price rises by more than the fall in supply, and hence total revenue increases. We summarize these facts in Table 37-7.

In the market for primary commodities farmers or producers act as perfect competitors. They take price (or expected future price) as given and make their production decisions, assuming that their own supply will not affect market price. They are, of course, correct because each producer con-

TABLE 37-7

INELASTIC DEMAND IMPLIES THAT PRICE AND REVENUE MOVE TOGETHER

	PRICE	REVENUE
Bumper crop	Falls	Falls
Harvest failure	Rises	Rises

FIGURE 37-2 A BUFFER STOCK STABILIZES COMMODITY PRICES. The buffer stock scheme tries to stabilize the price to final demanders of the good. When supply is large, for instance, on supply curve SS_1, the buffer stock buys an amount of goods equal to AB, thereby stabilizing price for the producers. When the crop is small, as shown, for instance, by supply curve SS_2, the buffer stock sells goods out of its inventories, maintaining the stability of price and revenue received from demanders. This stabilizes total export earnings for the economy.

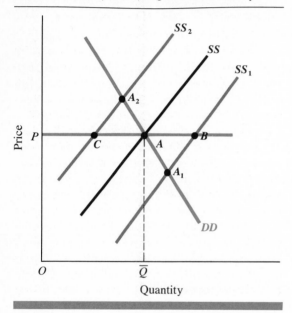

Quantity

low. It would ensure that the supply facing final consumers (or industrial users) stays as close as possible to SS and that therefore price and incomes of producers stay stable. Thus when there is a bumper crop, the buffer stock managers buy an amount AB, and when there is a crop failure, they sell from the stock an amount AC at the established price P. Price for consumers thus stays at P. In principle a buffer stock seems like an excellent solution to the problem of price instability.

But there are problems with a buffer stock. The first problem concerns uncertainty. How do we know that the price that is being stabilized is in fact sustainable in the long run? For example, in the case of rubber the long-run real price has been falling, but a buffer stock, in ignorance of the facts, might have kept buying to try to keep the price high. This problem is serious because producers want not only stable prices but also high prices. There may be a tendency to convert price stabilization into price supports. But of course, price supports above the equilibrium level involve accumulation of stocks, and someone has to be willing to pay for the program.

Price stabilization programs also involve the serious problem of organizing not only the producers in a given country but also in various countries that are actual or even potential producers of the good. There is always the temptation for a producer to stay out of the agreement and enjoy the advantage of the price umbrella to push its own exports. This is the same difficulty that is encountered in domestic cartels. Thus LDCs are seeking the assistance of developed countries in policing these agreements.

The difficulties in organizing commodity programs make it clear why there have been so few in operation. At present the main programs are those for coffee, cocoa, tin, and above all, oil. OPEC's success at

stitutes only a very negligible part of the market. But supply decisions by all producers together do affect price. If all producers, acting jointly, withheld part of a bumper crop, market price would not fall, nor would each farmer's revenue.

Figure 37-2 shows how a commodity buffer stock can operate to stabilize prices and income.

> A *buffer stock* is an organization set up to stabilize a commodity market. It tries to sell when price is high and buy when price is low.

As supply shifts between SS_1 and SS_2, the free market moves between prices at A_1 and A_2. A buffer stock organization would buy when supply is high and sell when supply is

pushing up price through supply restriction is a monument to the economics of monopoly in primary commodity markets. The success of OPEC is certainly part of the reason why in the context of the NIEO, the developing countries have once again raised their demand for participation in and financing by developed countries of comprehensive commodity price stabilization and support schemes. The proposed schemes are designed not only to promote stability of price and revenue to producers but also to keep prices high and thus transfer income from the industrial consuming countries to the poor producing countries.

These schemes are one of the key elements in the LDCs' views of the new international economic order.

3   TRADE IN MANUFACTURES

A sharp fall in world prices of traded goods can exert a major depressing effect on an entire economy. This was, indeed, what happened on a vast scale in the 1930s. The unemployment and recessions in industrialized countries led in the 1929–1932 period to a collapse of world trade in primary commodities. Trade in these commodities fell to only 35 percent of its earlier level. Countries in Asia, Africa, and Latin America that had developed themselves as suppliers of raw materials for Europe and the United States suddenly found themselves without export markets. In response to the export collapse, many countries, especially in Latin America, started an industrialization drive geared to producing for the home market.

Industrialization

Under heavy tariff and quota protection these countries built up domestic industrial capacity. By the mid-1950s industrialization through import substitution was taking place.

Import substitution is a policy of replacing imports by domestic production under the protection of tariffs and quotas.

One reason for the import substitution policy was the view that raw materials prices are bound to decline in the long run relative to the prices of industrial goods. Industrial goods, it was argued, were the sectors where employment, good jobs, and rising real incomes could be found.

Moreover, even though industrialization might run counter to comparative advantage, two facts had to be taken into account. First, comparative advantage had to be considered in a dynamic perspective. Given enough time and experience, LDCs could achieve efficiency in these sectors and thus ultimately justify initial protection. Second, industrialization, while perhaps costly in terms of resource allocation, has a major stabilizing influence by reducing dependence on single crops or products in the world economy. The 1930s would not be repeated.

Import substitution as a development strategy remains very controversial. Many economists from developed countries stress the wasteful aspects of high tariff barriers and inefficient production. The fact remains, though, that industrialization in the LDCs has been taking place on a large scale and that many of these countries have turned from import substitution as the growth strategy and toward an export-led growth pattern.

Export-led growth stresses production and income growth through expanded exports rather than displacement of imports.

NICs

Among the LDC exporters of manufactures, five stand out because of their export size and growth performance. They are called the NICs (newly industrializing countries). Table 37-8 shows some of their statistics.

TABLE 37-8

SOME STATISTICS OF THE NICs

	AVERAGE REAL GDP GROWTH, 1970–1979, %	SHARE OF MANUFAC-TURES IN EXPORTS, %		SHARE OF WORLD TRADE, %	
		1960	1977	1970	1980
Brazil	8.9	3.0	26.0	1.0	1.1
Mexico	5.4	12.0	29.0	0.5	0.8
Hong Kong	9.4	80.0	96.0	0.9	1.0
Korea	10.0	14.0	85.0	0.3	0.9
Singapore	8.9	26.0	44.0	0.5	1.0

Sources: World Bank, *World Development Report, 1981,* and IMF, *International Financial Statistics, Yearbook,* 1981.

The NICs all showed high real growth rates in the 1970s, between 5 and 10 percent, whereas growth in the industrialized countries averaged only 4 percent. Over the last 20 years manufactures have become an increasing share of total exports of these countries. Of course, there remains a large dispersion of the export shares of manufactures. Brazil and Mexico have major primary commodity exports (coffee and soya in one case, petroleum in the other), whereas Hong Kong, for example, is almost completely specialized in manufactures exports. Finally, the NICs now have a share of world trade of about 1 percent each. These shares are to be judged against the 6 to 12 percent share of countries such as the United Kingdom and the United States. By these standards the NICs are small. Yet they have larger trade shares than Austria, Denmark, Ireland, or Sweden, and they are now as important in world trade as Australia.

What makes the NICs especially interesting is their strong export performance in manufactures and their ability to widen their market share rapidly in world trade and in the markets of industrialized countries. These characteristics have given rise to the question of whether continued growth by the NICs will ultimately pose a significant adjustment problem for industrial countries.

There are two extreme views on that subject and a range of opinions in between. One view is that the NICs will ultimately (and it might not even take long) cause the extinction of an entire range of labor-intensive production in developed countries. Such a development would bring with it a problem of structural unemployment in industries where inport competition is particularly strong. The other view is complacent. It points out that the NICs, and all LDCs together, command only a negligible share of world trade and that they are far from being a threat even in individual industries. We shall look at the facts in a moment.

But it is useful to discuss the performance of Japan over the last 30 years to gain some perspective. In 1954 Japan's exports accounted for 1.9 percent of world trade. In 1980 Japan's share of world trade was 7.1 percent. The Japanese example makes the simple point that within a relatively short period—30 years—a country can move from a position of only 1 or 2 percent of world trade to becoming a major exporter with important impacts in other countries' markets. The argument that the NICs account for "only" 5 to 6 percent of world

TABLE 37-9

SHARE OF IMPORTS IN CONSUMPTION OF MANUFACTURED GOODS IN INDUSTRIALIZED COUNTRIES: MAJOR PRODUCT GROUPS, 1979
(Percent)

	SHARE IN CONSUMPTION OF:		GROWTH RATE OF MARKET SHARE, ANNUAL AVERAGE, 1970–1979:	
	All imports	LDCs' imports	All imports	LDCs' imports
All manufactured goods	16.8	3.4	5.1	8.1
Food, beverages, and tobacco	10.8	3.9	2.4	2.1
Clothing, textiles, and leather	23.8	9.6	7.8	14.8
Paper and printing	8.7	0.4	3.1	13.4
Chemicals	14.9	3.4	3.1	5.2
Nonmetallic minerals	9.3	1.0	5.0	13.2
Metals	18.4	3.5	2.2	1.4
Machinery	21.9	2.0	8.0	21.8

Source: H. Hughes and J. Waelbroek, "Can Developing Countries' Exports Keep Growing in the 1980s?" *The World Economy,* June 1981, Table 2.

trade thus is very misleading. They may account for 10 to 15 percent only 10 years from now.

The composition of LDC exports by major product group is presented in Table 37-9. In most categories the LDCs account for a small fraction of consumption and 10 to 30 percent of all imports. The one big exception is clothing, textiles, and leather, where the LDCs' share in consumption reaches nearly 10 percent and where the LDCs' share in imports is 40 percent. Clothing, textiles, and leather are areas in which LDCs have already made their impact on trade in a major way. In most product groups, most LDC market shares are growing more rapidly than those of industrial countries. The most striking growth rate as well as the most interesting one is in machinery—21.8 percent. This includes everything from automobiles to transistors and television sets. It is not an area which we would have associated with LDCs 20

years ago, but today it indicates the impact the LDCs could have on industry in the developed countries.

The New Protectionism

We return to the question whether industrial countries should view the growing industrial penetration from LDCs with apprehension or whether they should take a consumer's view, welcoming the availability of cheaper imports. The proper response to cheaper imports is to reallocate factors of production toward those sectors where we continue to have a comparative advantage. In this manner our resources are used most efficiently and our real income as consumers is maximized. This is the view behind the policy prescription of maximum openness to international competition, both among industrial countries and from LDCs.

However, the perception that LDCs (as well as Japan) are making major inroads in a market that is overcrowded with suppliers is leading to sharply increasing protectionism. In a world where tariffs among industrial countries have been negotiated down to negligible levels, there is now a reemergence of protectionism through quotas, voluntary export restrictions, and nontariff barriers. Restrictions on trade in textiles and clothing go back to the 1960s. Former areas of restriction are rapidly reemerging, for example, leather goods, cars, and steel. Much of the restrictive activity does not receive general publicity.

The rise of the new protectionism has a counterpart in programs to provide assistance to those damaged by import competition. Studies have shown that the costs of protection are very large compared with the benefits derived by the protected industries. A recent review of the costs of protection notes that

> For every $20,000-a-year job in the Swedish shipyards, Swedish tax payers pay an estimated $50,000 annual subsidy. Protection costs Canadian consumers $500 million a year to provide an additional $135 million of wages in the clothing industry. And when Japanese consumers pay eight times the world price for beef, Japanese farmers are not made eight times better off. It costs them that much more to produce it.[3]

Considering these large costs, it becomes reasonable to pay labor and entrepreneurs in an industry to adjust, phasing out production of inefficient plants and allowing increased growth of imports.

In a society that recognizes both the interests of consumers and its responsibility for those put in difficulty in the pursuit of a higher common interest (fighting inflation, import liberalization, etc.), a compromise must be struck that avoids costly protection but at the same time distributes the adjustment burden. As LDC growth brings the

prospects of growing areas of conflict, it becomes important to strengthen mechanisms for adjustment assistance so as to avoid being swamped by the claims for more protection.

4 EXTERNAL BORROWING

The third complaint of the LDCs is that borrowing terms are too tough. LDCs have traditionally been borrowers in world markets. They spend more than their incomes, or in terms of macroeconomic concepts, investment plus the budget deficit in these countries exceeds saving. With not enough domestic saving, external borrowing must finance the current account deficits. This pattern of external borrowing was sharply reinforced during the 1970s as a consequence of the oil shock. LDCs did not adjust very much to the higher import prices of oil by spending less on other imports and by reducing their oil consumption. For quite a while they allowed their deficits to grow, and they financed them by borrowing abroad.

The changes for non-oil-producing LDCs that have taken place as a consequence of the oil shock are shown in Table 37-10. The current account deficits are more than eight times larger today than before the oil shock in 1973, and the external debt—amounts owed to foreigners—is nearly five times larger. Of course, prices of most goods have about doubled in that period, but even

TABLE 37-10

CURRENT ACCOUNT DEFICITS AND EXTERNAL DEBT OF NON-OIL-PRODUCING LDCs (Billions of Dollars)

	1973	1982
Current account deficit	12	97
External debt	97	505

Source: International Monetary Fund, *World Economic Outlook, 1982.*

---

[3] World Bank, *World Development Report, 1981,* p. 33.

with that adjustment there is very substantial increase in the LDCs debts to other countries. To understand how this has come about we look at the current account.

We remind ourselves that we can look at the current account in one of three ways:

Current account deficit = imports minus exports of goods and services

= expenditure minus income

= decline in net foreign assets or increase in net external liabilities   (1)

The first line helps us understand that higher oil prices and declining prices of primary commodities have raised import spending relative to export earnings and therefore have widened the current account deficit. The second line explains the larger deficit by showing that higher oil prices and lower prices received for primary commodities imply higher spending and lower income receipts and therefore a larger deficit. The third perspective, finally, tells us that a deficit must be financed. A larger deficit implies larger external borrowing to finance it. It also suggests that we ask whether the deficit is sustainable or must soon be eliminated because of a country's inability to increase indebtedness on a large scale.

Current Account Financing

Table 37-11 shows how the group of non-oil-producing LDCs have financed their current account imbalances. The table focuses on the three sources of financing: borrowing, direct investment flows, and aid transfers. We comment on each of these categories after looking at the data.

In the period 1973–1981 the non-oil-producing LDCs experienced a *cumulative* current account deficit of $431 billion. Most of the deficit (69.2 percent) was financed by borrowing from foreign governments, official institutions, and private institutions including commercial banks. This major part of financing was long-term, meaning that the deficit countries borrowed for periods of several years rather than a month or half a year. While long-term borrowing accounts for the major part of the current account financing, there are three other sources. Direct investment accounts for 13.5 percent. Here we are talking about firms from developed countries as well as OPEC countries investing directly (meaning that they acquire a controlling share of a firm) in LDCs. They may be purchasing a major package of shares in an existing firm, or they may set up or expand new firms in LDCs. Interestingly, direct investment is a very small part of current account financing.

A larger share of current account financing comes from transfers and aid from developed countries and OPEC to the non-oil-producing LDCs. This source accounts for nearly 18 percent. The presence of these aid payments reflects the fact that some of the

TABLE 37-11

FINANCING CURRENT ACCOUNT DEFICITS OF NON-OIL-PRODUCING LDCs
(Cumulative, 1973–1981, Billions of U.S. Dollars)

CUMULATIVE CURRENT ACCOUNT, 1973–1981		BORROWING		DIRECT INVESTMENT		AID RECEIPTS
$438.7	=	$286.3	+	$64.6	+	$87.8
100%	=	65.3%	+	14.7%	+	20.0%

Note: Figures don't add up to totals because of rounding.
Source: International Monetary Fund, *World Economic Outlook, 1982.*

very poor LDCs can sustain their deficits only because they receive aid and that any cut in aid would, on their part, have to be matched by a 1 for 1 reduction in their deficits. We return to the question of aid below.

Debt

We have singled out the oil-price increases and the associated world recessions as sources of current account problems of LDCs. But in part these problems, once they exist, have their own evolution. Real interest rates in the world are positive and in fact have been high since 1980. Every year in which debtors do not set aside a current trade surplus large enough to pay the interest on their debts, these debts will grow. They grow because more must be borrowed to finance the interest. Thus without trade surpluses the external debt grows by itself, gets larger and larger, and ultimately leads bankers to stop lending or leads countries to default.

We now pursue the borrowing issue by looking at the increase in external debt by the non-oil-producing LDCs. Table 37-12 shows the size of the long-term debt in 1973 and in 1982. There are two statistics commonly used to measure the importance of a country's debt. The absolute dollar amount does not mean much if we don't know whether we are talking about a large or a small country. Therefore, we express the debt either relative to GDP or relative to exports. On both measures there has been a substantial increase in indebtedness. External debt for non-oil-producing LDCs is now equal to one-quarter of their GDP and more than 100 percent of their exports. The size of these debts, and especially their concentration in a few heavily borrowing countries, has become a continuing concern of the lending banks.

What would happen if new shocks made it impossible for LDCs to service these debts and defaults started happening? This

TABLE 37-12

EXTERNAL DEBT STATISTICS OF NON-OIL-PRODUCING LDCs
(Billions of U.S. Dollars)

	1973	1981
Total Debt:	96.8	505.2
To governments and official institutions, %	50.0	39.5
To private creditors, %	50.0	60.5
Ratio of debt to GDP	16.6	25.2
Ratio of debt to exports	88.7	109.1

Source: International Monetary Fund, *World Economic Outlook, 1982.*

happened on a large scale in the 1930s. In a number of cases outright default has been avoided in the last 20 years by rescheduling of debts, which means that a new and longer timetable for repayment was negotiated. For example, Chile and India in 1975, Peru in 1978, and, among others, Turkey in 1980 and Mexico in 1982 had reschedulings of their debts.

It is clear that defaults by all LDCs together would have a very substantial impact on financial institutions in the lending countries, just as defaults by some large corporations would. Whether the world financial system would collapse depends on what governments and central banks in the developed countries do to help the LDCs. In the end, governments in the industrial countries are likely to act as lenders of last resort to prevent financial collapse.

5 AID

Many of the complaints of the south come down to the view that the north should provide more aid to the south. What economic arguments can be given for aid? Why is the amount of borrowing countries can do from commercial sources not the right amount?

There are two separate questions here. The first is whether private institutions do a good job of lending, at market interest rates, to the developing countries. In other words, given the interest rates at which borrowing takes place in the world capital markets, is too little funding going to the south? There is little evidence that good investment opportunities in the south are not being funded because the private capital markets are too risk-averse. Indeed, it is often argued that the private banks are too easy in their lending. Several countries that have borrowed heavily probably will have trouble paying back their loans.

Once a country (or a person) has borrowed, much of the initiative in the transaction passes to the borrower. The borrower has the lender at his mercy, since it is now up to the borrower to repay. If he doesn't, the lender loses. Under these circumstances, there is usually an incentive for lending banks to keep relending to countries that are in trouble in order to enable them to keep making the payments on debts. This is already happening for several developing countries.

The second issue is whether the north should provide the south with loans at special rates or with other forms of assistance. Although the focus is on loans at low interest rates, this is just one sort of subsidy or form of aid; the general question is whether and how aid should be provided.

The basic issues involved in the aid question are the same as those which arise when redistributive questions are discussed within the developed countries. Does the U.S. government have the right or the duty to provide its poorest citizens with more resources than the market generates for them, with the resources paid for by other citizens? Typically, though not always, the answer given by governments (and the societies in which they operate) is yes. Do residents of a rich country have the right or duty to provide extra resources to people in other countries who are very poor? Here again the issue is a moral one. The moral issue is made more complicated by the argument of the south that part of the prosperity of the north has resulted from past unfair use of southern resources, when the countries of the south were colonies.

Aid and the Recipient Countries

Suppose a person feels that the poor people of the south should be helped. Does that mean aid should be given in the form of transfers of food, cheap loans, or grants? Are there better ways?

Probably the most important single form of aid is to provide access for the developing countries to the markets of the developed countries. The slogan of some aid critics is "Trade, not aid." Economic development based on profitable trade is likely to be more effective than relationships based on gifts from the north to the south. Relationships in which each side has something to offer—as in trade—are more lasting than relationships in which one side does all the giving.

It is also argued by some critics that the north would do more for the south by insisting that governments in those countries follow sensible policies than they would by providing them with aid. Governments in developing countries frequently intervene extensively in their economies, not allowing prices to adjust to clear markets. Free market critics suggest that aid merely reinforces governments in their policies and prevents needed adjustments in those countries. For instance, those who want reciprocity of trade arrangements with the south say that without this reciprocity the south will stay behind high tariff barriers, protecting inefficient local industry rather than forcing their industries to compete.

Along the same lines, it is argued that aid programs do more for the elites of the developing countries than for the poor residents. Typically we think of aid as taking money from a rich American and giving it to a poor resident of the south, but it may be that the transfer is from a poor American to a rich inhabitant of a poor country.

To prevent this, the donor government may try to make sure the aid is used correctly at the other end. For instance, if food aid is provided, the donor stipulates that it go to the poorest people rather than to wealthy food distributors.

But here the realities intrude. Governments dislike foreigners telling them what to do. It is usually necessary to work through foreign governments, doing the best that can be done to make sure the aid is distributed in a reasonable way.

Whenever aid and redistribution are discussed, it is useful to recall the leaking bucket analogy of Arthur Okun.[4] When transfers are made, it is like transferring water in a leaky bucket. Some of the water leaks out (the aid process is highly imperfect), but some makes it to the other end. Whether the process is worth carrying out depends on how fast the water leaks and how urgent it is to get water transferred. Of course, at the same time, we should be looking for buckets with fewer holes.

Aid and Migration

The quickest way to equalize the world distribution of income would be to permit free migration. The residents of poor countries could go elsewhere to look for higher incomes.

The massive movements of population

from Europe to the Americas and colonies in the nineteenth century and early twentieth century represented an income-equalizing movement of this sort. To some extent a similar movement, largely in the form of migrant workers, has taken place since World War II. Payments sent from workers in Europe to their families in Turkey and Yugoslavia are major economic factors in those countries. Similarly, Egypt, India, and Pakistan receive significant transfer payments from workers in other countries (especially the Persian Gulf) sending payments back to their families. Mexican workers in the United States play an important economic role in both countries.

Nonetheless, there is no free immigration to the rich countries today. Indeed, many migrant workers are illegal immigrants. One difference between the present situation and that of the nineteenth century is that there are now extensive welfare and public health and educational systems in the rich countries. Opponents of immigration say it would lead to immigration purely for the sake of going on welfare. Those who favor more immigration suggest that immigrants not have rights to use welfare until they have been in the receiving country for a specific number of years, say, 3 or 5. It does not seem likely that any country is about to open its doors to immigration. It is a fascinating question whether countries should open their doors and what the consequences would be (after all, the United States grew very fast when it had large-scale immigration), but the discussion is largely academic.

---

[4] We discuss the analogy at greater length in Chapter 38.

SUMMARY

1   The call for a new international economic order (NIEO) results from the attempt of the developing countries to get a larger share of the world's wealth and income for themselves. The current distribution of income in the world is extremely uneven. Average income per

annum for over half the world's population was \$230 in 1979. Other welfare indicators, including energy consumption, life expectancy, and caloric intake, all show substantial inequality between countries.

2   The call for an NIEO is put in terms of a north-south dialogue. This emphasizes the differences between high-income and low-income countries regardless of their political organization.

3   The south's complaints are that (*a*) the markets for their primary products are controlled by the north, (*b*) the prospects of their being able to industrialize and thus grow fast are hampered by northern protectionism, (*c*) financing for the south is too expensive, and (*d*) it is a matter of justice that the north take practical steps to close the enormous gaps that currently exist between north and south.

4   Primary commodities pose two problems. First, there is the volatility of prices. The volatility derives from the fact that supply and demand disturbances act on markets that are very unresponsive to price in the short run. Second, it is argued that the prices of primary commodities have a downward trend.

5   The possibility of a downward trend in the real price of LDC export commodities arises because world income growth may not generate enough growth in the demand for their exported food and materials to keep price from falling. At the same time synthetic substitutes for many primary commodities are being developed. In fact, prices of some primary commodities have been falling while others have been rising.

6   To stabilize commodity prices governments can organize stabilization programs that buy when price is low and sell when price is high. The main problems are financing the costs of the stocks and agreeing on a realistic price that can be stabilized.

7   LDCs are increasing their exports of manufactures. In the last 10 years their growth performance has been better than that of industrialized countries. But their current share in the production of manufactured goods in the industrial world is still only 3.4 percent.

8   The growth of LDC manufactures exports poses serious problems of protectionism in industrial countries. Nontariff barriers and quotas are rising in areas where LDCs are particularly successful. This new protectionism needs as a counterbalance more emphasis on adjustment to import competition.

9   LDCs have run large current account deficits since the 1975 oil shock. These deficits have been financed largely by external borrowing in the world capital market. There is now much concern whether there has been excessive lending and whether debt default is likely.

10 The opening up of trade to the south is an important mechanism for making the south better off. Observers of some developing countries argue that aid should be used as a lever to induce the governments of those countries to adopt sensible economic policies, though this is not easy to do.

11 More migration would be one means of equalizing world incomes more rapidly. The prospects for such migration are slim.

KEY TERMS

New international economic
  order (NIEO)
International Monetary Fund (IMF)
World Bank
Price volatility
Buffer stocks

Import substitution
Export-led growth of production
  and income
New Protectionism
Migration

PROBLEMS

1 Discuss in detail two factors that work in the direction of reducing the long-run real price of agricultural raw materials.

2 Use a demand and supply diagram to show the short-run and the long-run adjustment to the discovery of synthetic rubber. Discuss carefully each consideration.

3 Discuss the effect of a world boom on an economy specializing in the production of copper.

4 Use the theory of comparative advantage, which was discussed in Chapter 36, to explain why LDCs have been particularly successful as exporters of textiles, clothing, and leather footwear.

5 "LDCs' export growth in the U.S. market is no threat because the income they receive from selling to us is spent on our goods, and thus in turn creates employment for our export industry." In what way, if any, is this argument unsatisfactory?

6 "In many LDCs exports are produced at low wages, unfair to the foreign workers and unfair to our home competitors. On both counts we should deny these goods access to our markets." Discuss.

7 Discuss the advantages and disadvantages that you see in an ambitious program of import substitution in a small LDC.

8 Consider a country that experiences a doubling of the cost of its oil imports. Discuss two strategies of adjustment: increased exports and a cut in the budget. How would you bring the adjustments about, what are their side effects, and what are their respective disadvantages?

9 What are the complaints of the developing countries that have led to their call for an NIEO?

10 (a) Describe how a buffer stock commodity price stabilization scheme would work. (b) What could go wrong? (c) Why

don't private speculators smooth out the prices of primary commodities more than they do at present? (*d*) How does your answer to (*c*) affect your thinking about the desirability of commodity price stabilization schemes?

11 Discuss the economic arguments for and against aid from the rich countries to the poor countries. Be sure to include a discussion of the view that what is needed is "trade, not aid."

In 1972, the latest date for which these statistics are available, 643,000 Americans had assets in excess of $500,000 and 1 percent of the U.S. population—the top wealth holders—owned 20.7 percent of all personal wealth in this country. At the other end of the economic ladder, more than 5.3 million families, or 9.1 percent of U.S. families, lived below the poverty level.[1]

This chapter discusses how to define and measure inequality and poverty and examines the factors determining the distributions of income and wealth in the economy. These are important issues with which every society must deal. Every society decides how much inequality to accept: whether to let the market determine income distribution or whether to intervene actively to relieve poverty and change the distribution of income. The decisions are made piecemeal. The progressivity of the tax system, specific programs such as food stamps that allow eligible families to buy food at reduced prices, and the public school system all involve decisions made by society that have powerful effects on poverty and inequality.

The evaluation of inequality is not an area in which the economist has a lot to offer. Economics does not tell us how to judge a world in which a few people own most of the economy and some are starving compared with one in which each citizen owns an equal share independently of skill, privilege, or effort. But there are issues of economics to be discussed, related in part to the measurement of distribution, equality, and poverty and in part to alternative strategies to alter income distribution through education or taxation.

38

Income Distribution and Poverty in the United States

In the United States, income distribution and especially the role of the government in redistributing income are sharply debated. The 1930s and the 1960s were periods when the federal government assumed increased responsibility for those deemed underprivileged, developing an increasing array of programs to wage a "war on poverty." The time that has passed allows us now to look back at the changes that have occurred and judge whether the war on poverty has been won or whether, as many conservatives would claim, leaving matters to the free market might have done more to improve living standards for the poor.

[1] The poverty data refer to 1979. Details are given in later tables in this chapter.

In discussing the distribution of income, we are looking at the way society solves its "for whom" question. Leaving aside government for the moment, each individual's income—and therefore his command over resources—comes from ownership of factors of production. Each individual is endowed with a certain amount of human capital, varying across individuals, at the moment of birth. Education and experience augment the human capital. For many people, human capital is almost the only source of income. Some individuals own factors of production other than labor, namely, the capital and land used in production. They acquired ownership of these factors through inheritance or by saving out of their income.

In the absence of government, and in a market economy, the distribution of income would be determined by the initial distribution of abilities among individuals and by the rules governing the passing on of wealth. The distribution would not be the same in a society where, for instance, first sons inherit all as it would be in a society where all children share parents' assets equally. Given the pattern of ownership of factors of production, we could study how marginal productivities determine the distribution of income. We could also ask questions like those discussed in Chapter 14, for instance, whether discrimination affects the distribution of income.

Once government comes into the picture, it may play a major role in determining the distribution of income. Inheritance taxes may be imposed, and public education, income taxes, and transfers all change the distribution of income. The state could perhaps take a neutral role in determining income distribution, but certainly the modern welfare state does not stay out of the income distribution business.

In this chapter we start from the functional distribution of income.

> The *functional distribution* describes the distribution of income among different factors of production, particularly capital and labor.

The functional distribution is the place to start thinking about the distribution of income if society can be divided neatly into two groups: the working class (labor) and the owners of resources (capitalists). But in the modern economy it is certainly not true that those who own property receive no income from labor or that those who earn salaries and wages receive no income from capital.

For that reason, we focus more on the personal distribution of income.

> The *personal distribution of income* is the breakdown of aggregate income among individual economic units: persons, families, or households.

The personal income distribution describes how income is distributed among you, us, the Du Ponts and others. In discussing the personal distribution of income, there is no reason to worry about the functional distribution directly. Of course, underlying the personal distribution are the marginal productivities of the factors of production owned by different individuals, which for many is mostly their labor. But as we shall see, the distribution that would be determined by factor markets is heavily modified by government taxation and transfers.

1 FUNCTIONAL DISTRIBUTION OF INCOME

In this section we discuss the determinants of income distribution between capital and labor. We proceed as if both factors were homogeneous. This is, of course, a simplification. In practice, labor includes workers of differing skill levels and professional qualifications, while capital includes a vast range of assets from oil-drilling equipment to dentist chairs to urban land.

The Theory

The functional distribution of income is the breakdown of income among factors of production. In particular, we shall be examining the share of labor in total income.

$$\begin{aligned}\frac{\text{Labor's share}}{\text{in income}} &= \frac{\text{labor income}}{\text{total income}} \\ &= \frac{\text{wage rate} \times \text{labor supply}}{\text{total income}} \quad (1)\end{aligned}$$

We start by discussing the effects on the share of labor of changes in the supply of labor, changes in the capital stock, and changes in production technology. After we develop the theory, we turn to the facts to examine how the share of labor has changed over time, and we interpret those changes in the light of the theory.

Labor Market Equilibrium Suppose the economy has a given amount of capital. In Figure 38-1 we draw the demand schedule for labor that we have already encountered in earlier chapters. The schedule now represents the economywide labor demand, given the technology and the economywide stock of capital. The demand schedule for labor LL_D is drawn against the real wage. The lower the real wage, the larger the quantity of labor firms want to employ. With low real wages, firms find it advantageous to use relatively labor-intensive processes and therefore, given the capital stock, demand a lot of labor. Conversely, when the real wage is high, the quantity of labor demanded is low.

At any point in time there is, along with the capital stock and technology, also a given labor supply. The labor supply is shown in Figure 38-1 as the vertical schedule LL_S. We assume for simplicity that labor supply is independent of the real wage. Given the demand for labor and the supply of labor, there is an equilibrium real wage w_0 at which the labor market clears. This is shown at point E. The equilibrium at point

FIGURE 38-1 EQUILIBRIUM IN THE LABOR MARKET DETERMINES THE REAL WAGE AND LABOR INCOME. For given technology and a given capital stock, the schedule LL_D represents the economywide demand for labor. The lower the real wage, the more labor using the techniques firms wish to use, and hence the larger the quantity of labor demanded. With a given labor supply LL_S, the equilibrium real wage is w_0. Labor income is equal to the shaded rectangle, or the wage rate times the quantity of labor employed.

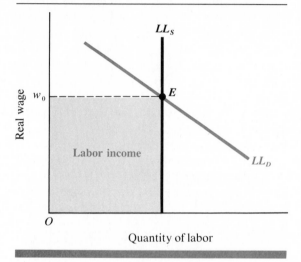

E implies a labor income equal to the shaded rectangle: the real wage times the labor supply.

An Increase in Labor Supply We now examine how labor income and labor's share in income are affected by changes in the supply of labor. We want to determine whether an increase in the supply of labor results in an increase or a fall in labor income and examine the share of labor in total income.

A shift in the labor supply schedule to LL_S' in Figure 38-2 raises the available supply of labor, but with the given capital stock, firms will not want to hire more labor unless the real wage falls. The real wage drops to w'.

What does an increase in the labor supply do to the share of labor? With un-

FIGURE 38-2 THE EFFECT OF AN INCREASE IN THE SUPPLY OF LABOR. A shift in the labor supply schedule to LL'_S lowers the equilibrium real wage at which the labor force will be employed. Firms have to be induced to employ more workers per unit of capital by a decline in the relative cost of labor or a fall in real wages. Total labor income may rise or fall depending on the elasticity of the labor demand schedule. With demand very inelastic, labor income must fall.

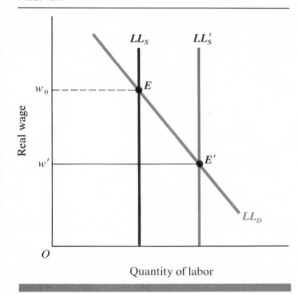

changed capital and technology and a higher labor supply, the economy will produce a larger output. Therefore, the denominator of equation (1) will rise with labor supply growth. What happens to the share then depends on the behavior of labor income. If labor demand is inelastic so that labor income falls when supply rises and the wage falls, labor's share in income must fall since total income is up and labor income is down. If labor's share falls, the share of capital rises.

What happens is that labor's marginal product falls sharply with the level of employment, because there are nearly fixed proportions in production. The fixed proportions mean that two workers per machine produce hardly more than one person per machine. Since labor is paid its mar-

ginal product, which falls sharply with the increased supply of labor, the total income of labor falls when the supply of labor rises.

By contrast, if capital and labor are very highly substitutable, wages may fall very little because the marginal product of labor hardly changes. Labor income actually rises, both absolutely and relative to total income. The income of capital also rises because the rental on capital has increased. But capital income does not rise as much as total output; hence, capital's share in income falls. In summary, then, the effect of labor supply changes on income distribution depends entirely on the ease of substitution between capital and labor. If they are very poor substitutes, labor loses absolutely and relatively. If they are extremely good substitutes, labor gains absolutely and relatively, while capital gains absolutely but is left with a smaller share of a larger pie.

An Increase in the Capital Stock It will not come as a surprise that the same analysis applies to an increase in the capital stock, given labor supply. With more capital around for firms to employ, there will be an excess supply of capital and an excess demand for labor. The rental on capital falls and the real wage rises as firms compete for labor to operate the now abundant capital. If substitutability is high, relative factor prices change very little. If substitutability between factors is very poor, however, it takes large changes in factor prices to induce firms to change production techniques, and then the factor that has increased in supply may lose both absolutely and relatively.

Figure 38-3 shows the effects in the labor market of an increase in the economywide capital stock. An increase in the capital stock increases the marginal product of labor and shifts the labor demand curve to the right. The shift in labor demand leads to a rise in the real wage from w_0 to w' and therefore to a rise in labor income. Thus an

FIGURE 38-3 AN INCREASE IN THE CAPITAL STOCK SHIFTS THE DEMAND FOR LABOR. An increase in the capital stock raises the marginal productivity of labor, since each worker now has more capital to work with. The demand curve for labor moves to the right, from LL_D to LL'_D. The real wage therefore rises. The increase in the real wage is larger the less substitutable are capital and labor.

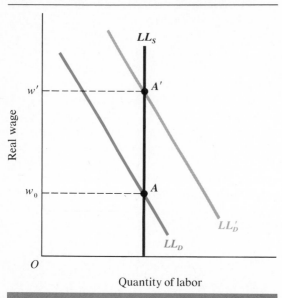

discussion by looking at the effect of an increased capital-labor ratio—more capital per worker—on wages, the rental of capital, labor income, income of capital, and labor's share in income.

Changes in Technology The effects of technological change on income distribution are less (or even less) clear-cut. Technological change may be neutral between capital and labor use, or it may promote the use of capital or labor at the expense of the other factor. We shall not discuss in detail the various possibilities but simply note that changes in technology can affect income distribution in either direction.

The U.S. Experience

What has been the actual growth of capital and labor in the U.S. economy? Estimates of the capital stock and labor input over the past 90 years give the growth rates in Table 38-2.

The table reveals that the long-term pattern has been one of capital growing faster than the labor input. Over the period 1889–1929 and in the period since 1929, capital grew on average more than a percentage point faster than labor. Thus over time capital per worker increased. Our model predicts that this pattern, in the absence of nonneutral technical change, will lead to a rise in the real wage and a fall in the rental on capital and to changes in the distribution of income between capital and labor that depend on the ease of substitutability.

Unfortunately, we do not have exact

increase in the capital stock must raise the real wage and labor income. It is not clear, though, whether labor income increases more or less than total output. That depends on the substitutability between capital and labor and hence on the rise in equilibrium real wages.

Because the analysis of changes in capital and labor is entirely symmetric, we can talk about the effects of changes in the capital-labor ratio. Table 38-1 summarizes the

TABLE 38-1

THE EFFECTS OF AN ECONOMYWIDE INCREASE IN THE CAPITAL-LABOR RATIO

	REAL WAGE	REAL RENTAL OF CAPITAL	LABOR INCOME	INCOME OF CAPITAL	LABOR'S SHARE OF INCOME
Substitutability:					
High	+	−	+	+	−
Low	+	−	+	−	+

TABLE 38-2

GROWTH RATES OF CAPITAL AND LABOR INPUT, 1889–1980
(Average Annual Percentage Growth Rates)

PERIOD	CAPITAL	LABOR	CAPITAL-LABOR RATIO
1889–1929	3.1	2.0	1.1
1929–1980	2.3	1.0	1.3

Sources: U.S. Department of Commerce, Long-Term Economic Growth, 1860–1970. Federal Reserve System, Balance Sheets for the U.S. Economy, 1945–1980, and Economic Report of the President, 1982.

TABLE 38-3

SHARES IN NATIONAL INCOME
(Percent)

	1929	1950	1960	1970	1981
Compensation of employees	60.3	65.2	70.9	75.5	75.6
Proprietors' income	17.7	16.3	11.4	8.2	5.7
Property income	22.0	18.5	17.7	16.3	18.7

Source: Economic Report of the President, 1982, Table B-21.

data with which to consider the predictions of Table 38-1. Table 38-3 looks at the distribution of income among three factors: labor (compensation of employees in wages and salaries), income from property (corresponding to income from capital in terms of this section), and proprietors' income. The last category is the source of the trouble. It shows the income of unincorporated businesses (farms, owner-operated shops, and income of self-employed people such as doctors or artists). But these unincorporated businesses yield an income that is partly a return on the capital involved in the business (the shop, the dentist's drill, and the farmland or livestock) and partly a return to the labor effort of the owner. We therefore cannot tell what part of proprietors' income to lump with employees' compensation as labor income and what part to lump with income from property. The lack of a more complete division of proprietors' income makes it difficult to develop a precise historical perspective on the shares of capital and labor income.

Even so, the data in Table 38-3 are of interest. Employee compensation has shown a very substantial increase, rising from 60 to more than 75 percent of national income. Property income (dividends, interest, and rent on land), by contrast, declined from 1929 to 1970, although there has been a recent increase.[2] Do these data support the notion that an increase in the capital-labor ratio, which has occurred since 1929, raises the real wage and labor's share in income? Or do they confirm the long-standing belief that economic growth—capital, labor, and technology improvements—leaves income distribution unchanged?

Suppose that all of proprietors' income in fact was labor income and that the income of capital in these businesses was neg-

[2] The recent increase from 15.5 percent to 18.7 percent should not be interpreted as a gain for capitalists. Rather it reflects improper accounting procedures that include the inflation-induced increase in interest rates as part of capital income. But this "inflation premium" in interest rates does not, in fact, belong in the income statistics. We deal with these questions in greater detail in Chapters 31 and 32.

ligible. Then we could add the first two rows in Table 38-3, calling them labor income. Labor's share, on this accounting, has risen from 78 percent to 81.3 percent over the period. Conversely, if all of proprietors' income was income from capital, labor's share would increase from 60.3 percent to 75.6 percent. Thus, unless the capital-labor income distribution within unincorporated businesses changed a lot over the period, the data suggest that labor's share in income over the period increased. Given that the capital-labor rose over the period, this means that substitution between capital and labor was low or that technical progress favored labor.

The most significant result of Table 38-3 is that there is *no* evidence that labor's share has been falling and much evidence to suggest that labor's share of GNP has increased substantially since 1929 and even since 1950.

2 THE PERSONAL DISTRIBUTION OF INCOME

In this section we discuss how total income in the economy is distributed among its members.[3] We introduce the discussion

[3] Separate data from surveys and from estimates are available on the distribution of income by persons and by families. The data on distribution by families represent direct evidence from surveys. The data on the distribution by persons are not from surveys, and are estimates.

with the basic tool of the personal distribution of income, the Lorenz curve.

The Lorenz Curve

Data are available in the U.S. economy for the distribution of total income among families. The typical information, referring to the years 1960 and 1979, is summarized in Table 38-4. Here is how to read the table. In 1960 the poorest fifth (20 percent) of families received only 4.8 percent of total U.S. income. In 1979 their share was 5.3 percent. By contrast, the top, or richest 20 percent, of households received more than 40 percent of total income. The table thus gives some indication of the inequality of the distribution of incomes. For instance, the bottom 20 percent of families have only 5 percent of total income, while the top 20 percent have eight times as much.

The data of Table 38-4 are also presented in Figure 38-4. The *Lorenz curve* in Figure 38-4 represents the cumulative distribution of income. It is designed to answer at a glance such questions as, What part of income accrues to the bottom 60 percent of families? Here is how the schedule is constructed. On the vertical axis we plot percentages from zero to 100 percent, representing the shares in income. On the horizontal axis we also plot percentages from zero to 100 percent, representing the cumulative fraction of families. Each point in the diagram is a combination of a given

TABLE 38-4

DISTRIBUTION OF AGGREGATE MONEY INCOME AMONG FAMILIES

PERIOD	% OF TOTAL INCOME RECEIVED BY FAMILIES					
	LOWEST FIFTH	SECOND FIFTH	THIRD FIFTH	FOURTH FIFTH	TOP FIFTH	TOP 5 PERCENT
1960	4.8	12.2	17.8	24	41.3	15.9
1979	5.3	11.6	17.5	24.1	41.6	15.7

Note: Money income is income *before* deduction of income and Social Security taxes.
Source: Statistical Abstract of the United States, 1981, Table 370.

FIGURE 38-4 THE U.S. LORENZ CURVE, 1979.
Note: Money income of families and unrelated individuals. (*Source: Statistical Abstract of the United States, 1981*, Table 370.)

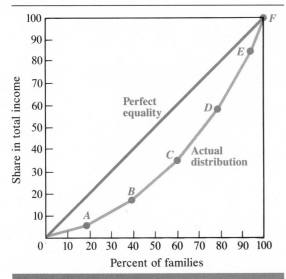

What shapes can the Lorenz curve take? There are two extremes we can think of. One is that a tiny fraction of families receives all income. In that case the Lorenz curve would practically coincide with the horizontal axis and then run up to 100 percent of income near the top 98 or 99 percent of families. (Draw such a schedule for yourself to visualize it better.) Alternatively, income distribution could be totally equal. Every family earns an equal share in the economy's total income. Hence the bottom 20 percent of families have 20 percent of income, the bottom 40 percent of families have 40 percent of income, and so on. In this case, plotting the points *A*, *B*, *C*, we would find that the Lorenz curve is a straight line running from *O* to *F*. The actual Lorenz curve for the U.S. economy sits somewhere between those extremes. Income is not perfectly equally distributed, nor is there extreme inequality where one family owns everything and everybody else owns nothing.

The Lorenz curve suggests a simple way of looking at equality. The closer the actual Lorenz curve is to the diagonal, the more equal the income distribution. Figure 38-5 makes the point by comparing income distribution in the United States and in Mexico. In neither country is distribution either perfectly equal or extremely unequal. But it is clear that in the United States the distribution is more equal; the Lorenz curve is closer to the line of perfect equality than it is in the case of Mexico.

Qualifications

We are interested in income distribution (and wealth distribution) because income represents purchasing power over goods and services and thus gives some indication of the welfare or well-being of people. The indicator may be very crude, and it is no doubt difficult to compare the happiness that one individual derives from an extra

fraction of families with the fraction of total income they receive. The schedule *OABCDEF* plots the data recorded in Table 38-4 for 1979.

Consider first the poorest 20 percent of families. They receive 5.3 percent of income. We show this as point *A*. Next we ask what part of income the bottom 40 percent receive. From the table we see that they receive 16.9 (5.3 + 11.6) percent of income. Point *B* represents the observation that the lowest 40 percent of families receive 16.9 percent of income. Next, point *C* records the fact that the poorest 60 percent of families receive 34.4 (5.3 + 11.6 + 17.5) percent of total income. Point *D* shows the share for the bottom 80 percent as 58.4 percent. Finally, point *E* shows that the bottom 95 percent receive 84.3 percent (100 percent − 15.7 percent) of total income, leaving "only" 15.7 percent for the top 5 percent of households. Connecting all the points, we have the Lorenz curve *OABCDEF* for the U.S. economy.

FIGURE 38-5   THE LORENZ CURVES FOR THE UNITED STATES AND MEXICO. (*Source: World Development Report, 1981,* Table 25.)

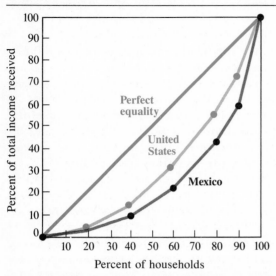

ployment benefits, retirement benefits, and public assistance. But the income measure does not include income in kind (owner-occupied housing, for example) or transfers in kind (such as food stamps or free medical care). One correction would be to use a more comprehensive concept of income that includes income and transfers in kind.

A second correction concerns taxes. The income measures considered include transfers but do not deduct personal income taxes and Social Security taxes. These taxes, because they are progressive, affect the distribution of income. Indeed, the progressivity is designed to make income distribution more equal. One study reports that the adjustment for income taxes does move the Lorenz curve toward more equality—but not very much so—as shown by the data in Table 38-5. The table shows that the bottom 80 percent gained nearly 2 percentage points in income lost by the top 20 percent. Thus the tax system does redistribute income, although the extent of redistribution is small.

A third correction to the income distribution data involves family size. To give a reliable indication of potential welfare we want to be sure that the family sizes at the low- and high-income ends are roughly equal. But this is not the case. At the high-income end the number of family members is nearly a third higher than at the bottom

dollar of income as compared to another. Even so, the distribution of income is one of the few available indicators of relative well-being. But there are important qualifications that have to be noted before we use it.

The income distribution reported in Table 38-4 comes from the U.S. Census. The income that is recorded includes income from current work effort or from property and also transfers. These transfers include Social Security payments, unem-

TABLE 38-5

BEFORE-TAX AND AFTER-TAX INCOME DISTRIBUTION OF FAMILIES, 1972

	SHARE IN TOTAL FAMILY INCOME, %				
	BOTTOM FIFTH	SECOND FIFTH	THIRD FIFTH	FOURTH FIFTH	TOP FIFTH
Before tax	4.9	11.6	17.2	23.6	42.7
After tax	5.4	12.3	17.7	23.9	40.8

Source: D. Radner, "Federal Income Taxes, Social Security Taxes and the U.S. Distribution of Income: 1972," U.S. Social Security Administration, Washington, D.C., Research Paper No. 7, April 1979.

TABLE 38-6

THE INCIDENCE OF POVERTY, 1979
(Percent of Group)

ALL PERSONS	WHITE	BLACK	MALE	FEMALE	AGE 65+
11.6	8.9	30.9	10.0	13.2	15.1

Source: *Statistical Abstract of the United States, 1982,* Tables 746, 748, and 749, U.S. Bureau of the Census, Series P-60, number 130, 1979, Tables I, II.

lation. As much as 13.2 percent of the female population lives in poverty, whereas only 10.0 percent of the male population does. Finally, we note that for old people the incidence of poverty exceeds the nationwide average of 11.6 percent.

The data on poverty leave little doubt that long-standing patterns of discrimination, which are reflected in lasting inequality of opportunity, education, quality of jobs, seniority, and all the attributes that lead to high incomes, have favored whites and males instead of blacks and females. The counterpart is the exceptionally high incidence of poverty among blacks and women.

In a study of poverty for particular stereotype groups, it was found that the probability of poverty for a family with specific characteristics might be as high as 40 to 70 percent. For example, a family of five with a female, black head of household with 9 to 12 years of education and living in a northwestern central city without a spouse and working part-time has a probability of poverty of more than 70 percent. That means, on average, 7 out of 10 such families have incomes below the poverty line.[4]

But the incidence of poverty is also very severe for old people, especially for unrelated individuals as opposed to heads of families. The severity of poverty—more than one out of every two aged blacks and one in four whites of age 65 plus—is a frightening reminder of what happens to individuals who have lost the ability to earn an income and cannot rely on the help of relatives for their support.

The Poverty Pool

In any one year a fraction of the population —currently about 11.6 percent—has incomes below the poverty line. It makes a difference to the way we view the poor whether the composition of this group changes very much or whether, on the contrary, the same people stay poor year after year. Unfortunately, there is no good information on the inflows into and outflows from this pool of people in poverty. Still, some points can be made. For old people who are poor, especially if they are unrelated individuals, there is very little chance of escaping poverty. There are no opportunities that open up for old people. The opposite is true for young people. A couple in college may have an income below the poverty level, but within a year of graduation, with each having a job as a high school teacher or an engineer, they are well beyond poverty.

For some people poverty is probably a transitory status associated with the sudden loss of a job. For others it may become a permanent status, starting with being born into a poor family and never receiving the opportunity to acquire training, motivation, and opportunity.

[4] See I. Garfinkel and R. Haveman, "Economic Capacity, Economic Status and Poverty," in M. Moon and E. Smolensky (eds.), *Improving Measures of Economic Well-Being,* Academic Press, New York, 1977.

If we want to do something about poverty, it is necessary to identify the sources of poverty. The appropriate policies are entirely different for old people and for students, for job losers in an economywide recession and for job losers in a permanently depressed area of the country. They are also different for female heads of households with dependent children. The unemployed need a fully employed economy to recover from poverty. People in depressed areas need migration or job retraining. Women with dependent children require child support or day care centers or both so they can go to work.

The War on Poverty

In the mid-1960s the Johnson administration decided to wage a war on poverty in America. In the *Economic Report of the President* for that year the administration set the target:

> There will always be some Americans who are better off than others. But it need not follow that the "poor are always with us." In the United States we can see on the horizon a society of abundance free of much of the misery and degradation that have been the age-old fate of men. Steadily rising productivity, together with an improving network of private and social insurance and assistance has been eroding mass poverty in America. But the process is far too slow. It is high time to redouble and to concentrate our efforts to eliminate poverty.[5]

The attack on poverty took place on a broad front, including programs of economic assistance, education, and welfare. There also was an effort to end discrimination and inequality of opportunity. One way to look at the progress that was achieved is to study the data on the fraction of the population below the absolute poverty line. Whereas in 1960, 22.0 percent, or nearly

one in four Americans, had incomes below the poverty line, by 1965 the fraction had declined to only 17.3 percent. By 1970 and 1978 the fraction was down to the 11 to 12 percent range. Clearly, the 1960s and 1970s showed a sizable reduction in the overall incidence of poverty. But we also must ask how that reduction was achieved.

Was poverty in the last 20 years reduced through improved equality of opportunities, reduced discrimination, and better education? Or was it reduced not at the roots but by papering over inequality through transfer payments, thus eliminating poverty but by no means the causes of inequality? A study for the year 1976 finds that much of the reduction in poverty was not due to improved earnings but rather to various kinds of transfer payments. Table 38-7 reports some of the details.

Taking into account only income from labor and property, and excluding both transfers and taxes, we have the income definition reported in the first row. By that definition 27 percent of families are below the poverty line. The share is so large because the data exclude all transfers accruing to retired and disabled people. The more common definition of income, employed in the U.S. Census investigations and used in the earlier tables in this chapter, is listed in the second row. Here we include all *cash* transfers, which includes retirement income, unemployment and veterans benefits, Social Security receipts, public assistance, and welfare. With this augmented income concept, only 13.5 percent of all families are below the poverty line. We see already what a large part transfers play in affecting the level of income.

A third adjustment is made in the third row, where we also include benefits in kind —hospital care, housing, and food stamps. These in-kind transfers produce a further large reduction in poverty status: 5.4 percentage points for all families but as much

---

[5] *Economic Report of the President, 1964*, p. 55.

TABLE 38-7

FAMILIES BELOW THE POVERTY LEVEL UNDER ALTERNATIVE INCOME DEFINITIONS, 1976
(Percent of All Families in the Category Shown)

INCOME DEFINITION	ALL FAMILIES	WHITE	BLACK	AGE 65+
Income before taxes and transfers	27.0	24.7	43.8	59.9
Income after cash transfers	13.5	11.4	28.9	16.7
Income after cash transfers and in-kind transfers	8.1	7.1	15.9	6.1
Income after taxes and all transfers	8.3	7.3	16.1	6.1

Source: Statistical Abstract of the United States, 1980, Table 770.

as 13 percentage points for black families and 10 percentage points for families headed by persons age 65 and over. The last row shows that adjusting incomes for taxes raises the incidence of poverty somewhat, although not substantially. The change from the third row to the fourth row is small because the poor do not pay high taxes.

Table 38-7 makes the significant point that on the basis of their own earnings—the income definition in the first row—a quarter of all U.S. families are below the poverty line. But transfers, including social programs and Medicaid, make a dramatic difference in reducing the incidence of poverty. The war on poverty succeeded to a large extent in eliminating poverty by transfer payments rather than by enhancing opportunities and earnings. The largest of these programs are food stamps and Medicaid.

4 LUCK, MERIT, AND MOBILITY

To what extent does economic status—being rich or being poor—persist within a family from one generation to the next? Do the poor stay poor without much possibility of escaping into the middle class or even moving to the top? Of course, we know plenty of stories about people who have made it, but perhaps there are an even

larger number of stories about people who could not escape from the poverty in which they grew up.

Table 38-8 suggests a way of thinking about socioeconomic mobility. Suppose we have two equally large income groups: the poor and the rich. In the vertical column we place the status of the parents, and in the rows we show the status of the children. In each of the cells we place a percentage which shows the probability that a child with a given background will reach a given status. In the table we show a case of low social mobility: A child with poor parents has a 90 percent chance of staying poor and only a 10 percent chance of moving into the rich group. Likewise, the children of the rich have a 90 percent chance of staying rich and only a 10 percent chance of becoming poor. By contrast, the case of perfect mobility is one where everybody has the same chance

TABLE 38-8

SOCIAL MOBILITY TABLE

	PROBABILITY OF CHILD BEING:	
	Poor	Rich
Parents:		
Poor	90%	10%
Rich	10%	90%

of being rich or poor, independent of the economic status of the family. In that case, the numbers in the two rows of the table would be the same.

Now we have to ask what the factors are that shape the probabilities in the social mobility table, or what makes the probabilities 90 percent to 10 percent rather than 50/50. Is it primarily a question of rank privilege, inheritance taxes, and connections, or is it a matter of personal motivation, individual achievement, and willingness to do hard, serious work? Or is it just plain luck?

In an effort to identify the factors that lead to economic success or failure we can separate three elements: family, achievement, and luck. We do not have much to say about how to be lucky, and therefore we concentrate on the other two determinants. Family background helps determine socioeconomic status in three separate ways. First, there are possible hereditary factors or genetic effects. To the extent that the children of smart parents tend to inherit that attribute genetically, the children will automatically be better placed, other things equal, than children of less smart parents.

The second channel through which family background works is environmental effects. Growing up in a hardworking, middle-class family may give a child motivation and orientation that would not be received by a child growing up in a family wealthy enough that no one in it works. The third channel involves direct economic benefits related to the family background. Children of rich people "automatically" receive advanced education independently of talent, while for children from slums, advanced education is the exception and occurs at best on the basis of unusual talent. This third channel also involves less well-defined benefits such as connections and access to opportunities on the basis of family ties and background. Being in the club definitely helps.

The other important determinant of socioeconomic success is personal achievement—push and drive. Of course, personal achievement is hard to measure and even harder to separate from some of the factors already mentioned in connection with family background. Other things equal, we would look here at such measures as educational achievement (years of schooling completed) and test scores.

Among people of the same background we expect these measures to be a reasonable screening device to determine ability, motivation, and likely success. But for people with different backgrounds, the test scores tend to overestimate the ability and potential of those who have already come further. Education remains one of the central screening devices in our society. Therefore, programs that provide access to education for people from poor family backgrounds are one of the main mechanisms for making the race for socioeconomic progress more fair and the probabilities for achievement more equal.

We do not have actual data to fill in Table 38-8. Claims that there is a "culture of poverty" in the United States, with children of welfare recipients being likely themselves to become welfare recipients, suggest that the data would be closer to 90/10 than 50/50 for at least those groups. There is also some evidence in the other direction, concerning the incomes and wealth of fathers and sons in Utah in the late nineteenth century.[6] The finding was that high-income fathers tended to have sons with higher income and wealth than average but that the effect was not large. What effect there was came from the fathers passing on their wealth at death rather than from the sons earning higher incomes on their own.

---

[6] James R. Kearl and Clayne L. Pope, "Intergenerational Effects on the Distribution of Income and Wealth: The Utah Experience, 1850–1900," National Bureau of Economic Research, Cambridge, Mass., Working Paper No. 754, 1981.

The widely held view of the United States as a land of social and economic opportunity and mobility is more consistent with the 50/50 probabilities than with 90/10.

5 EQUALITY, EFFICIENCY, AND THE GOVERNMENT

Income distribution is a sharply divisive issue. Some believe that the distribution generated by the market is best; others believe that the market-generated distribution needs, and should receive, substantial correction to enhance equality. Still others believe that capitalism has to be destroyed to generate a much more pervasive equality. We limit ourselves in this chapter to a discussion that takes as given a basically capitalistic society which makes decisions about the extent to which the tax and transfer system is used to change, or not change, the market-determined distribution of income.

The starting point of the discussion is to recognize that there is *no* commonly accepted argument for equality, or no standard by which we can determine how much inequality society should or should not accept.[7] Of course, at the extremes most people would feel that there is something deeply wrong about a society in which some people cannot feed their children while others cannot even count their fortunes. But most people also believe that hard work and effort should be rewarded by *extra* income, status, and opportunity and that those working less should not by right share on an equal basis. The problem is to reconcile in practice these widely held views.

Few would argue today that the market brings about an income distribution that is necessarily right, fair, just, or ethical. Even fewer would go so far as a leading conservative, Irving Kristol, has.

> I think status differentials testify to real differentials of character, ability, and talent, that they are deserved, and that we should have as many of them as possible.[8]

There is a basic skepticism among liberals who claim that many of the status differentials are acquired not on the basis of merit and contribution but rather on the basis of privilege and market failure. Such imperfections can indeed be identified, it is argued, and they should be compensated for by direct intervention in the income distribution process through a redistribution of income by taxes and transfers.

The disagreement is long-standing and has no solution, as society cannot wait for liberals and conservatives to find a solution or compromise. In the meantime the political process determines some degree of income redistribution through three channels: the tax system (primarily income taxes and gift and estate taxes), the social welfare system (cash and in-kind programs for the needy), and special legal and economic programs to promote equal opportunity and nondiscrimination.

We have already examined various transfer programs that form part of the second-round redistribution by taxes and transfers. The other part of redistribution is the progressive income tax structure that is in place in the U.S. economy. Table 38-9 shows the average tax rates—taxes as a percentage of taxable income—for various income groups as well as the percentage of taxable returns in each group.

But the redistribution of income that takes place does not come without generating waste and inefficiency. On this point

---

[7] A very accessible and readable account is Arthur Okun, *Equality and Efficiency: The Big Tradeoff,* Brookings Institution, Washington, D.C., 1975. For a discussion, see Part 1 of C. D. Campbell (ed.), *Income Redistribution,* American Enterprise Institute, Washington, D.C. 1976, which reports a diversity of political positions.

[8] I. Kristol in Campbell, op. cit., p. 62.

TABLE 38-9

AVERAGE FEDERAL TAX RATES AND DISTRIBUTION OF TAXPAYERS BY INCOME GROUP, 1978

INCOME GROUP	AVERAGE TAX RATE, %	% OF ALL TAX RETURNS
All income groups	18.3	100
Less than $15,000	10.2	51.4
$15,000–25,000	15.2	28.8
$25,000–50,000	20.3	17.2
Above $50,000	36.4	2.6

Source: Statistical Abstract of the United States, 1980, Tables 450 through 452.

Arthur Okun states that

> With very few exceptions, this second-round redistribution cannot be carried out cost-lessly: as I like to put it, we can transport money from the rich to the poor only in a leaky bucket. . . .
>
> Given (1) a social preference for equality (or at least for more equality than market determined incomes provide) and (2) a cost of altering the market determined distribution, society faces a trade-off between equality and efficiency. The resulting optimum will normally be a compromise.[9]

Where does the bucket leak? The most important point is the conflict between the provision of welfare benefits for those in need and incentives to work. If people are assured that their basic needs will be taken care of, their incentive to work is reduced. In detail, the important question involves the marginal effect on income in deciding to work. If welfare and unemployment benefits are reduced substantially when someone takes a job, the incentive not to work is strong. Indeed, it is possible that after-tax earnings from working may be less than the income received when not working.

The problem is one of eliminating the conflict between the income safety aspects of the social welfare program and the incentive effects that should encourage people to move out of poverty. This is a difficult problem, and it is also the key to the problem of the leaky bucket.

Other inefficiencies are involved in the administration of social welfare programs that require resources or in the payment of in-kind rather than cash benefits. But the inefficiencies do not show up exclusively in the poor dropping out of the labor force. They are also present when the progressive income tax system leads companies to pay their top executives with various kinds of amenities such as luxurious offices and when taxation affects saving and investment.

Waste in social welfare programs and disincentive effects of a progressive tax structure—the leaks in Okun's bucket—as well as a simple aversion to sharing with the anonymous poor lead to recurrent moves to reform the welfare program and the tax structure. Supply side economics in the early eighties represents the latest appearance of this attempt to reduce the role of government in reducing inequality. Eligibility for some welfare programs was reduced and high marginal tax rates were reduced so as to increase incentives for saving, capital formation, and work effort.

This example is a clear case of society making a choice: Increased inequality (through reduced progressivity of taxation) is tolerated for the benefit of a better-performing economy. But of course, such a

---

[9] A. Okun in Campbell, op. cit., p. 21.

move is not without controversy. Many have claimed that the tax cuts primarily made the rich richer and only secondarily and in a small way enhanced the efficient operation of the economy. Proponents of the policies, on the other hand, argued that the improvements in the economy—growth, innovation, and capital formation—would do more for the poor than any amount of public programs.

This view is certainly part and parcel of the conservative heritage and has been well summarized by Irving Kristol:

> The trouble with any massive scheme of income redistribution as a way of "abolishing poverty" is not merely its impact on marginal tax rates and hence its negative effect on efficiency and economic growth—an effect that is generally conceded even if its importance is debatable. One could contemplate, in good conscience, a somewhat lower standard of living for the average American family if this would result in a more contented political community. But the evidence is clear that trying to abolish poverty through income distribution results in nothing of the sort. The evidence is also clear that when poverty is abolished through economic growth, something real and desirable has occurred.[10]

The Negative Income Tax

We are nowhere near agreement on the desirable extent of government intervention in the redistribution of market-determined incomes. There is as much disagreement on how to reshape the existing programs.[11] But among the programs that have been advocated, particular attention has been focused on the negative income tax proposal first advanced by Milton Friedman. The proposal would substitute a comprehensive cash payment to low-income families and thus replace many specific programs. But it would avoid the work-disincentive effects of needs-tested programs by not reducing welfare payments 1 for 1 or even more when incomes are earned.

The simple idea of negative income taxes is as follows. The government gives *everybody* a check for $8000, which is the poverty line level of income. Thus we have insured that all people are placed at or above the poverty line, even if they do not have *any* earnings other than the government payment. Next we tax all incomes with a progressive income tax schedule. For people with incomes near $15,000, there already are significant tax liabilities, and hence their net receipts from the government are small—they in fact return a good part of the transfer as taxes on their earned incomes. People with incomes at the high end, of course, will be net payers of taxes.

The negative income tax would avoid the disincentive effects that now face people on welfare who think of taking a job but do not do so because they would lose their welfare benefits. Under the negative income tax, all citizens automatically get the $8000 check. They do not lose it if they take a job. Rather, they pay income taxes on what they earn in the job but keep the $8000 already in their pockets.

The concept of a negative income tax has received substantial public interest. It has even been experimentally applied in a number of projects to study the exact trade-off between earnings and transfer dollars (the amount of the check to be sent to everyone). It is an idea that strikes a balance between the need for income support programs on the one hand and the wide preference that those poor who can hold jobs should be in the market on the other hand. It is an idea that is waiting for the combination of economic stability and a political promoter.

---

[10] I. Kristol in Campbell, op. cit., p. 38.
[11] For a discussion, see Congressional Budget Office, *Welfare Reform: Issues, Objectives and Approaches*, July 1977, and Henry Aaron, *Why Is Welfare So Hard to Reform?* Brookings Institution, Washington, D.C., 1973.

The Flat Rate Tax

An alternative simplification of the tax system has also been suggested frequently. This is the flat rate tax, which would have a constant marginal rate of taxation of all incomes, with no deductions at all. The argument behind the flat rate tax is that the current tax system is so complicated that it is a waste of resources. A flat rate tax could be as low as 19 percent and raise the same amount of revenue as the current income tax.

What about the progressive feature of the current income tax? Proponents of the flat rate tax say the evidence is that the current tax system hardly affects the distribution of income, despite the apparently progressive taxes. To see that they have a point, look at Table 38-5, where the tax system produces very little change in the distribution of income.

There is no reason why the negative income tax and the flat rate tax should not be combined. Every family could start with its $8000 check from the government and then pay 19 percent on all its other earnings. In the early eighties the flat rate tax has attracted much attention and support from politicians, including perhaps President Reagan. Thus there may be some changes in the tax system in this general direction. The changes will probably increase inequality, reducing the mildly progressive structure of the current tax system.

SUMMARY

1   The functional distribution of income deals with the distribution of national income between different factors of production: labor, self-employed people, and property. The personal distribution deals with income distribution among individuals or families.

2   The data on the functional distribution of income are complicated by the presence of proprietors' income, which is the combined income accruing to property *and* self-employed labor in unincorporated businesses. But even taking into account the complication arising from property income, there appears a clear trend for labor's share to be rising over time.

3   Theory predicts that the movement in the relative shares of capital and labor over time depends on three factors: any bias in the rate of technical progress, the direction of change in the economywide capital-labor ratio, and the degree of substitutability of capital and labor as factors of production.

4   With neutral technical progress and a rising capital-labor ratio (as all industrialized countries have experienced), the share of labor in national income will rise if substitutability between capital and labor is low. Conversely, it will fall if substitutability is high.

5   The personal distribution of income is uneven in all countries. The Lorenz curve summarizes the degree to which the distribution is uneven by showing what fraction of the population receives what

share of income. An economy in which 1 percent of the population receives 60 percent of the income would be considered highly unequal. Conversely, an economy in which everybody receives the same share has full equality. The Lorenz curve allows comparisons of the degree of inequality across times or across countries.

6 In the United States the top 5 percent of families receive about 16 percent of all income while the poorest 20 percent of families receive only 5 percent of all income.

7 We cannot move directly from the distribution of income to a judgment about the distribution of welfare. Families may differ by size and by work effort. The income distribution data are also imperfect in that they do not make adjustments for income in kind as well as for taxation.

8 There are two common definitions of poverty. One, referred to as absolute poverty, identifies a level of income below which a person cannot maintain a specified subsistence level. The other—relative poverty—identifies a threshold level of income equal to one-half the median income level. Absolute poverty deals with subsistence and survival. Relative poverty is concerned with the economic status of people who are not threatened by starvation but who are poor among the rich.

9 Poverty is highly concentrated among particular groups: blacks, women with dependent children, and the aged. The war on poverty, intensified with many social programs in the 1960s, attempts to attack poverty by direct transfer programs in cash and in kind. These programs range from food stamps to supplemental income support for families with dependent children.

10 There is an important trade-off between equality and efficiency in the economy. Even if it were widely agreed that inequality is undesirable, we would still find that measures to reduce inequality through taxes and transfers impair efficiency and interfere with resource allocation. Thus there is a double obstacle to the use of taxes and transfers to redistribute income. There is, first, no consensus on the desirable degree of equality. Second, there are possible inefficiencies generated by tax/transfer policies to redistribute income.

KEY TERMS

Personal income distribution
Functional income distribution
Proprietors' income
Lorenz curve
Absolute and relative poverty levels

Socioeconomic mobility
Okun's leaky bucket
Equality and efficiency trade-off
Negative income tax
Flat rate tax

PROBLEMS

1 Use Figure 38-2, which develops the equilibrium in the labor market, to show the effect on income distribution of an increase in the labor supply accompanied by an increase in the capital stock by the same proportion. (*a*) What happens to wages, capital income, and the shares of capital and labor in income? (*b*) How would your answers differ if the labor force increased proportionately more than the capital stock?

2 Until the middle 1930s there was a firm belief that labor's share in income tended to be stable and near constant over time. Does the U.S. experience in the last 20 years support or contradict that belief?

3 The accompanying table shows income distribution data for the United Kingdom for two years, 1949 and 1979. (*a*) Draw in one graph the Lorenz curve for both years. (*b*) Which year shows more equality?

	BOTTOM 50%	51–60%	61–70%	71–80%
1949	26.5	9.5	10.5	11.9
1979	26.2	9.3	11.3	13.5

	81–90%	TOP 10%	TOP 1%
1949	14.5	27.1	6.4
1979	16.3	23.4	3.9

Source: Central Statistical Office (U.K.), *Economic Trends,* May 1978 and February 1981.

4 The table below shows data for the before-tax and after-tax income distribution in the United Kingdom. (*a*) Draw a Lorenz curve for each of the series in the same diagram. (*b*) Does the tax system increase or reduce equality?

5 Consider the socioeconomic mobility table (Table 38-8). Discuss three economic measures (legal arrangements or specific government programs) which would increase mobility.

6 Discuss why in an economy where everybody has adequate food and shelter, there may still be a poverty problem.

7 Identify the manner in which a progressive income tax adversely affects incentives for (*a*) the poor, (*b*) the middle-income earners, and (*c*) the very rich.

8 It has frequently been argued that the market-determined distribution of income should be accepted and not tampered with. Present and evaluate arguments for and against this view.

9 Consider education, or investment in human capital. Suppose there are two groups, the rich and the poor. The former can borrow at 10 percent interest; the latter, because they have no assets as collateral against the loans, have to pay 12 percent interest. (*a*) Discuss the effects of this difference in the cost of loans on the amount of education for individuals of equal ability from the two groups. (*b*) Is this an instance of market failure? Why or why not? (*c*) If there is a market failure, what specific government program could improve matters?

10 Income distribution data often show that young people are counted among the poor. Can you present an argument why students, for example, should not be counted among the poor even if their annual earnings place them below the poverty line?

11 Evaluate arguments for and against the negative income tax and flat rate taxes.

BEFORE-TAX AND AFTER-TAX INCOME DISTRIBUTION IN THE UNITED KINGDOM

	BOTTOM 20%	2D 20%	3D 20%	4TH 20%	TOP 20%	TOP 1%
Pretax	5.9	10.3	16.5	24.7	42.6	5.3
Posttax	7.0	11.5	17.0	24.8	39.7	3.9

Source: Central Statistical Office (U.K.), *Economic Trends,* May 1978 and February 1981.

One-third of the world's people—among them the Chinese, Russians, Eastern Europeans, Vietnamese, and Cubans—live in socialist or communist economies. These economies are marked by two main features: productive capital is mostly owned by the state, not by private individuals, and there is extensive central planning or direction of the economy. The economies are marked, too, by their claim that their economic organization is based on the theories of Karl Marx.

In this chapter we describe Marx's economics and Marxian economics, as well as the economic organization of the economies of the socialist or communist bloc. Although the distinction between capitalism and communism is convenient, the countries of the world do not fit themselves neatly into one group or the other. Modern western economies, such as those of the United States, West Germany, and Sweden, are *mixed* economies in which much capital is owned by the state (the roads, some schools, some industries) and in which the state plays a large role in economic life. Some countries in the communist bloc, such as Hungary and Yugoslavia, permit private ownership of some capital and give a large role to managers of firms in making production decisions. The most useful criterion for distinguishing economies as either modern capitalist or modern communist is the extent to which markets are used. Markets are used to some extent in all economies, including the Soviet Union, but they play a less important role in the centrally directed communist economies than they do in the western economies.

39

Alternative Economic Approaches and Systems

We will be asking in this chapter how Marxian economic analysis differs from the economics we have learned in the rest of the book. We examine how the centrally planned economies solve the economic problems of what, how, and for whom. We will compare the economic performance of those economies with the economic performance of the western economies. And we will ask where the economies are heading. Is there, as many used to argue, a convergence process in which the economies grow more like each other, approaching some happy common form of economic organization, each from a different starting point? Or are the western economies, with the elections in the late seventies and early eighties of conservative governments in Britain, the United States, Sweden, and elsewhere, moving back toward a purer capitalism and away from the mixed economy?

1 MARX AND MARXIAN ECONOMICS

Karl Marx (1818–1883) was the most influential economist who ever lived. He was born in Prussia and lived in Paris and Brussels. He edited newspapers in all three places that were closed by the government soon after he took them over. In 1849 he moved with his family to London.

Marx did not have an academic appointment or other regular job. He made some money writing for newspapers, including the New York *Tribune*. But during most of his life in London he lived in poverty. His coauthor, Friedrich Engels, a successful businessman, supported him while he did research. Later in his life, Marx received an inheritance that improved his financial lot. Marx spent most of his time in London in the library of the British Museum, studying for and writing his major economics book, *Das Kapital*, written in German (*Capital* in the English translation). Only the first volume was published while he was alive. Engels edited Marx's manuscripts and notes to produce the other two volumes.

Although Marx's economic analysis is contained mostly in *Capital*, many of the elements are present in the famous *Communist Manifesto*, which he and Engels wrote in 1848. Extracts from the *Manifesto* are given in Box 39-1. The *Manifesto* reflects most of Marx's important themes. Foremost is Marx's view that all recorded history was the history of class struggles. Marx interpreted economic life as a contest between classes and capitalism, in particular, as a contest between the bourgeoisie (the middle classes and the capitalists) and the proletariat (the workers). Where Adam Smith

---

BOX 39-1 ▰▰▰▰▰▰▰▰▰▰▰

THE COMMUNIST MANIFESTO

The *Communist Manifesto* was written by Marx and Engels in 1848 as a platform of the Communist League, an association of workers. The *Manifesto* is both an analysis of the forces responsible for the state of the society and the direction in which they believed it was moving and a call to fight the existing society. Instead of summarizing the *Manifesto,* we present extracts that give the sense of Marx's analysis in his own rhetoric. (The *Manifesto* was originally written in German.)

THE INTRODUCTION
A spectre is haunting Europe—the spectre of Communism. . . .

ANALYSIS OF ECONOMICS AND CLASS RELATIONS
The history of all hitherto existing society[1] is the history of class struggles. . . .

Our epoch, the epoch of the bourgeoisie, possesses, however, this distinctive feature; it has simplified the class antagonisms. Society as a whole is more and more splitting up into two great hostile camps, into two great classes directly facing each other: Bourgeoisie and Proletariat. . . .

The bourgeoisie, during its rule of scarce one hundred years, has created more massive and more colossal productive forces than have all preceding generations together. . . .

Owing to the extensive use of machinery and to division of labor, the work of the proletarians has lost all individual character, and, consequently, all charm for the workman. . . .

In proportion, . . . as the repulsiveness of the work increases the wage decreases. . . .

But with the development of industry the proletariat not only increases in number; it becomes concentrated in greater masses, its strength grows and it feels that strength more. . . .

The development of Modern Industry, therefore, cuts from under its feet the very foundation on which the bourgeoisie produces and appropriates products. What the bourgeoisie therefore produces, above all, are its own grave diggers. Its fall and the victory of the proletariat are equally inevitable.

THE PROGRAM OF THE REVOLUTION

1 The abolition of property in land and application of all rents of land to public purposes.

2 A heavy progressive or graduated income tax.

3 Abolition of all right of inheritance. . . .

5 Centralization of credit in the hands of the State, by means of a national bank with State capital and an exclusive monopoly.

6 Centralization of the means of communication and transportation in the hands of the State.

7 Extension of factories and instruments of production owned by the State. . . .

When in the course of development, class distinctions have disappeared, and all production has been concentrated in the hands of a vast association of the whole nation, the public power will lose its political character. . . .

In place of the old bourgeois society, with its classes and class antagonisms, we shall have an association in which the free development of each is the condition for the free development of all.

THE CONCLUSION

The Communists disdain to conceal their views and aims. They openly declare that their ends can be attained only by the forcible overthrow of all existing social conditions. Let the ruling classes tremble at a Communist revolution. The proletarians have nothing to lose but their chains. They have a world to win.

Working men of all countries, unite!

COMMENTS

The *Manifesto* was written earlier than Marx's *Capital.* In 1872, Marx and Engels, in a preface to a new edition, stood by the general principles while suggesting that some details could be improved if the *Manifesto* were rewritten then—but, as Engels noted, it was by then a historical document.

We can now see that the major mistake in the analysis of the industrial economies was the belief that the wage would fall and that workers would become poorer as industrialization proceeded. In fact, the living standards of workers in the developed economies have increased more rapidly since the middle of the nineteenth century than they ever did before. The workers of the developed world have far more to lose than their chains. No doubt, if Marx had foreseen the increasing living standards of workers and the development of the modern mixed economy, he would have written a very different analysis.

---

[1] A footnote from the original is omitted.

saw the self-interest of the individuals leading them to produce results that benefited all, Marx saw the self-interest of capitalists leading them to produce results that impoverished the workers and thereby produced the grave diggers of capitalism.

Note that Marx thought of the bourgeoisie as responsible for more massive development than in all of previous history. He admired the tremendous vitality and power of the development of the world economy set off by the European countries in the eighteenth and nineteenth centuries. But he was also sure that wages would fall in those countries and that this would lead eventually to revolution.

Why did Marxian analysis lead to the prediction that wages would fall? The prediction came from Marx's analysis of competition among capitalists. He argued that the wage is determined by how much it takes to keep workers alive and productive. Suppose that in any given year, say, 1850, it takes 7 hours of work per day for workers to produce enough so that firms can pay them the needed wage. But workers will work more than 7 hours, say, for 10 hours. The capitalists will only employ workers if there is some gain from doing so, and since the capitalists own the factories and control the jobs, they determine the hours of work: the worker has to work to keep body and soul together.

The total of 3 hours of extra work is called *surplus value*. That surplus value is the source of profits. Marx assumed that capitalists, by their nature, ceaselessly accumulate capital, saving from their profits. Modern economists would expect that the new capital tends to increase labor productivity and the wage, moving it above the bare subsistence level. At the same time, we would expect the rate of return to capital to fall as more and more capital is accumulated, because capital is subject to declining marginal productivity.

But Marx emphasized technical innovation under capitalism. Capitalists fight against the falling profit rate by trying to innovate, to produce new products, and to produce old products more cheaply. Ceaseless innovation is an essential part of capitalism and is responsible for the great success of the bourgeoisie in developing the world economy.

Why should the wage fall as more capital is accumulated? The reason is that innovation is in the direction of labor-saving machinery. Capitalists try to find machines to replace workers; they try (ultimately in vain) to protect profits by reducing labor costs. The labor-saving machinery reduces the demand for labor and thus prevents the wage from rising. As the demand for labor falls, more and more workers become unemployed. *A reserve army of the unemployed* develops. The unemployed are willing to work for even lower wages than those needed to keep workers alive and productive, and the condition of the workers worsens.

Marx did not see this as a smooth process. He believed that capitalist economies were bound to generate trade cycles and that things could even get better for the workers in a period of recovery and boom. But depressions were inevitable, as was the long-run downward trend of both wages and the rate of profit.

Table 39-1 shows real wage rates per hour in manufacturing in the United States since the 1890s.[2] The trend has certainly not been downward. And that is the major empirical fact that confronts the Marxian analysis.

---

[2] Note that real wages in manufacturing were *higher* in the thirties than in the twenties; that is, they were higher in the Great Depression than in the prosperous twenties. Of course, these were the wages of those employed—the unemployed did not get to enjoy the high wages of the thirties. Reasons for the rise in real wages and the role of the high real manufacturing wage in the Great Depression are still debated.

TABLE 39-1

REAL COMPENSATION PER HOUR AT WORK FOR MANUFACTURING PRODUCTION WORKERS (1967 = 100)

DECADE	INDEX	GROWTH RATE PER ANNUM OVER THE PREVIOUS DECADE, %
1890–1899	17.3	
1900–1909	20.2	1.6
1910–1919	24.4	1.9
1920–1929	30.4	2.2
1930–1939	40.3	2.9
1940–1949	58.7	3.8
1950–1959	78.2	2.9
1960–1969	96.5	2.1
1970–1979	106.6	1.0

Sources: U.S. Department of Commerce, *Long Term Economic Growth, 1860–1970*, pp. 222–223; U.S. Department of Labor, *Handbook of Labor Statistics, 1980*, p. 185.

Other Themes

Marx's major economic prediction of falling living standards for the working class turned out to be wrong, and therefore his political predictions based on the increasing misery of the working class also turned out to be wrong. But there is more in Marx than predictions about communist revolution.

The Labor Theory of Value   Marx's microeconomics was based on the labor theory of value.

> The *labor theory of value* states that the value of goods is derived from the amount of labor embodied in them.

This theme is an old one in economics. It is found in the writings of both Adam Smith and David Ricardo, the great early-nineteenth-century English economist to whom Marx owed much of his economics.

Marx argued that profits made by capitalists are the result of exploitation of the workers and are not a reward for their in-

novation and for the rental of the machinery they own. The reason is that the machinery itself owes its existence to the labor that went into making it and to the labor used to make the machines used in making it, and so on. Labor, not capitalists, should be earning the profits, Marx argued. Modern economists agree that very little in Marx really depends on the labor theory of value and that he could easily have reached most of his conclusions without relying on it.

The Marxian insistence on the labor theory of value created difficulties in the running of the Russian economy. The planners of the economy did not want to include as part of the costs of producing different goods a charge for the amount of capital used in production. Such reluctance leads to systematic underpricing of goods whose production is capital-intensive, since prices are based only on the amount of labor used in production. Since it was obvious that not charging for the use of capital led to distortions in pricing and production, means around the prohibition against charging for the use of capital have now been found.

We might ask how the theory of value we have learned in this book differs from the labor theory of value. We say that the prices of goods depend on both demand and supply rather than on just the costs of production. And we include in costs of production the opportunity costs of *all* factors used in production, including capital.

Monopolies, Bigness, and Alienation Writing in the 1850s and 1860s, before the modern corporation became the dominant form of business, Marx nonetheless predicted that firms would become bigger and that the biggest firms would come to dominate their industries and the economy. Marx believed capitalism would produce monopolies. Up through the end of the nineteenth century, he seemed to be right, at least for the United States. But then trust-busting became the policy of the government, and the trend toward monopoly stopped.

Marx also predicted that as the organization of production under capitalism became more sophisticated and complicated, the workers would feel less interested in their jobs and more like machines themselves. This was the phenomenon of *alienation.* Alienation is referred to, though not by name, in a quotation in Box 39-1: "the work of the proletarians has lost all individual character, and, consequently, all charm for the workman."

In the mid-1970s, "alienation" was a fashionable word, particularly in connection with the experience at a factory set up by General Motors in Lordstown, Ohio. The factory was opened with much hope that the ultramodern machinery would lead to high productivity. The experience at Lordstown turned out to be very different from the hopes. Workers disliked the factory, absenteeism was high, and productivity was low. The problem was blamed on alienation.

In a bid to avoid similar problems, Volvo of Sweden experimented with getting rid of the assembly line altogether. It allowed small teams of workers to each be responsible for building complete cars. After some initial success, this experiment to fight alienation failed, as productivity levels fell for the non-assembly-line production.

Socialism and Communism   There is a distinction between socialism, in which the state owns the means of production and directs economic activity, and communism. The socialist program is outlined in points 1 through 7 in Box 39-1 (there are 10 points in the original). Private ownership of land will be abolished, inheritance will be abolished, heavy progressive income taxes will be imposed, and so on.

The state dominates socialism. But communism was seen by Marx and Engels as an almost mystical condition in which the state

has withered away ("the public power will lose its political character") and everyone freely cooperates. Marx was not explicit about how communism would work. But in the *Communist Manifesto* and elsewhere he did give more details about how he believed a socialist economy would be run. As we shall see, much of what he said accurately describes today's nonmarket or communist-bloc economies.

In Marxian terms, the economies we think of as communist are really socialist, for in none of them has the state withered away—instead, the state dominates economic life.

Was Marx Almost Right?

In the early 1930s, with the United States in a deep depression, it seemed to many that Marx was right and that capitalism was indeed doomed. But gradually the U.S. economy moved out of the depression. Progress was slow, and full employment reemerged only in World War II. But since then the economies of the developed countries have performed better than at any previous time in their histories.

But the modern economies of the United States, Germany, and France, for example, are different from the pure capitalist economies Marx was analyzing. The state has assumed increasing responsibility for economic stability and is playing a bigger role in economic life. The *mixed economy* is a modern development, and it is the mixed economies that have shown that the Marxist predictions were wrong.

To say that the economies in which we live are different from the capitalist economies Marx was analyzing is to recognize that history does not stand still—for Marx or for us. The modern U.S. economy is not the economy we will have a century from now. Nor is the modern Russian economy the economy the Russian people will have in the 2080s. As technology develops and views about the role of government in economic life change, the economy will change.

2 RESOURCE ALLOCATION IN A COMMAND ECONOMY

From Marxian theory we move on to the organization of socialist or communist economies. Recall that these are marked by state ownership of productive capital and by only a limited use of markets. In this section we describe how resources would be allocated by a central planner. The central planner is responsible for deciding what goods should be produced, how they should be produced, and for whom. In this section we assume that he does not rely on markets in any way. All decisions are made by decree.

This is the situation in a command economy (defined in Chapter 1). In fact there is no such economy. In the next section we discuss the possibility of market socialism, in which markets are used to solve the economic problems. In the remainder of the chapter we describe how resources are in practice allocated in the Soviet Union, in China, and in other communist-bloc economies.

Figure 39-1 describes the problem solved by the planner. The PPF shows the goods the economy can produce. The choice is between consumption goods (food, clothing, tennis rackets) and machines. The more machines that are produced, the higher is the investment in the economy today, and the higher is future production—but the lower is consumption today.

To solve the what problem, the planner chooses a point on the PPF. Suppose he chooses point A. On what basis is such a choice made? Probably the planner is choosing a point that he believes (or that his political party believes) is good for the nation. If A means that a large part of the GNP is devoted to investment, then the planner

FIGURE 39-1   THE CENTRAL PLANNING PROBLEM. Given the economy's production possibilities, the central planner has to choose the point on the PPF at which society produces. This is shown by point A, with the output of machines equal to *OM* and the output of consumption goods equal to *OC*. Corresponding to point A is an allocation of the factors of production among industries and among firms in the economy. And the planner also has to decide how the consumption goods are to be distributed among the individuals in the economy.

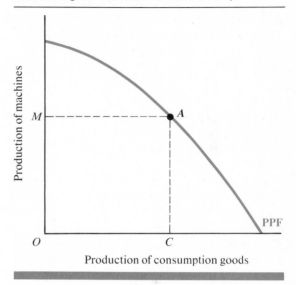

Production of machines / Production of consumption goods

is trying to get the economy to grow fast by increasing the capital stock rapidly. But that means curtailing current consumption. Perhaps the planner believes he is choosing what the consumers would choose if they had the choice. In any event, the planner, not the consumer, chooses to be at point A.

By choosing what to produce, the planner has already to some extent decided for whom to produce. If the output of machines at A is high, then the plan cannot also provide for a high level of consumption per head today. The total consumption to be shared this year is at level OC. There is also the question of how today's total consumption is to be split up among different people. Perhaps everyone gets the same amount so that every citizen is entitled to precisely the same amount of bread, candy, tennis rackets, and meat. Or perhaps the planner takes into account that there have to be incentives for people to work and decides that people get more the harder they work. Perhaps government officials get more. The central planner has to specify the for whom.

And then he has to specify how. For each point on the PPF there is an allocation of factors of production. This ensures that the economy will produce the right amounts of consumption goods and machines. Labor has to be sent to the right factories. The machinery has to be in the right place. The central planner has to work out how the production is to be allocated among different factories in each industry, and he has to be sure each factory has the factors of production it needs to meet the production required of it.

All this is complicated. But now think of the fact that Figure 39-1 simplifies the situation enormously by focusing on only two goods. In reality, there are hundreds of thousands of goods to produce and millions of workers to assign to workplaces and among whom to allocate the consumption goods that are produced.

Two facts make planning not totally impossible. First, the problem does not have to be solved afresh every day. There is an economy operating already, able to produce certain goods, with labor and capital allocated among factories and industries in a particular way. The planners can start from the existing situation and decide which way they want to move. Maybe the production of machinery should be increased. That means taking labor and some machines out of existing consumption goods uses and shifting them to the production of machines. Total consumption will therefore have to be reduced today. That can be done by reducing the amount each worker is entitled to.

Second, the plan does not have to be made all at once and forever. There may be a so-called iterative (repeating) process in which the planner sends out a set of plans to the factories and then modifies them according to the responses. Perhaps the managers will say that a plan does not give them enough capital to produce the specified output. The planner will try to judge the validity of the complaint and perhaps adjust the plan.

Corrections may be possible after the plan has started. For instance, if machinery production is not meeting target levels, more labor can be moved into the machinery industry and away from consumption goods.

Nonetheless, running an economy entirely by command and in full detail is impossible. There are too many decisions to be made. In practice there has to be extensive *decentralization*, even in a centrally planned economy. Factories and farms are given production targets, but the method of production—the how—is left up to them. This method, too, has its problems, because it is extremely difficult to state the targets. For instance, if a shoe factory is told to produce 1 million pairs of shoes a year with given amounts of labor, machinery, and raw materials, it will probably produce children's shoes. They are easier to make and require fewer raw materials. Or suppose the manager of a nail factory is told to produce 50 tons of nails this year. A Russian cartoon shows a factory shipping out one 50-ton nail. This meets the target. But it is not of much use to anyone.

Perhaps prices can be introduced to help solve the allocation problem.

3   MARKET SOCIALISM

There are two characteristics of socialist or communist economies: the state owns the productive capital, and there is little use of markets. But while it is essential for socialism that the capital stock not be owned by individual capitalists—that it be owned by the state or the people—it is not essential that there be little use of markets. There is in principle nothing that requires a socialist to believe in the command economy rather than an economy in which prices are used to allocate resources.

How would this be done? The planner, instead of issuing commands about what, how, and for whom, works out prices that produce the desired allocation of resources. These are the prices and wages that ensure that the goods are produced in the right amounts, that labor is available in the right amounts, and that the income is earned by those who should get it.

Given the prices, consumers are told to spend their incomes as they wish. Firms are told to maximize profits. Workers are told to work where they want. If the prices are right, the allocation of resources is the allocation desired by the planner.

Now in what sense do prices help solve the planning problem? After all, the planner has to figure out what prices to announce in the first place, and that means he has to figure out what supply and demand would be for each good and each factor. If he can do that, surely he can issue commands about how much to produce.

There are two reasons why the use of prices makes a difference. First, it is very easy to adjust prices. Suppose that the prices that are chosen are wrong to begin with. Then there will be excess supply in some markets and excess demand in others. The planner has only to raise prices in the markets where there is excess demand and lower them in markets with excess supply. Then he can readjust them if supply and demand are still not equal.

Second, the use of prices sets the right incentives for firms. If the manager of the shoe factory is told to maximize profits, he will produce the profitable shoes. If there is a surplus of children's shoes, there is no point in producing more of them. And if prices are adjusted to make the quantity supplied equal to the quantity demanded, the shoe factory will eventually end up pro-

ducing the mixture of shoes that consumers prefer.

There is one complication in this story. It is not clear what allocation of resources is to be chosen. Suppose that the central planner wants rapid investment and thus would prefer relatively little production of consumption goods. Then some means has to be found to ensure that the total demand for consumption goods does not exceed the supply. One simple procedure is to put a sales tax on the consumer goods. Or the consumers' income can be taxed. Either way, consumer purchasing power is reduced to make sure that the right amount of machinery is produced.

How does a socialist economy differ from a capitalist economy or a mixed economy if prices are used to allocate resources? The essential difference is the ownership of capital. In a capitalist economy, capital—the machinery, land, and buildings—is owned by private individuals. The owners are the shareholders in the corporations. Anyone who wants to start a new firm can try to borrow the money; he can go to a bank or sell bonds or stocks in the capital markets. In a socialist economy, productive capital is owned by the state. No one becomes rich by striking it lucky in the stock market because there is no stock market. Someone with a good idea for a new product does not have an opportunity to open up a new business to exploit his idea for his own account. Perhaps he will explain the idea to someone in the planning agency who is responsible for new products, and perhaps he will be given a medal for the good idea. Perhaps, also, he will be given a higher salary. But there is no notion that he should go out and develop the idea for commercial purposes on his own.

Most communist and socialist economies fall between the extremes of the command economy and market socialism. But in some of the Eastern European countries, there are also capitalist elements, particularly in agriculture, where the farmers manage their own (small) farms. They own the capital equipment and act just as an American farmer would.

We now turn to socialist economies in practice.

4 THE SOVIET UNION

The Soviet Union was the first country to organize its economy on Marxist (and Leninist) lines, and it is the first country to have undertaken serious central planning. Partly for those reasons, but also because of the competition between the countries, there has long been intense interest in the United States in the development of the Soviet economy. That interest intensified after 1957, when the Russians launched Sputnik, the first space satellite, and in 1959, when Nikita Khrushchev, the Russian leader, visited the United States and promised that the Russians would soon bury the United States —by outproducing it.

History of Soviet Planning
In the two decades before World War I, czarist Russia was industrializing very fast. Total output in Russia grew at an average rate of 8 percent per year from 1890 through 1913; in those years U.S. growth averaged 4 percent, which is itself extremely rapid. But the level of GNP in Russia in 1913 was way behind that in the United States; it was equal to only about 17 percent of U.S. GNP. In 1913, Russia was still a largely agricultural economy, with 80 percent of the population in agriculture. The U.S. figure was 34 percent.

Immediately after the Russian Revolution in 1917, banks and factories were confiscated from their private owners and nationalized, or taken into state ownership. Russia had already been in World War I for 3 years in 1917 and then faced 4 more years of fighting in a civil war, which ended in 1921. By 1921, the economy and the coun-

tryside were devastated. Industrial output was down to one-third of its 1913 level, and agricultural output was at 60 percent of the 1913 level. People were starving.

The response of the Bolshevik government, headed by Lenin, was entirely pragmatic. Capitalism was called in to rescue communism. The *New Economic Policy* (NEP) was introduced. Heavy industry and banking remained as state-owned and -controlled. But light industry and particularly agriculture were operated by their owners for private profit. That is, there was a limited reintroduction of capitalism. And it worked. By 1928 output was back to the 1913 level.

During the period of the NEP, there was intense discussion of what to do next. In 1928 the first comprehensive economic plan was introduced. It had one main aim, which was to rapidly change the backward, largely agricultural Russian economy into a modern industrial economy. As Stalin, Lenin's successor, put it:[3]

> . . . we are fifty or a hundred years behind the advanced countries. We must make good the distance in ten years. Either we do it or they crush us.

The procedure for reaching this aim was also simple. Invest a large proportion of output in heavy industry, coal, steel, and power generation. The consumption level would have to be kept low to make the rapid investment possible. Workers would have to be brought out of agriculture and into industry. And food would have to be obtained from the agricultural sector to feed the workers in industry.

There are two basic plans in operation in the Russian economy. There is a 5-year plan—the first one was introduced in 1928, and the eleventh is currently in operation.

---

[3] Quoted in George Dalton, *Economic Systems and Society,* Penguin Modern Economics Texts, Baltimore, 1980, p. 114.

This sets broad goals for the growth of the economy over a period of 5 years, and it also sets goals for the individual sectors of the economy. All these goals are supposed to be consistent. Then there are annual plans, which give the targets for output for each year to the managers of each firm and factory.

The Development of the Economy

The 1928 plan made two major changes in the economy. First, there was a shift in the share of private consumption in the economy toward investment and military expenditure. In 1928, private consumption came to about 65 percent of GNP in the Soviet Union; for the next 40 years it was close to 50 percent.[4] Second, agriculture was collectivized. The land and the livestock were taken away from the peasants, and attempts were made to set up collective farms belonging to the state.

The collectivization of agriculture was a disaster for agricultural output. The peasants killed their livestock for sale and eating instead of handing the livestock over to the collective farms. Brutal methods were used to force the peasants and their possessions into the collective farms and to make the peasants deliver their output, and many peasants were killed. Agricultural output, particularly of livestock, fell sharply.

Soviet agriculture has been a perennial problem. Although large amounts of resources were devoted to agriculture, particularly after 1950, and although there has been substantial growth in agricultural output in the Soviet Union, Soviet agricultural productivity is still well below U.S. levels. And Soviet agricultural productivity is growing more slowly than American agricultural productivity.

But the industrialization strategy worked. During the period 1928–1940, GNP in the Soviet Union grew at about 6 percent a year.[5] This was the period of the Great Depression in the United States, and so Russian economic growth in the first 10 years after planning was introduced was spectacular in comparison with U.S. economic growth in the same period.

World War II brought massive physical destruction to the Soviet Union, but by 1948 output was back to the prewar level. The basic pattern of the 5-year plans continued. A large share of GNP was devoted to investment (over 25 percent),[6] and consumption was not allowed to grow fast. One potentially important change in the planning system took place in 1956: workers were allowed to quit their jobs and look for better ones. Up to that point, workers had been assigned to jobs. Now firms have to go out to find the labor force they need.

How are wages set, and what is the distribution of income in the Soviet Union? Wages are formally determined as part of the plan. Wages are set for each skill level. But the actual wages paid in a firm are not entirely fixed, since the firm has some freedom to decide what position a worker will fill. Also, workers are sometimes paid at piece rates (i.e., according to the amount of output they produce), and it is possible to vary the amount paid. Thus there is some limited flexibility in wages, and firms can use this to attract workers when they need them. In addition, there are higher wages for working in remote areas.

There are no good data on the distribution of income in the Soviet Union. There is a sizable range of wages. Artistic stars supposedly earn thirty times the minimum wage. Further, the political elite have special privileges—they are permitted to shop

---

[4] The comparable U.S. figure is close to 62 percent.

[5] There are a variety of estimates of rates of growth in the Soviet Union. The Russians calculate the GNP differently than we do, omitting service industries. The estimates we give are western estimates of Soviet GNP, calculated on the same basis as U.S. GNP.

[6] For much of the postwar period, Japan invested a larger share of its GNP than did the Soviet Union.

FIGURE 39-2   SOVIET GNP RELATIVE TO U.S. GNP. Over the period since 1955, Soviet GNP has risen relative to U.S. GNP from about 40 percent of the U.S. level to about 58 percent. Soviet growth slowed in the late seventies, when U.S. GNP grew more rapidly than Soviet GNP. (*Source:* Imogene Edwards, Margaret Hughes, and James Noren, "U.S. and U.S.S.R.: Comparisons of GNP," in *Soviet Economy in a Time of Change, Vol. I,* Joint Economic Committee, 1979, p. 383, updated by the authors on the basis of data in CIA, National Foreign Assessment Center, *Handbook of Economic Statistics, 1980,* p. 28.)

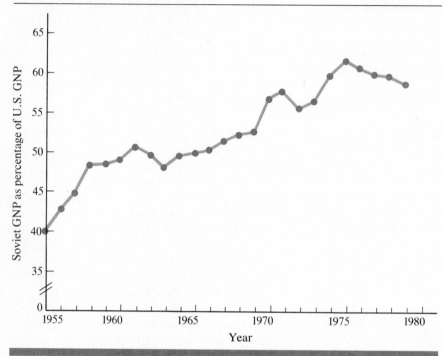

in stores available only to them. Even so, income is almost certainly more evenly distributed than in the United States. This is because there are few people who own large amounts of capital.

Goods are allocated within the Soviet Union in part by prices, in part by bureaucrats, and in part through the system of waiting in line. Housing is rented at low rates by the state. Education and medical care are provided by the state. Individuals can own some private property—a car, consumer durables, even a house in the country. But the goods they want to buy may not be readily available in stores. For some goods, people may wait on line. For others, like cars, there is a waiting list. The prices that are charged

are not equilibrium prices. The small amount of attention given to the consumer in the plans is also reflected in complaints about the poor quality of goods.

How well has the planning system performed? For most of the period since World War II, the Soviet Union has grown faster than the United States, though not faster than Japan. Figure 39-2 shows that since 1955 Soviet GNP has been increasing in relation to U.S. GNP; it is now about 60 percent of the U.S. level.[7] Because the popula-

---

[7] We repeat the warning that comparative GNP data cannot be exact. The comparison between U.S. GNP and the Soviet GNP comes out differently depending on whether Russian or American prices are used to value the goods produced. Do you know why?

TABLE 39-2

SELECTED INDICATORS FOR SOVIET (AND U.S.) ECONOMIES
(Growth Rates, % per Annum; U.S. Data in Parentheses)

	1965–1970	1970–1975	1976–1980
GNP*	5.3 (3.2)	3.8 (2.6)	2.8 (3.3)
Gross fixed capital	7.6	7.0	3.5
Consumption per capita	5.0 (2.7)	2.9 (2.0)	1.6 (2.1)
Employment	2.0 (2.0)	1.8 (1.8)	1.1 (2.8)
"Factor productivity"	1.3	−0.1	−0.3

* The CIA regularly provides estimates of Soviet GNP.
Source: Abram Bergson, "Can the Soviet Slowdown Be Reversed?" *Challenge,* November/December 1981, p. 35.

tion of the Soviet Union is larger, the per capita GNP is about half the U.S. figure.

The Slowdown in Russian Growth

Will the Soviet Union bury the United States economically? The answer is probably not. The Russians are beginning to experience slower growth. Selected data on their performance since 1965–1970 are shown in Table 39-2. Comparative U.S. data are shown in parentheses.

What has caused the slowdown in Soviet growth?[8] One factor is that the labor force is now growing slowly. Employment is expected to rise only 0.5 percent per year for the next 5 years. Second, the transfer of population from agriculture to industry is slowing. By now only 15 percent of the labor force is in agriculture, compared with 40 percent only 20 years ago. As workers move into industry, the overall productivity of labor tends to rise because the output per worker is higher in industry than in agriculture. But when the influx of labor slows, productivity growth slows too. Third, agricultural productivity continues to be low. Dependence on imported food has been increasing.

Many observers, including some in the Soviet Union, argue that the planning process is not suited to the development of a modern economy. Planning did well when the development strategy was simple: to build steel plants and power plants. But now innovation has become more important, and the planning system does not handle innovation well—it is not flexible. Without prices, there are increasing misallocations of resources.

The Soviet planning system does not stand still. There continue to be reforms and experiments in an attempt to improve the system. But underneath all the minor changes is the major question of whether loosening control over the economy will mean loosening control over political life. And thus reform is likely to be limited.

Because political factors inevitably intrude, it is difficult to reach a balanced judgment about the lessons of Soviet economic development. Critics point out that in 1913, Russia had one of the fastest-growing economies. It was industrializing rapidly and moving toward European standards of living. Now, 70 years later, it is indeed a major economic power, but its living standards are still well below those of other industrialized economies, and its economy is in trouble. In addition, its citizens suffered greatly from the disruption of the economy, from loss of property, and from loss of freedom.

[8] The Soviet slowdown happened at the same time as the slowdown in growth in other industrialized economies.

Others point out that since 1913 the Soviet Union has experienced physical destruction in two world wars and a civil war. It now provides all its citizens with the basics of life: food, education, medical care, and shelter. Since 1928, it has grown rapidly. Further, through the choice of its rulers, it has become one of the two major powers.

What is the balanced judgment? From 1928, the Soviet planning system undoubtedly succeeded in forcing the economy to grow faster than would otherwise have been possible. But that success came at a heavy price in terms of life and freedom.

5 CHINA

During the sixties and early seventies, China was widely regarded as the prime example of successful economic development. In 1949, when the Communists under Mao Tse-tung established control over all of China, the country had been at war with foreigners and in civil war for 12 years, and it had suffered political instability since the nineteenth century. Wartime destruction was widespread, and per capita income was about $150 per year (in 1980 dollars).

By the early seventies, the Communists had brought the entire economy and the population of 1 billion under central direction. Starvation had been eliminated. The Chinese economy was growing very fast. Reports described a society in which everyone worked hard and enthusiastically for the sake of the revolution and in which equality was an important goal. Chairman Mao led the way with a simple lifestyle that contrasted with the luxuries the leaders of the Soviet Union permitted themselves.

At the same time, very little was known about China. Economic data and details of the planning of economic life were not available. It seemed that development plans changed often, but the conflicting pressures that led to radical shifts in policy were not well understood. China was admired as much in ignorance as from knowledge.

Since then, China has opened itself up much more to the rest of the world. With the growing contact has come an increased understanding of what Chinese Marxist economic development has achieved, what the shortcomings are, and what the political process underlying development was.

The Historical Record

The record of Chinese development since 1949 is one of rapid growth, particularly in industry, with repeated disruption. Unlike the Russians—who, after establishing control over their territory and deciding on a development strategy in 1928, have stuck to their strategy ever since—the Chinese have repeatedly changed their minds about how to dévelop their economy. For all that, their economy has, on the average, developed very fast—the average growth rate for the period 1949–1979 was almost 7 percent per year. The growth of per capita real GNP averaged about 5 percent.

The economy in 1949 was almost entirely agricultural. Even today, 80 percent of the work force is in agriculture, though agriculture accounts for only about one-third of GNP. In 1949, agriculture accounted for about 60 percent of GNP.

In 1953, following reconstruction, the first 5-year plan was introduced. This followed Russian planning strategy. The emphasis was on industrialization. There would be heavy investment in industry and not much investment in agriculture. Farms were to be collectivized. During the period, real GNP grew at a rate of 7 percent, with industrial output growing by 13 percent per year and agricultural output by 5 percent per year. This was a period of cooperation between Russia and China, and the natural assumption was that China would thereafter follow the Russian plan of increasing industrialization.

Then came one of the two dramatic episodes of Chinese communist development —the *Great Leap Forward*. Chairman Mao decided to try to accelerate the development process by using China's most visible natural resource, its giant population, as the basis. Instead of concentrating entirely on heavy industry, the work force would develop small-scale, labor-intensive industry. The symbol of the Great Leap Forward was the backyard steel furnace. At the same time, agriculture was to become totally collectivized into communes of up to 50,000 people. And all this had to be done quickly.

The Great Leap Forward was a failure. Backyard steel furnaces are not adequate for making steel. By 1961, the GNP was 14 percent below its 1957 level. The most serious failure of the Great Leap Forward was that of agriculture. There were 3 years of bad weather, but equally important, the agricultural communes did not work. Peasant farmers who used to work for themselves or in small groups where it was easy to see the connection between work and return did not produce as well in a very large unit. The Great Leap Forward was abandoned, though not the notion that China should follow its own path to development.

The period 1961–1965 saw a return to a more orthodox communist development strategy for industry, along with the abandonment of the large-scale collectivization of agriculture. By 1965 GNP was 60 percent above its 1961 level. Again all seemed to be well—China apparently was headed for rapid economic development, with industry taking the lead.

Then came the second dramatic period —the *Cultural Revolution*. The leadership decided that the country needed shaking up, because it was settling too much into its bureaucratic ways. Schools and universities were closed. Young people, the Red Guard,

were encouraged to question all existing institutions and authority figures. City dwellers and particularly intellectuals and bureaucrats were sent into the countryside to work with the "real" people. The GNP fell between 1966 and 1968; it came back on track only in 1969, when the Cultural Revolution ended.

Once again the economy returned to a more normal planning process. And once again output grew fast—at an average rate of nearly 7 percent for the seventies. During this period, China once again changed its development approach. It is now trading with the rest of the world, allowing its citizens contact with the outside world, and drawing heavily on outside technical expertise and resources.

The Chinese revolution and development were marked by insistence on equality and continuing reluctance to use material incentives to encourage production. People were supposed to work because working for the country was good. They were not supposed to work only to make themselves better off. With the opening up of the Chinese economy has come a shift to the use of individual incentives.

The Prospects

The Chinese have declared their goal of building a modern socialist economy by the year 2000. For this, they say, they need to modernize in four areas: defense, the economy, political organization, and the educational system. They hope to maintain industrial growth of over 10 percent a year through the end of the century and growth in agricultural production of 4 percent. Whether these extraordinary rates of growth can be attained in an economy without the driving force of a recent revolution and tight central control remains to be seen. The growth of the last 5 years has been at rates a bit below those projected or, more likely, hoped for for the rest of the century.

How Fast Is Chinese Growth?

The growth rates recorded by China and the Soviet Union during their development are extremely high by any standards. But they are not the only such cases. For a long time Japan has been growing faster than both Russia and China. And Korea and Taiwan grew more rapidly than China in the sixties and seventies.

But China has the biggest population. In this connection, the growth of China and the growth of India have often been compared. Both countries have enormous populations and very low income levels. Both are heavily agricultural, and in 1949 both were recovering from the struggle for independence. China was communist, and India was democratic.

The comparison between China and India was seen by many as a contest between democracy and the communist system. If China could grow faster than India, that would show that the communist path to development was better. Actually, India also had 5-year plans and a large amount of state intervention in the economy, but in addition, it had a large private sector.

China grew about 2 percent per year faster than India over the sixties and seventies. But growth of the Indian economy increased at the end of the seventies, helped by good rainfall. It is not obvious what the faster growth of China's economy proves. India's people have more freedom but also more inequality and starvation. Those who favor capitalist development argue that India's difficulties are a result not of too little state intervention in the economy but of too much state interference with a productive private sector.

6 OTHER COMMUNIST-BLOC ECONOMIES

The Soviet Union and China are the two largest of the centrally directed socialist or communist-bloc economies, but they are also among the least market-oriented. Other Eastern European economies, Yugoslavia in particular, give prices and individual initiative a larger role in economic life than does the Soviet Union.

The distinguishing feature of the Yugoslav economy is that firms are managed by their workers, who also share the profits. When a firm is set up, the state makes a loan for its initial operations. The firm pays interest on this loan. The workers elect a workers' council, which hires managers and can fire them. Firms determine their own output levels, prices, and investment plans. In principle, a firm belongs to society rather than the workers, but since the workers get some share of the profits (which are also taxed by the state), ownership is partly in the hands of the workers. Firms can borrow from banks to finance their investment.

Most workers are employed in the socialized sector of the economy. But there are many small private firms, particularly in the service industries, such as barbershops and laundries. They can employ no more than five workers. There is substantial private ownership in agriculture—85 percent of the land is privately owned and cultivated.

Yugoslavia differs from Russia and China, too, in the extent of its foreign trade, particularly with the western economies. Any small country such as Yugoslavia is bound to be more dependent on foreign trade than large countries such as China and Russia. But Yugoslavia differs from the other countries in Eastern Europe by having refused to join Comecon, the Council of Mutual Economic Assistance, which was set up by the Soviet Union in an attempt to integrate the Eastern European economies into an interdependent trading group. For a long time Yugoslavia has been trading quite freely with the western economies; 65 percent of Yugoslavia's trade is with noncommunist countries.

The Yugoslav economy is a mixed economy, with private ownership of some productive capital and room for private initiative in business decisions. However, markets in Yugoslavia do not work freely. Enterprises get together to fix prices, and the state also controls some prices. In addition, it is not known how much freedom workers in firms actually have to choose their managers and operate as they see best.

Growth in the Yugoslav economy has been rapid, at nearly 6 percent per year, on the average, over the period 1969–1979. This rate is about the same as the rates of other Eastern European economies, and it is similar to the growth rates of the more successful middle-income European countries, such as Greece and Portugal. The Yugoslav economy has suffered more from inflation than the other communist-bloc countries, which control prices directly.

Hungary, too, has allowed a greater role for prices in the allocation of resources than have other Eastern European countries. The Eastern European economies, being small, have to rely substantially on trade. In the sixties and seventies trade with the west increased, though in no case except that of Yugoslavia was more than 50 percent of the trade done outside the communist bloc. Central planning has been used in all the communist-bloc economies, starting with the Soviet style of planning. At times there have been experiments with more market-oriented approaches. Growth has been rapid but not extremely so. The communist-bloc economies are not catching up with the western economies. In some cases, such as that of Poland, the economic and political systems are under severe stress.

7 THE MIXED ECONOMIES

The economies of the industrialized non-communist world vary widely in their organization. The state plays a large role in economic life in all these countries, regulating the allocation of resources, while still allowing an important role for market forces.

In France and Scandinavia, economic plans are published by the government. In France, plans are for 4 years. They are called "indicative plans" because they indicate to the private sector the likely or hoped-for development of the economy over the next 4 years. The plans are drawn up by a planning commission, which consults extensively with private businesses and other economic interests. The government uses its control over the banking system, as well as taxes and investment incentives, to move the economy in the desired direction.

Major sectors of industry are state-owned in France, including the coal, gas, and electricity industries, the railroads, and the banking system. The firms in these industries nonetheless run with much independence. Indeed, the nationalized firms frequently diverge further from the 4-year plans than firms in the private sector.

Since 1945 the performance of the French economy has been highly successful. Per capita GNP growth during the sixties and seventies averaged 4 percent. Toward the end of the seventies, though, unemployment rose, and the economy seemed to be in some trouble, as the state had to face up to the problem of eliminating unprofitable large firms. The economic discontent was in part responsible for the election of a socialist president; he promised a greater role for the government in fighting unemployment and more nationalization of industry.[9]

In the sixties West Germany was thought of as the miracle of capitalist development. After World War II, Germany operated for several years with price con-

---

[9] In 1982, the French government nationalized more firms. It now owns firms producing 23 percent of the GNP.

trols, and the economy stagnated. In 1948, price controls were lifted, and central direction of the economy was reduced. Growth of the German economy became extremely rapid. In part, this was because the United States, through the Marshall Plan, provided financing for the rebuilding of Western Europe.

Despite its image as the essential dynamic free-market economy, West Germany experiences large-scale government intervention. The state takes over 40 percent of the GNP in taxes of various forms. There is close cooperation between the state, the workers, and the industrialists. Workers have representatives on the boards of directors of corporations.

Japan has the true wonder story of economic development. From 1960 to 1979, per capita GNP grew at an average rate of 9.4 percent. At this rate, income doubled in less than 8 years. Rapid economic growth in Japan is not just a recent phenomenon. Since 1868, when it decided to build a modern economy, Japan has usually grown faster than other countries. Japanese income levels are now close to those of the United States.

What is the secret of Japanese growth? There are many factors. Some credit goes to the managers of the Japanese corporations, for they plan the introduction of new products over long periods. Some critics complain that the Japanese government, which works closely with industry, provides unfair advantages for Japanese exporters. Credit for Japanese growth certainly goes to the devoted work forces, whose loyalty to the company is foreign to American ways of thinking. That loyalty is, however, reciprocated by the companies, which essentially give their male workers lifetime tenure. Workers are not fired when business is bad. Since part of the annual wage is paid in the form of a bonus that is dependent on profits, the Japanese firm in effect faces flexible real wages. These make it easier to continue to keep workers on the payroll during a recession.

What is the point of all these fragmentary stories about different countries and economies? Only this: although countries have the same economic problems to solve —the problems of what, how, and for whom —they solve them in many different ways. Some rely largely on markets and some hardly at all on markets. The historical record of growth does not show that centrally planned economies are bound to grow faster than economies using markets to allocate resources. Nor does the use of markets ensure rapid growth. It does seem that the centrally planned economies that have grown fast have done so more through investment in heavy industry at the expense of consumption and that these economies have not succeeded in giving to their workers the benefits of the higher consumption that growth should make possible.

As the industrialized economies, centrally planned and mixed, enter the eighties, all are suffering from slower growth than they experienced in the sixties and seventies. Whether and how this situation will be turned around remains to be seen.[10]

8 SOCIALISM AND DEVELOPMENT

Many of the developing countries describe themselves as socialist. The socialism is reflected mainly in heavy government intervention in economic life. In many cases the state owns large firms, licenses production and importing, and often fixes the prices of basic commodities.

The appeal of socialism lies in its apparent promise of a more equitable distribution of wealth and income during the development process and in the belief that the

---

[10] For a view from the side of the mixed economy, see Moses Abramowitz, "Welfare Quandries and Productivity Concerns," *American Economic Review*, March 1981.

Russian and Chinese examples show that planning and government intervention are essential for rapid growth.

However, the experience of the developing countries with large-scale government intervention and ownership has not been good. Chile under Allende and Portugal after the 1974 revolution are examples. The developing economies that are growing most rapidly are those that have relied heavily on the use of markets and particularly on private ownership of productive capital. These successful developing countries are Korea, Taiwan, Singapore, Brazil, and Hong Kong.

9 THE CONVERGENCE HYPOTHESIS

Are the socialist and capitalist economies heading for the same point, with the western economies gradually accepting a larger role for government intervention and planning and the socialist economies allowing a greater role for markets?

This is the *convergence hypothesis,* the notion that over time, economies will become increasingly similar. There is no way of knowing whether that will happen. But it certainly is not happening in the short run. Many western economies have been moving away from the mixed economy and toward a greater reliance on markets and a lesser role for the state. Britain and the United States are the leading examples. And the communist-bloc countries in economic trouble show no signs now of permitting more freedom in economic life.

The convergence hypothesis is probably a reflection of a lack of imagination. If the world is viewed as being divided into two types of economies, each of which has some advantages, it is natural to think that each will pick up the good features of the other. But we should try to think of new developments that may affect the organization of economies. Here the implications of the extraordinary development of computer technology and data management are crucial. Decentralizing the locations of production becomes increasingly possible as the ability to use computers to interact with others increases. Perhaps the future is one of individual initiative, with work done largely at home. Or perhaps improvements in data processing will make central planning more efficient. Or perhaps the slowdown of growth in the communist-bloc countries will lead them to move to some new type of organization in which workers' councils or representatives play a genuine part in determining the allocation of resources and the state becomes comparatively less important. This is what Poland tried in 1981.

SUMMARY

1   The socialist or communist economies are marked by two main features. Productive capital is owned by the state, not by individuals, and there is very limited use of markets to establish the prices of goods and factors of production and to determine the allocation of resources.

2   Karl Marx saw all history as the history of class struggle and capitalism as the struggle between the bourgeoisie (professionals and capitalists) and the workers. Marx predicted that capitalism would destroy itself as labor-saving technical progress reduced the demand for labor, creating unemployment and lower real wages. This prediction proved to be wrong.

3   Marx used the labor theory of value as the tool of his economic analysis. The labor theory of value states that the value of a good is derived from the amount of labor represented by the good, both the labor used to produce the good and the labor used to produce any machines used in its production. Marx argued that labor should get all the proceeds from the sale of goods. Profit represented exploitation of the workers.

4   In a fully planned economy a central planner, meaning the government, decides what is to be produced, how, and for whom. In practice the allocation of resources cannot be undertaken entirely by central direction; substantial decentralization is necessary.

5   Under market socialism, prices are set to produce the desired allocation of resources. Consumers are then free to buy what they want, and the managers of firms are told to maximize profits. The firms are owned by the state. If prices are set incorrectly and result in excess supply or demand, the prices can be changed until the desired allocation of resources is brought about.

6   Central planning was introduced in the Soviet Union in 1928. There are two basic plans. One is a 5-year plan; it sets broad goals for the economy and the sectors in it. The second is the annual plan, which is more detailed and sets production targets for individual firms. The beginning of planning in 1928 was accompanied by an attempt to collectivize agriculture in which individual peasant farmers were moved into collective farms.

7   The Soviet Union has grown very fast, particularly in industry. But its growth slowed down severely at the end of the seventies. Reforms in the direction of a greater use of markets have been suggested by observers within the Soviet Union and outside. But the political authorities are afraid that any relaxation of economic control could lead also to a loosening of political control.

8   The Chinese economy developed very rapidly from 1949 on. Industrial output growth averaged above 10 percent per year. Chinese development was not smooth, however. Both the Great Leap Forward of the late fifties and the Cultural Revolution of the late sixties disrupted the economy. The disruptions were introduced by Chairman Mao, in part because he wanted to prevent the development of a large bureaucracy with substantial differences in living standards between citizens, and particularly between urban and rural dwellers.

9   Other communist-bloc economies are more market-oriented than China or Russia. Yugoslavia permits private ownership of small firms and most of agriculture, and workers manage the firms.

10   The convergence hypothesis is the view that communist and capitalist economies are becoming more like each other. Recent evidence does not support the hypothesis.

KEY TERMS

Mixed economy

Reserve army of the unemployed

Labor theory of value

Alienation of workers

Socialism

Communism

Capitalism

Command economy

Central planner

Market Socialism

New Economic Policy (NEP)

Convergence hypothesis

PROBLEMS

1 (*a*) Name six economies that are socialist or communist and six that are capitalist. (*b*) On what basis are you distinguishing between the two types of economies?

2 When the French government provides credit at low cost for companies that invest in particular industries, we say that it is using policy to help implement the economic plan. Would you say the same thing when the U.S. government provides an investment tax credit, encouraging investment and future growth?

3 (*a*) Why did Marx expect the real wage to fall under capitalism? (*b*) Why did it not fall?

4 Why might it be more difficult for a poor country such as China to invest 25 percent of the GNP than for a richer country?

5 What might be the benefits of market socialism as compared with the command economy?

6 Suppose that you are setting production targets for a factory producing 500 different sizes and types of screws. How would you go about setting the targets? What does this tell you about the ease or difficulty of detailed central planning of an economy?

7 There are two ways of thinking about Soviet planning. One is that it hasn't delivered the benefits of growth to the citizens. The other is that it is remarkable that something so difficult as planning had been done at all and even more remarkable that for a long time the economy grew fast. Discuss these two views.

8 By what total percentage would Chinese per capita income rise in the next 20 years if it grew at 5 percent per year? Given that U.S. per capita income is now about twenty times the Chinese level, how long would it take China to reach the U.S. income level if U.S. per capita income were to remain constant from now on?

9 One element of modern mixed economies is that the state has taken responsibility for the welfare of poor and badly off citizens—through medical aid, social security, food stamps, and a host of other programs. There is currently an argument in the United States about the desirability of cutting back these programs. Discuss the case for reducing the benefits, and then consider the case for not reducing them. Be sure to explain in your answer what facts you would like to know to make a correct decision.

10 How likely is it, do you think, that the Soviet and U.S. economies will one day look very similar?

Index

Key terms appear in **boldface** type.

BASIC INDICATORS OF THE WORLD ECONOMY

	POPU-LATION, millions, mid-1980	AREA, thousands of square kilometers	GNP PER CAPITA DOLLARS 1980	GNP PER CAPITA AVERAGE ANNUAL GROWTH, %, 1960-1980*	AVERAGE ANNUAL RATE OF INFLATION, % 1960-1970†	1970-1980‡	ADULT LITERACY, %, 1977§	LIFE EXPECT-ANCY AT BIRTH, years, 1980
Low-income economies	2,160.9	30,714	260	1.2	3.2	11.2	50	57
China and India	1,649.9	12,819	270	—	—	—	54	59
Other low-income	511.0	17,895	230	1.0	3.1	11.2	34	48
Chad	4.5	1,284	120	−1.8	4.6	7.8	15	41
Bangladesh	88.5	144	130	(.)	3.7	16.9	26	46
Ethiopia	31.1	1,222	140	1.4	2.1	4.2	15	40
Nepal	14.6	141	140	0.2	7.7	8.6	19	44
Burma	34.8	677	170	1.2	2.7	11.2	70	54
Mali	7.0	1,240	190	1.4	5.0	10.1	9	43
Rwanda	5.2	26	200	1.5	13.1	14.2	50	45
Upper Volta	6.1	274	210	0.1	1.3	10.1	5	39
Zaire	28.3	2,345	220	0.2	29.9	32.2	58	47
Malawi	6.1	118	230	2.9	2.4	9.8	25	44
Mozambique	12.1	802	230	−0.1	2.8	11.2	28	47
India	673.2	3,288	240	1.4	7.1	8.5	36	52
Haiti	5.0	28	270	0.5	4.0	9.4	23	53
Sri Lanka	14.7	66	270	2.4	1.8	12.6	85	66
Tanzania	18.7	945	280	1.9	1.8	11.9	66	52
China	976.7	9,561	290	—	—	—	66	64
Guinea	5.4	246	290	0.3	1.5	4.4	20	45
Pakistan	82.2	804	300	2.8	3.3	13.5	24	50
Uganda	12.6	236	300	−0.7	3.0	30.4	48	54
Niger	5.3	1,267	330	−1.6	2.1	12.2	5	43
Madagascar	8.7	587	350	−0.5	3.2	10.3	50	47
Sudan	18.7	2,506	410	−0.2	3.7	15.8	20	46
Middle-income economies	1,138.8	41,614	1,400	3.8	2.7	13.2	65	60
Ghana	11.7	239	420	−1.0	7.6	34.8	—	49
Kenya	15.9	583	420	2.7	1.5	11.0	50	55
Indonesia	146.6	1,919	430	4.0	—	20.5	62	53
Yemen Arab Rep.	7.0	195	430	4.5	—	16.1	21	42
Senegal	5.7	196	450	−0.3	1.7	7.6	10	43
Angola	7.1	1,247	470	−2.3	3.3	21.0	—	42
Honduras	3.7	112	560	1.1	2.9	8.9	60	58
Zambia	5.8	753	560	0.2	7.6	8.1	44	49
Bolivia	5.6	1,099	570	2.1	3.5	22.3	63	50
Egypt	39.8	1,001	580	3.4	2.6	11.5	44	57
Zimbabwe	7.4	391	630	0.7	1.3	8.8	74	55
El Salvador	4.5	21	660	1.6	0.5	11.3	62	63
Thailand	47.0	514	670	4.7	1.8	9.9	84	63
Philippines	49.0	300	690	2.8	5.8	13.2	75	64
Nicaragua	2.6	130	740	0.9	1.8	13.1	90	56
Papua New Guinea	3.0	462	780	2.8	3.6	8.8	32	51
Morocco	20.2	447	900	2.5	2.0	8.1	28	56
Peru	17.4	1,285	930	1.1	10.4	30.7	80	58
Nigeria	84.7	924	1,010	4.1	2.6	18.2	30	49
Jamaica	2.2	11	1,040	0.6	4.0	17.0	90	71
Guatemala	7.3	109	1,080	2.8	0.3	10.4	—	59
Ivory Coast	8.3	322	1,150	2.5	2.8	13.2	41	47
Dominican Rep.	5.4	49	1,160	3.4	2.1	9.0	67	61
Colombia	26.7	1,139	1,180	3.0	11.9	22.0	—	63
Ecuador	8.0	284	1,270	4.5	—	14.4	81	61
Tunisia	6.4	164	1,310	4.8	3.6	7.7	62	60
Syrian Arab Rep.	9.0	185	1,340	3.7	2.6	11.4	58	65
Jordan	3.2	98	1,420	5.7	—	—	70	61
Turkey	44.9	781	1,470	3.6	5.6	29.7	60	62
Korea, Rep. of	38.2	98	1,520	7.0	17.4	19.8	93	65
Malaysia	13.9	330	1,620	4.3	−0.3	7.5	—	64
Panama	1.8	77	1,730	3.3	1.6	7.4	—	70
Algeria	18.9	2,382	1,870	3.2	2.7	13.3	35	56
Brazil	118.7	8,512	2,050	5.1	46.1	36.7	76	63